831 A$167·00

A History of European Integration

A HISTORY OF EUROPEAN INTEGRATION

by
WALTER LIPGENS

VOLUME 1
1945–1947

The Formation of the European
Unity Movement
with contributions by
WILFRIED LOTH and ALAN MILWARD

Translated from the German
by
P. S. FALLA and A. J. RYDER

CLARENDON PRESS · OXFORD
1982

Oxford University Press, Walton Street, Oxford OX2 6DP
London Glasgow New York Toronto
Delhi Bombay Calcutta Madras Karachi
Kuala Lumpur Singapore Hong Kong Tokyo
Nairobi Dar es Salaam Cape Town
Melbourne Auckland
and associates in
Beirut Berlin Ibadan Mexico City Nicosia

Published in the United States by Oxford University Press, New York

Originally published as *Die Anfänge der europäischen Einigungspolitik 1945–1950, 1. Teil: 1945–1947*
© Ernst Klett, Stuttgart, Bundesrepublik Deutschland, 1977
ISBN 3-12-910330-9

© *English edition Oxford University Press 1982*

All rights reserved. No part of this publication may be reproduced, stored in a retrieval system, or transmitted, in any form or by any means, electronic, mechanical, photocopying, recording, or otherwise, without the prior permission of Oxford University Press

British Library Cataloguing in Publication Data

Lipgens, Walter
A history of European integration.
Vol. 1: 1945–1947
1. European federation
I. Title II. Die Anfänge der europäischen
Einigungspolitik 1945–1950. English
321.02'094   D1060
ISBN 0-19-822587-3

Typeset by Cotswold Typesetting Ltd.
Printed in Great Britain
at the University Press, Oxford
by Eric Buckley
Printer to the University

Preface to the English Edition

'Law must derive its power and observance from a definite source, and in studying this problem I am driven to ask: Will law be observed, if it is arrived at only by treaty and promises and decisions by governments as at present arranged? In all the years this has broken down so often... Will the people feel that the law is their law if it is derived and enforced by the adoption of past methods, whether League of Nations, concert of Europe, or anything of that kind?... Where does the power to make law actually rest? It is not even in this House, it is certainly not in the Executive, it is in the votes of the people. They are sovereign authority... [The original thirteen states in North America] decided, for the purpose of conducting foreign affairs, taxation, defence and the regulation of commerce, that they would create a federal body and in that body there would be direct representation of the people. [Similarly in South Africa,] in the end, to get peace and development there had to be a federal parliament, and it had to rest on the votes of the people direct to that parliament... It was the same in Australia... I think it right to let the country see exactly where the surrender of sovereignty leads us. The fact is, no one ever surrenders sovereignty; they merge it into a greater sovereignty'.

(Ernest Bevin, House of Commons, 23 Nov. 1945)

'We had better face the realities of the situation, which are that between these two great federations of Soviet Russia, on the one hand, and the United States, on the other, fortified by their satellite powers..., the smaller nations of Western Europe, of whom we are one, cannot hope to survive, politically or economically, in isolation. Unless we get together in pursuit of a common political and economic policy, we shall inevitably, sooner or later, be absorbed into one or other of these two great economic and political blocs which surround us, one in the East and the other in the West. Much lip-service has been paid in this country to the principle of federation; but when it comes to action it is a rather different matter'.

(Robert Boothby, House of Commons, 20 Feb. 1946)

vi *Preface to the English Edition*

The two basic convictions which gave birth to the historical process of European integration after World War II are well articulated in the declarations, quoted above, by two leading British statesmen. Firstly, international anarchy and what Kant called the 'lawlessness in the relations between states which always creates wars' can only be overcome by means of federal systems and a merging of sovereignty under one common authority by popular vote. Secondly, the lesson of history is that what remains of Europe after the shattering effects of two world wars must enter into a 'union or federation' (alternative terms which have prevailed simultaneously since the Hague Conference of 1948) if it is to be capable of dealing on more equal terms with Moscow and Washington in the new era of continental superstates.

This volume deals with the beginnings and first tentative steps towards 'union or federation' which took place in the West-European countries between 1945 and 1947. The progress of the movement for European integration is comparable with that of liberal democracy in the nineteenth century. Extending over a period of several decades, the movement began with individuals, writers, and associations which developed into pressure groups and finally into a transnational movement which penetrated the parties and political élites. At a later stage governments began to react, became increasingly influenced by the idea, and eventually started to put it partially though not wholly into effect.

In Western Europe, with which this book chiefly deals, the stage of government interest and support was not reached until the end of 1947. In an agreed outline of the proposed History of European Integration of which the present work forms a part (*Journal of Common Market Studies*, Vol. xvii, p. 90) it was laid down that: 'If the government majority of a country declares for years that it cannot or will not take part in the process of European integration, this fact and its reasons should be reported, but the record of its divergent foreign policy should not be enlarged upon'. Accordingly, while the present volume records the fact that governments did not support the idea of integration in this period, and explains the reasons for their attitude (in Chapter I, sections 3 to 7), the main emphasis is on the forces and associations which kept the idea alive until governmental interest was aroused. In Volume 2, which covers the years 1948–50, the centre of gravity shifts to parties and governments.

The forces and associations in question were especially strong in countries which had suffered total collapse as a result of the war, and this first volume is therefore written predominantly from a Continental viewpoint. Federalists on the Continent saw no hope for their countries other than in closer unity, whereas a majority of the British public was still capable of envisaging other alternatives. The reader will, I hope, appreciate the value of a full examination of the sources from the Continental point of view. It would serve no purpose to play down the strength of feeling represented by the Continental

Preface to the English Edition vii

movement; it is rather the historian's task to present it in all its fullness, and so contribute to mutual understanding in the continuing dialogue between Britain and Continental Europe.

The present volume left the press in the original German edition in April 1977. Clearly it could not be rewritten in full, though many structural refinements and corrections of errors which slipped into the German text have been made; above all, three passages have been amended and are thus different in the present edition. For Chapter I/3, I have been able to study the Foreign Office documents, which have meanwhile become available in the Public Record Office, concerning Bevin's policy towards Europe in 1945-7. On pp. 270-4 I have substituted a clearer presentation of the reasons which prevented the European governments from taking up the idea of union in 1945-7. Finally, Professor Alan Milward of the University of Manchester Institute of Science and Technology has contributed a section reflecting his expert knowledge of the economic situation and making use of the documents, which have now also become available, of the sixteen-power conference in Paris from July to September 1947.

I express my sincere thanks to Professor Milward for his contribution, and to Mr John Pinder and Professor Donald C. Watt for suggesting that the book be published in translation. For the present edition all quotations, English and other, have been furnished to the translators in the original languages; for a part of the volume, I received valuable help in this from Dr W. Kulla while at the European University Institute in Florence. I am indebted to Inter Nationes, Bonn, for a grant towards the cost of translation, and to the Commission of the European Community for additional help in this matter, as well as for archive missions carried out by Professor Milward in Europe; this assistance was furnished through the good offices of the European University Institute. Many thanks should go to the Volkswagen Endowment which enabled Professor Milward to take three-months' leave for research in American archives; and thanks are also due to Miss W. M. E. Bruseker, Mme C. Costes, Mr H.-W. Norman, and Mr H. Paulsen for their help during the completion of Professor Milward's chapter. Finally, I express my special gratitude to Mr P. S. Falla and Dr A. J. Ryder, who have translated the original text and sources from so many languages with expert understanding and personal interest. While the translators have worked in consultation, Dr Ryder is responsible for the Introduction and Chapter I, and Mr Falla for Chapters II and III and for general revision.

I trust that this account of the beginnings of the joint effort to create a European community may, in its English edition, contribute to a shared historical understanding of the process of integration.

W.L.
Florence/Saarbrücken, Sept. 1979

Acknowledgements from the German Preface

As a starting-point, the late Wilhelm Cornides placed at my disposal the rich collection of the *Europa-Archiv* containing material about German and supranational European associations. During my years as Associate Professor the University of Heidelberg enabled me to do research on this subject in major archives outside the German Federal Republic... The year 1966–7 spent at the Institute for Advanced Study at Princeton, NJ, deepened my understanding of the global aspects of the subject. After my appointment to the University of Saarbrücken, the granting of a research semester by the Saarland Ministry of Education in the winter of 1974–5 and above all the generous help of the Volkswagen Endowment, including funds for assistants and sabbatical leave in the winter of 1975–6, enabled me to visit the remaining West-European archives and to complete the work. I wish to thank all the owners of the archives named in the Appendix and all those who were active in the European associations between 1945 and 1950 and who helped me to examine their collections, often at considerable sacrifice of their time and with full understanding of the needs of historical research; I am particularly indebted to the late Ernst von Schenck and to Hans Dieter Salinger, Henri Brugmans, Alexandre Marc, Lord Duncan-Sandys, and Altiero Spinelli for their valuable help and suggestions. The chapters on Italy would have been far less informative without the untiring help of Andrea Chiti-Batelli and Professor Sergio Pistone. A special bonus during the final phase at Saarbrücken was the ever closer collaboration with my assistant, Wilfried Loth: without his unflagging aid several chapters would not have achieved their present form, and at least two are so predominantly his work that they appear under his name. In the collection of source material Hans Geib, Klaus Lorig, Christoph Stillemunkes, and Gerd Toscani were staunch helpers. While the final draft was being written Hellmuth Auerbach and Professor Hans-Peter Schwarz provided most valuable criticism and suggestions at a special seminar on the subject. The typing of the fair copy, lasting two years, was carried out by Frau Müller-Truschel with her usual care. Finally I thank the Wissenschaftliche Gesellschaft des Saarlandes and the Fondation Européenne de la Culture for generous subsidies. Above all I thank my wife, to whom the book is dedicated, for her unwavering moral support and co-operation.

I am, of course, solely responsible for any mistakes and shortcomings

Acknowledgements from the German Preface

which may remain despite the help I have received; and I am conscious that this first attempt at telling the full story of the European movement needs further critical underpinning at many points. But the attempt had to be made to present a considered and comprehensive account of the decline into which Europe had sunk and the development of an idea capable of rescuing it. My aim is to illustrate the clear-sightedness and wealth of ideas shown by those who responded to the challenge in the early phase of the breakthrough, and at the same time to bring home to people how far the reality still falls short of the ideal. In addition the present work will, it is hoped, assist the steadily developing European Community to acquire a well-founded consciousness of its own history.

W.L.
Saarbrücken/Florence, 29 Sept. 1976

Contents

Note on Contents of Volume 2 and on Volume of Documents

INTRODUCTION

Basic Factors of the European Situation in 1945

1.	The Decline of Europe and the Rise of the Superpowers	1
	(a) The Major Political Consequences of the Second World War	2
	(b) Europe's Economic and Social Losses	6
	(c) Territorial Losses: the Balkanization of Europe	11
2.	Europe's Self-Awareness: I. The Unity of Civilization and Economic Necessity	18
	(a) Redefining European Civilization	19
	(b) The Frontiers of European Civilization	25
	(c) The Beginnings of the Political Unification Movement, 1914–39: the Economic Imperative	35
3.	Europe's Self-Awareness: II. The Triumph of the Supranational Principle in the Resistance	44
	(a) The Resistance Movement against 'Hitler's Europe'	45
	(b) The Need for Supranational Authority	48
	(c) Motives for European Unity, the Summing-up by the Geneva Conference of Resistance Fighters	53
	(d) The Extension and Limits of Europe's Self-Awareness	58
4.	Forces of Opposition: I. The Post-war Planning of the World Powers	62
	(a) British and American Regional Plans	63
	(b) The Soviet Union as an Opponent of European Federation	68
	(c) Roosevelt's 'Four Policemen': Acceptance of the Soviet Standpoint	72
	(d) Yalta and the Beginnings of US Involvement in Europe	76
5.	Forces of Opposition: II. National Governments	81
	(a) The Key Problem: Governmental Attitudes	81
	(b) Temporal and Geographical Limits of the Present Work	86
	(c) Methods, Sources, and Structure of the Work	89

I. EUROPE'S MOOD OF RESIGNATION DURING THE PERIOD OF APPARENT RUSSO–AMERICAN CO-OPERATION (MAY 1945- MAY 1946)

1.	The Superpowers, the European Vacuum, and the Hope for a World-Wide Security System	93
	(a) Beginnings of Co-operation and Confrontation between the Superpowers	94

xi

	(b)	Foundation of the Organization for World Peace and its Limited Power: San Francisco	98
	(c)	No New Order in Europe: Potsdam	102
	(d)	Verbal Co-operation: London, Moscow, and again London	104
2.		Early Associations of Federalists in the Spirit of the Resistance Movements	107
	(a)	The Movimento Federalista Europeo	108
	(b)	The Swiss Europa-Union	117
	(c)	The Comité Français pour la Fédération Européenne	124
	(d)	Europeesche Actie	131
	(e)	Federal Union	142
3.		Britain's Aloofness under the Labour Government	154
	(a)	Conditions affecting British Policy in Europe in 1945	155
	(b)	The Stages of Bevin's Foreign Policy, 1945–1947	166
	(c)	Motives and Alternatives	189
4.		De Gaulle's Attempt to revive Nationalist Policy	201
	(a)	Conditions affecting France's New Foreign Policy	201
	(b)	Stages of de Gaulle's 'Policy of Greatness'	208
	(c)	The 'Other France' as Criticism and Alternative	214
5.		Pro-European Trends in Occupied Germany	230
	(a)	The Victorious Powers in Germany: the Administration of Chaos	231
	(b)	States and Parties. The Revival of Political Activity	234
	(c)	Rejection of Nationalism and Awareness of the Idea of Europe	237
6.		Countries in a Weak Situation: Italy, Belgium, and The Netherlands, *by Wilfried Loth*	246
	(a)	Italy's Problems before the Peace Treaty	247
	(b)	Italy's Commitment to Europe and its Helplessness	252
	(c)	Belgium. Spaak's Frustrated Efforts	258
	(d)	The Aloofness of the Netherlands; the Benelux Question	263
7.		Summary: 'Our Situation is like that of the Early Christians . . .'	268
	(a)	Reasons for Loss of Heart and for the Weakness of the European Associations	270
	(b)	An Illusory Alternative: The MFE in 1946	274
	(c)	Clear Assessments of the Situation	278

II. REVIVAL OF PLANS FOR FEDERATION: THE 'THIRD FORCE' AS AN ELEMENT IN THE ORGANIZATION OF WORLD PEACE (JUNE 1946–MAY 1947)

1.		Beginnings of Visible Crisis in the Joint Policy of the Superpowers	282
	(a)	The Preventive Policy of the USSR	283
	(b)	Hardening of US Policy	286
	(c)	Beginnings of Public Controversy: the Council of Foreign Ministers in Paris	291
	(d)	Renewed Co-operation: the Council of Foreign Ministers in New York	294

2.	Contacts among Federalist Groups in Western Europe		296
	(a) Increased Activity and Contacts in the Summer of 1946		298
	(b) The Hertenstein Conference of European Federalists		303
	(c) The Luxemburg Conference of European and World Federalists		310
	(d) The Basle Agreement for the Establishment of the UEF		314
3.	Churchill's Zurich Speech; Foundation of the United Europe Movement and the ELEC		317
	(a) Churchill's Appeal for 'a kind of United States of Europe'		317
	(b) Foundation of the United Europe Movement		323
	(c) Foundation of the European League for Economic Co-operation		334
	(d) Federalist Reactions to Churchill's Plan		341
4.	Revival of Federalist Ideas in France		346
	(a) The Comité International pour la fédération européenne (CIFE)		347
	(b) Integral Federalism I: La Fédération		349
	(c) Integral Federalism II: Cercles socialistes, fédéralistes et communautaires pour une république moderne (CSFC)		355
	(d) Smaller Federalist Groups		358
5.	The Union Européenne des Fédéralistes and its 'Third Force' Programme		361
	(a) Foundation and Development of the UEF down to March 1947		362
	(b) Meeting of the Enlarged Central Committee at Amsterdam: Design for Europe and Proposed Strategy		369
	(c) Organization and Working Methods of the UEF		376
	(d) Initial Conception of a 'Third Force' comprising the Whole of Europe		380
6.	The First European Federalist Groups in Germany		385
	(a) Paneuropa-Union (Hamburg and Freiburg), Paneuropa-Bund (Berlin)		388
	(b) Local Groups in the British Zone. Europäische Volksbewegung (Hamburg), USE-Liga (Ascheberg), Föderalistische Union (Cologne), Europäische Gemeinschaft (Münster)		399
	(c) Local Groups in the US and French Zones: Union-Europa-Liga (Munich and Coblenz), Europäische Aktion (Stuttgart)		410
	(d) The German Europa-Union up to the Eutin Congress, and the First Attempts to amalgamate the Various Groups		415
7.	Reactions in Western Europe; Consultation of Parliamentarians; Signs of East-European Interest		431
	(a) Reactions of the West-European Press		432
	(b) Coudenhove-Kalergi's Poll of Parliamentarians		435
	(c) East-European Interest in Federalism and European Union		441

xiv *Contents*

III. LIMITATION TO WESTERN EUROPE; EFFECTS OF THE DEVELOPING EAST-WEST CONFLICT (MAY–DECEMBER 1947)

1. Breakdown of Co-operation between the Superpowers; Effect on their Attitude towards European Union ... 458
   (a) US Foreign Policy comes to favour a Regional Security Organization ... 459
   (b) The Americans begin to endorse Plans for European Unity ... 467
   (c) The Soviet Union again rejects Plans for European Unity ... 478
   (d) The Preliminary Paris Conference on the Marshall Plan, and Moscow's Veto ... 481
2. The West-European Governments and the Impulse given by the Marshall Plan, *by Wilfried Loth* ... 488
   (a) The British Reaction: Delay instead of Leadership ... 489
   (b) France: a Change of Course, but with Hesitations ... 495
   (c) First Steps in Italy, Belgium, and the Netherlands ... 500
   (d) A New Quality of Unification Policy ... 506
3. The Committee of European Economic Co-operation (CEEC) and the Advent of the Customs Union, *by Alan S. Milward* ... 507
   (a) The Nature of the Paris Conference ... 507
   (b) The Problem of Germany ... 518
   (c) The Payments Problem ... 523
   (d) Labour and the Manpower Conference ... 535
   (e) The Decisions of CEEC in September ... 538
   (f) The Advent of the Customs Union ... 548
4. Decisions at the Montreux Congress of the UEF ... 569
   (a) The Concept of a Federal European Society and Economy ... 571
   (b) The Decision to make a Start with Western Europe ... 579
   (c) The World Federalists' Congress at Montreux ... 585
   (d) Position of the UEF after Montreux ... 590
5. Federalist Groups among Parliamentarians; Foundation of the European Parliamentary Union ... 599
   (a) Federalist Groups in the West-European Parliaments ... 601
   (b) Creation of the European Parliamentary Union, and its Congress at Gstaad ... 607
   (c) Federalist Parliamentary Groups in the Benelux Countries and Italy; the All-Party Europe Group in the House of Commons ... 614
6. Formation of National Federalist Associations in Western Europe ... 622
   (a) French Federalist Groups and the Conseil français pour l'Europe unie ... 623
   (b) Revival of the Movimento Federalista Europeo after Montreux ... 628

	(c)	Dissensions among Belgian Groups	633
	(d)	Creation of the Dutch Beweging van Europese Federalisten	638
	(e)	Unification of European Federalist Groups in the Western Zones of Germany	644
7.		The International Committee of the Movements for European Unity	657
	(a)	Foundation of the Liaison Committee in Paris, 20 July 1947	659
	(b)	Tension between Federalists and 'Unionists'	665
	(c)	Decisions of the Committee at its November/December Meetings	674

Position at the End of 1947   685

APPENDIX

List of Archives consulted	689
Abbreviations of Names of Parties, Organizations, etc.	695
Associations for European unity as at the end of 1947	700
Index of Proper Names, to Vol. 1	703

IN PREPARATION

Volume 2: 1948-1950
The Emergence of European Unity Politics

This will comprise the following four main parts:
Chapter IV: Attitude of the Political Parties towards the Concept of European Federation
Chapter V: Beginnings of West-European Co-operation, and the Demand for a European Constituent Assembly (1948)
Chapter VI: Failure of the First Attempt: the Council of Europe as a Governmental Compromise (1949)
Concluding Assessment of Concepts, Methods, and Aspects of European Federation
Vol. 2 will also include a full Bibliography, list of interviews and archives.

Forthcoming Documentary Volumes

A collection of source material used in this book, consisting of the most important documents from the archives listed in the Appendix on pp. 689-94, will in all probability be published by the European University Institute in Florence in a series *Documents on the History of European Integration*. The volume *Europa-Föderationspläne der Widerstandsbewegungen 1940-1945*, edited by W. Lipgens, and often quoted in the present work, will be published in a much enlarged English edition as volume 1 of this series under the title *Continental Plans for European Union, 1940-45*. It is in the process of translation by P. S. Falla.

Abbreviations used in the footnotes for German scholarly periodicals

HZ = Historische Zeitschrift (Munich)
VfZG = Vierteljahreshefte für Zeitgeschichte (Stuttgart)
(for abbreviations of names of parties, organizations, etc. see the Appendix, pp. 695-8.

INTRODUCTION

Basic Factors of the European Situation in 1945

1. The Decline of Europe and the Rise of the Superpowers

The Second World War caused far-reaching changes throughout the world; its result was a completely new alignment of forces. Nowhere was this truer than in Europe. A clear grasp of the basic factors in a radically altered Europe is essential both for an understanding of the groups which between 1945 and 1950 declared in favour of European unification and in order to follow the beginnings of this unification policy. These factors were already in existence by 1945 (before the outbreak of the East–West conflict); in the following years they emerged even more conspicuously. The aim of this introduction is to outline them as concisely and accurately as possible.

The concept of European union did not, of course, owe its origin to the change in the world's political scene that became apparent in 1945. It arose at an earlier date, as will be seen, partly in consequence of a revulsion against nationalism, partly from a deeply felt rediscovery of Europe's common interests, and partly from the peace movement that had grown up inside Europe as a force in its own right.[1] But within a few months of the end of the war the champions of European unification were clearly aware of the political decline of Europe, which they saw initially as a serious obstacle to their aims, then as the additional external challenge and stimulus which in fact it was—this must be emphasized in view of later and unrealistic tendencies to gloss over the importance of the change in Europe's status.

---

[1] Cf. Section 2, 'Europe's self-awareness', p. 18 ff. The object of this 'Introduction' is strictly defined in each of its sections by the heading 'Basic Factors . . . 1945'. It is not designed to present a history of Europe during the inter-war period or to provide in a nutshell the still unwritten scholarly volume on the antecedents and beginnings of the movement for unification since the First World War. As an introduction to the volume dealing with the years 1945 to 1950 it aims simply at summarizing the major results of the epoch that began in 1914 as they appeared in 1945. For this reason reference is made only to the most essential documentary evidence out of the mass of available material on the inter-war period and the Second World War.

2   *Introduction*

(A) THE MAJOR POLITICAL CONSEQUENCES OF THE SECOND WORLD WAR

These can be summed up in one sentence: in May 1945 the two former peripheral powers and new world powers, Russia and America, driven to reshape the world by their opposing political ideologies, and meeting in the heart of the devastated Continent of Europe, decided on the formal restoration of its shrunken nation states and divided it *de facto* between themselves into spheres of influence. That set the stage for the immediate post-war period and in essentials has not changed – since no union of Europe in fact has come about – especially as the two superpowers, whose spheres of influence met in close proximity at many points across the world, soon found themselves so locked in conflict that it appeared impossible for either to yield to the other any part of the European assets. The capabilities and resources of these continental unions—for this is what the new world powers, America and the Soviet Union, were – showed that the scale of technological and political power had in the meantime outstripped the capacity of a European nation state. The Europeans also had to realize that the Second World War, which had begun as the last war of its kind between sovereign European nation states, had done as much to accelerate the independence movement of the colonial peoples over whom they ruled as had the spread of technology and industry beyond Europe's boundaries. 'Hitler's Europe', the latest of many attempts by one Continental nation to dominate the others, had finally brought to an end any prospect of European hegemony once Hitler had been conclusively defeated by the advancing armies of Russia and America.[2]

The Second World War thus ended a process that had started with the catastrophe of the First World War. Up to then the European states had directly or indirectly dominated the world for at least three centuries; it was in Europe that military might, economic superiority, and intellectual progress were all concentrated. Under Europe's leadership between 1870 and 1914 the world, having undergone an industrial revolution, had experienced an unprecedented transformation of its mode of living and a vast increase in production, trade, and investment under the aegis of economic liberalism and internationalism. Within the monarchical state the doctrine of 'sovereignty', conceived in an earlier age as an antidote to the civil wars of religion, was now used by the conservative opponents of the liberal–democratic movement in order to break it up and divert it, and on both sides, as traditional Christian values lost their power, people came to accept hypercharged nationalism as a substitute religion; it had degenerated into the dogma of an eternal and absolute national sovereign state,

[2] Cf. especially H. Holborn, *The Political Collapse of Europe*, New York, 1966; L. Dehio, 'The Passing of the European System' in *Germany and World Politics in the Twentieth Century*, London, 1965; R. Salvadori, *Le Origini del processo d'integrazione dell'Europa occidentale 1940–1950*, Parma, 1974, especially the chapter 'Europa "dominante" ed Europa "passiva" ' (pp. 5–9) and 'Il Declino dell'Europa' (pp. 55–60).

responsible to no one and nothing except the policy of national imperialism and expansion. 'As a global concern Europe could only lose its hitherto unchallenged hegemony in the economic, financial and political spheres if the states which were partners in it were to wage a suicidal war against each other.' It was their compartmentalized power politics – in contrast to their growing economic interdependence and the international character of world trade—which, once they had failed to resolve the tensions between them, drove them into four years of mutual destruction in the First World War.[3]

In the most critical year of the war – 1917 – the United States and Russia, which had long since outstripped the Europeans and in the nineteenth century had colonized their vast open spaces, entered world politics with decisions of revolutionary significance. Both powers had become known in the nineteenth century as exponents of rival political creeds: the United States as a bastion of democracy and self-determination, a magnet for immigrants, Russia as a bastion of the principle of absolutism. And since about 1870 both had comprised territorial empires – from the Atlantic to the Pacific, from Warsaw to Manchuria – which covered respectively twice and five times the area of all the European states put together. But in 1917 for the first time they put forward programmes with a worldwide message; the USA by its decision to intervene in the European war to help democracy defeat autocracy; Russia, after the Bolshevik seizure of power, by its endeavour to promote a Communist world revolution – Lenin on the one hand and Wilson on the other both presented global programmes which were clearly directed against the existing regime of European national and colonial empires. Their effects were felt in many ways: in the first place, it was America's entry into the war, not a European coalition on its own, which tipped the balance of the war against the Central Powers; in Paris Wilson established the principle of a League of Nations for the rational and collective arbitration of future conflicts. Communist forces were active in the various post-war revolutions. But the direct influence of both powers was, as yet, short-lived; internal factors – which lie outside the scope of the present work – pulled them both back into isolation soon after the end of the war; for the majority of European states the victory of the democratic idea of the state remained ephemeral; the USA refused to join the League of Nations and repudiated any responsibility for the European status quo. Russia's internal troubles forced Lenin and later Stalin to concentrate on 'building Socialism in one country'. The one power did not want to play a

[3] Cf. the most comprehensive treatment (in its way still unsurpassed) in J. von Salis, *Weltgeschichte der neuesten Zeit*, vol. 2, Zurich, 1955 (quotation on p. 259); W. J. Mommsen, *Das Zeitalter des Imperialismus* (Fischer Weltgeschichte, vol. 28). Frankfurt, 1969; on the German contribution, esp. A. Hillgruber, 'Zwischen Hegemonie und Weltpolitik. Das Problem der Kontinuität von Bismarck bis Bethman Hollweg' in *Das Kaiserliche Deutschland, Politik und Gesellschaft 1870–1918*, Düsseldorf, 1970, pp. 187–204; for more detail on the view suggested here, W. Lipgens, 'Zum Geschichtlichen Standort der Reichsgründung 1870/71' in *Geschichte in Wissenschaft und Unterricht*, vol. 22 (1971), pp. 513–28.

leading role in Europe, the other was unable to do so.[4] Europe was given one more chance.

This chance was indeed almost inexplicably squandered by the Europeans between 1919 and 1939. The balance sheet of the First World War was soon realized: Europe had lost its position as leader of the world; the independence movement had become active among the colonial peoples; Great Britain had to concede full freedom of action to her Dominions even in foreign policy; Europe's resources had been exhausted, victors as well as vanquished were impoverished and had become debtors to the new world creditor nation, the United States. Many European statesmen were well aware that their countries, lying between the rising continental-size states, had been granted only a temporary respite in which to come to their senses and to unite; but their wish for future peaceful close co-operation in Europe did not go far enough to make them will the necessary means. With the setting-up of the League of Nations they had agreed on an initial international organization to 'guarantee international peace' and had taken a first step towards the transformation of international relations as a counterpart in principle to the democratic movement in domestic politics: to doing away with the existing inter-state anarchy which Kant had earlier condemned as 'a state of lawlessness which contains nothing but war'. But in the League of Nations unanimity was required for any major decision; all resolutions could only be presented to the member states as 'recommendations', that is, the League was given no power of its own over the states. In contrast to numerous warnings from a considerable proportion of the European intelligentsia that the time had come to devise a supranational legal framework, the nation states, knowing that the majority of their population showed no understanding of the new ideals, insisted on thinking in nation-state categories and upholding national sovereignty. A way was admittedly found of avoiding a direct relapse into the kind of inter-state anarchy, exemplified by the Rhine and Ruhr policy practised by Poincaré, yet renewed efforts at a collective organization for peace and at a rational community of states had no success. Statesmen like Briand and Stresemann did try to pursue a 'policy of understanding' with a European objective, but with 'preservation of sovereignty' and giving priority to national self-interest. In Locarno France saw at least a definitive if partial acknowledgement of Versailles, while for Germany it was the price to be paid for a successful policy of treaty revision in Eastern Europe. In the Briand–Kellogg Pact war was solemnly renounced, yet neither the threat of sanctions nor the demand for disarmament was made binding. Basically France was

[4] Cf. Holborn (n. 2), pp. 90–110, Mommsen (n. 3), pp. 340–64; E. Angermann, *Die Vereinigten Staaten von Amerika* (dtv Weltgeschichte des 20. Jahrhunderts, vol. 7) Munich, 1969², p. 35 ff.; K. H. Ruffman, *Sowjet-Russland* (ibid.; vol. 8), Munich, 1967, p. 184 ff.; K. Schwabe, *Deutsche Revolution und Wilson-Frieden*, Düsseldorf, 1971; F. T. Epstein, 'Aussenpolitik in Revolution und Bürgerkrieg, 1917–20' in *Osteuropa-Handbuch, Sowjetunion, Aussenpolitik 1: 1917–55*, ed. D. Geyer, Cologne/Vienna, 1972, pp. 86–149.

unwilling to give up her one-sided claim for hegemony based on the Treaty of Versailles; Germany was unwilling to accept the defeat she suffered in her first bid for world power; and Great Britain, preoccupied in preserving the Commonwealth, had no other plan for the Continent but 'balance of power'. In this way Europe persisted in a situation which Carl J. Burckhardt had accurately defined in 1922: 'We shall have to wait a long time for nationalism to subside ... Its hypnotic power continues to increase. In that respect we have long been in the position of the Greeks after the first Roman victories, perhaps we too shall have to experience occupation.'[5]

The most serious direct results of this obdurate nationalism occurred in the economic sphere. The European states clung to the policy which they had adopted during the First World War of pursuing economic 'autarky' as a supposed remedy for their economic decline. The fall in the European demand for foreign imports and the doubling of the export of manufactured goods by the United States and Japan to overseas countries between 1913 and 1929 together caused European exports to those countries to decline by about half. Every attempt in the 1920s to restore a liberal world economy proved fruitless because the European countries reacted to their reduced ability to import from each other by throttling back trade inside Europe by raising tariffs along frontiers which the Treaty of Versailles had lengthened by about 20,000 kilometres. The national economies, fragmented and artificially restricted, stagnated; in consequence of economic nationalism they were unable to produce anything like the domestic prosperity they desired; while in the same period in spite of crises the United States and the Soviet Union opened up and industrialized their countries and thus developed their production and markets to a formidable size.[6]

Economic, political, and intellectual developments, though not understood by the European peoples, were in fact working towards large-scale communities; the European nation states, already dwarfed in size, could not achieve the welfare they all sought. It was this very failure which, on the contrary, produced the reactionary movements that opposed the devaluation of the state and the repudiation of war, and sought to uphold 'national sovereignty' by every means in their power. Thanks to the misery caused by the world economic crisis, which led to a complete retreat into economic isolationism that in turn only aggravated the crisis, various

---

[5] H. von Hofmannsthal/C. J. Burckhardt, *Briefwechsel*, Frankfurt, 1956, p. 92. For warnings by intellectuals about the need for unification, cf. pp. 36 f. For general accounts, see esp. P. Renouvin, *Les Crises du XXe siècle*, vol. i: *De 1914 à 1929*, vol. ii: *De 1929 à 1945 (Histoire des relations internationales*, vols. 7 and 8, Paris, 1957 and 1958; J. R. von Salis, op. cit., vol. 3: 1919–45, Zurich, 1960; F. P. Walters, *A History of the League of Nations*, London/New York, 1960²; H. Graml, *Europa zwischen den Kriegen* (dtv. *Weltgeschichte*, vol. 5) Munich, 1969; Jon Jacobsen, *Locarno Diplomacy, Germany and the West, 1925–29*, Princeton, 1972.

[6] Cf. as an introductory survey the chapter on 'Europe and the world economy' in R. A. C. Parker, *Europe, 1919–45*, London, 1969. For more details including figures, see p. 8 f.

forms of Fascism came to power in almost half the states of Europe, and saw in their countries' 'struggle for survival' a higher value than peace.[7] The German form of Fascism, culminating in a last attempt of one nation to achieve hegemony in Europe, and intensified by Hitler's ruthless and total application of the slogan 'My country right or wrong' into a brutal late form of national imperialism, plunged Europe into the Second World War. By defeating all the other Continental states Nazi Germany imposed an effective economic and military unification of the Continent but by a dictatorship which provoked the opposition of every vital force still left in Europe, even though it took the intervention – this time a final one – of the two new world powers to bring the regime down. At the end of this war all real authority on the European Continent lay in the hands of these two superpowers, who along made decisions about frontiers, political institutions, and economic affairs; who, in a formal sense – and this must be repeated – decided in favour of systematically restoring the national states, while in fact dividing the Continent between themselves into areas of control or spheres of influence. Whatever in subsequent years the two world powers in their respective spheres would – very differently – initiate,[8] the 'Roman occupation' foreseen by Burckhardt had arrived. The European system of national states which had once dominated the globe had been replaced by a bipolar system of global hegemony jointly exercised by the United States and the Soviet Union.

(B) EUROPE'S ECONOMIC AND SOCIAL LOSSES

The exact figures of losses show how completely adverse Europe's balance sheet of the Second World War was. From 1945 to 1950 everyone was conscious of this through personal suffering and loss, and – apart from the later, partial recovery helped by the world economic boom after 1950 – it was in every respect of crucial significance for our subject.

First, the number of deaths: Europe (excluding Russia), which in the First World War had lost rather more than 6 million dead, had to suffer over 17 million dead in the Second World War. The highest losses in relation to numbers of population were borne by the countries of Eastern

---

[7] The interpretation, here emphasized, of the various forms of Fascism having originated in nationalist reaction against the tendency towards excessive division of labour in Continental unions, seen in E. Nolte, *Three Faces of Fascism*, London, 1966, esp. pp. 429–54, has been unjustly neglected in more recent discussions on Fascism, cf. R. Kühnl, 'Theorien über den deutschen Faschismus' in Walter Grab (ed.), *Jahrbuch des Instituts für Deutsche Geschichte*, vol. 3, Tel Aviv, 1974, pp. 313–47. On the validity of this interpretation cf. K. Hildebrand, *Deutsche Aussenpolitik, 1933–1945*, Stuttgart, 1971, and A. Hillgruber, *Hitler's Strategie, Politik und Kriegsführung, 1940–1941*, Frankfurt, 1965.
[8] The possibilities which existed and the state of Allied planning are sketched in the penultimate section of this Introduction, p. 62 f.; the actual power relations and growing East–West confrontation between 1945 and 1950 are analysed throughout the book at the beginning of every chapter as far as is necessary for understanding the consequent European reaction, taking into consideration the special position of Great Britain etc.

Introduction 7

and South-Eastern Europe up to the Russian border, which in the Second World War lost about 7.5 million people (about 1.2 million military casualties, 4 million murdered Jews, 2.3 million other civilian casualties) – almost 9 per cent of their population in all. Germany, which in the First World War had lost about 2.3 million people, lost about 5.5 million in the Second World War (of whom 3.6 million were soldiers killed or missing, 400,000 civilians killed in air raids, 220,000 murdered Jews, and 1.3 million killed or missing in the Reich territory East of the Oder–Neisse line) – roughly 8 per cent of the population living within Germany's 1937 frontiers. Only the West-European countries, especially France and Great Britain, suffered relatively fewer losses in the Second World War, altogether about 1.7 million, in consequence of the absence of trench warfare.[9] The United States, by comparison, had 259,000 servicemen dead or missing; in the Soviet Union, which has never published exact figures, between 7 and 14 million are estimated to have died; in the rest of the world, especially the Japanese theatre of war, between 14 and 16 million died, in both cases almost half of them civilians. The disaster caused by Europe's system of nation states, which in the First World War had caused a total of about 9 million losses, had cost the lives of over 45 million people in the Second World War.[10] Still greater was the number of injured and disabled.

As a result of the lack of men and machines, agricultural output in all European countries except Great Britain and the neutrals had fallen far below the pre-war level; in Europe as a whole it amounted in 1946–7 to only 75 per cent of the volume of 1938; the cultivated area was down by 20 per cent, the amount of grain was only 70 per cent of pre-war (with a mere 20 per cent of world grain production compared with 35 per cent in 1938); in animal fats and meat only about two-thirds of pre-war output was

---

[9] From H. Arntz, 'Die Menschenverluste im Zweiten Weltkrieg' in *Bilanz des Zweiten Weltkrieges*, Oldenburg, 1953, pp. 441–7; W. Köllmann, *Bevölkerung und Raum in Neuerer und Neuester Zeit* (= Bevölkerungs-Ploetz, Part 4) Würzburg, 1965[3], pp. 203, 208, and 189. The German war losses are often made to include the approximately 1.3 million killed or missing ethnic Germans from the countries lying east of the Reich frontier of 1937 between the Baltic Sea and Romania; but these figures are, in part at least, already included in the statistics of war losses for the East-European countries. The losses of the West-European countries (not including the fall in the number of births) were as follows:
Great Britain 1914–18, c. 800,000, 1939–45, c. 400,000
France   1914–18, c. 1.6 m., 1939–45, c. 700,000
Belgium   1914–18, c. 130,000, 1939–45, c. 80,000
Netherlands   1914–18, NIL   1939–45, c. 120,000
Italy   1914–18, c. 1.3 m., 1939–45, c. 400,000
Cf. Köllman, op. cit., pp. 149, 154, 159, and 167.

[10] Cf. H. Arntz (n. 9), pp. 444–7; Köllmann (n. 9) pp. 270, 227, and 232. Estimates of the losses of the Soviet Union are especially questionable: Stalin's statement at the Potsdam Conference that it 'had lost over 5 million people in this war' (*Foreign Relations of the United States. Diplomatic Papers: The Conference of Berlin*, vol. ii, Washington 1960, p. 386, cf. p. 299) only reflected provisional returns; on the other hand, the 13.6 million military casualties mentioned by a Russian Colonel Kalinov in 1948 (possibly with some exaggeration?) should not be added to the 7 million dead mentioned by Stalin on 13 March 1946, which may be an accurate figure (Arntz, p. 444). Because of this discrepancy, the total number of casualties for the world as a whole is uncertain.

produced.[11] As a UN Commission estimated in the summer of 1946, over 100 million Europeans had to live on a daily intake of fewer than 1,500 calories, i.e. they had to go hungry. Europe's grain imports rose from 19 million tons in 1938 to 27 million tons in 1946,[12] but its ability to export industrial goods in exchange had fallen sharply.

The European states had only managed a total growth of industrial production between 1919 and 1939 of about 40 per cent – compared with a rise of 150 per cent in the United States (and about 600 per cent from a low starting base in the Soviet Union) in the same period. The war caused a still further decline. In spite of all the American loans and of a restored European transport system, by the end of 1940 total industrial output amounted in Great Britain and Scandinavia to 105 per cent, in France and the Benelux countries 89 per cent, in South and East Europe about 60 per cent, in Germany 40 per cent of the pre-war total – whereas in the same period, 1938–46, industrial output in the USA rose by 210 per cent, i.e. more than trebled, and it now accounted for over half the world's production.[13]

The losses were apparent in the per capita distribution of the national income. Between 1938 and 1946 it had risen per head of population from an average of $420 to $580 in Great Britain, Switzerland, and Scandinavia, and had fallen from an average of $290 to $260 in France and Benelux, and in South and East Europe from $120 to $90. In the United States, however, it had risen from $550 to $1,260; that is, in round figures in Europe it had sunk from being about half the American average to a quarter.[14] Even more ominous were the figures of losses in the balance of trade. As early as 1938

---

[11] Grain production in 1946–7, compared with the pre-war level, was in Great Britain 156 per cent, in France 59 per cent, in Italy 68 per cent, in Germany 64 per cent. In Europe as a whole (ie. not including the Soviet Union) production of milk had fallen by 27 per cent, of butter by 30 per cent, of eggs by 37 per cent, all figures from: United Nations, *Economic Report 1945–1947*, New York, 1948, pp. 148–50. Cf. more details in O. Philip, *Le Problème de l'union européenne*, thesis, Paris, 1950, p. 45 f.

[12] United Nations, *Preliminary Report of the Temporary Sub-Commission on Economic Reconstruction of Devastated Areas* (E/156), New York, 1946, p. 26 f. Only for the West-European countries was a daily intake of 2,500 calories given as the average (85 per cent of the pre-war average), for the United States the average was 3,450 calories; Senate Foreign Relations Committee, *The European Recovery Program. Basic Documents,* Washington, 1947, pp. 12 and 20.

[13] Europe's coal production (including that of Great Britain, up by 7 per cent) amounted in 1946 to barely 73 per cent of the pre-war output (only 28 per cent of world production compared with 43 per cent); production of steel was only 55 per cent of pre-war. All figures from: *A Survey of the Economic Situation and Prospects of Europe, prepared by the Economic Commission for Europe,* UN Economic and Social Council, Geneva, March 1948, pp. 1–5, 10–12, and 124–30; and from United Nations, *Economic Report 1945–1947,* New York, 1948, pp. 124 and 131–41. Between 1941 and 1945 the Soviet Union had high rates of increase in its unoccupied eastern territories, which however were more than offset by dismantling or destruction in the occupied western territories, so that its total output in 1945 is estimated at about 90 per cent of pre-war (*A Survey . . .* p. 154 f.).

[14] This was a result of the rise of American production as well as of the fall of European. US figures in: *Economic Report of the President transmitted to the Congress,* Washington, Jan. 1948, pp. 109 and 113; Figures for the European countries in: *Foreign Assets and Liabilities of the United States and its Balance of International Transactions,* a *Report to the Senate Committee on Finance* by the National Advisory Council on International Monetary and Financial Problems, Washington, Dec. 1947 (pub. 1948), p. 131, and *Economic Report 1945–1947* (n. 13), p. 133 f.

the whole European balance of overseas trade showed a deficit of 2.1 billion dollars, and Europe had received an exactly equivalent sum from its overseas investments and services (especially shipping), so that its trade account was in balance. But in 1947 there was not only a trade deficit (in terms of the 1938 dollar) of 3.3 billion dollars (that is, a rise of over 50 per cent, less because of a rise in imports and decline in exports than because of a rise in the world price of raw materials); but a much more serious loss became apparent: many overseas investments were liquidated to pay for the cost of the war, the overseas services had for the most part ceased to exist (40 per cent of shipping had been sunk), so that in 1947 these invisible trade figures, instead of balancing the deficit on visible trade, were themselves a minus quantity; hence there was an enormous deficit in the European balance of trade.[15] Even though Marshall Aid and after 1948 economic co-operation in the OEEC would lead to a gradual closing of the dollar gap and to recovery in the traditional economic sectors, such a series of losses could not be recouped. When the atomic bombs dropped on Japan in August 1945 demonstrated the technological progress made in the meantime outside Europe, it was evident that none of the European countries after a loss of assets on that scale could on its own find the resources for the basic technology of the nuclear age.

There is no need for any lengthy explanation of the social consequences of these losses. The surviving population of the European Continent saw that it had suffered a severe set-back in its economic, social, and political progress. The fall in the per capita share of the national income already referred to shows the over-all extent of impoverishment in the decade 1938–48. The great movement in favour of civil rights, constitutional government, and social reform which had begun at least a century before and which had been strongly influenced by the effects on society and the standard of living produced by the industrial revolution had almost come to a standstill in Europe. Economic development, already stagnating between the wars, was regressive, and consequently little in the way of economic surplus was available for social purposes. The lack of progress was particularly evident in one of the chief indicators of the stage of development of an advanced industrial system with its division of labour, namely the proportion of those employed in agriculture on the one hand and those gainfully employed in modern service industries on the other: in almost all European countries the proportion of employed persons in agriculture was almost as high in 1948 as it had been in 1938 (24 per cent in what was to be the German Federal Republic), while the proportion of those employed in

---

[15] Two years after the end of the war in Europe the deficit reached the total of 16.7 billion dollars (according to the 1947 value of the dollar), a formidable amount by comparison with the gross national product; figures and facts in: *A Survey of the Economic Situation* (cf. n. 13), pp. 56–65; described by S. E. Harris, *The European Recovery Program*, Cambridge, Mass., 1948, pp. 46–52, 95–132; excellently summarized in E. Bonnefous, *L'Europe en face de son destin,* Paris, 1952, pp. 70–3. For the resulting 'dollar gap', balance of payments crisis of 1947, etc., in greater detail, see pp.157 f. and 470 f.

service industries had fallen (from 20 per cent to 17 per cent in the later Federal Republic). The middle classes were further impoverished; and the advance of the workers and white-collar employees to a middle-class standard of living was blocked.[16]

The extent and social consequences of the violent movements of population brought about by the Second World War need special emphasis. For two centuries the idea of linking changes in political borders to expulsion of the population had not been carried out in Europe because it was felt to be barbarous and a violation of human rights. Hitler, reviving the practice as a matter of course, reintroduced it on a large scale. In 1939–41 about 1.2 million Poles were 'resettled' from the Polish Corridor to the 'Generalgouvernement' (rump Polish territory including Warsaw and Cracow). 230,000 Slovaks and Czechs were transferred for the sake of 'racial purity' to the new Slovakia, 172,000 Bulgarians and Romanians were exchanged between North and South Dobrudja in the name of 'racial purity', 190,000 Serbs and Croats were exchanged between Serbia and Croatia, about 850,000 Germans were transferred from the East-European countries to the Polish Corridor, in the West 100,000 Lorrainers were expelled to France, 70,000 South Tyrolese were resettled away from their homeland. By the beginning of 1943 Germany had mobilized an army of about ten million men on all fronts. About 6.2 million people were evacuated from the big cities that were the targets of air raids. The number of prisoners of war working in Germany added to the total of foreign workers, most of whom were recruited as forced labour, exceeded 6 million by 1943 and in 1944 reached a peak of 8 million. Towards the end of the war, in a reverse process, millions of Baltic peoples fled from the advancing Soviet army or were deported by it; 2 million Poles moved from East to West. Then came the flight and expulsion of Germans from what in 1937 had been the German provinces East of the Oder–Neisse line, about 7 million of whom reached the Soviet and Western Occupation Zones (4.5 million in the later Federal Republic); and the flight or deportation of ethnic Germans from East-European countries, about 5 million of whom (more than half of the total being Sudeten Germans) reached the Soviet or Western Occupation Zones (3.1 million in the later Federal Republic). It is estimated that altogether in the areas of Europe affected by the war (that is, almost everywhere except Great Britain, Scandinavia, and the Iberian Peninsula) between 1940 and 1946 a total not far short of 50 million people were flung hither and thither as soldiers, resettlers, or deportees, a process 'which was unprecedented in scale and which produced

---

[16] Even after the recovery of the next two decades thanks to OEEC and EEC (almost a trebling of the gross national product per inhabitant, with in 1971 8.2 per cent of the population employed in agriculture, 25.7 per cent in service industries in the German Federal Republic), America's lead could not be overtaken. Cf. F. Below, 'Natürliche und soziale Strukturmerkmale Europäischer Völker' in: *Europa-Archiv*, 11 (1956), pp. 9290–5; R. Lepsius, 'Sozialstruktur und soziale Schichtung in der BRD' in: R. Löwenthal and H. P. Schwarz (ed.), *Die Zweite Republik*, Stuttgart, 1974, pp. 263–72; Statistical Office of the European Community, Luxemburg, 1972, pp. 22–6.

changes in the ethnic map of this quarter of the Old World such as had not been seen there since the *Völkerwanderung, c.*AD 375–675'.[17] Though this fate was sometimes described as 'a higher kind of mobility', yet the great majority of those displaced were socially uprooted after losing their homeland and cultural environment, their houses and possessions; and countless social communities were destroyed. They were the hardest-hit victims of the collapse of the nation states and the decline of Europe.

(C) TERRITORIAL LOSSES: THE BALKANIZATION OF EUROPE

The economic decline of Europe was also an important factor in bringing about a further major loss which Europeans came to realize as an irreversible consequence of the Second World War. From the seventeenth to the nineteenth century their technological superiority enabled Europeans to rule over the coloured races, and from this domination Europe's central role in the world evolved. In the First World War, however, European solidarity *vis-à-vis* the peoples of Asia and Africa was shattered; the native élites, though still small, had grasped the originally European principle of national self-determination as well as that of self-development. On American insistence Article 22 of the Covenant of the League of Nations in 1919 had spoken of the 'sacred trust of civilization' to lead all nations towards self-government, and had first promised the A Mandate states in the Near East that their existence as independent nations could be provisionally recognized 'subject to the rendering of administrative advice and assistance by a Mandatory until such time as they are able to stand alone'.[18] A Europe that had continued to prosper and had been politically united would have made it possible for self-government to develop on a federal basis and could at the same time have initiated a comprehensive programme of investment and development and have brought about cooperation in the interests of both sides. On the other hand, because Europe during the inter-war period clung against all reason to its nationalist antagonisms, was bogged down in economic division, could not afford to carry out its development programmes, and finally plunged into the Second World War, the movements in favour of self-determination and economic progress among the former colonial peoples were transformed into a struggle for revolutionary independence. In the second World War the political and military weakness of the then European major powers became obvious

[17] A. Toynbee, 'Introduction' in A. and V. Toynbee, *The Realignment of Europe (Survey of International Affairs, 1939–1946,* vol. 9), London, 1955, p. 4. Figures in E. M. Kulischer, *Europe on the Move,* New York, 1948, esp. table on p. 302 f., also Köllman (n. 9), pp. 204 f. and 185–8; on the Germans involved, see esp. W. Nellner, 'Grundlagen und Hauptergebnisse der Statistik' in E. Lemberg and F. Edding (ed.), *Die Vertriebenen in Westdeutschland,* 3 vols., Kiel, 1959, vol. i. For the wider implications of and conclusions to be drawn from this purely factual balance, see pp. 48–62 below.
[18] Text of the Covenant in *Nouveau Recueil général de traités,* série, iii, vol 11. Leipzig, 1922, pp.331–49, and in English in A. B. Keith (ed.), *Speeches and Documents on International Affairs, 1918–1937,* Oxford University Press, 1938, vol. i, pp. 9–23; quotations on pp. 334 and 344 of *Nouveau Recueil,* above.

(Singapore captured by the Japanese!). An additional factor was their rapidly deteriorating economic situation: the cutting-off of European industrial exports for over five years drove already independent or Commonwealth countries such as Brazil, Canada, South Africa, and Australia, but also European administrations in still dependent countries such as India, Morocco, and Nigeria, to press on with the building-up of their own industries, so that by 1946 all of these countries combined produced close on 10 per cent of the world's industrial output. Very little of the capital needed came from Europe, which on the contrary had liquidated its overseas investments to pay for the war and had had to let many of its invisible exports (shipping, insurance, banking) pass into non-European hands, most of which relied on American capital. But above all the two new world powers which dominated Europe came down on the side of the independence movements and managed to insert Article 73 into the United Nations Charter, which in principle promised free political institutions and self-government to all dependent territories.[19] The restored European governments failed for some time to realize which of these decisions were more than paper promises. Great Britain granted independence to India, Burma, and Ceylon in 1946, while overrating those Commonwealth links which remained. In Malaya, the Gold Coast, and Cyprus, as by France in the case of Indo-China, Madagascar, and Morocco, military force was used against independence movements. Two years later the countries of the Near East had virtually gained independence and the Netherlands, with some diplomatic urging from the Americans, had had to give up Indonesia. Yet as late as 1950 the European colonial powers (Britain, France, Belgium, the Netherlands, and Portugal) were still governing about 55 million Asians and about 115 million Africans, altogether about 174 million people or half as many again as the population of the mother countries. Their sense of being colonial powers prevented these countries in the first decisive years of the European unification movement from understanding what had become inevitable.[20] A decade later, however, all their possessions, with a few minor exceptions which were almost more of a liability than an asset, had disappeared. It is

---

[19] On this international development of first-rate importance for the twentieth century, which is indicated here only as a background factor and in broad outline, and to which little reference can be made in subsequent chapters, see summary in R. von Albertini, *Dekolonisation. Die Diskussion über Verwaltung und Zukunft der Kolonien 1919–1960*, Cologne, 1966; F. Ansprenger, *Die Auflösung der Kolonialreiche* (dtv Weltgeschichte des 20ten Jahrhunderts), Munich, 1973²; R. von Albertini, *Moderne Kolonialgeschichte* (= NWB 39) Cologne, 1970, p. 33, rightly emphasizing the role of the two world wars as 'accelerating factors'.

[20] Cf. the books mentioned in n. 19. During the war some authors active in the Resistance movements who supported a European federation urged early liberation for the colonies (cf. Lipgens, *Föderationspläne*. See 'Colonies' in Index, e.g. Romein in No. 104: 'Beibehaltung unmöglich und unrechtmässig'); the few voices raised in opposition to European federation had objected mainly by referring to colonial possessions (e.g. No. 107: 'How is it proposed to force a country like ours [the Netherlands], whose territory is spread over four continents, into the strait-jacket of a European Confederation?'). For contributions to the sequel to this discussion by European federalists from 1945 to 1950, cf. the Subject Index (in vol. 2) under the heading 'Colonies'.

fruitless to speculate how much more smoothly European unification in its first decisive stage would have proceeded if the almost total loss of empire had occurred, and had been seen to occur, at the same time as all the other losses arising from the Second World War, instead of taking a further fifteen years to complete. The fact is, however, that as a result of the war, the overseas areas ruled by Europeans were rapidly escaping from their control, and the Europeans were pushed back to the territorial limits which had been theirs at the beginning of the modern age.

A more depressing liability in the balance sheet of 1945 was the severe loss of Europe's own territory, the forcing back of its eastern border, a process of reduction whose ultimate limits no one at the time could foresee. The results of its cultural expansion eastwards, which had begun centuries before its overseas expansion, were almost completely reversed, wiped out, or suppressed. Its frontiers – as will be shown in more detail – particularly on the eastern flank had been fluid, not fixed. Ever since the tenth century the Western Slav tribes, the Scandinavians, and the Hungarians had been full members of the European cultural family. And even beyond the frontiers of Eastern Poland and the Carpathians not only was the influence of Europe felt in at least two epochs, between the tenth and the twelfth century and between the sixteenth and the nineteenth, but its culture had been effectively extended to the neighbouring Eastern Slav territories.

In the tenth and eleventh centuries unmistakable early European beginnings of a Christian urban culture, social differentiation, and urban self-government had developed on an economic foundation of trade and handicraft, in the Eastern Slav territory occupying the depression of the Upper Dnepr and the Northern Lovat and extending from Novgorod to Kiev and particularly in the Kievan state under Varangian rule – whereas to the east of that area, in the basin of the Don and the Upper Volga (the later Moscow region), the nomadic Asiatic peoples of the Avars, Khazars, and Meria were predominant. Hemmed in by these tribes on the South-East, Eastern Slav princelings had colonized the Upper Volga area in the twelfth century, while the kingdom of Kiev had fallen into political disunity and urban decay. But in the thirteenth century this whole budding civilization had collapsed under the catastrophe of the great Mongol invasion. In the second wave of invasions, between 1237 and 1240 'the tidal flood in the end covered almost the entire territory of the Russian princes', made them a part of the Tatar–Eurasian kingdom, and cut them off for centuries from all cultural links with the West; and the rule of the Mongols, which lasted 200 years in North Russia and 500 years in South Russia, had 'far-reaching influence', 'most lasting consequences' especially for the country's political and social structures, including on the whole a 'development of the Eastern Slavs away from Europe', combined as it was with a narrowly nationalist version of the Byzantine imperial idea.[21] On the other hand, the Baltic lands were not only permeated with a Catholic form of Christianity and a more

[21] Quotations from the two most important summaries: B. Spuler, 'Die Goldene Horde und Russlands Schicksal' in *Saeculum,* 6 (1955), pp. 399 f. and 406; G. Stökl, 'Russland und Europa vor Peter dem Grossen' in *Historische Zeitschrift (HZ),* 184 (1957), pp. 536 and 544. For Kiev Russia, cf. the most recent account by M. Hellmann, with list of the most important literature, in C. Goehrke, M.

14 *Introduction*

stratified European type of urban culture, but after the weakening of Mongol rule the Lithuanian–Polish Jagiellonian kingdom from the end of the fourteenth to the end of the eighteenth century had included the western part of White Russia and the Western Ukraine, converted most of the population to the Uniat Church, and reunited these territories up to the eastern border of Vitebsk along the Dnepr as far as Kiev with the European civilized world. But even in the rising Grand Duchy of Moscow (officially a Tsardom from the sixteenth century onwards), situated in the territory formerly colonized by Eastern Slavs, contacts with the West had gradually been resumed. This involved the extension of European cultural influence, not only through growing colonies of settlers from the West but also through indigenous if rudimentary elements of Reformation, Counter-Reformation, and Humanism. The later acquisition of European skills in the reign of Peter the Great amounted altogether to a confrontation of European and non-European influences. It is true that political structures in particular had remained consistently 'un-European' in consequence of the 'brutal destruction of all attempts to develop a society based on regional power' and the permanent ban on self-governing estates or towns by the absolute autocracy of the Tsar. Yet largely because of Russia's westward expansion, including her annexation of Baltic and Polish territories between 1721 and 1795, the Tsars, with the willing assistance of the Baltic and Polish nobility, had encouraged the cultural Europeanization of the small aristocratic upper class and called on Baltic and German settlers to help with the opening-up of Russia. Thus by the nineteenth century the impact of European civilization had reached as far as the lower Volga region thanks to enlightened noblemen's estates and communities of immigrant settlers.[22]

It is well to remember these facts if only to avoid any possible misconceptions, such as the view that the Eastern Slav regions should be seen as completely outside the borders of historic Europe, or refusal to recognize their early membership of Europe along their frontier with the people of the steppes. Nor would one wish to deny the strength of the Europeanizing forces in Tsarist Russia – just the opposite. Yet however much importance is ascribed to the historic 'mediatory' role of the original Eastern Slav heartlands on the Upper Dnepr and to the later process of Europeanization – it all came to an end in consequence of the Bolshevik Revolution. During the Revolution of 1917 and the subsequent civil war the 'Westernizers', the thin upper layer of the aristocracy and upper middle class, who had been the main source of European influence, were almost entirely uprooted. Moreover, all 'bourgeois elements', substantial farmers, men of property, and believing

---

Hellmann, R. Lorenz, and P. Scheibert, *Russland* (Fischer, Weltgeschichte, vol. 31), Frankfurt, 1972, pp. 30–75 (esp. also the maps on pp. 28 and 66). On the consequences of the Mongol invasion, see p. 27 for further details.

[22] The quotation is from Stökl (n. 21), p. 549. A brief and instructive introduction to these marginal problems is given by O. Halecki, *The Limits and Divisions of European History,* London and NY, 1950, esp. Chapter V: 'The Geographical Limits: (b) The Great Eastern Isthmus', pp. 85–101. Halecki's general thesis, however, is that the eastern frontier of Poland coincides with that of historic Poland and Uniat Christianity, whereas we are concerned here to emphasize the extension of European culture to include the Eastern and Orthodox Slavs. For a more detailed analysis, which can be undertaken only after it has been shown how that culture was understood and redefined in our decades, see pp. 25–32.

Christians were eliminated as further potential 'transmission points' of European influence. Under Stalin any remaining European liberal and Christian values were completely replaced by a totalitarian type of Asiatic despotism, an autocratic regime ruling over masses completely deprived of civil rights, a closely integrated Soviet empire whose basic features did not meet the most elementary requirements of European civilization in any essential respect.

The reality of Stalin's regime showed that nothing whatever remained of the measures taken under the Tsarist government to introduce liberal human rights, representative institutions, freedom of learning, and the beginnings of a pluralistic society. Instead, they had all been rejected on principle. As will be made clear, no champion of the concept of European unification during the inter-war years or the period 1945-50 considered the Soviet empire a potential member of a European union. This was ruled out by the very nature of European civilization, as was obvious to any observer.[23]

Having said that, it must be recorded that the area included in Stalin's empire at the beginning and still more at the end of the Second World War was vastly extended and the area remaining to Europe was correspondingly reduced. In 1917, reacting against the October Revolution, all the East-European territories previously annexed by Russia – the Baltic states, Poland, and Finland – which for years before had organized their own passive resistance to the policy of Russification – declared their full independence as democratic nation states. Their ability to maintain that independence resulted from their successful wars of defence between 1918 and 1921. Thus they escaped Soviet rule and remained within the bounds of European civilization, with Poland recovering White Russian and Ukrainian territories up to a frontier-line which more or less corresponded with that of the Second Partition of 1793. But in 1939 Stalin had seized the opportunity of reverting to the power politics of Imperial Russia. Hitler, who in historical perspective appears as his accomplice, took the decisive step towards surrendering Europe's eastern frontier when he agreed to let the Soviet Union have Estonia, Latvia, the eastern half of Poland, and Bessarabia. The process was completed by Stalin when he managed finally to incorporate all these territories, together with the whole of Lithuania and the northern

---

[23] Cf. below, sections 2(A) 'Redefining European Civilization' and (B) 'The Frontiers of European Civilization'. Let anyone who has doubts on this important point read these sections carefully and then come back from the arguments there presented to the statement about Stalin's empire quoted above and he will, it is hoped, find it justified. What has been said about retrogression in the USSR does not, of course, apply to purely technical industrialization, which has taken place also in Japan and the ex-colonial territories; on the other hand, it is not out of the question that elements of Europeanization which have been driven underground may reassert themselves at some time in the future. For a general interpretation, cf. esp. G. Stökl, *Russische Geschichte von den Anfängen bis zur Gegenwart,* Stuttgart, 1973³.

half of East Prussia, into the Soviet Union.[24] The ethnic map was made to agree with the new frontiers by the wholesale expulsion of populations, thus putting an end to the degree of Europeanization that already existed.

Estonians, Latvians, and Lithuanians as well as Germans from East Prussia and the Baltic, those who had not already fled across the Baltic or into what remained of Germany (about 2 millions), were deported *en masse* into the interior of Russia and replaced by settlers from Great Russia, so that their national life was almost extinguished. Like 450,000 Finns from Karelia (which was annexed to the Soviet Union), about 2 million Poles (including those from the Ukraine) were driven westwards. In the whole of the Ukraine 'western' elements were persecuted (at the end of 1945 over half the 2,700 priests and bishops of the Ukrainian Catholic Church were in prison). If one adds the westward shift of Poland enforced by Stalin so as to include the German eastern provinces up to the Oder–Neisse line, and the expulsion of about 7 million German citizens from this territory, the total result was, in Arnold Toynbee's words, 'to cancel the ethnic effects of a thousand years of German, Polish and Lithuanian conquest and colonization and to restore the ethnic map to something like the status quo *ante* AD 1200'.[25]

With these expulsions of what had been European populations Europe in 1945 experienced in the most direct way the pressure of an extra-European empire in the East, the reversal of an expansion which had lasted almost exactly a thousand years, and the loss of the frontier territory in the Baltic, White Russia, and the Western Ukraine, which had, with scarcely any interruption, formed part of European civilization. Europe's eastern frontier had been forced back to a line starting at Danzig (Gdańsk) and continuing slightly east of Warsaw as far as the Carpathians. Europe's land area had been narrowed and reduced by an area measuring on an average 400 km wide and 2,000 km long from the Gulf of Finland to the Black Sea. Moreover, Russia's imperial and hegemonistic claims went even further; between 1945 and 1949 the East-European countries, as a result of an enforced take-over of power in stages, were brought completely under Russian influence and bolshevized up to a line about another 750 km further west running from Stettin (Szczecin) to Trieste; in consequence no European in 1945 could be sure how far the European traditions of those countries would be able to survive.[26]

[24] Cf. for a general survey E. Lemberg, *Osteuropa und die Sowjetunion,* Stuttgart, 1950; H. Roos, *A History of Modern Poland,* London, 1966; C. A. Macartney and A. W. Palmer, *Independent Eastern Europe,* London, 1962; J. Rothschild, *East Central Europe between the two World Wars,* Seattle/Washington, 1974. For further details of allied wartime diplomacy and Soviet post-war planning in the Second World War, see p. 68 f. below.
[25] Toynbee, 'Introduction' (n. 17), p. 7. Cf. N. D. Czubatyi, 'Ukraine between Poland and Russia', in *The Review of Politics,* 8, 1946, pp. 331–53 (numbers of priests on p. 352); statistics of population in E. M. Kulischer, *Europe on the Move,* New York, 1948, p. 302 f.
[26] Cf. H. Seton-Watson, *The East European Revolution,* London, 1950; E. Birke and R. Neumann, *Die Sowjetisierung Ost-Mitteleuropas,* Frankfurt/Berlin, 1959; G. Bartsch, *Revolution und Gegenrevolution in Osteuropa 1948–1968,* Bonn, 1971, all with detailed booklists on sovietization of the East-European countries. For Soviet policy in more detail, see esp. chap. II/1, pp. 283–6; for Europe's self-defence

What remained of Europe, however, now occupied by the two new world powers, was a divided power vacuum compared with the potential and resources of these continental-sized powers. For the first time in its modern history Europe suffered an overwhelming loss of territory. Furthermore, inasmuch as the two world powers (in the Russian case most deliberately) restored Europe's traditional political system of small national states, Europe seemed in the long run doomed to remain a divided no man's land of the Balkan type, the object of a sphere-of-influence policy exercised by the two extra-European powers. This was the real situation with which Europeans had to come to terms. Although it was not yet fully understood in London or Paris, and although the Soviet Union was not yet a world power of fully equal standing with the United States, the actual predominance of the two new superpowers was a fact beyond doubt. It had taken only one generation between 1914 and 1945 for what had been the most prosperous and powerful continent to arrive at a state of complete impotence, brought about by itself.

The essential facts of 1945 were incisively summed up by Toynbee in 1945:

After the First World War the vast area in Central and Eastern Europe that was now occupied by a mosaic of weak successor states was, in fact, one enormous power vacuum; and the question how this vacuum was eventually going to be filled was the fundamental question of European power politics between the two world wars ... Germany and the Soviet Union were the only two great powers of the day whose geographical location and native strength gave either of them a chance of being able to make itself still stronger by incorporating the whole cluster of successor states in its own body politic ... The disintegration of Hitler's Europe ... created a far greater power vacuum in Europe than had been produced by the events of 1875–8, or even by those of 1912–18. The vacuum now extended over the whole of Continental Europe ... divided into two camps, each under the command of an extra-European world power. Thus the realignment of Europe after the Second World War was a change from the unity that had been imposed by German conquest to a partition into two spheres; and this partition was the consequence of the victorious powers' inability to maintain the unity of the Continent that had been their defeated adversary's sole, but signal, constructive achievement. Hitler's forcible military, political and economic unification of Europe had been a practical answer to Europe's most pressing need ... it was, nevertheless, a grave misfortune for Europe that part of the price of her release from German tyranny should have been the loss of the one great benefit that this tyranny had brought with it. The misfortune was the greater considering that, in all the European countries, except Finland, that found themselves on the Russian side of the line by which Hitler's Europe was partitioned into two spheres, the change was merely the substitution of a Russian tyranny for a German one. But the greatest misfortune of all was that the new alignment of

---

and the beginning of the impulse for European unification in the East-European countries, see esp. chap. II/7, pp. 441–57.

Europe, resulting from the victory of Germany's adversaries, disappointed the hopes that had sustained Hitler's victims and opponents throughout the war...[27]

2. Europe's Self-Awareness:

I. The Unity of Civilization and Economic Necessity

Europe's decline within one generation from the hitherto most powerful continent to an impotent land mass, severely truncated in the East, internally divided, and partitioned into spheres of influence between the two new superpowers, was by 1945 an accomplished fact and the main political result of the two world wars. It coincided, however, with another development – the Europeans' growing sense of unity, a sentiment hardly recognized and categorically ignored by the world powers in 1945, but clearly something of fundamental importance for anyone with a long-term view, particularly a view taking into account the events of the years 1942 to 1947. Millions of Europeans had experienced in their own lives their continent's rapid decline. The inability of the nation states to provide welfare and security within their own borders had been shown during the inter-war period. Moreover the second ordeal of a still more terrible European civil war had completely shattered the ideal of the nation state and had confirmed the view, already voiced by a growing number of intellectuals, that the European nations, outclassed in military technology, economically impoverished, and dwarfed by the new superpowers, were bound to unite. Only if they combined could the nations of Europe have a future.

This self-examination had initially begun among a small group of European intellectuals during the First World War. Appalled by the catastrophe – a wholly new kind of experience – they had developed a new kind of answer. This should not be construed as simply a continuation of earlier European plans for unification.[28] Rather it arose from a passionately renewed awareness, at a time of acute external threat, of the centuries-old unity of European civilization and its values. The starting-point of this intellectual renewal must be briefly described, if only to indicate the direction in which answers should be sought to questions crucial to the theme of European unity which, however, cannot be treated at any length in this book. Thanks to recent research, the redefinition of Europe as a civilization has enabled us to speak with fresh conviction about its boundaries. There also grew up between the wars a political movement in favour of European unification in the form of organized pressure groups. This movement reached a peak when it spelt out its objects in considerable detail in docu-

---

[27] Toynbee, 'Introduction' (n. 17), pp. 16 f. and 19. Unfortunately few historians have summarized the main result of the Second World War with such force and clarity. On the hopes of the Resistance groups, cf. pp. 44–62.
[28] For these, see Section 2(C), p. 35, n. 46.

ments produced by the Resistance movement during the Second World War. Here too the insights and arguments produced by this European self-examination as it had evolved since 1914 must be looked at closely.

(A) REDEFINING EUROPEAN CIVILIZATION

The outbreak of the First World War left many people horrified at the bloodbath it caused among the civilized and supposedly progressive nations, and they demanded better guarantees of peace for the future. One of the first to react in this way was Jules Romains, who in 1915 called 'this war ... an armed conflict at the heart of a homogeneous civilization' and spoke of a 'fratricidal war'.[29] Yet only after the war was over did people become conscious of the full extent of the catastrophe, realizing that the war had brought a loss of welfare and security for winners as well as losers, and that it meant the same thing for all European nations. No one put it more forcefully than Paul Valéry, whose book, *La Crise de l'esprit*, published in 1919, was widely read and was translated into every major language.

> We civilized peoples of Europe now know that we are mortal. We had heard of entire worlds that disappeared completely, of empires that suddenly foundered with all their inhabitants and artefacts ... their gods and their laws ... But these disasters, after all, did not concern us. Elam, Nineveh, Babylon were only glamorous names ... Now we see that the abyss of history has room for everyone ... Everyone is aware of the danger. An unprecedented shudder has seized Europe to its very marrow. Europe has felt in its nerve-centres that it has become unrecognizable, that it has ceased to resemble itself, that it was about to lose consciousness ... Then, as if in desperate defence of its very nature, its physiological substance, the fullness of its memories came flooding back in confusion ... In response to this same anguish, civilized Europe has experienced the swift revival of its inexhaustible wealth of ideas ...[30]

There had thus begun among the more thoughtful intellectuals a passionate search for a self-awareness of Europe, a look back at the past, and a thorough investigation into what European civilization really consisted of, a conscious rediscovery of the unity of European values as an indispensable preliminary to the political unification which was beginning to seem imperative. Valéry himself, speaking at Zurich in 1922, gave his well-known formulation of the essential basis of European unity: what had enabled the small European part of the human race, living on a narrow

---

[29] The quotation from Romains and much else is in G. Bonneville, *Prophètes et témoins de l'Europe. Essai sur l'idée d'Europe dans la littérature française de 1914 à nos jours*. Leyden (Aspects Européens A/5), 1961, p. 142 f. Cf. brief summary of opinions which already began to demand Europe's political unification during the First World War, see Section 2C, n. 48.

[30] P. Valéry, *La Crise de l'esprit*, Paris, 1929, quoted in D. de Rougemont, *Europa vom Mythos zur Wirklichkeit*, Munich, 1962, p. 307; similar passages in the latter's chapter 'Everyone felt the decline', pp. 303–16; special emphasis is given in A. Demangeon, *Le Déclin de l'Europe*, Paris, 1920; the English title of O. Spengler's well-known work is *The Decline of the West*, London, 1934.

segment of the globe compared with the total habitable area, to achieve for over a thousand years and by its own efforts all the essential progress of civilization was the combination of Greek rationalism, Roman law, and the striving for individual responsibility inculcated by the Christian Gospel. Many people began, like Keyserling in his *Spectrum of Europe,* to understand 'the different elements shown by the spectrum as essential components of a single body... in view of the growing proximity and overwhelming numbers of non-European humanity'.[31] In opposition to nationalist parochialism there evolved in various fields of knowledge a European point of view: it cropped up here and there in the 1920s and after the Second World War it made considerable headway. It was manifested in law in the efforts to subordinate a sovereignty based on positivism to a common law of nature, in theology in a *rapprochement* between the Church and secular civilization, in the rise of the ecumenical movement, and in other ways.[32]

Historians began to point out that the decentralized aristocratic society of Europe in early centuries had shared common values and a common social structure before the slow emergence of nations as language-based entities; that Europe, with all its intellectual currents, styles, and achievements, social structures and developments, had formed a civilized community for centuries; and that its educated classes had always been conscious of this before the growth of nationalism in the second half of the nineteenth century caused people to speak in a retrograde fashion of separate 'national cultures'. In liberating itself from an anachronistic, pre-dated view of history based on nation states, historical science has since shown how much European history since its inception has consisted of fruitful exchanges between ideas and realities common to the whole Continent on the one hand, and local or regional peculiarities and realities on the other.[33] One

---

[31] P. Valéry, *Variétés,* vol. i, Paris, 1924, pp. 35 ff. (1922 speech); Count A. Keyserling, *Das Spektrum Europas,* Stuttgart, (1928) 1931, pp. 371 and 373. Hitherto the most useful existing anthology of these opinions drawn from all countries of Europe, specially those of Jules Romains, Hugo von Hofmannathal, Guglielmo Ferrero, Christopher Dawson, and others, is in de Rougement (n. 30), pp. 317–400. Also L. Ziegler, *Der europäische Geist,* Darmstadt, 1929; J. Benda and others, *L'Avenir de l'esprit européen,* Paris, 1934, and many others. Cf. the titles of books which continue this basic line of thought in the years 1945–50, in chap I of this book, nn. 308–17.

[32] Cf. H. Kelsen, *Das Problem der Souveränität und die Theorie des Völkerrechts,* Tübingen, 1920; A. Weber, *Die Krise des modernen Staatsgedankens in Europa,* Stuttgart, 1925 (very forceful); H. Jahrreis, *Europa als Rechtseinheit,* Leipzig, 1929 (still with some reservation); the renewal of Christian natural law in the books by J. P. Steffes, H. Rommen, etc.; R. Guardini, 'Das Erwachen der Kirche in der Seele' in *Hochland,* 19 (1921/2), p. 257, the substantial collection of essays: *Wiederbegegnung von Kirche und Kultur in Deutschland* (for K. Muth on his sixtieth birthday), Munich, 1927; K. Kraus and the Brenn Circle, etc. Needless to say between the wars nationalists in history, positivists in jurisprudence, and the 'narrowly orthodox school' in theology etc. remained in the majority.

[33] E. Rosenstock-Wittig, *Das Alter der Kirche,* Berlin, 1927; R. Wallach, *Das abendländische Gemeinschaftsbewusstsein im Mittelalter,* Leipzig, 1929; J. Fischer, *Oriens-Occidens-Europa. Begriff und Gedanke 'Europa' in der Spätantike und im frühen Mittelalter,* Wiesbaden, 1957; G. Tellenbach: *Kaisertum, Papsttum, und Europa im Hohen Mittelalter,* and O. Brunner, *Das innere Gefüge des Abendlandes,* both in *Historia Mundi,* 6 (1958), pp. 9–103 and 310–85; W. Fritzemeyer, *Christenheit und Europa. Zur Geschichte des europäischen Gemeinschaftsgefühls von Dante bis Leibniz,* Munich, 1931; F. Chabod, *Der*

thing became clearer: from Castile to Poland and from Scotland to Hungary there circulated during the Middle Ages and since, through the centuries of the modern age, a stream of connections and developments, of styles and phases, of art and literature, of philosophical and political ideas, of unity and diversity. All the great intellectual and social currents continually flowed through all the peoples who formed part of this civilized world; they were common to all Europeans, and to them only. In music, painting, and sculpture, in poetry and learning all important forms, materials, and themes, appearing in various parts of Europe, were modified to suit national differences and transmitted in a similar cycle of style and development. In this sense too of exercising a common influence Europe remained a unity even when, during the nineteenth century, some of the educated classes ceased to base their values on Christian beliefs, while as one of the consequences of the industrial revolution the franchise was extended to the mass of the population. Just as in the past all the great movements had, each in its day, swept through the whole of Europe – Cluniac reform of the monasteries, Scholasticism, the Crusades, the founding of cities, humanism, the Reformation, the Enlightenment, and the scientific revolution – this is no less true of the movements and schools of thought of the nineteenth century which apart from temporary delays were able to range freely across the whole of Europe. Such were liberalism, conservatism, and Socialism, romanticism and realism, industrialization and democratization, loss of faith or recovery of faith, and finally nationalism, which was least of all a 'national speciality', but rather an international phenomenon that affected the whole Continent.

As early as 1929 Ortega y Gasset was able to conclude:

If we were to take an inventory of our mental stock today – opinions, standards, desires, assumptions – we should discover that the greater part does not come to the Frenchman from France, nor to the Spaniard from Spain, but to both of them from the common European stock. Today in fact we are more influenced by what is European in us than by what is special to us as Frenchmen, Spaniards, and so on ... four-fifths of the average European's spiritual wealth is the common property of Europe....[34]

Europagedanke, Stuttgart, 1963; D. Gerhard, 'Regionalismus und ständisches Wesen als ein Grundthema europäischer Geschichte', *HZ,* 174, (1952), pp. 307-37; J. B. Duroselle, *L'Idée d'Europe dans l'histoire,* Paris, 1965. Cf. also n. 38.

[34] J. Ortega y Gasset, *The Revolt of the Masses,* London, 1961 (reprinted), p. 137. Instead of mentioning a large number of single titles the reader is referred to a monumental compendium now in process of appearing: T. Schieder (ed.), *Handbuch der Europäischen Geschichte,* vols. 1-7, Stuttgart, 1968 ff., in which parts of each volume emphasize common European features (with numerous references). The reader is also referred to the comprehensive histories of European art, architecture, drama, ideas, the theatre, law, etc. which appeared in the 1920s, and again in the 1950s in great profusion. On the other hand, it must be borne in mind that in the political sphere the development of the territorial and monarchical nation state led to particularisms which left little room for the intellectual and cultural unity of Europe to express itself politically. Nevertheless federalism and a supranational order always remained as future tasks of which people were conscious even in the political sphere: cf. p. 35 f.

But more important than the rediscovery of Europe's common heritage in all its many facets were the efforts to grasp the essential values and seminal ideas which lay at the root of this diversity. The following four basic principles can be described as the most generally accepted European standards. They are certainly shared by the whole of humanity, but as standards have shaped European civilization alone for over a millennium despite periodic reverses. European writers know well enough that there have been periods of their history when one or other of these standards has not been upheld, but their restoration was always demanded by subsequent generations. Consequently they were of crucial importance for Europe's image of itself and for the self-understanding of the movement for unification after 1945.

1. Respect for the human personality, the freedom and dignity of the individual; the principle of individual responsibility constantly enjoined by Christian teaching, developed into a concept of personal freedom in voluntary association, freedom of the will and of vocation, expanded into the principles of pluralism and tolerance, democratic government and self-determination – all concepts unknown in Asia and Africa except as the result of European influence. As Montesquieu observed in his *Lettres persanes* – a book in other ways so critical of Europe – 'Outside Europe no power of imagination can help one to understand that anything except despotism exists on this earth' (Letter 131). This point was especially emphasized in the Resistance movements against Hitler: it was a question of freedom and human rights against totalitarianism, and this necessarily applied as well against the Soviet Union. When after the Second World War five European states in the Brussels Pact of 1948 for the first time assured one another of their 'close community of interests' and the 'need to unite', the governments concerned – again for the first time – included in the preamble such significant definitions as the following: they promised 'to strengthen and reaffirm their belief in fundamental human rights, in the dignity and worth of the human personality, to fortify and preserve the principles of democracy, personal and political freedom and the constitutional traditions and the rule of law which are their common heritage'. One of the principal aims of the movement for European union, the protection of individual rights to an extent not known in other parts of the world, led to the adoption of the European Convention on Human Rights as the first piece of legislation enacted by the Council of Europe at Strasburg.

In her widely read book *The West at Bay* (1948) Barbara Ward put it like this:

> In European civilization there emerges for the first time the concept of man as a supreme being, unique in his personality ... it was this revolutionary conception of human personality that succeeded, little by little, in establishing the no less revolutionary doctrine that government existed for the citizen, not the citizen for the all-powerful state. The sense of the unique character of each human spirit reinforced the notion of his rights derived from a superior natural law and was the

driving faith behind the origins of modern democracy. From it was also derived the belief hardly found outside the brief span of Western society, that men should be associated with their own government and should achieve true freedom by being governed, in so far as government was necessary, by themselves. . . .[35]

2. Respect for small communities and their right to self-government; a basic regard, inherited from the early Germanic tribes, for a politically vigorous regionalism based on Europe's rich diversity of peninsulas, islands, mountain ranges, and valleys; the principle of the interdependent rights of the estates of the realm, organized and represented for centuries – something recognized, as has been shown, even in 'absolute' monarchies, and that of self-governing towns which by way of city states became part of the democratic representative system; the acknowledgement of inherent rights which were to be exercised 'as far down the scale as possible' within the framework of regional government and estates and which formed a barrier against totalitarianism. As the Theses of the Dutch federalist movement, Europeesche Actie, which formed the basis of the Hertenstein Programme, stated in 1946: 'Europe's mission does not lie only in the intellectual sphere; it lies just as much in the sphere where political and economic life is shaped. It is part of its very essence that one has to seek the wealth of diversity and to reject the overwhelming pressure in favour of uniformity . . . ; that one rejects the postulate of a tyrannical community as much as one rejects the kind of abstract individualism which would like to release man from all communal ties. The political expression of this attitude is federalism.'

At what was its real founding congress in Brussels at the beginning of 1949 the 'European Movement', made up of both federalists and 'unionists', issued the following statement:

All of us believe in a rule of law which is independent of the State and which at the same time provides the foundations and fixes the limits of State authority. We believe that human personality is sacrosanct and that the fundamental liberties attaching to it must be guaranteed against all forms of totalitarianism. We further believe that the individual exists only in relation to his fellows and as a member of organic communities. Such communities must, within the limits of their competence, enjoy a considerable degree of autonomy, provided always that the necessary

---

[35] The Brussels Five-Power Treaty of 17 March 1948 in *United Nations Treaty Series*, vol. 19, No. 304, pp. 51–63, quotation p. 52 f.; European Convention for the Defence of Human Rights and Basic Freedom, text, ibid., pp. 515–32; for the origins of both, cf. chap. V (in Vol. 2). B. Ward, *The West at Bay*, London, 1948, pp. 224–5; she adds: 'The deep sense of the necessary limitations of government, which Western society has usually exhibited, springs from another fundamental concept of the Western world – that man is fallible as well as magnificent and that the dignity of the human person is only equalled by its capacity for sin . . . [There is also] the existence of an order of right and wrong, and good and evil, from which these rights are derived and which transcends man and society. These ideas have been among the principal ferments in Western society, making it the most rich and expansive and dynamic society mankind has ever seen.'

24   *Introduction*

collective discipline is maintained. Finally, we believe that the concept of democracy implies freedom of criticism and therefore the right of opposition. . . .[36]

3. Respect for objective truth, the belief, deeply rooted in Christian and Greek conviction, that truth can be objective; the will, derived from that conviction, to arrive at objective truth in all spheres and to subject all scientific knowledge to unceasing criticism, among the fruits of which were both technical research and the Enlightenment; a devotion to truth, already present in the work of Thomas Aquinas, developed in the flowering of the sciences and in the methods of thinking and judging which distinguish the European spirit from all other civilizations: the principle that the standard of truth and consequently the obligation to tell the truth has precedence over any kind of party or group discipline.

As the Brussels Congress of the 'European Movement' in February 1949 declared:

> Love of freedom, hostility to totalitarianism of every kind, the humble and conscientious search for truth, and, above all, respect for the human personality and for the individual as an individual – these are essential characteristics of the true spirit of Europe. From them there springs, not a grudging toleration of diversity, but a glad recognition of its merit. These moral values, which are the product of two thousand years of civilization and were reaffirmed in the resistance to Nazism and Fascism, must inspire the organisation of Europe. . . .

4. The sense of social responsibility for the weak springing from respect for the individual; the basic principles of help and protection, of justice and human brotherhood; hence the awareness of Europe's mission, a universalism that seeks to understand and penetrate the civilizations of other peoples and includes as its final goal the unification of mankind; a willingness to give and to create, applied to a world in which most other civilizations have rested on the wholly contrary principles of immutable castes, which no one is allowed to leave or enter, of closed frontiers and xenophobia.[37]

---

[36] On the Theses of Europeesche Actie, cf. more detailed treatment in chap.| 1/2, pp. 137–41. Published as leaflet: European Movement, *Principles of European Policy*. Statement adopted at the meeting of the International Council, Brussels, February 1949 (4 pp., printed New Southgate). In the historiography, see esp. (with book-list) D. Gerhard, 'Regionalismus und ständisches Wesen als ein Grundthema europäischer Geschichte' in *HZ*, 174 (1952), pp. 307–37. As early as the beginning of 1940 the Swiss Europa-Union in a striking definition of the 'basic elements' of the European 'unity of civilization and destiny' emphasized as second only to the idea of individual freedom and the idea of humanity that: 'The development of Western civilization springs from the free, true community, which in forming its political will was dependent on the free moral sense of responsibility of individual members of the community. It was on the basis of original popular freedom that the communities of citizens in the small state of the ancient world and of the Middle Ages became capable of their achievements in building up civilization.' (W. Lipgens, *Europa-Föderationspläne der Widerstandsbewegungen 1940–1945*. Munich, 1968, p. 345). Cf. the incisive definitions of D. de Rougemont and the UEF Congress at Montreux, 1947, in chap III/4 at nn. 309 and 313.

[37] EM Archives, Bruges, Minutes of Brussels Congress, 28 Feb. 1949. The basic concept of Europeanness, as redefined after the First World War, cannot be treated exhaustively in this

In such terms as these European civilization and its standards were redefined, and in any full-length study of the European unification movement they need to be expounded in some detail. In recognizing them, the movement was determined to draw a clear distinction between itself and any other kind of unification, whether Asiatic or Hitlerite. Unfortunately, however, much of this spirit has evaporated since 1950.

(B) THE FRONTIERS OF EUROPEAN CIVILIZATION

As with any great civilization, Europe's frontiers are fluid, not rigid and fixed. On this question recent research has provided a fairly complete and unequivocal answer. Europe was the area where the prevailing theories, standards of behaviour, and so far as possible the actual conduct of human society, as already described, were based on certain basic ideas, common to the whole Continent, and its frontiers extended as far as did this way of life. It was more or less between the seventh and tenth centuries that a clearly distinct cultural, ideological, and social unity was established thanks to the diffusion and assimilation first of classical and then of Christian civilization. This was done initially by the Germanic peoples who invaded the Roman Empire. Later, to the North and East of this 'older Europe' the process was continued and completed through conversions to Christianity carried out in the ninth century by expansionist Germanic tribes, and in the tenth century by Slavonic and Scandinavian tribes and Hungarians. But even in this early phase of its growth European civilization suffered its first reverse and loss of territory in the South caused by the advance of Islam, which finally cut off the North-African territories as potential fields of expansion for European civilization, and in 711 managed to conquer almost the whole of Spain except for some small Christian principalities which survived precariously along the North Spanish coast and in the Pyrenees. The 300 years of Arab rule in Central Spain left many traces, but Spain was more deeply stamped by the long-drawn-out *Reconquista*, the reconquest of the Iberian Peninsula. By the eleventh century the area won back reached as far as Toledo and the banks of the River Tagus; by the thirteenth century it included Seville and Cordoba. Wherever they went, the conquerors deliberately set up social structures of a European type, including a constitution providing for the three states of the realm and urban self-government. After the conquest of Granada in 1492 the whole of Spain was reunited with European civilization, whose southern

---

introduction, but only described as a factor present in 1945. For a fuller account the reader is referred to the works mentioned in nn. 33 and 38 as well as to Chap. X. 'The Basic Problems of European History' in Halecki, op. cit. (n. 22), pp. 166–85; C. Dawson, *Understanding Europe*, London, 1952; many documents in the collection by D. de Rougemont, op. cit. (n. 30).

frontier along the Mediterranean was never subsequently challenged.[38] Later there followed Islam's second great advance, this time led by the markedly oriental despotism of the Ottoman Empire in the Balkans. This advance caused a much greater long-term loss to European civilization: the 500 years of rule by the Sultan in Bulgaria and Northern Greece (1393–1908) and in Serbia, Bosnia, and Albania (1460–1878) – in contrast to the relatively brief Ottoman occupation of Hungary, Croatia, and Transylvania, territories which in a cultural sense remained clearly a part of the European area – had such far-reaching consequences that between Croatia and the Bosphorus European influence was almost obliterated. More debatable was the question of Europe's eastern border with its ebb and flow of population, and her overseas frontier in the Western Hemisphere.

There can be no serious doubt that the decision made by geographers at the end of the nineteenth century, in their search for an agreement to fix the borders of the five continents, to take the North–South line of the Ural Mountains as the geographical boundary between Asia and Europe never made sense in terms of the realities of cultural or political history. The Urals were chosen because of the desire for a frontier that would be geographically visible, and because of the prevailing notion that only seas or mountain ranges were suitable for that purpose. Yet the Urals are far from lofty, a mere chain of hills with many deep depressions, and only occasionally do they reach even the altitude found in the Black Forest. Historical and political movements of every kind have constantly crossed the Urals in both directions. They form no effective barrier. Moreover European civilization has never extended so far (about 1,500 km East of Moscow). The limits to which it did extend were defined by specialists on Eastern Europe in a carefully worded consensus agreed at an International Conference in Warsaw in 1933, which deserves to be better remembered than it is among politicians.[39]

In the tenth and eleventh centuries European civilization had begun to expand in an easterly direction across Poland and Hungary into the Eastern Slav region along the Upper Dnepr. In the principality of Kiev it had begun to develp such unmistakable features as centres of Christian culture, social differentiation, and urban self-government. But in the middle of the thirteenth century all these foundations were swallowed up in the catastrophe of the Mongol invasion, which turned practically the entire territory into

---

[38] On this point a reference to major works may suffice: C. Dawson, *The Making of Europe*, London, 1932; G. de Reynold, *La Formation de l'Europe*, 7 vols., Paris, 1947–57; H. Brugmans, *Histoire de l'Europe*, Vol. i: *Les Origines*, Liège, 1958; H. Dannenbauer, *Die Entstehung Europas. Von der Spätantike zum Mittelalter*, 2 vols., Stuttgart, 1959 and 1962. Among basic works R. Konetzke, *Geschichte des spanischen und portugiesischen Volkes*, Leipzig, 1939; A. Castro, *The Structure of Spanish History*, Princeton, 1954 (emphasizing the break caused by the Arab conquest); also R. Konetzke, 'Islam and Christliches Spanien im Mittelalter' in *HZ*, 184 (1957), pp. 573–91. Cf. Ortega y Gasset, *Stern und Unstern, Gedanken über Spaniens Landschaft und Geschichte*, Stuttgart, 1952; H. Livermore, *The Origins of Spain and Portugal*, London, 1971.

[39] See the records of the VIIth International Congress of Historians (Warsaw, 1933) in *Bulletin d'information des sciences historiques en Europe orientale*, Vol. 6 (1934). Cf. Oskar Halecki, 'Der Begriff der osteuropäischen Geschichte', in *Zeitschrift für osteuropäische Geschichte*, vol. 9 (1934), pp. 1–21.

part of a Tatar–Eurasian empire that was to rule North Russia for over 200 years and South Russia for over 500 years. To the West, in the Baltic lands and in Great Novgorod, which escaped Tatar rule, European ways of life and urban development of the Hanseatic type prevailed; and through the Polish–Jagiellonian kingdom with its graded structure of estates, city constitutions based on Germanic law, and what was for the seventeenth century a very liberal franchise, even the White-Russian and West-Ukrainian territories as far as the Dnepr were reunited with European civilization. To the East, however, in the lands ruled by the Tatars, it was, as recent research, especially that of Günther Stökl, has shown, three factors above all which set the Eastern Slavs on an 'anti-European' course.

1. Under Tatar domination, cut off for centuries from European influences and subject to the conditions of Russia's newly colonized North-East, the local principalities became so backward that the princes tolerated no regionally based estates of the realm and only towns dependent on themselves 'with limited economic scope and lacking in any political life of their own'. In the fourteenth century the princelings 'as a result of marked servility ... won the confidence of the khans ... to such an extent that they were raised to the dignity of Grand Dukes, that is were given the overlordship of all Russian princes together with the right of collecting tribute for the Tatars'. In the second half of the fifteenth century Ivan III subjugated the last of the remaining princelings, conquered Novgorod (expelling its patrician class), and put an end to the payment of tribute to the 'Horde', which in the meantime had disintegrated and embraced Islam.

2. Among the princes living under Tatar rule 'oriental despotism had been established as a model for their own relationship towards their boyars and other subjects ... as had the despotic form of state and the diplomatic and court ceremonial that went with it'. In the second half of the sixteenth century Ivan IV (the Terrible) completed this process by depriving the boyars of power and by subordinating the great part of his empire, lying along the lower Volga, to the oppressive 'Oprichnina' government exercised by the lower service nobility. In theoretical writings too he argued that despotism was the only possible alternative to anarchy.

3. The Moscow form of government was underpinned by a garbled interpretation of a *Translatio Imperii* which proclaimed Moscow as the successor to Byzantium. Byzantine Christianity was unable to oppose the autocratic principle because it lacked the European tension between Church and State as two coequal authorities, for the main reason for the Byzantine schism had been the Church's surrender to the power of the emperor. Moreover the way in which the idea of the Byzantine Empire was taken over 'was bound to lead from universalism to imperialism because of the extent to which it was nationalized and restricted ... The 'Third Rome' (i.e. Moscow) was the embodiment of perfection on earth, thought of by those whose conceived the idea and secured its acceptance as the absorption of the state by the Church. In reality it turned out to be the absorption of the Church by the state, but in any case it was always seen as the model of an ideal world and the appointed means of salvation. This idea was far too narrow to appeal to the world as a whole, it could only try to compress as much of the world as possible within its own narrow limits ... hardly a climate in which the European spirit can flourish.'

28 *Introduction*

After the end of the Tatar domination and the resumption of Russia's relations with the West (even before the reign of Peter the Great) counter-impulses were at work: indigenous support for the ideas of the Reformation or Counter-Reformation, as is shown by the trials of heretics whereby the established Church tried to suppress these influences. It was none other than Ivan IV who set up a provincial assembly on the Lithuanian–Polish model, which, however, remained 'politically sterile because the provincial nobility lacked the gift of leadership and practical experience of regional autonomy', so that it felt itself to be nothing more than a tool of the government and ceased to exist three decades later.[40] As a whole in the seventeenth century, the empire, which now included Siberia, remained outside the creative influence of Europe, whether judged by intellectual standards, principles of social organization, or styles in literature and art.

But in the eighteenth century there began a westward expansion of the Moscow realm started by Peter the Great. At the end of the Northern War the main Baltic lands, Estonia and Livonia (which up to then had been ruled by Sweden), were left in his possession. That these territories had been to a large extent Europeanized was bound to have some effect. Peter himself was above all an admirer of the West – though what he, like developing countries in a later age, wished to adopt was western skills, such as production methods and shipbuilding. By employing European technicians he increased the number of Russian factories from 13 old-fashioned ones to 178 new ones, and put in hand a modernization and quadrupling of the army; this resulted in placing further charges on the already overburdened peasants, who were held in strict serfdom by the landowning class.

Meanwhile the Orthodox Church, following the abolition of the Patriarchate and its subordination to an organ of the state administration, became a mere support for the autocracy; and attempts to introduce corporate self-government into the aristrocracy (by the election of provincial councils) and into the towns (by the election of municipal councils) proved a failure. Only in Petersburg, the new imperial capital in the conquered territory of Ingermanland (Ingria), a city built with a great deal of foreign help in a formal French style, did an elected council come into existence. And in Estonia and Livonia Peter in the capitulation treaties of 1710 had assured the orders of German knights and town councils that their

---

[40] Cf. the two basic summaries: G. Stökl, *Russland und Europa* (n. 21), including quotations on pp. 536, 538, 545, and 550; and B. Spuler (n. 21), the third quotation on p. 404. On the Tatar period a basic work is B. Spuler, *Die Goldene Horde. Die Mongolen in Russland 1223–1502*, Leipzig, 1943; G. Vernadsky, *The Mongols and Russia*, New Haven, 1953; for a survey of the whole period with most recent list of sources C. Goehrke, 'Die Moskauer Periode', in the collection of essays by C. Goehrke and others (n. 21), pp. 76–174; G. Stökl, 'Russland 1462–1689' in T. Schieder (ed.), *Handbuch der Europäischen Geschichte*, vol. 3, Stuttgart, 1971, pp. 1136–69. On ideology H. Schaeder, *Moskau das dritte Rom*, Darmstadt, 1957²; W. Lettenbauer, *Moskau das dritte Rom*, Munich, 1961; H. Neubauer, *Car und Selbstherrscher*, Wiesbaden, 1964; J. H. Billington, *The Icon and the Axe. An Interpretative History of Russian Culture*, NY, 1966; on Byzantium's fundamental surrender to the principle of imperial power: H. Rahner, *Kirche und Staat im frühen Christentum*, Munich, 1961, esp. pp. 283–375.

status would remain unchanged. In the following decades the court often employed advisers and specialists from these and other European countries, while the suburb of Moscow inhabited by foreigners expanded. From the time of the Northern War onwards Russia played a part in the concert of Europe simply because – unlike the declining Ottoman Empire – it was militarily so strong that no other state could afford to ignore it.

From the position of strength so obtained, Catherine II managed to complete the second major stage of westward expansion in the second half of the eighteenth century. After annexing the former Polish provinces north of the River Dvina and east of the Dnepr in 1772, she acquired the White-Russian and West-Ukrainian provinces through the Second Partition of Poland in 1793. The Tatar Khanate of the Crimea was also conquered about this time. The Third Partition of Poland in 1795 added Courland, Lithuania, and East–Central Poland. This meant that Russia's western frontier had advanced to a depth of about 400 km into the lands belonging to European civilization.

In the newly acquired territories (in contrast to what happened in Estonia and Latvia) there were no capitulation treaties of any importance, and soon a policy of gradual Russification began. As a result of the Napoleonic wars Alexander I acquired Finland (1809) and Central or Congress Poland (1812) including Warsaw; both Finns and Poles were promised constitutions and self-government. The consequences were not unlike those in the Balkan lands occupied by the Turks, where Moldavia, Wallachia, and Transylvania, thanks to treaties guaranteeing their autonomy, were more successful in preserving their European traditions than Byzantine Bulgaria and the Southern Slavs converted to Islam, who had no such treaties.

Catherine II also called on the Baltic and Polish aristocracy, Baltic and German citizens and settlers to help with the colonization of the interior of Russia. Yet at the same time 95 per cent of her subjects, the peasants, who could be sold apart from the land they worked on, were treated in law like mere chattels. Once again, but in vain, Catherine tried to introduce into Russia European ideas of self-government by the nobles and the towns, but 'without succeeding in making up for the missing tradition of corporate independence'.[41]

---

[41] Summaries in R. Wittram, 'Russland von 1689–1796', in T. Schieder (ed.), *Handbuch der europäischen Geschichte*, vol. 4, Stuttgart, 1968, pp. 476–510 (quotations on p. 508), and the relevant portion of C. Goehrke, 'Das Petrinische Kaiserreich', in C. Goehrke *et al.* (n. 21), pp. 175–206 (both with book-lists). On the lack of European motives and styles in earlier Russian literature and on the spread of the Enlightenment under Catherine the Great, cf. A. Stender-Petersen, *Geschichte der Russischen Literatur*, 2 vols., Munich, 1957. On the degree to which the incorporated East-European territories were part of European civilisation, cf. R. Wittram, *Baltische Geschichte*, Munich, 1954; M. Hellman, *Grundzüge der Geschichte Litauens*, Darmstadt, 1966; O. Halecki, *Borderlands of Western Civilization, A History of East Central Europe*, New York, 1952, 1957; H. Roos, 'Polen von 1668–1795' in Schieder (ibid., vol. 4), pp. 690–752; on the constitution, esp. J. K. Hoensch, *Sozialverfassung und politische Reform. Polen im vorrevolutionären Zeitalter*, Cologne/Vienna, 1973.

Alexander I in 1818 promised a similar measure, but abandoned it a year later. At the same time, the fruits of European civilization, the Enlightenment, romanticism, and the intellectual movements which followed began to filter into the interior of Russia thanks to a tenuous link of 'westernized' landed noblemen and leading merchants' families, French governesses, tutors, etc., but the pioneering impulses got lost somewhere between the Dnepr and the Volga, similarly to what happened in the Ottoman Empire between Croatia and the Bosphorus. The line of the Volga may be regarded as the extreme limit reached by European influence, which among the small upper social strata gradually produced a blending of European and non-European elements.

In 1825 officers of the imperial guard, imbued with European ideas, tried to gain their constitutional objectives in the Decembrist revolt. Nicholas I (1825-55), who began his reign by crushing the revolt, clung obstinately to the strictest exercise of traditional autocracy, the simple social structure of service nobility and serfs, anti-European censorship, intellectual repression, and arbitrary police powers. Under this regime the number of 'Westernizers' grew among the aristocracy and rising intelligentsia. Under Alexander II (1855-81) they managed to secure the legal abolition of serfdom (even though the land which the peasants could not pay for remained the property of the landlords, worked by the peasants in return for services) and a reform of the judicial system which replaced the existing bureaucratic and secret procedure by an open and independent process of law. This time genuine organs of self-government were created: thanks to the Zemstvos, district and local assemblies which met once a year, albeit indirectly elected on an unequal franchise weighted in favour of the nobles, and elected town councils, at least in Northern Russia people started to become accustomed to liberal and democratic ideas.

Nevertheless, apart from the annexed East-European provinces, this extension of European ideas failed to reach 95 per cent of the peasant masses, as the young students who went out into the countryside as 'friends of the people' found for themselves. It was entirely confined to the nobility and to the élitist military and bureaucratic upper class, who formed a mere 3-5 per cent of the population. Moreover it provoked an independent counter-movement which, invoking the native tradition, protested critically and militantly against 'imported European doctrines' and the attempts to swamp Russia with foreign influences since the time of Peter the Great. Fired by romanticism, the Slavophiles took up politics in the form of Panslavism, whose 'bible', Danilevski's *Russia and Europe* (1869), saw these two concepts as opposites. Russia as a rising empire was assigned the task of deposing Europe, depicted as decadent, from its pedestal.

Pan-Slavism opposed the existing regard for European traditions in the Western provinces with a tough, centralizing, 'Great Russian' policy. Already in the reign of Alexander II cultural Russification was enforced, not only in Poland, through abolishing what remained of self-government; in 1876 the printing of books (except *belles-lettres*) in Ukrainian was forbidden. A Russian claim to be the leader of the Slav peoples of Austria-Hungary and Turkey who aspired to liberation was proclaimed and had its repercussions in the war of 1877-8. The reactionary regime of the two following Tsars relied on the Moscow Pan-Slavs headed by Katkov, who though he started with liberal inclinations had become a champion of the old Russian autocracy. The guaranteed rights of self-government in districts and towns were practically abolished: censorship rules were tightened; the Russification of education and administration was carried further in the Baltic provinces and in Finland; a racial form of nationalism caused a sharp revival of special laws against the Jews and in South Russia led to pogroms.

Thus in Tsarist Russia repeated attempts at Europeanization suffered severe set-backs. Neither the unambiguously European character of the Baltic territories acquired 150 years earlier and the Polish and White-Russian lands incorporated 100 years earlier, nor the Europeanizing influences to which they gave rise were able, despite periodical encouragement from the Tsars, to bring about any real change in the interior of Russia or in its social and political structures. On the contrary, they provoked nationalist reactions, a policy of Russification, and a new Pan-Slav, markedly anti-European ideology. Only twice, and then briefly, did it appear that European influences might be victorious: in the revolution of 1905, in which congresses of the Zemstvo deputies (hitherto debarred from power) played a leading part, the 'Westerners'' liberal constitutional party temporarily won the upper hand; yet shortly afterwards manipulation of the elections to the Second Duma restored the initiative to the Orthodox and pro-government forces. Once again the 'Westerners' regained the upper hand under Kerensky after the revolution of February 1917; but they were overthrown a few months later by the Bolshevik Revolution of October 1917.[42] During this and during the subsequent protracted civil war the 'Westerners', the thin upper layer of noble families and of the upper middle class who had been the main sustainers of European influence, were almost completely eliminated. With the abolition of all that had been done in Tsarist Russia towards guaranteeing individual human rights and pluralist self-government so far as they had ever existed

---

[42] Cf. the survey chapter by G. von Rauch, 'Russland vom Krimkrieg bis zur Oktoberrevolution 1856–1917' in Schieder (ed.), *Handbuch der europäischen Geschichte*, vol. 6, Stuttgart, 1968, pp. 309–52, with bibliography. On the 'Westernizers', cf. A. von Schelting, *Russland und Europa im russischen Geschichtsdenken*, Berne, 1948; R. E. Pipes (ed.), *The Russian Intelligentsia*, Columbia UP, 1961. On the slavophiles N. Riasanovsky, *Russia and the West in the Teaching of the Slavophiles*, Harvard UP, 1952. Texts of Russian authors in D. Tschizewskij and D. Groh (ed.), *Europa und Russland*, Darmstadt, 1959; H. Kohn, *Die Slawen und der Westen*, Vienna/Munich, 1956; on the policy of Russification, *The Cambridge History of Poland*, vol. 2, Cambridge, 1951; Wittram, op. cit., n. 41; E. Jutikkala, *Geschichte Finnlands*, Stuttgart, 1964; L. Greenberg, *The Jews in Russia*, 2 vols., New Haven 1944/51. W. Lettenbauer, *Russische Literaturgeschichte*, Frankfurt/Vienna, 1958. E. Nolte, *Deutschland und der kalte Krieg*, Munich, 1974, pp. 105, 217 f., and *passim* shows that Marx and Engels, reflecting European views of the nineteenth century, considered Russia a decidedly non-European power.

in Russia, there arose the absolute autocracy of Stalin. With (at least) 10 million killed for political reasons and 25 million deported to inhuman labour camps, with the social structure reduced to an all-powerful centralist bureaucracy at the top and the terrorized masses below, with the cynicism of its political trials and its political police, this regime far surpassed any previous despotism. The original system of Soviets was superseded by a bureaucratic network, the originally dominant internationalist party by the chauvinist Russian party; the purely technical aim of industrialization was pursued by the state's 'accumulation of capital', largely based on inhuman methods of forced labour without the restraints that would have come from a free workers' movement or free trade unions.

In the older parts of Europe too there were social structures which had nothing in common with deeper European values. One need only mention Hobbes's theory of despotism, French anti-regional centralism, and the profoundly un-European dictatorship of Hitler's SS State – against which European influences and norms of freedom and human rights, regional self-government, scientific knowledge and Christian charity had to be maintained and reasserted. But in the area originally colonized from Europe, where the vast spaces of Eurasia were as unfavourable to Western political and social ideas as were the Tatar domination and the Pan-Slav version of the 'Third Rome' ideology, the duration and severity of Stalin's despotism meant the final negation of earlier attempts at Europeanization.

From what has just been said about Europe's cultural unity and the values for which it stood, of which the European intelligentsia had become increasingly aware, it is clear that Stalin's Russia was a tyranny which had no legitimate claim whatever to be regarded as European: on the other hand it was a powerful self-contained empire on a continental scale, and any idea of dividing it at the Ural Mountains was inconceivable. The formidable westward expansion of the Soviet empire at the beginning and still more at the end of the Second World War has already been mentioned. The Eastern-European countries, which had long resisted Russification, had renewed and maintained their independence as nation states between 1919 and 1939 and had thus remained part of European civilization, but Russia's second expansion westwards in 1945 engulfed all the Baltic lands, East Prussia as far as Königsberg, Eastern Poland, and Bessarabia, while in addition a belt of territory extending 750 km further west up to a line running from Lübeck to Trieste was gradually brought under Soviet control between 1945 and 1949. Not until 1956, as a result of the Hungarian and Polish risings, and again after the 'Prague spring' of 1968, was it clear that underneath the Russification of Eastern Europe and despite all Moscow's efforts, European traditions were capable of survival and recovery.

The early advocates of a European federal union in the years 1945–50, who are the subject of this book, never had the slightest doubt that Stalin's empire did not belong to Europe but that the Europe for which they strove should in principle comprise the ancient heartland of civilization from the Atlantic to the Eastern borders of Poland and Romania. The Theses of Europeesche Actie which soon afterwards became the main basis of the Hertenstein Programme summarized the position in June 1946: 'The frontier of a federally united Europe ends where people begin to treat a human being as important only so far as he is a member of a collective group.' It was a painful process for the European federalists to have to learn in 1947 that in consequence of the occupation of Eastern Europe by the Soviet Union 'the work of building up could be started only in Western Europe'; the congress of Montreux then gave the assurance that 'the UEF would never accept the division of Europe into two hostile blocs as an accomplished fact'.[43]

Finally, since the beginning of the modern age European civilization had begun to exert its influence on overseas continents. Its landward expansion to the East had been no more than a part of the 'projection of Europe' in the wider world, whose main efforts were directed rather to the overseas territories. At this point a distinction must be made between two principal stages of this process. By the end of the eighteenth century Europeans had opened up the world's oceans in daring voyages of discovery and established trading stations and missions along many distant coastal routes, but only in America and in South-East India were forms of government set up whose authority extended into the interior of other continents (in 1800 the United States had only about 6 million inhabitants). Not until the population of Europe started to double (from 160 million to 320 million) during the nineteenth century, when the first stages of industrialization occurred, did Europeans begin to occupy large parts of the overseas continents, whose inhabitants were no match for European superiority in all branches of knowledge and in arms. A distinction must be made between the territories which were entirely formed by European immigration, in which there was a genuine expansion of European values and civilized characteristics, e.g. in America and later Australasia, and on the other hand all the territories in which European government, lasting barely a century, remained a mere veneer, concentrated in a few key points

---

[43] On the westward expansion of the Soviet empire, on the corresponding forcing-back of Europe and its sovietization, cf. nn. 23-7. On the quoted texts, see pp. 137 (Theses of Europeesche Actie) and 582 (Resolution of Montreux, 31 Aug. 1947); Moltke's comprehensive definition of 1941 in n. 79 (below); esp. clear also the chapter 'L'U.R.S.S. n'est pas européenne' in M. Mouskhely and G. Stefani, *L'Europe face au fédéralisme,* Strasburg/Paris, 1949, pp. 65-72. When a working party of the UEF in Dec. 1948 discussed possibilities for relaxing the tensions caused by the Cold War through a federation of the whole of Europe (including Eastern Europe), and at the same time refused to admit Ukrainian exile groups to the UEF on the grounds that Poland's Eastern border was also that of Europe, the President, H. Brugmans, answered on 8 January 1949: 'If the Soviet regime was not totalitarian, one could ideally consider the Ukrainians as having double membership – in the federation of the USSR and in the European federation.' (BEF Archives, Brugmans Correspondence.) To my knowledge, this was the furthest expansion to the East ever proposed by a European federalist.

34 Introduction

round mining centres, and which, as their post-liberation history has shown, in essence acquired little beyond the adoption of imported technical know-how.

As Valéry wrote, modern science 'became a means of power, of material domination and the creation of wealth . . . Knowledge, which had been prized as something to be enjoyed, became prized as something to be exchanged. Its usefulness makes knowledge a commodity ... This commodity will accordingly be found in different forms [and] distributed to an ever wider public, it will become an object of trade, in the end something which is manufactured and produced almost everywhere.'[44]

On the other hand, the territories with a wholly or mainly European population such as the United States, Canada, and Australia developed in their intellectual achievements and standards as a 'new Europe' to which those basic definitions of European civilization apply in full measure – to a far greater extent than they ever did in Russia. In the history of America during the nineteenth century there were absolutely no ideas which did not come from Europe. The principles of individual freedom, the right of regional self-government, the obligation to tell the truth, the duty of mutual help all became an accepted part of the national philosophy which has been more consistently honoured in America than in Europe itself, since the Americans distrusted state power even more deeply than did Europeans.[45] In fact in the 1960s, after the failure (politically speaking) of the first two attempts to unite Europe, the founding of an Atlantic Community as a political entity became a goal for many people who felt that Europe had become too small. But for the champions of a united Europe in the period 1945–50, which is the subject of this book, the United States counted as a continental union of its own, which with its federal structure could nevertheless serve as a model for a European federation. This self-sufficiency of the USA seemed so obvious to the European federalists that their associations did not even expressly discuss the matter (except for a few British supporters of the Atlantic conception of Clarence Streit). From the Resistance movement they had inherited a special emphasis on human rights, which was bound to be directed against the Soviet Union; but they had also inherited the aim of a mainly 'left-wing' social order which they saw as a contrasting alternative to American 'capitalism'. Thus their objective was a united and neutral Europe which would steer a third course between both world powers. They still believed that Europe was strong enough to pursue such a policy.

[44] P. Valéry, *La Crise de l'esprit*. Deuxième Lettre, quoted in Valéry, *OEuvres*, I. i, Paris, 1957, p. 998.
[45] Here let it suffice to refer to the following basic works with their bibliographies: E. Sieber, *Kolonialgeschichte der Neuzeit*, Berne, 1949; F. Mauro, *L'Expansion européenne 1600–1870* (Nouvelle Clio, vol. 27), Paris, 1964; L. Diez del Corral, *Le Rapt de l'Europe*, Paris, 1954 (interpreted as the 'outpouring of Europe'); J. Höffner, *Kolonialismus und Evangelium. Spanische Kolonialethik im Goldenen Zeitalter*, Trier, 1969²; R. Konetzke, *Süd-und Mittelamerika*, i (Fischer, *Weltgeschichte*, vol. 22), Frankfurt, 1965; R. R. Palmer, *The Age of Democratic Revolution*, 2 vols., Princeton, 1964; G. Mann, *Vom Geist Amerikas*, Stuttgart, 1961³; Halecki (n. 22), pp. 46–54.

So much by way of a brief sketch of the fundamental factors, the redefinition of European civilization, its values, its unity, and its frontiers as seen by its most enlightened minds in the perspective of its decline and as elaborated by scholars of many European countries, in what Paul Valéry in words already quoted described as a 'desperate defence of its very nature'. Once again Europe received a new lease of life from 'the sum total of its memories' as a basis for and principal justification of the movement in favour of unification to which the reader's attention must now be directed.

(C) THE BEGINNINGS OF THE POLITICAL UNIFICATION MOVEMENT, 1914–39: THE ECONOMIC IMPERATIVE

The movement to unite Europe politically did not really get under way before the First World War. Those Europeans who were most anxious to recover the sense of the unity of their civilization realized that their history had consisted largely of interaction between factors common to the whole of Europe and those which belonged to particular regions, and that plans for European political unity had been drawn up in past centuries in almost forgotten profusion. Yet all such plans, which were especially numerous between the seventeenth and nineteenth centuries, remained for fairly obvious reasons paper projects and were never important enough to influence policy (except, perhaps, and then only briefly, during the Napoleonic Empire).

Some of these plans, beginning with one proposed by Abbé Dubois in 1306, were only a disguised form of a claim for hegemony put forward by one power or another. Other plans, especially since the seventeenth century, inspired by the consciousness of a common civilization and increasing concern at the growing lawlessness of sovereign states, had called for an end to the struggle for power and the setting-up of a European organization for peace. Yet individual authors had never been able to form political parties or influence practical politics in the way they desired. The gradual concentration of autonomous regions into what at the same time were large-scale national states temporarily satisfied the demands of technical progress; and since the wave of Islamic–Turkish expansion had subsided there had been no external enemy to make European unification a vital necessity.[46] But ever since the middle of the nineteenth century the ascendancy of Russia and

---

[46] On the plethora of plans for political union drawn up between the fourteenth and the nineteenth centuries, still waiting for historians to make them truly a part of our historical consciousness, see J. ter Meulen, *Der Gedanke der Internationalen Organisation in seiner Entwicklung,* 3 vols., The Hague, 1917, 1929, 1940; C. Lange (vol. ii with A. Schou) *Histoire de l'internationalisme,* 2 vols., Oslo, 1929, 1954; K. von Raumer, *Ewiger Friede. Friedensrufe und Friedenspläne seit der Renaissance,* Munich/Freiburg, 1953; T. Ruyssen, *Les Sources doctrinales de l'internationalisme,* 3 vols., Paris, 1954–61; C. Curcio, *Europa. Storia di un' idea,* 2 vols., Florence, 1958. For Germany, esp. H. Gollwitzer, *Europabild und Europagedanke. Beiträge zur deutschen Geistesgeschichte des 18. und 19. Jahrhunderts,* Munich, 1964; F. Dickmann, *Friedensrecht und Friedenssicherung. Studien zum Friedensproblem in der Geschichte,* Göttingen, 1971; R. Vierhaus, 'Überstaat und Staatenbund. Wirklichkeit und Ideen internationaler Ordnung im Zeitalter der französischen Revolution und Napoleons', in *Archiv für Kulturgeschichte,* 43 (1961), pp. 329–54; for a more popular treatment, R. H. Foerster, *Europa. Geschichte einer politischen Idee,* Munich, 1967.

36   Introduction

America had been foretold by far-sighted observers, and at the very time when the co-operation of Europeans in the world economy should have made them give priority to political security, the divisions caused by nationalism and the struggle for power reached their climax. It was then that Nietzsche felt moved to complain: 'Thanks to the morbid hostility which the madness of nationality has created among the nations of Europe ... the unmistakable signs proclaiming that Europe wants to unite are overlooked.' And the 'peace movement' had to face the fact that at the Hague peace conferences of 1899 and 1907 the powers were not even ready for agreements on disarmament or arbitration. All they were prepared to do was to codify some humanitarian modifications of the laws of war.[47]

It was only after the resistance of the various European nationalisms to economic internationalism and to the opportunities offered by large-scale technology had plunged them into the catastrophe of the First World War that a reaction took shape in the form of a movement for unification, initially supported by a small section of the intelligentsia, but marked by great determination and operating through a number of groups and committees. Horror at the four-year blood-bath caused by 'civilized' European nations and at the decline which it portended led in every country between 1914 and 1919 to a passionate debate on how peace could be safeguarded by institutions using supranational legal sanctions, and how the anarchy of interstate relations could be overcome by a league of nations (the term most often used in 1914–16 was the 'United States of Europe'), democratically based on the principle of self-determination.

An association called Neues Vaterland was founded in Berlin in November 1914. Its members included not only the leaders of the existing 'peace movement' such as Schücking and Quidde but the economists Lujo Brentano and Leopold von Wiese, the physicist Albert Einstein, the historians Max Lehmann and O. Nippold, and the former ambassadors Count Mons and Prince Lichnowsky among others. The object of the association was defined in Article 1 as 'Promotion of all efforts likely to imbue the policy of the European powers with the civilized notion of peaceful competition and supranational unification...' The Union for Democratic Control founded about the same time in London by Ramsay MacDonald, Charles Trevelyan, and Norman Angell declared in its first manifesto that: 'Policy should no longer be aimed at a balance of power but should be directed to establishing a European federation of states'. A whole host of books published in Switzerland urged European union as a condition and basis of lasting peace and saw the European civil war as 'the war of European unification', since it would force Europeans to learn their lesson. The foundation manifesto of the

[47] Cf. G. Barraclough, 'Europa, Amerika und Russland in Vorstellung und Denken des 19. Jahrhunderts', in *HZ*, 203 (1966), pp. 280–315; W. Faber, 'Victor Hugo als Vorkämpfer der Vereinigten Staaten von Europa', in *Die Friedenswarte,* 41, 1941, pp. 166–76; P. Renouvin, *Les Idées et les projets d'union européenne au XIXe siècle* (Carnegie Publication de la Conciliation Internationale, Bulletin, 1931, No. 6), Paris 1931, pp. 27–47 (2nd edition, Oxford, 1949); Ter Meulen (n. 46), vol. II/2: 1867–1889, The Hague, 1940; the quotation from Nietzsche, *Beyond Good and Evil,* London, 1907, pp. 217–18; cf. the books mentioned in n. 3 (above), H. Fried, *Handbuch der Friedensbewegung II (1889–1913),* Berlin, 1913; P. Zorn, *Die beiden Haager Friedens-Konferenzen von 1889 und 1907* (Hdb. des Völkerrechts, vol. 5(1)), Berlin, 1915.

Netherlands Committee 'De Europeesche Staatenbond' at the end of 1914 called for Europe to become 'a closely united league of states or a federal state'. A Spanish committee urged European federal organization. In France, where J. Barthélemy and A. Thierry developed elaborate arguments on how to achieve European unification, Jules Romains described the war as 'an armed conflict in the heartland of a homogeneous civilization ... in its nature less a war than a civil disorder ... a crisis of unification [showing] among the peoples of Europe an unappeased longing for unity'. In 1916–17 Hugo von Hofmannsthal travelled through the capitals of Northern and Western Europe making a series of speeches in which he described nationalism as 'not only something limited but something unethical' which confirmed Grillparzer's prophecy: 'From humanity through nationality to bestiality'. In 1918 Walther Rathenau called on Germany's youth 'to replace international anarchy by a voluntarily accepted higher authority'.[48]

The debate that had been going on in these various groups between 1914 and 1916 had as virtually its sole objective a future federal organization of the European countries. It repeatedly affirmed with surprising determination the need to merge or to get rid of national sovereignties. The one thing it could not do was to convert the belligerent governments. It was President Wilson who, from the summer of 1916 onwards, incorporated in the programme of the United States government the idea of 'an association of nations', the replacement of the existing balance of power by a 'community of power'; he appeared determined at all costs to win over the European governments, which at first only declared themselves 'ready to discuss' the idea in general terms. Hence it was generally assumed in most of the European groups and plans that the future league would include the United States as well as the few independent states which then existed outside Europe. Not many people saw clearly enough to criticize the fact that since the league was planned as a world body and therefore rather loosely organized, the more tightly organized prospective Union of Europe would remain unrealized, though historically it was overdue.[49] In the bitterly austere winter of 1918–19 hopes of a real League of Nations 'warmed millions of human hearts', as a very critical observer wrote at the time, but the statesmen did not make the sacrifices needed to create a legal

---

[48] As it is impossible to quote all the evidence (much of which is very similar) let these few examples (references, etc. for which are given in every case in W. Lipgens, 'Europäische Einigungsidee 1923–1930 und Briands Europaplan im Urteil der deutschen Akten', in *HZ*, 203 (1966), pp. 49–51) serve as proof that a response to the new kind of challenge was forthcoming in due time among the intelligentsia. Any comprehensive history of the European unification movement would have to begin by developing this point at some length. For this purpose there is ample material in Lipgens, loc. cit., works already mentioned, esp. *Les Français à la recherche d'une Société des Nations*, Paris, 1920; more recently the abundance of source references in U. Fortuna, *Der Völkerbundsgedanke in Deutschland während des I. Weltkrieges* (Zürcher Studien zur allg. Geschichte, vol. 30), Zurich, 1974.

[49] Thus, for example, G. Agnelli and A. Cabiati, *Fédération européenne ou Ligue des Nations?*, Paris, 1918. More evidence on the Continental versus global debate in H. Wehberg, 'Ideen und Projekte betr. die Vereinigten Staaten von Europa', in *Die Friedens-Warte*, 41 (1941), for 1914–1919, pp. 101–8; Fortuna (n. 48), op. cit., 160–79. The subject continued to be debated in the Resistance movement, see p. 48 f. below.

community of nations. Under Article V of the Covenant, decisions of the Assembly or of the Council required the agreement of all member states represented at the meeting, so that the League remained dependent on the veto or goodwill of each member state and lacked any power of its own.[50]

After 1919 the continuance of the system of national states was assured and the absence of a decision in favour of some kind of unity showed that the lesson of the great catastrophe had not been learnt. And when from 1920 onwards people became conscious of the depressingly negative result of the war for everyone, victors as well as vanquished, and of the inadequacy of the League of Nations, a renewed demand for an effective league of European states as a reaction against the prevailing nationalism steadily gained support, especially among some sections of the intelligentsia. After 1923 whole staffs of periodicals, associated pressure groups in many countries, and at least two dozen books published every year pursued this aim. The primary objective of preserving peace within Europe, and the second objective of renewing Europeans' awareness of belonging to a common civilization, were now reinforced by a third incentive: the necessity of a European economic union. A steadily growing number of economic experts pointed out in the 1920s that in consequence of the drive for autarky developed during the war and the continuing rise of tariff barriers along national frontiers, European economic life, broken up into unviable fragments, was heading for permanent stagnation. This moreover was at a time when in view of rising exports from America and Japan the disappearance of overseas markets called at the very least for a market the size of Europe; only through unification could the European nations thrive and maintain their place in the world.[51] Yet the major powers responsible for the peace treaties had actually abolished the 'Supreme Economic Council' set up in 1919 when it arrived at a similar conclusion in 1920, and they allowed the problems of tariffs and the ruinous drive for autarky to smoulder on, without taking any serious steps towards a solution. The results, in the form of rising prices, lack of outlets, and general stagnation, boded ill for the future and forced many sections of the economy to realize

---

[50] 'Critical witness' (later a champion of a resolute 'policy of revision' in the German Foreign Office), B. W. von Bülow, *Der Versailler Völkerbund*, Berlin/Stuttgart, 1923, p. 1 f. ('They behave like people who have sworn an oath in the hour of danger which they then fail to honour.') Cf. Léon Blum, *For All Mankind*, London, 1946. As general studies, D. H. Miller, *The Drafting of the Covenant*, 2 vols., NY, 1928; F. P. Walters, *A History of the League of Nations*, London, 1960²; the bibliography referred to in n. 5.

[51] Cf. – to mention only a few major works – the book by the former Italian Prime Minister F. Nitti, *The Wreck of Europe*, Indianapolis, 1922; J. Caillaux (leader of the Radical-Socialist party) *Où va la France? Où va l'Europe?*, Paris, 1922; Edo Fimmen, *Labour's Alternative: The United States of Europe or Europe Limited*, London, 1924; W. Woytinski, *Die Vereinigten Staaten von Europa*, Berlin, 1926; J. Christu, *L'Union douanière européenne*, Paris, 1928. Cf. books mentioned in n. 52 and periodicals in n. 54. For a general view, cf. introductory surveys with references to bibliographies and to the most important works: C. Pegg, 'Der Gedanke der europäischen Einigung in den zwanziger Jahren' in *Europa-Archiv*, 17 (1962), pp. 749–58, 783–90, and 865–74; also Lipgens (n. 48), esp. pp. 54–62.

ever more clearly the need for a European economic community. Analyses of the necessity of a single European market were often combined with references to the expanding large-scale markets of continental-size states in both the eastern and western hemispheres; but the other motives already mentioned also played their part.

Among a mass of similar evidence, at least five books deserve emphasis for their thoroughness, cogent arguments, and convincing analyses, which were to be particularly influential among many supporters of the movement for unification between 1945 and 1950. Two published in France, by Demangeon and Delaisi, contained the most effective and unsparing analysis of the losses suffered by Europe through the war, the 'de-Europeanizing of the world', and the intellectual, social, and economic necessity of European unification. The book *Paneuropa* (1923) by the twenty-nine-year-old Austrian Count Coudenhove-Kalergi presented the comprehensively argued thesis that the unification of the nations of the European subcontinent with its diminished importance 'will either come about voluntarily through the formation of a European federation or will be forced on Europe by a Russian conquest. Whether the European question will be solved by Europe or by Russia, in neither case can the European system of small states be maintained alongside the giant empires of the future.' A fourth contribution was Alfred Weber's analysis of the 'Crisis of the Modern State idea in Europe' with its conclusion: 'Nothing is so urgent as the creation of ideal, realistic and political conditions for a European federation.' Fifthly there was the inspired, comprehensive analysis called *The Revolt of the Masses* by Ortega y Gasset, which ran through many editions in nearly all European languages. Its famous fourteenth chapter argued incisively that Europe 'has arrived at a new stage in its existence where everything has increased, but the institutions surviving from the past are dwarfed and have become an obstacle to expansion ... It would be useless to change individual constitutions, for it is not the constitution which is failing but the state itself; it has become too small ... Only the determination to construct a great nation from the groups of peoples of the Continent would give new life to the pulses of Europe.'[52]

Several private organizations came into existence which sought to propagate the idea of European unity among the general public, to acquire influential members, and to win political influence by means of all-party committees. Among them the Pan-Europa Union, founded by Coudenhove-Kalergi at the end of 1923 as an all-party mass movement in favour of European unity, developed the best organization and had the greatest impact.

Every copy of Coudenhove-Kalergi's book contained a membership form with an invitation to the reader, if he agreed with its aims, to become a member of the

---

[52] A. Demangeon, *Le Déclin de l'Europe*, Paris, 1920; F. Delaisi, *Les Contradictions du monde moderne*, Paris, 1925 (560 pp., 3rd edition, 1932); R. N. Coudenhove-Kalergi, *Paneurope*, New York, 1926; A. Weber, *Die Krise des modernen Staatsgedankens in Europa*, Stuttgart, 1925 (quotation on p. 165); J. Ortega y Gasset (n. 34), pp. 96–141, chap. XIV (quotations on pp. 114 and 139–40). What European unity ought still to mean today – and the degree to which the concept has been diluted – cannot be fully understood without studying these books. Cf. n. 51.

Pan-Europa Union. First a strong Austrian branch was formed, with both the Federal Chancellor Seipel and the Socialist Vice-Chancellor Renner on the executive committee. Thanks to the tireless travels of Coudenhove-Kalergi, and as a result of the success of the First Pan-European Congress in Vienna in October 1926, in which over 2,000 European politicians, educationalists, business men, lawyers, and journalists took part, the Pan-Europa Union became an impressive supranational organization with national committees in all the major European capitals. Coudenhove's programme, temporarily accepting the inevitability of Great Britain's abstention, demanded the 'political and economic unification of all states from Portugal to Poland'. The process was to start with a treaty for compulsory arbitration to prevent the outbreak of war between any two European nations, a Pan-European defensive alliance against the Russian danger, and a customs union to promote economic recovery, and was ultimately to develop into a 'United States of Europe on the model of the United States of America'. From modest beginnings the Union finally became well known to all politicians. The President of the German Reichstag, the Social Democrat Paul Löbe (after a visit to the United States in the spring of 1926), the President of the Democratic Party, Koch-Weser, and the former German Minister of Agriculture, Joseph Koeth, joined the executive of the German section; in 1927 the veteran French Minister of Commerce, Louis Loucheur, the Socialist leader Léon Blum, and Joseph Barthélemy were on the executive of the French section, while Foreign Minister Briand became president of the Pan-Europe Union as a whole.[53]

Another association had become a centre for those who regarded a customs and economic union of the European countries as the most urgent and most attainable goal. Under the presidency of Stern-Rubarth, Charles Gide, and the Hungarian Professor of Economics, Elmer Hantos, the 'European Customs Union', as this association was called, became a solidly based organization with three periodicals and national committees in the major capitals of Continental Europe.[54]

Among other groups was the Association for European Co-operation founded at Geneva in 1926, which, though its proclaimed goals of 'co-operation with the League of Nations' and 'no step without Britain' were less ambitious, yet wished to go further than a mere 'policy of understanding'. It had committees in Berlin, Paris, and London, and in Germany it was headed by a Democratic Member of the Reichstag, Wilhelm Heile.[55]

Yet influential as this unco-ordinated movement, containing as it did outstanding economists, publicists, and politicians in every country, had become by the end of the 1920s, it did not succeed in making headway

---

[53] There is as yet no monograph based on its archives. The programme is quoted from Coudenhove-Kalergi; *Paneuropa*, Vienna, 1923, pp. 25 and 150 f.; the association's periodical *Paneuropa* (Vienna, vols. 1–14, 1924–38) is a mine of information. See also Coudenhove-Kalergi, *An Idea Conquers the World*, London, 1953.
[54] E. Stern-Rubarth, *Europa-Grossmacht oder Kleinstaaterei*, Bielefeld, 1951, pp. 8 f. and 12–17; a lot of material is contained in the three periodicals, *Europäische Wirtschaftsunion* (published by the Central Committee, ed. by C. Günther, The Hague), *L'Europe de demain* (published by the French Group, Paris), and *Europa-Wirtschaft* (published by the German Group, ed. by W. Grotkopp, Berlin).
[55] On this subject there is a recent article by K. Holl making exhaustive use of Foreign Ministry files, 'Europapolitik im Vorfeld der deutschen Regierungspolitik. Zür Tätigkeit pro-europäischer Organisationen in der Weimarer Republik' in *HZ*, vol. 219 (1974), pp. 33–94.

against the national sovereign state, still very much of a reality both as an institution and in the mind of the public at large. The associations managed to form thriving branches, made up mostly of intellectuals, but they gained little support among the mass of the population. The idea of Europe, although it was well enough known after 1927 to be the object of sharp attacks by extremists of both Right and Left, remained very much a minority concern by comparison with the strongly entrenched idea of the sovereign national state. Left-wing liberal and social-democratic party conferences began to vote for the 'formation of the United States of Europe', but in every country the nationalist Right dominated the field.[56]

This was clearly shown by the first attempt made between the wars to raise the campaign for European unity to the level of government negotiations. Worried by the failure of the 'policy of understanding' to break out of its impasse, Briand – apart from Seipel the only statesman in office who had managed to think out all the implications of actual unification – dared in carefully chosen words to propose to the Assembly of the League of Nations in September 1929 the project of a European federal union. The other European Foreign Ministers asked him with varying degrees of enthusiasm to express his thoughts in a memorandum. In the preceding months almost fifty books had appeared in various countries of Europe, demanding unification ever more insistently and realistically; and the associations redoubled their efforts to prepare the ground for the reception of Briand's memorandum.[57] But when in May 1930 the memorandum 'on the organization of a Europe federal union' reached the various governments, not only did it bear traces of the views of right-wing members of the French cabinet, and not only had the world economic crisis aggravated the situation with its mounting figures of unemployment; but, above all, the proposal was met with a complete lack of comprehension from most of the ministers and diplomats, unable as they were to think outside the categories of national sovereignty. 'Briand's intention to stabilize the present status quo in Europe', Brüning for example declared, 'must be opposed by a German demand for adequate and appropriate living space'. The possibility that thinking in terms of frontiers and rivalries could be made meaningless by the new concept of a political union was seriously considered only by a few governments – those in the smaller countries. The answers of the other governments, particularly of Great Britain and

[56] There are characteristic attacks on the European idea in *Hitler's Secret Book*, intr. by T. Taylor, NY, 1962, p. 29 f. and pp. 103–8; W. Borgius, *Der Paneuropa-Wahn*, Berlin, 1927; A. Dix, *Schluss mit Europa*, Leipzig, 1928. List of the resolutions of party conferences, including the quotation from the SPD's Heidelberg Programme of 1928, in Pegg (n. 51), p. 872 f.

[57] Cf. A. Fleissig, *Paneuropa*, Leipzig, 1930; F. Funk, *Die Vereinigten Staaten von Europa*, Aarau, 1930; E. Herriot, *Europe*, Paris, 1930 (translated into English and German in the same year); F. T. Gualtierotti, *Europa unita*, Milan, 1930; G. Quartara, *Gli Stati Uniti d'Europa e del mondo*, Turin, 1930 (both immediately translated into French), etc. Reports of the Second Pan-Europe Congress (17–19 May 1930 in Berlin) in *Paneuropa*, 6, June/July, 1930, pp. 201–71; and of the Congress for a European Customs Union (June 1934 in Paris) in *L'Europe de demain*, 11 October 1930, pp. 1–57.

of Fascist Italy, amounted to what the German Foreign Minister Curtius, referring to his own government's Note, described as 'a first class funeral for Briand's initiative'.[58] This made it certain that the concept would be condemned and relegated to the history of ideas, but it also meant that Europe missed the last chance to respond to the historic challenge by its own efforts before it was carved up between the new world powers. None of the lessons learnt by the disastrous experience of the First World War had any practical effect against the revival of nationalism. The peoples, longing for peace but bogged down in their divisions, were offered no common, fruitful alternative for the future. There had been no decision in favour of a final, institutional guarantee of peace and union in Europe which would have created a defensive bastion. Thus the way was free for reactionary Fascism in its various guises to uphold 'national sovereignty' with all the means which made Europe's downfall inevitable.

In the subsequent period of nationalist reaction, which many observers saw as a prelude to the Second World War, the idea of European unity appeared to be completely impracticable. In Germany the pro-European associations were banned as 'pacifist' from 1933 onwards. But even in the democratic countries they could only helplessly try to survive the 'epoch of Fascism'. In France the French section of the Pan-Europa Union and particularly of the European Customs Union, with its longer title L'Union Économique et Douanière de l'Europe, under Yves le Trocquer, Henri de Jouvenal, and Lucien Coquet, remained active both in publishing and in holding congresses, half hoping for an eventual understanding with Hitler's Germany; Blum's Socialists, on the other hand, were much readier to acknowledge that Hitler had to be adamantly opposed. What was more important for the future was the emergence of a group of young authors (of whom Denis de Rougemont, Robert Aron, and Alexander Marc were prominent) working for the periodicals *Esprit* and *L'Ordre nouveau*. Repudiating all forms of state-worship and starting from a position of Christian personalism, they advocated a federalism built on family, professional and local communities as the formation of a 'true European and federal new order'.[59] And for the first time, under the shock of the world economic crisis and the revival of nationalism, there came into

---

[58] Cf. with list of sources W. Lipgens, 'Briand's Europaplan' (n. 48), pp. 316–63; analysis of the memorandum, pp. 316–25; quotations from the cabinet meeting which drew up the German refusal, pp. 339–41. For Briand's proposal for European federal union, 1 May 1930, and the attitudes towards it of the governments concerned, see *Documents on British Foreign Policy, 1919–1939*, Second Series, vol. 1, 2nd impression, London, 1968, pp. 314–51. Cf. biographies, most recently, for example, K. von Klemperer, *Ignaz Seipel*, Princeton, NJ, 1972; F. Siebert, *Aristide Briand*, Erlenbach/Zurich, 1973.

[59] Cf. H. Truchy, *L'Union douanière européenne*, Paris, 1955; H. de Jouvenel, *Le Réveil de l'Europe*, Paris, 1938. For the Personalists, cf. E. Mounier, *Manifeste au service du personnalisme*, Paris, 1936 (e.g. p. 221 f.); A. Marc avec R. Dupuis, *Jeune Europe*, Paris, 1936; R. Aron, *La Fin de l'Après-guerre*, Paris, 1938 (esp. pp. 81 and 179). Creative original works by authors inspired by the European spirit are important: J. Romains, *Les Hommes de bonne volonté*, Paris, 1933; J. Benda, *Discours à la*

existence in Great Britain in 1932 an association called 'The New Commonwealth Society', whose many publications between 1933 and 1939 urged a reinforcement of the League of Nations by the creation of a compulsory court of arbitration and a strong international body of troops under the League to enforce its decisions. The thinking behind this was still in global terms and assumed that decisions would be made by individual states and not by a federation, but to a large extent it followed the lines of Harold Laski's pithy pronouncement in 1933: 'If you want peace you cannot contemplate setting up an international order based on sovereign states.'[60] But the British and other western governments, deceived like the German people by Hitler's emphasis on revision of the peace treaty, spent too much time thinking of a Europe that would be pacified by satisfying German demands and would return to co-operation within the League of Nations, but would still not be united. The same was true to some extent of the anti-Fascist resistance in Italy and Germany during the 1930s.[61] At the end of 1932 Coudenhove organized a 'third Pan-Europe congress' in Basle with resolutions which among other things called for a European party, but it was obvious to the much reduced number who took part that it could not be realized. In 1933 a pro-European group at Basle merged with the Swiss section of the Pan-Europa Union to form a new and independent association called 'Europa-Union' – a Swiss movement for the unification of Europe, which, as will be seen, was to exercise considerable influence in the 1940s. After fruitless efforts to enlist the support of Mussolini for his movement (as well as for preserving Austrian

---

nation européenne, Paris, 1933; R. Martin du Gard, *L'Eté 1914*, Paris, 1937; G. Bernanos, *Les Grands Cimetières sous la lune*, Paris, 1937 (with a searing indictment of the 'nationalist simpletons'), cf. G. Bonneville, *Prophètes et témoins de l'Europe. Essai sur l'idée d'Europe dans la littérature française de 1914 à nos jours*, Leiden, 1961.

[60] The major impulse behind the New Commonwealth Society came from Lord (David) Davies, *The Problem of the Twentieth Century*, London, 1931; an informative pamphlet in the principal languages called *The Aims and Tasks of the New Commonwealth* (signed by the President of the Society, G. N. Barnes, and the Vice-Presidents H. de Jouvenel, E. Jäckh, O. T. Crosby, and Lord Davies), London, 1932, p. 4: 'When we speak of an international authority, we mean a partly remodelled and rejuvenated League of Nations, which will have the power to alter public law and to make sure that it is put into effect.' H. Laski (deputy chairman of the Labour Party), *The Intelligent Man's Way to prevent War*, London, 1933. The British section of the NCS had as its president Winston Churchill, the French section had Georges Scelle, the German, Major General Haslmayr, with among others Fritz Gerlach, Prof. Herbert Kraus, and Carlo Schmid as members. On the shift of emphasis in the NCS in 1939 from global policing to European union, to the founding of Federal Union and finally of a British section of *Paneuropa* in 1939, see n. 101 f.

[61] The policy of appeasement is incisively analysed in M. Gilbert and R. Gott, *The Appeasers*, London, 1963, *passim*. On the anti-Fascist resistance before 1939, cf. W. Lipgens, *Europa-Föderationspläne deutscher und italienischer Widerstandsgruppen* in *Von der Diktatur zur Demokratie* (Schriftenreihe des Internationalen Schulbuchinstituts, vol. 17), Brunswick, 1973, esp. pp. 12–15. More outspoken demands for European federation at that period came from people in exile: C. Sforza, *Gli Stati Uniti d'Europa*, Lugano, 1930; C. Roselli in Paris (Lipgens, *ibid.*, p. 13); Fritz von Unruh, *Europa erwache*, Basle, 1936; O. Strasser, *Europäische Föderation*, Zurich, 1936.

independence), Coudenhove, before withdrawing to a Chair at Columbia University in New York, bluntly declared in 1938:[62]

'We prefer to postpone European unification to a later date rather than see it accomplished in the near future under Hitler's tyranny ... Paneuropa has room for monarchies as well as for republics ... what it cannot accept is states which do not recognize human rights.'

3. Europe's Self-Awareness:

II. The Triumph of the Supranational Principle in the Resistance

During the inter-war period European-minded writers had given prophetic warnings that, unless unity was achieved in time, the selfishness of national states would plunge Europe into a new war. And this war, unleashed by Hitler in 1939 in a bid for German supremacy in Europe, was now a cruel reality which brought suffering to millions of families and expanded into a global conflict. Writers had earlier warned that Fascist nationalism would develop into totalitarian rule: and after the majority of European states had been defeated in less than a year, the peoples, including the Germans, experienced the reality of a totalitarian Nazi regime such as the civilized world would never have believed possible, a barbarous and anti-European dictatorship comparable only to that of Stalin. Many saw it as Moltke did in a letter to Lionel Curtis in 1942: 'The tyranny, the terror, the collapse of all values, is greater than I could ever have imagined.'[63] Writers had also earlier warned that the old Continent, situated as it was between the rising continental-sized unions of the United States and the Soviet Union, had been granted only a brief time-limit in which to unite; and now the Europeans, as the war progressed, experienced for themselves the advance of these empires, which respectively comprised twice and five times as much of the earth's surface as the countries of Europe combined. Between the wars the challenge to Europe to unite had been issued by those who had foreseen these threatening developments (for up to 1939 only the weakening and economic stagnation of the European countries had actually come about). Now in the middle of the war, the threats having become a reality, the challenge was felt in the shape of harsh facts.

---

[62] Reports of and resolutions passed by the Third Paneuropa Congress in Oct. 1932 in *Paneuropa*, 8 Nov. 1932, pp. 225–94. For more details about the Swiss Europa-Union, see below pp. 117–24. R. Coudenhove-Kalergi, *Kommen die Vereinigten Staaten von Europa?* Glarus, 1938, pp. 20 f. and 96.

[63] L. Curtis (ed.), *A German of the Resistance. The last letters of Count Helmuth James von Moltke*, London (1946¹) 1948², p. 26.

(A) THE RESISTANCE MOVEMENT AGAINST 'HITLER'S EUROPE'

The First World War, fought in trenches lying to a greater or lesser extent along national frontiers, was a war which (apart from the Habsburg Empire) did not bring about the wholesale collapse of states. Consequently at European level its impact was felt chiefly by small groups of intellectuals. The six years of the Second World War, by contrast, were a harsh and unforgettable experience for the great mass of the population and caused the total collapse of almost every state on the Continent. The experience of the inter-war period had shown that Europe's states were too small to solve by their own efforts the problems of a modern economy, and the outbreak of a new war in 1939 proved the failure of all the attempts made since the First World War to set up a collective peace-keeping organization. Then for most Europeans came a still greater shock: by 1940–1 every European state north of the Pyrenees, with the exceptions of Great Britain, Sweden, and Switzerland, had been destroyed by Hitler's brutal lust for power, in a process which finally led to the destruction of the Italian and German states. All these governments had shown themselves incapable of guaranteeing their peoples the minimum of security and independence which it is the first duty of any government to provide.[64]

During the war people had to put up with the effective domination of practically the entire Continent by the German occupation forces, the humiliation of their own governments, and the mobilization of all resources irrespective of existing frontiers. This was the day-to-day reality which lasted for four years. The object lesson provided by the collapse and conquest, and by the creation of a single centrally controlled economy, did more to accustom the public at large to think in Continental terms than the whole Coudenhove-Kalergi movement a decade earlier; and because of the cynical use of the slogan 'Europe' by Nazi propaganda many soldiers, both German and, for example, volunteers in Hitler's forces, honestly believed that they were fighting for Europe. But such illusions prevailed in spite and not because of Hitler's nationalist conception of a 'Germanic Empire'. Still ignorant of the real aims and methods of Nazi leadership, idealists and fairly large numbers of ordinary people in the eastern and western parts of Central Europe as well as opportunists showed a readiness in the period immediately following defeat to co-operate with the Germans in establishing a genuinely 'New Order'. But in the course of time they all became increasingly aware that in reality the Nazis had no acceptable answer to the willingness of the peoples to learn the lesson of

---

[64] The fundamental importance for most Continental European states of the experience of defeat followed by long occupation by foreign troops is something which will often have to be reverted to, cf. esp. pp. 58 and 160. The fact that Great Britain, Sweden, Switzerland, Portugal, and Spain were the only countries not to share this experience is essential for an understanding of post-war history.

the collapse of their states, that for Hitler a remodelling of Europe in which the non-German peoples would co-operate as equals was inconceivable, that he was prepared to tolerate non-Germans merely as subordinates. He was, they saw, simply pursuing the old nationalist and imperialist ends with the most ruthless means.[65] The more plainly the totalitarian character, contempt for legality, and racial arrogance of Nazism were shown in action, the more people came to their senses and returned to the true European tradition. In course of time everyone with any real European convictions joined the opposition to the Nazi regime. 'Against the horrifying background of a Europe lying in ruins we shall be able to bear witness at the bar of mankind to the appalling consequences of old-fashioned theories of nationalism carried to excess.'[66]

For the Resistance groups which sprang into existence in Italy, Germany, and the occupied countries paramilitary resistance operations were impossible until the last few months before the Allied landings, at least in central and western parts of Europe, because of the efficient police system. Mental resistance was for a long time the only possible and in fact the most important form of resistance. The difficulties and obstacles in the way of even an adequate response to the challenge were inconceivably great; yet despite pressures of every kind the men of the Resistance (of course only a small minority) risked their lives not simply against something which already existed, but above all for something which they wished to put in its place. In a dangerous situation and facing a formidable challenge, they still succeeded in saying what a better future might look like.

The majority of the underground leaflets, distributed every week by the hundred, even by the thousand, contained accusations of coercion, injustice, and disregard for human rights perpetrated by the Nazi regime. But hardly ever in the non-Communist Resistance – which was the original and for most of the war the predominant type of resistance

---

[65] For the phase of willingness to collaborate in a European spirit as a consequence of the experience of defeat, which should be carefully distinguished from the collaborationism of the later war years, the best authorities are: P. Kluke and L. de Jong in: *Das Dritte Reich und Europa,* Munich, 1957, pp. 114–22 and 133–52; also S. Hoffmann, *Collaborationism in France during World War II,* and J. A. Armstrong, 'Collaborationism in World War II: the Integral Nationalist Variant in Eastern Europe', in *JMH,* vol. 40 (1968), pp. 375–95 and 396–410. On the real intentions of Nazi leadership, see P. Kluke, 'Nationalsozialistische Europaideologie', in *VfZG,* 3 (1955), esp. pp. 244–68; L. Gruchmann, *Nationalsozialistische Grossraumordnung* (Schriftenreihe der *VfZG,* No. 4), Stuttgart, 1962, esp. pp. 75–121; A. Hillgruber, *Hitlers Strategie, Politik und Kriegsführung, 1940–41,* Frankfurt, 1965 (concerning the struggle against the USA for world mastery after Hitler had created his Continental empire). For a general view, the sketch 'Zusammenbruchs-Erlebnis und Hitlers Europa' in Lipgens, *Föderationspläne* (see n. 67), pp. 6–11.

[66] *Föderationspläne,* No. 73 (E. Janvier, 20 Nov. 1943). There is plenty of other evidence showing how erroneous is the view put forward by Communists and also by some individuals on the Right that the Resistance movement as a whole was in favour of the nation state. On the contrary, the true Resistance saw as the basic obstacle to a European community 'the false necessity of totalitarianism, a necessity which is purely the invention of exacerbated nationalism' (ibid., No. 78, P. Viannay, Jan. 1944).

everywhere – did any underground newspaper or leaflet favour a return to the pre-war system of national states. 'Who', asked *Franc-Tireur* in 1944, 'would dare to suggest that the popular forces which have risen against Nazi tyranny are fighting for return to a past whose grave faults and irrevocable collapse they understand only too well?'[67] They wanted 'no return to the Balkanization of a continent in which each people would be enclosed behind its economic and political barriers' and in which the sense of human liberty would be enfeebled or perverted. On the contrary, these accusations were linked with the realization, expressed in an increasing number of ways, that human dignity is more important than the interests of the state, that the totalitarian claims of every state and nationalism must be resisted, and that the key question was how in future human rights, peace, and welfare could be better safeguarded. One of the basic themes of the Resistance, expressed in many documents, was the repudiation in principle of intellectual totalitarianism, state-worship, and nationalism.

The loss of the old obligations based on natural law, wrote Moltke in a memorandum of April 1941 prepared for the Kreisau Circle, had in recent times led to the 'creation of sovereign states' as unifying centres for limited purposes; yet their 'demand for the whole man had been shown to be an abuse of secular power, and this abuse led in turn to the loss of the sense of membership' and with it a loss of freedom. The opportunity to reshape Europe now existed because the national states, by the excesses to which they had been brought by Fascism, had carried the system to absurd lengths. At the same time, the 'Manifesto di Ventotene', one of the basic publications of the Italian Resistance, written in the spring of 1941 by Spinelli and Rossi, argued consistently for a federal conception of Europe. It saw the principles of freedom and human dignity threatened because national states, formed only a century or two before out of smaller units for purposes of self-protection, were no longer perceived simply as 'the most expedient way of organizing community life within the framework of human society'. On the contrary, national sovereignty had been exaggerated into a kind of 'divine essence,' into an 'organism concerned only with its own existence and its own development, with scant regard for the harm that others might thereby suffer'. But against these consequences a deep desire for freedom and international solidarity was now, the

---

[67] The volume edited by W. Lipgens, *Europa-Föderationspläne der Widerstandsbewegungen 1940–45* (Schriften des Forschungsinstitutes der deutschen Gesellschaft für Auswärtige Politik, vol. 26) Munich, 1968, 547 pages (quotation from Document No. 81, 1 March 1944), offers comprehensive evidence for what in the following pages can only be conveyed in a severely abridged form. In this work are published, mostly for the first time, a large number of the more elaborate 'foreign policy' blueprints of as many Resistance groups as possible in as many countries as possible, with an Introduction for each country and a commentary on each passage. An English edition is in preparation: see p. xvi.

This evidence shows that no national differences of any importance can be detected in the programmes as a whole: for each of the passages cited below, in what is necessarily a very limited selection, many parallel passages could be quoted from any of the others, irrrespective of the country of origin. The total volume of such evidence must be taken for granted as far as this part of the Introduction is concerned as the most important foundation of the European unification movement after 1945.

Manifesto added, making itself felt.[68] The most widely circulated Netherlands underground newspaper wrote in 1943: 'Countries in which the most elementary human rights are violated constitute dangerous sources of infection which the international community has the right to oppose.' It had been proved, a member of the Italian Resistance had written, that in the hands of the national states 'the power to decide over war and peace, the power to command national armies, ... the power to divide the world into closed economic areas, the power of individual countries to turn themselves into despotisms, without being disturbed by intervention from outside ... turned those states into instruments of disaster', and that their powers should be taken away and transferred to a higher level of authority.[69]

Many Resistance pamphlets demanded, following the logic of their case, decentralization within national states, with more power placed in the hands of self-governing local communities of manageable size. By making people accustomed to a free kind of democracy in Europe (such pamphlets argued, using similar language despite their independent origins), by making the democratic principle of self-government from below a reality, 'effective guarantees would be set up against the creation of an absolutist, centralizing and bureaucratic power of the national sovereign state'.[70] But, living as they did through a period of absolutist state power, the authors of these pamphlets knew that interstate federation could not in itself overcome the totalitarian claims of existing states, but that a supranational authority must be established to safeguard peace, democratization, and human rights.

(B) THE NEED FOR SUPRANATIONAL AUTHORITY

The attempt to answer people's first and most pressing question during the miseries of war and occupation – how to safeguard peace in future – led in the literature of the Resistance to the further question which was put in many different ways: Why had the organization for collective security set up after the First World War failed? So horrified had the statesmen been at the loss of their security and prosperity, and at the decline of Europe by comparison with the rest of the world, that they had tried through the

---

[68] The quotation is from the Moltke memorandum 'Point of departure, aims and tasks', first printed (with biographical details about all members of the group, pp. 55–209) in the pioneering work of Ger van Roon, *German Resistance to Hitler. Count Moltke and the Kreisau Circle*, London, 1971, pp. 317–28; extracts from the 'Ventotene Manifesto' with details of its origin, authors, etc. in W. Lipgens, *Europa-Föderationspläne deutscher und italienischer Widerstandsgruppen im II. Weltkreig* (n. 61), esp. pp. 15–27.

[69] Quotations from *Vrij Nederland*, Sept. 1943; and from the foundation resolution of the MFE, Milan, 28 August 1943, quoted in full in Lipgens, *Föderationspläne*, No. 103 and no. 10; cf. parallel passages shown in the Index there, under 'Interventionsrecht in innere Angelegenheiten zur Verhinderung totalitärer Regime'.

[70] Quotation from Rollier in *L'Unità Europea*, No. 4, Milan, May 1944. For the important point in the programme (to which it was not possible to do full justice in this Introduction) concerning the internal decentralization of the existing national states, cf. the parallel passages indicated in the Index in Lipgens, op. cit., under the heading 'Innerstaatlicher Föderalismus'.

Covenant of the League of Nations to create a law to prevent war that would have been unthinkable in the decades before 1914. Why was it that, only twenty years later, 'the first dream of world peace had dissolved in blood'?[71] Men of the Resistance in every European country gave the answer independently of each other, indeed without even knowing of each other, in what turned out be astonishingly similar terms. Two major reasons were identified: 1. The League of Nations failed not for this or that accidental reason, but because, as all the evidence quite plainly showed, it had been set up as an institution in international law consisting of sovereign states. Therefore it was inhibited by its very structure from performing the task assigned to it, whatever the nature of that task might be. The League had failed, as Léon Blum, at the time a prisoner of the Vichy government, wrote in 1941 in a passage that influenced the whole French Resistance: 'because it was not a sovereign power in its own right, independent of and superior to national sovereignties; because to implement its decisions it possessed neither the political authority nor the material power that would have prevailed over that of individual states.' It failed, wrote Einaudi, leader of Italy's underground liberals in 1943, like all mere alliances or confederations 'because it had no legislature and executive power of its own, but depended on the unanimous votes of its member states'. The same kind of arguments were used in the other languages of Europe, though there is no space here to go into detail.[72]

2. The other reason why the League failed, as documents of the Resistance continually emphasize, is that it could neither meet what were supposed to be its global responsibilities on the one hand, nor concentrate on Europe on the other, but fell between two stools. Thus the leading Dutch Socialist underground newspaper declared that the League 'had been over-ambitious' by 'attempting to create an organization that spanned the globe while Europe was still in chaos'; it had 'built the roof before the building was there to support it'.[73] The most discerning analysts explained that this second shortcoming made the first, that is the League's powerlessness, almost inevitable. The United States and the Soviet Union, leading world powers since 1917, had remained outside the League, while the non-European states which were members of the League had often made the solution of purely European questions more difficult.[74] Against the renewed

[71] Lipgens, *Föderationspläne*, e.g. Nos. 71, 73, and *passim.*
[72] Léon Blum, 'A l'Echelle Humaine' (July 1941), reprinted in *L'OEuvre de Léon Blum*, vol. 5, Paris, 1955, p. 477; Luigi Einaudi, 'Per una Federazione economica Europea' (Sept. 1943), reprinted in L. Einaudi, *La Guerra e l'Unità Europea*, Milan, 1950², pp. 50–1. Cf. the attempt to summarize the aspect of the Resistance programmes (from which in the following pages some formulations have been borrowed), W. Lipgens, 'European Federation in the Political Thought of Resistance Movements during World War II', in *Central European History,* vol. 1 (1968), pp. 5–19.
[73] *Föderationspläne*, No. 104 (Romein, 10 Sept. 1943); also No. 71, Jurgensen, Sept. 1943.
[74] F. P. Walters, *A History of the League of Nations*, London/NY, 1960, shows how between 1929 and 1938 the problem 'global or regional' was in effect an issue in countless particular cases: how frequently problems of a regional kind arose which only concerned one continent (usually Europe)

demand for a 'united states of the world' put forward by many writers with the aim of safeguarding world peace, the point was made that, to quote *Libération*, the organ of the second largest French Resistance group, in a passage written in 1943 which is typical of many similar passages in all the occupied countries: 'Abolition of war could not be achieved all at once on a world scale.' Therefore 'a gradual and piecemeal solution must be tried', and a distinction drawn between two problems. 'One solution consists of forming unions or federations which would allow states with close territorial or cultural ties to abolish their currency, customs and defence barriers and to manage their resources in common', so that nationalism and war between them would in future be impossible.

The other solution was to strive for world-wide 'international laws, whereby clashes of self-interest between the federations could be settled and a common code worked out in the sphere of morality and law'.[75] The final goal remained, in the words of the umbrella organization of all Resistance groups in the Lyons region, a definite outlawing of war and the 'unity of all nations in a federal world organization', but 'this immense and long-term task can only be undertaken with any prospect of success if in the first place a solution is found for the problem of Europe, which has been the starting-place of so many appalling catastrophes'.[76]

The Resistance writers were realistic enough to judge that both the extra-European world powers would be ideologically and economically self-sufficient, and would have enough resources to ensure their own internal peace, prosperity, and self-defence, in other words they would see no necessity to give up their sovereign rights in favour of any world organization that might be set up over them. Accordingly, on a global level, the only kind of organization that would exist would be one like the League of Nations, functioning between, not above, the member states, with powers only of recommendation. The nation states in the much reduced Continent of Europe, on the other hand, would obviously not be able to guarantee peace and prosperity from their own resources because they would be outclassed in terms of technology, economy, and defence. Only by pooling their sovereignty could they safeguard peace, prosperity, and human rights against the totalitarian claims of the former national states. The leader of

---

and about which the members from the other continents did not wish to commit themselves; how diplomats and journalists in Geneva discussed the necessity of founding, in addition to the largely European League of Nations, an 'American League of Nations' and an 'Asiatic League', the latter to have both the United States and the Soviet Union as members (p. 360). This was incidentally one of the reasons for Briand's proposal in 1930; the idea was, by founding a 'European Federal Union' under the supervision of the League of Nations, to enable the latter to become more global in character; cf. Lipgens, 'Briands Europaplan' (n. 48), pp. 317 and 360 f,

[75] *Les Idées politiques et sociales de la Résistance (Documents clandestins 1940–1944)*, ed. by Henri Michel and Boris Mirkine-Guetzévitch, Paris 1954, pp. 395–6 (Libération-Sud, Sept. 1943).

[76] Ibid., No. 89 (Mouvement de Libération Nationale, Région Lyon, Aug. 1944). This Lyons programme – distributed as a leaflet and poster in almost all the towns in Southern France – was substantially a summary of the Geneva Declaration drawn up by the clandestine conference of Resistance fighters from nine European countries in the spring of 1944 (cf. n. 87).

Combat, which until shortly before the end of the war was the largest French Resistance group, put it in a nutshell: 'History teaches us that frontiers are always being extended. The United States of Europe – a stage on the way to world unity – will soon be the living reality for which we are fighting.'[77]

In this way the future voluntary European federation came to occupy a dominant position in the programme of the non-Communist Resistance groups in every country. There were countless descriptions of how this federation was to be created in detail. Within the Resistance there were, probably in every country, small right-wing groups which for special reasons were not in the collaborationist camp, such as the Goerdeler group in Berlin, the 'Organisation civile et militaire' in Paris, and others. These acknowledged the need for a binding international legal order and for economic unification, but they wished to preserve a degree of independence for individual states in their foreign policy. They spoke of a 'European directorate' and an 'economic council' which would need machinery to implement their decisions, but nevertheless sought solutions which would leave states their freedom to make basic decisions and would be confederal rather than federal in character.[78] The great majority of Resistance writers, however, opposed any special consideration for national sovereignty in the sphere of foreign policy, economics, and defence. This time care was to be taken to avoid the chief mistake of 1919, which was the institutional weakness of the League of Nations. War between European states would have to be made absolutely impossible by the establishment of a strong

---

[77] *Föderationspläne*, No. 64 (Bourdet, Frenay, Hauriou, Sept. 1942): the preceding summary is based esp. on Nos. 10, 71, 89, 104, and 136, and on the Geneva Declaration by Resistance fighters from nine countries (with all the facts that have been ascertained about this conference: cf. op cit., pp. 379–400); for its importance as the point of departure for post-war federalists, cf. p. 57 f. For details of the problem of the relation between the 'World Federation' and the 'European Federation', see W. Lipgens, 'Innerfranzösische Kritik an der Aussenpolitik de Gaulles, 1944–46' in *VfZG*, 24 (1976), p. 152 f.

[78] e.g. *Föderationspläne*, Nos. 50, 62, and 100. No Resistance movement was so marked by a spirit of delaying caution as the German one, which, on the one hand, still had to take the plunge of breaking with its own nation state and, on the other hand, after Hitler's wholesale destruction of the Left was sociologically more strongly conservative-minded, whereas the Resistance groups in the other European countries which demanded unity were overwhelmingly Socialist. Within the Conservative-nationalist Goerdeler group Goerdeler himself (though not always its other members – see *Föderationspläne*, No. 39 for example in the case of Beck) passed from an originally opportunistic conception of Europe to one based on principle, in a remarkable intellectual evolution between 1942 and 1944. In a memorandum written at the end of 1941 he had expected the German nation to be the leader of the European bloc, but by the autumn of 1943 he was planning a 'union', a permanent league of peace . . . in which neither Germany nor any other power shall claim dominance', and which was to be equipped with a 'European foreign ministry' as well as a 'European economic ministry' and a 'European army'. At the beginning of 1944 he demanded an 'organic unity of federal states'. Quotations from *Föderationspläne*, Nos. 34, 50, and 53. On the ideas of the Kreisau Circle and the Goerdeler group as a whole there is a good account in H. Graml, 'Die aussenpolitischen Vorstellungen des deutschen Widerstandes', in *Der deutsche Widerstand*, ed. by W. Schmitthenner and H. Buchheim, Cologne, 1966, esp. pp. 19–72: Graml however was at the time unacquainted with the quoted documents, which throw further light on Goerdeler; on this extension to our knowledge, see in more detail Lipgens, *Europa-Föderationspläne deutscher und italienischer Widerstandgruppen* (n. 61), p. 19 f.

European federal government. This can be clearly illustrated by quotations from each of the leading countries.

Delegates of three or four of the main 'illegal' parties in the Polish Resistance drew up a basic programme which contained a single point dealing with foreign policy. It ran as follows: 'The Polish Republic will be a member of the Federation of Free European Peoples', and within it 'would strive to promote as much cohesion as possible and a federal authority powerful enough to protect the federated nations from external aggressive nationalism'. The fundamental document on which the German Kreisau Circle formed their plans began with the sentence: 'Europe is a federal state with one overall sovereignty.., Foreign affairs, defence, planning on a European level fall within the competence of the federal government.'[79] The leading Dutch underground newspaper declared: 'A new higher authority must be set up in Europe ... a European federation which will possess the means to put its will into effect and impose it on the various nationalities.' The programme of an Italian Resistance group declared: 'The preservation of freedom and peace on the whole Continent must be exercised exclusively by the European federation and its executive, legislative and judicial organs.'[80]

A test agreed by the umbrella organizations of all the Resistance groups in the Lyons region effectively summarized the views of many similar documents: 'The nation states ought to federate and transfer to the common federal state the right to manage the economic and commercial life of Europe, the sole authority over its armed forces and the right to take measures against any attempt to re-establish a fascist regime. The federation must also have the right to manage foreign relations and to administer colonial territories not ripe for independence, and the right to create a European citizenship in addition to national citizenship. The government of the federal state is to be chosen not by the nation states but by democratic and direct elections by the peoples.'[81] It was in such terms that the basic insights of innumerable writers were expressed at a time when Continental Europe was lying prostrate. For them it was completely unthinkable that the old system of European sovereign states should be restored once again after the experience of Fascism and world war to which that system had led.

[79] Polish basic programme in *Föderationspläne*, No. 114 ('Program Polski Ludowej'), Dec. 1941; published in full in *VfZG*, 21 (1973), pp. 107–11. For plans of the Kreisau Circle, *Föderationspläne*, No. 32 (Moltke, 'Ausgangslage und Aufgaben'), 9 June 1941: for the first version of this memorandum, see n. 68. In ibid., the limits of Europe are defined as follows: 'The federal state shall be bounded on the north and west by the Atlantic, on the south by the Mediterranean and Black Seas, on the east by the eastern frontiers of Romania, former Poland, the Baltic states and Finland'.

[80] *Föderationspläne*, Nos. 100 (Heuven Goedhart in *Het Parool*, 12.12.1942) and 10 (Programme of the Movimento Federalista Europea, 28.8.1943). Cf. in each case evidence of the organization's representative character and commentary.

[81] *Föderationspläne*, No. 89 (cf. n. 32 above). As to 'many similar documents', cf. the earlier specialized works: C. H. Pegg, 'Die Résistance als Träger der europäischen Einigungsbestrebungen in Frankreich während des II. Weltkrieges', in *Europa-Archiv*, 7 (1952), pp. 5197–206; C. F. Delzell, 'The European Federalist Movement in Italy. First Phase 1918–1947', in *JMH*, 32 (1960), pp. 241–50; H. Halin, *L'Europe unie, objectif majeur de la Résistance* (preface by P. H. Spaak), Paris–Brussels, 1967; also more recently the country-by-country survey by A. Chiti-Batelli, 'Il Federalismo nella Resistenza', in M. Albertini, A. Chiti-Batelli, G. Petrilli, *Storia del federalismo europea*, Turin, 1973, esp. pp. 125–204.

(C) MOTIVES FOR EUROPEAN UNITY, THE SUMMING-UP BY THE GENEVA CONFERENCE OF RESISTANCE FIGHTERS

The motives and theoretical arguments which the leaders of the Resistance put forward in favour of a European federation were surprisingly similar in all European countries, even though, if only for reasons of brevity, they were tersely expressed in underground leaflets and not developed in scholarly detail. In the following paragraphs they are arranged in order of the importance assigned to them by the Resistance writers themselves.

1. The basic and major justification for their plans for European unification in the case of nearly all the Resistance writers was defined as taking up an ideological stand against worship of the state, against the 'terrible' compulsion towards totalitarian rule, as it is inevitably forged by nationalism'. The system of nation states which had brought on mankind so much suffering, and in its extreme form of Fascism had been carried to absurd lengths, was felt to be unworthy of preservation. What was needed, instead, was to safeguard true values, personal freedom, religious and political rights, etc. against state nationalism by a European federation which should prevent the return of nationalism and Fascism in its member states. This conviction was reinforced by the experience of a common struggle against injustice and slavery by the Resistance groups of all the occupied countries, a feeling of Europeanness that was especially marked in the French group known as *Combat*, but was also summed up by Moltke when he wrote: 'After considerable difficulty we are in touch with Christian groups in the various occupied territories', and their 'effective opposition on grounds of principle' means 'a great addition of strength for us'.[82]

2. An equally fundamental argument, and one which was put forward by almost every author during the ordeal of war, was that the unity of Europe would make it impossible for the nation states to plunge the peoples of Europe into war in generation after generation. If the first argument stemmed from the degeneration of the nation state, the second argument was based on the experience of the League of Nations, whose purely intergovernmental machinery was unable to prevent war between European nations. Only a European federal union could put an end for good to 'European civil wars' and make peace secure once and for all. Not another loosely structured League, only a supranational federal authority could finally overcome nationalism and, being directly elected by the people and under their watchful eye, could exercise those common powers over foreign

---

[82] Moltke to Lionel Curtis. Cf. nn. 63 and 68; on *Combat*, cf. *Föderationspläne*, No. 77 (Frenay, Résistance – espoir de l'Europe, 12 Dec. 1943). The phrase 'terrible compulsion' from *Föderationspläne*, No. 78 (Viannay, 'Le Combat pour une cité libre', Jan. 1944), see n. 66 above. Cf. all the parallel passages listed in the Index, ibid., p. 542 under 'Souveränität, nationalstaatliche, Ablehnung der'.

54   *Introduction*

policy, security, and economic planning which could be effective only on a European scale.[83]

3. All those documents were characterized by a remarkable transformation of people's attitude to Germany. The Resistance writers shared the worldwide anxiety to make any recurrence of German aggression impossible. The question was how this was to be done without continual constraints, occupation, reparations, etc., which would only breed a new spirit of nationalism, and without enforcing the dismantlement and reduction of industry to a point where Germany would become an economic disaster area in the heart of Europe, with adverse effects on its neighbours. Unlike those planners who proceeded from the assumptions of nationalism and military power, they answered that the 'German problem' could be solved only by Germany's becoming a full member of the European federation. Distinguishing between the Nazi leaders and the German people, Claude Bourdet, for example, wrote in March 1933 in *Combat*, the leading Resistance organ in Southern France, that 'the revolutionary spirit of resistance unanimously looks to the Europe of the future and this Europe cannot be built without Germany'. Of course for some years to come Germany would have to be 'placed under tutelage in a political as well as a cultural sense', but this could be 'tolerated if at the same time all the nations of Europe renounced a part of their national sovereignty in favour of a European federation ... We do not forget that it was the German resistance which first raised its head and produced the first martyrs.' On the German side the deteriorating military situation brought similar insight. 'The main advantage of integrating Germany into Europe', wrote Theodor Steltzer, a member of the Kreisau Circle, to a friend in London in July 1944, 'as opposed to a policy of pure suppression would lie in the fact that in the first case all the constructive forces would be applied to co-operation under the lead of a German government, whereas the handling of the security problem has much less prospect of success through an isolated system of formal controls'. The statement issued by the International Conference of Resistance Fighters at Geneva in the spring of 1944 put the

---

[83] Cf. the writings mentioned in nn. 71–81, also the parallel passages referred to in Lipgens, *Föderationspläne*, Index: under 'Friedenssicherung', p. 532. A point particularly to be emphasized is that the persecuted Christian Churches, true to their duty to preserve supranational values, firmly opposed the 'false conception of the unfettered authority of the state': Pope Pius XII in the Encyclical *Summi Pontificatus* in 1939 called it 'pernicious ... because it destroys the supranational community', and declared that the 'alleged absolute autonomy of the state' 'is in clear contradiction to the natural order' in the sphere of international relations as well. The Pope's Christmas messages between 1940 and 1944 urged with mounting insistence the creation of supranational institutions 'whose authority must be real and effective *vis-à-vis* the member states' (Lipgens, *Föderationspläne*, Nos. 121, 124, 126, and 138). Likewise the General Secretary of the World Council of Churches, Willem A. Visser't Hooft, expressed the unanimous opinion of the member Churches that: 'The anarchy of mutually competing and unlimited national sovereignties must be overcome, and an international authority must be created which will establish the law and enforce it'.' (Memorandum, Jan. 1943, ibid., No. 128).

point incisively: 'Only a federal union will permit the German people to take part in European life without becoming a danger to other nations.'[84]

4. In all the Resistance documents the justification for a common market as an economic necessity emerged more strongly than the few quotations possible here would suggest. As *Liberté* wrote in November 1941: 'Europe is the smallest continent in which some twenty-eight nations tread on each other's toes. These frontiers have become intolerable as a result of the international division of labour, which has made every nation dependent on the others, and of the development of transport. They must be abolished'.[85] But this had been taken for granted ever since the economic crisis of 1930, and in the Resistance literature was used only as an additional argument to the first three just considered. For the rest the objection was not to the economic unification of Europe brought about by Nazi rule as such, but to its coercive character.

5. The fifth argument emerged towards the end of the war: Europe would only be able to retain its own kind of civilization and make its political voice felt if it united as a federation. 'From two directions', wrote Father Delp in his condemned cell at the turn of the year 1944–5, 'we are being invaded by forces foreign to our soil and unaware of our problems: Russia and America'.[86] Only through federal union would Europe be able to make sure of its future between them. But this last argument, which easily lent itself to misunderstanding, was used only cautiously and in isolated instances, for the Resistance leaders wanted – and as far as they were concerned practised – an end of power politics. Thus nearly all these writings urged the need for a global peace organization, into which a European federation was to be built as an essential substratum, cornerstone, and driving force. For obviously the establishment of an effective organization for world peace presupposed something like a global balance of power, in which the more obvious disparities would be eliminated because, in addition to the already existing continental-sized powers America and Russia, equally viable combinations would be formed in other parts of the world which were still divided and potential sources of war, such as the Far East and Europe.

[84] The quotations are taken in sequence from: *Föderationspläne*, No. 82 (Bourdet, 'Future Allemagne?.', March 1944; also published in G. Ziebura, 'Die Idee der Demokratie in der französischen Widerstandsbewegung', in *Festgabe für Hans Herzfeld*, Berlin, 1958, p. 372 f.; also Ziebura, *Die deutschfranzösischen Beziehungen seit 1945*, Pfullingen, 1970, p. 29 f.; *Föderationspläne*, No. 54 (Steltzer, Memorandum to British Friends, 15 July 1944) and No. 136 (Declaration of 20 May 1944 by the Geneva Conference of Resistance Fighters, Declaration II, 20.5.1944). Cf. the Index ibid. for parallel passages under 'Deutschland, Zukunft von' (p. 528).

[85] *Liberté* (a predecessor of *Combat*), No. 9, 15 Nov. 1941. Cf. too *La Marseillaise* of 14 July 1944: 'The different regions of Europe have become so dependent on each other economically that the economic barriers are today as artificial and irksome as the road tolls and customs barriers were in France under the *ancien régime*' (ibid., p. 247). For parallel passages, see Index in ibid. (p. 546) under 'Wirtschaftlicher Zusammenschluss Europas'.

[86] A. Delp (a member of the Kreisau Circle), 'Meditations on Europe on New Year's Eve, 1 Jan. 1945' (a month before his execution), *Föderationspläne*, No. 56. Cf. also Nos. 79, 87, and 89.

56 *Introduction*

These themes were taken up by Resistance groups in country after country with an astonishing degree of unanimity, though without knowledge of what the others were doing. Yet even before the end of the war representatives of the Resistance in nine different countries managed to arrange a meeting on Swiss soil at which a large measure of agreement was seen to exist. The fact that for reasons of expediency Hitler had allowed that small country to remain free, surrounded as it was by territory which he had occupied, enabled refugee members of the Resistance with or without an official mandate from their groups to meet secretly, although the Swiss authorities had banned public meetings in order to give Hitler no excuse of a breach of neutrality. Among them two names were especially noteworthy, those of E. Rossi and A. Spinelli, both of whom had escaped after spending years in Mussolini's political prisons. As will be seen later, they had founded the Movimento Federalista Europeo inside the Italian Resistance, and in the autumn of 1943 arrived already convinced that the Resistance all over Europe should accept a future programme of the same kind, and that the time had come to sum it up. From November 1943 onwards they tried to distribute an invitation to other refugee Resistance groups suggesting that the time had come in view of their common experience of resistance to work together for a 'United States of Europe', and appealing for help in co-operating for a 'preparatory congress' aimed at drawing up an agreed 'solemn declaration of our common aims'. The large number of contacts, often made with great difficulty, during the winter of 1943–4 led to the formation of a more closely knit group consisting of three Italians, three Frenchmen, two Germans, two Dutchmen, a Czech, a Yugoslav, a Pole, a Norwegian, and (for a time) a Dane, some of whom were refugees acting as official representatives of their own Resistance groups, while others had established contact without any direct mandate. In the home of Visser't Hooft, who was also a contact man between the Dutch Resistance and their government-in-exile, clandestine meetings of a formal character were held on 31 March, 29 April, 20 May, and 6–7 July 1944. The most important of these was the meeting of 20 May.[87] It was then that the draft of a declaration of the European Resistance movement was drawn up and sent with an accompanying letter, preceded by a declaration of solidarity, to the Resistance groups of all nine countries so far as they could be

---

[87] For the situation in Switzerland, see A. Mayer, *Anpassung oder Widerstand*, Frauenfeld (Switzerland), 1965; on Rossi and Spinelli and the foundation of the Movimento Federalista Europea, chap. 1/2, pp. 108–17; full text of the letter of invitation in Nov. 1943 to 'all anti-Fascists' in Lipgens, *Föderationspläne*, No. 131 (pp. 379–81); this work contains all the documents which have come to light, names, and facts about the preparation and proceedings of this Geneva conference of Resistance fighters, to which those seeking more detailed information are referred. Besides Rossi and Spinelli, who were officially nominated as representatives for this conference by most of the revived Italian political parties, and Visser't Hooft, those worthy of special mention as the most active in preparing the declarations were François Bondy as representative of French Socialist Resistance groups, Jean-Marie Soutou, a member of the group 'Témoignage Chrétien', Hanna Bertholet from the SPD in exile, and the Yugoslav (Titoist) representative; cf. ibid., n. on p. 389.

reached. The draft dwelt with some emphasis on the need for a federal union of all the nations of Europe. An excerpt from this document will show the determination with which unity of a federal kind was demanded as an irreducible minimum, and the deliberateness with which it was described as a supranational statement of Resistance aims.

1. Resistance to Nazi oppression, which unites the peoples of Europe in a common struggle, has forged between them a solidarity and a community of aims and interests ...

2. The lack of unity and cohesion which still exists between different parts of the world will not allow the immediate creation of an organization containing all the world's civilization in a single federal government ... At the end of this war it will be necessary to establish a world-wide organization of a less ambitious kind ... That is why, within that universal organization, the European problem must form the object of a more direct and more radical solution.

3. European peace is the key to world peace. In the space of one generation Europe has been the epicentre of two world wars, whose origins lay in the existence on this Continent of some thirty sovereign states. What is needed is to put an end to this anarchy by creating a federal union among the European peoples. Only a federal union will permit the German people to take part in European life without being a menace to other peoples. Only a federal union will enable frontiers to be drawn in areas of mixed population, which will thus cease to be the object of foolish national jealousies and will become simple questions of territorial delimitation, of pure administrative competence. The federal union will not be empowered to limit the right of each member state to solve its own problems in accordance with its ethnic and cultural characteristics. But in view of the experience and frustration suffered by the League of Nations, the states will have to surrender irrevocably to the federation those aspects of their sovereignty which concern the defence of their territory, relations with other powers outside the federal union, international exchanges and communications. Most importantly, the federal union will have to possess:

1. a government responsible not to the governments of the various members states but to their peoples, through whom it will have to exercise direct jurisdiction within the limits assigned to it;

2. an army subject to the orders of this government and excluding any other or national army;

3. a supreme court for trying all questions concerning the interpretation of the federal constitution and for settling disputes that may arise between the states and the federation.

By means of clandestine frontier crossings and courier services this clear summary of 21 May 1944 was sent from beleaguered Switzerland to as many Resistance groups in as many countries as possible in order to get their agreement to the preparation of a European conference of Resistance leaders immediately 'after the end of hostilities'. But the attempt, made as it was in the confusion of a war that was nearing its end, ran into enormous difficulties. Wherever the messages eluded the clutches of the German occupation authorities they found the Resistance groups waiting in some excitement for the advance of the Allied armies. This helps to explain why not all parts of the declaration were as enthusiastically received as they would have been a year before. It was only too obvious that the victorious world powers had other plans, and the responses remained meagre even after the Geneva group at its final session on 7 July had released the message to the entire area then occupied by the Allies. It was unable to find a place in the Allied plans which determined the shape of the post-war world.[88] Nevertheless Resistance fighters from nine of the most important European countries had managed to put on paper a programme for the future which was jointly championed by all their non-Communist Resistance groups. That they had done so in the midst of the still uncompleted tragedy of the war and in a supranational spirit made it a memorable achievement.

(D) THE EXTENSION AND LIMITS OF EUROPE'S SELF-AWARENESS

The question remains how far these plans were representative of the underlying attitude of the European population. Three qualifications have to be made which were all of decisive importance for an understanding of post-war history.

1. The population of Great Britain, the four neutral countries, and the majority of political emigrants who, like de Gaulle, had managed to escape in time from the débâcle on the Continent, had not experienced the war and Hitler's totalitarian rule in the same way as the population inside the disaster area. The British in particular had resisted attack all alone for over a year, from the fall of France until the summer of 1941, and in the end had actually survived as the only European 'victor nation', thanks to the intervention of Russia and America. In deference to the obviously different ideas of America and the Soviet Union little was said or done in favour of European unification.[89] The populations of Switzerland and

[88] Cf. further details given in the notes on the covering letters which Visser't Hooft sent with the Declaration of 21 May to the Dutch Resistance and on 1 Sept. to the Netherlands government in exile. in Lipgens, *Föderationspläne*, pp. 398–401. By 7 July declarations of agreement had been received from North-Italian Resistance groups and from the Comité Français pour la Fédération Européenne; and by the end of August the agreement and simultaneous manifesto of the Lyons Mouvement de Libération Nationale and a guarded answer from the Political Committee of the Dutch Resistance had arrived. The secretary of the London Socialist Vanguard Group, David Floyd, sent on 29 Sept. what appears to have been the first positive answer from Britain to Geneva: 'We are all in complete agreement with the programme set out in the Declaration.' Eichler's Information Service 'Europe Speaks' issued an English translation on 11 Oct. 1944 (cf. the texts in Lipgens, *Föderationspläne*, Nos. 86, 89, and 154). The most important British expression of agreement: Sir Walter Layton, *The British Commonwealth and World Order* (Sidney Ball lecture, March 3, 1944), London (Oxford UP), 1944 (19 pages), with extensive quotations from the Declaration. But it came too late to influence the Allies. On its further influence, cf. n. 56 in chap. 1/2.
[89] For the mood of 1940, cf. p. 63 below, and evidence in *Föderationspläne*, pp. 405–37. See n. 112 (below) for Churchill's last attempts in 1943 to retain the concept of European regional unity in Allied post-war planning. On the fading-out of plans for Europe in the confrontation between their remaining

Sweden, like those of the two Iberian states, which Hitler had for various reasons allowed to remain neutral, had also been spared the experience of seeing their nation states collapse; and there the thought of closer ties with the ruined heartland of the Continent was understandably hardly urgent.[90] So, because they had experienced a different kind of war, there was a small group of countries, led by Great Britain, in which the 'people' had considerably less reason to draw radical conclusions from radical disasters. In such countries only reasoned reflections about Europe's weakness between the world powers could in the long run lead to the thought of European unity, in contrast to those Continental countries which had felt the catastrophe at first hand. This fact was of decisive importance for at least the first twelve years of Europe's post-war history (up to the Suez crisis of 1956, which opened the eyes of many British people) and for the fate of the European unification movement during those years. For a long time the other Continental nations found it as hard to understand this mentality, based on a different experience of war, as the British and Scandinavians did the discrediting of the nation state on the Continent.

2. The second qualification arose from the fact that the Communist Resistance groups, no doubt on Moscow's orders, unanimously opposed the plans and the conclusions drawn by the non-Communist Resistance in so far as they affected Europe. The Communists, who in accordance with the Hitler–Stalin pact had preached collaboration with the Germans up to the summer of 1941, had had trouble in forming their own Resistance groups because their double about-turn had confused their own supporters (Tito and the ELAS organization in Greece were exceptions for special reasons). Not until the final months of the war, when many people quickly switched to the winning side, were the Communists able to expand their groups rapidly; until then they had formed no more than 8 per cent to 10 per cent of the Resistance in any one European country, apart from the two exceptions just referred to.[91] In view of the obvious preponderance of the major land victor on the Allied side, and because of the hopes placed in it as a liberating power, by the end of the war the programmes announced

---

advocates (e.g. Layton) and Eden's lack of understanding, cf. *Föderationspläne*, pp. 509–15. The effect of different experiences during the war is accurately described, for example, by the British author W. Clark, in 'Towards a More Perfect Union' in *The Twentieth Century*, vol. 152, No. 907, Sept. 1952, p. 213.

[90] In Denmark and Norway too disappointment over Germany and France predominated during the war, and hopes turned to Britain and the Atlantic Community; both countries, wedged in between the influence of Britain and that of Sweden, turned to this group, thus foreshadowing the later EFTA. Yet in those countries the necessity of a fundamental renunciation of sovereignty in favour of a supranational authority was widely recognised; cf. *Föderationspläne*, p. 27, and excerpts from Swedish newspapers, p. 334 f. For the fact that the majority of politicians in exile, especially those from Western Europe, lacking as they did the direct experience of living in a defeated country, inclined more to this group than to the European federalists, cf. p. 66.

[91] Cf. for example H. Michel, *Les Courants de pensée de la Résistance*, Paris, 1962, p. 705 ff.; C. F. Delzell, *Mussolini's Enemies, the Italian Anti-Fascist Resistance*, Princeton, 1961, p. 493 ff.

by the Communist Resistance groups acquired an importance which they had previously lacked. Without exception, they declared in favour of restoring the pre-war system of nation states, interpreted the Resistance movements as nationally inspired, and tried as far as possible to revive the phraseology of nationalism and to saddle the Germans rather than the pre-war system with guilt for all the misery that had been suffered.[92] Since then, for more than two decades they worked for the retention of the division of Europe into nation states and tried to keep alive atavistic nationalism among their supporters, including the most ignorant elements of society.[93]

3. The results of sociological research show that there is a further qualification to be made, one which can in fact be taken for granted, namely that there is always a non-political part of the population which ignores the lessons of history and resists any abandonment of existing structures. For this reason too the ideas of small, illegal resistance groups, inevitably few in number as they were, failed to become the common property of the European population as a whole.[94]

Yet on the Continent it was the negative aspect of the Resistance programmes from which we have quoted that had most influence on the lower social strata. The peoples had seen for themselves that their own state was unable to fulfil its primary duty of defending them. Every state had been overrun and conquered, often more than once, and in the end this happened to the Germans and Italians also. Inevitably these experiences of defeat had losened traditional loyalties and aroused among ordinary people nagging doubts about the value of national 'sovereignty'. In any case, the majority of nations, including the Germans, were subject to a severe conflict of loyalty between 'legal' and 'legitimate' governments, often represented in the conflict between collaborationist governments and governments in exile, between positivist law and true justice. Hundreds of thousands of Europeans had deliberately given up their national loyalty and sided with those who were officially their enemies against their fellow-

---

[92] On the uncompromising struggle of Stalinist leadership in the Soviet Union against any attempt to create a European federation, cf. pp. 70, 170, 223, and *passim;* on probable instructions to the Communist Resistance groups, see *Föderationspläne,* Nos. 13 and 84 (Declaration of the Central Committee of the French Communist Party against supranational unions, 25.4.1944).

[93] Cf. contribution to this important basic aspect of European post-war history shown in the Index under Communist Parties and Soviet Union. The fact that the Soviet Union failed to recognize or ignored the extent to which European federation was represented by the so-called Left in the Resistance movement revealed the neo-imperialist character of Moscow's power politics and robbed it of a golden opportunity to exert a strong influence on the entire left. The repudiation of European federalism by the European Communist parties proved more than anything else their subservience to Moscow and indifference to the real interests of the workers; the only role left to them was that of accomplices of what remained of the nationalist 'right'.

[94] Moltke, for example, complained of: 'Non-political people, those who at heart are undecided or neutral, who do their duty as specialists and are not interested in politics or for reasons of prudence don't want to become interested. They, especially in the Officers' Corps, form the majority.' (Memorandum, Dec. 1943, quoted in van Roon, op. cit. (n. 68), p. 583).

countrymen and officials. The result was an erosion of national solidarity, a moral collapse of the nation state that had dominated Europe for a hundred years, with consequences from which everyone finally suffered. It was impossible for the system of nation states to plunge the nations into war for the second time without making people ask themselves what the purpose of the nation state was and by that criterion questioning its right to exist. Just as after the First World War the desire felt by the majority of the population to 'reject war' had produced the 'policy of understanding', in much the same way the far greater suffering caused by the Second World War had led on the Continent to rejection of the existing state system as the cause of this suffering. An equally profound change of attitude had occurred in the last phase of the wars of religion in the seventeenth century: hitherto existing fronts and ideals, religious denominations in the one case, nationalism in the other, lost their power to attract because of the consequences they brought in their train.[95]

People longed for liberation, the restoration of human rights, democracy, and a Europe worth living in, but for the rest were open-minded about the future. The discrediting of current images was shown in the transformation of the party system throughout Europe in the first post-war elections, as the 'national right' which before the war had been universally predominant was replaced by parties traditionally internationalist in outlook.[96] In view of all the disasters and suffering, the losses, and the occupation of devastated Europe by the new, extra-European world powers, one thing was obvious. That was that the pre-war kind of state could no longer be the highest

[95] Documentary evidence for this negative major result of the Second World War in the mind of the public on the European Continent is amply provided in the following chapters. For the generation which consciously experienced defeat the systematic restoration of the nation states, ordered from outside, did not succeed in healing the rift with the past and restoring to the nation state the position of supreme value. The state of mind of that generation was probably most vividly described, as far as non-European observers during the war were concerned, by Vera M. Dean, the American editor-in-chief of the Foreign Policy Association, who, having sounded the opinions of Europeans about 'the recognized need for some form of unification of Europe', in Jan. 1943 summed up as follows: 'The fear inevitably arises that the first whiff of victory may be bringing to the fore, in Britain and the United States, the elements who hope that once the war is over the world can be restored to some semblance of what it was before 1939. . . . Yet to overlook the changes wrought among the peoples of Europe by the sufferings they have endured [would be to act] . . . just like Pitt and his supporters in England at the end of the eighteenth century [when they failed] to grasp the permanent changes that were being wrought in the fabric of Europe by the French Revolution. The conquered peoples have placed their trust and their hopes in the capacity of the United Nations, and especially the United States, to understand the crisis. . . . To betray this trust and frustrate these hopes would be one of the greatest acts of treason known to history.' *Foreign Policy Bulletin*, vol. XXII, no. 13, 15 Jan. 1943, p. 1 f.).

[96] For the first post-war elections, in which the 'nationalist right' on the whole Continent was reduced to below 10 per cent of the votes, cf. the beginning of chap. IV (in vol. 2). The same result is shown by numerous questionnaires, beginning with 73 per cent of Yes votes as the French national average in July 1945 for a democratically elected European federal government (cf. chap. 1/4, n. 258). These results could only have had their origin in the depth of wartime experience. (Admittedly, this positive aspiration, unlike the sense of disillusionment with the nation state, was, for obvious reasons, unable to survive with the same intensity for more than a decade without being turned into a political reality.)

form of political organization in Europe, that what remained of Europe, whatever the circumstances might be, could have a future only if it acted as a whole, that there must be a single authority over those states which had been so much reduced in status and often too in size. There is no doubt that if the advancing world powers had incorporated this European self-awareness and the plans of the non-Communist Resistance into their own policies and had installed in power authorities on a European basis they would have met hardly any serious opposition. On the contrary, they would have found the great majority of Continental Europeans only too willing to co-operate.

4. Forces of Opposition:
I. The Post-War Planning of the World Powers

The domination of Europe by Hitler and his collaborators in the various Fascist parties was overthrown by the extra-European world powers, not by the Europeans themselves. The question was whether the latter, as the Geneva conference of Resistance leaders from nine European countries had wished, would take 'all steps needed between the end of hostilities and the establishment of peace with reference to the need for a federal union'. Resistance writers had for some time been at pains to point out the advantages of such a union, while the Americans found the 'continual tensions and wars between the European nations incomprehensible. If in the end Europe finds the way to political unity, America can have only one response: At last!'. Yet it had to be recognized on the other hand that the 'formation of a federated Europe was supposed to give every assurance to Russia, for in the first place it would mean the prevention of any kind of plutocracy on the Continent' and secondly 'lasting peace would be created along Russia's western borders'.[97]

A specific idea of how the Allies ought to act in the opinion of the Resistance was expressed on many occasions: At the end of the war all European territory, as soon as it was liberated from Hitler's control, should be placed under a Supreme Allied Administration. The latter would then step by step restore economic life, freedom of political activity, and regional government with limited powers; it would then organize a general election for the convening of an all-European constituent assembly, and finally hand over its powers to a European federal

---

[97] *Föderationspläne*, No. 136 (Geneva Declaration), 110 (Salinger, autumn 1944, Part VI), and 79 (*Cahiers politiques*, Jan. 1944). As an objective *vis-à-vis* the USA: 'The United States of Europe are the only form in which our continent can really co-operate with the United States of America for a just and lasting peace' (No. 5, Ventotene Group, Dec. 1942); and *vis-à-vis* the Soviet Union: 'Let not Europe, still covered with ruins and stained with blood, become the arena and prize of a struggle between rival influences; [to prevent] this is the object we wish to achieve by federation and no one should see in it any cause for alarm' (No. 79). The tone of this and many other similar passages shows the extent to which the magnitude of the European catastrophe and of the accretion of power by the two new superpowers was underestimated.

Introduction 63

government which would result.[98] But the men of the Resistance had good reason to say at this time: 'There is a vague feeling about that we are not understood by the other side [meaning the Allies].'[99]

(A) BRITISH AND AMERICAN REGIONAL PLANS

Between the outbreak of war and the spring of 1943 the idea of a regional union or closer form of European unity played an important part in British and American planning for the post-war period. Not until a dramatic change occurred in that year was it abandoned.

Before the occupation of France, during the 'phoney war' winter of 1939–40, Daladier and Reynaud had proposed special European authorities within the framework of the League of Nations, but there was no time for this proposal to be included in Allied wartime plans before France passed into the hands of the Vichy government.[100] Developments in Great Britain had more bearing on the future: there, ever since the Sudeten crisis of 1938, the proposition that the League of Nations had been inadequate, and that a really powerful international organization, with a more compact and durable union of European states, must be created, was widely discussed and largely accepted. In the New Commonwealth Society before the war, and even more so during the war, the view had prevailed which Lord Davies had summarized in 1940 in his book *A Federated Europe*. Europe's most urgent need, he wrote, was to overcome the existing anarchy by forming a United States of Europe as a regional grouping within the League of Nations (the USE would include the British Dominions but not the Soviet Union), with foreign policy and defence reserved for the regional authorities.[101] The aims of Federal Union, a movement started in the autumn of 1938, went further than just a strengthened League of Nations.

---

[98] Cf. *Föderationspläne*, Nos. 12, 22, 86, 104, 136, and *passim*; in agreement with proposals in Britain, cf. ibid., Nos. 168 and 173. In other statements, however, the transitional period was not specified but left to the Allies; others again evidently thought that the European Union should only be formed by national governments restored to their full sovereignty.

[99] Statement from *Föderationspläne*, No. 109 (Netherlands Resistance, 21.8.1944). In fact the plans of the Resistance were probably never known to the leading statesmen, especially of the USA, because of the fact, which has often been deplored, that the Allied Intelligence Services in contact with the Resistance groups were interested only in military reports. Cf. *European Resistance Movements 1933–1945*, vol. ii: *Proceedings of the International Conference . . . held at Milan 16–29 March 1961*, London/NY, 1964, esp. pp. 72 ff., 262–392, 528–630.

[100] Cf. the collection of French declarations in *Die Friedenswarte*, 40, 1940, pp. 79–85; V. Depuis, *Vers un fédéralisme européen*, Paris, 1940; P. Reynaud, *Au cœur de la mêlée 1930–1945*, Paris, 1951; Lipgens, *Föderationspläne*, pp. 183 f. and 418 f.

[101] D. Davies, *A Federated Europe*, London, 1940 (1st edn., May, 2nd edn., October). Here, however, as in most of the articles in the periodical (*New Commonwealth Society*), the federal institutions were still thought of as consisting of representatives of the member states (irrespective of the political or economic regimes of these states), which – without counting the vote of the accused or defaulting state – were supposed unanimously to pass resolutions that would be binding on states rather than on the individual citizen. A democratic structure and/or a federal legislature was hardly envisaged – this was the most important difference between this project and Federal Union, see n. 102. The New Commonwealth Society had branches by the end of the 1930s in all English-speaking and West-European countries. In 1940 the President of the British group was Winston Churchill,

64   Introduction

Federal Union received strong backing and real momentum from a book called *Union Now*, first published in New York in March 1939. Its author, Clarence B. Streit, was the Geneva correspondent of the *New York Times*. It called for not merely a confederation but a democratic–federal union of nations along the Atlantic seaboard as the first step towards a federal world government; and as the bestseller of its year it made the principle of supranational federalism a subject for discussion by the Anglo-Saxon world. In the years when Britain was under greatest stress (1940–1) a large number of books and articles – including particularly studies by the London Federal Union Research Institute[102] – took up and publicized these basic ideas, with virtually no contradiction, either in the form of a league of states as in the 'New Commonwealth' or in the form of a federation of nations as advocated by Federal Union.[103] These policies were given a place in the statements on war aims issued by the British political parties, and came closest to realization when in June 1940 Churchill's government proposed to France a merger between the two countries with a common parliament as the nucleus of further European federation.[104]

Churchill, however, when the Soviet Union and the United States had become his *de facto* allies in the summer of 1941, failed, for reasons not easy to fathom, to discuss with them any definite plans for the post-war world. In 1942, which was a decisive year from this point of view, he openly declared that no planning for the future 'should divert our thoughts or our combined energies from the task of saving the nation'. Even when in the autumn of 1942 he heard for the first time of Roosevelt's idea of keeping world peace by 'four world policemen' he reacted only with a letter to Eden saying that he considered the idea too simple; he hoped that the European family of nations might act as a unity under a council of Europe, and he 'looked forward to a United States of Europe', but ended with the sentence: 'Unhappily the war has prior claims on your attention and on

---

the Vice-President Duff Cooper. For their programme of war aims, see full quotation, p. 159. Finally on 2 June 1939 a 'British parliamentary section of the Paneuropa Union' was formed; its members included, among others, Duff Cooper, Sir Walter Layton, Sir Arthur Salter, Sir Evelyn Wrench, L. S. Amery, and Harold Nicolson – but subsequently little was heard of it. (Cf. Coudenhove-Kalergi, *An Idea Conquers the World* [n. 53], p. 219).

[102] The two most important were: M. Channing-Pearce (ed.), *Federal Union* (Symposium of twenty-two studies), London, 1940, and P. Ransome (ed.), *Studies in Federal Planning*, London, 1943. C. K. Streit, *Union Now*, NY, 1939 (French edn., Paris, 1939); a more popular version by W. B. Curry, *The Case for Federal Union*, London, Penguin Books, 1939, was particularly influential in the rise of Federal Union as an organization. The most important work was R. W. G. Mackay, *Federal Europe, being the case for European federation, together with a draft constitution of a United States of Europe*, London, 1940.

[103] Cf. esp. L. Robbins, *The Economic Causes of War*, London, 1939; I. W. Jennings, *A Federation for Western Europe*, Cambridge, 1940: J. M. Garnett, *A Lasting Peace*, London, 1940; R. Dell, *The Geneva Racket 1920–1939*, London, 1940, H. R. S. Greaves, *Federal Union in Practice*, London, 1940.

[104] Cf. Lipgens, *Föderationspläne*, Nos. 141 and 144. For statements in similar vein by political parties and for the richness of British plans for Europe in 1939–41. see the selection of texts, collected by J. Pinder and Ph. Bell, in *Documents on the History of European Integration*, vol. ii, ed. by W. Lipgens (forthcoming).

mine',[105] and did nothing. Not until March 1943, by which time the very different notions of the Soviet Union and of the American government had largely taken shape, did Churchill in a public broadcast and subsequently in Washington speak out in favour of his own ideas – but by then it was too late.[106]

Yet ever since the beginning of the war and without any help from diplomatic representatives a good many British and French voices had been heard in the United States urging a future union of all the nations of Europe as the only possible answer to the Second World War. These plans for European union, both the ones which emerged from inside Europe and those put forward by Europeans in exile, were carefully scrutinized in the United States by private and semi-official commissions for the study of a future world at peace, as well as by the State Department's Committee for Post-War Planning, where they were favourably judged by those specifically involved in the assessment, including the Under-Secretary of State, Sumner Welles. The Advisory Committee of the State Department had in May 1940 become convinced, largely in consequence of a tour of Europe by Sumner Welles, that 'There must be in Europe such derogation to the sovereignty of states that quick and decisive action' on the part of a supranational European authority would be possible. The latter would have to be in charge of all European air forces, and alongside the Organization of American States there should be a more closely knit organization of the European states, with a third regional union for the Asian states. A global organization was not yet envisaged.[107]

---

[105] Public statement in the spring of 1942, with severe criticism of this standpoint, in *The New Statesman and Nation*, 11 April 1942, p. 235 f. Text of letter to Eden of 21 Oct. 1942 in W. S. Churchill, *The Second World War*, London, 1948–54, vol. iv, p. 504; on its origin see Woodward, *British Foreign Policy in the Second World War*, London, 1962, pp. 433–4 and 437 f.

[106] Cf. p. 73. One of the reasons why Britain failed to win over its allies for post-war planning in Europe, during the period when its weight in the alliance had not fallen hopelessly behind that of the Soviet Union, was the attitude of Foreign Minister Eden, whose traditional and conservative opinions remained (in contrast to those of his Prime Minister) consistently cool towards the idea of Europe. So far as is known, Churchill had previously only once, on 30 Jan. 1943, after talks with ministers in Turkey, recorded his 'morning thoughts', though again only as a note for his private file: 'An instrument of European government will be established [as part of a world organization for the preservation of peace] . . .' Obviously he was thinking not of full federation but at most of a confederation: cf. W. S. Churchill, *The Second World War*, London, 1948–54, vol. iv, p. 636.

[107] Text in H. A. Notter, *Postwar Foreign Policy Preparation 1939–45*, Washington (Dept. of State Publ.), 1949, pp. 458–60. Welles' proposal that Europe should be so constituted that besides the five major states (Britain, France, Germany, Italy, and Poland with the Baltic lands) there should be four equally strong federations of small states (the Iberian, Scandinavia, Danubian, and Balkan states) showed a sense of reality (cf. identical planning of such subfederations by the Resistance, collected in Lipgens, *Föderationspläne*, p. 300). The 'executive committee' for the whole of Europe, consisting of one representative each of nine member countries, would be 'capable of functioning provided that sovereignty could be . . . so far restricted that it would give way to a decision by the committee arrived at by a simple or two thirds majority'. It must be emphasized that planning in the State Department started from the principle of continental unions (it was only to co-ordinate trade policy that a commission 'with worldwide responsibilities' was envisaged, cf. Notter, ibid., p. 460).

66 Introduction

Among the important private commissions the Commission to Study the Organization of Peace (March 1941) was the first to demand a strong world-wide authority. The Commission considered it essential that in Europe a greater proportion of state sovereignty should be given up than in other continents. The New York Council of Foreign Relations had in September 1942 submitted a memorandum in favour of European economic unity. The Foreign Policy Association had urged 'some form of unification of Europe after the war'.[108] Similarly, as early as the end of 1941, the Catholic Association for International Peace had declared that 'Some kind of voluntary European union is a primary need', while the Commission to Study the Basis of a Just and Lasting Peace, set up by the Council of the Evangelical Churches of America, had in March 1943 called for European co-operation within the framework of a world peace organization: 'The degree of co-operation should be exactly proportionate to the degree of interdependence.' All commissions of any importance set up in the United States to work out a peace programme had by the spring of 1943 agreed in principle to support a global peace organization made up of continental unions.[109]

Exiled politicians from the European countries, who in view of the collapse of their own states supported a powerful international organization to provide future protection against any renewal of nationalist Fascism and to promote European unity, had rallied round American and especially British champions of that idea. That in all this the exiled East-European governments were the more active partners was due to their particularly harsh experience of nationalist divisiveness in their part of Europe during the inter-war years. Representatives of the exiled governments of Poland, Czechoslovakia, Yugoslavia, and Greece had in November 1941 signed a declaration couched in general terms promising future 'solidarity'. At the special prompting of the Polish Prime Minister in exile, Sikorski, who unequivocally advocated the unification of the whole of Europe and as the first step proposed a federal union with Czechoslovakia, a Polish–Czechoslovak

---

[108] Report of the 'Commission to study the Organization of Peace' in *International Conciliation,* No. 369, NY, April 1941, pp. 195–204, quotation on p. 202. Among the sixty-eight signatories from all camps were J. F. Dulles, J. T. Shotwell, and C. Streit. The second analysis mentioned in this paragraph is quoted by Max Beloff, *The United States and the Unity of Europe,* Washington, 1963, p. 2; for excerpts from the third analysis, see n. 95. Before the end of 1942 George F. Kennan in the State Department had produced a memorandum suggesting that the partial economic unity created by Hitler should not be destroyed but carried over into a future voluntary Union of Europe (information from G. F. Kennan to the author, 11 Oct. 1966). Even US Vice-President William H. Wallace had declared again in favour of European and other Continental authorities: 'Purely regional questions should remain a regional responsibility. In this way only the general and basic problems of a federated world organization would remain.' (Quoted by L. W. Holborn, *War and Peace Aims of the United Nations,* vol. 1: 1939–42, Boston, 1943, p. 149.)

[109] Excerpts from the conclusion of the Catholic Association are given by L. W. Holborn, op. cit., pp. 631–3. The 'Six Pillars' of the Evangelical Council, formulated under the chairmanship of J. F. Dulles, were publicized by the London *Times* and by the World Council of Churches at Geneva. Cf. the comments of von Trott zu Solz from a European point of view, in Lipgens, *Föderationspläne,* pp. 162-5. The Commission's findings as a whole expressed the realistic attitude towards world affairs of right-wing Democrats and sophisticated Republicans on the East Coast who were strong in the higher ranks of the Administration, as against the views of the Rooseveltian 'progressive' Democrats on the one hand and isolationists on the other.

confederal treaty was signed in January 1942, with modifications insisted on by Beneš. About the same time a treaty of union was signed between Greece and Yugoslavia.[110]

Among the West-European governments in exile only those of Belgium and Luxemburg tried in similar fashion to make a start in implementing the principle of regional union; but only a treaty for a customs union between Belgium, the Netherlands, and Luxemburg actually resulted. The Netherlands government, mainly because of its preoccupation with its East Indian empire, was as unfavourable to the notion of European union as was the Norwegian government, which supported a strong peace organization for the world as a whole; while de Gaulle, acting in the name of the Free French Committee, was completely opposed. Yet many others among those in exile, including personalities from France, Italy, and Germany, expressed their support for a future European union or federation in a large spate of publications.[111]

All these plans seemed to have been summed up, and, as radio listeners on the Continent of Europe still believed, to have won acceptance at the highest level, that of the Big Three, when at last in March 1943 Churchill in a broadcast to the world held out the hope that 'under a world institution embodying or representing the United Nations, and some day all nations, there should come into being a Council of Europe...' They must endeavour, Churchill said, to create 'a really effective League, with all the strongest forces concerned woven into its texture, with a High Court to adjust disputes, and with forces, armed forces, national or international, or both, held ready to impose these decisions'. At a later stage, he suggested, a 'world council' might be established consisting of the Big Three (Britain, the US and Russia) and representatives of continental unions (Europe,

---

[110] Text of the Declaration of Nov. 1941 in L. W. Holborn (cit. n. 108), p. 414 f.; continuation in the work of the Central and Eastern-European Planning Board, NY, appointed by the same four governments (cf. Feliks Gross, *Crossroads of two Continents*, New York, Columbia UP, 1945). For Sikorski, cf. the first Polish draft aimed at federation, in Lipgens, *Föderationspläne*, pp. 445-8), also his declarations on all-European federation by Holborn (n. 108), p. 454 and *passim*; on the hesitating attitude of Beneš and his readiness, which fatally divided the governments in exile, to defer at once to the first Soviet objections, cf. ibid., pp. 425-30 and *passim*. Both treaties in ibid., pp. 467-9 and 535-8. Best account in P. S. Wandycz. *Czechoslovak-Polish Confederation and the Great Powers, 1940-1943*, Bloomington, Indiana, 1956.

[111] On the efforts of the Belgian government in exile (esp. of its foreign minister, P. H. Spaak), see Holborn, op cit., vol. 2. *1943-45*, Boston (World Peace Foundation), 1948, pp. 970-2; on all governments in exile, see ibid., *passim*. On de Gaulle, see the summary on pp. 203-7 below. In addition to numerous declarations by individuals or groups (*Föderationspläne*, p. 416 f. the 'Deutsche Freiheitspartei', p. 441 f. Luetkens, p. 470 T. Mann, p. 515 Maritain, and others), cf. two bodies which declared with special emphasis in favour of European unification, the 'Congress of Free Italy' (1942, ibid., p. 462) and the 'Union deutscher sozialistischer Organisationen in Grossbritannien' (1943, ibid., p. 498 f.); also the resolutions of the international bodies, the Socialist Vanguard Group (ibid., p. 456 f.) and Count Coudenhove-Kalergi's 5th Paneurope Congress, NY, 1943, with its 'Draft Constitution of United States of Europe' (A. J. Zurcher, *The Struggle to unite Europe, 1940-1958*, NY, 1958, pp. 213-23).

68   Introduction

Asia, etc.).[112] These proposals were obviously more rational and more cautious than the plans drawn up by the Resistance leaders, inspired as the latter were by the experience of defeat and by a positive desire to limit 'sovereignty'. Yet if these proposals from the English-speaking world had become a definite part of Allied post-war planning, they could have been integrated with the programmes of the Resistance. Churchill, however, only came down in favour of them at a time when Britain's weight in the alliance had fallen well below that of the Soviet Union. It was one of the most obvious signs of the decline of this last European power (Britain) that she was wholly unsuccessful in making her point of view prevail against the very different post-war plans of the Soviet Union and the American top leadership.

(B) THE SOVIET UNION AS AN OPPONENT OF EUROPEAN FEDERATION

The Soviet Union was the source of very different demands and kinds of post-war planning. On 19 August 1939 Stalin after long hesitation had decided in favour of the non-aggression pact with Hitler. He did this in the first place because Hitler unscrupulously offered to divide the states of Eastern Europe into a German and Russian sphere of influence, and in practical terms had agreed to the incorporation into the Soviet Union of Estonia, Latvia, and the eastern half of Poland, later of Bessarabia and Lithuania. Secondly, because non-intervention by the Soviet Union on the side of the western democracies offered in Stalin's view a better prospect of the European states exhausting each other in the long-expected war between the capitalist nations. The decision was consistent inasmuch as it conformed to the ideologically conditioned thinking of Soviet foreign policy under Stalin, and indeed at other times too, with its categorization of states into friends and enemies. The 'only Socialist state', the Soviet Union, was seen as facing the unyielding hostility of the capitalist states, the differences between which had to be exploited as far as possible. In 1939 Stalin considered the group of 'have' states to be economically and militarily stronger than the group of revisionist 'aggressive Fascist states', and his pact with Germany was meant to ensure a better balance between the two groups. By strengthening the German position he hoped to incite the 'imperialist' powers against each other in order to weaken them both:

---

[112] Text in *British Speeches of the Day,* April 1943, pp. 1–10; on the origins of the speech, see Woodward (n. 105), p. 439 f. Churchill's first public advocacy, after long delay (see n. 105 above), vague as it was in its commitment and intending real unity to apply only to the smaller states, was for many months given too much practical importance by Resistance leaders on the Continent. For the failure of Churchill's attempt to get his idea accepted in Washington in May 1943, cf. n. 125.

the Soviet Union would gain both freedom of action and an increase of power in the role of an unscathed observer until the war was over.[113]

This calculation, which had underlain Soviet foreign policy for almost two years and rested on the assumption that Hitler would not turn on the Soviet Union before ending his war against the West, was completely upset by the attack on Russia launched on 22 June 1941. Notwithstanding the German advance to the gates of Moscow and the threat of total Soviet defeat, Stalin in his first contacts with his new, involuntary Western allies had made it clear that his primary aim was the full retention by the Soviet Union of at least the territorial gains assured to him by Hitler. His overriding purpose was to resume the westward expansion of Russia begun during the eighteenth century and to persuade his new allies to agree to the cession of territory acquired from Hitler. Immediately after the military situation in front of Moscow changed to his advantage in December 1941 Stalin had demanded recognition by the British Foreign Minister, Eden, of the Russian frontiers of 22 June 1941 (i.e. the annexation of Eastern Poland, the Baltic states, Bessarabia, and North Bukovina), and agreement to the annexation of the Finnish province of Petsamo and to the establishment of Soviet bases in Romania. The first meeting between Stalin, Roosevelt, and Churchill at Tehran in November 1943 eventually brought *de facto* recognition by the West, but with the difference that, in contrast to the frontiers of 1939, this time the Bialystok district was to remain in Poland, while Russia was to get the northern part of East Prussia including Königsberg.[114] Moreover Soviet diplomacy began to press for the setting-up of 'pro-Soviet' regimes to the west of this new border, forming a belt of countries in which Soviet influence would be paramount.

Stalin pursued the second main purpose of his European policy with equal coolness and energy: the preservation or restoration of a group of states west of the intended sphere of Soviet influence, divided as far as possible by nationality and other differences. In order to increase the number of such states he had demanded from Eden in December 1941 that not only Austria but also Bavaria, the Rhineland, and a North-German rump state should be established as separate and autonomous

---

[113] Cf. the following summaries, with bibliographies: A. Hillgruber, 'Der Zweite Weltkrieg, 1939–45', in *Osteuropa-Handbuch, Sowjetunion*, section on Foreign Policy, I, 1917–1955, Cologne/Vienna 1972, pp. 270–342 (esp. pp. 281–91 'Partnerschaft mit Deutschland'). On the basic approach of Soviet foreign policy (a hostile picture of all other states), see esp. G. F. Kennan, 'The Sources of Soviet Conduct' in *Foreign Affairs*, 25, 1947, pp. 566–82; A. Dallin (ed.), *Soviet Conduct in World Affairs*, NY, 1960; M. D. Shulman, *Stalin's Foreign Policy reappraised*, Cambridge, Mass., 1963; J. F. Triska and D. D. Finley, *Soviet Foreign Policy 1917–1967*, London, 1968; L. Fischer, *The Road to Yalta: Soviet Foreign Relations 1941–1945*, NY, 1972.

[114] Resumption of territorial expansion to the West, cf. p. 15 above. On Eden in Moscow in Dec. 1941 and in Tehran: A. Eden, *Memoirs*, vol. 2, London, 1965, p. 289 ff., and E. L. Woodward (n. 105), p. 190 ff.; relevant chapters of the basic study by W. H. McNeill, *America, Britain and Russia. Their Co-operation and Conflict 1941–1945 (Survey of International Affairs)*, London, 1953; H. Feis, *Churchill, Roosevelt, Stalin. The War they Waged and the Peace they Sought*, Princeton, 1957.

units. As soon as news came of British and perhaps also Continental ideas for European federation, and more particularly when the treaties signed by the East-European governments-in-exile in January 1942 disclosed the serious efforts being made in this direction, Soviet diplomacy began vigorously to oppose a federation of European states in whatever guise, conveniently recalling Lenin's pronouncement in 1915 that 'The slogan of a United States of Europe is incorrect.'

A United States of Europe, Lenin had written, would be possible only as an 'agreement between the European capitalists', but 'only for the purpose of jointly suppressing Socialism in Europe'; even the 'temporary' realization of European union with all its definite economic and political advantages should be allowed only under Communist auspices; otherwise, he had added, writing as a Russian politician, 'it may be wrongly interpreted to mean that the victory of Socialism in a single country is impossible; it may also create misconceptions as to the relations of such a country to the others' – that is, it would have to 'confront the rest of the capitalist world'. The language in which Stalin in 1930 had campaigned against the Briand Plan and had described all desire for a European federation as a 'bourgeois movement for intervention against the Soviet Union' was also resurrected.[115] The Soviet embassy in London at once brought influence to bear on politicians in exile by suggesting that it would be 'unrealistic' for them to fight for the restoration of independence and at the same time to be willing to give up independence in favour of any union. Molotov had personally argued with Beneš in London in June 1942, and Beneš as the weakest link in the chain was informed on 16 July 1942 of the Soviet Union's uncompromising veto: 'You Czechoslovaks have no need of a union with the Poles to safeguard your future.'[116]

Yet such plans still appeared to have the backing of the Western allies, nor had the latter in any way yet agreed to the Soviet proposals for territorial gains and the dismemberment of states. So Stalin, after the victory of Stalingrad had added decisively to the weight of the Soviet Union within the alliance, unleashed in the spring and summer of 1943 a diplomatic offensive in the course of which he broke off relations with the pro-federationist Polish government-in-exile, went so far as to recall his ambassadors in Washington and London, and threatened to make a separate peace with Hitler. It is possible that he seriously considered such a move (especially in his offer to Hitler of 3 September 1943) in order to restore the situation of

---

[115] V. I. Lenin, *Selected Works* in twelve volumes, London, 1960–70 (translated from the Russian and issued by the Marx–Engels–Lenin Institute, Moscow), vol. v (*Imperialism and Imperialistic War (1914–1917)*, pp. 138–41, quotations on p. 140 f. For Stalin in 1930, cf. Lipgens, 'Briand' (n. 48), pp. 85 and 327 (quotations); K. Toernudd, *Soviet Attitudes towards Non-military Regional Co-operation*, Helsingfors, 1963²; G. Zellentin, *Die Kommunisten und die Einigung Europas*, Frankfurt, 1964, esp. pp. 13–30.

[116] Details in P. S. Wandycz (n. 110), pp. 75–83. Beneš (who, unlike Hodža, Feierabend, and others had always been an anti-federalist nationalist) complied at once and broke off the negotiations for a federation; Lipgens, *Föderationspläne*, pp. 316–30 (the Polish underground complained that this was a victory for the Soviet Union) and 453. Cf. J. Kühl, *Föderationspläne im Donauraum und in Ostmitteleuropa*, Munich, 1958, p. 106 ff.; appropriate sections of works cited in n. 114.

Introduction 71

1939–41 and the mutual destruction of the capitalist states.[117] By means of this threat and through a number of publications and pronouncements issued about the same time, he was testing whether the Western powers would accept Soviet territorial demands and abandon their support of the plans for federation.[118] At the first joint conference of foreign ministers in Moscow in October 1943 – which took place only after considerable pressure on the part of the Western allies – Eden did not, as Churchill had enjoined him, put forward the latter's general concept of a world organization based on continental unions including a "council of Europe", but proposed for debate "the question of a confederation of the smaller European states with special reference to the Danubian area'. Molotov answered by reading 'a statement which emphatically criticized the idea of planning federations of small nations at this time ... Some of the plans reminded the Soviet people of the policy of the "*cordon sanitaire*" directed in earlier years against the Soviet Union.' At the subsequent conference between Stalin, Roosevelt, and Churchill at Tehran at the end of November 1943 Churchill used the debate on the break-up of Germany to renew the proposal to form a viable Danubian federation that would include Bavaria, Baden, Württemberg, and the Palatinate. Stalin's absolute rejection of this proposal and of all the other proposals concerning Europe was summed up a few days later by Charles Bohlen, a member of the United States delegation at Tehran, in the following apt conclusion:[119]

Stalin's opposition to federations is sufficiently clear to afford a glimpse of the Soviet idea of post-war Continental Europe. Germany is to be broken up and kept broken up. The states of Eastern, South-Eastern and Central Europe will not be permitted to group themselves into any federation or association. France is to be stripped of her colonies and strategic bases beyond her borders, and will not be permitted to maintain any appreciable military establishment. Poland and Italy will remain approximately their present territorial size, but it is doubtful if either will be permitted to maintain any appreciable armed force. The result would be

[117] McNeill (n. 114), p. 323, f.; B. Meissner, *Russland, die Westmächte und Deutschland, 1943–1953*, Hamburg, 1954, pp. 12–20; (more detailed) P. Kleist, *Zwischen Hitler und Stalin*, Bonn, 1950, pp. 235–84. In addition, for the founding of the National Committee 'Freies Deutschland', cf. J. von Puttkamer. *Von Stalingrad/zur Volkspolizei. Geschichte des Nationalkomitees*, Wiesbaden, 1951, p. 40 ff.; cf. Hillgruber (n. 113), p. 307. *Istoriya Diplomatii*, ed. by A. Gromyko and others, Vol. iii: *Since 1917*, Moscow, 1965², as usual gives no references and hence no means of verification (one would not even know from it that Stalin existed, only that 'the Soviet Union was the only power that pursued a peace-loving policy'.) Cf. *AHR*, 72 (1967), p. 1041.

[118] For threats and pressure on different levels, cf. Feis (n. 114), pp. 131–43, 166–76, 191–216; e.g. *What is behind the East European Federation Scheme?* Information Bulletin of the Embassy of the USSR in Washington, No. 94, 24 Aug. 1943, p. 6 f.; daily abuse of the exiled governments in the Communist *Daily Worker*, NY, which in Dec. 1943 celebrated the Beneš–Stalin Pact as a 'nail in the coffin of reactionary federation, which could have turned against the USSR' (W. C. Bullitt, *The Great Globe Itself*, NY, 1946, pp. 260–5).

[119] Molotov's statements in Moscow as reported in *The Memoirs of Cordell Hull*, NY, 1948, vol. 2, p. 1298 f.; minutes of the final session of the Tehran Conference and summarizing memorandum by C. Bohlen in: *Foreign Relations of the United States, The Conferences at Cairo and Tehran, 1943*, Washington, 1961, pp. 600–2 and 845 f.; on the American attitude in Moscow and Tehran, cf. p. 74 below.

72   Introduction

that the Soviet Union would be the only important military and political force on the Continent of Europe. The rest of Europe would be reduced to military and political impotence.

All this without any doubt amounted to a massive example of neo-imperialism, which saw its future security not as yet in the co-operation of prosperous nations in a world that had become indivisible, but, as in the past, in its own strength augmented by territorial gains at the expense of neighbours who would be kept as small, weak, and divided as possible, according to the ancient maxim of 'Divide and rule'.[120]

(C) ROOSEVELT'S 'FOUR POLICEMEN':
ACCEPTANCE OF THE SOVIET STANDPOINT

In a situation in which Great Britain on the one hand and the Soviet Union on the other presented such widely differing proposals for the reshaping of post-war Europe, the decisive question was what the attitude of the United States would be. This question had already been answered by the time of the conferences at Moscow and Tehran. Between spring and autumn 1943 President Roosevelt, for a number of very complex reasons, persuaded the chief members of his government that America, in contrast to the post-war planning carried out up to that time by the State Department, must fully accept the Soviet standpoint. Concerned as he naturally was to keep intact the wartime alliance with the Soviet Union, Roosevelt did not even try to counter Stalin's threats, for he did not expect that Hitler would make a separate peace on any terms that Stalin would accept. It was rather that in Roosevelt's mind progressive internationalism, designed to give every nation self-determination and freedom from Fascism and colonialism, had long been combined with left-wing sympathies for the Soviet Union as a progressive country which had had to endure a great deal of suffering from European conservatism. This kind of politico-ideological thinking, frequently met with among left-wing intellectuals, resembled Soviet thinking in that they both shared an out-of-date attachment to power politics. Another crucial factor for Roosevelt was his profound disappointment at the rapid collapse of the European democracies when faced by Hitler.[121]

[120] Cf. H. J. Morgenthau, *Politics among Nations*, NY, 1960, p. 178 f.; T. Schieder, 'Imperialismus in alter und neuer Sicht' in *Moderne Welt*, 1 (2), 1960, pp. 3–18, esp. 15 f. Colonialist subjugation of Eastern Europe and opposition to the idea of European union together constituted the neo-imperialist *Machtpolitik* of the USSR, to which all chances of advantageous co-operation with the European (and American) Left were sacrificed. On the commitment of the Communist parties in Western Europe to reactionary nationalistic defence of 'national sovereignty', cf. p. 59 f. Cf. E. Schulz, *Moskau und die europäische Integration*, Munich/Vienna, 1975.

[121] On the idealistic terminology, intended for public consumption, cf. W. Besson, *Die Politische Terminologie F. D. Roosevelts*, Tübingen, 1955. Roosevelt believed in the proclaimed goals of progressive internationalism, cf. R. E. Osgood, *Ideals and Self-Interest in America's Foreign Relations*, Chicago, 1953, p. 410; yet subordinated them pragmatically to the demands of *Machtpolitik* at any given time, cf. R. Hofstaedter, *The American Political Tradition and the Men who made it*, NY, 1948; E. E. Robinson, *The Roosevelt Leadership 1933–1945*, Philadelphia, 1955; summary in H. P. Schwarz, *Vom Reich zur Bundesrepublik. Deutschland im Widerstreit der aussenpolitischen Konzeptionen in den Jahren der Besatzungsherrschaft 1945–1949*, Neuwied/Berlin, 1966, pp. 41–6.

Introduction 73

In his view American intervention against the possibility of permanent Fascist hegemony in Europe and Japanese hegemony in the Far East was vital to the interests of the United States, and he saw the Soviet Union, whose strength had been underestimated, as the indispensable ally, whose aspirations must be satisfied. As early as the autumn of 1941, in the Soviet Union's hour of distress, Roosevelt agreed to Stalin's plea for massive aid without demanding in return the smallest concession such as assurances about the future settlement of Europe.[122] In the autumn of 1942 Roosevelt – for the first time, according to the available evidence – had declared in a confidential talk his 'basic idea in world politics' that in future 'there should be four policemen in the world – the United States, Great Britain, Russia and China – charged with the responsibility of keeping the peace. The rest of the world would have to disarm... Russia would be responsible for preserving peace in the Western hemisphere, the United States and China would be responsible for preserving peace in the Far East.'[123]

However, it was far from obvious that such a barefaced division of the world between power blocs would be accepted by the progressive left wing of the Democratic Party on which Roosevelt depended and by its spokesman, his Secretary of State, Cordell Hull. Hull's ideal, the goal of his life's work, was the creation with American help of a new, really world-wide and effective League of Nations, an organization for world peace in which – as he tried to convince Roosevelt – the smaller nations as well as the Big Four must have a say. As has been seen, the planning committees inside as well as outside the US government had advised the setting-up of this world organization by grouping together the smaller states in continental unions. Unfortunately, however, Hull had never really understood this idea, but had seen it as a possible source of future weakness in a global organization.[124] Rather late, in May 1943 Churchill spoke in Washington for the first time officially in favour of this concept: all problems 'the solution of which could not be achieved by regional councils would automatically fall within the competence of the world council'.[125] Details of the

---

[122] Cf. McNeill (n. 114), pp. 48–56; Bullitt (n. 118), pp. 11–14; R. H. Dawson, *The Decision to Aid Russia, 1941: Foreign Policy and Domestic Politics,* Chapel Hill, NC, 1959; R. H. Jones, *The Road to Russia: United States Lend-Lease to the Soviet Union,* Norman/Oklahoma, 1969; also in a balanced summary taking into account the 'revisionist' debate, J. L. Gaddis, *The United States and the Origins of the Cold War, 1941–1947,* NY, 1972 (esp. p. 135 ff.).

[123] *The Roosevelt Letters,* ed. by E. Roosevelt, 3 vols., London, 1949–52, vol. ii, p. 1366 f. On Roosevelt's idea of 'Four Policemen', cf. Gaddis, op. cit. (n. 122), p. 257; Fischer, op. cit. (n. 113), pp. 103–5.

[124] On Hull's mistaken belief that regional union would completely overshadow the global organization, involve the USA directly in European affairs, and raise barriers against American exports, cf. Hull, *Memoirs,* ii, 1943–6, pp. 1614 f. and *passim*. For the proposals of the planning commission, cf. p. 66 (above).

[125] In detail, however, apparently only at an Embassy lunch with Vice-President Wallace, War Minister Stimson, Interior Minister Ickes, Under-Secretary of States Welles, and Senator Connally; Europe was to consist of about twelve states or federations, which would form a 'council of the United States of Europe'. (W. S. Churchill, *The Second World War,* iv, pp. 717–21). It was probably at the suggestion of this group that Hull agreed to the setting-up of a 'sub-committee on the Problem of European Organization' within the framework of the 'Advisory Committee of the State

arguments in Washington have not yet been explored by historians. The 'Advisory Committee' put forward on 14 July a 'Draft Constitution of an International Organization' which as a compromise measure proposed by Roosevelt provided for 'four policemen' as an 'executive committee', but held to the idea of a specialist body consisting of the four great powers and five continental unions (South America, Europe, the Middle East, the Far East, and the British Dominions) as the appropriate legislative 'council' of the future world organization. The decisive step was taken in August–September 1943, certainly not without taking into account further Soviet protests. Hull discarded the draft of 14 July, dissolved the Advisory Committee, appointed a new, purely inter-departmental advisory committee and demanded that it produce plans which no longer provided for regional sub-organizations of the world peace organization, but assumed that the dominant role would be played by the four world powers.[126] That was evidently the price which Hull had to pay to persuade Roosevelt to keep to the idea of a world peace organization as a forum where the Big Four would co-operate with representatives of the smaller states. In this form the world organization could no longer be a danger to the predominance of the world powers projected by Roosevelt.

Roosevelt had explained with perfect clarity what he had in mind in a private conversation in this same month of September 1943: 'The plan is to get agreement between the Big Four. Accordingly, the world is to be divided into spheres of influence: China will get the Far East, the United States the Pacific, Great Britain and Russia will get Europe and Africa. But because Great Britain's interests are mainly colonial, it must be assumed that Russia will predominate in Europe.' The President harboured no illusions about the Soviet Union's desire to dominate and the probable harshness of its domination: 'Of course the European countries will have to undergo enormous changes in order to accommodate Russia ... The people of Europe will simply have to outlast Russian domination in the hope of being able to live on good terms with the Russians in ten or twenty years' time.'[127]

Roosevelt was thus consciously willing to hand over the 'people of Europe' to the Soviet Union for the sake of lasting peaceful co-operation

---

Department', which met on 4 June 1943 and studied plans for a European federation for some months, until it was overtaken by events (H. A. Notter, *Postwar Foreign Policy Preparation 1939–1945*, Washington, 1949, pp. 146–8).

[126] Text of the 'draft constitution' by which the advisers attempted for the last time to keep the principle of regional unity, even if only in a reduced form, in Notter, op. cit., pp. 472–82. Last Soviet protests: cf. n. 118; Hull's drastic decision and Churchill's final agreement: cf. Notter (n. 125), p. 167 ff.; McNeill (n. 114), p. 322 f.

[127] 'Communist regimes will spread, what can we do against it?' Note by Cardinal Spellman of a conversation lasting several hours with the President, who was on friendly terms with him, in R. I. Cannon, SJ, *The Cardinal Spellman Story*, NY, 1962, pp. 222–5. The document fully reveals Roosevelt's motives at Tehran; it forms the conclusive link between his utterances in 1942 (see n. 123) and 1944 (see n. 131); it reveals that illusions about the nature of the Soviet system were far from being responsible for his attempts at an American–Soviet axis. Quoted with bibliography, summary and analysis in Schwarz (n. 121), pp. 47–63.

between Russia and America. One major reason for this was obvious, namely his belief that a permanent American military presence in Europe would be unacceptable to the American public, and for him it was axiomatic that a war against the Soviet Union could not be won. Then too his basic dislike of Europeans as empire-builders can hardly be overrated. Roosevelt's anti-colonialism was deeply rooted. Finally it seemed to him that the lasting peace which he sought through a global balance of power could be secured only by really satisfying Russia's desires.

Roosevelt's conclusions were confirmed by an analysis made by the American General Staff in August 1943 of the balance of power in post-war Europe; at the end of the war the military preponderance of the Soviet Union would be inevitable; consequently the American government must strive for a policy of far-reaching concessions to the Soviet Union in order to seal the agreement between them.[128] Starting with the conviction that co-operation with the Soviet Union must be maintained in all circumstances, Roosevelt saw no chance of opposing Stalin's goals: the only remaining problem for him was how to justify letting Stalin have his way to the American public.

As a result of the sudden change in American post-war planning decided on by Roosevelt in 1943, in October of that year the leaders of the two new world powers were united in the intention, even before they informed each other, not to allow Europe any weight of its own in the future peace organization. The remaining war years brought only the logical consequences of these mutually agreed decisions, modified to some extent by the opposition of other members of the wartime alliance. The decision against the idea of a European union was evident, as has been shown, at the first American–Russian–British foreign ministers' conference at the end of October 1943 in Moscow. In answer to Eden's attempt to start a debate on the scheme for a Danubian federation, Hull gave a negative reply – the important thing, he said, was to reach agreement on the general principles of international co-operation – even before Molotov could read his statement that federal plans involving European states were in principle unacceptable to the Soviet Union. In view of this joint opposition by Hull and Molotov, Eden could only say that Molotov's statement was very emphatic and so he would not insist any further.[129] Pleased by this, Stalin

---

[128] Cf. R. E. Sherwood, *Roosevelt and Hopkins*, NY, 1948, p. 162, and K. R. Greenfield, *American Strategy in World War II. A Reconsideration*, Baltimore, 1963, pp. 3–10. This judgement was no doubt influenced by the battle of Kursk, which proved the superiority of the Russian army over the German, at a time when American troops had scarcely set foot on European soil.

[129] C. Hull, *Memoirs*, vol. 2, (n. 119), p. 1298 ff.; Molotov's declaration, p. 71 (above). On the Moscow Conference, see also: A. Eden, *Memoirs*, vol. 2 (n. 114), p. 411 ff., and Woodward (n. 105), p. 244 ff. It is not clear how Churchill, in 'Observations by the Prime Minister for the Foreign Secretary, London, 11 Oct. 1943', could still describe as the most important point of discussion for the Moscow Conference that 'We hold strongly to a system of a League of Nations, which will include a Council of Europe, with an International Court and an armed Power capable of enforcing its decisions' (Churchill, *The Second World War*, vol. v, p. 251), although he had agreeed in August 1943 at Quebec to the abandonment of the principle of regionalism (McNeill [n. 114], p. 323).

thereupon agreed that a first summit meeting of the Big Three to be held at Tehran at the end of November 1943 should approve these unexpectedly favourable results. At Tehran Roosevelt did everything to convince Stalin of his pro-Soviet intentions; he left it to Churchill to negotiate with the Russians about the limits of the extension of their power. The Russians were promised the frontiers of 1939 which they had previously demanded, and were assured by Roosevelt that Poland would be shifted westwards. A further attempt by Churchill to negotiate for at least a Danubian federation in return for these huge concessions failed through lack of support from Roosevelt, who obtained only Russian assent to a new League of Nations, that is to the foundation of the United Nations Organization desired by Hull, once the right of veto and leading position of the new world powers in it had been secured.[130]

Fortunately for the West Europeans, Roosevelt had not let it be clearly known at Tehran in 1943 that he was prepared to hand over the whole Continent of Europe to the Soviet sphere of influence. After Tehran, and increasingly in the course of 1944, he continued to hope that the Soviet Union would declare itself satisfied with direct influence in the eastern half of Europe alone and would be content to leave a power vacuum between itself and Great Britain. Yet instead of considering how to fill this vacuum with an independent federation of European states, Roosevelt's grand design remained to keep the Soviet Union satisfied by sacrificing any independent political role for the Europeans and by winning over the Russians – as he honestly believed – for future co-operation with America in the interests of world peace.[131]

(D) YALTA AND THE BEGINNINGS OF US INVOLVEMENT IN EUROPE

At the Moscow conference of foreign ministers Eden had managed to get agreement on the setting-up in London of a European Advisory Commission. This was not, as the British would have liked, the prototype of a supreme Allied administrative authority for Europe, but, if the Soviet and American leaders had had their way, would have been used only to draw the boundaries of the future zones of occupation. Nevertheless a body of experts had been created on which British and American officials who did not share Roosevelt's indifference to the fate of the European peoples

---

[130] Cf. the basic account by Feis (n. 114), pp. 240–87; also, using the American and Soviet documents published in 1961, G. Zieger, *Die Tehran-Konferenz, 1943,* Hanover, 1967, and G. Kolko, *The Politics of War, Allied Diplomacy and the World Crisis, 1943–1945,* London, 1969. The Communist *Daily Worker* acknowledged: 'The State Department is no longer a great incubator of anti-Soviet rumours ... Mr Hull's attitude is particularly praiseworthy ... Things are going very much better' (quoted in Bullitt [n. 118], p. 268. More details on the UN on pp. 79 and 98–101 below).
[131] Cf. esp. Forest Davies's account of Roosevelt's Russian policy, corrected and approved by the President himself in *The Saturday Evening Post,* May 1944, quoted in Bullitt (n. 118), pp. 16–20; Admiral Leahy's memorandum of 16 May 1944 in *Yalta Papers,* Washington, 1955, p. 107 f.

could try to mitigate the catastrophe now becoming apparent. Above all, they attempted to draw up plans to preserve European economic cooperation, but their proposed foundation of a European Economic Committee was summarily rejected by both Washington and Moscow; and in October 1944 they were unceremoniously forbidden by Roosevelt to draft any further plans for Europe's post-war economy.[132]

Further efforts by Great Britain to oppose the extension of the Soviet sphere of influence and the reconstruction of the European Continent on Soviet lines had little success. Churchill sought in vain by diplomacy and by personal intervention to prevent the progressive weakening and liquidation of the leading cadres of the Polish Resistance and political parties. From the formation of the Lublin Committee in July 1944 and the deliberate Soviet decision to let the Warsaw insurgents bleed to death, to the unilateral recognition of the Lublin Committee as the Provisional Polish Government in January 1945, Churchill was obliged to look on helplessly while the tragedy unfolded. In Moscow in October 1944 he tried to reach agreement with Stalin to divide the Balkans into spheres of influence: in Romania 90 per cent Russian predominance, 10 per cent Western; in Greece 90 per cent British predominance, 10 per cent Russian; in Yugoslavia and Hungary Russia and the West 50 per cent each; in Bulgaria 75 per cent Russian and 25 per cent Western. Yet this arrangement to limit the extension of Russian power remained without effect wherever Soviet troops were stationed. At the beginning of 1945 Churchill pleaded in vain for the setting-up of a Balkan federation including Turkey. Only Churchill's move to raise France to the status of an occupying power was agreed to at Yalta.[133]

The expansion of the Soviet sphere of influence in Europe was really only held up by the fact that with the landings of massive American and British armies in Western and Central Europe – since August 1943 they had been advancing in Italy, in August 1944 they had liberated France – America's political leaders saw that they were increasingly involved in the political and economic problems of the old Continent. Also, with the unexpected military success of the Soviet Union on the German eastern front after June 1944 and the equally unexpected and unprecedented

---

[132] It is significant that the American representative on the EAC, John G. Winant, was hardly informed of Roosevelt's real intentions; cf. the extremely informative book by Winant's economics expert E. F. Penrose, *Economic Planning for the Peace*, Princeton, 1953, esp. p. 151 ff., 194–9, 312 f., 262 f.; also the accounts by Gaddis, op. cit. (n. 122), pp. 105–14; Fischer, op. cit. (n. 113), pp. 194–7; Feis, op. cit. (n. 114), pp. 213 ff., 221 f., 312, 354–65, 420 ff., 612–26. All the same, the UNRRA organization for aid was set up to serve the whole of Europe; the EAC on the other hand was confined to working out plans for the dismemberment of Germany and instruments of surrender.

[133] On Churchill's famous 'percentage' proposals for South-Eastern Europe, cf. his *Second World War*, vol. vi, pp. 198 and 201 f., also Feis (n. 114), p. 448 f.; G. Kolko (n. 130), pp. 142–52, is reliable on Churchill's early efforts at 'containment' despite the author's revisionist interpretation; on Churchill's effort to get at least another European state, France, nominated as an occupying power, see W. Lipgens, 'Bedingungen und Etappen der Aussenpolitik de Gaulles 1944–1946' in *VfZG*, 21 (1973), pp. 52–102, especially 55–8.

severity of Soviet rule in the 'liberated' territories, a growing number of American leaders doubted whether the preservation of peace as desired by Roosevelt was compatible with the further growth of Soviet power. Even Roosevelt – with an eye to public opinion in his own country, but also recognizing America's interest in Europe as a field for investment and trade – now deemed it necessary to persuade the Soviet leaders to tolerate non-Communist forces in the countries they occupied. Since Roosevelt at Tehran had not let the Soviets realize how inclined he had been in 1943 to abandon the 'people of Europe' to Soviet rule, when the Big Three met for the second time, at Yalta in February 1945, at the urging of Great Britain and of many senior American officials the fact that the Western Allies were in military occupation of Western Europe was allowed to weigh in the balance.

Averill Harriman was Roosevelt's ambassador in Moscow and one of the advocates of a closer American commitment. In words which illustrate the emergence of a corrective trend within American policy and also the optimistic assumptions underlying it, he wrote: 'I believe we should make them [the Russians] understand patiently but firmly that we cannot accept their point of view and that we are prepared to take the consequences if they adhere to their position. In such cases, I am satisfied that in the last analysis Stalin will back down.'[134]

Stalin respected the realities of military and political power; he forbade the Communist parties in the parts of Europe occupied by the American and British forces to seize power by revolution. On the other hand, he fully intended to put a Leninist gloss on the 'Declaration on Liberated Europe' to which he had assented at Yalta, as far as the Russian-occupied part of Europe was concerned. Thus developments in fact seemed to point to the alternative of either a co-imperium over Europe or its partition. At first, as the results of the important war conference of Yalta early in February 1945 show, both superpowers tried to exercise their rule over Europe jointly, on the basis of the power relationship already established by Allied troops.[135] In the words of the final communiqué: 'Our meeting

---

[134] *FRUS* (n. 119), 1944, iv, p. 997. On the beginnings of American involvement in Europe while Roosevelt was still President, cf. Kolko (n. 130), pp. 161–71, and Gaddis, op. cit. (n. 122), p. 114 ff.
[135] On the spate of books etc. on the Yalta Conference, cf. as an introduction the classic analysis by Feis, op. cit. (n. 114), pp. 497–558, and J. Wheeler-Bennett and A. Nichols, *The Semblance of Peace, The Political Settlement after the Second World War*, London, 1972, pp. 188–250; from a markedly revisionist point of view Kolko (n. 130), pp. 343–69; moderately revisionist D. S. Clemens, *Yalta*, NY, 1970; a more recent account in L. A. Rose, *After Yalta, America and the Origins of the Cold War*, NY, 1973; all, however, agree that there was a temporary co-imperium. For Stalin's restraint at the beginning of 1945 in Finland and Greece, also his refusal to countenance a Communist seizure of power in Italy, France, and Belgium, see the summary by W. Wagner, *Teilung Europas*, Stuttgart, 1959, pp. 129–52.
[136] Last (ninth) section of the immediately published *Report on the Yalta Conference* in *FRUS: The Conferences at Malta and Yalta, 1945*, Washington, 1955.

here in the Crimea has reaffirmed our common determination to maintain and strengthen in the peace to come that unity of purpose and of action which has made victory possible and certain for the United Nations in this war.'[136]

The unity referred to had indeed taken shape in regard to certain urgent questions. The Soviet Union, the United States, and Britain had agreed at Yalta that they would jointly occupy and control Germany after it had been forced to surrender unconditionally. The three victorious powers would each occupy a separate zone of Germany; and on British insistence a fourth occupation zone, for France, would be carved out of the American and British zones. Co-ordinated administration and control would be exercised through a Central Control Council with headquarters in Berlin. German militarism and Nazism would be destroyed; all German industry that could be used for military purposes would be eliminated or controlled; all Nazi and militarist influences would be removed from public office; and the occupying powers would 'take in harmony such other measures' as might be 'necessary for the future peace and safety of the world'.[137] But towards the other countries too the three Allies had undertaken 'joint obligations' and had promised 'jointly to assist the people in any liberated state or former Axis satellite state in Europe... (a) to establish conditions of internal peace; (b) to carry out emergency measures for the relief of distressed people; (c) to form interim governmental authorities broadly representative of all democratic elements in the population and pledged to the earliest possible establishment through free elections of governments responsive to the will of the people; and (d) to facilitate where necessary the holding of such elections.'[138] It would have been logical, and consistent with their declared 'unity', if the three powers had established a joint supreme authority for the remainder of Europe on the model of the Allied Military Government in Italy. But Roosevelt had refrained from putting forward for discussion at Yalta a similar project supported by the State Department for establishing a 'High Authority for the Liberated Territories', doubtless out of consideration for Stalin's known opposition to any kind of all-European institution.[139]

The co-operation of America and Russia was most clearly expressed in the agreement on the foundation of the United Nations Organization which, in conformity with the wishes of Roosevelt and Hull, was supposed,

[137] From the second section 'Occupation and Control Council' of the *Yalta Report, FRUS* (see n. 136).

[138] From the fifth section 'Declaration on Liberated Europe' in the Report, whose sixth section specified Poland as an example of 'agreement reached', stating that 'the provisional Communist government which holds office in Poland at present ... is to be remodelled on a broader democratic basis with the inclusion of democratic leaders in Poland itself and from Poles living abroad', and that 'as soon as possible, free and unfettered elections should be held'. It was plainly on the strength of these assurances that the United States and Great Britain definitely accepted the Curzon Line as the Western frontier of the Soviet Union and promised to support at the future peace conference Poland's western frontier on the Oder and the cession of the northern part of East Prussia to the USSR. Cf. the sources given in n. 135 above and E. R. Stettinius, *Roosevelt and the Russians, The Yalta Conference*, London, 1950, pp. 84–8 and 216–33.

[139] Plan for a 'European High Commission on Liberated Territories' prepared by the Department of State, 18 Jan. 1945, given to Roosevelt before he went to Yalta, in *Yalta Papers*, pp. 97–100; cf. p. 76 above.

80 Introduction

according to the Yalta communiqué, to guarantee peace and security. However, the United States, having conceded to the Soviet Union the right of veto, now made a further important concession, one already demanded by the Soviet delegate A. Gromyko at the preliminary conference at Dumbarton Oaks. This was that the Security Council members' right of veto should also apply to questions 'directly affecting one of these countries' as far as military measures were deemed necessary. They thus made sure that the world organization could not take decisions contrary to Soviet interests.[140] Nevertheless, at the heart of all these declarations made to the world in general lay the idea of joint rule or co-imperium, to be exercised by the superpowers over Germany and the whole of Europe for a transitional period at least, leaving a definite statement about the final outcome to one or more future peace conferences.[141]

In the event, the new superpowers which met on the soil of the devastated old Continent made no formal decision except to return to the former system of nation states. The intellectuals of the European Resistance and even, with modifications, those of Great Britain and those among the Europeans in exile had with a remarkable degree of unanimity realized that the European nations could have a future only as a single community. Yet the system of nation states was reimposed on them by the will of the Soviet Union. The extra-European powers decided according to their own real or supposed interests; Europe, according to the old doctrine of the state, which was still accepted by those powers, had no claim on them to represent its interests. It was thus thrust back into hopeless disunity, so far as the Russians were concerned in the clear expectation that what was by the new global standards a Balkan-like power vacuum would at least confirm the thesis of the inevitable collapse of the capitalist states.[142] This basic decision to prevent the diminished European countries forming regional associations or unions, and consequently to deny them any weight of their own in the future balance of power, had been made by the Americans in 1943 to appease the Soviet Union for the sake of Russo-American co-operation. It soon proved, however, to be one of the reasons why the attempt at a co-imperium was increasingly unsuccessful and gave

---

[140] In addition to the sources named in n. 135, cf. esp. A. Dallin, *The Soviet Union at the United Nations*, London, 1962; F. C. Pogue, 'The Big Three and the United Nations' in J. L. Snell (ed.), *The Meaning of Yalta*, Baton Rouge, 1956, p. 167 ff.; F. Donovan, *Mr Roosevelt's Four Freedoms: The Story behind the UN Charter*, NY, 1966.

[141] Cf. the definition by Verdross (*Völkerrecht*, 1937, p. 132) 'Co-Imperium bedeutet Gemeinschaftsherrschaft auf fremdem Gebiet, Con-Dominium Gemeinschaftsherrschaft auf eigenem Gebiet', quoted by E. Menzel, 'Deutschland, ein Con-Dominium oder Co-Imperium' in *Jahrbuch für Internationales und Ausländisches öffentliches Recht*, i, 1948, p. 75. The description given by Menzel (p. 75 f., quoting further authorities on international law) is valid, if the essential characteristics of 'Herrschaft' (rule, domination) are strictly applied not only for Germany but for the whole of Continental Europe in 1945–6, whether occupied by the Russians or the Americans.

[142] Cf. also P. Quaroni, *Die Stunde Europas*, Frankfurt, 1959, p. 49 f.; W. Conze, 'Nationalstaat, Weltrevolution, Welteinheit', in *Offene Welt*, No. 65, 1960, p. 25.

place to the division of the Continent into a Soviet and an American sphere of influence, based on the disposition of their respective military forces at the end of hostilities.

5. Forces of Opposition: II. National Governments

There were thus two major lines of development which, having evolved since the First World War, came into their own during the Second World War, when they met in what was at first sight a somewhat unexpected fashion. On the one hand, there was the rise of the superpowers and their military preponderance over the ruined Continent; on the other, Europe's self-awareness and the unification movement born of its defeat. The coincidence of these two very disparate lines of development constituted one of the key problems in Europe's post-war history. It was further complicated by the fact that a second group of opposing forces within Europe had arrived on the scene: national governments and parties, which would either have to be gradually educated into sympathy with the unification movement, or which were opposed to a united Europe on principle. Only by first glancing at the further complex relationship between these developments and forces can we establish the limits and methodology of this book for the period 1945–50.

(A) THE KEY PROBLEM: GOVERNMENTAL ATTITUDES

In terms of power politics initially the sole decisive line of development was the rise of the new superpowers, the arrival of Russia and America as independent leaders on the world stage, each with its own global programmme. By comparison with the rise of both continental unions, each of which possessed a potential exceeding that of all the European states put together, the latter even during the inter-war years had sunk to the status of medium or small states, and the relapse into reactionary nationalism had finally brought about the military preponderance of both new superpowers. In this process the advance of the Eastern superpower, which managed to extend its westward frontier as far as the line Lübeck–Trieste, played a fundamental part. It was this power, too, which succeeded in getting all attempts to include European unification in Western post-war planning sacrificed to its implacable veto, with the result that the superpowers did not make a start in creating European institutions, as the main Resistance movements desired, but formally decided to restore the twenty-six small state sovereignties, while *de facto* partitioning the old Continent into spheres of influence.[143]

The other development, at first a purely ideological one, was Europe's self-examination, the attempt to frame a European answer to recent

[143] On this summing-up, cf. with supporting evidence pp. 1–6 and 69 f. above.

political and economic events, the decline of Europe and the rise of the new superpowers. Among the leaders of the Continental countries there had grown up a desire to build a common future transcending the sovereignty of the nation state which had caused so much unhappiness. This desire had developed in stages, beginning with the shock of the First World War, and had gained a large measure of acceptance in the non-Communist Resistance against Hitler during the Second World War; it was a product of the will to give Europe, which had suffered so much from the system of state sovereignties, a common future. The realization was expressed in forceful terms: the European nations must unite in view of the totality of technological warfare, the results of nationalism, economic impoverishment, and the rise of the extra-European powers. While plans put forward by British writers and by politicians in exile between the wars and at the beginning of the 1940s had emphasized the need for close co-operation and security through institutions of a confederal nature, the future plans of practically all non-Communist Resistance movements had categorically declared that only a voluntary union of the European nations in a federal state could answer the need. Only political unity, not simply loose machinery for consultation, such as the impotent League of Nations had been, could in the end make war between European nations impossible. Only economic unity, achieved through a common market, division of labour, and freedom of movement, would create the prosperity which would make possible a high standard of welfare and social services. Only by means of such unity could the German question be solved by abolishing one-sided restrictions without causing damage to Germany's neighbours, but actually to the advantage of the wider community. Only a united Europe, instead of a continent which was no better than a Balkanized no man's land, could still make its voice heard among the world powers. This answer was the only positive and constructive idea produced by a civilization in decline, and no serious alternative idea was put forward.[144]

The confrontation of these two lines of develoment in 1945 was necessarily a meeting of very disparate elements: on the one hand, the military prowess of the superpowers, Russian or American troops in almost every country of Continental Europe, the decisions of the 'great' on the future of Europe taken at the conferences of Yalta and Potsdam; on the other hand, the helpless European nations still struggling against great hardships, with all the understanding they had gained, their rejection of the past, and their desire for change. The question was whether the forces of Europe's self-awareness and readiness to unite would ever, as it were, succeed in setting foot on one square yard that was not directly or indirectly dominated by Russia or America. Had the two world powers remained united in their *de facto* co-imperium and in their rejection of the idea of a united Europe,

---

[144] Cf. with supporting evidence pp. 35–62 above.

Europe would have stood no chance. In reality it was obvious to any historically minded person that the historic moment for voluntary, independent unification had already passed, that any subsequent effort would represent little more than a posthumous enterprise: in other words, it could be done only with the permission of at least one of the superpowers.[145] When the war ended on 8 May 1945 with the capitulation of Germany nearly every country had its organized groups, mostly emerging from the Resistance, which proclaimed the idea of European unity in clearly conceived and well-drafted programmes. But they were soon obliged to realize that they had little prospect of success in a situation dominated down to the smallest detail by the two superpowers, both of whom opposed the European idea, and between the summer of 1945 and that of 1946 they had to accept the fact that their efforts were an abysmal failure.[146] After the miseries of war the populations showed complete readiness to accept the future imposed on them by their liberators, and all their hopes turned to the new, permanent peace organization promised by the superpowers. The restored national governments were preoccupied with the struggle to overcome chaos, and they too recognized the predominance of the Russians and Americans.[147] This state of powerlessness was the primary reason for the weakening of the movement for European unification.

When in the summer of 1946 European public opinion became anxious lest the two superpowers might fail to reach agreement over the peace settlement to which they had pledged themselves, rapidly growing groups were again formed in all the major towns to propagate the idea of a European federation as the Europeans' own solution. They knew that, as one of the symptoms of Europe's decline, every step taken towards partial unification depended on the approval of one of the superpowers, every expectation of all-European unity depended on the approval of both. The groups accordingly divided into two categories: those who, like Churchill, stood for partial unity within the sphere of influence of one superpower, and those like the Union Européenne des Fédéralistes (UEF) who remained faithful to the idea of an all-European 'third force' which it was hoped would be approved also by the Soviet Union.[148]

The disunity of Europe, on the other hand, had become a problem for the superpowers, even though they were the authors of it, for increasingly it aggravated their relations with each other. The existence of a power vacuum, especially in Germany, the test-case for co-imperium, called for

---

[145] Cf. the 'Conclusion' written in 1949 by H. Gollwitzer, *Europabild und Europagedanke*, Munich, 1951, p. 413: 'A large number of the most urgent problems can no longer be solved within the framework of Europe. Moreover, the Europeans can no longer conceal from themselves that their present attempt to establish European unity is in many respects a posthumous enterprise, an action of which Europe showed itself incapable when it was still independent.'
[146] Cf. chapter I, sections 2 and 7 for details.
[147] Cf. the survey of each major country in chapter I, sections 3 to 6.
[148] Cf. chapter II for details.

decisions on which they could not agree and drove them into confrontation, the very thing they had wished to avoid. It was impossible for either of them, having regard to its own interests, to expose its own share of Europe's resources to possible seizure by the other; each sought to organize its own sphere, the Western power after April 1947 by taking up and approving the idea of European unity, the Eastern power by a still more emphatic rejection.[149]

The onset of the Cold War between the superpowers imposed a severe geographical restriction on the movement for European unification. America's acceptance and promotion of the idea of a federation helped the movement to the extent of bringing about the first multilateral treaties between Western-European states, but only after the Soviet Union had insisted on cutting off Eastern Europe. This division and the assignment of countries to one or other of the new power blocs was in the long run the second reason for the weakening of the European unification movement. For European federalists it was far from easy to acknowledge that a practical move towards unity was possible only if it was sponsored by one superpower and at the cost of accepting the existing division of Europe. Yet at the Montreux conference of 1947 they agreed, after much wrestling with the problem, 'to make a start with the federal construction of Europe where a start can be made'.[150] This start in Western Europe meant after all the inclusion of over three-quarters of Europe's population. Yet this decision was also the reason why the federalists clung for more than two years to the view, which until then had not been regarded as of equal importance, that Great Britain and Scandinavia must at all costs be included within the narrower union. Having been forced for the time being to act without the co-operation of the Eastern-European nations, those in the proposed federal area were all the more anxious not to leave out any eligible part of Western Europe. Understandable as this point of view was, it nevertheless made the pace of the first move depend on Britain, whose population, like those of the few countries that had remained neutral during the war, was not yet ready to pool its sovereignty.

The beginning of the Cold War and of American support for the idea of European unity also revealed, however, the existence of opposing forces inside Europe which seriously impeded the work of unification. Until the spring of 1947 the most ardent leaders of the European federalist associations complained that the European governments, especially the British and French, did not even acknowledge the idea of European unity in words or by making initial contacts; but they realized that in 1945–6 these governments were silent on the subject of European unity because of the declared hostility of the two superpowers at that time, the latter having refused to allow advantage to be taken of 'Zero Hour' at the end of the

[149] Cf. the introductory sections in each case, in chapters I, II, and III.
[150] Cf. chapter III for details.

war and having decreed the restoration of the nation state. It was also clear that the idea evolved during the war by the leaders of the Resistance would in the normal course need a period of 'incubation', of penetration into practical politics, of spreading the word, winning influence in the political parties, building up contacts between the national associations, etc. The Belgian government under Spaak and the Italian government under De Gasperi had made proposals aimed at unification as early as 1945 which had been rejected in London and Paris. From the spring of 1946 onwards the British and French governments could have attempted steps in that direction, but such steps would have been risky in view of the opposition of the superpowers, and the result would have been uncertain. People realized that the governments were overburdened with the most urgent tasks involved in the overcoming of chaos, and in view of the Russian occupation of Eastern Europe wished to do nothing for their part to promote the division of the Continent. The situation changed completely, however, when the United States came out in favour of the idea of European unification and when the Cold War began. From then onwards in the larger half of Europe the idea of unity was no longer vetoed by the dominant power, but its implementation depended on the West-European governments, which now appeared as a second opposing force.[151] It is true that from the summer of 1947 onwards publicity and penetration of the political parties was more rapid, and the first moves towards implementing the idea occurred with what was really astonishing speed in the years 1948–50, thanks to its power to convince people, from the alliance of 1948 to the first general assembly in 1949 and the plan for a first supranational authority in 1950. Yet the federal idea never achieved the real breakthrough to success because besides the Soviet Union the British government too, followed by those of Scandinavia and later France, rejected and opposed it. In the upshot (and this is still true) the centres of the historically oldest nation states, London and Paris, proved bastions of stubborn nationalist traditions and illusions which refused to face realistically such facts as the decline of Europe, the preponderance of the new superpowers, and the need for European unity. Provincialism, a decline in civilized standards, and nihilistic fatalism made up the third reason for the weakening of the European movement.

Yet these purely European obstacles and opposing forces remained bound up in many ways with the root problem – the clash between the unity movement and the superpowers' rivalry, particularly the antagonism of Russia. In a general sense, the division of Europe that had already taken place, the cutting-off of Eastern Europe, and the incorporation of the Western states into the framework of NATO all had an inhibiting effect.

---

[151] Cf. esp. the analysis at the end of chap. I/7, p. 279 f., also in chap. III, which describes this change-about as a whole, III/2, p. 488 f., and Spinelli's trenchant analysis at Montreux, p. 582.

86 *Introduction*

The enfeebled forces of the nationalist Right, for example, would have been less effective in slowing down the process of European unification had they not been assisted in this by the uncompromising, pro-Moscow hostility of the Communist parties (particularly in France), with the Communists forming an unholy alliance with the old 'right' wing throughout Western Europe. Communist opposition, in turn, had some influence, thanks to the myth of the 'Marxist fraternal parties', on the left wing of the Social Democrats and reduced the number of pro-Europeans among them.[152] Thus Europe's subjection to a bipolar system dominated by Russia and America remained a key problem, containing as it did the possibility that at any time the superpowers might come to an understanding in their search for agreement, again at the expense of Europe. Hence we must continually take into account the reciprocal influence of the movement for European unification and the rivalry of the superpowers.

(B) TEMPORAL AND GEOGRAPHICAL LIMITS OF THE PRESENT WORK

The chapters of this book should be understood as studies for the understanding and recording of the process whereby the conception of European unity, starting from the basic premisses of the European situation of 1945 as already sketched, was able despite the supervention of the two new superpowers to hold its own during the difficult years of 1945–6, and then between 1947 and 1950 to advance in Western Europe to the level of parties and governments and to achieve some success in terms of political institutions. Thus the years 1945–50 include the decisive incubation phase, in which the unification movement, that hitherto had figured 'only' as part of the history of political ideas, managed in spite of adverse circumstances to exert a strong influence on parties and governments in the larger part of Europe and to make a real start towards unity in practice. There are already a number of good monographs on the organizations based on the method of supranational functionalism for partial (economic) integration (ECSC, EEC, EURATOM);[153] and various phases of development in the years after 1950 (Haas, Baring, Camps, etc.);[154] but a large gap in our knowledge remains inasmuch as there is no general analysis of the formative phase of the movement and of the beginnings of European policy between 1945 and 1950, which should include the history of several West-European countries and of the movement in both its national and supranational

---

[152] Cf. chap. IV (vol. 2).
[153] Summarized with comprehensive bibliography in H. P. Ibsen, *Europäisches Gemeinschaftsrecht*, Tübingen, 1972; at present the handiest 'Bibliographie raisonnée' is P. Buchrucker, *Bibliographie zur Europäischen Integration*, instituted by G. Zellentin, Cologne, 1970³.
[154] E. B. Haas, *The Uniting of Europe, Political, Social and Economic Forces, 1950–1957*, Stanford, 1968²; A. Baring, *Aussenpolitik in Adenauers Kanzlerdemokratie* (pocket edn. in 2 vols.), Munich, 1971; M. Camps, *Britain and the European Community 1955–1963*, Princeton, NJ, 1964, and others. See n. 163 below for important monographs on the years 1945–50.

aspects. In the words of Hans-Peter Schwarz 'the European movement still awaits its historian', especially 'for the particularly important initial period of 1945–49', and it is above all the 'lack of historical research that explains the absence of a theory to match the process of integration'.[155] Since the few works already published which go beyond the limits of a nation state have so far been concerned only with the later and obviously limited functional and partial achievements in the economic sphere and with the interlude of the EDC, the important period of general ideas and discussion about methods before the whole subject was narrowed down to functional and partial integration has remained uninvestigated.

Although for this reason this survey has been limited to the formative period of the European movement, the incubation phase which marked its first impact on practical politics, it must be admitted that neither 1945, the beginning of our period, nor 1950, its end, marks a turning-point in world history. In terms of world history the really decisive dates are 1943 and 1947. 1943 was the year of decision for the war, and also the turning-point when the new superpowers reached a basic understanding that in future Europe should cease to count as an independent power. But the year 1947 saw the climax of the next major political change which for some months had been envisaged by both superpowers: the end of American–Russian co-operation across the world, the outbreak of the Cold War, and in consequence of this breach the completion of the partition of Europe. For the United States this meant the partial revival of the pro-European post-war plans which Washington had shelved in 1943. As far as world politics was concerned the year 1945 brought only the fulfilment of the decisions made in 1943; it was simply the year in which the consequences of the change in the world situation reached Europe, which felt the effect of decisions made by the world powers two years before. In much the same way, the years 1948–50 in Europe, seen in a world perspective, were essentially a period when Europeans had to wrestle with their reactions to the change of direction by the superpowers in 1947. Any analysis of post-war history will constantly have to bear in mind that from then onwards European attitudes lagged behind global developments, that it was the superpowers which would make the running: Europe would react to events, not shape them.

There is, nevertheless, something to be gained by starting this book in the year 1945 because it marked the close of an era for the population of Europe. The end of the war meant that Europeans were free to react to events as they chose, subject to the limits explained in this Introduction. The choice of 1950 as the terminal date obviously needs more justification. The crucial period is between the spring and August of 1950: in other words the analysis will continue to the point at which the decision was

[155] H.-P. Schwarz, 'Europa föderieren – aber wie? Eine Methodenkritic der europäischen Integration' in *Demokratisches System und politische Praxis der Bundesrepublik, Festschrift für Th. Eschenburg*, Munich, 1971, p. 378 f.

reached that the Council of Europe, created with such high hopes, would not be developed into a constituent assembly. On the other hand our survey will not include the Schuman Plan, still less the beginning of government negotiations over the treaty which founded the ECSC, with which a new stage opened. By the middle of 1950 two things had been achieved:

1. The movement for European unity had taken shape; all its members had formed their own associations which were represented at international level with definite programmes. The hard-core federalist associations in particular could point to a well-thought-out policy, precise ideas for every field of political activity, a strongly militant basis, and a ceaselessly active lobby. Round them were grouped, equally self-contained as regards programmes and organization, the more 'unionist' associations; and they were all included in the highly organized umbrella organization known as the 'European Movement', which in the spring of 1950 succeeded in adopting a programme of advance by stages which embodied the federalist principle. Nothing of any substance was added to this after 1950.

2. The concept of European unity had by this time achieved recognition within the official channels of public opinion, the political parties; and as a result of interaction between the pro-European pressure groups 'from below' and the stimulating effect on governments of international events 'from above' (such as the encouragement given by the United States) the first moves were made towards integration, albeit still in theory only, such as the Brussels Pact, OEEC, and the Council of Europe. Going beyond that, groups of parliamentarians and the federalist associations had demanded the calling of a European constituent assembly which would agree upon the decisive step of political federation. Finally 'Operation Federal Treaty' launched by UEF in the winter of 1949–50 also urged the convening of a European constituent assembly. But between the spring and August of 1950 it became evident that the majorities even in the West-European parliaments were not yet ready to take this step.[156]

The attempt, begun in May 1950, to make progress within the narrower framework of the Six through partial integration of a supranational, federalist kind clearly marked a new stage which needs to be studied on its own (as it has been to some extent).[157] Moreover today, some thirty years

[156] Cf. on both points chapters IV–VI as a whole, also the 'Concluding Summary' (in vol. 2). Treating the year 1950 as the end of one stage and the beginning of another has a practical argument in its favour, though one of secondary importance: during the years when the European associations were making their way into active politics they were of such importance to our story that their archives enable us to follow all major developments very closely; not until the summer of 1950, when governments had at last taken a hand in the movement towards unity, does the inaccessibility of ministerial files present a real obstacle to historical research.

[157] Cf. esp. Haas (n. 154) and Ipsen (n. 153) with bibliographies. The European federalists themselves hardly experienced 1950 as a watershed, but threw themselves at once into the struggle for the ECSC and EDC, convinced that functionalist and partial integrations would bring about political unity, and that unity within the geographically limited circle of the Six would in the end bring the whole of Western Europe with it. So it was not until 1954, the year marked by the failure of the EDC and EPC, that they felt there had been a temporary set-back even within the

Introduction 89

later, it is plain that the functionalist partial integrations achieved as much as they could; that economic integration does not automatically lead to political integration; that, on the contrary, the Common Market threatens to crumble away if it is not reinforced by a complete economic and currency union, which again is inconceivable without political union. Thus the original goal reappears, and has been proclaimed under the slogan 'Political Union by 1980'. In this way, however, the European movement finds itself facing essentially the same decision as in 1950, when it evaded it by opting for partial integration. For this reason it is politically as well as historically important to recall to mind, and to provide for those involved in the recently revived debate on ends and means, information about the wide-ranging discussion on ideas and methods which took place between 1945 and 1950.[158]

For the period 1945–50 it was unfortunately necessary, not merely for purely technical reasons, to continue to treat of Europe in the narrower sense. For it was only the West-European nations living in the American sphere of influence which still had relative freedom to make their own response to the challenge presented by the outside world. The suppression of all approaches to the European unity movement in Soviet-dominated Eastern Europe is sketched in two sections below but cannot be described in detail.[159] In Western Europe limitations of time, energy and availability of sources necessitated the omission of the Scandinavian countries, whose European associations, for reasons already mentioned, were slow in being formed, as well as the beginnings of the movement in Greece and in the Iberian peninsula. For these reasons this book concentrates on the history of the idea of European union or federation, of the associations formed to further it, and of its rise to the level of practical politics in the territory of the West-European states which had experienced defeat in war and which later constituted the Six, together with Great Britain.[160]

(C) METHODS, SOURCES, AND STRUCTURE OF THE WORK

As far as method is concerned, the most important decision to be made in preparing this book was that the analysis of the idea of European unity as

---

Community of the Six. Yet in retrospect, the preoccupation with the narrower affairs of the Six which occurred between 1950 and 1954 clearly emerges as constituting a second phase in its own right, in which the associations were already becoming less important.

[158] Cf. Schwarz (n. 155), esp. pp. 424–33; W. Lipgens, 'Europäische Integration', in *Die Zweite Republik, 25 Jahre Bundesrepublik Deutschland—eine Bilanz,* ed. by R. Löwenthal and H. P. Schwarz, Stuttgart, 1974, pp. 519–53.

[159] Cf. chap. II/7 and chap III/2, which also deal with the pro-federation groups from the East-European countries in exile.

[160] In this way the central aspects of the problem – the West European states that had experienced defeat, Great Britain, and the global situation – are covered by the survey. The merely occasional consideration given to the Scandinavian states and Greece and to pro-European stirrings in the Iberian Peninsula is due to the fact that enquiries relating to this early phase yielded practically nothing: and it was not practicable to visit the archives in those countries as well as in all the others. On the other hand, full use was made of material belonging to the Swiss Europa-Union.

it was championed and developed, of the formative phase of the European movement and of the beginnings of European policy between 1945 and 1950 should not be based on the sources and viewed through the experience of any one nation. On the contrary, the work was intended to draw on the sources and experience of the European associations of at least the seven nations already mentioned, especially the four major nations, Great Britain, France, Italy, and Germany, as well as those of all the supranational umbrella organizations concerned. One could hardly expect that a result relevant in terms of history and method on the vital question of European unity could be produced by a study of the files of only one nation or the files of the umbrella organizations alone; only by treating the subject as both multinational and supranational was it possible to achieve the desired effect. What makes the majority of historical and political studies of this question unsatisfactory is precisely that (except for works by E.B. Haas and his school for the period since 1950) they have looked at matters from the point of view of a single nation state.[161] In this work, therefore, an attempt has been made in the case of the seven nations to provide equal investigation of the sources and to give each a proportionate share of the narrative and analysis, as well as to interweave the material drawn from particular nations with that of the European movement as a supranational movement. In other words, the author has deliberately preferred to lay himself open to the possible accusation that the book, which demands almost too much from one individual, deals inadequately with this or that detail rather than to be charged with a lack of clarity or courage in the attempt, both in theme and method, to master the problems which arose in the period 1945–50.

On many aspects of the subject it has been possible to make grateful use of research already carried out, as will be readily understood in view of the wealth of studies that have been undertaken as to the post-1945 period. Thus the introductory sections which outline the confrontation between the superpowers as it existed at a particular time and those sections which describe the original attitudes of national governments and part of the chapter on parties are based on secondary sources, to which references are given in every case. On the subject in its narrower sense, the history and programmes of the European associations and their influence on practical politics, there exist: (1) first attempts at general surveys (from Schöndube/Ruppert and Brugmans to Albertini and Mayne)[162] which, for lack of

---

[161] Cf. Schwarz (n. 154), p. 378; K. Kaiser, 'L'Europe des Savants. Die europäische Integration und die Sozialwissenschaften', in *Integration*, i, 1968, p. 12.

[162] C. Schöndube and C. Ruppert, *Eine Idee setzt sich durch*, Hangelar, 1964; H. Brugmans, *L'Idée européenne, 1920–1970*, Bruges, 1970³; D. W. Urwin, *Western Europe since 1945*, London, 1968; M. Albertini, A. Chiti-Batelli, and G. Petrilli, *Storia del federalismo europeo*, Turin, 1973; R. J. Mayne, *The Recovery of Europe, 1945–1973*, Garden City, 1973. No attempt has been made in the sections dealing with the European associations to record in the notes anything like all the references to particular events in the many early studies which were valuable in their time (e.g. H. Fischer, *Der Weg nach Europa. Übernationale Gemeinschaften und der Europarat*, Munich, 1953; W. Wehe, *Das Werden Europas, Zeittafel der europäischen Einigungsbestrebungen 1946–1955*, Frankfurt, 1955, etc.); these studies

previous work on the earlier phases, devote only one or two dozen pages to the period 1945-50, but which raise stimulating questions; (2) useful pioneer studies of single associations in one country (Cornides, Philip, Levi/Pistone, and Grailsammer)[163] which are based on the publications of these associations. There is no doubt, however, that substantial progress and a solid foundation for the history of the associations became possible only by embarking on what was a pioneer study of their widely scattered archives. With the help of many former leaders of the associations in the years 1945 to 1950 who are still alive, and in the course of many journeys to the seven countries and to Switzerland, if has been possible to discover a number of previously unknown archival sources. The author was not able to use them all since they also extend to the regional and local associations, but I have drawn on all the key archives of the national and supranational associations as far as I could find them, as well as on the private papers and collections of documents of the principal chairmen of the associations at the time, until all the links of historiographical value were clearly recognizable.[164]

The overwhelming mass of source material (as is usually the case with contemporary history) demanded strict concentration on essential developments and features, leaving on one side countless minor issues and details of a technical nature. On the other hand it was essential for reasons of method to scrutinize and evaluate the sources from many points of view in what became a multi-disciplinary study: the interplay and interpenetration of so many diverse sources and levels of activity – the history of the associations as pressure groups, including their sociological basis, the arguments between parties and their right or left wings, the relationship between domestic policy and the changing political situation on the world scene – all this demanded a correspondingly varied and many-sided application of scholarly techniques drawn from the study of associations, parties, ideas, and diplomacy.

Just as Europe's self-awareness and willingness to unite, despite the initial hopelessness of the situation, remained steadfast in the minds of individuals and groups, as it rallied and found its way into political parties

---

are only cited when, for example, they provide information about a conference and do not simply record that it took place.

[163] W. Cornides, 'Die Anfänge des europäisch föderalistischen Gedankens in Deutschland 1945 bis 1946' in *Europa-Archiv*, 6 (1951), pp. 4243-58; O. Philip, *Le Problème de l'Union Européenne*, thesis, Paris, 1950; L. Levi and S. Pistone, *Trent'anni di vita del movimento federalista europeo*, Milan, 1973; A. Grailsammer, *Les Mouvements fédéralistes en France de 1945 à 1974*, Paris, 1975.

[164] Cf. the list of public and private archives used in the appendix, pp. 689-98; supplemented by a list of 'Eye-Witness accounts and Interviews' (in vol. 2). It would be tedious in this Introduction to describe the situation and content of each Archive. In the volume of documents, which is intended to provide for the first time a comprehensive selection of the most significant texts, a report on archives will be included by way of introduction. There has been no attempt here to anticipate comment on publications contemporary with the Archives, some of which are of great value as sources; they will be evaluated at appropriate stages as the account proceeds.

and finally led to political action, so this book divides naturally into two parts, which have come to constitute two volumes. The first part analyses in three chronological stages, from 1945 to 1947, the crisis and survival of the European idea during the initial period of Soviet–American harmony, its subsequent revival, its restriction to Western Europe, and the development of the European Movement at the outset of the Cold War. During those years the European idea could not be implemented because at bottom it was vetoed by both superpowers. The second part begins by sketching in cross-section the attitude of the various political parties, and thus analysing the reasons for the purely European obstacles which now come into the foreground. It goes on to describe in two chronological stages between 1948 and 1950 the arrival of the European idea on the main political scene, the democratic programme for a European constituent assembly, the dilution of the idea by the governments, and at the same time the first moves towards its implementation. The final summary then focuses on all the elements which made up the spectrum of the idea of federation, the discussions on methods, the constraints on the effectiveness of pressure groups, the willingness of parties, and the forces which helped or hindered the idea.

In view of the predominance of the superpowers, to which the Europeans could only react, each of the chronological chapters will begin with a (necessarily) short section outlining the world situation and the development in relations between the superpowers. The ensuing sections will then describe the reactions of European federalists to the world situation during the period in question. It will be shown how they responded by carrying their ideas further and by adjusting their tactics this way or that as proved most effective. Between these two poles in the story there will be brief descriptions of the parties and governments and of their basic attitudes to foreign policy both in planning and execution, including detailed attention in every case to their positive or negative reaction to the idea of European unity.[165] For – in contrast to the subsequent stage which began in May 1950, when important initiatives came from governments and federalist pressure groups counted for less – during the period 1945–50 it was the associations of European federalists which with all their shortcomings were guardians of the European idea, the connecting link between the insights of the Resistance and the later partial adoption of those insights by the governments, the true authors of the European response during the first difficult post-war years.

[165] Each of these chapters thus deals with the subject on three levels: first the 'challenge' presented by the world situation is broadly outlined; then the attitudes of the various national governments are examined; finally the main emphasis is placed on the lowest or ground level, viz. the history of the unofficial associations. The course of the narrative will, it is hoped, make clear that what at first sight appears a complicated method of procedure was in fact the only one adequate to describe the progress of the European unity movement from theory to practice.

CHAPTER I

Europe's Mood of Resignation during the Period of Apparent Russo-American Co-operation (May 1945-May 1946)

1. The Superpowers, the European Vacuum, and the Hope for a World-Wide Security System

In the first year after the war, from May 1945 to May 1946, Europe's position in the world was marked by two principal characteristics: first, the intention of both superpowers to achieve their respective aims in Europe by co-operation, as they had so successfully done during the war, in spite of a lack of wholehearted willingness to place common interests above their own particular interests; and secondly the discrepancy between this tentative co-operation and the trend towards delimitation, even confrontation. In spite of the serious difficulties which, as we now know, were already emerging within the framework of provisional co-operation in the European sphere, we should not overlook the fact that during this period we can speak of symptoms and origins but not yet of the beginning of the cold war. In particular – a decisive point for our subject – the European peoples remained almost unaware of (and the media were silent about) what might be going on in the way of mutual recriminations at the highest level of world politics and the first signs that the wartime coalition was about to break up. For Europeans, struggling against elementary hardships and the chaos of the immediate post-war period, when some fifty million people were on the move and the only things that worked were those connected with the Allied military establishment, while everything else – the economy, transport, and administration – was in ruins, the only remaining hope was that the two superpowers would have the sense to build a lasting peace. This hope was strengthened by the Allies' declarations assuring the world of their readiness to co-operate and of their joint desire to assume responsibility for the policy of 'One World'[1] – although at bottom neither the United States nor the Soviet Union set a higher value on the goal of peaceful co-operation than on the pursuit of their own special interests,[2] and although they had arrived in Europe without a common plan for the future of the Continent. They came equipped simply with fragments of an occupation policy and with an unspoken agreement that, measured by the new standards of power, the confused conglomerate of states in the old Continent should not play a political role of any importance.[3]

(A) BEGINNINGS OF CO-OPERATION AND CONFRONTATION BETWEEN THE SUPERPOWERS

The contradiction between the basic aims of the superpowers and their tactics gave rise to the key question on which the future of all Europeans and the fate of their hopes depended: Would the United States and the Soviet Union be able to attain their respective objects or at least view them as attainable by means of co-operation, and would, therefore, the construction of a 'One World' system and of a co-imperium over Europe succeed; or would the fulfilment of their aims lead to confrontation and thus bring about a bipolar system of tension between East and West?

Among factors which favoured a continuance of peaceful co-operation were the interest of both sides in military disengagement, in the American case as a result of political pressure at home, in the Russian case through exhaustion caused by the war; and the experience of interdependence in defeating the Nazi imperium. A lot of people in the United States believed in a kinship with Soviet Russia based on their own revolutionary tradition and hoped for the liberalization and 'maturing' of the Soviet system; while in the Soviet Union there was a tendency to define Socialist internationalism more and more in terms of the collaboration of all progressive forces. Speaking of his conversations with Roosevelt, Harry Hopkins, one of the President's closest confidants, said later: 'We really believed in our hearts that this was the dawn of the new day we had all been praying for and talking about for so many years. We were absolutely certain that we had won the first great victory of the peace – and by "we" I mean *all* of us, the whole civilized human race. The Russians had proved that they could be reasonable and farseeing and there wasn't any doubt in the minds of the President or any of us that we could live with them and get

---

[1] Cf. the Yalta declarations referred to in nn. 134–8 to the Introduction and the statements quoted in nn. 24 and 26 f. to this chapter.
[2] The upshot of the debate on revisionism, which has almost ceased to be a matter of controversy, can perhaps be expressed in these terms, if it is granted that the Americans hardly realized at this time the divergence between their own interests and universalist principles (cf. note 2 to chap. II).
[3] Cf. pp. 76 and 80. In the following pages events at superpower level are only described in broad outline to give the background to European reactions.

Europe's Mood of Resignation 95

along with them peacefully for as far into the future as any of us could imagine.'[4]

What militated against further peaceful co-operation was a fundamental antagonism in power politics, which in turn was indissolubly connected – and this contradicted the supposed ideological affinity – with the very real differences in history, social structure, and ideological claims. America's interest in security suggested the establishment of a world-wide system of free trade which would conform to its own liberal principles and at the same time guarantee the further expansion of the United States as the strongest economic power. Russia's interest in security saw it as essential to mark out spheres of influence and especially to create a belt of friendly, not anti-Soviet states in the territories bordering the Soviet Union, as a safeguard against any repetition of an attack on their own system such as the one which had so recently been defeated at such heavy cost. The two powers' security interests thus clashed in their ideological implications. The Open Door policy presupposed the existence of liberal and democratic, or at least liberal and capitalist states; the Soviet policy presupposed, by contrast, 'anti-fascist, progressive' if not Communist states that would be pro-Soviet and would not interfere in the Soviet Union's internal affairs. The two security interests collided, especially in Europe, which was both part of the Russians' defensive glacis and the Americans' most important trading partner. Hence it was to be expected that a struggle between the superpowers would break out in the European sphere and that it would initially appear as a struggle between ideologies.[5]

It was the Soviet attempt in the winter of 1944–5 to create in Eastern Europe a political order that met their particular security requirements which proved the immediate (and not, as 'traditional' Western historians have claimed, the underlying) cause of the rivalry which by the end of the war was beginning to take shape, even though the differences were still hardly apparent to the general public. The refusal of help to the Polish national rising in Warsaw and the launching of the 'Lublin Committee' as the new Polish government were followed at the Yalta conference by lip-service to the Western Allies' demands for democracy and the Open Door. In the remaining months of the war from February to May 1945, however, the Soviet leadership imposed their interpretation of the policy of security and of the Yalta resolutions without any regard for American wishes. As late as February 1945 they established by force a Communist-dominated government in Romania; on 14 March they unilaterally transferred sovereignty over the German territory east of the Oder–Neisse line to the provisional

---

[4] R. E. Sherwood, *Roosevelt and Hopkins. An Intimate History*, NY, 1948, p. 870.
[5] For the historical and ideological causes of the Cold War, cf. esp. L. J. Halle, *The Cold War as History*, London/NY, 1967; P. Dukes, *The Emergence of the Superpowers: A Short Comparative History of the USA and the USSR*, London, 1970; also the penetrating analysis by E. Nolte, *Deutschland und der Kalte Krieg*, Munich, 1974.

Polish government; instead of the latter being reconstructed, as Stalin had promised the Allies, 'on a broad democratic basis', only two non-Communists were given office and on 28 March sixteen leading personalities of the Polish democratic Resistance were deported to Moscow. In April Poland and also Yugoslavia, which after the victory of the national Communist partisan movement sought closer ties with Moscow, were linked to the Soviet Union by treaties of alliance which ensured the establishment of a 'democratic' structure as a matter of international law. In June Czechoslovakia, which had had a similar treaty relationship with the Soviet Union since the end of 1943, was obliged to cede Ruthenia (Sub-Carpathian Ukraine) to the USSR; at the same time the Soviet Military Administration in Germany started the transformation of society in the Russian-occupied Zone by licensing democratic parties only within the framework of the 'anti-fascist bloc'. The 'friendly' orientation of Eastern Europe was consolidated by Draconian measures including the punishment and expulsion of 'dissidents'. All this happened without consulting the Western powers, whose influence in the Allied Control Commissions in Romania, Hungary, and Bulgaria remained virtually negligible.[6] Stalin interpreted the strategic guarantee of his new western boundaries by his Allies at Yalta as the recognition of his political expansion; he was not content with political hegemony over the neighbouring East-European states, but strove by dictatorial means (as in his own country) to impose within their borders a 'pro-Soviet' state of mind, an irreversible degree of Sovietization. In April 1945 he told a visiting Yugoslav delegation: 'This war is not like wars in the past; whoever occupies a territory imposes on it his own social system. Everyone imposes his own social system as far as his army can reach.'[7]

As far as the Western powers were concerned, Britain under Churchill had tried to counter these manœuvres before it was too late by military operations (such as the plan for liberating the Balkans from the south), by preparing to safeguard Western interests, and by a policy of spheres of influence; but Roosevelt rejected out of hand such a policy as thwarting his 'grand design' for world-wide co-operation with the Soviet Union based on mutual trust. Nevertheless in Italy from 1943 onwards, on British insist-

[6] W. McNeill, *America, Britain and Russia – Their Cooperation and Conflict 1941–1946*, London, 1953, p. 574 ff., B. Meissner, *Russland, die Westmächte und Deutschland 1943–1953*, Hamburg, 1954, p. 55 ff. For the East-European Pact System see Kazimierz Grzybowski, *The Socialist Commonwealth of Nations, Organizations and Institutions*, New Haven, 1964. For events in the context of the different countries, cf. the relevant sections in E. Birke and R. Neumann (ed.), *Die Sowjetisierung Ost–Mittel-Europas. Untersuchungen zu ihrem Ablauf in den einzelnen Ländern*, Berlin, 1959; for a summary, Jörg K. Hoensch, 'Sowjetische Osteuropapolitik 1945–1955', in *Osteuropa-Handbuch Sowjetunion, Aussenpolitik I*, Cologne–Vienna, 1972, pp. 382–447, and esp. pp. 384–405.

[7] M. Djilas, *Conversations with Stalin*, London, 1962. Cf. M. D. Shulman, *Stalin's Foreign Policy Reappraised* (Russian Research Center Studies, 48), Cambridge/Mass., 1963; B. Meissner, 'Wesen und Eigenart der sowjetischen Aussenpolitik' in *Europa-Archiv 24* (1969), pp. 639–50; M. Geiling, *Aussenpolitik und Nuklearstrategie. Eine Analyse des konzeptionellen Wandels der amerikanischen Sicherheitspolitik gegenüber der Sowjetunion 1945–1963*, Cologne/Vienna, 1975, pp. 9–17.

ence but with the support of the local American army chiefs, the pursuit of Western interests was given priority over co-operation with the Soviet Union to the extent that the Soviet representatives were only in a formal sense involved in the occupation of Italy and did not in fact share in decision-making. The Soviet request of 3 January 1945 for a credit of six thousand million dollars, which would have reduced the disparity between the superpowers' resources, was, as Ambassador Harriman had recommended, handled in a procrastinating way in order to show the Russians 'how lack of co-operation with our legitimate demands will adversely affect their interests', and was eventually rejected by Congress as part of a general veto on further war credits.[8] At the Potsdam conference and in the following months President Truman considered it advisable, in view of Soviet *faits accomplis* in Eastern Europe, for the time being at least to provide the Soviet Union with no more power of leverage; he refused to give firm guarantees on the question of German reparations and on the Soviet claim for a share of control over the Ruhr. The West's refusal to give co-operation precedence over the protection of their own interests meant the first delimitation of spheres of influence. At the Moscow conference of foreign ministers the Soviet Union had to be content with a nominal share in the occupation of Japan instead of the real share which it sought, and also undertook, in fulfilment of its promise of 1943, to evacuate the northern part of Iran by the beginning of March 1946. The Americans for their part gave up any further objections to the inclusion of Romania and Bulgaria in the Soviet-dominated sphere.[9]

Yet the course of both the Potsdam and Moscow conferences showed beyond doubt that these first approaches to a policy of delimitation by the US government were undertaken only as emergency moves and to tide themselves over an intermediate phase until such mistrust and tension as existed could be overcome for good. Within the US Administration the predominant assumption continued to be that the Russians were undergoing a change of heart because of the war-time alliance and because of the understanding shown by the West for the security needs of their Eastern ally, and that it only remained to expose differences of opinion as misunderstandings and patiently put forward compromises in order to achieve long-term co-operation with the Russians. The Americans refused to abandon their basic belief that this time they would succeed in bringing about an international order of universal peace. The strength of the expectation,

---

[8] Cf. L. R. S. Harris, *Allied Military Administration of Italy 1943–1945,* London (UK Military History Series), 1957. For Harriman see: *FRUS 1945, Diplomatic Papers, Stalin's Correspondence with Churchill, Attlee, Roosevelt and Truman, 1941–1945,* London, 1958, p. 822 (telegram of 6.4.1945); for resolution by Congress to stop all further war credits to the USSR, see n. 140 below.

[9] Cf. McNeill (n. 6), pp. 704–12; Meissner (n. 6), p. 78; H. Feis, *From Trust to Terror, The Onset of the Cold War 1945–1950,* pp. 53–5; I. L. Gaddis, *The United States and the Origins of the Cold War, 1941–1947,* NY, 1972, pp. 276–81; Sir J. Wheeler-Bennett and A. Nicholls, *The Semblance of Peace: The Political Settlement after the Second World War,* London, 1972, pp. 490–2.

born of the sacrifices of war, that this time, in contrast to what had happened in Wilson's case after the First World War, the American dream of a future peaceful world in which all nations would live happily together could come true, accounts for the patience and care with which the United States clung to Roosevelt's conception of lasting co-operation with the Soviet Union as an acknowledged world power.[10] It was with this purpose in mind that the American delegation at Potsdam expressed its *de facto* acceptance of Soviet *faits accomplis* and deferred all controversial decisions until later conferences. For the same reason, the US government refrained from trying to use its monopoly of atomic weapons to exert effective pressure on the Soviet Union.[11] Whereas Truman did from time to time begin to see the situation without illusions, the foreign policy conducted by Byrnes and supported by the Democratic majority of 'progressive internationalists' insisted on ignoring the realities of Soviet antagonism in terms of both ideology and power politics; it continued Roosevelt's 'policy of postponement' in all controversial questions, especially the problem of Germany, and adhered to the course of negotiating patiently in order to throw away no chance of a possible agreement with the Soviet Union.[12] In any event, it was only the leaders on both sides who had any knowledge of the signs of impending confrontation; considering the countless joint declarations of harmony the public in the world at large and especially in Europe could hardly doubt that the positive signs of co-operation between the superpowers were more important than their differences.

(B) FOUNDATION OF THE ORGANIZATION FOR WORLD PEACE AND ITS LIMITED POWERS: SAN FRANCISCO

The European public, which heard from enthusiastic broadcasts and press reports of the negotiations leading to the foundation of the United Nations as the new organization for world peace, received it as proof of successful

---

[10] For a particularly telling description of the 'American dream' see J. W. Spanier, *American Foreign Policy Since World War II*, NY/Washington, 1972⁴, pp. 14–23; also W. L. Neumann, *After Victory: Churchill, Roosevelt, Stalin and the Making of the Peace*, London, 1967; also works mentioned in n. 5.

[11] In reply to Gar Alperovitz, *Atomic Diplomacy: Hiroshima and Potsdam*, NY, 1965, J. L. Richardson, 'Cold-War Revisionism. A Critique', in *World Politics*, 14 (1972), p. 595, convincingly sums up: 'He fails to establish his central hypothesis that American diplomacy from May to July 1945 was shaped by a coherent strategy of settling the outstanding issues through a diplomatic confrontation ("showdown") after the dropping of the bomb. . . . There was in fact no showdown over Eastern Europe; it seems evident, moreover, that there was no planning of a showdown. . . . It would be more plausible to interpret American diplomacy in the early months of Truman's Presidency in terms of keeping options open, postponing final decisions until the situation was clearer, than in terms of "strategy" of the kind which Alperovitz postulates.' Cf. the books mentioned in n. 12, which agree with this judgement.

[12] Even the 'revisionists' (W. A. Williams, W. La Feber, G. Kolko), interesting as they are in their comments on single events, find it hard to distort or explain away the basic fact that the 'One World' idea was taken seriously for a long time. Cf. the account by Halle and Dukes (n. 5), 1966; Lukacs, *A History of the Cold War*, Garden City, NY, 1966², etc. Byrnes's biographer too came to the conclusion that 'A study of the circumstances leads to the conviction that Byrnes went to the limit to conciliate

co-operation and the beginnings of the promised 'One World'. The establishment of the UN seemed to Europeans more significant than the few visible signs of mistrust between the superpowers. The organization was set up at an international conference held in San Francisco between 25 April and 26 June 1945. Although the differences in objectives between the two superpowers were considerable, in fundamental questions affecting the UN Charter the US and Soviet delegations showed almost unclouded harmony. The superpowers had agreed at Dumbarton Oaks to allow no substantial restriction of their own sovereignty, and at Yalta the right of veto of the five permanent members of the Security Council (the Soviet Union, the USA, Great Britain, France, and China) had on Soviet insistence been so extended that it applied in all cases except preliminary measures for the peaceful settlement of disputes to which they were not a party.[13] At San Francisco both superpowers continued to defend this restrictive policy.

At the conference, where the representatives of some fifty states (of which only twelve were European) were allowed to join in the consultations, the many small states fought hopeless battles for weeks against this right of veto for the great powers. The latter's case was put by Gromyko, who in the name of the Soviet Union demanded the right of veto even against preliminary measures for the settlement of disputes in which a Great Power might be involved. The case for the other side was argued by Dr Evatt, the Australian minister for external affairs, who, in the name of the smaller states, after making an unsuccessful general attack on the right of veto, moved a resolution which would have prevented its applying to preliminary measures for the settlement of disputes of any kind. In the decisive vote on 12 June 1945 10 states voted for the Australian motion and 20 abstained, so that only 20 of the 50 states supported the US–Soviet formula as agreed at Yalta.[14] It was thus decided that the future world organization not only left the dogma of the indivisible sovereignty of individual states intact, but could only function as a mediator in disputes and take steps to prevent aggression if all five permanent members of the Security Council were in

---

the Russians even in the face of criticism of his willingness to "appease". And it should be remembered that this position accorded well with American popular opinion in the immediate postwar years.' (G. Curry, 'James F. Byrnes' in *The American Secretaries of State and their Diplomacy*, ed. by R. H. Ferrell, vol. xiv, NY, 1965, pp. 87–317; quotation, p. 312).

[13] Cf. p. 79 above and a basic survey in H. Feis, *Churchill, Roosevelt, Stalin. The War they Waged and the Peace they Sought*, Princeton, 1957, pp. 550–60.

[14] For instructive contemporary reports cf. C. Eagleton, 'The Charter adopted at San Francisco' in *American Political Science Review*, 39, Oct. 1945, pp. 935 ff.; W. F. Fox, 'The Super-Powers at San Francisco' in *The Review of Politics*, 8 Jan. 1946, pp. 115–27; J. B. Reston, 'Votes and Vetoes' in *Foreign Affairs*, 25 Oct. 1946, pp. 13–22; report by F. Dehousse (a member of the Belgian Delegation), *Cours de politique internationale*, Brussels, 1945 (esp. the vote on the Australian resolution, p. 112). For an over-all view: R. B. Russell, *A History of the United Nations Charter*, Washington, 1958, *passim*. After receiving a personal message from Truman, Stalin again concurred in the Yalta formula, which Gromyko had called in question probably by way of a tactical counter-attack.

agreement. It was they who were to decide what measures to take if peace was threatened (Article 39), without consulting the General Assembly unless they wished (Article 12). The concurrence of all five permanent members of the Security Council was required for all peaceful and preliminary measures in disputes to which they were not a party, and for more serious moves even in disputes in which they themselves were involved (Article 27). The UN can thus enforce peace against small aggressor states (which is progress compared with what could be done by the League of Nations); but whenever the five permanent members are in disagreement it is paralysed and powerless.[15]

At San Francisco the representatives of the smaller states were only able to win acceptance for a number of improvements on the Covenant of the League of Nations in secondary matters. The obligation of all states to keep the peace was firmly stated in the preamble. The powers of the Secretariat were considerably strengthened; far-reaching possibilities for fruitful international co-operation in many fields were opened up for the Specialized Agencies to be created. Moreover the smaller states were also willing that resolutions of the General Assembly should for most purposes require not unanimity but a simple majority (a definite gain compared with the Covenant of the League of Nations); yet because the principle of sovereignty remained intact such resolutions could, as before, only take the form of recommendations to the member states.

It was particularly the South American states which, on the basis of agreements concluded at the Pan-American conference at Mexico City in March 1945, and on this occasion with the support of the United States, succeeded in getting included in the Charter Articles 51 and 52, which expressly approved regional pacts and organs for keeping the peace as well as the 'inherent right of individual or collective self-defence', and states were required to endeavour to achieve 'pacific settlement of local disputes through such regional arrangements or by such regional agencies before referring them to the Security Council'. In this way the regional principle, against which Hull had fought so hard, was nevertheless given a secure place in the Charter – albeit too late for the Allies to be able to introduce it in the case of Europe[16] – just because the United Nations Security Council would obviously be unable to function in crucial cases.

---

[15] Cf. the books already mentioned, also analyses from the point of view of international law in E. Menzel, *Völkerrecht*, Munich, 1962, pp. 415 ff. etc.; Ernest A. Gross, *The United Nations, Structure for Peace*, New York, 1962; H. A. Schwarz-Liebermann von Wahlendorf, *Mehrheitsentscheidung und Stimmenwägung*, Tübingen, 1953, pp. 121–87.

[16] Text of UN Charter in L. M. Goodrich, E. Hambro, and A. P. Simons, *Charter of the United Nations, Commentary and Documents*. Third new Revised Edition, NY/London, 1969, p. 358. For the debate on regionalism at San Francisco, cf. H. Bodensieck, *Provozierte Teilung Europas*, Opladen, 1970, pp. 63–72. On the influence of the smaller states, details in L. Kopelmanas, *L'Organisation des Nations Unies*, vol. i: *L'Organisation constitutionnelle des Nations Unies*, Paris, 1947; as one example, S. J. P. van Campen, *The Quest for Security. Some Aspects of Netherlands Foreign Policy 1945–1950*, The Hague, 1958, pp. 15–22 and Documents 163–79; Netherlands Proposals at San Francisco. On the Specialized Agencies, especially the ILO, analyses in E. B. Haas, *Beyond the Nation-State. Functionalism and International Organization*, Stanford, Cal., 1964. Useful collections of material on individual topics in N. J. Padelford, L. M. Goodrich (eds.), *The United Nations in the Balance: Accomplishments and Prospects*, NY, 1965; J. L. Claude, *Swords into Plowshares: The Problems and Progress*

The Charter was signed by all fifty states on 26 June 1945 and within four months was ratified without amendment and came into force. It was bound to disappoint all those who had hoped for a final guarantee of peace. As an American writer asked at the time: 'After all the catastrophic events that followed the foundation of the League of Nations, is it really necessary to create another League – a hotbed for coming global wars – to prove that it cannot work? Are not the first and second world wars enough experience? Do we really need a third global war to understand the anatomy of peace and to see what causes war in human society and how it can be prevented? Let us be clear about one thing. A league of sovereign nation-states is not a step, neither the first step nor the ninety-ninth, toward peace. Peace is law and justice.'[17] Altogether Allied post-war planning had got itself into a vicious circle. In 1943 the principle of an organization for world peace based on continental unions had been rejected in favour of a single, really powerful global organization; the United Nations was supposed to ensure the lasting co-operation of the superpowers; yet now the superpowers had simply approved a UN Charter according to which the organization for world peace could function only *if* the superpowers co-operated. The regional principle, approved as it was in the end, could be of use only in America or the Commonwealth, whereas the Europeans and Asians were unable by their own efforts to make it a reality. The territories of Europe and Asia, divided into so many states as they were, were bound to become areas of rivalry in which friction between the superpowers would almost inevitably give rise to conflict. Yet in spite of everything most delegates left San Francisco with the hope that at future United Nations conferences the Charter might soon be substantially improved; and world opinion, amid the joy of victory and relief at the end of the war, was insufficiently aware of the Charter's weaknesses.

---

of International Organization, New York, 1964. Cf. also H. W. Schlüter, *Die politische Funktion des Sicherheitsrates der Vereinten Nationen von 1945–1950,* Bonn, 1970; id, *Diplomatie der Versöhnung. Die Vereinten Nationen und die Wahrung des Weltfriedens,* Stuttgart, 1966; for a general survey K. Hüfner and I. Naumann (eds.), *Zwanzig Jahre Vereinte Nationen, Eine Einführung,* Düsseldorf, 1974.

[17] E. Reves, *The Anatomy of Peace,* NY (July) 1945, p. 273 f.; cf. the Open Letter from twenty leading Americans including Owen Roberts, Albert Einstein, Thomas Mann, and Senators J. W. Fulbright and E. Thomas in the *New York Times,* 14 Oct. 1945: 'How long will the Charter of the United Nations endure? With luck one generation? A century? Is it enough to have peace by luck? Peace by law is what the nations of the world can have if they want it and now is the time to get it. The Charter of San Francisco is a tragic illusion if we are not prepared to take the further steps necessary to organize peace. We must aim at a federal constitution of the world – a working world-wide legal order – if we hope to prevent atomic war' (quoted in *Federal News,* No. 128, Nov. 1945, p. 4). The writer of the leading article in *Le Monde* passed a similar judgement: 'The public feels in a muddled way that the institution [the UN] as it is at present conceived contains, as the League of Nations did, the seeds of its own destruction. . . . Is it not a paradox that an institution whose main use should be to limit the effects of national sovereignty in this way puts a premium on that sovereignty?' (André Istel, *Le Monde,* 5.6.1945, p. 1 f.).

(C) NO NEW ORDER IN EUROPE: POTSDAM

When news of the results of San Francisco reached West Europeans at the end of June 1945 it led to a revival of the idea of a European regional pact, both as an example of the way in which the world organization needed to be adapted in order to keep the peace at least in Europe, and to create the conditions in which Europe could hold its own against the superpowers with their far-reaching claims. On the very day when the United Nations Charter was signed the head of the French delegation, Joseph Paul-Boncour, recommended as the only possible European answer a 'Western pact to include France, Great Britain, the Netherlands, Belgium, an Italy purged of Fascism, and Spain as soon as it has returned to the ways of democracy'. The London *Economist* wanted to include Denmark and Norway in the pact: these countries could only safeguard their security as well as their economic recovery by acting in common; a shared General Staff and a customs union with stable currencies was essential, and for the superpowers a prosperous union of 120 million inhabitants would be a better neighbour than a fragmented Europe. At the end of July *Le Monde* in Paris followed with an analysis which stated: 'The essential conditions appear to exist which make it possible to hope for the setting-up ... of a "third world" organization, comparable in importance to the United States of America and the Soviet Union ...' Even de Gaulle in an interview with *The Times* on 10 September joined in this general trend; he spoke in approving terms of the possibility of forming an *'ensemble économique'* of the West-European countries, which he believed was desired in London and Brussels.[18] Soon, however, less was heard of such schemes, and they were dropped altogether when the Soviet media reacted with several weeks of invective against the 'threat of a reactionary and aggressive Western bloc'. Léon Blum, one of the promoters of the idea of European unity, was described by Radio Moscow in September as a 'sinister henchman of sinister ideas', namely the dream of a 'union directed against the USSR'. The West-European Communist parties soon followed with denunciations of so-called 'threats of an anti-Soviet Western bloc'.[19] Once again it was evident that Europeans by themselves were no longer in a position to put into effect their own ideas of a peace settlement even as far as their own Continent was concerned.

[18] J. Paul-Boncour, Interview for AFP, in San Francisco, 26.6.1945, quoted in *Le Monde*, 27.6.1945, p. 1: *The Economist,* quoted in *Le Monde,* 17.7.1945, p. 1, f.; *Le Monde,* 31.7.1945, p. 1 (leading article by H. Beuve-Méry); de Gaulle, statement to *The Times* Paris correspondent, in *The Times,* 10.9.1945, p. 4; de Gaulle, *Mémoires de guerre,* vol. 3, Paris, 1959, pp. 558–62. For more details about the debate on a Western bloc in the summer and autumn of 1945, see W. Lipgens, 'Innerfranzösische Kritik der Aussenpolitik de Gaulles 1944–1946' in *VfZG,* vol. 24 (1976), pp. 169- -73.

[19] Commentary by Radio Moscow on 15.9.1945; French translation in *France-Soir,* 16.9.45; cf. Léon Blum, 'Le Bloc Occidental', in *Le Populaire,* 16.9.45; many references of a similar kind from that period quoted in Lipgens, ibid., (n. 18), pp. 171 f.

All the greater were the hopes they placed in the last of the wartime conferences of the Big Three, which met at Potsdam on 17 July 1945. In the meantime the superpowers had increasingly shown their inability to agree on joint action for peace-making in Europe. The Soviet *faits accomplis* and the stiffening American attitude to which they gave rise placed such a burden on the negotiations that a crisis seemed to be looming. Yet agreement was still not ruled out, and to the outside world the appearance of unity was completely preserved. Only two things resulted, however; firstly *de facto* recognition of the changes that had occurred, but particularly of the Soviet *faits accomplis*, and secondly a dilatory treatment of the real points of controversy.[20]

The Western powers did not insist on the 'Declaration on Liberated Europe' being put into effect as a condition of their assent to the westward shift of Poland up to the Oder–Neisse frontier; they agreed that the territories east of the Oder and of the Western Neisse (not only of the Eastern Neisse, as envisaged at Yalta) should remain under Polish administration as a provisional settlement until the peace conference; they accepted the expulsion of millions of Germans by Poland and Czechoslovakia – all in order to strengthen co-operation with the Soviet Union. On the question of how to deal with Germany they agreed upon negative decisions, such as complete de-Nazification, demilitarization, partial deindustrialization, etc. – the general ideas of both superpowers so far as Germany was concerned were broadly similar, if vague – but they could not agree on the question of Germany's future organization as a state. It was indeed confirmed that 'Germany was to be treated as an economic unity', yet taken singly the agreements showed a tendency to seal off the occupation zones on both sides. Once again it became obvious that the superpowers had no specific plan for post-war Europe, and Western public opinion began to realize with a shock that Stalin's Soviet Union was still a dictatorship whose methods took no account of the principles of human rights. The judgement passed by *The Economist* in its issue of 11 August 1945 on the Potsdam conference was severe: 'Above all it has in it not a single constructive idea, not a single hopeful perspective for the postwar world. At the end of a mighty war fought to defeat Hitlerism, the Allies are making a Hitlerian peace. This is the real measure of their failure.'

What was of most immediate concern and hardly comprehensible was the fact that the Allies as a whole, and particularly the Western Allies, had no plan for the continuation or restoration of Europe's economic life. Statements issued before 1944 by the European Resistance and by the

[20] Cf. McNeill (n. 6), p. 615–30; Meissner (n. 6), pp. 60–76; G. Kolko, *The Politics of War*, NY, 1968, pp. 568–93; Gaddis (n. 9), pp. 238–43; Feis (n. 9), pp. 36–55; id., *Between War and Peace;* G. Ressing, *Versagte der Westen in Jalta und Potsdam? Ein dokumentierter Wegweiser durch die alliierten Kriegskonferenzen*, Frankfurt, 1970. A summary of the decision and recommendations was signed on 2.8.1948 as a 'Protocol of Proceedings', but only an abridged version was published as a communiqué, in which eight of the twenty-two sections were missing, viz. those concerning Romania, Iran, the Straits, and other controversial points likely to betray tensions between the superpowers. The full Protocol was, however, made public on 24.5.1947 as a Dept. of State Press Release. Text, for example, in *The Conference of Berlin,* Washington, 1961, vol. 2, pp. 1477–98.

Allied governments had envisaged the creation of a common market as a *conditio sine qua non* of Europe's economic future, putting an end once and for all to the 'allotment garden' fragmentation of the Continent. But what happened in and after 1945 was the destruction (without putting anything in its place) of the economic unity already established over most of the Continent by the Nazi dictatorship, without any constructive idea of what to do next for the European economy. Equally ignored at the Potsdam conference was the fact that a harsh programme of dismantling and curtailing production in Germany, the heart of Europe, would be bound to have the most crippling effect on the European economy as a whole. Since there was no general Allied plan, each government in the restored nation states was obliged to try to reactivate its own economy according to the old idea of autarky which was now revived.[21] This in turn aggravated the division of Europe decreed by the superpowers, whereby the European power vacuum became an essential cause of conflict. After the First World War the dissolution of the Habsburg Monarchy had created a Balkan-type power vacuum of small and weak states, with the result that the two powerful neighbours of this defenceless area, Germany and the Soviet Union, inevitably divided it between themselves twenty years later. In 1945 'the disintegration of Hitler's Europe created a far greater power vacuum ... it extended over the whole of continental Europe' – and it was inevitable that the new great powers should sooner or later come into conflict over this vacuum.[22]

(D) VERBAL CO-OPERATION: LONDON, MOSCOW, AND AGAIN LONDON

From Yalta until the spring of 1946 the superpowers did their best to preserve the appearance of their 'complete unity of aims', 'common obligations', and success in organizing peace – because the confrontation between them was not yet final, and because to world public opinion the

---

[21] In this they were given a great deal of help by the American military governments, which often found really ingenious partial solutions and from whom came the first impulse towards the restoration of European co-operation. The 'Solid Fuels Division' of Supreme Headquarters (SHAEF) tried during the advance to organize the transport and power resources of the conquered or occupied countries, and was afterwards developed, being found objectively necessary, into a European Central Inland Transport Organization (ECITO, Sept. 1945) and a European Coal Organization (ECO, Dec. 1945). In addition, the UNRRA organization, founded in 1943, performed a great service in the liberated countries by overcoming economic chaos, looking after emergency areas, and supplying urgently needed agricultural and other machinery to reactivate the economy. Countries with colonies, viz. France, Belgium, and the Netherlands, were excluded from its operations by an earlier decision, but in Italy and throughout Eastern Europe its unselfish and hard-working staff managed to overcome countless hardships and revive production. Altogether 3.5 billion dollars (of which over 70 per cent came from the USA) was chanelled by UNRRA into these countries. Cf. D. Wightman, *Economic Co-operation in Europe*, London, 1956, pp. 9, 12–16, and the authoritative work on all aspects of UNRRA: A. Woodbridge (ed.), *UNRRA: The History of the United Nations Relief and Rehabilitation Administration*, 3 vols., NY, 1950.

[22] Toynbee, *The Realignment of Europe*, pp. 14–17 (quoted at greater length on p. 17).

thought of a new global struggle for power which might end in war was simply too appalling to contemplate.

The press had been excluded from the Potsdam conference; thus the public had to rely on the official 'Communiqué on the Tripartite Conference', worded so as to suggest unanimity, and, for example, on Truman's reassuring broadcast of 9 August. The victorious powers were 'determined to remain united and strong. We must not allow any aggressor in future to be clever enough to divide us ... It was in this spirit that the Berlin [Potsdam] conference took place. This spirit will govern all future peace agreements.'[23] In September and October 1945 there met in London the Council of Foreign Ministers set up at Potsdam for the purpose of working out peace treaties. At its very first session it broke up without agreement because differences over the meaning of 'democracy' had made it impossible to deal with peace treaties with Germany's former allies, and the attempt to set up common administrative authorities in occupied Germany had failed because of a French veto.[24] Nevertheless in the course of October President Truman in a number of key speeches announced his firm intention to bring about co-operation in spite of the difficulties; 'We can't stand another global war; we can't ever have another war unless it is total war, and that means the end of civilization as we know it.'[25] On 31 October Byrnes declared that the United States continued to sympathize with . . . the effort of the Soviet Union to draw into closer and more friendly relations with her Central and Eastern European neighbours. We are fully aware of her special security interests in those countries and we have recognized those interests in the arrangements made. . . . We can appreciate the determination of the people of the Soviet Union that never again will they tolerate the pursuit of policies in those countries deliberately directed against the Soviet Union's security and way of life. But 'the Soviet Union has also declared that it does not wish to force the Soviet system on its neighbours'; as before, world peace depended on the superpowers' success in co-operating reasonably; 'We cannot have the necessary form of co-operation necessary for peace in a world divided into spheres of influence and special privilege.'[26]

The modest compromises on spheres of influence which Byrnes, Bevin and Molotov agreed on during the Moscow Conference of Foreign Ministers at the end of December 1945[27] must have given Allied propaganda in favour of 'One World' new credibility and have renewed hopes of extending the powers of the United Nations, because they clearly marked a relaxation of the existing tension. There seemed therefore to be ample

[23] H. S: Truman, *Public Messages, Speeches and Statements of the President. April 12th to Dec. 31st, 1945*, Washington, 1961, p. 203 f.
[24] Cf. McNeill (n. 6), pp. 696–704; L. A. Rose, *After Yalta. America and the Origins of the Cold War*, NY, 1973, pp. 116–33; Gaddis (n. 9), pp. 263–75; Wheeler-Bennett/Nicholls (n. 9), pp. 420–9.
[25] Truman's speeches of 3, 7, and 27 Oct. 1945 in *Vital Speeches of the Day*, Vol. xii, Oct. 15, 1945, p. 3; ibid., quotation of 7 Oct. 1945, p. 9; and Nov. 15, 1945, p. 68. Cf. also the report of 5 Oct. 1945 on the London conference by Secretary of State Byrnes in *Vital Speeches of the Day*, Vol. xii, Oct. 15, 1945, pp. 3–7.
[26] Speech by Byrnes in New York City, 31 Oct. 1945 in *Vital Speeches of the Day*, Vol. xii, Nov. 15, 1945, p. 69.
[27] Cf. the books on the conference mentioned in n. 9 above.

justification for the hopes placed in the first General Assembly of the United Nations, which met in London from 10 January to 16 February 1946. On 22 November 1945 Eden had voiced certain misgivings in the House of Commons: 'At an early date, in my judgement, the United Nations ought to review their Charter in the light of the discoveries about atomic energy which were not before us when the Charter was drawn up. Nothing showed more clearly the hold that nationalism has upon us all than the decision of that Conference to retain the power of veto.'[28] Prime Minister Attlee, in his address at the opening of the General Assembly, expressed himself as host not quite so incisively: he spoke of the need to overcome the selfishness of nation states and said that 'the United Nations must become the overriding factor in foreign policy'. Many speakers from the smaller countries, continuing their unsuccessful struggle at San Francisco, urged that the United Nations should be strengthened by restricting the right of veto, while Byrnes in his speech of 14 January called for 'the establishment of a commission to deal with the problems raised by the discovery of atomic energy, ... inseparably linked with the problem of security ... We must not fail to devise the safeguards necessary to ensure that this great discovery is used for human welfare and not for more deadly human warfare.'[29] Only four days later, however, Gromyko as leader of the Soviet delegation made a statement which disappointed all hopes of a further development of the Charter: 'Voices are being heard in some quarters suggesting that the Charter has already become obsolete and needs revision. Such allegations must be decisively rejected by all those who, not merely by words but by action, are trying to build up strong and effective machinery for the maintenance of security. Such allegations are dangerous, and under certain conditions may lead to serious consequences.'[30]

An additional reason for disappointment was that, in the four controversial questions discussed by the Security Council in its first session, the Soviet Union on each occasion insisted on interpreting the right of veto in its own way.

It distinguished between a 'dispute' and a 'situation', and argued that in the case of a vote on a 'situation' and during the preceding vote to determine whether it was a 'situation', all permanent members of the Security Council must be

---

[28] For details of the House of Commons debate, see p. 173. *Parl. Debates, House of Commons*, vol. 416, column 613.

[29] Speeches at the opening of the General Assembly in *Vital Speeches of the Day*, vol. xii, 1945/6, pp. 239–46 (quotations from Attlee and Byrnes, p. 241, f.).

[30] Gromyko at the opening of the General Assembly, ibid., vol. xii, p. 261. Radio Moscow had declared on 10 January: 'Some people seem to see the UN more as a prelude to what they call a World Parliament which, according to them, should be elected by the nations of the entire world, should promulgate world laws, reduce the sovereignty of its member states, and so on.' These ideas were 'reactionary': such people 'demand the abolition of what they call the right of veto. Their purpose in doing so is to make the UN a tool of one power or group of powers and so destroy the Organization; they are out to undermine the very foundation of the new Organization' (quoted in *Federal News*, No. 131, Feb. 1946, p. 4).

unanimous.[31] What this amounted to was that the Soviet Union was trying to modify the compromise reached in the Yalta formula so as to widen the potential application of the veto; it became a defender of the existing unsatisfactory Charter, the determined opponent of its further development. It agreed to the establishment of a commission for the international control of atomic energy, but, as became apparent during the decisive sessions of the commission in June 1946, it sternly rejected any effective control from outside, since international supervision was incompatible with its closed dictatorial system.[32] At the General Assembly it became clear that the American recipe for security was bound up with principles applying to the world as a whole, the Soviet method with national and autarkic principles. Yet both clung to the veto, the means by which they were able to prevent an effective UN majority from thwarting them.

However, for the benefit of world public opinion Secretary of State Byrnes, speaking at the conclusion of the General Assembly, tried to dispel any rising doubts. Frank discussion was required 'between great powers of the things that give rise to suspicion ... Only an inexcusable tragedy of errors could cause serious conflict between us in the future ... We must live by the Charter. That is the only road to peace.'[33] Yet the world as a whole was still unshaken in its belief that the superpowers which had emerged victorious from the recent war were engaged in creating effective and permanent arrangements for peace.

2. Early Associations of Federalists in the Spirit of the Resistance Movements

The remaining sections of this chapter deal with the question: What happened to the idea of European unification within the global situation described above, after the military take-over by the superpowers and during the first post-war year (May 1945 to May 1946), marked as it was by the slow and difficult restoration of government at every level and with the economy on the verge of collapse? The purpose of the present section is to take stock: Which *coherent* associations, i.e. not simply scattered expressions of individual opinions but organized groups with explicit programmes, were there at the end of the war which publicly championed

---

[31] Cf. the concise analysis of the four controversial questions (Iran's complaint against the Soviet Union, Soviet complaint against British troops in Greece, Ukrainian complaint against the Netherlands in Indonesia, complaint by Syria and the Lebanon against French and British troops in their country) by A. Balazs, 'Das Vetorecht auf der ersten Session des Sicherheitsrates' in *Die Friedens-Warte*, 46, 1946, pp. 222–7.

[32] For more detail see p. 285 f.; summarized by H. Wehberg, 'Amerikas Plan einer internationalen Kontrolle der Atomenergie' in *Die Friedens-Warte*, 47, 1947, pp. 5–31 and pp. 71–92; for further information see the list of books mentioned in nn. 9–11.

[33] Byrnes, 28 Feb. 1946 in *Vital Speeches of the Day*, Vol. xii, p. 327 f. Churchill's Fulton speech followed on 5 March 1946. The Western powers' change of style from emphatic declarations of co-operation to the official policy of 'patience with firmness' was starting at this time, as will be shown at the beginning of chapter II; cf. p. 286 ff.

the 'alternative line of development',[34] the concept of European unification as it had been worked out in the wartime planning of the non-Communist Resistance; and how did these bodies develop and spread the idea in practice in 1945?

In this section we are not yet concerned with the question of the attitude of the restored national governments to the idea of European unification, or the degree of support it found among the newly emerging parties and in public opinion. Apart from the already existing groups of European federalists there was a much wider body of opinion in favour of European unity at party conferences and in party programmes, in the press, and in articles or books by individual authors. The extent and nature of such manifestations, like the attitude of the national governments (or their counterparts in the German situation) will, as already indicated, be outlined in sections 3 to 6 in a country-by-country survey of Western Europe. Section 7 will then summarize the reasons for the difficulties experienced by the existing associations and their resigned attitude to this in the first post-war year.

(A) THE MOVIMENTO FEDERALISTA EUROPEO

Among the five large associations active at the end of the war, with programmes already worked out and with a more than local network of branches independent of each other and consisting mostly (except of course in Switzerland and Britain) of former Resistance groups,[35] the Italian Movimento Federalista Europeo (MFE), founded as early as 1943, stands out for the clarity of its aims and the strategy of its leadership. Often enough in the anti-Fascist Resistance and among Italians living in exile the view was expressed that after Fascist reaction had been defeated it would be essential to create a 'United States of Europe'.[36] But a systematic elaboration and broadening of the concept of federalism, based wholly on this thesis, had been launched in 1941 by a group of members of the Resistance who were interned on the island of Ventotene, led by Altiero Spinelli,[37] Ernesto Rossi,[38] and Eugenio Colorni.[39] In the first half of 1941

---

[34] Cf. Introduction, section 5, p. 81.

[35] Other smaller groups are mentioned in the course of the survey of countries, chap. I, sections 3–6. I have several hundred type-written or printed pages of material on each of the five groups. Section 2 of chap. I could be expanded into a full-sized book. Here, as in the following sections, only the more important points can be emphasized.

[36] Cf. C. F. Delzell, 'The European Federalist Movement in Italy. First Phase 1918 to 1947' in *The Journal of Modern History*, vol. 32 (1960), pp. 241–50; W. Lipgens, 'Europa-Föderationspläne deutscher und italienischer Widerstandsgruppen im II. Weltkrieg', in *Von der Diktatur zur Demokratie* (Schriftenreihe des Internationalen Schulbuchinstituts, Vol. 17), Brunswick, 1973, p. 12 f.

[37] Altiero Spinelli, born 31.8.1907, joined the Communist Party in 1924 when a law student, being attracted by its 'internationalism'; three years later he was sentenced to twenty years' imprisonment; after ten years' cogitation he declared that he had left the Communist Party since he wanted all his fellow human beings to be free and saw the real enemy in state sovereignty and totalitarian tendencies, whatever their origin. Cf. Delzell (n. 36), p. 243, also Spinelli's autobiographical study: 'Pourquoi je suis européen', in *Preuves*, no. 81, November 1951, pp. 33–9.

[38] Ernesto Rossi, born in 1897 at Caserta, joined two Florence professors, Gaetano Salvemini and Piero Calamandrei, to edit the first anti-Fascist underground periodical 'Non Mollare!'; as an

a statement, based partly on a reading of the Marxist classics on the one hand and partly on the 'Federalist Papers' of Hamilton, Madison, and Jay on the other, as well as on the group's own discussions, was produced and in July 1941 smuggled to Rome. Written by Spinelli and Rossi and known as the 'Ventotene Manifesto', it caused a considerable stir in many opposition groups during the following months and because one of the basic documents of the European federalist movement.[40]

The central thesis of the 'Manifesto' ran: 'The real foundation of modern civilization, the principle of freedom' and human dignity is threatened by the fact that the nation states, reduced in size as they are, can no longer satisfy the 'claims of the various social groups', and therefore resort to a 'maximum of centralization and autarky' and finally dictatorship. The cure must begin with the central problem: 'The first problem to be solved, and without whose solution progress of any kind is just an illusion, is the final abolition of the division of Europe into nation states.' As events had shown, immensely destructive wars could not be prevented by a League of Nations 'which claimed to guarantee international law, while lacking the military power capable of enforcing its decisions and allowing the 'absolute sovereignty' of member states to remain intact'. And all the problems of frontiers, minorities, access to the sea, etc. which would find the easiest solution in a European Federation, would otherwise remain insoluble. To bring federation about, all those 'who intend to create a firmly based supranational state as the major task' must before the war was over join together in a truly progressive 'revolutionary party', and at the moment when Hitler's regime collapsed must seize the leadership in as many European countries as possible 'in the brief but intense period of general crisis in which the nation states lie broken and prostrate and the mass of the people wait anxiously for a new slogan', and lead them to federation.[41]

To make his ideas more explicit Spinelli wrote a second memorandum in the autumn of 1941, which also soon circulated in Italy, entitled, 'The United States of Europe and the different political trends'. Its main object was to explain why existing political forces could hardly solve the problem of international anarchy, and what kind of union would be needed.

---

economist he also published critical studies in Einaudi's periodical *La Riforma sociale* and was imprisoned in 1930. Cf. C. F. Delzell, *Mussolini's Enemies. The Italian Anti-Fascist Resistance*, Princeton, 1961 (references in the Index), also Rossi's own autobiographical notes in typescript.

[39] Eugenio Colorni, born 1909 in Milan, Tutor in Italian at Marburg University in 1932-3, received a doctorate for a dissertation on Leibniz; belonged to the illegal hard core of the Italian Socialist party and was arrested in 1938. (He was shot on 28.5.1944, according to information from Mrs Ursula Spinelli-Hirschmann on 27.4.1964.)

[40] After being distributed in typescript on the Italian mainland from the autumn of 1941 onwards the manifesto was printed for the first time, clandestinely, in 1943: *Manifesto del Movimento Federalista Europeo, Quaderni del Movimento Federalista Europea*, No. 1, p. 1 (Milan, 1943): reprinted in Rome during the German occupation: A. S. and E. R., *Problemi della federazione europea, prefazione di Eugenio Colorni*, Rome, Jan. 1944, pp. 9-30. The other basic texts of 1941 are those of Léon Blum in France, Count Helmut Moltke in Germany, and R. W. G. Mackay in Britain.

[41] Quotations from the first printed version, Milan, 1943 (n. 40), p. 8 f., 13 f., and 12. It is impossible to do justice here to the wealth of the text, only the leading ideas can be indicated; detailed interpretation by e.g. A. Humonda and L. Levi in: *Quaderni della crisi*, vol. 4, no. 3, Aug. 1963, p. 67-76.

Racism – it was argued – ended with the model of the 'rule of the master race' and the 'military colonization' of the other races; democrats unfortunately did not 'apply their ideals to relations with foreign countries', but slid into the 'foreign policy of their ancient régimes and would in future of their own accord bring about little more than a new League of Nations'. Communism 'continues to believe that the major question is the abolition of capitalism', although nationalized economies create more international problems and 'leave the whole anarchic system of national states with their "sacred egoisms" untouched'. The effective abolition of this anarchy could come only through a federation, 'which removes from the sovereignty of all member states the means whereby the latter give effect to their own particular egoisms'. In a list of powers to be assigned to a federal authority, the memorandum stated that it must have 'the exclusive right to recruit and pay armed forces (which would also have the task of keeping internal order); to conduct foreign policy; to determine the administrative frontiers of the member states . . .; the right to provide for the total abolition of all protectionist barriers and to prevent their return; the right to issue a common federal currency; the right to assure full freedom of movement to all citizens within the frontiers of the federation'. To accomplish these tasks 'the federation must have at its disposal its federal civil service, its own administrative machinery, independent of all the individual states, the right to levy direct from the citizens the taxes which it needs in order to function, legislative and supervisory bodies based on the direct participation of the citizens and not representing the states'.[42]

In a third memorandum in the winter of 1941–2 Spinelli summed up the root evils of European society under the heading 'sectionalism'. The 'worst sectionalism' lay in the division of the world into sovereign states. So long as this evil was not removed, there was no hope of countering industrial and geographical sectionalism (the formation of monopolies in industry and the ownership of large estates in agriculture) by Socialist reforms. 'The federalists intend', ran the concluding sentence, 'to form the nucleus of a progressive governing party' and thus 'to defeat the reactionary forces which intend to keep the privileges of the sovereign states, selfishness and parasitic wealth'.[43]

Yet when on 25 July 1943 Marshall Badoglio arrested Mussolini, assured the Germans in Italy that the alliance would be maintained but abolished the Fascist régime and freed the political prisoners, it was evident how far the ideal of European unification had already spread. Spinelli's manifesto had been in circulation since July 1941, and other groups had independently come to similar conclusions. Colorni, who in 1942 had managed to escape from prison, was one of the leaders of the illegal PSIUP in Rome, and he

---

[42] Distributed in typescript in Italy in 1942–3 and first printed clandestinely in the periodical cited in n. 40, Rome, Jan. 1944, pp. 31–74; reprinted in A. Spinelli, *Dagli stati sovrani agli Stati Uniti d'Europa,* Florence, 1950, pp. 7–57.

[43] *Politica marxista e politica federalista,* first printed clandestinely in Rome, 1944, pp. 75–125, reprinted in A. Spinelli, *Dagli stati sovrani . . .* op. cit., pp. 59–116. The Ventotene Group agreed with the Resistance groups of all the occupied countries in supporting a substantially progressive social policy as well as in the idea of forming a new party from its own ranks.

persuaded his colleagues to recognize the European idea. Already in May 1943 he had had the first number of a new underground newspaper printed with the title: *L'Unità europea. Voce del Movimento Federalista Europeo* containing an appeal and a reprint of part of the Manifesto. In the second number, issued in Rome in July 1943, he advised against the founding of a specifically 'European party', because all anti-Fascist groups had already acknowledged the need for a European federation. In fact the newly drawn-up programmes of all the parties, except the Communists, which circulated during the forty-five days of Badoglio spoke of European unification.[44] Spinelli and Rossi for their part discovered the Partito d'Azione (PdA) led by the Milan Resistance leader Professor Ferruccio Parri, which to judge by its programme and leadership was strongly in favour of a European federation. They joined this party and were able to try and mould it into a party of revolutionary leadership as they conceived it, heading for European federation.[45] Among the twenty or more persons who on the night of 27–28 August 1943 gathered in the house of the chemist and theologian Mario Alberto Rollier there were active politicians from almost every party, though the majority of course came from the PdA; they all decided to found a supranational movement, whose members in all parties would work for the co-ordination of their European aims.

In the light of the statements approved at the foundation conference of the Movimento Federalista Europeo and of the additional declarations made by the central committee or its leading members between 1943 and 1945, the basic ideas, organization, and activities of the MFE can be summed up as follows:[46]

1. *Design for Europe*. The Theses of the founding conference ran:

> Militarism, despotism, and war can be abolished only by a European federation, to which will be transferred the sovereign powers concerned with the common interests of all Europeans, the same powers as lie today in the hands of nationalist states and so are purely destructive. It will take over arms production, freedom of international trade, money, adjustment of national boundaries, the administration of colonial territories not ripe for self-government, intervention against possible attempts to re-establish authoritarian régimes – in short, responsibility for

---

[44] For Colorni, cf. Lipgens, *Föderationspläne* (Introduction n. 67), p. 63 f. For the programmes of the various political parties, see the section on Italy, chap. I, section 6, pp. 252–7.

[45] Spinelli was for a time head of the North Italian secretariat of this party; cf. Lipgens, *Föderationspläne*, p. 54 f., 60 f., and 97 f.

[46] In the following chapters each group will be described separately in terms of its programme, organization, etc. under the same five headings. (1) 'Design for Europe' indicates what kind of European unity was desired, (2) 'Europe in the World' discusses the group's attitude to the superpowers, (3) 'Plan of Campaign' tries to establish how the goal was to be reached, with brief quotations from the main programmes (many details on future constitutions, social order, etc. are omitted to keep the survey within bounds, so that further specialist studies will be needed); (4) describes the nature of the organization, and (5) its various forms of activity. Notes draw attention to changes during the period 1945–50, to be described later. The 'Conclusion' in vol. 2 will provide a systematic summary.

freedom and peace on the whole Continent must be exercised solely by the European federation and its executive, legislative and judicial bodies. In the whole area of federal sovereignty the inhabitants of the different states must, in addition to their national citizenship, be citizens of the European community, that is, they must have the right to elect the members of the federal government and to call them to account, while themselves being subject to direct federal law . . .

As for the internal policy of such a federation, 'the MFE is not in any way committed to a federation in which the proportions between collectivism and capitalism, democracy and authoritarianism are laid down in advance'. Only one thing is 'absolutely certain, namely that a federal order excludes any form of totalitarianism, just as it does any other kind of preponderance or a bogus federation which is in fact controlled by a totalitarian régime'.[47]

Within the leadership G. Peyronel, supported by Rollier, emphasized the principle of inter-state federalism: 'There exists a complementary relationship in the Movement between freedom at the top level (federation) and at the bottom level (autonomy) . . . The local autonomies (parochial, regional, cantonal and those of ethnic and linguistic minorities) will offer supranational federalism not only the guarantee of sufficient decentralization of the nation state, but a firm foundation for the creation of a unity within the most varied diversity.' Spinelli on the other hand laid most stress on the removal of 'despotic tendencies' of nation states by the 'union of several states and the transferring of their state powers to a common superior political organ. A healthy democracy can emerge today in Europe only on a European scale through the creation of a federal European union.'[48]

2. *Europe in the World.* On this point the founding conference declared: The Federation of Europeans 'will thus lay the foundation-stone for the still distant goal of world federation'. A preliminary draft from the Milan group on the Geneva Declaration made hopeful assumptions: The Europeans 'count on the approval of the great powers or on their friendly co-operation in the task of constructing Europe. Above all they count on the readiness of the British Labour Party to establish federal relations with the rest of Europe. They count on the economic and political support of America and the friendship of Russia for a peaceful federation of the European nations.'

Rossi said in July 1944: 'We must always insist that we are not thinking of a federation in an anti-Russian sense, that on the contrary a federation of Europe would be the great guarantee of peace for Russia too; but we must say equally clearly that, if the Soviet government thinks it must keep Europe divided in order

---

[47] Resolutions of the founding conference of the Movimento Federalista Europea, Milan, 27–8 August 1943; first printed in Italian in *L'Unità europea*, No. 3, Milan, beginning of Sept. 1943, p. 3 f. A copy was sent to France in particular, as Rossi and Spinelli annexed it to their invitation sent from Switzerland in Nov. 1943 to all Resistance movements that could be reached. Cf. Lipgens, *Föderationspläne*, pp. 379 and 381.

[48] Articles by Peyronel in *L'Unità europea*, No. 4 (Milan), June 1944, and Spinelli in *L'Unità europea*, No. 5 (Swiss edn.), Aug. 1944.

to pursue an imperialist and expansionist policy, it will always find us and all progressive forces in Europe against it.'[49] The central committee of MFE told the CFFE (Comité Français pour la Fédération Européenne) in August 1944: 'If the European nations show themselves at loggerheads and incapable of overcoming the political anarchy which has already lasted far too long in this world, it would be only natural for the great powers to return to the old and fatal policy of balance of power, alliances and spheres of influence in order to try and minimize the dangers which would continue to exist on our Continent.'[50]

3. *Plan of Campaign.* The genuine achievement of the Ventotene group was that they had not only a goal but a clear tactical and strategic idea of how to reach it. 'The collapse of most of the states of Europe under the German steam-roller', in the words of their Manifesto, 'has involved them in a common fate; they were all subject to Hitler's domination and after his overthrow they will all find themselves in a revolutionary crisis from which they will not re-emerge as solid state structures, distinct and intact'. The Theses of the foundation conference continued: 'Once the war is over, when the short period of extreme national and international crises has arrived, during which the structures of the various nation states will fall apart or at best hardly survive', the federalist movement must fight with all its resources 'to give firm support to the state or states which are trying to help to create federal organizations, and to mobilize popular forces in every country so that they apply all their strength to achieve the federal solution ... while the memory of the horrors of war is still fresh in everyone's mind'.[51]

When the problem of the preponderance of the extra-European powers gradually appeared on the horizon, the Milan group wrote in April 1944: 'We must bring to power governments which proclaim the federation of Europe as their programme: that offers the only chance of being more than just the object of influence for the world powers, of ourselves being able to exert some influence on the views of the

---

[49] Milan Group in *L'Unità europea*, No. 4, p. 3; Rossi in *L'Unità europea*, No. 5 (Milan edn.), Aug. 1944, p. 3. The Ventotene prisoners wrote to Count Sforza in Dec. 1942: 'America could not help becoming a militarist state in its turn if Europe remained divided into militaristic, autarkic states... The United States of Europe are the only form in which our Continent can collaborate effectively with the United States of America.' (Printed in C. Sforza, *O federazione europea o nuove guerre*, Florence, 1948, pp. 103–10, quotation on p. 110).

[50] *L'Unità europea*, No. 6 (Milan), Sept.–Oct. 1944, p. 4 f. All these expressions of opinion (as A. Spinelli, *L'Europa non cade dal cielo*, Bologna, 1960, p. 22, confirms in retrospect) clearly assumed that after the war Europe would be an autonomous centre of world politics; America would withdraw across the Atlantic and Russia behind its own frontiers, once the Europeans achieved a peace settlement. This point soon had to be reconsidered, taking into account the full extent of the European catastrophe. Cf. chap. I/7, p. 278 and chap III/6, p. 628–33.

[51] 'Manifesto' quoted from the first printed edn., 1943 (see n. 40), p. 13, for the 'Theses' see p. 47. Spinelli's article on 'Political Trends', there referred to, contained a detailed description (seven pages) of the 'favourable circumstances' in which the federal movement would have to give a lead at the end of the war, 'when all the countries of Europe will face the problem of settling the Continent's affairs', and nationalism would be deeply discredited (see n. 42). The expectation that one or two countries would take the initiative towards a federation applied partly to Britain but even more to France; on this see the quotations at the beginning of sections 3 and 4 of chapter I, p. 159 and 203.

major allies.' The Geneva Declaration of May 1944, mainly the work of Spinelli and Rossi, contains the statement: 'The Resistance movements which are signatories to this Declaration recognize the need for the active participation of the United Nations in the solution of the German problem but expect that all measures to be taken between the end of hostilities and the establishment of a peace settlement will pay due regard to the necessity of a federal union of this kind.'[52]

4. *Purpose and Character of the Organization.* The founding conference decided: 'The MFE is not just an alternative political party ... Since the programmes of all the non-Communist parties came out in favour of European federation, the MFE aims at being the movement above parties which within every party rejects the persistent error that the important thing is first to establish national independence, democratic freedom and social justice, and in the end the fraternization of peoples will come about of its own accord. It sees this as an illusion and the priority of aims to be just the opposite. National independence, freedom and Socialism only bring benefits or are capable of survival if the federation – which is a political structure and guarantees peace and international justices – precedes them and does not simply follow them. If we succeed in laying the foundations of European federation, it will pave the way for the fulfilment of all the other progressive aims of our civilization.'

The decision (in its negative aspects too) was most clearly argued in a letter from the central committee of the MFE to the CFFE in August 1944: We cannot consider forming a federalist party at the moment because it would have no prospect of attracting enough popular support with an understanding of the actual priority of European problems over national problems. A party, that is to say an organization created by democratic means to win power in the state presupposes the existence of a state. So long as there is no federal state and consequently no federalist democratic political struggle, there can be no federalist party ... We must form an association to provide every democratic and progressive party with its international political programme. We must explain to every party, every movement, that they can attain their democratic, Socialist, libertarian and national ideals only to the extent that in foreign policy they help to build the federation of Europe. On the question of organization they wrote in July 1944: We announce that the Italian national central committee consists for the time being of militants of the 'Party of Action' and the 'Italian Socialist Party', and that the local federalist committees in the various cities consist of members of different progressive tendencies without regard to whether or not they belong to a party or whether in the committees they represent a cross-section of the parties. The only proviso is that they all agree that the most important problem is the federation of Europe.[53]

[52] 'Milanese' (probably Rollier) in *L'Unità europea*, No. 4, June 1944, p. 3; Geneva declaration in Lipgens, *Föderationspläne*, p. 397. For an explanation of the failure of this idea, cf. chap I/7, p. 278 f., for the later strategic ideas of the MFE see chap. III/6, p. 631 f.
[53] Foundation conference and letter of the Central Committee, see references in nn. 47 and 50. Information on the form of organization in *L'Unità europea*, No. 5 (Milan edn.), July–Aug. 1944, p. 1, where the passage continues: 'Thus, for example, at the time of liberation the local committee in Rome consisted of three Socialists, one Christian Democrat and one Republican; the local

5. *Forms of Activity.* These, though limited at first by the need to act clandestinely, were marked during the whole of 1945 by far-reaching division of responsibility based on mutual trust. Ten days after the Milan conference Badoglio's military cabinet fled to the South of Italy, which was occupied by the Allies, and the Germans took over direct command of the front line as far as Naples. Yet some of the founders of the MFE remained behind in Rome as a pressure group to commit the party leaders who had remained there in hiding to the aim of a European federation: Leone Ginzburg, Rossi-Doria, Colorni (whom Nenni had made chief editor of the underground Socialist-party newspaper *Avanti*), Altiero Spinelli, and others.[54] The second major group, in Milan and Turin, led by Mario Rollier and with the later help of Guglielmo Usellini, one of the founding members of MFE, continued to produce the association's periodical *L'Unità europea*, illegally from No. 3 (Sept. 1943) to No. 8 (Feb. 1945), then legally from No. 9 (29 April 1945) to No. 17 (28 July 1945). After the liberation it was responsible for the broadcast known as 'La Voce dei federalisti', transmitted by Radio Turin for the first time on 15 May 1945 and from then on at regular intervals, to propagate its views. From the summer of 1945 onwards it was especially active in recruiting new members.[55] Spinelli and Rossi meanwhile had gone to Switzerland soon after the founding conference, and despite very serious difficulties had sought contact with the Resistance groups of as many countries as possible. They had finally succeeded in getting 'active fighters in the Resistance movements of France, Holland, Italy, Norway, Poland, Czechoslovakia, Yugoslavia, and Germany' to meet in Geneva between March and May 1945, where they jointly adopted the famous Geneva Declaration of the European Resistance Movements in favour of European Federation.

Thanks to the confidence they inspired in the Swiss journalist François Bondy and the General Secretary of the World Council of Churches, Visser 't Hooft, they had been given the Swiss addresses of many Resistance movements and in November 1943 had sent them an invitation suggesting that the Resistance should

---

committee of one North Italian town, two militants from the Partito d'Azione and one non-party man; that of another town, one socialist and two members of the Partito d'Azione. The federal movement works together with all progressive parties . . . but is directed by none.' For the organization, statutes, etc. of the MFE after its reconsolidation, cf. the analysis in chap. III/6, p. 631 f.

[54] Colorni managed to get the Ventotene documents published clandestinely in Jan. 1944 (cf. nn. 40 and 42), and the proposal for a pro-European resolution accepted by the PSIUP in Feb., before he was shot by the Germans (as was L. Ginzburg) on 28.5.44, a few days before the liberation of Rome. Colorni's successor as editor of *Avanti* was the equally European-minded Ignazio Silone (cf. Lipgens, *Föderationspläne*, p. 55 f., 63 f., and 77 f.).

[55] Nos. 3–11 of *L'Unità europea* were published under the editorship of M. A. Rollier, nos. 12–17 under that of A. Spinelli, until at the end of July 1945 lack of paper supplies forced publication to be suspended. It was resumed by the Piedmont branch of the MFE in Turin with *L'Unità europea*, Vol. 2, No. 1, Turin, 10 Oct. 1945 under the editorship of Prof. Augusto Monti. No. 13, Turin, 20.4.1946, p. 1 contained a report on broadcasts.

work together for a 'United States of Europe' and inviting them to a 'preparatory congress'. For this purpose Rossi wrote a summary in forty pages called 'L'Europe de Demain', which in three chapters described the decline of European civilization in consequence of political anarchy and the failure of the League of Nations through lack of supranational authority, and in a further five chapters described the 'federalist solution'. After April 1944 some 10,000 copies of this were distributed in French. As a result of the conference of Resistance fighters from nine countries which met three times at monthly intervals, the Geneva Declaration was passed on 20 May 1944 and distributed with a preceding declaration of solidarity from Resistance fighters of all the nine countries. It explained in urgent language the necessity for federal union and demanded unequivocally that a European federal government be given supreme authority over foreign policy, the economy, and defence. Thus the programme for the future, which had been worked out on similar lines by the Resistance groups of so many countries, was the expression of widespread supranational opinion.[56]

Yet in the confusion of the last months of the war the Geneva Declaration made less impact than had been hoped, and above all it had no influence whatsoever on the planning of the superpowers, whose preponderance in Europe became more and more obvious. 'Since up to now', Spinelli wrote after his return to German-occupied Milan in September 1944,

there exists not the smallest embryo from which a body to represent the peoples of Europe could emerge, there is no hope of forming a European constituent assembly overnight ... The European Federation will not come into existence as simply as the United States of America. The road will probably be much more tortuous ... The majority of citizens ... will be too preoccupied with rebuilding their normal national life ... The success or failure of the making of a European federation will above all depend on the goodwill, perserverance and intelligence of the political leaders of the individual countries.

From the beginning of January until the end of April Spinelli was still trying to help to make the movement 'take off' at least in Lyons and Paris;

---

[56] Cf. facts, names and documents on the preparation and course of this Conference in Lipgens, *Föderationspläne* (n. 40), pp. 379–81 (letter of invitation), pp. 383–8 (Rossi's article), and pp. 388–401 (declarations of the Conference and circular). The declaration in favour of European federation certainly strengthened many people's convictions in the years 1944–5. But it belongs to the Resistance period (cf. Introduction, at n. 87), and will not be considered in detail at this point, because no permanent group was formed by the participants at the conference. They did appoint a 'Provisional Committee for European Federation' with Rossi and Jean M. Soutou as the most active members, which issued one number of a periodical (*L'Europe fédéraliste*, No. 1, Geneva, Oct. 1944) and also (using the name 'Centre d'action pour la Fédération Européenne') the book *L'Europe de demain*, ed. Baconnière, Neuchâtel, March 1945. This contains on pp. 19–66 a reprint of Rossi's pamphlet, on pp. 67–107 pro-European statements, mostly by the French Resistance, and on pp. 108–203 similar statements made in Britain; for quite a long time it was the only book giving information about federalist views in the Resistance. But soon after the end of the war all non-Swiss participants returned to their own countries; some citizens of Geneva who remained as a '*centre d'action*' under Dr René Jaccard joined the Swiss Europa-Union before the end of 1945 (see n. 71). The proposed 'international congress of federalists to be held at the end of the war' took place (on a smaller scale than originally intended) in March 1945 at the invitation of the CFFE (cf. p. 127–30 below).

using the pseudonym 'Antonelli' he was a co-organizer of the federalists' conference in Paris.[57] With brilliant insight he then drew up the 'balance sheet' in June 1945 in these terms: 'Our vision of a Europe in which all state structures would have collapsed, but the peoples would be free to decide their destiny in freedom, has not materialized ... The troops of the superpowers have occupied the defeated countries and placed them in tutelage.' These and other perceptive remarks of Spinelli and of other members of MFE in 1945–6 described the situation as a whole so accurately, and the confused reactions of other sections of the MFE from the autumn of 1945 onwards were so characteristic of the first post-war year, that they will be discussed more extensively at the end of this chapter.[58]

(B) THE SWISS EUROPA-UNION

This body was of special importance in that it was the only European association which by 1945 could look back on a decade of lively activity at cantonal and local level, with thousands of paid-up members and a programme worked out in committees which had spent months on the task, without the handicap of illegality. It had sprung up in 1933 from the merger between a group known as 'Jung Europa. Bund für die Vereinigten Staaten von Europa',[59] which had been particularly active in Basle and its neighbourhood, and the Swiss branch of the Pan-Europa-Union, which had turned its back on Count Coudenhove and his attempt in the autumn of 1932 to found his own party. The Europa-Union, after a period of difficulty when a new war was seen to be inevitable in 1939, had experienced a continuing upsurge, having its own monthly magazine, a steadily rising membership, and a regular programme of lectures in every town, especially in German-speaking Switzerland. Its long-standing president was the Basle editor, Dr Hans Bauer, who led the association with as much foresight and integrity as tactical skill and humanity and who was regularly re-elected president until long after 1950.[60] In the winter of 1939–40 an

---

[57] Article in *L'Unità europea*, No. 6, Milan, Sept.–Oct. 1944, p. 1; also in Spinelli, *Dagli stati sovrani agli stati uniti d'Europa*, Florence, 1950, pp. 157–66. For hopes built on France, cf. p. 203; on the parallel organization of the Paris conference of federalists in March 1945, see p. 126 f.

[58] Spinelli's 'Bilanco federalista nel giugno 1945' in *L'Italia libera* (organ of the Partito d'Azione), June 1945, repr. in *L'Unità europea*, No. 12, Milan, 17 June 1945, p. 1, and in Spinelli, *Dagli stati* ... (n. 57), pp. 173–7. More about these views and the difficult situation of the MFE in chap. I/7, p. 274–8.

[59] The President of its 'Swiss Bureau for Action' was Hermann Aeppli. It was in liaison with a 'Belgian Bureau for Action' (E. Didier), a 'French Bureau for Action' (R. Mangin), and a 'Dutch Bureau for Action' (J. H. Schultz van Haegen). It already gave emphatic support to the idea that 'every nation must give up part of its sovereignty' in favour of the United States of Europe; and it demanded that the 'European Movement' should remain 'neutral in a party political sense' on economic matters so that 'co-operation between members of all political camps would remain possible'. Cf. H. Aeppli, *Wir fordern Europa* (Jung Europa Verlag), Basle, 1933, p. 21, 24 f., and 37.

[60] Hans Bauer, born 10 July 1900, doctor of political economy, was the author of the booklet: *Vaterland und Völkergemeinschaft, Ein Manifest ... am Europatag 17.5.1933* (Jung Europa Verlag, Basle, 1933 and so presumably a product of this group). For his other books, see next footnote. For an appreciation of his leadership see E. von Schenck, 'Zentralpräsident Dr Hans Bauer zum 60. Geburtstag', in *Europa. Organ der Europa-Union*, vol. 28, No. 7, July 1961, p. 1. Cf. n. 73 on Bauer's articles in every number of this periodical since 1935.

'Action Committee' had circulated a comprehensive statement of its aims in the fields of politics, culture, and the economy, unequivocal in its commitment to a federal unification of Europe. This was adopted as 'Guiding Principles for a New Europe' by an assembly of delegates on 4 February 1940 in Berne, as the basic programme of Europa-Union, which remained valid for the whole of the period with which this book is concerned. Since Hitler never occupied Switzerland, not only did the extremely active life of the association continue, but leading members were able to publish detailed studies of the programme in book form. The titles alone showed how deep-rooted was the belief, shared by the great majority of members, that multilingual Switzerland with its mixture of peoples and its decentralized form of government, while preserving federal authority for the few matters which were essentially federal, could and should serve as a model and hope for the future to the other Europeans suffering from the troubles of the nation state.[61]

According to the resolutions passed by further assemblies of delegates in addition to the 'Guiding Principles', and to the declarations and reports of the central committee between 1944 and 1946, the key ideas and activities of this association may be summarized as follows:

1. *Design for Europe.* 'Europe by reason of its historical development represents a spiritual and cultural unity with a common destiny' which is now 'threatened with the undermining of its civilization by totalitarian regimes'. 'Curbing the overweening will to power of modern states', preserving the fundamental 'ideas of individual freedom and human kindness ... and thereby saving Western civilization is actually possible only by limiting the sovereignty of the individual state and forming a European federal state'.[62] The 'Bases of a European Federation' are

[61] H. Bauer and H. G. Ritzel, *Von der eidgenössischen zur europäischen Föderation*, Zurich/NY, 1940 (cf. the same authors' *Kampf um Europa. Von der Schweiz aus gesehen. Mit Beiträgen von A. Siemsen, O. Brogle und L. Klaesi*, Zurich/NY, Jan. 1945); Léon van Vassenhove, *L'Europe helvétique. Étude sur les possibilités d'adapter à l'Europe les institutions de la Confédération Suisse*, Neuchâtel, 1943 (cf. the same author's *Le Préjugé de la guerre inévitable*, Neuchâtel, 1945); A. Gasser, *Gemeindefreiheit als Rettung Europas*, Basle, 1943; J. J. Kindt-Kiefer, *Europas Wiedergeburt durch genossenschaftlichen Aufbau*. Berne, 1944. Also worthy of note are R. Silva, *Au service de la paix*, *L'idée fédéraliste*, Neuchâtel, 1943; E. Privat, *Trois Expériences fédéralistes. États-Unis d'Amérique, Confédération Suisse, Société des Nations*, Neuchâtel, 1943. For further historical inquiry: E. Rotten, *Die Einigung Europas. Sammlung von Aussprüchen und Dokumenten aus einenhalb Jahrhunderten*, Vorwort von J. R. von Salis, Basle, 1942; L. Ledermann, *Les Précurseurs de l'organisation internationale*, Neuchâtel, 1945.

[62] Summary of the first part of the 'Leitsätze für ein neues Europa' printed in: *Der Europäer. Organ der Europa-Union*, vol. 6, No. 1, Basle, Jan. 1940, p. 1 f.; also in *Die Friedens-Warte*, 40 (1940), pp. 109–13, and in Lipgens, *Föderationspläne* (n. 40), pp. 345–51 (this quotation on p. 345). This first part was a summary of the pamphlet written by the co-founder of EU, a frequent public speaker who was also a lecturer in history at Basle University, Dr Alfred Gasser: *Der Kampf um das europäische Freiheitsideal in Geschichte und Gegenwart* (Verlagsgenossenschaft der Europa-Union), Basle (n.d., c.1938, twenty pages), an appeal to uphold the Europe of freedom and federal democracy against the Asiatic danger arising from the totalitarian one-party states, Communists as well as Fascist. In 1942, in an article entitled 'Dreierlei "Neues Europa" ', Gasser argued that the only solution worth aiming at was neither Hitler's totalitarian Reich nor a Europe divided into blocs of States as the Allies clearly intended, but a confederal Europe (*Der Europäer*, vol. 9, No. 2, Feb. 1942, p. 1 f.; reproduced in Lipgens, *Föderationspläne*, pp. 361–5.)

described in eighteen points: '1. The European Federation shall promulgate a federal constitution. The sovereignty of the individual members of the Federation (i.e. states) shall be restricted as far as is required by the security of Europe as well as by the freedom of human beings to develop economically, socially, and intellectually.' The states shall remain autonomous in all questions (including the form of government), but the following areas must become 'exclusively federal matters': 'Foreign policy ... the right to declare war and make peace ... customs policy ... a single currency ... control over the entire arms industry'. Further, 'Matters for federal legislation according to the constitution' are 'the equality of all citizens, sexes and languages, the introduction of one language as a link between the peoples, a guarantee of the right to freedom of all citizens, freedom to settle in any part of the federal area, the drawing-up of a code of civil law for all Europeans'.[63]

To exercise these combined powers the constitution must create 'legislative, executive and judicial' bodies. 'The federal parliament shall consist of two Chambers. The Senate shall be elected by the governments of the individual states. The Chamber of Deputies shall be elected by men and women of the individual states who are entitled to vote, in proportion to the size of the population. The task of the federal parliament shall consist in safeguarding the general legal community of the member nations, in safeguarding the financial and military power of the federal institutions, and in deciding the federation's foreign policy.' To preserve its own power the federation 'shall create its own financial sovereignty, based preferably on certain federal monopolies and customs'; also a federal police. 'The federation shall take over from the individual states the whole range of heavy weapons, tanks, aircraft etc., as well as munitions and accessories. The states shall be forbidden to have such weapons themselves or to produce them for their own purposes.' 'The federal government shall consist of a cabinet of federal councillors elected by the federal parliament for a given period. The federal councillors shall be responsible for their actions to the federation alone and not to the state from which they have come.' To protect the federal constitution and 'to regulate differences a federal court of justice shall be set up, whose decisions shall be binding on all member states. The functions of the federal court will be modelled on the long and well-tried experience of the Swiss federal court. The decisions of the court of arbitration shall be binding in law. Their enforcement shall lie with the federal

---

[63] Part II in 18 points (essence of the 'Leitsätze'), points 1–3, 9 f., and 12–15 quoted here; also reprinted in *Der Europäer,* vol. 7, no. 7, July 1941, and vol. 10, no. 7, July 1943. French translation ibid., vol. 7, no. 7, July 1944. The above text follows Lipgens, *Föderationspläne,* pp. 346–8. Part IV (p. 349) actually stated: 'As soon as possible total abolition of tariffs (if necessary in stages) between individual European states and import duties ... in a new single currency, to be levied only at the frontiers of the new customs union.' Part III (p. 348 f.) called for 'reform of the present school system with a view to educating young people to be pro-European and pro-democratic', with its administration 'simultaneously in the hands of the government and of the cultural authorities ...; the whole university world will be self-governing'. All these points are elaborated in H. Bauer and H. G. Ritzel, *Kampf um Europa ... 1945* (n. 61), where Ritzel (pp. 238–41) also proposed 'economic democracy' and a large measure of self-government by means of a 'European economic council'.

executive. Members of the arbitration court shall be elected by the federal parliament.'[64]

2. *Europe in the World.* The 'Guiding Principles' of 1940 had laid down two basic principles on this subject: 'All European powers pledge themselves to transfer to a European federation those of their colonies which are not self-governing (i.e. those which have never had a government appointed by the population itself for independent and unfettered government) as a possession of the federation.' The colonies were to join the federal customs union, which was to be open to all citizens of the federation, and should cease to be the cause of disputes and inequality between the members of the union. For the rest 'more active moral support for Europe by the USA can be expected only if the Europeans . . . unite in following the example of the USA but also following the example of Switzerland', and aim for 'close co-operation with the USA in the economic and cultural spheres'. A third principle was added by a meeting of delegates on 28 November 1943, after the emergence of plans for a global peace organization: 'This world order can, however, only be federal, and must rest on regional and continental unions of states. The bridge of understanding between the nations across the world must be supported by intermediate pillars, and therefore the Europa-Union supports the formation of European Union within the framework of a global union.'

A resolution passed in April 1944 added that the Europa-Union saw European federation 'as an essential constituent element of a genuine world union. As further elements of a world union it sees the Pan-American Union, the British Commonwealth, closely linked through Britain with the European Union, the Soviet Union, the Asian Organization proposed by some responsible statesmen, later perhaps an Arab federation ... According to the federal principle of organic growth upwards from below, the Swiss Europa-Union would consider it a mistake to transfer the existing tensions of particular continents to a world league of nations for solution. For the protection of the smaller European states Europa-Union demands European unity as part of a world union.' The meeting of delegates on 22 April 1945 was more explicit: 'Europa-Union sees in a world union without intermediate structures the greatest possible number of areas of friction', whereas by contrast in Europe 'areas of friction can be reduced to a minimum through a European federation ... Europa-Union regards the formation of a European police force of limited size and a European federal constitution guaranteed by the world union as

---

[64] '*Leitsätze*', ii, here points 4–8, 11 and 18. Detailed interpretation in terms of the Swiss federal constitution in Bauer/Ritzel, *Kampf um Europa,* pp. 139–45; especially urgent plea for extension of the Swiss confederal idea into an 'open' European Community as an 'intermediate pillar' of the organization for world peace by H. Bauer, 'Die Eidgenossenschaft und Europa' in *Stimmen aus der Schweiz zu Europas Zukunft,* Zurich, 1945. A 'draft constitution for a United States of Europe' (in ninety clauses) was published later in *Europa. Organ der Europa-Union,* vol. 15, no. 7, July 1948, pp. 3–5. This was based on the '*Leitsätze*' of 1941/2 and was mainly the work of W. Hoegner and H. G. Ritzel; it was discussed and amended at eighty sessions of the Basle branch of Europa-Union before reaching its final form.

the minimum programme for unifying Europe and the best way of overcoming militarist thinking among the German people'.[65]

3. *Plan of Campaign.* Europa-Union did not develop a political strategy as to how federation could be brought about. This was connected with its basic educational approach (as will be seen in point 4 below). 'The European idea', Hans Bauer had written when announcing the 'Guiding Principles' in 1940, 'must fill the hearts and minds of war-suffering humanity like a new gospel, so that it can then be put into effect by all the different countries, lay a solid foundation for the work of future diplomats and provide a compelling sense of direction'.

At the time of the armistice in May 1945 Hans Bauer wrote an article 'Der Krieg in Europa ist zu Ende – der Kampf um Europa beginnt!' which was very much to the point: 'The world powers are masters not only of Germany but of Europe. The old world has become a kind of protectorate. That is the result of Hitler's "struggle for Europe" … America and Asia meet on the Elbe and in Austria.' Yet all he could do about this momentous fact was to repeat: 'Only European self-determination, which must remind us of our common destiny in the world and of our common will to live after the catastrophe in which we have all been involved, can save us.' The first signs of a tactical plan were developed in a 'programme of action' prepared by H. G. Ritzel and approved by a Commission on 29 December 1945. 'A. The European nations, their parliaments and governments, must pledge themselves to outlaw war by an oath to be taken openly in all public bodies, and this oath must become a part of the official oath taken by all public servants; B. An 'International Penal Law', on the basis provided by the Nuremberg trials, 'must be codified, so as to make all statesmen, politicians, journalists, and economic leaders, but also those engaged in education and youth leadership, who encourage war and the war spirit liable to arrest under criminal law'; C. 'A European court of arbitration is to be set up as a constituent part of the International Court of Justice provided for by the United Nations Charter, and as soon as, after a transitional period of uncertain duration, the occupying troops of the United Nations have left Germany, the establishment of a European police

---

[65] 'Leitsätze', parts V and VI, quoted in Lipgens, *Föderationspläne,* p. 350 f.; resolutions of 28 Nov. 1943 and April 1944, ibid., p. 382 f.; resolution of 22 April 1945 in *Der Europäer,* vol. 12, no. 5, May 1945, p. 2. In *Kampf um Europa* by Bauer and Ritzel, Bauer in 1945 specially emphasized the following point: 'The most zealous supporters of direct unification in the "United States of the World" usually turn out to be people who are not themselves acquainted with the world in its multifarious variety, and who are too near to their own continent to know it as it really is' (p.41). Europe is a danger to the world in two ways: 'by its divisions and self-mutilation, which are the denial of a common European destiny, but no less by forming a bloc against the rest of the world' (p. 43). Not Continental nationalism but a united Europe, open to the world, should be aimed at as the foundation of world union: 'Between national and global problems there are definite regional problems which need regional solutions, European as well as American, Asian as well as Australian. Why should Europeans suddenly interfere in the government of America, or Asians in Europe? A larger organization is only justified in interfering where the size of its task extends far beyond the borders of a smaller area; only when a European union cannot cope with certain of its functions or fails to perform the tasks expected of it should the global union intervene' (p. 47 f.).

force as an executive organ and for the maintenance of peace is to be put in hand.'[66] Yet here too no details were given as to how the states were to be induced to take these preliminary steps.

4. *Purpose and Character of the Organization*. Every publication of the Europa-Union carried the sentence: 'Europa-Union works as an independent Swiss movement, but in common with like-minded people in all parts of the world, for a federation of free states, united on the basis of equality.'[67] Stress was laid on the principle of educating people and endowing as many of one's fellow-citizens as possible with insight, for decisions for the future must be made in the heads and hearts of individuals; according to the constantly quoted saying of C. G. Jung: 'The individual alone makes history, it is in him alone that all great changes begin, and both the future and the history of the world originate in the last analysis in the hidden springs of the individual.'[68] The organization of the association was as clear as it was democratic. Each local branch sent delegates in proportion to its number of paid-up members to the annual spring meeting of delegates, which was held at the time of the Swiss Trade Fair; this meeting elected new members to the central committee of twenty-six (as death or retirement made necessary) and also its president.

About half of the central committee was composed of the chairmen of the most active branches, the rest being co-opted professors, business men, and members of town and national councils. From its ranks the Committee appointed the chairmen of the specialist committees and of any special branches that might be necessary.[69]

[66] Bauer on the 'Leitsätze' in *Der Europäer*, vol. 6, no. 1, Jan. 1940, p. 1; Bauer's views in May 1945 in ibid., vol. 12, no. 6, June 1945, p. 1, 'Europäisches Aktionsprogramm' in ibid., vol. 13, no. 1, Jan. 1946, pp. 1 and 4. Also 'D. Overcoming the war spirit', with proposals for 'democratization', 'principles of European education', 'exchange of lecturers', etc., and 'E. Removing the causes of war'; for the rest, 'Comprehensive struggle against the impoverishment of the peoples of Europe . . . gradual abolition of customs barriers . . . creating a new European currency', etc. – *Der Europäer* performed a special service (for the plan of campaign also) by publishing several articles, including one in each of its issues for 1945, on 'The other Germany', urging respect for the values of the German nation which had been led astray and arguing that the 'German question' could be solved only by Germany's inclusion in a European federation.

[67] These words appeared in every number from 1943 to 1948 at the head of the column headed 'News of the Movement'. After Nov. 1948 an amended version (approved by the UEF congress in Rome) ran: 'works for the federal union of the peoples of Europe with a view to a federal union of the world'; from June 1950 onwards the wording was: 'is a foundation member of the UEF in the Association of the European Movement and works for a decentralized democratic federal state of the free peoples of Europe as an intermediate stage on the road to the hoped-for world federation'.

[68] C. G. Jung quoted in the New Year Appeal of the Central Committee, *Der Europäer*, vol. 9, no. 1, Jan. 1942; ibid., headed 'Good ideas are like natural forces'; ibid., vol. 7, no. 7, July 1941, under a banner headline: 'Conviction, that is the rudder which guides us. Jakob Burckhardt'; also vol. 10, no. 10, Oct. 1943, motto: 'In the long run the sword is always defeated by the spirit. Napoleon.' By way of summary Hans Bauer wrote: 'With our convictions and our behaviour we all decide the spirit which will decide our future. . . . We cannot for ever expect that someone else will give us a better world . . . it will come if we contribute our share. . . . Such is the meaning of democracy. And such is the deep conviction of Europa-Union when it turns unceasingly to the individual to call the world to its senses through the combined force of many individuals' (ibid., vol. 13, no. 1, Jan. 1946).

[69] Every number of the monthly periodical contained in the column 'News of the Movement' a list of office-holders. Standing committees from 1940 onwards were: economic questions (chairman E.

Dr Hans Bauer (the Basle editor) was regularly re-elected central president; so was O. Brogle (headmaster, Menziken), as vice-president: the next vice-president until 1947 was L. Klaesi (business man, Zurich); the vice-president from 1947 onwards was H. Genet (engineer and city councillor, Lausanne). The branches which made most impact in publicizing the Europa-Union's message were in German-speaking Switzerland and in the Ticino.[70] A branch known as 'Section du Léman, Lausanne' founded in June 1945 was such a success under H. Genet as president and Ernest B. Steffan as secretary that Bauer assigned to it the task 'd'organiser l'expansion du mouvement en Suisse Romande'. At the end of 1945 the remainder of the Geneva 'Centre d'Action' joined the Union. By 1949 French-speaking Switzerland was covered with energetic branches.[71] Until the end of 1947 H. G. Ritzel in Basle ran the General Secretariat, E. B. Steffan in Lausanne succeeded him in the summer of 1948.[72]

5. *Forms of Activity.* The most important means of propagating the idea and preserving unity in the ranks of the association was its monthly periodical *Der Europäer* (known after 1946 as *Europa*) which has appeared without a break from May 1935 to the present; its articles with their wide mental horizon and lucid style commented on political events and expounded the federal answer to them.[73] In the local branches these articles would be discussed at the weekly meeting of members (every Wednesday, for

---

Ernst, an editor in Zurich); customs and currency questions (chairman Dr A. Gelpke, a lawyer in Winterthur, after the death in March 1945 of Dr Georg Wettstein); constitutional questions (Dr E. Henseler, a lawyer in Lucerne); cultural questions (Rektor O. Brogle, Menziken); women's affairs (Frau Dr H. Dünner, Zurich); language questions (L. Klaesi). There was also a central management committee (chairman H. Schiess, a business man in Aarau) and the finance committee (chairman H. Krattiger, Basle). For special sections formed from time to time, see n. 74.

[70] The largest and most active branches, according to reports under 'News of the Movement', were Aarau, Basle, Berne, Biel, Burgdorf, Liestal, Locarno, Lucerne, Olten, Eastern Switzerland, Rheinfelden, Solothurn, Winterthur, Wynen- und Seetal, Zug, and Zurich.

[71] This task was assigned to the Lausanne branch. See *Der Europäer*, vol. 12, no. 9, Sept. 1945, p. 4, and no. 11, Nov. 1945, p. 3. The remainder of the 'Centre d'Action' group (cf. n. 56) joined the Europa-Union first as an 'autonomous group', then as the ordinary Geneva branch, ibid., vol. 13, no. 1, Jan. 1946, p. 4. The other active sections were: Lausanne, Geneva, 'Groupe Fédéraliste Européen du Jura, Reconvilier', Neuchâtel, and Valais.

[72] Heinrich Georg Ritzel. Born 10.4.1893, mayor of Michelstadt (Odenwald) in 1919, was an SPD member of the Hessen Landtag from 1924 to 1930, member of the Reichstag from 1930 to 1933, an official of the League of Nations administration in the Saar from 1933 to 1935, then a writer in Switzerland (see n. 61). From 1940 to Dec. 1947 head of the central secretariat of Europa-Union in Basle; in 1948 a 'delegate of the central committee for German-speaking foreign countries' (cf. p. 420); after Sept. 1949 a member of the Bundestag. Ernest B. Steffan was secretary at the headquarters of Europa-Union in Lausanne from Sept. 1948 to Oct 1951 (the main secretariat was then transferred back to Basle).

[73] *Der Europäer, Organ der Europa-Union,* vol. 1, no. 1, May 1935 (edited at first by H. Aeppli, later by H. Bauer) to vol. 12, no. 12, Dec. 1945. From 1 Jan. 1946, vol. 13, no. 1, it was called *Europa. Organ der Europa-Union. Organe de l'Union Européenne* with a note explaining that the name had to be changed to make it bilingual; as a result of its distribution in French-speaking Switzerland the journal was henceforward a model of bilingualism. Every number ran to between four and eight pages, the size of a daily newspaper: every member of Europa-Union was a subscriber, but there were others as well. Exact numbers for both sets of subscribers are not available but are believed to have been in thousands. The column headed 'From the Movement' in every number was a mine of information, and the facts which follow are based on it.

example, in the usual pub); every branch tried to offer a public lecture at least once a month; while introductory courses on the 'Guiding Principles', each of forty hours, were organized for members at regular intervals. Influence on governments, though, existed only to the extent that if, for example, Attlee, Paul-Boncour, Truman, or one of the Swiss Federal Councillors made a more or less pro-European statement, the central committee would send him a telegram expressing gratitude coupled with encouragement to go on promoting European unification.

It was obvious that this association, which had emerged from the war stronger and unscathed, would be bound to play an important part in the reconstruction of European federalist groups in the neighbouring countries and in establishing contacts. As early as June 1945 the central committee assigned special branches to this task.[74] Yet even in 1945–6 its chief problem was that, faced with the military take-over by the superpowers, it had no political answer to the problem of how to set in motion the process of federalizing the whole of Europe.

(C) THE COMITÉ FRANCAIS POUR LA FÉDÉRATION EUROPÉENNE

Lyons was the city where, from the end of 1941 until shortly before the end of the war, the strongest and best organized group of the French Resistance, known as Combat and led by Henri Frenay, published its underground newspaper (also called *Combat*) which in almost every issue spoke of the future federation of European peoples. Lyons, being the conspiratorial centre of the Resistance, was also the place where the Mouvement de Libération Nationale (MLN) was founded as the umbrella organization of the eight non-Communist Resistance groups, all of which in their publications described a European federation as the goal of their future foreign policy. By the beginning of June 1944 (at latest) the 'Theses' of the Milan founding conference of MFE (and perhaps the Declaration of the Geneva conference of Resistance fighters as well) were known in Lyons. Leading personalities of MLN, expecially Albert Camus, editor-in-chief of *Combat*, André Ferrat of *Franc-tireur*, Gilbert Zaksas of *Libérer et fédérer*, and others – as they revealed in a secretly printed 'Déclaration ... Juin 1944' – 'resolved

---

[74] A 'German Section' (at first under the chairmanship of Dr J. Kindt-Kiefer, later under Ritzel) consisting of Germans living in Switzerland, was charged with the task of getting a parallel group set up in Germany itself. There was also a 'Section for the Danubian and Balkan countries' (under a member of the Central Committee, a Berne business man named Walter Kocher) which soon reported (and continued to do so until August 1947) that 'necessary measures have been taken to spread the idea in the Balkan and Danubian countries'; and a Spanish section (under Luis Neumann of Basle). A relief operation known as 'Parcels Campaign, Social Aid by Europa-Union', was organized to send parcels to distressed areas, especially in Germany, and appealed for contributions. In *Europa*, vol. 13, No. 3, March 1946, H. Schiess urged 'taking the initiative for a meeting as soon as possible to set up a committee to co-ordinate efforts in every country. This Committee, together with annual congresses, must be the umbrella organization to which our Europa-Union should belong.' On preparations for the Hertenstein conference see p. 298 f., below.

for their part to form a French Committee for European Federation' as a body especially designed to further this common purpose.[75]

The 'basic ideas' of this 'Déclaration du CFFE' were as follows: 1. It is impossible to build a prosperous, democratic and peaceful Europe so long as the jumble of sovereign states remain divided from each other by political and customs barriers ... 2. Any attempt to create prosperity, democracy and peace by a league of nations in the form of a league of states is doomed to fail ... 3. Europe can only evolve along the path of economic progress, democracy, and peace if the nation states become a federation and transfer to a European federal state the following powers: the economic and commercial organization of Europe, the sole right to possess armed forces and to intervene against any attempt to reinstate an authoritarian régime, control of foreign affairs ... 4. The national governments will be subject to the federal government only in respect of matters which concern the federated states as a whole.[76]

In conclusion the Committee appealed to all Resistance groups 'to endorse, individually or collectively, the key ideas of its programme and to support them wholeheartedly'.

A few days before their city was liberated from German troops on 3 September 1944, MLN Lyons drew up a programme which was circulated as a leaflet immediately after the Germans' departure and was displayed in most of the towns of Southern France. In the section dealing with foreign policy there was a brief summary:

Since we therefore consider it impossible to construct a happy, democratic and peaceful Europe as a collection of sovereign, individual states, divided from each other by political frontiers and customs barriers, and since moreover a league of nations consisting of sovereign states is nothing more than a sham, we are fighting for the creation of a democratic European federation ... Only such a federation can by its example lead the nations of the world towards a world federal organization.

Some weeks after the liberation Francis Gérard became secretary of CFFE, which late that autumn began to send out invitations to a projected

---

[75] The 'Déclaration du Comité Français pour la Fédération Européenne', June 1944, was distributed as a pamphlet and is also in *L'Europe de demain*, Neuchâtel, March 1945 (cf. n. 56), pp. 75–8; German text in Lipgens, *Föderationspläne* (n. 44), pp. 244–6, the third part of which, 'European Plans of the French Resistance', pp. 177–250, must be read as preceding the Declaration (e.g. the programmes in *Combat* in ibid., pp. 190 f., 197 f., 227–30, 236 f.; 238 f.; in *Franc-Tireur*, p. 235 f.; and in *Libérer et féderer*, pp. 195 f., and 232–5).

[76] Point 5 of this Declaration was taken word for word from the Milan 'Theses' (cf. n. 47): 'But while the democratic, Socialist, Communist patriots often think that their goals should first be reached in each country separately, and that at the end of the day an international situation will come about in which all peoples will be able to fraternize, the Movement for European federation warns against that illusion.' An exactly opposite procedure must be followed. In a Europe divided into sovereign states, such national movements were doomed to fail or fade away; they could only succeed in a Europe already federated. *L'Europe de demain* (n. 75), p. 77 f. The Declaration of the CFFE, which also reached Milan in August 1944, was warmly welcomed and endorsed in an Open Letter from the MFE to the CFFE in August (ibid., pp. 90–2, .cf, quotation in n. 53).

126 Europe's Mood of Resignation

'conference of European federalists'.[77] Early in January 1945 Ursula Hirschmann and Altiero Spinelli (using the cover name Antonelli) made their way across the Alpine front in order to take part in preparations, at first in Lyons and later in Paris, for the projected conference, finally arranged for March. Public attention was still focused on the war, which continued for another six weeks in Central Europe; but Paris and the greater part of France had been liberated for six months, and the organizers felt there was no justification for postponing the conference if they were to exert any influence on the shaping of post-war policy in France. By way of preparation CFFE published at the beginning of March 1945 the first 'Cahier de la fédération européenne' which for the first time made available to the reading public of Paris the programmes of MFE, CFFE, and the Declaration of the Geneva conference of May 1944.[78]

At the federalists' conference, which met at the 'Maison de la Chimie' in Paris between 22 and 25 March 1945, 'numerous French personalities were seen to be present: several members of the Assembly (MM Baumel, Guérin, Mayer, Philip, Zaksas[79]) took part in the work, also the editors or proprietors of newspapers and periodicals (*Combat, L'Aube, Lyon libre, Liberté, Témoignage chrétien, Libertés, Esprit*, etc.) and well-known members of the Socialist Party, the Mouvement de la Libération Nationale, the Christian Democrats, and other Resistance groups'; also federalists from Italy, Switzerland, Austria, Germany, Great Britain, Spain, and Greece.[80] The

[77] In Milan, still under German occupation, a similar invitation from the CFFE was received in early Dec. 1944 (information from Spinelli on 2.5.1964). The programme of the MLN Lyons was also reprinted in *L'Europe de demain* (n. 75), p. 88 f. – Francis Gérard, a naturalized German Socialist who had lived in France since 1929, was converted by Léon Blum's book, *A l'échelle humaine* (Lipgens, *Föderationspläne*, pp. 185–90, July 1941) to the idea of European federation and championed it in a pamphlet written in 1943 (ibid., pp. 218–22, Nov. 1943). He became acquainted with the Ventotene Documents as an officer in the Psychological Warfare Department of the US Army during its advance to Rome (n. 40; information from Gérard on 18.3.1964).

[78] *Cahier de la fédération européenne* [No. 1], published by the Comité français pour la fédération européenne, Paris, March 1945, after a brief declaration that France must stand at the head of a post-war European movement (p. 5 f.) contained in the first part an article 'Pour l'Union démocratique des peuples d'Europe' by André Ferrat (pp. 7–18), and an unsigned study by Spinelli of 'La tâche européenne des forces progressives' (pp. 19–22); these formed the basis of the two speeches introducing the conference (cf. n. 81). The second part (pp. 25–32) contained the programme texts of the CFFE, the Geneva conference, and the MFE (n. 75, 56, and 47).

[79] Jacques Baumel was general secretary of the MLN and as representative of the metropolitan Resistance a frequent speaker in the Assembly (later he became a Gaullist). Maurice Guérin, who had been a member of the Sillon group and co-founder of the *Jeunesse Ouvrière Chrétienne* and Catholic Action (cf. M. Fogarty, *Christian Democracy in Western Europe, 1820–1953*, London, 1957, p. 310), was a co-founder of the MRP and in 1945–6, together with Paul Coste-Floret and Henri Teitgen, was a leading MRP spokesman in the constitutional committee of the Constituent Assembly (cf. B. D. Graham, *The French Socialists and Tripartisme 1944–1947*, London, 1965, p. 190). The leadership of the French Socialist Party was especially well represented with Daniel Mayer (General Secretary, 1943–August 1946) and André Philip (member of the Central Committee, minister of economics and finance in de Gaulle's first cabinet); also with the declaration of support by Auriol and Verdier, cf. n. 80. Gilbert Zaksas too was a delegate of the SFIO.

[80] According to the hectographed *Compte-Rendu de la Conférence Fédéraliste de Paris, 22–25 mars 1945* (Spinelli Archives), p. 1. A report on similar lines by W. G. Eichler in *Europe Speaks*, London, 24.4.1945, named as co-operating editors Albert Camus of *Combat*, Emmanuel Mounier of *Esprit*, Michel Collinet

main speech at the opening of the debate was made by André Ferrat, a member of the executive committee of MLN, president of SFIO in Lyons and publisher of *Lyon libre*. He started not with a theory about the federal ideal, but with an analysis of the predominance of the two superpowers, which had been apparent since Yalta and which in future would be the determining factor in the international situation.

At Yalta the superpowers had in a formal sense declared themselves against the policy of 'spheres of influence' (which had in fact already begun) and in favour of a common organization for world peace. But they would have great difficulty with this organization until the real causes of war in Europe were recognized and abolished; so long as Europe remained a trouble-spot, and Europe did not put an end to its own anarchy, the need for constant intervention in Europe would remain and there would always be an excuse for outside interference, with the probability of rising tension between the intervening powers. The only alternative to a policy of uniting Europe was to divide it into zones of influence. The prospects of effective agreement between the superpowers, on the other hand, would increase in proportion as the European nations themselves became united and eliminated the most serious national antagonisms within their Continent. In the other main speech Spinelli pointed out how unsuccessful the progressive parties had been in consequence of their past 'concentration on domestic policy'. Because inside the smaller nation states the prerequisites were lacking, the democratic forces had been unable to achieve their goal, but had succumbed to the various nationalisms. What was now required was to create the prerequisites for political and economic unity which alone would enable the progressive forces to succeed.[81]

After three days of discussion the participants summed up the results in a Manifesto and in a resolution consisting of five parts on the basis of which the design of CFFE can be systematically described:

1. *Design for Europe*. The cause of Europe's catastrophic decline – the 'European anarchy' which meant that within the Continent, small as it had become, every state claimed 'sovereignty', relations between states were governed by the 'primitive law of the stronger', and the economy and education were made to serve the various nationalisms – could only be overcome by the creation of a European federation. 'The dogma that the nation state is the highest political form of organization for mankind must be swept away.' 'Only the establishment of a federation, subordinat-

---

of *Volonté*, Brizon of *Liberté*, and André Ferrat of *Lyon Libre*. Both reports stated that Minister Henri Frenay, as well as Vincent Auriol and Robert Verdier of the Central Committee of the SFIO, were unable to take part but that they were in agreement with the resolution. Debarred by transport difficulties from attending, Sir Walter Layton (cf. his appeal in 1944 for a federation of Continental Europe, see note 136) and the London 'Socialist Vanguard Group' sent messages expressing solidarity; Lipgens, *Föderationspläne,* p. 456. The Labour Party was represented by John Hynd, MP, and the SPD in exile by Willi Eichler.

[81] Reports of both speeches in the *Compte-Rendu* and in Eichler's concurrent report (n. 80); printed preliminary drafts in no. 1 of *Cahiers de la fédération européenne* (cf. n. 78). Both urged that advantage be taken of the current crisis of the European system. Ferrat moved the draft resolutions on which the discussion was based.

ing problems of common concern to all Europeans to a common democratic authority' could guarantee the future protection of human rights, bring about a general revival of the economy, and reduce problems of frontier-drawing in areas of mixed population to the level of pure administrative convenience. 'The federation will not be allowed to encroach on the right of every member state to solve its own particular problems according to its domestic and cultural traditions. But all states must irrevocably hand over to the federation their sovereignty, the defence of their territory, their relations with outside powers, and international traffic and transport matters. The federation 'must above all include the following bodies: a government responsible not to the governments of the individual states but to the peoples... an army subject to the orders of this government ... a supreme lawcourt with power to deal with possible disputes between the federation and the member states'.

As to the 'German problem', it was stated that more repressions or 'the annexation of German territory by other countries' would 'inevitably drive the Germans into a new, violent nationalism'. Instead 'the democratic forces among the German people must be helped to transform the unitary and centralized Reich into a group of federated states... Only a European federation can initially keep a check on the new kinds of state in Germany, in order gradually to integrate them into the federation on the basis of equal rights and duties for all European states.'[82]

2. *Europe in the World.* The CFFE welcomed the attempt 'to set up world assemblies and councils where representatives inspired by the spirit of peace will endeavour to settle their disputes by arbitration'. This, however, would succeed only so far as the states were ready to show understanding. For Europe, 'the starting point of two world wars in one generation', such a method was certainly inadequate. Only 'if the states of Europe federate will a decisive advance be taken towards world peace, and the example of Europe will inspire other countries to join in advancing towards a federation of the world'.

The recent declarations of the Yalta conference about joint guarantees for the liberated nations were taken at their face value, hence the comment: 'The great world powers which have pledged themselves jointly to guarantee the democratic

---

[82] Part II (European anarchy), Part III (European federation), and Part IV (the German problem) of the resolutions passed by the European federalists' conference in Paris on 25.3.1945 were first hectographed and distributed, then printed in *Cahiers de la fédération européenne*, No. 2, 1945 edn., pp. 36--40; English translation in *Resistance speaks: United States of Europe*, ed. by Federal Union, London, 1945, pp. 11–16. The reported discussion noted differences of opinion on the 'German problem', as some participants 'felt it to be an injustice and an anachronism to demand the complete disintegration of Germany while all other states were to retain their national unity. But the majority felt that the break-up of the Reich was inevitable', since (after Yalta and before Potsdam) that seemed to be the unanimous intention of the Allies: the partition would only be 'reactionary and impracticable if Germany's neighbours were allowed to retain their complete sovereignty. If, however, the German states were integrated into Europe on a completely equal footing this would be a step forward for the German people and at the same time the way to dispel all distrust against the Germans on the part of the other nations.' (Report by Eichler in *Europe Speaks*, n. 80).

development of the whole of Europe were obliged to recognize that Europe's fate is indivisible and that this continent cannot be broken up into spheres of influence. Therefore the responsibility of choosing between a system of rivalry and one of peaceful and democratic co-operation has now again become one for the Europeans themselves.'[83]

3. *Plan of Campaign.* 'The European Federation ... can only be the result of a free decision by the peoples, who in this way express their will to save their common democratic civilization.' 'During the brief space of time in which we find ourselves today, with the horrors of war' and the collapse of the nation states still a vivid memory, all progressive forces must join to prevent any recurrence of nationalist foreign policy and to promote federal union. 'If we allow traditions and special national interests to entrench themselves once again, if Europe remains fragmented and at the mercy of its own quarrels, then the patriots, the democrats and the Socialists will have fought in vain.'[84]

4 & 5. *Purpose and Character of the Organization.* The participants at the Paris conference set their committee in March 1945 an exacting task which extended far beyond France. It was expressed in the resolution to rename the existing CFFE the 'Comité International pour la Fédération Européenne'. Albert Camus, Jacques Baumel, André Ferrat, Gilbert Zaksas, Robert Verdier, Maurice Guérin, John Hynd, Altiero Spinelli, and Willi Eichler were invited to join its central committee. It was emphasized that 'CIFE does not intend to form new parties or a new International, but is meant to bring together the different Socialist and democratic parties to take joint action with federation in mind, whatever their divergences on other questions may be.' In marked contrast to the Swiss Europa-Union, no word was said about rallying popular support, forming local branches, educating the public, etc., nor was any mention made of any organized body below the level of the central committee. This committee was given the following tasks:

---

[83] From Part I of the resolution (Europe in the world setting) and Part V (The struggle for European federation) (cf. n. 82); cf. the opening speech by Ferrat (n. 81) and, as regards the Yalta Declaration, n. 136 to the Introduction. Reports on the discussions indicate that this was the second controversial point: many people stood out for an immediate world federation, but the majority were convinced that the superpowers still thought themselves able to solve their own problems and saw no reason to submit to 'a World Parliament or any kind of international government. The same, however, does not apply to the European countries', whose problems could only be tackled in common, i.e. by some kind of 'supra-national authority'. (Report by Eichler, also in the *Compte-Rendu*, cf. n. 80).
[84] Summary of Part V of the resolution (n. 82), which thus endorsed the expectations of the earlier MFE and followed Spinelli's speech (cf. n. 81) in respect of priorities for the political parties. 'If attention is paid only to the domestic political, social and national problems of each individual country, the reasons for rivalry, militarism, rule of force and war remain. National sovereignty is bound to produce new nationalisms.' All progressive parties must, 'on the contrary, put the struggle for the unity of Europe in the forefront of their efforts'. There was specific agreement at the conference that 'for the time being it is France which must promote the initiative for creating federal European institutions' (*Compte-Rendu*, n. 80, p. 6).

130 Europe's Mood of Resignation

1. To establish links with progressive parties and movements in all European countries in order to brief them about the struggle for European federation; 2. to prepare for a federalist congress of delegates and representatives of all parties and movements that are fighting to establish a democratic European civilization; 3. to organize widespread federalist propaganda forthwith by means of publications and federalist news bulletins in France and other countries.[85]

The difficulties which stood in the way of accomplishing that task soon became apparent. At the time of the conference and for a month and a half afterwards, for example, the North of Italy and the Netherlands were still under German occupation, while the hopes placed in the United Nations reached their zenith as its founding conference met on 25 April 1945 in San Francisco. Seeking contacts with parties in other countries could hardly produce results in these few months in which parties everywhere (like the members of the CIFE committee themselves) were fully preoccupied in struggling to rebuild their strength, winning favourable vantage-points for the first local government elections, etc.; and in any case the prevailing feeling was that all foreign-policy questions of any importance would be decided by the superpowers. The more clearly the conferences of San Francisco, Potsdam, and London revealed the character of the Allies' decisions on Europe and the fact that they had not the slightest intention of helping to bring about a European federation, the more obvious it became that the prerequisites for a programme of European federation, which in March had been taken for granted, in fact simply did not exist. And in France itself de Gaulle had not only deprived the Resistance organizations of their power, but even in 1945 he was thinking of outmanœuvring the parties and steering French foreign policy, which he considered his personal prerogative, back to the old Clemenceau line, which could not have been more remote from the spirit of the European federalists.[86] The latter's conference of March was one of the factors which kept the idea of a European federation alive all through a difficult year, so that, for example, in May 1945 a Europe number of the periodical *Esprit* appeared in defence of the idea and there was more of that kind of support during the summer. The secretariat of CIFE itself published for the second and last time the 'Cahiers de la fédération européenne' containing some impressive articles.[87] For financial reasons it limited itself from then on-

---

[85] Quotations from the *Compte-Rendu* (n. 80), p. 6 f.: they summarize the appeal to all parties drawn up at the end of the conference and printed in *Cahiers de la fédération européenne*, No. 1, Paris, Aug. 1945, p. 34 f. For the names mentioned, cf. nn. 79 and 80. Apart from Baumel and Guérin they were all Socialists; André Ferrat was also elected to the SFIO executive on 1.9.1946 (cf. Graham, n. 79, p. 212). The task of co-ordination would have been formidable even if limited to France, and would have called for participation from a broader range of parties.

[86] More about France during de Gaulle's first Presidency in section 4 of this chapter, pp. 201–8. The difficulties facing the European associations and the reasons for their weakness in 1945–6 are summarized and analysed in section 7, pp. 269–74.

[87] For the Europe number of *Esprit* (no. 110) in May 1945 (with articles by M. Collinet, J. Lacroix, and A. Philip) as well as other federalist literature in France in 1945, cf. W. Lipgens, 'Innerfranzösische Kritik der Aussenpolitik de Gaulles 1944–1946' in *VfZG*, vol. 24 (1976), esp. pp. 167–9. CIFE: *Cahiers*

wards to a duplicated edition of a very useful 'Documents de la fédération européenne'. In a pamphlet published in November 1945, many copies of which were printed and distributed, it protested 'against the division of Europe into zones of influence and against the formation of opposing blocs', and commended unreservedly 'the unification of the states of Europe into a federation'.[88] But as regards its appointed task of co-ordinating the pro-European federalist activities of all Socialist and democratic parties CIFE remained without the slightest importance, because in this first postwar year there was nothing to co-ordinate. Also it had no connection with other existing groups of French federalists, particularly the hard-core supporters of 'integral federalism' associated with the periodical *La Fédération*. Not until December 1946 did it join these groups to found the UEF.[89]

(D) EUROPEESCHE ACTIE

In the leading Netherlands underground pamphlets too, every article which dealt with future events wrote of the need to limit national sovereignty in favour of an order based on international justice and future communities of nations. Although most of the newspapers with small circulations, which tended to support the Right, envisaged a global organization, the two newspapers which were by far the most important mouthpieces of the Netherlands Resistance, the Socialist weekly *Het Parool* and the progressive Christian monthly *Vrij Nederland*, had since 1942 urged the need for a federal community of European nations as an essential stage on the way to organizing world peace. The first draft proposals for the European 'Continental community' with lists of powers were put forward by (among others) the historian Jan Romein, and both the periodicals just mentioned stated in a joint manifesto, as the only point concerned with foreign policy: 'The Netherlands, once they are free again, must work for the closest

---

de la fédération européenne (No. 2), Paris, Aug. 1945, contains in particular, besides the resolutions of the March conference (pp. 34–40), articles by A. Altier, 'Les tâches de la politique extérieure française' (pp. 7–12, appealing for understanding and federation with Germany); A. Spinelli, 'Le problème allemand' (pp. 13–19); G. Scelle, 'Méditations fédéralistes au lendemain de San Francisco' (pp. 19–21); F. Bondy, 'L'Europe se tourne vers l'Angleterre' (pp. 22–4, cf. n. 143 below), and a report by P. Brizon on a public opinion survey in France, July 1945 (cf. n. 258).

[88] Cf. the 'Documents de la Fédération Européenne', which are especially informative for 1946-7, as shown in the Index. The leaflet printed on one side headed 'The sole means of saving Europe: Federation' (*Gérard Archives*) demanded without qualification 'Economic unity: gradual removal of customs barriers within the Continent for commodities and raw materials. Harmonization of the basic factors of economic legislation in the various European countries and the creation of a single European currency. Political unity: a federal police force will replace the national armies. Abolition of national diplomatic services and creation of a federal ministry of foreign affairs. Election of a European representative assembly.'

[89] Cf. pp. 349–55 for this association (initially concerned almost exclusively with federation within states), with its periodical *La Fédération* from Oct. 1944; for the joint foundation of the UEF see p. 362 f.

possible union with the other states of Western Europe ... and in doing so must be prepared to give up some of their sovereignty.'[90]

There too a group of Resistance fighters (independently of any other group) saw the goal of European unity as an urgent future necessity, worked it out in joint discussions into a detailed plan and by the end of the war formed a European association for the post-war period. Their leader was a specialist in economic law, Dr Hans-Dieter Salinger, who had emigrated from Germany in 1936. The group met almost every week at his office in The Hague from the summer of 1942 onwards.[91] The group's most important member, apart from J. S. Carmiggelt, was Willem Verkade, according to whom 'If Salinger was the inspirer ... and the author of most of the script, yet the working-out of the ideas would not have been so complete and elaborate had it not been for a group of seven people, subsequently rather more, from different walks of life, who met regularly for two years and discussed in great detail every aspect of the post-war situation with all its dangers and opportunities.'[92] To escape arrest

[90] The joint manifesto of *Het Parool and Vrij Nederland*, distributed clandestinely, in 60,000 copies, reprinted in *Het Woord als Wapen. Keur uit de Nederlandse ondergrondse Pers 1940–1945,* The Hague, 1952, p. 310; German text in Lipgens, *Föderationspläne* (n. 40), p. 284.

[91] Hans-Dieter Salinger, born in 1889, the son of an East-Prussian judge (later Counsellor of the Reich Supreme Court); enlisted as a volunteer in 1917 and was awarded the Iron Cross, first class; member of the *Freikorps*; studied law and political economy; civil servant in Reich Ministry of Transport; adviser to industry on cartel matters. He himself declared that his loyalty to Europe had a threefold origin: (1) to purge the clear, rational ('Prussian') idea of the public weal from contamination by populism, '*Deutschtum*' and 'racism'; (2) to remedy the absurdity of economic nationalism whereby export premiums were as high as 50 per cent and goods from neighbouring countries paid up to 50 per cent customs duty ('In this way we were making certain of our own poverty and slamming the door against wealth'); in 1935 he founded in Berlin the 'Association of European industries producing household equipment', with the object of stimulating remedial measures through direct talks between industries of different countries; (3) as a Jew deprived of nationality by the Nuremberg Laws, he was invited by the Netherlands Minister of Economics to continue to direct his association from The Hague. From then on he became more than ever determined that his former and his adopted country and all the nations of Europe, once the madness of the War was over, must form a single state which would be more like what a state ought to be. Arrested by the Gestapo because he refused to wear a Star of David, but set free at the end of 1941 by the head of the German Arms Inspectorate, he intensified his contacts with the underground and his own acts of resistance. (Information from Salinger, 25.4.1964).

[92] W. Verkade, 'Unite Europe as a protest against the Greater German Reich' (in Dutch) in *Nieuw Europa: Maandblad van de Europese Beweging*, vol. 17, no. 11, Nov. 1964, p. 199; also in the BEF pamphlet *Europa in Beweging,* The Hague, 1968, p. 9. According to this the most important members of the group were: Jan S. Carmiggelt, Socialist economics editor, arrested in 1944 for supplying members of the Resistance with ration cards, died in Vught concentration camp; Anton P. W. van der Lugt, a member of the Catholic Employers' group, arrested in 1944 for distributing *Christofoor,* died in Neuengamme concentration camp; Pastor O. T. Hylkema; Jan F. Sligting, head of the research department of the Netherlands steel industry; C. J. de Korver, member of the *Parool* group in Leiden (all ibid.), and Willem Verkade himself. Before the war Verkade had headed the Refugees Committee of the 'non-denominational Christian movement in the Netherlands' and helped many members of the German Bündische Jugend (e.g. Hans Ebeling); he considered the war a European civil war and from the middle of 1943 onwards edited the right-wing Socialist Christian Resistance paper *Je Maintiendrai.* From 1946 to April 1949 he worked for the Netherlands Institute for International Politics, and from May 1949 to 1951 he was UNESCO representative in the British Zone of Germany. (Information from Verkade, 27.9.1974).

Salinger was obliged to go underground in October 1943, and thus found the time to record his thoughts and the group's discussions in the most comprehensive and compact manuscript on Europe that was produced by the underground movement in any country, *Die Wiedergeburt von Europa* (The Rebirth of Europe).[93] The wealth and aptness of his reflections in six chapters can only be briefly indicated here:

'1. The world on the threshhold of peace' (pp. 4–18) is about to repeat the mistakes of 1918: 'Liberation for what? Silence on this question' in regard to Europe proves the 'failure of the Allies' political strategy'. In fact 'there is no basic problem in Europe which is confined to a single country... every major political or economic question in Europe... has become a European problem'. In failing to recognize this the Allies seem bent on restoring 'the status quo of the same nation states' and, as in 1918, 'in the stifling air of the modern ruins of the old structures of state and society... they seem bent on condemning Central Europe to become a source of anarchy for the entire Continent'.

'2. The prospects of the peace' (pp. 18–34) proposed by the Allies, 'that Britain, Russia, and the US together keep the rest of the world at peace and will do so if necessary by force' prove at once the weakness of the projected United Nations Organization: it refuses to allow the 'other nations' equality of obligations and is unable to reduce serious tensions between the major Allies, so that the latter must pile up armaments on the frontier between Russia and the Anglo-Saxon countries. Externally Europe 'faces the threat of being squeezed between two massive millstones', while internally 'the economic impoverishment of Germany threatens the material recovery of all the other European countries'. 3. The United States of Europe as the Way Out (pp. 35–78). 'The federal union of all European countries from the Atlantic to and including Poland' would make it possible to base the organization for world peace on two continental unions more or less equal in strength;[94] reduce tension between Russia and the Anglo-Saxon countries; 'rule out any future war between the nations of our continent'; replace Allied occupation troops in Germany by a 'European federal army'; re-establish the idea of the federal state in its true and original sense and one which meets the needs of modern life, by dissociating it from the idea of the nation; and get rid of poverty 'caused by customs and currency barriers'. 'Only a federation of European countries' will

---

[93] This pamphlet: 'Die Wiedergeburt von Europa. Der Sinn dieses Krieges für Europa. Ein Kontinent sucht nach seiner Lebensform und seiner Weltgeltung. Von Hades' (pseudonym of H. D. Salinger) was clandestinely hectographed in Sept.–Oct. 1944 and distributed in several hundred copies in German. (For the Dutch version, cf. n. 97). In date it belongs to the Resistance rather than to the period covered by this book. A sixteen-page summary of its ideas is in Lipgens, *Föderationspläne* (n. 44), pp. 290–306. It must suffice here to outline the general principles of this document, which was of great intellectual importance for the work of the Dutch group.

[94] The recommendation, as so often in the writings of the Resistance, was that the future League of Nations should be composed of Continental federations (cf. Lipgens, *Föderationspläne*, pp. 21, 210, 230, 243, 279 f., 295, 382); of these the USA, the British Commonwealth, and the Soviet Union were existing examples, and it was supposed that a European federation would soon be followed by one of the South- and Central-American countries and another comprising the countries of the Far East. For Great Britain, which culturally belonged to Europe, a close alliance with a federated Europe was envisaged, but not membership of it so long as Britain saw herself as the keystone of the Commonwealth.

be strong enough to reduce social tensions and solve problems of large-scale development.

'4. The picture of European Unity' (pp. 79–116). To rule out the unacceptable possibility of the hegemony of a single nation, it was 'urgent for the European federation to be based on territorial units of a certain size which could safeguard the balance of power better than the rivalry of large and small states'. Thus about ten subfederations seemed indicated: a Balkan league, a Danubian league, and a league centred on the River Vistula; also leagues for Scandinavia, North-West Europe, France, Prussia with Saxony, the Alps, an Italian and an Iberian league. 'Each group of states would be able to send not more than 30, but not less than 20, deputies to the European parliament.' '5. Thoughts on a European charter' (pp. 116–99) demanded that each group of states, like each of the member countries, should have a free hand in drawing up its constitution and in electing its parliament and government; but European federal law must (1) prohibit dictatorial forms of government of any kind (2) guarantee civil rights and political freedom. The federation would have to have complete authority over foreign policy and the diplomatic service (whereas the consular service would remain subject to the individual states), the armed forces, European citizenship, trade policy and communications, the preservation of unity, and the federal budget. The main authorities would be: 'The President of the United States of Europe, the European parliament ... the cabinet ... the ministers in charge of departments ... the federal supreme court for settling any disputes within the federation.'[95]

'6. The Way through Reality' (pp. 200–51) must be feasible, since the US, which regarded 'the continuing tensions and wars between European nations as simply incredible', could have only one answer: 'At last!'. As for the USSR, 'the neutralization of Europe in the event of tension between the Anglo-Saxon powers and Russia ... would be a guarantee of the safety of the Soviet Union'. Danger threatened from the ranks of the former leaders of the 'nations of the occupied countries who delude themselves that they are on the winning side in this war'; the peoples themselves knew better: 'What failed completely in the past needs more than cosmetic treatment', and we need men who 'are free from the pettiness that allowed our life to become so wretched'.

Some months before the Netherlands were liberated from German occupation, those of the original associates who had not been arrested, Hylkema, Sligting, Salinger, and Verkade, persuaded a courageous notary to sign an affidavit recording the founding of Europeesche Actie with headquarters at The Hague. 'This', it was explained in Article 2 of the document, 'is an inter-European association whose object is to work for the creation of the United States of Europe as a political and economic

---

[95] These original ideas, which 'Hades' reinforced with detailed proposals concerning scope, methods of election, etc., required special interpretation. The idea of a president and 'cabinet of regency' for each group of states (to be elected by a large majority), with the task of 'directing political strategy ... without being burdened by administrative detail', was not afterwards maintained by the group (or anywhere else in the European movement), but is of practical interest for any future planning of a 'European Union'.

unity by all appropriate and morally justified means'.[96] On 15 December 1944 Salinger and Verkade had discussed with the publishing-house of Brill the publication of 'The Rebirth of Europe' in book form in Dutch, French, German, and English, and the issue of a periodical to be called *Europa*. As early as the summer of 1945 Verkade's Dutch translation appeared as Brill's first post-war publication. The manuscript must have circulated before the end of the war and was seen by, among others, a group which met in the house of the banker Jonkheer François W. L. de Beaufort at The Hague to talk over post-war problems. 'Salinger and I were able to win over this group fairly quickly for the ideas in *The Rebirth of Europe*', wrote Verkade.[97] On 22 May 1945, three weeks after the liberation, Beaufort, Sligting, Salinger, and Verkade registered an 'Endowment for the promotion of Europeesche Actie' to provide a financial basis. During the following months a number of new members were acquired, but there was also a good deal of disappointment over the lack of 'renewal'. Priority was given to those who returned from exile, the old party machinery was reinstated, the purge of collaborators proved slow and sluggish, and the economic chaos had to be overcome – altogether it was felt to be a 'difficult period'.[98] The group gained one important advantage towards the end of 1945 when the leading Dutch renewal movement, the 'Nederlandse Volksbeweging', which had been founded in May 1945 by the group in charge of the Resistance newspaper *Je Maintiendrai*, to which Verkade belonged, and which was already on bad terms with the older parties, was undermined by internal dissension. In the elections held early in 1946 it

[96] The actual document of 29.1.1945 could not be traced in the *BEF Archives*, but there is plenty of evidence of its existence: e.g. Article 1 of all later reprints of the Statutes, which formed an essential part of the memorandum of association, runs: 'The Union dates from 29 January 1945'; cf. the pamphlet *De Europeesche Actie*, The Hague, n.d. (*c.* Dec. 1946), p. 6. One copy of 'Statutes of Europeesche Actie' dated 1 May 1945 contains in Article 2, immediately after the sentence just quoted, a short sketch of the programme: to avoid any one group becoming predominant, 'groups of states of approximately the same size' should join to form a 'United States of Europe'; the world organization should consist of 'continents or groups of equal standing'; in the European Federation political rights, 'a single customs and currency area', and 'European civil rights' should be safeguarded (*Verkade Archives*). In the Statutes as they stood from the summer of 1946 onwards we read: 'The principles of Europeesche Actie are laid down in the "Theses" ' (cf. n. 107). There invariably followed: 'Article 3: Europeesche Actie recognizes individual membership and that of organizations. Article 4: Membership is open to citizens of any European country and to any stateless person who lives in Europe . . .'

[97] W. Verkade, 'Bij een oude stichtingsacte' in *Nieuw Europa*, vol. 23, No. 4, 1970, pp. 71–90 (quotation on p. 82, with the additional sentence: 'In particular Jonkheer de Beaufort, who I suppose was at least sixty, remained a true and active member after the Liberation.') The final minutes of the discussion with the Brill publishing house, dated 15.12.1944, with the original signatures, made provision for a payment of 2,000 florins by the publisher and 1,000 each by Salinger and Verkade (*Verkade Archives*). Only the Dutch translation (by Verkade) appeared as *De Wedergeboorte van Europa. De les van dezen Oorlog voor ons Wereldeel (The Rebirth of Europe. The Lesson of this War for our Continent)*, Leiden, 1945, 176 pages. Salinger himself was arrested on 19.3.1945 and identified as the author of the book; but the head of the Gestapo at The Hague, after reading it, spent nights discussing it with Salinger, and, although the death sentence was passed, took him into the woods and set him free. (Information from Salinger, 25.4.1964.)

[98] Information from Salinger, 28.9.1974. Notarial deed of 22.5.1945 establishing an Endowment to promote Europeesche Actie (*BEF Archives*); cf. Verkade (n. 97).

136   Europe's Mood of Resignation

failed to win a single seat.[99] Among those who in these circumstances turned to Europeesche Actie was Dr Henri Brugmans, who wrote later: 'European federalism came to us as a message of liberation ... The national renewal had failed, because it had no chance of success ... We had been mistaken in believing that a democratic revolution can take place in an obsolete framework ... European federalism enabled us to make a new start.'[100] Events soon showed that the European federalist movement had thus acquired a leader of high intellectual powers and outstanding eloquence.

In the autumn of 1945 contact was made with another group representing a somewhat younger generation, which had also been formed at The Hague towards the end of the war. Its main inspiration came from Clarence Streit's *Union Now* and other publications of the British Federal Union. Its name was Federale Unie, and its spokesmen were two lawyers, Dr Hans R. Nord and Dr R. F. Wery. In a duplicated news-sheet called *De Federalist* their aims were described as: 'proclaiming the federal principle as the solution of all international problems; urging that the United Nations Organization should be extended so as to become a world government; urging the European nations to accept the federal solution as soon as possible'.[101] On 28 February 1946 Dr Nord as president of Federale Unie and Dr Salinger as general secretary of Europeesche Actie informed their

---

[99] Cf. *Je Maintiendrai,* Liberation number, May 1945, p. 5: Manifesto of the Netherlands People's Movement, it spoke of 'the need for a radical renewal of our national life' based on 'personalist Socialism' and was signed by the periodical's contributors P. J. Schmidt, H. Brugmans, W. Verkade, and others, as well as by F. J. Goedhart of *Het Parool,* de Quay, Wijffels, and other Catholics; among the thirty-three names was that of Prof. Dr W. Schermerhorn, who on 24.6.1945 became, as a Socialist, the first Dutch post-war prime minister (till 17.5.1946). Failure at the elections: information from Brugmans, 23.4.1964.

[100] H. Brugmans, 'Het begin van een beweging' in *Europa in Beweging,* The Hague (BEF), 1968, p. 12. 'Salinger's proposals, of which Verkade wrote, were attractive to us because they put the German problem in the centre and showed convincingly that there was no solution for it except a united Europe' (ibid., p. 11). Henri J. Brugmans, born at Amsterdam on 13.12.1906, became a Socialist and follower of Jaurès while a student (in Amsterdam and at the Sorbonne). A humanist, patriot and lover of peace, he read Proudhon ('I was a federalist before I was a European'), and obtained a doctorate in French language and literature at Amsterdam University in 1934. Director of the Netherlands Institute for Workers' Education, 1935–40, in 1939 he became a deputy in the Second Chamber for the Socialist SDAP; prisoner in Camp Geisel from May 1942 to 20.4.1944, then worked in the underground with *Je Maintiendrai*; during the war embraced the Catholic doctrines of natural law and subsidiarity; from 24.6.1945 state secretary for press and information under Prime Minister Schermerhorn; in Dec. 1946 president of the UEF; 1947–51, professor of French language and literature at the State University of Utrecht; 1950–72, principal of the Collège d'Europe in Bruges (information from Brugmans, 23.4.1964); see also Index.

[101] The programme was given special prominence by being 'framed' in *De Federalist. Orgaan van 'Federale Unie' in Nederland,* April 1946, ed. G. W. Willems (seventeen pages, hectographed); only this number has survived out of probably several (*Gérard Archives*). It contained a review of E. Reves, *The Anatomy of Peace,* a speech by O. J. Roberts of the American Society for International Law, and an article by an enthusiast for Esperanto. On its origin there is a report by Miss F. L. Josephy: 'On 26th April 1945 the first European Branch of Federal Union was formed – in the Netherlands. We were informed of this in a letter signed G. Westerhuf, C. H. Clemminck and A. Leenhouts' (*Josephy Archives,* Report J, p. 47). Cf. H. Nord (then chairman of the BEF), 'Tien Jaren' in the pamphlet: *BEF, Tien Jaren, 1947–1957.* The Hague, 1957, pp. 7–17, quotation on p. 10.

members in a joint circular that an exchange of views between Nord and Wery on the one hand and Beaufort, Verkade, and Salinger on the other had shown that the two associations 'start from different points but have part of their field of activity in common'. The differences were emphasized at first, but in the end 'it was seen to be possible to arrive at common attitudes by both sides modifying their point of view'.

The starting-point of Europeesche Actie was the statement: 'Europe is in a kind of anarchy.' This and the general impoverishment 'can only be overcome by the creation of a European federation' which at the same time 'would put an end to its powerlessness in face of actual or possible arbitrary behaviour by the three great powers'. The global federation needed to preserve peace 'can only develop soundly if its members are not a collection of large and small countries but political units of approximately equal importance. Only a European federation, an Ibero-American federation etc. will be able to hold their own with the USA, the British Empire and Soviet Russia.'

Federal Unie 'propagates the federal idea throughout the world', 'would like to see the UN extended to become a world federation, and advocates a federation in Europe as an important part of its policy'. Yet it considers it dangerous to start with an impoverished and conquered Continent whose aim must be to win back power, for 'it is possible that a European form of nationalism may thereby be created, which would differ in degree, but not in fundamentals, from the nationalism of the past'.[102]

A 'small committee' was appointed to 'deepen the discussion' and work out proposals 'for the basis on which merger could be arrived at'. It consisted of Nord and Wery on the one hand and Hylkema, Salinger, and Verkade on the other, with Dr Brugmans as the chairman elected by both sides, and it studied the thorny problems with great care at a number of weekly meetings. On 28 March the 'small committee' was able to report that 'all the material collected for the Theses of Europeesche Actie, that is to say Brugmans's and Verkade's drafts ... must be boiled down into a single document', but even as things were there was 'no longer any reason for Europeesche Actie and Federale Unie continuing to exist side by side'. 'The "Theses of Europeesche Actie" draft contains all the ideas which

[102] Joint circular letter of 28.1.1946 from Nord and Salinger to the members of both associations, The Hague, hectographed (*Brugmans Archives*), pp. 1–4. A second discussion on 26.1.1946 was also attended by F. Jas and G. W. Willems, representing Federale Unie, and Dr Brugmans and Pastor Hylkema for Europeesche Actie; here the differences were identified still more clearly. 'The world', maintained Federale Unie, 'under the shadow of the atom bomb cannot take the risk of bringing about a world federation through continental groups only, because this might involve war between them'. At least there must be a simultaneous move to develop the UN into a world federation in order to remove the danger of 'European nationalism'. 'The expectation', Europeesche Actie wrote, 'that in the foreseeable future ... the UN will adopt the federal principle as its own must to some extent be seen as Utopian. ... The struggle for a united Europe is far more realistic than efforts to bring about a world federation'; of course every kind of 'Chauvinism is a symptom of degeneration. The European movement is supposed to provide only the foundation for the development of a healthy European common sense'. Nevertheless, the 'Small Committee' mentioned later was set up to work out 'common attitudes' (ibid., pp. 5–8).

inspire the representatives of Federale Unie, while on the other hand those members of Federale Unie who are present have become convinced that the creation of a federal Europe would form a favourable basis for publicizing the idea of a world government, starting in Europe and proceeding outwards.' 'Committees for the creation of a world government' should be set up in every local branch for those especially interested. Their members would elect similar committees at regional level and to the central committee, whose chairmen would automatically be members of the local regional and central committees, but 'at any rate for this purpose all members of Federale Unie can count as members of Europeesche Actie'. On 30 April 1946 Salinger sent the theses which had been prepared in the meantime, together with the commission's proposals, to the central committees of both organizations and invited them to a joint general meeting on 14 May.[103] At this or a further meeting in June – the records are incomplete at this point, but in any case by the middle of June 1946 the integration of Federale Unie (and also of another association) into Europeesche Actie took place on the basis of the commission's proposals and the Theses, and Dr Brugmans, who had headed the commission so successfully, was elected chairman.

The 'Association for the study of the Future of the Netherlands' *(Neerlands Toekomst)*, which was also absorbed in 1945, called for the annexation of certain North-German territory and was opposed by the EA with the slogan 'Federation, not Annexation'; but the Association's first bulletin in March 1946 had described its aim as 'promoting the idea of a North-West-European Federation'.[104] In the second half of May 1946 (or possibly in August 1945?) Verkade and two other

[103] Letter from Dr Salinger (Europeesche Actie, general secretariat), The Hague, 30.4.1946, to all members of the Central Committee (*Verkade Archives*); the report of the 'Small Committee' enclosed as Appendix I and dated 23.3.1946. Also enclosed as Appendix II the 'Theses', completed in April, and the German translation enclosed as Appendix III with the request that it be approved as 'an authorized statement of principles in the German language' (*Verkade Archives*). It was also announced that 'representatives of the association called Neerlands Toekomst, with which negotiations for merging with Europeesche Actie had reached an advanced stage', had joined the talks (cf. n. 104). The integration of Federale Unie in Europeesche Actie strengthened the commitment to work for a world federation (cf. n. 107); the other point which needs emphasis is the personal unselfishness with which Nord, Wery, etc. agreed to the absorption of their association in the EA. The Theses were printed in *Je Maintiendrai. Weekblad voor Personalistisch Socialisme*, 14.6.1946.

[104] Information sheet, *Neerlands Toekomst, De Lage Landen, Uitgave van het Studiegenootschap Neerlands Toekomst*, No. 1 (probably the only number), Amsterdam, March 1946 (*Verkade Archives*). According to this newspaper their main spokesman was S. J. van Embden; one of the speakers at their meetings was W. Verkade, who acted as the main intermediary. A leading article by Dr P. van der Kooy urged that the Netherlands, Belgium, and Denmark should press for North-West Germany to be reconstituted in such a way that 'the former state of Hanover should be revived and the establishment of an independent Rhineland encouraged. When the time is ripe, one can proceed to establish a federation of North-West European states' of which 'the two Low Countries would form the nucleus' (ibid.). See 'Slogan' in H. Brugmans's retrospect (n. 100), p. 12. It was presumably in opposition to Brugmans's scepticism concerning the division of Germany into different subfederations of the European federation ('I personally have never believed in such an arrangement', ibid., p. 12) that Salinger and Verkade encouraged the accession of this group. (Information from Verkade, 27 Sept., 1974).

Dutchmen, having been entrusted with a fact-finding mission by the Dutch Prime Minister Schermerhorn and War Minister Meynen, spent a fortnight in the British Zone of Germany. Wearing uniform, they drove in a Netherlands army staff car and were accompanied by Salinger and Alfred Mozer in civilian clothes. In Cologne, Hanover, Berlin, Hamburg, and Emden they had long discussions with as many Germans as possible and gained valuable information about the future balance of political forces and the readiness to accept a united Europe.[105] Alfred Mozer's energetic co-operation as a new member of the EA, and soon afterwards as head of the foreign-policy department of the Dutch Socialist Party, meant as much to the EA as the addition of a new group. Salinger, Verkade, Brugmans, Nord, and Mozer were able to proceed to the Hertenstein Conference in complete agreement.[106]

In the light of the Theses which had been so thoroughly worked over, and contained a wealth of detail which cannot be explored here, the policy of the EA can be summed up as follows: As the Theses based their argument on global needs, we have to start with

2. *Europe in the World.* The appalling risks arising from the technology of modern war made it imperative to 'create a legal order valid and effective for all nations'. Now was the time to do this, for 'the risks of transferring sovereign rights to an international organization are insignificant compared with the risks of an atomic war'. Nevertheless, 'the essential prerequisite of a just international order is the creation of a counterpoise against the present trend towards the formation of two steadily growing power groups, which in their rivalry threaten to absorb or crush anyone who is weaker. There would be such a counterpoise if in addition to the existing great powers a European federation, an Ibero-American federation etc. could be formed as equal partners.'

For the sake of its future development Europe must 'seek with great determination to have the UN expanded into a federal organization for the world. It is true that present-day Europe lacks the necessary authority to achieve this purpose. But Europe can only regain this authority by itself setting an example of how the most

---

[105] According to information from Salinger on 25.4.1964 and 28.9.1974 and from Verkade on 27.9.1974, the journey took place in May 1946. Karl Barth and Cardinal Frings were receptive, Adenauer sceptical *vis-à-vis* the European idea; Schumacher nationalistic, the editors of *Die Zeit* especially helpful; cf. W. Verkade, 'Het Europa van het verzet' in *Europa in Beweging*, The Hague (BEF), 1968, p. 9. L. A. V. Metzemaekers, *Alfred Mozer, Uitgave van de Europese Beweging in Nederland* (Festschrift, The Hague, 1970), dates the journey to August 1945; the articles of 9.3.1946 and 9.8.1946 by Mozer on the German question (not available to me) would supply dates and further information.

[106] Alfred Mozer, born in Munich in 1905, the son of a Hungarian immigrant worker, later moved to Kassel where he worked for a Socialist newspaper; from 1925 editor of the SPD newspaper in Emden, elected a member of the town council; opposed Nazism and in 1933 fled to Holland, where he worked in the Amsterdam office for German refugees. He was a member of the Netherlands SDAP and a confidential contact man of Koos Voorrink with the opposition groups in Germany and the Socialist International. During the war lived underground; in 1945 editor of the SDAP weekly *Paraat*; since 1946 senior director of the foreign-policy secretariat of the SDAP; from 1958 to 1970 *chef de cabinet* of Dr Mansholt in the EDC Commission (information from Metzemaekers, n. 105). For his journey to Hertenstein, see chapter II/2.

difficult problems can be solved in practice.' In doing so it must 'avoid any *arrière-pensée* of European chauvinism'.[107]

1. *Design for Europe*. The tradition to which Europe must be loyal 'lies not only in the intellectual sphere, but just as much in the shaping of political and economic life. It is essential to its nature that the "centralizing urge" in favour of uniformity has to be resisted; that the value of personality is respected ...; that the postulate of a domineering society is rejected as much as that of an abstract individualism.' The federalist belief based on this attitude 'shows the only way between regimentation and fragmentation'. That is why on its eastern border Europe ends at the point 'where people begin to treat a person as significant only as part of a collective organization. In the West, Britain belongs unmistakably to Europe in an intellectual and cultural sense', but the initiative for joining a European federation – whose existence was thus clearly postulated – lay with Britain and 'depended on whether her role as the centre of an empire meant more to her than her role as a European country'.

The federation should not be a mixture of large and small states but should consist of (a) areas of considerable size, formed by the smaller countries with close ties combining to form regional federations; (b) the larger German states being reconstructed on a federal basis, because the 'revival of a centralized German Reich would represent a permanent threat to the balance of power in Europe'.[108]

The design was summed up in the last Thesis (No. XI): 'The complete blueprint for the formation of a federation would have to include the following: (a) the creation of a common European currency (b) the introduction of a European citizenship in addition to the legal citizenship of the individual countries; (c) the setting-up of a European parliament as a legislative body (a federal European government was envisaged in Thesis X); (d) the creation of federal European

---

[107] Pamphlet, *Theses of Europeesche Actie*. Six pages with additional material: General Secretariat, The Hague, Nassauplein 19 (office of Dr Salinger; for authorized German translation, cf. n. 103), based on the Dutch original in *De Europeesche Actie,* pamphlet (with the statutes as revised in autumn 1946), The Hague (Dec. 1946), pp. 1–5, containing Theses II, III, V, and VIb (both printed in the *Salinger, Verkade, Schenck and Bernhard Archives,* etc.). The belief held by Federale Unie in the urgency of a federal world organization was fully endorsed and at the same time logically combined with the original viewpoint of EA by the proposition that a European federation was the 'essential prerequisite' and blueprint for a global one. The predominance of the superpowers, which in 1946 was in most quarters a source of discouragement, was thus transformed by EA into a major argument in favour of a federated Europe.

[108] Ibid. (n. 107) These IV, VII, and VIII; IX; only when 'all national aspirations can be fully satisfied as far as culture is concerned' will 'every task which belongs purely to the state be performed within the actual framework of a supranational order'. The demand (as originally put forward in the 'Hades' pamphlet) for a break-up of Germany into various 'sub-federations' evidently remained controversial: the final sentence quoted from Thesis VIII can be interpreted (as by Brugmans, see n. 104) as meaning that a 'decentralised' federation of German states would no longer represent a 'permanent threat': yet in the 'crash programme' proposed by Thesis X (presumably by Salinger, Verkade, and representatives of 'Neerlands Toekomst', cf. n. 104) the 'creation of regional federations, such as the establishment of a North-West European federation, a Scandinavian, Balkan federation, etc.' was revived.

jurisdiction, with the appropriate judicial bodies: (e) the unification of European foreign policy and the co-ordination of the foreign representatives of the European countries.

3. *Plan of Campaign.* The Theses appealed on the one hand to every individual not to increase the danger of anarchy by giving up hope: 'From Christian conviction as well as from a purely human sense of responsibility, everyone must make his own contribution to the political world around him'; but they appealed also to the various governments: 'The European countries must together seize the initiative to develop a plan for the economic and political reconstruction of Europe on a federal basis.' Their special value, however, lay in the fact that Thesis X contained for the first time a catalogue of practical details showing how the process of federalization was to be accomplished.

'Co-ordination of the basic foreign policy of the European countries'; 'creation of a European police force ... to replace the Allied occupation troops in Germany and in the former German vassal states'; 'co-ordination of the economic planning offices of the European countries'; 'federalization of the German state railway as the first step to the setting-up of an all-European state railway'; 'unification of European transport policy'; 'federalization of the fuel resources of the Rhine and Ruhr districts as the first step to a federal administration of the energy resources of the whole of Europe'; 'creation of a common European trade policy within the framework of world trade'; 'unification of the foreign-exchange policy of the European countries'; 'systematic exchange of European university teachers and students; to strengthen Europeans' self-awareness'. Quite apart from the declaration of aims, all this amounted to a detailed and concrete 'emergency programme' based on real needs (followed by the 'further programme' on the formation of a federation in Thesis XI which has already been quoted from).

4. *Purpose and Character of the Organization.* The EA proceeded in a redraft of its statutes to describe itself as an 'inter-Europe association', definitely non-party, whose purpose was 'to promote the creation of a United States of Europe as a political and economic unity'. The individual members of a district (parish or locality) would elect the members of the district committee and appoint the district secretary (who was also responsible for financial aspects); the members of the district committee elected their chairman and his deputy, and representatives of the district committees elected the executive committee for the Netherlands as a whole.

After adopting these revised statutes (which it did in September–October 1946, soon after the Hertenstein conference) the EA regarded itself as the prospective umbrella organization for federalist groups throughout Europe. For this reason a 'central executive' (according to the statutes it was later to be elected by a 'European congress') was envisaged, to which (before the June conference) Dr Brugmans (chairman), Dr Salinger ('general secretary'), Verkade, Dr Nord, van Embden, and four others belonged. The executive of the 'Netherlands Section' consisted at first of eighteen persons including de Beaufort (chairman), Hylkema, and Mozer, and also some from the groups which had been absorbed. The historian J. Meilof Yben (formerly of *Neerlands Toekomst*) was secretary.[109]

5. *Forms of Activity*. EA intends on the one hand 'to popularize the unification of the countries of Europe on a federal basis by means of the press, lectures, conferences, and pamphlets', and on the other hand 'by making contacts with politicians and authorities to promote all inter-European projects in the economic and cultural fields. It also intends to prepare the ground through working parties who will co-ordinate the different interests of the countries of Europe in a wide variety of fields.'[110]

The great merit of this Dutch group was that during the discouraging first post-war year it was the first to react to the disappointing situation with an appropriate response, while continuing to absorb like-minded associations and to work on its programme. 'The same energy as was shown in resisting tyranny must be displayed in the struggle against defeatism', against the passive acceptance of European anarchy and the possibility of a confrontation between the superpowers on European soil. It is this response which accounts for the leading role played by Europeesche Actie during the realignment of the European federalist associations that began in the autumn of 1946.

(E) FEDERAL UNION

Federal Union was founded in Britain in November 1938 by Derek Rawnsley, Charles Kimber, and Patrick Ransome. With a panel of advisers that included such well-known personalities as Lionel Curtis, Lord Lothian, Wickham Steed, and Barbara Wootton, it reached the height of its effectiveness in 1940–1, having grown with astonishing speed (by June 1940 it had 225 branches with 12,000 members) and produced an equally astonishing output of books and pamphlets. The movement's initial publications included Lord Lothian's pamphlet *The Ending of Armageddon*, June 1939, W. B. Curry's *The Case for Federal Union*, issued as a Penguin special in the autumn of 1939, a symposium edited by M. Channing-Pearce entitled *Federal Union*, and L. Robbins's *The Economic Causes of War*,

---

[109] The names are in the pamphlet: *De Europeesche Actie,* The Hague (Dec. 1946), p. 5 f.; the statutes, articles 2–10, ibid., pp. 6–14 (cf. n. 96, version of May 1945). It was also provided that between the national sections and the central committee 'groups of countries', each consisting of several sections, would be formed, corresponding to the proposed European subfederations. When the statutes were revised in Oct. 1947, these and the central committee were dropped, and only one national association was envisaged for what was to be the Netherlands association within the framework of the UEF (cf. chap. III, n. 445 f.).

[110] In the pamphlet already mentioned (n. 109), p. 5. From autumn 1946 onwards there was a drive to attract new members and form new groups etc. 'Working committees' (as provided by Article 11 of the statutes, that is, one for each district and combining to form sectional working committees) were set up for the proposed world federation (cf. n. 103), for the question of Germany etc. (cf. Chap. II/5, nn. 176 and 185). In 1947 *Nieuw Europa* began to appear (as it still does) as a monthly periodical.

Sept. 1939. In this first phase of the movement, the principal theme was that national sovereignty creates 'international anarchy' and war, and that the prevention of war depended upon the establishment of a federal government which could manage common affairs between nations. In this phase, before an Annual Conference met to formulate an official programme on a democratic basis, a 'statement of aims', formulated in the spring of 1939 by eminent members, declared:

> National sovereignty leads to competition in armaments, economic self-sufficiency and internal regimentation, and thus inevitably to war, imperialism, poverty and loss of individual liberty, because where sovereign States fail to agree there is no remedy save resort to violence in the form of power politics or war. No international order based on co-operation between sovereign States will prove either efficient or durable, since all sovereign States in the last resort seek their own national self-interest. Nothing less than a union of the peoples can end this anarchy and give peace, justice and freedom to all.
>
> Accordingly we advocate:
> I. A Federal Union of those nations which hold that the State exists for the freedom and responsibility of man, and that government must be conducted with the consent of the governed.
> II. That this constitutional Union will assure national self-government to all units within the Union in those affairs which are solely of national interest, and will establish legislative, executive and judicial organs representative of and responsible to all the citizens of the Union for such common affairs as defence and order, currency, trade, communications and migration, and will possess the taxation and borrowing powers necessary to finance its own activities.
> III. As a first step a Federal Union of the established democracies to form a nucleus of the future world federation; such a nucleus to be open to accession by other nations which accept its basic principles, and to act as a loyal member of any larger organizations designed to promote international co-operation.[111]

The general formulation in favour of a union of democracies had thus been proposed and defined, though not as yet politically focused upon an area which might actually federate in practice. This gap was soon filled by the work of the Federal Union Research Institute, set up at Oxford in March 1940 under the direction of Sir William Beveridge with Patrick Ransome as Secretary, which suggested that a manageable area for this post-war

---

[111] 'Statement of Aims' printed in Lord Lothian, *The Ending of Armageddon*, London (Federal Union), June 1939, p. 16 f. According to Channing-Pearce, *Federal Union*, London 1940, the statement was formulated by a number of eminent members of Federal Union. On all activities, the numerous meetings etc., detailed information can be found in the Association's periodical *'Federal Union News'* which appeared weekly from May 1940 (the editor from Sept. 1939 to Feb. 1944 was C. Kimber). A selection from all main Federal Union documents and publications, collected by J. Pinder, will shortly be published as part of a Documentary Series dealing with wartime plans for European Union. On the early heyday of Federal Union, with its renewal of the concept of federalism in Britain, a special monograph is needed. The subject is apparently dealt with in chapter 3, 'Federalism and European Unity', of a thesis by N. Forman: written under the supervision of Prof. R. Pryce: *The European Movement in Great Britain 1945–1954* (Dissertation Manuscript, Univ. of Sussex, 1966, 438 pp.), but it is not accessible to the public and I was unable to make use of it.

federation should initially comprise Britain, France, Germany, and the smaller European democracies. The proposal was subsequently developed in a flow of publications printed in 1940, at a time when Barbara Wootton was Chairman of Federal Union's Executive Bureau. Among them were *A Federation of Western Europe* by Ivor Jennings, Sir William Beveridge's pamphlet *Peace by Federation,* and R. W. G. Mackay's book *Federal Europe,* containing a draft constitution, concentrated on a Western-Europe Federation as the nucleus of a future world government. The first Annual Delegates' Conference of Federal Union, held in February 1940, presented a draft programme entitled *'Aims and Policy'*, which was finally adopted by the Federal Union Council on 31 March 1940. This focused on a federation of 'the Allies' with the emphasis on a nucleus of Britain and France, but with the future accession of Germany explicitly foreseen. Thus, while the general goal of the movement repeated the need for a 'common government' of 'free peoples' as a first step towards 'ultimate World federation' and a 'secure peace', the specific policy of Federal Union was formulated as:

1) To work for an Allied Statement of Peace Aims challenging the idea of race superiority with a declaration of the rights of man, and the method of aggression with a declaration of readiness to federate with any people whose government is prepared to recognise these rights.

2) To welcome any steps towards such a federation of the Allies or any other groups of peoples, provided that at the time of its formation the federation is declared open to accession by other nations, including Germany.[112]

A deeper study and further elaboration of this programme was accomplished at regular meetings of the Constitutional, Economic, and Colonial Committees of the Federal Union Research Institute. The results were propagated in *Federal Tracts* published during 1941, when Mackay was Chairman of the Executive Bureau. These included: *Economic Aspects of Federation* by Lionel Robbins; *The Colonial Problem and the Federal Solution* by Norman Bentwich; *What Federal Government is* by K. C. Wheare; *The Philosophy of Federalism* by C. E. M. Joad; *Socialism and Federation* by Barbara Wootton; and *Federation and the Colonies* by Lord Lugard.

This is not the place to describe in detail the heyday of Federal Union (1940–1), which was fertile in enterprising ideas and dynamically effective.

[112] 'Aims and Policy', *Federal Union News,* No. 29, 6 April 1940, pp. 2, 3; reprinted in a leaflet entitled *Federal Union,* with a foreword by Sir William Beveridge, 12 June 1940, London (Federal Union), 1940, p. 3. Of the persons so far named (cf. J. R. Butler, *Lord Lothian,* London, 1960, and J. Harris, *William Beveridge,* Oxford, 1977, esp. pp. 367–70) by far the most important during 1945–50 was Ronald W. G. Mackay, born in Australia in 1902, lecturer in Philosophy, History, and Economics at Sydney University; settled in England as a solicitor in 1934, Labour Party parliamentary candidate, 1935–1942. His book *Federal Europe* (1940) provided the most thoughtful analysis, with a detailed constitutional draft, of a 'United States of Europe' with a close definition of the federation's 'exclusive' and 'concurrent' legislative powers, built around the nucleus of a British–French–German federation. From 1942 to 1945 he worked in the Ministry of Aircraft Production; from 1945 to 1950 he was Labour MP for North-West Hull, in 1950–1 for Reading North; 1947–9 vice-president of the European Parliamentary Union (see also Index); died 1960.

It is a theme which lies outside the scope of this book and deserves a separate study. The *'Aims and Policy'* document with its principles of pooling sovereignty and a federation of nations remained valid for the next decade, but their development and effectiveness were interrupted by the impact of the war. With the collapse of France the movement lost much of its impetus and began to waver about its aims. Kimber wrote in the *Federal Union News* of 22 June 1940: 'Europe is now dominated by the Germans ... We must launch a crusade for the world beyond Hitler ... a union of free peoples.' Britain's complete concentration on the war not only brought leading members of FU, who hitherto had been able to give their time to the association, into government posts (Lord Lothian as ambassador to Washington, Lord Beveridge as chief of the Planning Staff, and Mackay to the Ministry of Aircraft Production); it made it increasingly difficult to divert the public's attention from the war, to resist the tendency to draw a sharp distinction between friendly and enemy nations, and to speak of a future federation that would include Germany. Another trend in Federal Union, caused by the series of defeats on the Continent, dependence on the United States, and growing uncertainty about the future, was revealed in an article published in September 1941 which urged 'the setting up of permanent joint institutions with the United States' and 'preparation for a postwar conference of authoritative representatives from the Commonwealth, the United States and the European nations to discover which nations were prepared to federate with us and to draw up a constitution'.[113]

At Federal Union meetings, where she was the most effective speaker, the Liberal politician Miss F. L. Josephy did her best to dispel these doubts and to prevent the fading-out of a European federation as a practical goal. From August 1941 till September 1945 she succeeded Mackay as Chairman of FU's Executive Bureau. At first she tried to clarify the association's programme by setting up a 'Peace Aims Committee' to which she, Kimber, Joad, and Zilliacus belonged.[114]

---

[113] Article (probably by Kimber) in *Federal Union News*, No. 71, 13.9.1941; this and the preceding facts quoted from: *Josephy Archives*, Report J., pp. 5–11, a collection of material written about 1970 by Miss F. L. Josephy on the history of FU from 1938 to 1948. Questions were even asked in the House of Commons, where in Nov. 1941 Churchill was asked by Sir W. Smithers 'whether, in view of the fact that the declared policy of the organization known as Federal Union is to surrender sovereign powers to a federal government, he will take the necessary steps to stop the activities of FU as being inimical to our war effort'. Churchill answers: 'I am advised that the activities of this body have not so far called for such action as the Honourable Member suggests.' The Home Secretary, Herbert Morrison, replied to a similar question in Dec. 1941 that the special powers conferred on him were not intended 'to be used for the purpose of restricting the expression of opinion' on a matter of 'improving the organization of international co-operation after the war' (ibid., p. 14).

[114] Miss F. L. Josephy, born about 1910, studied French and German language and literature; as a member of the Liberal Party she was a British delegate (often the only one) at meetings of the Liberal International in the inter-war years and thus became acquainted with Continental problems. Between 1939 and 1959 she was a Liberal parliamentary candidate six times; she joined FU after attending a Liberal Summer School in Aug. 1939 at which P. Ransome explained its principles, and a FU meeting in Hampstead where Joad and Brailsford did the same. Because of her

Yet the *'Peace Aim – War Weapon'* report subsequently submitted to the main Annual Conference in Easter 1942 remained an evident compromise between the two emerging wings in Federal Union, as Josephy and Joad pressed for an emphasis upon European federation plans, while Kimber and Zilliacus insisted upon the overall confederal world order into which regional federations should be fitted. Thus, although the initial part of the report seemed to indicate a consensus in favour of a federal rather than a confederal order as the best theoretical form for combination between states, at a practical level the overriding need for a broader 'intergovernmental' approach was also conceded. Hence the report started from the assumption that 'Experience of confederations in general and of the League in particular has proved that the only effective form of international government is supranational government – that is, a federal government to which the member States have surrendered jurisdiction over certain specifically defined matters, and which is elected by, responsible to, and has a direct claim on the loyalty of the citizens of the federating States' but that at a global level not all states at the end of the war would be ready for federation. Accordingly, 'a World Confederation containing a Federation of Democracies' was proposed (a confederation being defined as 'an association or league of independent States which have signed a treaty pledging them to co-operate for certain purposes; such co-operation is through conferences of government delegates'). Similarly, the report at first repeatedly stressed that a 'Federation of Democracies' was the 'distinctive proposal' in the plan and would serve as the 'distinctive contribution' to a general peace, since as one unit it would form the 'most important part' of the broader confederation. But the text as a whole clearly gave weight to the proposal for a new world order and stressed that a federal initiative should not take place independently or outside of the overall confederal design: 'It will be seen that the world government envisaged after the war comprises two essential features: (1) a Federal Union of Democracies; (2) the World Confederation of States of which it would be the nucleus. Both must be established as parts of a single treaty.'[115]

---

gifts as a speaker, using only the briefest notes, she was elected to the executive office in May 1940 and soon became a speaker at almost all meetings arranged by FU. From 1941 to 1946 she was employed as a lecturer by the British army. In one of her first speeches for FU on 16.5.1940 she said: 'If you can make the separate interests of Germany, France and Britain the common interest of all the three, war in Western Europe is finished for all time. The structure that we want to build ... is a federation which will include the democracies and a de-Nazified Germany. (*Josephy Archives*, Report J., p. 4a, and information from Miss Josephy on 30.11.1974).–Cyril Edwin M. Joad, born at Durham on 12.8.1891, was from about 1920 to 1930 an official in the Labour Exchange Department of the Board of Trade; from 1930 head of the Philosophy Department at Birkbeck College, London; from 1939 a member of the Executive Office of FU, 'British Brains Truster No. 1', and in 1945 Professor of Philosophy at the University of London. His books included *Decadence* (1948) and *The Recovery of Belief* (1952); he died on 9.4.1953.

[115] In this compromise form, the report was passed by the FU General Meeting on 28 March 1942 and subsequently published as a leaflet entitled: *Federation: Peace Aim – War Weapon – The Peace Aims Report of Federal Union issued with the authority of the Annual General Meeting held at Easter 1942,* June 1942 (sixteen pages), distributed with *Federal News,* No. 88. The report in addition stressed that several federations were envisaged within the World Confederation, namely: a European Union (including Britain), an American Union (possibly embracing Australia), a Far-Eastern Union and a Eurasian Union (the USSR). The final goal was the transformation of the World Confederation into a World Federation, though, as the report also stressed: 'Meanwhile, it is not the least of the merits of the "combined" system of world-government, that is an "open" Democratic Federation as an integral part of a World Confederation, that it is extremely flexible. It permits of all sorts of half-way houses and intermediate arrangements between Federation and Confederation, in accordance with circumstances and the desire of the States concerned.'

Meanwhile, on a proposal by Miss Josephy, an 'International Bureau' was added to the Executive Bureau for the purpose of making contacts with groups of federalists in other countries, a 'European Committee' being attached to the Bureau as a subcommittee. On this committee in 1942–3 there sat, besides Miss Josephy as chairman, exiled politicians from sixteen European countries including the Belgian General M. de Baer, Císař and Vojaksch of Czechoslovakia, Eyriey and J. Métadier of France, Gottfurcht and Westphal (= H. A. Kluthe) of Germany, Gardini and Luzatto of Italy, Kronsten and Szapiro of Poland, and others. This committee produced in July 1943 two memoranda which recommended continued support for European federation as a matter of urgency.

The Memorandum on Foreign Policy stated: 'We recognize that supranational government will not be possible on a world scale or even for all the United Nations, but we believe that it should apply to the European Council proposed by the Prime Minister... The European Council, if it is to be successful, must be a legislature whose decisions have constitutional authority... a European government with definite but limited power.' According to the second memorandum 'Tomorrow's world will be centred around two mains poles of attraction: the USA and the USSR ... A divided Europe would be a mere toy between these two giants. Only a *united* Europe can hope to make her voice heard tomorrow...'[116]

Federal Union's annual general conference in August 1943, at which Miss Josephy was able to announce that the number of members had stabilized (moving up slightly from 2,810 at the end of 1941 to 3,131 at the end of 1942, with 130 branches), took favourable note of both memoranda, but no resolution was passed. The European Committee with Miss Josephy in the chair drafted a resolution in the form of a request, but in more pressing language: 'FU should encourage the establishment of any federations and international organizations which tend to lead to ultimate world federation.' Kimber resigned as editor of *Federal Union News*, which since the middle of 1942 had appeared monthly, and Miss Josephy herself took over the editorship of the periodical, which was renamed *Federal News* in March 1944 and kept this title until after 1950. It published a series of articles on the French and Italian Resistance urging the formation of a federal Europe: 'Underground Europe is asking for it, but a lead from Britain is essential.' Against the wishes of a bare majority of the Executive Bureau, from which Curry, Wootton, Ransome, and Kimber immediately resigned, Josephy as chairman sent a memorandum to all members of the next annual general conference describing the choice that lay before them:

[116] Memorandum 'On Foreign Policy' and another memorandum, 'Federation and the Four Freedoms', which in other respects, especially in its concern for Freedom from Want, recommended a more markedly Socialist policy: 'A central economic plan must direct economic life in the whole federation. The federation itself must have sufficient control of the key industries' (*Josephy Archives*, Report J. List of members of the 'European Committee', p. 26 f.; the memoranda, p. 27, f.).

FU can say (a) that, because world federation is not practicable at the end of this war, FU has no political function and must become a purely educational organization, or (b) that WF is not possible at the end of the war, but that if it is ever to be attained the loose world organization that will have to be set up must be able to function ... Twice in 25 years a war has broken out in Europe; Europe is at a point of development at which its people can elect a Federal Parliament; therefore ... the immediate job of FU must to be press with every means in its power for the inclusion in the postwar settlement of a provision setting up a European Federation, open to accession by other nations, as the most urgent first step to World Federation.

At the annual general conference on 23 and 24 September 1944, following a searching debate, a resolution to amend Federal Union's basic guide-lines was proposed by Philip Edwards, a member of the Executive since July 1939, supported by Mackay, Joad, John Parker MP, and others, and passed by a two-thirds majority. The amendment embodied the following statement of objectives:

'(a) World Federation as the long-term aim; (b) educating the public in the meaning of and need for federation; (c) immediate aim the promotion of a democratic federation of Europe as part of the postwar settlement.'[117]

This decision, which cleared away many doubts, was conveyed to all members in a personal letter from the re-elected chairman headed 'Clearing the Decks for Action'. The work of the association thereupon took on a new lease of life with a series of meetings to publicize what a FU report for 1944 described as 'really practical policy'. It began with a meeting at Caxton Hall, Westminster, on 30 November 1944, billed as 'United Europe – the Key to Peace'. An audience of 1,300 heard Tom Horabin, MP, Lord Huntingdon, Professor Joad, Miss Josephy, and Commander Stephen King-Hall expound the need for Europe to form a federation including Britain. A new series of booklets with the same message was started.[118] The series of meetings continued until the summer of 1945. The annual general conference of 29–30 September 1945 declared that: (a) the

[117] All facts and quotations from *Josephy Archives,* Report J., pp. 30–6. The value of this resolution lay in its rejection of the illusory belief in the progressive character of the policy of the Big Three and in the endorsement of the principles developed by the FU, including their practical application to Europe despite the absence of Allied support at that date (1944).
[118] *Josephy Archives,* Report J., pp. 37–41. The FU Report for Sept.–Oct. 1944, referring to the renewed acknowledgement of a European federation as an 'immediate objective', stated that 'There had been an encouraging response both inside and outside the movement, and a number of well-known people who had thought FU was too Utopian decided to join' (ibid., p. 37). A number of new publications appears, including F. L. Josephy, *Europe – the Key to Peace.* London, Oct. 1944 ('Europe, containing 27 separate sovereign states, presents the greatest danger area. . . . For the sake of our own security, as well as for the sake of world peace, we must have a government which will be ready and anxious to join with the new governments of Europe in creating a democratic European Federation'). Other new publications were *Federal Union, Federation – Target for Today,* London, Nov. 1944 ('The future of Europe as a whole can be safeguarded only within the framework of a federation which includes Britain, France and all other democracies'); and *Federal Union, Resistance Speaks,* London, May 1945 (an impressive collection of statements from the French, Italian, etc. Resistance urging a federation of Europe, including the Geneva Declaration, cf. n. 56 above, and the Resolution of the Paris Federalists' Conference, see n. 82 above).

existence of the atom bomb underlined 'the imperative need for a World Federal Government' and that (b) 'the advocacy of a democratic federation in Europe is part of Federal Union policy'.[119] In the light of this, FU's policy may be defined as follows:

1. *Design for Europe*. The undisputed conviction of Federal Union was that peace and welfare could be ensured only by a federation of nations, as the failure of mere co-operation as tried by the League of Nations had shown. The first official programme, 'Aims and Policy', adopted by Federal Union at its first annual conference in 1940, formulated the following clear list of powers which should be exercised by the 'common Federal Government': 'The Federation would control foreign policy, Armed Forces and armaments. It would have substantial powers over tariffs, currency, migration, communications and similar matters. It would also have power to ensure that colonies and dependencies were administered in the interests of the inhabitants and not for the benefit of any particular country.'[120] From 1941 to 1944 there was controversy about whether to aim in the first instance for a federal Europe as an essential step towards a wider federation. In September 1944 this course was confirmed and given detailed justification:

European Federation is needed primarily for five reasons: (i) as a framework for Germany; (ii) as the only way of preventing the smaller European states from endangering peace because they cannot defend themselves against potentially predatory neighbours; (iii) to prevent a clash between the Great Powers of East and West over backing rival ideologies in Europe; (iv) to give Europe a common voice in world affairs and make a common contribution to world defence; (v) to raise living standards by supra-national planning.[121]

A report from the 'Federal Power Committee' adopted by the annual general conference in August 1943 had defined the minimal powers required by a federal

---

[119] Report of the Annual General Meeting, 29 and 30 Sept. 1945 in *Federal News*, No. 128, Nov. 1945, p. 12. This basic programme then remained unchanged until 1950 and even later. Cf. nn. 130 and 131 for a falling-off in the number of meetings in the second half of 1945 and 1946, and for further resolutions passed by the AGM of 30.9.1945 etc.

[120] Official programme of Federal Union *Aims and Policy*, see footnote 112. It was entirely in this spirit that, for example, at a Brains Trust held in London on 12.3.1945, the FU point of view was explained by Prof. Joad, Miss Josephy, and Sir Walter Layton as 'the people of each federating state elect two sets of Members of Parliament – one to the home parliament to deal with matters of purely national concern such as housing, health services and marriage laws; the other to the Federal Parliament to deal, in conjunction with the other members from all the other federating states, with matters of common concern to all the peoples, such as control of armed forces, foreign policy and trade relations' (quoted from *Federal News*, No. 122, April–May 1945, p. 10).

[121] Leading article (probably by Josephy) in *Federal News*, No. 116, Oct. 1944; cf. the texts quoted in nn. 116 and 117. At the Brains Trust on 12.3.1945 it was stated: 'Great Britain dare not stand out, for her own safety . . . Germany should be invited to join the Federation as soon as the German people are in a position to elect their members to the Federal Parliament, and as soon as she can genuinely accept and maintain the Charter of Rights . . . Unfortunately we cannot wait until Socialism is adopted by every nation before setting up an organization to prevent war, even if Socialism in itself were a means of preventing war, which does not necessarily follow. Socialist solidarity up to now has never stood the test of war.' (*Federal News*, No. 122, April–May 1945, pp. 10 and 12).

government as follows: 'A Federal Judiciary, with Courts of First Instance in the federated states and a Federal Supreme Court', would be responsible for 'maintenance of the political rights set out in the Federal Charter' and would decide cases of dispute, but 'there must be individual right of appeal'. The Federal Parliament would have oversight of defence forces and of the 'Federal Police Force', and would decide basic questions of foreign policy; it would supervise the Federal Government in its handling of economic policy and would introduce a 'common second language, to be taught compulsorily in all schools in the Federation from the earliest stages'.[122]

2. *Europe in the World.* FU always emphasized the fact that it was a European federation as an integral part of a future world federation and, meanwhile, as an essential contribution to the organization of world peace. In a telegram to Eden on 21 April 1945 the Council stated that FU 'strongly urges the formation of a democratic federation of European countries as a first step to ultimate world federation. We believe this will prove the only basis for European reconstruction and will eliminate the danger of future wars breeding in Europe.'

The Federal Union Brains Trust was realistic and more specific: 'Federalists have never suggested that federation will prevent war except within the area federated. That is why their ultimate objective remains World Federation. European Federation is proposed merely as the first necessary step ... But the world organization, which for many years to come can probably be nothing better than a League, will have a greater chance of functioning if the great powers on whom it mainly rests are not torn asunder by European quarrels leading to world war.'[123]

3. *Plan of Campaign.* This for FU was always strictly democratic. 'Federal Union will be achieved only by the power of public opinion. There are too many vested interests concerned for it ever to be offered from the top.' When the next general elections were held after the war 'it will be for those

---

[122] It was stated that the Federal Government would need the following Departments:
1) Foreign Office
2) Ministry of Defence
3) Ministry of Justice
4) Ministry of Internal Security
5) Ministry of Education (... to control the teaching of ... federal civics ...; Federal Universities ...)
6) Ministry of Trade
7) Ministry of Planning
8) Ministry of Communications
9) Mandates Board
10) Ministry of Finance (... to raise taxes to pay for the federal forces ...)

See Report of the Federal Powers Committee (set up on 11.9.1942 with Prof. Joad, Keeton, Kimber, and Josephy), printed in *Federal Union News*, No. 101, July 1943.

[123] Telegrams to Eden quoted in *Josephy Archives*, Report J., p. 46 f. Cf. the quotations in nn. 116, 117, and 121 ('To give Europe a common voice in global questions'). At the Federal Union's Brains Trust (quoted from *Federal News*, No. 122, April–May 1945, p. 11), members of the audience asked if the Soviet Union was to be included in the United States of Europe; Lord Strabolgi, in a first reply, said Yes; but the chairman of the FU, Miss Josephy 'did not think that Russia should, or would wish to, be included, as she already is a federation of states and her economy is based on a system totally different from anything European' (ibid., p. 9). As for the Dominions, they 'would decide for themselves whether they wished to become members of the European Federation because Britain was a member, or whether for defence and economic planning they would prefer to be attached to some other world unit. In any case the loose organization known as the Commonwealth would still be bound together by its present ties' (ibid., p. 12).

who believe that federation is necessary for the winning of the peace to ensure that only federal-minded M.Ps. are returned to Parliament'.[124]

After having sought and obtained by means of general elections a general mandate to ratify the draft federal treaty as an integral part of the peace treaty setting up a World Confederation, the national parliaments and governments concerned should put into practice the Federal 'Constitution' which would be based upon 'democracy, social justice and racial equality', along with a 'Charter of Rights', a 'common democratically elected Parliament and a common government', and a 'single defence system'.[125]

4. *Purpose and Character of the Organization.* Great stress was laid in FU policy on the principle of educating the public so as to form a mass movement transcending party ties, with such influence on the electorate that as many federal-minded MPs as possible would be elected to parliament. The annual general meeting, at which every branch was represented in proportion to its number of members, met for a weekend in the autumn (usually with about a hundred persons present), decided on the broad lines of policy, and elected new members of the National Council of thirty-one as vacancies occurred through death or retirement. The National Council met two or three times a year between the annual general meetings, decided what course to take on important political issues, and managed the financial side; it also elected from its own ranks the real governing body, the Executive Committee of twelve which met every fortnight to take practical decisions within the framework laid down by the guide-lines.[126]

These decisions were prepared by two committees, one for finance and general purposes with de Peyer as chairman, the other for meetings and publicity with Miss Newlands in the chair. Other members of the National Council sat on these committees, for example Ota Adler on the former and Professor Joad on the latter. Other committees were set up as necessary:

[124] Federal Union's Brains Trust. ibid., p. 13. 'It has never been suggested that the European Federation could be set up all at once. The first stage should be a union of the existing democracies; the second, the adherence to that Union of the other European states as they become democracies; the third stage will be the incorporation of Germany when she too has a democratic government' (ibid., p. 11).
[125] Official programme of Federal Union (1942) *Federation: Peace Aim – War Weapon,* see n. 115.
[126] Cf. reports on the Annual General Meeting in *Federal News*; complete collection of minutes of all meetings of the National Council and the Executive Committee in *Federal Union Archives* (with the help of which a detailed history of the association could be written). At the AGM in Sept. 1945 Miss Josephy announced her resignation as chairman of the executive 'as she could no longer afford to spend practically every day in the office as full-time voluntary chairman' (*Josephy Archives*, Report J., p. 50). Philip Edwards was elected as the new chairman; he had been a member of the executive and secretary of the organization since July 1939. The executive from autumn 1945 onwards was composed as follows: P. Edwards (chairman), S. F. Sheridan (deputy chairman), R. B. Bucknell and Monica Wingate (*ex officio* chairman and deputy chairman of the National Council), E. E. V. de Peyer (*ex officio* hon. treasurer of the National Council), Miss F. L. Josephy (editor of *Federal News* and chairman of the International Bureau), Keith Killby (the new secretary), the newly elected MPs John Hare, Col. E. M. King, and H. C. Usborne, also Cmdr. Innes Hamilton and Miss H. M. L. Newlands (cf. minutes of the executive, 7.12.1945 at the House of Common, *FU Archives*).

e.g. between January and July 1945 there was an elections committee for questioning and influencing the views of all parliamentary candidates, and so on. In addition, in 1945 as a successor to the FU Research Institute an independent 'Federal Research and Educational Trust' was formed.[127]

5. *Forms of Activity*. These were briefly summarized in a circular letter sent out by Miss Josephy for the new phase of Federal Union which began in October 1944: 'large public meetings, press advertising, a parliamentary pressure group, by-election activity, preparation for the forthcoming general election, co-operation with other national or international bodies with similar objects,' etc. *Federal News*, FU's monthly periodical, was important as a means of keeping the association united; it made forceful comments on political events from a federalist point of view, as did pamphlets in so far as financial resources, derived wholly from members' contributions, made possible their publication.[128]

A special source of strength for FU was its public meetings, organized not only in the British fashion with several speakers, but mostly in the form of brains trusts: with a neutral chairman, two speakers for Federal Union would debate against two more or less anti-federalist invited MPs on questions put to them by the audience.[129]

For years FU had emphasized the need for a federation of nations, and since 1944 it had once more explicitly made a federation of Europe its immediate aim. It is not surprising that for a number of reasons the association was in the doldrums in the second half of 1945: the lack of any prospect of this aim being realized in the foreseeable future in a Europe occupied and divided by the two superpowers, the relative ineffectiveness of Federal Union's attempt to influence the 1945 general election, and finally the renewed awareness that they were a tiny minority. Another disadvantage was that Miss Josephy herself was away for several months

[127] For Subcommittees, cf. for example the minutes of the executive of 5.10.1945, p. 3. For the re-establishment of a 'Federal Research and Educational Trust', especially thanks to the co-operation of Mackay and the services of D. W. Sanders (member of the National Council for South-West England and first trustee), cf. the minutes of the Council of 13.1.1945, p. 3 (decision that the Trust should be financially independent with its own office etc.). Revision of the 'federal tracts' and new federalist publications, in which P. Ransome and C. Kimber were again to co-operate, were planned (cf. minutes of the executive meeting of 7.12.1945, p. 2; all in *FU Archives*).
[128] Josephy, 'Clearing the Decks for Action', quoted from summary in *Josephy Archives*, Report J. p. 41. According to the minutes of the executive meeting of 7.12.1945 Jack Fidler (temporary editor of *Federal News* in the absence of Miss Josephy, see n. 130) was anxious to bring the number of copies printed to 10,000; hence the total must have been somewhat less. New publications were also discussed: 'Policy Leaflet', a revised edition of 'Questions and Answers', and a new pamphlet explaining federation (*Federal Union Archives*). For the number of members, cf. p. 147 in this chapter and n. 86 of chap. II.
[129] For example H. M. L. Newlands, 'Fun with the "Brains" ', in *Federal News*, No. 122, April–May 1945, pp. 9–13; at this meeting of 13.2.1945 Leslie Mitchell, a member of FU and 'well known to film-goers as chief British Movietone News commentator', acted as chairman. B. Baxter, a Conservative MP, Lord Strabolgi (Labour), Sir W. Layton, Prof. Joad, and Miss Josephy took part in the discussion. Summer Schools for members, lasting between one and three weeks, were also influential; they were resumed in the summer of 1946, according to Council minutes of 27.4.1946.

and it took time for the other members of the executive to replace her effectively. In October a mass meeting that had been planned had to be cancelled 'owing to the difficulty of obtaining speakers'.[130] Yet in September Miss Josephy herself had shown how the association, despite the temporary frustration of attempts to form a European federation, could point to the unleashing of atomic energy as a reason for urging the case for a world federation even more strongly: 'EF, though still an essential part of the whole, is no longer enough even as a first step, WF, far from being a utopian dream, becomes at one jump a practical necessity. The atom is a world force, and a world organization is needed to control it.' Accordingly, the annual general meeting at the end of September 1945 underlined as 'a re-statement of Federal Union policy ... the imperative need for a world federal government' as well as 'the advocacy of a democratic federation in Europe'.[131] By restoring equal weight to both aims the Executive Bureau was able to get the organization moving again in December 1945, to assign new tasks to new members, to win back former members, and gradually to reactivate the programme of meetings for both objectives in 1946. This was the position when, from the autumn of 1946 onwards, the revival of Continental federalism brought the European objective back into the foreground, while, in February 1948, the Communist coup in Prague ended all present hope of establishing a world federation.[132]

---

[130] In the election campaign of June–July 1945 every candidate was to be asked: '1. Are you in favour of a United States of Europe? 2. If elected, are you prepared to advocate the establishment of a democratic federation of Europe, including this country, as part of the new world order?' – but the results were clearly disappointing. Only nine FU members sat as 'federalist M.P.s' in the new House of Commons: Boyd Orr, Gruffydd, Horabin, Mackay, Parker, Scolefield Allen, Usborne, Zilliacus, and John Hynd (*Josephy Archives*, Report J., pp. 47 and 51; cf. n. 87 to chap. II on the growth of this group). Miss Josephy, already in June and July busy as prospective parliamentary candidate for Devizes, was 'abroad lecturing to the Forces' between Nov. 1945 and May 1946, first with British troops in Italy, then in Ceylon, Singapore, and India, finding genuine interest everywhere in the idea of federation (ibid., p. 51, f.). The results of the October meeting are given in the minutes of the executive of 5.10.1945, p. 2 (*FU Archives*).

[131] Josephy in *Federal News*, No. 126, Sept. 1945, p. 1; AGM resolution of 30.9.1945 in *Federal News*, No. 128, Nov. 1945, p. 12. Perhaps Miss Josephy herself believed for a time that reason would prevail in the sphere of world politics: 'In a few years', she wrote in *Federal News*, No. 127, Oct. 1945, 'if not in a few months, at least all the Great Powers will have found out the secret for themselves. If we and America offer it to them now with World Federation ... as a quid pro quo, the price paid will be a million times worth the sacrifice ...' A memorandum of the 'European Committee of Federal Union', of which she was the chairman, demanded direct election of the UN General Assembly so as to be able to control a Security Council which would have atomic weapons at its disposal (Report J., p. 51). Yet in view of the unwillingness of the superpowers to act, this demand soon became for her, as it did for the majority of the executive bureau, simply another tactical move in order to leave the world federalists some scope inside FU. (Information from Miss Josphy, 30.11.1974).

[132] Between the autumn of 1945 and 1947 the bulk of the membership and of those who attended the annual general meetings were no doubt world federalists of unimpeachable goodwill; but the most intelligent and active members (such as Bucknell, Joad, Miss Josephy, Mackay, and Killby) considered it futile to hope that the United Nations would develop into a world government, and urged that a start be made with what was possible, a federation of Western Europe (information

3. Britain's Aloofness under the Labour Government

'The establishment of a European federation will depend above all on the good will and intelligence of the political leaders of the individual countries.' This was one of the conclusions drawn by Spinelli from the fact that neither did the Allies on their arrival provide for the future unification of Europe under its reinstated national governments, nor did the potential leaders of a supranational federation with influence on those governments emerge from the Resistance. All the associations described in the preceding chapter were nevertheless, as can well be imagined, so convinced of the rationality of their diagnosis of the causes of the collapse of Europe, the common nature of the material problems facing the whole continent, and the overwhelming case for a federal solution, that they assumed that the majority of those competent to judge would come to a similar conclusion and would act accordingly.

In the following sections the countries of Western Europe will be considered in terms of the question: What view did the political leaders, parties, and governments in each country take of the idea of European unification? Having looked at the upper stratum of international politics and also at the lower level on which the associations presented an alternative policy for Europe, the middle stratum of leadership within the individual nations must now be examined. In doing so we must particularly notice what differences existed between them in spite of their common destiny, and how far such differences formed an obstacle and a handicap to the policy of European federation.[133] In the situation of 1945–6 there was no doubt from the outset that only the support of the British and/or French governments, the only European governments whose opinion still counted for anything at that time, could have kept alive the thought of European unification and brought it to the attention of the superpowers. Neither the defeated Axis powers, waiting for a dictated peace, nor the smaller states, but Britain, still officially one of the 'Big Three', and France, now accepted

---

from Ota Adler, 8.10.1974). – With this section on Federal Union all the fully organized pro-European groups of any importance that existed in 1945 have been introduced to the reader. A number of smaller groups are mentioned in later sections of the book, where the attitudes of the governments and parties in each country are briefly described. Similar trends in Germany did not lead to the formation of associations in the first post-war year because of the incomparably greater losses suffered by German Resistance groups and the disapproval of the occupying powers: cf. section 5 of this chapter, p. 243.

[133] For Spinelli's words quoted in the preceding paragraph cf. n. 57. It will be appreciated that the following country studies will necessarily concentrate more on the differences in the basis of their foreign policy than on the similarity of conditions due to their common defeat, of which enough has been said; and that attention will be focused on their attitudes to the idea of European unity rather than on their diplomacy as a whole. Once the archives are open specialized studies will be needed to do justice to the complexity of the material available for research. As the various governments were preoccupied until the spring of 1947 with the most urgent tasks of reconstruction and did not pursue the idea of a united Europe, the survey will take in rather more than the first post-war year and will for the most part apply to the period up to April 1947. Cf. chapter III, Section 2, p. 488 f.

as an occupying power in Germany thanks to Churchill's efforts at Yalta and ranking since May 1945 as a permanent member of the Security Council, really bore the main responsibility for Europe at that crucial period.

(A) CONDITIONS AFFECTING BRITISH POLICY IN EUROPE IN 1945

Britain's policy towards Europe from 1945 onwards had to start from three main premises, of which British public opinion was well aware. They were much discussed, and, as will be shown, people reacted by drawing markedly differing conclusions. The premises were as follows:

1. Within the wartime alliance of the Big Three, the longer the war lasted (and even more after it was over) Britain's political importance was clearly in decline compared with the United States and the Soviet Union. The 'parity of status' with America which Britain had struggled to preserve during the inter-war years had progressively changed into a junior partnership as a result of her long dependence on America for economic and military aid. In the great strategic and political decisions Britain, in view of the increasing power of both the major allies, had been unable to press her own policy where it differed from theirs but in practice had been obliged to submit to the policies of both the USA and the USSR as reconciled by Roosevelt. During the war Commonwealth ties had been loosened as Canada, Australia, and New Zealand learnt to depend on the United States and India had to be promised independence. The question was whether Britain, supported by her African empire and other Commonwealth territories, would be able to continue playing the part of a third world power or if she would have to accept relegation to the role of a purely European power.[134]

A memorandum for the Prime Minister headed 'Stocktaking after VE Day', written on 11 July 1945 by O. G. Sargent, who was shortly afterwards promoted by Bevin to be his Permanent Under-Secretary of State, shows that some people

[134] The state of historical work on British policy towards Europe from 1945 onwards presents a similar picture to that of European post-war history in general. As far as later years are concerned, when attitudes had begun to crystallize – e.g. between 1957, when Britain changed her mind about the EEC, and her first application for entry in 1961 – there are already a number of excellent studies (notably by M. Camps, H. Schneider, R. Pfaltsgraff, R. J. Lieber, and others); but hardly anything has yet been published on the early period when British foreign policy-makers, political parties, and others were first coming to grips with the idea of European union. The only specialist study which seeks to deal with the subject from 1945 onwards (H. Heiser, *British Policy with regard to the Unification Efforts on the European Continent*, Leiden, 1959) contains only some of the relevant documents – with substantial gaps between them for the years 1945–50 (with incorrect dates, for example, on pp. 23 and 30) – and becomes more detailed only for the 1950s. Existing accounts of British foreign policy between 1945 and 1950 make a point of studying relations with other countries such as the USA and the USSR, but mention questions of European unity only in passing (the same is true of the books mentioned in n. 135). The most comprehensive treatment of Bevin's foreign policy to date is M. A. Fitzsimons, *The Foreign Policy of the British Labour Government 1945–1951*, Notre Dame, Indiana, 1953.

in the Foreign Office were aware of the decline in British power, but that others regarded this interpretation as false. The memorandum urged maintenance of co-operation between the three Great Powers, which in principle was also desired by the USA and the Soviet Union; 'but the fact remains that in the minds of our big partners, especially in that of the United States, there is a feeling that Great Britain is now a secondary Power and can be treated as such'. Sargent called this 'a misconception which it must be our policy to combat'. But in the next sentence he virtually admitted it to be a fact and urged that Western Europe should be included to strengthen Britain. 'Because we are numerically the weakest and geographically the smallest of the three Great Powers, it is essential that we should increase our strength in not only the diplomatic but also the economic and military spheres. This clearly can best be done by enrolling the Dominions and especially France, not to mention the lesser Western European Powers, as collaborators with us in this tripartite system. Only so shall we be able in the long run to compel our two big partners to treat us as an equal.' Two weeks earlier Oliver Harvey, whom Bevin was soon to make his Deputy Under-Secretary of State, had come to the same conclusion: 'Faced by such prospects it seems common sense for us, if not a necessity, to get the French to co-operate with us on the most intimate terms. By standing together, we neither of us sacrifice anything. Nor can France stand alone without declining to secondary status. We had hoped indeed to combine with her in organizing a Western Regional Group based on an Anglo-French alliance.' But he had at once pointed out the main obstacle: 'Because of de Gaulle and Syria, however, this has never materialized ... without going into the past, it is clear that we cannot hope ever to reach satisfactory relations with France while he is in power.'[135]

2. The problem of chaos on the Continent could not be solved by washing one's hands of it. As one of the most respected politicians in Britain, Sir Walter Layton, put it: 'The anarchic politics of Europe have led to two world wars. It is vital, not only to Europe, but also to the world that this anarchy should cease.' At the outset, admittedly, 'peace will be preserved by the authority of the Big Three. But this is a very provisional measure both for the policeman and for those who are policed. The great powers have other fish to fry, and a Europe which is not her own guardian will never be truly free. A beginning must be made with the task of preparing the European authority to whom responsibility for security can be handed over.' Otherwise Europe would inevitably become the object of division

---

[135] *Public Record Office,* Prem. 4, 31/5, O8851: O. G. Sargent 11.7.1945 ('Stocktaking after VE-Day', p. 320); FO 371, 49068/05354: O. Harvey 26.6.1945 (p. 208). See also E. L. Woodward, *British Foreign Policy in the Second World War,* vol. 3 (1944–5), London, 1971; D. Taylor, *The Years of Challenge. The Commonwealth and the British Empire, 1945–1958,* London/New York, 1959; F. S. Northedge, *British Foreign Policy. The Process of Readjustment, 1945–1961,* London, 1962 (especially its enumeration of the reasons for the 'decline in British power', pp. 13–20). R. B. Bucknell, President of the National Council, told the annual general meeting of FU on 29 Sept. 1945: 'Britain is extremely insecure, but she is not very worried about it. She is beginning to realize that she is a second-rate power, but she is not very worried about it', and concluded: 'She is now in the best possible position in the world to take a moral lead' (*Federal News,* No. 128, Nov. 1945, p. 12).

into spheres of influence and a source of tension between the superpowers.[136] Non-participation, which meant closing one's eyes to the confusion in Europe, could not be a policy of any permanence.

3. The economy demanded European solutions. Ronald Mackay stated in October 1945:

> In the changed circumstances of 1945 this country can only survive economically in co-operation with the other states of Europe. On the basis of pre-war trade, with tariff barriers and other restrictions, we cannot build up sufficient exports to pay for our overseas imports which we require to live ... Approximately 80 per cent of the trade of the independent states of Europe before the war was with one another... Europe, with a population of 300 millions and with resources about as great as those of the USA and USSR, and under one government as they are, could bring prosperity to all its people.[137]

Admittedly Britain's economic situation was more favourable than that of the Continental countries because in her case the damage directly due to the war was less than in France, the Netherlands, Germany, or Eastern Europe. Britain industrial production in 1946 was on average 5 per cent above that of 1938, not far below as it was elsewhere in Europe.[138] Yet in a more fundamental, structural sense the economic situation in Britain was if possible more catastrophic than on the Continent. For six years the whole national economy had been concentrated on the needs of the war. Total exports in 1945 amounted to only 42 per cent of the 1938 level. Yet even before the war exports had been far from balancing the necessary imports of food and raw materials, and between 1925 and 1929 the average annual trade balance had shown a deficit of £370 million. The difference was made up by the earnings of British investments and

---

[136] W. Layton, *The British Commonwealth and World Order*, London (Oxford Univ. Press) 1944 (Sidney Ball Lecture, 3 March 1944, at Oxford, 19 pp.), quotation p. 13; cf. his emphatic endorsement of the Geneva Declaration in the *News Chronicle* of 4 Jan. 1945. Sir Walter Layton (1884–1966), editor of *The Economist*, 1922–38, and for a time Director of the Economic and Finance Section of the League of Nations, Chairman of the Joint War Production Staff 1942–3, from 1931 onwards Chairman and Publisher of 'News Chronicle Ltd.'; in 1947 he became Baron Layton of Danehill, Vice-President of the Liberal Party, and leader of the Liberal Party in the House of Lords until 1955. Like Churchill, Layton supported at this time the establishment of 'a European federation or union' with British co-operation, but without British membership; later he was firmly committed to British membership.

[137] 'Thus, a federation of Europe is the first step towards the economic stability of Europe and the first step towards the political stability of the world' – the case for the latter was stated first, but since 'one cannot expect to create a world government on a federal basis today because the different continents of the world are at different stages of political development and political thought', Europe, following the examples of the USA and the USSR, must at least 'take a significant step towards removing war and securing law and order in Europe' by uniting itself: The Federation of Europe is priority number one in foreign affairs.' R. W. G. Mackay (see n. 112 for biographical details), 'Where do we go from here?': in *Federal News*, No. 127, Oct. 1945, p. 8 f. Mackay wanted Great Britain to be a founding member of a 'real federation of Europe on a democratic basis' (ibid.; cf. n. 204).

[138] Cf. Introduction, section 1(b), 'Europe's Economic and Social Losses', p. 8, esp. nn. 13 and 14.

services overseas, the wealth accumulated in the course of two centuries. During the war the huge deficit caused by the decline of exports (which in 1944 were only 31 per cent of the pre-war figure) was largely covered by the massive payments and supplies provided by the US under the Lend-Lease Act of March 1941 (totalling together between 1941 and 1945 some 31,393 million dollars), given by Congress, however, only on condition that the receiving country exerted itself to the full. In Britain consumption was drastically reduced by rationing and high taxation; the funds needed in the usual way for reinvestment were almost completely unavailable. Above all, those overseas investments which (especially before the beginning of Lend-Lease) could be realized were requisitioned and sold in the US and Canada for a total of £1,118 million (almost five billion dollars, a quarter of the nation's pre-war wealth). And for the balance of commodities needed for the war Britain had incurred debts, especially to the Commonwealth countries, of the fantastic order of £3,555 million (£3,700 million by December 1946). What had once been the world's greatest creditor nation had become its greatest debtor.[139]

Britain's ability to pay for its future imports at the new, higher world prices of raw materials, after the loss of a quarter of its pre-war wealth and a quarter of its merchant navy, had been catastrophically reduced. When the Lend-Lease Act was extended for the last time in April 1945 President Truman had to promise the Senate that this unrequited aid would cease immediately hostilities ended. On 21 August, in fact, immediately after Japan's capitulation, Truman informed all the states in receipt of Lend-Lease that payments and supplies would be stopped; as a gesture he allowed the final date to be 2 September, the day of the formal armistice with Japan. British Treasury experts calculated that in the ensuing twelve months Britain if unaided, would have to pay some £2,100 million (almost nine billion dollars) for imports and debts over and above what it earned (that is, having for over a century enjoyed the profits of empire, the country would now be living beyond its means); and that in the most favourable circumstances this sum could only be reduced by 1949 to an annual deficit of £1,250 million (above five billion dollars) by the strictest limitation of imports, promotion of exports, etc.).[140] Such was the economic predicament of the island kingdom, which its foreign policy was bound to take into account.

[139] For a most instructive survey with list of sources see R. G. Hawtrey, 'The Economic Consequences of the War', p. 36 ff., in A. Toynbee (ed.), *The Realignment of Europe (Survey of International Affairs, 1939–46*, vol. 9), London, 1955. On the Lend-Lease Act, see Vol. 8 of the same *Survey:* W. H. McNeill, *America, Britain and Russia. Their Co-operation and Conflict, 1941–1946*, London, 1953, p. 773 ff. Further statistical material in the Appendix to R. G. Mackay, *You can't turn the Clock back*, London, 1948, pp. 339–54 (for the pre-war adverse trade balance, see p. 344); also HMSO, Treasury: *Statistical Material Presented during the Washington Negotiations* (autumn 1945), Cmd. 6707, London, 1945.

[140] For the termination of Lend-Lease, cf. Hawtrey (n. 139). p. 42 f. and McNeill (n. 139), pp. 673–8 and 784–8; calculation by Treasury experts quoted in H. Dalton, *High Tide and After, Memoirs 1945–1950*, London, 1962, p. 71 f.; much additional material in G. D. Worswick and P. H. Ady (ed.), *The British Economy 1945–1950*, Oxford, 1952 (p. 153 f.). On the resulting approach to Washington, cf. p. 174 below.

No sensible observer could fail to recognize the constraints which these three basic facts placed upon Britain foreign policy as it entered the post-war era. Yet the conclusions drawn by, for example, Layton and Mackay were far from being generally accepted by the British public as a whole – the situation in this respect was entirely different from what it had been in 1939–40. At the earlier date the British people, like their leaders, had been fully conscious that the fate of Britain as a part of Europe was determined by what happened on the Continent, that the attempt between the wars to establish a lasting peace in Europe had failed, and that the country was once again being drawn into a war whose outcome no one could foresee. A flood of newspaper articles, pamphlets, and books, statements by politicians, parties, and associations had deplored the ineffectiveness of the League of Nations as a major cause of yet another war with all its attendant misery, and had proclaimed that at the end of this new war an authority must be created with power over the individual states and the military means to ensure lasting peace in Europe.

In November 1939 Attlee had given the Parliamentary Labour party the famous slogan 'Europe must federate or perish', and Prime Minister Chamberlain had spoken of 'machinery for a new order in Europe'. The programme of the New Commonwealth Society, whose president was Winston Churchill, contained a passage concerning post-war aims: 'When we allude to an international authority, we mean a reconstituted and revitalised League, possessing the power to alter the public law and to enforce it. As an illustration of the procedure by which this change may be effected, there is the transformation of the confederate into the federal constitution of the United States ... The time has now arrived when the members of the League should face the task of amending their Covenant.' As first steps 'the Society advocates (1) the establishment of an International Tribunal empowered to deal with all disputes threatening the peace of the world; (2) the creation of an International Police Force under the control of an international authority, as a sanction of international law'. Federal Union, which, as has been seen, demanded a full federation at least for Britain, France, and Germany, had reached the zenith of its growth. Its policy seemed about to be put into effect when on 16 June 1940 Churchill's all-party Cabinet proposed to France an 'indissoluble union' in such bold and forthright wording as had never been seen in a diplomatic document. 'The two governments declare that from now onwards France and Great Britain shall no longer be two nations but one Franco-British Union. The constitution of the Union will provide for joint organs of defence, foreign, financial and economic policies. Every citizen of France will enjoy immediately citizenship of Great Britain; every British subject will become a citizen of France.' And on 21 March 1943 Churchill, in a special broadcast heard all over the world, had again spoken of 'the earnest hope ... that we shall achieve the largest common measure of the integrated life of Europe that is possible ... We must try – I am speaking of course only for ourselves – to make the Council of Europe, or whatever it may be called, into a really effective League, with all the strongest forces concerned woven into its texture, with a High Court to adjust disputes, and with forces, armed forces, national or international, or both, held ready to enforce these decisions and prevent renewed aggression and the preparation of future wars.'[141]

All this had aroused hope and expectation on the Continent and in many Resistance circles that Britain, as the sole victorious European nation, would take the lead at the end of the war in building a European Union. As late as July 1944 Rossi had declared: 'We must always keep in mind the offer of 16 June 1940 for a Franco-British union – that is of immense significance for us.' The words of Attlee and Churchill were endlessly quoted in underground leaflets, and the conclusion was drawn that Britain had recognized the needs of the hour and would provide leadership in the advance towards European unity. This was especially expected of the Labour Party.[142]

In 1944–5, however, the British people and their leaders were under the impact of two other experiences, very different from those of 1940, and suggesting very different conclusions. Since the shock of France's rapid fall they had seen almost all the other Continental states collapse, whereas their own national institutions had stood the crucial test in the hour of supreme danger – and this had strengthened the nation's pride in itself. To this was added the realization, which people shared in varying degrees, that Britain had been spared the shock of defeat thanks to the entry into the war of Russia and America as her allies – that is, her fate had been decided by the non-European great powers. Both experiences had understandably caused British public opinion to turn away from the idea of a united Europe. Readiness to throw in their lot with Europe, which had been widespread in 1939–40, was now superseded in the popular mind by the idea that Britain with the Commonwealth would still remain a world power, and that it should not tie itself too closely to the chaos on the Continent but should seek its salvation in the flattering circumstance that

---

[141] Quotations from C. R. Attlee, *Labour's Peace Aims,* London, Jan, 1940, p. 12; Chamberlain in *The Manchester Guardian,* 27 Nov. 1939 (quoted in R. W. G. Mackay, *Federal Europe,* London, 1940, p. 23); *The Aims and Objects of The New Commonwealth Society,* Pamphlet Series A/1, rev. ed., London, 1937, p. 10 f.; for the Declaration of an Anglo-French Union, see W. S. Churchill, *The Second World War,* vol. ii, *Their Finest Hour,* London, 1949, pp. 183–4 Churchill's Speech, 21 March 1943, in *The Times,* 22 March 1943. Cf. Introduction, nn, 101–4: on Federal Union, see p. 142 ff; for more detail about Attlee, see n. 154.

[142] E. Rossi in *L. Unità europea,* No. 5 (Milan edn.), Aug. 1944, p. 3. The leading group of MFE, themselves mainly liberal Socialist, had expressed themselves as having 'no confidence in the Conservatives'; 'they are only thinking of how to serve British interests' (ibid., No. 3, Sept. 1943, p. 4); but 'we count on the readiness of the Labour Party to establish federal relations with the rest of Europe' (ibid., No. 4, June 1944, p. 3, quoted in n. 49). The book issued by the Geneva Centre, *L'Europe de demain.* Neuchâtel, March 1945, contained about eighty-five pages of documents from the Resistance, about ninety-five pages of British documents about Europe (cf. n. 56), among them (obviously exaggerating its importance) Federal Union's Report dated Easter 1942 (cf. n. 115). Other Resistance writers considered Britain's membership unlikely as long as she saw herself as the centre of the Commonwealth, but expected from her friendly encouragement of Continental unity. Both schools of thought underestimated the extent to which British enthusiasm for Europe had waned since 1941.

it was still a member of the Big Three. These considerations undoubtedly explain the aloofness of Britain's attitude to Europe in the post-war years.

At the end of May 1944 Foreign Secretary Eden declared in the House of Commons: I think it may be desirable to have close, intimate and friendly relations with other countries of Western Europe, but ... on such a foundation alone such lasting security could not be founded. We have to stretch wider to ensure this: there must be close political and military co-operation between the United States, the Soviet Union, the British Commonwealth and China; ... and consequently the world organization should be constructed on and around the four great powers'– thus making clear the connection with Roosevelt's idea of restoring the old world of nation states with four powers predominant (the 'four policemen'). When on 6 February 1945 Lord Huntingdon in the House of Lords introduced a motion asserting the urgent need for a federal union of all European states including Britain on the model of the USA, the government spokesman, Lord Cranborne, answered him: 'I am bound to say that Lord Huntingdon's proposal for an immediate federation of European democracies seems to me to be so far from the realm of reality that I find considerable difficulty in framing a government reply to it. We should not rule it out as an extremely long-term policy.'[143]

In 1945–6 only a few of the organized groups and associations clung to the views they had held in 1939–40 and concluded from their knowledge of the new circumstances of British foreign policy that a union of the European countries had become more, not less urgent. Among these associations, which no doubt were representative only of tiny minorities, Federal Union, described in the previous chapter, with its 130 branches was still the most important. Since September it had proclaimed as its 'short-term aim ... the creation of a democratic European federation'.[144] Publicity for the same objective was also carried on by a small 'New Europe

---

[143] Eden on 25.5.1944, *Parl. Debates,* House of Commons, vol. 400, columns 1040–55; Huntingdon on 6.2.1945 in House of Lords. François Bondy's experience is revealing: 'Shortly after the Paris conference [of federalists in March 1945, cf. p. 126]]I tried on a visit to England to get a clear idea of the attitude of British Socialists and progressives to these questions. I found two things: firstly that many British personalities, including well-known economists, who in 1940 had supported the idea of a European federation and encouraged our enthusiasm by their writings, have since lost their whole interest and their whole belief in this solution. Secondly, the majority of those who favour a common solution of common European problems reject political solutions and urge "functional" ones' (F. Bondy, 'L'Europe se tourne vers l'Angleterre' in *Cahiers de la fédération européenne,* No. 2, Paris, Aug. 1945, p. 22). Any Continental politician who in the following years stubbornly refused to take 'any step' without England could have ascertained this at any time.

[144] Cf.n. 117. In connection with this second point *Federal News,* No. 122, April–May 1945, p. 6, quoted with approval a passage in the *Observer* of 18 March 1945: 'The liberation of Europe will be an unfinished task if it results merely in a return to the chronic economic anxieties, the gluts and shortages, the restrictive, frontier-ridden outlook of the inter-war years. The Nazis are challenging the Allies to improve on Hitler's New Order; the Allies have to show that free men can do far better.' On this FU commented: 'Europe united under a federal government for common affairs, such as defence, economic planning, maintenance of civil liberties, and equal rights for all irrespective of race, creed or their minority or majority status, would provide a very different New Order from Hitler's empire of serfs, and one in which free men would have opportunity, liberty and lasting peace.'

Group', by the 'Socialist Vanguard Group' – important as a rallying-centre for internationally minded Socialists – and by an equally left-wing Socialist 'European Federation Campaign Council'. A post-war foreign policy oriented towards Europe could have found support in all these groups, as Churchill's United Europe Committee did at the end of 1946.

Unlike Federal Union, the New Europe Group existed only in London. Its membership included leading representatives of the arts and sciences. Soon after its foundation by the Serb philosopher Dimitrije Mitrinović it had produced in 1929 a policy document entitled 'The Federation of the states of Europe'. It was perhaps the first real European–federal group. Its 'integral' conception of federation urged the pooling of foreign policy, defence, and currency, depriving the nation state of its political functions and leaving it simply cultural autonomy with decentralization so as to give more power to the regions and a share of management for workers in industry. With remarkable consistency it had championed this idea between 1932 and 1935 in the periodicals *New Britain* and *The Eleventh Hour*, and in 1947 under the Chairmanship of Professor Soddy (Nobel Prizewinner in Chemistry) it joined UEF, being represented at the latter's congresses at Amsterdam, Montreux, and Rome by Professor David Shillan and the Labour MP Niall MacDermot.[145]

The Socialist Vanguard Group, consisting of leading Socialists from every country in Europe, continued in 1944–5 to repeat the basic facts in its fortnightly *Socialist Commentary*: The League of Nations had failed because the nation states would not transfer to it any of their sovereignty; the US and the Soviet Union were still unwilling to make any such transfer; the federal union at least of Europe, as demanded by the Resistance movements on the Continent, was an urgent political necessity for Europe and the world.[146] In the autumn of 1944 young members of the Independent Labour Party, prominent among whom was Norman J. Hart, founded a European Federation Campaign Council and zealously publicized their aims by means of two groups which met regularly in east London. At the end of 1946 they joined Federal Union and through that the UEF.[147]

As far as political parties were concerned, the situation was as follows. In the case of the Conservatives it may be taken as certain that their

---

[145] After migrating to Britain in 1914 Dr Mitrinović (who died in London in 1953) founded the International Society for Individual Psychology (the 'Adler Society'); the 'New Europe Group' originally sprang from this. Its archive, now owned by the new Atlantis foundation, was not available to me as the group is planning to publish its own history. The account in the text is based on information from D. Shillan, 31.1.1975). Cf. also 'Associations et revues fédéralistes' in *Cahiers du monde nouveau*, vol. 3, 1947, p. 309.

[146] The 'Socialist Vanguard Group' in which Willi Eichler spoke for the German Socialists, Louis Lévy and Felix Gouin for the French, and George Green for the British Socialists, came into existence in 1934 as a 'Militant Socialist International' in protest against the inactivity of the official 'Socialist International' in face of the Fascist regimes, and during the war advocated European union at a number of congresses and in its programmes. It now did so with special emphasis in its fortnightly eight-page publication, *Europe and World Peace*, London, 1944. It was, however, evident that most of its members were foreign immigrants.

[147] The EFCC had previously considered Federal Union 'too bourgeois': information from N. Hart, 7.10.1974; unfortunately he was unable to trace any documents of this group, one of the earliest of its kind and (like FU) evidently purely British in composition.

undisputed leader, Winston Churchill, in 1944–5 still stood by his own conviction, expressed as early as 1930, frequently proclaimed between 1940 and 1943 and publicized again after September 1946, that Europe could achieve peace and prosperity only if it abandoned the old policy of rival blocs and succeeded in closely integrating the Continental states. This conviction was linked in his mind with the three basic premisses already referred to. No one knew better than Churchill Britain's relative loss of power compared with the USA and the USSR; no one described more forcefully the wretchedness and danger of chaos and a power vacuum on the Continent. Besides the need – to which he probably attached less importance – for economic integration, from 1944 onwards he realized the need to set limits to Russia's advance. His belief was that in the long run only a close union of the Continental states could prevent the entire Continent from being dominated by the superpower in the East.[148] He certainly envisaged, as will be seen in the chapter on Churchill's appeals to Europe in 1946–7, a special and separate role for Britain as head of the Commonwealth and junior partner of the US: she would not be an ordinary member of a united Europe like the other countries (to this extent he shared the prevailing view), and in contrast to the federalists he thought in terms of co-operation and confederation even for the Continental states, not of federation or integration. But, with his strong feeling for the unity and former greatness of Europe and the new threat to European civilization, he saw equally clearly that one of Britain's most urgent tasks was to play a leading part in encouraging the Continent towards such integration and to be the 'sponsor' of its unity.[149] In 1944 he explained the essential elements of his design to the Canadian Prime Minister, as the latter noted in his diary: 'Churchill began with our own Commonwealth and Empire keeping together in friendly co-operation ... having the fraternal association with the United States perpetuated at all costs ... for a United States of Europe, which would preserve the culture of separate nations and which could

---

[148] Cf. the quotations from Churchill from 1940 to 1943 in Introduction, section 4, pp. 64 and 67, and n. 134 to this chapter; also his article in the *Saturday Evening Post* of 15.2.1930 (already containing the gist of his later idea) and his speeches of 1946–7 in chapter II, section 3, pp. 317–22 below, which are considered in the general context of his idea of Europe (on which there has not yet been an adequate monograph; this is to be expected from the latter part of Dr Martin Gilbert's monumental biography, two volumes of which have taken the story to 1915). An incisive sketch, stressing the containment of Soviet expansion as the dominant motive from 1944 onwards, is in H. P. Schwarz, *Vom Reich zur Bundesrepublik*, Neuwied/Berlin, 1963, pp. 150–3. The most revealing picture of Churchill's anxiety, concern, and tactics is furnished by his telegrams to Truman of 11 and 12 May 1945 and the report of 12.6.1945 by the US ambassador extraordinary, Joseph E. Davies, in *FRUS, Diplomatic Papers: The Conference of Berlin*, vol. i, Washington, 1960, pp. 6–9 and 64–70.

[149] Cf. the detailed analysis of Churchill's ideas in chap. II, section 3, pp. 317 ff. (at this point they are relevant only so far as they form part of the background to Bevin's foreign policy). The word 'sponsor' was used in his Zurich speech, 19.9.1946, see p. 319. It would of course have been a helpful clarification for Continental Europeans if he had stated unambiguously that Britain would not join the Union herself, though she desired and encouraged unity for the Continental countries.

164 Europe's Mood of Resignation

make its contribution to the world; he thought it might be made so complete and secure that it might itself become a bar to Russian encroachment.' It was obviously in the light of such opinions that Lord Alanbrooke, Chief of the Imperial General Staff, wrote: 'Therefore foster Germany, gradually build her up and bring her into a Federation of Western Europe. Unfortunately this must all be done under the cloak of a holy alliance between England, Russia and America. Not an easy policy!'[150] Had Churchill been returned as Prime Minister in the general election of July 1945, no doubt he would have tried to introduce this policy at an early stage and would have persevered with it.

The difficulties which in the months immediately before and just after the end of the war stood in the way of Churchill's design, particularly the predominance of the US and the Soviet Union, both of which rejected the idea of an independent union of Continental European states, made its realization in 1944–5 quite impossible. That was why in September 1944 Foreign Secretary Eden put forward a considerably modified version in the House of Commons. After the European governments had been reinstalled Britain would be able to put into effect the agreements already reached with the governments in exile, since 'we for our part are ready to enter into association with them, as they are with us, to guarantee the future peace of Europe and to play our part in dealing with our common problems'. A customs union between France, the Benelux states, Norway, and the entire Commonwealth could be the first step. This version bore some resemblance to Smuts's idea of an association of West European states with Britain and the Commonwealth in order to provide the latter, as one of the Big Three, with a potential comparable to those of the USA and the USSR.[151] An essential prerequisite of either policy, a close understanding with the government of liberated France, was lacking. On 11 November 1944 Churchill had offered to conclude an Anglo-French treaty of alliance, but was unwilling to accept de Gaulle's condition – the permanent subjection of the whole of the left bank of the Rhine as far as Coblenz and Cologne to French rule, a move that would have made Franco-German reconciliation, which meant so much to Churchill, impossible for the foreseeable future. A month after this rebuff from de Gaulle, who instead made a pact with Moscow, the Belgian Prime Minister Spaak proposed close co-operation

---

[150] Diary of Mackenzie King, Canadian Prime Minister from 1935–48, concerning a conversation in 1944; in J. W. Pickersgill, *The Mackenzie King Record,* vol. i, Toronto, 1960, p. 672, f.; notes by the Chief of the Imperial General Staff in A. Bryant, *Triumph in the West 1943–1946. Based on the Diaries and Autobiographical Notes of Field Marshal The Viscount Alanbrooke,* London, 1965, p. 193; both quoted in H. P. Schwarz, *Vom Reich zur Bundesrepulik,* pp. 49 and 727. Support could be expected from other prominent politicians who did not belong to Churchill's immediate circle, such as Leslie Hore-Belisha, Minister of War in Chamberlain's Cabinet, from May to July 1945 Minister of Supply in Churchill's Cabinet. He said in August 1944: 'The present war has shown that Britain cannot afford to neglect the Continent of Europe. She will not enjoy security against the risk of a third world war until there is a United States of Europe as firmly founded and knit as the United States of America' (quoted in S. D. Bailey, *United Europe,* London, 1947, p. 28 f.).

[151] Eden on 29.9.1944 in *Parl. Debates, House of Commons,* vol. 403, col. 706; remarkably close in his views to the proposal of J. C. Smuts, South African Prime Minister, in his speech in London of 25.11.1943; text in L. W. Holborn (ed.), *War and Peace Aims of the United Nations,* vol. ii, Boston, 1948, pp. 712–16.

between Britain and Belgium, which 'must be compatible with co-operation with the Netherlands and France', but received no response.[152] But it can be taken as certain that in the very different (and from Churchill's point of view more favourable) circumstances that prevailed in the spring of 1946, by which time de Gaulle had resigned and America was showing growing resistance to the Soviet Union, a Churchill in office would have done his best to realize his designs.[153]

Meanwhile during the inter-war period the Labour Party had acquired a considerable reputation as a champion of the idea of collective security and of the League of Nations. It is true that since 1931 no Labour politician responsible for foreign policy had had to give practical effect to the much publicized slogans of international co-operation and collective security. Shortly after the outbreak of war Clement Attlee, the party leader, had, however, gone further by urging that 'there must be acceptance of the principle that international anarchy is incompatible with peace, and that in the common interest there must be recognition of an international authority superior to the individual states and endowed not only with rights over them but with power to make them effective, operating not only in the political but in the economic sphere. Europe must federate or perish.' The party's official statement on war aims in February 1940 had demanded that 'the peace settlement shall establish a new Association or Commonwealth of States whose collective authority must transcend, over a proper sphere, the sovereign rights of the separate States'.[154] On this point of the surrender and/or pooling of sovereign rights on the part of Britain as well as other states, Labour seemed ready in the spirit of Socialist internationalism to go further than the Conservatives, who were more wedded to the retention of an independent British people. During the

---

[152] For de Gaulle's rejection of Churchill's offer of alliance on 11.11.1944, with sources, see W. Lipgens, 'Bedingungen und Etappen der Aussenpolitik de Gaulles, 1944–1946' in *VfZG*, vol. 21 (1973), pp. 82–4, also the present work, p. 208; for Churchill's lack of interest in Spaak's proposal for a pact, cf. P. H. Spaak, *Combats inachevés*, vol. i, p. 164, also n. 372. Cf. Report of the US Ambassador Extraordinary J. E. Davies fo 16.6.1945, 'As far as France was concerned, Churchill was annoyed. He had had more than enough of de Gaulle.' *FRUS, Diplomatic Papers: The Conference of Berlin*, 1945, vol. i, Washington, 1960, p. 64 ff., the quotation on p. 67.

[153] For the altered circumstances in the spring of 1946 see p. 181 below, and for an analysis of Churchill's initatives, beginning with the Fulton speech of 5.3.1946, see p. 317 ff. below. It is there argued that the aloofness of Churchill's last government (that of 1951–5) towards the EDC does not invalidate the above analysis of his attitude towards Europe (chap. II, n. 76).

[154] Attlee's speech of 8.11.1939 to the Labour Parliamentary Party printed in C. R. Attlee, *Labour's Peace Aims*, London, Jan. 1940, p. 12 f.; for the Party's official war aims, *Labour, the War, and the Peace*, London, 8.2.1940, p. 7. The best analyses, to date, of the attitude of the Labour Party towards foreign-policy problems are: W. P. Maddox, *Foreign Relations in British Labour Politics*, Cambridge, Mass., 1934; W. R. Tucker, *The Attitude of the British Labour Party towards European and Collective Security Problems 1920–1939*, thesis, Geneva, 1950; E. Windrich, *British Labour's Foreign Policy*, Stanford, Cal., 1952 (rich in documentary material of the period 1914–44 in the first eleven chapters); and E. J. Meehan, *The British Left Wing and Foreign Policy*, New Brunswick, NJ, 1960 (pp. 1–65 for the pre-war and war periods). But the programme entitled 'The Old World and the New Society', London, 1942, felt no need to go beyond the assurance that 'Labour's first aim . . . [was] to continue the closest possible Anglo-American–Russian Co-operation' (quoted in Windrich, op. cit., p. 166).

spring and summer of 1945 and especially during the election campaign the idea of a 'socialist foreign policy' was given concrete meaning by the argument that a Labour government would be able to ensure future cooperation with the Soviet Union in a spirit of confidence.

In the Labour general-election manifesto describing the domestic and foreign policy which the party intended to follow, the only passage dealing with foreign affairs ran as follows: 'We must consolidate in peace the great wartime association of the British Commonwealth with the USA and the USSR.'[155] At the pre-election party conference at Blackpool in May 1945 Hugh Dalton put the point most emphatically: 'The peace will be won only if we co-operate with Russia. You cannot settle the problem of Europe by long-distance telephone calls and telegrams. Round the table we must get, but do not present us with *faits accomplis* when we get there.' Bevin closed with the unexpected appeal not to belittle the work of the League of Nations but to continue it so that 'the dream of a world parliament can perhaps be realized'. Towards the end of the conference a resolution introduced by MPs of the extreme Left was passed, to the effect that a Labour government should 'oppose the crystallization of power politics into a so-called League of Nations consisting only of the victorious powers and struggle for the establishment of a United Socialist States of Europe as the only means of ensuring a just and lasting peace'.[156] The ensuing general election was fought with charges that the Conservatives shared the guilt for the war and were the 'last-ditch defenders of capitalism', as well as with the foreign-policy slogan 'Left understands Left'. Bevin assured his election audiences: 'With a Labour government in office, which would be believed and understood by Russia and other countries, the whole international situation would be changed.'[157]

(B) THE STAGES OF BEVIN'S FOREIGN POLICY, 1945–7

The general election, which the Conservatives decided to hold before it was due and a mere eight weeks after the end of the war in Europe, began on 5 July and ended with the count on 26 July. It gave the Labour Party for the first time in British history an overwhelming majority of votes and seats. About twelve million people voted for them, barely ten million for the Conservatives, and 2.2 million for the Liberals. In accordance with the British system the victory was still greater in terms of parliamentary seats: Labour obtained 394, the Conservatives 212, and the Liberals 12. This massive swing showed the basic similarity of political trends in Britain and on the Continent. After an election campaign which had concentrated on

---

[155] Labour Party, 'Let us face the future', London, Feb. 1945 (edited by Herbert Morrison as chairman of the 'Special Campaign Committee'), quoted in D. N. Pritt, *The Labour Government 1945–1951*, London, 1963, p. 23.

[156] *Report of the 44th Annual Conference of the Labour Party*, London, May 1945, p. 104 (speech by Dalton, on whom see n. 160 below), pp. 107 f., and 115 f. For Bevin's speech, see Bullock, *The Life and Times of Ernest Bevin*, vol. 2, 1940–5, London, 1967, pp. 382–5 and p. 112 (resolution moved by the left-wing spokesman Leigh Davies).

[157] Quoted by Pritt (n. 155), p. 58; cf. ibid., p. 28; similarly in Sir S. Cripps's election speeches, cf. R. B. McCallum and A. Reachman, *The British General Election of 1945*, London, 1947, p. 137.

the problems of reconstruction, the party of the Right (which had also been in power between the wars in every Continental country, and had failed to avert the catastrophe) suffered a humiliating defeat, whereas the Leftist parties with their promises of more democracy at home, socialization of the economy, and international co-operation abroad, made enormous gains everywhere. Despite their consciousness of having won the war, the British people formed no exception.[158] The result also showed the strength of hopes that a Socialist government would succeed in establishing a new international order including, in particular, friendly relations with the Soviet Union, and would 'win the peace' by persuading it to co-operate (which Churchill by this time considered to be a forlorn hope). In historical retrospect, the most valuable result of this general election is seen to be that Labour was given the opportunity to exert all its efforts to secure this co-operation, but that the Soviet Union plainly could not be persuaded to respond.

The Labour government which took office on 27 July 1945 was overwhelmingly preoccupied with domestic policy, healing the scars of war, and applying Socialist principles to the economy and society. Attlee's primary concern as Prime Minister – a task for which he was particularly well suited – was to hold together the divergent forces of the party. These included the gradualists of the Fabian Society, the Marxists, the Cooperative Movement and the Christian Socialists, the Trade Unions, which controlled three-quarters of the votes at the party conference and at that time were realistic and moderate, and the constituency Labour parties, who were then more extreme.[159] Attlee himself considered foreign affairs to be a matter for the Foreign Secretary: 'It is in my view a mistake for a Prime Minister – save in exceptional circumstances – to intervene personally.' After briefly considering Hugh Dalton for the post he entrusted the Foreign Office to Ernest Bevin.[160] As organizer of British war industry

---

[158] Cf. the tables of votes and seats for the House of Commons, 1919–45 in D. Sternberger and B. Vogel, *Die Wahl der Parlamente*, Berlin, 1969, vol. i, p. 637 f.; and F. Boyd, *British Politics in Transition, 1945–1963*, London, 1964 (with an analysis of the reasons); D. W. Urwin, *Western Europe since 1945*, London, 1968, pp. 65–7, emphasizes that the most important reason for Labour's victory was that the country had become accustomed to a planned economy under the Labour ministers in Churchill's cabinet. For the effect of the first post-war elections in transforming relations between the parties in all European countries, see the analysis at the beginning of Chapter IV in vol. 2.

[159] Cf. M. A. Fitzsimons, 'British Labour in Search of a Socialist Foreign Policy' in *The Review of Politics*, vol. xii, 1950, p. 198 f.; Boyd (n. 158), pp. 66–76; H. Pelling, *A Short History of the Labour Party*, London, 1972; P. Adelmann, *The Rise of the Labour Party 1880–1945*, Harlow, 1972.

[160] C. R. Attlee, *As it Happened*, London, 1945, p. 169. Since Bevin's Blackpool speech (cf. n. 156) Attlee had had him in mind for the Foreign Office. However, on 26 July a left-wing attempt led by Harold Laski, chairman of the Executive, to substitute Morrison as Party leader was defeated by Bevin's steadfast loyalty to Attlee. For this reason, and because Bevin himself wanted the Treasury, for the space of one day Attlee was disposed to give the Foreign Office to Dalton as Bevin had suggested – a move which, in view of Dalton's egocentricity and hidebound insularity, would hardly have had fruitful results. But on 27 July Attlee returned to his original decision to make Bevin Foreign Secretary, not least thanks to the King's advice, inspired by Churchill, that a strong personality like Bevin was needed to cope with the Russians. Cf. J. Wheeler-Bennett, *King George VI*, London,

in Churchill's War Cabinet, Bevin had become without any doubt the second most important Labour minister and had proved a straightforward, robust, and absolutely trustworthy colleague. As founder and head of what was by far the largest trade union he occupied the most influential place in the party next to Attlee, and as Foreign Secretary was always able to get his policy accepted by the Cabinet. Attlee aptly described him as a man 'who is not the slave of abstract theory but a practical man of affairs seeking to get things done'.[161]

Bevin's earlier statements on foreign policy had certainly been undoctrinaire and changeable. After a visit to the United States in 1926 he told the Trades Union Congress in 1927: 'We have got to teach the people of Europe that their economic interests, their economic development have to transcend merely national boundaries'; what was needed was a union of European countries including 'their colonial empires', 'an indivisible united nation spreading from the borders of Russia to the borders of France'. But in 1930 he agreed with a TUC economic report which rejected British membership of a 'European bloc' but called for 'as full a development as possible of the economic relations between the constituent parts of the British Commonwealth'. In 1920, in order to assist the Red Army he had organized a boycott of arms supplies to Poland and to British troops intervening in Russia. But when the Communists tried to split his trade union he told the Soviet ambassador point-blank: 'I have built up the Transport Union and if you try to break it I will fight you.'[162] Altogether he approached the problems of British foreign policy, especially in Europe, in a forthright way, from the point of view of increasing exports and giving the British worker economic security.[163]

1958, pp. 636–8; Bullock (n. 156), pp. 390–5; Dalton (n. 140), pp. 8–14. For Dalton's egocentricity, see ibid., p. 4 f. and *passim*. As Chancellor of the Exchequer he 'stood out as an opponent of any association with the continent of Europe' (A. Nutting, *Europe will not wait. A Warning and a Way Out,* London, 1960, p. 4).

[161] Attlee in *Parl. Debates, House of Commons,* vol. 430, 18.11.1946, col. 590. Ernest Bevin, born at Winsford, Somerset, rose from humble circumstances by attending evening classes while working as a carter. In 1910 he organized the carters of South-West England into a branch of the Dockers' Trade Union, becoming its secretary-general in 1911. Founder and chairman of the powerful Transport and General Workers' Union, formed by the merger of a number of independent unions (14 up to 1923, 22 by 1929, and 28 at a later date), he was Labour MP for Central Wandsworth from 1940 to 1950. In May 1940 he joined Churchill's War Cabinet as Minister of Labour and National Service, and as organizer of manpower in the war economy soon became one of the three most influential ministers in the 'inner Cabinet'. Cf. F. Williams, *Ernest Bevin,* London, 1952, and the admirable biography by A. Bullock, *The Life and Times of Ernest Bevin,* vol. i, 1881–1940, London, 1960; vol. ii, 1940–1945, London, 1967. The third volume dealing with his career as Foreign Secretary is still awaited. Bevin nearly always got his way in the Cabinet, according to Nutting (n. 160), p. 39: but 'in those closing months of his reign at the Foreign Office he was both physically ill and mentally exhausted'. He died in London on 14.4.1951.

[162] Bullock, vol. i, (n. 161), p. 360 f., 387 f., and 440 f.; Northedge (n. 135), pp. 13–32; R. Blackburn, 'Bevin and his critics' in *Foreign Affairs,* vol. 25 (1947), p. 239 f. (Bevin's quotation from *Report of the 45th Annual Conference of the Labour Party, Bournemouth, 1946.*)

[163] Fitzsimons (n. 134), p. 27, quoted a characteristic expression of this basic attitude from a speech by Bevin (*Report of the 46th Annual Conference of the Labour Party,* London, 1947, p. 176): 'Reference was made by one speaker in connection with the Middle East to the fact that we ought to hand this over to an international concern. I am not going to be a party to voluntarily putting all British interests in a pool and everybody else sticking to his own. The standard of life and the wages of the workmen of this country are dependent upon these things.'

True to the slogan (used by him also) 'Left understands Left', Bevin made great efforts to bring about close co-operation between London and Moscow as promised during the election campaign. Having gone to Potsdam on his first day as Foreign Secretary, he tried during the last third of the conference to establish a direct man-to-man relationship with Stalin and Molotov by speaking frankly and honestly. Bevin's subsequent remarks make it quite clear that he had no illusions about the dictatorial character of Stalin's system; but the conference minutes show equally clearly that on every question he tried his utmost to reach firm and unequivocal agreements, being ready to compromise as far as humanly possible in order to safeguard the permanent co-operation of the Big Three on a basis of full understanding. The sign of co-operation which he wanted from the Soviet leaders was willingness to guarantee democratic freedoms to the population of the Eastern-European countries as promised by the Yalta conference. He obviously trusted Stalin's assurances on this point. In his first major foreign-policy statement in the House of Commons after his return from Potsdam on 20 August, Bevin said that the Soviet Union had agreed that free and secret elections would be held in Poland not later than the beginning of 1946. All democratic parties would be allowed to take part and would be able to draw up their own programmes and put up candidates; freedom of speech and assembly would be guaranteed to all political parties.

Bevin added that in Romania, Bulgaria, and Hungary Britain likewise could not accept the governments installed in power as representative of the majority of the population, and he criticized elections which disfranchised considerable sections of the population and presented the remainder with only a single list. 'We shall not be able to regard as representative any government resulting from such elections.' Bevin's human and deeply democratic convictions showed clearly when he said that it was a tragedy for suffering humanity that 'one kind of totalitarianism is being replaced by another'; yet Stalin's assurances gave cause for hope.[164] The Council of Foreign Ministers was still expected to accomplish the major task of concluding peace treaties with all the nations of Europe at the forthcoming conference in London.

Yet Bevin's expectations were deeply disappointed at the first Conference of Foreign Ministers in London in September 1945. Molotov made it clear that wherever in Eastern Europe its troops were stationed the Soviet Union intended to remain and to impose its permanent domination by means of governments imposed by its authority. He went on to make demands concerning the right to station troops and exercise control in the

---

[164] Bevin in *Parliamentary Debates, House of Commons*, vol. 413, 20.8.1945, col. 291 f. For Bevin's searching questions demanding precise and binding agreements at Potsdam, cf. Minutes of the 10th-13th sessions in *FRUS, Diplomatic Papers: The Conference of Berlin*, vol. 2, Washington, 1960, pp. 459-595. The latest specialist study by Charles L. Mee, *Meeting at Potsdam*, London, 1975, pp. 249-54, 261 ff., 271 ff., gives a more critical view.

Mediterranean, the Straits, and Cyrenaica as well as in Iran. He declared that the Soviet Union would be ready to discuss the terms of the peace treaties only if its right to share in all Allied Control Councils including Japan was recognized, and so on. Molotov showed no readiness to compromise on any of these questions, until finally he forced the conference to break up and refused even to approve the minutes of what had been agreed.[165] Simultaneously the Moscow news media launched a propaganda campaign lasting several weeks against the idea that West-European countries might form closer links with each other. Because a conference of the French Socialist Party on 15 August proposed a 'Franco-British alliance' as the basis of a European organization for peace within the framework of a 'world-wide organization for collective security', and because on 10 September de Gaulle too had spoken of an 'economic grouping' (*ensemble*) of the West-European countries, Moscow applied the same methods as it had used in 1942 to frustrate plans for an Eastern-European federation. It declared that any closer co-operation on the part of the countries of Western Europe could only be intended as a bloc directed against the Soviet Union and would be seen by it as a hostile act – to the consternation of the West Europeans for whom, after the recent terrible war, nothing could have been further from their intentions.[166]

This campaign by the Soviet press, which denounced in advance any designs for West-European co-operation as a 'Western bloc', was viewed by the Foreign Office with alarm and taken very seriously. The documents now accessible in the Public Record Office show how quick Bevin was to disavow any intention to form a West-European association and to keep open only the possibility of an Anglo-French treaty of the traditional kind. In discussion with Molotov on 23 September, Bevin, after firmly rejecting Soviet territorial demands in the Mediterranean, explained the British desire for a 'treaty with France. We did not want to create – and he rejected the term – a Western bloc. He would say so in the House of Commons.' In reply to a direct question whether he had 'any objection to such a treaty', Molotov said he had not. To Bevin's further question 'whether the Soviet Union had any objection to such a treaty?' Molotov replied 'that he would report to his government and that he would like to be able to tell them that the purpose of the treaty would be the same as that of the Anglo-

[165] Cf. the works cited in n. 24, especially McNeill, pp. 696–704; J. F. Byrnes, *Speaking Frankly*, NY, 1947, pp. 94–104. According to J. F. Dulles, who took part, 'Molotov treated him [Bevin] as a banderillero treats a bull' (J. F. Dulles, *War or Peace*, NY, 1950, p. 28).
[166] Manifesto of the 37th Congress of the SFIO in *Le Populaire* of 16.8.1945; de Gaulle in *The Times* of 10.9.1945. Warnings from the Russian side had already been given, e.g. by B. J. Yermashev, 'Blocomania' in *Soviet News*, No. 1179, London, 12.6.1945, p. 1; they were now repeated by *Krasnaya Zvezda:* 'Travaillistes Français essaient de réaliser le plan britannique d'un bloc occidental', Moscow, 24.8.1945 (quoted in French in Blum's riposte, 'L'Étoile rouge fait fausse route', in *Le Populaire*, 28.8.1945, and reprinted in *Œuvre*, vol. vi, pp. 175–7; also Radio Moscow on 15.9.1945, *Krasnaya Zvezda*, 14.9.1945, *Pravda* 17.9.1945, *Trud*, 23.11.1945, etc.; 'Western Bloc or Allied Unity' in *Soviet News*, No. 1217, London, 25.9.1945, p. 1.

Soviet Treaty – that was to say against German aggression. He did not foresee any kind of objection.' Bevin did not ask if there was any Soviet objection to a multilateral Western group, and the possibility of this was not even mentioned. On the contrary, at its meeting on 25 September the British cabinet on the one hand considered the possible break-up of the Council of Foreign Ministers if the Soviet Union continued to insist on the exclusion of France and China, while on the other hand noting that 'care would have to be taken to avoid any action which might bring us under the suspicion of attempting to set up a Western bloc'.[167]

In Foreign Office Harvey on 6 November submitted a 'Draft Cabinet Paper on the proposed Anglo-French Treaty' which clearly defined the limitations of which Molotov had already been notified. In accordance with Molotov's stipulation the treaty was to 'follow closely on the lines of the Anglo-Soviet treaty and be limited to action against German aggression. An alliance conceived on any other or wider basis would be certain to encounter Soviet suspicion.' As regards the other West-European countries the draft observed: Whilst the desire for closer relations between the smaller Western countries has been frequently expressed both by their leaders and in their press, the Communist party and certain sections of the Socialist parties, notably in Belgium, have evinced opposition on the familiar ground that it would consistute an anti-Soviet bloc ... Moreover, the Soviet press have increasingly denounced the policy of the so-called Western bloc which they misrepresent as a move against Eastern Europe. The US Government and press are also critical. For these reasons I doubt the wisdom of pursuing for the present any further negotiations other than those for an Anglo-French Treaty, to which the Soviet Government do not object. The conclusion of an Anglo-French Treaty itself will mark British interest in Western Europe as a whole and so partly satisfy the need of the smaller Western countries for leadership and help orient them towards this country. Later on it may prove to be in our interest and capacity to organize a wider formal association'. In this way the latter was postponed in the Foreign

---

[167] *Public Record Office* (henceforward PRO), Cab. 129, vol. 3 ('Conversation between the Secretary of State and M. Molotov on 23rd September 1945', record by A. Clark Kerr) p. 56, and Cab. 128, vol. 3 (Cabinet meeting 25 Sept., confidential annex), p. 16. According to the record of a second conversation with Molotov before the meeting ended, Bevin assured him: 'He did not want France to be the tool of a Western bloc or an Eastern bloc. He wanted her to have full voting power ... if France, therefore, were admitted as a full member to the Council of Foreign Ministers all suspicions would be dispelled. He could assure M. Molotov that so long as he was in office His Majesty's Government would do nothing consciously to injure Russia, but they would expect the same treatment from the Soviet Union' (Cab. 129, vol. 3, 'Conversation at the Soviet Embassy on 1st October', record by A. Clark Kerr, p. 16).

The following pages have been revised and amplified by the incorporation of material from the records of the Foreign Office and Cabinet meetings between 1945 and 1947, which have become accessible since the German edition of this book went to press. I am grateful to Mr Michael Reece for his help in scrutinizing and copying documents from Collection FO 371 (Foreign Office from Aug. 1945). As far as the cabinet files are concerned I have confined myself to looking at Cab. 128 (minutes of the Cabinet meetings Aug. 1945–Dec. 1947, eleven volumes) and Cab. 129 (Cabinet papers in twenty-two volumes). The correspondence of the Prime Minister (Prem. 8), the papers of the Cabinet Committees, those of the Deputy Under-Secretary of State Oliver C. Harvey, and Bevin's own papers (which are expected to be made available in 1982) will provide further sources for specialist research in depth such as could not be undertaken within the scope of this book.

172   *Europe's Mood of Resignation*

Office to a problematical occasion some time in the future. But no memorandum on the 'Anglo-French Treaty' was presented to the Cabinet; Bevin noted on the draft of 6 November 1945: 'Will study it later as soon as Levant is settled.'[168] In fact the Cabinet did not receive a memorandum on the more limited subject of an Anglo-French Treaty until February 1947 – a delay of some sixteen months.

By way of contrast to this initial reaction and this diplomatic accommodation to the Soviet point of view as shown in the records, Bevin in addressing the House of Commons on 7 November 1945 tried to assert more freedom of manœuvre. He drew two conclusions as to how Britain should react to Soviet wishes. On the one hand, he indicated that he was ready to abandon his efforts to uphold democratic freedom in Eastern Europe: 'We will take no steps, we will do nothing nor allow any of our agents or diplomats to do anything which will stir up hatred, or provoke or create a situation detrimental to Russia in the Eastern European countries' – in the same way as 'we also recognize the Monroe Doctrine in the Western hemisphere'. But this could not mean 'to close the door and prevent entry or any contact with those peoples for trade'. On the other hand:

Neither am I prepared to accept the contentions so often blared from Moscow radio, that Russia claims the right to have friendly relationships with her near neighbours ..., while I am to be regarded as a criminal if I ask to be on good relations with other countries bordering on the British frontier. What am I doing wrong? I am doing nothing to injure anybody, and I am not prepared to accept that position from any other country in the world. What His Majesty's Government are willing to give, they claim the right to have for their part with France, with Holland, Belgium, Scandinavia or other countries – not a Western bloc for war purposes.[169]

---

[168] PRO, FO 371, 59952/05595, Harvey: 'Proposed Anglo-French Treaty'. On this draft a tougher attitude is shown in a minute by Cadogan (Permanent Under-Secretary of State until Jan. 1946): 'If we are arranging insurance against Germany, it seems to me only reasonable to bring in the other Western Powers. These, individually, are not impressive. The only way in which they could be enabled to make a useful contribution would be to integrate them in a Western system, politically, economically and militarily. That might provide a fairly good insurance against Germany. If Russia chooses to regard it as insurance against herself, and if the cap fits, let her wear it. If Russia maintains her present status and strength, she cannot really be afraid of any aggression from the West. If, on the other hand, she is contemplating any aggression herself, we had better take such precautions as we can.' But such clear-sighted reflections were not followed up in the Foreign Office until 1947. The position in the autumn of 1945 was summarized by the officer for French affairs in the Western Department, A. Rumbold, with reference to a Parliamentary question on 22 October: 'The smaller Western allies are not likely to be unduly disappointed when we in due course tell them that we are not at present going to take the lead in the formation of a Western group, provided that we can tell them at the same time that we have concluded or are about to conclude an alliance with France. But there is no doubt that they would be very discouraged if they were to learn, either through a statement in the House of Commons or by any other means, that we had dropped the idea of a Western group, before they were in receipt of any such information about our intentions with regard to the Anglo-French Treaty. We cannot therefore say anything in public now about the idea of a Western group.' (PRO, FO 371, 49070/05435, p. 45 f.).

[169] Bevin in *Parl. Debates, House of Commons*, vol. 415, 7.11.45, col. 1337 f. Cf. the article entitled 'The Schism of Europe' in *The Round Table*, vol. 36, pp. 3–8 (quoted in Fitzsimons (n. 134, p. 33): 'To Western eyes it appears obvious that a main buttress of European peace must be a close associa-

Thus even at this early date Bevin drew what for so many reasons was the obvious conclusion that could have led to Britain playing a helpful and leading part in the movement towards European unity, although *vis-à-vis* Molotov and within the four walls of the Foreign Office it had been decided that Britain did not want to make any use of this 'right' in deference to 'Soviet suspicion'.

A fortnight later Bevin told the House of Commons the result of his further reflections on this point. 'His Majesty's Government must go on with the task of building up friendships with our immediate neighbours economically, and assisting in the well-being of all of us.' But besides adding this qualifying word 'economically' he added: 'I can only say that we shall not, in any arrangements that we make, commit any unfriendly act towards any other nation' – the question remained whether it would be left to the Soviet Union to decide what would be an 'unfriendly act'. Bevin recalled that as early as 1927 'I moved a resolution at the Trade Union Congress, and succeeded in carrying it, declaring that the policy of that movement should be an attempt to create a United States of Europe, the object being to prevent any one country dominating another, and to confer the benefit of a great free trade area.' He welcomed the fact that 'today that idea is being revived', because 'I cannot see a single frontier of Europe today that is economically sound.' He agreed with the previous speaker (Eden) that 'the coming of the atomic bomb and other devastating instruments has caused offensive action to jump ahead both of defence and of the machinery of diplomacy'. He also agreed to a 'remedy'. Eden had 'called it the surrender of sovereignty. I do not want to use that word'; but 'in studying the problem I am driven to ask: will law be observed, if it is arrived at only by treaty and promises and decisions by governments as at present arranged? In all the years this has broken down so often.' The example of the USA deserved to be borne in mind, where the Thirteen States, after tough disputes, 'then decided, for the purpose of conducting foreign affairs, taxation, defence and the regulation of commerce, that they would create a federal body and in the body there would be direct representation of the people, not through the thirteen states, but direct from the people to the federal Parliament of the country'. Much the same thing had happened in South Africa and Australia: 'In the end, to get peace and development, there had to be a federal parliament ... I think it right to let the country see exactly where the surrender of sovereignty leads us. The fact is, no-one ever surrenders sovereignty; they merge it into a greater sovereignty.' Did Bevin say this so clearly (in more specific terms than any other speaker) in order to draw the conclusion that for the time being Britain could not back it? Whatever the reason, his speech, some passages of which sounded like the plea of a European federalist, suddenly, without adding another word about Europe, changed direction, as he went on to say: 'We need a new study for the purpose of creating a world assembly elected directly by the people of the world as a whole, to whom the governments who form the United Nations are responsible and who, in fact,

---

tion of powers led by Great Britain, with France as second member, including the kingdoms of Scandinavia and the Low Countries, eventually perhaps Portugal and a liberalized Italy, and having an eastern outpost in Greece; with a powerful friend across the Atlantic, the degree of whose future interest in purely European affairs remains problematic.'

make the world law which they, the people, will accept.'[170] This implied federalism on the global scale – which after the dropping of the first atomic bombs seemed to many absolutely vital – yet a realist like Bevin could not have been blind to the fact that the Soviet Union at least would certainly never agree to a parliament of the world. But by speaking of what was very much a utopian and long-range objective he diverted attention from the application of the federal principle to Europe.

At that time, in fact (November–December 1945), not even the minimum pre-conditions existed for a policy of co-operation and association between the European countries. In France de Gaulle was still in office. He had not forgotten Syria and wished to have nothing to do with a British alliance. It was also still uncertain if the United States would not obstruct such a policy by continuing to act on the principles laid down by Roosevelt;[171] yet it was only with American help that Britain could expect to avert the threat of national bankruptcy. To cover the huge annual deficit, estimated by Treasury experts at £2,100 million, resulting from lower exports, higher prices for essential imports, and the continuing fall of invisible exports (income from overseas investments, etc.) there was clearly no alternative to asking America for more aid. As the new Chancellor of the Exchequer, Dalton, afterwards summed it up: 'Now we faced, not war any more, only total economic ruin.'[172] Since 11 September a British delegation led by Lord Keynes had been negotiating in Washington, initially in the hope of getting six billion dollars as a gift without interest or strings; but the American experts were bound by Congress to negotiate about credits, no longer as during the war about gifts, and they were also anxious to abolish existing barriers to free trade across the globe. By the Anglo-American financial and trade agreement signed on 6 December 1945 the US granted credits amounting to 4,400 million dollars on extremely favourable terms: interest at 2 per cent (to be remitted in any year when Britain did not have enough foreign currency at its disposal) and repayable in annual

---

[170] 'I am willing to sit with anybody, of any party, of any nation, to try to devise a franchise or a constitution – just as other great countries have done – for a world assembly . . . with a limited objective – the objective of peace.' *Parl. Debates, House of Commons,* vol. 416, 23 Nov. 1945, col. 3, 761 f. and 781–6. Two months earlier Bevin had passed a very cautious judgement on the idea of a world parliament: 'The idea of world government is something which must be carefully nursed in order that the right atmosphere may be created. It is not something that can be imposed from the top. but must be the result of a period of growth.' *The Times,* 17.8.1945, quoted in Fitzsimons (n. 134), p. 39.

[171] For de Gaulle, cf. pp. 204–14, John Foster Dulles, adviser to Secretary of State Byrnes, declared in a speech in New York on 6.10.1945 that 'there would be no bloc of Western powers if the United States can avoid it', but admitted that if disagreement with the Soviet Union continued 'it would lead to different nations carrying out their ideas in particular areas, which might not necessarily be a permanent disaster' (*The Times,* 8.10.1945 quoted in Fitzsimons (n. 134), p. 33. Yet in both countries the prospects and conditions for West-European co-operation were to be considerably more propitious only four months later; cf. n. 178.

[172] Dalton (n. 140), p. 68. Cf. analysis of Britain's economic situation in 1945 in nn. 135–7, with references. Attlee reported to the House of Commons on 24.8.1945 with great reserve on the 'very serious financial position'; according to Boyd (n. 158) Dalton had difficulty in convincing his ministerial colleagues of the seriousness of the situation and the need for economizing.

Europe's Mood of Resignation   175

instalments within fifty years of 1951. Canada granted a credit of 1,250 million dollars on similar terms.

In return Britain pledged herself to adhere to the Bretton Woods Agreement of July 1944, to uphold as far as possible the principle of non-discrimination embodied in it, and to co-operate in the foundation of the International Currency Fund and World Bank at the end of 1945. America's concern for the removal of discrimination against its own exports ran parallel to the economists' belief that the elimination of all political obstacles to a free but jointly regulated system of world trade was essential to avert economic war, promote prosperity, and guarantee peace. Britain had to agree to make sterling convertible within fifteen months (which proved impracticable in 1947), and in no circumstances to raise Commonwealth preferences, but rather to endeavour to reduce them by stages. Finally the agreement forbade the use of any part of the dollar credits to pay back debts to Commonwealth countries (which it took the British over twenty years to pay off by instalments).[173] There were no other strings to the Agreement, which nevertheless clearly bound Britain's interests closely to those of the US.

Meanwhile the American Secretary of State Byrnes, anxious to retrieve something from the wreck of the London Conference of Foreign Ministers, let it be known that he was urgently interested in getting the Big Three to agree on definitive peace treaties. By so doing he increased the bargaining power of the Soviets, with whom he agreed that a three-power conference would be held in Moscow at the end of December. It was there, as Bevin foreshadowed on 7 November, that the two Western foreign ministers yielded to the Soviet Union's inexorable desire to consolidate its hold over Eastern Europe. The only concession they received in exchange was Russian acceptance of free elections in Austria and Hungary and – in return for giving Soviet delegates a place on the Allied Advisory Commission in Japan – the appointment of British and American delegates to a Commission designed to ensure that two leaders of non-Communist parties would be allowed to join the cabinet in Romania and Bulgaria. By accepting these useless (except in the case of Austria) and barely face-saving concessions as a quid pro quo for diplomatic recognition of the East-European governments, the Western powers abandoned *de facto* the

---

[173] Text of the Agreement of 6.12.1945 in Cmd. 6708 and 6709, London, Dec. 1945. Cf. R. F. Harrod, *The Life of John Maynard Keynes,* New York, 1951, pp. 586–623; Dalton (n. 140), pp. 70–81; T. Balogh, 'The International Aspect' in Worswick and Ady (n. 140), pp. 476–510; for a brief account McNeill (n. 139), pp. 676–84; Hawtrey (n. 139), pp. 43–7; R. Mayne, *The Recovery of Europe 1945–1973,* Garden City, 1973², pp. 88–90. On 13.12.1945 the Agreement was approved in the House of Commons by 345 votes (including 319 Labour) against 98. 23 Labour left-wingers voted against it, 44 abstained because they opposed the ties with America; 72 Conservatives voted against it, and 118 abstained because they were in favour of creating a Commonwealth economic bloc (to which Keynes objected that that would be a bloc with countries to which Britain owed more debts than she could pay, which could lend her no more money, and which wanted to buy goods that she could not supply; see Boyd (n. 158), pp. 103 and 106). The huge credit was just enough to cover the deficits of 1945–7; real improvement in the national economy was slight; for 1948 an increased deficit of 1,000 million dollars was expected which only the Marshall Plan was capable of offsetting (cf. chapter III, n. 70).

Yalta insistence on democratic freedom in Eastern Europe. Yet even this did not prevent them from being violently attacked by the Soviets at the first meeting of the UN General Assembly, which took place soon afterwards, over the few issues (Greece and Iran) on which they had not given way. Did Bevin, for his part, in accordance with his statement of 7 November, do his best at the Moscow Conference to make the Soviet Union understand that the West-European countries too must be allowed to establish closer ties with each other? The brief provided on this subject by the Western Department of the Foreign Office ran:

> The Secretary of State might inquire whether Mr Molotov's attitude of non-opposition to an Anglo-French treaty had been endorsed by the Soviet Government ... I do not know whether the Secretary of State, if he gets a favourable reply from Mr Molotov about the Anglo-French treaty, would want to go further and say anything about the possible Western Regional Association. He might perhaps be able, without committing himself in any way, to test Mr Molotov's reactions and see whether the Soviet Government are really so hostile to the idea as their newspapers make out.

During the official sessions of the Moscow Conference between Byrnes, Molotov, and Bevin there was evidently no room for this question; at any rate it does not figure in the 'minutes of the meetings of the three Foreign Secretaries'. But on 19 December Bevin had a private conversation with Stalin in which he concentrated on three major issues: the withdrawal of Soviet troops from Iran, the rejection of Soviet claims to Turkish Armenia and the Dardanelles, and the wish to include India in the discussion of draft peace treaties. Only at the very end of the conversation did Bevin mention the question of a Western bloc, but evidently no real discussion took place. The final paragraph of the record of the meeting runs:

> Before leaving, Mr Bevin said that he wished to touch on one other question, that of the Western bloc. He explained that the United Kingdom must have some security arrangement with France and the other neighbouring countries, just as the Soviet had with her neighbours, to which he raised no sort of objection. But he was resolved to do nothing against the Soviet Government and would not do anything without telling the Generalissimo and explaining it to him. Generalissimo Stalin said 'I believe you'.

Basically, Bevin had thus left open only a vague future possibility, and had made even that subject to the good pleasure of the Soviet Union. In his long report of 1 January 1946 to the Cabinet on all the issues raised at the Moscow Conference, he apparently did not once raise the question of a Western association.[174] Yet in the House of Commons as well as in the

[174] Brief for Moscow (by Hoyer Millar), 12 Dec. 1945, FO 371, 49070/05435, p. 143; 'Proceedings of the Conference between the Foreign Secretaries of the United Kingdom, the United States and the Union of Soviet Socialist Republics, held at Moscow from 16 December to 27 December 1945, together with the records of certain private conversations'; including on pp. 116–19 'Record of a meeting at the Kremlin on 19 December' (quotation on p. 119), FO 371, 57093/07732; Meeting of

Foreign Office there were those who considered it necessary and vital to initiate a policy of bringing together the European countries and who criticized Bevin for dilatoriness and lack of interest.

During the House of Commons debate of 20-1 February 1946 the chief Conservative spokesman, Harold Macmillan, tentatively asked: 'May it not be that the apparent chauvinism of Soviet policy is a form of insurance, not of expansion, that security not imperialism is their instinctive goal?' Had the Soviet Union forced its smaller East-European neighbours under Communist rule in order, while the world was still in a state of exhaustion, 'to seize and fortify bastions against foreign aggression? All this is very wrong and very dangerous, but if this interpretation of Russian motives should be right, it need not be fatal', for in that case it should be possible to remove the fear and reach reconciliation 'by personal and direct negotiations' in the weeks that would follow. The first speaker to urge Britain to get closer to Europe was Wilfrid Roberts, a Liberal: I do not think appeasement ever achieves the result that I want to see, and that is a good understanding. The Russians are much too realistic to have any respect for a country that does appease ... We shall reach a better understanding with the Russians if we make perfectly certain that our own policy is a very positive foreign policy. I do not want to see this country abstaining from positive action in foreign affairs because the Russians may object. For instance, it is highly desirable that we should have the closest understanding with the Western liberal and social democratic countries who mean by democracy the same as we mean. 'We should respond' to the cries for help from Europe. As for Russia's objection, 'We should not take any notice of it. It is not for any negative reason of balancing Russia that I want such an understanding, but for practical positive reasons.' These were the co-operation of those who believed in democracy and the urgent need for economic co-operation.

During the debate a Conservative MP, Robert Boothby, spoke with great emphasis on federation: We had better face the realities of the situation, which are that between these two great federations, that of the Soviet Union on the one hand and the USA on the other, fortified by their satellite powers – because that is all you can call them either in South America or in Eastern Europe – the smaller nations of Western Europe, of whom we are one, cannot hope to survive, politically or economically, in isolation. Unless we get together in pursuit of a common political and economic policy we shall inevitably, sooner or later, be absorbed into one or other of these two great economic and political blocs which surround us, one in the East and the other in the West.[175]

---

the Cabinet, 1 Jan. 1946, Cab. 128, vol. 5, pp. 2-5. Bevin, in his statement to the House of Commons on 21 Feb. 1946, seems to have much exaggerated the extent to which he pressed the issue of a Western bloc in Moscow. He told the House: 'Nothing has percolated through with greater acrimony than the question of a Western bloc. I deliberately raised this question in Moscow. I said, "You want friendly neighbours. Well, in my street I want friendly neighbours, too. I am entitled to have them, but I will do nothing that injures you." ' (*Parl. Debates, House of Commons*, vol. 419, 21.2.1946, col. 1349.) For the Moscow conference, cf. the references quoted in n. 10, also Fitzsimons (n. 134), p. 37 f.

[175] *Parl. Debates, House of Commons*, vol. 419, 20.2.1946, col. 1166 f. (Macmillan), 1183 (Roberts), and 1252 (Boothby); the latter argued that 'the absence of any effective economic co-operation on a regional basis' had ruined Europe during the inter-war period (1247); now Britain should 'take the

In the Foreign Office too voices began to be heard expressing concern and criticism at the dilatory way in which the matter was being handled. One occasion for this was that in the House of Lords a motion was to be introduced by Lord Vansittart to the effect that 'It is necessary to proceed without further delay to the closer integration of Western Europe.' The Foreign Office had twice asked Lord Vansittart to agree to a postponement of the debate on his motion 'because we felt it undesirable for such a motion to be debated now', but on 24 January 1946 this objection was waived. Again, in connection with the attendance of Foreign Ministers at the forthcoming opening session of the UN General Assembly, the head of the Western Department of the Foreign Office, Mr Hoyer Millar, urged in a memorandum dated 1 January 1946: 'We should try to clear our minds as to where we stand in regard to the "Western bloc" ... We have never, I think, really decided whether the conclusion of some kind of Western Regional Association would or would not be desirable and in our interests.' Meanwhile the problem of whether Britain was willing to support French plans for the Ruhr was causing 'still further delay in the conclusion of an Anglo-French Treaty and, therefore, a further prolongation of the present feeling of uncertainty about the relations between this country and our Western European Allies. Any such further delay is, I think, likely to be both unfortunate and embarrassing for us.' For example, as regards Spaak's request for Anglo-Belgian co-operation on military matters and the Dutch request for an exchange of scientific information, 'the position would, of course, be very much easier if we had some clearly defined policy to guide us'. Sir Nigel Ronald, a senior Assistant Under-Secretary of State, who as early as November 1945 had advocated the idea of a Western group, reinforced these criticisms with a memorandum dated 4 January 1946 and arguing that, in accordance with Articles 52–4 of the UN Charter, 'one of the natural groupings for the maintenance of international order will consist of the States of Western Europe'.

It would 'become apparent that these states, acting as a group with defined responsibilities suitably apportioned, will be better able to discharge the obligations devolving on all of them individually from the Charter than if each attempted to discharge his obligations separately on the basis of his own national resources alone'. That applied to their duties as a 'defence group'; but in the same way 'regional arrangements in such fields as monetary co-operation, the promotion of full employment, the co-ordination of national policies on food and agriculture, the maintenance of labour standards and the development of educational and cultural relations will be

---

lead, for which many countries are now looking, to build up a regional economic bloc in Western Europe . . . It is manifestly absurd to suggest that such a federation would be directed against anyone, and no one knows that better than the Kremlin, which has done precisely and exactly the same thing in Eastern Europe already. On the contrary, a united Western Europe would provide a far more substantial and stable market for primary producing countries' (1251). Cf. R. Boothby, *Recollections of a Rebel*, London, 1978.

necessary.... In so far as the countries of Western Europe can take concerted measures for their rehabilitation at once they should clearly do so.' In this connection there was also 'a manifest community of interest among the Western powers that Germany shall not become for all time a festering economic sore on their borders'. The only strong objection came from the Soviet Union: The weaker and more vacillating the Governments of Western Europe are and the less they hang together, the easier it will be for the Soviet Government, through the agency of national Communist parties, to ensure that, far from thwarting, the Western European governments actually serve the ends of Russia, political, economic and even ideological ... If the attitude of Russia is in fact of this nature, how far can the United Kingdom afford to allow herself to be deterred from proceeding further with such plans for a Western European group as she regards as calculated to serve her vital interests? May it not be that, Russia's objective being what they are, this is in itself an added reason why the United Kingdom should go ahead with her Western European plans? The right way of proceeding towards this goal 'should be that the group should grow by accessions to an initial Anglo-French Pact'.

However, a meeting of senior officials of the Foreign Office on 4 January, chaired by the Permanent Under-Secretary of State, Sir Orme Sargent, concerned itself solely with the question whether, as the prerequisite for an Anglo-French treaty, 'a compromise could be worked out on the issue of a West European association which would also take account of French plans for the Ruhr'. Sargent's report to Bevin on this meeting contained the advice: 'Until we have had the matter out further with the French, and see where we stand, you will, no doubt, agree that it would be wise to be very non-committal' towards the wishes of the Belgian and Netherlands governments. In these circumstances this meeting did not go beyond advising that 'some way ought to be found of avoiding a public debate on the Western bloc. Lord Vansittart has a motion down ... It would be better if we could avoid having to answer the question at all.' The officer responsible for French affairs in the Western Department, A. Rumbold, rightly minuted: 'The questions asked by Mr Hoyer Millar were not really touched upon at this meeting.'[176] But de Gaulle's resignation from power removed what was either an obstacle or an excuse for inaction, and the number of critical voices in the Foreign Office and Foreign Service increased. The British ambassador in Paris, Duff Cooper, pointed out in a strongly worded dispatch, dated 19 March 1946, that in the summer of

---

[176] Lord Vansittart's motion in *Parl. Debates, House of Lords*, 24.1.1946, col. 1089–101; requests for postponement from Foreign Office, 24.10., 17.11. and 9.12.45; memo. from Hoyer Millar, 1.1.1946, and from Sir N. Ronald, 4.1.1946; Sargent's report to Berlin on the meeting of 4.1.46 – all in FO 371, 59911/08703. Lord Vansittart described the answer which he received on 24 January as follows: 'I am disquieted by the lethargy and timidity surrounding and obscuring the issue ... The Government's reply was not even a masterpiece of evasion, but an uneasy shuffle' – on which Hoyer Millar remarked: 'I think that we all have a great deal of sympathy with Lord Vansittart and would agree with many of his remarks' (22.2.1846, ibid., FO 371, 59911/08703).

1944 he had advised Bevin's predecessor, Eden, that the democrats of Western Europe shared a 'community of interests, similarity of colonial problems and a mutually inherited tradition of civilization which, combined, should form the surest basis of enduring friendship and even of future federation'. Eden had rejected the suggestion at the time with a reference to the fears of the Soviet Union, and 'I had the temerity to reply to Mr Eden's despatch and to suggest that the arguments in favour of doing nothing were similar to those which had been advanced before the war in favour of the appeasement of Germany.' In the meantime the Soviet Union had imposed its own regime on the countries of Eastern Europe. In France a growing number of people

are frankly puzzled as to the attitude of Great Britain, just as they were puzzled for twenty years between the two wars. Members of my staff and I are plied with questions to which we find difficulty in replying. Do we want an alliance with France? Why do we do nothing about it? ... Only a few days ago M. Bidault said to me that he feared we considered France 'a lost country'. Uncertainty about the policy of Great Britain and anxiety about the future of France are producing a mood of pessimism that verges upon despair ... The time has come, I submit, to count our friends, to fortify them and to bind them closely to our side ... An Anglo-French alliance would form a potent magnet for others who are now looking round rather wildly in search of security and salvation.

The ambassador's appeal reinforced similar efforts of officials in the Western Department. As Rumbold observed in a memorandum of 18 March: 'The time has come once more to consider' how urgent the conclusion of the Anglo-French treaty was, constituting as it did 'an essential preliminary to the organization of a Western European system of security, assuming that that still remains our ultimate aim'; the Soviet Union's main fear was that 'a Western group under predominantly socialist leadership would strengthen the Social Democratic forces throughout Europe'. In a further memorandum of 22 March he referred to the need to support the 'moderate parties' in the June elections in France against the advance of the Communists by providing economic aid and by immediate 'negotiation of the much delayed treaty of alliance; this is probably the easiest step of all, because it would cost us nothing, it would be popular in France and it would bring immediate credit to M. Gouin and M. Bidault. Perhaps even over the Ruhr we could make a concession.' The head of the Department, Hoyer Millar, supported all these views in a minute dated 24 March, suggested a new meeting of senior officials, and summed up his criticism of the existing delay in the following words:

I am afraid that if we continue to turn a cold shoulder to these approaches, we shall end by discouraging the Belgians and the Dutch and so lead them to think that there is no use looking to us for support. Since we seem to arouse Russian suspicions even when we do nothing, I would hope that if we are really agreed that it is in our own interests to go ahead, not only with the Anglo-French alliance, but with the subsequent military agreements with Belgium, etc., we need not be unduly deterred by the fear of Russian opposition and criticism.[177]

Thus in the spring of 1946 Bevin's foreign policy was faced with the question whether or not to go on deferring to Soviet displeasure at any kind of closer contact with the states of Western Europe. Did Bevin still want to acquiesce in what he had trenchantly described on 7 November as 'the contentions blared from Moscow radio' to the effect that any closer relationship between the countries of Western Europe would be 'criminal', or did he prefer to give effect to the conclusions he had himself drawn from the abandonment of the countries of Eastern Europe to Soviet control, and initiate close co-operation and association with all those European countries which, despite loss of status, were still free to pursue such policies? In the spring of 1946 (in contrast to the autumn of 1945) the minimum prerequisites for such a policy undoubtedly existed. Firstly, the shock caused to America's political leaders by Soviet intransigence at the Moscow Conference and the United Nations General Assembly had broken the spell of Roosevelt's policy. Truman had written in January 'I'm tired of babying the Soviets.' In February Byrnes (like Vandenberg too) had announced that he was going to take a firm line, and Churchill in his speech at Fulton – made, as we now know, after consultation with Truman – spoke of the need for the Western world to combine, adding 'The safety of the world requires a new unity in Europe.' Secondly, had Britain made a decision for Europe at that time it would have come just after de Gaulle's resignation: the French Socialists with Prime Minister Gouin were then trying to bring about a change in their country's foreign policy in favour of European co-operation, a move that could well have achieved something had the British responded.[178] Also, from the Socialist

---

[177] Letter (No. 218) from Duff Cooper, 19 March 1946 to Bevin in the original and in reproduction in FO 371, 59952/05595; Rumbold's memoranda of 18 and 22 March with attached notes by Hoyer Millar of 24 March in FO 371, 59953/05727. At the subsequent meeting of senior officials called by Sargent on 29 March it was decided to propose to Bevin 'that we should press the US and Soviet governments to agree to very early discussion of the French Ruhr and Rhineland proposals with a view to a settlement; that we should decide to offer an Anglo-French alliance as our contribution towards a settlement', also economic aid; that, on the other hand, negotiations about a 'regional association of Western European countries' would have little meaning: 'There would be little prospect of the present caretaker French government, which includes Communists, embarking on such a course, to which the Soviet government have always been bitterly opposed' (Minutes of meeting on 'Policy towards France', 29 March 1946 in FO 371, 59952/05595). Rumbold noted on 3.4.1946 as a further result: 'We should *not* offer to enter into staff conversations with the Dutch or the Belgians at least until after we have concluded our alliance with France' (FO 371, 59953/05727). But this time too no treaty with France came about (cf. n. 180).

[178] For the beginning of the American shift towards a policy of firmness, with quotations from the sources named, cf. nn. 10–12 at the beginning of chap. II. The US government had not yet decided what form co-operation should take, but European proposals to this end would have found a ready hearing from the spring of 1946 onwards. For the efforts of the French Socialists after de Gaulle's resignation (which took place on 20.1.1946), see p. |228. A British initiative would have enabled Gouin to go for the alliance with Britain rather than continue Gaullist policy.

point of view, such hopeful co-operation between British and French Socialists would have given Social Democracy in Western Europe the vital stimulus it needed instead of leaving the initiative by default to the Christian Democrats. The moment of decision – and of failure – is easily identified. Bevin decided to do nothing, to accept the Soviet veto, to take no initiative in bringing the Europeans together, and to continue the policy of appeasement towards the Soviet Union. In the House of Commons debate of 4 June 1946 he explained:

'I do not think that it will be impossible for us (the Big Three) at our next meeting to arrive at agreed conclusions. There is no real and insurmountable division. If all parties will try, Europe can revive and security for all can be provided. But they must try; we can and we must, if everybody is willing, bridge the gap now existing between the East and the West ... Not only must we meet, we must understand and learn to co-operate. It is my belief that mutual respect and confidence is now in the process of formation.'

In the same debate the Conservative spokesman on economic affairs, R. A. Butler, criticized the absence of any initiative in European policy and encouraged Bevin to act to overcome the chaos in Europe. The development of closer links with France and the reconstruction of the German economy must be the main stages in the creation of a 'co-operative society' of the West-European countries which should develop on the basis of a common cultural tradition. Robert Boothby again called for a federal union in which the economic and political integration of Western Europe, including Great Britain, could be brought about. In this way the Commonwealth, united with the West-European democracies and their colonies, could become a powerful factor for security and peace in the world. But from the government there came not the slightest reference to the problem or to the first major question, whether Britain would either help the Continent towards co-operation and union without itself being a full member (as envisaged by Churchill, Layton, and others) or whether it would become a full member of a federation (as proposed by Boothby, Mackay, and others). The government passed over the whole issue in silence.[179]

Since Bevin remained determined to arrive at 'agreed conclusions' as discussed at the Moscow Conference, he was uninterested in the early conclusion of an Anglo-French treaty, which Foreign Office officials saw as the prerequisite of possible future regional associations. He did indeed instruct Harvey on 4 April to find out what Gouin had meant when, five days earlier, he had spoken of the possibility of such a treaty. But, after the

---

[179] *Parliamentary Debates, House of Commons*, vol. 423, 4 June 1946, col. 1850 (Bevin), 1859 f. (R. A. Butler), and 1949 f. (Boothby); cf. further quotations from Boothby's speech at n. 205 below. Towards the end of his speech Bevin urged an agreement in the near future between the Big Three, but began by refusing to discuss alternatives: 'It is obvious that the world cannot be left in this undecided state. We cannot be forced to acquiesce in an indefinite stalemate. We must regularize our relations with the ex-enemy countries. It cannot go on very much longer. There have been, in the course of these difficulties, other ideas promulgated, but I will not pronounce an opinion upon them now. I propose to make another effort at agreement before deciding on any final or alternative form' (ibid., col. 1847).

French Cabinet had declared on 5 April that it adhered to its policy regarding the Ruhr and the Rhineland and wished for Franco-British talks to include 'all outstanding questions between the two governments', Bevin on 11 April answered brusquely that he could only consider an 'alliance without conditions';

> In view of the French Government's communiqué, I propose to take no further action in the matter or to make any statement myself until such time as M. Bidault approaches me in regard to his proposal that all outstanding questions between the two governments should be discussed ... It must however be remembered that the question of the future of Germany's Western frontier is a matter which concerns all four occupying powers.

No such approach took place. When on 15 May 1946 Bevin and Bidault met for a private conversation at the end of the fruitless first round of negotiation at the Council of Foreign Ministers, according to Bevin's record 'M. Bidault said that he wished he could revive the proposal for common citizenship made by Mr Churchill to M. Reynaud in 1940, but he feared that it was too late to carry the proposal or, at least, too soon to revive it ... If we wanted an alliance tomorrow, we could have it, but he thought our view was that it was to wait to settle these matters until after the French elections. That was also his view.' But six weeks after those elections, during an urgent visit by Duff Cooper to London, Harvey, noted on 25 July: 'There are further French elections in October, whilst in November the Big Four will begin their German talks in earnest. Having waited until now, there is much to be said for waiting until a German settlement has been reached, or at any rate its outline, and a more stable political set-up has appeared in France.' Actually the question of an Anglo-French treaty lay dormant for the rest of the year. And at the Paris Peace Conference of twenty-one states which met from 29 July to 15 October 1946 and, not without difficulty, prepared for signature peace treaties with former allies of the Axis, there was no mention of a European regional association in any shape or form.[180] However, at a Foreign Office meeting in August Bevin declared that it would be useful for all eventualities to put up to the Cabinet a paper requesting authority to initiate a 'study of the

---

[180] Report by Duff Cooper (No. 141), 4 April 1947 on his and Harvey's conversations with Bidault and Gouin; reports by Duff Cooper (no. 202), 5.4.1947 and (no. 206) 9.4.1947 with communiqués from the French Cabinet – all in FO 371, 59952/05595. Bevin's instruction (No. 765 – draft by Hoyer Miller with hand-written corrections by Bevin) of 11 April to Duff Cooper (circulated to the Cabinet, with copies sent to Washington, Moscow, Brussels, The Hague) in FO 371, 59953/05727. Bevin's memorandum on his 'Conversation with M. Bidault' in Paris, 15.5.1946; Note by Harvey of 25 July – both in FO 371, 59954/05762. According to information kindly supplied by Mr Reece (cf. n. 167), the Foreign Office records on the Paris Peace Conference, 29 July – 15 Oct. 1946 (FO 371, 57341-393) clearly show the growing divergence between the Western powers and Russia; 'nothing about European union, however, no mention of it at all'. Bevin was able to say of it what he had told the House of Commons on 7 Nov. 1945: 'All this chopping and changing of frontiers over hundreds of years has made people very little richer' (*Parl. Debates, House of Commons*, vol. 415, col. 1342).

possibilities of close economic co-operation with our Western European neighbours'.

A paper on these lines was drafted by Roger Stevens, discussed with the Departments concerned, and shown to officials of the Board of Trade and the Treasury. After their amendments had been included it was submitted to Bevin on 10 October 1946 and circulated with his approval to members of the Cabinet on 18 October. The paper advanced two reasons why it would be useful to set up a study-group as suggested. Firstly, Britain favoured the 'maximum possible expansion of world trade' as laid down in the Anglo-United States Financial Agreement of 6 December 1945, but it was not impossible 'that the United States' sponsored plan for an expansion of multilateral trade will break down'. Secondly, Britain was trying 'to prevent, if possible, the division of Europe ... into exclusive economic blocs', but the danger was growing 'not only that the Eastern half of Europe will be excluded altogether from the general free expansion of trade, but also that the USSR will seek to extend its political and economic influence into Western Europe. We shall prevent this only if we are prepared with measures which, involving close economic ties, would bind Western European countries politically more closely to ourselves.' Should it be necessary, for both these reasons, 'to strengthen our ties with Western Europe we may be faced, therefore, with the necessity of taking a single plunge into a full customs union, which has always been exempted from the operation of the most-favoured-nation clause, and is expressly permitted under the United States proposals on commercial policy. Such a step would need the most careful consideration. It raises great practical difficulties connected with the position of the Dominions and the status of the respective colonial empires. Moreover, for its successful working over any length of time some measure of concerted industrial and commercial planning with other members of the Union would be necessary. It would be impossible, without extensive preliminary study, to determine whether in fact, on balance and in the circumstances envisaged, it would be economically of advantage to the United Kingdom.' Accordingly, the Cabinet was asked 'to sanction' without prejudice to any ultimate decision, the most complete possible study by the departments concerned of the practicability and desirability of: (i) a full customs union (ii) some special economic regime, falling short of a full customs union', either with France alone or with 'Western Europe as a whole', either in the event that the US proposals for an International Trade Organization came into operation or in the event that they failed to do so.

The establishment of a study-group of this kind was intended to be decided at a Cabinet meeting on 25 October 1946. On 23 October Deputy Under-Secretary of State Hall-Patch feared opposition from the Board of Trade on balance-of-payment grounds and on the pretext of the difficulty of making officials available for the study, to counter which a suggestion might be made to 'farm out part at least of this work to a number of university economists'. Whether for this or another reason, Bevin himself at the Cabinet meeting withdrew his proposal to set up a study-group: 'The Foreign Secretary said that, on reflection, he had decided not to ask the Cabinet to consider this proposal until after the forthcoming elections in France. The Cabinet agreed to defer consideration of the proposal.'[181] Sir Nigel Ronald once more had reason to complain on 11 November 'that HMG have never finally made up their minds what they did really think about the utility of a Western Group', that 'that idea has never received any sort of formal blessing by the Foreign Secretary or the Government', and that 'the Foreign Secretary is very dubious about a Western Group'. Yet a meeting of all the Assistant Under-Secretaries and Heads of Departments concerned with European questions, held on 5 December to discuss a draft paper in which Sir Nigel Ronald again urged the creation of a 'Western European Security System', showed clearly that the majority of these senior officials were equally 'very dubious about a Western Group'.[182]

Meanwhile Bevin had for the first time stated emphatically that the results of the New York meeting of the Council of Foreign Ministers had been unprofitable for the West; the Soviet Union had secured the peace treaties it wanted with the East-European satellites, but he, Bevin, had tried without success to persuade the Russians to make less use of their veto at the United Nations. 'We in Britain are now at the point where we

[181] Roger Stevens on 10 October to Bevin, submitting draft of a paper with brief review of the background (Fo 371, 53008/08587). Steven's first draft, dated 5 September (for which the third Deputy Under-Secretary of State, Sir Edmund Hall-Patch, was responsible), the correspondence with J. R. C. Helmore of the Board of Trade and E. Rowe-Dutton of the Treasury, the inclusion of their sceptical and varying approaches in the draft (points 8–11) in FO 371, 53007/08292. Minutes of 23 October by Hall-Patch, to Bevin's private secretary in FO 371, 53008/08587. Cabinet paper (46) 386 in Cab. 129, vol. 13; Conclusions of Cabinet meeting, 25 Oct. 1946, in Cab. 128, vol. 6. Not until 18 Jan. 1947 was the 'Proposal for a Study of the possibilities of close economic co-operation with our Western European neighbours' laid before the Cabinet 'with only slight amendments' and with the additional argument: 'The French Government has suggested that it would like to pursue informal discussions about the possibility of closer economic integration on the basis of the Monnet Five-Year Plan. It is my belief that an examination of British and French economic plans, with a view to preventing conflicts between them, could usefully take place . . . and M. Blum during his recent visit was informed accordingly' (C.P. [47] 35, Cab. 129, vol. 16). Not until February 1947 was a start made in forming subcommittees of a study-group of that kind, so that, before any political proposals could emerge from this project, it was overtaken by Marshall's initiative.
[182] Sir. N. Ronald on 11 Nov. (obviously 1946) in handwriting to Sir O. Sargent; memorandum by Sir N. Ronald on 4 Dec. 1946; Record of meeting on 5 December (two versions) – all in FO 371, 59911/08703. According to the record the main counter-arguments were: 'Without the participation of the United States there was thought to be only a small chance of the countries of Western Europe being able to withstand a Russian attack . . . Our initial approach would have in any case to be made to the Americans.' Yet it 'would be quite fatal', for 'it would excite in the Americans all their old prejudices against exclusive spheres of influence; the Russians would profess to see in the proposals an attempt to set on foot a 'Western bloc' in its most pernicious form; the French would regard it as an attempt to inveigle them into an Anglo-Saxon combination against Russia. . . . If a scheme was unacceptable to the Russians because it appeared to them to constitute an attempt to create a Western European group divided against Russian interests, it would be unacceptable to any French government for the same reason.' However, 'Ronald's cockshy' could be sent to the ambassadors in Washington, Moscow, and Paris for comments. A note from R. M. A. Hankey of the Northern Department displayed the greatest measure of support: 'I am coming more and more to the conclusion that the real Soviet aim is to disintegrate the Western countries and particularly to isolate ourselves. In my view the best answer to this is to go quietly ahead and organize Western Europe' (ibid.).

must establish our general policy. We had hoped that the debates here would allow us to tell the British people that we are prepared to base our policy on the United Nations. Unfortunately, as things stand, this will be impossible.' At this juncture, the coincidence of three events indicated the direction in which a 'forward policy' could at last be launched.

The elections in Poland – important for Britain and for Bevin personally – were held on 19 January 1947, a year later than promised, and were turned by the Soviet Union into a performance that had nothing in common with the 'free and unfettered voting' that had also been promised. The ballot took place after a series of arrests lasting several months and in an atmosphere of terror, of which the Polish Socialist leader Zygmunt Zulawski, who had earlier approved the principle of co-operating with the Communists, said: 'They were not elections at all, but a display of organized violence against the voter and his conscience.' In a protest note Bevin condemned the whole process as a flagrant breach of the Yalta and Potsdam agreements, and clearly thereafter felt freer to make his own independent decisions.

Two days before, on 17 January 1947, the United Europe Movement had been launched in London with a cautious Declaration of Principles initiated by Churchill; to emphasize its all-party character, the committee of the Movement was composed of politicians of all parties in proportion to their importance and of leading personalities in the Churches and in cultural life. Clearly the only possible objective of an independent British foreign policy could no longer be left to the Conservatives alone.[183] When, on 15 January 1947, Léon Blum, the 'grand old man' of Continental Socialism, visited London as French Prime Minister, it was almost certainly not just to plead for the sort of Anglo-French treaty that Bevin was in the end willing to agree to: it can be assumed that Blum as a convinced supporter of European unity asked for further moves to be made in that direction.

Yet what soon turned out to be Britain's last chance of launching an independent foreign policy with the object of rallying the peoples of Europe left Bevin quite unmoved. A decision to offer closer co-operation and association to the countries which were ready and able to respond could have set in motion efforts to unify Europe as an enterprise undertaken by the Europeans themselves. Instead it was the US Congress which acted two months later, with the result that the movement in favour of unification acquired a more restricted character and was represented as a corner-stone of the Western alliance in the developing Cold War. In view of Bevin's dominant position in the Cabinet there is no doubt that from this time on

---

[183] Bevin's statement in the *Observer*, 24.11.1946 (quoted in Fitzsimons (n. 134), p. 89). For the Polish elections on 19.1.1947, cf. p. 461. (The quotation from Zulawski in J. Braunthal, *Geschichte der Internationale*, vol. 3, Hanover, 1971, p. 134). For the founding of the United Europe Movement on 16.1.1947, see p. 325 f. (where the names of members of the committee who belonged to the Labour Party are given). For Léon Blum, see Index of Persons.

he stubbornly continued to oppose a close association with the Continent. Even before the end of January 1947 the Executive Committee of the Labour Party warned members of the party not to take part in the United Europe Movement because it was 'an embarrassment to Britain's Labour government, which was trying to avoid anything that would tend to embarrass its relations with the Soviet government'.[184]

In reply to an urgent motion in the House of Commons (which, signed by seventy-two MPs, urged the government 'to affirm Britain's readiness to federate with any other Allied nations willing to do so on the basis of a federal constitution'),[185] Bevin deputed his Parliamentary Under-Secretary of State Christopher Mayhew to explain rather patronizingly: 'The question of European unity has, however, cropped up from time to time ... We have noticed, too, a great deal of talk outside this House on this subject, and we see, too, suspicions in the minds of our Soviet friends that these proposals are tending in fact to develop against the Soviet Union' – without a word to suggest that the suspicions were unfounded, or that Europeans were entitled to take steps to overcome their political and economic disunity.[186]

In this way the Soviet Union in addition to its legally established right of veto in the United Nations, which Bevin had tried to curb, acquired so patently a *de facto* right of veto in Western Europe, where it had no legal standing, that one can hardly help wondering whether Bevin was not using a pretext to defend a policy on which he had already made up his mind. Whether his attitude should be ascribed to his own reluctance or to deference to the Soviet Union, Bevin obviously desired to reduce the treaty with France – which, in view of the insistence of the French Socialist government and of the British parliament, he could no longer refuse – to

---

[184] For the decision by the United States Congress at the end of 1947 to promote a 'United States of Europe', cf. p. 470 below. The veto of the Labour Party's Executive Committee, quoted from the *New York Herald Tribune* of 21.1.1947, is confirmed by E. Windrich (n. 154), p. 188 (members of the Labour Party were warned not to join the United Europe Movement because it was too much of a challenge to the Soviet Union) and Heiser (n. 134), p. 28.

[185] Cf. verbatim report on this motion, evidence, etc. in chapter II, n. 87; for the sponsoring group and names of signatories see chapter III, n. 360.

[186] Moreover Mayhew went on to explain immediately after the quoted passage: 'It is easy enough at first sight to feel sympathy with almost any proposal for diminishing the unfettered sovereignty of the nations of Europe in an atomic age. Such sovereignty in the circumstances of today is surely an anachronism, and many people . . . would welcome the merging of the nations simply on the grounds that sovereignty in itself is bad.' Yet one could not simply welcome a United States of Europe 'merely because it aimed at the elimination of sovereignty. We ought first to ask ourselves how it will work out in practice. What countries will in fact support it? Will it in fact unite Europe, or accentuate divisions? Has it got the appropriate leadership? These are the questions we must ask before we can give such schemes our blessing, and the view of my right honourable friend is that at present these schemes are premature and more likely to lead to disunity than to unity in Europe.' (*Parl. Debates, House of Commons*, vol. 433, 27.2.1947, col. 2405). Can Bevin, after his experience of Soviet stubbornness in imposing its authority in Eastern Europe, have seriously believed, as many Continental federalists such as Vassenhove did, in a real possibility of uniting Europe, including Poland; or was his clear perception that sovereignty would have to be pooled the real reason for his renunciation of the idea? One can only eagerly await Bullock's investigation of this point when his third volume on Bevin appears (n. 161), and publication of the relevant documents.

little more than a polite allusion to the historic past which had nothing to do with taking the first step towards European co-operation. The treaty was signed with Bidault at Dunkirk on 4 March 1947.[187] Not until 15 May did Bevin inform the House of Commons of the 'happy event', with the clear intention of playing down its significance: 'In signing that Treaty we have confirmed that, while Germany may be down and out at the moment and is not a danger, we do not forget what France has suffered ... As anyone who reads this Treaty will see, its purpose is to provide for mutual assistance in the event of any renewal of German aggression.'

Lord Hinchingbrooke, MP, aptly commented: 'He spoke of it, if I may say so without offence, in a rather old-fashioned Foreign Office sense ... Those were the terms in which treaties were written before the war.' There was, he observed, no specific agreement for economic co-operation with France or indeed (as Eden had already pointed out) with other European countries. Kenneth Lindsay, a Labour MP, spoke with restrained bitterness of the 'little gleam of hope' that Bevin would at last realize the 'realities of Europe' and the rapid 'deterioration of the respect in which this country is held ... Now we are literally part of the Continent.' 'It is time we realized that where we cannot obtain Russian co-operation we must go ahead on our own and with those who will act ... Because the people of this country believe that if we do not go ahead ... there will be not only a feeling of deep frustration on the continent but a feeling that their own austerity and economic conditions are never going to improve.' Anthony Nutting, a Conservative MP, summed it up: ever since the war the British government had scrupulously avoided anything 'which could be regarded as hostile, or in any way opposed to Russia. For two years we have avoided making any counter-bloc to that of the Slav group' until now they faced 'the danger of total collapse of Western Germany and through her of democracy in Europe ... Where Soviet collaboration is not and cannot be obtained ... we must concentrate all our energies on restoring Western and Mediterranean Europe ... the last chance to save Europe from the slow death with which it is now threatened.'[188]

[187] The memorandum to the Cabinet C.P. (47) 64 (Cab. 129, vol. 17) dated 26 Feb. 1947 emphasized that the Anglo-French treaty 'follows the general lines of the Anglo-Soviet and the Franco-Soviet treaties'; to enter any further into the details of the record would go beyond the scope of this book. The contracting parties pledged themselves 'in the event of any threat to the security of either of them arising from the adoption by Germany of a policy of aggression' to take, after appropriate consultation, 'such agreed action ... as is best calculated to put an end to this threat' (Art I). 'Should either of the High Contracting Parties become again involved in hostilities with Germany, either in consequence of an armed attack' by Germany ... or as a result of agreed action taken against Germany under Article I of this treaty, or as a result of enforcement action taken against Germany by the United Nations Security Council, the other High Contracting Party will at once give ... all the military and other support and assistance in its power' (Art. II). There was also a vague promise of 'constant consultation on matters affecting their economic relations with each other' (Art. IV), and the whole treaty was 'without prejudice to any arrangements that may be made between all the powers having responsibility for action in relation to Germany under Article 107 of the Charter of the United Nations' (Art. I). Text in *United Nations Treaty Series*, vol. ix, 1947, p. 188 f. As anyone who had grasped the potential of the new superpowers would realize, this treaty 'faced the past rather than the future' and 'fell far short of the type of leadership of all Western Europe which people like Paul-Henri Spaak were seeking from Great Britain' (Nutting [n. 160], p. 17).
[188] *Parl. Debates, House of Commons*, vol. 437, 15.5.1947, col. 1742 (Bevin), 1790 (Hinchingbrooke), 1751 (Eden), 1786–9 (Lindsay), and 1816 f. (Nutting). E. M. King (Labour) spoke of having reached a 'moment in history when a real appeal for a degree of functional unity, if not of organic

Bevin remained deaf to all these arguments. His great service in the year 1945–6 was that he made every effort to get co-operation with Stalin and then realized that it was impossible. His most serious limitation was that at the moment when he recognized this he clearly perceived a constructive political idea but did not dare or wish to translate it into reality – either because he considered Britain had already become too weak to conduct an independent European policy, or because the idea of close association with the Continent was simply uncongenial to him (a point which will be examined later). For over nine months from March 1947 he left it to the United States to make the running for European unification (ignoring the European federalists). Not until 22 January 1948 did he take a stand of his own, and even then the main burden of his speech was to prevent co-operation developing into full unification.[189] He had refused to make Britain the spokesman for Europe and to give a lead to the Continental peoples in fulfilling their vision of Europe's future.

(C) MOTIVES AND ALTERNATIVES

It is easier to grasp the motives behind this refusal if they are seen in contrast to the various alternative policies put forward in Britain, as well as in relation to Bevin's arguments against these alternatives. They were, in essence, three possibilities, each divisible into two or more variants, and they were all proposed both inside and outside parliament by well-known politicians opposed to Bevin's foreign policy, which was seen to be sterile as early as February 1946.

The first alternative was championed from the spring of 1946 onwards at party conferences and in the House of Commons by a section of the left wing of the Labour Party led by Harold Laski, Richard Crossman, Michael Foot, and Konni Zilliacus. Its belief was that the difficulties of co-operation with the Soviet Union, which had become apparent at the end of 1945 and were debated in the House of Commons after 21 February 1946, had arisen because Bevin was too mistrustful and reserved in his approach to the Soviet Union. Specialized studies of this period which have so far appeared (by Fitzsimons, Windrich, Meehan, and Schwarz) have concentrated almost exclusively on this first alternative and have assessed Bevin's foreign policy by that criterion.[190] The left-wing group

---

union, in Europe could be made. . . . We unite against no-one, but in order to preserve our lives against economic and political ills which can be removed in no other way' (Col. 1822).

[189] For Britain's reaction to the Marshall Plan, cf. chapter III/2, pp. 488–95, which takes up the story of Britain's attitude to the question of Europe. There is a clear distinction between Bevin's positive attitude to the offer of economic help and his negative attitude to the appeal for unity connected with it. For the speech of 22.1.1948, cf. chapter V/1 in vol. 2.

[190] Cf. the books mentioned in nn. 134, 154, and 148 (H.P. Schwarz in the chapter 'Die Labour-Bewegung im Zwiespalt: "Britische Interessenpolitik oder sozialistische Aussenpolitik"?', pp. 156–65). In specialist studies of this subject the section of the Labour left wing which urged an independent policy for Europe has not hitherto been given the attention it deserves (cf. nn. 197–200).

complained with mounting bitterness that Bevin did not try with sufficient determination to put into effect the 'socialist foreign policy' promised in the election campaign of 1945, especially friendship with the USSR, but had reverted to the old and dangerous path of power politics, and in practice was carrying out a Tory policy. This group criticized the British policy of intervention and support for free elections in Greece, the policy of non-intervention in Spain, gullibility towards 'Yankee imperialism', and lack of confidence in the Soviet Union. Criticism reached its first climax at the annual conference at Bournemouth in July 1946, when a resolution was moved that the conference 'calls on the government (a) to maintain and strengthen an attitude of sympathy and trust towards the Soviet Union ... (b) to reject any proposal likely to make the British Commonwealth a satellite of American monopoly capitalism'.[191]

Criticism from this group reached its second and final climax when they launched a revolt after the speech from the throne in October 1946 and moved an amendment urging the government to follow a more pro-Russian and less pro-American policy. Crossman urged in the debate of 18 November: 'Only a Labour government could mediate fairly between Russia and America ... only a Labour government would want genuine friendship with America and genuine friendship with Russia ... – That was the centre-piece of foreign policy on which the government fought the general election.' Accordingly, the important thing was 'to co-operate fully with Russia and America, refuse all exclusive commitments on either side, and remain really independent, even at economic cost to ourselves, and through that independence exert moral influence which alone can save the world'. These words appeared to point to the Utopia that was envisaged in much the same terms by French and German neutralists (the Nauheim Circle for example), with the idea that any one of the diminished European nation states could play the part of a mediator or 'third force' (a role which only a united Europe might have been capable of playing). But the amendment went on to show a different emphasis by expressing 'the urgent hope that His Majesty's government will so review and recast its conduct of international affairs as to afford the utmost encouragement to, and collaboration with, all nations and groups striving to secure full socialist planning ...', on which Hans-Peter Schwarz pertinently remarks: 'This kind of language shows clearly that in spite of all the professions of friendship with both camps, the heart was more inclined towards the planned economy of the Soviet Union.'[192] The amendment was withdrawn by the group after incisive criticism

[191] *Report of the 45th Conference of the Labour Party*, London, 1946, p. 157. At the same conference Harold Laski said: 'Let capitalist governments mistrust one another; that mistrust is inherent in capitalist society. But governments like the Russian and our own are the surest hope of peace when they find the road to the same ends' (ibid., p. 106). A comprehensive collection of similar utterances by left-wingers is to be found in E. J. Meehan, *The British Left Wing and Foreign Policy*, New Brunswick, NJ, 1960, pp. 66–114 (dealing with the years 1945–6).

[192] *Parl. Debates, House of Commons*, vol. 430, 18.11.1946, col. 527 f. (Crossman) and 526 (amendment), analysed by H. P. Schwarz (n. 148), p. 158. The Fabian International Research Group in November–December 1946 resolved to draw up 'the outlines of a Socialist foreign policy for Great Britain', but at the beginning of 1947 published instead a pamphlet entitled *Foreign Policy: the Labour Party's Dilemma* – a significant change of title. In this publication Leonard Woolf argued that Britain must support peace and collective security even though these were not specifically

Europe's Mood of Resignation

by Attlee. At the party conference as well as in the House of Commons Bevin's foreign policy was approved by large Labour majorities. The doctrinaire intellectuals of the Left, after once again rejecting Britain's connection with the US in a pamphlet entitled 'Keep Left' which appeared at the beginning of May 1947, sank into insignificance in the next few months when faced with the harsh reality of Russia's abuse of power.[193]

In 1945 Bevin's own attitude had not been far from the left-wing point of view, as was indicated by the resolution at the party conference urging the government 'to maintain and strengthen an attitude of sympathy and trust towards the Soviet Union'. With his genuinely democratic outlook he could not turn a blind eye to the fact that the Soviet Union was a totalitarian police state; but for the sake of peace between the Big Three he did his best, at least until January 1946, to co-operate with the Soviet Union and made it his first priority. Throughout 1946, moreover, he kept open the way for Soviet co-operation with the West by formally recognizing the Soviet Union's 'Monroe Doctrine' in Eastern Europe and by respecting its veto on the strengthening of ties between the West European countries. His main achievement was the proof, which Churchill would hardly have sought at such a cost, that the policy did not work. For that reason the bulk of the Labour Party were convinced of the rightness of Bevin's policy when, in speech after speech, he described all that he had offered the Soviet Union without getting any response. In the words of his Parliamentary Under-Secretary Christopher Mayhew: 'Our efforts to extend the Anglo-Soviet Treaty, our attempt to increase Anglo-Soviet trade, our well-intentioned cultural initiatives such as our suggestion for a mass exchange of teachers and pupils with the Soviet Union, our patient attitude at the United Nations and on the Allied Control Commission in Germany – all these things failed to win Soviet co-operation.' On the contrary: 'More and more of the Yalta Agreement was violated, more satellite states established. In Germany quadripartite government became bogged down. The Cominform was founded. The Soviet veto stultified the work of the

---

Socialist aims, and must realize that it had become 'a second-class power' which must steer clear of the power politics of the USA and the USSR. W. N. Ewer, on the other hand, urged close co-operation with the US. Laski in his Introduction condemned both views (quoted in Fitzsimons [n. 134], p. 52 f.).

[193] The pamphlet *Keep Left*, London, 1.5.1947, mainly by Crossman, Michael Foot, and Ian Mikardo, opposed 'the Tory idea of bolstering up the British Empire with American dollars' and all 'spheres of influence'. The Labour Party Congress at the end of May 1947 witnessed only a mild echo of left-wing revolt; after the decisions taken in the spring of 1948 'ideological criticism persisted, but the critics, thereafter, were or appeared to be Communist fellow-travellers' (Fitzsimons [n. 159], p. 212 f.). Cf. the summary in the chapter 'Socialist Foreign Policy: Reductio ad Absurdum' in Fitzsimons (n. 134), pp. 50–4. Crossman later became a supporter of NATO (ibid., p. 54) but Michael Foot remained incorrigible, as did D. N. Pritt (at that time a member of Labour's left wing), whose book *The Labour Government 1945–51*, London, 1963, in pp. 53–80 continued to criticize Bevin for his failure to show unqualified friendship for the Soviet Union.

Security Council.'[194] Those members of Labour's left wing who refused to see the point were a small minority even at the two peak periods of their revolt. It may have suited Bevin to placate the group stating that he would not do more to promote the idea of European unity because it would displease 'our Soviet friends', but he was far from having to act in this way because of their susceptibilities. His negative attitude and lack of support and understanding for a policy of European unification must have had other causes. He did not, it should be noted, allow the Left to deter him, in and after the spring of 1946, from working for an increasingly close association with the Americans, whose friendly approach, in contrast to that of the Russians, and their wealth, applied to economic recovery, were in themselves convincing arguments. Bevin welcomed with relief the US agreement, announced on 4 June, to co-operate in the occupation of Germany for twenty-five years, and he lectured the House of Commons on 22 October after Byrnes's speech in Stuttgart: 'It cannot be too often repeated that the continuance of American interest in Europe is vital to the peace of Europe.' He agreed to the merging of the British and American Zones in Germany. When in February 1947 the Treasury announced that United States credits would be exhausted in twelve months, when British troops evacuated Cairo and Attlee announced that they would be withdrawn from India by the end of the year, Bevin sent his famous telegram to Washington (not Moscow!) declaring that Britain could no longer bear the cost of aid to Greece and Turkey. But, as Anthony Nutting pithily expressed it in 1960, Bevin preferred for Britain at this time 'the comfortable role of junior partner of America to the challenge and responsibility of being the senior partner of Western Europe'.[195] Why?

For this is what the *second alternative*, as has been seen, had increasingly urged, though up to now special studies of the period have mentioned it only in passing. Initiatives should be taken to build up close economic and political co-operation and association with and among European states which were willing to do so; Britain, as the only victorious European nation, should give the Continent the expected lead towards co-operation and unification, without herself being completely merged in it and without

---

[194] C. Mayhew, 'British Foreign Policy since 1945' in *International Affairs,* vol. 26, 1950, pp. 477–86 (quotation on p. 479). Similar views can be found in each of Bevin's speeches already quoted. Cf. the explanation by Mayhew (ibid., p. 480); 'Our suspicions became confirmed that the Soviet Government, blinded by false dogmas – in particular, I believe, a conviction that the economic collapse of the West was inevitable and that the West was bound, by its nature, to be irreconcilably hostile to the Soviet Union – had reached the disastrous conclusion that it had more to gain by weakening and undermining the regimes of the West – by hastening their inevitable collapse – than by trying to co-operate with them.'

[195] Bevin on 4.6.1946 (*H.C.,* vol. 423, col. 1842 f.) and 22.10.1946 (*H.C.,* vol. 427, col. 1510). The events of February 1947 are excellently summarized by Mayne (n. 173), pp. 105–9; Nutting (n. 160), p. 12. Attlee in his memoirs (n. 160), p. 170, encapsulates the whole process in one laconic sentence: 'While this friction with Russia increased, we naturally drew closer to the United States' – without even mentioning the possibility of an association with Europe.

any constitutional strings. This second alternative to Bevin's policy was in principle supported by two very different schools of thought, one in the Conservative and the other in the Labour camp. The cause of European association was supported in the course of 1946 by a rapidly growing section of the parliamentary Conservative party, a development which cannot be described in detail here. In 1945, when circumstances still precluded the feasibility of such a policy, Churchill himself remained silent. Only his friend and confidant L. S. Amery, in an article in *The Times* at the end of November, proposed the goal of a 'European Association or Commonwealth based on mutual co-operation' – albeit with the rider that Europe would not follow a *laissez-faire* policy in the style of the American economy during the preceding century, but needed a good deal of planning and control to achieve economic recovery. But as soon as de Gaulle's departure and America's switch to the policy of containment created more favourable conditions, Churchill returned to the public eye with his long-cherished design, now ripe for realization, for overcoming Europe's chaos and reviving the fortunes of the devastated Continent through co-operation and unity. The intention was not only to form the free states into an anti-Soviet bastion, but to enable the civilized world to save itself by signing a definitive peace and by co-operation among all its members, making possible the readmission of Germany – a point on which Churchill, unlike Bevin, set much store – into a free, democratic system of European states. The sense of commitment and the deep conviction that show in every sentence of his carefully thought-out speeches in 1946 and 1947 admit of no doubt: a Churchill in office would not have hesitated and procrastinated as Bevin did even in 1948 but would have seized the initiative in 1946 and fought tooth and nail for the realization of his design, including the creation of a Council of Europe. 'Anything', he exclaimed in the House of Commons debate of 5 June 1946, 'is better than this ceaseless degeneration of the heart of Europe. Europe will die of it!' Since Churchill was thinking not of a constitutional federation but of a Commonwealth kind of association with moral rather than legal ties, Europe would not have escaped the later dispute between federalism and functionalism.[196] But the phase of co-operation would have been started in the spring of 1946 instead of two years later, and would have been sponsored by a European country at the very time when Bevin's policy was running out of ideas.

[196] L. S. Amery in *The Times*, 27.11.1945 (quoted in Fitzsimons [n. 134], p. 36); for Churchill's idea, see n. 145 f. above, and at greater length in the analysis of his speeches on Europe in 1946–7 in Section 3 of chapter II, pp. 317–30, for the more favourable external conditions from the spring of 1946 onwards, see n. 178. A growing number of Conservative MPs spoke in a similar vein (see nn. 179 and 188 above). For Churchill, see *Parl. Debates, House of Commons*, vol. 423, 5.6.1946, col. 2039. In view of this, the charge made by a section of the Labour Left that Bevin was basically conducting a Conservative foreign policy needs in my view much more qualification than the verdict of 'not far wrong' in Schwarz (n. 148), p. 161. Schwarz's judgement may be true of Bevin's growing reserve towards Moscow and his closer association with Washington, but it is far from being true of his policy *vis-à-vis* Europe.

A policy of rallying and uniting the West European countries (though without linking them by any federal constitution) was at the same time being urged on Bevin by a group of the Labour Left, namely those elements which, at the party conference of May 1945, had carried the resolution opposing world domination by the great powers and advocating a 'United Socialist States of Europe'. This group argued that Britain's economic recovery and political future in the long run essentially depended on the recovery and co-operation of the whole of Western Europe; that democratic Socialism would only be able to hold its own against the totalitarian Soviet Union (which had a Socialist planned economy but no democracy) on the one hand, and against the capitalist USA (which had freedom and democracy but no Socialism) on the other, by forming a 'third bloc' of Socialist states between the two colossi of America and Russia. An article in the *New Statesman* in August 1945 declared that parliamentary democracy was unlikely to spread east of Prague and Vienna because the necessary social and economic conditions were lacking: 'It is only in Western Europe that we can hope to see the restoration of parliamentary government and the building of Social Democracy in the immediate future.'[197] The well-known Labour author and Oxford professor, G. D. H. Cole, was active as a propagandist for this group in his innumerable writings and at party conferences, arguing in favour of 'the unity of Western Europe on a socialist basis, which would enable the nations of Western Europe, instead of being under the thumb of the United States on account of their divergences and economic weakness, to face the American capitalist pressures on much more equal terms'. What was essential for this purpose, he explained in a pamphlet published during the crucial spring of 1946, was 'full-hearted co-operation' under a 'supra-national political and economic plan' which could be agreed and carried out only by like-minded Socialist or predominantly Socialist 'governments such as exist already in Norway and Sweden as well as in Great Britain, and could exist in France, Holland and Belgium and probably elsewhere if only Great Britain would give the right lead'. 'I claim that the problems of Western Europe are insoluble except on supra-national lines.' The demand for a common economic policy entailed 'no need for a common constitution or a common parliament even of a federal type. The whole thing could be done by treaties filled out by agreements for close economic co-operation'; similarly to Churchill's Council of Europe, 'the political machinery could be no more than a periodically-meeting West European Congress'.[198]

[197] The resolution of May 1945 is quoted at n. 154 above. The unsigned leading article 'Britain and Europe' appeared in the *New Statesman* of 25.8.1945, p. 119 (quoted in Schwarz [n. 148], p. 730).
[198] G. D. H. Cole, *On Labour's Foreign Policy* (*New Statesman* pamphlet), London, April 1946, pp. 12 and 14 f. As regards Cole, who was associated with the co-operative movement inspired by Proudhon, cf. A. W. Wright, 'Guild Socialism revisited' in *Journal of Contemporary History*, vol. 9 (1974), no. 1, pp. 165–80. Cole's principal work, known throughout the world, was his *History of Socialist Thought* (five books in seven vols., London, 1953–60).

The decisive thing, Cole explained shortly afterwards, was to put an end to the hopeless attempt to base Europe's revival 'on an obsolete basis of national sovereignty and purely national economic effort ... Tariff and currency barriers need taking down, so as to constitute a free trading area with a market comparable in extent with those of the United States and the Soviet Union.' The treaties needed to take the place of a constitution would have to guarantee as a minimum: full freedom of movement and residence for the citizens of all the participating countries in all countries belonging to the group 'to the extent of acquiring full legal and voting rights'; common regulations for patents, employers' and trade union rights, double taxation, and social insurance; lastly 'a truly common currency'. On the other hand 'any sort of military alliance among the countries of Western Europe' should be strictly avoided; 'emphasizing at the same time their joint renunciation of interference in the affairs of Eastern Europe, the Soviet Union would be confronted with a group that it would have to treat with respect and could no longer regard as a potential instrument of American capitalism'. Moscow would then allow the Communist parties ('which indeed have served well the purpose of keeping Western Europe from achieving any sort of unity') to co-operate in creating the Western-European group so as to ensure that it would be Socialist and not dependent on coalitions with the Christian Democrats.[199] Apart from this last speculation, which was not shared by the Dutch and German Socialists, the basic idea of a united Socialist Europe with the opportunity of developing into a 'Third Force' was very popular and widely championed in all the Continental Socialist parties between the autumn of 1945 and the spring of 1947, and in many respects it formed a parallel to the basic policy of the UEF. All the Socialist leaders, especially Mollet and Spaak, considered the vital prerequisite to be that the British Labour government should seize the initiative and so enable them to gain power at the next elections in their own countries. Yet in 1948 Cole's *History of the Labour Party*, representative of much current thinking, was to pass the following retrospective judgement: 'British Labour government failed, in 1945 [1946] when the chance was greatest, to give the lead to the forces of democratic socialism in Europe.'[200]

Why Bevin made no move in that direction, urged on him though it was in general terms by a section of the Conservatives and in a specifically Socialist form by his comrades in the Labour Party, why he refused with ever increasing stubbornness to take any step in favour of the European

---

[199] Using similar wording to that of the pamphlet published in April 1946 (n. 198), this argument was spelt out in G. D. H. Cole, *The Intelligent Man's Guide to the Post-War World*, London, 1947, pp. 1054–6 and 1032 f. (for the quotations, written before Feb. 1947, cf. p. 1032). This idea of a 'third' block of Socialist states was publicized to a large extent and in similar terms by Richard Löwenthal, at that time a correspondent in Germany of the London *Observer*, who, under the pen-name Paul Sering, was the author of *Jenseits des Kapitalismus. Ein Beitrag zur sozialistischen Neuorientierung*, Lauf bei Nürnberg (first edn., Feb. 1947). He saw the connection between the Socialist-governed British Empire and the West-European states as constituting a powerful neutral buffer, dominated by neither America nor Russia, which could prevent a clash between the two colossi and make it possible to carry out a Socialist policy in domestic affairs (ibid., p. 251; cf. the analysis by H. P. Schwarz [n. 148], pp. 568–72).

[200] G. D. H. Cole, *A History of the Labour Party from 1914*, London, 1948, p. 468. Cf. numerous examples of similar expectations on the part of Continental Socialists in the section headed 'Party Attitudes' in chapter IV, section 1 (vol. 2). For the concept of a 'Third Force', see pp. 380–5 below.

idea – on this matter the available sources, including official records which have now become accessible, provide no completely satisfactory information, and perhaps there is no logical explanation. He seems, however, to have been influenced by five reasons which can be inferred on broad lines from the sources and may be summarized as follows.

1. The explanation which Bevin himself emphasized between February 1946 and February 1947 must be taken seriously, at least for the first half of that period. It was not for the sake of the first mentioned group within the Labour Left, but for the sake of the Soviet Union that he eschewed any initiative in favour of a European policy which the Soviet Union would have regarded as 'an unfriendly act'. The records show clearly how frequently it was repeated in Foreign Office papers that Britain must put out of her mind the thought of a Western Group. To do nothing which might be embarrassing or vexatious to the Soviet Union was his main concern until the Paris conferences in the summer of 1946, as he still seriously hoped that these would produce some concession on the part of the Soviet Union – although the passivity and appeasement displayed by the British government was obviously not productive of either respect or compromise. This motive, however, cannot have continued to be a major factor from the time when Bevin was not afraid to 'provoke' the Soviet Union by taking a determined stand in favour of association with the United States of America, approving Bizonia, and handing over Greece and Turkey to 'American imperialism'. These moves at the same time showed that Bevin considered it more important to strengthen relations with the US than with Europe – perhaps believing, though wrongly as it turned out, that the two aims were mutually contradictory.

2. Since a policy of organizing and uniting the Europeans was invariably recommended by its advocates with the argument, among others, that it was the only way of safely reincorporating the Germans into the European family, Bevin's dislike for the Germans, shown by his constant warnings that they should not be treated too leniently, must have gone some way to turn him against the idea; this aspect has been well brought out by the studies of Hans-Peter Schwarz. Bevin declared it to be his main anxiety that Germany might succeed in becoming a powerful country again as a result of differences between the great powers.[201] Yet in his speeches one looks in vain for a single really understanding, cordial remark about Dutchmen or Frenchmen or any other European nation, apart from the usual platitudes about wanting to be a good neighbour to everyone.

3. Although Bevin never acknowledged it, at least in 1946–7, a basic feeling for Britain's world-wide links, its traditional aloofness towards the Continent in contrast to the ties of kinship with the Commonwealth, was obviously an important counter-influence. On average only a third of

---

[201] Cf. Schwarz (n. 148), pp. 162 f. and 731 f.

Bevin's major speeches in the House of Commons were concerned with Britain's relations with the USA and the USSR, while the German and from time to time other European problems were dealt with in that context; two-thirds of the speeches, on the other hand, dealt with the Dominions and what was left of the Empire. The colonies had been promised progress towards self-government; these promises would of course be kept, and for economic reasons a 'reduction of commitments' was unavoidable, but British overseas interests must also be safeguarded and clearly had priority over any initiatives in Europe.

The essence of British policy, as summed up in 1950 by Christopher Mayhew, Parliamentary Under-Secretary of State at the Foreign Office from October 1946, 'consisted in the firmness with which we have maintained that the unity of the West must be broadly based. The emphasis has been on the ties between Europe, Africa, America and Asia, rather than on the ties between individual countries composing these regions. This attitude ... arises inevitably from the universality of Britain's ties and commitment in the Western world.'[202]

4. On one of the few occasions on which Bevin defended himself against the criticism that he had not seized the initiative in rallying Europe before America did so, he told the House of Commons on 19 June 1947: 'What did I have to organize it with? What could I offer? I had neither coal, goods nor credit ... I cannot be accused now of not taking a line to help Western Europe. I have nothing with which to do it. I have not had one ton of spare coal to ship to Western Europe to help in rehabilitation.' These sentences prove Bevin's awareness of Britain's weakness and inability to give direct economic help, but even more his complete failure to understand that what the Continental Socialists and European federalists hoped for from Britain was not money but a political initiative and leadership in the direction of European unity.

In much the same way, a year earlier (June 1946) Bevin's then Parliamentary Under-Secretary of State, Hector McNeil, had lamented: 'We are without any cash and with very little credit. If this government had the resources which governments had in the nineteenth century, what development would not be possible in Europe?' And the guiding principle of his successor as Parliamentary Under-Secretary, Christopher Mayhew, was that 'The planning of Europe's defence, trade and economic development seemed to make little sense without active United States participation.'[203] What was lacking on the part of the British govern-

---

[202] 'No other country has a foot in so many camps, and consequently is liable to fall between so many stools' Mayhew (n. 194), p. 483; cf. the chapter 'The Reduction of Commitments' in Fitzsimons (n. 134), pp. 55–86. Yet it must be emphasized that Bevin and his colleagues in their statements opposing a European initiative (known to few at the time) never used the Commonwealth as a counter-argument, as was done after 1950 – despite the continuing transformation of the Commonwealth and the effective sovereignty of its individual states – by both Labour and Conservative politicians in their rejection of European federation (cf. Nutting [n. 160], pp. 105–12).
[203] *Parl. Debates, House of Commons,* vol. 439, 19.6.1947, col. 2354 (Bevin); vol. 423, 5.6.1946, col. 2129 f. (McNeil); C. Mayhew (n. 194), p. 483.

ment, however, was the political will to throw in their lot with Europe and to have confidence in its possibilities of recovery as a co-operative community – for which purpose, as Bevin knew at the very latest when he sent his telegram about Greece, a request for American credit facilities would not have been turned down.

5. The Labour programme in Britain itself, including the nationalization of key industries, constituted a further argument against a pro-European policy. A policy of state Socialism was bound to protect its credit and full employment policies against international influence. Moreover the co-existence of a number of state Socialist economies was logically conceivable in two ways only: either as involving merely the exchange of information plus, at most, the harmonization of national economic plans, or as requiring joint European institutions for the direction of the national economies – an unthinkable degree of centralization. Bevin may have doubted whether the Western-European countries would prove to be Socialist enough, but even if they were, he may have doubted with even better reason whether, if they lacked a constitutional framework (as they would have done under Churchill's Council of Europe or Cole's West-European Congress) they would really have formed a coherent structure with a common economic policy. But would this have been a reason, in Bevin's eyes, for advocating a stronger measure of constitutional integration in Europe?

Such integration was precisely what the *third alternative* proposed. In 1946–7 this had the support, it is true, of only a small minority in Britain, perhaps not even of all the 3,000 members of Federal Union, but it was backed with impressive logic by important representatives of both the major parties: a real federation under a common government, full unity with the European countries ready for it, so that the result would be a viable community. Among Labour MPs Ronald Mackay stood out as an unwavering protagonist of the view expressed in his article of October 1945, already quoted, that Britain like the rest of Europe could only survive 'as a state in a federation of Europe with a common currency, and no tariffs or restrictions and complete freedom of trade'. As a back-bencher with a considerable reputation among his parliamentary colleagues for legal and economic expertise, Mackay was absorbed during 1946 in the parliamentary preparation of the Coal Mines Nationalization Bill and refrained from challenging Bevin's foreign policy. At a press conference in New York on 2 April 1947, however, he tried to get the Americans to understand that the USA would be choked by its own capacity to overproduce if other economic communities of equal capacity did not develop; that the states of Europe, reduced in importance as they were, must form a federation for their own salvation as well as America's, not 'an association or league of states, but a federation with real power, which will mean that the states of Europe will drop out of UNO, the USE becoming the member state. Such a development is the only way to solve the economic problems of Europe today, for neither Britain nor Italy nor France can solve their economic problems on their own, but they can solve them by coming together.' He described Churchill's proposals for a United Europe as wholly inadequate 'because he does not hold that the states of Western Europe should surrender sufficient sovereignty to establish such a federation'. Mackay's conception, as argued and worked out in detail, will be more closely examined in connection with the important part he played after the end of 1947 as founder of the Europe Group in the House of Commons, as vice-president of the European Parliamentary Union, and as sponsor (together with Boothby) of the motion, signed in March 1948 by no fewer than 190 MPs, in favour of a European constituent assembly.[204]

Among the Conservatives it was Robert Boothby, one of their most outspoken MPs since 1924, who alone urged the most radical course in 1946–7. Both the basic assumptions made towards the end of the war, he declared in the House of Commons debate of 4 June 1946 – viz. 'that unity of purpose and outlook existed between the Big Three' and that 'a world dictatorship by the Big Three' could guarantee lasting peace – had proved mistaken. It was intolerable to insist that 'all other nations should not have any say in making the peace', while Britain had 'no positive policy at all' and the Soviet Union had taken eleven East-European nations under its rule. 'There is only one way out: a Western Federal Union, by which I mean the political, cultural and economic integration of Western Europe', including West Germany. 'The democracies of Western Europe are too small to survive as independent political or economic units in this modern world.'

'Flanked as they are by the vast federations of the Soviet System and the United States, they cannot survive, they cannot hope to raise their standard of living in isolation. They are dependent to an exceptionally high degree on trade with one another.' They would only accept decisions of the Security Council 'if you have a federal union represented in the Security Council, and the countries of that union have played a full part in the framing of the policy that is put forward in the Council'. The basic idea of the Schuman Plan was anticipated: 'The productive industries of the Rhineland should be placed under the control of an international commission and co-ordinated with the productive industries of Luxembourg, the Saar, Lorraine and Belgium into one great heavy industrial unit which could and should produce the necessary steel and coal for the reconstruction of Western

[204] R. W. G. Mackay (for biographical details, see n. 112), article of Oct. 1945 quoted in n. 137 above, press conference in New York on 2.4.1947, and his attitude to Churchill's movement quoted in his principal work, *You can't turn the Clock back* (London, July 1948, pp. 4 f. and 269; for an analysis of this work, together with the foundation of the British EPU Group and the motion for a constituent assembly, see chapter V/2 (in vol. 2). Of Bevin he wrote: 'Some of us may be critical of Mr Bevin's foreign policy, but we are in a minority . . . I think our international policy has been a disaster. In the field of foreign affairs we have tried to play the part of a great power, which we no longer are' (ibid., p. 105). Nevertheless in February 1947 there were some seventy-two MPs, mostly of the Labour Left, who in a resolution in the House of Commons urged 'Britain's readiness to federate . . . on the basis of a federal constitution' (cf. for details n. 87 to chapter II).

Europe.' Objections by the Soviet Union could not be accepted. 'The Cold War will not stop until Western Europe is securely established and has no longer any need to struggle for survival, or to be frightened of its own immediate future. Fear – that is the trouble in Europe.'[205]

But such an advance towards federation went far beyond anything intended or desired by Bevin. In his speech of 23 November 1945 he had seen the possibility more clearly than others, but like the majority of the House of Commons he did not want it. Moreover, after Marshall's offer of aid and the appeal for European unity made by the Americans – whose co-operation he had earlier described as the missing *sine qua non* – there emerged, as the sixth and probably most important reason of all, his rejection of any pooling of sovereignty with the other countries of Europe because it seemed to him too risky to link Britain's fate irrevocably with the future of the devastated Continent. Attlee's only remark on the subject in his memoirs (1954) expresses the same idea: 'I am on record as having said that Europe must federate or perish, but to bring such ideas into the region of the practical is a very difficult proposition. Every state has its old traditions'; 'old-established communities' could not be brought together like 'the federation of the thirteen American Colonies'.[206]

The British government in 1945–7 – and this remains hard to understand in spite of all the reasons enumerated – had neither fully realized that Britain was no longer a world power nor understood that it was being offered the leadership of Europe. The government disappointed all the hopes of Continental Europeans, and especially the Social-Democratic parties, that the idea of European unity would be proclaimed by Britain as a European power and would thus enable Europe to save itself by its own effort; instead, the European idea was made an issue of governmental negotiation by the US and was inextricably bound up with the Cold War. Thus the British took the lead in adopting the illogical and defeatist posture by which the European governments on the one hand passively accepted their decline to the status of small or medium-sized

---

[205] *Parl. Debates, House of Commons*, vol. 423, 4.6.1946, col. 1944–54). Robert J. G. Boothby, born 1900, educated at Eton and Oxford, read for the Bar; 1924–58 Conservative MP for East Aberdeenshire, was from 1926 to 1929 Parliamentary Secretary to the Chancellor of the Exchequer, Winston Churchill; 1940–1 Parliamentary Secretary, Ministry of Food, 1949–57 delegate to the Consultative Assembly of the Council of Europe; author of *The New Economy* (London, 1943), *I fight to live* (London, 1947), *Western Union* (London, 1949); *My Yesterday, Your Tomorrow* (London, 1962); *Recollections of a Rebel* (London, 1978).

[206] Attlee (n. 160), p. 172 f., adding a sentence which claimed a superior position for Britain *vis-à-vis* the Schuman Plan: 'We could not enter into engagement to the full extent possible to the Continental powers.' This remained the attitude of Bevin, who spoke in a mercantile and cynical tone of the lack of 'assets' on the Continental side. In September 1948 he said in answer to an interruption in the House of Commons: 'I have often said that I amalgamated a lot of unions into one union, but the first thing I looked at was the assets' (*Parl. Debates, House of Commons*, vol. 454, 15.9.1948, col. 105). For a general view, cf. also Stanley Henig, 'The Europeanization of British Politics' in C. Cook and J. Ramsden (ed.), *Trends in British Politics since 1945*, London 1978, esp p. 183 f.

states, truckling to the Soviet Union or begging the US for credits, while on the other hand trying to uphold the old claim of 'national independence' vis-à-vis one another and to avoid the pooling of sovereignty.

4. De Gaulle's Attempt to revive Nationalist Policy

There were numerous reasons why France rather than Britain could have become the spokesman of the defeated Continental countries in 1945 and of the idea of political unity, as she eventually did after following a false trail between 1944 and 1947. Like the other Continental nations but unlike the British, France had seen the collapse of its national institutions, four years of foreign occupation, and finally the entry of victorious Allied troops. In all the groups belonging to the non-Communist Resistance, which was more important than the Communist one until the end of 1943, European federation had been proclaimed as a future goal. The Resistance had planned a total change of French domestic and foreign policy: Socialist and decentralized at home, France was to become part of a voluntary federal union of European nations. Only the Communist wing of the Resistance, following Moscow's instructions, had since 1944 called for a sharply contrasting policy of national sovereignty, the dismemberment of Germany, and a pact with the Soviet Union.[207] A determined effort by France's post-war government, in conjunction with the non-Communist Resistance of the other European countries, would have had the best chance not indeed of reaching the goal of European unity, but at least of impressing on the victorious superpowers that the Europeans had decided to make it their aim in the epoch then beginning. Contrary to expectations, too, France received exceptionally preferential treatment as compared with the other Continental countries.

(A) CONDITIONS AFFECTING FRANCE'S NEW FOREIGN POLICY

After being occupied by German troops for over four years France was finally liberated by American, British, and Canadian troops with the participation of some Free French divisions, in much the same way as the other countries which Hitler had defeated between 1939 and 1941. In contrast to what happened in Poland, Norway, the Netherlands, and Belgium, there was no government in exile to make common cause with the Allies, for the legal French government had been the collaborationist

---

[207] Cf. pp. 50 f. and 59, also references in the section on France in Lipgens, *Föderationspläne* (n. 44), pp. 177–250; for the ideas of the Communist wing, see esp. ibid., p. 239 f. and H. Michel, *Les Courants de pensée de la Résistance*, Paris, 1962, pp. 705–10.

regime of Vichy. France's weakness at the time of its liberation was plain for all to see.[208]

However, the more clearly Churchill from the spring of 1943 onwards perceived the growing power of the Soviet Union as the major victor in the land war, the global aspirations of the US as its strength developed, and the relative decline of Britain between the two giants, the more he began to wish to include at least one other European partner in the projected international institutions so as not to be alone in facing the extra-European powers. In the nature of things only France was a suitable candidate: it could not be one of the smaller countries or Italy.[209]

These considerations were strengthened by Churchill's determination to oppose point-blank the inveterate conviction of Roosevelt and his advisers that the war must put an end to the colonial empires of the European states. During the first meeting of the Big Three on 28 November 1943 at Tehran Stalin had vouchsafed that after the war no important territories outside its own boundaries could be entrusted to a France which was for practical purposes in league with the Germans. Roosevelt in reply developed his favourite idea of an international trusteeship for all colonial territories. Churchill alone fought for allowing France to keep her colonial possessions – and in doing so he was indirectly fighting for the British Empire.[210] He had good reasons for expecting to find in France a fellow champion of the principle of upholding colonial rule, even if the two countries might differ as to how this should be done.[211]

When, in September 1944 France's military liberation was almost complete and it was clear that de Gaulle's National Committee (installed in power in Paris after co-opting representatives of the national Resistance)

---

[208] For French foreign policy in 1945, cf. details in A. W. DePorte, *De Gaulle's Foreign Policy, 1944–46*, Cambridge, Mass., 1968, and analysis of the basic problems in W. Lipgens, 'Bedingungen und Etappen der Aussenpolitik de Gaulles, 1944–1946' in *VfZG*, vol. 21 (1973), pp. 52–102. Some passages from this article, which in essence is an early and more detailed version of section 4 of this chapter, have been incorporated in the following summary. Cf. also G. Ziebura, *Die deutschfranzösischen Beziehungen seit 1945*, Pfullingen, 1970.

[209] As early as March 1943, when Roosevelt expressed the opinion that France would need no armed forces to speak of and that its overseas bases should be transformed into military bases of the United Nations, Eden cautiously replied that 'England would probably be too weak to face Russia alone diplomatically': R. E. Sherwood, *Roosevelt and Hopkins*, NY (2nd ed., revised), 1950, pp. 709, 712, 716, and 721.

[210] *FRUS, Diplomatic Papers, The Conferences at Cairo and Tehran*, 1943, Washington (DC), 1961, pp. 256, 310, 345, 484 f., 568 f., 872 f.; the first part of the article by W. Cornides, which unfortunately was never completed, referred to this aspect in 'Die Illusion einer selbständigen französischen Deutschlandpolitik' in *Europa-Archiv*, vol. 9, 1954, pp. 6733–5.

[211] At the conference of French governors of Equatorial Africa on 31.1.1944 de Gaulle expressly denied 'any idea of autonomy and any possibility of development outside the bloc of the French Empire'. Cf. De Gaulle, *Memoirs*, vol. 2 (*Unity, 1942–1944*), London, 1959, p. 188; also the accounts by R. von Albertini, *Dekolonisation, Die Diskussion über Verwaltung und Zukunft der Kolonien 1919–1960*, Cologne, 1966, pp. 419–30, and F. Ansprenger, *Auflösung der Kolonialreiche*, Munich (dtv Weltgeschichte, no. 13), 1966, p. 157 f.

was going to prevail,[212] Churchill in his Notes to Roosevelt of 14 and 22 October and his simultaneous negotiations with Stalin in Moscow favoured recognizing de Gaulle's administration as the 'provisional government' of France.[213] In November, after repeated references to the fact that 'there will be a time not many years distant when the American armies will go home', he persuaded Roosevelt to agree to increase the armed strength of a 'French occupation force', and in January 1945, Roosevelt also fell in with his suggestion at Yalta that France should be given a Zone of Occupation in Germany.[214]

That France should thus occupy a superior position to all the other defeated and subsequently liberated Continental countries was due solely to the repeated advocacy of Britain and to the acquiescence of America and Russia. It did not affect the underlying realities of the balance of power in the world. When Stalin asked Roosevelt at Yalta why he wanted to give France a zone, 'Roosevelt replied that he favoured it only out of kindness. Both the Marshal and Molotov in vigorous tones said that this was the only reason to give the French a zone.' And when soon afterwards British diplomacy managed to get France a permanent seat on the Security Council, Admiral Leahy, Roosevelt's Chief of Staff, spoke of the 'fiction of France's great power status', which had been created in the interests of Britain and would only cause difficulty in the relations with other states and with the real great powers.[215]

A new French government after the Liberation could, nevertheless, have taken its stand on the achievements of the Resistance, the latter's rejection of nationalism and its 'European' vision of the future. The

[212] Cf. p. 205. The recognition of de Gaulle's committee (on 23.10.1944) was facilitated by the fact that he had managed to convince Roosevelt in July that he did not wish to impose it as a future government; in view of this Eisenhower on 25.8.1944 entrusted the committee 'as the de facto authority' with the civil administration of liberated territories in the rear of the Allied forces, on condition 'that as soon as the military situation permits, the French people will be given an opportunity freely to exercise their will in the choice of their government' (*FRUS, Diplomatic Papers, 1944*, vol. iii, *The British Commonwealth and Europe*, Washington, 1965, pp. 715-24; DePorte (n. 208), pp. 52-4.
[213] W. Churchill, *The Second World War*, vol. vi, *Triumph and Tragedy*, pp. 213-17; for Roosevelt's last-minute precipitation over recognizing de Gaulle's government, see M. Viorst, *Hostile Allies. FDR and Charles de Gaulle*, NY, 1965, p. 220 f. De Gaulle reacted with ironic disdain at a press conference on 25.10.1944: 'Le gouvernement français est satisfait qu'on veuille bien l'appeler par son nom' (de Gaulle, *Mémoires de Guerre*, vol. iii, *Le Salut, 1944-46*, Paris, 1959, p. 44; henceforth quoted as *Mémoires*, iii).
[214] Churchill even proposed that de Gaulle be invited to Yalta for the points on the agenda which concerned France, but Roosevelt refused: 'It would merely introduce a complicating and undesirable factor' (16.12.1944); Churchill, vi (n. 213), p. 226; *FRUS, Diplomatic Papers, the Conferences at Malta and Yalta, 1945*, Washington, 1955, pp. 283 f., 294 f., 300 f. For Churchill's efforts to obtain for France a zone of occupation in Germany and eventually a seat in the Allied Control Council, cf. E. R. Stettinius, *Roosevelt and the Russians. The Yalta Conference*, NY, 1950, pp. 126-9 and pp. 162-71; R. Feis, *Churchill, Roosevelt, Stalin, The War they waged and the Peace they sought*, Princeton, 1957, p. 531 f.; F. R. Willis, *The French in Germany 1945-49*, Stanford, Cal., 1962, pp. 8-13.
[215] Stettinius (n. 214), p. 101 f.; W. D. Leahy, *I was there*, London, 1950, pp. 354 and 379.

government could have continued and strengthened the process of rethinking that had already begun in France, and might have become the spokesman of the whole European consciousness. The important point, wrote an Italian Resistance group to French friends in August 1944, was to convince the parties which had arisen since the Liberation that their democratic, Socialist, and other aims could be achieved only within the framework of a European federation. If this could be done, 'especially if it is successfully carried out in France, then there is an excellent chance of success, because France's voice certainly has more authority in the eyes of the great powers than that of any other Continental country'.[216] The foreign policy envisaged by de Gaulle, however, who entered Paris with the American army as head of the Free French Provisional Government late in August 1944, was diametrically opposed to constructive planning for a future Europe. His design was an uncompromising return to the very nationalism which the non-Communist Resistance had just overcome.

This conception depended on certain key principles which Charles de Gaulle had imbibed from the tradition of the nationalist Right long before the war.[217] The foundation of all de Gaulle's political ideas was belief in an ideal, eternal France, representing for all practical purposes the highest value. Every sentence at the beginning of his Memoirs was meant to be taken literally as it was written: 'All my life I have had a certain idea of France ... like the Madonna of the frescos or the Princess in the fairy story ... I felt called to a sublime and unusual destiny ... Providence created France for complete success or exemplary sorrow ... France is not France if it is not in the first place ... In short, I believe that without grandeur France cannot be itself.' With his notion of the state as an absolute value, the perfect product of history, above which there could be no higher authority, de Gaulle was the classic example of a nationalist. France had to be in the 'first place' because it set an example to the whole of humanity, but also as an antidote to the lurking forces of discord inside the country. In the most revealing chapter of his Memoirs entitled '*Le Rang*', the words '*rang*', '*prestige*', '*honneur*', '*dignité*', '*pouvoir*', and '*grandeur*' rise in ceaseless crescendos. From his conviction that the sovereign state would for ever remain the highest reality in history, de Gaulle drew the conclusion that history consists of a never ending 'struggle for national existence and national self-preservation'. Ideologies, coalitions, plans for international peace were (he believed) nothing but a masquerade or passing illusion in the eternal game of power politics, whose final outcome would only be decided by the sword,

[216] Letter of the Movimento Federalista Europeo to the Comité Français pour la Fédération Européenne (CFFE). At the Paris Conference of federalists of 22–5 March 1945 'there was agreement that the main responsibility for setting up common European institutions rests with France' (report by Willi Eichler in *Europe speaks*, London, 24.4.1945, p. 4). On CFFE and the Paris federalists' conference, cf. pp. 126–30.

[217] Cf. H. Lüthy, 'De Gaulle, Stil und Politik' in *Aus Politik und Zeitgeschichte*, vol. 32, 11.8.1965, pp. 3–10; in their conclusions, apart from differences of emphasis, the two basic books on de Gaulle are in agreement: A. Baring and C. Tautil, *Charles de Gaulle, Grösse und Grenzen*, Cologne, 1963; and J. Lacouture, *De Gaulle*, Paris, 1969; an excellent summary by G. Ziebura, 'Gaullismus', in H. J. Schultz (ed.), *Politik für Nichtpolitiker. Ein ABC zur aktuellen Diskussion*, Stuttgart–Berlin, 1969, vol. 1, pp. 176–84; see also Lipgens (n. 208), pp. 64–70.

'for the sword is the world's axis'.[218] It never occurred to him that this exaltation of the military nation state could itself be an ideology. One example of what this belief meant in practice was the basic and – at this time – axiomatic conviction of inevitable enmity between France and Germany, derived from de Gaulle's education and from many years' study of nationalist authors from Jacques Bainville to Charles Maurras. Of all enmities this was the least likely to change because in geo-political and strategic terms France's eastern frontier was the least defensible and most exposed, and also because the supposed antagonism between the national characters of *Gaulois* and *Germains* compelled them to be perpetual enemies. History and geography taught that the only guarantee against this danger was a Germany divided into as many states as it had been after the Treaty of Westphalia, with France vigorously maintaining a forward defensive glacis. It was with this purely Poincarist conception of foreign policy that de Gaulle came to power in 1944.[219]

Since de Gaulle remained in his basic approach a man of the Right, committed to the doctrine of '*grandeur*' and to the slogan '*La France seule*', he had no understanding of schemes for a European federation such as had arisen during the war in the French and other Resistance movements, and was unable to seize the opportunity of becoming the spokesman of such views. On the contrary, being a traditionalist and thinking in terms of the alliance between France and Tsarist Russia, he envisaged Europe divided into two spheres of influence, one under Soviet leadership, the other under French, which should hold the balance by mutual agreement – an astonishing failure to recognize the realities of power. The re-establishment and if possible expansion of France's own power by means of French-dominated border territories was the essential preliminary to what de Gaulle pithily described as France's goal: 'The return of a great power to its place as a great power by way of war and the use of force.'[220] It was questionable how far de Gaulle would succeed with a programme of this kind at the end of the Second World War, for all his pragmatic skill and the favourable start created for him by Churchill. There was far less doubt, on the other hand, that this kind of programme was both highly

---

[218] Charles de Gaulle, *Vers l'armée de métier*, Paris, 1934. Cf. de Gaulle, *Le Fil de l'épée*, Paris, 1932 and 1959, p. 10, extolling military power in lyrical language as 'recours de la pensée, instrument de l'action, condition du mouvement . . . Berceau des cités, sceptre des empires, fossoyeur de décadences, la force fait la loi aux peuples et leur règle leur destin.' This is why Baring/Tautil (n. 217), p. 89, call him a 'secret Nietzschean . . . terrified of tranquillity and full of distrust towards peace'. The best sketch of his 'indifference to ideology' is in Lüthy (n. 217), p. 5 f.

[219] Best brief account, with quotations, in Ziebura (n. 208), pp. 32–6. Georges Bidault in *Resistance: The Political Biography of Georges Bidault*, London, 1967, p. 88, writes in retrospect: 'I knew it was pure romanticism to try applying seventeenth-century politics to a twentieth-century situation. The "wind of history" had not yet blown away the jargon of another age.'

[220] Speech at the final meeting of the first session of the Assemblée Consultative, 25.11.1943 in Algiers: de Gaulle, *Discours et messages*, vol. i, *Pendant la guerre, 1940–1946*, Paris, 1970, p. 349. For quotations on how the Soviet Union and France should 'as balancing factors . . . establish their relations on a basis of equality' in order to reject an international system ('systems so extended that one is in danger of getting lost in them') etc., cf. Lipgens (n. 208), pp. 66–8.

traditional and popular in France, and that by using his power and the weapons of state propaganda in its favour de Gaulle might hope to consolidate nationalist thinking which in recent years had become unsure of itself. His policy would also redirect the justified longing for security into anti-German channels instead of into forms of international organization, and would to a large extent revive the Versailles mentality – especially since the extreme Left (as instructed by Moscow) added its voice to the chorus. Thus it was possible to arrest the process, begun during the Resistance, of coming to terms with the real changes that had taken place and adapting to the new international situation.

In the autumn of 1944 de Gaulle, thanks to an artful arrangement with the Communists, succeeded in weakening and outmanœuvring the non-Communist Resistance parties. Three reasons accounted for the defeat of the latter. Firstly, while the leaders of the Resistance groups had lived in hiding under assumed names, constantly on the run from the police and so unknown to the population as a whole, de Gaulle as the symbol of Free France possessed undisputed moral authority and prestige. Secondly, this authority was of decisive importance to the Supreme Allied Command, which needed a smoothly functioning administration on French soil; hence the Allies' *de facto* recognition of de Gaulle as President of the Provisional Government on 25 August. The third factor was the Soviet Union's interest in ensuring that the effectiveness of the Second Front was not endangered in the middle of the war. Despite the opposition of local militia groups of the Resistance, Maurice Thorez, the head of the French Communist Party, on his return from Moscow in January 1945 gave his support to de Gaulle's dissolution of the patriotic militia and the placing of the Liberation Committees under the authority of the government.[221] De Gaulle, not least in response to Allied pressure, convened an enlarged Consultative Assembly on 7 November 1944, but declared that he was in no way bound by its recommendations.

In fact he acted against the Assembly's decisions on many important issues, in spite of its protests and no matter how large the majority might be. Still less did the Cabinet mean a reduction of power for de Gaulle, who considered himself its sole proprietor; the ministers, in his view, were only assistants, especially in foreign policy, as Bidault testified: de Gaulle 'allocated to himself all major matters and dealt with them himself. One was lucky if one received not even perhaps a statement but some information about decisions that had been taken and the direction in which we were supposed to be going.'

For a whole year – until the meeting of the first elected assembly on 6 November 1945 – de Gaulle possessed what was in fact unlimited,

---

[221] Cf. J. E. Sawyer, 'The Re-establishment of the Republic in France, The de Gaulle Era 1944 to 1945' in *Political Science Quarterly,* vol. 62 (Sept. 1947), pp. 354–80; for an incisive criticism of de Gaulle's obstruction to the programme of the Resistance, see P. Tesson, *De Gaulle Ier. La Révolution manquée,* Paris, 1965; for a basic account in considerable detail, see R. Aron, *Histoire de la Libération de la France, juin 1944–mai 1945,* Paris, 1959[1], 1966[2]; for a summary, Lipgens (n. 208) pp. 70–4.

'Bonapartist' power, the only constraint being that he had to promise the Allies to reintroduce parliamentary democracy and hold a general election 'after the prisoners of war come home'.[222] Re-elected President of the Provisional Government by the Constituent Assembly on 13 November, he endured its superior authority, which he could henceforth hardly challenge, for little more than two months. When at the beginning of January 1946 it cut the army budget and on 15 January criticized his foreign policy, he resigned. Yet the year during which he had exercised autocratic power was enough to put French foreign policy, as he conceived it, back on the old Poincarist lines.

Among the factors of which de Gaulle took too little account, France's economic situation was the most serious. The material damage caused by the war was devastating in all the Continental countries: large numbers of factories, stations, bridges, and harbours were destroyed, and only 40% of pre-war railway-engines were undamaged. The index of industrial production in January 1945, five months after liberation, was still only 29% of the pre-war level; by the end of that year it had risen only to 65%. As a result of wartime occupation costs the amount of money in circulation had more than quadrupled, the price index (1938 = 100) rising to 260 by January 1945. Since de Gaulle decided against currency reform the index by December 1945 went up to 455, in other words rampant inflation had begun.[223] Inflation, an almost complete lack of exports to balance a heavy demand for imports, and, though to a lesser extent than in the case of Britain, the sale of overseas investments caused serious shortfalls in the French balance of trade and budget. In this case too it was only thanks to an enormous loan of capital from America, which by an agreement of 28 February 1945 supplied raw materials and consumer goods to the value of 1,675 million dollars, that the gaps were filled and a collapse of the franc averted.[224] But by the end of 1945 this huge sum was almost exhausted, and the indispensable minimum of imports was possible only because the United States in December 1945 granted a further credit of 550 million dollars through the Export–Import Bank. Besides this, France received as part of the winding-up arrangements of Lend-Lease (analogous to the Keynes agreement in the case of Britain) credits to the extent of 720 million

---

[222] Cf. de Gaulle, *Unity*, p. 233: 'If my power had been increasingly recognized it was to a large extent because of this commitment: to refuse to fulfil it now would stamp my mission with a fraudulent seal. But it would also turn against me the nation, which would no longer distinguish the reasons for this despotic action.' The best factual account so far is J. Chapsal, *La Vie politique en France depuis 1940*, Paris, 1966, pp. 74–110, esp. p. 88; DePorte (n. 208), p. 57 f.; Lacouture (n. 217), p. 138; Bidault (n. 219), p. 63.

[223] Cf. tables in *L'Année politique, 1944–1945*, Paris, 1946, pp. 520–5; more detailed information in Lipgens (n. 208), pp. 76–8.

[224] The aid procured by Jean Monnet in Washington under the Lend-Lease Acts was granted for thirty years at the extremely generous rate of interest of $2^{3}/8\%$; moreover, the US promised further manufactured goods to the value of 900 million dollars on the same terms in return for a pre-payment of 20% of the purchase price: *L'Année politique, 1944–1945*, p. 127 f.

dollars. Even so, in May 1946 a further loan of 650 million dollars had to be sought from the Export–Import Bank.[225] One of the criticisms most frequently made by French opponents of de Gaulle's foreign policy was that in complete disregard of these facts the General was trying to play the part of an independent great power that was wholly incompatible with the country's modest economic strength compared with that of the new superpowers.

(B) STAGES OF DE GAULLE'S 'POLICY OF GREATNESS'

De Gaulle began to carry out his intention to restore France 'as a great power to its place as a great power'[226] by advancing traditional demands for the Rhine to become Germany's western border, for the territory on the left bank to be transferred to French control, for the remainder of Germany to be split up into a number of loosely connected states, and for the Ruhr to be placed under international control with a considerable part of its production earmarked for France. These demands, first expressed in confidential memoranda, were made known to the French public around the end of January 1945.[227]

His diplomatic efforts for an agreement between the Allies began on 11 November 1944 during Churchill's visit to liberated France. Churchill for one was not prepared to back de Gaulle's territorial and economic claims. When asked for British support for them he answered that he was against any transfer of territory in principle, and that in any case nothing could be decided in advance of the peace treaty. Meanwhile, he suggested early talks should be held for an Anglo-French treaty of alliance.[228] In a general review of other world problems Churchill referred to the necessity of terminating the French mandates in Syria and the Lebanon in accord-

---

[225] Cf. *L'Année politique, 1944–1945,* p. 387 f.; R. G. Hawtrey, 'The Economic Consequences of the War' (in *The Realignment* quoted in n. 139), p. 45 f. In addition, Canada lent France 240 million dollars, cf. R. Mayne (n. 173), p. 89. The sole but excellent French monograph by Jean Godard, 'L'Aide américaine à la France' in *Revue de science financière,* vol. 48 (1966), pp. 438–59, unfortunately starts only with the period 1948–54.

[226] Speech of 25.11.1943, cf. n. 220. Best existing summary of de Gaulle's demands on Germany as the principal means of his 'status' demand for France in H. P. Schwarz, *Vom Reich zur Bundesrepublik,* Neuwied–Berlin, 1966, pp. 180–8 and Ziebura (n. 208), pp. 32–40.

[227] Initially at a press conference on 25.1.1945; to the public at large in a broadcast on 5.2.1945, during the Yalta conference, to which he had not been invited: 'I can be specific once again and say that the definite presence of French power from one end of the Rhine to the other – the separation of the territories of the left bank of the Rhine and of the Ruhr district from whatever becomes of Germany or the German states . . . are the conditions which France considers necessary.' *L'Année politique 1944–1945,* p. 101, and *Discours* (n. 220), p. 518. Cf. the collection of relevant quotations in Lipgens (n. 208), pp. 78–82.

[228] Cf. the French record of this conversation, *Mémoires,* iii, p. 356; but de Gaulle omits, replacing them with dots, several parts of the record relating to his own demands and to the British offer of alliance. Also, Churchill's account to Roosevelt (in *FRUS . . . Malta and Yalta* [n. 214], p. 284) gives only a vague assurance that, contrary to press reports, nothing else was decided. *Mémoires,* iii, p. 50: 'Still less did they [the British] allow themselves to envisage anything definite with us about the future form of government of the German *Länder,* about the Ruhr, Rhine, Saar etc.'

ance with the promises given in 1941.[229] De Gaulle, obviously annoyed by this reference to the Levant and Churchill's refusal to back his demands for the Rhine and the Ruhr, simply acknowledged the British offer of an alliance. In restrospect he noted that in contrast to 'what seemed logical and right to us, the British saw fit to approach matters in terms of empiricism and compromise'. And when Churchill on another visit to Paris in January 1945 again offered an Anglo-French alliance, de Gaulle rejected it and indicated that an alliance of that kind would only be considered if Britain first agreed to the Rhineland demands and left France a free hand in the Levant.[230]

De Gaulle, who after the *de jure* recognition of his government had invited the British Prime Minister and the American President to Paris, himself went to Moscow a fortnight later: his first visit abroad was to Stalin. For one who wished to re-establish France's independent role in international politics it was an obvious move, at a time when France was occupied by and dependent on American and British troops, to seek an invitation from the Soviet Union and to give proof of independence by talks with the third great ally – an independence which, in de Gaulle's eyes, could only be preserved if France succeeded in reducing Anglo-American influence on the Continent.

In his first discussion with Stalin, in Moscow on 2 December 1944, de Gaulle declared his own ambitions quite frankly; but he was told at once that Stalin was not prepared to back them. In reply to the proposal that Moscow and Paris should agree on the principles of a German settlement in a 'direct understanding' and then propose them to the other allies, Stalin 'laconically' replied that every question must be examined with the other allies. Thereupon de Gaulle, feeling that in view of Soviet territorial demands in Eastern Europe he could put his cards on the table, made his specific claims: '*La frontière géographique et militaire de la France est constituée par le Rhin et . . . l'occupation de cette ligne est nécessaire à sa sécurité*' (according to the French account) – or, according to the Soviet report: 'De Gaulle said that it would be a wise decision to detach the Rhineland from Germany and reunite it with France', while the Ruhr, also to be detached from Germany, could be put under international administration. Stalin answered equally drily that 'the Anglo-American troops are in charge of military operations in that area and . . . it is necessary to hear the opinion of the British and Americans before that question can be decided'. And when, despite this rebuff, de Gaulle gave his assurance (two months before Yalta and eight

---

[229] For the French mandatory government in Lebanon and Syria the chief work is I. Lipschits, *La Politique de la France au Levant, 1939–1941*, Paris, 1963; for the declaration of 8.6.1941 in which General Catroux, the general officer commanding, promised independence at the end of the war in the name of the Free French committee, see *L. Année politique, 1944–1945*, p. 50. For the situation in the Levant at the time, cf. DePorte (n. 208), pp. 126–52.

[230] De Gaulle, *Salvation* (Eng. translation of *Mémoires*, vol. iii), p. 57; *L'Année politique, 1944–1945*, p. 99 and (from the broadcast of 5.2.1945), p. 533 f.

months before Potsdam) that France would have no objection to the detachment and transfer to Poland of the territory east of the Oder–Neisse line to compensate for her loss of territory east of the Curzon Line, Stalin refused to make any comparable commitment in regard to France's territorial wishes in the West.[231] The only concession he made was that Bidault and Molotov could examine the possibility of a Franco-Russian pact in the next few days.

In substance, then, de Gaulle had reached the same point with Stalin as he had with Churchill; but, while he refused throughout 1945 to conclude an Anglo-French treaty unless Britain recognized French demands in the Rhine and the Ruhr, he remained eager to sign an agreement with the Soviet Union although it too had not accepted his demands. The treaty signed by Bidault and Molotov on 10 December offered the Soviet Union a good many advantages. In the first place it was bound to benefit from Article 3, which contained reciprocal assurances of far-reaching rights of intervention against the slightest possibility of German aggression. Should such aggression nevertheless occur, under Article 4 both partners to the treaty guaranteed each other all possible help. Beyond that they pledged themselves '*à ne pas conclure d'alliance et à ne participer à aucune coalition dirigée contre l'une d'elles*' (Article 5). The practical effect of this was a promise of French neutrality in case the Western Allies opposed the Soviet urge to expand in Europe.[232] De Gaulle secured the one advantage that this treaty recognized that France was again a great power and entitled to a say in the future control of Germany; but this concession was dearly bought with the rejection of any idea of a Western bloc, with the exchange (even if unofficial) of representatives with the Lublin Committee in Poland and with the recognition of Soviet domination in the whole of Eastern Europe. Above all, de Gaulle's attempt to link recognition of the transfer of East German territory to the Soviet Union with recognition of the (proposed) transfer of West German territory to France was flatly rejected by Stalin.

[231] Ministerstvo inostrannykh del SSSR. *Sovetsko-frantsuzskie otnosheniya vo vremya velikoy otechestvennoy voyny 1941–1945. Dokumenty i materialy*, Moscow, 1959, No. 197, Soviet record of the conversation between Stalin and de Gaulle on 2.12.1944, pp. 339–47 (quoted in A. J. Rieber, *Stalin and the French Communist Party 1941–1947*, NY, 1962, p. 120). The French text is in 'Les Entretiens de Gaulle–Stalin des 2, 6 et 8 décembre 1944' in *Recherches internationales à la lumière du Marxisme*, No. 12, Paris, 1959, pp. 43–50; the French version is in substantial agreement, with only slight deviations: Record by Roger Garreau of de Gaulle's conversation with Stalin on 2.12.1944 in *Mémoires*, iii, pp. 364–7. Cf. the abridged account by de Gaulle in *Mémoires*, iii, p. 62 f. and Stalin's telegram of 3.12.1944 to Churchill and Roosevelt: 'As I expected, de Gaulle demanded the French frontier on the Rhine and the conclusion of a Franco-Soviet mutual assistance pact', quoted in *Stalin's Correspondence with Churchill, Attlee, Roosevelt and Truman, 1941–45*, 2 vols., Moscow, Foreign Languages Publishing House, 1957, and London, Lawrence and Wishart, 1958, vol. 1, p. 171; confirmed by 'Les Entretiens . . .', p. 45 f. For the reasons why de Gaulle stood by his recognition of the Oder–Neisse frontier despite the fact that Stalin rejected his demand for the Rhineland, cf. the passage in *Salvation*, p. 88: 'We believe that this solution will exclude any possibility of agreement between Germany and Poland.'

[232] Text of treaty in *L'Année politique, 1944–1945*, p. 528 f.; 'Les Entretiens . . .' (n. 231), pp. 99–101; *Salvation*, p. 171.

Moreover de Gaulle was soon made to realize that while Stalin signed the treaty for the sake of the advantages mentioned, he was far from accepting France as a partner 'on an equal basis'. At the end of February 1945 Bidault was told in London that Stalin at Yalta had only reluctantly agreed to the assignment of a zone of occupation to France and had categorically refused to accept France as a member of the newly formed Reparations Commission.[233] When the French ambassador in Moscow asked for his government to be given a seat on the Commission Stalin replied that he could only agree if Poland and Yugoslavia were also given places. In reply to the plea for Soviet support for French claims in the Rhineland Stalin answered: 'I repeat that the Soviet Union is not in any way committed as regards the Rhineland.' The ambassador rightly concluded: 'The Soviet Union behaves towards France as if the alliance did not exist.'[234] De Gaulle's ploy with the Franco-Soviet Pact virtually came to an end when Stalin ignored an Anglo-American application of 11 April for France to be included in the Dismemberment Committee, and in his broadcast speech of 9 May following the German capitulation openly declared: 'The Soviet Union celebrates the victory although it does not intend to dismember Germany.' The assumption that de Gaulle and Stalin were at one in their policy towards Germany proved to be no longer correct. It was by Stalin's wish that France was excluded from the Potsdam conference.[235] The notion of strengthening a non-Communist power in Western Europe and sharing power with it over the Continent in any shape or form was simply out of the question.

Even before the middle of April 1945, when the failure of all the hopes raised by the Moscow pact was more than obvious, there could be no doubt that for French aspirations to be fulfilled the goodwill of Britain and America was essential. It was all the more incomprehensible, to be explained only by de Gaulle's exaggerated desire for prestige, that he embarked on a series of open and deliberate snubs to the Western Allies, which had continuing repercussions in the debate on foreign policy in France throughout the rest of the year. First of all de Gaulle reacted to Roosevelt's proposal to meet him at Algiers on his way back from the Yalta conference with the remark that 'it would be impossible for [de Gaulle] to go to Algiers at short notice'; he would be glad to welcome the President in Paris; but if Roosevelt nevertheless wished to break his journey at Algiers,

---

[233] *L'Année politique, 1944–1945*, p. 132; Rieber (n. 231), pp. 194–7; on Yalta, the references in nn. 135–6 to the Introduction, esp. *Foreign Relations . . . Malta and Yalta*, pp. 572 f. and 623. Since Churchill's efforts to have a zone of occupation assigned to France had already begun in the middle of November 1944, while Stalin announced his opposition on the first evening of the Yalta conference, the Yalta decision favouring the French case cannot be said to have been the result of Western reaction to the Franco–Soviet treaty.

[234] G. Catroux, *J'ai vu tomber le Rideau de fer*, Paris, 1952, pp. 63–8. Rieber (n. 231), pp. 197 f. and 202 f., inferred from Soviet newspapers and periodicals that the chief reason why the Kremlin considered the Franco–Soviet treaty to have been 'constantly violated and in the long run destroyed' lay in its grievance at the French delay in giving full diplomatic recognition to the East-European governments installed by the Russians.

[235] P. E. Mosely, 'Die Friedenspläne der Alliierten und die Aufteilung Deutschlands, Die alliierten Verhandlungen von Jalta bis Potsdam' in *Europa Archiv*, 5 (1950), p. 3039 f.; B. Meissner, *Russland, die Westmächte und Deutschland*, Hamburg, 1954, pp. 47 and 57.

would he please inform de Gaulle in time so that the Governor of Algeria could be given the necessary instructions.[236] Roosevelt was not only annoyed by this answer but deeply injured. In his speech to Congress of 2 March on the results of Yalta he made an unmistakable reference to 'a great many prima donnas in the world who want to be heard'.[237] A second incident was more dramatic. Towards the end of the war de Gaulle arranged for units of the French army to cross the Alpine frontier into the North-West Italian province of Cuneo, with the intention of incorporating into France 'the former Savoy cantons of Tenda and Briga, and if possible also Ventimiglia' and the Val d'Aosta.[238] When the commander of the American Fourth Army Corps wanted to establish the military government for the area, de Gaulle informed him on 2 June through General Doyen that he had given orders to prevent the setting-up of an Allied military government 'in the territory occupied by our troops and administered by us' by every means and *without any exceptions*. It was only when President Truman cut off supplies to the French troops and issued a sharp protest against the French commander's threat to have his troops fight the Americans that de Gaulle gave way.[239] He went even further when his attempt to re-establish French influence in Syria and the Lebanon in spite of the 'independence and sovereignty' promised in 1941 led to a direct confrontation with British troops. On 29 May 1945, with the war in Europe hardly over, serious fighting broke out in Damascus between French troops and Syrians; the Syrian and Lebanese governments appealed for help to the British forces in those countries, whereupon on 2 June the British interned the French in their quarters.[240]

Neither at the last wartime conference of the Big Three at Potsdam in July and August nor at the first meeting of the four-power Council of Foreign Ministers in London in September and October was any serious consideration given to de Gaulle's main demands – detachment of the Rhineland, internationalization of the Ruhr, and the break-up of Germany. This was a result not only of France's weakness but also of Stalin's contemptuous attitude and the annoyance felt by the British and

---

[236] Sherwood (n. 209), pp. 859–61; *Mémoires*, iii, p. 87 f.

[237] From the Roosevelt Archives at Hyde Park, NY, in Viorst (n. 213), p. 233; cf. *Mémoires*, iii, p. 89; the press releases of both sides are cited in *L'Année politique, 1944–1945*, p. 120 f.

[238] *Mémoires*, iii, p. 180. Cf. the detailed study by Suzanne Bastid, 'Le rattachement de Tende et de la Brigue' in *Revue générale de droit international public*, July–Dec. 1949, pp. 321–40.

[239] Text of Truman's Note (with communications from Doyen) in French in *Mémoires*, iii, pp. 537–9; cf. *Mémoires*, iii, p. 182 f.; Truman, *Memoirs: 1945, Year of Decision*, vol. i, NY, 1955, Signet Book edition, NY, 1965, p. 269 f.; Churchill, vi (n. 213), pp. 493–4; Leahy (n. 215), p. 373 f. The withdrawal of French troops began a few days after Truman's protest of 7 June; for the cutting-off of American arms supplies, cf. M. Vigneras, *Rearming the French* (United States Army in World War II, Special Studies), Washington, 1957, pp. 360 f. and 367–72.

[240] Main references for the Levant crisis: *Mémoires*, iii, pp. 186–98, 508–21, and 530 f.; Churchill, vi (n. 213), pp. 489–93; Truman (n. 239), p. 270 f. Of other accounts, esp. G. Kirk, *The Middle East in the War* (part volume of the *Survey of International Affairs, 1939–1946*, ed. A. Toynbee), London, 1952, pp. 272–306, and DePorte (n. 208), pp. 126–52.

Americans.[241] In vain did de Gaulle concede, in an interview with *The Times* of 10 September, the possibility of forming an '*ensemble économique*' of the West-European countries, which he assumed was the wish of London and Brussels; it was too clearly meant as a cloak for his prior aim, French control of the Rhineland. There remained for de Gaulle only one last, destructive weapon: on 1 October for the first time he used the French veto against all plans for an all-German administrative authority so long as no decision had been made to sever the Rhineland and the Ruhr from Germany.[242] But even this policy of obstructiveness failed. When at the end of December the Moscow Conference of Foreign Ministers met without a French representative, it was clear that because of de Gaulle's behaviour France had gradually been forced to step down from the level to which Britain and the United States had tried to raise it at Yalta.[243]

In retrospect there is no doubt about the external failure of de Gaulle's foreign policy in 1945. Once again he had sought to secure for his nation the role of a 'first-class power' by demanding a considerable share of German assets and by making this the alpha and omega of his foreign policy. But the two superpowers had seen no reason to satisfy the desires of the diminished French nation state. 'The disparity between wish and ability ... was so obvious that neither for the Soviet Union nor for the Anglo-Saxon powers could a possible separate alliance with France be more than a secondary consideration, taking into account France's exaggerated hankering for prestige.'[244] French foreign policy had arrived at a hopeless impasse when de Gaulle, partly for that reason, resigned on 20 January 1946. It remained for Foreign Minister Bidault to struggle for over a year towards the same goal, but without success, before, in view of the Cold War, he reluctantly accepted the need to fall into line with American policy towards Germany and Europe. The internal effects for France were more serious: once again de Gaulle had bolstered nationalism among wide sections of French society, once again he had narrowed their view of foreign policy to the old stereotypes dating from the seventeenth century, which after 1919 had already proved so hopelessly impractical. How far he succeeded in the fateful policy of once more imbuing French public opinion with a nationalist mentality (with enthusiastic help from

[241] Cf. H. Feis, *Between War and Peace, The Potsdam Conference*, Princeton, 1960, pp. 128–32, and the Notes of 7.8.1945 on the Potsdam communiqués, hardly disguising the French Government's disappointment; French text in *Documents français relatifs à l'Allemagne*, Paris, 1947, pp. 7–11.
[242] De Gaulle in *The Times* of 10.9.1945, p. 4, emphasized his territorial claims in the Levant and in the Rhineland; the 'European' theme was hardly touched on. The diplomatic Note and statement by the French representative at the Allied Control Council on 1.10.1945 were not divulged to the French public, but first appeared in 1947 in *Documents français*, op. cit., (n. 241), p. 16.
[243] Cf. Catroux (n. 234), pp. 131–6 and 147–9; J. F. Byrnes, *Speaking Frankly*, NY, 1947, pp. 109–22, fully documented in DePorte (n. 208), pp. 136–44.
[244] A. Hillgruber, 'Eine Bilanz des Zweiten Weltkrieges aus der Sicht der kriegführenden Mächte' in Hillgruber, *Grossmachtpolitik und Militarismus im 20. Jahrhundert*, Düsseldorf, 1974, pp. 53–67, this quotation, p. 56.

the French Communist Party) can be seen more clearly in the light of an examination of the more enlightened views which were prevalent in France, as elsewhere, after the Second World War.

(C) THE 'OTHER FRANCE' AS CRITICISM AND ALTERNATIVE
In France, as in other countries, even in the age of nationalism internationalist and federal ideas had their forerunners and established a tradition. It is enough to recall the internationalism of the French liberals associated with Victor Hugo; the Socialist federalism of the school of Proudhon; the large number of distinguished Frenchmen in the nineteenth-century peace movement such as Gratry, Frédéric Passy, d'Estournelles de Constant, and others; the consistent rejection of the Treaty of Versailles by the French Socialists under Léon Blum and the early Christian Democrats associated with Marc Sangnier; Briand's ten-year struggle for a policy of reconciliation; the strength of the French section of the Pan-Europa Union, etc.[245] During the inter-war years such pioneers were in the minority, as in all the neighbouring countries. But from the experience of defeat and occupation there had emerged in the non-Communist French Resistance, as forcefully as in other Continental countries, a deep-seated awareness of changes in the power structure of world politics, the conviction that the age of the nation-state had passed and that an international community must be created if peace and prosperity were to be assured in future. All such thinkers had described the merging of essential sovereign rights in supranational federal institutions as the decisive step towards overcoming international anarchy; only so could a lasting solution of the German problem be found.[246] This whole trend of French internal opinion away from nationalism and towards plans for a European community was voiced emphatically by a host of writers from the autumn of 1944 onwards and during the first post-war years.[247]

[245] Cf., e.g., A. Schou, *Histoire de l'internationalisme*, Vol. 3: *Du Congrès de Vienne jusqu'à la 1ère guerre mondiale (1914)*, Oslo, 1963; B. Voyenne, *Le Fédéralisme de P.-J. Proudhon*, Paris, 1973; A. Wild, *Baron d'Estournelles de Constant. Das Wirken eines Friedensnobelpreisträgers für die deutsch-französische Verständigung und europäische Einigung*, Hamburg, 1973; G. Bonneville, *Prophètes et témoins de l'Europe. Essai sur l'idée d'Europe dans la littérature française de 1914 à nos jours*, Leiden, 1961; G. Ziebura, *Léon Blum. Theorie und Praxis einer sozialistischen Politik*, vol. i, 1875–1934, Berlin, 1963; F. Siebert, *Aristide Briand 1862–1932. Ein Staatsmann zwischen Frankreich und Europa*, Erlenbach–Zurich, 1973; W. Lipgens, 'Europäische Einigungsidee 1923–1930 und Briands Europaplan . . .' in *Historische Zeitschrift*, no. 203 (1966), pp. 46–89 and 316–63.

[246] Cf. the brief account 'The Idea of the non-communist Resistance', with quotations from all nine important Resistance Groups, in Lipgens, *Bedingungen* . . . in *VfZG*, (n. 208), pp. 58–64; similar outline by Ziebura (n. 218), pp. 24–32; for a more comprehensive collection of documents, see W. Lipgens, *Europa-Föderationspläne der Widerstandsbewegungen* (n. 44), pp. 180–250; to complete the story, Daniel Mayer, *Les Socialistes dans la Résistance*, Paris, 1968, *passim*.

[247] These conclusions emerge from an analysis of the foreign-policy debates of the Assembly, Nov. 1944–Jan. 1946, and of views on foreign policy expressed by the parties and in the media, in a study originally written for the section which follows but, in view of its length, published as W. Lipgens, 'Innerfranzösische Kritik der Aussenpolitik de Gaulles, 1944–1946' in *VfZG*, vol. 24 (1976), pp. 136–98. The detailed analysis of sources there covers sixty-three pages; in this book space allows only a summary of the main conclusions.

The strength of French revulsion against nationalism and the turning towards internationalist and federal ideas was even reluctantly admitted at times by de Gaulle. During the first foreign-policy debate in the Consultative Assembly in November 1944 he observed that when he had spoken 'specifically of the Rhine, the Saar and the Ruhr', the parliamentarians had hardly paid any attention; 'towards such problems of foreign policy as frontiers, security, and balance of power, they adopted doctrinaire attitudes which impressed public opinion but were as nebulous as they were sentimental'. It is significant that he attributed this attitude to a minority, saying that he did not understand them, but nevertheless admitted that they made an impact on public opinion. Recording that *'la plupart des éléments organisés pour se faire entendre'* had disapproved of his refusal to meet Roosevelt in Algiers, he added: 'I was obliged to discover that my idea of France's standing and rights was hardly shared by many people who swayed public opinion.' Moreover de Gaulle found himself 'on the Levant issue without effective support from the leading political circles in France. My handling of it roused criticism among almost all influential personalities. On this occasion I became aware of the whole depth of the gulf which on questions of foreign policy separated me from the political parties.'[248] There must have been good reasons, apart from the desire to emphasize his own influence on events, which induced him to make such admissions, contradicting as they did his conviction that he represented 'the nation'.

Among the re-emergent political parties it was the Socialist Party round which the non-Gaullist, non-nationalist idea of 'security through federal organization' crystallized. In the spirit of Léon Blum's criticism in 1941 of the Europe of national sovereignties and his support for an effective federation of sovereignty-pooling states within which, 'by including the German nation', a solution of the German problem could be found, the programme of the underground SFIO under its general secretary Daniel Mayer had called in December 1943 for *'une communauté internationale constituée d'abord par les États-Unis d'Europe et aboutissant, en fait, à des États-Unis du Monde'*. A consensus of all non-Communist post-war planners was expressed in the formula coined by Vincent Auriol: *'La Fédération européenne complétée par la Confédération internationale'*.[249] Immediately after liberation the newspapers reported the opening of the Dumbarton Oaks conference; federation on a global scale seemed more attainable, especially since, as people were often reminded, 'the Soviet Union was an opponent of regional federations'.

---

[248] De Gaulle, *Salvation*, p. 60.
[249] Basic reading for this is L. Blum, *A l'échelle humaine*, esp. chapter 7, written in July 1941. (English translation *For all mankind*, London, 1946.) For the development of the SFIO programme (quotation from D. Mayer [n. 246], p. 235), frequent use of Auriol's formulas and agreement with the other Resistance groups, cf. Lipgens, 'Innerfranzösische Kritik' (n. 247), p. 152 f., with detailed references. The maximum goal of a world federation and the more limited goal of a European federation were not seen as opposites, but as being equally necessary to preserve peace through the pooling of sovereignty.

And so the first extraordinary congress of the SFIO drew up a manifesto which articulated the federal principle in global terms and, rejecting Gaullist plans for breaking up Germany, insisted on its being applied to that country also. A lasting peace would depend on

'collective security in a world-wide organization based on justice. This organization must not be dominated by one or several great powers, but must take the form of a federation of free nations, each of which gives up part of its sovereignty to a superior body with its own leadership, its own budget and armed forces adequate to guarantee the security of every individual and of the whole community.' Economic and social organizations with a record of service in the international field must be placed at the disposal of this body. 'Only within a framework of all these institutions will the measures be successful which are envisaged to enable a Germany, changed both in its structure and its mentality, to take its place in the community of civilized peoples.' The guilty must be punished, but 'the Socialist Party considers it necessary to draw the nation's attention to the dangers of vengeful nationalism that would be caused by any break-up of Germany and any annexation of indisputably German territory.'[250]

This basic approach prevailed, however, far beyond the ranks of the Socialist Party. Proof of this will be given not so much by citing individual authors as by quotations from the frequent debates on foreign policy in the first year after the war, especially the concluding *'ordres du jour'* which recorded the Assembly's basic convictions. When the Consultative Assembly met for the first time in Paris (with twice as many seats as before) on 7 November 1944 and held its first foreign-policy debate on 21 and 22 November, only three speakers clung stubbornly to the old ideas of national security, a defensive glacis in the Rhineland and so on: Florimond Bonté for the Communist Party, Maurice Schumann, de Gaulle's former press officer in London, and Louis Marin, a veteran right-winger. Apart from these the debate was dominated by the ideas of 'international organization', a 'federation of free peoples'.

The leader of the Christian Trade Unions, Gaston Tessier, urged that the new world organization should immediately admit the defeated nations to membership and should 'give up the outdated dogma of absolute state sovereignty'. Daniel Mayer was emphatic in describing the 'federation of peoples' as the principal task, and he somewhat ambivalently linked together a European federation with an organization spanning the globe. France had 'a mission to help in the reconstruction of Europe and of the world ... The Europe we propose is a federation of free peoples [applause] ... which through economic co-operation will succeed in under-

---

[250] For the newspapers in the autumn of 1944 cf. C. Pegg, 'Die Résistance als Träger der europäischen Einigungsbestrebungen in Frankreich' in *Europa-Archiv*, 7 (1952), p. 5204; the unanimously adopted manifesto 'Le Parti Socialiste au Peuple de France' in *Le Populaire* of 14.11.1944, quotation here from sections 6 and 7. Part of the text is given in French in a basic study analysing the foreign-policy ideas of the SFIO during the 1940s by my colleague Wilfried Loth, *Sozialismus und Internationalismus. Die französischen Sozialisten und die Nachkriegsordnung Europas, 1940–1950*, Stuttgart, 1977, p. 49 f.

standing one another, helping each other and building up a complex and many-sided relationship which will lead them to federate and create an international community.' Other deputies also spoke in favour of a strong world-wide organization; even the Communist Bonté, though he added that the decision was one for the victorious powers and that alliance with Russia was a matter of urgency. Louis Saillant agreed, adding: 'We must support the creation of a permanent international army, not only an air force, in the service of the new international authority.'

At bottom all these expressions of opinion, following as they did the experience of defeat and the diminished prestige of the nation state as it had hitherto existed, pointed to what was the only conceivable future for Europe; but these conclusions were also applied, somewhat heedlessly, to the world as a whole despite the fact that the two superpowers, being themselves continental-size unions, knew perfectly well that their safety and prosperity could be guaranteed by their own strength. The motive behind the Europeans' line of thought was to do everything possible, after the suffering caused by the war, to ensure a lasting peace. The final resolution approved unanimously by the Assembly made no mention of proposals for ceding the Rhineland or breaking up Germany, but called on the government (1) to prosecute the war vigorously, (2) to remain in close co-operation with the Allies, and above all

'(3) to prepare an international organization which will lead the community of states towards a federation of free peoples within which the regional unions will not be in danger of giving rise to hostile blocs; (4) to follow an international policy based on the peoples themselves and taking account of their wish for freedom and international democracy'.[251]

The Assembly thus clearly approved the principle of international democracy, i.e. federation involving a parliament of peoples as against the inter-governmental diplomatic methods of the former League of Nations. It postponed the 'regional', i.e. European, union which it really wanted in deference to Soviet objections to a 'western bloc', but used these objections to press the case for a global federation of a truly supranational kind.

It was at first only as steps towards this goal that the Assembly welcomed bilateral treaties. De Gaulle kept to himself the fact that he had rejected a treaty offered him by Churchill on 11 November because Britain would not support his Rhineland demands. Bidault publicly assured the Assembly that the 'very great day' had shown that 'our heart has not changed. We have renewed the old ties with Britain; we have become friends again and,

---

[251] *Journal officiel de la République Française. Débats de l'Assemblée Consultative Provisoire* [henceforward *J.O. Débats*], séance du mardi, 21 Nov. 1944, p. 309 opens with a non-committal statement by Bidault: 'France can only state the position it will take up when it knows exactly the choices that have been made by its great allies'. The speakers quoted in the text are p. 311 Bonte, p. 314 f. D. Mayer; session of 22 Nov., p. 321 Tessier, p. 322 Saillant, p. 324 Schumann, and p. 333 Marin. For the *ordre du jour*, see p. 330.

as we hope, for ever... An alliance with the West, of course. How could it be otherwise? But an alliance with the East as well. We too are interested in questions which extend beyond the West.' It was on this basis that the Assembly welcomed the treaty with the Soviet Union. In the debate on ratification on 21 December 1944 André Mutter declared on behalf of the right-wing parties: 'It would be a mistake and an injustice to think that the Franco-Soviet Pact has priority in our friendship. It must be emphasized that France has the same respect, the same trust, the same friendship for all the nations which have helped to liberate it.' And speaking for the Socialists André Philip declared:

> We believe that the pact with Russia is the beginning of a whole series of mutual-assistance treaties into which France, Russia and Britain will draw all the nations of Europe that are united to us by long-standing ties, both moral and material ... But this pact, if it is the first of a number of agreements on mutual friendship and defence, which we hope will embrace the whole Continent, must – as the Foreign Minister has reminded us – find a place within the framework of our efforts for an international organization. Alliances are not a substitute for an international organization [applause]; they are a preparation for it, they create the basis on which it can be established ... First [there must be] political organization by the setting-up of an international body, which – and this is vital – will limit the sovereignty of all nations; then [will come] the creation of economic and social institutions.

Although the Franco-Soviet Pact was welcomed as a sign of recognition that France had returned to the ranks of the great powers, none of the non-Communist speakers in either of the two foreign-policy debates regarded it, like de Gaulle, as a means of putting pressure on the West; they welcomed it as one of the first steps towards the construction of a world-wide organization. It was in this spirit that a resolution was passed unanimously at the end of the December debate that the Assembly 'fully approves the Franco-Soviet treaty ... but desires that it be supplemented by a series of similar pacts which will show France's solidarity with the other United Nations and, in the aggregate, form an essential stage towards the future international organization for security and peace'.[252]

When de Gaulle in his broadcast of 5 February 1945 for the first time openly indicated that it was he himself who had refused to sign a treaty with Britain unless the latter supported his Rhineland policy, the first emphatic protests against such a policy were raised. On 7 February the

[252] *J.O. Débats*, 21.11.1944, p. 309 Bidault; 21.12.1944, p. 590 A. Mutter, p. 591 A. Philip, and p. 595 *ordre du jour* (comprising only these two sentences). For the British offer of alliance and the treaty with the Soviet Union, see Lipgens, 'Bedingungen' (n. 208), pp. 82–9. The post-war Congress of the Radical-Socialist Party unanimously passed a resolution on 21.12.1944 saying that the future League of Nations 'devra être réellement issue d'une fédération des peuples' (*Le Monde* report, 22.12.1944). The MRP, formed from a number of groups, held its foundation congress on 26.11.1944, when it adopted its statutes. Its first statement on foreign policy was made on 8.4.1945 (cf. n. 260).

Socialist *Populaire* started a series of articles which lasted a month, in the course of which every leading member of the Party in turn warned against such a reversion to the policy of inter-state rivalry. Paul Rivet wrote that the impression could not be avoided that at that juncture, '*exceptionnel et de courte durée*', when the creation of an organization for world peace was a possibility, the government was leading France back to the politics of international rivalry 'on the pretext of pursuing a policy of prestige'. The majority of the French people, however, wanted 'the government to follow a policy not entirely dominated by narrow-minded nationalist ideas'. Vincent Auriol, president of the Assembly's foreign-affairs committee, followed with a series of articles in which he described the Rhineland demands as '*de fragiles protections territoriales*'; to insist on their acceptance as the pre-condition of a Franco-British alliance and thereby jeopardize the idea of collective security was 'a bad mistake which tarnishes France's good name, involves it in risks and damages its true security'. People were impatiently hoping for negotiations that would at last lead to an alliance, 'but for us alliances can and should be nothing but integral parts of a federal organization of Europe and the world', failing which there would again be crisis, war, and defeat 'whether we have favourable frontiers or not'.[253]

In March 1945 the view began to be expressed once more that the superpowers, being continental unions, would not as yet be willing to give up sovereignty and accept federal unity on a global scale; but a world peace organization which thus remained inter-governmental would run into great difficulties in dealing with a Europe that could not put an end to its own anarchy and presented a constant temptation to intervention from outside. At the conference of European federalists held in Paris from 22 to 25 March by the Comité français pour la Fédération Européenne these basic ideas were worked out with much care, with leading Socialists such as D. Mayer and A. Philip, and the editors of such well-known periodicals as *Liberté, Témoignage chrétien,* and *Esprit* playing an active part.[254] But the political party organs and the Assembly at that date, on the eve of the foundation conference of the United Nations at San Francisco, remained

---

[253] Paul Rivet, 'Le rôle humain de la France', *Le Populaire*, 7.2.1945; Vincent Auriol, 'La sécurité française' and 'Le vrai réalisme', ibid., on 18 and 20.2.1945. At the same time the secretary-general of the SFIO, Daniel Mayer, underlined Auriol's statements in 'Brumes à dissiper' in *Le Populaire* of 21.2.1945. At the end of the series Albert Gazier wrote: 'Our foreign friends might well suppose from statements by the head of our government that we were thinking of unleashing an ambitious policy of annexations. They wonder if they are not witnessing a resurgence of Poincarism.' (*Le Populaire*, 27.2.1945.) Quoted by Loth (n. 250), p. 58.
[254] Cf. detailed account of the CFFE and the federalists' conference in Paris in March 1945 in section 2 of chap. 1 above: drafts of reports to the conference can be found in *Cahier de la fédération européenne* (No. 1), Paris, March 1945, pp. 7–22. It was then that the painstaking work of building up from below was initiated by the groups associated with *La Fédération* and *La République moderne*, cf. section 4 of chap. II, pp. 349–58.

true to the course they had adopted the previous November. In the debate on 27 March on the line to be taken by the French delegation at San Francisco, many speakers emphasized once again the provisional nature of the peace settlement, which had set up no supranational authority to uphold it, and regretted that for the sake of unity among the Allies the right of veto must presumably be accepted for the time being. These sentiments were closely reflected in the final resolution moved by the foreign-affairs committee and approved unanimously by the Assembly, which once again declared its readiness for a supranational organization to be set up at San Francisco, but combined it with a proviso that unity among the Allies must be preserved.

'Convinced that a durable peace presupposes the establishment of international justice and an international authority superior to the nation states and largely independent of them, but also concerned to take account of realities and to strengthen the bonds of trust and friendship among the great powers as well as to gather round them all the democracies of the world, the Assembly approves as a whole the plan drawn up at Dumbarton Oaks and charges the government to improve it by trying to ensure the adoption of the additional provisions contained in the memorandum addressed [by the French government] to the United Nations.' In this memorandum in question (even in de Gaulle's much abridged version) the two main sentences in the preamble ran: 'France considers that a lasting peace presupposes an international organization which will be both wider and stronger, and demands the establishment of justice and of an international authority superior to that of individual states. For its part it will be prepared to commit itself beyond the scope envisaged at Dumbarton Oaks and to accept more far-reaching restrictions on its sovereignty in exchange for more effective international organization.'[255]

The Assembly showed severe displeasure when, hardly a fortnight after the fighting in Europe had come to an end, de Gaulle risked a military confrontation with Britain over the question of spheres of influence in Syria, thus again spoiling the chance of an alliance which was an essential element in the arrangements for global as well as for European peace. In the debate on the subject which lasted from 15 to 19 June, many deputies thought that part of the blame for the crisis probably lay with the British, but apart from Maurice Schuman all the speakers saw the real cause of the trouble, as André Viénot observed on behalf of the Socialist Party, in de Gaulle's refusal to confer on Syria and the Lebanon the independence which they had been promised. André Hauriou remarked that if the British

---

[255] Text of the final resolution (*Ordre du jour*), *J.O. Débats*, 27.3.1945, p. 786. Government Memorandum in *Documents of the United Nations Conference on International Organization*, San Francisco, 1945, 22 vols., NY/London, 1945–55, vol. iv, p. 522; summarized in *L'Année politique, 1944–1945*, p. 180 f. cf. Lipgens, 'Innerfranzösische Kritik' (n. 247), pp. 158–60 for more details and supporting evidence about this debate in the Assembly and about the Memorandum prepared by a commission chaired by J. Paul-Boncour. This contained far-reaching federalist proposals which were severely reduced in Cabinet, de Gaulle allowing the two sentences in the preamble to go through because he thought it obvious that the superpowers would not agree to any curtailment of their sovereignty.

Colonial Office had been able to assert any influence it was only because French policy, 'hesitant and sometimes even contradictory' had lagged behind events and adopted 'the style (*allure*) of a conservative policy'. This must not be allowed to diminish 'the chances of a close understanding between France and Britain, which we see as an essential foundation of inter-allied co-operation and therefore of world peace'. For the Radicals Pierre Cot spoke of an 'almost incredible series of errors and blunders' and said that the methods employed by the French government in Syria had frequently been condemned by the Allies and by the Resistance organizations. Turning to de Gaulle he declared: 'There has been no lack of warnings, but you have paid about as much attention to them as you have to the views of this Assembly.' At the end of the debate the Assembly unanimously adopted a final resolution which left no doubt of its rejection of Gaullist foreign policy:

> The Consultative Assembly, in consternation . . . urges the government to agree to discuss all the agreements or treaties with Syria and the Lebanon, recognized as independent and sovereign states, in the spirit of trust and friendship, and in the same way to discuss any proposal which the British government may make to it on the basis of the Declaration of 13 June. It urges the government to redouble its efforts to negotiate a Franco-British Pact which, together with the Franco-Soviet Pact, will be one of the European foundations of the collective structure of world peace.[256]

When in the same month (June 1945) the results of San Francisco became public, showing as they did that the great powers had achieved their objective of setting up a world organization which would be able to keep the smaller powers, but not the great powers, in check, and which through the right of veto put the smaller powers at the mercy of the great, the meaning of the new international situation began to be realized. The way was open for what many commentators on the UN Charter pointed out as the logical sequel: since at global level there was no more than a consultative body fettered by the right of veto, it was up to the regions to make their own arrangements, and for Europe at least the opportunity for putting the supranational principle into practice seemed to have arrived. The recommendation to this effect made by Paul-Boncour on the day the Charter was signed was reported by *Le Monde* with as much approval as was the London *Economist*'s proposal that the Western-European countries should set up a General Staff and a customs union, as even for the two

---

[256] *J.O. Débats.* 15.6.1945, pp. 1118–21; A. Viénot, pp. 1121–4; M. Schumann as the only deputy supporting de Gaulle, pp. 1124–6; Georges Gorse as second spokesman for the SFIO heaping reproaches on the government, pp. 1127–9; F. Bonte for the French Communist Party, at that time still faithful to its anti-colonialist tradition, voting on this issue, exceptionally, against de Gaulle's foreign policy as well; on 19.6.1945 p. 1135 f. Hauriou, p. 1137 P. Cot, p. 1148 *Ordre du jour.* De Gaulle said of the resolution: 'The Assembly . . . voted for a motion lacking all vigour and expressing nothing but renunciation. I was obliged to declare that the text was not binding on the government.' *Salvation*, p. 195.

superpowers 'a prosperous united Europe would be a better neighbour than a fragmented one'. A series of pamphlets developed the same argument, none more forcefully than *L'Âge des empires* by Raymond Aron. His thesis was that the post-war world would be dominated by the two extra-European states because they alone were of the size needed by human societies to match the development of industrial technique and large-scale production; Europe would be 'completely divided into spheres of influence by the extra-European powers' if it did not achieve unity, 'without which a Balkanized Europe is doomed'. On 31 July the editor of *Le Monde,* Beuve-Méry, wrote in a leading article:

> In view of the unmistakable loss of power by Britain and other states in comparison with the world powers, all the essential conditions seem to exist which make it possible to hope for the creation – necessarily slow and difficult – of a third organization in the world, comparable in importance with the USA and the Soviet Union ... The Soviet Union completely rejects the idea of an organization which it suspects of anti-Sovietism and of becoming sooner or later an instrument of war against the USSR. The objection is serious ... The Western-European Association or Union is indeed only possible and desirable if it preserves the same understanding for both America and Russia and the same independence of both.[257]

One step in that direction, including the means to make it effective, was – to their credit – understood and approved by the French people as the only conceivable solution. This was shown by a questionnaire drawn up by the French Office for Public Opinion Research 'using the methods of the Gallup Institute' and published in July.

The following question was put: 'There is talk of arranging Europe into a federation of states, which for administrative purposes (police, justice, education, etc.) would be autonomous, but in all matters of common concern (industrial production, agriculture, transport, defence of the Continent, etc.) would be subject to a democratically elected "federal government". Do you consider the creation of a European federation desirable in these circumstances?' The answers were as follows:

	Yes	No	No opinion
Urban communities	71 per cent	20 per cent	9 per cent
Rural communities	75 per cent	14 per cent	11 per cent
Whole of France	73 per cent	17 per cent	10 percent [258]

[257] J. Paul-Boncour, interview for AFP, 26.6.1945, in San Francisco, *Le Monde,* 27.6.1945, p. 1; L. Dor, 'L'Union occidentale vue de Londres', *Le Monde,* 17.7.1945; R. Aron, *L'Âge des empires et l'avenir de la France,* Paris, July 1945, p. 345 f. and (partly dated June 1945) pp. 366–8; H. Beuve-Méry, 'France-Angleterre', *Le Monde,* 31.7.1945, cf. reference in DePorte (n. 208), pp. 195–7. Among the Catholic section of opinion a special European number of *Esprit* edited by E. Mounier prepared the ground: to solve the German problem it was essential 'for Europe to be created' (Jean Lacroix); the differences between the continents were still too great for a world federation to be possible, but within Europe 'common sufferings' had created a measure of agreement which made it possible 'at last to create a human community that could hold its own with the forces of the modern world. This we call the United States of Europe'. (Michel Collinet; both in *Esprit,* 13/6 [No. 110], 1.5.1945, pp. 772 and 783.)

[258] L'Institut Français d'Opinion Publique: *Sondages,* No. 17, Paris, July 1945. A 'personal statement' by Pierre Hervé, co-director of the French Gallup Institute and the only Communist on

In September Léon Blum, the Socialist leader released from a Nazi concentration camp, prudently bearing in mind the Soviet Union's well-known mistrust of 'blocs', spoke in favour not of the immediate setting-up of a European federation but of 'an alliance between France and Britain which would certainly attract the present and future democracies of the West'. His caution did not prevent him being attacked by Radio Moscow as a 'sinister accomplice' of a 'union aimed against USSR', whereupon Blum explained that what he had in mind was a 'Western family' of nations, each of which lacked an adequate home market and which were thus economically dependent on each other, *'une famille ... préexistant entre des peuples formés par des siècles d'histoire et de civilisation commune'* – far from being an anti-Soviet bloc. The Socialists thus tried to show the way while still paying heed to Soviet objections.[259] It was all the more important that at this juncture Christian-Democratic voices began to speak out more firmly in favour of a federation of Europe. 'The coming of a global society and of a perfect world', as envisaged by Blum, was certainly desirable, wrote Bertrand de la Salle in *La Nef*; but San Francisco had proved that it was for the time being unattainable, and the example of the League of Nations showed that an organization of governments could not guarantee peace; the urgent task was therefore 'to federate ... the countries of Western Europe'. A process of rethinking was going on inside the MRP, as the first resolution on foreign policy passed by the party's national congress in December 1945 emphatically declared that 'there will be no real peace as long as the dogma of national sovereignty has not been overcome', and in Europe 'no political settlement has any chance of being respected if the conditions for a healthy economy have not been created'. Jean Gauvin writing in *Esprit* was even more outspoken:

'In Moscow they continue to condemn European federalism ... This attitude is hard to understand after two world wars which resulted from the excesses of

---

the board, was annexed to the Report. According to Hervé, the federation of Europe was 'a cosmopolitan, Trotskyite and anti-communist idea', a sinister machination of the City of London which recalled the declamations of the Nazis about the need to 'create Europe'. (Quoted by P. Brizon in *Cahier de la fédération européenne*, No. 2, Aug. 1945, p. 26, with the comment: 'Pierre Hervé overlooks the fact that, a few pages earlier on, the same volume shows that his own carefully worded inquiry brought 73 per cent of "yes" answers drawn from all over France. Is he aware that his anathema applies to three quarters of the French population...?' Hervé, Brizon pointed out, had not questioned the reliability of the poll.

[259] L. Blum, 'L'Étoile rouge fait fausse route' in *Le Populaire*, 28.8.1945; L. Blum, 'Le "Bloc occidental"' in English in the *Daily Herald* of 15.9.1945, in French in *Le Populaire* of 16.9.1945; more explicitly at a press conference in London, 18.9.1945, reported in *Le Populaire* of 19.9.1945. Radio Moscow's comment in French in *Paris-Soir*, 16.9.1945; protests in *L'Humanité*, esp. on 11, 12, and 20.9.1945, in *Krasnaya Zvezda*, 14.9.1945, *Pravda*, 17.9.1945, *Trud*, 23.11.1945, etc.; for more details of Blum's conception, Loth (n. 250), pp. 72–86. A decisive assurance was given in the *Cahier de la fédération européenne* (No. 2), Aug. 1945, by Paul Brizon, 'La Fédération est-elle anti-soviétique?' (ibid., p. 28); The charge that 'the European federation would constitute an anti-Soviet bloc is unproven, unprofitable and irresponsible: if no constructive idea is offered, but divided Europe is left as an arena between the superpowers, an anti-Soviet bloc is more likely to emerge from this chaos than from a democratically organized community'.

nationalism in Europe. How is one to try to guarantee peace without a genuinely international organization making it possible to eliminate outdated rivalries and create multinational groups?' Since the failure to do this at San Francisco 'nothing would be more appropriate than to establish a federation at least in Europe, the starting-place of so many wars'.[260]

Yet however forcefully the views of the 'other France' were expressed in the summer, autumn, and winter of 1945, and however logical it was to apply the supranational principle to Europe after its rejection in the United Nations Charter, it was equally obvious that much of the enthusiasm for federalism, as far as Europe was concerned, had evaporated or was permeated with a feeling of resignation and frustrated by opposing influences which were growing in force. There were two main reasons for this. First, the victorious superpowers, especially the Soviet Union, had clearly not only rejected the supranational, federal principle in relation to the UN as a global organization, but, as was already clear, had also opposed its application to Europe. Secondly, de Gaulle's government not only took no initiative in favour of European unity but also, in defiance of majority opinion in the Assembly, continued to put forward out-of-date territorial demands in the Rhineland and Syria, the precise details of which were not disclosed to the French public but which were couched in terms of militant nationalism. De Gaulle first made his official demand for the Rhine and the Ruhr to be detached from Germany at the Council of Foreign Ministers on 14 September 1945. He clung to it stubbornly, though without making it public, and his government's declaration of 23 November paid lip-service to 'international organization' in the style of Socialist-party speakers without actually favouring it.[261] The

---

[260] Bertrand de la Salle in *La Nef,* Vol. 2, No. 11, Oct. 1945, p. 124 f.; J. Gauvin, 'L'U.R.S.S. et l'Europe' in *Esprit* 14/1 (No. 118), 1.1.1946, pp. 65 f. and 73. In MRP's first statement on foreign policy: General Motion, adopted by the first National Council on 7 and 8 April 1945 (p. 1 of the leaflet), there was some ambivalence. 'Security depends in the first place on real protection on the Rhine. It depends especially on the organization of true collective security with institutions capable of forestalling a future conflict by the compulsory arbitration of international differences and by decisive sanctions against a possible aggressor . . . France, like other countries, must be ready to accept a limitation of its sovereignty in proportion to the actual power possessed by the world organization and must take part in the establishment of an international armed force . . .' The greater emphasis on the second course in the quoted text is in *IIe Congrès National du M.R.P.,* 16.12.1945; Motion on foreign policy, p. 7 of the leaflet. For the gradual development of the foreign-policy aspect of the MRP see Lipgens, 'Innerfranzösische Kritik' (n. 247) at nn. 37, 47, 62, 82, 97, and 112; cf. section 2 of chapter IV of vol. 2 of this book.

[261] On de Gaulle's tactic of concealing his nationalist foreign policy, an important factor explaining the weakness of the 'other France' in the autumn and winter of 1945, cf. with detailed evidence Lipgens, op. cit. (n. 247), pp. 142 and 186 f. The Note of 14.9.1945 obstructing Allied policy in Germany was not published until 1947. The government declaration of 23.11.1945 did not contain a word about Germany or a specifically national security policy, because de Gaulle had to win the Socialists' support, against Communist claims, for a cabinet coalition of Communists, Socialists, and MRP. In the debate no one could oppose a policy which was not included in the government declaration, and the Socialists hoped that the commitment to an international organization signified a change of heart (cf. esp. Lipgens, op. cit. [n. 247] n. 100).

Assembly's foreign-policy debate from 15 to 17 January 1946 brought to light the anger and disappointment of progressive pro-federal elements as well as the revival and consolidation of narrow-minded nationalist forces as a result of the general situation and de Gaulle's tactics. The debate was opened on 15 January by two well-known exponents of the 'other France'. Once again the secretary-general of the SFIO, Daniel Mayer, speaking 'in the name of the Socialist parliamentary group', explained the basic idea which they had taken over from the Resistance:

'Before reconstructing the world, you must first reconstruct Europe ... The Europe we propose [in contrast to Hitler's attempt to establish the predominance of a single country] is a federation of free peoples.' Round the Rhine and Danube valleys 'free peoples, co-operating for economic purposes, are beginning to understand one another, help each other and build up close and many-sided relationships which will lead them on to federate and form an international community'. To make this possible, 'each state will have to give up part of its sovereignty to a higher authority that will have its own government, its own budget and system of justice and means of enforcement ...' He added by way of criticism of Gaullism: '*La France seule* is the slogan of people, some of whom are sitting on these benches, who imagine that France's security lies in its military potential, in the number of soldiers in its barracks, the power of its guns ... – these people forget, by the way, the atomic bomb – or still more in the number of miles which will separate the Germany of tomorrow from the left bank of the Rhine. Our real security lies in none of these things, but in the gradual build-up of federal communities.'

The second speaker, Ernest Pezet of the MRP, gave an assurance that the applause for his predecessor 'showed that my friends, in whose name I am speaking here, share his views unreservedly'. They were horrified by the 'tragedy of distrust' between the two superpowers, who had fallen back into the policy of zones of influence because of the old-style 'defence glacis' created by the USSR in Eastern Europe and its objections to regional federations.

'In Eastern Europe there are already *de facto* agreements, but people don't want to hear about regional agreements in the West. We must nevertheless have the courage to speak about this quite frankly.' Pezet rejected the restoration of the pre-war system of 'balance of power, zones of influence and intervention' – so why should they be accused of 'wishing to create a Western bloc to which aggressive intentions are gratuitously ascribed?' 'France must remember that the right of veto means the unanimity rule of 1919 ... and that the organic formation of a real League of Nations requires federalism.' Very different arguments were used by Bidault and his MRP supporters, but at the end of the debate Jules Catoire repeated that the one thing needful was 'a European federation ... There will be no real peace until the sovereign nations have agreed to give up part of their rights and their pride in favour of an international organization which will represent – we are not afraid to use the word – a true superstate.'[262]

[262] *J.O. Débats*, 15.1.1946, pp. 3–5 D. Mayer, pp. 5–8 E. Pezet; 17.1.1946, p. 107 J. Catoire. The other Socialist speakers demanded the application of these principles to the German question as

This idea of the 'other France' was opposed by two groups, who received more support from outside events than they had so far had during the debates of the Assembly. One group consisted of the Communist speakers, who utterly condemned any idea of a supranational order involving renunciation and pooling of sovereignty in favour of any kind of union as a betrayal of the national principle; they advised France to seek its security in loyalty to the pact with the Soviet Union and in keeping Germany permanently in check. They were supported by Pierre Cot of the Radicals and by the older right-wing nationalists like Louis Marin. The second group consisted of sections of the Radicals, right-wingers, and the MRP led by Bidault, whose blinkered and Poincarist way of thinking made them incapable of envisaging any alternative to the policy of separating the Rhineland from Germany.[263] So for the first time at the end of that debate the result was an *ordre du jour* which was almost meaningless despite the fact that it had majority (not unanimous) backing. The Assembly wanted 'to safeguard peace by collective security while respecting [the rights of] all nations' – but the internationalists were for the first time unable to get a motion passed in favour of supranational pooling of sovereignty. As for policy towards Germany, it was simply stated to be the removal of 'those people and institutions that are helping to preserve traces of National Socialism and Fascism'; territorial changes were not even mentioned.[264]

---

well; instead of the separation of the Ruhr – intolerable for Germany – they wanted economic internationalization of the Ruhr industrial complex in preparation for the inclusion of Germany in a European federation (16.1.1946, pp. 52–4 Grumbach, p. 55 f. Lapie). Of the MRP deputies Pezet, Catoir and Marcel Poimbœuf urged that every country should give up 'part of its sovereignty in favour of the international organization' (15.1.1946, p. 17); Jean Palewski spoke of the need to renounce economic autarky and to create an international economic authority for this purpose (16.1.1946, p. 38). B. Ott favoured an economic authority which could provide joint administration for the Ruhr, Rhine, Saar, Luxemburg, and Lorraine and serve all Europe's industrial needs; it was unnecessary to make political or territorial demands if peace could be guaranteed in that way (16.1.1946, p. 48 f.).

[263] Bonte, again the chief Communist speaker, opposed 'the seductive formulas of a world parliament or the abandonment of national sovereignty . . . a return to the methods of the Tower of Babel, where every language would be spoken but there would be no understanding' (*J.O. Débats*, 15.1.1946, pp. 9 and 11). Jacques Duclos declared that France would not agree to something which it had refused to Hitler; Leagues of Nations were impossible 'without the prior disappearance of the capitalist regime' (17.1.1946, p. 102 f.). Pierre Cot (16.1.1946, p. 37); Louis Marin (ibid., on p. 43 f.). The chief burden of these utterances was that de Gaulle's German policy was welcome to the Soviet Union because it caused controversy between the Western countries. Alfred Oberkirch of the MRP urged: 'West Germany's unity must be smashed once and for ever' (16.1.1946, p. 50, f.); Bidault wanted the definite separation of the Ruhr district, while 'the Rhineland should belong politically to neither Germany nor France' (17.1.1946, p. 80).

[264] Text in *J.O. Débats*, 17.1.1946, p. 107. To quote one more voice of the 'other France': 'A policy predicated on local economic or military conflicts of the Franco-German type threatens to engulf us in an anachronism which is increasingly the besetting sin of the French intelligentsia. . . . It is not only the methods of this policy which seem out of date, it is the very idea of a German danger. A conflict between powers which are not first-class powers, but still important enough for their disputes to be more than mere local incidents, can only take place in future within the framework of a conflict between the "great" powers . . . In a world still divided into small isolated economic

To sum up. The significant feature of the remarkably frequent debates on foreign policy held during this period (November and December 1944, March, June, and November 1945, and January 1946) is that in none of them was the Gaullists' idea of a purely national security policy, of *de facto* French control of the Rhineland, whenever it was suggested by a deputy, allowed to pass uncontradicted; nor was it included, in spite of their wishes, in even one of the six *ordres du jour* which ended the debates and summarized the Assembly's views. The Assembly accepted the 'federation of free peoples', the principle of supranationality, the urgency and importance of the pact with Britain and the 'extension of collective security' while 'respecting all nations', but never once did it accept the detachment of German territory. Consistently with these statements of principle the Constituent Assembly passed by a substantial majority Article 46 of the Constitution which ran: 'Provided there is reciprocity, France agrees to the limitation of its sovereignty so far as that is necessary for the organization and defence of peace.'[265]

The Socialist Party as a whole had proved to be de Gaulle's severest critic. Led for two decades by Léon Blum in a spirit of internationalism which during the Resistance had been embodied in an avowedly supranational, federal programme under leaders committed to that programme, it took a firm stand against nationalism and power politics and in favour of supranational pooling of sovereignty in a 'federation of free peoples' on both a Continental and a global level. During the foreign-policy debate the Socialists were joined by sections of the Radical-Socialist Party and by right-wing Republicans who belonged to the Briand tradition. Especially on such controversial issues as the pact with Britain, the organizing of world peace, and the federal principle they were joined by sections of the MRP, so that between the autumn of 1944 and the autumn of 1945 the Assembly passed a number of concluding resolutions which were unequivocally federal and internationalist. The Communist Party proved equally staunch in support of the traditional idea of nationalism, 'continuing', as Jean Maigne wrote at the end of 1944, 'to make use of patriotic feelings' as they had done in the Resistance; but above all following the decision of the Soviet Union which from 1945 onwards asserted that any attempt to strengthen the ties between West European countries would mean a threat to itself. Apart from this attempt to set up a *cordon sanitaire* in

---

units, neither France nor Germany would stand much chance of recovering its prosperity ... The prerequisite for a constructive policy of this kind is that French diplomacy should cease to be exclusively preoccupied with a return of the German danger and should understand that for France and Germany there can in future only be a common destiny *vis-à-vis* the "great" powers.' (J. Rovan, 'Politiques en Allemagne', *Esprit* (No. 118), Jan. 1946, p. 147 f.)

[265] This Article, which had been demanded by the Socialists since their 37th Congress in Aug. 1945, was adopted by the Constituent Assembly on 11.4.1946 (*J.O. Débats*, 11.4.1946, p. 1728); it was taken over unchanged into the second Constitution on 29.9.1946, which on 13.10.1946 was voted for by the electorate, and thereafter was often hopefully cited by European federalists.

reverse, the main feature of Moscow's West European policy was to arouse nationalist passions and proclaim the slogan of the sacredness of national sovereignty. A kind of alliance on foreign-policy questions was formed by the Communists on the one hand and, on the other, a group consisting mainly of the majority of the MRP grouped round the pro-Gaullist leadership of Bidault and Schumann, with some support from Radicals and right-wing nationalists like Marin, especially because they hoped for Soviet backing for de Gaulle's claims on Germany. From the autumn of 1945 onwards traditional nationalism was strengthened when the Western powers rejected a world peace organization based on supranational principles, while de Gaulle rejected the Franco-British Pact, as he did any other approach to Western integration, and made his demand for the separation of the Rhineland an official aim of French diplomacy.[266]

With de Gaulle's departure in January 1946 there began a change of direction in French foreign policy; but several other factors were also at work, so that the process lasted a year and a half before the full effect was felt. The new head of government, Félix Gouin (SFIO), used ambivalent expressions in his initial policy statement, which differed only slightly from those of his predecessor.

But the demand for internationalizing the Ruhr and the rejection of a central administration in Germany, when voiced by Gouin, had different implications from the same demands put forward by de Gaulle. In a series of articles between 12 and 17 March Léon Blum urged that the policy of separating the Rhineland from Germany, which was bound to fail, should be replaced by the much more promising policy of placing the economy of the Ruhr under international control. Gouin declared in a speech at Strasburg on 24 March, with equal clarity, that no one wanted to annex any territory, but that the Ruhr district, 'the possible means of Europe's recovery', must not 'for the third time become the main instrument of its destruction'. An international solution of this problem should be sought by the creation of an international consortium. An extraordinary congress of the SFIO on 31 March 1946 unanimously supported this idea, which aimed at putting into practice, in part at least, the ideas about Germany which the Socialists had advocated since France's liberation.[267] If Gouin had managed to win support for

[266] A general reference to Lipgens, 'Innerfranzosische Kritik' (n. 247), must suffice here; its conclusions can be applied for example to the excellent chapter on political parties in A. Grosser, *La IVe République et sa politique extérieure*, Paris, 1967, pp. 103–41. For the Socialists, a useful study is that by W. Loth (n. 250), which deals also with their later crisis caused by Guy Mollet. The quotation in the text is from Jean Maigne, 'La Résistance comme expérience et volonté' in *Esprit*, 13/1 (no. 105), Dec. 1944, p. 10. In Jan. 1947 the French Communist Party decided to stay in Ramadier's new Cabinet solely in order to support Bidault's policy towards Germany for as long as possible (cf. B. D. Graham, *The French Socialists and Tripartisme, 1944–47*, London, 1965, p. 258 f.).

[267] Government declaration by Gouin in *J.O. Débats*, 1946, p. 153; Series of articles: Oreste Rosenfeld (but writtten by L. Blum, cf. *Œuvre*, vii, p. 451) 'L'internationalisation de la Ruhr' in *Le Populaire*, 12, 14, and 17–18.3.1946; F. Gouin on 24.3.1946 quoted in *L'Année politique, 1946*, p. 533; resolution of the extraordinary party congress of the SFIO at Montrouge, 31.3.1946: 'Opposed to any dismemberment and any annexation, as well as to maintaining the division of Germany into four occupation zones, the party demands that international occupation continue until there is total

his policy in the French cabinet he would certainly have been able to carry it out in view of the generally favourable attitude of the then British government towards Socialist policies.

Two obstacles, however, delayed the change. One was that Gouin was obliged to form a tripartite government, in other words to include the Communists, who insisted on a nationalist foreign policy. Secondly, since a shift of opinion inside the MRP was as yet unable to prevail against Bidault, Gouin was also obliged to keep him, hitherto de Gaulle's right-hand man and the interpreter of his thinking, as foreign minister.[268] Like most Christian Democrats Bidault's career had been in Catholic social work before he entered politics, and he was almost entirely unfamiliar with foreign policy questions; as he himself said, he had 'spent three years in a closed community and knew hardly anything about the changes that had taken place in the world'.[269] He believed that it was his duty to stick rigidly to the demands of nationalist *raison d'état* as he had learnt to do under de Gaulle. Thanks to a secret alliance the Communists and the right wing of the MRP ensured that the nationalist policy should continue for a further year. To win concessions over the German question they preferred to fall in with Soviet ideas rather than make any move in the direction of West-European solidarity.

Not until the battle for a new Constitution was over and relations between East and West deteriorated did a real transformation come about. As Prime Minister of the last transitional government before the inauguration of the Fourth Republic, Léon Blum, in a surprise visit to London on 15 January 1947, paved the way for the conclusion of the overdue Franco-British alliance; the Treaty of Dunkirk was signed on 4 March, but thanks to the views of Bidault and Bevin it embodied little of the co-operation that had been intended.[270] Only after the Foreign Ministers' meeting in Moscow in April had convinced Bidault of France's dependence on the West was he ready to be more co-operative, and only after Prime Minister Ramadier dismissed the Communist ministers on 4 May was the way clear for the pro-European forces to advance – and even then only one step at a time.[271] It was a tragedy for Europe that the

---

denazification and economic internationalization . . . of the Ruhr.' (*Bulletin intérieur*, No. 12, April, 1946, p. 6.) Evidently what was here envisaged was a nationalization which could lead to a European High Authority in quite a different sense from that of de Gaulle, for whom such a solution was the last and worst, to be resorted to only if a nationalist one could not be obtained. However, when questioned in the National Assembly about his speech at Strasburg, Gouin had to give an assurance that the general direction of foreign policy remained unchanged (*J.O. Débats*, p. 2081) – for reasons which will be seen later.

[268] Cf. *L'Année politique, 1946*, p. 372; for Gouin's unsuccessful move, see the comprehensive account in Loth (n. 250), pp. 94–7.

[269] G. Bidault, *Resistance: the Political Autobiography of Georges Bidault*, London, 1965, p. 59.

[270] For the origins of the Treaty of Dunkirk, cf. R. J. Guiton, *Paris–Moscow*, Stuttgart, 1956, p. 162–70, and Loth (n. 250), Chapter IV.3. Cf. J. Freymond, *Western Europe since the War*, New York (Praeger), 1964, p. 39. For Bevin's playing down of the treaty, see p. 188.

[271] Cf. sections 1 and 6 of chapter V in vol. 2 of this book.

only one of its states which by its domestic situation and through the opportunities presented to its foreign policy could, in 1945, have done much to set the movement for European unification in train, instead reverted to the old nationalist groove and remained stuck there for over two years.

5. Pro-European Trends in Occupied Germany

Unlike France, Germany after 1945 had no chance whatsoever of playing a leading and active part in the shaping of a new Europe. On the contrary, the collapse of the Third Reich meant the end of Germany as an independent political entity; the country and its inhabitants were at first nothing but the property of the victorious Allied powers, they no longer had any say in international policy. Yet even in defeat the German state continued to be a central object of these powers' plans and actions; Germany was for the time being a chaotic power vacuum, but the victors were bound, each in its own way, to make use of German resources, especially industrial resources, in pursuit of their national objectives in the post-war period. The clash of interests between the Allies would thus inevitably come to a head over the 'German question', if at all. For the Germans themselves the prospects of regaining any political independence in future depended on the extent of co-operation or confrontation between the new superpowers at any one time.

Nevertheless, to understand the new phase of German politics which began in 1945 and which eventually gave birth to the Federal and to the Democratic Republic, it is essential to realize that the first steps taken by German statesmen in this new process of adjustment were not determined solely by the balance of power between the victorious powers and the decisions taken by them, but that they also had their roots in the Germans' own traditions and political reassessments. For the idea of a European federation had also gained support in the German Resistance;[272] and in contrast to what happened in the neighbouring states, in Germany the reaction against nationalism was not obscured by the superpowers' restoration of the nation state, but was deepened and extended after that state's destruction. The constraints imposed on the Germans' rethinking by the victorious powers, the conditions to which the Germans in their defeat were subject, and their own basic inclinations set the scene for a new era in German politics.

---

[272] Cf. Lipgens, *Föderationspläne,* pp. 100–76; summarized in Lipgens, 'Europa-Föderationspläne deutscher und italienischer Widerstandsgruppen im II. Weltkrieg' in: *Von der Diktatur zur Demokratie, Deutschland und Italien in der Epoche nach 1943,* Brunswick, 1973, pp. 11–27; also section 3 of the Introduction to this book.

(A) THE VICTORIOUS POWERS IN GERMANY: THE ADMINISTRATION OF CHAOS

From spring 1945 to spring 1947 Germany presented the unique spectacle of a modern community stripped of its statehood.[273] The occupying powers had taken over power from the highest level to the lowest, in accordance with the 'Declaration regarding the Defeat of Germany and the Assumption of Supreme Authority with respect to Germany' dated 5 June 1945.[274] Germany no longer existed as an independent state; its future depended entirely on the pleasure – but also on the responsibility – of the occupying powers. This followed the unconditional surrender of the German forces on 8 May, in accordance with the demand formulated by Churchill and Roosevelt at the Casablanca conference, and the arrest of the 'Acting Reich Government' headed by Grand Admiral Dönitz, which the Russians had demanded and which occurred on 23 May. In addition the occupying powers issued announcements on 5 June on 'the machinery of control', on 'zones of occupation in Germany', and on 'consultation with governments of other United Nations'.[275] Supreme power in each zone was exercised by the Commander-in-Chief, who was subject to orders from his government. On questions affecting Germany as a whole the supreme authority was the Allied Control Council consisting of the four Commanders-in-Chief. Decisions of the ACC had to be unanimous, and if unanimity was not achieved there was no way of ensuring uniformity between the zones. The fact that supreme power was thus exercised on two levels – directly in the zone and higher up through the ACC – meant that the zones were able to develop on different lines because there was no authority capable of preventing any one occupying power from pursuing its own aims without regard for the requirements of other zones.

Military governments, set up immediately in the rear of the advancing armies, issued strict rules about reporting to the police, curfew, the surrender of arms, etc., and tried to restore the public services needed by the troops such as light, water, and communications. Their instructions were obeyed with surprising willingness by a listless and famished population.

---

[273] It is not the purpose of the following section to retrace Germany's domestic history from 1945, but merely to recall the circumstances under which German pro-European thinking had to make a new start. The following books may be cited as general accounts of Germany's development: W. Cornides, *Die Weltmächte und Deutschland, Geschichte der jüngsten Vergangenheit 1945–1955*, Tübingen/Stuttgart, 1961²; E. Deuerlein, *Deutschland nach dem Zweiten Weltkrieg 1945–1955*, Constance, 1964; T. Vogelsang, *Das geteilte Deutschland* (dtv-*Weltgeschichte des 20. Jhs.* vol. 2), Munich, 1966¹, 1973⁵; A. Grosser, *Germany in our Time: a Political History of the Postwar Years*, London, 1971; A. Hillgruber, *Deutsche Geschichte 1945–1972. Die deutsche Frage in der Weltpolitik*, Frankfurt/Berlin/Vienna, 1974.
[274] Text in *Nouveau Recueil général de traités*, Greifswald/Aalen, 1944–69, Série III, vol. 41, pp. 919–23.
[275] Ibid., pp. 923–5.

What faced the military governments was utter chaos;[276] Germany was a landscape of ghosts. About a quarter of all dwelling-houses were completely destroyed, a further quarter partially destroyed, and the total quantity of rubble was estimated at 400 million tons. When Harry Hopkins saw Berlin on his way to Moscow in May 1945 he exclaimed: 'It's a second Carthage!', and an American journalist reacted similarly: 'This is more like the face of the moon than any city I had ever imagined.'[277] Over half of Germany's railway-engines, trucks, and bridges had been destroyed; such railway-lines and post offices as were still intact were for months reserved for the Allies. For the time being there was no question of contacts between different parts of the country or of organizing political groups. Most of the population were barely able to exist on inadequate rations, and crowds of people stood outside the kitchens of the occupying forces begging for scraps of food. People were obliged to spend most of their time 'organizing' extra food supplies from the countryside or the black market. The mark lost virtually all its value and was largely replaced by cigarettes. Those who occupied responsible posts in the public service inevitably saw their overriding and at first sole duty as keeping the population alive. Divided families tried to reach home by trekking on foot for weeks on end. Prisoners of war also came back, 3.4 million from American captivity, most of whom were soon released, the last in July 1946; they were followed by 3.2 million in British captivity. The release of prisoners of war from Russia was not completed until 1955. Some 11 million foreign workers ('displaced persons') and ex-prisoners of war thronged the towns for months. They were joined in the general confusion by refugees and expellees from Eastern Germany: 6.8 million from the eastern provinces (within the 1937 frontier) arrived in the four occupation zones, while a further 1.4 million perished in the course of their flight. Added to them were 6.3 million expelled from their homes in German-populated areas of Eastern Europe, almost 3 million of whom came from the Sudeten districts of Czechoslovakia. Altogether over 13 million human beings had to be taken in and provided for.

Germany as a whole showed every conceivable sign of total military, political, and economic collapse, from the vast areas of war devastation to the breakdown of ordinary human institutions.[278]

In contrast to 1918, the completeness of the catastrophe had sunk deep into the consciousness of every single person; the Germans could not doubt the finality of the defeat, nor that in a sense it was logical and necessary. Accordingly, the officers, soldiers, and employees of the occupying armies were strictly forbidden by the ban on fraternization to shake hands with a German or hold any conversation with German people – a drastic prohibition, which was gradually relaxed in the first nine months of 1946, and was not applied in the Soviet Occupation Zone. The basic

[276] Cf. the graphic descriptions in V. Gollancz, *In Darkest Germany,* London, 1947; O. Müller-Marein, *Deutschland im Jahre I, Panorama 1946–1948,* Hamburg, 1960; G. Siemer, *Deutscher Exodus – Vertreibung und Eingliederung von 15 Millionen Ostdeutschen,* Stuttgart, 1974, and in the collection of essays edited by H. Dollinger, *Deutschland unter den Besatzungsmächten, 1945–49,* Munich, 1967.
[277] Hopkins retranslated from Deuerlein (n. 273, p. 3); the journalist quoted in J. Gimbel, *The American Occupation of Germany, Politics and the Military, 1945–49,* Stanford, 1968, p. 6.
[278] Vogelsang (n. 273), p. 15.

directive JCS 1067 issued by the American Chiefs of Staff to the occupation troops defined the 'principal objectives of military government in Germany' as follows: 'It should be brought home to the Germans that they cannot escape responsibility for what they have brought upon themselves.'[279] In the world-wide debate concerning Germany and the Germans, hatred and repugnance predominated. President Roosevelt expressed the attitude of the victorious powers: 'All Germans should feel that the entire nation has taken part in a criminal conspiracy against the laws of decency of modern civilization.'[280]

This somewhat superficial anti-Fascist ideology, much encouraged by the Allied demand for unconditional surrender, became the basis of the joint German policy of the victors and especially the two superpowers. Tension inside the Allied Control Council increased slowly at first, more rapidly from the summer of 1946 onwards, until on 20 March 1948 the Soviet Military Governor walked out of the Council and thus brought about its demise. Nevertheless, it should not be forgotten that at least during the first post-war year, from summer 1945 to summer 1946, the Council functioned to a large extent effectively and unanimously. Wholesale de-Nazification was vigorously put in hand, the trials of war criminals began, the press, publishing, and broadcasting were restarted on a new footing, and finally a comprehensive policy of 're-education' was attempted.[281]

Only gradually did disagreements in the Allied Control Council become obtrusive. At first, in the winter of 1945–6, it was mainly the French who used their veto against any move that would prejudice the question of German unity, having in mind their own demands for the separation of the Rhineland and the Ruhr. They thus prevented the establishment of the central government agencies for Germany envisaged in the Potsdam Agreements. Only in the months that followed the adoption of the Level of Industry Plan in March 1946 did the problem of reparations divide the Americans and British from the Russians. While the former were anxious for their zones to be self-supporting, if only to pay for the huge imports of food, the Soviets increased the Western Zones' adverse balance of payments by appropriating part of the current production of their zone as reparations, instead of sending it to the West as the Western powers insisted they were obliged to do by the Potsdam Agreements. When on 3 May 1946 the American Military Governor, General Clay, ordered the suspen-

[279] JCS 1067, full text in B. Ruhm von Oppen (ed.), *Documents on Germany under Occupation, 1945–1954*, London, 1955, pp. 13–27.
[280] Roosevelt to Cordell Hull on 26.8.1944, quoted in Deuerlein (n. 273), p. 67.
[281] Cf. G. E. Gründler and A. von Manikowsky, *Das Gericht der Sieger*, Oldenburg, 1967; J. Fürstenau, *Entnazifizierung*, Neuwied, 1969, I. Niethammer, *Entnazifizierung in Bayern, Säuberung und Rehabilitierung unter amerikanischer Besatzung*, Frankfurt/Main, 1972; K. F. Bungenstab, *Umerziehung zur Demokratie? Re-education-Politik im Bildungswesen der US-Zone 1945 bis 1949*, Düsseldorf, 1970 also the general accounts of occupation policy referred to in n. 282.

sion of all further reparations deliveries to the Soviet Union, and the British and French followed his example, a decisive step had been taken towards the economic division of Germany. French and Russian attempts to use German economic assets to compensate for their own serious war damage nullified the common economic policy agreed at Potsdam and aggravated the existing chaos.[282]

(B) STATES AND PARTIES.
THE REVIVAL OF POLITICAL ACTIVITY

In all four occupation zones the Allies found themselves, even in the first few weeks, unable to overcome the confusion and rebuild the minimum of government without the co-operation of the German population. In the Russian Zone government agencies with authority over the whole zone (at first, of course, under Russian officers) were set up with the help of the 'Ulbricht group' who had arrived together with the Russian forces. In the three Western Zones the largest administrative unit that was left was the rural district of *Landkreis*, with the *Landrat* as the most senior German official.[283]

The realization that to master the chaos larger governmental units with more power were needed led to the creation in the American Zone in September 1945 of the states or *Länder* of Bavaria, Württemberg–Baden, and Hessen. In this process the American authorities took care to build on traditional territorial loyalties as well as to strengthen federalist tendencies. A Council of States in the US Occupation Zone (*Länderrat des Amerikanischen Besatzungsgebietes*) to co-ordinate policy between the *Länder* was established in Stuttgart as early as October 1945. The powers of the *Land* governments were gradually expanded.

The *Länder* of the British Zone – North Rhine–Westphalia, Lower Saxony, Schleswig–Holstein, and Hamburg – were, on the other hand, given much less autonomy. In North Germany, as a result of Prussia's past predominance, federalist traditions were less in evidence, and the British were anxious to organize their zone as effectively as possible. The result was the establishment of central authorities for the zone before the states were formally created. In February 1946 a Zonal Advisory Council (*Zonenbeirat*) consisting of German administrators and political leaders was

---

[282] For the economic situation, cf. G. Stolper, *Die deutsche Wirklichkeit*, Hamburg, 1948; for occupation policy in general, M. Balfour and J. Mair, *Four-Power Control in Germany and Austria, 1945–1946*, London, 1956; K. F. Latour and T. Vogelsang, *Okkupation und Wiederaufbau. Die Tätigkeit der Militärregierung in der Amerikanischen Besatzungszone Deutschlands 1944–1947*, Stuttgart, 1972; T. Vogelsang, 'Die Bemühungen um eine Deutsche Zentralverwaltung 1945/46' in *VfZG*, vol. 18 (1970), pp. 510–28; J. Gimbel (n. 277); F. R. Willis, *The French in Germany, 1945–49*, Stanford, 1962; E. Deuerlein, 'Frankreichs Obstruktion deutscher Zentralverwaltungen 1945' in *Deutschland-Archiv*, vol. 1 (1971), pp. 455–91.

[283] Cf. the studies of occupation policy in n. 282; a concise summary of developments in the different zones in Vogelsang (n. 273), pp. 50–62.

set up in Hamburg. The occupying power, however, kept responsibility in its own hands to a greater extent than in the American Zone, and the Zonal Advisory Council possessed only advisory powers until 1947.

The French were the last to hand over a share of administrative and political power to the Germans in their zone, and their reluctance to do so was in keeping with de Gaulle's policy of avoiding any commitment to a united German state and of encouraging the greatest possible dismemberment of Germany. No central government agencies of any kind were set up, and *Länder* were created relatively late in the day. At first they existed simply as 'administrative units', to which governmental powers were gradually handed over; there ensued on 30 August 1946 – without any regard for traditional territorial ties – the formation of *Land* Rhineland-Palatinate. Baden and Württemberg–Hohenzollern followed as late as 1947. Already in May 1945 the Saar territory was cut off from occupied Germany; in December 1946 it was incorporated in the French economic and currency system and separated from Rhineland–Palatinate by a customs barrier.

The four *Länder* established in the Soviet Zone were allowed even less autonomy than those in the French Zone;[284] they remained mere instruments of the Soviet Military Administration at Karlshorst near Berlin. Immediately after the Potsdam conference the Soviet officials embarked with speed and determination on the social transformation of their zone on the Soviet model. One step towards this was land reform, which began in Saxony with an order dated 3 September 1945 decreeing that all landed property larger than 100 hectares and indeed all real estate must be given up without compensation. By April 1946 a third of all agricultural land and forest had been taken over. Similarly an order of 30 October 1945 'regarding the confiscation and temporary appropriation of certain types of property' heralded the nationalization of almost the entire assets of industry. At the same time dismantling and reparations deliveries were enforced on a much larger scale than in Western Germany.

Hand in hand with the formation of the new administrative structure went the founding or refounding of political parties – and it was here that the different objectives of the various Allies in their German policy showed up most clearly. Preliminary political gatherings were allowed at an early stage of the Occupation so that the process of forming parties could get under way in accordance with the 'democratization' laid down at Potsdam. Social Democrats, Christian Democrats, and Communists, anti-Fascist parties which had been banned and persecuted for twelve years, were the first to arrive on the scene; after that liberal parties and still later conservative parties were licensed.

[284] For the separate development of the Soviet Zone, cf. H. Weber, *Von der SBZ zur DDR,* vol. i, 1945–55, Hanover, 1966; E. Deuerlein (ed.), *DDR 1945–1970. Geschichte und Bestandsaufnahme,* Munich, 1970[1], 1971[3] (with further bibliography).

236 Europe's Mood of Resignation

First of all came the establishment, according to a well-prepared plan, of central offices of the political parties in the Soviet Zone,[285] which in accordance with Soviet policy regarded themselves as headquarters for the whole of Germany. As early as June 1945 the KDP (Communist Party) under Pieck and Ulbricht and a 'Central Executive Committee of the German Social Democratic Party' headed by Fechner, Gniffke, and Grotewohl was licensed, the leaders of the SPD being especially chosen by the Soviet Military Administration on the strength of their long-standing support for a policy of co-operation with the KPD on 'Popular Front' lines. There followed in July the licensing of a Christian–Democratic Union of Germany under Andreas Hermes and Jakob Kaiser, and of a Liberal–Democratic Party under Külz and Schiffer. Both had to promise to accept an 'anti-Fascist bloc system' and co-operation with the KPD. From November onwards the KPD pressed for union with the SPD.[286] After elections in Austria and Hungary clearly showed that the Communist parties could not win majority support from the population, Social Democracy was expected – in the words of Kurt Schumacher – to become the 'blood-donor to the anaemic body of the Communist Party',[287] in order to provide the latter with an organization large enough for the leading role designed for it. The proposed unification of the SPD and KPD throughout Germany broke down because of the opposition of Kurt Schumacher and of the party leaders in the Western Zones. SPD conferences held on 6 and 8 January 1946 at Frankfurt and Hanover for the US and British Zones respectively rejected the proposed merger. A preliminary referendum in West Berlin organized by the SPD on 30 March resulted in a vote of 82 per cent against and only 12.4 per cent in favour. A unification conference was nevertheless held in East Berlin on 21–2 April; the SPD and KPD became henceforth the 'German Socialist Unity Party' (SED), in which, despite parity of numbers, it was the Communists who called the tune.

In the three West-German Zones, on the other hand, the formation of political groups at grass-roots level proceeded, without the participation of the occupying powers, slowly and laboriously between June and October 1945, handicapped further by the lack of communications; in the French Zone, owing to the restrictions imposed by the authorities, the process was delayed until the beginning of 1946. All the groups, however, were at one in rejecting the claims to leadership put forward by the so-called Reich Committees in the Eastern Zone, which were established gradually by direction from above. Dr Schumacher's office in Hanover tried tirelessly to restore the links between the various SPD groups in parishes and rural districts.[288] In October 1945 it organized with British approval a first 'all-German conference' of the SPD at Wennigsen, supported by the executive council

---

[285] Cf. N. Mattedi, *Gründung und Entwicklung der Parteien in der sowjetischen Besatzungszone Deutschlands, 1945–1949*, Bonn/Berlin, 1966; H. Laschitzka, *Kämpferische Demokratie gegen Faschismus. Die programmatische Vorbereitung auf die antifaschistische Umwälzung in Deutschland durch die Parteiführung der KPD*, Berlin (East), 1969.

[286] Cf. A. Kaden, *Einheit oder Freiheit, Die Wiedergründung der SPD 1945/46*, Hanover, 1964; K.-P. Schulz, *Auftakt zum Kalten Krieg. Der Freiheitskampf der SPD in Berlin, 1945/46*, Berlin, 1965.

[287] Quoted in Vogelsang (n. 273), p. 55.

[288] Cf. besides Kaden (n. 286), T. Pirker, *Die SPD nach Hitler*, Munich, 1965; L. J. Edinger, *Kurt Schumacher, A study in Personality and Political Behaviour*, Stanford and London, 1956; f. Heine, *Dr Kurt Schumacher. Ein demokratischer Sozialist europäischer Prägung*, Göttingen, 1969; conspectus in S. Miller, *Die SPD vor und nach Godesberg*, Bonn/Bad Godesberg, 1974.

of the SPD in exile in London (this body was allowed to return to Germany early in 1946). The conference rejected the claim of the Berlin 'central committee' to lead the party, committed itself to pluralist democracy and political freedom as the main priority, and spurned a merger with the Communists. The Christian-Democratic groups that sprang up in many places[289] were inspired by the wish, even before they contacted one another, to create an interdenominational Christian party, the watchword being the need to escape from the exclusiveness of the old *Zentrum* (Catholic) Party. The main centres of the movement were the Cologne district, where Adenauer played a leading part, and Munich, where the leaders were Müller and Schäffer. Among the new liberal groups, which met under a variety of names, the Liberal Democrats at Stuttgart, led by Reinhold Maier and Theodor Heuss, were particularly important.[290] While other new political groupings, such as the German Party in Lower Saxony and the Economic Reconstruction Party in Bavaria, remained strongest in certain regions, Christian Democrats, Social Democrats, and Free Democrats were to be found in all parts of Western Germany from the beginning of 1946 onwards.

By the middle of 1946 it was obvious that the Soviet Occupation Zone was going to develop on the Soviet pattern, while in the Western Zones the machinery was being created to express the political will of the electorate. In both parts of Germany the population depended entirely on the victors and their military governments, but within the prescribed limits German politics were able to begin a new lease of life.

(C) REJECTION OF NATIONALISM AND AWARENESS OF THE IDEA OF EUROPE

Some accounts exaggerate the extent to which people in Germany sank into complete apathy as far as public life was concerned.[291] No doubt this was true of that section of the population which normally 'goes along' with current trends; it had 'gone alone' with Hitler and suffered in consequence, and now it just wanted to be left in peace. But, generally speaking, interest in politics had tended to increase since 1945. Questionnaires about political meetings, once the Allied ban on them was lifted, showed that the percentage of those who considered such meetings worthwhile and useful rose from 60 per cent in November 1945 to 72 per cent in March 1946. During the same period the number of 'Don't knows' fell from 29 per cent

---

[289] H. G. Wieck, *Die Entstehung der CDU und die Wiederbegründung des Zentrums im Jahre 1945*, Düsseldorf, 1953; ibid., *Christliche und Freie Demokraten in Hessen, Rheinland-Pfalz, Baden und Württemberg 1945–1946*, Düsseldorf, 1958; A. J. Heidenheimer, *Adenauer and the CDU. The Rise of the Leader and the Integration of the Party*, The Hague, 1960; L. Schwering, *Frühgeschichte der Christlich-Demokratischen Union*, Recklinghausen, 1963; W. Conze, *Jakob Kaiser, Politiker zwischen Ost und West 1945–49*, Stuttgart, 1969.

[290] J. M. Gutscher, *Die Entwicklung der FDP von ihren Anfängen bis 1961*, Meisenheim/Glan, 1967; Wieck, 1958 (n. 289).

[291] H. G. Wieck, *Die Entstehung der Christlich-Demokratischen Union in der Britischen Besatzungszone und in Berlin und die Wiederbegründung der deutschen Zentrumspartei in West-Deutschland im Jahre 1945*, Dissertation, Hamburg, 1952, pp. 29–31, has collected impressive evidence of this passivity.

to 12 per cent.[292] An appreciable proportion of the population reacted to events with keen interest.

If the expression 'inner emigration' means anything it stands for the hundreds of thousands of individuals, their families and friends, who for years lived in anticipation of the day when they would be able, as it were, to return to the liberated homeland and rebuild it. The fact that Germany at the end of the war was a country without a state suited their sentiments. People who were hardly acquaintances would read political manifestos to each other when they met over peppermint tea. Deep despair gave rise to an emotional desire for reform.[293]

All over the country little groups, especially of young people, met to discuss Germany's past and present and how a new start could be made on the basis of democracy and natural law. The number of such groups will never be known with any certainty because little evidence has survived for historians, and research on this subject would be a topic in itself. What all these discussions had in common was a profound emotion which was more intense, widespread and lasting than any other feeling, and considerably more so than the preoccupations of everyday life. It had no special name, but was reflected in the overriding imperative by which all Germans were constrained during the post-war period, and what it said was: 'Never again' ... And since this profound feeling was not just an emotional mood but had an intellectual meaning, it was transformed into a number of strongly felt demands about which there was almost complete unanimity: Discover the sources! Look for firm ground! Make a new start.[294]

One example of this was the Social Republican Working Group founded in Frankfurt am Main in December 1945 by some enterprising young people about the age of twenty five. It invited people to lectures in unheated rooms where the audience would number about fifty. All the talks were meant to satisfy the ordinary person's concern to find his bearings in the catastrophic situation, the extent of which, as the speakers invariably emphasized, had been seriously underrated. A common theme running through all the discussions was the idea of a social and political transformation, which seemed to be the only way whereby the complete disarmament imposed on Germany could be made into something positive. Wilhelm Cornides, for example, who during the war had been in touch with the Austrian Resistance through Otto Molden and with the German Resistance through Alfred Delp, made a speech on 11 December 1945 urging that the democratic ideals of equality and freedom should be firmly applied in the economic sphere. He rejected the choice between 'Potsdam and Weimar', for humanism itself had proved too weak as a moral counterweight. The true antithesis in the modern age lay in the choice between Caesarism and federalism based on natural law. It would doubtless be better for no German state to exist for some years and for no parties to be allowed, rather than to have yet again a political clique running

---

[292] Cf. K. H. Niclauss, *Demokratiegründung in Westdeutschland,* Munich, 1974, p. 89 f.

[293] Cf. W. E. Süsskind, 'Der politische Rohstoff' in *Deutscher Geist zwischen gestern und morgen, Bilanz der kulturellen Entwicklung seit 1945,* ed. by J. Morras and H. Paeschke, Stuttgart, 1954, p. 16.

[294] E. Nolte, *Deutschland und der Kalte Krieg,* Munich, 1974, p. 191. Altogether Nolte provides (pp. 190–6) an impressive survey of the literature that emerged from Germany's 'Year Nought'.

amok and repeating the mistakes of 1870 and 1914, 1918 and 1933. If for a few years there are no politics in Germany, it would perhaps enable us to acquire a better understanding of the new Europe and of a world organized on democratic lines and to make a fuller commitment to them.[295]

Publications which began to appear in 1946 and consisted largely of material discussed at group meetings show how seriously the traditions in German history which were opposed to the power of the state were being revived. Such books and articles reflect only part of what was going on in people's minds at that time – the part that was not banned by the military censor; yet that does not detract from the urgency and comprehensiveness of the rethinking in progress. Here there is room only for a brief survey. Innumerable writings tried to articulate the basic ideas of democratic state-building after twelve years of totalitarian rule.[296] Historical works, sometimes of ephemeral importance as contributions to scholarship but of lasting ethical value, sought to highlight the errors made by Germany since 1866 in terms of power politics and nationalism.[297] Germany was aided in overcoming its enforced isolation from the mainstream of European intellectual life by the writings of Wilhelm Röpke in Switzerland, which had a wide circulation among the leading groups in West-German politics. In his book *The German Question*, which was published in 1945 and by 1948 had reached its third impression, he offered an analysis of Germany's development in which faith in authority and collectivism, inhuman severity on the one hand and instability on the other, were shown to be specially characteristic of the Prussian mentality, and the distortion of the Christian and humanist traditions of Southern and Western Germany by the centralizing Bismarckian Empire was seen as the root cause of the catastrophes of 1933 and 1945. As against nationalism, collectivism, authoritarianism, and the worship of power, Röpke pleaded for a social doctrine in which 'personalism, acknowledgement of the natural laws of economic life, acceptance of the essential values of Western ethics and freedom' were the guiding principles.[298] Another work of the

[295] *Cornides Archive*, file on the 'Sozial-Republikanischer Arbeitskries'. This group heard talks on 9.1.1946 by Eugen Kogon on 'Youth and the national problem', on 30.1.1946 by Werner von Trott zu Solz on 'Marxism and the current situation', and on 27.2.1946 by Leo Bauer on 'The political aims of Communism'; it dissolved once its members had established themselves in their careers. Written accounts of many similar groups would be worth collecting.
[296] Cf. for example D. Sternberger, *Dreizehn politische Radioreden*, Heidelberg, 1946; W. Körner, *Zur Verfassungsfrage*, Berlin, 1946; E. Wiechert, 'Rede an die deutsche Jugend', 1945, in Wiechert, *An die deutsche Jugend, Vier Reden*, Munich, n.d., pp. 87–138; F. A. Kramer, *Vor den Ruinen Deutschlands*, Coblenz, n.d.; W. Röpke, *Die deutsche Frage*, Zurich, 1945.
[297] Cf. E. Fischer-Baling, *Feinde ringsum*, Berlin, 1946; F. Meinecke, *The German Catastrophe*, London, 1950; G. Ritter, *Europa und die deutsche Frage*, Munich, 1948; L. Dehio, *Gleichgewicht oder Hegemonie*, Krefeld, 1948; R. Ingrim, *Von Talleyrand bis Molotow, Die Auflösung Europas*, Zurich, 1968; E. Lemberg, *Geschichte des Nationalismus in Europa*, Stuttgart, 1950. Cf. also R. Wittram, *Das Nationale als europäisches Problem*, Göttingen, 1954, with extensive bibliography on pp. 214–44.
[298] Four books by W. Röpke were much read: *Die Gesellschaftskrise der Gegenwart*, Zurich, 1942; *Civitas Humana*, Zurich, 1944; *Internationale Ordnung*, Zurich, 1945; and *Die deutsche Frage*, Zurich, 1945. For a basic interpretation: H. P. Schwarz (n. 318), pp. 393–401; quotation in the text, ibid., p. 395. Cf. also Röpke's collection of essays *Gegen die Brandung*, ed. by A. Hunold, Zurich, 1959.

same kind, also from Switzerland, which was avidly read was *Grundsätze und Richtlinien* by Joseph Wirth, Otto Braun, Wilhelm Hoegner, and others, who argued for a German 'federal republic' and its inclusion in a 'federation of European states and a peaceful community of nations'.[299] The 'federation of European states' was seen as very much a thing of the future.[300] The most urgent task was described as recalling the link with the revolution of 1848 as an example of historical continuity best preserved by the Socialists and Catholics, restoring a proper conception of the individual and a system of social order, and reinstating jurisprudence on a basis of natural law influenced by Christianity. In short, the common intellectual heritage of the European spirit as defined in the Introduction to this book was to be recovered and developed after the twelve-year lapse during which it had been neglected and betrayed.[301]

Once the universities had reopened, awareness of this common cultural and intellectual heritage was developed by lectures and studies which built on the ideas of Western civilization as the Weimar Republic had tried to do. The object of the address given at Tübingen in 1946 by Theodor Steinbüchel was to see the ethical and philosophical values which were usually described as Western anchored in 'Europe as an intellectual unity'.[302] A whole series of writings was devoted to this theme, accompanied by suggestions of a religious revival as usually happens after a war, and often by somewhat nebulous reflections on the collapse of civilization.[303] It was all the more important that other scholarly and analytic works, such as those of Wilhelm Schubart, defined with some precision the relationship between Christianity and the West,[304] and traced the evolution of Western thought as the nucleus of a truly comprehensive cultural synthesis.[305] Thanks to such studies as these, the notion of Europe as an intellectual community acquired a definiteness and a wealth of ideas which went far beyond anything that had been achieved in the days of Weimar. Thinkers in the liberal religious tradition such as Karl Jaspers sought the same kind of integration of intellectual forces.[306] His lecture in Geneva

---

[299] J. Wirth, O. Braun, W. Hoegner, J. Kindt-Kiefer, and H. G. Ritzel, *Das demokratische Deutschland, Grundsätze und Richlinien für den deutschen Wiederaufbau im demokratischen, republikanischen, föderalistischen und genossenschaftlichen Sinn*, Berne, 1945.

[300] It is significant that the book by H. Bauer and H. G. Ritzel, *Kampf um Europa*, Zurich, 1945, containing detailed proposals for the creation of a United States of Europe, at first gained little support. An illuminating book on the situation as a whole is E. von Schenck, *Europa vor der deutschen Frage, Briefe eines Schweizers nach Deutschland*, Berne, 1946; German edn., Franfurt am Main, 1947.

[301] K. Jaspers, *Vom europäischen Geiste. Vortrag, gehalten bei den Rencontres Internationales de Genève*, Munich, 1947; R. Schneider, *Die Heimkehr des deutschen Geistes*, Baden-Baden, 1946, cf. Introduction, section 2, p. 19 f.

[302] *Europa als Verbundenheit im Geist*, Tübingen, 1946.

[303] The following works were of some note, however: H. Zbinden, *Die Moralkrise des Abendlandes. Ethische Grundlagen europäischer Zukunft*, Berne, 1947; E. Przywara, *Vier Predigten über das Abendland*, Einsiedeln, 1948; F. J. Hylander, *Zur Kulturkatastrophe des Abendlandes*; J. Plenge, *Die Altersreife des Abendlandes*, Düsseldorf, 1948.

[304] *Christentum und Abendland*, Munich, 1947.

[305] F. Adams v. Scheltema, *Die geistige Mitte. Umrisse einer abendländischen Kulturmorphologie*, Munich, 1947; K. Muhs, *Geschichte des abendländischen Geistes, Grundzüge einer Kultursynthese*, Berlin and Munich, 1950; also various lectures in *Erbe und Zukunft des Abendlandes. Zwölf Vorträge*, Berne, 1948.

[306] *Vom europäischen Geist*, Munich, 1947 (given at the Rencontres Internationales at Geneva, 1946, cf. account of further speeches in EA, 1, 1946–7, pp. 318–20). Cf. K. Jaspers, *Europa der Gegenwart*, Vienna, 1947.

'On the European Spirit' contained the following pronouncement: 'If the question is asked what, if anything, Europe would be without the Bible, given its pre-Biblical and pre-Hellenic origins, one thing is evident again and again. What we are, we are because of the Bible and the various forms of secularization based on the religion of the Bible, from the foundations of humanism to the themes of modern science and the impulses of our great philosophies. This is undeniable: without the Bible we sink to nothingness. We cannot abandon our historical origins.'[307] Other writers tried to synthesize Europe's common intellectual heritage, stimulated in their search for binding ethical standards by the experience of living in a totalitarian state and by the desire to prevent its recurrence by implanting firm convictions about man's duty to be free and to accept moral obligations.[308] Whatever the degree of emphasis, the heart of the message as it emerged was everywhere the same: Europe is older than the nations that have evolved from it and have brought about its collapse by destroying their common heritage.

Such reflections were politically relevant during the first post-war year (May 1945–May 1946) inasmuch as representative democracy was now accepted as the only system appropriate to the European tradition, and also in the more specific sense that internal federation was seen as an essential counterpoise to the power of the nation state. Countless books and articles pointed out the lessons of the abuse of state power: that it was vital to prevent any restoration of an authoritarian and centralized state in Germany and to re-establish by means of the *Länder* the old European principle of federal autonomy, which was also grounded in natural law.[309] At the first post-war conferences held to found or refound the political parties – from September 1945 onwards in the US Zone and from September 1946 onwards in the British and French Zones – the programmes presented laid stress on federal principles, a theme to which we shall return in due course.[310] At first only the Communists acted as advocates of the centralized nation state. F. A. Kramer and Adolf Süsterhenn wrote a series of articles in the *Rheinische Merkur* from April 1946 onwards in which they revived the ideas of Constantin Frantz and Benedikt Schmittmanns, who regarded Prussian centralism as the cause of Germany's aberration and argued in favour of reconstructing Germany on federalist and centrifugal lines.

According to this view the German catastrophe had begun with the subordination of the German lands to Prussian centralism; by developing into a nation state

---

[307] *Vom europäischen Geist*, op. cit., p. 28.
[308] W. Meyer, *Grundlagen eines neuen Europa*, Zurich, 1946; O. Kossmann, *Warum ist Europa so? Eine Deutung aus Raum und Zeit*, Stuttgart, 1950; D. de Rougemont, *Europa und seine Kultur*, EA 5, 14/1950, pp. 3183–6; ibid., *Freiheiten, die wir verlieren können*, Berlin, 1951; S. de Madariaga, *Europa eine kulturelle Einheit* (Publications of the European Movement), Brussels, 1952. H. Loebel (ed), *Europa: Vermächtnis und Verpflichtung*, Frankfurt am Main, 1957, is an important collection of essays by German scholars, summarizing their common approach in many fields.
[309] Cf. W. Ferber, *Der Föderalismus*, Augsburg, 1946; and especially Heile's great speech of 19.5.1946 to the first annual conference of the FDP: *Deutsche Demokratie und europäische Einigung*, printed in W. Heile, *Abschied von der FDP*, Syke, 1947.
[310] Cf. p. 245 f. and, in connection with the analysis of political parties, chap. IV (vol. 2).

based on power politics Germany had lost its intellectual open-mindedness and erected barriers against the common heritage of European civilization. To refashion German life after the débâcle of the German nation state it was necessary to turn to the principles of natural law and to reject a superficial but for that very reason dangerous legal positivism. It was particularly important to apply the principle of subsidiarity as found in Catholic social doctrine, viz. that 'functions which smaller and subordinate communities can perform effectively' should not be taken out of their hands by 'larger and dominant communities'. Hence there follows a new definition of the community as something which emanates from the individual. 'The individual exists, lives and will continue to live. His or her natural origin is the family, the primitive cell of all society. The local community (*Gemeinde*) is the first and most important political association. Peoples (*Stämme*) and countries (*Länder*) exist in their own right prior to the state. States form groups with their neighbours, and in the aggregate they form a community of states.' 'Each of these natural social groups has its natural right to exist and to perform its function. Thus the state is built up from below, which means that the constitution should be federal.' If the *Länder* insist on maintaining their own independence and statehood they are not indulging in separatism, but providing the necessary scope for 'the political form of Germany as a civilized nation and thus enabling the Germans and their European neighbours to live in peace and security'. 'Only if constitutional theory rests on federal foundations is there no obstacle to the transition from the state to a community of states, so that domestic and foreign policy share a common centre.' Only a federal Germany would be able to discover its affinity with France and Britain and continue to develop with them their common European heritage.[311]

The *Rheinische Merkur* became the centre of the movement for *Land*-based federalism in Germany, a movement related to 'integral federalism' in France and the trend towards decentralization in Italy. Its articles aroused a widespread response, and can be shown to have had a direct bearing on the constitution of the Federal Republic as it was elaborated in discussions at the Herrenchiemsee monastery.[312]

It was, however, impossible for Germans in the first twelve months after the war to apply this new understanding to the political reshaping of Europe and thus contribute towards Europe's unification. Ignorance based on Germany's complete isolation and the ban on postal communications, and also a sense of shame prevented them from speaking out in favour of an idea which also concerned other nations. Associations whose aim was to unite Europe only came into existence in Germany in June

---

[311] Cf. a number of articles in *Rheinischer Merkur*, 1946. Quotations from (1) Quadragesimo Anno according to A. Süsterhenn, 'Freiheit und Recht', No. 9, 12.4.1946; (2) F. A. Kramer, 'Die Zukunft Deutschlands', No. 18, 14.5.1946; (3) A. Süsterhenn, 'Zur deutschen Frage', No. 40, 30.7.1948; (4) F. A. Kramer, 'Die Zukunft Deutschlands', No. 18, 14.5.1946. The Rhineland has always been considered an example of a German region with its own tradition, its claim for separate statehood, and its links with the supranational European community.

[312] 'Moreover, success has confirmed beyond all expectation that our youth is thirsting for righteousness and that the great majority of the population, in good health and attached to their native soil, want to return to the true sources of their life.' (F. A: Kramer, 'In eigener Sache', *Rheinischer Merkur*, No. 29, 21.6.1946). For Herrenchiemsee, cf. chap V/4 in Vol. 2.

1946, and then only because by that time the superpowers were seen to be at loggerheads. These associations will be examined in chapter II of this book, where it will also be seen that the attitude of the occupying powers presented a further difficulty in that only discussions of a very general and theoretical kind were allowed. No association could function without permission from the military authorities, but the first licences were granted by the British only in September 1946, and by the Americans and French – after considerable hesitation – in the second half of 1947. Although the military governments all followed a policy of re-educating people to think in international terms, they prohibited any German participation in the congresses of European federalists that took place in 1946 and 1947. Those Germans who approached the Education Branch of military government with plans for uniting Europe invariably met the most stubborn opposition from left-wing elements in the branch concerned; they were rebuffed as 'anti-Communists' and admonished that there must be no playing off of the West against the East.[313] To avoid any infringement of the 'anti-Fascist united front' of the victorious powers, the American occupying authorities turned a deaf ear to proposals to put into effect the unification plans of the German Resistance, which Dr von Trotha and Horst von Einsiedel presented to the Americans when they entered Berlin in the summer of 1945. Only one American official, Allen Dulles, head of American Intelligence in Europe, went so far as to ask them for a memorandum which he forwarded to the State Department.[314] As far as is known only one book appeared on this subject in Germany in 1946, entitled *Europa 1975* and cautiously prophesying a 'United States of Europe' by that date. Walter Dirks's appeal in the April 1946 issue of *Frankfurter Hefte* remained isolated in its appeal to work for a European confederation:

'We proclaim the end of the sovereign nation state ... The European nations have become too small. They cannot cope with the crisis, they will not succeed if they persist in relying on their own efforts.'[315]

One periodical with a special interest in political questions was *Die Gegenwart*, which first appeared in November 1945. In its first two years it reported on the United Nations Charter but had nothing to say about a united Europe. People were still preoccupied with finding their ideological bearings and with uncertainty about what would happen to Germany once it was let out of quarantine and readmitted to the international community. 'The worst outcome would be the rise of a new centralism in

---

[313] Information from Cornides on 19.8.1960; *Cornides Archive*, File 'Gründung des Europa-Archivs'. For the German associations from June 1946 onwards see section 6 of chap. II, p. 385.
[314] Letter from Dr von Trotha to Herrn von Mangold on 7.12.1948. I am grateful to Frau Dr Margarete von Trotha for kindly letting me see the relevant files. She informs me, however, that the memorandum to Allen Dulles cannot be traced.
[315] L. Emrich, *Europa, 1975. Die Welt von morgen*, Freiburg, 1946; W. Dirks, 'Die Zweite Republik' in *Frankfurter Hefte*, vol. 1, no. 1 (April 1946), pp. 12–24 (quotation on p. 17).

Berlin. The best would be the establishment of a new political structure for the whole of Europe.'[316]

The leaders of the German Resistance movement had been victims of Nazi persecution to a much greater degree than those in other countries. It was therefore all the more significant that some leaders of the newly emerging democratic parties committed themselves to the idea of a United States of Europe. For between six months and a year they anticipated leading politicians in the neighbour countries by proclaiming the idea of European unity as the German answer to the disaster brought about by Nazism and war, and in so doing they made sure that there would be support for a foreign policy of this kind in the German democracy still to be created. Kurt Schumacher declared in his first policy statement at the SPD conference at Wennigsen on 5 October 1945: 'In order to establish European economic unity it is as important for Germany as for the rest of the world to create the appropriate political structures.'[317] It was therefore incumbent upon the Social Democrats to play their part in 'making Europe into a social and economic unity of interdependent parts, in which German workers would be able to win for themselves the same position as workers in other countries ... We want to see Germany not as a national and independent entity but as part of a peaceful and united Europe.'[318] Such statements remained vague as to the form a united Europe should take, and bore obvious traces of anxiety about the economic chaos in Germany and consequently in Europe as a result of the Allies' policy of dismantlement; however, Schumacher explained himself in more detail in the spring of 1946 in connection with ideas on the kind of new constitution Germany should have. It was important from the outset, he urged, 'to bear in mind and encourage the possibility of international co-operation, that is to say of a United States of Europe'.[319] A European federation would be 'the ultimate fulfilment of our desires',[320] assuming, of course, that Germany would have the same status as all the other member nations and that such a Europe would put Social-Democratic aspirations into effect in the social order. The 'political programme' approved by the SPD's first annual congress on 11 May 1946 summarized the position: 'German Social Democracy aims to bring about a United States of Europe, a democratic and Socialist federation of European states. It desires a Socialist Germany

---

[316] *Cornides Archive,* File 'Gründung des Europa-Archivs', Note of 12.9.1945.
[317] Quoted in O. K. Flechtheim (ed.), *Dokumente zur parteipolitischen Entwicklung in Deutschland seit 1945,* vol. 3, Berlin, 1963, p. 6.
[318] Speech at the district conference of the SDP in Düsseldorf, 1.12.1945, *SPD Archive,* Bonn, Kurt Schumacher, 'Reden 1945/46', quoted in H. P. Schwarz, *Vom Reich zur Bundesrepublik. Deutschland im Widerstreit der aussenpolitischen Konzeptionen in den Jahren der Besatzungsherrschaft, 1945–1949,* Neuwied/Berlin, 1966, p. 528.
[319] *Die Welt,* 25.6.1946.
[320] *Die Welt,* 19.7.1946 and 30.7.1946.

in a Socialist Europe.'[321] Adenauer, the CDU leader, likewise expressed at an early stage his basic conviction that only a European union could arrest the decline of Europe, which he felt keenly, and halt the advance of what he called the 'Russian colossus'. Two themes stood out clearly in a letter which he wrote at the end of October 1945, just after being dismissed for the second time from his post as Lord Mayor of Cologne.

> Russia is withdrawing more and more from co-operation with the other great powers and acts entirely as it chooses in the territories over which it rules. In the area which it dominates, quite different economic and political principles prevail from those in the rest of Europe. The partition of the Continent into Soviet-dominated Eastern Europe and Western Europe is a fact. The part of Germany not occupied by Russia is an integral part of Western Europe ... It is in the best interests not only of the part of Germany which is not occupied by Russia, but also of Britain and France, to unite Western Europe under their leadership.

This analysis of the situation, the accuracy of which was soon to be demonstrated, indicated in sober language that the sights should now be fixed on 'making a start in Western Europe'. For the rest it was a question of finding a permanent answer to France's desire for security and thus settling the questions of the Rhineland and the Ruhr: 'The only way of fully satisfying the French desire for security must in the long run lie in the economic interlocking of West Germany, France, Belgium, Luxemburg and Holland. If Britain decided to take part ... it would go a long way to bring about the ultimate objective of a union of the states of Western Europe.'[322] In a number of speeches made during the Occupation Adenauer spoke of this 'organic solution' by economic interlocking, without being more specific about the institutional form it should take, but often using the term 'United States of Europe' to designate the final goal while waiting pragmatically for the chance to make a start. He appealed more than once to the occupying powers to pursue a truly European policy by creating a 'United States of Europe' including Germany.

> The United States of Europe is the best, safest and most lasting guarantee for Germany's Western neighbours ... We may and must hope, and everyone must make his own contribution to this, that such a community of nations, a real community, will come about, and one which is not dominated by a few great

---

[321] Quoted in Flechtheim, op. cit. (n. 317), p. 22 f. For Schumacher's idea of Europe after the end of the war see in more detail H. P. Schwarz (n. 318), pp. 528–32.
[322] Letter of 31 Oct. 1945 in K. Adenauer, *Erinnerungen 1945–1953*, Stuttgart, 1965, p. 39 f. Evidence of Adenauer's awareness of the decline of Europe and his fear of further Soviet expansion is assembled in the comprehensive analysis by H. P. Schwarz, 'Das aussenpolitische Konzept Konrad Adenauers' in R. Morsey and K. Repgen (ed.), *Adenauer-Studien I*, Mainz, 1971, pp. 71–108, esp. p. 79 f.; cf. too Schwarz (n. 318), p. 443–54; the continuation of this attitude during the 1950s is documented in A. Poppinga, *Konrad Adenauer. Geschichtsverständnis, Weltanschauung und politische Praxis*, Stuttgart, 1973, pp. 63–77 and 129–33.

powers. I believe that a unification of the states of Europe in such a community is the appropriate policy.[323]

Most of the newly formed CDU associations at *Land* level shared these views. In February 1946 a sentence was added to the CDU programme in the British Zone: 'Germany's aim must be to share on equal terms in international co-operation within a union of nations.' The 'basic programme' of the Christian Social Union or CSU, the Bavarian counterpart of the CDU, described Europe as a supranational, living community and supported the 'creation of a European economic and monetary union'. The (Catholic) Centre Party's programme, drawn up at Soest in 1945, declared its readiness for European federation; even those on the party's left wing, such as the group associated with the *Frankfurter Hefte* who usually opposed Adenauer, were early enthusiasts for a federal Europe.[324]

Even a politician so reserved in his attitude to Europe as Jakob Kaiser noted in June 1946 that 'The demand for a United States of Europe ... has cropped up in recent weeks in speeches by German politicians';[325] and this aspiration was in fact a *leitmotiv* in statements of foreign-policy objectives by the new democratic forces in Germany. Yet in 1945–6 at any rate German politicians were not yet in a position to express their views about how the generally desired objective should be attained, partly because of uncertainty about the fate which the victorious powers had in store for them, and partly from well-founded reticence in view of all that their neighbours had suffered at German hands.

6. Countries in a Weak Situation: Italy, Belgium, and the Netherlands

by Wilfried Loth

Among the other West-European nations there was none in which the European idea failed to find an echo in this first year of peace, but none had a government that was in any position to inaugurate the process of unification. In Soviet-dominated Eastern Europe the former ruling groups were struggling for survival, and seeds of federalist ideas in regard to

---

[323] First quotation from Adenauer's speech on 24 March 1946 in the great hall of Cologne University, published as No. 8 of the series of pamphlets of the Christian Democratic Union in the Rhineland, Cologne, 1946 (p. 24 of the pamphlet); similarly, Adenauer (n. 322), pp. 39–47. Second quotation from Adenauer's speech on 5 May 1946 at a CDU rally in the town hall at Wuppertal-Elberfeld, *Adenauer Archive* R II 19b, quotation p. 16: similarly his speeches of 29 May 1946 in Hamburg and of 2 June 1946 at Mönchengladbach, both in *Adenauer Archive*.

[324] 'Party programme' of Neheim-Hüsten, 27 Feb. 1946, quoted in Heidenheimer (n. 289), p. 68 f.; 'foundation programme' of the CSU quoted in Flechtheim (n. 317), vol. 2, pp. 53 and 218; 'Soest Programme' of 14 Oct. 1945, ibid., p. 245. *Frankfurter Hefte*, esp. W. Dirks, 'Die Zweite Republik' (cf. n. 315), 'Das Abendland und der Sozialismus', *Frankfurter Hefte*, no. 3 (June), pp. 67–76.

[325] J. Kaiser, speech at the Berlin congress of the CDU, 15–17 June 1946, in *Deutschland und die Union. Die Berliner Tagung 1946*, in the series entitled 'Wege in die Neue Zeit', No. 4, Berlin, n.d.

Europe as a whole were, as will be seen later, suffocated.[326] In the West there remained, within the limits imposed on this work, Italy, whose position more or less resembled Germany's as a defeated, ex-Fascist state waiting for whatever peace terms the victors might impose; and finally Belgium and the Netherlands, which, under governments that had returned from exile in London, were, of course, among the victorious countries, but were in no position to make a start where Britain and France were unwilling to do so.

(A) ITALY'S PROBLEMS BEFORE THE PEACE TREATY

The example of Italy shows how little the European nation states, in their reduced importance, were able, despite widespread awareness of Europe's need to federate, to transform this state of mind into policy and action. In Italy, which had suffered the Fascist seizure of power ten years before Germany, the idea of European unity had won a remarkable degree of support among the intelligentsia during the last years of the war; moreover, this idea was taken up by the great majority of the newly revived political parties to an extent unmatched by any other European country.[327] But Italy, like Germany, besides having to wait for a dictated peace, had first to contend with serious internal problems. Compared with Germany, however, her lot was alleviated by three circumstances.

First, on 25 July 1943 after the conquest of Sicily by British and American troops, the army chiefs in Rome, led by Marshal Badoglio, staged a coup d'état against Mussolini and otherthrew him without outside aid. After forty-five days of political manoeuvring these military chiefs took refuge with the Allied forces in the southern tip of Italy and were granted recognition as a co-belligerent government, with limited authority to administer liberated territory. Secondly, Badoglio while still in Rome had allowed groups of the new anti-Fascist parties to assemble in Rome and Milan. These included Communists, Socialists, Christian Democrats, the Partito d'Azione which had emerged from the Resistance, the Liberals and Republicans. All these parties now joined in organizing an active 'Resistenza Armata' against the Germans, who had meanwhile taken over the government in North and Central Italy. Their efforts show what might have been achieved in Germany if the attempt on Hitler's life on 20 July had succeeded and been followed by effective action against remaining Nazi concentrations of troops etc. In the third place, Italy was favoured by the circumstance that Allied Military Government (AMGOT) was exclusively Anglo-American. True, there were differences of opinion in that the British wanted to extend Badoglio's powers and particularly to preserve the monarchy, whereas the Americans, more reserved towards Badoglio,

---

[326] Cf. section 7 of chap. II, pp. 441–57. Greece was in the throes of civil war, while Spain and Portugal were under regimes whose affinity to the Axis powers discredited and isolated them. In the Scandinavian countries – which, as mentioned in the Introduction, p. 88 f., could not be included in this survey – at first the sole prevailing wish, in view of disappointment over Germany and the collapse of France, was to develop closer ties in foreign policy with Great Britain and, if possible, with the USA.

[327] For more details on this point, cf. the beginning of the next section, pp. 252–5.

shared the party leaders' desire for a republic. (After the liberation of Rome in June 1944 the Americans brought about the appointment of a cabinet headed by Bonomi which enjoyed the support of the six anti-Fascist parties and lasted a year.) But at least in the government of Italy there were no Frenchmen bent on annexations or Russians with Sovietizing intentions, for the participation of these nations in AMGOT was purely nominal.[328]

The German surrender and the freeing of the active anti-Fascists in Northern Italy were followed in June 1945 by the formation of a new cabinet under F. Parri, a supporter of European federation and former leader of the partisan groups of the Partito d'Azione, with De Gasperi as foreign minister. The government convened a temporary parliament, tried to stimulate the economy, presented the choice between monarchy and a republic in such a way as to favour the latter, and attempted to make a clean sweep of all remaining Fascists. The Liberal ministers, however, opposed the purge as too drastic and in the end resigned in protest, so that in December 1945 a new government was formed with De Gasperi as Prime Minister, an office he was to retain until 1953. The distribution of posts within the cabinet reflected the balance of power among the electorate: the Christian Democrats (DC), Socialists (PSIUP), and Communists (PCI), representing 35.1 per cent, 20.7 per cent, and 18.9 per cent of voters in the election to the Constituent Assembly in June 1946, decided on Italy's future in much the same way as the corresponding parties did that of France until the beginning of 1947.[329]

As in every other European country politicians were at first almost wholly preoccupied with the struggle for a new order, staking out claims, establishing links, and calculating prospects on the one hand, and on the other hand tackling the immediate and formidable problem of food supplies and reviving economic life. Initially public discussion was dominated by constitutional questions. Christian Democrats, Socialists, and Communists were united in desiring to abolish the monarchy in favour of a republic. Yet supporters of the dynasty – who were particularly numerous in the agrarian South – in spite of the discredit caused to the monarchy by Victor Emmanuel's pact with Mussolini, calculated that they still had a chance of carrying the day when the king abdicated at the beginning of May 1946 in

---

[328] Cf. for a general survey of the transitional period: N. Kogan, *Italy and the Allies*, London, 1956; C. R. S. Harris, *Allied Military Administration of Italy, 1943–45*, London (UK-Mil. Series), 1957; F. Chabod, *Die Entstehung des neuen Italien, Von der Diktatur zur Republik*, Reinbeck bei Hamburg, 1965; L. Valiani, 'Vom Widerstand zur Republik' in *Von der Diktatur zur Demokratie, Deutschland und Italien in der Epoche nach 1943* (a book containing much useful information, published as No. 17 of the *Schriftenreihe des Internationalen Schulbuchinstituts*), Brunswick, 1973, pp. 55–63.

[329] The Liberals received only 6.8 per cent, the Uomo Qualunque movement 5.3 per cent, the Republicans 4.4 per cent, the Partito d'Azione 1.5 per cent, other groups altogether 5.5 per cent. Cf. G. Mammarella, *Italy after Fascism. A Political History, 1943–1965*, Notre Dame, Indiana, 1966, p. 116, also, for the early years of the Republic, N. Kogan, *A Political History of Post-War Italy*, NY/Washington, 1966; G. Vaccarino, 'Die Wiederherstellung der Demokratie in Italien (1943–1948)' in *VfZG*, vol. 21 (1973), pp. 285–324; S. J. Woolf, *The Rebirth of Italy, 1943–50*, London, 1972.

favour of his son Umberto. In a referendum on 2 June 1946 the Italian people decided in favour of a republic by a relatively narrow margin (12.7 million votes against 10.7 million). The elections to the Constituent Assembly confirmed the predominance of the three large parties; they were joined by the aggressively anti-monarchist republicans as a new coalition partner.[330]

A matter of special urgency for post-war Italian governments was how to deal with the economic emergency. All branches of the economy had suffered heavily during the war.[331] Losses in industry amounted to about 450 million lire, the equivalent of a fifth of the total value of all industrial plant in 1939. Output of electricity had fallen by 35% compared with its highest level in 1941. The worst losses in the industrial sector occurred in Central and Southern Italy, where the fighting on Italian soil had been going on longest. In calculating the fall in productivity of Italian industry it has to be remembered that 'only' 20 per cent of the fall was caused by direct war damage, whereas approximately 57 per cent was due to decline over a much longer period. Altogether industrial production in 1945 was down to about 25 per cent of its 1938 level.[332]

Public buildings and installations were particularly hard hit. 60 per cent of the major roads had become unusable and over 8,000 bridges had been destroyed. Only about a third of the ports and about 60 per cent of schools, hospitals, and railway stations were serviceable. The railways had suffered damage estimated at about 900 billion lire, a sum almost equal to the value of all their fixed assets. 60 per cent of all rolling-stock and 80 per cent of the electrified lines were in ruins, while Italy's merchant fleet, in 1938 the fourth largest in Europe with 3.5 million registered tons, had shrunk to a mere 450,000 tons. In the private sector more than two million dwelling-houses or flats had been destroyed and another 1.8 million severely damaged, amounting altogether to about 10 per cent of Italy's pre-war housing stock. Agricultural production in 1945 was only 40 per cent of the 1938 level; livestock had been reduced by 75 per cent. Total losses in agriculture amounted to 550 billion lire. Lack of manure and shortage of human labour during the war caused grain yields to fall from an average of 56 bushels a hectare in 1938 to 45 bushels in 1945. Falls in production, losses in material, and the cost of the war produced an enormous deficit in the Italian treasury. The national debt, which in 1939 amounted to 145 billion lire, had risen by the end of the war to about 906 million lire, while the deficit in the budget for 1945–6 reached 380 billion lire. A further problem was inflation. The quantity of paper money

---

[330] On this, see esp. G. Romita, *Dalla monarchia alla repubblica*, Pisa, 1959, and Mammarella (n. 329), pp. 61–70 and 106–118.

[331] For the following sketch of the economic situation, cf. Mammarella, p. 121 ff., S. Bernstein/P. Milza, *L'Italie contemporaine. Des Nationalistes aux Européens*, Paris, 1973, p. 365; B: Clough/S. Saladino, *A History of Modern Italy*, NY/London, 1968, p. 536 f.; F. R. Willis, *Italy chooses Europe*, NY, 1971, p. 15.

[332] Figures in Mammarella (n. 329), p. 122; in identical terms in Bernstein/Milza (n. 331), p. 365, where industrial production in 1945 is estimated to have been only 23 per cent of the pre-war level. The depression was due to the wearing out of plant and machinery; disputes between workers and management which broke out after the liberation, and transport difficulties, which led to shortages in the supply of raw materials and hindered the distribution of finished products.

250 *Europe's Mood of Resignation*

increased steadily, for the Treasury could only meet its huge obligations during the first phase of economic recovery by printing more and more notes. The general price index (1938 = 100) stood at 2,392 in 1945, while at the same time wages, allowing for regional variations, had fallen to between 50 per cent and 75 per cent of what they were in 1938. A further problem that the government were powerless to solve was the mass of unemployed. Their numbers rose by leaps and bounds as prisoners of war returned home, and by 1946 over two million people were registered as out of work.[333]

The situation was so hopeless that Italy could only survive with foreign aid. The US had helped out by supplying the most essential foodstuffs until the end of the war, and in the summer of 1945 had given a credit of over a million dollars for the further purchase of necessities. In January 1946 the Italian government signed a treaty with **UNRRA** (the United Nations Relief and Rehabilitation Administration) providing for financial help; this followed a grant of 50 million dollars from UNRRA (73 per cent of whose revenue came from the US) in the previous year. Altogether UNRRA aided Italy with sums amounting to about 435 million dollars between January 1946 and June 1947. The volume of goods supplied, especially food, coal, and machinery, exceeded ten million tons.[334]

The social tensions caused by economic distress were aggravated by the traditional cleavage between the Mezzogiorno (the South) and the Northern provinces.[335] The poverty of the soil in the South (which had once been fertile), the often inhospitable landscape, the lack of communications and the scarcity of water, compared with the fertile plains and navigable rivers of the North, produced a gap between North and South Italy the extent of which is vividly illustrated by the following statistics:[336]

	South	North
Income per head (Italy as a whole = 100)	58.2	126.1
Consumption of electricity (kw per head)	153.1	683.1
Consumption of meat in kg (Italy as a whole = 13.4)	7.6	17.1
Number of workers in industry	709,788	3,456,466
Average earnings per hectare of land, in thousand lire (Italy as a whole = 265)	230	290
Number of illiterates (over age 6) per 100 inhabitants	24.3	5.7

[333] Figures from Mammarella (n. 329), pp. 121–4; similarly Clough/Saladino (n. 331), p. 536 f. Willis (n. 331), writes: 'At the end of World War II Italy was one of the poorest countries in Europe' (p. 103).
[334] Cf. Bernstein/Milza (n. 331), p. 365. After the ending of UNRRA aid in June 1947 and before Marshall Aid began, Italy received industrial goods direct from the US in accordance with the AUSA Programme (Interim Aid from the United States of America).
[335] The Mezzogiorno comprises all territory south of the line Rome–Pescara, including the islands, that is to say the following regions: Abruzzi, Molise, Campania, Apulia, Basilicata, Calabria, Sicily, and Sardinia. It amounts to 42 per cent of the country's area, but contains only a third of the population.
[336] Source: SVIMEZ, *Statistiche sul Mezzogiorno d'Italia 1861–1953*, Rome (Svimez), 1954, quoted in Mammarella, p. 225 f. Although the figures are those for 1951, they give a true picture of the relations between North and South for the post-war period as a whole.

The new Constitution called for 'special subsidies ... for the economic development of Southern Italy and the islands',[337] but it was not until March 1950 that the government introduced the necessary legislation in parliament. The country's economic plight and its sharp division pointed to structural problems which could not be solved by the nation state's own resources; consequently the quest for a solution became a major theme in Italy's European policy.

During the war representatives of the Movimento Federalista Europeo (MFE) had called for a solution of these problems by the inclusion of Italy in a federally organized Europe on the one hand, and by the reduction of the central government's powers in favour of decentralization on the other.[338] Federalism between states and within the individual state went hand in hand in Italy as elsewhere. The strength of the general desire for a new deal in Italy is shown by the success of the programme for domestic federalization in the constitutional debate which the Italians were free to conduct without foreign interference. The Christian Democratic Party (DC) proved to be a particularly ardent champion of internal decentralization and federalization.

The party's first national congress, held in Rome on 27 April 1946, urged in Section G/VI of its programme, entitled 'Decentralization, Autonomy, Regionalism', not merely 'administrative decentralization' and 'reform of the bureaucracy', but 'a state which is institutionally decentralized'. The programme continued: 'Local self-government must be developed to the maximum ...' This was 'the cornerstone for reform of the character of the state ... Each region will be a self-governing entity ... Relations between the regions and the central government must be regulated by the principle of promoting as far as possible local self-government within the general framework of the state.' The aim of 'renewing the state on a regional basis' was to 'facilitate the direct participation of the people in public life' and reduce 'the inflated organs of state bureaucracy ... to a healthy size', while countering 'separatist and quasi-federalist tendencies' and preventing totalitarian adventures.[339]

These principles put forward by the DC received a remarkable degree of support in the new Constitution which was adopted in December 1947 by a large majority and came into force on 1 January 1948. Article 5 states: 'The Republic recognizes and promotes local self-government; it applies

---

[337] Text of the Constitution with commentary (the best by contemporary writers) in P. Calamandrei, *Commentario sistematico alla costituzione italiana*, Florence (Barbera), 1950; C. Lavagna, *La Costituzione italiana commentata con le decisioni della Corte Costituzionale*, Turin (Unione Tipografico–Editrice) 1970; V. Falzone, F. Palermo, and F. Cosentino, *La Costituzione della Repubblica Italiana. Illustrate con i lavori preparatori e corredate da note e riferimenti*, Milan (Mondadori), 1976. English translation in A. Blaustein and G. Flanz (ed.), *Constitutions of the Countries of the World* in vol. vii; G. Flanz and C. Figliola, *Italy*, New York (Oceana), 1973 (section on the Constitution of the Republic of Italy, pp. 1–41).
[338] Cf. e.g. the article 'Federalismo, autonomia locale, autogoverno' in *L'Unità europea*, No. 4 (Milan), May–June 1944, p. 3; Federalismo e Autonomia', ibid., no. 5 (Milan), July–August 1944, p. 2; 'Federalismo Integrale', ibid., no. 8 (Milan), Jan.–Feb. 1945, p. 3.
[339] The programme of the Christian Democrats is reprinted in Aldo Moro (ed.), *Atti e documenti della Democrazia Cristiana, 1943–1959*, Rome, 1959, p. 212 f.

252 Europe's Mood of Resignation

the fullest measure of administrative decentralization in services dependent on the State.' 'The Republic is divided into Regions, Provinces and Communes' (Article 114).[340] 'The regions are constituted as autonomous territorial units with their own powers and functions...' (Article 115). They are responsible for, among other things, local police, public health and welfare services, education, agriculture, forestry, handicrafts, and public works (Article 117). Their institutions are financially autonomous (Article 119) and are represented in the Senate, which is the Republic's federal Second Chamber (Article 57).

(B) ITALY'S COMMITMENT TO EUROPE AND ITS HELPLESSNESS

For the Italians, however, the most important conclusion to be drawn from the Fascist–nationalist adventure, the sufferings caused by the war, and the country's material ruin was the argument in favour of supranationalist federalism, the notion of a federated Europe. As has been shown, this idea spread among the political parties thanks to the Ventotene Manifesto and found widespread support such as existed in no other country before the onset of the Cold War in 1947.[341] The parties must be briefly considered in turn.

The Partito d'Azione (as it was called from January 1943 onwards) consisted of remnants of the former party known as Giustizia e Libertà, university groups anxious to combine Socialism with political liberalism, and radical republicans of the North Italian cities led by the Milan Professor Ferruccio Parri. Its composition thus answered to Spinelli's desire for a new party embodying the principles of the Resistance. The original group of leaders put forward a programme with a single clause concerning foreign policy, drawn up as early as December 1941: '7. Creation of a European federation of free democratic states within a framework of world-wide co-operation.'[342] The final version adopted at the party's foundation conference in January 1943 similarly urged

---

[340] The regions involved are the following (Art. 131): Piedmont, Val d'Aosta, Lombardy, Trentino-Alto Adige, Venezia, Friuli–Venezia Giulia, Liguria, Emilia–Romagna, Tuscany, Umbria, the Marches, Latium, Abruzzi, Molise, Campania, Apulia, Basilicata, Calabria, Sicily, Sardinia. Of these Sicily, Sardinia, Trentino–Alto Adige, Friuli–Venezia Giulia and Val d'Aosta were granted forms and conditions of autonomy as provided by special constitutional statutes (Art. 116). The articles of the Italian Constitution are taken from the English translation in A. Blaustein and G. Flanz: Constitutions (n. 337), pp. 2 and 29 f. The authoritative work on its origin, by the President of the Commission for the Constitution, is M. Ruini, *Come si è formata la costituzione,* Milan (Giuffre), 1961.

[341] For details of the Ventotene Manifesto and the foundation of the Movimento Federalista Europeo, see chap. 1/2, pp. 108–17. On the Italian Resistance as a whole a basic study is C. F. Delzell, *Mussolini's Enemies. The Italian Anti-Fascist Resistance,* Princeton, 1961; a more recent survey is Leo Valiani, 'La Resistenza Italiana' in *Rivista storica Italiana,* vol. 85 (1973), pp. 64–102; on Resistance plans for the future see also E. Collotti, 'La solidarietà europea e prospettive di un nuovo ordine internazionale nel pensiero della resistenza italiana' in *Annali della facoltà di lettere dell'Università di Trieste,* vol. ii, Trieste, 1966.

[342] Cf. Delzell (n. 341), pp. 29–32, 169–73 and 213 f.; history of the rise of the Partito d'Azione by its first secretary-general, Leo Valiani, *Dall' antifascismo alla resistenza,* Milan, 1959; ibid., 'Il Partito

the bringing about of a European federation of free democratic countries ... which decisively rejects the principle of absolute state sovereignty, advocates the renunciation of all purely territorial claims, and favours the creation of a legal community of states with the necessary institutions and the means to establish a regime of collectively organized security.

At the party's first national congress, held from 4–8 February 1946, Parri pleaded in favour of 'a federation of European nations', Spinelli urged Italy to make a 'committed contribution to the democratic rebirth of the world', and Fancello spoke in favour of 'a Europe united in the spirit of democracy' as the only safeguard against 'new adventures': Fascism, he believed, could not be defeated within the framework of the nation state.[343]

Ignazio Silone, the acting secretary of the Partito Socialista Italiano (PSI), had circulated a statement in September 1942 in the name of the PSI's foreign-affairs department in Zürich. This document stated that for Socialists the 'basic demand in regard to the future government of Europe' was that 'the unity of European society which already exists must be buttressed by political union. The old and reactionary systems of national sovereignties must be abolished.'[344] Colorni, chief editor of the party newspaper *Avanti*, who was in close touch with the federalist groups, wished to distribute this programme to the Partito Socialista Italiano di Unità Proletaria (PSIUP), the broadly-based party of all Italian Socialists founded under Nenni's chairmanship on 12 August 1943.[345] It was mainly due to Colorni's influence and the efforts of Silone, who succeeded him as editor of *Avanti* after Colorni had been murdered by the Germans at the end of May 1944, that the PSIUP at its first congress in November 1944 declared in favour of 'encouraging the formation of a federation of European nations'.[346]

Accordingly, the Socialist parliamentary party in a declaration issued on 18 July 1946 advocated 'that the party should give firm support in foreign policy to the European Federalist Movement (MFE) ... since this movement in its efforts to

---

d'Azione' in Valiani–Bianchi–Ragionieri, *Azionisti, Communisti e Cattolici nella Resistenza*, Istituto Nazionale per la storia del Movimento di Liberazione in Italia, Milan, 1971.

[343] For the foundation programme of the Partito d'Azione see *L'Italia libera*, No. 1, Jan. 1943; the part of the programme dealing with foreign policy is reprinted in *L'Unità europea*, No. 1, (Rome), May 1943, p. 4; speeches at the Feb. 1946 congress in *L'Unità europea*, No. 9, Turin, 20.2.1946, p. 3. After the end of the Partito d'Azione in the elections of 1947 Parri became for over twenty years President of the group of European federalist parliamentarians in the Italian Senate; cf. in the series of MFE publications F. Parri, *Per l'unità federale europea*, Rome, 1952.

[344] Ignazion Silone, 'Nel Bagaglio degli esuli' in *Esperienze e studi sozialisti*, Florence, 1957, p. 301 ff.; translation in *Europe speaks* (ed. W. Eichler), London, 3.11.1942, p. 5 f. On the party's politics during the Resistance, cf. O. Lizzadri, *Il Regno di Badoglio*, Milan, 1963; P. Nenni, *La Politica del PSIUP*, Rome, 1944; for the party's ideas on Europe, E. Gencarelli, 'Dalla Resistenza l'impegno per un'Europa socialista' in *Mondo operaio*, vol. xxv, no. 4, April 1972, pp. 27–38.

[345] Cf. his draft resolution submitted to the party leadership, ibid., p. 77 f.

[346] Text in *L'Avanti*, 30.11.1944, reprinted in *L'Unità europea*, No. 7, Milan, Nov.-Dec. 1944, p. 3.

build a democratic Europe united by federal ties would rescue our country from the dangers arising from the clash of opposing political blocs'.[347]

However, the pro-European section of the PSIUP was faced from the outset by an anti-federal wing which, in its anxiety to re-establish the 'unity of the working class' as the sole guarantee against the return of Fascism, was determined to respect Soviet wishes in regard to foreign policy and was therefore content with vague references to the 'anti-Fascist alliance of the United Nations'. This group managed to gain a majority in the party by the summer of 1945, and at the congress at Florence in April 1946 the commitment to European federation was not repeated. Not until the party conference in Rome in January 1947, when the minority led by Giuseppe Saragat seceded in order to found the PSLI, was the way clear for Socialist politicians to take a pro-European line.[348]

As regards the Christian Democrats, Alcide De Gasperi, the last secretary-general of the Partito Popolare, had drawn up a draft programme which was in circulation in North Italy in the spring of 1943 and which called upon nations to accept 'restrictions on their sovereignty in favour of overall solidarity'. The foundation programme of Democrazia Cristiana, made public on 25 July 1943 (the day of Badoglio's coup) after a long period of preparation, was explicit:

A federation of freedom-loving European states – an expression of the solidarity of all peoples – within a revived League of Nations. Direct representation of peoples as well as of governments ... Armed forces and voluntary recruitment under the sole control of the international community. Nations to be allowed to choose their own legal system and to have European as well as national citizenship.[349]

The programme adopted at the party's first congress on 27 April 1946 did not specify the exact geographical limits of the federation they hoped to create, as by this time the general frustration of 'European' initiatives had set in; however, it committed itself unreservedly to the principle of limitations of sovereignty, which must 'be accepted so far as they are required to enable the international community to function properly'.[350] 'We Christian Democrats', declared Giuseppe Grosso in November 1945, 'can enthusiast-

---

[347] Text in *L'Unità europea*, No. 15/16, Turin, 25.8.1946, p. 1.
[348] For the argument between opponents and supporters of common action with the Communists for the period up till 1947, see esp. W. Hilton-Young, *The Italian Left: A Short History of Political Socialism in Italy*, Italy, 1949; M. Grindrod, *The Rebuilding of Italy, Politics and Economics, 1945–1955*, London/NY, 1955; also A. Forlani, *Il PSI di fronte al comunismo dal 1945 al 1956*, Rome, 1956. More details in section 1, chap. IV, vol. 2.
[349] De Gasperi, Idee ricostruttive ... (spring, 1943) and Il Programma di Milano (27.5.1943) in A. Moro (ed.), *Atti e documenti* (n. 339), pp. 9 f. and 12 f.; cf. De Gasperi, *Studi e appelli della lunga vigilia*, Rome, 1946. De Gasperi's father, a police constable in the Trentino under the Habsburg Monarchy, had helped to found the Italian branch of the (Catholic) Christian Socialists at Trent; he and his son were in favour of autonomy for all nationalities, but under a Habsburg or other European government; they were consistently anti-nationalist and pro-European; cf. L. Valiani, *L'Avvento di De Gasperi*, Turin, 1949, and P. Scoppola, *La proposta politica di De Gasperi*, Bologna, 1977.
[350] Text in *Atti e documenti della Democrazia Cristiana, 1943–59*, Rome, 1959, p. 194.

ically join a movement which, standing above parties, aims at becoming the champion of a European federation'.[351]

Among the smaller parties the Republican Party (PRI) had a long tradition of support for federalist aspirations. At the party's first post-war conference, held in Rome on 9–11 February 1946, the acceptance of this principle was taken for granted; the only question for debate was whether in the existing situation a European or a world-wide federation was to be preferred.[352] The Movimento Democratico Italiano, founded in Rome in the spring of 1943, contained an assurance in its programme that the party 'will raise no obstacle to a possible international community or an eventual democratic European federation, but on the contrary is determined to further them'.[353] Luigi Einaudi (who became President in 1948), the most important of those who refounded the Liberal Party, was the author of a pamphlet entitled 'Per una Federazione economica Europea' which appeared in Rome during Badoglio's forty-five days. It urged the creation of a supreme European authority with power not only over the economic and monetary systems but also equipped with armed forces and executive bodies, and a European legislation elected directly by the people[354] – a programme that went too far for the majority of the party with their traditional attachment to property and the monarchy, even if they had no alternative to set against it.[355] Even in the Communist Party there were internationalists inclined to federalism who still hoped, like Picardo Orazio in August 1946,

'that before proletarian internationalism has become acclimatized and put down roots in every country, and before it has united the nations of the whole world in brotherhood, a European federal republic will already have done away with the most evil kind of nationalism and helped to give full effect to the principles of democracy'.[356]

To the extent that the PCI conformed to Moscow's European policy such voices were, indeed, bound to be silenced. Even so, its official foreign-policy line up to 1947 held firmly to 'collaboration and ever closer political, economic and cultural ties with all the European democracies'.[357]

---

[351] *L'Unità europea*, No. 3, Turin, 20.11.1945, p. 3. For the Christian Democrats and the development of their pro-European aspirations, cf. in more detail, with references, chap. IV/3 in vol. 2.

[352] Cf. the comprehensive account in *L'Unità europea*, No. 9, Turin, 20.2.1946, p. 4.

[353] Together with other similar declarations by Socialist Resistance groups in Rome in the spring of 1943, this document was printed by E. Colorni in May 1943 in the first number of a clandestine newspaper, *L'Unità europea. Voce del Movimento Federalista Europeo*, vol. i, p. 4. This newspaper was welcomed in *Combat* (Lyons) on Dec. 1943, so that by then it must have circulated as far as Lyons (cf. Lipgens, *Föderationspläne*, n. on p. 230).

[354] Together with another pamphlet written by Einaudi in Switzerland for the MFE (Lugano, 1944), this is reprinted in L. Einaudi, *La Guerra a l'unità europea*, Milan, 1950², pp. 35–78.

[355] Cf. the testimony of the Liberal federalist Gastone Cottoni in *L'Unità europea*, No. 10, Turin, 5.3.1946, p. 3. For more about the Liberals, see chap. IV/4 in vol. 2 of the present work.

[356] P. Orazio, 'Comunismo e Federalismo Europeo' in *L'Unità europea*, Nos. 15–16, Turin, 25.8.1946, p. 2.

[357] Declaration by the PCI in Nov. 1944. Text in *L'Unità europea*, No. 8, Milan, Jan. 1945, p. 8.

To sum up, all anti-Fascist groups of any importance which appeared as founders of parties in Italy's future democracy, with the sole exception of the Communists, had urged, in a multiplicity of statements which all agreed on fundamentals, the establishment of a supranational authority to safeguard peace. As in the German and French, Polish, and Dutch Resistance movements, so also in Italy all non-Communist forces had learnt the need for a European federation from the experience of defeat and the totalitarian excesses of nationalism.

However, the first independent post-war governments headed by Bonomi, Parri, and De Gasperi, which quickly succeeded each other between 1944 and 1946, had scarcely any opportunity of conveying their views to their European neighbours or to the victorious Allies. 'The project of a European federation on the lines we have in mind', Ivanoe Bonomi admitted at the end of the war in 1945, 'has no chance whatsoever of being implemented'.[358] Italy, as a former Axis power, had first to recover a place in the international community before it could gain a hearing for its own views on how post-war Europe should be run.

Although Italy had taken part in the war against the Germans with slender forces of its own, and Italian partisans could take some of the credit for the liberation of Northern Italy, these efforts were not enough to dispel anti-Italian feeling or to give the country any real political weight. While Churchill made no secret of his antipathy towards Italy, Stalin demanded reparations, supported the Yugoslav claim for Trieste, and wished to make the former Italian colony of Libya into a Russian 'trust territory'. De Gaulle tried to enforce his claim to the Val d'Aosta by using troops, and it was only the US government which showed any interest in Italy's return to democracy and to a place on the international stage. At Yalta Roosevelt put pressure on Churchill in this sense, and at Potsdam Truman was able to get a resolution adopted whereby a treaty with Italy would be given priority at the forthcoming peace negotiations.[359] Thus the basic conditions of an independent foreign policy were provided, though it was clear that the new Italy owed its international position entirely to the US and was dependent on its patron's goodwill.

So it was an almost forlorn hope, more an avowal of principle than a serious political move, when Alcide De Gasperi as foreign minister of the Parri government tried to gain a hearing for the pro-European views of the Italian parties at his first meeting with the Allied Council of Foreign Ministers in September 1945. Italy, he declared, was ready to make sacrifices for European solidarity and help to build a better world; as Italian Foreign Minister he was the 'protagonist of a new, federated Europe'. His audience reacted with reserve, almost hostility; only the US Secretary of State, Byrnes, openly showed sympathy, and this was due more to De

---

[358] Quoted from L. Salvatorelli, *La Guerra fredda 1945–1955*, Venice, 1956, p. 126.
[359] Cf. H. S. Hughes, *The United States and Italy*, Cambridge, Mass., 1965²; N. Kogan, *The Politics of Italian Foreign Policy*, New York, 1963; F. Roy Willis, *Italy chooses Europe*, 1971, esp. pp. 12–18; Atti del convegno *Italia e Stati Uniti durante l'amministrazione Truman*, Milan, 1976.

Gasperi's record as a victim of Fascism than to his vision of a post-war Europe. The meeting showed beyond any doubt that decisions about the government of post-war Europe lay solely in the hands of the superpowers, and that these were not responsive to the views of the Europeans themselves.[360]

Disappointed by the attitude of the great powers and especially by the nationalistic policy of the French government, on whose sympathy people in Italy had built many hopes, all that remained for Italy's democratic politicians as far as the European ideal was concerned was a mood of resignation not unmixed with bitterness. 'France', De Gasperi declared to the Constituent Assembly in June 1946, 'has preferred to look back at the past rather than turn to the future. We had hoped to convince it that our friendship would be of more value to its European mission than a few of our most remote mountain fortresses...'[361]

On this issue, too, however, the Italians did as much as they could within their own borders. After a searching debate the Constituent Assembly adopted what became Article 11 of the Constitution, which embodied the 'essence of federalist doctrine' with regard to the preservation of peace: 'Italy ... agrees, on conditions of equality with other states, to such limitation of sovereignty as may be necessary for a system calculated to ensure peace and justice between nations; it promotes and encourages international organizations having such ends in view.' 'All of us in this Chamber', declared Ruini, chairman of the committee which drafted the Article, 'are animated by a common desire, namely to condemn war and to work for an international organization'. This, he continued, was no obstacle to the creation of European unity; on the contrary, it was an essential prerequisite. 'The effort for European unity is a supremely Italian principle: Italian thinkers have emphasized that Europe is our second fatherland. It has nevertheless been considered right at this historic moment that an international settlement can and must extend beyond the frontiers of Europe.'[362]

Yet in the first two years after the war Italy had no choice but to aim for a lenient outcome of the negotiations for a peace treaty and for other conditions which would enable it to exert some influence on the still fluid post-war situation. From the beginning successive Italian governments tried not to attain Utopian goals but to put up with inevitable sacrifices, while warning the Allies not to make unreasonable demands if the Italian

---

[360] Cf. the testimonies of C. Sforza, *Cinque anni a Palazzo Chigi: La politica estera italiana dal 1947 at 1951*, Rome, 1952, p. 18; J. F. Byrnes, *Speaking Frankly*, New York, 1947, p. 141; P. C. Adstans, *Alcide de Gasperi nella politica estera italiana*, Milan, 1953, p. 33 f.

[361] *Atti dell'Assemblea Costituente, discussioni*, 12 vols., Rome, 25 June 1946 to 31 Jan. 1948, this quotation from vol. i, p. 29. For de Gaulle's small-minded annexationist policy towards Italy and its critics in France and elsewhere, cf. Lipgens 'Bedingungen und Etappen' (n. 208), p. 93 f. and Lipgens, 'Innerfranzösische Kritik' (n. 247), n. 102.

[362] This argument was used to reject a proposal to include the objective of 'European unity' in the Article in question. Cf. the whole discussion in: *Atti i documenti dell'Assemblea Costituente* (n. 361), esp. vol. iii (4 March–15 April 1947); Ruini's arguments in vol iii, p. 2432 f.; the resulting Article 11 quoted from A. Blaustein and G. Flanz, *Constitutions* (n. 337), p. 3.

people were to be won for co-operation in the new global settlement and in making democracy work.[363] These tactics met with little understanding on the part of the Allies; on the contrary, the attitude of the Soviet Union over the question of Trieste and the Allies' unanimous refusal to return Libya, Eritrea, and Somaliland to Italian rule led to a revival of nationalism, especially among the right-wing parties and the Communists. There was general disappointment that Italy was given hardly any credit for its struggle against Nazi Germany, which had lasted almost two years. It was far from easy for De Gasperi as Prime Minister and his Foreign Minister Count Sforza (who succeeded Pietro Nenni in 1947) in the National Assembly, and Luigi Einaudi in the Senate, to win a majority for the peace treaty, which placed the greater part of Trieste (Zone A) under international administration and assigned the remainder (Zone B) to Yugoslavia.[364]

Only the prospect of once more becoming a sovereign nation and thus occupying a better vantage-point from which to further the overdue consolidation of Europe, together with the prospects opened up by the announcement of the Marshall Plan, enabled Italy to accept the treaty negotiated in Paris, which was ratified by the Italian parliament on 31 July 1947.[365]

(C) BELGIUM: SPAAK'S FRUSTRATED EFFORTS

Belgium suffered less material damage from the war than its neighbours, and after its rapid liberation by Allied troops in September 1944 was able to return to economic normality quite smoothly. Since the disaster of 1940 the Belgian people had shown their awareness of the interdependence of Western Europe in terms of both economics and security: after the

---

[363] G. Petrilli, 'La politica estera e europea di De Gasperi', type-written article of fifty-one pages, Turin, 1975, p. 8.

[364] The final terms of the treaty involved a considerable reduction in the size of the armed forces and in armaments; the army was restricted to 185,000 men, the air force and navy 25,000 each. The exorbitant Soviet demand for an indemnity of 600 million dollars having been rejected, Italy had to pay reparations of 125 million dollars to Yugoslavia, 105 millions to Greece, 100 millions to the USSR, and 5 millions to Albania. The other most difficult problem was the territorial question of Venezia Giulia, which was only provisionally solved by the peace treaty. Trieste with its surrounding district was divided into two zones: Zone A (including the town itself) was to be under Anglo-American military administration, Zone B (the whole of Istria) under Yugoslav military administration, a provisional arrangement which remained in force until Oct. 1954. Italy was allowed to keep South Tyrol (Alto Adige) but had to grant it a wide measure of self-government; this region was also to be officially bilingual. Italian text of treaty in *La Legislazione italiana (coordinata da M. Fragali)* vol. iv, 1947, Milan (Giuffre), 1947, pp. 760–97. Translation in *United Nations Treaty Series*, vol. 49, NY, 1950, pp. 126–235 (No. 747). Cf. J. B. Duroselle, *Le Conflit de Trieste, 1943–1954*, Brussels, 1966; B. C. Novak, *Trieste 1941–1954*, Chicago, 1970.

[365] The result of the vote was: of 410 deputies present 262 voted yes, 68 no, while 80 abstained. It was of some interest that 78 out of 104 Communist deputies abstained, in other words the great majority of PCI deputies did not vote against the treaty although they could have been expected to do so after the debates of the previous weeks (see *Atti dell'Ass. Cost.* [n. 352], vol. vi, p. 6572 ff.). For the ratification and the revival of 'European' hopes in the wake of the announcement of the Marshall Plan, cf. chap. III/2, p. 500 ff.

unhappy experience of the inter-war years, the majority were ready to take part in plans for integrating the whole of Europe, even if at first that had to be under German leadership.[366] As they came to realize the true character of Nazi rule the Belgians, during the years of Resistance, looked for ways of bringing about a new European order without the Germans. They were clear about one thing: the country could not revert to its traditional neutrality. Realists advocated a close relationship with Britain in future; the far-sighted also grasped that Belgium's inclusion in a new, international order would require willingness to renounce sovereignty.

The committee of the clandestine Socialist Party (PSB), one of the few political groups which actually managed to put down on paper detailed plans for the post-war period, drew up a programme in the spring of 1942, the foreign-policy section of which called for the limitation and reduction of sovereignty in all states in favour of international law and international arbitration backed by a police force, and added to this proposals designed to promote international economic solidarity.[367] As appears from the regular reports on public opinion by Paul Struye, the Louvain professor who was founder and editor of the most important Belgian underground newspaper, *La Libre Belgique*, this programme reflected views widely held by the general population. He wrote, for example, on 1 February 1944, that the majority wanted 'the integration of our country in a huge military and economic complex which would preserve intact our sovereignty for domestic purposes'; they had so often been told 'Europe must organize' that they had become complete converts to that principle.[368]

Paul Henri Spaak, a leading member of the Belgian Socialist Party, endeavoured to promote these views while Foreign Minister of the Pierlot government, which had escaped to London in 1940. In his contacts with the exiled governments of Poland, Czechoslovakia, Norway, the Netherlands, Luxemburg, Greece, and Yugoslavia, and later especially in negotiations with Eden and Churchill, Spaak tried to create conditions that would make it possible to unite the states of Europe at the end of the war.

> In the world of tomorrow [he wrote in 1942], especially in the Europe of tomorrow and, more particularly, the small countries of Europe, the problems of security and prosperity will be inseparable. The formula 'United in war but isolated in peace' did not apply yesterday and it will be completely inapplicable tomorrow. We must reconcile the rebirth of nationalism with an internationalism which will be essential ... If we try to cling to old formulae we shall achieve nothing worthwhile. The experience of the League of Nations demonstrates this point. Its rule of unanimity, its deference to national sovereignty, was one of the principal reasons for its failure. Tomorrow there will be international, regional, European

---

[366] Cf. the testimony of P. Struye, *L'Évolution du sentiment public sous l'occupation allemande* (Documents pour servir à l'histoire de l'occupation allemande en Belgique, vol. i), Brussels, 1945, relevant date here 15.12.1940, p. 20. For Belgian hopes of future European union between 1940 and 1945 see Lipgens, *Föderationspläne*, pp. 250–61.
[367] Full text in *Belgium* (New York), 2.4.1942; still more specific is the programme of the Socialist underground newspaper, *Le Peuple*, of 1.5.1942.
[368] Struye (n. 366), Report of 1.2.1944, p. 173.

or world organizations, it does not matter which. But they are doomed to failure from the outset if their participants do not accept that the body must be superior to its individual members.[369]

Convinced that Belgium must become a member of a much larger grouping and that the new authority to be created must have supranational powers, the Belgian foreign minister, who despite numerous ministerial changes remained in office after his government's return to Brussels until 1949, continued to take a flexible line on the question of geographical boundaries and political organization and thus on the general plan of campaign for unification.

In accordance with the new balance of power in the world, in 1944–5 Spaak worked for an 'organization of Western Europe under British leadership'[370] which would include at least Belgium, the Netherlands, Luxemburg, and France, leading to close co-operation in the political, economic, and military fields and finally integration. However, when at the end of 1944 Spaak on a visit to London put his proposals to Eden and Churchill[371] he met with uncomprehending rejection. 'The idea of an organization of Western Europe did not appeal to [Churchill]. My plans for economic integration seemed to him, I believe, a pipe-dream.'[372] When Churchill was succeeded by a Labour government, Spaak was even less successful; even his proposal at the end of 1945, at least to make a start with close military co-operation, was treated in a dilatory fashion by his new opposite number, Bevin.[373] He experienced a similar disappointment in Paris: negotiations which the Belgian ambassador, Count de Romrée, began with de Gaulle's caretaker government in the autumn of 1944, and which Spaak himself tried to animate in May 1945, proved completely fruitless.[374] Thus the first and, apart from Italy, the only post-war government which was ready to take up the views of the Resistance movements in favour of European unification and to incorporate them in government proposals was doomed to see its efforts wrecked by the opposition of the leading European powers. By not even making use of the chance left to them by the superpowers to remould Europe, albeit within diminished borders, the French and British governments condemned the smaller European states to abandon plans that had emerged from the Resistance tradition.

[369] P. H. Spaak, *Combats inachevés*, I, *De l'independance à l'alliance,* Paris (Fayard), p. 149, quoted from abridged English translation, P. H. Spaak, *The Continuing Battle. Memoirs of a European 1933–66.* (Weidenfeld and Nicolson), 1971, p. 77 f.
[370] Quoted from Spaak, *Combats*, p. 157, *The Continuing Battle* (n. 369), p. 82.
[371] Text of Note handed to Sir Alexander Cadogan, Permanent Under-Secretary of State in the Foreign Office, *Combats,* pp. 160–3 (not reproduced in the English edition); for Spaak's visit to London as a whole, ibid., pp. 159–64.
[372] Spaak, *Combats* (n. 369), p. 164 (not in English edition). Cf. n. 152.
[373] Spaak, *Combats,* p. 164; *The Continuing Battle,* p. 85 f.
[374] Spaak, *Combats,* pp. 109–71; *The Continuing Battle,* p. 89 f. For the whole subject see also J. Willequet, *Paul-Henri Spaak. Un homme des combats,* Brussels, 1975, pp. 134–7.

Spaak's double rebuff by Britain and France left him a deeply disappointed man as far as the question of a new kind of Europe was concerned. In the following two years he saw no opportunity for a political initiative in this direction, and thought he could best serve internationalist principles by playing a part at the UN whose first General Assembly, meeting in London early in 1946, elected Spaak its president. In the absence of any practical means of making a start the desire for European unity could only evaporate in a basic but nebulous commitment to internationalist principles. Thus Spaak's party, the PSB, at its 'Congrès de la Victoire' on 11 June 1945, passed a resolution on foreign policy urging that: 'To guarantee its safety, Belgium, like other nations, should give up part of its sovereignty in order to enter into treaty commitments or obligations as a member of an international organization'; but no specific moves were suggested except that 'Belgium should enter a customs union or, failing that, a multilateral economic treaty which should also include at least the Netherlands and France.'[375] The Christian Social Party (PSC) in its 'Christmas 1945 Programme' urged in firmer and more explicitly European terms, but equally fruitlessly, that all nations 'should be free in accordance with their affinity and natural interests to form regional and other kinds of groups, the existence of which should be recognized by the international community'.[376] The one and only federalist association founded in Belgium soon after the end of the war, the Union Fédérale Internationale (Section belge), was thus virtually unable to take any initiative as far as Europe was concerned.

The founding committee of this organization met on 1 December 1945 at the house of the Belgian deputy Ernest Demuyter (a member of the Liberal Party or PLB) on the initiative of D. H. Bridgeman, a member of the British Federal Union. Among its forerunners was the Institute of European Economy, whose director, Dr van der Ghinst of Brussels, had suggested in 1939 that European states could be 'obliged to follow the example of the USA and create a political structure more in conformity with modern technique and civilization'. The forerunners also included a group of ex-concentration-camp inmates and Resistance fighters led by Requille, who in the summer of 1945 issued a manifesto warning that 'A conspiracy is afoot against peace' and denounced secret diplomacy, Soviet and British policies of domination, and nationalism. Under Demuyter's chairmanship the new group sought close co-operation with Federal Union.[377] By 1947 a number of other

---

[375] *P.S.B., La Ligne politique du parti. Textes adoptés par le Congrès de la Victoire des 9, 10 et 11 juin. 1945.* Brussels (Ed. Soc.), June 1945, quotations on p. 10.

[376] The 'Christmas Programme' was printed in: Centre International Démocrate-Chrétien d'études et de documentation (ed.): *La Doctrine social-chrétienne en Europe occidentale,* Rome, 1963, quotation on p. 18. For a general description of parties in liberated Belgium, see F. E. Oppenheim, 'Belgian Political Parties since Liberation' in *The Review of Politics,* vol. xii, No. 1, Jan. 1950, pp. 99–119; for the period after 1947, see also G. Marchal-Van Belle, *Les Socialistes belges et l'intégration européenne,* Brussels, 1968.

[377] Cf. Bridgeman's Report in *Federal News,* No. 131, Feb. 1946, p. 11 f. (quotation, ibid.); for Federal Union, see pp. 142–53 above. Antoine Allard took part as representative of *Union Fédérale* at the International Meeting of Leaders of the Peace Movement (Geneva, 12–14 Sept. 1946), convened by the British National Peace Council (director Gerald Bailey) and the Swiss Council of the Peace

federalist groups had come into existence in Belgium – the Centre international d'Amitié, the Rassemblement Fédéraliste, the groups associated with the periodicals *Synthèses, États-Unis d'Europe,* and *La Relève,* and those associated with the *Cahiers socialistes* and the *Documents de l'Action Catholique*;[378] yet none of them had any influence on Belgian foreign policy before mid-1947.

The disappointment of the European federalists in Belgium was aggravated by the fact that the country was soon involved in an acrimonious argument about its national identity. The controversy, which increasingly came to dominate all political discussion, was sparked off by the more or less collaborationist attitude of King Leopold III, after the German victory in 1940. His claim to return to the throne after having been a prisoner of war in Germany split the royalist Flemings and Catholics from the Socialists and Liberals, who called for Leopold to renounce the throne and whose main support came from the Walloon part of the population. The king, who in the past had held the balance between Flemings and Walloons and represented the unity of the state, had become the major subject of controversy between the two groups, whose clash for that reason became all the more acute.[379]

A government composed of representatives of all parties was formed by the Socialist van Acker in February 1945 following the resignation of Pierlot, the Prime Minister of the government-in-exile, who had become unpopular at the end of the war because of supply difficulties; but the coalition broke up in June 1945 when King Leopold announced that he was about to return from his exile at Salzburg. The cabinet asked the king's brother, Prince Charles, who had been appointed Regent by parliament, to depose Leopold. Socialists and Liberals called on Leopold to abdicate at once, while the Catholics prepared to form a new government. Not until Leopold had assured the presidents of both Houses of Parliament of his willingness to wait for the next general election before deciding on return or abdication did the van Acker government resume office, though not before the ministers belonging to the Christian Social Party had resigned. The remaining government parties got parliament to pass a law making the king's return depend on the vote of the people's elected representatives; Leopold, on the other hand, declared, to the applause of the Catholics, that he would give way only to the decision of a referendum. In the first post-war general election, held on 17 February 1946, the royal question was the overriding issue and exacerbated

---

Movement (secretary-General Léopold Boissier). Cf. 'Associations et revues fédéralistes' in *Cahiers du monde nouveau,* vol. 3, no. 6, 1947, p. 303 ff. For Allard's co-operation at subsequent congresses of federalists, see Index.

[378] Cf. analysis of these groups in chap. III/6 at nn. 430–5.

[379] For Belgium's early post-war history, cf. surveys by F. E. Eyck, *The Benelux Countries, An Historical Survey,* Princeton, NJ, 1959, and W. Wagner, *Europa zwischen Aufbruch und Restauration* (= dtv *Weltgeschichte des 20. Jhs.,* vol. 14), Munich, 1968, pp. 204–19. The valuable survey of Belgian history since 1830 by J. E. Helmreich, *Belgium and Europe, A Study in Small Power Diplomacy,* The Hague/Paris (Mouton), 1976, traces its further evolution in the chapter 'International Cooperation', pp. 380–91. A pioneer monograph on this subject is T. Luykx, *Politieke Geschiedenis van België van 1789 tot heden,* Amsterdam/Brussels (Elsevier), 1973, especially Part 4: 'Na de Tweede Wereldoorlog (1945–1973)', pp. 399–608.

existing divisions. The anti-Leopold parties kept their majority in the Chamber of Deputies – the Socialists won 69 seats, the Communists 23, and the Liberals 17 – but the Catholics with 91 seats were by far the largest party. The pro-Leopold groups were also able to claim that van Acker had denied voting rights to women as well as to about 300,000 Belgians suspected of wartime collaboration – both groups were known to be overwhelmingly monarchist. Henceforward the king's supporters constituted the Opposition, and van Acker formed a new cabinet consisting of Socialists, Liberals, and Communists.[380]

The two major parties, the PSB and the PSC, remained at loggerheads over the royal question until March 1947; the issues on which they were agreed, including internationalism, were shelved as far as practical politics were concerned. Instead, the Socialists continued to be part of what – apart from opposition to the king – was an extremely heterogeneous coalition, marked by ceaseless internal wrangles about the course its policy should take. If Spaak had had the courage to continue the attempts he made in 1944–5 to bring about a Western Union his efforts in any case would have been frustrated by the veto of the Communists, who were his partners in the coalition.

The paralysis of Belgian politics did not come to an end until the Christian Social Party decided to postpone the royal question for the time being in order to form a broadly-based coalition with the Socialists, excluding the Liberals and Communists, and so at last to provide an opportunity for carrying out the joint programme they had agreed on in 1945.[381] Rebuffed for two years by the leading European governments and hampered by the resurgence of the problem of national identity, Belgium's European policy was in the same position as it had been in at the end of the war – the only difference being that in the meantime considerable changes had occurred in the international scene.

(D) THE ALOOFNESS OF THE NETHERLANDS; THE BENELUX QUESTION

The Belgians' willingness in principle to give up traditional neutrality in favour of closer co-operation with their European neighbours; their impotence, as a small state, *vis à vis* the superpowers and the negative attitude of France and Britain; their political effectiveness handicapped by unresolved problems surviving from the national past – all these factors, though with differences of emphasis, were paralleled to a remarkable degree by the Dutch situation in the immediate post-war years.

The Dutch Resistance, which between 1941 and 1944 had a markedly ideological character, had in its great majority urged the need for a federal community of the nations of Europe as one of the major post-war

[380] Cf. Wagner, ibid.
[381] Cf. chap. III/2, p. 504 f.

objectives. A joint manifesto issued in April 1944 by representatives of the two largest Resistance groups, the pro-Socialist *Het Parool* and the progressive Christian *Vrij Nederland*, summed up a large number of policy documents by declaring:

The Netherlands must aim at the closest possible combination with the other Western European states and also co-operate loyally with the other nations of the world, especially in organizing a new League of Nations. In so doing the Netherlands must be ready to accept a limitation of their sovereignty, as every nation should be asked to do after this war in the interests of an organization standing for international justice.[382]

Progressive and internationalist circles, anxious for the heritage of the Resistance movement to bear fruit in Dutch post-war politics, helped to found the Partij van de Arbeid (PvdA), which was supposed to overcome the outworn divisions of the past.[383] Those former Socialists, Liberals, and progressive members of the denominational parties who wanted to unite persuaded Queen Wilhelmina to call on Professor Willem Schermerhorn to preside over a cabinet of 'national unity' in which the representatives of the Resistance had a preponderant voice. By this time the war was over and the northern part of the country, which had remained in German hands until February 1945, had been liberated. Some politicians who, during the Resistance, had recognized the need for the Netherlands to become part of a united Europe had now joined the government, among them Henri Brugmans as Director-General of Information and Sicco Mansholt as Minister of Agriculture. In its domestic policy the government aimed at reducing class tensions and bringing about a comprehensive social partnership. At the suggestion of Dirk Stikker a 'Labour Council' consisting of representatives of the trade unions and the employers was set up to help develop an even-handed policy towards labour and social questions. In foreign policy the government was in favour of internationalism, which, as long as there was still hope that the prospective United Nations organization might be a more effective institution than the League of Nations, was expressed in a commitment to give it wider powers. The Netherlands government replied to the draft proposals formulated at Dumbarton Oaks with a memorandum favouring a limitation of the right of veto and adding to the powers of the smaller states: in particular it urged that 'the right of veto in a power's own cause be not insisted on by any state'.[384]

[382] *Manifesto* of 15.11.1944 (pamphlet); frequently reprinted. For the European plans of the Dutch Resistance, see Lipgens, *Föderationspläne* (n. 44), pp. 263–310.

[383] For the Dutch party system, cf. G. Geismann, *Politische Struktur und Regierungssystem in den Niederlanden*, Frankfurt and Bonn, 1964, and W. Verkade, *Democratic Parties in the Low Countries and Germany, Origins and Historical Developments*, Leiden, 1965 (with more emphasis on the historical side); ibid., p. 225 ff. for the most revealing survey yet published of domestic developments in the Netherlands.

[384] From 'Suggestions presented by the Netherlands Government concerning the proposals for the maintenance of peace and security agreed on at the Four-Power Conference of Dumbarton Oaks, as published on October 9th, 1944'; full text in Campen (n. 16), pp. 163–79. Cf. also the analysis ibid., pp. 15–19.

As soon as the war was over other ex-Resistance fighters tried to gain a hearing for their pro-European views through two groups, Europeesche Actie and Federale Unie; both began on a modest scale, but after their merger in June 1946 the organization developed and grew in importance.[385]

The Schermerhorn government, like most of those in which Resistance personalities were prominent, envisaged a federation of Europe or at least of Western Europe as part of the international peace settlement still in the making. The Foreign Minister, Van Kleffens, who had held that post in the government-in-exile in London, declared in a parliamentary debate on foreign policy on 30 October 1945 that in principle his government supported regional unions in Europe. It must, however, be realized, he added, that such unions, though their objects might be admirable, also carried a risk of endangering rather than maintaining the international balance. There must not be a 'Western bloc', only a regional grouping with the proviso that it must not be directed against one or more friendly states. Should a regional grouping be formed in Western Europe, it should be within the framework and under the control of the United Nations, which alone could deal with dangers of that sort.[386]

Like all those who were federally minded, the Dutch government found itself placed in an inescapable dilemma by the superpowers' aloofness or hostility towards European union. On the one hand, their experience of pre-war instability and the collapse of the national state during the war obliged the Dutch to favour a policy of pooling the rights of sovereignty at regional level as well as world-wide; on the other hand, the superpowers obstructed the establishment of the kind of international peace-keeping organization for which the Dutch had hoped, with the result that the regional groupings which they also hoped for would become potential instruments of traditional power politics and a threat to peace. Seeking a guarantee of peace by means of an international organization, but simultaneously dependent on the victorious powers in order to get it, the Netherlands government had to be content with vague appeals for international co-operation, addressed especially to the Allies. As late as March 1947 the Beel government, which succeeded that of Schermerhorn, emphasized that any question of a Western-European Union was purely academic so long as the major Allies had not agreed on a settlement of the German problem; accordingly, the Netherlands could only go on waiting.[387]

Two developments in domestic politics helped to increase disillusionment and accelerate a return to the country's traditional foreign policy. In the first place, the retention of the Dutch colonial empire in Indonesia was, against all the lessons of history, seen by almost the entire population as

---

[385] Cf. the detailed account in chap. I/2, pp. 131–42.
[386] Second Chamber, 30.10.1945, p. 143, summarized in Campen (n. 16), p. 21
[387] First Chamber, 12.3.1947, p. 7; summarized in Campen (n. 16), p. 33. For the change in the Netherlands' European policy after 1947, cf. Campen p. 57 ff. and chap.III/2, p. 504.

essential to the national interest; and in this way the Netherlands became involved in a struggle with the Indonesian liberation movement which almost monopolized the nation's energies.[388]

Dutch prosperity before the war was essentially based on the products of the colonial territories, which in area were sixty times as large as the home country. The general belief was that if, as the superpowers clearly desired, the colonies were given independence, the miserably low standard of living in the Netherlands in 1945 would be perpetuated. Except for the Communists, all parties regarded the Indonesian nationalists led by Ahmed Sukarno as rebels. In August 1945 the 'Republic of Indonesia' was proclaimed; that autumn Dutch and Indonesian troops were fighting each other in Java; in September 1946 more Netherlands forces landed at Djakarta. In November 1946 the moderate wing of the independence movement was obliged to sign an agreement providing for the formation of a 'United States of Indonesia' within a 'Netherlands Commonwealth'; in July 1947 a police action was mounted against Jogjakarta, the capital of Sukarno's Republic, which opposed the agreement, and this finally led to the intervention of the UN Security Council.

The second development was a revival of traditional and conservative forces, stimulated by the colonial war and frustration in the field of foreign policy. The first post-war general election, held on 17 May 1946, proved a bitter disappointment to the Resistance groups. The PvdA, created three months before, received only 29 per cent of the votes and 29 seats in parliament instead of the 40 per cent of votes estimated on the strength of the pre-war poll of its constituent parties. The Catholic People's Party (KVP) became the largest party with 32 seats, while the veteran Protestant parties – the Anti-Revolutionary Party (ARP) and the Christian–Historical Union (CHU), with 13 and 8 seats respectively – had emerged from the war with their voting strength intact.[389] The victory of the KVP did not necessarily mean any abrupt change in government policy: Professor Louis J. M. Beel, one of the most prominent leaders of the KVP's progressive wing, became prime minister and the PvdA agreed to a 'black–red' coalition of the two largest parties, so that the Socialist and internationalist policy could be continued, albeit in a more cautious fashion. The return of public opinion to a more conservative frame of mind was, nevertheless, clearly shown by the election.

A good example of the cautious foreign policy of the Beel government was its attitude to the German question. The Netherlands followed the same line as the French Foreign Minister Bidault in calling for Germany to be broken up into a confederation of loosely connected states, with a special statute for the Ruhr and the Rhineland and the economic incorpo-

---

[388] For the following passage cf. A. M. Taylor, *Indonesian Independence and the United Nations*, London, 1960; G. McT. Kahn, *Nationalism and Revolution in Indonesia*, Ithaca, NY, 1952; C. Smit, *De liquidatie van een Imperium. Nederland en Indonesië 1945–1962*, Amsterdam, 1962.
[389] Cf. Verkade (n. 383), pp. 230–2.

ration of the Saar territory into France. Yet, in contrast to the French government, in a memorandum dated 14 January 1947 the Dutch also insisted on the need for German economic recovery as an essential prerequisite for the revival of its European neighbours and thus of Europe as a whole. No other European government drew attention so outspokenly to what was shortly to be spelt out in the Marshall Plan, namely the economic and thus also the political interdependence of the European countries including Germany.

No other European government called so unequivocally as the Dutch for 'the recovery of the national economy and ... prosperity of Germany in so far as this is essential to European and world prosperity'. The Netherlands government warned the Allies against seeing the German problem in isolation and solely as a problem of security: 'It is a matter for consideration whether the outline for a general economic co-operation in Europe, including Germany, should not be concomitant with the conclusion of the peace treaty with Germany. Any arrangements relating to the structure of German industry and the extent of German production, import and export, will then have to be fitted into the framework of this European co-operation.'[390] It was particularly necessary for Germany's smaller neighbours to take part in working out a common Allied policy for Germany. These demands fell far short of the plans for European unity which had been drawn up by the Resistance groups and taken up by the Dutch federalists,[391] but they had one thing in common: they regarded the European Continent as an interdependent whole.

The negotiations and agreements which led to the formation of the Benelux Union took place within the same framework of cautious co-operation, inspired by a basic awareness of economic interdependence but facing immense difficulties with the outside world still thinking in terms of nation states.[392] During their wartime exile the governments of Belgium, the Netherlands, and Luxemburg had agreed, despite British and French objections to a Western-European Union, that they would try to bring about at least an economic union of their countries, which were already closely interlinked in many ways. As the first step, on 21 October 1943 they decided to harmonize their currency policies, and on 5 September 1944 they agreed to create a customs union, with almost complete free trade among themselves and common external tariffs.

[390] Memorandum of the Netherlands government on Allied policy with regard to Germany, full text in Campen (n. 16), pp. 230–43, quotations on pp. 230 and 236, summary pp. 44–56. On 28 Jan. 1947 a Netherlands delegation clarified the memorandum at the London conference of Allied deputy foreign ministers convened to prepare for the Conference of Foreign Ministers in Moscow, at which the peace treaty with Germany was to be discussed.
[396] In the April number of the *Action fédéraliste européenne* Henri Brugmans made the following comment on the Netherlands memorandum on Germany: 'Malgré notre joie à souligner tant d'idées justes, nous avons trouvé, sur ce dernier point encore, cette même lacune ... l'absence d'un fédéralisme européen, consciemment accepté comme idée-force. Et c'est ce qui rend la note néerlandaise moins claire, moins vigoureuse qu'elle n'aurait pu l'être.' (H. Brugmans, 'La note du Gouvernement néerlandais sur la question allemande' in *L'Action fédéraliste européenne*, vol. 2, no. 5, April 1947, quotation on p. 42. f.)
[392] Cf. J. E. Meade, *Negotiations for Benelux: an Annotated Chronicle 1943 to 1956*, Princeton, 1957; M. Weisglas, *Benelux*, Amsterdam, 1969.

'Desiring, at the moment of liberation of the territories of the Netherlands and the Economic Union of Belgium and Luxemburg, to create the most favourable conditions for the ultimate formation of a complete and durable Customs Union and for the restoration of economic activity', the governments-in-exile agreed on a joint Administrative Council on Customs Duties, which was to work out proposals for unifying tariffs in the Netherlands and the already existing Economic Union of Belgium and Luxemburg. It was to be reinforced by a joint Commission on Customs Disputes, responsible to the ministers concerned, with a power of veto over the subordinate national authorities, a co-ordinating Administrative Council for the Control of Foreign Trade, and a Commercial Agreements Council for negotiations with third countries.[393]

When the three countries were liberated, these agreements had to run the gauntlet of objections from the experts concerned. Business interests, traditionally geared to the nation state, and feeling the pressure of competition aggravated by the general depression and the crippling lack of dollars, allowed the goal of economic union to recede into a distant future. One obstacle to implementing the customs union was the difference in wage levels between Belgium and Luxemburg on the one hand and the Netherlands on the other. The relatively low level of wages in the Netherlands was bound to penalize Belgian products on the home market and Dutch exports to third countries. Despite all these difficulties the three governments, at a meeting at The Hague on 17 and 18 April 1946, confirmed their resolve to put into effect what they had decided while in exile. A commission was appointed to revise the joint tariffs agreed on in London in order to modify the starting differences between the two economic areas. This commission on tariffs completed its work in January 1947, two months later than had been expected, so it was agreed that the standardized tariff should come into force on 1 January 1948. In the meantime commissions had been working on proposals for economic standardization and integration in other sectors. Yet only when the Marshall Plan opened up the prospect of a large-scale solution for Western Europe as a whole did these commissions manage to make decisive progress in overcoming the many difficulties arising from different national traditions.[394]

7. Summary: 'Our Situation is like that of the Early Christians . . .'

For Europe the balance sheet of this first post-war year to the end of summer 1946 was depressingly negative in almost every respect. It caused deep disappointment and dismay, as has been seen more than once in the preceding sections, among those who had built their hopes on the insights gained during the war as to the need for a united Europe. During the

[393] Text of the Customs Union Agreement in Campen (n. 16), pp. 296–9.
[394] Cf. Meade (n. 392), pp. 10–23; on the decisive stimulus given by the Marshall Plan, see chap. III/2, p. 505 f.

months when Europe was being gradually freed from German occupation (in the autumn of 1944 and during the following winter) grateful enthusiasm and hopes for a permanent peace settlement predominated. The first free expressions of opinion assumed, without evidence, that the Resistance's own aversion to power politics and the claims of sovereignty was shared by the Allies. The Russian and American liberators, it was thought, could not possibly pursue a policy of force like Hitler, but would set their sights on a true peace settlement with the necessary preconditions. But in the autumn of 1945 it became increasingly clear that the superpowers were far from having lost faith in the categories of power politics, that they were restoring the system of small, weak nation states and were altogether behaving as if the Resistance movement and the new understanding of Europe to which it had given birth did not even exist.[395]

Shortly before and after the end of the war some prominent European statesmen tried to make unification the subject of official negotiations: Spaak with his proposals in London in December 1944 and in Paris in March 1945; De Gasperi at the Council of Foreign Ministers' meeting in London; Blum in Paris, and others. But because the only two European governments that could have acted with any prospect of success, those of Britain and France (de Gaulle), flatly refused, deferring to Soviet objections to the idea of a 'Western bloc', these voices relapsed into silence.[396] Five large non-governmental associations, whose programmes and organization made them of more than local importance, tried from 1945 onwards to act as pressure groups for a European federation. But there was no debate of any kind, and when they realized that the superpowers were adamantly opposed to the concept of Europe, while France and Britain were unwilling even to discuss it, they were disheartened and in some cases even retraced their steps. In April 1946 one of their journals wrote: 'In recent months a marked lull has come about in the activity of federalist groups throughout Europe ... The Italian MFE has had to cease publication of its weekly *L'Unità europea*. Money is running short. The CIFE in Paris is no longer active. These are distressing facts to admit.'[397]

---

[395] Illusory hopes in relation to the superpowers, shown in publications after the Liberation and to some extent even in Resistance documents, were typical of the disappointments often experienced by the public of small countries. The superpowers decided according to their own real or supposed interests. The false expectations on the one hand and the actual behaviour of the superpowers on the other were proof of the correctness of the statement so often found in other Resistance documents, that the 'state of development' of the various continents was still so diverse that the unity of the world was not yet a possibility (cf. p. 50).

[396] Cf. sections 3 and 4 of chap. I, esp. pp. 171 and 223; for the initiatives by Spaak and De Gasperi, see pp. 260 and 256.

[397] Declaration in *De Federalist. Orgaan van 'Federale Unie' in Nederland,* April 1946, p. 1, which, however, ended: 'Propagate the principles, recruit new members in your environment. Remain active, persevere!' Spinelli, with some exaggeration, said on 6.1.1946: Since the superpowers 'have deprived the European nations of the right to decide their own fate over the whole field of international relations ... a political movement towards European federalism, that is one capable of doing something concrete to bring it about, cannot exist for the time being. As you know, in Italy as

(A) REASONS FOR LOSS OF HEART AND FOR THE WEAKNESS OF THE EUROPEAN ASSOCIATIONS

A number of reasons, some rooted in local or national politics, have been mentioned in the preceding pages; but the end of this chapter on the first post-war year is a suitable point at which to summarize the reasons why the understanding expressed so clearly in the writings of the Resistance was so ineffective politically during that period, and why during the winter of 1945–6 it was almost reduced to silence.

1. The first reason, exacerbated by the hungry winter of 1945–6, was the vast extent of the economic and administrative chaos on the European Continent, and the time needed to deal with it. Practically everyone was preoccupied with the search for food, fuel, and somewhere to live. Postal services and communications were restored only slowly; travelling on the few undamaged railway lines was a risky business. The absolute priority, for towns and states as for individuals, was the revival of economic life, food supplies, rubble-clearing, and the reconstruction of administration with largely untrained staffs. The task of purging Fascists and collaborators used up a lot of valuable energy, as did the replacement of discredited constitutions by new ones.[398] Too much effort had to be spent on recreating normal conditions in which national institutions could function, and little was left to spare for the peace settlement in Europe, which in any case, as everyone knew, would be decided by the superpowers and/or such bodies as the Allied Council of Foreign Ministers.

2. The most important reason for the weakness of the European idea in the first year after the war was that the victorious superpowers, whose troops were stationed in every European country except the four neutrals, and who made the decisions on all important questions, were flatly opposed to unification. They had not come, as the Resistance hoped they would, as supporters in the battle against nationalism and fragmentation as causes of war, but – as everyone in 1945 could very soon see – with the intention of establishing world-wide Russo-American co-operation with no assistance from the Europeans. Consequently the former Resistance leaders, who had championed the cause of Europe, quickly lost prestige and influence, while the politicians who returned from exile with plans for the full restoration of the small nation states were in a much stronger position. Anybody from one of the Resistance groups, for example, who approached the US military authorities in order to put the case for European federal union was rebuffed and admonished not to repeat the attempt to undermine

---

elsewhere the movement is either in course of dissolution or unable to come into existence' (in *L'Unità europea*, 7, Turin, 20.1.1946, p. 2 f.).

[398] In his Section 'L'échec des résistants', 'Naissance d'une politique fédéraliste' in *Cahiers de Bruges*, 7 (1957, 1, 'L'Europe en 1947'), p. 54 f., H. Brugmans stresses the urgency of reconstruction and rubble-clearing as well as the fourth and fifth reasons mentioned in the text.

friendship between America and Russia.[399] It was some time before people were fully aware of the unpalatable and devastating truth that the superpowers had no policy for Europe except restoration of the nation states, abandonment of one-third of the Continent to Soviet rule, and a new version of the ineffectual League of Nations.

3. The governments of the shrunken European nation states, burdened as they were with the most urgent tasks of reconstruction and with economic worries, did not take up the idea of unification. The British and French could in theory have done so with some prospect of being listened to, but this was not true of the defeated or the very small countries. But, apart from Anglo-French discord over the Rhineland and Syria (dramatized by de Gaulle), which blocked what could have been the nucleus of the Anglo-French treaty, they were all constrained by the diplomatic framework which, based on the wartime alliance, had taken shape at Yalta, San Francisco, and Potsdam, and which was predicated on Roosevelt's idea of Russo-American friendship. The predominance and pre-eminence of the two superpowers were acknowledged *de facto*, and no European government could contemplate endangering the success of the long hoped-for peace settlement by the Council of Foreign Ministers. Above all, the British government, whose leadership was considered indispensable for bringing about European unification on the Continent, deliberately avoided any action which, in view of Soviet protests against the idea of a 'Western bloc', could stand in the way of agreement over a peace settlement and cooperation between the Big Three. The Foreign Office records show how often the need for Great Britain to exclude any notion of a 'Western group' was reiterated in deference to 'Soviet suspicion'. Not until February 1946 did the minimum conditions exist which would have enabled the British and French to reach agreement on a circumspect advance in the direction of European unity: viz. de Gaulle's resignation, the French Socialists' readiness to co-operate, and the beginning of the US policy of containing the Soviet advance. But even then the British and French governments clung strictly to the diplomatic structures established at Yalta and Potsdam, from fear of the rising power and expansion of the Soviet Union and because, so soon after the war and after all the outrages committed by Germans, they found it impossible to conceive of including Germany in a united Europe. Their policy was influenced most of all, however, by the way in which people in general reaccustomed themselves to thinking in terms of nation states.[400]

[399] Information from Cornides and Spinelli; similarly the rebuke to Carlo Schmid, quoted in Schwarz, *Vom Reich zur Bundesrepublik* (n. 318), p. 712, n. 94 (Schmid's conversation with General L. Clay).

[400] Cf. review of the Western-European governments' attitude to the idea of European unity in sections 3 to 6 of chapter I. On the key position of the British and French governments, in contrast to that of the defeated and the smaller countries, cf. the beginning of section 3 of chapter I (p. 154 and n. 133), also n. p. 246 f. Cf. Foreign Office Papers, p. 171; for the prospects after February 1946, see esp. p. 181 and n. 178. For the persistence in thinking in terms of the nation state, see also p. 274.

4. Those members of the non-Communist Resistance groups who had written about and propagated the theme of European unity found themselves at the end of the war, so far as they survived, in a completely new situation. The German and Polish groups in particular had been decimated by the Gestapo and the abortive Warsaw Rising; for many survivors the physical and nervous strain of the years of struggle, even if they had not been in a concentration camp, had been so great that afterwards they were incapable of making the effort needed. Others, who had proved their worth in the Resistance, were less suited to peacetime politics, or had to concentrate first on their own livelihood. Those who were able to go into political life had to compete with professionals of the older generation. In no country was the Resistance able to organize and maintain itself as an independent and united post-war party, partly for such reasons as these, and partly because during the war the various groups, minimizing contacts between one another for reasons of security and differing in their ideas concerning post-war reform, had seen themselves primarily as the fighting fronts of traditional anti-Fascist parties. This was particularly true of the Communists, but it also applied to the Socialists and Christian Democrats, who proceeded after the war to reconstruct their parties on the old model. The most significant attempts to form a peacetime Resistance party as such were Parri's Partito d'Azione in Italy, the Union Démocratique Belge under Paul M. G. Lévy, and the Nederlandse Volksbeweging. But events showed that to make Europe the goal of their foreign policy, as the first two of these did, was not enough to establish a viable party, while their domestic programme, combining humanist and Christian traditions with Socialism in the spirit of the Resistance, struck people as a somewhat incongruous mixture. These parties never won more than 3 per cent of the poll in any country in the first post-war elections, because it seemed safer to vote for one of the traditional internationalist parties against the Right. And in France de Gaulle prevented the formation of a party reflecting Resistance ideas by using Maurice Schumann to bring to heel the MRP, which at first showed signs of developing along those lines.[401]

5. The Communist parties in particular were quick to re-establish their monolithic party structures; they endeavoured to sabotage as far as possible any post-war organization of Resistance members which they could not dominate as a subordinate unit of their own party, and did their best to claim the whole Resistance myth for themselves, while at the same time reinterpreting it as a purely national movement in each country. They opposed the idea of European unity, in Eastern Europe with strong-arm methods and in Western Europe with every conceivable nationalist slogan, and exploited the fact that post-liberation euphoria could only find an

---

[401] Cf. nn. 43–5, 99, 221, and 345 f. to this chapter; summaries in H. Brugmans, *L'Idée européenne 1918–1965* (= Cahiers de Bruges N.S. 12), Bruges, 1965, pp. 82–4; D. W. Urwin, *Western Europe since 1945*, pp. 8–13 and 17 f.

outlet in nationalist channels. The superpowers offered no alternative, and this in turn was due to the Soviet attitude towards European reconstruction.[402] In most liberated countries the Communist party was part of a government coalition up to 1947, and its ministers did their best to veto any discussion about uniting Europe.

6. The most successful move, relatively speaking, was the support given to the European idea by Resistance fighters within the democratic new party groups that had taken shape in 1943-4, when the prestige of the Resistance was at its height and hopes of a federal Europe after the war had not been dashed. A surprising number of Social Democratic, Christian Democratic, and Liberal groups and programmes proclaimed the need to unite Europe and readiness to hand over sovereignty to international institutions. Former members of the underground who were in favour of a federal Europe managed to win a majority in the leadership of the French Socialist Party when it was refounded by Daniel Mayer and others, and also in the leadership of Italy's Democrazia Cristiana with De Gasperi and his colleagues. But since, in view of the superpowers' inflexible opposition, these policies had to remain on paper with no prospect of being put into practice, and since it was imperative to bring order into the economic and administrative chaos and to carry on with home politics in every sense of the word, including jockeying for position in the forthcoming elections, the pro-Europeans with their plans found themselves in a kind of vacuum.[403]

Either the pro-European politicians had to go through almost two years of 'hard sledding' while engaged in the Sisyphean task of national restoration (like De Gasperi), or they lost the leadership of their party (like Daniel Mayer in the autumn of 1946). The older professionals regained the upper hand – either those who, having avoided both collaboration and resistance, now wanted to be back in the centre of the stage, or their colleagues who had returned from exile (especially in the Netherlands, Belgium, and Gaullist France). The most that the supporters of European unity could achieve at this time was the resolution in which the French Assembly unanimously requested the great powers to form 'an international organization which will lead the community of states towards a federation of free nations within which regional unions will not run the risk of giving rise to antagonistic blocs.'[404]

7. Since there was no sign of European unity coming about, even in a rudimentary form, because of superpower opposition with the acquiescence of the British and French governments, and because urgent priority had to

[402] Cf. pp. 59 f. and 69 of Introduction, also pp. 441-56 with supporting evidence.
[403] Cf. pp. 227 f. and 252 f. for the foreign-policy parts of the programmes and declarations of the French and Italian parties and their situation. More detailed analyses of party structures and ideologies in the various countries will follow in chapter IV. An instructive article is G. A. Almond, 'The Resistance and the Political Parties of Western Europe' in *Political Science Quarterly*, No. 62 (Columbia, New Jersey, 1947), pp. 27-61.
[404] Cf. n. 253 to this chapter; for a more detailed interpretation Lipgens, 'Innerfranzösische Kritik' (n. 247), pp. 152-8.

be given to economic revival, the great majority of the population fell back into traditional modes of thought. Up to the end of the war, thanks to the defeat of the nation states and the years of occupation, there was a lack of confidence in traditional political models and a readiness to accept change. But since in Europe's 'Year Zero' not even the suggestion of any practical alternative was permitted, it inevitably happened that (as right-wing, Gaullist, and Communist forces desired) nationalist thinking, which had for a time lost faith in itself, began to recover its hold. In fact the parties and the reinstated governments, which had to bow to the superpowers on questions of the peace settlement, had no choice but to adapt themselves realistically to the arrangements which those powers imposed.

The established pro-European associations could still hope that in the long run the whole process of Europe's self-awareness and the plans put forward by the Resistance could not be stifled so easily, but until the autumn of 1946 they had to accept defeat in their efforts to co-ordinate the pro-European forces in every party, and to realize that they had underrated the time and trouble needed for a true understanding to win the day against inveterate mental habits, particularly when such habits were supported by powerful external vetoes.

(B) AN ILLUSORY ALTERNATIVE: THE MFE IN 1946

It is not surprising that in these very unpropitious circumstances illusory ideas prevailed for a time in the Italian MFE, which had been especially optimistic as to the possibility of a European federation being imposed on the post-war *tabula rasa* at an early date. Altiero Spinelli, the leading personality among the founders of the MFE, managed in the first few weeks after the war – and this was his second great achievement – to reject this self-deception as far as he himself was concerned and to acknowledge that hopes of imminent success were misleading because of the attitude of the two superpowers. Spinelli also recognized that thinking in terms of nation states had proved much more tenacious than had been expected, and that a campaign of painstaking attrition would have to be carried on inside the states and parties if the old modes of thought were to be overcome. A minority of perceptive people in the association agreed with his diagnosis;[405] but it was naturally difficult for the rank and file of an association of this kind to have to admit that the fulfilment of their ideal was, for the time being at least, quite outside the bounds of possibility.

Immediately after the German surrender MFE made a significant advance in both numbers and organization. This was especially true of North Italy, where it opened a number of 'permanent offices in Milan, Turin and various provincial towns. It produced the weekly paper *L'Unità*

---

[405] For the foundation and activity of the MFE up to the summer of 1945, see chap. 1/2, pp.108–17, Spinelli's views are given in detail at the end of this chapter, p. 278 f.

europea. It received many applications during the first few weeks of liberation ... Quite spontaneously and all over the country federal groups are being formed which come and ask for advice and want to affiliate to the MFE.'[406] Old and new members of the Milan and Turin branches of MFE held a conference at Milan on 9–10 September 1945 with representatives of an 'Associazione Federalisti Europei' formed in Bologna and Florence under the leadership of a Resistance fighter named Paride Baccarini, together with one representative from Aosta. The Associazione joined MFE *en bloc*, its branches becoming local branches of MFE. A policy resolution proposed by Aldo Garosci in the name of the original members, including Spinelli, was passed by a majority. A draft supported in the main by new members and sponsored by Umberto Campagnolo, professor at the University of Padua, was narrowly defeated; this called in militant language for the masses to be mobilized and for an avant-garde to be formed to carry out a 'federalist revolution'. Garosci's resolution, by contrast, since the setting-up of a federation was not practical politics in the existing state of the world, provided for (a) the creation of a study-centre for a closer examination of the problem; (b) 'mobilization of public opinion' – a concession to Campagnolo, but qualified by the words: 'in support of federalist activities undertaken by the political parties'; (c) pressure on parties and governments in favour of federalist solutions of current questions. Spinelli defended this programme on the ground that:[407]

As it was 'impossible to put federalist ideas into practice for the time being', they should 'not try to mobilize the masses, for once we had won their backing we should not be able to find anything for them to do right away'. Rather, 'Our main task is to win over the leaders of the progressive parties for the federalist programme by co-operating with their commissions for foreign affairs and, in due course, with the Consultative and Constituent Assemblies.'

Partly because Spinelli, Rossi, and others of the original founders thought it best in the prevailing situation to withdraw from active co-operation in MFE and devote themselves entirely to working for the Partito d'Azione, of which Spinelli became secretary-general in 1946,[408] the Campagnolo wing managed to organize an MFE conference in Florence

---

[406] Letter from the General Secretariat of the Partito d'Azione (probably by Spinelli, cf. n. 408), dated 7.8.1945, to the CIFE, Paris; English translation in *Federal News*, No. 127, Oct. 1945, p. 9 f.; confirmed by appropriate documents, forms of membership, applications, etc. in *MFE Archive*, Turin. Cf. also p. 277 for numbers of members.

[407] Report on the conference, with texts of both resolutions, by Prof. Francesco Lo Bue, Turin, a member of the Campagnolo wing, in *L'Unità europea*, No. 1, 10.10.1945, p. 3; the journal was able to resume production after three months of non-appearance thanks to Lo Bue and to Augusto Monti. A temporary committee was formed which reflected the balance of opinion, half of those chosen being from the original group of founders, half from elected representatives of the branches. Garosci's text is in the following passage with Spinelli's gloss; see his letter of 7.8.1945 to the CIFE (cf. n. 406).

[408] The object was to concentrate on the struggle for a republican form of government and to get Italy's conditions for a European democracy accepted. Cf. L. Levi and S. Pistone, *Trent'anni di vita del Movimento Federalista Europeo*, Milan, 1973, p. 78.

on 8 and 9 January 1946 and so arranged its composition that they commanded a majority. The main speech, delivered by Campagnolo himself, urged the peoples of Europe to mobilize their forces in order to establish a federation and not to rely on the governments, which were as inept as they had been after the First World War. In this spirit the majority adopted a four-point resolution: (1) the movement must be strengthened by having a bigger mass impact, (2) pressure should be brought to bear on the parties to adopt measures favouring federation, (3) awareness of Europe was to be intensified among the public at large, (4) support must be recruited from all social classes.[409] The ideas behind this resolution are evident from Campagnolo's writings:

In 1938 he had published a book in Paris which denied the possibility of international law so long as there existed as many kinds of international law as there were states, each believing itself to be the supreme authority.[410] In *Repubblica federale europea*, written in February 1945, he had concluded that states could never establish a peaceful world order because they were 'evil by nature, striving for conquest and war'; they must therefore be replaced by a republic embracing the whole of Europe. 'The formation of a federal state implies the radical negation of the legality of member states' (p. 61). This federal union would be the expression of a true human society which had abolished the barriers formed by states; it should be divided not into member countries but into all-European parties. The federation could not be set up by the nation states but must grow from the revolutionary will of the people. The understanding of Europe possessed by a few must be converted into the political desire of the majority by means of a network of periodicals and newspapers, which must also bring about the unity of international parties; the latter would then organize a European plebiscite and convene a constituent assembly. The initiative must in any event spring from the people, even if it meant going against the wishes of politicians. Here was obviously a passionate Europeanism, but one not free from contradictions, and, as reviewers pointed out, of an excessively centralist kind.[411] A further problem was that Campagnolo with equal

---

[409] Report on the conference in *L'Unità europea*, no. 7, Turin, 20.1.1946, p. 1 f. To prepare for the national congress a committee of eleven, chaired by Campagnolo, Prof. Dal Pra, and Dr G. Usellini, was appointed to direct the movement, the study-centre in Florence, and the organizational centre in Milan until the congress met. This amounted to a take-over by the Campagnolo wing, since only Usellini belonged to the founding group. Cf. MFE, Organizing Committee, Circular No. 4 (on the results of Florence, from the MFE Archive, Turin): 'What is of vital importance, in fact the only task which we have to tackle at the moment, is to increase the number of members as much as possible.'

[410] U. Campagnolo, *Nations et droit ou le développement de l'état*, Paris, 1938. review by H. Wehberg in *Die Friedens-Warte*, no. 38, 1938, p. 262.

[411] U. Campagnolo, *Repubblica federale europa. Unificazione giuridica dell'Europa*, Milan, 1945, 130 pp. Cf. the generally critical reviews: P. V. in *Die Friedens-Warte*, no. 45, 1945, p. 503 f.; A. Monti in *L'Unità europea*, No. 11, Turin, 5.6.1946, p. 1 ('a remedy which, taken without care, can kill rather than cure the patient'); A. Chiti-Batelli in *Il Ponte*, Oct. 1946, pp. 912–14. For a summary of Campagnolo's arguments, see *L'Action fédéraliste européenne*, No. 1, July 1946, pp. 54–61, in which the editor L. van Vassenhove also commented that he did not agree with Campagnolo's premiss of 'indivisible sovereignty', since it was the reverse of federalistic.

enthusiasm advocated the membership of Russia as well as of Britain, in other words the Soviet Union as a state would have to be demolished by its own people.[412]

Campagnolo's committee having made the preparations, the MFE's first national congress met in Venice from 5 to 7 October 1946, and an argument between the two wings soon developed. A minority argued strongly for cultivating good relations with as many party leaders as possible, so that the Italian government would in the end announce its readiness to hand over many of its sovereign rights to a European federal regime. Campagnolo's supporters, on the other hand, contended that the goal could be reached only if the politicians had their hands forced by the mobilized masses, i.e. by a popular opposition movement. By presenting this argument as one between 'minimalists and maximalists', 'conservatism and progress', and suggesting that the conservatives 'did not appear to be genuine federalists at all', Campagnolo's group once again won a majority for its 'maximalist' programme.[413] For the rest, the congress spent most of its time working out constitutional statutes for the association which would be acceptable to both sides. A national steering committee of twelve was then elected, which, having a pro-Campagnolo majority, appointed him to the post of secretary-general. A report on organization showed that the association at this time had something over 6,000 paid-up members in at least a hundred towns.[414] which made it by far the largest body of its kind. But while its aims were clearly defined, it possessed neither tactics nor strategy; it was radicalism without any realistic policy in relation to the existing situation, which it completely ignored. So from the autumn of 1946 to the middle of 1947 the MFE was unable to make headway. When, on top of that, Campagnolo failed to recognize the transformation of the international situation brought about by the announcement of the Marshall Plan and continued to call for the abolition of Western as well as Eastern statehood by means of a 'European revolution', a policy which had absolutely nothing to do with reality, signs of dissolution appeared. Individual branches broke

---

[412] Cf. U. Campagnolo, *Speech at the Conference of the Ivrea Branch of the MFE on 4.11.45* (leaflet in *MFE Archive*, Turin), p. 15 f.; 'Russian civilization is basically European . . . Democracy [there] is not developed as it is in our country, but it is not apostate.' Campagnolo also appeared at Hertenstein; H. Brugmans in 'Het begin van een beweging' (n. 100) ('The Beginning of a Movement'), p. 15, recalls that: 'He advocated a completely unitary Europe. He didn't last long at our congress . . . to nobody's great regret.' An acquaintance described Campagnolo as an imposing figure who, however, indulged in wild talk and took any criticism personally. (Information from Pistone on 10.11.1974.)
[413] Cf. detailed report on the congress in *L'Unità europea*, No. 19-20, Turin, 25.10.1946; the categories quoted are mentioned in the introduction to it by A. Monti. A Spinelli in his later introduction to the first volume of his collected writings (*Dagli stati sovrani agli Stati Uniti d'Europa*, Florence, 1950, p. 4) put it most succinctly '. . . that European federation will either be the work of the political leadership or it will not come about at all'.
[414] Cf. the booklet *The First National Congress of the MFE in Venice, Survey of Proceedings, 5-7.10.46* (seven pages in MFE Archive, Turin) with the text of the statutes (to which we shall return in connection with the reorganization of the association on p. 632) and with the report on organization delivered by De Col about the state of membership (p. 7).

away from the MFE, four other Italian federalist groups were formed, and so on, until in September 1947 Spinelli set about reorganizing the association with the help of its original founders.[415]

(C) CLEAR ASSESSMENTS OF THE SITUATION

On 6 January 1946 Spinelli addressed an 'open letter' to Campagnolo's MFE conference at Florence. In retrospect this letter is seen to have been a remarkably sober and realistic analysis of the situation at that time. The majority of the conference were unable to emulate Spinelli's realism, but the terms of his letter, supplemented from other documents, may stand here as an appropriate summary, in brief and clear language, of the almost insuperable difficulties which faced the European federalists during the first post-war year.

'If we do not want to become a small clique of people with our heads in the clouds, we must frankly acknowledge that our prediction and consequently our programme have proved to be mistaken.' This prediction, so emphatically expressed by the foundation group of the MFE in 1941–3, but also to be found in many Resistance texts in other countries, was that when the German armies that had crushed most of the Continental states themselves collapsed, Europe would find itself in a crisis situation in which hardly any state structures would survive; consequently the clear-sighted men of the Resistance, supported by popular repugnance against the former system of national states which had caused so much suffering, would be able, free and unencumbered from outside, to establish a federal organization for peace in Europe.[416] In much the same way, the Socialists of 1849 had seen their expectations suddenly dashed;

'or, to take a more august analogy, our situation is like that of the early Christians when their prediction of the imminent end of the world, and thus their original programme, came to nothing. Our vision of a Europe in which all state structures would have collapsed, but the peoples would be free to decide their destiny in freedom, has not materialized. The great powers have preserved the old state structures except in the case of Germany, and together have deprived the European nations of the right to decide their own destiny over the whole range of international relations, in part even over their domestic affairs.'[417]

[415] On this point see the continuation of the section on Italy in chap. III/6, pp. 628–33. Cf. the pamphlet by E. Rossi sent to all other branches in the name of the Rome branch, preparing them for changes within the association, entitled *Il Movimento federalista europeo in Italia* (two pages, end of Sept. or beginning of Oct. 1947, *Spinelli Archive*): 'In this way propaganda for the federalist idea, having lost all relevance to the present international situation, has for a year or two had virtually no appeal to politicians, who alone could make it a reality.' Cf. also the report in A. A. Young, 'Federalism in Italy' in *Federal News,* No. 148, July 1947, p. 8.

[416] Compare the passages quoted in nn. 51 and 52 to this chapter under the heading 'Plan of Campaign'; also the later reference by Spinelli (*L'Europa non cade dal cielo,* Bologna, 1960, p. 22): The European federalists in the Resistance movement had naturally assumed that after the war Europe would continue to be an autonomous centre of world politics, the USA withdrawing across the Atlantic and Russia behind its frontiers.

[417] A. Spinelli, *Il Movimento federalista europeo e la realtà politica dell'ora.* Open letter to participants at the MFE convention in Florence, dated 6.1.1946, printed in *L'Unità europea,* No. 7, Turin, 20.1.1946, p. 2.

These words were a realistic acknowledgement of the first major factor in the European situation after May 1945: viz. the predominance of the two world powers, which controlled the frontiers, the economies, and the fate of the European countries and were not in the least interested in their unification. Spinelli continued:

In broad terms Europe can be said to be at present divided into: 1. an Eastern Europe directly ruled by the USSR, 2. a Western Europe predominantly under American influence, 3. a weakened and inward-looking Britain which is attempting to construct a Socialist economy, and 4. a Germany split into four parts, none of which can survive on its own. In these circumstances it is meaningless to speak of European federal union, for Europe lacks any centripetal force.[418]

Earlier, in June 1945, Spinelli had analysed the situation as follows:—

The liberated countries have not been allowed to manage their own affairs, but have been systematically occupied, controlled and put in tutelage by the three great powers, which ... have in every case restored the states to what they were before the Nazi aggression. The great powers too have for the time being deprived them *de facto* or *de jure* of any possibility of developing their own foreign policy. The consequence of this tutelage exercised on the Continent by the USSR, the USA and Britain is that the European countries have at present no opportunity of exercising any initiative. The first acts of Europe's post-war history will be performed not by the European nations but by the concerted action of the three great powers, and anything attempted without them would be no more than a storm in a teacup ... That is why the integration of the European nations into one free community can take place only when the great powers have reached a settlement which allows the European nations, or at least a considerable number of them, to regain some freedom of action, so that they can give thought to joint efforts to achieve their common destiny.[419]

---

[418] Ibid. Clear assessments of this kind are to be found also in other contemporary authors: e.g. Raymond Aron in an essay dated May 1945 expressed even more emphatically Europe's growing domestic and intellectual dependence. Europe was henceforth dominated by the extra-European continental-size states; in the European countries domestic policy had become a mere reflection of the 'great powers', for 'there is a tendency to associate every great power with this or that ideology or social system, these or those men and parties. As a result the struggle between ideologies, men, parties and systems is bound to appear, so to speak, as a microcosm of global relations between the super-powers. Agreement between the great powers means internal peace for the small, and the converse is equally true. . . . Compromise between the divergence influences of the Western empires and the Russian empire will come about in a different way in each particular case. The forms of democracy – elections, multiplicity of parties – will provide the framework: according as the countries concerned are neighbours of Russia or situated close to British bases, the pluralism will be more or less genuine, the rights of minorities or of the opposition will be more or less respected, the left or right wing parties more or less strong'. (Published in R. Aron (ed.), *L'Âge des empires et l'avenir de la France*, Paris, July 1945, pp. 363 and 366 f.).

[419] A. Spinelli, 'Bilancio federalista nel giugno 1945' in *L'Unità europea*, No. 12, Milan, 17.6.1945, p. 1 (repr., see note 58 to this chapter). Soon afterwards F. Bondy (*Cahier de la fédération européenne*, No. 2, Paris, August 1945, p. 22 f.) concluded similarly as follows: 'If Europe's anarchy is not got rid of by Europe itself, there will always be an excuse for foreign intervention, which will only increase tension between the intervening powers.' This fact might be an inducement to the superpowers to permit Europeans to unite. 'Will the superpowers do so? If their real aim is peace, which is in their own interest, they must be perturbed by the re-establishment of a Europe based on balance-of-power principles. To re-establish Europe as an anarchy of different nationalisms or a pattern of satellite states means creating a battlefield for the next generation. Peace must be built

The second major factor, if possible an even more stubborn threat to the concept of federal integration, was, Spinelli argued, the relative ease with which so many people in the parties and governments accepted the restoration of the nation-state. The real obstacle lay not in the 'more or less temporary phase of tutelage, in which the Continent now finds itself' but in 'the difficulty of getting the European nations and above all their governing classes to regard national problems as aspects of the whole European community, instead of which, by an automatic reflex, they see problems of international co-operation as merely aspects of their own national power'.

In spite of all the convulsions brought by the war, 'it is, for example, difficult to find people in France who set themselves the task of achieving peaceful co-operation with a revived Germany and are not simply concerned with occupying the Rhineland and the coal-mines of the Ruhr; or anyone in Italy or Yugoslavia who is prepared to play down the importance of the frontiers instead of agitating about Trieste and making it an apple of discord.' What Europe needed was an earthquake of the spirit. 'It is true that deep fissures already exist in the minds of all politicians of the different countries and of the masses who follow them. But these are fissures that are not yet visible, and of which people themselves are hardly aware. Time will be needed to bring them to the surface. Today everyone is anxious to improve this or that aspect of national life, but they fail to recognize that national problems can only be solved on the basis of supernatural premisses ... The chief task of the federalist movement is to liberate men's political consciousness from rigid nationalist traditions so that they can understand events properly and build on them with federalist vision.'[420]

Finally, as against the hypnotic attraction of the 'One World' concept as an answer to the longing for peace, Spinelli already saw in the burgeoning East–West conflict a growing obstacle to European unification. Unlike other clear-sighted observers such as Röpke, he was in no hurry to equate the concept of federalism with that of policy for the West, although this inevitably meant a further trial of patience for the federalist movement.

'Today one can only speak of federation in Europe if one means a federation of the Western countries, leaving the whole area east of a line from Trieste to Lübeck

---

into the very structure of Europe in such a way that it does not have to be imposed by continual arbitration or last-minute intervention.'

[420] A. Spinelli, 'Bilancio' (note 419): similarly in the Open Letter (note 417): 'In our view federalism as a method is more alive today than ever . . . limitation of national sovereignty is the major postulate of any further development of civilization. The task of the federalist movement must be to form a federal political consciousness which is destined to supersede the existing national consciousness.' A striking example of clear-sightedness was given by Daniel Villey, professor at the faculty of economics, Poitiers, in his 'serenade without hope' written on 23 October 1945 to a friend who had been elected a member of the French Constituent Assembly: 'Follow a right-wing economic policy, create a radical [i.e. liberal] constitution, pursue a socialist foreign policy and an MRP domestic policy. . . . The best constitution in my view would be as follows: Article 1. The French Republic makes the sovereign decision to renounce its sovereignty, in order to federate with the other nations of Western Europe.' (D. Villey, *Redevenir des hommes libres*. Paris, 1946, p. 290)

to be organized under the Soviet aegis. But this would mean reconciling ourselves in advance with what is certainly a grave threat, but not yet a certainty... Nothing should be left undone at the present time to bring about a peaceful *modus vivendi* between the USA and the USSR: the European contribution to this must consist in turning Europe into a neutral zone between the two or three great powers, and enlarging this zone as much as possible. It is dangerous to interfere in the diplomatic efforts that are still going on by putting forward premature plans for federation which would only have the effect of stiffening Soviet opposition.'[421]

These words summed up what was to become the decisive question of the second post-war year.

---

[421] From Spinelli's Open Letter (note 417). On the idea of Western integration as formulated in the spring of 1945 by W. Röpke, cf. in detail H. P. Schwarz, *Vom Reich*... (note 318), esp. p. 398 f.

CHAPTER II

Revival of Plans for Federation: the 'Third Force' as an Element in the Organization of World Peace (June 1946 – May 1947)

1. Beginnings of Visible Crisis in the Joint Policy of the Superpowers

While the press and public opinion, especially in Western Europe, were still largely convinced of the 'unity of purpose' of the superpowers, their sharing of a co-imperium over Europe and their plans for a peace-keeping organization, awareness of a crisis in their mutual relations began to spread at the top level, though the expressions of this awareness did not become public in the first half of 1946. It began to be realized that postwar planning had only led to meagre results and chiefly to agreement on negative matters, such as punitive measures against Germany (in a 'transitional' period) and the policy of preventing the UN from acquiring supranational authority: the functioning of the world organization had been made dependent on co-operation between the superpowers, but the latter had not made co-operation the primary basis of their policy. The first General Assembly of the UN in January 1946 had clearly demonstrated this weakness and also the large number of contentious issues, the solution of which was no easier now that the common enemy had been destroyed.[1] Voices were soon heard like that of the World Council of Churches at its first post-war congress: 'Mankind's hopes for a better world have not been realized. Millions have to undergo intolerable suffering. The nations do not seem able to cope with the vital problems of international order.' Voices such as these remained isolated, however, and

---

[1] Cf. above, chapter I/1, pp. 93–107, the outline of the situation resulting from the policy of the two superpowers is here extended for a further period of twelve months. For the term 'co-imperium' cf. Introduction, n. 141. The message of the World Council of Churches, issued at its Geneva congress of 23 February 1946, is back-translated.

it was generally hoped that the peace conferences and treaties announced for the early summer of 1946 would mean final success in the organization of peace. Only when this hope proved illusory and the differences became public in July 1946 did the European public experience the shock and consequent reactions described in further sections of this Chapter.[2]

(A) THE PREVENTIVE POLICY OF THE USSR

Around the turn of the year 1945/6 the US and Soviet leaders began to realize that co-operation between the victors of the Second World War might not be long-lived and that the symptoms of crisis that had already appeared in their relationship, from Yalta to Moscow, were perhaps not transient but were based on permanent interests and opposing attitudes that it would not be easy to reconcile. Either despite or because of Byrnes's conciliatory behaviour at the Moscow conference, it was the Soviet leaders who, at the beginning of 1946, apparently first came to the conclusion that while co-operation might work for a while, it was unlikely to be long-lived. The Russians began to base their policy on the idea that confrontation with the Americans was inevitable, with the result that some members of the US Administration likewise came to expect a confrontation with the USSR and to adopt a tougher line in consequence.

The Soviet Union, brought by the war to the brink of economic collapse, saw itself confronted by a strong America and an American economy expanding on a global scale; and the events of 1945 had shown that the Americans would not go out of their way to assist Soviet recovery or accept without question Soviet methods of safeguarding their interests in Eastern Europe. These facts seemed to confirm the latent belief, always present in the minds of the Soviet leaders, that 'capitalist' states were warlike and aggressive by nature. The dictatorial Soviet regime was, moreover, imbued with a craving for security, a kind of persecution mania brought about by the experiences of the Civil War, the traumatic effect of the great purges, and the German attack of 1941. The result of all this was that Stalin and his associates, analysing the world situation at the end of the

---

[2] On the general development of East–West relations in 1946 see relevant chapters of J. Lukacs, *A History of the Cold War*, Garden City, NY, 1966[2]; M. F. Herz, *Beginnings of the Cold War*, Bloomington, Ind., 1966; E. O. Czempiel, *Das amerikanische Sicherheitssystem 1945–1949*, Berlin, 1966 (esp. pp. 131–85); A. Fontaine, *Histoire de la guerre froide*, 2 vols., Paris, 1965/7; H. Feis, *From Trust to Terror, The Onset of the Cold War 1945–1950*, New York, 1970. For the 'revisionist' viewpoint, see W. A: Williams, *The Tragedy of American Diplomacy*, New York, 1962; W. La Feber, *America, Russia and the Cold War 1945–1966*, New York, 1967; J. and G. Kolko, *The Limits of Power. The World and United States Policy 1945–1954*, New York, 1972. 'Realistic' and more balanced: L. J. Halle, *The Cold War as History*, London/New York, 1967; J. L. Gaddis, *The United States and the Origins of the Cold War 1941–1947*, New York, 1972; A. B. Ulam, *The Rivals. America and Russia since World War II*, London/New York, 1974[2]. For a critique of the sometimes crude political argumentation of some revisionists, see J. L. Richardson, 'Cold-War Revisionism. A Critique' in *World Politics*, 14 (1972), pp. 579–612; Robert J. Maddox, *The New Left and the Origins of Cold War*, Princeton (UP), 1973. For a review of the state of the discussion, see bibliographical notes in R. S. Kirkendall (ed.), *The Truman Period as a Research Field. A Reappraisal 1972*, Columbia, Mo., 1974.

war, drew the conclusion – as far as their motives can be judged without first-hand evidence – that the Soviet Union was once more threatened, potentially if not acutely; that its defensive capacity must be restored, and that it must establish itself in the most favourable strategic positions in case a new confrontation took place [3] The five-year plan for 1946–50, and the Soviet government's presentation of it to the Russian people in the spring of 1946, were inspired by these three considerations.

As Molotov explained in an electoral speech in Moscow on 6 February 1946, it was not only a question of rebuilding the country but of 'overtaking and surpassing economically the most developed capitalist countries of Europe and the USA'. There must be vigilance against all enemies of peace, since 'in order finally to accomplish this major task we need a lengthy period of peace and of ensured security for our country'. Stalin, in his electoral speech on 9 February, referred still more clearly to the defence aspects of the recovery programme. To protect the Soviet Union against 'any accidents' would require 'perhaps three new five-year plans if not more. But this task can be accomplished, and we must accomplish it.' The plan in fact provided that by 1950 the pre-war level of industry and agriculture must at least be recovered, and rearmament must be pressed forward without respite. With this aim in view it was made clear to the Soviet population in the spring of 1946 that the exertions of war were not to be followed by a period of relaxation, but that all the nation's energies must once more be deployed to the uttermost.[4]

In addition to restoring the defences of the Soviet Union itself, attempts were made to extend as far as possible the outposts of Soviet security not only in Eastern Europe but also in the Middle East, the Mediterranean, and the Far East. In northern Iran Soviet forces were stationed for the duration of the war under a British–Soviet–Iranian treaty of 1942, which provided that they were to be withdrawn not later than six months after the cessation of hostilities. In the autumn of 1945, when the time for withdrawal was close at hand, these forces began to foment and encourage a northern Iranian separatist movement. Troops sent by the Tehran government to suppress the movement were hampered by the Soviet forces. On 1 March 1946 the Soviet government announced its intention of keeping its troops in Iran after the agreed withdrawal date 'until the situation is clarified'; meanwhile the 'Autonomous Republic of

---

[3] Cf. in particular M. D. Shulman, *Stalin's Foreign Policy Reappraised*, Cambridge, Mass., 1963; a basic historical account in A. B. Ulam, *Expansion and Coexistence. The History of Soviet Foreign Policy 1917–1967*, London, 1968; the best systematic analysis in J. F. Triska and D. D. Finley, *Soviet Foreign Policy*, New York, 1968; a comprehensive view in D. Geyer, 'Von der Kriegskoalition zum Kalten Krieg' in *Osteuropa-Handbuch, Sowjetunion Aussenpolitik Bd. I (1917–1955)*, Cologne/Vienna, 1972, pp. 343–81.

[4] V. M. Molotov, *Problems of Foreign Policy. Speeches and Statements, April 1945–November 1948*, Moscow, 1949, pp. 26–36; *Speeches by J. V. Stalin and V. M. Molotov delivered at Election Meetings in Moscow in February 1946*, Soviet News, London, 1946, pp. 17, 26 f. For the efforts involved in the completion of the Five-Year Plan, 1946–50, see *Geschichte der Sowjetunion, 1917–1957*, Berlin, 1960, pp. 659–75 (original: *Istoriya sovetskogo obshchestva v vospominaniyakh sovremennikov 1917–1957*, Moscow, 1958–61; no English translation exists).

Azerbaijan' and the 'Kurdish People's Republic' had been proclaimed with Soviet connivance. While thus asserting its influence in the Middle East, the Soviet Union renewed its claim to bases in the Straits and also demanded from Turkey the cession of the East–Anatolian districts of Kars and Ardahan. In the Greek civil war, which entered an acute phase in March 1946 with partisan activity in the northern part of the country, the Soviet Union not only countenanced the provision of military aid to the Communist partisans by Tito's Yugoslavia but also gave propaganda and diplomatic support to the rebels. As far back as the Potsdam conference the Russians had laid claim to a trusteeship over the former Italian colony of Tripoli and to major units of the Italian fleet. Altogether, the southern flank of the Soviet empire was to be strategically secured by a Near Eastern and Mediterranean policy on classical Tsarist lines.[5] The Soviet Union also intensified its policy of safeguarding military interests in Asia. In Korea the Soviet troops refused to allow the Americans any say in the administration of their zone, and soon shut off the northern area against any political or economic influence from the south. In Manchuria the Soviet leaders used their troops to transfer huge quantities of industrial plant to the Soviet Union; under a Soviet–Chinese agreement the troops were supposed to be withdrawn in November 1945, but they did not in fact leave, after many postponements, until the beginning of May 1946.[6]

Above all, from February 1946 onwards Stalin took intensive measures to complete the subjection of the East-European states to the Soviet Union – the more so as, in the next two months, he had to yield to increasing American opposition in the Mediterranean and Iran. In the occupied countries of Eastern and South-Eastern Europe the key positions, especially the ministries of the interior, were already safely in the hands of Moscow-trained Communists. A few 'loyal' representatives of the opposition parties, without real influence, were allowed to remain in office or were even co-opted at a later stage, in accordance with a promise made to the Americans in Moscow in December 1945; this was ostensibly to demonstrate Russo-American co-operation, but in fact it discouraged the anti-Communist opposition. Then came increasingly ruthless pressure on the non-Communist parties and other organizations by the secret police, under Soviet control and backed by the Red Army, which trampled

[5] Cf. D. Geyer, *Die Sowjetunion und der Iran*, Tübingen, 1955; J. E. Kovac, *Iran and the Beginning of the Cold War. A Case Study in the Dynamics of International Politics*, Ph.D. thesis, University of Utah, 1970; M. Sokolnicki, *The Turkish Straits*, Beirut, 1950; M. P. Caboiaux, 'La Turquie et ses relations avec l'Union Soviétique: Antécédents historiques et incidents sur l'engagement dans l'affrontement est–ouest' in *Chronique de la politique étrangère*, 19 (1966), pp. 619–730; S. G. Xydis, *Greece and the Great Powers, 1944–1947*, Thessaloniki, 1963; E. O'Ballance, *The Greek Civil War 1944–1949*, New York, 1966; P. Hiltebrandt, *Der Kampf ums Mittelmeer*, Stuttgart, 1953.

[6] Cf. M. Beloff, *Soviet Policy in the Far East 1944–1951*, London, 1953; Youn-Soo Kim, 'Die Teilung Koreas am 38. Breitengrad' in *Politische Studien März-April 1970*, pp. 164–71; F. C. Jones, H. Borton, and B. R. Pearn, *The Far East 1942–1946* (= *Survey of International Affairs 1939–1946*, Vol. 7), London, 1955; C. B. McLane, *Soviet Policy and the Chinese Communists 1931–1946*, New York, 1958.

human rights underfoot and deliberately created an atmosphere of terror. A phase of economic exploitation and the dismantling of productive capacity in the satellite countries was followed by an attempt to rebuild their economies on a Socialist basis and to consolidate them by planning, while attacking the middle class at its roots by expropriations of all kinds. A systematic policy of Sovietization was put in hand so as to destroy the variety of institutions and ideologies that still existed, and to make it possible for early 'elections' to show the desired degree of unanimity.[7] This whole process, in which the ousting and exile of non-Communist politicians played a major part, was closely connected with new waves of purges in the Soviet Union itself. As part of the effort to mobilize all the nation's forces, and for fear of the effects of Western ideas and ways of life, whole sections of the population were deported or arrested: 'deviationists' of all kinds, soldiers who had fought in the West, and the inhabitants of areas that had been under German occupation. Penal and labour camps were enlarged and multiplied, and before long the number of inmates reached a permanent figure of over ten million.[8] Naturally all these measures were kept as secret as possible; public opinion in Europe and elsewhere was assured that nothing of the kind was taking place, and much propaganda was devoted to extolling the democratic qualities of the East-European regimes. Stalin, who at this time did not want a major confrontation but was more concerned to consolidate his greatly expanded empire, lost no opportunity of reiterating his loyalty to the principle of co-operation and harmony among the 'Big Three'.

(B) HARDENING OF US POLICY

Stalin's policy of transforming the Soviet Union into a fortress capable of withstanding all dangers, and protected by a broad glacis of countries under direct Russian control, provoked American reactions of precisely the kind that it was his object to prevent. The sharp language of Molotov's and Stalin's election speeches, the increasing ruthlessness with which the Soviet Union consolidated its direct rule in Eastern and South-Eastern Europe, the ease with which it felt able to foment a revolutionary move-

---

[7] Cf. the comprehensive review in Geyer (n. 3), pp. 363-9, and detailed account in J. K. Hoensch, 'Sowjetische Osteuropapolitik 1945-1955' in *Osteuropa-Handbuch, Sowjetunion Aussenpolitik I*, Cologne/Vienna, 1972, pp. 382-447, especially 384-95. For the elections and further sovietization, see n. 22, and chap. II/7, pp. 446-55. The revisionist attempt to see all this as a policy of 'security' and not expansionism can only relate to the question of motivation, which was a complex one. It should not be allowed to conceal the fact that what actually took place was a tremendous expansion of Soviet power and the subjugation of neighbouring peoples, 'justified' of course, as in all such cases, on defensive grounds: e.g. Bismarck's annexation of Alsace-Lorraine 'so that French aggressive moves would have to start from further back', Poincaré's Rhineland policy as a glacis against the 'German threat', and so on.

[8] Cf. Z. Brzezinski, *The Permanent Purge*, Cambridge, Mass., 1956; M. Fainsod, *How Russia is Ruled*, Cambridge, Mass., 1963[2]; A. Dallin and G. Breslauer, *Political Terror in Communist Systems*, Stanford, 1970; R. A. Medvedev, *Let History Judge*, ed. D. Joravsky and G. Haupt, London, 1972.

ment in Iran, the ambitions it showed to establish positions of strength in the Mediterranean and Far East – all this was out of keeping with the picture of a Soviet system evolving towards democracy and realism, which had led opinion-forming circles in the US to support the idea of co-operation and 'one world'. It began to be suspected that the Soviet aim of world revolution was more than a mere empty formula. Pressure from strong groups of *émigrés* and exiles from Eastern Europe helped to give US public opinion the impression that the Truman administration had so far been too co-operative towards the Soviet Union and too careless of its own legitimate interests, and had shown undue readiness to abandon the cause of democracy and human rights in Eastern Europe.

Such voices of criticism and suspicion, however, clashed with expectations that had grown during the long years of war, encouraged by the Roosevelt administration and the Democratic majority of 'progressive internationalists', and that still dominated US public opinion at this date, barely six months after the end of the war. The hope was that the new international organization of the United Nations would bring about the realization of the American dream of a 'One World' system of peace and security in which the old 'European' tradition of power politics would no longer have a place, as conflicts would be resolved by a new type of international co-operation. The Democratic majority, including Secretary of State Byrnes, who had been an intimate of Roosevelt's for many years, was still determined to secure the co-operation of the Soviet Union by emphasizing its respect for the latter's security interests; its policy, while patiently endeavouring to remove 'misunderstandings', was to postpone decisions on controversial issues or, whenever possible, to settle them in the Russians' favour.

In a broadcast talk on 30 December 1945, after his return from the Moscow conference of Foreign Ministers, Byrnes gave a typical account of his policy of appeasement. Preparation for the peace conference was still less than ideal, 'but the departure from the ideal standard is more in the form than in the substance'. The agreements concerning Romania and Bulgaria were not all that could be desired, but they represented 'a substantial improvement in the democratic character of these governments'. The Foreign Ministers had reaffirmed 'the policy of non-interference in the internal affairs of China' and had in fact reached agreement on all questions except Iran. As to this: 'I do not wish to minimize the seriousness of the problem, but I am not discouraged.'[9]

One of the first members of the Administration who protested against this kind of self-deception and complaisance was President Truman, who,

[9] Text of Byrnes's broadcast in *Dept. of State Bulletin,* xiii (Dec. 30, 1945), pp. 1033–6. For the 'American dream' of a world peace organization superseding power politics, and for the persistence of Roosevelt's conception of 'One World', see works listed in chap. I/1, nn. 10–12, and the persuasive interpretation by M. Geiling, *Aussenpolitik und Nuklearstrategie. Eine Analyse des konzeptionellen Wandels der amerikanischen Sicherheitspolitik gegenüber der Sowjetunion 1945–1963,* Cologne/Vienna, 1975, pp. 17–25.

having studied the record of the Moscow conference, rightly came to the conclusion, as he later wrote, that 'the successes of the conference were unreal'. He wrote in his own hand a long 'Memorandum for conversation with Byrnes' and, according to his subsequent recollection, read this document out to Byrnes at the White House on 5 January 1946. In it he declared that he would not renounce the Presidential prerogative of taking key decisions in foreign policy; he complained that Byrnes had kept him insufficiently informed during the conference, and ended with an incisive criticism of the expansionist policy of Stalin and Molotov:

'I think we ought to protest with all the vigour of which we are capable against the Russian programme in Iran ... It is a parallel to the programme of Russia in Latvia, Estonia and Lithuania ...' At Potsdam he (the President) had been compelled by circumstances to accept Russian *faits accomplis*, although these were a 'high-handed outrage'. The Soviet proceedings in Iran were still more impudent. 'I do not think we should play compromise any longer... I'm tired of babying the Soviets.'

These critical words were subsequently much quoted, but it is overlooked in most accounts that Truman evidently did not utter them in this form on 5 January. We may believe Byrnes's later statement that 'Of course, such a letter was never sent to me, nor read to me. Had this occurred, with my deep conviction that there must be complete accord between the President and his Secretaty of State, I would have resigned immediately. My first knowledge of the "memorandum-letter" came with its appearance in the Hillman book.'[10] The most likely explanation of the discrepancy is as follows. Truman's political prestige in his first few months as President was not very great, partly because of the circumstances in which he had taken office, and he had no experience at all of foreign policy. No doubt he intended to convey to Byrnes the substance of the memorandum in which he expressed frustration at Soviet intransigence, and subsequently, after his acrimonious breach with Byrnes, he imagined he had actually done so. But in January 1946 he apparently expressed his discontent to the spokesman of the Democratic majority of 'progressive internationalists' in such a mild form that Byrnes, while promising to keep the President better informed in future, left the White House without realizing that Truman disapproved of the whole tenor of his policy.

In the same way, most accounts assign too early a date to the effect of the important 'long telegram' which George F. Kennan, counsellor at the American Embassy in Moscow, sent to the State Department on 22 February

[10] J. F. Byrnes, *All in One Lifetime*, New York, 1958, p. 402 f.; referring to W. Hillman, *Mr. President: The First Publication from the Personal Diaries, Private Letters and Revealing Interviews of Harry S. Truman*, New York, 1952, pp. 20–3. (Hillman remarks on p. 46 that Truman often wrote letters 'which he never sent but wished he had sent'.) See, on the other hand, H. S. Truman, *Memoirs*, Vol. i: *Year of Decisions, 1945*, New York, 1953, pp. 550–2, with full text of the 'Memorandum' of 5.1.1946 and author's comments. Cf. G. Curry, *James F. Byrnes* (= *The American Secretaries of State and their Diplomacy*, Vol. 14), New York, 1965, pp. 186–90.

1946. Washington had expressed surprise at indications that the Russians were unwilling to secure a promise of large-scale credits by adhering to the World Bank and the International Monetary Fund. In reply Kennan set forth a penetrating analysis of the 'sources of Soviet conduct' as evidenced by all Moscow's utterances.

'The U.S.S.R. still lives in antagonistic "capitalist encirclement" with which in the long run there can be no permanent peaceful coexistence ... Internal conflicts of capitalism inevitably generate wars.' It did not matter that this Soviet belief had 'little to do with conditions outside of Russia'; it arose 'mainly from basic inner-Russian necessities' and was the rationalization of an 'instinctive fear of the outside world' which a cruel dictatorship 'clothed in trappings of Marxism'. On all levels and in all questions, as Kennan showed in detail, the Soviet Union endeavoured to strengthen its own power and autarky and to diminish that of all other countries. 'We have here a political force committed fanatically to the belief that with the U.S. there can be no permanent *modus vivendi*, that it is desirable and necessary that the internal harmony of our society be disrupted, our traditional way of life be destroyed, the international authority of our state be broken, if Soviet power is to be secure.' Soviet power, however, unlike that of Hitlerite Germany, was not 'adventuristic' and was 'highly sensitive to the logic of force. For this reason it can easily withdraw – and usually does when strong resistance is encountered at any point.' What the European hoped for from America was 'guidance rather than responsibilities. We should be better able than the Russians to give them this.'

Kennan's analysis was circulated among senior members of the State Department, and in the atmosphere of growing uncertainty as to Soviet intentions it helped gradually to prepare the way for a change in America's foreign policy. It is unusual nowadays for a report from a fairly junior diplomat to have so much influence on events. In the spring of 1946, however, as one insider pertinently put it, 'The Kennan cable was harsh and disillusioning doctrine, much too disillusioning for early 1946 when the United States was not even ready for Churchill's Iron Curtain speech. Only during the succeeding months, as the Soviet acted ever more plainly the dark role which Kennan had assigned to it, did his words begin to count.'[11]

A stronger direct influence in the spring of 1946 was that of a speech by Senator Vandenberg, the foreign-policy spokesman of the Republican opposition. Addressing the Senate on 27 February, he drew sceptical conclusions from the proceedings of the first General Assembly of the UN. After outlining the course of Soviet expansionism since the war he put the question 'What is Russia up to now?' and urged that Soviet ambitions, which were evidently world-wide, must be met with firmness – with

---

[11] G. F. Kennan, *Memoirs 1925–1950,* Boston, 1967, pp. 292–5 for the circumstances, pp. 547–59 for verbatim extracts from the telegram. For the comment quoted in the text, see E. F. Goldman, *The Crucial Decade: America 1945–1955,* New York, 1955, p. 70 f. For Truman's change of attitude, which was only completed at the beginning of 1947, and for Kennan's part in it, cf. chap. III/1, pp. 463 f. and 475 f.

patience, but not with wavering irresolution. Under Vandenberg's influence a 'realist' group took shape within the Republican party; its powerful chairman, Senator Robert A. Taft, was a former isolationist and still advocated a 'free hand' policy, i.e. in practice he supported Byrnes's 'policy of postponement'. On the following day, however – the day before that on which Soviet troops were supposed to withdraw from Iran – Byrnes himself made a speech containing a surprisingly firm warning to 'our Soviet ally'. The US could not ignore 'a unilateral gnawing away at the *status quo*'; they did not wish to contribute in any way to dividing the world into blocks or spheres of influence, but 'we will not and we cannot stand aloof if force or the threat of force is used contrary to the purposes and principles of the UN Charter'. Byrnes expressly denied that the Great Powers had any right to maintain troops on the territory of other sovereign states without the latter's consent.[12] When the Russians declared on 1 March that they would nevertheless keep their troops in Iran, Byrnes permitted Churchill, the British opposition leader, who was then visiting the US, to give a clear indication of the position. Speaking at Fulton, Missouri, on 5 March, in Truman's presence and from a text which Byrnes had read beforehand, Churchill described the widespread disquiet aroused by Soviet policy and introduced the metaphor of the 'Iron Curtain':

> Nobody knows what Soviet Russia and its Communist international organization intend to do in the immediate future, or what are the limits, if any, to their expansive and proselytizing tendencies ... From Stettin in the Baltic to Trieste in the Adriatic, an iron curtain has descended across the Continent ... The Communist parties, which were very small in all these eastern states of Europe, have been raised to pre-eminence and power far beyond their numbers and are seeking everywhere to obtain totalitarian control ... I do not believe that Soviet Russia desires war. What they desire is the fruits of war and the indefinite expansion of their power and doctrines ... From what I have seen of our Russian friends and allies during the war, I am convinced that there is nothing they admire so much as strength, and there is nothing for which they have less respect than for military weakness.

This, however, did not mean that the US concurred in Churchill's assessment of the situation. Many representatives of American public opinion were shocked. A shower of protest came from pro-Roosevelt Democrats, senators, and the press. Three days later Byrnes stated at a press conference that he had not been 'consulted' about the speech, and, when asked whether the US 'associated itself' with Churchill's views, he replied that the US had nothing to do with them.[13]

---

[12] For Vandenberg's speech of 27.2.1946, cf. *The Private Papers of Senator Vandenberg*, Boston, 1952, pp. 246–9. For an excellent account of Taft see J. T. Patterson, *Mr. Republican: A Biography of Robert A. Taft*, Boston, 1972. Byrnes's speech of 28.2.1946 in *Dept. of State Bulletin*, xiv (10 March 1946), pp. 355–8.
[13] For Churchill's Fulton speech of 5.3.1946 see *Vital Speeches of the Day*, Vol. xii, No. 11 (15 March 1946), pp. 329–32 (and, for its conception, cf. chap. II/3, p. 318 f.). Speech read beforehand by

The line pursued by Roosevelt and after him by Byrnes had been called in question, but not replaced by a different policy. The idealistic belief that it was only necessary to dispel 'misunderstandings' to reach full unity of purpose with the Soviet Union began to fade away in the light of ruthless Soviet expansion; no other doctrine took its place, however, and irresolution made itself felt more and more. Under pressure from public opinion, the run-down of American forces continued; Truman had to put up with the 'frenzied demobilization' of over seven million men by August 1946, and was unable to persuade Congress to accept his plan for a new national security system with militia-type training for all men of military age. Thus by the end of 1946 the US army consisted of only about a million inexperienced troops, mostly young draftees, while the Soviet Union had under arms a good six million, mostly battle-seasoned troops. Churchill had put forward the idea of a joint 'Western' policy of containing the Soviet Union, but American policy in 1946 offered no support for such a plan, still less for the idea of European unity. From spring 1946 onwards the US government was resolved not to permit any significant further extension of the Soviet sphere of influence; but this new 'firmness' was no more than a vague reluctance, scarcely defined except in the case of Iran, to give in to further pressure, and did not amount to a new foreign policy.[14] Byrnes held fast to a policy of 'patience with firmness', the ultimate aim of which was, as before, reconciliation with the Soviet Union.

(C) BEGINNINGS OF PUBLIC CONTROVERSY: THE COUNCIL OF FOREIGN MINISTERS IN PARIS

Stalin reacted sharply to Churchill's Fulton speech in an interview on 14 March 1946, in which he called Churchill a 'warmonger' and compared him with Hitler. On the 22nd and the 25th, however, he gave further interviews that sounded accommodating and conciliatory, denying that there was any danger of war and maintaining that all differences were soluble.[15] The unexpectedly firm and unanimous reaction of other members of the Security Council on the question of Iran, and the unwelcome opposition to which it pointed, induced him to 'shorten the front' on this sector, and within barely a month the Soviet troops were withdrawn. It became evident, however, that Stalin was only disposed to yield on a point which

---

Byrnes, and by Truman on the journey to Fulton: see Curry (n. 10), pp. 203 and 369. Widespread condemnation of Churchill, see D. F. Fleming, *The Cold War and its Origins,* vol. i. New York, 1961, pp. 351–3. Byrnes's disavowal, see Curry, p. 204.

[14] For a comparative summary see Halle (n. 2), pp. 108–13, with demobilization figures on p. 110. These are given more precisely in A. Buchan and O. Windsor, *Arms and Stability in Europe,* London, 1963. The summing-up, 'Byrnes went to the limit to conciliate the Russians' is by his biographer Curry (n. 10), p. 312, already quoted more fully in chap. I/1, n. 12, similarly Geiling (n. 9), pp. 25–35.

[15] Answers to *Pravda* correspondent, 14.3.1946, and to E. Gilmore, 22.3.1946, in *J. V. Stalin on Post-War International Relations,* Soviet News, London, 1947, pp. 3–8 and 9–10; Russian text in Stalin, *Sochineniya,* Vol. 3 (xvi), Stanford, Calif., 1967, pp. 35–43 and 45 f.

the Americans clearly found unacceptable, and not in regard to other areas of Soviet expansion. The pace of Communist domination of the East-European countries was speeded up, and in the Soviet Zone of Germany the merger between the SPD and the KPD, which had been forced on since November 1945, was finally concluded on 21 April.

At the second meeting of the Council of Foreign Ministers, which began in Paris on 25 April 1946, the opposing attitudes clashed so openly that the public became aware of them for the first time. The Soviet Union pressed for high reparations claims to be embodied in the peace treaties with the ex-enemy states – Italy, Romania, Bulgaria, Hungary, and Finland – and for extensive Soviet rights of control to be sanctioned by international law. Both these demands were largely opposed by the American delegation and pressed with equal firmness by the Russians.[16] Once again it proved impossible to reconcile the American interest in free trade and the Soviet security in Eastern Europe, the American interest in long-term economic stabilization in Europe and the Russian interest in the direct use of reparations to rebuild the Soviet economy, and finally the strategic interest of both powers in Trieste. The first round of negotiations broke off on 15 May without any real progress having been achieved.

On the Western side the debates were not based on any more positive viewpoint than that of the struggle for control of borderline areas, disarmament, rights of colonial administration, and the object of enabling individual states to assert their right of self-determination against Soviet control. In the second round of negotiations, from 15 June to 12 July, an agreement was reached concerning the peace treaties with the former Axis allies on lines which differed as between Italy and the four East-European states, in accordance with the delimitation of American and Russian spheres of influence.[17] A uniform draft without too many controversial points was submitted to the peace conference of the twenty-one belligerents which met in Paris on 29 July. None of the parties, however, put forward any conception which transcended the division into spheres of influence. The discussion was purely in terms of nation states; no reference was made to a European peace organization or to the future of Europe as a whole. From this point of view the Paris meetings were as devoid of conceptional policy-making as Potsdam had been.

As a result, the confrontation in the sphere that affected both world powers, viz. the question of a peace treaty with Germany, was all the more violent. The dispute over the interpretation of the reparations provisions of the Potsdam Protocol had already led, in May 1946, to the suspension

---

[16] Cf. Second Sessions of the Council of Foreign Ministers, First Part, Paris, April 25–May 16, 1946, in *Foreign Relations of the United States (FRUS)*, Diplomatic Papers, 1946, Vol. 2, Washington, 1970, pp. 88–440; V. M. Molotov, *Problems of Foreign Policy* (n. 4), p. 37 f.; W. Cornides, 'Der Weg zur europäischen Friedenskonferenz' in *Europa-Archiv*, i (1946/7), pp. 3–21; id., 'Die Pariser Konferenz von 1946', ibid. pp. 187–208.

[17] Cf. nn. 21 f.

of all reparation deliveries from the Western Zones to the Soviet Union.[18] It now became clear that each of the superpowers intended to reshape the whole of Germany according to its own design.

Molotov rejected as wholly insufficient an offer by Byrnes that Germany should be treated as an economic unity and its demilitarization guaranteed by a twenty-five-year period of control by the Great Powers. He demanded a forty-year period and insisted that the Western powers should first carry out democratization in their zones as had already been done in the Soviet Zone, which alone had carried out land reform and destroyed the economic basis of Fascism. A central German government must then be set up, and only with it could a peace treaty be concluded. Asked by Byrnes what the Soviet Union really wanted, Molotov admitted that its chief objective was for Russia to take part in a four-power control of the Ruhr, on the model of that in Berlin. The Soviet Union thus showed a clear desire to extend its influence over the whole of Germany. Byrnes for his part declared on the last day of the conference that the US would no longer take responsibility for the chaos caused by the division of Germany into four economic zones; he invited the other occupying powers to unite their zones with the American one so that Germany might be administered as a single economic unit.[19]

After the failure of the Paris Council of Foreign Ministers the two superpowers endeavoured to make each other appear responsible for the break-up of the wartime alliance. By appealing to world opinion to judge between them on this point, they laid the basis for the end of co-operation and brought it about all the more speedily. How fragile the alliance had become by the summer of 1946 is shown by the fact that they appealed to the German people, which had only just been defeated, to bear witness to the good faith of their respective policies. Molotov gave the signal on 10 July with a press statement which represented the Soviet Union as the Germans' only true friend, the sole champion of democratic recovery and German unity, and conjured up the bogy of an American 'Carthaginian peace' on the lines of the Morgenthau plan. Byrnes, who was clearly alarmed, replied with a speech in Stuttgart on 6 September in which he emphasized America's interest in German recovery.

The victorious powers, he said, had 'learned that peace and well-being are indivisible and that our peace and well-being cannot be purchased at the price of the peace or the well-being of any other country'. After describing in detail the measures that would be taken to improve the economic situation and develop the autonomy of the *Länder,* the speech ended with the following assurance. 'The U.S.

---

[18] Cf. chap I/5, pp. 233 f.
[19] Cf. The Second Session of the Council of Foreign Ministers, Second Part, Paris, June 15–July 12, 1946, in *Foreign Relations* (n. 16), pp. 493–940; Molotov (n. 4), p. 59 f.; P. A. Nikolayev, *Politika Sovetskogo Soyuza v germanskom voprose 1945–1964 (Policy of the Soviet Union on the German Question),* Moscow, 1966, p. 61 f.; B. Meissner, *Russland, die Westmächte und Deutschland, Die sowjetische Deutschlandpolitik 1943–1953,* Hamburg, 1954², pp. 83–94. Page 87 of this work records the important offer of a guaranteed US presence for twenty-five years, which Molotov refused because it would have been contrary to the Soviet Union's true aims: cf. chap. III, n. 18. For the Paris Peace Conference, 29 July–15 Oct. 1946, cf. chap. I, n. 180.

cannot relieve Germany from the hardships inflicted upon her by the war her leaders started. But the U.S. has no desire to increase those hardships or to deny the German people an opportunity to work their way out of those hardships... The American people want to help the German people win their way back to an honourable place among the free and peace-loving nations of the world.'[20]

The appeal to unite the German zones of occupation was, in the face of economic chaos, a logical consequence of this proclaimed readiness to see Germany rebuilt. As only the UK government responded, it led to an agreement of 2 December 1946 for the creation of Bizonia as the first unit transcending zonal boundaries.

(D) RENEWED CO-OPERATION: THE COUNCIL OF FOREIGN MINISTERS IN NEW YORK

The break-up of the meeting of Foreign Ministers on 12 July and the violently opposed press statements on Germany brought home to world opinion for the first time that the tension between the world powers was not merely transitory, but that they appeared unable to agree on any of the key questions affecting the European peace treaties or, above all, on policy towards Germany. At this time and in the ensuing weeks the press reported US–Soviet differences in the Security Council and the UN disarmament and atomic-energy committees, the Greek civil war, tension in China, etc. For good or evil, therefore, European and world opinion in the summer of 1946 had to take seriously the possibility that the promised progressive organization of world peace by the two superpowers might not succeed and that the tensions between them might become increasingly acute.

At first, however, world opinion refused to recognize the scale of the confrontation – a psychological attitude that is only too understandable in view of the intensity of hopes for a lasting peace. After the Paris crisis the superpowers themselves reverted to the attempt they had made at the Moscow meeting of foreign ministers in December 1945 to settle their differences by compromising over spheres of influence. The Russians were prepared to do so because they were able sufficiently to establish their domination of Eastern Europe and wished to avoid further direct confrontation with the strongest world power; the Americans, because they gave up Eastern Europe as a lost cause and thought they saw signs of a weakening of Soviet expansionism in other areas. At all events, Byrnes was able to reaffirm his policy of 'conciliation' as far as the 'progressive internationalists' were concerned. At the third meeting of the Council of Foreign Ministers, held in New York from 4 November to 11 December 1946, both sides

---

[20] Molotov's press statement in Molotov (n. 4), p. 218 f.; Byrnes's Speech in *Department of State Bulletin, September 15, 1946*, pp. 496 f. J. Gimbel (in 'Byrnes' Stuttgarter Rede', *Vierteljahreshefte für Zeitgeschichte (VfZG)*, 20 (1972), pp. 39–62) suggests that Byrnes's speech was intended as a warning against French policy in Germany. This draws attention to an aspect of America's German policy in 1946 which has certainly been neglected, but in my opinion it overlooks the importance of Molotov's speech as the main cause of Byrnes's public statement.

reached agreement on the terms of the peace treaties with Italy, Finland, Hungary, Romania, and Bulgaria, which had been revised in Paris and were now presented in final form.[21] The Russians abated their claims in regard to reparations and control arrangements, especially as regards Italy, which they accepted as belonging wholly to the American sphere of influence; in the former Axis countries which were now part of their imperium, they could in any case achieve any purpose they wished. The US and the other signatories, however, agreed that with the conclusion of the peace treaties the Allied Control Commissions in Romania, Bulgaria, and Hungary would be dissolved, which meant that non-Communist forces in those countries could no longer be supported by a Western presence; the treaties recognized the existing governments and, the Yalta Declaration notwithstanding, gave *de facto* sanction to the Soviet domination of Eastern Europe.

The Soviet Union had hastened developments in the East-European countries with an eye on the New York timetable. In Bulgaria the peasant and bourgeois parties, although represented in the government by individuals approved by the Communist Party, were so terrorized that after the elections of 27 October 1946 only 99 out of 465 deputies were non-members of the Fatherland Front under Communist leadership. In Romania elections held on 19 November resulted in 347 seats going to the Communist-controlled 'bloc of democratic parties', only 33 to the Peasant Party, and 3 to the Liberals. Similar developments were imminent in Poland and Hungary. The Americans gave up Eastern Europe so completely, in accordance with Byrnes's renewed policy of co-operation and the careful delineation of spheres of influence, that they even terminated, as from the end of 1946, their economic–humanitarian programme of aid through UNRRA. 'The Western Allies sanctioned this development [in Eastern Europe] by their signature of the peace treaties on 10 February 1947 ... They recognized that real power and control over all important political posts in the East-European countries was in Communist hands. The democratic forces were defeated.'[22]

Significantly, in anticipation of this development the governments of Poland and Czechoslovakia – which, though already to a large extent ruled by native Communists, were still anxious to preserve a remnant of independence – in August 1946 placed on the agenda of the UN Economic and Social Council the plan for a United Nations Economic Commission for Europe (ECE), which should co-ordinate the national recovery programmes into a general European one and help towards its realization.

[21] Cf. Third Session of the Council of Foreign Ministers, New York, November 4–December 12, 1946, in *Foreign Relations* (n. 16), pp. 965–1566; H. Volle, 'Die Aussenministerkonferenz in New York vom 4.11. bis 11.12.1946' in *Europa-Archiv*, i (1946/7), pp. 321–9; id., 'Die Friedensverträge mit den ehemaligen Verbündeten Deutschlands', ibid., pp. 483–90. For texts of the treaties, see UNTS microfilmed: Bulgaria, Vol. 41, No. 643; Hungary, Vol. 41, No. 644; Romania, Vol. 41, No. 645; Finland, Vol. 48, No. 746; Italy, Vol. 49, No. 747.

[22] Hoensch (n. 7), p. 396 and (for the quotation) p. 398. For the cessation of UNRRA aid and the withdrawal of its numerous staff, who had provided valuable moral and practical help to liberal democratic circles in Eastern Europe, cf. the concise account with sources in G. Zellentin, *Die Kommunisten und die Einigung Europas*, Frankfurt, 1964, p. 33 f.

296 Revival of Plans for Federation

The idea was welcomed by the Americans but opposed by the Russians on the ground that Europe was not an economic unit; however, the Soviet delegation was persuaded by the Poles and Czechoslovaks to abstain on the vote once it was made clear that the Commission would have no important powers. The Commission was set up on 28 March 1947, with the task of 'facilitating concerted action for the economic reconstruction of Europe'. It was the first, and is still the only, economic commission for Europe as a whole; but its terms of reference lay down that 'it takes no action in respect to any country without the assent of the government of that country'.[23]

Altogether the results of 'Russo-American co-operation' were so favourable to the Soviet Union, especially the *de facto* recognition of its domination of Eastern Europe, that Stalin saw advantage in advocating a continuance of this policy. In interviews with Elliott Roosevelt and Harald Stassen in December 1946 and April 1947 he declared that harmony still prevailed among the Big Three as regards the basic objectives of their policy, and that the existence of different social systems was a challenge to peaceful competition and not to confrontation. To abuse one another as 'monopolists or totalitarians' was mere propaganda and stood in the way of necessary co-operation.[24] Thus it appeared that a delimitation of interests in regard to Germany, on the lines of Moscow 1945 and New York 1946, was still possible; the attempt to agree on a peace settlement for Germany at the fourth meeting of the Council of Foreign Ministers, set for 10 March 1947 in Moscow, was not altogether hopeless; and a section of world opinion could still cherish hope of a security organization on a 'One World' basis.

2. Contacts among Federalist Groups in Western Europe

As a result of press reports, scanty though they initially were, of such matters as the crisis over Iran, the failure of the first session of the Council

---

[23] The ECE, comprising European countries who were members of the UN, held its first session, with Soviet participation, at Geneva in May 1947. Not only could its decisions be vetoed by any member country, but the Americans never provided a financial basis that would have enabled it to work effectively. It has nevertheless often been useful as the sole clearing-house for economic data as between Eastern and Western Europe. It is excellently described in D. Wightman, *Economic Co-operation in Europe. A Study of the UN Economic Commission for Europe,* London, 1956: pp. 6–18 give an account of its origins, including the facts cited above. As it played virtually no part during the first years of the 'Cold War', it is not mentioned again in the present account. It may have a future as a link between COMECON and the EEC.

[24] Interview with E. Roosevelt, 21.12.1946, in *J. V. Stalin on Post-War International Relations* (n. 15), pp. 18–22; Russian text in *Sochineniya* (n. 15), pp. 65–70; interview with H. Stassen, 9.4.1947, *Sochineniya,* pp. 75–92. For Truman's reaction, cf. the continuation of this sketch of East–West relations in chap. III/1, p. 460 f.

of Foreign Ministers in Paris on 15 May and of the second, amid mutual recriminations, on 10 July, the European public, which took an interest in world politics despite food shortages and grave economic difficulties, began in the summer of 1946 to be seriously alarmed by the possibility that the superpowers, after making such a show of taking in hand the problem of organizing world peace, might find the task too much for them and come into conflict with each other; tension might, it was feared, increase to the point where a third world war threatened to break out barely a year after the second had ended. To the European federalists, who had been in a state of profound resignation for the past twelve months, this widespread anxiety afforded an opportunity, from outside as it were, to point out with fresh vigour, and with renewed hope of finding a response, that they themselves had a different programme to offer: the ideal of European federation as the fruit of reflection by Europeans on the lessons of the war and the collapse of Europe. As the dispute between the superpowers became public knowledge, the concept of federal Europe presented itself as a contribution to the solution of many of the problems which the world powers evidently could not master.

Thus in the summer and autumn of 1946 all the federalist groups which had been founded or been active at the end of the war, and had for the past year been in a state of hopeless disappointment and resignation, began to revive: they sought and found new supporters and contacts with one another and with groups that now came into existence for the first time. The previous motives and arguments for European federation – keeping the peace in Europe, the need for economic union, supranational protection of human rights against the claims of the nationalist state – were now supplemented by a new basic theme: European union was necessary so as to prevent a Russo-American line of confrontation running through the middle of Europe; it would, moreover, constitute a regional organization that would strengthen the UN and altogether make a decisive contribution to world peace. From this time on the idea of European union took on a fresh lease of life within political parties also, though more sporadically and slowly than among the federalist groups.[25]

---

[25] The remaining sections of chapter II, and also chapter III, are chiefly concerned with the revival of the federalist pressure groups; the texts referred to in nn. 26–35 below illustrate abundantly the effect on the latter of the increasingly evident crisis between the two superpowers. The evolution of thought within the political parties was slower on account of their preoccupation with the day-to-day problems of reconstruction, and because they had learnt to concentrate on internal affairs; a summary for each party will be given in chap. IV (in vol. 2). From the point of view of method it is preferable to analyse the progress of the European idea with reference to each party's outlook and the development of its programme. (In the following sections, which only cover short periods in various countries, parties are referred to summarily and by abbreviations.) As to the European governments, they made no response before May 1947; cf. chap. I/3–6, and chap. III/2.

(A) INCREASED ACTIVITY AND CONTACTS IN THE SUMMER OF 1946

Hans Bauer, the president of the oldest federalist group, the Swiss Europa-Union, wrote in the journal of his organization as early as May 1946 'A year after VE day we must acknowledge with regret that ... for 365 valuable days an incalculable amount of energy has been wasted in the great powers' struggle for positions.' In the June number he wrote more sharply: 'No one will dispute the greatness of the great powers, but equally we cannot ignore the fact that the combined efforts of several great powers, with their claims to have the chief say in how the post-war world is organized and governed, have so far scarcely achieved even small results.' It was unendurable that the powers should engage in the pointless, outdated activity of shifting frontier posts that represented spheres of influence in Europe, while the peoples concerned were in a state of starvation and chaos.[26] In both his articles Bauer laid fresh emphasis on the need for European union in order to prevent the Continent from becoming an apple of discord between the two superpowers.

Before discussing methods, however, it was necessary to decide two questions of basic policy, each of which implied several further decisions. Should the concept of European unity in its revived form:

1. As the plans of the Resistance movements had assumed, envisage as a matter of course the unification of the *whole* of Europe *between* the world powers, i.e. with America and Russia withdrawing from the Continent; or, taking account of the Russian occupation of Eastern Europe, should plans be limited to the unification of the West-European countries?

2. Likewise in accordance with the plans of the Resistance movements, should the objective be a federal union in which nation states were subordinated to common federal authorities; or, now that these states had been fully restored, should a more modest start be made with confederal plans such as those devised between the wars and by politicians in wartime exile?

It soon became clear that all the associations which had existed since the end of the war were emphatically in favour of the first answer in each case. The second alternatives were put forward somewhat later by entirely new groups of politicians who had not experienced the collapse of Europe at first hand during the war.[27]

---

[26] Leading article in the monthly *Europa. Organ der Europa–Union*, Vol. xiii of *Der Europäer*, No. 5; May 1946, p. 1 (with the further comment: 'Up to 8 May 1945 everyone knew what they were fighting *against*. A year later it is still an open question what they were fighting *for*'); also June 1946, p. 1. For details of the Swiss Europa-Union, see chap. I/2, pp. 117–24.

[27] The following part of section II/2 describes the unification of older associations and their endorsement of the first alternative in each case (continued in II/4 and II/5), while section II/3 describes the creation of new associations devoted to the second alternative. The difficult implications of both main questions are discussed there in the light of sources: cf. pp. 329 f., 371–5, and 380–5.

The first of the existing organizations to take up a position on these questions was the Dutch Europeesche Actie: on the occasion of the accession of other groups between 14 May and 14 June 1946 this body agreed on a six-page formulation of its aims which gave a clear answer on both points. As we have already seen, the Theses produced under the intellectual leadership of Salinger and Verkade, Brugmans and Nord were a well thought-out and forceful expression of the association's new aims in the light of its disillusionment with great-power policy.[28] The document may be summarized as follows. The federal concept put forward by the Resistance movements was preserved intact as an ultimate aim, but was modified to take account of the restoration of national states that had taken place meanwhile. The steps to be taken were divided into (1) an 'urgency programme' for the immediate period during which a 'federal European government' (to be set up by a conference of European governments, with genuine but still limited authority) would in the first place co-ordinate state functions, especially in the economic sphere, and (2) a long-term programme for the creation of a common parliamentary and judicial system and the complete unification of economic, financial, and foreign policy. Emphasis was laid on the additional motivation that this European federation would 'point the way to world consolidation' and afford an 'example' for the necessary development of the UN; it would furnish a pattern of regional organization and remove the risk, due to anarchy, of war between the intervening world powers. In particular the European federation would ease the dangerous confrontation of the superpowers in Europe and enable them to withdraw to their respective hemispheres, while a 'European police army ... would replace the allied occupation forces in the German lands and Germany's former vassal states', i.e. Italy and Eastern Europe.[29] Thus, as regards the other basic question of policy, an 'acceptance' of the Russian occupation of Eastern Europe was firmly rejected; European federation was seen as a pre-condition of, and a decisive step towards, disengaging the two superpowers and ensuring world peace.

The May 1946 issue of the Europa-Union journal was unequivocal on this point also. Why had

two European wars been fought and won ... if the most important problem, namely Europe, the root cause of these wars, is to remain unsolved? ... What is the use to these peoples of their new-won freedom if they are not given a chance to form themselves, politically and economically, into a stable Continental union? ...

[28] On Europeesche Actie and the persons named, see above, chap. I/2, pp. 131–41, for its programme and Theses, ibid., pp. 139–42; for editions of these, chap. I, n. 107.
[29] The expressions 'Federal government' and 'European police army' both occur in the 'crash programme' (Thesis X). In view of the basic importance of the Theses for the Hertenstein programme (cf. n. 43 f.) we quote Thesis III once again: 'It is an essential precondition of the creation of an international order based on law (*Rechtsordnung*) to create a counterweight to the present development of two power groups which are steadily becoming larger and which, in their contest for power, threaten to absorb or crush any state that is weaker than they.'

Even Russia cannot in the long run afford to have on its Western border a fragmented, unorganized Europe in which some minor event may at any moment touch off a first-class crisis. Such a fragmentation of Europe could only be regarded by the Russians as an ideal state of affairs for their purposes if they were openly bent on conquest

– which the writer was reluctant to believe, in view of the 'peaceful intentions they have themselves proclaimed'.[30]

From the outset of the period of reactivation of federalist plans it was urged that as a 'first stage', now that the worst disorganization of postal and other communications was over, the associations should make contact and co-ordinate their efforts for the joint struggle. In the same May issue of *Europa-Union* Dr Léon van Vassenhove, a French journalist living in Berne and a member of the association since 1940, wrote: 'What is the European federal movement at the present time? It exists, it is alive and active ... Federalists and groups of federalists are to be found in many European countries.' But 'un mouvement fédéraliste européen, ce n'est pas une addition de mouvements fédéralistes nationaux: c'est leur collaboration, leur conjugaison, leur interpénétration, leur union'. On 27 May 1946 a meeting took place at Basle between Dr van Vassenhove, Dr Hans Bauer, and Prof. Umberto Campagnolo representing the Italian MFE, which at that time was uncompromisingly in favour of a strictly supranational federation including Eastern Europe. The parties signed the 'draft of an alliance' whereby Europa-Union and the MFE were to form the nucleus of the European federal movement. Van Vassenhove was to seek the accession of the French, Belgian, and Czechoslovak federalists, and the MFE that of Federal Union and Europeesche Actie; Europa-Union would seek to persuade Scandinavian federalists to join (Art. 1). The object of the alliance was to unify the principles and co-ordinate the actions of the participating movements (Art. 2). A joint congress of as many groups as possible was to be held in Switzerland in September for the purpose of working out the statutes of the alliance.[31] There ensued a difficult period of seeking contacts, during which not everything happened on the lines planned on 27 May, while the chief burden of preparing for the congress fell on the well organized secretariat of the Swiss Europa-Union.[32]

It was an important advantage at this time that Léon van Vassenhove

---

[30] A. Laragnini, 'England, Russland und die Einigung Europas', *Europa* (n. 26), May 1946, p. 3.

[31] Cf. L. van Vassenhove's federalist convictions expressed in *L'Europe helvétique. Étude sur les possibilités d'adapter à l'Europe les institutions de la Confédération Suisse*, Neuchâtel, 1943, and *Le Préjugé de la guerre inévitable*, Neuchâtel, 1945. His article in *Europa* (n. 26), May 1946, p. 1 had already appeared in the *Gazette de Lausanne*, 12.4.1946. For Campagnolo and his programme, temporarily adopted by the MFE, cf. chap. I/7, esp. p. 276 f. Text of the 'draft alliance' in *MFE – Comitato nazionale organizzativo*, record of monthly session, May 1946 (typescript in *MFE Archives*, Turin).

[32] Announcements in *Europa* (n. 26), May 1946, p. 3, and Aug. 1946, p. 1. For the role of the Swiss EU, cf. also C. Gasteyger, *Einigung und Spaltung Europas 1942–1965*, Frankfurt, 1965, p. 35; on the difficulties of contacts and invitations see nn. 37–40.

succeeded in July in publishing the first number of a new journal, *L'Action fédéraliste européenne*, devoted entirely to providing information, discussion, and a meeting of minds among federalists throughout Europe. An introductory article pointed out that many journals already published useful essays by federalists in the different countries, but that a forum was also needed to provide a conspectus of the development of the federal idea in Europe as a whole.

To pursue, step by step, the development of the federal idea in Europe, to help the national movements to co-ordinate their activities, and to bring about a comprehensive and thorough discussion of all questions connected with the creation of a federated Europe – this should be the best way of promoting the necessary synthesis of federalist ideas.

The first number of the journal, like its successors, did justice to the proposed task. It included an appeal by Schuschnigg, the former Austrian Chancellor, who invoked the example of the United States of America and declared that 'to create a truly European constitution would be a less thankless task and one more in accordance with justice than to dictate new frontiers of the Balkan type'. Other contributions were an article by Bauer on the programme of Europa-Union, one by Campagnolo on the MFE, and much information about federalist activities in Europe.[33] Above all, an essay by van Vassenhove himself entitled 'Pourquoi, quand et comment fédérer l'Europe?' painted a vivid picture of the need for federation in face of the imminent threat of war between the two great powers.

European history, the essay declared, was a march towards an abyss, the brink of which had now been reached (p.9). The risk of war was never greater than when people believed war to be possible. President Truman had said in April that next time America might be the first target. Stalin, in his order of the day for 1 May, had proclaimed in still stronger language than before that international reaction was forging new war plans. Byrnes had said on 21 June that if it was not possible to achieve co-operation in organizing peace on an indivisible basis, the US might be forced into a third world war (p.11). This danger of war, van Vassenhove went on, was the cause of a paralysing pessimism, but it also inspired determination, in view of the centuries of European social and cultural unity (pp. 14–20), at last to create a political federation of European peoples as a peace zone between the world powers. Russia, as a signatory of the UN Charter, must allow this: 'A federated Europe is a guarantee to the Soviet Union of peace and order on its western frontier' (p.28). A renewed democratic Germany should be a

---

[33] L. Vassenhove, 'Préambule: Un organe d'action et d'information', *L'Action fédéraliste européenne*, No. 1 (July), 1946, p. 3 f.; K. von Schuschnigg, 'Le Courage de penser neuf', ibid., pp. 5–9 (quotation on p. 9); H. Bauer, pp. 49–53; U. Campagnolo, pp. 54–61; E. Rotten on a children's village as a European federation in miniature (pp. 62–5); news of European associations, pp. 66–72. The journal was published (like *L'Europe de demain* in 1945: cf. chap. I, n. 56) by the firm de la Baconnière, Neuchâtel, which did so much for the European cause. In succession to the two numbers of *Cahiers de la fédération* (Paris, March and Aug. 1945; cf. chap. I, nn. 78 and 85), the federal movement thus again possessed a representative monthly journal, alongside the excellent fortnightlies *Federal News* and *L'Unità europea* and the Swiss monthly *Europa*.

part of the federation (pp. 29–34). The question from now on was one of method. 'So far there has been no apparent link between the theoreticians and the architects of European federation' (p. 35). 'Governments are national institutions whose task is to find out what their people want and to defend their interests' (p. 38). 'The first step is to create a European federal movement which will take root in people's hearts' (p. 39). It was urgently necessary to create (1) a 'federalist European agency' and (2) a 'European University' to study all the relevant problems thoroughly. These two institutions should systematically encourage and intensify the aspiration of all European peoples towards unity.[34]

There were further signs of a revival of the concept of European unity in view of the clash of Russo-American peace plans in the summer of 1946. In Brussels a weekly journal called *Les États-Unis d'Europe* began to appear; its editor, the Belgian journalist Ram Linssen, declared in a leading article that 'federalism is above all opposed to "spheres of influence", the disquieting intervention of non-European powers ..., antagonistic interests which are only too well placed to exploit the chaos of Europe'. The University of Milan circulated to Italian professors a 'Manifeste des universitaires italiens pour la fédération européenne' which stated that: 'All attempts to solve European problems have shown that only such a federation can put an end to the present grave crisis ... Awareness of European federal principles can nowhere be better developed than in the universities'; to give effect to them, all progressive forces must work for the creation of a 'European constituent assembly'.[35] At the 'Rencontres Internationales' organized by the City of Geneva from 2 to 14 September, at which nine well-known authors and philosophers spoke on the subject of the "European spirit', the Swiss author Denis de Rougemont described federal aims with especial clarity.

'Nationalism, the romantic disease of Europe', which had been the Continent's ruin, was still rampant. 'Physically hemmed in by the two great empires whose

---

[34] L. van Vassenhove, 'Pourquoi, quand et comment fédérer l'Europe?', in *L'Action fédéraliste européenne*. No. 1 (July), 1946, pp. 10–48. As far as I know, this (pp. 42–5) is the first occasion on which the idea of a 'European university' was put forward. Subsequent issues of the journal also fulfilled their purpose admirably, and it is quoted from on many occasions in this work. The serial numbers and dates, however, show that it seldom appeared at regular monthly intervals: No. 2 is dated October 1946, No. 3 November 1946, No. 4 January 1947, No. 5 April 1947, No. 6 July 1947, No. 7 August 1947, No. 8/9 October/November 1947, and No. 10 – the last as far as I know – February 1948. The cessation of the journal was probably connected with the failure of hopes for a federation including Eastern Europe, an aim for which van Vassenhove struggled untiringly. He could not participate in the execution of the Montreux decision: cf. chap. III/4, especially n. 319. An excellent assessment of No. 2 by Jean Bareth appeared in *La Fédération*, Paris, Nov. 1946, p. 24.

[35] Ram Linssen, leading article quoted from *L'Action fédéralists européenne*, No. 2, Oct. 1946, p. 63 (further information should be obtained about this Belgian weekly). The 'Manifeste des universitaires italiens' is quoted from ibid., No. 3, Nov. 1946, p. 64 f.; by October 1946 it was signed by 266 professors of the Universities of Milan, Genoa, Turin, Padua, Rome, and Naples (ibid.). Mention should be made of Max Picard's book *Hitler in uns selbst*, which was published in Zurich in the summer of 1946 and by the autumn had been translated into French, Italian, Czech, Dutch, Swedish, and Danish. This work, which did much to lessen hatred of Germany, condemned nationalism as one of the omnipresent factors which made a revival of Nazism appear possible.

huge shadows meet threateningly over it, the Continent is being eroded at the edges; it is desolated and morally shut in on itself. More than that: I can see how Europe, for the benefit of those two empires, is exhausted by certain ambitious efforts, dreams and doctrines which originated on European soil and seemed at one time to constitute its proper genius. Our dream of progress, for instance, has, as it were, abandoned Europe and taken up its abode in America and Russia. This is an idea which fades as rapidly with us as it flourishes with our neighbours ... Nationalism, on the one hand, stifles living diversities under the pretext of unification, where there can be no question of harmony because there is nothing left to harmonize. On the other hand, it proclaims the nation, thus unified, to be the seat of sovereignty, and the nation presents itself to Europe as an autocratic group, in the alleged freedom of which a base individual is freed from any kind of restriction. In the same way Hitler destroyed the German parties so that the German nation might behave towards other Western countries like a party of the most unscrupulous type. Federalism, by contrast, wishes to achieve unity but not uniformity. Just because it respects the rich variety of internal groups, it is prepared to accept the most comprehensive form of union ... A federation of Europe is only thinkable with the ultimate object of a world federation. Peace and the future can only be envisaged in the light of efforts to create a genuine world government.'[36]

(B) THE HERTENSTEIN CONFERENCE OF EUROPEAN FEDERALISTS

The secretariat of Europa-Union in Basle was unable to contact all the reviving federalist groups in July/August 1946, as addresses were lacking; Campagnolo and van Vassenhove were unsuccessful with those they had undertaken to reach,[37] so that neither the British Federal Union nor some of the new French groups were invited in time. Nevertheless the conference in September was the most important gathering of European federalists since the Resistance conference in Geneva, including as it did the two strongest organizations at that time, the Dutch Europeesche Actie and the Swiss Europa-Union, as well as representatives of the Belgian Union Fédérale, the Italian MFE, and the French CIFE. The most important contact from the point of view of bringing the conference about and of its practical outcome was effected by Ritzel, who wrote at the end of July to Dr Ernst von Schenck, president of the Deutsch-Schweizerischer Kulturbund: 'On the occasion of your visit to the Netherlands we request you to make contact on our behalf with Dutch organizations who, like us, are

---

[36] D. de Rougemont (b. Neuchâtel, 1906), 'Die Krankheiten Europas' in *Merkur, Deutsche Zeitschrift für europäisches Denken*, Year 1, No. 1, March 1947, pp. 17–26 (quotations from pp. 19, 21, and 23 f.). For other speakers at the Rencontres Internationales in Geneva, 2–14.9.1946, see report in *Europa Archiv*, i (1946/7), pp. 316–18.

[37] Cf. the agreement of 27.5.1946 quoted in n. 31 above. Campagnolo also did not trouble to contact the Dutch, and in the end, to the disappointment of the Swiss, he was the only Italian to appear at Hertenstein (cf. n. 40). The Hertenstein conference and its programme are mentioned in the familiar short accounts of the European unity movement, from Fischer and Koppe to Rohn and Wehe, in the sections dealing with 1945–50. It is not necessary to enumerate these short factual accounts here: cf. Introduction, n. 162.

working for the unity of Europe on a federal basis.'[38] In the second half of August von Schenck, who was then in The Hague, was able to discuss the work of the conference on general lines with Brugmans (who had just returned from an exploratory trip to Paris), Salinger, Verkade, Nord, and Mozer; von Schenck himself, moreover, was to become in the future an important co-operator with the federalist movement.[39] When the Hertenstein conference opened on 15 September 1946 (the first two days' sessions being held in Berne), altogether seventy-eight persons were present, most of them representing various federalist groups in thirteen European countries. H. G. Ritzel described its composition as follows:

'About eighty foreign representatives accepted the invitation, and the Swiss were generous in granting entry visas. The fact that only thirty-six attended from outside Switzerland was due in a few cases to obstacles of a personal nature, but mostly to exit visa difficulties. In particular the Germans and Austrians who had accepted were unable to come for this reason. A strong team of Greek federalists were also prevented for unknown reasons. However, one Englishman attended, 4 Frenchmen, 13 Dutch, 4 Belgians, 2 Americans, 2 Greeks, 1 Italian, 1 Austrian, 1 Hungarian, 1 Pole, 1 Spanish Republican, 1 Liechtensteiner, 5 Germans living in Switzerland, and one stateless person. In addition 41 Swiss attended at different times, so that the conference consisted altogether of 78 representatives from 14 countries.'[40]

[38] Letter from H. G. Ritzel (Central Secretary of Europa-Union from 1940 to the end of 1947, cf. chap. I, n. 72) to E. von Schenck, Basle, 31.7.1946 (*von Schenck Archives*, UEF files, 1946/7). Ernst von Schenck, who in this way became an adherent of the European federal movement, soon played an important part in its development in Germany. As a student in Berlin before 1933 he was a strong sympathizer with the left-wing Socialist group around Dr Landauer, which had already advocated a world order based on 'the community of communities of communities' and 'the federation of federations of federations'. During the war von Schenck built up the 'Aktion nationaler Widerstand', organized on a cell basis, as a means of strengthening the Swiss population's will to resistance in the event of a German occupation (information from *von Schenck*, 23.8.1961). As editor of *Schweizer Annalen* he wrote in the May 1946 number of that journal an article on 'Europe and the Third World War' calling for a joint European administration of the whole industrial area of Eastern France, Belgium, Luxemburg, the Saar, and the Ruhr, as a 'vote of confidence' in the future union of Europe (*Europa,* June 1946, p. 2). He was the author of one of the best books on Germany, *Europa vor der deutschen Frage. Briefe eines Schweizers nach Deutschland,* Berne, 1946.

[39] Von Schenck declared that these talks, and those at Hertenstein and Amsterdam, had been a great experience for him, revealing the complete unanimity and federalist determination of French, Dutch, Belgian, German, and other representatives (information from *von Schenck,* 28.4. and 23.8.1961). On 14.8.1946 Brugmans thanked Francis Gérard for 'notre longue et si vivante conversation de l'autre jour' in Paris and advised him to contact Ernest Pezet, whom he had come to know as a 'fédéraliste européen convaincu' (*BEF Archives,* Brugmans correspondence), but Gérard was notified of the conference too late to get a visa (information from *Gérard,* 18.3.1964). Von Schenck, who was previously not a member of the Europa-Union, became one of its most active speakers from Oct. 1946 (cf. correspondence with Ritzel on organizing lectures, *von Schenck Archives,* UEF files, 1946/7). For his general outlook, see especially E. von Schenck, *Angst um die Welt. Zwölf Versuche zur Humanität heute,* Cologne, 1952.

[40] H. G. Ritzel, 'Der Geist von Hertenstein', *Europa* (n. 26), Oct. 1946, p. 1. Cf. information from *Verkade,* 2.9.1954: 'We tried in vain to get Germans to come to Hertenstein from Germany: the occupation authorities would not give exit permits'. Correspondence showing who was invited has not been preserved. Of the '5 Germans living in Switzerland', those most often mentioned are Ritzel, Count von Kanitz (a former diplomat, who died a year later), and Prof. Dr Anna Siemsen. The latter was a writer who emigrated to Switzerland in 1934 and worked there for European union;

Although the conference was not representative of the whole of Europe, it included the whole leadership of the Dutch and Swiss associations. It opened on 15 September, a date chosen for its connection with the traditional peace movement which had upheld the cause of international understanding during the decades before and after the war of 1914-18. On 11--14 September there had in fact been a meeting in Geneva of the 'Dirigeants du Mouvement pour la Paix' and the International Peace Bureau, both of which had welcomed the federal idea; on the 15th the Aktionsgemeinschaft schweizerischer Friedensvereinigungen organized a joint session between those bodies and the Europa-Union, at which Hans Bauer pointed out that Article 52 of the UN Charter recognized the concept of European union as a regional component of world peace.[41] At the first working meeting, at Berne on 16 September, Léon van Vassenhove spoke on the 'Creation of a European unification movement' and Henri Brugmans on 'Europe's mission'. The conference then moved to Hertenstein on Lake Lucerne, where on 18 September François Bondy and H. Nadai (Hungary) gave important addresses on 'The United States of Europe as a first step to world federation'. On 20 September Anna Siemsen, H. G. Ritzel, and H. Salinger spoke on 'The solution of the German problem within the framework of European federation'. The principle of internal federation was the subject of an address by Adolf Gasser on 'Democracy based on a system of free local communities'. On the 19th a public manifestation was held in Lucerne, and on the 22nd the conference concluded with a 'Rütli demonstration for Europe'.[42]

As a result of their discussions the participants published a statement of principles on 21 September. On the basis of the Principles of the Swiss Europa-Union and the Theses of Europeesche Actie, Brugmans proposed a draft formulation of the essential common principles of federalism and

---

she had for a long time belonged to the SPD and to the circle of Joseph Bloch's *Sozialistische Monatshefte* (information from *Brugmans, Verkade,* and *von Schenck*). Cf. A. Siemsen, *Zehn Jahre Weltkrieg* (her diary, 1935-45), Olten, 1946.

[41] Cf. H. Wehberg, 'Reorganisation des Internationalen Friedensbüros und Tagung der Leiter der Friedensbewegung', *Die Friedens-Warte,* 46, 1946, pp. 325-7. (Van Vassenhove addressed the session on federalism, and the resolution of the Peace Bureau stated, though with some reserve, that 'especially in smaller countries . . . there is much sympathy for the idea of organization on a federal basis': ibid., p. 325). Cf. report by 'Les dirigeants du mouvement pour la paix' in *L'Action fédéraliste européenne,* No. 2, Oct. 1946, pp. 71 f. The joint session in Berne inaugurating the Hertenstein conference was broadcast by Swiss Radio: cf. report by H. Bauer in *Europa* (n. 26), Oct. 1946, p. 1.

[42] Cf. the programme printed by Europa-Union: *Tagungsprogramm der Réunion europäischer Völker in der Schweiz vom 14. bis 22. Sept. 1946 in Bern und Hertenstein.* (In accordance with this title the opening date of the conference is generally given as 14 Sept., but in fact this was only the date on which delegates were expected to arrive. Copies in *EU Archives, Basle,* Central Committee files, 1945-57; *von Schenck Archives,* UEF file, 1946/7; *Brugmans Archives,* etc.). The addresses are summarized in the report by L. van Vassenhove, 'La Réunion des Peuples Européens' (he also gives the date '15-22 Sept.') in *L'Action fédéraliste européenne,* No. 2, Oct. 1946, p. 64. The demonstration at Lucerne was addressed by O. Brogle and Prof. Volpelière (France), M. Cosyn (Belgium), and Capt. Abraham (presumably the Englishman mentioned by Ritzel (n. 40); nothing is known as to his membership of Federal Union). For the Rütli demonstration, see n. 47.

its role in the organization of peace; after critical remarks by the Swiss and especially Salinger, this was amended to form a clear statement in twelve points.[43] The text avoided going into political detail, but presented an all the more vivid picture of agreement on essential aspects of federation. It defined no institutions and, unlike the Theses, did not prescribe the successive steps to be taken, but left all these matters for future determination; it confined itself to an attractively simple and precise statement of the need for European federation as a means of preserving democracy and a contribution to the organization of world peace. The text was thus approved 'unanimously' and 'in a fine display of solidarity'; under the name 'Hertenstein programme' it was subsequently adopted by all European federalist associations as a basic programme, and is still regarded as their fundamental manifesto.[44]

Although deliberately kept to general terms, the programme was uncompromising on three main points. (1) As to the sharing of sovereignty and the need for a federal authority: 'The members of the European Union shall transfer part of their economic, political and military sovereignty to the federation created by them' (Art. 4). The basic ethical attitude of the Resistance movements and the principle of internal federalism were formulated in Articles 6 and 7, which called for a 'declaration of European civil rights' and respect for small communities, while Art. 10 declared that sub-federations were 'admissible and even desirable'. (2) *All* European nations were urged to show by creating such a federal union that they desired 'themselves to settle disputes that might arise between its members' (Art. 2) and to organize their own 'planned recovery' and economic co-operation (Art. 8). 'The European Union is open to accession by all nations whose way of life is European and who accept its basic laws' (Art. 5); it 'renounces all power

---

[43] Information from *von Schenck*, 23.8.1961. For the criticisms see H. Brugmans, 'Het begin van een beweging', *Europa in Beweging*, The Hague, 1968, pp. 14 f., concerning 'the Swiss, with whom Salinger and we had some trouble', and also the abandonment of 'Salinger's original ideas. To him, Europeesche Actie was not a so-called popular movement with little departmens and congresses, but a conspiracy of people who intended and were able to achieve something; an international conspiracy, not a federation of national movements. All the same, it was impossible to get things going if one ignored already existing groups.' Confirmed by information from *Salinger*, 25.4.1964: 'At Hertenstein I began to be less interested in work with the associations.' The text was finally drafted by Brugmans, Salinger, Mozer, Bauer, Ritzel, Nord, and von Schenck, according to H. Brugmans, *L'Idée européenne 1920–1970*, Bruges, 1970³, p. 122; according to information from *von Schenck*, chiefly by Brugmans, Mozer, and von Schenck.

[44] 'Unanimously', see Ritzel's report in *Europe* (n. 26), Oct. 1946, p. 1, which was also the first official printing of the Hertenstein programme. 'Fine display . . .' in H. G. Ritzel, 'Die Aktion Europa-Union. Die Konferenz von Hertenstein', *Die Friedens-Warte*, 47, 1947, pp. 68–70, with text of the programme, on which most of the innumerable printed versions are based. The next 'Jahres-Landes-Kongress der Europa-Union' in Lausanne on 8.12.1946 'approved the Hertenstein decisions' and formally adopted the programme (*Europa*, Jan. 1947, p. 4); so did the general assembly of Europeesche Actie at The Hague, Nov. 1946 (pamphlet, *De Europeesche Actie*, Dec. 1946, p. 15, with Dutch text of the programme). Earliest French printed version in *Le Document Fédéraliste* (*publié par le CIFE*), No. 3, Paris, 15.1.1947, where it is indicated as having been signed by 'Le comité restreint: Dr. Brugmans (Hollande), Dr. Steffan (Suisse), Mme Volpelière (France), R. Linssen (Belgique)'. In subsequent pamphlet editions of the programmes of the UEF and its member associations the Hertenstein programme was printed first, followed by the later programme of the association in question: cf. nn. 163, 292, and 297.

politics, but also refuses to be a tool of any foreign power' (Art. 9); it alone can ensure 'the territorial inviolability and individuality of all its peoples' (Art. 11). (3) The beginning and end of the document emphasized that the European community was 'a necessary and essential component of any real world union' (Art. 1), that it 'inserted itself into the framework of the U.N. and was a regional body in the sense of Article 52 of the Charter' (Art. 3), and that Europe wished to 'contribute to recovery and a world union of peoples by proving that it can solve the problems of its own destiny in a spirit of federalism' (Art. 12).[45]

At that early stage it was a notable feature that Germans were invited to the conference and took part on an equal footing. The conference, moreover, unanimously approved a resolution proposed by the Netherlands delegation, which stated that only by the incorporation of Germany in the European Union could 'the German problem be solved without falling into particularism or permitting the creation of a "Fourth Reich". We believe that the fight against deplorable conditions and despair in Germany imposes a collective responsibility on Europe.' Economic experts of all European countries should 'reach agreement on German recovery within the framework of European reconstruction. The conference urges the speedy removal of the barriers which prevent intellectual contact between German-speaking peoples and the other European states, and which encourages nationalism.'[46]

Finally, on the basis of this agreed programme the conference achieved its other aim of organizing the national federalist associations into a single whole. On 21 September it was agreed that the associations should first be combined under an umbrella organization and then merged into a truly supranational organization, as had been laudably but unsuccessfully attempted at the Geneva and Paris conferences of federalists. Henri Brugmans was elected provisional president. The importance of the decision was underlined at the 'Rütli demonstration' on Sunday 22 September, a public affair with a crowd, music, and banners: on the historic plateau where, in 1291, the founding Cantons united in what was to become a federal, multilingual Switzerland, the first step towards European union was to be taken with the amalgamation of the national federalist associations. Impassioned speeches were made, and Ritzel solemnly read out the resolution:

> The representatives of European unity movements and individual personalities assembled at Hertenstein in Switzerland for the purpose of reuniting the peoples of Europe proclaim their determination to create jointly an effective organization in the interest of securing peace and bringing about European unity. This will first

---

[45] The text is at present most accessible in *Europa-Dok.*, vol. i, pp. 115 f.; Gasteyger (n. 32), pp. 42 f.; K. Koppe, *Das grüne E setzt sich durch*, Cologne, 1967, p. 184; Cl. Schöndube, *Das neue Europa-Handbuch*, Cologne, 1969, p. 157; W. Lipgens, *Die europäische Integration*, Stuttgart, 1972, pp. 26 f. For the interpretation, cf. p. 308 below.
[46] According to H. G. Ritzel, 'Die Aktion Europa-Union. Die Konferenz von Hertenstein', *Die Friedens-Warte*, 47, 1947, p. 69.

take the form of an umbrella organization covering existing national organizations, and will be converted as soon as possible into a merger of those organizations. The umbrella organization will be called 'Aktion Europa-Union, International Movement for the Unification of Europe and the World'. The existing movements for European unity in the various countries declare their willingness to belong to this umbrella organization on a basis of equal rights and to amend their statutes in the sense of the proposed co-operation. The provisional executive consisted, in addition to Brugmans as chairman, of Baron Allard for the Belgian Union Fédérale, Mme Volpelière (member of CIFE) for France, Anna Siemsen (who was shortly afterwards appointed to the Pädagogische Akademie, Hamburg) for Germany, and Heinrich Schiess for Switzerland.[47]

Although the resolution soon had to be considerably modified in view of the narrow personal basis of the Hertenstein conference and the accession of further associations, it unquestionably marked the first step towards the foundation of the Union of European Federalists (UEF). Above all, the conference presented the UEF with a programme which, while leaving many details to be fixed later, set forth the basic principles boldly and clearly. For the sake of Europe's future and that of its people the programme demanded that, German national sovereignty having been destroyed, other states too should now give up their rights of sovereignty. Clearly refusing to accept the division of Europe into a Russian and an American sphere of occupation, the programme declared that the Continent did not belong to either world power; as Hans Bauer put it in his report, 'To the divisive rivalry of blocs we oppose our allegiance to federation and European unity, the salvation of all European nations in the service of world peace.'[48] Europe was not to form part of any power bloc but to be a

[47] According to Ritzel's report, with text of the resolution, in *Europa* (n. 26), Oct. 1946, p. 1; the persons according to *Die Friedens-Warte*, 47, p. 69. Van Vassenhove's report, 'La Réunion' (n. 42), pp. 65 f., agrees in substance and emphasizes the Rütli symbolism. Brugmans's later report, 'Het begin' (n. 43), p. 15, confirms that there was general agreement for a merger, 'but Ritzel had thought up a name that he discussed with no one, Aktion Europa-Union. How he came to choose it was one of the many Ritzel riddles.' The plan was for a joint secretariat in two sections, one at The Hague under Salinger dealing with general co-ordination, political and economic matters, the other at Basle under Ritzel dealing with membership, organization, propaganda, and finance (pamphlet, *De Europeesche Actie*, Dec. 1946, pp. 14 f.). This plan had to be revised in Dec. 1946, as it was too closely linked to the two groups that had sponsored the Hertenstein conference.
[48] H. Bauer, 'Die europäische Stunde', *Europa* (n. 26), Oct. 1946, p. 1. Bauer expressed his view more fully in the same number after quoting Churchill's Zurich speech (on which see chapter II/3), which was interpreted by the Communist countries as an appeal for the formation of an anti-Soviet bloc. 'Against such a conception our Aktion Europa-Union must clearly emphasize that we envisage the federation not as a bloc opposed to other blocs but as a unifying community designed to put an end to power politics. If Russia wants peace and security it will find them best guaranteed in a peacefully united Europe in which big and small states co-operate in freedom and with equal rights, like large and small cantons. Russia's attitude to this conception of European unity will be a touchstone of Russian intentions. Britain and Russia will not let themselves be divided from Europe; both, with their special European interests, must appear as co-guarantors of a European federal constitution, while the British family of nations, like the Soviet one, in accordance with their inter-continental situation, will, like the United States of Europe, be regional organizations within the framework of the UN, under Article 52 of the San Francisco Charter. Thus a united Europe will be a regional bulwark of world peace, whereas a disunited Europe is a constant threat and danger to it. Russian opposition to a European union, an organization of pure self-preservation, could only be motivated by ill will, by a desire to divide and rule' (ibid., p. 3).

neutral third force keeping the West and East apart and thus ensuring world peace. Placed between the opposites of capitalism and Communism, it should make a fresh synthesis of these and so prevent the world being split into two hostile camps. This was the essence of the Hertenstein view of world politics.

How serious the participants were in their opposition to power blocs was shown by their reception, on 20 September, of the news of Churchill's speech in Zurich the previous day. A spontaneous proposal to send Churchill a telegram welcoming his support for European unity was defeated by a large majority. By dissociating itself from plans for a Western bloc the conference hoped to dissuade the Soviet Union from completing its occupation of Eastern Europe and to convince it of the advantage of having a firmly neutral European federation as part of the world federation.[49]

In the light of hindsight and of the East–West conflict as it developed in the ensuing years, it is easy to criticize the federalists – who maintained their objective of a Europe-wide union, holding the two blocs apart, continuously until the summer of 1947 – for lack of realism and for shutting their eyes to the *fait accompli* of Soviet domination in Eastern Europe. They certainly were unrealistic in this respect. But, just as the Hertenstein programme assumed that the US would withdraw and allow the Western half of Europe to work out its own salvation once more, and as this actually happened, so it was not unreasonable to expect the Soviet Union to do likewise.[50] The idea that one of the world powers that had freed the nations from Nazi imperialism would continue to occupy a line 1,000 kilometres west of its original western border, to which its troops had advanced in the closing phase of the war, and would subject the nations behind that line to its own imperialist rule, seemed so monstrous to those who had just gone through the sufferings of Nazi occupation that they very understandably refused to believe it. Although with heavy misgivings at times, they gave proofs of confidence to the Soviet Union in the hope of thereby inducing it to behave in the manner expected of an enemy of Hitler. Faced with the crisis of the allied peace-keeping organization, the federalists put forward the idea of European union with renewed courage, under the illusion that the world powers, like the European Resistance movements, had grasped the fact that the war was the *reductio ad absurdum*

---

[49] Information from *von Schenck*, 23.8.1961, confirmed by *Brugmans*, 23.4.1964; also noted in E. Friedländer, *Wie Europa begann*, Cologne, 1965, p. 59. Friedländer points out the relevance of the party political allegiance of the Hertenstein leaders (Brugmans, Mozer, and Ritzel were Social Democrats): 'Even though not committed to a party line in the narrow sense, most of them belonged to the Left.' For the federalists' attitude to Churchill's concept, cf. chap. II/3, pp. 341–5.

[50] H. Brugmans, in *L'Idée européenne 1920–1970*, Bruges, 1970³, p. 122, adds the realistic argument: 'Why indeed, they [the Hertenstein federalists] wondered, should Russia persist in turning the East-European countries under Red Army occupation into Soviet satellites, if the effect was to drive the West Europeans into the arms of the US? Before accepting the Iron Curtain as inevitable it was better at least to try to prevent a polarization into two blocs.' Cf. fuller exposition of the concept of a 'Third Force', with full quotations, in chap. II/5, pp. 380–5; the abandonment of this illusion in Aug. 1947 in chap. III/4, pp. 579–85.

of power politics in general. After stoutly defending their view for a year longer they were destined once more to be disillusioned.

(C) THE LUXEMBURG CONFERENCE OF EUROPEAN AND WORLD FEDERALISTS

It was not only the Swiss Europa-Union and the Dutch Europeesche Actie who were impelled by the evident crisis in allied post-war planning to reactivate the idea of European federal union and, as a first step, to bring about the union of federalist associations. The same idea was mooted by Federal Union in Britain, the European Committee of which, under Miss Frances L. Josephy, had proposed during the war that a conference of federalists from all countries should be held when the war was over, and which pursued this plan energetically in the summer of 1946. After the twelve months' discouragement of 1945-6 its plan for a conference of European federalists ran into difficulties of communication, and it failed to contact either Europa-Union or Europeesche Actie. Federal Union included a strong party of world federalists, and at the latter's wish approaches were made to world federalist groups in Europe and the US. At the suggestion of the secretary of the European Committee, Mrs Alison Koch – wife of Henri Koch, a Committee member of long standing from Luxemburg, who obtained financial aid from the Luxemburg authorities – Luxemburg was chosen as the seat of the conference and the groups were invited to meet there from 13 to 16 October.[51]

The federalists' principle – viz. the distribution of powers in accordance with the principle of subsidiarity, the exercise of authority 'as far down as possible' and 'as far up as necessary', in matters of foreign policy, security, and welfare which national states were no longer in a position to safeguard by themselves – was no less applicable to Europe than to the world as a whole. All the early federalist groups were convinced that the UN, founded as a meeting-place of sovereign states and liable to be blocked at any time by the veto of a permanent member of the Security Council, offered no sufficient guarantee of world peace. Nearly all the federalist groups in Europe wanted a fusion of powers on the European level and, as soon as possible, on a world scale; the two seemed equally necessary, for, as van Vassenhove put it, 'A European federation must be created so that the

---

[51] For Federal Union, cf. chap. I/2, pp. 142-53; especially p. 147 f. on its European Committee and p. 153 on its world federalist wing, which was strong in the autumn of 1945 and in 1946. Plan for a conference of European federalists, see F. L. Josephy, 'Full steam ahead. Report of the International Conference of Federalists at Luxemburg, October 13th to 17th, 1946', *Federal News*, No. 141, Dec. 1946, pp. 2 and 4. Henri Koch, b. Luxemburg 2.5.1906, a lawyer, from 1940 to 1946 head of a department in the ministry of information of the exiled Belgian government in London (responsible for the Congo, Sweden, and Switzerland), and an active member of Federal Union; Jan. 1947 to May 1948 Secrétaire-Général adjoint of the UEF (cf. Index); 1949-51 secretary-general of the European branch of world federalists (information from *Koch*, 18.11.1971); cf. H. Koch, *Sie boten Trotz. Luxemburger in Freiheitskampf 1939-1945*, Luxemburg, 1974.

European nations no longer make war on one another, and a world federation is necessary to prevent war between Europe and Asia or America.' The Hertenstein programme described European union as an 'essential component of true world union' and a step towards the 'world community of peoples'.[52] Opinions differed, however, as to priorities. Some, especially at this time the American federalists, emphasized the importance of an effective federalist world government, while others wanted to begin with the federal union of Europe, on the principle of 'building up from below' and in realistic awareness that neither the Soviet Union nor the US were prepared to relinquish sovereignty to a world government. There were of course possibilities of conflict here: while the European federalists believed world union to be impossible so long as Europe was not federated, there were world federalists who thought European union an obstacle to world union because it was anathema to the Russians.

The Luxemburg conference, while reflecting a common background of federalist conviction, was the first international gathering at which these conflicting views came into the open. On the evening of 13 October the participants were welcomed in the Hotel de Casino at Luxemburg by Col. Evelyn King, a Labour MP, on behalf of Federal Union. The invitations turned out to have reached many groups, especially French ones which had been newly founded or revived as recently as the autumn of 1946. Almost exactly as at Hertenstein there were 75 delegates from 12 countries, but 71 of these were non-Luxemburgers; 31 organizations were represented. As Miss Josephy reported:

The delegations varied enormously in size, from 19 Dutch, 18 British and 15 French, through 7 Americans and 4 each from Belgium and Luxembourg, to two apiece from Italy, Switzerland and the Basque country, and one each representing Australia, India, South Africa, New Zealand and Sweden ... The French delegation consisted of representatives from 7, the Dutch from 6, the American from 5, and the British from 4 different bodies, in our case the official representatives of Federal Union being supplemented by members of the National Peace Council, World Unity, and New Commonwealth.[53]

---

[52] Cf. note 45; L. van Vassenhove, 'Pourquoi ... ', article of July 1946 quoted in n. 34, p. 37. On the principles of federalism and their sources (subsidiarity, Proudhon, etc.), see chap. II/5, pp. 373 f., and Conclusions (in vol. 2).

[53] F. L. Josephy (n. 51), p. 2; for the New Commonwealth Society cf. Introduction, nn. 60 and 101. The seven French organizations are listed on p. 21 of *Federal News*, No. 141: La Fédération (J. Bareth, A. Voisin), Ligue pour la Défense des Libertés Humaines (Mme Finidori), Comité International pour la Fédération Européenne (R. Lhuillier), Union Économique et Douanière Européenne (G. Riou), Comité pour les États-Unis du Monde (P. Larmeroux), Union Fédérale Mondiale, Union Universelle pour la Paix (for details of these see chap. II/4). The six Dutch comprised four world federalist associations, the Europese Federative Beweging (J. van Dierendonck), and the no longer independent Federale Unie (cf. chap. I, nn. 101 f., and chap. III, nn. 443 f.). For other participating organizations, see nn. 54 and 55.

On 14 October, the first working day, two schools of thought soon became evident. Col. King, the chairman for that day, declared that it was the conference's task to set up a World Council of Federalists with its own secretariat, representing organizations all over the world which believed in a federal solution of world problems. Some delegates, taking their cue from this, endeavoured to confine the conference proceedings strictly to the creation of a World Council: this group was led by King and his fellow-MP Henry Usborne, the Americans, and Dr Max Habicht.[54] The other participants thought that before creating an organization it was essential to define its policy, and that it would be part of that policy to approve a European federation. This group was led by the more influential members of the French and Dutch delegations, the few who had also been at Hertenstein, and Miss Josephy,[55] who reported:

Never for one moment ... was there any difference of opinion between the two groups on the necessity for World Federal Government. The second group, however, felt that European Federation was an essential part of any effective peace-keeping organization, and believed that what they called the 'Twin Aims' – World Federal Government and European Federation – should be laid down as the basis of future activities. There seemed to be a fear on the part of Group I that if the Conference discussed policy there would be no agreement and it would break up without having set up the world organization of federalists. In addition the Americans, particularly Mr Tom Griessemer..., maintained not merely that European Federation would not be a step to peace, but that regional federations in themselves were a menace to peace. (I was driven to ask them in reply whether in that case they were prepared to go home and ask President Truman to dissolve the United States of America.) When they said they could not go home with a statement that mentioned Europe, we told them pretty plainly that the Europeans could not go home with a statement that did not. We assured them we were not asking America to work for European Federation; what we *were* asking was that they should not prevent *our* doing so, or refuse to allow the Europeans to know what was best for themselves.[56]

---

[54] Cf. the anonymous account of the day's proceedings, 'Federalists at Luxembourg', *Federal News*, No. 140, Nov. 1946, pp. 6–8; Josephy (n. 51), p. 4. The American organizations were: World Federalists Inc. (T. O. Griessemer), Student Federalists (F. Parmelee), Americans United for World Government (J. A. Migel), Campaign for World Government (Mrs G. Lloyd), Students for World Government (F. S. Carney); cf. a thesis on the world federalists by Frank Niess, begun under my supervision at Heidelberg and to be published shortly. Max Habicht of Geneva probably represented the only Swiss organization reached by invitation, the Mouvement Populaire Suisse en faveur d'une fédération des peuples (Dr P. Meyerhoffer, Geneva; this appears from Griessemer's letter of 9.12.1946 to Ritzel, *EU Archives,* Basle).

[55] Among those who were also at Hertenstein were M. Cosyn for the Belgian Union Fédérale, U. Campagnolo for the MFE, and probably H. Nord. In any case 'the Hertenstein Declaration was widely discussed by the conference' (Josephy to Salinger, 24.10.1946, *BEF Archives,* Brugmans corr.) and encouraged the second group to press for European federation.

[56] Josephy (n. 51), p. 4; fully confirmed by L. van Vassenhove, 'Congrès Fédéraliste', *L'Action fédéraliste européenne*, No. 3, Nov. 1946, pp. 66–8, who speaks of an 'assez vive controverse' and quotes Josephy's retort about dissolving the USA. M. Voisin of La Fédération, Paris, argued that federalism did not simply mean world government but should consist of a pyramid of communities with more extensive authority the higher one went, from municipalities to nations and from regional

Thanks to these vigorous arguments by the Europeans of the second group the conference, which had been in 'complete discord' on the evening of 14 October, resolved on the 15th, under Dr Habicht's chairmanship, that it was clearly necessary to set up two federalist associations. Two committees were appointed to work out the main lines of a world-wide and a European organization; their reports were adopted with few amendments on the 16th, under the chairmanship of H. Maas Geesteranus. A 'Movement for World Federal Government' was founded, open to any organization in the world which sought the creation of a world federal government. Griessemer was appointed its provisional secretary and was to set to work, first in New York and from the spring of 1947 in Geneva, to make arrangements for a world conference to be held in Switzerland in the summer; the provisional council of the Movement was to consist of one delegate from each country. On the recommendation of the second committee a 'Conseil des Fédéralistes Européens' was founded, on which each European federalist group was to have one representative; its 'provisional liaison officer' was Miss Josephy, who was to accept nominations of representatives from each of the European countries represented at Luxemburg for the smaller Executive Committee. This body was to hold its first session on 15th December in Paris, where a permanent secretariat would be established; the first meeting of the full Council would be held 'in Holland during the Easter holiday'. Also on 16 October, agreement was reached on a 'Declaration' to the press:

Recognizing that all the peoples in all the lands desire peace, we, Federalists from all parts of the world, meeting in Luxembourg in October, 1946, have decided to and do now bring into being an International Association uniting all organizations which seek the creation of a World Federal Government. Many of us advocate, as a step towards this end, the formation of Regional Federal Unions, and in particular the United States of Europe ... Conscious of the increasing perils which threaten mankind and of the functional incompetence of the Sovereign State to solve our difficulties, we appeal to men and women everywhere to join with us in this great campaign for the creation of a World Federal Government embracing all the peoples of the globe.[57]

Although the Declaration stressed the objective of world government, as common to both groups, the European federalists had successfully main-

---

federations to world government (ibid., p. 67. Confirmation also in H. Wehberg's short account, 'Der Zusammenschluss der pazifistischen Kräfte', *Die Friedens-Warte,* 46, 1946, pp. 394 f., and M. Plantier, 'Les Journées de Luxembourg', *La Fédération,* Paris, Nov. 1946, p. 20 f.

[57] Cf. record of the concluding day's proceedings in *Federal News,* No. 140 (n. 54), p. 8, and No. 141 (n. 51), p. 5. French texts of the committee reports and final declaration in *Le Document fédéraliste (publié par le CIFE),* No. 3, Paris, 15.1.1947; declaration only, in English, in A. and F. Boyd, *Western Union,* London, 1948, p. 71; German texts in Wehberg (n. 56) and *Mitteilungsblatt der Europäischen Föderalistischen Union,* No. 1/2, Cologne, March 1947. The announced conference of world federalists was held in Montreal in August 1947, cf. chap. III/4, pp. 585–90; the executive committee of the UEF, set up meanwhile, met in Paris on 15.12.1946, and its enlarged session was held in Amsterdam at Easter 1947, cf. chap. II/5, pp. 361–80.

tained their view at Luxemburg. The conference as a whole had not produced a notable statement on the lines of the Hertenstein programme, but it had done important organizational work by founding a world-wide union of world federalists and, within it, an autonomous union of European federalists. The latter constituted the second step, independent of Hertenstein, towards the foundation of the UEF.

(D) THE BASLE AGREEMENT FOR THE ESTABLISHMENT OF THE UEF

The last paragraph of the report of the European Committee adopted by the Luxemburg conference stated that 'The organizations represented at the Hertenstein conference in September are invited to express their views and to join the Conseil des Fédéralistes Européens.' Miss Josephy, as provisional liaison officer, accordingly wrote a week later to Salinger (having by then ascertained the address of Aktion Europa-Union) saying how much she regretted that they had not yet met, and 'how much we all hope you will agree to merge your provisional committee with the larger body'.[58] This was not altogether simple, especially as she mentioned in the same letter that the various Dutch groups were to appoint a single representative and that the secretariat was to be located in Paris. From Paris, however, where it no doubt seemed especially necessary to strengthen the European federal group, Francis Gerard wrote: 'Il faut évidemment à tout prix qu'il y ait unification des efforts'; he went on to say that he had heard from Mme Volpeliere that the executive of Aktion Europa-Union was shortly to meet in Switzerland, and made the helpful suggestion that he was prepared to attend.[59] Salinger wrote in this sense to Miss Josephy, who replied that she would accept the invitation to Basle on 9 December, as it was 'essential that the two organizations should be integrated as far as Europe is concerned'. Brugmans thanked her warmly, adding: 'From our side there will be no kind of "organization–nationalism" whatsoever, so I fervently hope we will achieve federal unity.'[60]

It was in this spirit that all-day discussions were held in Basle on 9 December 1946 – the day following the annual congress of the Swiss

[58] Report of the European committee, cf. note 57; Miss Josephy's letter (London, 24.10.1946) to Dr Salinger, The Hague, in *BEF Archives*, Brugmans corr.; she probably obtained the address from Dr Nord or another of the Dutch delegates at Luxemburg.

[59] Letter from Gérard (Paris, 28.10.1946) to Dr Brugmans, The Hague, in *BEF Archives*, Brugmans corr. Somewhat later Alexandre Marc must have written a similar letter (not preserved) on behalf of the French associations represented at Luxemburg, for Brugmans wrote to Ritzel on 18.11.1946, that Marc had enquired 'whether it would be useful for him to attend our Executive meeting in Basle. Personally I am convinced that we should have much closer ties with our French friends.' Ritzel replied on 23.11.1946: 'I entirely agree that Marc and Gérard should be invited' (ibid.).

[60] Letter from Josephy (London, 15.11.1946) to Salinger: 'sub-offices in The Hague, Basel, Prague' were possible, but the 'central office of the European Movement' must be in Paris. Letter from Brugmans, The Hague, 27.11.1946) to Josephy. A. Allard also wrote to Brugmans from Brussels on 16.11.1946, and U. Campagnolo from Milan on 30.11.1946, on the necessity of uniting the associations. (All in *BEF Archives*, Brugmans corr.)

Europa-Union[61] – between the full executive of Aktion Europa-Union, other members of its central committee, Miss Josephy representing Federal Union, Alexandre Marc representing 'all French federal movements', and U. Campagnolo for the MFE.[62] Brugmans began by asking whether 'after the Hertenstein and Luxemburg conferences ... it would now be a question of co-operation or antagonism'. After Miss Josephy had given an impassioned statement of the Federal Union view that there must be a global movement of which the European unity movement should be a part, there ensued a lengthy argument in which Campagnolo and van Vassenhove in particular expressed scepticism concerning a world federation; Brugmans, however, smoothed things over by pointing out that European union must naturally be seen in a world context from the outset and required, for example, a policy of friendship with Russia. Salinger declared that he saw no contradiction between the Luxemburg and Hertenstein resolutions, and the meeting unanimously endorsed this view. All those present, moreover, agreed on the necessity for the European Federalists of Hertenstein and Luxemburg to merge and thus unite their efforts for the cause of federation in Europe in the first instance.[63] Having expressed the desire for a single organization the meeting then discussed in general terms the question of a secretariat and agreed that a final decision on this could only be taken on 15 December in Paris.

The first question, viz. whether there should be a decentralized secretariat on the model of the Hertenstein resolution, with different functions performed in different places, or a joint general secretariat, was decided fairly quickly in the morning session; all except Salinger were in favour of the second solution. As to its location, Miss Josephy argued vigorously for Paris, which the French and Dutch also preferred; but Campagnolo, the Swiss, the Germans and Baron Allard, among others, advanced so many arguments for Geneva – a neutral country, more hope of influencing Eastern Europe, the presence of UN agencies, Switzerland

---

[61] 7/8.12.1946, Lausanne. At this congress the Hertenstein resolutions (cf. n. 44) were approved and H. Brugmans gave one of the principal addresses. 'S'unir est pour l'Europe moins une question d'idéal que de réalité, de nécessités concrètes ... L'Europe ne doit pas être un État-tampon, elle doit être un pont entre l'Ouest et l'Est. Européens de tous les pays, unissez-vous' (report in *L'Action fédéraliste européenne*, No. 4, Jan. 1947, p. 56 f.).

[62] *Protokoll über die Sitzung des Präsidiums der 'Aktion Europa-Union' am 9.12.1946*. Those present were: Dr. Brugmans, Holland, president; Mme Volpelière, Nîmes, France; H. Schiess, Aarau, Switzerland; Baron Allard, Brussels, Belgium; Dr Salinger, secretary-general, The Hague; H. G. Ritzel, secretary-general, Basle; also, in the afternoon, A. Siemsen, Germany, making the executive complete (cf. n. 47). Also present were Josephy, Marc, and Campagnolo, as mentioned, and members of the central committee: van Vassenhove, Hans Bauer, Count Kanitz, and (for Spain) L. Neumann. Eight pages of typed minutes in *EU Archives, Basle*, UEF files, 1.

[63] Minutes (n. 62), pp. 1–4. The main result was to provide for greater independence of the world federal organization than in Josephy's original formulation; this is well expressed by H. G. Ritzel in his short account in *Die Friedens-Warte*, 47, 1947, p. 70: 'The decision reflected the desire to make the Hertenstein and Luxemburg resolutions the basis of a common organization which would have European federation as its chief aim but would also support the desire for world federation through the individual associations and the movement as a whole.' A report in the same sense (but with the wrong date) is in *L'Unità europea*, Vol. 3, Nos. 1/2, p. 1 f.

as the core of a European confederation, etc. – that Miss Josephy finally leant towards the majority view. On the third question, as to who might be the secretary-general, Miss Josephy favoured Alexandre Marc, whose contribution to the discussions had been concise, sensible, and conciliatory; she and Ritzel did not wish to be considered for the post themselves; Campagnolo and Schiess proposed van Vassenhove and a vote was taken, during which Marc and van Vassenhove withdrew from the meeting.

At this preliminary sounding two votes were cast for van Vassenhove and all the rest for Alexandre Marc, save for one abstention.[64] The leadership of the European federalists was thus reinforced by one of the best-known *hommes de lettres* belonging to the French progressive Left and Renouveau Catholique, a member of the editorial staff of *Temps présent* and *Témoignage chrétien* and a theorist of federalism whose personality probably impressed most foreign federalists who met him in the same way as it did Brugmans: 'Meeting Marc was a revelation to me. A pupil of Proudhon, he had combined into a self-contained doctrine everything that we, during the occupation and immediately afterwards, had called personalism.'[65] Following the Luxemburg timetable, it was agreed that final decisions would be taken in Paris on 15 December.

The name of the joint organization had not yet been discussed, but Miss Josephy, disliking the word 'Conseil' used by the European committee at Luxemburg, had changed it to 'Union'. Before the Basle session, her invitations to the Paris meeting of 15 December were sent out under the letterhead 'Union Européenne des Fédéralistes – European Union of Federalists'.[66]

[64] Minutes (n. 62), pp. 4–7. In conclusion, on a proposal by Prof. Anna Siemsen a committee was set up to plan for a European College of Education, its members being Ritzel, Brogle, Siemsen, van Vassenhove, and the Italian minister to Switzerland; and, on Ritzel's proposal, it was agreed to draft a petition, to be signed by Brugmans, that German prisoners of war should be released or allowed to work on a voluntary basis in the Allied countries (ibid., p. 8).

[65] H. Brugmans, 'Het begin . . .' (n. 43), p. 16. Alexandre Marc, b. Odessa 1904, emigrated to Paris with his parents at an early age. According to his own account, his 'European' sympathies were first inspired by a visit to Germany in 1923, when he was a young student and had intensive talks with German students at Freiburg. Together with Otto Abetz, Walter Strauss, Jean Luchair, Philippe Lamour, and others he organized camp meetings for the promotion of Franco–German understanding, at Solberg in 1929, Rethel (Ardennes) in 1930, and near Frankfurt in 1931 with Denis de Rougemont and Harald Schulze–Boysen. In 1932–6 he was in contact with the 'Ordre nouveau' group including Robert Aron, Daniel Rops, and Arnaud Dandieu (with whom he wrote a book on the 'splendour and misery of the intellect') and the progressive Dominican journal *Sept*. After studying the theory of subsidiarity in natural law he evolved a comprehensive theologico-political conception of federalism, owing more to Proudhon than to Thomas Aquinas. He published two books on Péguy. In the Resistance, in the winter of 1940/1 he distributed *La Voix du Vatican* (French translation of anti-Nazi items from Vatican Radio); he also worked for *Combat*, the clandestine *Cahiers du témoignage chrétien*, and *Libérer et fédérer*. To escape imminent arrest he remained in Switzerland from the beginning of 1943 to the autumn of 1944. He wrote for A. Beguin's *Cahiers du Rhône* and published books: *Proudhon* and *Avènement de la France ouvrière* (Paris, 1945). In 1945/6 he was guarantor for the journal *La Fédération* and editor of the journals referred to in the text. (Information from A. Marc, 28.11.1963; see also Index.)

[66] Invitation dated 4.12.1946 (an original e.g. in Gérard archives); Miss Josephy had also used the word 'Union' in her report in *Federal News*, Dec. 1946 (n. 51). On the Paris meeting and further

3. Churchill's Zurich Speech; Foundation of the United Europe Movement and the ELEC

The federalists had as yet attracted little attention in the daily press. In the first months after the end of the war the idea of European union was frequently mooted by papers of consequence such as *Le Monde*, notably on the occasion of the London meeting of the Council of Foreign Ministers in September 1945;[67] but the general public lost sight of it during the twelve months' period of resignation, as the dictatorship of the two superpowers over Europe became evident. The federalist associations had their own journals, and their activities found an echo in some periodicals of note such as the London *Economist*; but in the ordinary press even the Hertenstein and Luxemburg conferences received, at most, a brief and inconspicuous mention. Then suddenly, in the last week of September 1946, almost exactly a year after the subject had been despondently abandoned, the idea of a 'United States of Europe' again hit the headlines on account of a single speech by a famous man, and politicians in office found themselves obliged, or able, to take notice of it once more.

(A) CHURCHILL'S APPEAL FOR 'A KIND OF UNITED STATES OF EUROPE'

The extraordinary importance of Winston Churchill's speech in Zurich on 19 September, and the attention it aroused throughout the world, were due to the fact that the plea for European unity was not a cry in the wilderness from some unknown member of the European Resistance, but came from one of the 'Big Three' leaders of the victorious coalition against Nazi Germany – a man who had proved himself to be a hard and realistic politician, whose political and military genius had saved Britain, and whose determination during his country's lone stand against Hitler in 1940–1 had earned him the reverent gratitude of all European lovers of freedom. Another reason for the effect produced by the speech was that the great statesman's call for European unity was made at a time of general uncertainty and bewilderment, when public controversy and mutual accusations by the two superpowers aroused fears that a world peace settlement could not after all be expected from them, and when politicians and the public were groping for a way out of the impasse. Churchill, however, did not address himself directly to what might be only short-term difficulties, but voiced convictions that had matured in his mind over

---

building-up of the UEF, cf. chap. II/5, PP. 361–80. The rather sudden founding or reactivation of several French federalist groups in Oct.–Nov. 1946 might properly be described at this point. But one of its causes was Churchill's Zurich speech, and is seems appropriate to analyse this speech first and examine its consequences. The revival of French federalism is therefore discussed in chap. II/4, pp. 346–61.

[67] Cf. examples in W. Lipgens, 'Innerfranzösische Kritik der Aussenpolitik de Gaulles 1944 bis 1946', *VfZG*, 24 (1976), pp. 167–73.

nearly two decades. Since the First World War he had felt the decline of Europe more deeply than most politicians, and had drawn the conclusion that an end must be put to Continental quarrels. Almost alone among British statesmen he had welcomed Briand's plan for 'European federal union', though, it is true, he envisaged the scheme as suitable only for the European Continent, without the adherence of Great Britain.

'How mighty Europe is, but for its divisions!' – Churchill had written in an article published in the *Saturday Evening Post* of 15 February 1930. 'The mass of Europe, once united, once federalized or partly federalized, once continentally self-conscious, ... would constitute an organism beyond compare ... We see nothing but good and hope in a richer, freer, more contented European commonalty. But we have our own dream and our own task. We are with Europe, but not of it. We are linked, but not comprised. We are interested and associated, but not absorbed.'[68] In 1939, as has been seen, Churchill as president of the New Commonwealth Society advocated a supranational peace-keeping authority in Europe; in 1940 he proposed an indissoluble union of Britain and France with a common parliament; and in 1942–4 he spoke several times of the need to unify Europe under a Council with power to enforce its decisions. In 1945, owing to the predominance of the two superpowers and to de Gaulle's non-co-operation, he had to fall back on defending Britain's interests.[69] Driven from office by the Labour victory in July 1945, in an address to both houses of the Belgian parliament on 17 November he reverted to the theme of united Europe which, although the 'one world' thesis was then at its height, was still dismissed as Utopian: 'I see no reason why, under the guardianship of a world organization, there should not arise the United States of Europe, which will unify this Continent in a manner never known since the fall of the Roman Empire, and within which all its peoples may dwell together in prosperity, in justice and in peace.'[70]

After the fiasco of the Paris meetings of foreign ministers, Churchill spoke in circumstances which ensured a world-wide response to his views. On 5 July 1946 he had expressed his feelings by exclaiming in the House of Commons: 'Anything is better than this ceaseless degeneration of the heart of Europe. Europe will die of it!' Earlier, in March, he had spoken at Fulton of the Iron Curtain behind which Eastern Europe was disappearing. While on holiday at Bursinel on Lake Geneva he was invited by Zurich University to delivery an address on 19 September, and there he spoke with urgency, in still plainer terms, of European unity as a remedy against

[68] Cf. extracts from this article in R. Coudenhove-Kalergi, *Eine Idee erobert Europa*, Munich, 1958, pp. 174–6 (English version, *An Idea Conquers the World*, London, 1953, p. 162 f.); also H. von Siegler, *Dokumentation der europäischen Integration*, vol. i, Bonn, 1961, p. xi (which also quotes, as one of the few British voices that then supported Churchill, his friend L. S. Amery speaking at the Second Pan-Europe Congress at Berlin in May 1930).

[68] Described more fully above, with quotations: cf. pp. 64 f., 67 f., 73, 76, 162–5.

[70] As regards Britain's destiny, Churchill said in his Brussels speech: 'It is evident of course that the affairs of Great Britain and the British Commonwealth and Empire are becoming ever more closely interwoven with those of the United States, and that an underlying unity of thought and conviction increasingly pervades the English-speaking world.' (*Winston Churchill, His Complete Speeches 1897–1963* (ed. R. R. James), vol. vii, 1943–1949, New York/London, 1974, p. 7253).

the dangers he foresaw.[71] Beginning with the simple but pregnant sentence: 'I wish to speak to you today about the tragedy of Europe', he went on to speak of the intellectual and cultural wealth which might be preserved if only the peoples of the Continent would cultivate their common heritage in peace and unity. Instead, Europe presented the spectacle of

a vast quivering mass of tormented, hungry, careworn and bewildered human beings, scanning the dark horizons for the approach of some new peril, tyranny or terror ... Yet all the while there is a remedy which, if it were generally and spontaneously adopted, would, in a few years, make all Europe, or the greater part of it, as free and happy as Switzerland is today. What is this sovereign remedy? It is to recreate the European Family, or as much of it as we can, and provide it with a structure under which it can dwell in peace, in safety and freedom. We must build a kind of United States of Europe. In this way only will hundreds of millions of toilers be able to regain the simple joys and hopes which make life worth living.

Churchill went on:

'There is no reason why a regional organization of Europe should in any way conflict with the world organization of the United Nations. On the contrary, I believe that the larger synthesis will only survive if it is founded upon coherent natural groupings. There is already a natural grouping in the Western Hemisphere. We British have our Commonwealth of Nations. These do not weaken, on the contrary they strengthen the world organization. They are in fact its main support. And why should there not be a European group which could give a sense of enlarged patriotism and common citizenship to the distracted peoples of this turbulent and mighty continent; and why should it not take its rightful place with other great groupings in shaping the destinies of men?' He did not wish to suggest an exact programme; 'ways and means can certainly be found. But I give you a warning. Time may be short. At present there is a breathing space. The cannons have ceased firing. The fighting has stopped: but the dangers have not stopped. If we are to form the United States of Europe or whatever name or form it may take, we must begin now ... The first step is to form a Council of Europe. If at first all the States of Europe are not willing or able to join the Union, we must nevertheless proceed to assemble and combine those who will and those who can ... In all this urgent work, France and Germany must take the lead together. Great Britain, the British Commonwealth of Nations, mighty America, and I trust Soviet Russia – for then indeed all would be well – must be the friends and

---

[71] Churchill, speech in House of Commons, 5.6.1946, quoted in chap. I/3, n. 196; Fulton speech, March 1946, quoted in chap. II/1, n. 13. For his summer holiday at Bursinel on Lake Geneva cf. Coudenhove-Kalergi, *An Idea* ... (n. 68), p. 267 f.; Coudenhove, who was revisiting Europe from America for the first time since the war, states that he lunched with Churchill on 14 September, five days before the Zurich speech, and found him 'ready to listen to advice and criticism'. According to an agency report at the time, Churchill, in keeping with the academic setting at Zurich, 'read his speech, which lasted seventeen minutes, from a manuscript, with simple, natural gestures, sometimes emphasizing a word or a short sentence in a calm, unemotional tone. The audience followed his words with continuous and growing interest' (AEP, 19.9.1946).

320 *Revival of Plans for Federation*

sponsors of the new Europe and must champion its right to live and shine. Therefore I say to you: Let Europe arise!'[72]

The statesman who had helped to determine the outcome of the Second World War and was one of the 'Big Three' who had fought it to a successful conclusion thus launched the slogan of the United States of Europe at a time of renewed uncertainty. The world paid attention, and in the ensuing days and weeks the speech aroused widespread repercussions in the press and in many government circles. Reactions were divided, however. The British Labour government let it be known that it had had no advance knowledge of Churchill's speech, which only represented his personal views. Innumerable press comments expressed hope and agreement with what Churchill had said, but to many others the call for an 'act of oblivion' in Germany's favour seemed premature. The Communists, as will be seen, rejected the speech with one accord.[73] The main theme of Churchill's speech, coinciding with the views of the European Resistance and the reviving federalist groups, was that Europe must unite and assume a position of its own between the two world powers as a regional body in the sense of Article 52 of the UN Charter, so that the organization of world peace might become a reality. The federalists could only be gratified at the enormous propaganda success which attended this proclamation of their own thesis. When the speech was looked at more closely, however, it appeared that on three points Churchill's ideas differed somewhat from those of the European federalists.

1. Churchill proposed a union that should begin with the reconciliation of France and Germany and include 'the European Family, or as much of it as we can'. He presented this as a means by which the old Continent could save itself through a lasting peace and co-operation among its member states. He did not expressly say anything adverse to the Soviet Union, which he mentioned only once, in the hopeful words of the penultimate sentence quoted above. But his allusion to 'dark horizons' and 'some new peril, tyranny or terror' were unmistakable. His realism and clarity of vision permitted no doubt as to the aims of Soviet policy in Europe. The majority of commentators were clearly right when they interpreted Churchill's reference to states 'not willing or able to join the

---

[72] Text of the speech in W. S. Churchill, *The Sinews of Peace, Post-War Speeches by Winston S. Churchill*, London, 1948, pp. 197–9; A. and F. Boyd, *Western Union*, London, 1948, pp. 109–12; H. Brugmans, *L'Idée européenne 1920–1970*, Bruges, 1970³, pp. 373–6. According to the report quoted above 'the audience thanked the British statesman with loud and prolonged applause. The students' choir concluded the ceremony with an impressive rendering of the national anthem by Hermann Suter. Churchill was applauded again as he left the hall' (AEP report, 19.9.1946).

[73] For the British government's disavowal (in the form of a Foreign Office statement), see *The Times*, 21.9.1946. For the reactions of European public opinion to Churchill's speech, the foundation of his United Europe Movement and the general revival of the European idea in autumn–winter 1946/7, see summary at the end of this chapter, pp. 432–5; for Soviet and American reactions, see chap. III/1, pp. 467–81. For the reactions of the inner circle of already convinced European federalists, see p. 341–5.

union' as designating the East-European countries, and drew the conclusion that he was arguing for a Western-European union in the first instance – especially when he warned the Europeans that they might have only a brief respite 'under the shield and protection of the [US] atomic bomb'. For some months to come the federalists were not ready to write off Eastern Europe in this way: they hoped desperately that the Soviet Union would relinquish its control over the satellites so that a neutral Europe might be constituted as a 'Third Force'. Churchill, as a visionary and a realist, well understood that the all-European solution would not be practicable for a long time to come, and moreover that the union of those European states which were still in a position to combine together was all the more essential because of the need to oppose a barrier to further Soviet expansion.[74]

2. In contrast to the traditional British policy of playing the Continental states off against one another, Churchill was far in advance of the greater part of British public opinion in urging the Continent to unite. But he reflected a typically British view when he made it clear, in the Zurich speech and elsewhere, that he did not think of Britain as a member of the 'kind of United States of Europe' which he was urging the Continental states, especially France and Germany, to form. 'We British have our own Commonwealth of Nations', he pointed out, and in his concluding words he spoke of Britain as one of the world powers which 'must be the friends and sponsors of the new Europe'. The federalists differed in their attitude to the question of British membership: not all of them were pleased with Churchill's idea that, while other countries should unite, 'we British' were a special case. The idea that Churchill was in favour of British membership arose later because the association founded by him, as will be seen, expressed itself differently on this point. But Churchill himself only varied for a while (1948–9) from the opinion he had expressed in 1930, that Britain – 'linked but not comprised' in Europe, 'associated but not absorbed' – was destined, as head of the Commonwealth, to play the part of a world power of the first rank, a link between the United States of Europe and those of America.

3. Churchill's appeal for European union was clear and urgent, but his indications as to its form and structure were extremely vague. This may have been connected with the two previous points: he did not want to prescribe in detail to the Continentals how they should unite, or to give the Soviet Union any ground for criticism; but the chief reason was no doubt his aversion to federal principles. He had a clear idea of what he expected European union to achieve; by talking of the 'United States' of Europe he invited comparison with America's strength, and he appealed for a 'structure' within which Europeans could 'dwell in peace' among them-

---

[74] Quotations in this and the next two paragraphs from the Zurich speech, cf. n. 72; for the federalists' divergent view on these points, cf. pp. 343 f. and 380 f.

selves and 'in safety' *vis-à-vis* the Soviet Union. But, like the founders of the League of Nations in their time and de Gaulle subsequently, he did not understand what means were necessary to bring about the desired objective. The nearest he came to a concrete suggestion was that there must be 'a sense of enlarged patriotism and common citzenship'. But he clearly envisaged the 'Council of Europe' merely as a regular conference of government representatives, not as an independent executive; otherwise he would have advocated a European parliament to supervise the Council's actions, which he never did. He definitely wanted much more than an alliance: he spoke of uniting and combining, but he did not want a federation; he wanted a really strong union, but gave no clear idea of how it was to be achieved.[75]

Despite all this, Churchill's speech was a turning-point – an expression of personal conviction, breaking the resigned silence which had prevailed for twelve months past. The victor of the Second World War made credible once again the idea of European unity which, in the eyes of many, had been discredited by Hitler's abuses. From now on the idea presented itself once more as a realistic plan and an answer to the manifest dissensions of the superpowers. Churchill's conviction of the need for Continental union was so evident, his personal devotion to the cause so emphatic, that there can be no doubt that, had he been in office, he would not, like Bevin, have waited till 1948 to take up a position, and then taken a hesitant and obstructive line; he would have begun in 1946 to display initiative and untiring energy in order to overcome the 'ceaseless degeneration' of Europe and lay the foundations of European union. This was so essential, in his view, to his main-purpose of containing Soviet expansion, and the prospects seemed so much improved by the signs of a 'firm' American policy and by de Gaulle's resignation, that in the winter of 1946/7 he would have used all his diplomacy and ingenuity to help forward the cause of union. In his capacity as 'sponsor' he would have seen to it that the phase of conferences and co-operation began in 1946 and not 1948; and in that case the impulses of 1948–50 might have led to a Continental federation, if Britain's intention to remain outside had been made clear from the outset.[76]

---

[75] One reason was no doubt that Churchill did not wish to tie his hands in case he should return to power. For a similar over-all interpretation see H. Brugmans, 'Legenden um eine europäische Grösse. Winston Churchill: ein früher Gaullist', *Europa-Union, Europäische Zeitung*. Vol. 22, No. 9 (Bonn), Sept. 1971.

[76] The lack of enthusiasm shown by Churchill's last government, from October 1951 to April 1955, does not seem to me to invalidate this view. 1. The disappointment of the Europeans was chiefly due to their erroneous belief that if Churchill were in office Britain would join in the process of unification. This was never Churchill's own intention (cf. his speech in *Parl. Debates, House of Commons*, Vol. 476, 27.6.1950, cols. 2157–62: Britain's role consisted first in leadership of the Commonwealth, second in her fraternal relationship with the US, thirdly in promoting Continental European union). 2. The degree of Continental unity and self-confidence that Churchill had pleaded for in 1946 was by now largely attained: Soviet expansion was curbed, the Council of

(B) FOUNDATION OF THE UNITED EUROPE MOVEMENT

Churchill, however, was not in office. In Zurich he had spoken of the 'resolve of millions of men and women' that was necessary to bring about union, and presumably also to prepare the ground for it. Returning to England at the end of 1946, he set about founding a non-party organization to mobilize British support for the cause of European unity. Being fully occupied with his duties as Leader of the Opposition, he delegated most of the work to his son-in-law Duncan Sandys, a sympathizer with the European cause, who had been a successful junior minister during the war but was now out of office, having lost his seat in the 1945 election.[77] A first-class organizer and negotiator, convinced of the danger of Soviet expansion, Sandys busied himself with the establishment of a committee of sympathizers.[78] For this purpose Churchill and Sandys were obliged to seek support from existing forces, either actual or potential allies, who, however, did not all share Churchill's view that Britain should remain outside the proposed European union. It was necessary in particular to seek a compromise with two groups which had long been working for European union in different ways:

1. One group wished to rescue Europe from disunity and impotence and help it to unite under British leadership – generally by way of associa-

---

Europe had been set up, Franco-German reconciliation was in progress; he had also welcomed the Schuman plan; if the Europeans wanted to advance further towards federation it was their affair, he would not interfere but would not do anything specially to promote it. 3. Churchill was 78–81 years of age and left a fairly free hand to Eden, his undisputed successor.

[77] Rt. Hon. Duncan E. Sandys (Lord Duncan-Sandys), b. 24.1.1908, educated at Eton and Oxford; diplomatic service 1930–4 (1930–3 at the British Embassy, Berlin), from which he resigned when his memorandum on Hitler's dangerous ambitions was rejected by the Foreign Secretary, Sir John Simon; 1935–45 Conservative MP for Norwood Division of Lambeth; after his election met and married Diana Churchill; loyal supporter of Churchill's fight against 'appeasement', even in 1936–8 when only two or three Members were on Churchill's side (cf. R. R. James, *Churchill. A study in failure 1900–1939*, London, 1970, p. 335 f.; James describes Sandys (ibid., p. 296) as 'a man of great seriousness of purpose . . . , a dogged persistence, coupled with an absolute personal integrity'). 1939/40 on active service, Expeditionary Force in Norway, disabled and discharged with rank of Lieutenant-Colonel; 1941–3 Financial Secretary to War Office; 1943–4 Parliamentary Secretary, Ministry of Supply; 1943–5 Chairman of Cabinet Committee for defence against German 'V' weapons. 1950 re-elected (and remained till 1974) MP for Streatham Division of Wandsworth; 1951–64 senior minister in all Cabinets, including Supply 1951–4, Housing and Local Government 1954–7, Defence 1957–9, Commonwealth Relations 1960–4, Colonies 1962–4 (*Dictionary of National Biography*).

[78] According to his own account Sandys, when still at Oxford (*c.* 1927) founded a 'British–German Club' to promote understanding between the two nations in a European spirit. In 1930–3, when a Secretary in the Berlin Embassy, he witnessed the rise of Nazism and understood its causes in the world economic crisis; in 1935–9 he nevertheless fought hard against 'appeasement'. After Churchill's Zurich speech he concentrated on the campaign to create a united Western Europe between the two world powers, his chief reason being that Communism was an even greater danger than Nazism – an ideology of world revolution as opposed to a German national imperialism which was essentially not exportable. Unlike Churchill, however, he believed that Britain should from the start be a member of united Europe which for Sandys became a commitment and ideal in itself (Information from *Duncan-Sandys*, 3.10.1974). For his views and co-ordination of all 'European' groups, cf. chap. III/7, pp. 659 f., esp. pp. 666–70.

tion with the British Commonwealth, a solution advocated by Field-Marshal Smuts in 1943 and favoured by Eden and other leading Conservatives. On 11 October 1946 Smuts, in an address to both houses of the Dutch parliament, expressed general agreement with Churchill's Zurich speech but added: 'I fear Europe cannot wait until there is a great change of heart in France and Germany', and pointed out that many were asking 'why Britain herself did not take the lead in this greatest of European interests'. He suggested that 'the smaller European states', whose respect, sympathy, and confidence Britain enjoyed thanks to her war record, might 'exercise some influence with her', in this direction.[79]

2. Federal Union, a body whose co-operation was expecially desirable since it had been advocating European federation since 1938 with considerable propaganda success, laid down three conditions which were difficult to reconcile with Churchill's ideas. It insisted on prior agreement that (a) Britain was regarded as part of Europe; (b) the 'United States of Europe' were to be the first step towards world government, and (c) it must be clearly understood that the 'United States of Europe' were not to form an anti-Soviet bloc.[80] The second condition of course implied that the European union must be of a federal character. No direct records are available concerning the discussions between the different groups, which cannot have been easy. Churchill tried to remove some of the difficulty by writing an article in December 1946 enlarging on what he had said at Zurich and making some concessions to the federalists:

As to (a), he stuck to his point that 'It is now for France to take the Germans by the hand and lead them back into the brotherhood of man.' He also insisted on Britain's special role, but expressed this in more forthcoming terms: 'The British nation, lying in the centre of so many healthy and beneficent networks, is not only the heart of the British Empire and Commonwealth of Nations, and an equal partner in the English-speaking world, but it is also a part of Europe and intimately and inseparably mingled with its fortunes.' To sum up: 'We must have the four great entities and contributors to world government' – the Soviet Union, the USA, the USE and the Commonwealth, and 'we must hope indeed that China will make a fifth – all playing their part in the world organization'. In this way

---

[79] For Smuts's programme, Nov. 1943, and similar statements by Eden, cf. chap. I, n. 151. Smuts's address at The Hague, 11.10.1946, in *The Times*, 12.10.1946. Only after making this appeal for British leadership did Smuts advocate that 'if none will venture to take the lead towards such a political regional solution', 'a start should be made on the economic plane.'

[80] *Mitteilungsblatt*, No. 1/2 of the Europäisch-föderalistische Union, Cologne, March 1947 (by Stocky, who was in regular touch with Federal Union, cf. e.g. Minutes of the Executive Committee of 28.3.1947, *FU Archives*). No date is given there, but since (1) the text is not identical with the FU press statement (which included points (b) and (c), cf. note 87); (2) at the time of the Zurich speech Miss Josephy wrote to *The Times* protesting against Churchill's 'exclusion of Great Britain from membership of the United States of Europe – from every point of view this would be a major calamity' (quoted in *Federal News*, No. 140, Nov. 1946, p. 6); and (3) the text agrees with Josephy's report (n. 82) – it may be regarded for these reasons as an accurate formulation of the points maintained by Josephy and E. King, MP, in the discussions with Sandys.

Churchill acknowledged the importance that Federal Union attached to their point (b). Churchill also for the first time gave a clear idea of the tasks, though not the constitutional structure, of the Council of Europe. It was to endeavour to remove tariff and trade barriers and bring about economic co-operation as a step towards economic unity; there must be 'a uniform currency' and 'some common form of defence which will preserve order among, and give mutual security to its members'.[81] As to point (c), Churchill declared: 'We are told this conception of a free, reviving, regenerated Europe is anti-Russian ... This is not true. The many peoples of Russia who are comprised in the Union of Soviet Socialist Republics, and who occupy one-sixth of the land surface of the globe, have nothing to fear and much to gain from the creation of a United Europe.' There might well be Communists 'enjoined to raise their voices in favour of keeping Europe divided, helpless, impoverished or even starving ... as an essential preliminary to world Communist domination ... But Europe and the great world around must find their own way through their troubles' and must not let themselves be deflected from their own policy and interests by an 'arbitrary veto'. Churchill continued to maintain this principle of self-determination.

In negotiations with individuals and groups in London in December 1946 and the first half of January 1947, Sandys obtained agreement on a statement of policy that was a masterpiece of compromise: it was simple and clear, yet the controversial points were so drafted that everyone could read his own meaning into them.[82] On 16 January 1947 the 'provisional British Committee to further the cause of a United Europe' held its opening session under Churchill's chairmanship and unanimously approved a declaration covering a single sheet of paper. It pointed out that 'the anarchy of Europe has already brought about two world wars in our time', and expressed the conviction that 'appropriate nations should be encouraged to group themselves together in larger units' with the ultimate objective of world government; more especially, a 'unified Europe' must be created. 'If Europe is to survive, it must unite' – this was the essential theme on which agreement was unanimous. As to point (a) the wording was ambivalent: 'Britain has special obligations and spiritual ties which link her with the other nations of the British Commonwealth. Nevertheless, Britain is part of Europe and must be prepared to make her full contribution to European unity.' Whether this meant she was to be a member of the European union – which was not Churchill's own intention at any

---

[81] 'Luckily coins have two sides, so that one side can bear the national and the other the European superscription. Postage stamps, passports' – all this would follow. Specific aims were at last mentioned in the shape of currency and defence. Churchill's article 'A United Europe. One way to stop a new war' appeared in *Collier's Weekly Magazine,* New York, for Christmas week, 1946, and in the *Daily Telegraph,* 30/1.12.1946; I have a seven-page offprint by St. Clements Press, London (*FU* and *EM Archives* and elsewhere).

[82] Miss Josephy informed the National Council of Federal Union at a special meeting on 26.1.1947 that 'Mr. Churchill's Committee would have issued a statement with or without the co-operation of the four federalists on it, but because of their co-operation the statement was very much more federal and in line with the policy of FU than it would otherwise have been' (Minutes of meeting, 26.1.1947, *FU Archives,* p. 2).

326   *Revival of Plans for Federation*

time – was left open, and this caused much misunderstanding. As to (b), apart from the polite reference to the 'ultimate ideal' of world government, matters were deliberately left vague: 'It would be premature to define the precise constitutional relationship between the nations of a unified Europe'; the main thing was to make a start with consultation and concerted action. As to (c), there was no critical reference to the Soviet Union; it was merely pointed out that 'United Europe' would have the status of a regional group under the UN Charter, and would 'naturally seek the close friendship and co-operation of the Soviet Union and the United States of America'.[83]

It was important to the founders that the Committee was a non-party body composed of eminent figures in political and cultural life, capable of promoting the European cause with authority in every sphere. Under Churchill's chairmanship it comprised twenty-two members, carefully chosen as follows:

3 Conservative Members of Parliament (Robert Boothby, David Maxwell Fyfe, Home Secretary from 1951, and Oliver Stanley, Colonial Secretary in the War Cabinet) and 3 other leading Conservatives (L. S. Amery, for many years Secretary of State for India, Ernest Brown, a former Minister of Labour, and Duncan Sandys); 3 Labour parliamentarians (Evelyn King, the Revd. Gordon Lang, and Lord Lindsay of Birker) and 3 more Labour representatives (George Gibson, former chairman of the Trades Union Congress, Victor Gollancz the publisher, and Commander Stephen King-Hall); 3 members of the Liberal party (Miss Josephy, Sir Walter Layton, and Lady Rhys Williams); Lionel Curtis, a well-known federalist (as were Miss Josephy and the two first-named Labour MPs); 3 eminent scientists, and 3 representatives of the Churches.[84]

The project, however, ran into opposition in a powerful quarter, the Executive Committee of the Labour Party. None of the party's chief leaders had shown willingness to support the European cause, and as soon as the UEC statement was published they forbade members to support the Committee on the ground that it was 'an embarrassment to Britain's Labour Government, which is trying to avoid anything that would tend to

---

[83] Text in *The Times, Manchester Guardian,* and *Daily Telegraph* of 17.1.1947 (also in *Federal News*, No. 144, March 1947, p. 6), with the comment, probably furnished by the Committee, that 'They think it essential that this country should give a lead, and believe that it will bring an immediate response from all parts of Europe. Many of them hold that only within the framework of a more closely integrated Europe will it be possible to achieve a final and peaceful solution of the future of defeated Germany. . . . It is felt that there is no reason why Eastern European States should not be associated with a United Europe while continuing to have a specially close relationship with Soviet Russia.' (Cf. also report in *L'Action fédéraliste européenne*, No. 4, Jan. 1947, pp. 58 f.)

[84] The three scientists were Dr J. J. Mallon, CH, Prof. Gilbert Murray, OM, and Earl (Bertrand) Russell, FRS; the three church leaders were W. R. Matthews, Dean of St. Paul's Cathedral, S. E. Ellis, Roman Catholic Bishop of Nottingham, and Dr S. Berry, Secretary of the Congregational Union. (Dr Mallon and Bertrand Russell were also members of the Labour Party). The names of the twenty-two are given in the sources cited in n. 83; also in S. D. Bailey, *United Europe. A short history of the idea*, London, (*c.* July) 1947, p. 33.

embarrass its relations with the Soviet Government'.[85] This did not cause any of the eight Labour members to resign from the Committee, but Attlee's disavowal meant that the Committee was henceforth mainly associated with the Conservative party, which was a grave handicap to the European movement.

It was all the more important that the leaders of the federal movement in Britain, whose position was still weak, decided to support the Committee actively even though the manifesto took insufficient account of their principles. On 24 January 1947 Miss Josephy submitted to the Executive Committee of Federal Union a letter from Duncan Sandys explaining that the United Europe Committee did not intent to build up an organization based on mass membership, but sought the friendship of Federal Union and its co-operation in organizing talks, etc. As a result 'it was generally agreed that Federal Union should co-operate with the Committee provided it did not lose its identity and stressed at all times its own wider policy'. At a special meeting of the National Council of Federal Union, despite objections to Churchill as 'leader of an anti-Russian crusade' and 'thoroughly reactionary' (Mr Wall) the prevailing view was that 'Churchill was too important a person to ignore' when his policy 'was in part that of FU', that by co-operating with the Committee it could be brought 'more on federal lines' (Miss Josephy), and that, while maintaining FU's own policy, they should take advantage of the 'opportunity to increase membership' (Mr Catlin, Mr Ransome, and others). By 20 votes to 3 the meeting adopted a decision on these lines, which was announced in a letter to *The Times*:

> The Council of Federal Union ... discussed the Manifesto ... The boldness and political vision of the statement was fully recognized, and the manner in which it is focusing attention upon the urgent need for political and economic integration ... We welcome the formation of the United Europe Committee and are anxious to collaborate with it, while continuing to emphasize our own conviction that peace on this planet will only be permanently assured on the basis of a world government elected by and responsible to the peoples of the World as a whole. Secondly, we are convinced that any European Union must be federal in character; and thirdly, that it must be ... without latent hostility to the U.S.S.R. or to any other group or nation whatsoever.[86]

---

[85] Quoted from *New York Herald Tribune*, 21.1.1947; the fact of the prohibition is confirmed by E. Windrich, *British Labour's Foreign Policy*, Stanford, 1952, p. 188. and H. Heiser, *British Policy with regard to the Unification Efforts on the European Continent*, Leiden, 1959, p. 28. This historically fateful *rifiuto* is attributable to the stalemate of Bevin's foreign policy (cf. chap. I, esp. pp. 181 f.), and probably even more to party political motives, viz. the fear that if Churchill's prestige were enhanced on the international plane it would also strengthen his position in home affairs. The suspicion that this was Churchill's own motive throughout is largely refuted by the fact that he had taken the same line when the war was still in progress.

[86] Minutes of Meeting of the Executive Committee, 24.1.1947 (with J. Fidler, F. L. Josephy, H. Usborne, MP, M. Wingate, and others, twelve in all), p. 1; minutes of Meeting of the National Council, 26.1.1947 (M. Wingate in the chair, twenty three present), pp. 1–5 (ibid., p. 5, statement by the secretary, K. Killby: 'Whereas in 1945 there had been only 368 new members, in 1946 there had

More important still, a group of MPs who were members of FU – H. Usborne, D. L. Lipson, J. Parker, A. S. Champion, E. Roberts, and E. Wills – tabled a motion which obtained the signatures of seventy-two members of the course of February 1947 and – while avoiding direct reference to Europe and the Committee, in view of the attitude of the Labour Executive – stated in emphatic terms that 'in order to raise the standard of living of the peoples of the world, and to maintain world peace, this House requests His Majesty's Government to affirm Britain's readiness to federate with any other nations willing to do so on the basis of a federal constitution to be agreed by a representative constituent assembly'.[87] Since the 'nations willing to do so' could in practice only be European ones (as was taken for granted in the government's negative response),[88] the number of signatories to the draft resolution, almost all of whom belonged to the Labour Left, showed how much support there was for the idea of a supranational federation including Britain. This, moreover, was the first time that anyone in a European parliament (albeit a minority in this case) had mooted the idea of a 'constituent assembly'.

The formal inauguration of the United Europe Movement (as it was now officially called) took place on 14 May 1947 in an impressive ceremony in the Royal Albert Hall, which was thronged for the occasion. Under the chairmanship of the Archbishop of Canterbury, Dr Geoffrey Fisher, who spoke a few words of introduction, addresses were given by Winston Churchill, George Gibson for the trade unions, Lady Violet Bonham Carter for the Liberal party, Victor Gollancz, the Revd. J. M. Richardson (Moderator of the Free Church Federal Council), Oliver Stanley, and Henri Barré, the last-named representing a delegation of French federalists who were present.[89] The audience in their thousands applauded unceasingly, and a resolution was adopted by acclamation

---

been 668'); both in *Federal Union Archives*. Text of letter in *The Times*, 29.1.1947; report on the meeting also in *Federal News*, No. 144, March 1947, p. 2. Similarly Josephy to Brugmans, 27.1.1947, in reply to his complaint (cf. n. 168): 'The presence of King and myself on the Group has meant that the final statement is very different from, and very much more federal than it would have been had we not been there. . . . It seems to me still that we could not possibly have refused to co-operate with Mr. Churchill when he came out with the policy which, in part at any rate, is our own' (*BEF Archives*, Brugmans corr.).

[87] As Usborne's motion was not mentioned at the FU meetings of 24/6.1.1947, although its text was sent by Killby to Brugmans on 31.1.1947 (*BEF Archives*, Brugmans corr.), it was no doubt drafted between those dates. Text also in Bailey (n. 84), p. 32, where the names of all the signatories are given as well as the six authors; they will be found in chap. III/5, n. 360.

[88] The reply was given by Mayhew, a junior Foreign Office minister; cf. chap. I, n. 186.

[89] Cf. United Europe Movement, *United Europe. Speeches at the Royal Albert Hall, 14th May, 1947*, London, 1947 (twenty-four pages). Ibid., p. 1: 'Under the dome hung a large banner bearing the words "Europe arise!" The great platform was filled with some two hundred prominent supporters, including leaders in almost every sphere of British public life. The French federalist movements were represented by a delegation from Paris, including French Members of Parliament of all the principal parties. The Royal Box was occupied by ambassadors and other diplomatic representatives of European countries.' Cf. Federal Union press release of 12.5.1947 on the arrival of the French delegation headed by A. Voisin with six deputies, also trade unionists and federalists including H. Brugmans and

'that this meeting believes that, in the interests of freedom and peace, the peoples of Europe must create unity among themselves and together make a positive European contribution to the progress of civilization and world order; and, recognizing that Britain must play her full part, pledges its support in the forthcoming campaign for a United Europe.'

Churchill had spoken with his usual eloquence and with obvious personal feeling:

'But what is Europe now? It is a rubble-heap, a charnel-house, a breeding-ground of pestilence and hate. Ancient nationalistic feuds and modern ideological factions distract and infuriate the unhappy, hungry populations ... Has Europe's mission come to an end? ... Are her peoples to go on harrying and tormenting one another by war and vengeance until all that invests human life with dignity and comfort has been obliterated? Are the states of Europe to continue for ever to squander the first-fruits of their toil upon the erection of new barriers, military fortifications, tariff walls and passport networks against one another? Are we Europeans to become incapable ... of even averting famine from the mass of our peoples? Are we all, through our poverty and our quarrels, for ever to be a burden and a danger to the rest of the world? Do we imagine we can be carried forward indefinitely upon the shoulders – broad though they be – of the United States of America? The time has come when these questions must be answered. This is the hour of choice and surely the choice is plain. If the people of Europe resolve to come together and work together for mutual advantage, to exchange blessings instead of curses, they still have it in their power to sweep away the horrors and miseries which surround them and to allow the streams of freedom, happiness and abundance to begin again their healing flow.'[90]

On the basis of the manifesto and the statements made at the Albert Hall assembly, the programme of the UEM may be summarized (in accordance with the schema we have adopted for other associations) under five main headings as follows.

1. *Design for Europe.* This was deliberately left vague: as Churchill said at the Albert Hall, 'It is not for us at this stage to attempt to define or prescribe the structure of constitutions. We ourselves are content to present the idea of United Europe, in which our country will play a decisive part and to

---

A. Marc (*BEF Archives;* cf. note 193). Text of speech by H. Barré (who gave general assurances that France would support 'cette nouvelle croisade en faveur des États-Unis d'Europe') in *La Fédération. Revue de l'ordre vivant,* No. 30, July 1947, p. 13. Members of the FU had '5,000 United States of Europe posters displayed in London before the Albert Hall meeting' (Exec. Committee 28.3.1947 and 19.4.1947, *FU Archives*).

[90] Text of resolution in the pamphlet cited in n. 89: *United Europe. Speeches . . . ,* p. 14; Churchill's speech, ibid., pp. 4–13 (passage quoted on p. 6; ibid., p. 1: 'The principal speeches were broadcast by the BBC on its Home and European services'); also in W. S. Churchill, *Europe Unite, Speeches 1947 and 1948,* London, 1950, pp. 77–85; French translation in *La Fédération* (n. 89), July 1947, pp. 2–7. H. Brugmans, 'Naissance d'une politique fédéraliste', *Cahiers de Bruges,* 7, 1957–I, p. 57, giving his impression on rereading the speech: 'On croit entendre à nouveau cette grande voix, pathétique et tempérée, à la fois truculente et sereine, ayant les accents d'un vieillard très cultivé qui exprime un grand idéal et d'un homme d'État qui surveille ses déclarations.' Further quotations from the speech in points 1–5 below.

which all can rally without being disturbed by divergencies about structure.' At Zurich and in the article in *Collier's Weekly* Churchill had spoken of a 'Council of Europe' and, while not defining its powers, had indicated that it should work towards unity in matters of defence, economics, and passport arrangements. None of this, however, was reflected in the manifesto, which merely said: 'The aim must be to unite all the peoples of Europe and give expression to their sense of being Europeans, while preserving their own traditions and identity': it was 'premature to define constitutional relationships'. In his speech at the Albert Hall Churchill only said that the European peoples must 'work together for mutual advantage' and that for all of them 'a welcome will be waiting at the European Council table'. There is no doubt that what was envisaged was a co-operative union and not a federation; this is especially clear in view of the British federalists' demand that the way should be left open to British membership, a demand which the UEM did not feature in its programme.

To the question 'Which countries will be in and which out?' Churchill gave a satisfactory reply in his Albert Hall speech. 'It is not our task or wish to draw frontier lines but rather to smooth them away. Our aim is to bring about the unity of all nations of all Europe. We seek to exclude no state whose territory lies in Europe and which assures to its people those fundamental personal rights and liberties on which our democratic European civilization has been created.' He wished to see as a beginning 'a Charter of Human Rights' for all, and hoped for 'a Europe where men of every country will think as much of being a European as of belonging to their native land'. These views were similar to his ideas and aspirations concerning the Commonwealth.[91]

2. *Europe in the world* This was the one point as to which objectives were clearly stated. As Churchill repeated in his Albert Hall speech, 'United Europe' was indispensable to the organization of peace and would 'form one major Regional entity' in accordance with the UN Charter. 'There is the United States with all its dependencies; there is the Soviet Union; there is the British Empire and Commonwealth; and there is Europe, with which Great Britain is profoundly blended. Here are the four main pillars of the world Temple of Peace.' He had once feared that the US or the Dominions might be against the plan, but they were in favour of it, for they were sick of seeing their young manhood bleed to death every twenty years in wars that sprang from European disunity. In the same way 'the Russian people should surely realize how much they stand to gain by the elimination of the causes of war and the fear of war on the European

---

[91] Cf. sources cited in nn. 83 and 90. Miss Josephy informed the writer that at that time she once asked Churchill what he meant by a United States of Europe; he gave a few puffs at his cigar and replied: 'A kind of Commonwealth' (information from *Josephy*, 30.11.1974; as she remarked, the Commonwealth was never a federation). L. S. Amery, one of Churchill's few close friends, spoke at the Swiss City Club on 8.10.1946 and in London on 16.10.1946 in favour of a united Europe on the model of the Commonwealth: cf. *Der Tagesspiegel*, 19.10.1946, and L. S. Amery, *My Political Life*, vol. 3, London, 1955.

continent'. Finally: 'Nothing will help forward the building of the world organization so much as unity and stability in a Europe that is conscious of her collective personality and resolved to assume her rightful part in guiding the unfolding destinies of man.'

Gollancz, a Socialist by conviction, said at the Albert Hall: 'The real enemy of peace is not a strong and united Europe, but a weak and divided Europe. Feebleness and chaos tempt the aggressor. By stabilizing Europe and making the continent immune to piecemeal exploitation from any quarter we shall prevent her from becoming a battle-ground of conflicting interests and clashing rivals.'[92] What was not perceived, however, was that all this could not be achieved on the basis of a vague, Commonwealth type of co-operation.

3. *Plan of Campaign*. This was scarcely dealt with at all. Churchill said at the Albert Hall: 'Far off, on the skyline, we can see the peaks of the Delectable Mountains. But we cannot tell what lies between us and them.' This was an understandable statement from a Leader of the Opposition who did not wish to commit himself in detail in advance of his return to office, but it was too vague to be the watchword of a political pressure group for European union. Churchill added that 'it is for the responsible statesmen, who have the conduct of affairs in their hands and the power of executive action, to shape and fashion the structure.' Similarly the manifesto had said that 'unity can only grow from free consultation' – sc. among statesmen.

4. *Purpose and character* of the United Europe Committee. 'It is for us to lay the foundation, to create the atmosphere and give the driving impulsion', said Churchill; 'until public opinion expresses itself more definitely, governments hesitate to take positive action'. Oliver Stanley added at the Albert Hall that 'through this movement we shall be able to ensure to the Government of the day wide support for any action which tends towards European unity. It is not our intention to set up any great mechanism of areas and branches, membership drives and intensive canvasses.' The original Committee needed 'a body of supporters, wide in their influence and varied in their interests'; but 'numbers are not the main consideration'. The centralist form of organization thus described took shape in the ensuing months: a 'high-powered club' of influential members of the élite, representing all parties and spheres of public life, with 'helpers' to popularize its aims but with no organization of members, no local branches with any degree of autonomy, no democratically framed resolutions that could be binding on the association's leaders.[93]

---

[92] Quotations from Churchill's speech in the pamphlet cited in 89, pp. 7, 10 f., and 13; V. Gollancz, ibid., p. 20. Churchill used Gollancz's argument in a letter in *United Europe, News-Letter of the UEM*, No. 1, London (March) 1948, p. 3: not a thriving, united Europe but a divided and Balkanized one was a threat to peace, as it offered an easy prey to the aggressor.

[93] Speech on organization by O. Stanley in the pamphlet cited in n. 89. Churchill wanted a 'high-powered club' unfettered by resolutions: information from *Pinder*, 29.11.1974. Application forms were attached to the pamphlet, but they read simply: 'Please enrol me as a Supporter and send me any free literature.' When groups of sympathizers were formed after meetings in provincial cities,

On 14 May 1947 the twenty-three members of the Provisional Committee, including Churchill and Duncan Sandys, were formed into the Executive Committee which was in practice the only directing body of the Movement of which Churchill was Chairman. Lady Violet Bonham Carter, the President of the Liberal Party, joined the Committee as its twenty-fourth member. To emphasize its all-party character L. S. Amery, G. Gibson, and Lady Violet were designated Vice-Chairmen and Lord Layton became Hon. Treasurer, while the Hon. Secretaries were Duncan Sandys and the Labour MP Gordon Lang. The 'Council' of the Movement, which scarcely ever met, consisted of the Committee plus fifty eminent 'supporters' who occupied the platform at the Albert Hall meeting, from Field-Marshal Viscount Alanbrooke and Admiral of the Fleet Viscount Cunningham toLord Beveridge, Sir Laurence Olivier, and the MPs Harold Macmillan and Sir Arthur Salter.[94] All the other 'supporters', especially outside London, merely assisted in distributing the propaganda material sent out by the central office. Unlike the European federalists, the UEM had no serious financial troubles to contend with.[95]

5. *Forms of activity*. Stanley declared in the Albert Hall that 'through great meetings such as this in the larger provincial centres, by small meetings elsewhere in the country, by discussion groups among those interested, and by the supply of literature through the channel of our supporters, we can make our ideas and progress readily available to all'. In the summer months of 1947 and from the spring of 1948 onwards large meetings on the lines of that in the Albert Hall were held in almost all the larger cities, with eminent UEM speakers and appropriate resolutions; local dignitaries were present, but Labour and the trade unions held aloof. From the summer of 1948 onwards an efficient service was organized in London whereby associations, clubs, schools, etc. could engage speakers

---

e.g. Manchester, Leeds, and Birmingham in 1948, they were called 'advisory committees'; composed of local dignitaries, their function was to help the propaganda work of the London office by their knowledge of local conditions. Cf. 'Developments in Great Britain' in *UEM News-Letter*, No. 4, July 1948, p. 42 f. Particularly successful was a UEM university group in Oxford, which grew to over 700 members between March and October 1948 and held numerous meetings (cf. ibid., p. 44, and No. 7, Oct. 1948, p. 3).

[94] Cf. p. 25 of the pamphlet cited in n. 89: list of members of Council and Executive Committee, the latter identical with the names given above (p. 326 and n. 84). Lady Violet Bonham Carter, 1946/7 President of the Liberal Party, which under her leadership adopted the Layton policy of supporting Continental union; cf. V. Bonham Carter, *Winston Churchill as I knew him*, London, 1965. A full list of the Council (then 84 persons, the Executive Committee being virtually unchanged) in *UEM News-Letter*, No. 1, March 1948, p. 11. The secretarial work was originally performed by Sandys; after G. Lang joined him as Hon. Secretary it was entrusted to a highly competent full-time officer, T. B. Martin, while Sandys concentrated almost exclusively on co-ordination with Continental groups (cf. chap. III/7); information from *Sandys*, 3.10.1974; reports by T. B. Martin to Sandys on organization of the UEM, 1947/8, in *EM Archives*, Bruges).

[95] E. Beddington-Behrens, a well-known banker, UEM supporter, and member of ELEC, in his autobiography *Look Back – Look Forward* (London, 1963, p. 179 f.) relates graphically what used to happen when the UEM, or later the European Movement, ran short of money: 'Lord McGowan, chairman of Imperial Chemical Industries, assisted by his new recruit from the Treasury, Paul Chambers, would gather together leaders of British industry at a luncheon in Sir Winston's honour, and would then ask for generous donations for the European cause. This was readily given in homage to the greatest Englishman of our time.'

to attend their meetings and talk about the European cause, which was thus widely popularized in a great many quarters; draft speeches on various subjects, often in question-and-answer form, were specially printed for members of the speakers' service. The most important publication was *United Europe. News-Letter of the United Europe Movement*, which ran to ten pages and appeared monthly from March 1948. It comprised summaries of all important activities and was sent regularly to 'supporters'; 2,000 copies were printed, and the number of supporters was presumably about the same.[96]

The movement was also advertised by means of posters, exhibitions, film shows, and radio talks. A later monthly publication was *The European Review* (also in a French edition, *La Revue européenne*), which did not contain news but essays, often of a general cultural type. In January 1947 a programme of 'restoring close contact with the like-minded individuals and groups on the Continent' was set on foot; thanks to Sandys's efforts the Conseil Français pour l'Europe Unie was founded in June 1947, its original title being Section Française du UEM.[97]

Nevertheless, Churchill's United Europe Movement reached its zenith with the inaugural meeting at the Albert Hall. Despite the self-sacrificing work of organizers and propagandists, the movement never again excited so much attention in the press and radio. As the Labour party refused to take part, the stimulus of internal debate was lacking; the opinions of Churchill and his associates were all too perceptible. Above all there was no development of the programme, which was vague and ambiguous on so many vital points; greater precision and readiness to take decisions would have given the movement a sharper and more attractive outline. Apart from the general thesis that Europe must cease to be a plague-spot and a breeding-ground of wars, and must unite to form a 'pillar of the world Temple of Peace', the clearest and, in the circumstances of the time, most realistic provision was that union should begin with the countries that were 'willing and able' to unite, i.e. for the time being excluding those occupied by Russia. But there was still complete vagueness as to what sort of unity or union was envisaged; indeed, statements on this

---

[96] For large meetings, see e.g. *UEM News-Letter*, No. 1, March 1948, p. 9; No. 2, April 1948, p. 20; No. 7, Oct. 1948, p. 5 etc.; for the speakers' service, see e.g. No. 4, July 1948, p. 44; No. 8, Nov. 1948, p. 70 etc. (a full set of communications to members of the speakers' service is in the library of St. Andrews University, Scotland). The size of the edition of *United Europe. News-Letter of the UEM* is stated in No. 2, April 1948, p. 19; this agrees with A. J. Zurcher's statement in *The Struggle to Unite Europe, 1940–1958*, p. 21, that the UEM had about 2,500 members. The *News-Letters* exist as far as No. 29, Oct. 1950, when the UEM virtually ceased to exist in Britain; the pages are numbered continuously from 1 to 342, and provide a wealth of information on the history of the association.

[97] As to poster advertising (with a prior competition) and the United Europe exhibition held in London from 17 Nov. to 4 Dec. 1948 and afterwards in other cities, cf. *News-Letter*, No. 2, Apr. 1948, p. 20; No. 4, July 1948, p. 43 f.; No. 8, Nov. 1948, p. 69; No. 9, Dec. 1948, p. 77. For extracts from talks broadcast by UEM from Radio Luxemburg every Sunday from March to July 1948, cf. chap. V/3 (in vol. 2). *The European Review – an independent international journal devoted to the cause of European unity* appeared in London (Nos. 1–50) from Nov. 1950 to Dec. 1954, outside the period covered by this book. For the foundation of the Conseil Français, cf. chap. III/6, p. 623 f.

point were even less precise than Churchill's speech at Zurich had been. This was because, under conflicting pressure from British nationalists on the one hand and British federalists on the other, the clear statement that Britain would be a sponsor but not a member of united Europe – a statement which would have been perfectly well understood on the Continent, and which reflected Churchill's own view and that of a majority of Britons – was abandoned in favour of vague but impressive-sounding phrases such as 'Britain must be prepared to make her full contribution to European unity'. In the long term, British federalists might congratulate themselves on having brought the UEM programme closer to that of the Continental federalists by securing a vague promise of British membership; but by blurring the edges of Churchill's position, which was to prove the more realistic for at least a decade to come, they raised false hopes within the West-European federalist movement as far as the next few years were concerned. The West Europeans thought they had only to wait for Churchill's return to power for Britain to become a full member of united Europe – which was far from being Churchill's own intention. Moreover, because of the hint at British membership, references in the UEM programme to the nature of the proposed union were so vague, cautious, and respectful of national sovereignty and the voluntary principle that it was unrealistic to suppose that such a loose association could succeed in enabling Europe to survive between the two world powers, or even do away with customs barriers and prevent future conflicts among European states.[98]

(C) FOUNDATION OF THE EUROPEAN LEAGUE
FOR ECONOMIC CO-OPERATION

At the same time as the UEM there came into being an association which introduced itself to the press on 7 March 1947 with a 'Memorandum Préliminaire' in which it was styled the Ligue Indépendante de Coopération Européene. In many ways it resembled the UEM: it did not seek mass membership but was still more distinctly intended as an élite group, more particularly of acknowledged economic experts; it realized at an early stage that union would have to be confined to Western Europe, and its ideas were based on co-operation and not federation. It differed from the UEM, however, in that it did not seek to popularize the idea of European unity in a single country, but to prepare the way for economic co-operation by international committee work.

In taking this line its founders were consciously following the precedent of the Union Économique et Douanière Européenne, instituted in 1926

---

[98] Cf. H. F. Sennholz, *How Can Europe Survive?*. New York, 1955, p. 116: the UEM was ineffective because its founders sought to apply the loose forms of the Commonwealth to Europe, whereas it was obvious that these forms were insufficient even for an economic union. Cf. the more detailed criticism by federalists, p. 344 f.

under Briand's patronage. This body, whose presidents were Stern-Rubarth, Charles Gide, and Elmer Hantos, had set up strong committees in most of the Continental capitals (the German one was called the Europäischer Zollverein) with the task of preparing detailed studies and persuading experts of the urgent need for a European economic union.[99] In 1945 the first of these committees to revive was the French one, which, under the chairmanship of Gaston Riou, set up subcommittees and began to issue publications. In 1946 a split took place, however: Riou favoured activity on a broader front and, taking with him some members of the main committee, founded the Union Économique et Fédérale Européenne. The more limited objective of reducing tariffs, and achieving free trade and economic co-operation was pursued by the most active subcommittee under Jacques Lacour-Gayet (President du Centre d'Etudes de Commerce) and Daniel Serruys (a senior pre-war official in the French Ministry of Commerce and a chairman of the Economic Council of the League of Nations); the subcommittee for this purpose turned itself into an independent body called the Comité d'Action Économique et Douanière.[100] The former Belgian Prime Minister, Paul van Zeeland, took part in meetings of economists organized by Serruys at the beginning of 1946, and in the spring of that year he wrote to prominent Belgian politicians, economists, and academic personalities urging that private groups should work for a European union and should make a detailed exploratory study of the economic problems involved.[101] He seems also to have written to some of his friends from the days of exile in London. In May 1946 Joseph Retinger, formerly General Sikorski's private secretary and a diligent organizer of wartime contacts, met him in Brussels, and they agreed that action must be taken to prevent the unthinking restoration of European national

---

[99] Cf. Introduction, n. 54; also E. Bonnefous, *L'Europe en face de son destin*, Paris, 1955, p. 59; O. Philip, *Le Problème de l'union européenne*, Paris/Neuchâtel, 1950, p. 146 f.

[100] On Gaston Riou and his UEFE with its federal inclinations, see below, chap. II/4, p. 360 f. The Comité d'Action Économique et Douanière, which in June 1947 became the French Section of the LECE (cf. n. 108), had its headquarters at 199, boulevard Saint-Germain. The organizational lists under both its titles show essentially the same composition, with Paul Naudin as director and L. de Sainte-Lorette as secretary-general under the chairmanship of D. Serruys (lists in *Brugmans Archives*). Among 'Publications' (initially by the old Union Économique et Douanière Européenne, then by the Comité d'Action, and collectively by Éd. SIPD, Paris) are listed: H. Alphand, *La Coopération économique en Europe libérée* (1945); E. Giscard d'Estaing, *Nationalisations* (1945); R. Picard, *La Reconversion économique aux États-Unis* (1945); H. Helbronner, *France et Occident européen* (1946); collective work, *Liens entre Nations* by J. Lacour-Gayet, D. Serruys, R. Dautry, L. Saillant, J. Rueff, L. Febvre, L. Noel, J. Hamel, P. Naudin (1947); E. Giscard d'Estaing, *Faillite du dirigisme* (1947).

[101] Cf. O. Philip (n. 99), p. 178; L. de Sainte-Lorette, *L'Idée d'union fédérale européenne*, Paris, 1955, p. 114 f. Paul van Zeeland (b. Zinik, 11.11.1893), a brilliant economist, had published, in association with the 'Europäischer Zollverein', a sharp attack on national protectionism when he was director of the Belgian National Bank: *A View of Europe 1932. An interpretative Essay on some Workings of Economic Nationalism* (Lectures at the Johns Hopkins University), Baltimore, 1933 (153 pp.). A member of the Catholic party, he was Belgian Prime Minister from March 1935 to Oct. 1937; he was not a member of the wartime government in exile, but served as Foreign Minister from Aug. 1949 to 1954. P. H. Spaak pays a tribute to his brilliant intellect in *Combats inachevés*, Paris, 1969, vol. i, p. 31.

economies and that the European idea should be developed first and foremost in the economic sphere through an international 'independent league' of experts.[102]

Preparations for the foundation of such a league went forward vigorously, thanks to Van Zeeland's and Retinger's international contacts and the fact that they were free from governmental duties. Van Zeeland persuaded the president of the Belgian Liberal party, Senator Roger Motz, to chair a committee of Belgian industrialists, trade unionists, and economists; a former minister, Guillaume Konsbruck, became chairman of a similar committee in Luxemburg, and in Italy the support of Ugo La Malfa was enlisted; an Italian Section was founded only in 1950, however, on the initiative of Senator Enrico Falck.[103] From Brussels Retinger went on to visit his wartime Dutch friend Senator Pieter Kerstens, formerly Minister for the Economy, who promised to set up a Netherlands Section; this took place, however, only in the autumn of 1948. In London General Sir Colin Gubbins, who had moved into the industrial world, established contact with the former director of the International Labour Office, Sir Harold Butler, who had just retired and who offered his services as chairman of the British Section; the nucleus of the British group was completed in the autumn of 1946 by Edward Beddington-Behrens and Lord Layton. At the same time Serruys expressed willingness to turn his committee into the French Section. Retinger also tried to obtain support in Eastern Europe, but a visit to Jan Masaryk for this purpose elicited a refusal, while a letter to Molotov, the Soviet Foreign Minister, through Ambassador Bogomolov remained unanswered.[104]

[102] Cf. Retinger's account in J. Retinger, *Memoirs of an Éminence Grise*, ed. John Pomian, Sussex University, 1972, p. 210. This book, about 40 per cent of which consists of Retinger's reminiscences, is edited in the form of a sensitive biography by Pomian, who was his secretary during the last twelve years of his life, from Sept. 1948, and gives a lively picture of all the phases of his adventurous career. Born at Cracow on 17.4.1888, he studied in Paris from 1906 to 1908 (*Docteur ès Lettres* at the Sorbonne) and in Munich and London from 1909 to 1912, 1912-14 director of the Polish Bureau in London, 1914-18 working in London for Polish independence, 1918-26 adviser in Mexico, then in London as agent for General Sikorski and the Polish Socialist Party in opposition to Pilsudski; from 1924 'imbued with the idea of the unity of Europe. (ibid., p. 68); 1940-3 close collaborator of Prime Minister Sikorski, especially engaged in planning for regional federations within a European union; Feb.-July 1944 clandestinely in Poland, where he contracted polyneuritis; 1945 organized dispatch of gifts from Britain to Poland. Spaak writes in the (abridged) English version of his memoirs (*The Continuing Battle: Memoirs of a European 1936-1966*, London, 1971), p. 265 f.: 'He knew everybody and no door was closed to him. During those years he was one of the best informed politicians. He helped to initiate the discussions we Poles, Czechs, Dutch, Norwegians and Belgians held.' As the conflict between the two world powers became evident, Retinger spoke on 7 May 1946 at the Royal Institute of International Affairs of the centuries-old cultural unity of Europe and Sikorski's wartime federation plans, and concluded: 'Mistrust can be overcome, the policy of spheres of influence replaced by economic cooperation, provided there is a free neutral area between the rivals . . . the European Continent an entity again.' In a 'Postscript, 30.8.46' he added that Russia would not agree to 'the obvious solution, a Congress of all the Continental Powers'; the West Europeans should 'initiate consultations' (J. H. Retinger, *The European Continent, An Address given on 7th May, 1946, with a Postscript 30.8.1946*, London, privately printed, e.g. in *EM Archives, Bruges*, ELEC Documents).

[103] Retinger, *Memoirs* (n. 102), p. 211 f.; O. Philip (n. 99), p. 178; pamphlet with lists and dates of foundation of national committees, published by the German Section (founded in 1950 by Hermann J. Abs, banker, and Richard Merton, industrialist), *Zehn Jahre LECE 1947-1957*, Frankfurt, 1957 (hectographed).

[104] Cf. Retinger, *Memoirs* (n. 102), p. 210 f. and 212 f. Conversations with A. Harriman (US Ambassador in London) and with D. Rockefeller, J. F. Dulles, and American industrialists in New

Thus by the spring of 1947 Sections of European-minded economists were already in being or in course of formation in Brussels, Luxemburg, London, and Paris. At the beginning of March the initiators and chairmen met at The Hague and formed themselves into a 'Comité Central provisoire'; they drew up the first written statement of their ideas and aims in a 'Memorandum préliminaire' and gave it to the Belgian press on 7 March. An accompanying communiqué stated: 'Certain international personalities have held several meetings in the past few months ... their discussions have led to a plan to set up a Ligue Indépendante de Coopération Européenne', and the provisional Central Committee at The Hague had formulated the aims and methods of the new organization. This date may be taken as marking the foundation of the League.[105] Three months later Secretary of State Marshall's offer gave the new group an ideal opportunity to submit concrete proposals for economic co-operation, and it was quick to respond by organizing meetings. On 20 June 1947 van Zeeland, Retinger, and the seven most active members of the London group produced a memorandum urging the necessity of accepting Marshall's offer, replying to it with a co-ordinated European plan and setting up a 'European Planning Board' for the purpose of combining the most urgent national needs into a single list and planning for the removal of the trade and customs barriers that were partly responsible for Europe's troubles.[106] The memorandum was further discussed in Paris on 30 June at a meeting at which all four national Sections were represented (the British and French with six members each); the references to free trade and the need to approach European unity by stages were strengthened, and the text was then sent to all European governments who were members of the UN.

York at the end of 1946, led to the formation of a US Section under Adolf Berle, Jr., which, however, decided in June 1947 to concentrate exclusively on supporting the Marshall Plan in the US. The British Section was especially active in the ensuing years thanks to the tireless activity of its Hon. Secretary, Lady Rhys-Williams, DBE, whose estate includes the extensive, still unclassified archives of the British Section; cf. also Beddington-Behrens (n. 95), p. 178 f.

[105] *Communiqué à la presse, Création d'une Ligue Indépendante de Coopération Européenne*, Brussels, 7.3.1947 (four typed pages); with memorandum and preamble (five typed pages) in *Brugmans Archives*. The ideas in the memorandum are discussed above. The date of foundation is more usually given in the literature as May 1946, evidently because Retinger in his later account of his Brussels meeting with van Zeeland wrote: '. . . thus we started the Independent League' (Retinger, *Memoirs* (n. 102), p. 210; this note was evidently known to D. de Rougemont when he wrote 'Hommage à un grand Européen: Joseph H. Retinger' in *Bulletin du Centre Européen de la Culture*, Geneva, 1960, No. 5, p. 43). As in the case of all associations, however, the date of foundation is not that of the first preliminary talks among individuals but that on which a governing body actually met and issued a statement of policy.

[106] *Independent League of European Cooperation. Action to be taken on Marshall's offer*: conclusions of a working meeting held in London on 20.6.1947 by van Zeeland, Retinger, Sir Harold Butler, E. Beddington-Behrens, Lord Layton, H. Macmillan, MP, Sir Henry Price, Sir Arthur Salter, MP, and H. V. Tewson (Trades-Union Congress), in *EM Archives, Bruges*, ELEC Documents (ten typed pages). The draft memorandum (pp. 8–10) was preceded by a discussion of 'Reasons for the Marshall offer', 'What are Europe's requirements?' 'Removal of economic barriers', and 'The difficulties' that might arise from lack of goodwill by Russia and France.

The memorandum had a decided effect on governments as the first expression of opinion by an independent body of experts in the light of the new situation in Europe.[107] The existence and function of the small but highly qualified association of experts, which in June 1948 presented itself for legal registration in the *Moniteur belge* under the more accurate name, already considered in Paris, of Ligue Européenne de Coopération Économique (European League for Economic Co-operation), were thus assured.[108]

On the basis of the memoranda of 7 March and 30 June 1947 the ideas and aims of the League may be summarized as follows:

1. The *design for Europe* was presented in extremely vague and cautious terms. The preamble to the March memorandum spoke of a 'double aim: firstly to increase and reinforce opportunities for co-operation among European peoples, and secondly to revive the traditions and forces which have made this small Continent great in the past and have brought about a civilization that has impressed its stamp on the whole world'. In order to reorganize economic life, the June memorandum added, and to respond to General Marshall's appeal, European governments must 'work together in framing without delay a comprehensive scheme for common action. By showing themselves capable of organizing European self-help they will provide the best justification for American aid.' The 'European Planning Board' which was to co-ordinate recovery plans must 'recommend measures to be taken by each individual country according to its own economic system. But in any case the Governments concerned must be prepared to delegate such executive authority as may be necessary to ensure the effective execution of the plan.' This provision, which was first introduced in Paris and therefore presumably by the French, foreshadowed the pooling of executive authority, but in the legislative sphere the plan did not go beyond 'recommendations' to the states.

Finally the March memorandum contained an echo of wartime plans for regional federation: 'The Europe we envisage is not merely a grouping (*groupement*) of nations but, in the full measure required by the facts, a grouping of regions. Every international edifice is based on the national state, but immediately above

---

[107] *I.L.E.C., Paris Meeting 30.6.1947 . . . Summary of Proceedings* (sixteen typed pages), with final text of the memorandum (four pages) 'signed by: Senator Paul van Zeeland, President, Dr Joseph Retinger, Secretary General, Sir Harold Butler, Chairman of the British National Committee, Daniel Serruys, Chairman of the French National Committee, Guill Konsbruck, Chairman of the Luxembourg National Committee, Senator Pieter Kerstens, Chairman of the Dutch National Committee, Senator Roger Motz, Chairman of the Belgian National Committee', *EM Archives, Bruges*, ELEC Documents. Other participants were, from Britain, C. Gubbins, E. Beddington-Behrens, Lod Layton, and H. Macmillan; from France, Charles-Roux, J. Chastenet, E. Giscard d'Estaing, Paul Naudin, and L. de Sainte-Lorette. Extracts from the memorandum in nn. 109 and 111.

[108] Cf. O. Philip (n. 99), p. 178. According to the minutes (*Paris Meeting 30.6.1947*, p. 14 f.) it was agreed to make contact with other pro-European associations, and to avoid misunderstanding in this connection H. Butler proposed that 'The League should at least introduce the word "Economic" into its title.'

that comes the region – for instance Western Europe, Scandinavia, the Balkans and the Slav states.'[109]

2. *Europe in the world.* The preamble to the March memorandum continued from the point quoted above: 'In the same way Europe must in its turn be integrated into a wider complex so that it may once again take its proper place in the mosaic of nations and regions, the unity of which is ensured by the United Nations Organization.' The memorandum went on to advocate the development of relations between Europe, thus consolidated, and the other regions of the world, especially the Atlantic region and the Western hemisphere on the one hand and the USSR on the other; this would strengthen the ties between national states and economic regions within the framework of the UN.[110]

3. As regards the *plan of campaign*, both memoranda point to a realistic attempt to take account of European conditions in the spring of 1947. The March memorandum stated that 'Our aim is to foster by every possible means economic collaboration between the countries or regions of which Europe is composed and, on the other hand, to emphasize, in its underlying unity and its manifold expressions, the essence of the civilization that has spread from Europe throughout the world.' The conclusion of the June memorandum added that once the benefits of economic co-operation were evident to all, 'the way may be opened to more far-reaching projects'.[111]

4. *Purpose and character of the organization.* The March memorandum stated that the policy of the League was (1) to promote closer understanding and develop the spirit of co-operation among European states; (2) for this purpose, to tackle problems from the cultural and economic points of view and, for the time being at least, to leave politics out of account. The June memorandum and all later statements concentrated on the objective of demonstrating the necessity of economic co-operation and proposing definite steps towards it. As to organization, the press communiqué which accompanied the March memorandum had stated that 'National committees will form the basis. The assembly of chairmen of the national committees will constitute the Central Council of the League, with the addition of some international personalities to be co-opted.'

---

[109] Brussels memorandum, 7.3.1947 (n. 105), preamble, p. 2 f.; Paris memorandum, 30.6.1947 (n. 107), p. 2 f. The texts quoted under (3) and (4) give a further idea of the League's aims for Europe.

[110] Brussels memorandum (n. 105), preamble, p. 3, and text, p. 5. The preamble went on to say that to improve co-operation in Europe was not only in the interest of Europeans but also in that of the whole world; 'for what country is not interested . . . in the material welfare of a continent where hundreds of millions of people live and work?' (ibid., p. 3).

[111] Brussels memorandum (n. 105), preamble, p. 4. The Paris memorandum of 30.6.1947 (n. 107), p. 4, concluded: 'If the economic life of Europe can be conceived on freer and more cooperative, more systematic and more organic lines, Europeans may achieve not merely greater prosperity, but a greater sense of common destiny than they have known in the past. Instead of being divided by ancient fears and rivalries they will be joined in a common enterprise, which will offer them a brilliant future and the sure prospect of peace on this continent.'

A publication by the British Committee in 1948 stated that 'ELEC aims to make its contribution to the ideal of European Unity by working out, step by step, the economic plans by which it can gradually be achieved. It is a non-party organization that does not seek large membership' but it was intended to consist of practical and theoretical economic experts, capable of making 'constructive proposals to meet present economic problems'. The lists of members of the British and French committees in fact contain about thirty names, and those of the other committees less than twenty each, so that the total membership at no time exceeded 150; this did not at all diminish the League's effectiveness, however, in view of the expertise and political influence of most of its members.[112]

5. *Forms of activity*: these are briefly indicated by the foregoing. Economic experts produced factual studies, analyses, or draft resolutions on concrete problems for the approval of the Central Council. Together with the memorandum on Marshall's offer the League drafted economic resolutions for the Hague Congress in the spring 1948 and, a year later, all the documentation needed for the economic conference of the European Movement at Westminster. The first of its series of publications, in 1949, was entitled *Propositions relatives à la convertibilité des monnaies européennes*.[113]

The effectiveness of the ELEC consisted in the fact that its members were recognized experts, occupying positions of responsibility, and that they concentrated strictly on a particular aspect of the problem of unity, viz. the promotion of economic co-operation in a given situation. By contrast with the pointless restoration of national economic autarky and state bureaucracies, they represented a progressive and co-operative outlook. The national committees also made it their business from the outset to consult trade-union economists and take their views into consideration. But the chief feature of their work was the extreme caution with which they limited themselves to pointing out the urgency of economic co-operation while 'leaving political aspects out of account'. A key to this lies in the fact that the nucleus of members of the ELEC consisted almost entirely of elder statesmen and economists of long experience, aged on the average over sixty and in many cases retired (e.g. Serruys and Butler); by contrast, the average age of federalist leaders who had emerged from the Resistance movements was at this time about forty. The older generation of politicians and economists had for the most part striven for European unity between the wars and been disappointed by the frustration of their efforts. Many of them were personally prepared to go further in the direction

---

[112] Memorandum of 7.3.1947 (n. 105), p. 5, and accompanying press communiqué, p. 2. Pamphlet (eight pages) by British Committee of ELEC, London, 1948, p. 3. Lists of members, ibid., in a similar publication by the Section Française, Paris, 1949, and in *Zehn Jahre LECE* (n. 103), pp. 5–14. From 1950, when the Belgian industrialist Baron Boel became chairman of the Conseil Central, valuable use was made of a system of supranational commissions on specific questions, staffed by experts from the national committees, so that these questions were discussed *ab initio* from a European and not from a merely national point of view (cf. *La Ligue Européenne de Coopération Économique*, published by Secrétariat International, Brussels, 1951, p. 5).

[113] Cf. p. 683, and chaps V/3 and VI/2 (in vol. 2).

of political and federalist recommendations, as Retinger had shown in 1942 and as van Zeeland was to show in 1949–54; but they were resolved not to get out of touch, as they had in the past, with the climate of opinion in the national bureaucracies; as Retinger put it in May 1946, 'We were most careful not to be carried away by unrealistic Utopianism.'[114] In its early years, moreover, the ELEC was clearly influenced by the preponderant activity of the British section, while the leading members of the other sections had mostly been in exile in London during the war and had therefore not experienced the collapse of the federal idea in the Nazi-ruled Continental countries. As the League restricted itself to the immediate aims of tariff reduction, currency convertibility, and economic co-operation among West-European states including Britain, it fitted well into the purely co-operative approach of the British UEM as the latter had developed, deviating to some extent from Churchill's ideas. The two organizations eventually dovetailed so successfully, in contrast to the federalists with their pan-European aspirations, that the Belgian, French, and other national committees of the ELEC figured as Continental outposts of the UEM.[115] The federalists, however, were greatly disappointed by the caution with which the ELEC experts limited their sights to the '*dévaluation des frontières*'. These influential older 'Europeans' were careful to avoid discussing the need for common political institutions, and their attitude no doubt strengthened the forces of conservatism in their belief that the most pressing objectives could be achieved without political federation.

(D) FEDERALIST REACTIONS TO CHURCHILL'S PLAN

The many who responded to Churchill's call for a united Europe can be roughly divided into two very unequal groups. Firstly the great majority of government ministers and party politicians who had not had any idea of European unity before 1946, or had resigned themselves to its impossibility;

[114] Retinger, *The European Continent* (n. 102), p. 6. In discussions with the Czechoslovak Government in exile in 1941/2 on the formation of a Central–East-European federation, to which a West-European parallel was envisaged, Retinger himself had emphasized the need for effective federal structures, a joint Foreign Ministry and parliament, etc. (cf. Walter Lipgens, *Europa-Föderationspläne der Widerstandsbewegungen 1940–1945*, Munich, 1968, p. 445 f.). Another example of the readiness of certain members to go further in a federal direction: Roger Picard, one of the most active members of the French section, Professor at the *Faculté de Droit*, Paris, in *L'Unité européenne par l'intercitoyenneté*, Paris, 1948 (in the series of publications by the Comité d'Action Économique et Douanière) proposed, in addition to economic co-operation, the institution of European citizenship as a step towards European political union. On the 'generation gap', see also chap. III/7, p. 670.

[115] As Beddington-Behrens recorded on 10.5.1948, 'The British Section of the League' actually 'decided in October 1947 to merge with United Europe on the understanding that the French Section and other sections of the movement would do the same. These fusions have, however, not taken place.' Consequently 'after discussions amongst the original members of the British Committee of the League at the Hague Conference, it was decided to re-create the British Section of the League, on the understanding that it would work in the closest association with United Europe . . .' ('Formal minute reconstituting the British Section of ILEC', London, 10.5.1948, sent by Beddington-Behrens to Sandys on 25.5.1948; *EM Archives, Bruges,* ELEC Documents).

a general description of their position will be given at the end of this chapter. Secondly, the small group of federalists who had long fought untiringly and sacrificed themselves for the cause and who, even in the first bitter year after the war, continued to see European unity as the only road to salvation; these were naturally stirred to their depths by Churchill's appeal.

The federalists could not fail to rejoice that a statesman whose voice was heard throughout the world had spoken so emphatically of the need for 'a kind of United States of Europe'. This feeling was expressed in reactions from every quarter, though some had more reservations than others. The October number of the Swiss *Europa*, which appeared a few days after the Zurich speech, proclaimed its gratitude to 'Churchill the European', who in long sections of his address had given utterance to aims that Europa-Union had long been advocating. Van Vassenhove declared that: 'Despite many essential reservations there is probably no European federalist who is not grateful to Mr Churchill for the fact that, in what may be a decisive hour, he has indicated to the peoples of Europe that union is the only road to salvation, and has insisted on the necessity of their uniting at once.' Three months later, Brugmans declared that it was Churchill's great merit to have recognized the need to depart from the centuries-old British policy of the 'balance of power' in Europe, and to have encouraged Europeans to unite instead:

For the first time in modern history, Britain seems interested in strengthening Europe instead of weakening it. The policy of 'dividing and conquering' European states would make them all dependent on the Soviet Union. Assuming the reality of 'Soviet imperialism', Mr Churchill's attitude is a logical one. In any case he is right to point out that British isolationism has had its day... We are happy that Mr Churchill advocates a policy of European responsibility, and we agree with him in desiring a federation of Europe, which is alone capable of rescuing us from our present stagnation.[116]

The 'essential reservations' did not, as a rule, relate to the question of British membership, which Churchill did not mention at Zurich. Van Vassenhove, who in this was typical of the European federalists, touched on the point in a single sentence: 'We have always thought that it is for the British alone to decide whether Britain should, as all European federalists keenly desire, be part of a federated Europe.' Before the Continental

---

[116] *Europa. Organ der Europa-Union*, Vol. 13, No. 10, Basle, Oct. 1946, p. 3; L. van Vassenhove, 'À propos du discours de Zurich de M. W. Churchill', *L'Action fédéraliste européenne*, No. 2, Oct. 1946, p. 6; H. Brugmans, 28.2.1947, to 'Reuter's special correspondent, Brussels', who had evidently asked his views on the formation of Churchill's United Europe Committee. In his comments (three typed pages, *BEF Archives*, Brugmans corr.) Brugmans said nothing about Britain's non-membership but dissented vigorously from Churchill's idea of beginning with the West-European countries, as it was to be feared that 'the united Europe advocated by him would in fact be, in his mind, a trump card in Anglo-Saxon strategy in case of a conflict with Russia'. The idea of a 'bastion against the East' was firmly rejected by the federalists because they hoped for an all-Europe federation with Soviet approval (cf. texts at n. 116 and nn. 197–201).

federalists realized that the East-European countries were lost to them, they were quite prepared to accept what had been Coudenhove's own view in the 1920s, that Britain had special obligations as head of the Commonwealth. The only group who protested strongly against this view were the British federalists. R. W. G. Mackay, writing in 1948, objected to 'Mr. Churchill's refusal to face the position of the British Commonwealth. If there is to be a federation of Western Europe, Great Britain must be a foundation member state. It must face its responsibilities to Europe, and only by joining to the fullest extent will it afford the federation the necessary confidence and stability.' Britain's remaining ties with the Dominions, which were already very loose, could in that event be 'transferred' to Europe.[117] The two main objections, however, that were raised by federalists in every quarter were that Churchill's proposal was for a Western bloc and not a neutral Europe, and that he evidently had in mind a loose association and not a true federation of European states.

The first objection was forcefully expressed in a letter addressed to all members of the Swiss parliament by Hans Bauer as president of Europa-Union and on behalf of its committee:

Winston Churchill's speech at Zurich with its call to European unity has left conflicting impressions in our country and elsewhere. Many have expressed fears that the idea, which is desirable in itself, is being put forward in the interest of a very one-sided conception of Europe. We of Europa-Union attach the greatest importance to pointing out that ... we insist on the reconciling character of European union as a link between East and West, and deprecate any leaning of Swiss public opinion, even on a purely ideological plane, towards one power bloc or the other. The Swiss people must not, for instance, make friends with a Western bloc even if that bloc calls itself Europe, any more than we made friends with Hitler's 'New Europe'.

Thus Bauer did not shrink from comparing proposals that 'smacked of an anti-Russian attitude' with the ideas of Nazi dictatorship. Gaetano Salvemini, at a mass meeting in the Teatro Eliseo in Rome, spoke with equal force against the attempt to 'draw Europe into a conflict between the Soviet and the Anglo-American system'. Churchill's appeal for European union was 'the worst disservice that we federalists have experienced in recent times'; for:

The European unity that Churchill pleads for after the dismemberment of Germany, which was partly the work of this same Churchill – the unity of Europe,

[117] L. van Vassenhove, 'À propos des articles de M. W. Churchill', *L'Action fédéraliste européenne*, No. 4, Jan. 1947, p. 5; cf. Bondy, ref. in Chap. I, n. 143. For Miss Josephy's protest against British non-membership, cf. n. 80; R. W. G. Mackay, *You can't turn the Clock back*, London, 1948, p. 267, where he continued: 'This means that Great Britain must recognize and acknowledge that the time has come for a change in the status of the British Commonwealth of Nations. The Commonwealth cannot continue as a political and economic entity in the modern world because it has not sufficient power to defend itself in all parts of the world. At present the Dominions have a loose political and economic arrangement with Great Britain. There is no reason why that arrangement cannot be transferred to Europe, once Britain becomes a member state of a European federation.'

to be supported by the unity of the British Empire which the same Churchill praises so highly – is nothing but an invitation to European countries to be kind enough to form a safety zone protecting the British Isles against bombs and air attack from Soviet-controlled central Europe. The Second World War has shown that France and the Low Countries are no longer a big enough glacis for Britain's safety, and so more European countries are now being called on to enlarge the safety zone ... We must hope that European federalists will have nothing to do with such unity and will make their position perfectly clear to British friends who attend their meetings. A federated, neutral Europe determined to defend its neutrality against all comers would be a much more useful and effective protection for the British Isles than a Europe, whether federal or atomized, that had been drawn by the Anglo-American bloc into its power struggle against the Soviet bloc ... The European federation must be created for peace and not in order to wage war in Europe. It must be neutral between the two systems, as Switzerland is neutral today in the heart of divided Europe.

Van Vassenhove commented in more moderate terms that Churchill was perhaps unjustly reproached with seeking to divide Europe into spheres of influence: he had only suggested pragmatically that a start should be made, 'comme un stade transitoire', with the countries that were willing and able to unite. But a 'half-Europe' of this kind was suspect to the USSR as a 'Western bloc', and for this reason the federalists stuck to their plan of offering the Soviet Union a neutral, undivided Europe. 'Russia wants friendly neighbours; we offer it something better, a whole friendly Europe.'[118] The federalists were not yet prepared either to renounce the hope of Soviet understanding and consent or, as they feared, to confirm the Russians in their negative attitude by making a premature 'beginning in Western Europe'.

The federalists' second basic objection was to the vagueness with which Churchill defined the degree of unity he had in mind, and the fact that to all appearances it was much less than the circumstances demanded. Campagnolo argued that when Churchill proposed a Franco-German 'partnership' as a first step he evidently contemplated 'Franco-German understanding in the form of a close alliance to which the other European states would accede so as to form a European union'; but this would never

---

[118] H. Bauer, 29.1.1947, to all members of the Federal Assembly in Berne (*EU Archives, Basle,* Central Committee Documents 1945–7; G. Salvemini, 'Problemi politici dell'unificazione europea', *Europa federata,* ed. E. Rossi, Milan, 1947, pp. 74 f. and 79; L. van Vassenhove, 'À propos du discours ...' (n. 116), p. 5 f. In 'À propos des articles ...' (n. 117) van Vassenhove wrote: 'Why should one, as he [Churchill] does, link the European question with the defence of Eropean society against Communism? ... We think it wrong to posit an antithesis between Federalism and Communism. ... The federation we envisage is neither Communist nor Socialist nor Catholic nor Protestant; it is democratic and must permit the free play of intellectual tendencies and free competition between them' (p. 7). Mackay (n. 117) also formulated as a basic objection: 'It is difficult to believe that ... Churchill has not been moved mainly by a desire to create a political organization against Soviet Russia. ... There can be no federation of Western Europe if it is founded upon such a negative conception' (p. 268 f.).

bring about the necessary federation, only 'an association of states like Coudenhove-Kalergi's or Briand's Pan-Europe', which was quite insufficient at the present time. R. W. G. Mackay put it succinctly: 'On Mr Churchill's proposals there can be no federation of Western Europe at all, because he does not hold that the states of Western Europe should surrender sufficient sovereignty to establish such a federation.' The Europeans must realize more clearly that the prosperity and success of the two great powers, the Soviet Union and the US, were due to the fact that they were an amalgamation of many states and peoples; their strength and prosperity were the result of that union and of the pooling of sovereignty by the states composing the federation. Van Vassenhove, again taking a more measured view, did not exclude the idea that when Churchill spoke of a 'United States of Europe' he meant something on federal lines, since he immediately called to mind the precedent of the USA. Van Vassenhove skilfully took as his text the later statements by Smuts and Amery suggesting a 'European Commonwealth', in order to point out that, if this was all that was being suggested, the experience of the war showed that it was not enough. 'The British Commonwealth is a colonial empire which has evolved happily towards a free association. But Europe had never been colonial or imperial for any length of time, and there was no analogy to the 'common allegiance to the British crown'; Europe, 'torn by a thousand years of warfare', could only find a peaceful future in a true federation.

The most elementary history books tell us that 'Europe' equals 'war'. And the ferment of this perpetual European warfare is the unrestricted sovereignty which the states of our Continent have never managed to give up. Realizing this, all Europeans who desired that Europe should signify peace, as it can and ought to do, have understood that they must combat the principle of state sovereignty and demand that it be restricted ... Any conception of European unity based on respect for the prejudice of sovereignty has been overtaken by the spiritual development of nations ... Europe can only be reborn and work effectively for world peace if it begins by eliminating the possibility of war among its own peoples. European security must be created as an essential pillar of world security, and this can only be achieved by creating a European sovereignty ... not a loose association of sovereign governments, and not a mere economic council.[119]

---

[119] U. Campagnolo, comment on Churchill's Zurich speech in *L'Unità europea*, Nos. 19/20, Turin, 25.10.1946, p. 5; Mackay (n. 117), p. 269; L. van Vassenhove, 'La parole est aux peuples', *L'Action fédéraliste européenne*, No. 3, Nov. 1946, pp. 6 f., 9, and 16 f.: all European peoples should be invited to accept a provision similar to that in the new French constitution, that 'France consents, on a reciprocal basis, to any limitations of sovereignty that are necessary for the organization and defence of peace.' There could be no doubt as to the outcome of such consultation; 'governments would pay attention, and the way would be open for the convocation of a European Constituent Assembly' (p. 19). Cf. the discussion of the federalist view on the two main questions at the conclusion of our analysis of the UEF viewpoint in chap. II/5, pp. 371-85.

4. Revival of Federalist Ideas in France

As the rift between the two world powers became manifest, as federalist movements in the smaller countries were reactivated and as Churchill's Zurich speech had its effect, European expectations were again concentrated on France, as they had been during the weeks of liberation in 1944–5. Churchill had urged France to take the lead towards European unity, and the prospects for her doing so seemed better after de Gaulle's resignation in January 1946 and after the debate over the new constitution had been resolved in the autumn of that year. In the winter of 1946–7, however, as already explained, the French government, with its three-party basis including Communist participation, was not yet able to make such a move.[120] It was even more vital, therefore, to see whether the revival of pro-European forces and ideas would take a stronger form in France and influence the course of internal politics. To federalists in the neighbouring countries it was especially important to know whether French thinking would develop on British 'unionist' lines or towards the federal principles of the Hertenstein programme. The programme and strategy of the reviving European-unity movement depended in a large degree on the reactivation of French pressure groups and the direction in which their influence was exerted.

The Russo-American dispute over the peace settlement in the summer and the autumn of 1946 led, in France as in the neighbouring countries, to a revival of the concept of European union. This trend was perhaps somewhat delayed during the summer by the general concentration on the constitutional problem, but the enthusiasm of new federalist groups was all the greater in that they were opposed by the most conscious of all the movements of nationalist restoration, that of France under de Gaulle. In France more than anywhere else in Europe, the year of reluctant acquiescence in the dictatorship of the world powers was also a year of resurgent nationalism and governmental centralism, and it was all the more necessary for those who held contrary views to take a stand on firm principles. Many did so on the basis of the strongly held views of the Resistance movements and the criticism of de Gaulle's foreign policy which became articulate at an early stage.[121] With the change in the world situation, those who felt this way in the autumn of 1946 could express their opinions with the hope of commanding increased attention, and organized groups began to form in rapid succession. The largest of these and, as it proved, the most significant intellectually, La Fédération, conducted an

---
[120] Despite the readiness of the Socialists, such a move was impeded by the foreign-policy alliance between Bidault and the PCF: cf. chap. I/4 at n. |268 f. For earlier hopes concerning France, cf. chap. I at nn. 216 and 361. For the gradual change during the spring of 1947, cf. chap. III/2, pp. 495–500. For the meaning of the following term 'unionist' in the Euopean context, cf. p. 665–9.
[121] Cf. W. Lipgens, 'Innerfranzösische Kritik der Aussenpolitik de Gaulles 1944–1946', *VfZG*, 24 (1976), pp. 136–98, and chap. I/4, pp. 214–30.

enquiry in November 1946, evidently inspired by its participation in the Luxemburg congress; this elicited responses from nineteen French federalist groups, and it was agreed to form a Comité français de Coordination des Mouvements fédéralistes. Initially conceived as a loose 'umbrella' organization, this developed within two years into the French section (Union Française des Fédéralistes – UFF) of the Union Européenne des Fédéralistes (UEF), the international body which had taken shape over the same period.[122] The nineteen associations varied a great deal in importance and in details of political outlook.

(A) THE COMITÉ INTERNATIONAL POUR LA FÉDÉRATION EUROPÉENNE (CIFE)

As has been seen, this Committee was founded in July 1944 and played a significant pioneering role in the first months after the Liberation, especially by organizing the first international federalist congress in Paris in March 1945.[123] By now, however, it was only of secondary importance among the nineteen, having become an outstanding example of the paralysis and exhaustion that afflicted the Resistance forces in the first twelve months after the war. During the year of discouragement there were no 'federalist activities by Socialist and democratic parties' to co-ordinate (cf. page 131 above); the Committee was in this sense premature, and its members, some of whom were persons of influence, returned to their professional work. Albert Camus edited *Combat*, which concerned itself chiefly with internal problems; Robert Verdier was political editor of the SFIO organ, *Le Populaire*; André Ferrat was a member of the directing committee of the SFIO. The chairman of the Comité International, Francis Gérard, was almost the only member who tried to carry on its work and enlarge its circle of membership to include subscribers to his bulletin *Le Document fédéraliste*. The only important step taken by the Committee in the second half of 1946 consisted in drafting 'Proposals to the Delegations at the Paris Peace Conference', which were submitted at the end of August. These were an attempt, foredoomed like others of their kind, to introduce federalist ideas into the peace settlement by the initial creation of special bodies concerned with European economic and nationality questions.

The memorandum submitted by the Committee to the delegations on 31 August 1946 suggested that these bodies should be concerned in the first instance with the affairs of Germany's former allies, but that their competence might afterwards be

[122] Cf. a survey by the first secretary of the Co-ordinating Committee, A. Voisin, chairman of La Fédération, 'Vers le grand rassemblement européen', *La Fédération*, No. 35, Dec. 1947, p. 31. For participation in the Luxemburg congress (13–16.10.1946) see n. 53 above; for the creation of the UFF in March 1948, see chap. V/5 (in vol. 2).

[123] Cf. chap. I/2, pp. 124–31. The Committee had been envisaged as a sort of headquarters which would 'co-ordinate the federalist activities of all Socialist and democratic parties' (ibid., p. 129); since for the next twelve months there were no such activities, on account of the Russo-American co-imperium, the Committee tended to wither away.

extended to cover the rest of Europe. For the 'economic reorganization of Germany's former satellites', the proposed European Economic Bureau was to have 'comprehensive powers as regards the economy of the states in question'. It was to consist of 'representatives of all the European countries concerned' – thus excluding the two superpowers – and to work out 'an overall plan for the economic reorganization of the five ex-satellites', to be approved by a two-thirds majority of the General Assembly of the United Nations and put into effect by organs of the Economic Bureau. The proposed Nationalities Bureau (Office européen des nationalités) was to protect minority nationalities and to be likewise composed of representatives of all the European countries concerned. It would issue, on demand, European passports to all members of a national minority (*minoritaires*) and would thus take them under its authority and protection. The final delimitation of the frontiers between the former enemy states would take place after the two Bureaux had begun to function.[124]

These proposals were clearly designed to get round the veto provision of the UN Charter and to offer a pragmatic and exemplary solution of two of Europe's acutest problems – especially affecting South-Eastern Europe – viz. economic Balkanization and the question of nationalities. The Bureaux would constitute, for the first time, authorities independent of national governments, and their competence could be extended by degrees. But the fact that they were devised as organs of the UN – and that the Committee in January 1947 added 'et mondiale' to its title – made clear that its leaders accepted with resignation that the European settlement was largely governed by extra-European interests and depended on a meeting of minds between the superpowers, which in the circumstances meant that the CIFE plan was doomed to failure.

The CIFE, consequently, was unable to develop any concrete activity, but it served to keep alive the ideas of Resistance leaders concerning the future of Europe and to convey them to the new associations which were in the course of formulating their own programmes. For this purpose it drew up a 'Declaration of Principles' which was approved at a 'General Meeting' of the Committee in January 1947 and communicated to the Comité de Coordination in reply to its enquiry as to the policies of member associations.[125]

---

[124] CIFE, 'Proposals to the Delegations at the Paris Peace Conference', dated 31.8.1946, published in the CIFE journal *Le Document fédéraliste*, No. 2, Paris, 1.9.1946, pp. 1–3. To ensure the supranational competence of the Bureau of Nationalities the memorandum provided for 'the establishment of a court of justice to try all cases relating to the violation of the rights of European nationals by individuals, groups or governments'. It also proposed that sanctions within the competence of the UN Security Council 'should be applied against any government which refused to carry out the court's decisions'.

[125] CIFE 'Declaration of Principles' published in *Le Document fédéraliste*, No. 4, Paris, 1.7.1947, p. 1 f., with other replies to the enquiry of the Comité français de Coordination concerning the policies of member associations (cf. nn. 134 and 158). As to the 'General Meeting' in Jan. 1947 no details of those present and no record of proceedings can be traced, so that presumably it was only a small meeting of sympathizers. Apart from Francis Gérard, the only active members of CIFE in the autumn of 1946 of whom I have found evidence are Mme Volpelière, who represented CIFE at

The design for Europe was governed by strictly supranational federal principles. 'The European federation ... must not be a bloc or an intergovernmental *entente*, but a union of European peoples' with a federal bicameral parliament and a federal government for foreign policy, economics, and defence; national governments were to confine themselves to 'areas not transcending national boundaries', which the statement defined very narrowly as 'purely administrative matters'. Only thus was it possible to overcome Europe's 'chronic weakness' and the threat it presented as 'the Balkans of world politics'. In addition, European federation would be a step towards world federation, and there could be 'no lasting peace without the federation of all peoples'.

In this way CIFE also indicated its attitude towards the problem of Europe in the world. The supreme aim of federalism was to ensure peace, and 'the European federation must be open to all European peoples without exception'. As long as the rest of the world was not united in a single federal security system, the federation might be regarded by the other powers as a threat; hence it was essential that other powers should view European federation with goodwill (which at present they did not), and better still that they should all join in a world federation. CIFE could find no way out of the vicious circle represented by the primacy of peace and the divergent policies of the world powers, especially the Soviet Union, and therefore it was unable to devise a political strategy for Europe. With its dwindling membership, moreover, CIFE did not possess sufficient intellectual capacity to rethink federal positions *ab initio* on the basis of a plurality of motivations.

(B) INTEGRAL FEDERALISM I: LA FÉDÉRATION

The group which emerged in winter 1946/7 as the most important French association for European federation started from quite different beginnings. It arose immediately after the Liberation, on 4 October 1944, under the name Centre d'études institutionnelles pour l'organisation de la société française; and its principal founders were members of Catholic social organizations who, after the experience of the war, wished to replace the national state run on centralist–Jacobin lines by a policy based on Christian natural law: 'All authority exercised as far down as possible, as far up as necessary.' The group was solidly based, with the Catholic industrialist Jacques Bassot as chairman (he also provided financial assistance) and with André Voisin in charge of organization. Its journal *La Fédération*, under the brilliant editorship of Jean Bareth and Max Richard, appeared from

---

Hertenstein (cf. at n. 47), and René Lhuillier, who represented it at Luxemburg (cf. n. 53 and M. Plantier in *La Fédération*, Nov. 1946, p. 21). Lhuillier, however, was from 1948 one of the leading members of the French section of the MSEUE. The Comité pour une Fédération Européenne et Mondiale (formerly CIFE) still appears in UEF lists in 1949, but the only representative mentioned is Francis Gérard; cf. E. Bonnefous, *L'Idée européenne et sa réalisation*, Paris, 1950, pp. 266–9.

November 1944 in mimeographed form and in print from January 1945.[126]

The group emphasized the principle of internal, decentralizing federalism, and favoured anti-*étatiste* strategy as against parliamentary action. The key to its success, as compared with CIFE, in enrolling a large membership (which numbered thousands within a short time after the end of the war) lay in the concreteness of its aims and the fact that it had an adversary to combat: the unimaginative Gaullist restoration of Jacobin-type centralism. Inspired by Proudhon's federalist ideas and the Christian social theories of René de la Tour du Pin, its chief aim was to oppose internal federation to national centralism. With organized sections in most parts of France and committees for all main professions, by 1945 it was already without question the most important grouping of French federalists, and its leaders – Robert Aron, Jean Bareth, Alexandre Marc, Bernard Voyenne, Gabriel Marcel, Bertrand de Jouvenel, and others – developed the principle of internal federation with all possible emphasis as the first step in their programme. As early as June 1945, however, there appeared in their *Circulaire intérieure* an article entitled 'La paix et le principe fédératif' which stated that it was also of course 'necessary to go a step further and work out similar federal arrangements and bases of international solidarity on a European and global level'. Federation was essential to natural, communal, and professional groups, 'because they represent the stable foundation on which Europe and France are called upon to build'.[127]

La Fédération strove to construct a blueprint for federal order in every aspect of French society. According to its statement of policy, 'La Fédération proposes federal structures based essentially on natural and historical groups at the human level, which alone can give the individual a firm basis and enable him to play his destined part in life and enjoy specific liberties. These groups are: the family, the local community, the region, his place of work and his trade union.' A new juridical order should be

---

[126] For a general review, cf. J.-P. Gouzy, *Les Pionniers de l'Europe communautaire*, Lausanne (Centre de Recherches Européennes), 1968, p. 26 f. For details of the origin and structure of the Fédération cf. A. Greilsammer, *Les Mouvements fédéralistes en France de 1945 à 1974*, Paris (Presses d'Europe) 1975, pp. 117–23 and 130. (This work suffers in places from its unhistorical arrangement; it is less full for 1945–50 than for later years, but is very informative on the Fédération.) On the group's theoretical origins cf. J. Bassot, *Travail et propriété. Actualité révolutionnaire de La Tour du Pin*, Paris, 1943 (288 pages). André Raymond-Marie Voisin, b. Neuilly 1912, a teacher and afterwards a journalist, came to La Fédération through the Justice Sociale group and the works of La Tour du Pin; he later served on the Executive Bureau of the European Movement and as adviser to the Chaban-Delmas cabinet. Max Richard, b. 1914 at Levallois, also began as a teacher; he was afterwards a journalist and active member of Justice Sociale, and later delegate-general of the European Movement (data in Greilsammer, op. cit., pp. 117 and 198 f.).

[127] Circulaire intérieure de la Fédération, Centre d'études institutionnelles pour l'organisation de la société française, Paris, June 1945, pp. 6 and 8. 'Cette construction ne pouvant être réalisée ni immédiatement, ni globalement, il est recommandable de réaliser tout d'abord des "Fédérations" régionales, groupant des nations manifestement complémentaires par leur situation géographique, la similitude de leurs positions politiques, le degré et l'esprit de leur culture, l'interdépendance de leurs économies' (ibid., p. 6).

created 'in which the family is considered as the primary cell of social life.' There should be

an administrative organization based on municipal autonomy and not on an all-powerful state; an economic system founded on functional syndicalism and the transformation of capitalist enterprise into an association of producers, within the framework of a professional organization independent of party and of public authorities, the latter's role consisting of general direction, co-ordination and arbitration.[128]

Within the limits of these basic convictions, the views of members of the association varied from moderate anti-centralism to rigorous opposition to *étatisme*. An idea of how they proposed to 'break the coercive power of the state'[129] is given by their appeal at the time of the municipal elections in October 1947. They urged citizens not to vote for any party, since 'what is taken by parties finally reverts to the state; municipal elections must therefore be depoliticized'. Instead, citizens should vote for direct representatives of self-government, 'so as to create federal communities. This means liberating the present municipalities from abusive administrative tutelage, ... making them autonomous in all matters affecting their own interests.'[130] A convenient summary of the internal federalist programme is given in a pamphlet published in the spring of 1947 entitled *Nous voulons*. This called for: a habeas corpus statute of individual rights, protecting men and women against arbitrary action by the police and all administrative bodies; autonomous municipalities, their liberties guaranteed by the recognition of a sovereign right to manage their own affairs; communal, regional, national, etc. federations, their powers restricted to the management of common interests. The state will be all the stronger and more authoritative as its competence is properly restricted. There should be communal enterprises, free from either capitalism or collectivism, diverse in structure but based on the syndical association of productive elements in accordance with justice and with the needs of sound management; public services, freed from *étatisme*, constituted co-operatively within the framework of federations appropriate to their nature, and free of administrative servitudes, selfish rivalries and political influences; economic federations, based on enterprises and occupations established in a given centre, which will bring back fair competition that has been stifled by trusts and state capitalism, humanize work conditions and multiply consumer goods by the use of modern techniques ... We shall achieve all this without party political action, thanks to each person's effort in the framework of

---

[128] Basic statement of policy, printed in most numbers of *La Fédération* in 1946/7 on the inside of the cover, and concluding with the words: 'La Fédération calls on all French people to establish everywhere realistic action centres, independent of all parties, at local and regional level: the Centres d'action fédérale.'

[129] P. Nicolas, 'Briser la contrainte et organiser la liberté', *La Fédération*, No. 25, Feb. 1947, p. 30. As a more fundamental justification, a sentence from Pius XI's encyclical *Quadragesimo anno* was frequently quoted (e.g. *La Fédération*, Nov. 1946, p. 2): 'It is an injustice, a grave evil and a disturbance of right order for a larger and higher organization to arrogate to itself functions which can be performed efficiently by smaller and lower bodies.'

[130] J. Bareth, 'Bientôt les élections municipales', *La Fédération*, No. 30, July 1947, p. 30. Understandably, from 1946 onwards the Fédération was able to form local groups in most French departments thanks to the adherence of many local government officers who had been deprived of their powers by Paris centralism: cf. n. 131 and, for examples, the reports 'Les Communes forestières', 'Chez les Maires d'Alsace', etc. in *La Fédération*, Nov. 1946, p. 22 f.

everyday communities; the creation of federal communes, centres of social, economic and cultural life, and primary political cells of the nation; the federation of communes in the region, regions in the nation, nations in supranational federations.[131]

The extension of the federal principle beyond the boundaries of the nation was intended from the beginning, as the above-quoted article of June 1945 shows, but little stress was laid on it in the first discouraging twelvemonth after the war. As the rift between the world powers and the crisis over the peace settlement became evident, however, *La Fédération* quickly began to devote more attention to the question of European federation. Max Richard, as chief editor, began with an article in May 1946 on the Swiss system as a pattern for Europe. Vital-Mareile argued that European federation was necessary to pave the way for world federation. Alexandre Marc, one of the most prolific contributors to *La Fédération*, argued elaborately in September 1946 that in the great battle against 'the reduction of everything to the level of the state', 'integral federalism' could only be achieved by a combination of 'internal federalism' and 'European federalism'. The first of these meant transferring to municipalities and trade associations all the functions they were capable of handling, while the second meant transferring to a European federal authority functions that could only be performed properly at a higher level, such as defence, foreign policy, and economic planning.[132] After the impetus given by participation in the Luxemburg congress in October 1946, every issue of *La Fédération* contained a discussion or statement of the principles of European federation.

In accordance with these and with the association's policy statements in winter 1946/7, we may summarize its aims as follows:

1. *European federation*: from the standpoint of integral federalism this was not merely an answer to the problems of peace and economic welfare, but was above all a means of curbing the absolutism of the national state. As Daniel Rops put it in a vehement attack on 'statolatry', federalism was based on the concrete reality of the *patrie*, viz. the parish or municipality, the region, and the 'living communities of society'. It developed

---

[131] Pamphlet, *Principes et méthode d'action* (Action fédérale series), Paris, 1947; the programme was also printed in *La Fédération*, No. 29, June 1947, p. 33. The association's first statement of principles – *France, terre de libertés*, Paris, 1945 – had contained a fuller justification of internal federalism against Jacobin centralism. Cf. also Robert Aron, 'Mission du fédéralisme en France', *La Fédération*, No. 24, Jan. 1947, pp. 13–15. A bestseller of 1947 was J. F. Gravier's protest, *Paris et le désert français. Décentralisation, équipement, population,* Paris (Le Portulan), 1947. Similarly A. Gasser, *L'Autonomie communale et la reconstruction de l'Europe* (Neuchâtel, La Baconnière, 1946) made much more of an impression in France than in Switzerland.

[132] M. Ricard, 'De la Suisse à l'Europe', *La Fédération*, May 1946, p. 6; Vital-Mareile, 'Sur le fédéralisme international', ibid., Sept. 1946, pp. 3–5; A. Marc, 'Le Fédéralisme Intégral', *L'Action fédéraliste européenne*, No. 2, Oct. 1946, pp. 44–56. On Alexandre Marc and his elaboration of the general concept in book form, cf. n. 65.

the national principle as a spiritual requirement (*exigence*) that might go beyond the bounds of the *patrie* but is neither aggressive nor narrowly exclusive. It assigns its proper role to the state while tending more and more to place it in a supranational setting, because the conditions of production and the functions that require to be performed call increasingly for a wider administration than that to which states are restricted by our present European frontiers.[133]

European federation, in the words of the pamphlet of spring 1947, was 'a necessary condition for the economic organization of the Continent and the defence of its common civilization, the only possible solution of the German problem, and the way to a world federation which may bring about world peace'.[134]

2. In terms of *world politics,* according to La Fédération, the function of a balanced European federation of this kind was to mediate between the two extra-European great powers (the Soviet Union was regarded throughout as basically non-European in its structure).[135] Europe was threatened by the conflict between the two world powers, the *'super-grands'*: between two 'materialist myths, both of which are completely alien to its spiritual inheritance'.[136] To meet this threat, Europe must unite; otherwise it risked being 'crushed between two measureless giants'. Only a united Europe could act as a bridge between two empires; it alone might bring balance into a world which had ceased to understand nothing but force.[137]

3. *The way* to such a federated Europe could hardly lie through the institutions of national *étatisme,* at any rate not through them alone. 'If states show themselves incapable of conforming to this necessity, we shall have to review the archaic bases on which their power rests. Otherwise men ..., acting across frontiers, will have to force them to behave as they should.'[138] Hence efforts towards internal federation were also a step

---

[133] D. Rops, 'Esquisse d'une leçon de vocabulaire', *La Fédération,* No. 24, Jan. 1947, pp. 5–7. Against the attempt to designate 'a single administrative organism as the sole reality that is to absorb everything else', against the 'monstrosity of the state', it was necessary to devise 'a mode of life based on a radical distinction between motherland, nation and state'. Cf. Salinger, p. 133 above.
[134] *Principes et méthode d'action,* Paris, 1947 (n. 131). Similarly the declaration presented in March 1947 to the Coordinating Committee of Federalist Associations: 'La Fédération distinguishes three spheres in which a federal order must be introduced: the national . . .; the European sphere, in which supranational institutions must be created on the basis of successively concluded regional agreements; and the world sphere, in which central authority must rest on the solid basis of local, national and regional authorities' (*Le Document Fédéraliste,* No. 4, Paris, 1.7.1947, p. 3). Many articles spoke of solving the German problem by 'German federation within a European federation' while overcoming the *'nostalgie de l'unité'* (i.e. the hankering after a centralized national regime) in all European countries: cf. *La Fédération,* Nov. 1946, pp. 7–9, March 1947, pp. 12–14, and elsewhere.
[135] A Joussain, 'La Fédération européenne et l'U.R.S.S.', *La Fédération,* No. 33, Oct. 1947, p. 22 f.
[136] *La Fédération,* No. 25, Feb. 1947, p. 1: leading article, hence representing all the leaders' views (Basset, Voisin, Richard, Bareth, and others).
[137] Manifeste des Responsables, drafted by Gabriel Marcel: 'Il faut faire l'Europe! Ruinées par la guerre, bouleversées dans leurs fondations, broyées entre deux géants sans mesure, les nations européennes savent que leur restauration propre est inexorablement liée à la restauration du continent' (*BEF Archives,* Brugmans corr.).
[138] From the leading article quoted in n. 136; to be read in the light of the texts cited in nn. 131 and 132.

towards supranational federation; and co-operation among federalists would bring about an international movement which, in the long run, would have a revolutionary effect on national sovereignty.

4. *Purpose and character of the organization.* In terms of this strategy, La Fédération was thought of as a movement embracing all elements that identified with federalism and were prepared to use their efforts to bring it about on the national and international plane. The membership forms attached to all the group's publications distinguished between (1) subscription to *La Fédération* and (2) membership of the association itself; the latter covered, in addition to the subscription, invitations to lectures under its auspices and the obligation to serve on specialized committees or regional or local *Centres d'action fédérale*. The number of full members in 1946/7 has been estimated as between 4,500 and 5,000, and to these must be added a certain number of subscribers only.[139]

In 1948, the year in which the European idea first recaptured the attention of a wide public, the total number rose above 9,000; for the end of 1949 O. Philip gives a figure of 15,000, no doubt including subscribers-only.[140] This made La Fédération unquestionably the largest French association in the early European movement, though it was not a mass movement on a scale to justify placing any hopes in revolutionary strategy; in practice, like the other groups, it did not amount to more than an influential lobby.[141]

5. *Forms of activity.* The practical nature of its aims enabled La Fédération to develop numerous forms of activity on the part of its members. Its monthly journal was well produced and of high intellectual quality; it published lively discussions and articles, not only by its own members but by prominent politicians like Paul Reynaud and Edgar Faure, and foreign federalists like Miss Josephy and Henri Brugmans.[142] Ten specialized commissions, which in principle all members were free to join, discussed all aspects of integral federalism, from its philosophical basis to economic problems and forms of international federation. In addition La Fédération founded and supervised sixteen special organizations on a regional basis or on particular subjects.[143] By means of 'direct action groups' La

---

[139] Date from Greilsammer (n. 126), p. 118. Application forms in every number of the journal (usually on inside cover); especially clear e.g. in the issue of Nov. 1946, p. 28. On committees, local groups, meetings, etc., see nn. ibid., pp. 122 f.
[140] Cf. appeal to recruit members to a total of 10,000 subscribers, No. 35, Dec. 1947, p. 22; total of 9,000 mentioned in No. 39, Apr. 1948, O. Philip (n. 99), p. 194.
[141] Greilsammer (n. 126) states on p. 119 that the Fédération was never designed as a mass movement, but this is only true in the sense that it never managed to become one; its strategy, however, postulated mass support.
[142] Cf. Greilsammer, ibid., p. 130. Permanent members of the editorial board were Daniel Halévy, Maxime Leroy, Gabriel Marcel, Robert Aron, Hyacinthe Dubreuil, Bertrand de Jouvenel, Thierry Maulnier, Paul Séraut, Georges Vedel, André Voisin, and Max Richard (chief editor).
[143] These organizations (some founded in later years) were:
Municipal:
(a) Les Jeunes Élus Locaux (JEL)
(b) Centre d'Information des Communes Rurales (CICOR)
(c) Mouvement National des Élus Locaux (MNEL)

Fédération achieved a uniform basis of country-wide support: its journal came by degrees to report the activities of more than fifty local groups.

The variety of these may be judged from the record, taken at random, for the month from December 1946 to January 1947. On 3 December Robert Aron spoke at the group's monthly press conference on conferences of European intellectuals; on the 8th, Jean Bareth spoke at Rouen on the principles of La Fédération; on the 10th M. Sicé, mayor of the 16th Paris *arrondissement*, gave a description of his duties; on the 19th Dr Morlaas spoke on humanism and medicine, on 9 January (at a press conference) Gaston Bardet on town planning, on the 14th MM. Robet and Martin on the Resistance and totalitarianism, on the 15th Alexandre Marc on principles of federalism.[144] In the spring of 1947 the emphasis shifted from internal to European federalism.

The dynamic nature of La Fédération naturally enabled it, as will be seen,[145] to take the lead among French federalist groups and to play an important part in the foundation and development of the UEF as a league of European federalists.

(C) INTEGRAL FEDERALISM II: CERCLES SOCIALISTES, FÉDÉRALISTES ET COMMUNAUTAIRES POUR UNE RÉPUBLIQUE MODERNE (CSFC)

Next to La Fédération, the second great collective movement of integral federalism in France was that known as Cercles socialistes, fédéralistes, et communautaires pour une république moderne. In its history, doctrine, methods, and significance it had much in common with La Fédération; there were many personal connections between the two groups, and they

---

Regional:
  (a) Mouvement National pour la Décentralisation et la Réforme Régionale (MNDR)
Economic and social:
  (a) Conseil National des Économies Régionales et de la Production (CNERP)
  (b) Comité Hyacinthe Dubreuil
  (c) Centre d'Études de la Socio-Économie
European:
  (a) Conseil des Communes d'Europe (CCE)
  (b) Cercle de Strasbourg
  (c) Bureau de Liaison Franco-Britannique
Youth:
  (a) Jeunesses Européennes Fédéralistes (JEF)
  (b) Mouvement National des Élus Universitaires
  (c) Centre d'Études de la Société Française (CESF)
The Fédération was also closely connected with the following movements:
  (a) Fédération Nationale des Femmes (FNF)
  (b) Union Nationale des Combattants (UNC)
  (c) Fédération Européenne des Anciens Combattants (FEDAC)
Cf. Greilsammer, ibid., pp. 122 f.

[144] Cf. the account in *La Fédération*, No. 24, Jan. 1947, p. 33. In addition to conferences and committees, La Fédération organized three-week training courses at an École de Cadres fédéralistes. French industrialists, especially Georges Villiers, the pro-European president of the employers' union, CNPF, helped to finance its many activities: cf. Greilsammer (n. 126), pp. 119–21, and the pamphlet *Action fédérale, principes et méthodes d'action*, Paris, n.d. (c.1947).

[145] Cf. the account in *La Fédération*, No. 24, Jan. 1947, p. 31; also pp. 362 and 626, and see Index under 'Voisin'.

were linked by joint activities. They belonged, however, to different traditions: in La Fédération the dominant principles were those of Catholicism, corporatism, and natural law, while the Cercles were concerned with renewing and developing the ideas of anti-*étatiste* Socialism.

The central figure of the Cercles was Claude-Marcel Hytte, a former Communist party member who had become a libertarian Socialist and was one of the leaders of the wartime Resistance group, Mouvement national revolutionnaire (MNR).[146] From 1945 he edited the monthly *La République moderne*, a continuation of the clandestine *Le Combat national révolutionnaire*, and organized a federalist movement consisting of social-democratic, syndicalist, and Proudhonist Resistance fighters. At the beginning of 1946 the movement was called 'Cercles d'amis de la république moderne', then 'Cercles d'études et d'action pour une république moderne'; finally at the beginning of 1947 it took the title 'Cercles socialistes' etc. With the eminent historian Robert Aron as political editor of its journal from April 1947, the movement became the second most important centre of integral federalism.[147]

Hytte and his associates described themselves as 'firm opponents of etatism' and advocated 'a humane and free Socialism, based on the communities within which men carry on their civic, economic and social activities: the home, the local community, the place of work, trade unions, cultural and intellectual groups etc'. On the economic plane they sought to replace *étatisme* by joint enterprises of self-administering producers; politically they called for 'direct representation in specialized bodies'; in other words, corporate instead of parliamentary representation.[148]

According to a manifesto issued by the MNR in October 1944, these 'intermediary communities' were necessary to protect the individual from the state and also to provide the political community with a solid basis.'The revolution we seek does not mean civil war, disorder or anarchy. What we wish to achieve by revolution is to restore order and liberty in France ... Not the capitalist and paternalist order, ... but the revolutionary order that gives everyone the place he is entitled to; ... not the freedom of the capitalist jungle ... but the true freedom that a nation can achieve by ridding itself of foreign interference and domestic tyranny.' At the beginning of 1947 René Lhuillier described this freedom: 'Producers must be free – politically, of course, but economically as well. And

---

[146] Hytte, b. 1902, was a journalist and, after his breach with the PCF, became secretary-general of the Socialist revolutionary Parti frontiste for the Paris region. Later he was secretary-general of the Union Française des Fédéralistes (UFF) and member of the Central Committee of the European Federalist Movement (MFE); cf. Greilsammer (n. 126), pp. 131 f.

[147] As a source for the history of the Cercles ..., see the collection of their regular publications in the Bibliothèque Nationale, Paris: *Le Combat national révolutionnaire*; then, from 1944, *Documents du M.N.R.*; from Document No. 6 onwards = *Les Cahiers de la République moderne*; from 15.11.1945, *Nouvelle Série: La République moderne*, monthly; from 1.10.1946, every two months.

[148] Declaration of principles of the Cercles Socialistes ..., 'Ce que nous sommes, ce que nous voulons', in *La République moderne, Suppl. aux Nos. 23–4* (beginning of 1947); reprinted in *Le Document fédéraliste*, No. 4, Paris, 1.7.1947, p. 2 f.

they can only be free if they are organized at the lowest level in autonomous cells, the totality of which constitutes the economic apparatus of the country. The state should intervene solely to co-ordinate the activity of the basic cells and fit it into the national economic plan.'[149] Like all forms of libertarian Socialism, the doctrine of the Cercles was both Utopian and concrete; without attempting to cover the whole complexity of life in a modern industrial society, it contained many suggestions as to how conditions might be modified in the short term.

The Cercles also maintained from the outset that, in the words of their declaration of principles at the beginning of 1947, 'this federal structure must also be introduced on the international plane'. Thus their

1. *Design for Europe* was clearly federal. They called for 'a federative organization of the European Continent, involving a surrender of sovereignty to the Federation in so far as tasks of common European interest are concerned'. It was not a question of making Europe but of restoring it, as it already constituted an economic whole and 'an inestimable store of cultural and intellectual values which must be preserved at all costs'.[150] Hytte and the Cercles saw libertarian Socialism as pre-eminently the fruit of a European tradition; to make Socialism a reality Europe must assert itself, and for that purpose it must unite.

2. *Europe in the world.* Replying to Communist accusations in the autumn of 1946, Hytte declared that a federated Europe would be in no way directed against the Soviet Union but would be 'a Third Force of equilibrium between the American and the Eurasian empire' and hence 'a substantial guarantee of peace'.

'This federal and united Europe must in turn be integrated into a larger, world-wide organization comprising all states or federations of states and thus constituting the United States of the World'; only thus could world peace be safeguarded. But such a 'world parliament' could not be achieved in the short run, as the American capitalists and the Russian dictators had different aims; so the objective must be pursued by stages. 'This [European] federation of the most intelligent and civilized peoples on earth would be an irresistible force that could prevent war by its very existence.'[151] The self-assertion of traditional Europe against the

---

[149] Charter of the MNR, 'Pour une République moderne', adopted at the MNR congress of 29.10.1944, published as MNR Document No. 3 of 10.11.1944. René Lhuillier, 'Socialisme et Fédéralisme', *La Fédération,* No. 27, April 1947, p. 15 f.

[150] First quotation from Declaration of principles, 1947 (n. 148); second quotation from C.-M. Hytte, 'Esquisse d'une politique véritablement française', *La République moderne,* No. 15, 15.11.1946, p. 3 f.

[151] First quotation from Hytte (n. 150); second quotation from Declaration of principles, 1947 (n. 148), third quotation from A. Bunet, 'Conditions de la Paix', *La République moderne,* No. 8, June 1946, p. 8 f. An unsigned article in the Supplement to No. 29 of *La République moderne* (spring 1947) stated that 'If Europe does not unite . . . it cannot escape economic or political subjection, and in that case, not only is its very existence threatened but its division will increase the likelihood of an East–West conflict, which must be avoided at all costs. United Europe will not be the work of the Americans or the Russians, but of the Europeans themselves. If the Americans sought to impede European unity, which we do not expect, it would none the less come about sooner or later, and perhaps in opposition to them. The same applies to the Russians, who have an interest in the emergence of a free, independent Europe.'

encroachment of the two new world powers, and its role as a pacemaker for world federation, were regarded by the Cercles as two sides of a single coin.

3. The *plan of campaign* followed logically from this. The integral federalists strove for world federation as a maximum objective, but in pragmatic fashion recommended partial measures, however small, towards federation at all levels.

We have better things to do than to start at once drawing the frontiers of this Europe and deciding which countries should be in and which out. Since there is no hope that a ready-made Europe will come into being one fine day of its own accord, the work of building it must be begun gradually. Countries which are prepared to form the nucleus of the new structure here and now should announce the fact and form a union. Others will join them before long, and in due course others still. The only ones left out will be those who so choose, or whose geographical position and interests require them to create other federations or join existing ones.

As a first step the Cercles vigorously supported the SFIO plan, evolved by Léon Blum, of the 'Western family' of France, Britain, Benelux, Italy, a democratic Spain, and, if possible, Switzerland. To achieve their aims on the European scale they hoped for a renewal of European Socialism by progressive minorities who 'know that Socialism can only succeed if it reaches a higher spiritual level than that of liberal capitalism or Bolshevism'.[152]

4. *Purpose and character of the organization; forms of activity.* The Cercles regarded themselves as one of these 'progressive minorities', working with other federalist groups in the trade unions, the SFIO, and finally the European Movement to bring about the renewal of Socialism in the spirit of integral federalism, and thus the renewal of Europe in the spirit of liberal Socialism. Membership of the Cercles rose rapidly from the moment of their foundation and was soon close to 5,000.[153] Their organ *La République moderne*, like *La Fédération*, had among its regular contributors Robert Aron, Alexandre Marc, and Bernard Voyenne. They played a prominent part in creating the European federalist union (UEF): Hytte was present at the early meeting of federalists at Hertenstein in September 1946.[154]

(D) SMALLER FEDERALIST GROUPS

Similar in aims and ideas, but of less weight, were a number of other federalist groups that revived in France from the autumn of 1946 onwards. Two of them, like the Cercles, grew directly out of the European movement of the Resistance.

---

[152] First quotation from 'Vers l'Est ou vers l'Ouest?', *La République moderne,* Supplement to No. 29 (spring 1947); second quotation from C.-M. Hytte, 'Une renaissance du Socialisme est-elle possible?', *La Fédération,* No. 27, April 1947, p. 17 f. For the concept of the 'Western family' cf. W. Loth, *Sozialismus und Internationalismus. Die französischen Sozialisten und die Nachkriegsordnung Europas 1940–1950,* Stuttgart, 1977, pp. 79–86; for the support of this conception by the Cercles . . . , see Bunet (n. 151).
[153] O. Philip (n. 99), p. 194.
[154] Cf. pp. 306 and 362, and see Index under 'Hytte'.

Union européenne was founded in Paris on 22 November 1944; its provisional headquarters was at Nice, however, where the Resistance groups were particularly strong. Its statutes proclaimed as its aim the

creation of a United States of Europe ... The association intends to promote the cross-fertilizing (*copénétration*) of the ideas of individuals of different nationalities so as to encourage an understanding of those forces which are committed to the cultural, social, juridical and economic progress of the peoples of Europe and to lead them towards a state of pacification (*apaisement*) and mutual understanding, in a democratic spirit and within the framework of an international organization of the Great Powers.

Like other federalist groups, Union européenne was scarcely active in the twelve months following the end of the war; it showed fresh signs of life in June 1946.[155]

Socialisme et Liberté was founded in July 1946 by Henri Frenay, leader of the important Resistance organization Combat, who was known for his European federalist views. The association was the successor of the wartime Mouvement de Libération Nationale (MLN), and aimed especially to rally the forces which opposed the integration of the MLN into the Radical Party and wished to maintain its libertarian Socialist orientation. Besides Frenay the original executive of Socialisme et Liberté included Claude Bourdet, who had also been a leader of Combat and now edited the newspaper of the same name, and Claude-Marie Hytte, leader of the Cercles socialistes.[156] In conscious opposition to the 'bureaucratization' of the Communist and Socialist parties, Socialisme et Liberté aimed at reviving the basic attitudes of libertarian Socialism: it advocated self-administration in freedom, democracy in economic as well as political matters, federal decentralization, and internationalism.

'Mankind is torn between two irreducible antagonisms', Frenay declared in his initial appeal; 'it can only be saved by setting up an ideological and political third force, which must be authentically Socialist and can only be located in our Western world, at present in danger of being crushed between two conflicting imperialisms ... Socialisme et Liberté appeals to you to create a federation of all forces in the service of justice and liberty, to build up a Federal French Republic of

---

[155] Quotation from Statutes of Union Européenne dated 22.11.1944, *EM Archives, Bruges*. Announcement of proposal to publish a 'Revue européenne', in *L'Action fédéraliste européenne*, No. 1, July 1946, p. 66.

[156] Other members were Charles Tanguy, Jean Gemaehling, Jeanne Bertrand, Jean Allardi, Brille, Pierre Chateau, Fortoul, Robert Dessailly, Beilhartz, Dr Rouzaud, Lienert, Mme Girard, Lerat, Jacques Lavigne, and Madeleine Rousseau. Cf. the inaugural 'Appel' in *Socialisme et Liberté = La République moderne*, Supplement to No. 10, and Henri Frenay's first circular of 27.7.1946 (*EM Archives, Bruges*): For the Combat organization cf. Introduction, n. 77. Frenay, b. 1905, an officer of the regular army, joined the Resistance in 1940 and soon became one of its key members as leader of Combat. Atfer the liberation in 1944 de Gaulle appointed him Minister for War Prisoners, but he soon relinquished his post on account of concerted Communist attacks. Cf. his war memoirs: H. Frenay, *La Nuit finira*, Paris, 1973. From he beginning of 1947 he was engaged in rallying pro-European left-wing Socialists. He took an important part in the formation of the Socialist European movement MSEUE: cf. chap. IV/1(c) (in vol. 2).

Socialist Communities as a first stage towards the United States of Europe and the United States of the world.'[157]

Another movement, Union économique et fédérale européenne (UEFE), under the chairmanship of Gaston Riou, grew out of Union économique et douanière européenne, which had existed since 1927. Daniel Serruys and his associates, who were more interested in working for economic co-operation on traditional lines, pursued their activity under the title Comité d'Action Économique et Douanière, while Gaston Riou (chairman), Henri Truchy (vice-chairman), Pierre Pasani (secretary-general), and others, with Herriot and Joseph Paul-Boncour as honorary presidents, emphasized the need for common European institutions, though they did not always go so far as federalism.

The UEFE, which was basically liberal in its approach, advocated 'a study of commercial, industrial, agricultural and financial relations among European countries with a view to substituting for the present regime a peaceful system of industrial and tariff agreements'. The nature of the proposed system was not clearly defined. Europe was to enjoy 'economic union' and a 'federal organization', but the concrete proposals for such organization amounted to no more than bilateral and multilateral inter-state agreements. True to pre-war tradition, as late as the spring of 1947 'Europe' was still envisaged as an independent union consisting of Western, Central, and Eastern Europe; the UEFE executive made approaches to Prague and Budapest as a matter of course. Putting an end to economic warfare within Europe would create conditions for stability and do justice to its economic interdependence. Even in the summer of 1947 the Union still hoped to rescue the East-European countries from final incorporation in the Soviet empire by developing their economic and politico-institutional ties with Western Europe. 'That', as Riou said to Duncan Sandys, 'is why Churchill's plan is unquestionably the right one'.[158]

While the UEFE sought to enlist the collaboration of important figures from the political and economic spheres, other groups of the incipient movement for a federal Europe worked on the principle of an 'élite minority' acting as an inspiring force in as many branches of social activity as possible. These included integral federalist groups like the Équipes fédéralistes françaises, the Union des Étudiants fédéralistes, and La Démocratie fédérative, headed by Philippe Serre. Some combined integral federalism with traditional pacifism and thus laid stress on world federation:

---

[157] 'Appel', ibid. (n. 156).

[158] Last quotation: Riou to Sandys, 5.6.1947, *EM Archives, Bruges*; remainder from declaration by the UEFE, presented to the Comité de Coordination in March 1947, printed in *Le Document fédéraliste*, No. 4, Paris, 1.7.1947, p. 3. Gaston Riou, a Radical deputy between the wars, published *Europe ma patrie* with a foreword by Aristide Briand; cf. O. Philip (n. 99), pp. 146 and 193; also, for the Union économique et douanière européenne, chap. II/3, at n. 100. After the 1946 congress the vice-chairmen of the group included many economic and political figures; Mme Kempf-Berthelot, Jacques André, Paul Benazet, Clauzel, Julien Durand, Fleury Thomas, Georges Hersent, Paul Jourdain, Lucien Le Foyer, Léon Lebrec, Armand Meggle, Georges Scelle, and André Siegfried; quotation from record of the general assembly, 1.7.1946, *EM Archives, Bruges*.

these included J. Larmeroux's Comité International États-Unis du Monde, M. Belley's Union Fédérale Mondiale, P. Benazet's Union Universelle pour la Paix; also the Ligue internationale pour la défense des Libertés Humaines, the Front humain des citoyens du Monde, the Centre d'action internationale, Rene Lhuillier's Fédération européenne, and Robert Margin's Ligue pour les États-Unis d'Europe.[159] While many of these groups were ephemeral, in union with the strong La Fédération they ensured that the European movement in France was responsive to the Proudhonist tradition of federalism, and at the international level they imparted a similar tendency to the nascent UEF.

Altogether, from mid-1946 onwards the French federalists developed the federalist principle in great detail and in conscious opposition to Gaullism. It was important that the French federalists, in particular, revived the attitude of the Resistance leaders as a matter of principle and, like them, placed in the forefront of their campaign the abolition of the absolute power of the state; their object was to safeguard human rights by restricting state power, on the basis of subsidiarity, to a supervisory function *vis-à-vis* the local communities which were the real centres of political life. It is especially true of the two main groups, the Fédération and the Cercles socialistes, that they were 'federalists' before they were 'Europeans'; this was an important factor in lending depth to their conception of Europe, as was also true of committed federalists in other countries. The fact that French federalism developed so vigorously in spite of de Gaulle's restoration of nationalism shows how deep-seated was the revulsion from nationalist thinking. Federalism made headway in political circles as early as 1946/7, and this was to be a determining factor of France's European policy in and after 1948.

5. The Union Européenne des Fédéralistes and its 'Third Force' Programme

The example of France showed once again how, owing to the rift between the Soviet and American peacemakers in the summer and the autumn of 1946, the idea of European unity took shape again in various cities and among different circles which were, at the outset, unaware of each other's existence. In all West-European countries federalist groups revived or were newly founded. After a year of resignation in the face of what seemed a *diktat* by the two world powers acting in concert, now that the latter's discord had become apparent, these organizations preached with renewed

---

[159] Cf. the various lists of federalist organizations in *Cahiers du monde nouveau*, 3 (1947), No. 6, p. 309 f. (in an instructive special number on problems of federalism and European union); *Federal News*, No. 141, Dec. 1946, p. 21; J.-P. Gouzy, *Les Mouvements pour l'unité européenne en France de 1945 à 1951* (unpublished MS); *Europe unie dans un monde uni,* UEF pamphlet, Geneva, n.d. (*c.*beginning of 1948), p. 11 f.

362   *Revival of Plans for Federation*

fervour the ideas which the experience of wars had implanted in European minds, and which they now saw as Europe's proper contribution to the peace settlement.[160] At the beginning of this period of reactivation, in July 1946, the journal *L'Action fédéraliste européenne* urged that the many local and national groups should unite in a European federalist movement so as to co-ordinate and strengthen their efforts *vis-à-vis* the national states; the watchword was 'federate the federalists!' In September, as we have seen, on the initiative of the Swiss Europa-Union and the Dutch Europeesche Actie, these two bodies united with the Belgian Union fédérale, the Italian MFE, and the French CIFE to form Aktion Europa-Union. At Luxemburg in October, although the British Federal Union had also invited the organizations devoted to world federation, the principal outcome was that the seven French associations headed by La Fédération had joined with the British, Dutch, and Belgian groups to form an independent Conseil Europeen des Fédéralistes. Finally, on 9 December 1946 the leaders of the two over-all associations decided at Basle to set up a joint organization; this was done formally at a session of the presidium of Aktion Europa-Union together with representatives of the Conseil.[161]

(A) FOUNDATION AND DEVELOPMENT OF THE UEF DOWN TO MARCH 1947

On 15 December 1946 the chairmen or authorized representatives of individual associations met, as agreed, for a full-day session at the office of La Fédération near the Paris opera house. They were: H. Brugmans (Holland) for Europeesche Actie; Miss Josephy (Britain) for Federal Union; A. Allard (Belgium) for Union fédérale; U. Campagnolo (Italy) for the Movimento Federalista Europeo; H. Koch (Luxemburg) for Union fédérale; and H. Schiess (Switzerland) for Europa-Union. As to the French associations, which were naturally in greater strength on the spot, La Fédération was represented by A. Voisin, La République moderne by C.-M. Hytte, CIFE by F. Gerard, Union économique et fédérale européenne by G. Riou, États-Unis du Monde by J. Larmeroux, and Union fédérale mondiale by M. Belley. With André Voisin in the chair and after hearing a report from Dr Brugmans on the Basle meeting, the assembled representatives officially set up the Union Européenne des Fédéralistes (UEF) as their common organization. Constituting themselves as its provisional Central Committee, they unanimously elected Henri Brugmans as its provisional chairman and Alexandre Marc as secretary-

---

[160] The same process of founding or reactivating European federalist groups began simultaneously in the German zones of occupation. It took place more slowly, however, being hindered by the occupation authorities, until it was stimulated by emissaries of the UEF. For these reasons, and because the early German groups were not in a position to help in the creation of the UEF, they are discussed in the next section this chapter, pp. 385–431.

[161] Cf. detailed account of these preliminaries to the foundation of the UEF in chap. II/2, pp. 300–16.

general. They decided that Paris should be the provisional headquarters of the secretariat and Geneva its permanent seat, that an 'enlarged Central Committee' should meet in April at Amsterdam to consider the programme and organization further, and that these should be adopted by a first regular congress of the UEF to be held in Switzerland in August 1947.[162] Such was the beginning of the supranational association of European federalist groups, which was soon co-ordinating in all West-European countries the activities of those who advocated a European federation; it united the former leaders of the non-Communist Resistance movements, and after three years of continuous expansion comprised over forty affiliated associations numbering over 100,000 paid-up members. Article 1 of the Statutes formulated in the ensuing weeks stated that:

The European federalist movements, assembled in Paris on 15 December 1946, have decided to form together an association named the European Union of Federalists. This shall be open to all European federalist organizations, that is to say groups, movements and associations that accept its general orientation as defined by the federalist declarations of Hertenstein and Luxemburg.[163]

It was a basic principle, as laid down by Art. 6 of the Statutes, that the UEF 'shall be composed solely of moral persons, i.e. associations, groups and movements (professional, syndical, co-operative, parliamentary etc.) which are fighting for the victory of federalism in Europe and the world'; individuals could only be members of affiliated regional or sectorial associations. Further decisions taken in Paris were: a plan should be worked out for a passport system for all European citizens, also designs for a uniform membership badge;[164] all member associations should help to finance the

---

[162] Concordant accounts of participators in the founding meeting in Paris, 15.12.1946: L. van Vassenhove, 'L'Union européenne des fédéralistes', *L'Action fédéraliste européenne*, No. 4, Jan. 1947, pp. 53–6; A. Voisin, 'Les Fédéralistes se fédèrent', *La Fédération*, No. 24, Jan. 1947, p. 31; H. Schiess, 'Es geht vorwärts!', *Europa*, xiv, vol. 1, Jan. 1947, p. 1 f. Others present at the meeting, though not officially representing associations, were René Lhuillier, L. van Vassenhove, and A. Marc. For the preliminary decision at Basle to establish headquarters in Switzerland and to appoint Marc secretary-general, see p. 316 above, with n. 65 concerning Marc himself, who personified ideally the combination of Christian traditions of natural law and the Socialist-Proudhonist tradition of federalism. For the first half-year J. Larmeroux provided the use of his Paris office at 12 avenue George V.

[163] When the Statutes were finally adopted at the first regular congress at Montreux on 31.8.1947 the words 'and by the Amsterdam and Montreux resolutions' were added. (Text in UEF, *Rapport du premier congrès annuel de l'U.E.F. 27–31 août 1947 Montreux*, Geneva, 1947, pp. 113–19). In his early review of the Paris decisions Marc added that it was the Hertenstein declaration which 'defined more particularly the European aspect of our efforts' (*Lettre-circulaire*, No. 2, 6.1.1947, p. 1; No. 5, 20.2.1947, p. 3, stated that in accordance with Swiss law the Statutes in their first draft were ready to be circulated for discussion at Amsterdam). This reflected the agreement of the Paris founders, not recorded in writing but formulated by van Vassenhove in the same issue: 'The creation of a European federal state bears its necessity in itself. . . . We see world federation as the crown of regional organizations. . . . We wish to create a united Europe that is ready to enter a world federation. . . . What we do not intend to do is to give up the idea of a federal Europe if world federation is delayed' (*L'Action fédéraliste européenne*, No. 4, Jan. 1947, p. 22 f.).

[164] A full list of decisions was given by A. Marc in *Lettre-Circulaire*, No. 2, 6.1.1947, p. 2. H. Schiess (cf. n. 162) was evidently particularly interested in the passport and badge ideas. In *Lettre-Circulaire*,

secretariat in such a way that each country provided altogether at least 100,000 French francs per annum;[165] van Vassenhove was to ask Count Coudenhove-Kalergi if he was prepared to bring his group into the UEF on the same terms as all other federalist movements; 'sub-secretariats' (specialized committees) were to be set up, and one on the German question was established at once, as it was considered urgent to adopt conclusions on this subject at Amsterdam.[166]

On the evening of 15 December the French associations entertained their foreign colleagues at a banquet to celebrate the foundation of the UEF; it was presided over by Gaston Riou, the veteran champion of Patrie Europe. Next morning, Monday the 16th, Henri Vergnolle, president of the Paris municipal council, gave a concluding reception at the Hôtel de Ville at which he made a heartfelt appeal for European federation: 'It is monstrous to suggest that a Western bloc is an instrument of war against any other bloc. Can it be thought that peoples who have suffered martyrdom twice in twenty years are desirous of uniting only to wage war? And how could another bloc prevent us from uniting and federating? If Europe does not federate it will die.'[167]

In the following weeks of winter 1946/7 – a time of extreme cold, privation, and despair throughout Europe – it was above all Alexandre Marc who, by his energy, managed in a short time to turn the provisional secretariat of the UEF in Paris into a centre of renewed hope for European federation. On 24 December he began to send out mimeographed circular letters at intervals of ten or fourteen days, addressed to leading personalities in all member organizations, other influential sympathizers, and newly

---

No. 5, 20.2.1947, Marc said that a passport plan 'by our Swiss friends' was 'unfortunately not feasible on account of state attitudes'; as to the badges, 'our Italian friends' had set up an artists' competition (p. 1, f.); nothing more was heard of these projects.

[165] *Lettre-Circulaire*, No. 2, 6.1.1947, p. 2; about 200,000 francs per month were needed for the secretary-general, a female secretary, and a shorthand-typist, office hire, stationery, etc. (ibid., p. 4). No. 4, 12.2.1947, complained that so far only 50,000 francs had come in from a single association and that work was possible owing chiefly to personal donations, especially 100,000 from the Swiss writer Raymond Silva (cf. n. 173). The associations made efforts, e.g. in March Miss Josephy secured a decision in London that the transfer of the promised £250 would have priority over any payments to the World Federalist Union (Meeting of the Executive Committee of Federal Union, 28.3.1947, p. 3, *Federal Union Archives*). However, *Lettres-Circulaires*, Nos. 10 and 11, 4. and 18.6.1947, once more appealed to associations to pay their annual dues. The situation improved following decisions by the Montreux congress, cf. III/4 n. 342.

[166] As Coudenhove was still teaching in New York he could only be consulted later, cf. p. 439 f. below. Francis Gérard was the provisional chairman of the committee on Germany; its other members were Ritzel, Larmeroux, Mass-Geesteranus, Verkade, and Campagnolo (*Lettre-Circulaire*, No. 2, 6.1.1947, p. 4; on its activity see n. 176). Other specialized groups, international in composition, were planned with provisional chairmen as follows: G. Riou for relations with world federalists, Lhuillier for trade-union matters, Dr Salinger for economic questions, Baron Allard for youth, and van Vassenhove for educational questions (ibid., p. 5), *Lettre-Circulaire*, No. 5, 20.2.1947, enquired why only the German committee had produced any results. The committees (in some cases differently composed) reported later, in preparation for Montreux: cf. p. 572.

[167] Cf. van Vassenhove's account (n. 162), p. 55 f., and A. Voisin (n. 162), p. 31 (whence the quotation). The mayor of Paris, a member of the SFIO, was also one of the most enthusiastic speakers at the Montreux congress: cf. *Rapport du premier congrès* (n. 163), p. 106.

formed federalist groups, and informing them of the activities of the president, the secretariat, etc.; he also issued numerous questionnaires, appeals for action, and requests for news of activities, publications and journeys, circulating the answers to all concerned and thus bringing about a lively interchange of information across all frontiers. Here is a typical extract from the second circular:

I ask all Federalists to reply to the following questions: (1) Do you know of any federalist organizations or federal-minded persons, in your country or elsewhere, who have not yet joined the UEF? ... (2) In particular, are you in touch with the following countries: Austria, Czechoslovakia, Hungary, Yugoslavia, Romania, Bulgaria, Poland, Denmark, Sweden, Norway, Finland? If so, please send names, addresses and details with a view to possible contacts. (3) Do you know of any publications (newspapers, journals, bulletins etc.), in your country or elsewhere, that support federalism or would print articles about it? Which are they? Can you take out subscriptions to them for the secretariat? ... What are the chief works you know of, inspired by the federal ideal and published since 1937? ... *Au travail!*[168]

Meanwhile Dr Brugmans travelled indefatigably, first in the Benelux countries and France, conferring frequently with Marc in Paris, contacting one federalist group after another, encouraging the formation of new groups in numerous cities, helping existing ones to recruit new members, and setting up committees to co-ordinate them at the national level. News of the formation of the UEM brought him speedily to London, as he saw in it a contradiction to his own ideas. In accordance with the Hertenstein programme Brugmans hoped for a federation of the whole of Europe including the Eastern countries, to be set free for the purpose by the Soviet Union; this federation would be strictly neutral between the two world powers. Churchill, however, had appealed at Fulton for a strengthening of resistance to Soviet expansion; now that he had founded a United Europe Movement of his own, would not this condemn all European movements in Soviet eyes and harden Soviet opposition to the idea of European unity? 'Theoretically you can explain', Brugmans wrote in agitation to Miss Josephy, 'that the Western Bloc is not our aim, but practically, if the Russians and the other Slavs don't believe you, the movement fails'; consequently 'I must say that I and my group will have to fight the Churchill Movement.'[169] Brugmans hoped that the Labour Party could be induced to take an initiative of its own for a neutral, Socialist, all-European

---

[168] *Lettre-Circulaire*, No. 2, 6.1.1947, p. 6 f. This refers at the beginning to 'No. 1 of 24 Dec. 1946', of which no copy seems to have survived. An otherwise complete run of this informative first series was supplied by Raymond Silva to the *CEC Archives, Geneva*, UEF Documents: viz. Nos. 2 (6.1.1947), 3 (18.1.1947), 4 (12.2.1947), 5 (20.2.1947), 6 (25.2.1947), 7 (24.3.1947), 8 (25.4.1947), 9 (29.4.1947), 'Aux membres du Comité Central' 12.5.1947), 10 (4.6.1947), 11 (18.6.1947), etc. (photocopied set in *DGAP Archives*, E 791.71). Most numbers are also in *EM Archives*, Bruges, UEF Jan.–June 1947. No. 5 (20.2.1947) contains an urgent request that 'All publications and pamphlets, all documents of member associations of UEF should please be sent in about 200 copies to the secretariat for redistribution.'

federation, so as not to leave the field entirely to Churchill, and that Churchill's committee might perhaps be got to repudiate the idea of a 'Western bloc' policy. With this double objective Brugmans, accompanied by Marc and by Dr Nord, deputy Chairman of Europeesche Actie, visited London from 1 to 9 February 1947. Their mission, however, was unsuccessful to an extent that they would not at first admit to themselves.

They had written beforehand to the editor of the *Daily Herald* and to Labour MPs, saying that many on the Continent were disappointed that on the question of European union, 'which many Europeans feel to be of the utmost importance, the only voice we hear from England should be that of Mr Churchill'. Such people hoped for a Labour initiative, especially for 'a social and economic programme which only a federal Europe will be able to carry into effect'. Brugmans and his colleagues had conversations to this effect at the *Daily Herald* office and with MPs, but elicited only polite interest.[170] On behalf of the UEF they presented to Duncan Sandys a six-point statement of objectives with a request for comment by members of the United Europe Committee. The points were: (1) 'No United Europe can be created if the members do not surrender certain elements of their sovereignties'; (2) as a move towards political union, 'an economic plan for European reconstruction should be worked out and social justice should be assured to all'; (3) 'To divide Europe into two parts represents in fact an attack upon her very life'; (4) therefore there must be no question of a 'Western bloc', and (5) all efforts must be concentrated on removing Soviet distrust; (6) if the UEM shared these views it could join the UEF like any other association. In reply, Duncan Sandys seems to have spoken in a friendly tone about the gradual progress of the European idea in Britain and the promise it offered for the future. Only after a visit to Paris in March did he give carefully qualified answers to the

---

[169] For this reason Brugmans deplored the fact that Miss Josephy had signed the Churchill group's manifesto. 'I met the Czech Ambassador in The Hague', he wrote in English. 'I proposed him to link us up with a personality of Eastern Europe, able to speak together with Mr Churchill. His answer was categoric: impossible.' The ambassador, who had been an *émigré* in the West during the war and personally admired Churchill, was 'excellently intentioned toward us' but was convinced 'that every so-called "European" movement is condemned with Mr Churchill' and unacceptable to Eastern Europe (Brugmans to Josephy, 21.1.1947, *BEF Archives*, Brugmans corr.; for her reply, see n. 86).

[170] Brugmans, 27.1.1947, to Percy Cudlipp, editor of the *Daily Herald*, and similarly on 27.1.1947 to Michael Foot and others with request for an appointment after 1 Feb. (*BEF Archives*, Brugmans corr.). Marc in *Lettre-Circulaire*, No. 4, 12.1.1947: 'We were received in the House of Commons and were able to talk to several members, who were clearly interested, about the aims and methods of the UEF.' The upshot may be judged e.g. from Brugmans's letter of 15.3.1947 to M. Foot: 'It was agreed that we should contact you again as . . . concrete plans in accordance with our principles' developed; he now invited Foot to come to the Amsterdam meeting for further information, but Foot sent a reply by his secretary that he was otherwise engaged (24.3.1947, *BEF Archives*, Brugmans corr.). Later, referring to his conversations at the *Daily Herald*, Brugmans wrote in 'Het begin . . .' (n. 43), p. 13: 'We fought for the ideal of a Socialist, pacifist United Europe under Labour leadership. . . . We were bitterly disappointed. . . . We tried in vain to convince the Labour journalist that it was not enough to argue against Churchill's Europe: there must be an alternative conception of our own. . . . Why should not London and Paris have made a joint proposal to the Prague government so as to bring about an initiative for close economic and political co-operation? Why not, indeed? Unfortunately the British Socialists then took the view that the East-European comrades must come to terms with the Communists because the latter were backed by the Red Army.'

first five points and declare his intention of attending the Amsterdam congress as an observer.[171] The UEF representatives gained the impression that more co-operation, at least, could be expected from him than from Labour circles.

Meanwhile Brugmans made a trip to Prague in February–March 1947 for the purpose of discovering how far it was possible to form pressure groups for European federalization in the East-European countries, or at any rate in Czechoslovakia to begin with. This was a natural outcome of the idea of federating the whole of Europe as a 'Third Force', but the objective exceeded the powers of the UEF even more than in the case of the London visit, and the results of his quest were not encouraging. He had more success on subsequent visits to Belgium and Holland to co-ordinate newly formed federalist groups in those countries.[172]

Following Marc's return from London, the secretariat in Paris concentrated increasingly on preparations for the Amsterdam meeting. Marc had the full-time assistance of Henri Koch, who moved to Paris at the beginning of February and took over much administrative work as deputy secretary-general. Further valuable help was afforded by the writer Raymond Silva, living in Geneva, who offered to assist in setting up an 'Agence de Presse et de propagande fédéraliste' to translate federalist material for books, the press, films, and broadcasting and to distribute it to all countries. Pending the creation of such an agency – the plan for which was revived several times by the UEF during the following decade – Silva offered his services as delegate for propaganda purposes.[173] Daily

[171] Brugmans/Marc/Nord to UEM, 3.2.1947 (*EM Archives, Bruges,* UEF Documents, Jan.–June 1947; points 3 and 4 are quoted more fully in n. 197 below, in the context of the 'Third World' concept). Marc wrote in *Lettre-Circulaire,* No. 4, 12.2.1947: 'In our dealings with the United Europe Committee we have used all necessary prudence. . . . We met with several of its members who, on a personal basis, showed a definitely favourable attitude towards the points in our letter. . . . All our endeavour was to encourage this progress to the fullest possible extent.' Sandys, writing to Marc on 26.3.1947, thanked him for what he had said in Paris and enclosed 'for the confidential information of yourself and a few of your most intimate colleagues, a statement of our views on the questions you raise'. As to point (1), states must of course agree 'in some measure to surrender elements of their sovereignty', but what elements and when could only be discussed later. As to (2), 'common action and mutual assistance in the economic as well as in the political field' were necessary; as to (3) and (4) it was clear 'that we are not working for the creation of a Western bloc', and as to (5) 'every effort must be made to remove the distrust' of the Soviet Union. On 17.2.1947 Marc had thanked Keith Killby, the secretary of Federal Union, for all his help during the London visit (Miss Josephy was in Egypt) and asked him to form a co-ordinating committee for all British groups interested in Europe (for both points see *EM Archives, Bruges,* UEF Documents, Jan–June 1947). Nothing more was heard of this committee, but Federal Union invited D. Sandys to go to Amsterdam as an observer (Executive Committee, 28.3.1947, p. 2, *Federal Union Archives*).

[172] *Lettre-Circulaire,* No. 3, 18.1.1947, p. 3, mentioned Brugmans's forthcoming trip to Prague and asked for addresses there. Unlike his second visit in July 1947, this one was not altogether unsuccessful: cf. chap. II/7, p. 447 f., in the East-European context. For attempts to co-ordinate new federalist groups on Belgium and Italy, cf. chap. III/6 at nn. 422 and 436, in the context of these countries.

[173] Cf. *Lettre-Circulaire,* No. 3, 18.1.1947, p. 2 f.: 'This agency, as an autonomous body on a commercial basis, would have as its aims: (1) to co-ordinate the efforts of all those who serve the federalist cause in books, the press, radio and even films; (2) to report federalist activities in all countries, especially published material which it would bring to the knowledge of a wider public; (3)

enquiries and correspondence with federalist groups in many countries showed that there was an urgent demand for two kinds of publication: a leaflet on a single sheet giving 'a dynamic résumé ... of our doctrine and activity', and a pamphlet of a dozen or so pages with 'information on the establishment of the UEF, its component associations, our joint propaganda ..., our plans, practical ways of helping us etc.'. Work on these was pushed forward rapidly; the draft of a leaflet entitled 'Pour sauver l'Europe', was circulated at the end of March and discussed in Amsterdam, and an abridged version of the pamphlet, drafted by Silva and entitled 'Fédérer les Fédéralistes', was circulated immediately after the congress.[174] Towards the end of February Marc sent out a four-day agenda for Amsterdam and a plan for the allocation of votes in proportion to membership. This took careful account of democratic principles and the claims of the many associations that composed the UEF, and allocated voting rights as fairly as possible – a policy very different from that followed by Sandys in the early years of the European Movement.[175] Much attention was also devoted to drafting a resolution on Germany.

Brugmans had prepared an analysis of the German situation in the middle of January; this set out principles but was too lengthy for resolution. Europeesche Actie set up its own committee on Germany, comprising three subcommittees on political and economic affairs and occupation problems; each of these was composed of fifteen members and included specialists who mostly represented the various

---

to provide federalist publications in different countries with unpublished material or translations; (4) to communicate federalist texts to the press of different countries; (5) to organize propaganda campaigns in collaboration with the Executive Bureau of the UEF.' Cf. later efforts by Kogon and others (in vol. 2). H. Brugmans, 'Het begin ...' (n. 43), p. 16: 'Silva's interest in everything was directly political and not ideological like that of Marc. He had lost his son in the war and himself fought with the French Resistance. His ideal, as stated in his book *L'Idée fédéraliste*, was to ensure permanent peace in Europe under a federal authority on the Swiss pattern.' For Silva's book, see chap. I, n. 61. For an impressive summary of federalist aims and a cogent condemnation of the idea of sovereignty, cf. R. Silva, 'Au-delà des souverainetés nationales', *Cahiers du monde nouveau*, vol. 3 (1947), pp. 150–65 (dated Jan. 1947).

[174] Plan, by Marc, of the leaflet and pamphlet in *Lettre-Circulaire*, No. 3, 18.1.1947 (quotations). The draft leaflet was sent out with *Lettre-circulaire*, No. 7, 24.3.1947 (copy, e.g. in von Schenck Archives, UEF Documents); after revision at Amsterdam the text was printed in May under the title *Pour bâtir l'Europe*, Paris, 1947, four pages. The draft pamphlet was hectographed and sent out from the end of April ('Fédérer les Fédéralistes', short version, six pages; von Schenck Archives, EM Archives, Bruges, DGAP Archives, and elsewhere). After the Montreux congress it was printed in a large edition in final form together with the text of the Montreux resolutions etc.: Union Européenne des Fédéralistes, Geneva, c. Feb. 1948, twenty pages (copies in all Archives). Both texts have been drawn on for the account of UEF aims in the following section.

[175] *Lettre-Circulaire*, No. 6, 25.2.1947, pp. 1–3 agenda and timetable (adopted with few alterations, cf. below at nn. 178–80, p. 5 voting system (*"Affectation des mandats"*): five votes for each individual association and thirty for each national co-ordinating committee; in countries with no such committee, the thirty votes are added to those of the separate associations. This arrangement was intended to respect and promote the formation of national committees (as in France), but also to give weight to the divergent opinions of individual groups (cf. explanation in *Lettre-Circulaire*, No. 7, 24.3.1947, p. 2 f.). The system was taken over with little change in the final version of the Statutes (Art. 18; cf. *Rapport du premier congrès* [n. 163], p. 117).

political parties. This elaborate machinery did not, of course, produce any conclusions by April. At the beginning of March Gérard produced a draft on behalf of the UEF, but this was not adopted as a basis for the Amsterdam discussion, probably because it laid too much stress on the partition of Germany. Instead the discussion was based on a short, very clear, draft resolution by von Schenck and van Vassenhove.[176] All these preparatory studies, however, agreed on the principle that the German problem could only be solved within a European federation.

(B) MEETING OF THE ENLARGED CENTRAL COMMITTEE AT AMSTERDAM: DESIGN FOR EUROPE AND PROPOSED STRATEGY

The Amsterdam meeting of the UEF from 12 to 15 April 1947 was an important step towards strengthening the organization and clarifying the objectives of the young association. Brugmans and Marc had expected an attendance of twenty or thirty, but there were in fact eighty delegates of member associations plus 'observers' from Britain (D. Sandys), Germany (M. Heidorn), Czechoslovakia (M. Britys), Hungary, and Yugoslavia; including journalists, over 100 people attended the three plenary sessions. The eighty delegates represented associations in eight countries: Belgium, Denmark, France, Britain, the Netherlands, Luxemburg, Italy, and Switzerland. Brugmans opened the conference on the morning of 12 April with a vivid description of the task that lay ahead:

'This Conference meets at a critical period in history, in a makeshift world, ... already engulfed in a war of nerves and anticipating with dread the outbreak of total war ... The control of Europe passes more and more into non-European hands; and the ideological strife between communism and capitalism becomes more and more evident and threatening.' But there was also in Europe 'a certain confidence, a belief in the value of peace, in humanity and in cooperation; a faith in federation. The UEF ... is the incarnation of that faith ... National defence has now become a farce. Economic need knows no frontier ... Only federation can bring the solution.'[177]

---

[176] On 25.1.1947 F. Gérard thanked Brugmans for sending his memorandum (*BEF Archives*, Brugmans corr.); this has not been traced, but was no doubt similar in content to Brugmans's essay 'L'Allemagne et le fédéralisme européen' in *Synthèses, Revue Bruxelles*, No. 8 of 1946 (reprinted in H. Brugmans, *Vingt ans d'Europe. Témoignages 1946–1966*, Bruges, 1966, pp. 17–30). As to the committee of Europeesche Actie on Germany we have a report by Verkade, its chairman, on the sessions of 25.1.1947 and 22.2.1947 (*Verkade Archives*) and a basic paper of 20.2.1947 with the names of all subcommittee members by its secretary J. C. Wesseling (*BEF Archives*, Brugmans corr.). Gérard's draft sent on 13.3.1947 by H. Koch to E. von Schenck (*von Schenck Archives*, UEF Documents) cannot be traced but no doubt followed the lines of his partition plan of 1943 (cf. Lipgens, *Föderationspläne* [n. 114], pp. 218–23). The counter-draft by von Schenck and van Vassenhove is printed in part in *Die Friedens-Warte*, 47, 1947, p. 178; information from *von Schenck*, 23.8.1961.

[177] Quotation from *Federal News*, No. 147, June 1947. For a list of the twenty-one member associations, see below at n. 190. Concurrent accounts of the Amsterdam meeting may be found in: A. Marc, *Lettre-circulaire*, No. 8, Paris, 25.4.1947; J. F. Kövér in *Die Friedenswarte*, 47, 1947, p. 175 f.; R. Czuczka, 'Grundsätzliches zum Kongress einer Europa-Bewegung', ibid., pp. 176–8; H. Brugmans, 'L'U:E.F. se réunit à Amsterdam', *Cahiers du monde nouveau*, Vol. 3, Nos. 5/6,

370 *Revival of Plans for Federation*

All reports go to confirm that the delegates, many of whom had left their own countries for the first time, were greatly impressed by the conference and by the way in which delegates who differed in nationality, ideology, party politics, and social origin were able in a couple of days to surmount real difficulties of mutual comprehension; their desire to save Europe by federation was so strong that, in spite of keen controversy from time to time, they managed to reach unanimous or nearly unanimous decisions on the most difficult questions. Miss Josephy was in the chair for the first day; the morning agenda included reports by Marc and Koch on organization and finance respectively, while in the evening representatives of countries or associations spoke for a quarter of an hour each on activity in their countries, the work of co-ordinating local groups, and various other problems. The local congress committee had arranged for a public rally to take place on the first afternoon; their boldness proved to be justified, as over 500 people besides the delegates crowded into the hotel reception room. A Swiss participant reported:

'Eight speakers from different countries, most of whom had never met before, despite their differences of language, temperament and outlook combined to deliver what was in essence a single speech lasting two hours: its theme was the need to federate Europe as the only way to preserve our corrupt and war-torn Continent from fresh catastrophes and the decline of its culture.' The audience applauded with increasing enthusiasm and showed 'how close the federal solution was to their hearts'.[178]

Next day, Sunday the 13th, was devoted to private contacts and preliminary committee sessions. In the evening Europeesche Actie entertained all the delegates at a banquet presided over by the mayor of Amsterdam, at which speeches were made by Henry Hopkinson, Léon van Vassenhove, Jean Larmeroux, and others. On the 14th, with André Voisin in the chair, the most difficult problems were discussed. The draft statutes were approved as a temporary 'règlement intérieur', to be revised for submission to the Montreux congress; a federalist definition of how the UEF should be organized was worked out on a motion by Killby and Voisin; a reorganization of the subcommittees was decided on and a new 'Central

---

May/June 1947, pp. 117–20 (reprinted in Brugmans, *Vingt ans* . . . [n. 176], pp. 31–5); L. van Vassenhove, 'La Réunion d'Amsterdam', *L'Action fédéraliste européenne*, vol. 6, July 1947, pp. 42–7. Further accounts in the May/June bulletins, journals, etc. of member associations, e.g. *Europe*, vol. 14, May 1947, p. 1; esp. A. Marc, 'European Action', *Federal News*, No. 147, June 1947, pp. 8–10. Ibid., p. 10 f., 'Summary of the opening speech by Dr H. Brugmans' (following quotation).

[178] Monthly *Europa*, vol. 14, Basle, May 1947, p. 1. According to Marc's report in *Lettre-Circulaire*, No. 8, p. 2, the *réunion publique* was presided over by M. E. Sassen, vice-chairman of the Dutch Catholic Party; the eight speakers were: the Jesuit Pierre Chaillet, Resistance leader and co-founder of Combat, editor of *Témoignage chrétien* and *Cahiers du monde nouveau;* Col. Evelyn King, British Labour MP, member of Federal Union and UEM; Robert Aron, the federalist thinker and editor of *Nef;* Ernst von Schenck, editor of *Schweizerische Annalen*; Anne-Marie Trinquier, French Senator; Thomas H. Olsen, Danish student, chairman of the newly affiliated group, Een Verden (One World); M. Britys, Czechoslovak observer; and H. Brugmans. Cf. also Vassenhove (n. 177), p. 46.

Committee' of twenty-one members was unanimously elected; the whole afternoon was devoted to an informed and lively debate on Germany, ending in a unanimous 'Resolution on the German question'.[179] On 15 April, with Heinrich Schiess in the chair, Dr Milo di Villagrazia spoke on behalf of two Italian associations. His review of the situation commanded much agreement, but lively opposition was aroused by his remark that Britain might wish to remain outside the federation. After a conciliatory suggestion by Vassenhove that Britain might belong to both the European federation and the Commonwealth, almost unanimous agreement was reached on a motion by Silva that 'Britain is an integral part of Europe'. A thorough discussion of general policy followed, and a text proposed by the political committee was recast to form two resolutions that were passed unanimously.[180] Altogether the UEF performed a remarkable amount of work and equipped itself for the supranational struggle with a degree of solidarity unusual in international congresses at that time.

In the light of the three resolutions and other decisions and texts agreed at Amsterdam, the ideas of the UEF may be summed up in accordance with our five-point scheme as follows.

1. *Design for Europe.* The picture that began to emerge at Amsterdam was already much more specific than that of the individual associations that have been so far discussed, not to speak of 'unionist' associations.[181] It owed much to the French integral federalists, but also went beyond them in many respects. Like the key documents of the non-Communist Resistance, it deduced the need for European union from the objective of safeguarding basic human freedoms and the rights of autonomous communities within the state; the system of state sovereignty should be dissolved and replaced by a pyramid of federalist communities leading up to the world peace-keeping organization. The concluding 'Appeal to the Public' ('*Motion finale*') took note 'that the attempts so far made to establish peace have been unsuccessful' and expressed that view 'that some of the territorial and economic claims put forward by the victorious nations will inevitably become the breeding-ground of future wars'. It affirmed

---

[179] These results and the gist of the preceding debates are described more fully below in the context of the analysis of the UEF's aims and methods: for the Resolution on Germany, see at n. 186 f.; for the nature of the organization, see at n. 189; for the new Central Committee, n. 190; for the specialized secretariats, n. 195.

[180] The discussion of Britain's position is reported most fully in Czucka (n. 177), p. 177. The three unanimous resolutions – Resolution on General Policy, Resolution on the German Problem, and Final Resolution (Appeal to the Public) – were published by the UEF secretariat in a leaflet, printed on both sides, to be found in all Archives; also in the May/June bulletins of member associations, e.g. English text in *Federal News,* No. 147, June 1947, p. 11 f. (Resolution on General Policy also in A. and F. Boyd, *Western Union,* London, 1948, p. 71 f.); French in *Cahiers du monde nouveau,* Vol. 3, Nos. 5/6, May/June 1947, p. 120 f., and No. 7, July 1947, p. 247 f., also *L'Action fédéraliste européenne,* vol. 6, July 1947, pp. 47–9; German in *Mitteilungsblatt der Europäischen Föderalistischen Union* Nos. 3/4, Cologne, May 1947.

[181] UEM and ELEC, cf. above, pp. 323–41. For the meaning of the term 'unionist' in the European context, cf. p. 665 ff.

that the material and moral welfare of free men can be assured neither by treaties nor by private alliances which, during a quarter of a century, have been powerless to prevent the two most terrible wars of all time, but only by the building of a world order for mankind, based at the same time on a universally accepted law and on absolute respect for federal institutions and legitimate self-government.

To avert the danger of another war, 'action for the federation of Europe [was] a matter of the first importance and urgency'. The 'Resolution on General Policy' declared

that the internal problems of Europe, notably those of material and moral rehabilitation, the co-ordination of economic resources and the reintegration of the German people into the community of nations – whilst excluding all danger of overlordship and aggression no matter from whence it may come – cannot be resolved without a Federal Union of the nations concerned.

'Europe is breaking asunder and threatens to drag the rest of the world into the abyss' – these were the opening words of the pamphlet *Pour bâtir l'Europe*. Europe's crisis and the starvation and misery of its people made clearer than ever 'the imperious necessity of supranational co-operation ... Having barely survived a conflict that has left it helpless and exhausted, divided in two and harassed by adverse forces, Europe is in danger of offering a pretext for self-seeking intervention that will again turn it into a battlefield.' The inter-war policy of understanding had inevitably failed because it was founded on ineffectual alliances between states entrenched in their own sovereignty and dominated by irreconcilable interests ... Problems can no longer be resolved on the national plane, and no international solution can be arrived at among sovereign states ... To embark on a fresh course we must first put an end to the ruinous and murderous system of state sovereignty.[182]

To the question what kind of Europe ought to be created instead, the UEF replied not merely by advocating union but by putting forward positive federalist principles as a basis for internal and social policies. As stated at the beginning of the Resolution on General Policy, the most pressing problems were 'the establishment of a real and lasting peace and the rational organization of production and distribution, guaranteeing to all the free development of human personality in all spheres of daily life'. For this purpose 'a new social structure must be built wherein men may enjoy, not only personal liberty, but justice and economic security'. Article 2 of the Statutes declared that 'in accordance with principles of decentralization and democratic organization from the bottom upwards, it is incumbent on the European community to resolve by itself any regional differences

---

[182] For the Resolution, see the sources quoted in n. 180. The leaflet (cf. n. 174) was further revised after Amsterdam and circulated on about 25.4.1947 to all members of the Central Committee for approval (n.d., e.g. in *von Schenck Archives*, UEF Documents); it was printed in the middle of May 1947: UEF, *Pour bâtir l'Europe*, Paris, 1947, four pages, and was enclosed in all communications thereafter (copies in all Archives). It bore as a motto the words: 'Unir sans unifier. Libérer sans désorganiser. Coordonner sans contraindre'. The draft of the larger pamphlet *Fédérer les Fédéralistes* had as its subtitle: 'Our aim is to create progressively, but as quickly as possible, a true European Federation, a constituent element of the future World Federation; and to promote a new social order in which men will enjoy personal liberty, justice and economic security.'

that arise among its members'. The pamphlet stated that federalism was 'the only way of ensuring that liberty is the principle of any and every organization', and went on:

'It signifies the transformation of our society, which is both disunited and over-centralized, into voluntary associations of political, economic and social collectivities, looking after their own interests in full autonomy but delegating some of their authority to "higher" bodies so that these may defend their independence, guarantee their essential liberties and act as trustees for their common interests. This means the practical affirmation of solidarity, ... the liberation of the individual within liberated collectivities ... the opportunity, in a Europe freed from administrative obstacles and those of tariffs and currency, to create a system of the production, exchange and circulation of goods which shall be of service to man instead of enslaving him.' The pamphlet called for 'a Europe whose boundaries and objectives are fixed not only by historical tradition and the facts of geography but also, and above all, by a "Bill of Rights" common to all European citizens, the keystone of a new social order. It must be a Europe, united under the sovereignty of Law, in which the harmonious edifice of a society made in man's image will comprise both the communities of everyday life and also the most comprehensive federal structures.'[183]

Clearly some of these formulas were directly influenced by Proudhon and can only be fully understood in terms of his system, while the UEF's assumptions and deductions in the field of social philosophy had still more in common with Catholic social doctrine. This appears, for instance, in the contention that the individual is ontologically superior to the community; that (in contrast to liberal–individualist social theory) he is obliged as a social being to serve the communities which, for their part, exist for the sake of man and his development in freedom (in contrast to collectivist theories of all kinds); that, corresponding to the multiplicity of tasks, there exists a multiplicity of communities – family, place of work, municipality, province, state, and supranational federation; and that every task must be performed at the lowest feasible level (with the more comprehensive bodies supporting the 'lower' ones, in accordance with the principle of subsidiarity) and also 'as high up as necessary' (it being the duty of the 'lower' bodies to refer upwards tasks that they cannot perform themselves). We need not go further into these matters here, but it should be pointed out that on the basis of the Amsterdam programme the UEF leaders produced a considerably more elaborate 'design for Europe' in the great resolutions of their first Congress at Montreux in August 1947, and that the proposed allocation of functions was set out in detail in the draft

[183] For the Resolution, see n. 180; for the Statutes, n. 163; for the leaflet *Pour bâtir l'Europe*, n. 182. The call for a declaration of European civil rights had figured in Art. 6 of the Hertenstein programme: cf. at n. 45 above. E. von Schenck, in his account of the results of the Amsterdam meeting ('Europa und die Sicherung des Weltfriedens', *Die Friedens-Warte*, 47 (1947), p. 137), added a further point: '7. At the level of internal politics European federation will be based on a charter of European civil rights, guaranteeing the inviolability of personal rights and the autonomy of communities.'

374 Revival of Plans for Federation

constitution and in the resolutions of the second congress in Rome in November 1948; a detailed analysis of the UEF concept would have to take account of these later documents also.[184]

As has been observed, the Amsterdam meeting devoted a special resolution to the question of Germany's membership of the European federation, declaring that the solution of the German problem, which had led to such dangerous disputes between the wars, was 'the basic condition of European reconstruction' and of lasting peace. At the instance of the Dutch delegates, regret was expressed that it was not possible 'to investigate this problem with the full participation of German federalists', since 'a German delegation, in spite of their wish to do so, were unable to take part in the work', having been refused permission to travel.[185] However, the resolution proclaimed as an 'essential principle' that, in the first place, 'there can be no constructive future for Germany except within a federated Europe' – this was the basic federalist assertion from the Resistance onwards. Secondly, it was dangerous and false 'to present the federalist solution ... as a punishment inflicted on the vanquished or as a measure favourable to the victors'.[186] Thirdly, only through a federal solution could Europe enjoy 'mutual trust, prosperity, stability and peace'; and fourthly, 'Only in European and world solidarity, achieved through federalism, can the German people realize that

---

[184] For Proudhon it must suffice to refer here to T. Ramm, *P. J. Proudhon. Ausgewählte Texte,* Stuttgart, 1963 (esp. pp. 193–264, extracts from *Du principe fédératif,* 1863) and to the most recent study by B. Voyenne, *Le Fédéralisme de P.-J. Proudhon,* Paris, 1973. On subsidiarity and Catholic social theory, summed up in classic form in Pius XI's encyclical *Quadragesimo anno* of 1931, cf., for contemporary analyses, P. Jostock, *Grundzüge der Soziallehre und der Sozialreform,* Freiburg im Breisgau, 1946, pp. 3–81 and 154 f., and Hedwig Maier, *Deutscher und europäischer Föderalismus,* Stuttgart, 1948, pp. 80–128. For the doctrinal evolution of the UEF at the Montreux congress, cf. chap. III/4, pp. 573–9, and for the Rome congress chap. V/7 (in vol. 2). The most thorough basic discussion is in A. Marc, *Dialectique du déchaînement. Fondements philosophiques du fédéralisme,* Paris, 1961.

[185] For the Dutch proposal, see von Schenck's account (n. 183), p. 136. The sources mention only one German participant, M. Heidorn, a Social Democratic member of the Hamburg parliament, who attended in his private capacity and not on behalf of an association. He is reported as having said that in Germany 'extreme national centralization' was condemned, but 'the German people could only welcome a renaissance of federalism if it could regard it as a step forwards to European unity' (van Vassenhove [n. 177], p. 43). Invitations addressed to Germans by the UEF Secretariat can be found, for instance, in the *Bernhard Archives* (to H. Bernhard and J. Sandner). Sandner, referring to the impossibility of obtaining permission to travel, wrote a four-page letter to Dr Salinger on 3.4.1947 in which he acknowledged the German people's share of guilt for Hitler and continued: 'This people which has given the world so much and owes it so much more, which has plunged the whole world in unspeakable misery, must be incorporated into a Europe which must enjoy the certainty that such a calamity can never be repeated. . . . The German problem with all its consequences can only be solved by Europe itself. We may leave it to the men in Amsterdam to find the right way to a united Europe.' (*Bernhard Archives,* Europ. Aktion Documents).

[186] In contrast to Czuczka's view (n. 177); p. 178, it appears to me that the final version of this second point; referring to victors and vanquished, was not basically altered but was merely expressed more precisely as compared with the Schenck/Vassenhove draft. It was one to which the UEF attached great importance: Brugmans (n. 177), p. 119, called it a 'cri du cœur'. 'Do not compromise the word "federalism" as if it meant the dismemberment of Germany. Do not expose the federal idea to the same fate as disarmament after 1919. . . . If people want to dismember Germany let them say so, but not bring in federalism, which has nothing whatever to do with it.' (Gérard's draft – cf. n. 176 – was rejected because it laid itself open to this misunderstanding: information from *von Schenck,* 23.8.1961).

economic, social and cultural revival which will give to the youth of Germany a new ideal in life.' Finally, 'Only by their spontaneous and active adherence to such a conception can the German people give proof that they have broken deliberately with National Socialism.'[187] By accepting the Germans without further reservation as members of a federated Europe the UEF went beyond Churchill's appeal and laid down an important principle of future policy.

2. *Europe in the world.* The object of creating a federation of all Europe in time to prevent the Continent being divided into blocs and to keep the two world powers apart was regarded by the UEF leaders during this first half-year as of the greatest importance; they saw it as the key to world peace and as an issue of no less importance than the necessity of federation as an answer to Europe's internal problems. For this reason we shall discuss their views fully in Section (D) below, entitled 'Europe as a Third Force'.

3. The UEF's *plan of campaign* was firmly democratic in character. In the final Resolution it appealed 'to everyone to spread the ideas of supranational and federalist co-operation for which it stands ... There is still time to act, but there is only just time.' The delegates proclaimed 'their decision to intensify their efforts to obtain the agreement of the peoples, and if possible of the governments, to all-out action to create an effective federal union'.[188] The Amsterdam texts did not call for a European constituent assembly: this was proclaimed only in later UEF texts as a short-term objective. The Amsterdam delegates took a broad view of all possibilities in the spirit of 'integral federalism' and democratic building from the bottom upwards, and aspired to create as a first step 'communities of daily life' in economic and social matters and internal politics, on the basis of which European institutions could be erected. This was made especially clear in the second section of Article 2 of the Statutes:

The UEF 'sees as its principal tasks (1) to help every European to recognize the necessity of uniting all European nations in a federation capable of working effectively for the organization of our Continent and of a united world; (2) to prepare and assist the creation of new economic, social, administrative and technical bodies to form the nucleus of federal structures, and of juridical institutions which may, when the time comes, give political sanction to this new state of affairs.'

---

[187] For the Resolution on the German Problem cf. n. 180; German text in *Europa*, Vol. xiv, No. 6, Basle, May 1947, p. 2. E. von Schenck insisted particularly on point 5, which was evidently expressed more strongly in his own draft; it was a 'prior condition' that the German should acknowledge their responsibility. The French Socialist Hytte vigorously opposed a formulation which suggested a pharisaical attitude towards the Germans. Agreement was achieved on a compromise proposal by Marc. Cf. Vassenhove (n. 177), p. 45, and Brugmans (n. 177), p. 120. Ernst von Schenck (cf. n. 38) was made responsible in the Executive Bureau (see below) for co-ordinating federalist work in the German-speaking countries. The annual assembly of delegates of the Swiss Europa-Union expressly endorsed the resolution: cf. *Europa*, Vol. xiv, No. 7, Basle, June 1947, p. 1.
[188] For the Final Resolution, cf. n. 180. Campagnolo's revolutionary 'hard line' of refusing to co-operate with governments (cf. chap. I/7) was thus rejected. Instead, after Amsterdam the UEF made special efforts to form parliamentary groups of federalists in all countries: see *Fédérer les fédéralistes*, p.4; cf. n. 196 and chap. III/6, pp. 604–7.

(C) ORGANIZATION AND WORKING METHODS OF THE UEF

The Amsterdam leaders were conscious of the fact that in the UEF, for the first time in history, over twenty independent national associations for the promotion of a federal Europe had united to form a single supranational association. They saw this 'federation of federalists' as a first step towards the 'federation of nations', and regarded the structure of their own organization as a model for the future constitution of the world. In the light of this we may examine the organization and working methods of the UEF in terms of our five-point system.

4. *Purpose and character of the organization.* Article 2 of the Statutes declared that 'The UEF proposes to work for the creation of a European federation which shall be a constitutive element of a world confederation, so as to ensure lasting peace on a basis of respect for human rights, fundamental freedom for all and social justice.' Among the principal tasks, in addition to the two already mentioned, were '(3) to co-ordinate and intensify the activities of different European movements and groups in a federalist spirit and with federalist methods, and without distinction as to nationality, religious denomination or political tendency'. It was a special achievement of the Amsterdam meeting to formulate in accordance with its own federal principles the relationship between the UEF and its member associations, and hence the character of the UEF, which had not been closely defined when it was founded in December 1946.

The UEF is neither a mere liaison body nor a 'super-movement'. Respecting the basic autonomy of the federalist movements of which it is composed and constituted, it in no way purposes to subordinate them to the central bodies that it wishes to see set up; on the contrary, its purpose is to place these bodies at the service of the associations. In other words, not only does the UEF intend to work for the realization of the federal ideal, but it intends to do so in a federal spirit and with federalist methods. The end, as we see it, dictates the means. Federalism signifies not merely co-ordination but also, inevitably, the transference of certain functions from basic groups to central bodies. This centralization can only be justified if it is required by the very nature of the functions in question and if, far from injuring fundamental initiatives and autonomies, it contributes to their development and harmonious expansion.[189]

What functions were transferred to central organs of the UEF can for the most part be seen from the following account of working methods. They were decided upon by the Central Committee of the UEF, composed of the chairmen or most active members of the constituent associations. At Amsterdam a new Central Committee of twenty-one members was elected, taking account of the respective importance of the associations and also of

---

[189] For the Statutes, cf. n. 163. The exemplary federalist definition of the relationship between the UEF and the member associations was 'due to a suggestion by Killby and Voisin, commented on and developed by other delegates, especially our friends Bassot and King', according to Marc in *Lettre-Circulaire*, No. 8, 25.4.1947, p. 3.

the quality of individuals available at the time; the Committee was empowered to co-opt members to make up for inequality of representation. The following alphabetical list of elected members also shows the fifteen most important member associations other than the MFE.

Allard (Antoine)	Union fédérale	Belgium
Brugmans (Henri)	Europeesche Actie	Netherlands
Buchmann (Jean)	Rassemblement fédéraliste	Belgium
Genet (Henri)	Union européenne	Switzerland
Gérard (Francis)	Comité international pour la Fédération européenne	France
Hopkinson (Henry L.)	Federal Union	Great Britain
Hytte (Claude-Marcel)	Cercles socialistes, fédéralistes, et communautaires	France
Josephy (Frances L.)	Federal Union	Great Britain
King (Evelyn M.)	Federal Union	Great Britain
Koch (Henri)	Union fédérale	Luxemburg
Larmeroux (Jean)	États-Unis du Monde	France
Maas Geesteranus (Henry)	Mouvement pour un gouvernement mondial	Netherlands
Marc (Alexandre)	La Fédération	France
Milo di Villagrazia (Antonio)	Associazione federalista Europea	Italy
Nord (Hans R.)	Europeesche Actie	Netherlands
Olsen (T. Hatt)	Een Verden	Denmark
Rifflet (Raymond)	Action européenne	Belgium
Riou (Gaston)	Union européenne économique et fédéraliste	France
von Schenck (Ernst)	Europa-Union	Switzerland
Schiess (Henri)	Europa-Union	Switzerland
Silva (Raymond)	Europa-Union	Switzerland

It was decided that the chairman of the Central Committee for each year should be a representative of the country in which the next annual congress was to be held, and the Swiss Henri Genet was elected for 1947.[190]

[190] For 1948, the year of the second Congress in Rome, the chairman was Ignazio Silone. On Genet (engineer and town councillor of Lausanne, cf. chap. I at n. 71), cf. Vassenhove's interview with him: H. Genet, 'L'heure du fédéralisme européen', *L'Action fédéraliste européenne*, No. 6, July 1947, pp. 33–7 ('Notre but, c'est la création de la souveraineté européenne, du peuple européen, de l' État fédératif européen', p. 35). List of elected members of the CC in *Lettre-circulaire*, No. 8, 25.4.1947, p. 4 f.; also J. Larmeroux, 'Bilan des Forces Fédéralistes Européennes', *Cahiers du monde nouveau*, Vol. 3, No. 7, July 1947, p. 248. The non-representation of the Italian MFE, which was in a state of crisis over Campagnolo, is to be noted. Although Campagnolo was present at Amsterdam (cf. Vassenhove [n. 177], p. 44) the delegates did not elect him to the Central Committee but were pleased to find another Italian of consequence, Dr Milo di Villagrazia, representing three groups that had split off from the MFE (cf. chap. III/6 at n. 416). The remaining groups, not directly represented in the CC, were the (London) New Europe Group (also represented by Federal Union), the Alliance spirituelle des Femmes pour la Paix, and the Union des Étudiants fédéralistes (represented by the five French delegates who formed the strongest national group in the CC, followed by four Swiss, and three each from Britain, Belgium, and the Netherlands); this completes the total of twenty-one associations. (Cf. list of the CC after Montreux in chap. III/4 at n. 339.)

Revival of Plans for Federation

At its first session on 16 April, on Marc's proposal to approve the past activity of the Secretariat, the Committee elected from among its members an Executive Bureau of five persons, each with a special sphere of action, who were to direct the activities and initiatives of the UEF in concert with the Secretariat; the Bureau as a whole was responsible to the Central Committee and to the annual congress. Its members and their duties were:

Chairman and delegate for East-European countries	Dr H. Brugmans
Secretary-General	A. Marc
Deputy Secretary-General and administrator	H. Koch
Delegate for propaganda and information	R. Silva
Delegate for English-speaking countries	F. L. Josephy
Delegate for German-speaking countries	Dr E. von Schenck

Brugmans and the three last-named declared themselves willing to devote the bulk of their time to the UEF without remuneration, asking only for the refund of travel expenses. None the less, finance continued to be a difficult problem.[191] In the following months the UEF was largely sustained by the self-sacrificing work of the six members listed above. Marc devoted himself in particular to organizing the specialized committees. In his circular letters 10 to 12 he spoke of the Secretariat as 'snowed under' with work, but was able to announce a signal success in the field of external organization: thanks to Silva's efforts and the support of the Swiss Foreign Ministry, the Secretariat was able on 1 July 1947 to take up its quarters in the League of Nations building in Geneva. On 16 July the Central Committee, sitting in Paris, released Marc from the office of Secretary-General and made him responsible for a 'Département Institutionnel (économique, social et politique)' for the purpose of working out 'urgent plans for concrete and co-ordinated action'. The Secretariat in Geneva was put in charge of Silva, who directed it with great success until November 1948.[192]

---

[191] Minutes of first session of the newly elected Central Committee, Amsterdam, 16.4.1947, 9 a.m. to 1 p.m. (hectographed), nine pages (*von Schenck Archives,* UEF Documents). Composition of the Executive Bureau also in *Lettre-Circulaire,* No. 8, 25.4.1947, p. 5, and Larmeroux (n. 190), p. 244. At this session the salaries of Marc, Koch, a female secretary, and a typist were fixed at about 100,000 French francs per month; office and stationery expenses, travel, and propaganda were estimated at a further 100,000 francs, so that the budget for the six months until the congress came to 1 million francs. At the suggestion of Bassot and Monnier a scale of contributions was fixed at *c.*35% each from France and Britain and 10% each from Belgium, Holland, and Switzerland. A finance committee was appointed, consisting of O. Adler (Federal Union), Bassot (La Fédération), and Ravey (Europa-Union). At the meeting of the National Council of Federal Union in London on 19.4.1947, which ratified all the Amsterdam decisions as reported by Miss Josephy, a committee was set up to organize a British contribution of £1,000, but the Council itself declined responsibility for this (p. 2 of minutes, *Federal Union Archives*).

[192] Cf. Brugmans, 13.5.1947, to Daniel Secrétan, head of the International Organizations department in the Swiss Foreign Ministry, expressing thanks for the 'sympathies solides et efficaces' which he had shown in arranging for the use of rooms in the Palais Wilson. The CC's decision of 16.7.1947 was announced by Silva in *Lettre-Circulaire,* No. 13, 22.7.1947, p. 1, when the agenda for the Montreux congress was sent out. A personal ground for the change is mentioned by H.

5. The *forms of activity* of the UEF were described in a report by Marc as '(1) Developing federalist action and propaganda, aiding member associations to increase their popular following as rapidly as possible, and creating federalist *"centres de rayonnement"* in specialized areas such as trade unions, co-operatives etc.' The latter objective was initially successful only within the range of French 'integral federalist' groups in the Proudhonist tradition, while the former was achieved primarily by means of propaganda and information pamphlets and by the circular letters which maintained a flow of information across frontiers. National associations continued to issue in their own languages such journals as *La Fédération, L'Unità europea, Europa,* and *Federal News.* '(2) Regular journeys to European countries in order to strengthen existing relations between member associations and the Executive Bureau, to ascertain the existence of other associations and facilitate their affiliation to the UEF, and to promote the foundation of federalist associations in countries where they do not yet exist, especially in Eastern Europe.'

The principal journeys undertaken in the weeks following the Amsterdam meeting were as follows. From 12 to 16 May a party of twenty-eight French federalists, led by André Voisin and accompanied by Marc and Brugmans, visited London, where they took part in the Albert Hall meeting of the UEM and had talks with Churchill, Sandys, Federal-Union leaders, and the Federalist Group of the House of Commons.[193] From 28 May to 15 June Brugmans and Marc visited Belgium, France, and Switzerland. On 21–2 June the whole Executive Bureau attended the congress of the Comité pour les États-Unis Socialistes d'Europe (EUSE) and expressed the hope 'that all national sections of the EUSE would join the UEF'. From 23 June to 1 July Brugmans visited Italy to organize a co-ordinating committee there. In the first half of July Dr von Schenck made a tour of Germany to contact federalist groups. On 17–20 July a British delegation was received in Paris. From 21 to 30 July Brugmans visited Prague for the second time.[194] These

---

Brugmans in 'Het begin . . .' (n. 43), p. 16: Marc and Silva 'were too different. Silva found Marc's revolutionary sympathies too vague, and Marc thought Silva was no more than a conservative pacifist. But the clash came, as always, over organizational matters. The upshot was that Silva became Secretary-General, a post he held very successfully until November 1948, when our "moderate" policy was rejected at the Rome congress.' Silva expressed gratitude to Marc in *Lettre-Circulaire*, No. 13: 'But for his tireless activity the UEF would not be what it is today.'

[193] Marc's description of activities in *Lettre-Circulaire*, No. 8, 25.4.1947, p. 7. Press statement of Federal Union, 12.5.1947, on the arrival of the group of French federalists, who included six parliamentarians of the Independent, MRP, and Socialist parties (*BEF Archives*, Brugmans corr.); report by A. Voisin, 'L'effort franco-britannique pour l'Europe', *La Fédération*, No. 30, July 1947, p. 2; for their attendance at the Albert Hall meeting, cf. n. 89. In a letter of thanks to Sandys, 21.5.1947, Marc wrote that the visit had not only promoted the cause of Franco-British understanding, on which Sandys had evidently laid emphasis, but also that of federalism; he was particularly grateful for the opportunity of meeting Churchill and 'expressing to him the admiration and gratitude that every Frenchman, whatever his political orientation, feels for that great, indomitable statesman' (*EM Archives, Bruges,* UEF Documents, 47).

[194] Summary of these journeys in *Lettre-Circulaire*, No. 11, 18.6.1947, p. 2 f. They will be discussed further in context: the visit to Prague in chap. II/7, von Schenck's tour of Germany in chap. III/6, etc. For the congress of the EUSE (later MSEUE), cf. chap. IV/1 (in vol. 2).

and other journeys represent an extraordinary achievement by the UEF leaders in overcoming difficulties of communication within Europe.

'(3) Appealing to experts and specialists in all countries to assist in forming large supranational committees capable of working out concrete proposals for the economic, social and political transformation of Europe in a federal perspective.' The organization of such committees was another major achievement of the UEF, since at the time they had no counterpart on the governmental level. Although funds were short and all the experts were overburdened with problems in reconstructing their own professional carreers, the UEF was amazingly successful in laying the foundation for congresses and preparing resolutions. Marc gave a more detailed description in a Circular Letter devoted entirely to these 'Commissions d'études supranationales':

Given the responsibility that weighs upon us we must not content ourselves with approximate solutions, still less with vague general ideas, however 'generous' they may be. If, as we are all convinced, federalism is destined to save Europe and the world, we must formulate precise answers to the burning questions of the hour; we must carefully work out unassailable and co-ordinated solutions so that the UEF could at any time assume effectively and with full knowledge the task of refashioning European structures on federalist lines.[195]

'(4) We are already making a start with the systematic preparation of our General Congress this autumn, which is to mark a new step forward in the effective development of European federalism.' Each of the successive Congresses did in fact mark such a step; they were the only large manifestations undertaken by the UEF itself, other public demonstrations being left to the member associations. '(5) We plan to create federalist parliamentary groups, such as already exist in some countries, to facilitate their closer co-operation across frontiers and to improve their co-ordination in effective day-to-day work.'[196]

(D) INITIAL CONCEPTION OF A 'THIRD FORCE' COMPRISING THE WHOLE OF EUROPE

It was clear within a few months that this first supranational federalist association with its specific design for Europe, itself organized on federalist lines and with an elaborate programme of activities, was capable of

---

[195] *Lettre-Circulaire*, No. 9, 29.4.1947, p. 1. Marc proposed committees on economic questions (production, circulation, distribution), politics ('timetable and ways of transforming disunited Europe into a federation, organization of liberties and powers in a European federation . . .'), and social questions (immigration, social security, Fundamental Charter of the Rights of Man and of Communities). All member associations were asked to provide details of specialists 'of unquestionable authority and competence' who were sympathetic to federal solutions, and to invite them to co-operate (ibid., pp. 2–4). For the economic, social, etc. resolutions of the Congress, cf. chaps. III/4 and V/7.

[196] Points (1) to (4) are as formulated by Marc; point (5) is quoted from the more explicit formulation in R. Silva's otherwise similar enumeration in *Fédérer les Fédéralistes,* May 1947, p. 4. For details of the formation of federalist parliamentary groups, see chap. III/5.

functioning successfully, even though it was obliged at Montreux to abandon or at least greatly modify its original idea that European federation could play a direct role in ensuring peace. But during the first six months of UEF's existence this idea that European union was essential in order to keep the world apart and prevent the formation of two hostile blocs was of such significance to the whole movement that it must now be discussed separately.

The idea was based on the conception of Europe, including Eastern Europe as a matter of course, as a single cultural unit, and on the mission of the UEF, representing the will of the Resistance organizations, to assert the basic rights of man and of small communities against the claims of national sovereignty and *étatisme*. As the Amsterdam Resolution on General Policy put it, 'The European Union of Federalists, wishing to avoid the division of the world into opposing blocs ..., declares that a European Federation is essential to overcome bloc politics and thus to avoid a new conflict which would be the inevitable result of the division of the world into spheres of influence.' Only such a federation could safeguard the freedom of individuals and small communities and ensure prosperity in Europe. Moreover, 'by the very nature of its principles such a federation is called upon, not only to co-operate with other powers, but also to play its part from the beginning in the functioning of world organizations and in the creation of a world federation'. The UEF pamphlet expressed the matter antithetically thus:

We do not want a moribund Europe, marked out as a victim for ambitions of every kind, and governed either by a pseudo-liberal capitalism that subordinates human values to the money power, ... or by some totalitarian system seeking, by fair means or foul, to exalt its idea of justice over the rights of man and communities. What we want is a Europe which shall be an open society, friendly to both East and West, prepared to co-operate with all and capable of incorporating a federal Germany without danger.[197]

In January 1947 Brugmans had already proclaimed the objective of keeping Europe out of the looming East–West conflict and had, as a consistent federalist, opposed the idea of polarization in world politics. 'We are increasingly menaced by the formation of two monolithic blocs.' Both these blocs sought to dominate half the world; the imminence of a catastrophe was obvious. 'We are invited to choose; but is either choice acceptable? Must we throw in our lot either with totalitarian Socialism or with anarchic capitalism?' To accept the necessity of a

[197] For the Resolution, see n. 180; pamphlet *Pour bâtir l'Europe*, n. 182. Brugmans, Marc, and Nord put the point strongly in their letter of 3.2.1947 to the UEM, hoping to provoke the latter into making its position clear. '3. We are convinced that to try to divide Europe into two parts represents in fact an attempt upon her very life and will inevitably result in a final clash between two hostile blocs; it follows, therefore, that any attempt to organize one part of Europe without taking the other part into account must be considered criminal. What is the view of the United Europe Committee on this point? 4. In particular we trust that, while fully recognizing the perfect legitimacy of freely formed regional and local sub-federations, consistent federalists will not hesitate to reject the policy of the "Western Bloc", no matter what pretext that policy might use to cover itself up. (*EM Archives, Bruges*, UEF; cf. n. 171 with Sandys's answer).

choice would mean reducing the diversity of the world to a single unbridgeable opposition. 'We must create Europe in such a way that there shall be "neutral" powers – not in the sense of indifference and disinterest, fear and passivity, but "neutral" in a precise, constructive, political sense ... The globe must not be divided in two; there must be other realities than that of the two potential belligerents with their "bridgeheads", "bastions" and respective vassals.' Ernst von Schenck summed up the position in *Europa*, the organ of the Swiss association: 'We are neither anti-American nor anti-Russian, we are pro-European.'[198]

This concept of a neutral federated Europe which, by uniting, should cease to be a bone of contention between the two world powers contained various implications and assumptions. These were clearly enough perceived by the UEF leaders, and we should not be too ready to dismiss their hopes as illusory. One assumption which they regarded as almost self-evident was that none of the European national states was able to ensure its own neutrality in the new world situation, let alone keep the world powers apart by its own efforts. But 'in order to be effectively neutral a country must possess the means of maintaining and ensuring its neutrality *vis-à-vis* the neighbours in respect of whom it wishes to be neutral'. With this argument Ernst von Schenck was still, at the beginning of 1948, advocating the idea of Europe as a Third Force.

Only Europe as a whole can, on a world scale, offer the great powers the assurance of a neutrality that would serve any purpose from the point of view of a future conflict. Only Europe as a whole can, by a well-founded active neutrality comprising various guarantees, so far exclude itself from being the object of a quarrel between great powers that at least this part of the globe could no longer provide the occasion for the final destruction of humanity. Only thus can the peoples of Europe for their part have the necessary guarantee that they can continue the organic development of their historical identity, and this guarantee may in turn give them the necessary inducement to renounce national sovereignty, which stands in the way of European unity.[199]

The UEF leaders were well aware, however, that the decisive question in 1947 was not whether the Europeans were or were not willing to 'choose', but whether the world powers that were in occupation of Europe would

---

[198] H. Brugmans, 'À l'échelle européenne', in the Paris newspaper *Réforme*, 25.1.1947, p. 2 f.; E. von Schenck in *Europa*, Basle, March 1947, p. 3. The idea is argued more fully in E. von Schenck, 'Europa und die Sicherung des Weltfriedens', *Die Firedenswarte*, 47 (1947), p. 133 f.: 'A monistic world power, which looms ever more clearly as a logical consequence of dualism. . . . is a usurpation and a mortal sin. . . . Why should history have developed in such diversity from one millennium to another, if in the end a single power is to give orders or take decisions for the whole world? . . . To all such possibilities we oppose the conception of a world federation to which all states on earth should give up a decisive part of their sovereignty'; however, 'everything that does not absolutely have to be regulated centrally must be left to the autonomy of the component parts. . . . A federal world organization presupposes regional sub-federations of neighbouring and historically related groups of states', and the present urgent need was for a European federation.
[199] E. von Schenck, 'Neutralität und europäische Zukunft', *Neues Europa. Halbmonatsschrift zur Völkerverständigung*, Vol. 3, No. 5, 5.3.1948, p. 20 f.: written to show that German neutrality was not feasible by itself and that neutrality on the Swiss or Swedish model was only possible in practice with the consent and under the protection of one of the world powers.

allow them to do so, or would surrender their respective zones of influence in order that a neutral Third Force could be created. 'Will the great powers accept such a solution?' asked Brugmans. In July 1947 he still hoped that, on a rational calculation, the Soviet Union would agree to it, if only by a realistic assessment of the 'lesser evil'.

I wonder if a truly united Europe does not at least offer the Russians a means of avoiding a worse solution for them, namely an American bridgehead on the Continent. Of course it would mean their giving up hope of a rapid Bolshevization, or rather Russification ..., but they would gain the certainty that their Western frontiers would be protected by a Europe that was friendly although not subservient, fully open to collaboration and 'neutral' in the strategic sense. The US for its part, would also have to give up the idea of 'using one part of Europe and abandoning the rest. It would have an organized, pacified, prosperous Europe to deal with. We shall fight for European independence, but the Americans will certainly find in us an excellent partner and a valuable market, once we have overcome our present destitution and disintegration.'[200]

Finally, the UEF leaders were firmly convinced that a united Europe would be 'friendly towards East and West alike'. They did not merely profess this belief because they thought the world powers would otherwise not consent to European union. Their background and their entire concept of federalism, based on abhorrence of war and the European nations' longing for peace after the sufferings they had undergone, imbued them with a deep conviction that a European federation could alone restore Europe's independence and, on the other hand, that such a Europe could not possibly engage in power politics. It was their constant contention that the centralism, *étatisme*, and power politics of the European national states had been the cause of their misfortune and ruin, that these states could no longer ensure their citizens' security, and that only federation could guarantee an independent future for Europe. They fully endorsed the conclusion of the Hertenstein programme that a European federation would 'renounce all forms of power politics but would also refuse to be the

---

[200] From H. Brugmans's article 'L'Unité de l'Europe', dated June 1947, in *Cahiers du monde nouveau*, Vol. 3, No. 7, July 1947, pp. 191–7 (quotation on p. 196; reprinted in Brugmans, *Vingt ans* [n. 176], p. 43). That the UEF leaders, as Kövér (n. 177), p. 174, was aware, 'deliberately sought contact with Moscow' in order 'to convince the Soviet leaders that their rooted objection was due to a suspicion that was no longer justified' is confirmed by Brugmans, who states that he had 'several conversations with a member of the Russian embassy at The Hague and tried to persuade him that a united Europe, East and West, would be much more desirable for the Soviet Union itself than a group of "satellites" under the latter's own control, ... which would inevitably mean that the Western, Atlantic parts of the Continent would fall under American hegemony. I am still convinced that this is true.' However, 'one fine day I could no longer get my Russian friend on the telephone; an Iron Curtain had fallen between him and me' (Brugmans, 'Het begin ...' [n. 43], p. 12). Cf. also letter of 29.4.1947 from the chairman of the Berlin Paneuropa-Bund, Bernhard Kolanczyk, to Jakob Kaiser: We have 'entered into close contact with the Eastern political authorities, i.e. also the Soviet political administration', as 'the Secretary-General of UEF, M. Alexandre Marc, requested us on 24 January 1947 'to make systematic efforts as soon as possible to make contact also with the East-European states"' (*Federal German Archives*, Kardorff papers, Vol. 72). For these contacts in Berlin, cf. chap. II/6, at nn. 223–8.

tool of any foreign power', whether Soviet or American. Hence, as von Schenck put it, they could promise the two world powers that a European federation would be 'both determined and able' to preserve its neutrality.[201]

Holding these views, they came to hope that a united and initially neutral Europe would in time become a 'bridge between East and West' and that the monomanic dualism of the two rivals might gradually be so far attenuated that understanding could be reached on a world confederation which would ensure lasting peace. Here, as in the Resistance, they expressed with great force and clarity a point that was later almost forgotten: the original link between the ideas of European unity and world peace.

This conception that European unity would remove the causes of European wars, facilitate the disengagement of the world powers, and provide a foundation for world peace was by no means confined to the UEF, but was widely shared throughout Europe. It was doomed to failure, however, as early as the time of the Amsterdam meeting, by the policy of the Soviet Union, which, in contrast to the US, showed its determination to exercise direct control over all the territories occupied by the Red Army during the last phase of the war. The degree of support and sympathy which the European federalists expected from Stalin, Molotov, and Zhdanov was so contrary to the dictators' mentality, grounded in fear and mistrust, and to the 'new order' they had created in Eastern Europe, that no amount of patience or persuasion could be of the least avail. As Brugmans admitted in retrospect: 'We still had illusions about Stalinist Russia; after all, American propaganda had persistently taught us to regard it as "radical-democratic" and nothing more... True, our proposals of those days sound rather Utopian, and indeed they were. But at least they prove that it was not out of fear of Communism that we advocated a European federation.'[202] No one will reproach the UEF leaders for having been slow to accept the bitter fact that, just as Nazi imperialism had sought to establish Germany's Eastern frontier from the Baltic to the Crimea, so

---

[201] Hertenstein programme, above at n. 45. E. von Schenck, in 'Europa und die Sicherung des Weltfriedens' (n. 198), p. 135, expressed the matter clearly and forcefully: 'Russia has a right, indeed its government has the national duty, to require every guarantee that the name of "Europe" is not used to create a bulwark of anti-Russian politics and strategy. Quite apart from all ideological differences we need Soviet good will towards the proposed European federation; indeed we depend on the Russian leaders' perceiving its desirability, just as we depend on the United States realizing that this European federation is both determined and able to remain neutral in the event of a world conflict.' Similarly Brugmans, Marc, and Nord in their letter to the UEM: 'In our opinion, the European federalist movements must be very specially bent upon removing the distrust with which the Soviet Union regards the effort to unite Europe; we recognize that the origin of this distrust may lie in attempts to maintain, under the pretext of European unity, non-European interests and privileges of a political, economic and social nature' (3.2.1947, *EM Archives, Bruges*). It is to be noted that copies of all the UEF *Lettres-Circulaires* of 1947, here quoted, were sent to Semenov as head of the Soviet political administration in East Berlin, and through him to the Kremlin (cf. at n. 225).

[202] Brugmans, 'Het begin...' (n. 43), p. 13 f. For the revision of the UEF's concept of foreign policy at the Montreux congress, cf. chap. III/4, pp. 579-85; for Soviet opposition to the revival of the European idea in the winter of 1946/7, see more detail chap. III/1, pp. 478-86.

the Soviet Union now aimed to secure permanent control of a glacis of almost the same size, from its Western border as far as the Elbe. By thus exaggerating its claims, Soviet imperialism has so far justified Churchill's conception and prevented the fulfilment of the original UEF design. The fact is not that the idea of European union was evolved because of the Soviet danger, but that the Soviet Union itself made that idea unrealizable. In this way Soviet policy missed a great opportunity. If one thinks of the extraordinary prestige that Russia enjoyed throughout Europe in 1945 as a victor over Nazi dictatorship, and the belief that it had fought against Nazism as such and not merely German aggression, it seems more than probable that if the Soviet leaders had shown more understanding of European economic and political aspirations they might have secured for themselves a prosperous neighbour with strongly pro-Russian and Socialist sympathies. Instead, they opposed those aspirations to the point of provoking the formation of an anti-Soviet 'Western bloc'. By the summer of 1947, the UEF had already modified its original 'foreign policy' on the basis of its federalist principles.

6. The First European Federalist Groups in Germany

Just as the increasingly evident discord between the two superpowers led to a revival of the idea of European union in France and the other West-European countries in the summer of 1946, a similar process took place, despite the relative dearth of public information, in the quarantine wards of the occupation zones of Germany. Groups arose spontaneously in various cities, often unaware of each other's existence to begin with, but with remarkably similar programmes. After the failure of the first round of negotiations in the Paris meeting of the Council of Foreign Ministers, when, as we have seen, federalist groups were revived or came into existence in many West-European cities, the same month of June 1946 saw the formation of the Europäische Föderalistische Union in Cologne, the Europäische Gemeinschaft in Münster, the Paneuropa-Union in Hamburg, and the Union-Europa–Liga in Munich. These associations, which were soon followed by others, were not at first allowed by the military governments to carry on propaganda activity. Permission to form associations with a political objective was first granted by the British authorities in October 1946 (and until May 1947 the scope of their activity was restricted to particular cities or rural districts), by the Americans in March 1947, and by the French in August of that year;[203] but the dates at

---

[203] Cf. *Mitteilungsblatt der Föderalistischen Union*, Nos. 3/4, Cologne, May 1947; and see n. 291 for an example of permission to form a branch of a federalist association in an urban district. Cf. information from von Schenck, 23.8.1961: he was still permitted to visit Germany only as president of the German–Swiss Cultural Association and not as chairman of the UEF commission for Germany. For a brief background description of the occupation in general, cf. chap. I/5, pp. 230–43.

which the movements were founded are nevertheless significant. Byrnes's speech at Stuttgart in September 1946, with the assurance that 'peace and well-being are indivisible' and that the German people would be helped 'to win their way back' into the fellowship of nations, and Churchill's appeal at Zurich for reconciliation and 'a kind of United States of Europe', were fully reported, although little discussed, in the licensed press;[204] both speeches contributed to the evolution of German thinking which passed through successive phases of a revulsion from Nazism and militarism, attempts to find a new philosophy, and the dawn of political hopes and planning for the future. Associations dedicated to European federalism continued to spring up, and in Germany as elsewhere they were only the outer expression of a deeper and more widespread hope. The atmosphere in Germany was described by Lord Beveridge in a broadcast on his return from a tour of the occupation zones in December 1946:

Everywhere, from young and old, came expressions of intellectual hunger for books and papers from abroad. And everywhere I was asked with a wistful hopefulness about Mr Churchill's speech at Zurich in which he proposed a United States of Europe. What were the prospects for getting this plan adopted? It seemed the one positive hope that had come their way. I cannot of course say what all Germans are thinking, but I am certain that there is in Germany a strong desire to be part of the peaceful family of nations again.[205]

As this description suggests, the European movement in Germany was distinguished by a motivation which operated more strongly than in other countries and tended to give its utterances a philosophical rather than a political flavour. After the barrage of disclosures about Nazi crimes, in the state of helpless bewilderment and uprootedness following the suicide of nationalism, the German people's conception of Europe was marked, more than elsewhere, by the longing to be part of human society once again. Even those in whose minds the European idea was directly linked with that of the recovery of 'equal rights' for Germany regarded supra-

---

[204] For Byrnes's Stuttgart speech, see above at n. 20; for an interpretation H. P. Schwarz, *Vom Reich zur Bundesrepublik,* Neuwied/Berlin, 1966, p. 115 f.; for Churchill's Zurich speech, pp. 317–22 above. Samples of the German daily press in winter 1946/7 indicate that the editorial staffs appointed and supervised by the occupying powers seldom ventured to express any views of their own on the European idea, for the most part merely reporting comments by the London, Paris, etc. press (cf. *Wiesbadener Kurier,* 18.10.1946, *Tagesspiegel,* 21.1.1947, *Wirtschaftszeitung,* 7.2.1947), and that they seldom took a line of their own on German external affairs; confirmed by Schwarz, loc. cit., p. 26 f.; H. Hurwitz, 'Die Pressepolitik der Alliierten', in H. Pross (ed.), *Die deutsche Presse seit 1945,* Berne, 1965.
[205] Broadcast of 27.2.1947, reprinted in the *Listener,* 6.3.1947, pp. 313–14. Ernst von Schenck recorded similar impressions after a tour of Germany in December 1946. He found the great majority of Germans weary of national and militarist traditions and sincerely pacifist; but it was precisely the best of them who repeatedly pointed out to him that the mood of negative rejection could only be overcome if there was hope for the future. 'Among these thinking individuals there are not many who consciously envisage a solution in terms of dependence on one of the victorious powers', but the idea of 'Europe' was constantly put forward (monthly *Europa,* Vol. xiv, No. 1, Basle, Jan. 1947, p. 3).

national union not as merely a matter of everyday politics but as a historical opportunity to escape from the predicament of the German collapse and embark, on an equal footing with other nations, on the creation of a new international entity. For many years, however, the strongest wish was to return to Christian and humanistic European traditions after the monstrous betrayal of those traditions by the Nazi regime. This desire was a major reason for the increasing firmness of German commitment to the European cause in the ensuing decade; but it also meant that that commitment did not at once find expression in any concrete political plans. The men of the German Resistance movement would no doubt have had ideas to contribute, but, unlike those in other countries, they had for the most part been executed before the end of the war; their absence was a great loss. As it was, those Germans who thought about these matters were careful to avoid giving specific advice to the victorious powers on international questions. Such a sober politician as Hermann Pünder declared at the opening of the *Kölner Kulturtage* in October 1946:

'Amid the horrors of destruction we have learnt to cling to the deepest foundations of our being' and to rediscover European values. 'At the moment when this tradition threatened to escape us, it became more precious in our eyes than ever... The essential condition of rebuilding is that European unity should be created on the political plane and that an end be put to the period of European civil wars... It is impossible for us as Germans to take an active part, let alone a leading one, in this process; we have no longer the necessary power, and a criminal leadership has deprived us of the moral right as well. Recently, since the Zurich speech of the great British statesman, who is also a great European and who expressed similar ideas, we have again experienced the deep mistrust with which we are regarded, and which we fully understand. To endeavour to dispel that mistrust is the only contribution we can make at this stage towards a united Europe. We cannot and must not neglect that duty, and the first thing we have to do is to teach our own people to understand the new ideal.'[206]

The pro-European groups which came into being in rapid succession in several cities in November and December 1946 had as a rule even more material difficulties to overcome than those in other countries. Their activities depended on the economic struggle for existence, on finding rooms in which to meet, typewriters and stationery, and on the favour or

---

[206] H. Pünder, *Von Preussen nach Europa*, Stuttgart, 1968, p. 447 f.; opening speech delivered by Pünder as Lord Mayor of Cologne in the great hall of the University on 18.10.1946. Similar utterances in periodicals, especially from the spring of 1947 onwards, are reviewed in chap. III/6. Pro-European statements by political parties were rare in the early days, as those concerned were occupied with the day-to-day problems of economic distress, relations with the occupying powers, etc.; they will be discussed in chap. IV in the context of the development of parties in Germany and other countries (cf. n. 25). In the present chapter we concentrate on the associations, our analysis may serve as a supplement to the monographic account of 'conflicting conceptions of foreign policy during the Occupation years 1945–1949' in H. P. Schwarz, *Vom Reich zur Bundesrepublik* (n. 204 above); cf. ibid., p. 702, n. 22.

otherwise of the local occupation authorities. Postal and other communications were in a parlous state, and contacts between the groups took a long time to establish. 'When, in spring 1947, the first contacts beyong Germany's frontiers became possible, there were at least a dozen federalist associations of varying sizes, some of them formed by the merger of several lesser groups.'[207] These will now be discussed individually.

(A) PANEUROPA-UNION (HAMBURG AND FREIBURG), PANEUROPA-BUND (BERLIN)

Two of the earliest associations were formed by individuals who had belonged to Coudenhove-Kalergi's Paneuropa-Union and who desired to continue the efforts of the inter-war period. They used the name 'Paneuropa' but were prepared to develop their activities on different lines, especially when Coudenhove-Kalergi dissociated himself from the new foundations.

The re-establishment of the Paneuropa-Union took place in June 1946 on the initiative of Heinz Dahlmeyer, a retired consul living in Hamburg, who had belonged to the Union since Weimar days and, being a business man, had the necessary funds, offices, and transport facilities. His chief associates were Dr P. Pulides (business manager) and Dr Friedrich Ablass (legal adviser). The group received a licence from the British military authorities soon after Churchill's Zurich speech. At the beginning of December it held a large public meeting in the Hamburg Schauspielhaus, which was attended by a British general and aroused much interest. An appeal, composed by Dahlmeyer, was printed shortly afterwards; it reflects the tenor of the speeches that were made and, while vague in content, bears witness to the strong psychological motivation of those concerned.

'The German people stands at a turning-point ... The misery and hardships of the time and the wretched state of mind in which we live must not cause us to feel that life has no meaning; we must, with God's help, address ourselves again to daily life'. That is why 'we have revived the Pan-European idea and brought into being the German Section of Pan-Europa-Union'. For 'today there is only one way to save Germany and the rest of Europe from the chaos in which our Continent is sunk', and that is 'the United States of Europe'.[208]

---

[207] Thus accurately described in an early account by W. Cornides, 'Die Anfänge des europäischen föderalistischen Gedankens in Deutschland 1945–1949', in *Europa-Archiv*, vol. 6 (1951), p. 4244; and an essentially similar account by A. Herpels, 'De Europeesgezindheid van West-Duitsland 1945–1949', in *Politica, Tijdschrift voor Staatkunde en Sociologie*, 9, March 1960, pp. 22–42. Both of them (cf. Cornides, loc. cit.) 'knew little about' the early history of the many associations prior to their merging in Europa-Union from 20.11.1947. Adequate source material is now available, mostly in the form of bequeathed papers, for the brief analyses given above, with particular emphasis on the associations' programmes. The full texts of these will be published in the forthcoming documentary volume.

[208] *Hamburger Allgemeine Zeitung*, 21.1.1947, headed: 'The executive of Paneuropa-Union, German Section, headquarters at Hamburg, has issued the following appeal by its chairman Heinz Dahlmeyer'; further extracts at n. 214; Dahlmeyer referred to 'the general enthusiasm at our first public meeting last month in the Deutsches Schauspielhaus'. On this and on the foundation of the Union, also information from Schinzinger, 7.8.1954.

Since the Hamburg association claimed continuity with the former Paneuropa-Union, its leaders offered the chairmanship to Count Coudenhove-Kalergi, who was in Europe during the summer and autumn of 1946; he had spent the war years in America, whence he returned permanently in 1947. However, in the autumn of 1946 and when approached later by Dr Rosenfeld, a member of the Hamburg executive, Coudenhove replied orally in reserved and non-committal terms. It was thus difficult for the Paneuropa-Union to maintain its claim to be the over-all association of Germans interested in European unity, as other such groups came to be founded in Germany. On 6 January 1947 it reacted with a sharp protest to press announcements of the foundation of the German Europa-Union and, alluding to the fact that the latter's leading figures belonged to the Freie Demokratische Partei (FDP), described it as unfortunate that 'the impression should be given that the great aim of achieving a United States of Europe was a party political matter'. It was

regrettable that individual party leaders ... were once more seeking to call hybrid movements into being. There is only one authorized body representing the cause of European unity regardless of party, and that is the German Section of Pan-Europa-Union with headquarters at Hamburg, which has for some time been approved by Military Government and has already established the necessary contacts with competent bodies abroad.[209]

On 8 January, however, Dr Ablass wrote to Wilhelm Heile that

our Paneuropa-Union is in no way directed by Count Coudenhove-Kalergi ... Contact has been made with the Count, but no discussions have taken place between him and us. We take the view, in any case, that the Pan-European principle can only be realized in accordance with present-day ideas, that is to say including Britain and the countries of Eastern or South-Eastern Europe, and if the Count disagrees we shall dissociate ourselves from him.[210]

As Coudenhove made no further communication to the Hamburg association, its leaders soon developed an independent programme of their own (see below).

---

[209] Deutscher Pressedienst (DPD), 6.1.1947 (*DGAP Archives,* E791.71D). On Coudenhove's hesitation, cf. chap. II/7, p. 436 f. On the one hand his circular enquiry addressed to parliamentarians introduced a different procedure from which Germany was excluded at the outset; on the other, towards the end of his first post-war stay in Europe he discussed with Churchill the foundation of a popular movement. On the establishment of Europa-Union under Heile and Hermes, see p. 415 f.

[210] Dr Ablass suggested a discussion between the leaders of the two associations (*Federal German Archives,* Heile papers, Vol. 73). This, however, failed to take place owing to Hermes's refusal (cf. n. 295), and Dahlmeyer therefore stated once again at a press conference on 10.2.1947 that: 'As Count Coudenhove-Kalergi had personally caused him to be informed, the German Section of Pan-Europa-Union was to be regarded as the authorized German organization of Pan-Europa-Union and had been recognized as the sole official agency of the pan-European movement. Count Coudenhove-Kalergi ... would return to Europe in about two months and, as president-in-chief, would take over the general direction of the European sections' (DPD, 10.2.1947). There was thus no written indication of Coudenhove's position. There was probably a divergence between Dahlmeyer's long-standing loyalty and the attitude of other members of the executive like Dr Ablass, which was resolved by the former's departure.

Meanwhile the membership of Paneuropa-Union grew steadily. At the beginning of March a group called Gesellschaft der Freunde des neuen Europa (Society of Friends of the New Europe) affiliated with it; this was founded by notable personalities of Schleswig–Holstein including Bishop Halfmann, minister Andresen, and trade-union leader Beyreis. The Union also held a large meeting at Düsseldorf with the object of establishing itself in the Rhineland, but was evidently unable to found a local branch. In and around Hamburg, however, it soon had over 3,000 paid-up members, an impressive achievement compared with party-membership figures at that time.[211] Dahlmeyer was obliged to resign the chairmanship for health reasons on 22 April, but on 9 June a general meeting of members elected a new committee of twenty-two, which on 26 July appointed a new executive: Kurt Rompf became chairman, Dr Pulides remained as manager, and the most active of the other members were Harald Absatz, Dr Ablass, Dr Behrens, and Dr Bobzin. A few days later this executive terminated the independent existence of the Paneuropa-Union, which from then on functioned successfully under the title Landesverband Hamburg des Europa-Bundes.[212]

In June 1946 a private scholar named Albert Schinzinger had begun to form a group of fellow-members of the old Paneuropa-Union at Freiburg im Breisgau, with Dr Pitsch, a chief medical officer, as his deputy chairman. At the end of 1946 this group made contact with the secretariat at Hamburg. As the group could not obtain a licence from the French military authorities they functioned from then on as a subsidiary of the Hamburg Paneuropa-Union and, on the strength of the latter's British licence, began to recruit members throughout Baden. From Freiburg groups were formed in the Rheingau, Bad Homburg, and Upper Bavaria.[213] Independent programmes of the Freiburg group have not survived; from the end of 1946 they evidently used the programmes and circulars of the Hamburg Section.

From these documents, the ideas of Paneuropa-Union may be summarized as follows.

---

[211] DPD, 6.3.1947, on the accession of the Schleswig-Holstein group; DPD, 15.6.1947, on the Düsseldorf meeting, 'predominantly attended by young people', at which Prof. von Grumbkow was the chief speaker; on the number of members, see n. 218.

[212] Cf. report in *Rundschreiben* (Circular) No. 2, Hamburg, 24.6.1947, with names of the twenty-two members of the main committee, nineteen of whom belonged to Hamburg; the exceptions were Broschkowski (Passau), Meinecke (Oldenburg), and Schmitz (Solingen); as to the 'most active members', especially in directing the specialized committees, cf. Rundschreiben No. 3, Aug. 1947 (both circulars in *DGAP Archives,* E791.71D). For the fusion into Europa-Bund on 1.8.1947, cf. p. 647.

[213] Schinzinger also tried to persuade Coudenhove to resume the presidency, but received a reply from the latter's agent, Generaldirektor Münch at Wolfsburg, that Coudenhove thought it was not yet time for such activities in Germany. (Information from Schunzinger, 17.7.1954; Dr Pitsch died in 1952, A. Schinzinger in 1957.)

1. *Design for Europe*. The January appeal linked up with the basic motif of the Resistance period: 'Equality of all citizens under a uniform system of European law to be established; personal liberty and inviolability of dwellings and property of the individual, freedom of religious belief and ideology, freedom of the spoken and written word and of political opinions'. The only further specific aim was 'the removal of all customs barriers in Europe so that Europe may become a single economic body'. Apart from this the objective was vague: 'We desire for Europe associations of states, a policy of peace and social freedom and a unified currency.'

The chief speaker at the Düsseldorf meeting advocated 'the formation of a confederacy (*Staatenbund*) which should develop into a federation (*Bundesstaat*) with a bicameral parliament'. The definitive programme of March 1947 was, however, couched in general terms and merely spoke of 'a Pan-Europe, an economic and political union of *all* European peoples, the United States of Europe'; a 'peaceful economic union of the states of Europe, which, in harmony with the UN, will afford European peoples the best possible guarantee of well-being, law and order, freedom, security and human rights'.[214]

2. *Europe in the world*. In agreement with the views of the West-European federalist groups and the UEF, it was stated that 'the Pan-European movement in no way welcomes a political split between Eastern and Western Europe. On the contrary, it wishes to form a bridge that will make it possible for all remaining differences to be overcome. It wishes to facilitate the evolution of a rational direction of Europe's affairs which can be integrated into a rational world government.'[215] Thus the Hamburg group did not see the Soviet Union as a member of 'Europe', but agreed with the UEF in closely associating the idea of united Europe with that of peace.

3. *Plan of campaign*. The nearest to this was the emphasis laid on a customs and currency union, together with Dahlmeyer's statement that 'a temporary European parliament (*Zwischenparlament*) should be set up in the next two years and prepare for the union of all European nations'.[216]

4. *Purpose and character of the organization*. 'Pan-Europa-Union is a non-party organization uniting men and women devoted to the European cause and belonging to all parties, denominations, races, professions and classes of the European peoples.' It 'has as its aim the intellectual preparedness and democratic maturity of the whole German people for the cultural, economic and political unity of all European states'. The organization emphasized its own 'democratic principles': the general meeting elected

---

[214] Dahlmeyer's appeal in *Hamburger Allgemeine*, 21.1.1947 (cf. n. 208); Prof. Grumbkow at the Düsseldorf meeting according to DPD, 15.6.1947; the actual programme of Paneuropa-Union, German Section, was sent out with recruiting literature on 3.3.1947 (*DGAP Archives*, E791-71D; collected, like the further circulars, by Cornides from the Radowitz papers, cf. n. 218).
[215] Recruiting circular attached to the Programme, 3.3.1947; cf., in the Programme, the underlining of '*all* European peoples' (at n.|214)|and Dr Ablass's letter (at n. |210).
[216] Dahlmeyer at his press conference, DPD, 10.2.1947.

the committee, and this elected the executive from among its own members.[217]

5. *Forms of activity.* The Union pursued an efficient recruiting policy, sending out literature which finally reached every household in Hamburg and organizing smaller public meetings in each district. A membership card issued on 29 April 1947 bears the number 3229. After the election of the executive, special committees were formed for legal and economic questions, culture and welfare, with subcommittees under the direction of academics from the respective faculties.[218] It was no doubt regarded as urgently necessary to work out in detail what the programme laid down in very imprecise terms.

In Berlin, according to a report in the *Berliner Kurier* of 26 May 1946, an application was made at that early date for a licence to form a new party called Europäische Demokratische Union; this was presumably refused, as no further trace of such a party exists.[219] Oberingenieur Bernhard Kolanczyk formed an association of members of the pre-war Paneuropa-Union; on 6 September 1946 he founded the Paneuropa–Bund,[220] consisting of himself and twenty-seven other members including Prof. Dr Hans Peters, an expert in administrative law, and the last chairman of the old Union, Dr Adolf Stauss. The statutes of the new association, annexed to the licence application that was presumably made shortly afterwards to the Four-Power Kommandatura of the City of Berlin, began with the following declaration:

> Europe has been so afflicted by the most terrible of all wars that it cannot rebuild itself by its own resources. Those whose help is needed will, however, only grant it if they are convinced that it will lead to a final unity that will prevent warlike conflict. The need for reconstruction itself makes union essential. From the German point of view we do not believe that we are as yet entitled to submit

---

[217] Programme of 3.3.1947; Circular No. 2, of 24.6.1947.

[218] Account of recruiting methods in Hamburg in Circular No. 4, Aug. 1947. From this it appears quite probable that '3229' was a true indication of the size of membership; the card was issued to Hugo Wendt von Radowitz, Frankfurt; the great majority of members, however, were in Hamburg, as the composition of the main committee indicates (n. 212). Description of specialized committees in Circular No. 3, beginning of August 1947; measures 'designed to help bring about a European community life' were to 'form the subject of memoranda which would (a) serve as reports to meetings of individual district and local groups . . . ; (b) form the basis of articles to be published in the press or in a possible future journal of our own; and (c) be used as documents for an exchange of view with like-minded foreign organizations' (all from *DGAP Archives*, E791.71D).

[219] Reported in *Die Friedens-Warte,* 46 (1946), p. 158, which adds: 'It has set itself the task of making propaganda for a United States of Europe.' However, when the applicant, Dr Gerber, developed his ideas at a meeting of the Liberal Democratic Party he was asked to leave on the ground that he 'saw no need for the restoration of a sovereign German national state'.

[220] Report of foundation in Kolanczyk's letter of 20.1.1947 to Frau Katharina von Kardorff-Oheimb (a prominent member of the Berlin LDP) inviting her to join the new association, which she did; he enclosed a list of the twenty-eight founder members (*Federal German Archives*, Kardorff papers, Vol. 72). Coudenhove wrote on 14.4.1954 to W. Cornides: 'Of former members of the executive of Pan-Europa-Union (Germany) I mentioned in the first place . . . Paul Löbe . . . , Hermann Münch . . . , Dr Adolf Stauss' (*DGAP Archives*, E 790/Korresp.).

concrete proposals. We regard ourselves in the first instance as an ideological advance guard whose primary purpose is to instil the Pan-European idea as deeply as possible into the hearts of the German people.

The prevention of wars within Europe thus figured as a dominant motive, as it had done with the Resistance movements, and also as a precondition of help from outside. These points were enlarged on in a commentary annexed to the statutes for the purpose of enlisting members (which could only be done on a private basis pending the issue of a licence by the Allied authorities), this stated that the association wished to:

'help the new Germany' to conduct an earnest 'self-examination and prepare itself to return as soon as possible into the family of the European democracies'. It was also necessary 'above all to achieve a deeply rooted relationship to all the ideas and forces which were and are based on the concept of Europe as an intellectual, cultural and historical unity', so as to 'give Europe a uniform customs and currency system and eventually unify it economically and politically', and 'to co-operate with these forces in creating a European federation'.[221]

Knowledge of pro-European activities outside Germany was improved by a correspondence between Kolanczyk and Miss Josephy, who passed on the address of the German association to A. Marc. The latter sent Kolanczyk all the UEF Circular Letters and on 24 January 1947 asked him, in accordance with the UEF programme, 'to make systematic efforts as soon as possible to establish contact with the East-European states as well'.[222] But this could not be done before the Kommandatura, and particularly the Soviet representative, had signified approval of the association by granting a licence.

At this point an offer of help was received from a new member, Wilhelm Kasting of Berlin/Pankow, who had access to the political department of the Soviet military administration (SMAD) at Berlin/Karlshorst. Kasting made no secret of the fact (which he later also acknowledged to Hermes and the UEF) that he was obliged to keep SMAD currently informed of

[221] Statutes of the Pan-Europa-Bund (four printed pages) and programme commmentary with membership application form (three printed pages); copies attached to Kolanczyk's letter of 20.1.1947 inviting Frau von Kardorff to join (*Federal German Archives,* Kardorff papers, Vol. 72). In my view, the careful phraseology and reference to the 'family of European democracies' show clearly enough that, in the tradition of the old Pan-Europa-Union, the purpose was to embrace the area of European civilization excluding the Soviet Union.

[222] Quotation from A. Marc's letter in Kolanczyk's letter of 29.4.1947 to J. Kaiser (*Federal German Archives,* Kardorff papers, Vol. 72); similarly in W. Kasting's letter of 14.4.1947 to Consul Stocky (*Mitteilungsblatt der Föderalistischen Union,* Nos. 3/4, Cologne, May 1947, p. 3). Kolanczyk wrote on 20.1.1947 to Frau von Kardorff (cf. n. 220): 'We are in close touch with the foreign Europe-organizations, especially our umbrella organization in London or Paris.' The enclosed commentary, printed at the end of 1946 (cf. n. 221), states that the Bund 'is a member of the European Union of Federalists in Paris', evidently on the basis of information from Miss Josephy; on 14.5.1947 Miss Josephy thanked Kolanczyk for 'several letters', explaining that she had not been able to answer them before as she had been abroad almost continuously since the beginning of February. She and Kolanczyk may have known each other from pre-war meetings of the Liberal International (cf. chap. I, n. 114). Kolanczyk's papers which might have thrown light on this have not been traced.

what the Paneuropa-Bund was doing; but since it depended largely on SMAD whether the licence was granted or not, and since the winning of Soviet confidence was of cardinal importance in the wider context of the UEF objective of a 'Third Force',[223] Kolanczyk accepted Kasting's offer and, around the beginning of April 1947, appointed him secretary-general of the association (a post he only held, however, for just over two months). In this capacity he addressed a circular on 14 April 'To all pan-European organizations in Germany', stating that:

> He had advocated 'supranational government' as early as the Weimar period; during the war he had prepared the way for the re-establishment of a 'pan-European organization', and soon after the end of the war 'I invited all the politicians of my acquaintance to a discussion at which the Soviet Kommandatura was represented by several officers. Everyone was enthusiastic about the idea ... Since then I have been in the closest personal contact with the Soviet military administration at top level, and have had eight friendly interviews of several hours each with its commander; the last of these was on 2 April 1947.' Having heard at the 'end of 1946' of the association founded by Kolanczyk, 'I at once renounced my own project and placed myself at the disposal of the Paneuropa-Bund', especially as the umbrella organization to which it belonged, 'the UEF, was opposed to the well-known idea of a Western bloc ... We believe that we have already dispelled the Soviet administration's mistrust of the UEF, and we should be sincerely glad if we could also remove its mistrust of the West German organizations.'[224]

It seems clear that Ambassador Semenov, head of the political department of SMAD, who was the 'chief exponent of a moderate policy aimed at winning over non-Communist forces', and also A. Smirnov, head of the German department of the Soviet Foreign Ministry, were inclined, after the set-back of the Berlin elections in September 1946, to adopt a more cautious policy in regard to Germany as a whole, and had

---

[223] Cf. the UEF's foreign policy programme in chap. II/5, pp. 380–5. No sources for W. Kasting's previous career have been found. On 25.6.1947 he wrote to Hermes advocating a pro-Russian attitude: 'As you know, I have to report to the UEF and to the Soviet political administration ... I have personally taken over responsibility for the Bund and, by so doing, have obtained approval for the Bund from the competent head of department' (*Federal German Archives*, Kardorff papers, Vol. 72). At the co-ordinating discussions in Hanover on 12.7.1947 he stated that the Paneuropa-Bund had been 'tacitly accepted as the only pan-European association, and many of its active members belonged to the SED' (Berlin *Kurier*, 14.7.1947). On 31.8.1947 he told the Central Committee of the UEF at Montreux that the Russians had 'not yet consented' to grant an official licence, but had approved (*favorisé*) his journey to Switzerland. 'It is incumbent on me to prove to the Soviet authorities that the UEF is in no way directed against them' (minutes of Central Committee, 31.8.1947, *DGAP Archives*, E 791.71).

[224] Circular of 14.4.1947, typescript in Kardorff papers, printed in *Mitteilungsblatt der Föderalistischen Union*, Nos. 3/4, Cologne, May 1947, p. 3 (with the wrong initial for Kasting, who in all sources gives Wilhelm as his first name). The earliest mention of Kasting in sources available to me is in Kolanczyk's letter of 10.4.1947 to Frau von Kardorff: 'I have a feeling that the Russians would like to "get in on" pan-Europe by way of the Pan-Europa-Bund in Berlin, as pressure from the West is becoming too strong for them. I am not afraid of these talks at all; I know what to say to the Russians. For the time being only a representative of mine has spoken to Herr Smirnov. I hope you and I may meet soon ...' (*Federal German Archives*, Kardorff papers, Vol. 72).

put Kasting up to joining the Paneuropa-Bund so as to keep them informed of the growing movement for European unity. As late as the end of 1947 the Soviet Union had hopes of extending its influence over the whole of Germany, and accordingly the occupation authorities tolerated the association in East Berlin and even allowed it, as Kolanczyk observed six weeks later, 'to win over important politicians of the SED Communist party for the idea of peace linked with that of Pan-Europe'.[225] This was an exception to the rule which strictly forbade the formation of pro-European associations in the Soviet Zone; but it was evidently important to the Russians to obtain information through Kasting concerning other associations in and outside Germany. Undoubtedly they received full reports, and from the point of view of global policy it is important to note that they were thus amply informed of the peaceful and neutralist views of the federalist associations and their opposition to the idea of a 'Western bloc'. Kasting, moreover, aroused the interest of the Soviet politicians by a view he put forward in May–June 1947 – or perhaps they themselves 'planted' him in the Paneuropa-Bund for the purpose of floating this idea: viz. he not only stated, rightly, that the UEF was firmly opposed to Churchill's notion of a Western bloc and wanted a federation of all Europe, but he also declared, incorrectly, that the UEF hoped the Soviet Union would join the federation. This, of course, was fully in line with Soviet expansionist policy, involving as it did a union of the superpower with all the small European countries 'from the Urals to the Atlantic, from the Balkans to the North Sea' (as Kasting put it, thus evidently excluding Britain); the Soviet Union was stronger than all the rest of them put together, and would thus obviously dominate the entire Continent.

: In May Kasting ventured on an 'appeal' to pan-Europeans in Germany: 'The advocates of a Western bloc want to unite all the West-European nations, excluding from Europe not only the Soviet Union but all the East-European peoples and also the Eastern Zone of Germany.' Pan-Europeans could only fear that such a partition of Europe 'would inevitably lead to a third world war in which Europe would be destroyed. What we want is a federation of all Europe including the Soviet Union ... Let everyone examine his conscience and decide to which of the two groups he belongs, as the UEF only wants convinced pan-Europeans in its ranks.' In a 'personal statement' at the end of June he explained to Hermes why it was imperative to 'include the Soviet Union in the United States of Europe',

[225] Kolanczyk to Consul Stocky, 23.5.1947 (*Mitteilungsblatt der Föderalistischen Union*, Nos. 5/6, Cologne, June 1947, p. 3 f.). On Semenov and the energetic Soviet efforts to ascertain and influence the formation of West-European public opinion in the spring of 1947 cf. M. Balfour and J. Mair, *Four-Power Control in Germany and Austria 1945–1946*, London (Oxford University Press), 1956, pp. 44 f. and,209; Schwarz (n. 204), pp. 264 and 266. Andrey A. Smirnov, with whom Kasting was in touch according to Kolanczyk (n. 224), was (according to *Who's Who in the U.S.S.R.*, London, 1966, p. 787) a deputy foreign minister of the RSFSR and head of the German Department in the ministry of foreign affairs in Moscow; in Nov. 1947 he was Soviet representative at the London meeting of deputy foreign ministers to prepare for the Council of Foreign Ministers' meeting in London in Nov. 1947; from 1956 he was the first Soviet ambassador in Bonn.

using *inter alia* the childish argument that 'Russia has enormous agrarian and industrial wealth, and must therefore belong to the federation on economic grounds alone.' He added that 'the political conflict between East and West ... is not the cause but the effect of the hermetic separation of peoples from one another', and therefore 'they will assimilate much more quickly if East and West live together under one roof, whereas an Iron Curtain will only deepen the rift.'[226] Apart from the question whether the Soviet system was not responsible for the 'separation', Kasting did not enquire whether 'assimilation' under one roof with a superpower would not inevitably turn to the latter's advantage.

In any case, Kasting's argument was never endorsed by Kolanczyk or the Berlin Paneuropa-Bund. Kolanczyk indeed complained in a letter to Jakob Kaiser that the other 'pan-European organizations' had so far 'tacitly ignored the cardinal question of what exactly our relations with Russia and the East-European states should be'. Like all Berliners he felt keenly the danger of a 'Europe divided into two parts. The Paneuropa-Bund has been founded for the purpose of working actively to prevent this tragedy. It has set itself the task of creating, politically and economically, a way of compromise between East and West', and it 'firmly rejected a Western bloc policy', as did the UEF. At no time, however, did Kolanczyk or the Paneuropa-Bund use such words as 'including the Soviet Union'; like the UEF, he stood clearly for a peaceful Europe between the two world powers, believing that a liberal Socialist European community should be established 'between Russian Communism and all-out American capitalism'.[227] This difference of view was no doubt the chief reason why the association broke with Kasting, who was removed from the post of secretary-general before the middle of June 1947. Kasting himself stated in a 'report' to A. Marc: 'I became aware that my views as regards independence of party ties differed essentially from those of the association. Another factor was the chairman's dictatorial attitude.' Furthermore 'the Soviet Union's confidence in the new UEF movement', which 'I originally managed to secure', had been 'completely changed' by the association's 'half-open, half-concealed anti-Soviet attitude'. Nevertheless Kasting

---

[226] 'Appell an alle deutschen Paneuropäer', signed W. Kasting, undated, but must date from May 1947; 'Die Stellung der Sowjetunion in Paneuropa', sent by Kasting to Hermes on 25.6.1947 with a covering letter stating: 'As I unfortunately had no chance to speak at Eutin about the role of the Soviet Union in a new Europe, I enclose a statement of my personal views' (each of these articles covers two closely typed pages; *Federal German Archives*, Kardorff papers, Vol. 72). By the latter date Kasting was no longer secretary-general of the Bund (cf. at n. 228). As to the first article, § 8 of the Statutes is relevant: 'The Pan-Europa-Bund is represented for legal and other purposes by its chairman or his deputy' – hence at no time by Kasting.

[227] Kolanczyk to Jacob Kaiser, 29.4.1947 (similarly to the headquarters of all licensed political parties), with a request to each party to appoint two representatives to form a 'Political Advisory Council of the Pan-Europa-Bund', in accordance with an annexed 'Organizational Plan'; an identically worded letter of 16.5.1947 to Frau von Kardorff, inviting her to join the proposed 'action committee' (*Federal German Archives*, Kardorff papers). The last quotation is from Kolanczyk to Miss Josephy, 30.5.1947; cf. further at n. 231, with reference to point 2 of the systematic analysis.

turned up as a representative of the Paneuropa-Bund at Eutin, Hanover, and Montreux, where he argued for the inclusion of the Soviet Union in 'Europe', with the result that the other German associations would not admit the Paneuropa-Bund into the Europa-Bund or the merged Europa-Union.[228] By a decision of the Kommandatura dated 28 February 1948 the Berlin association, which was no longer of interest to the Russians and was honeycombed with agents of all four occupying powers, was refused a licence on the ground of Soviet objection, and was thus obliged to terminate its activities.[229]

In the light of its official texts and statements by the chairman, the association's programme may be analysed as follows:

1. *Design for Europe.* In accordance with the statement in the preamble to the Statutes that 'we do not believe that we are as yet entitled to submit concrete proposals', no specific design was put forward. However, §3 of the Statutes stated that: 'The Pan-Europa-Bund sees it as its primary task to spread among the German people the pan-European idea as the ultimate guarantee of peace for Europe and the world. As a further task it believes that it should in due course help to formulate concrete proposals for a United States of Europe, or itself submit such proposals.'[230]

2. *Europe in the world.* The commentary on the programme said cautiously: 'The Pan-Europa-Bund desires to see a "United States of Europe" established within the geographical limits designated by the expression "European cultural area" (*europäischer Kulturkreis*).' Kolanczyk wrote in

---

[228] Kasting, 'Bericht über die deutsche Europa-Union und den Pan-Europa-Bund', undated, but noted as having been sent to A. Marc on 25.6.1947 in a letter of that date (deploring the failure of the Paris meeting of foreign ministers). The document stated further that 'when I proposed an SED parson as a member of the executive' the Bund refused him. The Europa-Union had chosen as its chairman W. Heile, who had been removed from the chairmanship of the LDP in Thuringia at the beginning of 1946 on account of his anti-Soviet attitude, and who at Eutin managed 'to keep me [Kasting] from the rostrum . . . The Soviet Union sees evidence of reaction and Fascism and therefore rejects both associations.' Nevertheless, in letters of the same date (25.6.1947), clearly confirming the breach with the Bund, to Hermes and to Dr Schmitz-Lenders of the Berlin branch of Europa-Union (cf. n. 292), and again to Hermes on 7.7.1947. Kasting tried to maintain his position as 'co-ordinator' between the Bund and the Union (all this in *Federal German Archives*, Kardorff papers). For his 'obscure' links with Karlshorst as the reason why the Bund was rejected from the two mergers, cf. information from *Schinzinger*, 7.8.1954, and *von Schenck*, 23.8.1961. Abandoned on all sides, Kasting wrote from Karlsruhe to the UEF on 15.10.1948: 'I was finally blacklisted in Berlin and had to leave the city for ever.' He appended an 'Appeal to all democratic people of the world', complaining bitterly that the Kremlin had 'totally enslaved Eastern Europe spiritually and politically', that its 'formal toleration of democratic parties' was a mere façade, and that it was 'turning the Eastern Zone of Germany into a Soviet republic' as a step towards the Sovietization of all Europe – 'unless it proves possible to unite the West into a solid democratic bloc' (*BEF Archives*, Brugmans corr.).

[229] *Tägliche Rundschau*, 12.3.1948; information from *von Schenck*, 23.8.1961. After the Berlin blockade Kolanczyk was once more selflessly active in forming a local section of Europa-Union, this time limited to West Berlin: cf. chap. VI/3 (in vol. 2).

[230] Statutes, cf. n. 221; the printed commentary (cf. ibid.) spoke of 'currency and customs union, an economic . . . unity' as well as the 'creation of a European federation'. In the 'Organizational Plan' sent to Jakob Kaiser (cf. n. 227), point 1 of the 'Principles' stated that 'the Pan-Europa-Bund aims at a federation of all Europe'.

May 1947: 'The proposed action committee must demonstrate to world opinion that the German people is firmly opposed to the partition of Europe and the resulting exclusion of the East-European states and the Eastern Zone of Germany, and wishes to see a unified Germany in a unified Europe.' Moreover: 'European union will be one of the final stages on the road towards a supranational world government, under which the internal independence and distinctive culture of all peoples will be fully respected.'[231]

3. *Plan of campaign.* There was no indication of the way in which the federation was to be brought about. The plan communicated to Kaiser merely said vaguely that the Bund itself was 'absolutely neutral and supra-national, and looks to the West as well as the East'.

4. *Organization.* The association, according to its Statutes, was democratically based. An assembly of members was to elect a presidium (executive committee), which would choose from among its own members a chairman and a 'director of working committees'. 'The assembly of members has a right of suspensory veto over all decisions by the presidium.' Kasting stated at Montreux that the association had 'as yet only 300 members', since he could not advertise it publicly until a licence was obtained.[232]

5. *Activities* were planned on a large scale, according to the commentary of December 1946. They included publications by the association itself, 'a fortnightly journal to publicize the European idea, a magazine in five languages and a weekly paper. More specialized interests will be catered for by the European Economic Bulletin and published reports by the working committees on their studies and researches.' In January 1947 Kolanczyk claimed to have 'assured financial help for periodicals to be issued by the Association in large editions and in several languages'. In May he compiled a 'specimen number' for licensing purposes. 'Meanwhile we are issuing a fortnightly press review.' Meetings in advance of a licence were prohibited, but one took place 'with the 15 foreign communities here

---

[231] Kolanczyk to Frau von Kardorff, 16.5.1947; the last-quoted sentence also in letter to J. Kaiser and other party leaders, 29.4.1947. When the chairman spoke of 'East European states' (*Oststaaten*) he definitely did not include the Soviet Union (though he could not say so openly lest it jeopardize his application for a licence), but had in mind a European 'Third Force' on UEF lines. This is shown by his letter of 30.5.1947 to Miss Josephy: 'I have already had occasion to point out in black and white to several gentlemen of the Eastern Zone that Mr Churchill would be very glad to include the Eastern states in his plans . . . I firmly believe that as between Communism in Russia and all-out capitalism (*Hochkapitalismus*) in America it would be possible to agree to a kind of co-operative Socialism for Europe, the principle of private initiative being amply safeguarded. Once negotiations were started, I am sure that I could prevail on the two great antagonists to accept this compromise.' (*Federal German Archives,* Kardorff papers, Vol. 72).

[232] Minutes of 31.8.1947 (cf. n. 223), p. 2 f. The 'Organizational Plan' sent to J. Kaiser (n. 227), which also refers to the Bund as 'completely non-party', envisaged (no doubt under Kasting's influence) the presidium as being enlarged into a 'national executive' (*Reichsleitung*) with an 'action committee' and a 'political advisory council' (of party representatives); organizations were to be formed in each of the German *Länder*, whose chairmen would 'belong to the enlarged Federal executive'.

in Berlin', in order to form 'a smaller committee as the very first beginning of a pan-European union'.[233] The fate of this small group of idealists in Berlin, and the way in which it was first penetrated and then vetoed by the Soviet military government, may serve as an indication of what probably happened to similar ventures in the East-European countries.[234]

(B) LOCAL GROUPS IN THE BRITISH ZONE: EUROPÄISCHE VOLKSBEWEGUNG (HAMBURG), USE-LIGA (ASCHEBERG), FÖDERALISTISCHE UNION (COLOGNE), EUROPÄISCHE GEMEINSCHAFT (MÜNSTER)

Among the groups which arose in the British Zone independently of one another, the Europäische Volksbewegung Deutschlands (EVD: 'People's Movement for the United States of Europe') was a special case, not only because of the very early date at which it came into being. It was founded at a meeting in Hamburg–Altona chaired by Herbert Ritter on 19 March 1946; thus it did not represent a reaction to the signs of growing US–Soviet dissension, nor was it the successor to a Resistance group. The EVD was granted a licence for the Hamburg city area on 10 October 1946 and at once declared, unlike all other groups of the kind, that it would in due course claim the right to parliamentary representation, i.e. it wished to develop into a political party.[235] From the unusually long and detailed programme, dated 6 October 1946, it is clear that the EVD is to be regarded as the first example of a movement making use of the idea of European unity as a means to German recovery and 'equality of rights' in the framework of a 'United States of Europe', which the group desired sincerely enough but without accepting all its implications.

The four-page preamble started from the premiss that 'the fruitful reconstruction of Europe requires the closest possible political and economic co-operation of all European countries'. This in turn required mutual confidence, and accordingly the EVD recognized that 'the National Socialist government is to be regarded as fully responsible for the outbreak of the Second World War'; at the same time, 'the idealism of large sections of the German people had been culpably abused', and the war was 'waged by the National Socialist government against the will of millions of Germans'. In order 'to demonstrate our sincerely peaceful intentions'

---

[233] For the commentary, cf. n. 221;| Kolanczyk to Frau von Kardorff, 20.1.1947, also 7.5.1947 and 16.5.1947 concerning the 'specimen number' (*Federal German Archives*, Kardorff papers, Vol. 72). Ibid.: *Zeitschriftenschau des Pan-Europa-Bundes*, No. 1, 1.1.1947–No. 5, 1.3.1947, each consisting of two closely typed pages with brief summaries of pro-European articles in German, British, and French periodicals. As to the meeting with the 'foreign communities' Kolanczyk informed Frau von Kardorff on 10.4.1947 that 'our session on Easter Eve was very pleasant and harmonious. We invited 16 foreigners, all of whom turned up. Altogether 40 people were present. I was very pleased to be able to welcome Herrn Schwennicke' (Berlin chairman of the LDP).

[234] Such information as could be obtained about these is in chap. II/7, pp. 441–57.

[235] DPD report, 27.10.1946. According to a biographical note in the *Neue Zürcher Zeitung* of 17.5.1950, Herbert Ritter was a member of the NSDAP (National Socialist party) in 1930–1; he afterwards emigrated to Austria and was arrested there in 1938, but was still to be regarded as belonging to the political Right (cf. n. 238).

the EVD solemnly declared that it 'permanently renounced any idea of re-establishing German defence forces on land or sea or in the air'; its leaders considered 'that this renunciation ... gives us the moral right to take advantage without hesitation of any possibilities of economic development that may present themselves in order to promote the peaceful existence of the German people'.

The EVD's *design for Europe* was partly obscure and partly conventional. 'As the only possible basis of a happy future for Germany ... the politico-economic form of the future European community must be a United States of Europe, indivisible for all time' (Art. 1). European states must be 'politically and economically united on the basis of respect for their complete independence and inviolability ... In the interest of the inviolable sovereignty of states, we repudiate all attempts of any kind to establish hegemony in Europe' (Art. 5). There should be 'treaties between Germany and the other European states for the purpose of a European customs union, ... a currency union, ... economic union and a European defensive alliance' (Art. 6).

The programme had nothing to say about *Europe's position in the world,* but in its second half (Arts. 7-10) it put forward a detailed plan for German recovery.[236] Earlier Articles stated that: 'The movement's chief objective is to bring about a healthy and efficient German economy as part of a future European economic unity' (Art. 2). The EVD would endeavour 'to awaken a conviction of the necessity of a United States of Europe among the broad masses of the German people' (Art. 3), and desired to function as soon as possible as 'a political organization with parliamentary representation' (Art. 4).[237]

Sincere as the desire for 'mutual understanding' and the renunciation of military power politics no doubt were, the EVD's programme clearly laid the principal stress on German economic efficiency. It is reminiscent of the 1920s, particularly in its echoing of Briand's contradictory appeal for union combined with inviolable national sovereignty. The fact that the Hamburg Pan-Europa-Union, which protested so strongly against the existence of the Europa-Union, saw no occasion to take exception to the EVD is a measure of the latter's unimportance in practical terms. In May 1947 the British military authorities banned Ritter from speaking in public

---

[236] The programme is printed in a pamphlet *EVD, Die Vereinigten Staaten von Europa,* Hamburg, Dec. 1946, pp. 9-22. Only the above-quoted Articles 1 and 5/6, pp. 13 and 15, relate to a policy for Europe; the 'preamble', pp. 9-13, was devoted to the 'German problem' and the whole of the second half, pp. 16-22, to specific proposals for German recovery. The programme approved the 'democratic political system' but condemned the 'fatal quarrels of narrow party politics'; it also approved 'private economic initiative . . . as opposed to Socialist objectives' and a 'social employment policy' with workers' councils that were to be secure against dissolution but 'independent of trade-union influence'. The many detailed provisions included the 'creation of a large German fishing fleet' and of a 'voluntary German labour service', and a 'guarantee of Germany's frontiers as they were on 1 March 1935'.

[237] The work of 'popular enlightenment' was to be pursued by means of: 'public political meetings and demonstrations . . . lectures . . . publication of daily newspapers, pamphlets and other literature . . . designed to promote understanding among European nations' (Art. 3). 'Once the political aims of the EVD have gained the assent of a broad section of the German people, application will be made to the respective Allied military governments to permit the movement to function as a political organization represented in parliament, like the political parties' (Art. 4, p. 15).

on account of his nationalist utterances. His 'People's Movement' is to be regarded as a precursor of the Nation Europa group, later founded by Priester. The other federalist organizations were prompt to denounce Ritter's association as 'neo-Nazi', and it ceased to exist during the summer of 1947.[238]

A small group, which lasted independently for a shorter time than any other, began from somewhat similar premisses but evolved in a genuinely federalist direction. This was the Deutsche Liga für Europäische Union, headed by Dr Wilhelm Freiherr (Baron) von Rheinbaben and founded 'on 7 August 1946 at Schwerte an der Ruhr by a group of inhabitants of Dortmund and Schwerte'. In the first version of its programme at the end of August von Rheinbaben referred to conversations with British and French personalities which has shown 'agreement on all sides as to the desirability of an understanding among European peoples' and as to the necessity for countries situated, as Germany was, 'between two fronts, East and West' to be 'given a chance to opt for the West'.[239] As a result of developing this political viewpoint and of contacts with Federal Union, the group changed its name into Deutsche Liga für föderalistische Union Europas. Under this title a second version of the programme was printed in about November 1946; it was essentially federalist, though not worked out in detail.

True, the programme still referred in a nationalist tone to 'pre-conditions' that must be met. 'A European union can only come about if each of the nations concerned has full confidence from the outset that it will be regarded and treated by all the others as a member of the union with equal rights.' Furthermore, 'All hostile criticism of another country, even if it was an enemy in the war, must in future be avoided' as it could only have a dangerous effect in 'exacerbating national feelings'; the same was true of 'separating national territory from the body of the nation (*Volkskörper*)'. Statements like these, and the author's connection with the former German National party, provoked charges that the group was a crypto-nationalist one;[240] but the rest of the programme indicated that its long-term aims were similar to those of the UEF.

---

[238] For disapproval of the EVD, cf. information from *Schinzinger*, 7.8.1954 (*DGAP Archives*, Documents E 790/corr.). Subsequently, when the US occupation authorities began to favour the idea of 'Europe', Ritter tried to refound his movement at Stuttgart; it was licensed for a time, but came to nothing; cf. DPD, 19.1.1948 and 16.6.1948. He then founded the Rechtssozialistische Deutsche Arbeiterpartei; on this and on Priester, cf. chap. IV/5 (in vol. 2).

[239] Quotations from first version of the programme (three typed pages), probably drafted in Aug. 1946, as it was sent on 12 Sept. to W. Heile; a covering letter invited him to join the Liga and declared that 'if there is still a way of preventing the collapse of the West, it must be based on my ideas' (*Federal German Archives*, Heile papers, Vol. 98). The first version stressed the point, omitted for brevity in the second, that 'all legal principles concerned with the defence of human rights' must be 'strictly enforced' in the proposed union.

[240] Quotations from the second version of the programme, printed *c.*Nov. 1946 on two sides of a leaflet, emphasizing twice that 'the Liga has established contact with Federal Union in London'; cf. a letter of 26.9.1946 to Heile, signed by Dr jur. Wilhelm Frh. von Rheinbaben and Friedrich Heinemann, stating that 'we have today been invited by the British Federal Union to send observers to an international conference to be held at Luxemburg in mid-October' (*Federal German Archives*,

1. *Design for Europe.* In order to 'make European wars impossible' and enable 'European countries to recover their prosperity speedily', there must be

a federation of states, the individual members of which should remain independent in all branches of state administration in so far as they are not subject to the federal government. The latter must in particular be wholly responsible for the control of military forces of all kinds, needed for the defence of the federation. The federal government must also be responsible for foreign policy and for those ministries whose competence is to be gradually extended to cover the whole federation. A peace-keeping ministry should be set up alongside these. The federal government must be supported by a federal parliament.

Although the details were left vague, a federal union was thus clearly intended.[241]

2. As to *Europe's position in the world*, the programme only stated that the union should 'prevent dictatorships from arising and make possible a policy of world equilibrium. It will reconcile conflicting economic interests by creating uniform conditions of production in the different European countries. The union must be closely linked with the other world democracies, and preserve from destruction the culture and civilization that has radiated from Europe.' Thus the union was chiefly designed as a means of protection and equilibrium *vis-à-vis* the over-mighty Soviet Union; there was no mention of world federation.

3. *Plan of campaign.* The first version spoke of 'preparing the German people' and expressed the hope that groups 'in all European countries' would be 'prepared to champion the idea of a union of all European countries ... All these associations should work in their own countries to spread the idea of a peaceful union of European states on a Christian and democratic basis and thus prepare the ground for political treaties.'[242]

Heile papers, Vol. 73). Wilhelm Freiherr von Rheinbaben, b. 1878, represented the Deutsche Volkspartei in the Reichstag from 1920 to 1930; he was for a time state secretary in the Reich Chancery, a member of the German delegation to the League of Nations, and subsequently of the NSDAP. On 7.7.1947 von Schenck wrote that 'the fact that Rheinbaben, though not gravely incriminated, had to be denazified is quite sufficient' to disqualify him for the new movement. Rheinbaben replied on 27.7.1947 protesting that the chaos of post-war Europe had turned him into a convinced federalist and that he now sincerely regarded it as his duty to 'win over to European ideas the nationalist circles which constituted a danger to peace after the First World War' (printed in *Informationsdienst der Europa-Union* 29.8.1947, *EU Archives*, Basle). Cf. his memoirs: W. Frh. von Rheinbaben, *Viermal Deutschland. Aus dem Leben eines Seemanns, Diplomaten, Politikers 1896–1954*, Berlin, 1954 (in which, however, he does not mention the Deutsche Liga).

[241] From the second version of the programme (n. 240). In the first version (n. 239) he laid more emphasis on the inter-war idea of arbitration: 'The European nations will remain independent in every respect; but they will submit any disputes that may arise among them to an arbitral court whose decisions shall be legally binding.' He also referred more specifically to the need for a customs union and a joint General Staff, 'to decide all military questions and in particular the establishment, armament and use of federal contingents. ... The federation's foreign policy will be conducted by the federal government, elected by the federal parliament. Members of the federal parliament will be appointed or elected by the parliaments of the individual states, as will the members of the joint federal council.'

[242] Programme, first version (n. 239), p. 3. The second version only contained the vague statement: 'This idea will be promoted by international discussions of men and women.'

Nothing was said about organizational plans. The Deutsche Liga as such did not receive a licence, and therefore carried on no activities until, on 6 February 1947, it merged with an explicitly federalist body, formed as a local group in the neighbouring area of Münster and known as the Bewegung Vereinigte Staaten von Europa – USE–Liga. This association, with its headquarters at Ascheberg (Westphalia), was of much greater intellectual importance than Rheinbaben's league; its leading spirit was Dr Theo Merten.[243] On 29 November 1946 the USE-Liga was licensed by British military government, its executive consisting of Hugo Merten (Theo's brother, a manufacturer at Ascheberg), Paul Haase, a merchant at Dortmund, and Kleinemeyer, a clergyman at Schwerte. Dr Merten, who styled himself 'honorary general manager', appointed as secretary of the association a retired civil servant, Werner Stefan, who had evinced European sympathies in Weimar days as secretary-general of Koch-Weser's German Democratic Party.[244] The USE-Liga issued its first appeal in mid-December 1946.

The appeal, distributed in the Münster area by the bulk mailing system, declared that: From the dire distress and unspeakable misery that has afflicted Europe we can be saved only by an idea which should inflame and inspire all nations and peoples of this much suffering Continent: that of drawing all Europeans into an indivisible political, economic and cultural union, a United States of Europe. Rallied under this banner ... let us show ourselves determined to prove that we are willing and prepared to atone for the evil that we have brought about.[245]

The USE-Liga grew rapidly in Westphalia and soon had branches in all the more important localities, starting with the southern part of the Münster area. Its members initially included personalities from the Frankfurt area, such as Dr Eugen Kogon, Prof. Dr Strecker of Giessen, and Dr Veit of Wiesbaden, director of the Hessische *Landesbank*; however, from the beginning of the merger negotiations with the other federalist associations, the USE-Liga regarded itself as the Westphalian section of the movement as a whole. On 6 February 1947, as already mentioned, it absorbed Rheinbaben's Deutsche Liga as a local branch, and its own

---

[243] Dr Theo Merten, b. 5 March 1899, publisher; in a statement written on 24.1.1945, before escaping from Potsdam, he wrote that 'there is only one possibility for Europe between Americanism and Bolshevism, viz. that the European countries should sooner or later devise forms of supranational cooperation' (*Merten Archives,* USE-Liga documents). He himself based his decision to work for European union on the Catholic and natural-law doctrine of subsidiarity and solidarity, and also on the profound effect of Churchill's Zurich speech (information from Merten, 2.10.1961) – an individual instance of the influence of this speech in Germany.
[244] Grant of licence and compostion of the executive reported in *Rundschreiben an die Vorsitzenden der Landesverbände, Bezirksgruppen, Ortsvereinigungen,* Ascheberg, 17.3.1947 (two hectographed pages), which added: 'The US authorities granted permission in January, and permission in the other two Zones has been applied for. . . . Press reports and broadcasts about our movement are evidently reaching a wide public and are constantly bringing us new members' (*Merten Archives,* USE-Liga documents). At the end of 1948 Werner Stefan was appointed by T. Heuss director of the Naumann Foundation (information from Merten, 2.10.1961).
[245] Christmas appeal, Ascheberg, Dec. 1946 (*Merten Archives*); reprinted in the Dec. 1947 number of *Europa. Mitteilungsblatt der Gemeinschaft Europa-Bund/Europa-Union.*

basic programme was printed about this time. On 8 March it reached agreement with the Hamburg Paneuropa-Union for 'closest co-operation with a view to an organizational merger'.[246] A fresh series of meetings from spring onwards led to the formation of local groups in the rest of Westphalia. On 7 July Maria Meyer-Sevenich addressed a mass meeting at Münster on the theme 'Peoples of Europe, unite!'; applications for membership were received in large numbers, and a group was formed to which almost all the local notabilities belonged, including Salzmann, the *Landeshauptmann* (head of provincial administration). Further local groups were formed as far afield as Bielefeld and Duisburg; Dr Merten regularly addressed up to three of these groups every Sunday. In this way, by the autumn of 1947 the USE-Liga brought about the accession to the Europa-Bund, and then to the merged Europa-Union, of what was probably the largest and best organized provincial association, representing Westphalia.[247] We may analyse its programme under the usual headings as follows:

1. *Design for Europe.* The programme of the Liga stated that 'The constitution of the confederation of Europe will be assimilated to the American federal constitution.' Its citizens would be 'subject to uniform civil, criminal, administrative and social legislation'. There would be a single currency and system of weights and measures; all national frontiers would be abolished, and the United States of Europe would form 'a single economic area with a central office for planning and economic matters'; there would also be a joint federal defence force. This clearly amounted to complete federation. A close relationship between Germany and France was postulated as the pre-condition of European unity.[248]

[246] Cf. Merten's *Rundschreiben* (Circular) of 17.3.1947 (n. 244); with information on members from the Frankfurt area and text of merger announcements, DPD, 6.2.1947 and 8.3.1947. It would appear from the report of 6.2.1947 that this was the first occasion on which the Ascheberg USE-Liga prefaced to its title the words 'Bewegung Vereinigte Staaten von Europa'. The programme was then probably printed in the following weeks of February. It is assessed in the next few paragraphs above.
[247] Cf. *Rundschreiben,* 15.4.1947, and *Europa-Liga. Mitteilungsblatt,* printed at Ascheberg, July 1947, with details (*Merten Archives*), DPD, 10.7.1947 on the meeting addressed by Maria Sevenich, in whom Dr Merten had secured one of the most effective speakers of the time (cf. M. Sevenich, *Unser Gesicht. Vortrag auf dem ersten Reichstreffen der Christlich-Demokratischen Union in Bad Godesberg 9.2.1946,* Recklinghausen, March 1946; this already called for the assertion of European cultural unity, based on religion, against pagan nationalism, but did not put forward a political programme for Europe). For Dr Merten's unselfish role in the merger negotiations see reference in the Index. In 1948 he was much concerned with organizing the celebrations, at Münster, of the 300th anniversary of the Treaty of Westphalia (cf. chap. V/4 in vol. 2); after the currency reform he had to look to his own career, and established a publishing firm at Darmstadt. His typical role as an initiator is illustrated by the fact that once the European cause was taken up by politicians he left it to them and devoted himself to the 'Third World', especially the Benedictine abbey of Toumliline in Morocco (information from Merten, 2.10.1961).
[248] Programme (two printed pages); *c.*Feb. 1947 (cf. n. 246); it was also proposed that all types of school should teach English compulsorily as an auxiliary language (*Merten Archives;* a copy addressed to Victor Gollancz, also in *EM Archives,* Bruges, File: Germany). A 'close relationship between Germany and France' was not mentioned in the programme but was emphasized in the circular of 17.3.1947, as being necessary 'if European unity is to be achieved and firmly based. The movement therefore attaches great importance to suggestions for the closest co-operation between Germany and France in political, economic and cultural affairs' (*Merten Archives*).

2. *Europe in the world.* 'The ultimate purpose of the United States of Europe is to prepare for a unified world economy and the safeguarding of world peace. The USE will be absorbed, when the time comes, by the general world organization that is to be set up.' The Christmas appeal stated: 'We deliberately abstain from thinking in terms of national frontiers or in narrow racial categories. We seek today the friendship of all European nations, and tomorrow the brotherhood of all inhabitants of the globe.' The 'Third Force' was one of the most frequent themes of Dr Merten's speeches: the European federation should exert such a power of attraction that Eastern Europe would free itself from the Soviet orbit and join the European community; the latter would be a neutral, intermediate entity, independent of the world powers and linking them together.[249]

3. *Plan of campaign.* The programme stated that 'Before the United States of Europe is set up, a provisional federal government will be established with its seat in Switzerland. In it, all member states of the USE will be equally represented. The provisional President of the USE will be elected by representatives of the member states from amongst their number.' The provisional federal government would take emergency measures to revive the economy, put an end to unemployment, etc. It was thus expected that governments would embark on the federalist path of their own accord. At the same time the Liga urged that all citizens should be convinced of the need for union; in July it appealed 'to the representatives of all political parties in the *Landtag* to support the passing of a resolution that in all schools and universities ... emphasis should be laid on inculcating supranational ideas and attitudes'.[250]

4. *Purpose and character of the organization.* 'Our movement is clearly and definitely a non-party one.' It was designed to be 'a powerful and vital movement expressing the will of all sensible, clear-minded Europeans; it represents a return to reason and to the only idea for which there is room and justification in Europe today, namely the creation of the USE'.[251]

5. *Activities.* As has been indicated, the principal strength of the Liga lay in its early concentration on Westphalia and its considerable success in forming groups in every locality of any size. Dr Merten made especially skilful use of press announcements and broadcasts, as well as stimulating

---

[249] Quotations from Programme (n. 248) and Christmas appeal, Dec. 1946 (n. 245); speeches according to information from Merten, 2.10.1961. It can be seen that the whole conception of the USE–Liga was in close accord with that of the UEF, though the two were not in contact at this time.
[250] Programme (n. 248) and DPD report, 28.7.1947; the latter added: 'The unity of European culture, history and ways of thought will be specially emphasized. Adult education will include special courses on the idea of Europe.'
[251] Circular, 17.3.1947, and programme (n. 248). Nothing is known of the formation of specialized committees or of the size of membership, nor have we information of organizational structure, ambitious plans for 'advisory councils', etc., as with the Pan-Europa-Bund. The USE–Liga evidently concentrated on the formation of efficient local groups, and was largely kept going by the selfless and universally appreciated, whole-time activity of Dr Theo Merten; financially it depended on members' subscriptions and subsidies from Hugo Merten's steam bakery at Ascheberg.

circulars addressed to local headquarters; it was planned to expand these into a regular weekly journal. The chief means of recruitment, however, were public meetings.

For example, a large rally took place on 14 June 1947 in Münster town hall, at which Prof. H. E. Stier spoke on 'The historic unity of the European proples', Prof. F. Klein on 'Overcoming the anarchy of international law', and Prof. H. Linhardt on 'The necessity for an economic union of our Continent'. Dr Merten summed up from the political point of view and Count von Galen, brother of the Bishop of Münster, spoke on the moral implications.[252]

In June 1946 a *Föderalistische Union* was founded in Cologne by Julius Stocky, a retired consul. It was approved for the Cologne area on 19 September by the British military government, and began to rally adherents to the cause of European and world federation. It called itself 'the first German branch of "Federal Union"', and the latter's objectives were repeated almost verbatim in its programme:

The Union has the double purpose of preparing the German people (a) for a democratic federation of European nations as an immediate aim, and (b) for the long-term aim of a world federation. The Union appeals to those elements in the German people who believe that close co-operation among European peoples within a world federation of all democratic nations is the only possible way to prevent the collapse of Europe, the home of our culture for the last thousand years.

In its Bulletin (*Mitteilungsblatt*) No.1 of March 1947 the Union already described itself as a 'local branch' of the UEF.[253] The next issue, however, in May 1947 reported a conversation with Emery Reeves, author of *The Anatomy of Peace*, which evidently made a lasting impression on Stocky: according to Reeves, a regional federation would only create a more powerful 'war machine' as a factor in inter-continental disputes, and therefore should not be regarded as a useful step towards world government.

In the same Bulletin Stocky expressed the view that 'Regional federations no doubt remove the risk of war between their member states, but they also increase it as between big federations ... Regional federations are no use for peace-keeping

---

[252] An instructive account of all these activities is in *Europe-Liga. Mitteilungsblatt,* Ascheberg, July 1947; this also records two very successful talks broadcast by Merten in July (Nordwestdeutscher Rundfunk); expansion into a weekly journal announced in an undated circular, *c.*beginning of May 1947 (*Merten Archives,* USE-Liga Documents). The whole output of this association shows a remarkable intellectual grasp of difficult problems.

[253] *Europäische Föderalistische Union. Union Européenne des Fédéralistes. Mitteilungsblatt der Zweiggruppe Köln, Föderalistische Union,* Nos. 1/2, Cologne, March 1947, p. 1; on p. 2 a reprinted extract 'From the Programme'; for similarity to the Federal Union Programme, cf. Chap. I at n. 117. For the licence date see *Mitteilungsblatt,* Nos. 5/6, June 1947, p. 2. The editor had championed the European idea a quarter of a century earlier in *Frei-Deutschland. Politische Wochenzeitung,* ed. by Julius Stocky, a lawyer at Düsseldorf; cf., e.g., Vol. 2, No. 23, 18.6.1922, J. Stocky 'To our readers': 'In all countries there is a need to convert men's minds from excessive national egoism to the idea of a European community of interests.... We owe it to our children not to look on helplessly as Europe sinks more and more deeply into hatred and violence and thus brings about its own destruction.'

except in the framework of a world federation.'[254] At a general meeting in Cologne on 3 June 1947 Stocky persuaded the members of the correctness of his change of mind, and an appeal was issued which stated that: 'An Eastern bloc opposed to a Western bloc is not a hopeful beginning for a European federation. To bring about a European federation which will ease the general situation instead of increasing tension, we must first set up a world government.' Stocky added that 'a regional organization is only safe in the framework of world government'.

Accordingly the meeting on 3 June decided on a change of name: the group was to be called Liga für Weltregierung (League for World Government), and a revised programme stated that its purpose was: '(1) to help the German people to find the spiritual basis for a reform of its political life so that Germany can be smoothly integrated into a future supranational world order; (2) to arouse the German people to the idea of a federal union of nations, to cultivate this idea and especially work for a world government'. It was agreed to endeavour to influence the press, radio, and universities with this purpose in mind.[255] From then on the group, in the light of its pacifist principles, placed the objective of world government firmly above the urgent needs of Europe – ignoring the fact that, as the negotiations for the foundation of the UN had clearly shown, the two superpowers and especially the Soviet Union were anything but ready to submit to a federal world government. Stocky's League continued to exert its influence in favour of supranational federal principles, but for the time being it no longer figured among the associations working immediately for a United States of Europe.[256]

It should be mentioned here that the principal inter-war pacifist association, the *Deutsche Friedens-Gesellschaft*, adopted a resolution at the beginning of April 1947, at the first joint meeting of its federal and *Land* executives, which declared: 'The German Peace Association, in accordance with its

---

[254] *Mitteilungsblatt der Föderalistischen Union.* Nos. 3/4, Cologne, May 1947. Emery Reeves's book *The Anatomy of Peace* (New York, 1945; cf. extract in chap. I at n. 17) was at this time highly regarded throughout the world. A full indication of its contents was given in *Mitteilungsblatt*, Nos. 5/6, June 1947, p. 4 (in part of the edition; the remainder contained the correspondence with Kolanczyk).

[255] Account of the meeting, appeal, new programme, and new plan of operation in *Mitteilungsblatt der Liga für Weltregierung* (Föderalistische Union), Nos. 5/6, Cologne, June 1947, pp. 1–3. From now on the Liga described itself as a member of the 'World Movement for a Federal World Government', the other umbrella organization of world federalists founded at Luxemburg, in October 1946 (cf. at n. 57). The following executive was elected: J. Stocky and Prof. Dr Hans C. Nipperdey (chairmen), Prof. Dr H. Corsten, and Dr R. Juchhoff (secretaries), and other members including Willi Eichler and the Cologne CDU trade unionist J. Albers (ibid.).

[256] For the argument over this point, cf. Miss Josephy's stand at Luxemburg (at n. 56 above). As a systematic introduction, analysis of all previous federal constitutions, etc. much use was made of H. Hörhager, *Föderalismus. Wesen und Praxis übernationaler Staatsordnung (Heft 1 der Schriften der Liga für Weltregierung)*, Oplanden, n.d. (end of 1947). This stated on p. 4: 'Federalism as a form of political organization presupposes a certain degree of political sophistication. Two great inventions, without which a federal state is unthinkable, had first to be evolved: democracy and parliament.' But the group would not at first draw the conclusion that the goal of world government was still too far away. It was not until 1950 that Stocky's journal *Die Welt von morgen* again came out unconditionally for European federation.

programme of international understanding, has worked since the end of the First World War for a United States of Europe and welcomes all efforts, both in and outside Germany, which contribute to that aim. We call for a Europe-wide solution, which cannot be achieved from either an Eastern or a Western point of view.'[257] Another inter-war association, the *Reichsarbeitsgemeinschaft Deutscher Föderalisten*, which had stood for federalism within Germany and would have been an appropriate organ of European federalism, had not yet been revived at the time we are dealing with. Its former chairman, Ludwig Alpers, circularized former members in December 1946 with the question 'Who is interested in renewing federalist activity?', but the association was not reformed until August 1947.[258]

Another group in the British Zone, called *Europäische Gemeinschaft*, took an especially clear line in favour of European unity, in harmony with the views of the Resistance movements. This group was founded in June or early July 1946 by students of Münster and Bonn universities. They addressed a memorandum of 'Basic Thoughts' (*Leitgedanken*) to Wilhelm Heile on 25 July; Clemens R. Amelunxen, son of the prime minister of North Rhine–Westphalia, signed on behalf of the Münster students, and Ursula Benninghaus for those of Bonn.[259] They applied for a licence as a 'non-party, non-denominational association', and wrote to Dr Salinger asking to be incorporated into Europeesche Actie. The letter stated that: 'Our founding committee includes members of many nations ... Our movement is primarily one of the younger generation, which has been horrified and revolted by the misery of war and is determined to do all in its power to save the peoples of the world from another such catastrophe.' The *Leitgedanken,* which were also sent to Salinger, were an eloquent expression of their motives.

'Deeply conscious of the warning example of all those who have ever had to suffer or die on account of their nationality, race, religion or other affiliations', the

---

[257] Quoted from *Badener Tagblatt,* 10.4.1947. Between the wars, the idea of a United States of Europe was not so unanimously approved as is here suggested, but was always contested by the 'globalists'. At the present time, however, the association was definitely in favour of it. This was in line with the expression of sympathy by the International Peace Bureau and the 'dirigeants' of the peace organizations outside Germany: cf. n. 41.

[258] Circular from Bremervörde, Dec. 1946 (one printed page); 'Federalism has suddenly become fashionable in Germany. Up to 1935 the Arbeitsgemeinschaft Deutscher Föderalisten was almost alone in advocating federalism (Constantin Frantz), after the collapse of the centralised unitary state ... almost all the parties spoke up for federalism.' Those who wished 'their organization to be built up again from the beginning' were asked to reply accordingly. (Sent to Heile on 5.1.1947 with a covering letter arguing against dispersing federalist forces: *Federal German Archives,* Heile papers, Vol. 73). For the refoundation in Aug. 1947, cf. chap. III/6, p. 652 f.

[259] To Heile, 25.7.1946, hoping for understanding 'in view of your speech at Münster' and asking for comments. Heile replied on 2.8.1946 that he had read the *Leitgedanken* 'with great pleasure'. Asked if he was in contact with Coudenhove, he reacted on 21.8.1946 with his old acerbity against 'the Little European idea of organizing the Continent without Britain'; he had always 'pointed out the shortcomings of this project' and urged the group 'to have nothing to do with that self-advertiser' (*Federal German Archives,* Heile papers, Vol. 73). Not surprisingly, the group did not pursue their contact with him either.

group expressed irrevocable hostility to the pernicious habit of thinking in terms of nations or races, which we regard as a projection of individual egomania ... We do not recognize the principle that nations are eternal. They are the result of historical development and are transitional forms preparing the way for new communities. We do not regard the nation as a supreme earthly good for which we are prepared to live and die without question. Nations in their present form have been outstripped by the development of history: a higher Continental community demands to be recognized. Recognizing the signs of the times, we seek the abolition of outdated national frontiers.'[260]

Salinger replied that he was 'much impressed', and rightly added that the *Leitgedanken* were forceful, 'clearly and concisely expressed ... What most encouraged us all, however, was the statement that your movement is one of the younger generation. The twelve years of misery were not in vain if such forces are now at work among German youth.'[261] The students' basic ideas were as follows:

1. *Design for Europe*: essentially in accordance with Resistance ideas. 'Convinced of the dignity of man as the conscious subject of intellectual and spiritual values, we rank human personality higher than nations, races and other groups. In order that it may be preserved and strengthened we call for the limitation of all forms of sovereignty and the abolition, to the utmost extent possible, of all warlike means of settling conflicts.' World government was unfortunately still only a 'long-term aim', but 'we believe that the pre-conditions for a "European state" are already fulfilled ... National differences recede far behind the European community, which has matured during the centuries in which the peoples of Europe have been living together.'[262]

---

[260] Letter of 24.9.1946 to Dr Salinger, signed by C. Amelunxen and U. Benninghaus, also by H. A. Guillaume and Helle Ambre, probably as non-German members of the founding committee; enclosing a version of the *Leitgedanken*, somewhat more precise in language and content than that of July; points 1 and 6 thereof are used here, the others in the following paragraphs.

[261] H. D. Salinger, 8.10.1946, to C. H. Amelunxen (five closely typed pages) with a full exposition of his idea. 'The longing for a united Germany (*Reichssehnsucht*) in the middle of the last century was nothing but a prelude to the longing for a united Europe. . . . From the point of view of Realpolitik, too, it is very important that German youth should cease to think in terms of the Reich', for 'especially after the experience of the last few years, this is a real bogy to the other peoples of Europe'. Europe, therefore, should be constructed of partial federations of more or less equal size (cf. his ideas in chap. I, p. 136 f.). Salinger also enclosed the Hertenstein programme drawn up fourteen days earlier and asked the group to keep in close touch (copy in *BEF Archives*, Brugmans corr.; further correspondence not preserved).

[262] Points 2 and 4 of *Leitgedanken* (*BEF Archives*, Brugmans corr.). Detailed indications as to political or social structure are lacking, but the general statement of motives clearly points to federal union, as is made explicit in point 5: To overcome the 'intolerable contradiction between the inner unity and external, political disunity of Europe; perceiving the urgency of large-scale political organization in the age of atomic energy and the conquest of space, which has long since turned the European states into mere provinces; looking forward to the great cultural and economic opportunities of a politically united Europe – we call for the external unification of the West in the shape of a United States of Europe (*Vereinigte Staaten von Europa*) as a preliminary to the European State (*Europäischer Staat*)'.

2. As to *Europe's position in the world*,

We call for the closest possible union between all peoples of the world, based on voluntary agreement and absolute equality of rights. A world federation is our long-term aim, but the spiritual unity of the world community which we regard as the necessary basis for such a union is not yet complete. Hence we regard as an immediate aim the political unification of the great areas of world civilization.

3. *Plan of campaign.* The young authors did not put forward any political proposals as to how the peoples and governments of Europe (and eventually the world) should achieve unity; they believed that the need for unity would speak for itself. This also appears from the

4. *Purpose of the organization.* 'We regard it as our task to strengthen the European sense of community, to promote awareness of the existing natural and cultural unity of the Continent, to deepen understanding of the need for a "European state" and the advantages it would bring, to instil determination to create such a state, and to prepare the way for consideration of its structure.'[263] Like other student circles in other universities, the group regarded intellectual preparation as its main task, and hence there is nothing to record as regards organizational plans or forms of activity. The actual work no doubt took place in student working groups. Europäische Gemeinschaft did not establish links with the other associations.[264]

(C) LOCAL GROUPS IN THE US AND FRENCH ZONES: UNION-EUROPA-LIGA (MUNICH AND COBLENZ), EUROPÄISCHE AKTION (STUTTGART)

The earliest initiative in the US Zone emanated from Carl Schmidt, a publisher in Munich, who on 19 February 1946 published an appeal for European political union; I have not been able to ascertain whether he was a former member of Paneuropa-Union or whether his action was a response to the catastrophe of the war just ended.[265] In June he was visited by Paul G. Kolwes of Coblenz and they agreed to establish the Union-Europa-Liga (UEL) to promote the idea in Germany. The inaugural

---

[263] Point 3 ('World Community') and 7 (Purpose of Association) in the *Leitgedanken*. In the letter to Salinger (n. 260) the group described themselves as 'non-party': 'We are not a German party or league; as a "European community" we avoid taking any part in day-to-day political conflicts inside Germany, and we already feel that we are, first and foremost, members of the great European nation.'

[264] Dr Merten informed H. Bernhard on 15.9.1947 of the theoretical and recruiting activity of the student group in Münster and Bonn under the general direction of Ursula Benninghaus, Kachtenhausen (*Bernhard Archives*, Europa-Bund documents). Not surprisingly, its members were little attracted by the squabbles of the other associations, and on leaving the university probably went on working mainly as individuals.

[265] Paragraph 9a of the Statutes approved at the inaugural assembly on 28.9.1946 runs: 'The basis of the UEL consists in more than twenty years' experience and activity, in and outside Germany, by its founder Carl F. Schmidt, and more particularly in his work *The Meaning of Heaven: Peace on Earth* and his memorandum *Proposals for a United States of Europe and International Peace*' (*Federal German Archives*, Kardorff papers, Vol. 72).

assembly was held in Munich on 28 September 1946; Carl Schmidt was elected chairman and Kolwes vice-chairman, and statutes and a manifesto were approved. Kolwes set up a branch in Coblenz on 28 January 1947, but could not make much progress at first for lack of a French licence.[266] The Munich group was more successful, as it evidently received a local licence from the US authorities in the spring; Schmidt, who died in May, was replaced as chairman by Edmund Wertheimer. A *Landesverband Bayern* (association for the *Land* of Bavaria) of the Union-Europe-Liga, founded on 1 June 1947, was based on at least three existing local groups, as those elected to its executive included 'Herr Geineder for Munich, Dr Binapfl for Regensburg and Herr Zanker for Augsburg'. Wertheimer remained chairman of the association as a whole, which was planned to extend beyond Bavaria; he represented the Union-Europa-Liga at the unification conferences, and brought the Liga into the Europa-Bund on 1 August 1947 and eventually into the amalgamated Europa-Union.[267]

After Schmidt's death and in view of the success of the Eutin congress of Europa-Union, Kolwes decided that he could make a better contribution as chairman of a *Landesverband* of Europa-Union for the Rhenish Palatinate. On 1 August 1947 he was granted a licence for the Europa-Union Rheinland-Pfalz with headquarters at Coblenz, the first licence issued by the French authorities to a 'European' organization.[268]

1. *Design for Europe.* The UEL, according to its statutes, aimed to set up 'the United States of Europe on a federal basis, with the abolition of all national and economic frontiers and with equal rights for all peoples, if possible with its seat of government at Strasburg as a link between France and Germany, the Latin and Germanic peoples, and all nations of Europe'. Thus the special importance of Franco-German relations was emphasized, but no further constitutional details were suggested.[269]

2. *Europe in the world.* 'The Union of Europe is to form a component part of the union of all nations.' A programme drawn up in 1947 called for a 'European federal state comprising all European states and peoples, as a historical mediator between the Eastern and the Western world. The mediatory role ... applies equally to the field of culture, political ideology

[266] According to the 'Memorandum by Paul Kolwes, 1957' (*DGAP Archives*, file 790 corr.); cf. *Tagesspiegel*, 23.10.1946. The statutes, dated 28.9.1946, were at once put into use as regards the programme section. As regards organization, Schmidt was to be chairman for five years and to have the exclusive right to appoint local chairmen, after which a general meeting was to be held (§9); all this, however, was invalidated by Schmidt's death in the spring of 1947.

[267] Cf. 'Report on the Founding Assembly of the Landesverband Bayern der Union-Europa-Liga, held in Munich on 1.6.1947' (*Federal German Archives*, Kardorff papers, Vol. 72). For Wertheimer's role in the unification conferences (he was elected to the executive of the Europa-Bund as well as to that of the amalgamated Europa-Union), cf. Index.

[268] 'Memorandum by Paul Kolwes' (n. 266).

[269] Statute of 28.9.1046, § 2a (*Federal German Archives*, Kardorff papers, Vol. 72). On the other hand, human rights were expressly mentioned as a basis (§ 2d): 'The intellectual, ethical and spiritual basis consists in inculcating strict respect for the sacred rights of man, in setting an example of true humanity and in maintaining pure, noble human dignity.'

and the economic system ... In particular the UEL expects that an economically united Europe will have a stimulating effect on the whole world economy which will also lead to political compromise and *détente*.'[270]

3. *Plan of campaign*. 'Federal Union in the shape of a United States of Europe will be pursued by way of the unification of European communications, economy, customs and currency.'[271]

4. *Purpose and character of the organization*. The UEL regards itself as an 'intellectual, cultural and economic study and action group'. It is 'non-party, non-denominational and non-national ... Its sole purpose is to see the United States of Europe established for the benefit of all peoples and in the interests of true humanity.' It wishes to enlist 'the co-operation of all sections of the people ... in the struggle for European unity'.

5. *Activities*: the statutes provided for 'an Association journal', and the UEL's objectives were to be 'elaborated and brought home to members and the general public by meetings, talks and lectures'.[272]

In the late autumn of 1946 there came into existence in Stuttgart a group called *Europäische Aktion. Landesverband Württemberg-Baden*: as its name suggested, it was linked to the Dutch Europeesche Actie. Its founder and chairman was a retired consul, Henry Bernhard, who had been *chef de cabinet* to Stresemann in 1923–9; he edited the *Stuttgarter Zeitung* from September 1945 and from June 1946 was vice-president of the Württemberg-Baden *Landtag*, in which he represented the (Liberal) Democratic People's party. His book *Finis Germaniae* (1945) concluded on the theme that the Germans must swallow their arrogance and 'adapt themselves to the community of nations'; there could be no 'rebuilding' of Germany, only a completely new start in changed conditions.[273] At an unusually early stage, at a May Day meeting of Stuttgart trade unions and parties in 1946, Bernhard had made a public declaration in which he said that:

---

[270] Statutes, § 2b; other quotations from a programme entitled 'Objects of the Union-Europa-Liga' (one typed page, undated but probably of 1.6.1947, as filed among papers of the foundation meeting of the *Landesverband* on that date). Bruno Maass, a member of the executive, spoke at the meeting on 'Tasks and purposes of the UEL' and looked forward to a 'Pan-European federation' as a mediator between the two 'world giants', the US and USSR, who would both be non-members (*Federal German Archives*, Kardorff papers, Vol. 72).

[271] From 'Objects' (n. 270). The Statute emphasized the importance of education (§ 2c): 'Education and life, like all thought and action, must be European and cosmopolitan, so that people may feel themselves to be Europeans.'

[272] Statutes (n. 268), § 1 and § 2 g-k' As regards organization nothing more is known than what is stated in nn. 265 and 266. The group's working methods and most of its statements are more suggestive of paternalism and didacticism than of a political pressure group.

[273] H. Bernhard, *Finis Germaniae*, Stuttgart, 1946, p. 328. Henry Barnhard, b. Dresden 1896, was trained by the Bund der Industriellen in Berlin from 1911 to 1914. On 29.9.1947 he wrote to Schinzinger about his fate in the Third Reich: 'Up to 1935 I worked as a journalist in Berlin. When that was no longer possible and every journalist was supervised by the Propaganda Ministry I opened a press cutting bureau which I ran until 1938. In 1939 I was taken on by the literary department of Daimler-Benz A.G. at Stuttgart-Untertürkheim.' In this way 'I managed to preserve my anti-Nazi attitude' (*Bernhard Archives*, Europa-Bund file). As licensee and chief editor of the *Stuttgarter Zeitung* from Sept. 1945 onwards (*Stuttgarter Nachrichten* from Nov. 1946) he had access to the news services of the world press.

As nationalism had destroyed Europe, 'we must renounce nationalist solutions of German problems in the European future, whatever reasons may be advanced for them. We must not only call for supranational solutions but must henceforth concentrate all our intellectual effort on securing them. We must realize that the age of national states is past and that the age of supranational construction must be created in Europe.' Like the union of North American states and that of the USSR, 'the future of Europe must and will consist in an organic union of European democracies, indissoluble for all time'.[274]

Bernhard himself does not seem to have thought of founding an association at the outset. In the autumn of 1946, however, Dr Salinger, one of the founders of Europeesche Actie and an old party associate of Bernhard's, visited him in Stuttgart with a copy of the Dutch Theses and urged him to form a German branch organization. Accordingly, in November or December Bernhard applied for a licence for his Landesverband Württemberg–Baden der Europäischen Aktion. In the spring of 1947, while the application was pending, he and Fritz Eberhard initiated a series of publications (*Schriftenreihe der Stuttgarter Rundschau*) under the general title *Werdendes Europa* (Europe in the Making): the first volume consisted of reflections by the editors on the 'road to peace' by way of 'uniting Europe', and the second contained an extract from A. Gasser's *Gemeindefreiheit* (Communal Freedom).[275] However, it turned out that Bernhard's editorial and parliamentary duties left him little time to act as chairman or to do more than provide the association with ideas.

After the licence was granted by the US authorities, Bernhard informed Dr Merten that the inaugural assembly of Europäische Aktion Württemberg–Baden would be held on 23 April in order (as Bernhard put it somewhat casually) 'to see to the formalities, elect an executive and whatever else is necessary'. This was done, and Dr F. Nothardt of Stuttgart Radio was appointed deputy chairman, but

---

[274] Printed leaflet of the May Day speech in *Bernhard Archives*, file of Speeches 1946/7; it ended with the appeal: 'Let us free ourselves from all the nationalist traditions of an outdated past; let us serve humanity by engaging all our strength with one accord so as to bring closer the day of a united Europe, working in unison for the good of the whole world!' In an article 'Germany and Europe' in the June 1946 number of the *Stuttgarter Rundschau* he had written: 'German–French relations are the key problem of modern times. Its solution will give mankind the certainty of peace. . . . Everything that is aimed at and consciously pursued in the UN organization must find its natural substructure in the creation of a unified Europe.' In the Sept. number he welcomed Churchill's appeal. He revered Stresemann's legacy, which he defined as the 'renunciation of nationalist dreams of power', and went beyond it in his advocacy of federal union (cf. at n. 278).

[275] *Schwerer Weg zum Frieden* (The Hard Road to Peace) (= *Werdendes Europa*, Vol. 1), Stuttgart, (c. Apr.) 1947; A. Gasser, *Aufbau von unten oder Zwang von oben* (Construction from below or Compulsion from above) (= *Werdendes Europa*, Vol. 2); Stuttgart, (May) 1947; both in a first impression of 5,000 copies. In the Principles (*Leitsätze*) attached with the programme and statute to the licence application he stated that the *Landesverband* was affiliated to the 'Mouvement Fédéral Européen', The Hague and Basle (*Bernhard Archives*, Europ. Aktion file); the document, which is undated, must therefore belong to the time between Hertenstein and the foundation of the UEF. As to the visit: information from *Salinger*, 28.9.1974; the latter could not remember the month, but probably on the way to Hertenstein, since reference is made to *Thesen der Europäischen Aktion* (cf. chap. I/2, pp. 137–42) but not to the Hertenstein programme.

not much was subsequently heard of the association's activity.[276] A branch in Carlsruhe (evidently the only one), founded by the industrialist Julius Sandner with the support of the Lord Mayor, showed greater energy; but its requests to Stuttgart for literature and other assistance remained unanswered for three months. On 30 June 1947, however, Bernhard began a series of talks on Stuttgart Radio, and in July a manifesto was drafted, which was intended to be produced in several thousand copies.[277]

Soon afterwards, however, the Stuttgart association was merged in the Europa-Bund, of which it became a *Landesverband* on 1 August 1947. It had remained small in size, but was important owing to Bernhard's intellectual and parliamentary prominence and to the definiteness of its programme. This embodied the gist of the Theses of Europeesche Actie together with certain additional 'Principles' (*Leitsätze*):

1. *Design for Europe*. 'The age of nation states is at an end. Economic needs demand the formation of large economic units ... Germany must be the first of the old European states to accept limitations on its own sovereignty for the sake of the supranational goal. A federal Germany is the first, indispensable step towards a European democratic federation.' Thus the need in each country for internal as well as international federation was clearly emphasized.

As to the European constitution, Bernhard said in his May Day speech that 'This union must be welded together by a joint foreign and economic policy, a customs union, a common social programme for the future and other joint institutions. Its object must be to remove all political and economic features of particular countries that are merely a question of national prestige.'[278]

2. *Europe in the world*. 'The federation of European democracies has no aim but the salvation and welfare of Europe, and must therefore not let itself be manœuvred into a position of hostility towards either of the extra-European great powers. It wishes to see Europe neutral between the great powers.'

3. *Plan of campaign*. The Stuttgart Principles do not say how the federation is to be achieved, although this subject was fully dealt with in the Hague Theses.

4, 5. *Activities*. 'Europäische Aktion, Landesverband Württemberg–Baden is completely independent of any party doctrine or party organization.'

---

[276] Bernhard on 17.4.1947 to Dr Merten (*Bernhard Archives,* Europ. Aktion file). The minutes of the founding assembly, and further information on the scale and activity of the Stuttgart group, have not survived. Of Dr Nothardt there is only an earlier invitation, dated 28.2.1947, to a discussion on 4 March in the Ministry of Culture on questions of founding a pro-European organization in Germany (*Federal German Archives,* Rossmann papers).

[277] Cf. Sandner on 28, 29, and 30 Apr. and 12, 15, and 18 May to Bernhard, ending with complaints at receiving no answer. Cf. Sandner's letter of 3.4.1947 to Dr Salinger with memorandum for the UEF congress at Amsterdam, n. 185 above. The first broadcast, on 30 June, was a paraphrase of the *Leitsätze* (n. 275). Sandner's letter of 16.7.1947 stated that the Carlsruhe group had approved the draft of the manifesto (*Bernhard Archives,* Europ. Aktion file).

[278] Speech of 1 May 1946 (n. 274); otherwise from *Leitsätze,* Nov./Dec. 1946 (n. 275).

It proposes to form groups throughout the country to 'spread the European idea in their areas', and to assist them 'by providing speakers, literature and discussion material'.[279]

The only association in the British Zone which addressed itself especially to young people was, as we have seen, the students' Europäische Gemeinschaft. In the US Zone Harry Wildc-Schulze, a friend of André Gide and editor of the Munich weekly *Echo der Woche*, undertook a well-planned campaign to acquaint the young generation with the European idea. He was helped on behalf of the Swiss Europa-Union by Ritzel, its secretary-general, who arranged for a team of speakers, headed by Ernst von Schenck, to visit Munich on 27 June 1947. A rally held next day, advertised only by wall-posters, attracted some 10,000 young people of both sexes. It was a new experience to them to be addressed by foreigners who spoke as civilians and not as representatives of the occupying powers, and the idea of European union aroused enthusiastic assent.[280] This was a field which lay open for penetration by the still unco-ordinated German groups, and to which it was time for them to turn their attention.

In the French Zone, the editorial staff of the youth magazine *Die Kommenden* had written to Brugmans at the beginning of 1947: 'As an organ of the young generation we have made it our special task to encourage all ways of thought that may lead to the actual establishment of a European federation. We share your view that if there is to be a future for Europe it can only be by overcoming nationalism and limiting state sovereignty for the benefit of Europe as a whole.'[281]

(D) THE GERMAN EUROPA-UNION UP TO THE EUTIN CONGRESS, AND THE FIRST ATTEMPTS TO AMALGAMATE THE VARIOUS GROUPS

At a comparatively late date, on 9 December 1946, a further group was founded in the British Zone, with an original membership of six. A press

---

[279] All from the *Leitsätze* (n. 275). Art. 11, the last of these, stated that 'a committee elected on democratic principles would subsequently draft a Statute based on the foregoing'. As to the adoption of the Theses of Europeesche Actie, Art. 2 stated that the Landesverband 'stood for the purposes of the parent organization'. Dr Salinger's Europeesche Actie evidently promoted the formation of further groups in Germany (cf. n. 261, also n. 294), e.g. one at Hamburg headed by a Dr Plato. The minutes of the session of the first amalgamated organization at Ascheberg on 26.4.1947 stated that: 'Herr Heile and Dr Merten were asked to establish contact between Dr Plato's group (Europäische Aktion) and the Hamburg *Land* executive of the Europa-Liga (*Federal German Archives,* Heile papers, Vol. 98). No material of this group could be found, however.

[280] Information from *von Schenck,* 23.8.1969. Ritzel's letter on difficulties of organization in *von Schenck Archives,* UEF documents 1946–9. Schenck stated that on their return journey the team held a similar meeting at short notice at Mainz University, at which an Indian prophesied that Germany would soon be as powerful as ever. This provoked wild applause, showing that it would take little to revive a national mass psychosis; the UEF speakers had the greatest difficulty calling the meeting to order.

[281] Editorial letter from *Die Kommenden* (published by Novalis, Freiburg im Breisgau), 25 February 1947, to Brugmans, referring to an article of his and proposing an 'exchange of views'. Brugmans replied on 29 April that he hoped soon to visit the French Zone and have a full discussion with the Freiburg group 'in a spirit of mutual confidence'.

announcement of 2 January 1947 stated that: 'A group of Germans in favour of the European idea have formed an association at Syke near Bremen under the title Europa-Union. Wilhelm Heile was elected chairman of its founding committee, while Wilhelm Hermes of Mönchengladbach is the chief executive of the association and effective director of its Central Bureau for Germany, located in that city.' The choice of name indicated, to those who were aware of it, a link with the Swiss Europa-Union.[282] Wilhelm Heile, a well-known and influential politician, had been a champion of European unity in Weimar days, when his Verband für europäische Kooperation competed with Coudenhove's organization. He was co-founder with F. Middelhauve of the Free Democratic party (FDP) in the British Zone; at its foundation meeting at Opladen in January 1946 he was unanimously elected its first chairman, and at its first congress at Bad Pyrmont in May he became president of the FDP for the British Zone. In his keynote address to the congress he advocated federalism in both internal and external affairs:

As we erect on German soil our German state, our German administration and self-government, let us devise that self-government in such a way that our federation of autonomous members of our nation can be a model for all peoples and that a European federation may develop directly from it. German unity will thus be a basis for the union of all European peoples in a United States of Europe; and on the day that happens, a firm foundation will have been laid for the United States of the whole world. That is Germany's mission.[283]

However, the executive of the FDP under Franz Blücher was more nationalist in outlook and did not share Heile's views about federalism or a broadly based middle-class party. It took advantage of the latitude allowed by him to express dissenting views at Pyrmont, and on 16 November 1946 urged him to resign as president of the FDP. On 8 December Heile

---

[282] DPD report of 2.1.1947. For the six participants in the founding assembly at Syke on 9.12.1946, cf. their minute at n. 289; for the actual influence of the Swiss Europa-Union, see n. 287. It was not a question of 'various groups uniting' as stated, e.g., by K. Koppe in *Das grüne E setzt sich durch* (Cologne, 1967, pp. 15 and 17); like all the instances already mentioned, it was a local foundation by individuals unaware of the activity of similar groups.

[283] Quoted from the full text in W. Heile, *Abschied von der FDP*, Syke, 1947, p. 54. Wilhelm Heile, b. 18.12.1881, a Lower Saxon of stubborn temperament and a friend of Friedrich Naumann; received severe head injuries in World War I. Co-founder of the German Democratic party. On his Verband für europäische Kooperation (1926–32), see Introduction, p. 40, and n. 55. In the summer of 1945 he was removed from the chairmanship of the Thuringian LDP (Liberal Democratic Party), which he had held for a short time, on account of anti-Soviet utterances; at the end of 1945 the British appointed him *Landrat* in his home town of Syke near Bremen (*Land* Hanover). From August 1946 he was minister without portfolio in the first government of *Land* Hanover (from 21 Sept. also minister of transport), until 8 December when the *Land* governments of Hanover, Brunswick, and Oldenburg were replaced by the first government of Lower Saxony, to which Heile did not belong. During this period, in addition to being the FDP leader in the British Zone, he cherished the idea of reviving his pro-European organization: 'I intend in the near future to go to London and then Paris, to renew old ties with leading "Europeans" and try to revive my old national committees for European co-operation' – he wrote thus on 3.10.1946 to W. von Rheinbaben and similarly on 2.8.1946 to C. Amelunxen (*Federal German Archives,* Heile papers, Vol. 73).

lost his post as a minister in the *Land* government at Hanover, and on the following day he founded Europa-Union.[284] In November he had fruitless talks with the leaders of the Hamburg Paneuropa-Union, so that his new association represented a revival of his old rivalry with Coudenhove.[285] At the outset his name carried considerable weight, but from July 1947 onwards he receded into the background – he was well advanced in years – and the balance of power shifted decisively.

The real driving force from the beginning was Wilhelm Hermes, who had been secretary-general of the FDP under Heile and was squeezed out of the party along with him. According to his posthumous papers, he and Heile decided on 25 November (no doubt after Heile received the demand for resignation from the party executive) to found a 'German organization of Europa-Union'. On the 27th he appointed 'responsible directors' of the organization for three *Länder* – Wilhelm Hellwig of Düsseldorf for North Rhine–Westphalia, Dr Walter Hasemann of Hanover for Lower Saxony, and Nicolaus Möller of Meldorf for Schleswig–Holstein – and invited them to a founding assembly at Syke. Hermes was a brilliant organizer, spurred on by political ambition and aided by financial independence; even the *Spiegel* weekly called him 'an able man of business and a seasoned interviewee'.[286] He did not profess to be an original thinker: the documents he submitted to the founding assembly consisted of material from the Swiss Europa-Union, hastily reprinted on paper headed 'Europa-Union.

---

[284] Mindful of the defeat of his party in Weimar days he had endeavoured, before the newly formed CDU (Christian Democratic Union) could gain ground, to make the new FDP a rallying-point for all bourgeois–democratic groups and in particular for all forces working for the reconstruction of Germany and Europe on federal lines. However, the executive was strongly critical of his negotiations with the Niedersächsische Landespartei, his advocacy of a right-wing democratic bloc, and his 'particularist' attitude; and the demand for his resignation was endorsed at the end of 1946 by an FDP arbitral court. Heile at first refused to comply, but on 21.3.1947 he joined the Niedersächsische Landespartei under Block and Hellwege, which shared his federalist views. Cf. *Parteien in der Bundesrepublik, Schriften des Instituts für politische Wissenschaft*, vol. 6, Stuttgart/Düsseldorf, 1955, pp. 289, 409, and 536. All sources on the dispute within the FDP, and text of Heile's letters to Hellwege, Steltzer, Adenauer, etc. on the need to unite all bourgeois–democratic forces, in W. Heile, *Abschied von der FDP*, Syke, (end of March) 1947, pp. 1 f., 7, and 68–81.

[285] References to conversations in November in letter from Dr F. Ablass (Hamburg) to Heile, 14.12.1946, Heile to Ablass, 20.12.1946, and Hermes to Ablass, 30.12.1946; continuing stress on the old rivalry with Coudenhove, cf. Heile to Amelunxen (quoted in n. 259), Heile to Rheinbaben, 3.10.1946, etc., against 'the old dangerous error . . . Coudenhove's Continental Little-Europe programme' (ibid., *Federal German Archives*, Heile papers, all in Vol. 73) – although the next five years were to bear out this very point of Coudenhove's.

[286] Wilhelm Hermes claimed to be a member of the German Resistance, to have been six times arrested by the Gestapo, and to have escaped death by the merest accident. The owner of a slate quarry in the French Zone and a distillery at Mönchengladbach, the management of which he left to relatives, he was able to devote himself to Europa-Union without any financial anxiety (*Der Spiegel*, Vol. 2, No. 9, 28 Feb. 1948, p. 4 f.). On 27 Nov. 1946 Hermes wrote to Hellwig, Hasemann, and Möller to arrange in their respective *Länder* for the 'formation of inaugural bodies of 5 members for each local centre'. He also thanked Möller for a contribution of 20,000 Reichsmark; 'I myself have put up an equal sum.' Also on 27 Nov. Hermes appointed the three first full-time local managers in North Rhine 'at an initial salary of 250 Reichsmark gross' (*Federal German Archives*, Heile papers, Vol. 73).

European Unity Movement. German Branch of the New Commonwealth Society ... German Central Bureau, Mönchengladbach': these texts constituted the 'directives' and 'programme' of the new organization.

The 'Directives' consisted of a slightly simplified version of Part 1 of the *Leitsätze* of the Swiss Europa-Union, dating from 1940, and the verbatim text of the Swiss resolution of April 1944 on 'European and World Union'; the 'programme' of Europa-Union, in eighteen points, was Part 2 of the Swiss *Leitsätze*, dating from 4 February 1940. Hermes evidently got these texts from H. G. Ritzel during the latter's tour of the Western Zones in May 1946; his acceptance of them *en bloc* explains why, in the following months, Ritzel gave exclusive support to Hermes's group.[287] Hermes himself contributed only the Statutes, full of organizational detail, which he brought to the meeting at Syke, also ready printed. None the less, he was sincerely devoted to European union. Later on, he was asked by the organizing committee of the Eutin congress to print a special postcard with the text 'He who cannot think internationally cannot act in a national manner'; Hermes, however, rejected this vague formulation and substituted a firmer though not exactly federalist version: 'National states must die so that Europe and the world may live.'[288]

The founding assembly at Syke on 9 December 1946 was attended by Heile, Hermes, Hellwig, Hasemann (these four constituted the 'founding committee' together with N. Möller, who was unable to be present), and two, already appointed 'regional managers', F. Drasdo and E. Rütten. The minutes stated that it was for the 'present founding committee' to decide concerning 'the addition of further founding committee members, who should if possible not be members of the FDP'. This appears to indicate that all the original members did belong to the FDP, a fact which was at first an obstacle to recruitment.[289] The committee further decided

---

[287] *Leitsätze* of the Swiss Europa-Union, first printed in *Der Europäer*, Vol. vi, No. 1, Basle, Jan. 1940, p. 1 f.; resolution on 'world union' ibid., Vol. xi, No. 4, Apr. 1944, p. 2 (both also in W. Lipgens, *Europa-Föderationspläne der Widerstandsbewegungen 1940–1945*, Munich, 1968, pp. 345–8 and 383 f.); cf. chap.I/2, pp. 117–23. Copies of Hermes's reprint (without indication of source), early Dec. 1946, in *Federal German Archives*, Heile papers, Vol. 73, and Kardorff papers, Vol. 72. H. G. Ritzel reported that 'on the occasion of a tour of Germany he had talked to Germans in the French, American and British Zones about the problem of European unity' (*Europa*, Vol. xiii, No. 6, June 1946, p. 3), and later that: 'The foundation of the German Europa-Union on 9.12.1946 was influenced from Basle' (ibid., Vol. xv, No. 2, Feb. 1948, p. 3); I know nothing of a visit by Ritzel 'in November 1945' as stated by K. Koppe (*Das grüne E setzt sich durch*, Cologne, 1967, p. 13). As to further support, cf. n. 293 f.

[286] *Lammers Archives*, Eutin congress file (cf. n. 316), correspondence of 3/4 June 1947. Hermes told *Der Spiegel* (Vol. 2, No. 9, 28.2.1948, p. 4 f.) that he hoped the whole of Europe would be like Switzerland in five years' time, with people of different languages living together in a federal state. Unfortunately no Hermes archives could be traced, as no reply was received to my enquiries or to one by W. Cornides on 10.8.1954.

[289] 'Summary record of meeting of the central inaugural committee at Syke, 9.12.1946'. None the less, Hermes on 21.12.1946 proposed three new members (who were elected at the next meeting on 8.1.1947), viz. Dr Karl Hoffman (Schönau, Black Forest), Herbert Kauffmann (Bochum), and Max Dominicus (Remscheid), on the ground that the last two were tried members of the FDP, while the first was a 'proved democrat' and in touch with the Swiss Europa-Union. On 23.1.1947 Drasdo reported candidly to Heile and Hermes: 'Success of activities: negative', because 'the

that 'pending the revision of the policy directives, which Herr Heile expressed willingness to undertake', the Swiss documents would be used as a 'basis for the application to be made to Military Government'; 'the Statutes proposed by Herr Hermes' were also adopted.[290]

In the next four months Hermes developed the organization at an astonishing rate. In a short time he had built up an efficient staff at Mönchengladbach, using for preference former military staff officers of suitably European sympathies. Local groups were rapidly formed in the Düsseldorf, Cologne, and Aachen districts, on the lines indicated in the fortnightly bulletin (*Informationsdienst*): 'A five-man founding committee is appointed for each local area; this body will submit the directives and statutes ... in three signed copies to the competent military authorities together with the licence application.' By 10 January 1947 *Informationsdienst*, No. 3 announced that applications were already pending from 60–70 groups in the British Zone.[291] On 20–3 January Hermes founded a 'Landesgruppe Berlin der Europa-Union, headed by Rudolf Bürgel ... to function for the time being in the British and US Sectors' of Berlin; he ignored the Paneuropa-Bund, just as he had ignored existing federalist groups elsewhere. On returning to the British Zone he found a copy of the Hertenstein programme awaiting him, and in the next bulletin declared

---

appointment of two well-known FDP leaders, Heile and Hermes' meant that branches could only be started with FDP members; he added that the 'directives' should be shorter and less influenced by party politics. Thereupon, on 30 Jan. Heile invited the chairmen of all German parties to become honorary presidents of Europa-Union. This, however, was a failure. Adenauer replied on 17.2.1947: 'I beg you to be kind enough to drop this idea for the time being. In my view Germany's external situation is not yet such as to make it desirable to set up in this country a firm organization, such as you have in mind, to propagate the European idea' (all in *Federal German Archives,* Heile papers, Vol. 73). The imbalance as between parties in the founding committee was only cured when it was enlarged for the second time, on 1 Apr. 1947: cf. n. 298.

[290] 'Summary record' (n. 289). The Statute, which had to be appended to the licence application, was on strictly democratic lines. The members of each local group elected an executive and a 'local council' (on which every twenty-five members had one representative) to supervise the executive. The local executives of each district elected the district executive, supervised by a district council on which every 100 members had one representative. The *Land* executive was similarly elected and supervised by a *Land* council (one representative per 250 members). Finally the *Land* executives elected a 'central directorate' of five members, supervised by the assembly of all *Land* councils. Pending this assembly, the inaugural committee was the 'supreme governing body'. To achieve this last result, Hermes had in March 1947 made an incongruous addition to the Statute: cf. n. 304. The 'summary record' added only the words: 'Europa-Union will only take part in elections in the British Zone if this should be absolutely necessary' – showing that at least one of those present, probably Hermes, wanted to leave open a loophole for such action, incompatible though it was with a non-party attitude.

[291] *Informationsdienst,* Z-1, probably to be dated 9.12.1946 (*Federal German Archives,* Heile papers, Vol. 67); Z-2 contained the resolutions of 9 Dec.; Z-3, dated 10.1.1947, recommended that, as had happened at Bonn, inaugural committees should include members of all four parties (hectographed, ibid., Vol. 98, as are all further numbers of *Informationsdienst*; from Z-5 onwards (beginning of March 1947) these consist of a sheet printed on both sides). Similar announcement by DPD, 16.1.1947. e.g. licence granted on 8.2.1947 by Headquarters Military Government, *Stadtkreis* Düsseldorf: 'Approval is hereby given for the formation of a branch of the Europa-Union in Stadtkreis Düsseldorf' (*Heile papers,* Vol. 73).

that it was 'likewise binding on our Europa-Union in Germany..., superseding our present directives and 18-point programme'.[292] Hermes thereupon went to Basle from 18 to 26 February for talks with the Swiss Europa-Union. After returning from Germany, Ritzel had built up in Switzerland from June 1946 an organization called 'Europa-Union Economic and Social Aid: Parcels for Europe', a charitable body through which Swiss citizens and other sympathizers paid for parcels of food and coffee to be sent to Germany and other distressed areas. Hermes was now able to arrange for his Central Bureau at Mönchengladbach and the *Landesverbände* of the German Europa-Union to be entrusted with the distribution of these parcels in Germany, which enormously enhanced the associations' recruiting appeal.[293] In addition, as Ritzel announced in the next number of *Europa,* published at Basle, the Swiss Europa-Union recognized its German namesake as the 'sole authorized movement in Germany for the unification of Europe. It has been nominated as a member of the inter-European Union Européenne des Fédéralistes.' Hermes's *Informationsdienst* announced at the beginning of March that the German Europa-Union had been 'recognized at the Basle conferences as the only authorized movement for European unity in Germany', and from then on it styled itself 'Europa-Union. German branch of the UEF'. Only when other member associations of UEF protested vigorously did the Swiss Europa-Union abandon this formula.[294] The same number of

---

[292] *Informationsdienst,* Z-4, of 27.1.1947, with text of resolution establishing *Landesgruppe* Berlin and also of the Hertenstein programme. Dr Bruno Schmitz-Lenders, a pro-European and head of a department in the Berlin City government, complained to Hermes on 28.1.1947 that it was 'inadmissible in Berlin conditions to set up Europa-Union only in the British and US Sectors'; the Allied Kommandatura had ruled that 'organizations of a political character must either be authorized for the whole city or not at all', and it had been improper simply to turn down his invitation to a discussion with the Pan-Europa-Bund (*Federal German Archives,* Heile papers, Vol. 73). The warning was justified, for shortly after the Bund was prohibited the Europa-Union received an order of 31.5.1948 from the Kommandatura stating that it was 'not permitted in Berlin. Its founders must therefore cease all activity in Berlin' (DPD, 1.7.1948).

[293] Especially as 'any surplus of income over expenses' was to be 'spent on sending more parcels': cf. monthly advertisements in *Europe,* Basle, every number from June 1946, esp. those of 1947. Information from *Schinzinger,* 17.7.1954, and *von Schenck,* 23.8.1961.

[294] Ritzel in *Europa,* Vol. xiv, March 1947, p. 4; Hermes in *Informationsdienst,* Z-5 (the first in printed form, *Federal German Archives,* Heile papers, Vol. 98); cf. DPD, 5.3.1947. The Swiss Europa-Union wrote to the UEF on 24.2.1947: 'We have the honour to inform you that the German Europa-Union . . . in co-operation with us has been recognized as the only authorized German movement for European unity. We hereby nominate this body . . . as a member of the inter-European Union Européenne des Fédéralistes. We . . . permit ourselves to state that, having thoroughly investigated conditions in Germany, it is our wish that no other German movement should become a member of the Union Européenne des Fédéralistes.' On 17 March Salinger on Brugmans's behalf requested Hermes to publish a correction: 'The statement that Europa Union . . . is recognized as the sole German movement for European union is based on a misunderstanding The correct position is that any German organization that pursues the same or similar aims to those of the Union Européenne des Fédéralistes can, directly or indirectly, become a member of that body.' For, he continued, Europeesche Actie also supported groups in Germany (*BEF Archives,* Brugmans corr.). Federal Union wrote similarly to the Swiss Europa-Union: 'Federal Union claimed the right to help new organizations about to set up, but did not claim to stipulate that they

Informationsdienst reported the formation of *Land* groups for the US Zone: Hesse (H. Rudloff, Frankfurt), Bremen (Arthur Buls), and Württemberg–Baden (Karl Steinhorst, Mannheim), and added: 'We hope to begin ... organizing very soon in Bavaria and in the whole French Zone.' It was increasingly clear that Hermes intended to establish his organization even in places where other 'European' associations, mostly of earlier vintage than his, were already active. As far as Europa-Union itself was concerned, he had made sure at an early date that he would be in charge of the merger discussions that must inevitably be held with other bodies.

On 5 December 1946, even before the founding meeting, he had listed the existing associations for Heile and remarked that, when the time came to discuss union with these, 'to avoid a repetition of the unhappy experience with the FDP I shall insist absolutely on the recognition of our directives and statutes. The political leadership must in all circumstances remain with you, and I for my part would like to keep the whole organizational side in my own hands.' When the Hamburg Paneuropa-Union proposed immediate conversations, Hermes wrote on 30 December to Heile in 'great anxiety': 'I have no intention of letting the management be wrested from me this time'; and he revealed his basic intention by continuing: 'We must at all costs go ahead as fast as possible with the announcement of fresh groups. When, as a result, the balance of forces has clearly shifted in our favour, it will be far easier for us to assert our claims.' Hermes indeed succeeded in preventing the first Hamburg approach from bearing any fruit. He had to take account, however, of Heile's views: the latter thought that 'We must on no account permit, let alone encourage, disunion within the European movement. I am doing and shall do all I can to bring about the earliest possible amalgamation of all pro-European organizations.'[295]

In February 1947 the Deutsche Liga (Schwerte) merged with the USE-Liga (Ascheberg), and on 8 March they reached agreement at Ascheberg with the Hamburg Paneuropa-Union for 'closest co-operation with a view to an organizational merger'. When, on 10 March, the Hamburg Union visited Hermes at Mönchengladbach he could not refuse, especially in view of Heile's attitude, to form a co-ordinating committee; he did arrange, however, that the crucial meeting would take place rather later,

---

were or were not sections' of UEF (Meeting of Executive Committee, 19.4.1947, *Federal Union Archives*): The Swiss accordingly drew in their horns, and replied to Salinger with a copy to Hermes: If 'other German organizations do not wish to co-operate with Europa-Union, which we have recognized as *our* representative in Germany, and prefer to notify their membership direct to the UEF, they are free to do so' (communicated by Hermes to members of the founding committee in a circular of 24 Apr., *Federal German Archives*, Heile papers, Vol. 98).

[295] Hermes to Heile, 5 and 30.12.1946. Cf. Dr Ablass's approach, n. 210 above; since no further correspondence exists, the Hamburg group seem to have shelved their proposal in Jan. 1947. Heile to Schmitz-Lenders on 12.2.1947, cf. n. 292. Similarly on 15.3.1947 he assured Axel Eggebrecht of the DPD that 'my friends and I want to unite Europe, and therefore we regard it as urgently necessary to unite all "Europeans" ... In a discussion with the Pan-Europeans we agreed to form a co-ordinating committee ... after all of us had expressly declared our basic readiness for union or at least for co-operation' (all in *Federal German Archives*, Heile papers, Vol. 73).

422 *Revival of Plans for Federation*

on 12 April, with the participation of other associations.[296] Meanwhile he continued to force the pace as regards forming new branches of Europa-Union. A revised version of the statute was printed in a large edition and distributed in March together with policy 'directives' drafted by Europa-Union itself. These, together with the 'obligatory' Hertenstein programme, 'took account of the special circumstances of Germany'; they will be reverted to presently.[297] Hermes made special efforts to form *Landesgruppen* in the US Zone, so that Europa-Union could present itself as the strongest association in all parts of the country. An important step forward, no doubt due to Ritzel's influence, was that Dr Wilhelm Hoegner, a Social Democrat and deputy prime minister of Bavaria, who had been won over to the European cause while an *émigré* in Switzerland, now declared himself willing to join the central founding committee of Europa-Union. At a meeting of this committee at Frankfurt on 1 April 1947 the eight original members co-opted nine others including Hoegner, Steinhorst, Ritzel, and Kilwes.[298] As regards the forthcoming merger negotiations Hermes expressed doubts concerning Dahlmeyer and Rheinbaben, but 'Herr Heile dissented, and believed co-operation ... to be absolutely necessary.' A 'large majority' of the committee was in favour of 'friendly conversations with all concerned', but Hermes none the less secured a decision to 'conduct negotiations with all groups in a dilatory manner while making ourselves as strong as possible'. The 'directives' were criticized; Dr Hasemann pressed for 'an appeal to be drafted' and also 'a pamphlet examining the question of European federation from various points of view'.[299] Finally

---

[296] DPD, 12.2.1947 and 8.3.1947 and USE–Liga circular of 17.3.1947 (*Merten Archives*). Hermes's *Informationsdienst*, Z-6, reported on about 20.3.1947 the discussion between 'Herren Heile, Hermes and Hellwig of our Europa-Union, and Herren Dahlmeyer, Hellmann, Meinecke and Müller-Wiemers of the Paneuropa-Union' and observed that 'agreement on the following points will be required: unified directives and statutes, a common name and headquarters, temporary leadership'. In the same number he announced that Europa-Union would organize a series of large public meetings from the end of April (*Federal German Archives*, Heile papers, Vol. 98).

[297] *Informationsdienst*, Z-5, beginning of March 1947, with which the revised statute ('approved by the central founding committee at its session at Mönchengladbach on 15.2.1947') was sent out in an edition of 2,000 copies; the 'directives', with the Hertenstein programme annexed, followed in about mid-March in an edition of 10,000 copies (*Federal German Archives*, Heile papers, Vol. 98; *DGAP Archives*, E791.71D). These are analysed in the five-point survey which follows.

[298] Cf. Minutes of meeting of 1 Apr. 1947 by Schumacher-Hellmold (*Federal German Archives*, Heile papers, Vol. 98). In addition to the previous members (Heile, Hermes, Hellwig, Möller, Hasemann, Hoffmann, Kauffmann, Dominicus, cf. n. 289), the meeting confirmed the appointment in March of Wilhelm Elfes (mayor of Mönchengladbach) and Karl Steinhorst (Mannheim), and co-opted Heinrich G. Ritzel (Basle), Dr Wilhelm Hoegner (Munich), Heinrich Kredel (Michelstadt), Otto Schumacher-Hellmold (Bonn), Dr R. Fecker (Trier), Benno Hein (Düsseldorf), and Dr Paul Kolwes (Coblenz). The non-party principle was emphasized by the addition of Elfes, one of the best-known CDU politicians at that time, and Hoegner, a prominent Social Democrat. Cf. also list of the seventeen in *Informationsdienst*, Z-7, 19.4.1947.

[299] Quotations from Minutes (n. 298). Hermes had little sympathy for these ideas, but replied by referring to his dynamic organization. Hermes's methods were emphatically criticized in a letter of 14.4.1947 to Heile from Helmut Fischer, chairman of the Cologne *Bezirk* since Jan. The first thing to do, Fischer argued, was 'independently of all organizational questions, to give our work the

the committee approved a somewhat naïve message to the Council of Foreign Ministers, then meeting in Moscow:

> The central committee of the German branch of Europa-Union, at its inter-Zonal meeting in Frankfurt am Main on 1 April 1947, has observed with concern that the negotiations in Moscow have been impeded by national reservations. Peace and security in Europe can only be guaranteed in the long term if a peaceful settlement is reached in accordance with a supranational conception of Europe. Europa-Union urges that the aspiration of all peoples towards supranational co-operation be supported and not hindered by imperialist aims.[300]

In analysing the views and objectives of Europa-Union it will be noted that Heile's 'directives', the only ones drawn up by the association itself, were couched in vague and somewhat old-fashioned terms, but were supplemented by the much simpler and clearer Hertenstein programme which was annexed to them ('Art. 4: The members of the European Union shall transfer part of their economic, political and military sovereignty to the federation created by them'). Nevertheless, the intellectual content appears somewhat thin in comparison with other associations.

1. *Design for Europe.* 'The appalling consequences of two world wars have turned Europe into a spiritual and economic wilderness and expose the Continent to the danger of complete collapse. A final and lasting peace and the economic and cultural recovery of Europe can only be brought about if all European nations are prepared to join in peaceful co-operation.' Our aim is 'the union of the whole of Europe; all European peoples and states must become members of the European confederation, provided they feel and acknowledge that they are European and belong to Europe'. 'Europa-Union regards it as premature to draw up a detailed constitution for the European confederation at the present time.'[301]

---

comprehensive ideological basis that it urgently requires'. There must first be 'a genuine change of mentality, a sincere intellectual and moral demilitarization' on a large scale; until that happened, it was wrong to 'seek to push our ideas through in the shortest possible time by means of a mass movement and every other conceivable means'. Over hasty organization was dangerous; 'transient tactical successes *vis-à-vis* other movements could not be claimed as an argument in favour of such methods' (*Federal German Archives,* Heile papers, Vol. 99).

[300] Text in Minutes, according to which Hermes even proposed 'that an application be made to attend the Moscow conference', an idea which the meeting thought decidedly unfeasible. Text also in *Informationsdienst,* Z-7, of 19.4.1947, which states that the message was 'forwarded to the Moscow peace conference via the Allied Control Commission'. The Commission no doubt refused to send it on.

[301] Directives, mid-March 1947 (cf. n. 297). While 'co-operation' and 'union' are here used imprecisely to mean more or less the same thing, 'confederation' (*Staatenbund*) means more than it says. In a written interview for DPD at this time Heile was asked: 'So nations would no longer enjoy full sovereignty?' Answer: 'No. The next step must be for sovereignty to reside, not in countries or national states but in the European confederation' (Heile to Eggebrecht, 15.3.1947, *Federal German Archives,* Heile papers, Vol. 73). 'Confederation' is evidently used here to mean 'federation' (*Bundesstaat*), as had been envisaged very clearly in the eighteen-point programme of the Swiss Europa-Union issued from Mönchengladbach three months earlier: cf. chap. I/2, p. 119 f.

2. *Europe in the world.* Just as the Pan-American Union, the British Commonwealth, and the USSR already exist, so there must be a European Union, including Britain. Moreover, Europa-Union hopes that 'Russia and the East-European states will join the movement for European union or at least give it their benevolent support'. It must not be allowed, however, 'that the work of peace in Europe should degenerate into a system of Continental power politics, an enlarged version of the national power politics of the past. Hence Europa-Union seeks the unification of Europe only in the framework of the world-wide peace mechanism of the UN.'[302]

3. *Plan of campaign.* All that was said on this was: 'Unification can only succeed on a basis of free speech and joint efforts.' Hermes no doubt thought in terms of political influence. Only in the concluding speech at the Eutin congress did Berringer speak of recruiting members and educating the public as the Union's principal tasks.[303]

4. *Purpose and character of the organization.* 'In co-operation with similar organizations in other European countries, Europa-Union aims to bring about the political and economic union of the peoples and states of Europe.' This was not merely 'an aim for the distant future', but 'the most important and urgent task of practical politics at the present day'. In working for this aim 'there must be no party-political differences'. As we have seen, organization was Europa-Union's strong point: 'The Union is organized in (a) local groups, corresponding to urban and rural districts (*Stadt- und Landkreise*) . . . ; (b) regional groups . . . corresponding to administrative districts (*Regierungsbezirke*); (c) *Land* groups (*Landesgruppen*) . . . ; and (d) the central association (*Zentralverband*) for Germany.'[304]

5. *Activities.* For some time the emphasis lay exclusively on personal recruitment by local representatives. At the Eutin congress, Hermes claimed a membership of 10,000. From April 1947 the fortnightly *Informationsdienst*, which was organized with great efficiency, was printed in 10,000 copies, so that, allowing for publicity copies, the actual number of subscribers may have been somewhat below this figure. Public meetings were

---

[302] On this point too Heile expressed himself much more clearly and in accordance with UEF views in his written interview for DPD (n. 301). 'We hope and believe that the Eastern and South-Eastern states which at present lean towards Russia will, together with Russia, see the European confederation as their best friend, unless indeed they join it as we would wish them to do' (implying, indirectly but clearly, that Russia was *not* expected to join).

[303] Cf. n. 317. *Informationsdienst* put the point more clearly in Sept. 1947: European economic union, it said, conveyed to the average person the idea of a German industrial come-back, with the slogan 'made in Germany' instead of 'made in Europe'. It was the first duty of Europa-Union, therefore, to teach people to be Europeans and to 'think European'.

[304] Statute, § 10. The elaborately democratic structure from the bottom upwards was unaltered in the revised version of Feb. 1947 and has been described in n. 290. The process of elections began in May. It was devalued, however, by a new § 23, which provided for an unelected governing body with very wide powers, to which 'all members of the central founding committee shall belong for life'. Comment is superfluous, especially as the merged Europa-Union later adopted a new statute after Hermes was removed from power.

organized from the end of April, and at Eutin it was decided to form specialized committees.[305]

A special operation was conducted in June, when Europa-Union asked all members of the *Land* parliaments in the British and US Zones whether they were in favour of a United States of Europe. Out of 1,144 deputies only 325, or 28 per cent, answered by 10 July, but 312, or 96 per cent of these, replied 'Yes'. There were only 6 Noes (from Communist deputies); 7 SPD and CDU deputies expressed no opinion.[306]

In the conversations that took place on 12 April 1947 and subsequently with a view to a merger among the German groups, the general aim was not a subject of argument. The respective programmes were in harmony on all main points (though some were vaguer or less detailed than others), and will be analysed as a whole in due course. The discussions were eased by this agreement on essentials and by the idealistic goodwill of all concerned. The large number of separate groups and their geographical dispersal was, after all, not intentional (except for Hermes's policy), but was due to the fact that the European idea had taken root spontaneously all over the country at a time when mail and transport were still disorganized and the occupation zones were hermetically divided from one another. As soon as the various groups learned of one another's existence, at the beginning of 1947, they made efforts to unite their activities in the common cause. Only the Europa-Union under Hermes took delaying action; on 12 April, however, the meeting agreed upon five weeks earlier took place in Hamburg. Those who attended, with full powers to effect a merger, were Hermes, Hasemann, and Hellwig for Europa-Union, Dahlmeyer and Hellmann for Paneuropa-Union, and Heinemann and Merten for the Vereinigte Staaten von Europa–USE-Liga; Merten was also empowered by Bernhard to represent the Stuttgart Europäische Aktion. On the same evening they were able to sign the following 'Circular to all members' of the associations concerned:

On 12 April 1947, in Hamburg, an amalgamation took place of the following organizations devoted to promoting the political, economic and cultural unity of Europe: Europa-Union (Mönchengladbach), Paneuropa-Union (Hamburg), Deutsche Liga für föderalistische Union Europas (Schwerte), USE-Liga (Ascheberg), and Europäische Aktion (Stuttgart). These associations, united by a common purpose, are at once proceeding to organize mutual co-operation under the new

---

[305] Information given at Eutin, from DPD, 27.6.1947; for the public meetings, see n. 315 below. The idea of specialized committees remained on paper for the time being; it was revived in *Informationsdienst,* Nov. 1947, on the valid ground that when the statesmen eventually met together they should find before them 'constructive plans, the fruit of thorough consideration of all questions by members of the European unification movements throughout Europe'.

[306] *Informationsdienst,* Z-10, of 12.7.1947. The highest percentage was from the Bavarian *Landtag:* 55 per cent of its members replied affirmatively, the proportion being almost uniform as between the four democratic parties. An impressive result for the first poll taken by a small private association. Cf. Coudenhove's parallel enquiry addressed to members of West-European national parliaments, pp. 437–41.

name 'Europa-Liga'. The central bureau of the joint association at Mönchengladbach will gladly furnish information on any questions that may arise. The following division of activity has been decided on: (1) Constitutional questions: Syke; (2) Management: Mönchengladbach; (3) Economy and Communications: Hamburg; (4) Press and Radio: Ascheberg; (5) Financial matters: Hanover; (6) Matters relating to Foreign Countries: Stuttgart; (7) Intellectual aspects: Schwerte and Frankfurt; (8) Culture and Education: Hamburg and Munich. Further details concerning the merger will follow shortly.[307]

Evidently Hermes had been won over by the others' enthusiasm for unity, plus the fact that they 'several times expressed the unanimous desire' – which was indeed no more than his due – 'to confide to Herr Hermes the direction of organizational matters and measures connected therewith'. At the same time it was agreed that the local, district, and *Land* groups should unite at their respective levels and elect joint executives, and that 'in accordance with the federal principle, the *Landesverbände* should be as autonomous as possible'.[308] A 'temporary central executive of the Europa-Liga' was appointed at Hamburg to hold office for a month. On 26 April it met at Ascheberg – those present being Heile, Hermes, *Assessor* Kurt Rompf (replacing Dahlmeyer, who was ill), Rheinbaben, and Merten – and performed useful work. 'The Hertenstein programme will be used as a basis of political activity. Herr Heile is entrusted with the task of drafting German directives to take account of the particular conditions in Germany'; Hermes was to draft the Statutes. 'A large measure of autonomy' was again 'guaranteed' to the *Landesverbände*, and 'the proposed working groups and their chairmen' were also to be given 'wide responsibility'. Agreement was also reached on the provisional exercise of authority in the *Landesgruppen*.[309] To all appearances a unified association had been created without sacrificing the liveliness of diversity.

[307] Text in USE–Liga circular of 15 Apr. (*Merten Archives*) and in *Informationsdienst der Europa-Union*, 19.4.1947; likewise in 'Minutes of meeting of the Coordinating Committee in Hamburg on 12.4.1947'. According to this last, Hermes 'repeatedly and emphatically argued for the name "Europa-Union" ', but the others present wanted a 'basically new name'; finally 'Herr Dahlmeyer's proposal of the name "Europa-Liga" was unanimously adopted. (*Federal German Archives*, Heile papers, Vol. 98).

[308] Minutes of Hamburg meeting, 12.4.1947 (n. 307). As to the composition of the 'presidium' which was to govern the Europa-Liga for the next three years, on Hermes's proposal it was decided that it should consist of 11 members: 5 elected by Europa-Union and 6 by the other four associations, each in accordance with its own statute. The election was to take place by 10 May.

[309] 'Minutes of meeting of temporary central managing executive committee of the Europa-Liga at Aschberg on 26 Apl. 1947'. For the temporary *Land* executives, in some cases a collegiate solution was adopted: *Stadtrat* Bernhard Broschkowski (Passau) and *Dipl.-Ing.* Joachim Berringer (Munich) for Bavaria; Bernhard and Steinhorst for Württemberg–Baden; Schinzinger and Hummel for Baden (French Zone). Europa-Union was to provide the temporary executive for Hesse, Lower Saxony, Schleswig–Holstein, and Bremen, and Paneuropa-Union for Hamburg. No agreement was reached at this stage regarding North Rhine–Westphalia, for which Hermes proposed Joachim of Dortmund; instead, Westphalia was assigned to Rheinbaben and North Rhine to a representative of Europa-Union. In addition 'Dr Merten was given full responsibility to examine and decide the question of publishing an Europa-Liga journal. Herr Hermes was similarly made responsible for the publication of newspapers' (*Federal German Archives*, Heile papers, Vol. 98). The implementation of all these decisions would have produced a very effective over-all organization.

Revival of Plans for Federation 427

But, before the unification had time to take full effect in the different local areas, Europa-Union withdrew from the merger. Although Hermes enjoyed a large measure of influence over the Europa-Liga thanks to his role of 'manager' at Mönchengladbach, drafter of the Statutes, etc., he must have realized soon after the meeting on 26 April that alongside such personalities as Merten and Rompf, Rheinbaben and Bernhard, and in view of the increased autonomy of local branches, committees, etc., his power would be a good deal less absolute than in the past.[310] At a meeting of the founding committee of Europa-Union on 10 May (Heile and several other members being absent) he agreed to the appointment of a five-man steering committee of Europa-Union, which was to have been a component part of the executive of Europa-Liga; this consisted of himself, Heile, Ritzel, Hummel, and Berringer, but, instead of the more conciliatory Heile being chairman, Hermes reserved this function to himself. What was more, he secured the passage of a resolution stating that 'The authorized representatives of all *Landesgruppen* of Europa-Union have refused their consent to the union' with other groups 'in the Europa-Liga'.[311] The reason initially given for this, and communicated to the press, was that 'the agreements arrived at [had] not been kept by the Hamburg Paneuropa-Union'.[312]

The chief argument used by Hermes at the meeting of 10 May was, however, that the central committee of the SPD had adopted a resolution at Bad Meinberg on 22 April forbidding SPD members to join the Paneuropa-Union because some Communist tendencies had allegedly shown themselves there. Hermes hastened to enquire at Hanover whether the ban also applied to Europa-Union; he was told by Ollenhauer (the SPD leader) that it 'related to the Paneuropa-Union with headquarters at Hamburg', and on 10 May he convinced those present that a union with the Hamburg group was out of the question. Rheinbaben protested

---

[310] On 29 Apr. he duly sent Heile a good draft of the Europa-Liga statute, under a newly printed letterhead 'Europa-Liga. Europäische Einigungsbewegung. Deutscher Zweig der UEF. Deutsches Zentralbüro M. Gladbach' (*Federal German Archives,* Heile papers, Vol. 121). On Hermes's real motives for torpedoing the Europa-Liga, see especially n. 314.
[311] 'Summary Minutes of meeting of the central founding committee of Europa-Union at Mönchengladbach, 10.5.1947' (*Federal German Archives,* Heile papers, Vol. 99). Of the seventeen members (since 1 Apr., cf. n. 298) only five were present, viz. Hermes, Steinhorst, Kolwes, Hellwig, and Hasemann. Hermes therefore began by co-opting Dr Müller (Berlin), Hans-J. Rudloff (Hesse), Karl Hummel (South Baden), and Joachim Berringer (Bavaria), all of whom were present, so that the decision could be represented as endorsed by all the *Landesgruppen*.
[312] 'Summary Minutes' (n. 311). On 6 June Hermes explained to Heile: 'Although it was expressly agreed at Ascheberg that all the member associations of Europa-Liga would refrain from setting up independent subgroups as from 26 April, on 29 April the Paneuropa-Union held a public meeting at Flensburg at which it set up a *Landesgruppe* Schleswig–Holstein.' Apart from the fact that there is no reference to any such agreement in the minutes of 26 April (n. 309), the Flensburg group had already explained (Dr Günther Wiedemann to Heile, 1 May) that the establishment of the *Land* committee had been planned for months past and the invitations had gone out weeks before; moreover they were perfectly ready to integrate themselves into a 'representative committee of the new over-all organization' (*Federal German Archives,* Heile papers, Vols. 98 and 73). If an error was committed it was a pardonable and insignificant one and in no way justified Hermes's action.

against this 'denunciation of the Hamburg agreement of 12 April', which was in any case inadmissible as a matter of form, and pointed out that 'the SPD forbade its members to join the Hamburg Paneuropa-Union because the latter had entered into relations with a pro-Europe organization in Berlin which, although the Paneuropa-Union did not know it, was thought to have been influenced by the Soviet authorities in an SED direction' (sc. through Kasting, see p. 396 above). But, he continued, since Dahlmeyer had resigned and the merger had taken place, 'the offending association had for practical purposes ceased to exist. It would have been easy to clear this matter up by enquiring of the SPD leadership.'[313] Hermes, however, had evidently seized on it as a pretext.

Hermes subsequently revealed to Heile his real reason for torpedoing the merger, and also made it publicly known: he hoped that a merger 'would indeed be possible eventually, but on different terms, which must above all take account of the relative strength of the individual associations', i.e. his own ambition to rule the roost.[314] In pursuance of his policy Hermes had since March been planning a series of large public meetings as a fresh activity on the part of Europa-Union. At the first of these, at Duisburg on 27 April, Heile once again called for the application of the federal principle both nationally and internationally: i.e. Germany must have a democratic and federalist form of government as a pre-condition of European federation. At a meeting on 1 May in the Kolosseum at Lübeck, Heile deplored talk of another war and said the Germans must be proud and courageous enough to remain disarmed while evolving towards the supranational organization of the future.[315] Finally a well-prepared 'Delegates' Congress was held at Eutin from 21 to 23 June 1947, attended by at least 300 delegates and about forty press reporters, so that for the first time practically all German newspapers in the Western Zones carried informative articles on Europa-Union. In an opening speech in the Schlosstheater Hermes said that the congress must show the world 'that

---

[313] For the party political context of the SPD's decision, cf. chap. IV/1 (in vol. 2). Copies of Hermes's enquiry of 28 April to Dr Schumacher and Ollenhauer's reply of 8 May were attached to the Summary Minutes of 10 May (n. 311); they were mentioned in Europa-Union's *Informationsdienst* of 16.5.1947 and quoted in the issue of 29.8.1947 and to Heile on 21.5.1947 (*Federal German Archives*, Heile papers, Vol. 67); without effect, as Heile took no action in spite of the way he had been treated by Hermes. Schinzinger stated that the Paneuropa-Union were able to persuade the SPD leaders to 'forget about their resolution, though it was never officially revoked' (information from *Schinzinger*, 7.8.1954).

[314] Hermes to Heile, 6.6.1947; similarly in *Informationsdienst*, 29.8.1947 (he also laboured the fact that Rheinbaben had not yet been de-Nazified). On 13.5.1947 he had written to Heile: 'I myself held out for "splendid isolation" because otherwise, sooner or later, our fine organization would only have served the ambitions of the Hamburg group' (*Federal German Archives*, Heile papers, Vols. 98 and 99). This was quite unjustified as far as the Hamburg group were concerned, but threw a revealing light on Hermes's own attitude.

[315] Cf. the DPD reports of 27.4.1947 and 1.5.1947. About this time Ritzel was again behind the scenes in Germany: in a letter of 14.5.1947 A. Ganz (Lucerne), replying to a message of Ritzel's that has not survived, wrote: 'I am glad you have managed to secure permission for Mönchengladbach' (perhaps the Zonal licence?). By 11.5.1947 Ritzel was back in Basle (*EU Archives*, Basle, 'World Federation' documents).

Germany is prepared, without any reservations, to integrate itself into the developing European community'; he described the expansion of Europa-Union and said that it was 'a member of the UEF in Paris, the only German body ... so authorized by the Swiss Europa-Union'. Heile, reviewing the current situation, said that: 'The Marshall plan to grant loans of several billion dollars in the next few years to European countries that are genuinely resolved on a policy of unity and co-operation is a proof of practical idealism' and not merely a policy of creating markets for America's benefit, since devastated Europe 'would hardly appear creditworthy to someone thinking in purely capitalist terms'; in any case, the Marshall Plan was a unique opportunity to bring about European union.[316]

Anna Siemsen spoke of the need to educate the young generation to be good Europeans: 'we have no time to lose, if Europe does not unite it will be torn in two and will become a colonial area'. Max Dominicus criticized the absurdity of economic frontiers in diminished Europe and deplored protective tariffs, attempts at autarky, and bilateral clearing agreements; the Marshall Plan had no chance of bringing about more than a temporary respite or illusory prosperity unless Europe 'can make up its mind to achieve a customs union and a Continental-scale economy'. Christa Koch, speaking on 23 June, declared that united Europe was a pre-condition of world unity and was not to be considered as an end in itself or a new power structure. Buchheister emphasized the peaceable disposition of German youth, and Berringer called for further working meetings to study the various problems more deeply. No policy resolutions were adopted – this was characteristic of Hermes – but a new 'managing presidium' was elected with Hermes as chairman, the other members being Ritzel, Hasemann, and Steinhorst;[317] from this time Heile was no longer a member of the leadership.

The torpedoing of the alliance was a shock to the other associations, but they were not daunted. On 21 June, while Europa-Union was holding its

---

[316] Cf. four-page DPD communiqué, 21/2.6.1947; reports also in West Berlin newspapers: *Der Kurier* 23.6.1947, *Neue Zeitung* 24.6.1947 (*Federal German Archives,* Kardorff papers, Vol. 72). Manuscript of Heile's speech, ibid., Heile papers, Vol. 73. Overcoming great difficulties, the chairman of the Eutin *Kreisgruppe,* Heinrich Lammers, managed, by appealing to the public, to secure accommodation for nearly 400 delegates and organized their subsistence and transport with the help of the Schleswig–Holstein ministries; he arranged for a special sub-post office and postmark, and decorated the town with the assistance of refugees. Records, including correspondence with Mönchengladbach, in *Lammers Archives,* file on Eutin congress. As regards the postcard which was to be specially franked, cf. n. 288.

[317] For speeches see the sources cited in n. 316; after a debate on the statute it was decided to refer it to a committee for study during the following months. Besides the 'managing presidium' which was actually functioning under Hermes, an enlarged presidium was created; the following were elected to it as representatives of their *Land* groups: Peter Fuglsang (Schleswig–Holstein), *Polizeipräsident* Erwin Barth (Lower Saxony), Wilhelm Hellwig (North Rhine–Westphalia), and Dr Ernst Müller (Berlin). The following were made chairmen of central specialized committees and consequently members of the enlarged presidium: Wilhelm Heile (constitutional matters), Prof. Dr Anna Siemsen of Hamburg (women's affairs), J. Berringer of Munich (transport), Max Dominicus of Remscheid (economic questions), and Duke Adolf Friedrich zu Mecklenburg (sport). According to *Informationsdienst,* Z-11, of 29.9.1947 Erwin Buchheister became chairman of a committee for young people's affairs and therefore a member of the presidium.

well-advertised congress, representatives of all the other bodies comprised in the Europa-Liga met together at Hamburg, and were joined for the first time by members of the Munich Union-Europa-Liga. They had before them a letter addressed to 'les fédéralistes allemands' by Alexandre Marc, secretary-general of the UEF, urging that associations with similar aims should unite and that others should form a co-ordinating committee. Those present agreed, with one exception, to form a combined association.[318] The next step in that direction was already suggested by an invitation, issued by the Berlin Paneuropa-Bund, to a conference of all associations for European federation, to be held at Hanover on 12 July. All the groups concerned – the Europa-Union, those still in the Europa-Liga, and others, particularly in the US Zone – vied with one another in protestations of readiness to bring about the long-awaited merger on that occasion.[319]

To sum up: in the West-German Zones as in other parts of war-devastated Europe, the second half of 1946 saw the spontaneous appearance in many cities, independently of one another because of communication difficulties, of groups advocating a union of European countries in order to safeguard their continued existence between the two world powers and to free the Continent from internal wars and the curse of nationalism. In the first half of 1947 these German groups increased their activities, gaining fresh members and moving towards unification whenever they became aware of one another's existence. Their programmes, while sometimes clumsily drafted, were essentially in agreement, apart from the Cologne Föderalistische Union, which dissented from the other associations' view that European federation was an important step towards world peace. All the programmes reflected a desire, on a deeper level than that of politics, to safeguard human rights by a 'European code of law' and to put a final end to the internecine wars that had turned Europe into a 'spiritual and economic wilderness'. All of them called for a union of European states under a unified constitution, a 'United States of Europe' invested with essential, communal rights of sovereignty. All were reluctant to make proposals on

[318] Europa-Liga bulletin, July 1947 (*Merten Archives*); DPD, 23.6.1947. Only the Europäische Volksbewegung Hamburg (cf. p. 399 f.), which was also represented, wished to remain independent as a 'parallel organization on a parliamentary footing'. According to Dr Merten the other associations at this time quoted this formula as a ground for refusing close co-operation with the Volksbewegung (information from *Merten*, 2.10.1961).

[319] Europa-Union *Informationsdienst*, 12.7 1947; Europa-Liga bulletin, July 1947. The expectations of the German public were a further reason prompting the associations to unite. For instance, the Westphalian industrial organization wrote to Dr Merten: 'Westphalian industrial circles are keenly interested in the efforts being made towards a United States of Europe. It is, however, felt to be regrettable that so many organizations are pursuing the same object.' If there were a unified association, 'we would be prepared to urge all our members to support the Pan-European movement'. But the movement 'could not be taken seriously as long as the various German associations which shared a common objective could not manage to unite among themselves' (quoted with approval in Europa-Liga bulletin of July 1947, *Merten Archives*). On the Hanover conference and further attempts at amalgamation in the second half of 1947, cf. chap. III, pp. 645–52.

constitutional details or the steps by which union should be achieved, realizing that it was not a fitting time for Germans to make political suggestions to other nations. All were convinced that only by uniting could Europe safeguard its own future and that of mankind by turning itself from a Balkanized powder-keg into a zone of peace. Everyone wanted Britain and Eastern Europe to be part of the union; they hoped for the consent, goodwill, and co-operation of the Soviet Union and the USA, and they saw it as the union's task to preserve world peace by keeping the superpowers apart and providing a means of reconciliation and compromise between them. All the associations saw it as their function to prepare the public mind as widely as possible for the idea of union by means of publications, meetings, and non-party membership groups. Most of the idealists, however, were apt to underrate questions of organization. Hermes was the exception, stressing as he did the importance of an efficient centralized machine, and it was this difference of approach that held up the merger process for some time.

On all the main points of their European programme, however, the associations were in agreement with one another and, it is important to note, with the other bodies affiliated to the UEF: they shared the latter's basic conceptions although they sometimes expressed them in more veiled and cautious language. In the first negotiations for a merger they had no difficulty in agreeing on the Hertenstein programme as a basis, and in later discussions too there was no dispute as to common aims.[320] As with all UEF associations, the objective of a pacific neutral Europe between the two world powers, uniting its own people and thus banishing war and misery within its frontiers, was inspired by horror at the way in which Europe had torn itself apart and at the suicidal exaggeration of the principle of state sovereignty, the effects of which were in everyone's memory.

7. Reactions in Western Europe; Consultation of Parliamentarians; Signs of East-European Interest

The fact that the two superpowers were unable to agree on a peace settlement, and that their relations in the summer of 1946 were visibly so strained as to threaten Europe with disruption, led to a revival of the ideal of European unity. Ideas that had found acceptance among outstanding leaders of the wartime Resistance movements, and in the weeks after liberation, but had been stifled by great-power opposition, were brought to life again in the

---

[320] Cf. n. 309 and information from Merten, 2.10.1961, confirmed by the course of the later negotiations for a merger (chap. III/6). Cf. especially also the Principles (*Leitsätze*) of the Europa-Bund, the effect of the first merger, p. 647 f. The above summary can be verified from all the five-point analyses in this chapter. The Amsterdam UEF resolutions of April 1947, as soon as they became known, were reported with approval and/or reproduced verbatim: Europa-Liga circular of 15.6.1947; *Informationsdienst*, Z-9, of Europa-Union, 3.6.1947; *Europa. Mitteilungsblatt des Europa-Bundes*, Aug. 1947.

winter of 1946/7 by spontaneous organizations which rapidly set about bringing them to the notice of a wide public. The present section discusses how strong an impression this revival made on European public opinion; the reaction of the two great powers will be described at the beginning of the following chapter.[321] The reactions of the West-European press will first be outlined within the limits permitted by the restriction of our sources, after which follows an account of the questionnaire addressed to members of the West-European parliaments by Count Coudenhove-Kalergi on his return to Europe in the winter of 1946/7. A final sub-section investigates what signs there were of a similar renewal of interest in the East-European countries.

(A) REACTIONS OF THE WEST-EUROPEAN PRESS

The revival of the idea of European unity, Churchill's speech at Zurich, the foundation of the UEF and other associations – all this at first met with a hesitant reception in the press of the Western countries, which, unlike that of the rest of Europe, was able to express itself freely. Between September 1946 and the spring of 1947, however, there was a swing over from predominant scepticism to predominant approval.

The reactions to Churchill's Zurich appeal in September 1946 reflected the uncertainty of European public opinion after the shock of 1945. The speech aroused much interest; it was headlined in all the papers, and quoted in full or extensively summarized; but its scope was so bold and so far beyond the journalistic horizon of the day, bounded for the most part by the detailed problems of the Paris peace conference, that many papers, especially those licensed in the German Zones of occupation, offered no comment on it whatever.[322] To many people the notion that the Soviet–American dispute might once more thrust a significant political role on the European nations came as too great a surprise, resigned as they had been to the idea that world history must in future be left to the world powers. Such press comment as did appear was mostly inspired by the principle, inculcated since 1945, of the Soviet–American community of interests and joint responsibility for peace, and was critical of what was taken to be Churchill's idea of a union of Western Europe only. In France especially, the first reactions were of alarm at the suggestion of Franco-German partnership. There were protests at the idea of a 'Fourth Reich', and the

---

[321] Cf. chap. III/1, pp. 468–87. The reactions of European federalists to Churchill's appeal, i.e. as it were within the pro-European camp, have been discussed, pp. 341–5.

[322] Thus the *Wiesbadener Kurier*, 20.9.1946; *Rhein-Neckar-Zeitung*, 21.9.1946. *Die Neue Zeitung*, Munich, 23.9.1946, confined itself to quoting 'political observers in London' to the effect that: 'Compared to the foreign policy that is actually being pursued by Bevin and Byrnes, Churchilll's speech is as far to the right as Wallace's was to the left. Churchill's, however, is much less calculated to bring confusion into international politics, as it was clear from the outset that he could only speak as a private person. Both speeches, however, are an example of the democratic freedom that permits everyone to advance his personal views as a basis of discussion.'

MRP organ *L'Aube* declared that only when and if France had 'the necessary guarantees in the East' could there be any question of a policy based, as Churchill suggested, on 'forgetting the past'. Rather than cite many instances of the cool reception of Churchill's speech in less important quarters we may quote the London *Times*, one of the few papers to comment at length:

After speaking of Churchill's 'courage' and 'imagination' and the 'sense of history enabling him to view the present "tragedy of Europe" as a stage in a developing drama', *The Times* went on to ask: 'But is the remedy Mr Churchill prescribes one to which Europe, in its present situation, will submit? It must be admitted that there are few signs of it.' ... The speech 'was in fact based on the assumption that Europe is already irrevocably divided between East and West', but 'British policy has not yet despaired of averting the division'; the 'first steps may prove to be best directed along the path of economics rather than politics', including the UN plan for an Economic Commission for Europe, and 'exchange and intercourse with Eastern Europe and above all the Soviet Union itself'. For the rest, 'Germany today is in no position to offer partnership to anyone.'[323]

While most journalists initially took a narrow view, the idea of a United States of Europe aroused enthusiastic echoes among the general public. Sixteen special files in Duncan Sandys's office, classified by countries, contained letters addressed to Churchill by ordinary citizens, architects, teachers, engineers, etc., many of them couched in moving terms and expressing confidence that he would continue to use his influence to bring about European federation as the only hope for the future.[324]

As for the press, its reactions became more varied during the hungry winter of 1946/7 and especially in the new year, after the foundation of the UEM in London and the UEF meeting at Amsterdam, as the Russians overplayed their hand and the need for a new way forward became increasingly urgent. On the Continent especially, more and more commentators saw the revival of plans for European federation as offering the only real hope. The Communist press naturally remained firmly hostile. In Britain, where Churchill's conception held the field as opposed to that of the UEF, favourable and unfavourable views were more or less evenly balanced.

In January 1947 the editor of the (Labour) *Daily Herald* criticized Churchill's 'attempt to play power politics' and declared that he was 'possessed ... by a fixed and violent phobia against Soviet Russia ... Let us avoid even the semblance of a

---

[323] *L'Aube* quoted from *Wiesbadener Kurier*, 24.9.1946. *The Times* article of 20.9.1946 conceded that 'If the British Government's hopes of maintaining a wider unity in Europe were to prove ultimately and unmistakably vain, then many minds in Western Europe would no doubt revert to Mr Churchill's project for a lesser but closer unity.'

[324] The writers often enclosed typed copies of projects of their own, some written in the course of the winter and others dating from earlier years when they were already in favour of European union. They did not receive personal replies from Churchill or Sandys, but were sent a routine letter signed 'for Hon. Secretary', thanking them and promising 'careful study'. (A collection from Sandys's office is in the *EM Archives, Bruges*, in sixteen blue files labelled by countries; none of the writers are well-known political names.)

defeatist anti-Russian grouping in Europe such as Churchill advocates.' *The Times* continued to warn against divisive political plans but argued that Europe needed mutual economic aid and a free-trade system, a start towards which had been made by the Anglo-French trade agreement; no one could see this as directed against the Soviet Union. The conservative *Daily Telegraph* said that the UEM Committee had been wise in not letting itself be deterred by the prospect of Russian or Communist hostility; 'if other nations prove to be favourable, something might be worked out which would in practice disarm Russian suspicions'. The *Observer*, following Churchill's original line which envisaged a European federation without Britain, declared that European unity was 'a major British interest as well as a Continental necessity'. Altogether there was a great deal of variation in British attitudes, which did not at this stage take account of the basically federalist views of the European Resistance movements as reflected by the UEF.[325]

On the Continent, however, the non-Communist press began to take an increasingly favourable view of the idea of unity. *Le Monde,* for instance, wrote: 'Churchill's plan will be welcomed with enthusiasm by many in France and throughout Europe, and many more will find in it food for thought.' Russia's fear that a united Europe might be anti-Soviet should be treated calmly: 'if the Russians find that this is not so and that Europe means peace, they will change their minds'. The global aspect was important: 'A United Europe in which all common interests and forces work together will be more independent of the US and the Soviet Union; the two great powers will be joined by a third which is hostile to neither of them but extends a hand to each.' This was clearly inspired by the UEF concept rather than Churchill's. The Paris *Liberté* declared that the evolution of the situation in Europe made the need for federal union more and more evident.[326] The increase of interest and response to the UEF's ideas was described by Raymond Silva a month after the Amsterdam meeting:

At many lecture meetings, especially in France and Switzerland, audiences have been invited to open debates by putting questions to the speaker. These discussions have shown that the idea of a European federal *entente* is gaining support in quarters that have hitherto been sceptical or reserved, especially in trade-union circles. The UEF has been the subject of more than 15 broadcasts by

---

[325] *Daily Herald*, 30.1.1947; *The Times* and *Daily Telegraph*, 17.1.1947; *Observer*, 19.1.1947. Further British press reactions to the foundation of the UEM were summarized in *Federal News*, No. 144, March 1947, pp. 8-11; several papers rightly criticized its statement of policy (cf. n. 82 f.) as unduly vague, 'a curiously indeterminate document' (*Spectator*, 24.1.1947). It was indeed not well calculated to produce a clear and enlightening discussion. The question most often mooted was whether a closer European union would strengthen or weaken the UN Organization.
[326] *Le Monde*, 19/20.1.1947. *Liberté* quoted from a large selection of similar views from the Swiss, Belgian, and French press in *Europa. Organ der Europa-Union*, Vol. xiv, No. 4, Basle, March 1947, p. 3. Even a large-circulation paper like *Samedi-Soir* urged the need to 'entrer dans cette fédération européenne dont on parle beaucoup et qui, précisément, rétablirait l'équilibre centre ces deux mastodontes que sont les États-Unis et la Russie soviétique'; and the Paris *Réforme*: 'Si nous voulons sauver la paix et organiser une future prospérité pour nos peuples, le fédéralisme s'impose.'

the BBC, Radiodiffusion française, Radio Sotten and Hilversum. We have been able to develop our views in broadcast debates and interviews. The press, as a whole, is very favourable to us. Over 200 papers and periodicals have published articles about the UEF and full reports on the work of the Amsterdam meeting. All these results justify our hopes.[327]

In the spring of 1947 the revival of federalist ideas still found no echo among governments; the French and British, on whom so much depended, did not begin to react until the time of Marshall's offer, reflecting the change of opinion in the US. But by February 1947 public opinion and that of political circles had already evolved to the point where Sumner Welles, writing in the *New York Herald Tribune,* could say that: 'One of the most heartening developments in Europe in recent months has been the rapid increase in the popular demand for the establishment of a European Federation.' He added that at a recent meeting of the Council on Foreign Relations at Cleveland he had been impressed by the 'sense of urgency' with which the Europeans present proclaimed their conviction 'that only a federated Europe could survive'.[328] The conviction was in fact shared by a steadily growing percentage, though not yet a majority, of the main political groups to which the members of West-European parliaments belonged: this was shown by an enquiry conducted at this time by Coudenhove-Kalergi.

(B) COUDENHOVE-KALERGI'S POLL OF PARLIAMENTARIANS

Richard Coudenhove-Kalergi, the founder of the inter-war Paneuropa-Union, spent the years from 1940 to 1946 in the USA. As a professor at Columbia University he endeavoured to uphold the idea of European union as against the prevailing climate of admiration for Soviet Russia; this had little apparent success, but sowed a seed that was to bear fruit a few years later. Returning to Europe from New York on 18 June 1946, he endeavoured to find out 'whether, after all the terrors of a long war, Europe was really prepared to accept a federal form of government'.[329] In

---

[327] Report by Silva as delegate-general of UEF for information matters, quoted in UEF *Lettre-Circulaire,* No. 10, Paris, 4.6.1947, p. 2. It should be recalled that, in accordance with our policy concerning the use of sources (cf. Introduction, p. 90 f.), we have not attempted to give a systematic analysis of press comment but merely a sketch based on available material. A full analysis would be a complete task in itself.
[328] 'Rising demand for federation of Europe called hopeful sign' article by Sumner Welles, former Under-Secretary of State, in *New York Herald Tribune,* 5.2.1947. Welles commented, however: 'Europe desperately needs some form of political and economic federation. But it cannot . . . be advanced until the present suspicions of the Soviet Union can be dispelled and unless the Soviet government can be convinced that its own enlightened interest will be best served by the construction of a European system founded upon political and economic federation rather than upon that anarchic conglomeration of clashing sovereignties to which so many of the ills which the people of Europe have suffered during the last thousand years can be directly ascribed.'
[329] For Coudenhove-Kalergi's life and opinions, see his *An Idea Conquers the World,* London, 1953 (cf. n. 68). The son of an Austro-Hungarian diplomat, descended from Brabant and Cretan forebears, and of a Japanese mother, Count Richard Coudenhove-Kalergi was born on 17.11.1894. He

March 1945, along with fifteen other *émigrés*, he had addressed to the US Congress a 'Declaration of European Inter-Dependence' in conformity with the idea, still dominant in *émigré* circles, that only a confederation was feasible as a first step.

The declaration urged Congressmen 'to support our efforts toward the establishment of a European Confederation', recognizing that the European nations constituted 'an inter-dependent region of the world' between the U.S.A. and the U.S.S.R.' and that only 'a Confederation can secure for Europe lasting peace, personal liberty and speedy recovery'. It should be constructed 'around a European Council and a Supreme Court, to coordinate the common political, military and economic interests of Europe'; it should have defence forces, a 'Bill of Rights', and a 'Bill of Social Rights'; it should create a 'single market with a common currency' and guarantee the 'national sovereignty, security and equality' of its members. These proposals were a repetition of the half-measures that had been advocated between the wars; reading the text in 1946, R. W. G. Mackay criticized it to Coudenhove in terms that may be taken as reflecting the views of Continental federalists. Such a 'Confederation', he said, was 'completely inadequate'; what was wanted was a 'federation' on US lines with a parliament 'elected on the basis of universal suffrage' and empowered to legislate on matters of foreign policy, defence, tariffs, and economic planning. The concluding provision about national sovereignty was 'a repudiation of anything that is worth while in the document. I want the sovereignty of the individual states considerably reduced, and that is the purpose of a federation ... I am afraid you are many years behind the times in your contacts over here.'[330]

But once Coudenhove-Kalergi returned to Europe he soon realized that there had been an essential change: 'the wave of nationalism which had caused two world wars seemed at last to have exhausted itself', and while 'there were certainly many people who refused to believe in the practical possibility of a European federation, there were few who opposed it on principle'. From the autumn of 1946 onwards he spoke only of 'Federation'. This was not the crux of his difficulties with the federalists, which will be discussed later. He now considered reviving the Paneuropa-Union as a matter of course; in mid-July 1946 he sent out invitations to a 'preliminary

---

founded the inter-war Pan-European movement (op. cit., p. 98 f.) and taught history at Columbia University, New York, as a lecturer from 1941 and a professor from 1944; with Prof. Arnold Zurcher he directed a 'Research Seminar for Post-war European Federation'. For the quotation in the text, see ibid., p. 261; for an account of developments from his viewpoint cf. A. J. Zurcher, *The Struggle to Unite Europe 1940–1958*, New York, 1958. Cf. above, Introduction, nn. 53, 62 (the inter-war period), and 111 (Fifth Pan-European Congress, New York, 1943).

[330] 'Declaration of European Inter-Dependence', New York, 14.3.1945, signed by Coudenhove-Kalergi, Fernando de los Rios (former foreign minister of the Spanish Republic), and fourteen other *émigrés* including A. Toscanini and F. Werfel. The constitutional project of 1943 (cf. Introduction, n. 111) was inspired by the Swiss Constitution of 1848 and the Articles of Confederation in early US history, i.e. it provided for a loose union of sovereign states. For Mackay's criticism of 25.11.1946 to Coudenhove-Kalergi, see *Mackay Archives*. On 20.5.1946 Coudenhove and F. de los Rios urged Trygve Lie, Secretary-General of the UN, 'to call a conference of the European Region in accordance with Article 52 of the UN Charter'; this, however, came to nothing (*EM Archives, Bruges*, file on member associations of the European Parliamentary Union).

conference' in September, but cancelled them in mid-August owing to 'deplorable impressions' received on a visit to Paris. At the end of October he visited Churchill at Chartwell and discussed 'the question of reorganizing the old movement under our joint leadership'. He suggested that 'Churchill [should] be our first president, whilst two vice-presidents would be chosen from the ranks of the Socialist and Catholic parties on the Continent. I was to act as secretary-general and Sandys as my deputy.' Churchill and especially Sandys, however, took delaying action on the ground that they wished first to set up a British national committee.[331] Coudenhove must have felt as a result of this discussion that the idea of 'joint leadership' of a 'movement' was unlikely to come to anything.

Instead, in November 1946 he took a step of great tactical importance. As he explains in his autobiography, 'Our main difficulty was that, whilst the people of Europe were clearly ready for federation, their governments, still tainted by pre-war ultra-nationalism, took a different view. Our task was therefore to bring pressure to bear on governments and thus induce them to take the initiative towards Pan-European federation.'[332] The first problem was to discover how many parliamentarians were actually in favour of European unity. In the first week of November Coudenhove began signing identical letters to the members of West-European national parliaments, who numbered about 4,000, explaining that 'We wish to know to what extent the representatives of European democracy approve, in principle, European Federation.' The members were asked to write 'Yes' or 'No' on a card attached to the letter, with the question 'Are you in favour of the establishment of a European federation within the framework

---

[331] Coudenhove-Kalergi (n. 329), op. cit., pp. 264–5 and 269. Mackay to Coudenhove, 19.7.1946, asking for 'more details about the preliminary conference in September'; 27.8.1946, regretting 'the deplorable impressions which you have brought back from Paris. I appreciate the need for putting off the preliminary meeting' (*Mackay Archives*). Sandys to Churchill, 11.10.1946, about Coudenhove's visit 'at the end of this month': 'There is a serious danger that the approaches which we are going to make to European personalities will become confused with Coudenhove's parallel activities. This could best be avoided by finding an honourable place for him within the framework of our new movement. . . . I do not, however, think that he should be offered a position which would give him control of the new organization' (*EM Archives, Bruges*). It was clearly already Sandys's idea that he himself should exercise such 'control'.

[332] Coudenhove-Kalergi (n. 329), p. 266. Nearer the time, in a document prepared for the EPU conference at Gstaad on 9.9.1947, he summed up his ideas as follows. Having discovered in the autumn of 1946 the wide extent of public support for union, he had asked himself: 'How realize the Union of Europe before it is too late? There were three answers to this question: Union by governmental agreements, Union by revolution, Union by parliamentary majorities. My first contacts with members of governments convinced me that it was useless to hope for the moment that governments would take the initiative of the United States of Europe without being assured beforehand of parliamentary support. Confronted with these hesitations of the governments and the dangers of revolutionary action, only the third solution was left: parliamentary initiative, based on the following steps: first, to mobilize parliamentary majorities all over Europe for the cause of Union; then, to organize and coordinate these majorities until they attain the strength necessary to impose their programme on their governments' (*Toward a Constituent Assembly for Europe*, EPU pamphlet, Gstaad, Sept. 1947, p. 7).

of the United Nations?'[333] The letter was addressed to all members of the national parliaments of Belgium, Denmark, Eire, France, Great Britain, Greece, Italy, Luxemburg, the Netherlands, Norway, Sweden, and Switzerland (in the case of Belgium, Denmark, France, the Netherlands, Sweden, and Switzerland it was sent to members of both Chambers). It was not addressed to parliamentarians in the East-European countries under Soviet occupation – not even Czechoslovakia or Hungary, where the elections had been relatively free – and not to German parliamentarians either, 'as there was no German parliament'.[334] Coudenhove-Kalergi, who returned to his teaching job in New York from November 1946 to mid-April 1947, drew up a memorandum in January 1947 (by which time 400 replies had been received) embodying a plan of action:

1. In every Parliament, the Members having given affirmative replies are invited to constitute immediately non-partisan Parliamentary Committees for European Federation, to study and promote the cause of European Union. 2. Each of these Committees ... should aim at attracting a majority of Members of its Parliament, to compel its Government to embrace the cause of European Union ... 3. To merge the activities of these various Parliamentary Committees, a European Congress is being organized for June 1947 at Geneva. 4. This Congress shall take the lead in the campaign for European Federation, ... recommend to the European Governments practical steps to be taken to promote the political and economic union of Europe, ... examine the organization of a European Plebiscite on the issue of Federation, ... [and] constitute itself as a permanent body, meeting periodically and representing a kind of preliminary Parliament for Europe.[335]

Answers to Coudenhove-Kalergi's letter at first came in slowly and in too small a number to justify firm conclusions. By the spring of 1947, however, after he had written to remind those who had not replied, at the same time informing them of the results so far, a remarkably high proportion of answers were received. From the beginning, over 90 per cent of

---

[333] Only some of the letters were signed personally by Coudenhove-Kalergi before he returned to New York on 10.11.1946 for the winter semester; cf. op. cit. (n. 329), p. 272 f. The rest were sent out during November, with a typed signature, by his secretariat at Gstaad, e.g. to Mackay on 20.11.1946 (*Mackay Archives*). To French-speaking and South-European addressees the question was: 'Êtes-vous en faveur de la Fédération Européenne dans le cadre de l'O.N.U.?'

[334] Letter of 14.4.1954 from Coudenhove-Kalergi to W. Cornides (*DGAP Archives*, E 790/corr.). Coudenhove's enquiry continued until the end of 1947; in August he addressed it also to members of both Austrian chambers, thus raising the total of those consulted to 4,387. There were elected *Landtage* in the US Zone of Germany from December 1946, in the British Zone from April 1947, and in the French Zone from May, but apparently Coudenhove gave no thought to consulting these German representatives. For his firm decision not to consult members of parliament in Soviet-occupied Eastern Europe, cf. at n. 338.

[335] 'Memorandum on the organization of a Parliament for Europe', New York, 27.1.1947 (two typed pages, probably sent to Sandys, as it is among his early papers in *EM Archives, Bruges*); also op. cit. (n. 329), pp. 274–5. The preliminary parliament was to 'Elect a Council of Europe, to serve as a permanent advisory body to the Governments and to the United Nations; this Council ... shall constitute the Continent's supreme moral authority'. Curiously, after these 'preliminary' provisions nothing is said about the actual federation, a constituent assembly, etc.; can Coudenhove have reverted to confederal ideas after his return to New York? For the partial endorsement of his ideas by the Gstaad conference on 9.9.1947, cf. chap. III/5, pp. 607–14.

those who replied were in favour; but the gradual increase in the number of answers was closely linked to events on the world political stage. Up to 20 January only 400, a bare tenth of those questioned, had replied; by 12 February, 550; by 8 March, 617, whereof 605 'Yes' and 12 'No'; by 28 April, 660, whereof 646 'Yes' and 14 'No'.[336] Then, in response to Coudenhove's reminder but evidently also to the failure of the Foreign Ministers' meeting at Moscow, the number of answers doubled by the end of May to reach 1,329, only 39 of which were 'Noes'. Coudenhove, who had returned to Europe at the end of April, announced this result in June to a press conference at Berne, with a table which showed that there were now substantial differences between the respective countries. The most enthusiastic deputies were those of the Italian Constituent Assembly, of whom 57 per cent had replied, all affirmatively. Then came a middle group:

France	Assemblée Nationale	44 per cent 'Yes'	1 per cent 'No'
Belgium	Chambre	44 per cent 'Yes'	0 per cent 'No'
Greece	Constituent Assembly	41 per cent 'Yes'	0 per cent 'No'
Netherlands	Second (Lower) Chamber	39 per cent 'Yes'	5 per cent 'No'
Switzerland	National Council (Lower House)	39 per cent 'Yes'	3 per cent 'No'
Luxemburg	Chambre des Députés	38 per cent 'Yes'	2 per cent 'No'

The percentage of replies from the Upper Houses or Senates was somewhat less throughout. The North-European countries showed decidedly less enthusiasm: the figures for Eire were 25 per cent Yes, 4 per cent No; for the UK 17 per cent Yes, ½ per cent No; for Denmark, Norway, and Sweden an average of only 8 per cent Yes, 2 per cent No. If the results thus attained by June 1947 were to be regarded as an 'indirect plebiscite', they did not as yet support Coudenhove's inference that 'the people of Europe were clearly ready for federation'; for northern Europe they rather proved the contrary. None the less, in the countries that later formed the European Coal and Steel Community about 43 per cent of those questioned had, by this date, seen fit to express themselves publicly in favour of a federation of Europe, and these included such prominent politicians as Vincent Auriol, the Italian President Einaudi, Paul Reynaud, Paul-Boncour, Bonomi, van Zeeland, Count Sforza, and others. As a good propagandist, Coudenhove made the most of the fact that 97 per cent of the replies were affirmative.[335] He was vexed, however, by searching questions put by Dr Brugmans at the press conference:

Brugmans asked, firstly, why the East-European countries had been left out: 'Don't you think that in this way you are, in effect, working for a "Western bloc"?

[336] Cf. DPD report, 23.1.1947; letter from Coudenhove to King-Hall, 12.2.1947; van Vassenhove, reporting information from Coudenhove dated 8.3.1947, in *L'Action fédéraliste européenne*, vol. 5, April 1947, p. 71; appeal of 28.4.1947 from 'on board the *Queen Elizabeth*', cf. chap. III, n. 366.

[337] Cf. Coudenhove-Kalergi (n. 329), p. 275. A typed table of the replies, dated 'Gstaad, 1st of June 1947', was evidently handed out by Coudenhove-Kalergi at his press conference on 20 June at the

... Is it right for pioneers of a United Europe to encourage people to regard the unhappy division of the Continent as a *fait accompli*?' His second question was probably even less welcome: 'Do you not think that your efforts ought, logically and practically, to be integrated into the federal movement as a whole, more especially the Union Européenne des Fédéralistes, which is today the body representing organized European federalism?' Coudenhove was evidently displeased, and on the following day wrote to Sandys: 'Brugmans behaved very unfairly at my Press Conference ... I had the strong impression that he stays with Russia aclose [*sic*] ..., trying to interpret my action as anti-Russian. I therefore don't wish to have anything to do with Mr Brugmans.'[338] Coudenhove, agreeing on this point with Churchill and van Zeeland, had in fact made up his mind from the start that it was only realistic to limit his movement to the West and accept that Soviet-occupied Eastern Europe must be written off for the time being at least. In the matter of desiring a genuine federation, as his subsequent conferences showed clearly, his thinking was much closer to that of the UEF, but he was divided from it by his attitude towards Eastern Europe and above all by his claim to leadership.[339]

After the announcement of the Marshall Plan, however, further answers to Coudenhove's enquiry were received, and by September 1947 the figures indeed amounted to a strong vote for federalism on the part of Continental West-European members of parliament. The total rose to 1,735, of which only 52 were 'Noes'. From the Scandinavian countries, it is true, only about 15 per cent of deputies had replied by this time, and only about 12 per cent affirmatively; from Eire 25 per cent answered 'Yes', and from the British House of Commons 26 per cent. It would have been well to pay serious attention to these low figures instead of concealing them in the unaltered average of 97 per cent 'Yeses'. But as far as devastated Continental Europe was concerned, the figures were certainly impressive: 64 per cent and 58 per cent of the Italian and Green Constituent Assemblies, 56 per cent of the Luxemburg deputies, 53 per cent of the Dutch, and 50 per cent of the National Assemblies of France, Belgium, and Switzerland

---

Palace Hotel, Berne (invitation to Brugmans, 14.6.1947; copy of table in *BEF Archives,* Brugmans corr.); this is not to be confused with the tabulation of the more nearly final results printed in Sept./Oct. 1947 (cf. n. 340). The interim results published on 20.6.1947 were reported in the *Neue Zürcher Zeitung,* 22.6.1947, and *Federal News,* No. 149, Aug. 1947, p. 10 (with somewhat different figures, as in the case of countries with two chambers a single total was given).

[338] Brugmans's questions were prepared by him as 'Trois questions à M. le Comte Coudenhove-Kalergi, Berne 20.VI.1947' (*BEF Archives,* Brugmans corr.). From Coudenhove's letter to Sandys, 21.6.1947, it appears that Léon van Vassenhove introduced Brugmans to him beforehand (*EM Archives, Bruges,* file on member associations of the EPU). Sandys was no doubt pleased that the incident made it more difficult for Coudenhove to join forces with the UEF.

[339] On the later conferences and further friction with UEF, cf. pp. 610 f., 664, and 680 f. Ernst von Schenck had the impression from conversations with Coudenhove that he regarded the UEF as positively sinister: he never understood its roots in the Resistance movements, and could not accept the fact that people like Spinelli and Frenay were nowadays more important to the unity movement than he himself (information from *von Schenck,* 23.8.1961).

had declared themselves in favour of European federation.[340] These percentages of replies to an enquiry from a private individual showed that to a majority of Continental deputies the idea of European federation as the proper lesson to be drawn from the catastrophe of World War II appeared no longer Utopian, but feasible as well as desirable.

(C) EAST EUROPEAN INTEREST IN FEDERALISM AND EUROPEAN UNION

For three main reasons it can be taken as certain that, at the period we are dealing with, the idea of European federation enjoyed considerable popular support in the East-European countries, although this was firmly opposed by the Soviet rulers of the area and was not allowed to express itself in the form of associations.

1. In the first place, the experience of the inter-war period and the conclusions drawn from it in the 1930s were fully present to the minds of thinking East Europeans in the aftermath of the Second World War. Before 1914 the inhabitants of this area, surrounded by Germans and Italians, Russians and Turks, were accustomed to living in multinational empires, organized to some extent on pronouncedly federal principles; and the most prominent representatives of the East-European national movements aspired to federal solutions rather than full sovereignty. The peace treaties of 1919–20, however, bestowed on the area the doubtful blessing of dividing it into ten sovereign states – Estonia, Latvia, Lithuania, Poland, Czechoslovakia, Hungary, Romania, Bulgaria, Yugoslavia, and Albania, with a total population of 99.3 million in 1930, flanked by Finland (3.4 million) and Greece (6.2 million). The Balkanization of the area was at first greeted enthusiastically by the dominant race in each country, and correspondingly lamented by millions of their subjects belonging to national minorities. The peasant parties, the intelligentsia, and the workers' parties, which were still narrowly based, made valiant efforts to create national democracies on the Western model; but these failed owing to the underdevelopment of the middle class and above all the economic fragmentation which stood in the way of industrialization and its modernizing social consequences. All these states except Czechoslovakia evolved

---

[340] Quoted from the most widely distributed printed table (in practically all archives) in R. Coudenhove-Kalergi, *Vers un parlement de l'Europe*, Gstaad, n.d. (end of Sept. 1947, general report on Gstaad conference, 8–10.9.1947), p. 3. There are three further versions of this table, differing according to dates: (1) position at the end of August, in *Rapport sur l'union parlementaire européenne*, Gstaad, 7.9.1947 (presented to the conference), when there were 118 fewer replies; (2) position at the beginning of December, in the English version of the report on the conference: *Towards a Constituent Assembly for Europe*, Gstaad, n.d. (Dec. 1947), p. 3 – with 37 more 'Yeses'; (3) position at the beginning of 1948, in Coudenhove-Kalergi, *Kampf um Europa*, Zurich, 1949, p. 267, with a further 55 'Yeses'; the affirmative votes from the Belgian Chamber and the French Assembly had now risen to 53 per cent. But the above-quoted version dating from the end of Sept. 1947 was the most widespread at the time.

by degrees towards semi-fascist regimes of an absolutist type, monarchical or presidential.[341] Progressive parties and the educated class had meanwhile come to realize that the division of the area into so many small states was a mistake and an obstacle to economic and social development. In 1924 the Communists of South-Eastern Europe, meeting in Vienna, put forward plans for a Balkan federation; from 1932 onwards the agrarian parties held federalist congresses and made plans for federations embracing the whole or part of Eastern Europe. Not only this, but Coudenhove's Pan-European Union and the plan for a European customs union, put forward by the Hungarian economist Elmer Hantos, were represented by larger associations of sympathizers in the East-European capitals than anywhere else. Even among the ruling oligarchies, although federalist ideas were long hindered by the 1919 division into victors and vanquished and by outdated dreams of 'Greater Poland', 'Greater Bulgaria', 'Greater Romania', etc., plans for union began at last to be considered: e.g. in March 1939 the Polish foreign minister József Beck and his Romanian opposite number Grigore Gafencu contemplated a federation of the whole of Eastern Europe. Thanks to the inter-war experience of these small national states and their collapse in 1939–40, the need for federal union was scarcely challenged as a basic assumption of political thinking.[342]

2. As a consequence of this, the East-European politicians and intellectuals who escaped into exile from German-occupied Europe in 1940–4, and the Resistance groups who went on fighting on home ground, emphasized their belief in European federation as the only solution for the future. Only a brief sketch can be given here; but the leaders in exile in Britain – Poles, Czechs, Yugoslavs, and Greeks – showed a stronger sense of urgency than the exiled West-European governments, and tried at an early stage to translate their ideas into practical suggestions. On 4 November 1941 the Polish Prime Minister Sikorski and his government put forward 'Theses for a Polish-Czechoslovak Federation' with a fully responsible federal parliament and a federal government for economic matters,

---

[341] Population figures from W. Köllmann, *Bevölkerung und Raum in Neuerer und Neuester Zeit* (*Bevölkerungs-Ploetz*, Vol. 4), Würzburg, 1965³, pp. 170, 202, 212, and 214. The most instructive sketch is still W. Conze, 'Die Strukturkrise des östlichen Mitteleuropas vor und nach 1919', *VfZG*, 1 (1953), pp. 319–38. Cf. K. Renner, *Das Selbstbestimmungsrecht der Nationen in besonderer Anwendung auf Österreich*, Leipzig/Vienna, 1918²; O. Bauer, *Die Nationalitätenfrage und die Sozialdemokratie*, Vienna, 1924²; W. Jaksch, *Europas Weg nach Potsdam. Schuld und Schicksal im Donauraum*, Stuttgart, 1958; detailed analysis by countries from 1919 to 1939 in L. S. Stavrianos, *The Balkans since 1453*, New York/Chicago, 1958, pp. 545–760.

[342] See the useful documentation in M. Hodža (Czechoslovak Prime Minister, 1935–8), *Federation in Central Europe, Reflections and Reminiscences*, London/New York, 1942; also especially F. Gross, *Crossroads of Two Continents. A Democratic Federation of East–Central Europe*, New York (Columbia), 1945, pp. 5–20 and 89–102 (texts); R. Schlesinger, *Federalism in Central and Eastern Europe*, London (Oxford University Press), 1945 (533 pages); J. Kühl, *Föderationspläne in Donauraum und in Ostmitteleuropa*, Munich, 1958, pp. 16–102; R. Wierer, *Der Föderalismus im Donauraum*, Graz/Köln, 1960, pp. 11–177 and 197 (Beck/Gafencu); L. S. Stavrianos, *Balkan Federation. A History of the Movement towards Balkan Unity in Modern Times*, Hamden, Conn., 1944.

defence, and foreign affairs; this was to be open to accession by other states, and was conceived as part of an equally desirable all-European federation.[343] At an ILO conference on the same day Yugoslav, Czechoslovak, Polish, and Greek delegates, representing governments, employers, and workers, signed and published a declaration of solidarity and co-operation. A Greek–Yugoslav treaty for a Balkan union was signed on 15 January 1942, and on 23 January the Poles and Czechs signed an agreement to form a confederation. At the same time all four governments set up a Central- and Eastern-European Planning Board in New York to prepare plans for an East-European federation as an element in a federation of all Europe. Beneš, who for reasons of internal Czechoslovak politics was the least federally minded of the exiled leaders, withdrew from co-operation in these activities after the Soviet government expressed its disapproval on 16 July 1942; at the end of 1943 he signed an alliance with the Soviet Union, the first link in the system of Soviet bilateral pacts with East-European countries. Meanwhile the Planning Board in New York continued its activities, which were paralleled by the 'Danubian Club' in London.[344] The exiled politicians were encouraged by many expressions of agreement on the part of Resistance movements in their home territory, from Yugoslavia, Poland, and Czechoslovakia. The Polish underground journal *Nowe Drogi* wrote: 'Federated Europe must be composed of federated regions'; an underground Czech paper added: 'The Polish–Czechoslovak union must not be allowed to become the basis for any imperialist designs. It must be one of the stable foundations of the future federation of free European nations, based on peace, security, and democracy.'[345] The Polish Resistance movement in particular laid stress on a future European federation.

The basic 'Programme for a national Poland', drawn up in 1941 by 'representatives of the workers' party, the peasants' party and the democratic intellectuals' of the civilian leadership of the Resistance has already been quoted: 'The Polish Republic will be a member of the Federation of Free European Peoples.'[346] In

---

[343] The Polish government's 'Theses' of 4.11.1941 were published for the first time in W. Lipgens, *Europa-Föderationspläne der Widerstandsbewegungen 1940–1945*, Munich, 1968, pp. 445–8, with commentary; ibid., pp. 445 n. and 477 f., statements by Sikorski and other Polish ministers showing their readiness for an *all*-European federation composed of regional sub-federations.

[344] For German texts of these treaties etc., with indication of original printed sources, see Lipgens, *Föderationspläne* (n. 1343), Appendix, Nos. 149–52, 155, 156, 165, 167, and 176, with commentary; analysis and fullest English version in Gross, *Crossroads* (n. 342), pp. 17–85 and 102–53 (texts); the most reliable summary in P. S. Wandycz, *Czechoslovak–Polish Confederation and the Great Powers 1940–1943*, Bloomington, Indiana, 1956; cf. also Kühl (n. 342), pp. 106–12; Stavrianos, *Balkan Federation* (n. 342); P. Jordan, *Central Union of Europe*, New York, 1944.

[345] All cited in Gross (n. 342), pp. 22–5. Gross, who was secretary-general of the Planning Board set up by the four governments in exile, added. 'These are typical of numerous quotations which could be cited from different underground papers, all stressing the fact that only through federation can the mutual problems of these states be solved.'

[346] Already quoted more fully in Introduction, n. 79. For a full German translation of the programme, based on the compilation *Z Pola Walki. Cele i drogi podziemnego ruchu robotniczego w Polsce*

444 Revival of Plans for Federation

February 1942 the Polish Socialist Party declared that: 'Almost every organ of opinion, whether official or underground, and every citizen of Europe, be he a German, a Pole, a Frenchman, a Belgian, a Croat or a Czech, today thinks in terms of a coming European Federation ... It is a task of our revolutionary movement to create solid foundations for a European federation ... The 'state' enclosed in a system of political and economic frontiers, fenced in by a system of laws and military power, is an idea that has had its day.' Other Resistance journals, large and small, took up the idea of federation, and a periodical entitled *Blok Środkowo-Europejski* (Central European Bloc) was created especially to popularize it: 'Central Europe' was seen in 1944 as part of 'a union of Europe to be created by the merging of separate blocs', an element in an all-European federation.[347]

After all the experience of nation states in Eastern Europe, and the unanimous conclusions drawn from it by leaders in exile and in the Resistance, it must be regarded as highly probable that, had it not been for the Red Army occupation and the subsequent Soviet hegemony, the members of any parliament freely elected in 1946 would have returned an even higher vote for European federation than did those of Western Europe – or Greece – in reply to Coudenhove's enquiry. As things were, however, Soviet hegemony soon developed into absolute domination; exiled politicians from the West were only permitted to return in exceptional cases; the non-Communist Resistance movements were disavowed and destroyed; minority Communist parties were enabled to seize power by 'national front' tactics; national enmities were deliberately fomented by the expulsion of minorities and the displacement of Poland to the west; and any rallying of forces in favour of federalism of any kind was rigorously opposed. 'In order to exploit to the full the national political structure of the Eastern bloc, all attempts to create a Danubian and Balkan federation, not to speak of a wider East-European federation including Poland, were to be stamped on'[348] – let alone any ideas of a federation embracing the whole of Europe.

3. Nevertheless – and this is a third set of relevant facts – various pieces of evidence from individual sources, small in themselves but collectively convincing, show that even at the worst period of Soviet domination in the

---

1939–1942 (From the Field of Battle. Aims and Ways of the Underground Workers' Movement in Poland), to which reference is made in Lipgens, *Föderationspläne,* p. 320, n. 3, see C. Klessmann, 'Das "Programm Volkspolens" von 1941', *VfZG,* 21 (1973), pp. 103–14 (cf. p. 104, n. 5).

[347] These references must suffice here; cf. 'VI. Europa-Pläne im polnischen Widerstand', Lipgens, *Föderationspläne* (n. 343), pp. 311–37, a compilation made possible by the fact that documents of the Polish Resistance reached London regularly via Sweden. Similar evidence for the Resistance groups of other East-European countries cannot be furnished, as the non-Communist organizations which predominated during the war were disavowed and denigrated after 1945; many of their documents were destroyed, and the rest are not accessible. The Geneva Declaration of May 1944 on all-European federation was the work, among others, of Polish, Czechoslovak, and Yugoslav (Titoist) Resistance groups: cf. chap. I/2, n. 56.

[348] Cf. the summary by B. Meissner, 'Sowjetische Hegemonie und osteuropäische Föderation', in G. Ziebura (ed.), *Nationale Souveränität oder übernationale Integration?,* Berlin, 1966, pp. 57–85, esp. p. 64 f. The following notes gives references for each country.

East-European countries, federalist sympathies still survived. At first they could be expressed in letters, conversations, and private meetings; but even in the first coalition governments the Communists regularly assured themselves of the ministries of the interior, justice, and information, so as to be able to use the police, law courts, and mass media against rival forces and ideas whenever necessary. It was a grave psychological handicap that bourgeois or Socialist groups who were traditionally sympathetic to federation clung to the hope that if they conformed completely to Moscow's line in foreign affairs they would still be allowed to play a part in domestic politics. Consequently they made no independent move on the international plane – an attitude which did not save them from political extinction in 1947–8.[349] None the less, we may record a number of significant indications. The Paris branch of the old Union Économique et Douanière Européenne (UEDE) had word that its branches in Prague and Budapest had been revived. Gafencu, the former Romanian foreign minister, who was in exile from 1941 onwards, declared at a press conference that 'The idea of a federated Europe has aroused the keenest interest in the countries of the East.' Professor Jászi of Hungary, who received a grant from the American Philosophical Society enabling him to tour the Danubian countries, reported that:

'After the collapse of Hitler's "New Order" there was a widespread desire for federal co-operation among the Danube countries. This was the view of all competent observers with whom I spoke on my travels. People understood that chaos and collapse would ensue once again if the nations followed their old policy of national rivalry', and would once more become 'tools of the imperialist powers'. These impressions were confirmed by S. Borsody: 'So many of us in Central and Southern Europe felt during the German occupation that the atmosphere was more and more favourable to a federation.' Many East-European *émigré* politicians wrote to the same effect in 1947.[350] The Swiss Europa-Union apparently received enough letters by the summer of 1945 to justify creating a 'Section for the Danubian and Balkan countries'; issues of its journal from December 1945 to August 1947 carried, under this heading, a routine statement that 'Measures were taken to spread the European idea in the Balkans and Danubian countries.'[351]

[349] Cf. above, chap. II/1, n. 9; H. Seton-Watson, *The East European Revolution*, London, 1950; E. Birke and R. Neumann, *Die Sowjetisierung Ost–Mitteleuropas*, Frankfurt, 1959; F. Fejtö, *Histoire des démocraties populaires*, Paris, 1952. Stalin's bilateral defence treaties with each East-European country forbade the signatories to enter into coalitions directed against the interests of the other party, so that Moscow could put a stop to any moves towards federation. On 29.10.1946 Stalin declared that the Soviet Union at that time had altogether sixty divisions in Germany, Austria, Hungary, Bulgaria, Romania, and Poland – excluding, of course, the hosts of secret police; cf. Hoensch (n. 7), p. 399.
[350] UEDE report in *Le Document fédéraliste*, No. 4, 1.7.1947 (*Gérard Archives*); Gafencu in *New York Times*, 28.10.1946. O. Jászi, 'Russia Balks Danube Unionists', *Freedom and Union* (ed. C. Streit), July 1948; S. Borsody, 'Let Free Danubian Federalists Unite', ibid., Feb. 1949; both articles were sent to all leading politicians of the Danubian countries who were in exile and were reprinted with their approving comments, ibid., Sept. 1950 (quotation from Jászi, p. 3, from Borsody, p. 7; back-translations in the text). Cf. chap. VI/2 (in vol. 2) on indications of support from politicians in exile.
[351] In every number of *Der Europäer. Organ der Schweizer Europa-Union* from Vol. 12, No. 6, June 1945 onwards, the column 'Aus der Bewegung' mentioned a Section for the Danubian and Balkan

The following paragraphs give a brief account of the situation in each country, which the combined efforts of many East-European historians may one day make it possible to complete.

In *Poland*, which Stalin was determined from the outset to keep under his thumb and which was initially treated like an enemy country, with a massive occupation force, wholesale arrests, and deportations, the Soviet grip was so firm that no evidence of pro-European sentiment can be adduced for the darkest period in 1945-7. The Nazis had decimated the Polish upper classes (one in every five adult Polish citizens was killed in the war) and aroused a universal hatred of Germany, which played into the hands of the Communists with their policy of submission to the Soviet Union. Those members of the Resistance who had not perished in the Warsaw rising were persecuted by the new rulers, and their leaders, after a show trial in Moscow, were sentenced to labour camps from which they did not return. Leaders of the Socialist and Peasant parties were tortured and murdered by the NKVD and its Polish henchmen. Mikolajczyk and his fellow-representatives of the London government-in-exile, who were taken into the new Polish government in July 1945 at the instance of the Western powers, could achieve nothing against the sixteen ministers who depended on Moscow; Mikolajczyk's Peasant Party was harassed by every method of terrorism until 1947, when faked elections sealed its doom and Mikolajczyk fled to the West.[352] No politician opposed to the regime could afford to risk what little freedom of action he still enjoyed by supporting federalist ideas which were known to be anathema to the Soviet Union. At most, those who travelled abroad might secretly express their sympathies. Brugmans, who applied for a Polish entry visa, did not even receive an answer.[353] Professor Wandycz, in his book published in 1956, could not do more than infer that as 89 per cent of the *émigré* Poles who were questioned on the subject were in favour of federation, the position in

---

countries, represented by Walter Kocher, member of the executive, Berne; from No. 12, Dec. 1945, the report included the statement quoted above; then, from Vol. 14, No. 10, Sept. 1947, all mention of the Section suddenly disappeared. It should also be noted here that the Berlin Paneuropa-Bund, after its meeting with East Europeans in Berlin (cf. n. 233) reported: 'We can state with certainty that the Eastern countries . . . are extremely interested in a federation of all Europe' (Bulletin of the Föderalistische Union, Cologne, Nos. 3/4, May 1947).

[352] H. Seton-Watson (n. 349), pp. 171-8; S. Mikolajczyk, *The Pattern of Soviet Domination*, London, 1948 (= *The Rape of Poland. Pattern of Soviet Aggression*, New York, 1948); G. Rhode, 'Polen als "Volksdemokratie" ', in *Osteuropa-Handbuch. Polen* (ed. Markert), Cologne, 1959, pp. 223-35; Z. K. Brzezinski, *The Soviet Bloc. Unity and Conflict*, Cambridge (Mass.), 1960, pp. 9-14; Hoensch (n. 7), p. 392 f.

[353] According to the then chief medical officer in Thuringia, several Polish doctors who came there in the autumn of 1945 to ask for antibiotics left behind by the Americans spoke with great earnestness in private of the need for European union (information from *Unger*, 7.12.1974). Brugmans was able to expound UEF principles to the Polish ambassador at The Hague in April 1947 and sent him documents on the subject on 6 May, but received no answer to his request of 14 June for a visa to enable him to visit Poland and organize a Polish delegation to the Montreux congress, although he referred to the UEF's opposition to 'Western bloc' ideas (*BEF Archives*, Brugmans corr.).

Poland itself could not be entirely different; this was confirmed by refugees from behind the Iron Curtain, but there could be no question of such ideas finding overt expression there.[354]

Czechoslovakia was treated much more benignly by Stalin up to the end of 1947. President Beneš, who when in exile had backed away from federation plans as soon as the Russians objected to them, lost no opportunity of declaring that Eastern Europe belonged to the Soviet sphere of influence and that he intended to be a true ally of the Soviet Union. He acted in voluntary anticipation of possible Soviet demands, when in Moscow in March 1945 he undertook to reserve a third of the seats in his post-war government for members of the Czech Communist party. Like many of his compatriots, he was motivated by the Western 'betrayal' of Czechoslovakia at Munich in 1938 and by gratitude to the Red Army for bringing 'liberation' from the east. The Communists under Gottwald's premiership initially pursued a moderate policy, bringing the army, police, and local 'National Committees' under their control without the use of terror; thanks to this and to their management of the allocation of lands in the Sudeten area from which the Germans had been expelled, they succeeded in polling 38 per cent of the vote in the free election of May 1946. The three other parties – the Social Democrats, the National Socialists (Beneš), and the Christian Democrats – were for close co-operation with the USSR but hoped to preserve their freedom in home affairs and to maintain relations with the Western countries, which still accounted for two-thirds of Czechoslovakia's trade.[355] These parties showed a cautious interest in the European idea as represented by the UEF. Brugmans twice received an entry visa through the Czechoslovak minister at The Hague in order to go to Prague and assist in founding a member association of the UEF. His first visit, from 1 to 4 April 1947, was 'promising' and led to many conversations.[356] Reporting on its success, he wrote:

'Anyone who starts a conversation in Prague on European unity' will find 'on the one hand lively agreement, but on the other a certain reserve ... Our Czechoslovak friends do not want to be cut off from the West; but the bitter experiences of 1938 are by no means forgotten ... People from the West are listened to, but the country's foreign policy is orientated Eastward ... What European federalism can offer Czechoslovakia' – this was evidently the argument

---

[354] Wandycz (n. 344), p. 122.
[355] H. Seton-Watson (n. 349), pp. 179–90; Brzezinski (n. 352), p. 18 f.; a thorough account in J. Korbel, *The Communist Subversion of Czechoslovakia 1938–1948*. Princeton, NJ, 1959. Early hopes typically expressed in an article by a leader of the Czech Christian Democrats, Frantisek Glaser, 'La Tchécoslovaquie, trait d'union entre l'Ouest et l'Est', *L'Action fédéraliste européenne*, No. 4, Jan. 1946, p. 32 f.
[356] Brugmans, 'Het begin ...' (n. 43), p. 14: 'We had received from Salinger some useful addresses of people then working for Pan-Europe', sc. in Prague. Cf. Salinger's letter of 21.3.1947 to Dr J. M. Kučera announcing Brugmans's visit 'to found a Czechoslovak Section of Europeesche Actie' (*BEF Archives,* Brugmans corr.).

used by Brugmans himself in Prague – 'is the following: there will be no attempt to detach the country from the USSR or Slav solidarity', but 'the object is to keep the Slavic world in Europe open in both directions and not confront these nations with a choice between Russia and the West. A United Europe will make it possible to work with both'; it was also the only answer to the German problem. This understanding approach on Brugmans's part evidently met with much agreement.[357]

In July, however, when all four parties in Prague declared for the acceptance of Marshall aid, Stalin showed how limited their freedom was by peremptorily ordering the Cabinet to reverse its decision. When Brugmans visited Prague for the second time on 3–7 August 1947, having announced his intention of discussing with Beneš 'European solidarity between the countries of the West and East', he found 'almost all doors closed. The country already seemed to be living under the threat of imminent disaster' – and, sure enough, the Communist seizure of power in February 1948 was the prelude to harsh measures in all fields.[358]

In *Hungary*, as in Czechoslovakia, Stalin began by ruling without the terrorist methods he had used in Poland, and tried to achieve his aims by 'popular front' tactics. Before the elections of November 1945, it is true, Marshal Voroshilov demanded that the four permitted parties submit a single list, but he yielded when the Smallholders' party stood out for a 'competitive' election. In a free vote that party scored 57 per cent of the poll, the Communists only 17 per cent, the Socialists (already infiltrated by crypto-Communists) 17 per cent, and the 'National Peasants' 7 per cent. In February 1946 Tildy, the Smallholders' leader, became the first president of the Republic, while Ferenc Nagy, also a Smallholder, became prime minister. There seemed to be a prospect of relative freedom and a chance for plural democracy, but this was frustrated when the Soviet occupation authorities insisted that the ministry of the interior in the new government – i.e. control of the police – should be given to a Communist. For the next eighteen months the Smallholders, despite their progressive

---

[357] H. Brugmans, 'Tsjechoslovakije: Raakvlak van twee Europa's', in *Je Maintiendrai. Weekblad voor Personalistisch Socialisme*, 2.5.1947. In letters of thanks dated 24.4.1947 to Dr K. Karnel (economic adviser to the People's Party), Dr W. Beneš (head of the UN department in the Prague foreign ministry), and Dr Milos Stransky (National Socialist, secretary of the Association pour les Relations Étrangères), Brugmans told them that he now understood much better the difficulty of 'convincing people that we really do not intend to form a kind of anti-Russian Fifth Column'. He thanks them for their understanding of his contention that 'only by the practical solidarity of our whole Continent can we prevent a policy of forming blocs', and hoped that a Czechoslovak delegation would take part in the UEF congress at Montreux. He also thanked Stransky for having been allowed to address the Central Committee of the Association (*BEF Archives*, Brugmans corr.).
[358] Quotation in Brugmans, 'Het begin . . .' (n. 43), p. 14; letters announcing visit to Stransky, 20 July, and Beneš, 29 July 1947, in *BEF Archives*, Brugmans corr. For the seizure of power in Feb. 1948, see H. Ripka, *Le Coup de Prague. Une révolution préfabriquée*, Paris, 1949 (= *Czechoslovakia Enslaved*, London, 1950); E. Taborsky, *Communism in Czechoslovakia 1948–1960*, Princeton, NJ, 1961; J. K. Hoensch, *Geschichte der Tschechoslowakischen Republik 1918–1965* (= Urban Bücher, Bd. 96), Stuttgart, 1966, Chap. VII, p. 129 f.

social policy, were harassed by methods of arrest and torture, forced 'confessions', trumped-up charges of war crimes, etc. Finally, in June 1947, Ferenc Nagy was compelled to resign on the strength of a faked 'confession', and the Communist seizure of power was rapidly completed.[359] Shortly afterwards Nagy, in exile, wrote that: 'If Hungary and the eastern European countries had received even a tiny share of the support which is now granted by the people of the United States to western Europe, then popular democracy could have victoriously resisted the Communist attempts at subjugation.' Nagy also declared himself to be in favour 'of a federation of the peoples of Europe', and this was evidently not a mere piece of hindsight.[360] During the period of relative freedom, at least until the summer of 1946, many Hungarian voices were permitted to speak out in favour of federalism; one of its most untiring advocates was Paul von Auer, chairman of the foreign-affairs committee of the Hungarian parliament.

In 1932–8 von Auer was chairman of the Comité Permanent pour le Rapprochement Économique des Pays Danubiens, on which Austria, Czechoslovakia, Hungary, Romania, and Yugoslavia 'were represented by outstanding statesmen'; an article he wrote at the time in the *New Commonwealth Quarterly* concluded with the words: 'The only constructive solution, in this author's opinion, is to unite the Danubian states in a federal system.'[361] On 2 October 1945 he argued for federation in an article in the Budapest newspaper *Új Magyarország* entitled 'Permanent Peace and Co-operation in the Danube Basin'. In January 1946 he argued in parliament in favour of establishing joint commissions of all the Danubian countries for the settlement of common problems, from which a subordinate organization of the United States of Europe might one day emerge; soon afterwards, he addressed the Budapest Foreign Affairs Society in a similar vein. In the *New York Times* of 20 February 1946 he urged the great powers not to miss the chance afforded by the forthcoming peace treaties but to abolish all customs and economic barriers in Europe, to set up a 'Danubian "Tennessee Valley" scheme' and to organize 'periodical meetings of foreign, finance and economic ministers

---

[359] Cf. Seton-Watson (n. 349), pp. 190–202. Abundant material for 1944–8 in S. D. Kertész, *Diplomacy in a Whirlpool. Hungary between Nazi Germany and Soviet Russia,* Notre Dame, Ind., 1953; for 1947–56 F. A. Váli, *Rift and Revolt in Hungary,* Harvard, 1961.

[360] F. Nagy, *The Struggle behind the Iron Curtain,* New York, 1948, p. 453 (where he adds that if a measure of support had been given, European democracy would today extend to the western frontier of the Soviet Union) and p. 460: 'Historically, economically and culturally, Europe is one and indivisible': international understanding, today prevented by Soviet oppression, must lead to a 'United States of Europe'.

[361] Cf. Kertész (n. 359), p. 32 f. (describing his conversations at the time with Beneš, Krofts, Hodza, etc.) and p. 202. P. von Auer, 'The Problem of Danubian Co-operation', *New Commonwealth Quarterly*, 3, No. 1, June 1937: 'The mistake of those responsible for the peace of 1919 was not so much the dissolution of Austria–Hungary, which was already taking place thanks to the activity of the various national movements, but their failure to realize that any future structure in the area would have to fulfil the functions of the old Empire to prevent the Balkanization of that part of Europe.' Cf. also P. von Auer, 'Das neue Mitteleuropa', *New Commonwealth Quarterly,* 4, 1938, p. 267 f. At the inaugural meeting of the Committee in Budapest on 12.2.1932 Gafencu, the Romanian foreign minister, expressly referred to the necessity of a federal system (information from von Auer, 13.6.1964).

and bank presidents as well as meetings of parliamentary delegations'. In April 1946, in the official Budapest journal *New Hungary*, he called for the realization of Kossuth's plan for a 'Danubian confederation' by way of 'institutional cooperation' in joint committees to deal with all important questions, with a 'Danubian Court of Arbitration' under UN supervision. Evidently as a result of this, the Soviet element of the Control Commission saw to it that Auer was removed to the post of Hungarian minister in Paris, where he became a political exile after Nagy's fall.[362]

The Ferenc Nagy government endeavoured, as far as it was allowed, to restore close relations with Hungary's neighbours; it made plans for customs unions, organized Hungaro-Romanian cultural weeks, etc. Sulyok, a politician expelled from the Smallholders' party under Soviet pressure in March 1946, was given permission to form a 'Freedom party' of his own, but this was temporarily revoked in July because he had dared to speak in parliament in favour of a United States of Europe.[363]

In *Romania* the government was taken over in March 1945 – at the behest of Vyshinsky, the Soviet deputy foreign minister, who paid a special visit to Bucharest – by the National Democratic Front, which was dominated by Communists but included left-wing Social Democrats and a liberal group headed by Tatarescu; the prime minister was the fellow-traveller Petru Groza. The Communists, as usual, had secured the ministries of justice and the interior, and used the weapons of police terror and charges of war crimes against their political enemies. Groza carried out agrarian reform, which was overdue, and, himself a Transylvanian, was interested in a harmonious peace settlement with Hungary and Romania's other neighbours. Tatarescu, as foreign minister, supported all plans for customs union etc. until he was forced from power by the Communists in November 1947.[364] The National Peasant party, still permitted in 1947, was led by Iuliu Maniu, who had been prime minister three times between 1928 and 1933 and 'never ceased repeating that there

---

[362] All information from *von Auer*, 13.6.1964, with documents: text of *New York Times* article of 20.2.1946 and P. von Auer, 'Hungary and the Danubian Basin', in *New Hungary. A Fortnightly Review for South-Eastern Europe*, Vol. i, No. 1 (Officina Press, Budapest), 15.4.1947, with the words: 'The initiative and assistance of the Big Three is definitely wanted for the reorganization of the Danubian basin.' All these hopes, especially those placed in the USA, were bitterly disappointed by the peace treaties: cf. chap. II/1, p. 294 f. For Auer's importance in the European Movement, cf. chap. VI (in vol. 2).

[363] For Sulyok, cf. Seton-Watson (n. 349), p. 194 f. A systematic study of the Hungarian parliamentary debates would no doubt produce further evidence. On the efforts of Nagy's government, cf. J. F. Kövér, 'L'idée fédérale dans la Région Danubienne', *L'Action fédéraliste européenne*, vol. 7, Aug. 1947, pp. 21–33, especially p. 30 f.: 'the reason why Danubian federation does not become a living reality is that the Russians mistrust the movement. . . . There is no lack of encouraging signs [from the countries themselves]. What is lacking is understanding between the Russians and the Anglo-Saxons' (p. 33).

[364] Cf. Seton-Watson (n. 349), pp. 202–11; Kövér (n. 363), p. 30. Basic study by G. Ionescu, *Communism in Rumania 1944–1962*, London, 1964 (Balkan federation pp. 24, 27, and 155); also S. Fischer-Galati (ed.), *Rumania (East Central Europe under the Communists)*, New York, 1957; id., *Twentieth Century Rumania*, New York, 1970.

was no salvation for European countries, big or small, except in union and a federal system'.[365] In July 1947, however, the Peasant Party was formally dissolved and Maniu, revered by most of his countrymen as the greatest living Romanian, was thrown into prison, where he died in 1952 (or so it was officially stated four years later). In November the Liberals were banned and the Socialist party was forced to merge with the Communists, while the king was forced to abdicate and the monarchy abolished; the political Sovietization of Romania was complete. At the same time 'the group of federalists in Romania was dissolved as part of the Russian campaign against all deviations from Moscow dogma'.[366] Gafencu and the other Romanian politicians in exile had no other course open to them than to set about 'organizing Europe' in the free West-European countries: 'Pour réaliser l'union européenne, seule une association anglo-française pourrait constituer un instrument.'[367]

The development of the federal concept in *Bulgaria* and *Yugoslavia* was more important, as a matter of practical politics, than anything that happened in the rest of the Soviet orbit, and was correspondingly unwelcome to Stalin. The Communist leaders Dimitrov and Tito, whose authority was undisputed in their own countries, espoused the idea of a federation of the whole of Eastern Europe and took energetic steps in that direction. What they envisaged was, of course, a Communist federation allied with the Soviet Union and not linked with the 'capitalist' countries of Western Europe; they did not, like the non-Communist politicians so far mentioned, regard a regional federation as a step towards the United States of Europe. Tito and Dimitrov were wholly orthodox Communists, and were no less ruthless in seizing power than their opposite numbers in the rest of Eastern Europe. In Bulgaria the Communist party joined with

---

[365] According to the competent testimony of the former foreign minister Gafencu, signed in Paris on 15.6.1948 by twenty-six leading members (in some cases former ministers) of the three chief parties (Liberals, Socialists, Peasants): 'Appel en faveur d'un groupement Roumain pour l'Europe Unie', (*UEF Archives,* Paris, 1948 corr.). For the appeal itself, cf. chap. VI/2, in vol. 2. The fact that it was signed by so many leading personalities, most of whom were not driven into exile until 1947, is evidence of the strength of the European idea in Romania in 1946.

[366] Thus there had already been an organized group of European federalists, as noted in the UEF pamphlet *Fédérer les Fédéralistes* (Paris, May 1947), p. 2: this mentioned a 'Grupul Federalist Roman', indicating that letters with this heading must have been received in Paris. Müller, in *Der Gedanke der europäischen Einigung und die Frage seiner Verwirklichung nach schweizerischem Vorbild,* p. 45 f., also mentions such a group and adds that its dissolution caused the UEF to finally give up hope of support from Moscow. An isolated piece of evidence is Brugmans's letter of 28.5.1947 to Prof. Dr Victor Deznai, Timişoara, Romania, thanking him for his interest in European federation and hoping for an early meeting, as he (Brugmans) intended to visit Romania (this visit did not take place; *BEF Archives,* Brugmans corr.). For the official announcement of Maniu's death, see Ionescu, op. cit. (n. 364), p. 136.

[367] G. Gafencu, 'Les Pays de l'Est et le projet d'une Confédération Européenne', *Cahiers du monde nouveau,* 3, April 1947, pp. 215–22, quotation, p. 217; the East-European nations should be invited, for without them Europe was incomplete (p. 218); but essential features of European union must be a political guarantee of human rights and the freedoms of plural democracy. 'C'est pour avoir perdu ces libertés que les pays de l'Est se sont aujourd'hui séparés de l'Europe' (p. 220).

the Social Democrats, Petkov's Agrarian Union, and the officers of the Zveno group to effect the *coup d'état* of September 1944 which brought Bulgaria into the war against Germany. The Communists at once took over the ministry of the interior and started a wave of purges which, especially after Dimitrov arrived from Moscow in November, were chiefly directed against the other politicians represented in the government. By July 1946 the generals of the Zveno group were in exile or in prison; during the summer fifteen members of the central committee of the Socialist party and thirty-five out of eighty members of the supreme council of the Agrarian Union were thrown into prison or concentration camps; terrorism was rife, especially in the countryside, and the Communists thus secured a majority in the October elections. Dimitrov took over the premiership, and in the next year or so the Socialist and Agrarian parties were liquidated; Petkov was executed in September 1947, and the monolithic dictatorship was complete by 1948. Dimitrov, however, had been a tireless advocate of Balkan federation since as far back as 1923.[368]

In Yugoslavia the National Liberation Front, firmly controlled by the nucleus of Communist Party leaders under Tito, had freed the country from the Nazis by its own efforts – the mountain areas by the summer of 1944, and the rest of the country a few months afterwards. It was the only East-European Resistance movement (apart from Greece and Albania) to succeed in this way without Red Army aid. By the end of the war all key political posts were held by Tito's Communists; some non-Communist pre-war politicians were allowed a measure of power as individuals, but the formation of new parties was not permitted. In the 'election' of November 1945 the regime secured 96 per cent of votes on a single-list basis; sporadic resistance to the party's dictatorship was silenced by political trials in the course of 1947. Apart from the population's war-weariness, the high percentage of support for the regime was due in large measure to Tito's personal achievement: both before and after the liberation he suppressed Greater Serbian aspirations and practised federal principles in internal affairs, as the only way of genuinely reconciling the five very different peoples who make up the Yugoslav federation.

During the Resistance period the centralized administrative machine was dismantled and replaced by national committees built up from below, on the local, district, and provincial level. The Constituent Assembly elected in November 1945 was composed, on federal lines, of a people's chamber (called the Federal

---

[368] Cf. Seton-Watson (n. 349), pp. 211–19; L. A. Dellin (ed.), *Bulgaria (East Central Europe under the Communists)*, New York, 1957; J. F. Brown, *Bulgaria under Communist Rule*, London, 1970. George Dimitrov was elected secretary of a 'Communist Balkan federation' in 1920 by the Communist Parties of Bulgaria, Yugoslavia, and Greece; from 1924 he advocated a political federation of the Balkans; hero of the Reichstag fire trial at Leipzig in 1933, he was for many years secretary-general of the Comintern; cf. Ruth Fischer, *Stalin and German Communism*, London, 1948, p. 307 f.; Kähl (n. 342), pp. 28–31 and 94 f.

Council) and a Council of Nationalities; on 31 January 1946 it enacted the first Constitution of the Federal People's Republic of Yugoslavia (FPRY). Article 1 provides that the FPRY is a community of nations enjoying equal rights, which in the free exercise of their right of self-determination have agreed to live together in a federal state. The federation consists of five People's Republics which are ethnically more or less homogeneous – Serbia, Montenegro (both Serbian), Croatia, Slovenia, and Macedonia; the ethnically mixed People's Republic of Bosnia–Hercegovina; and the ethnically mixed provinces of Vojvodina and Kosova-Metohija, which are autonomous parts of the People's Republic of Serbia (Art. 2). The sovereignty of the People's Republics is limited only by the rights assigned to the federation by the constitution (Art. 9). There is a general guarantee of the progressive structure of representative bodies from local National Committees up to the Council of Nationalities, the respective powers being prescribed at each level (Art. 6). The federal bodies are responsible for foreign policy, defence, transport and finance, legislation concerning currency and taxes, also commercial, procedural, and criminal law, and the general principles of economic legislation, insurance, and civil law (Art. 44).[369]

This progressive and successful application of the federal principle in internal affairs, as a means of reconciling the Yugoslav nationalities, gave Tito at an early stage the idea of applying it to a larger area as well. He first took up the notion, to which Dimitrov had long been devoted, of a Balkan federation. In discussions with the Bulgarians which began at the end of 1944 and of which Moscow was kept informed, he proposed a federal state consisting of the six Yugoslav republics plus Bulgaria as a seventh, the Macedonians of Yugoslavia and Bulgaria being joined into a single republic. In response to this proposal, which could be interpreted as reflecting expansionist Yugoslav ambitions, Dimitrov suggested a more confederal arrangement which would also include Albania. As agreement could not be reached on the main issue, Tito and Dimitrov agreed in secret talks at Bled in July–August 1947 that the Macedonian question would be left in suspense for the time being and that, while continuing to aim at a union of all the East-European peoples' democracies, in order to preserve freedom of action *vis-à-vis* the USSR they would ostensibly confine their plans to a Bulgaro-Yugoslav pact of mutual assistance with a customs and monetary union, which they believed Stalin would accept. Lively diplomatic activity led to remarkably quick results. Tito, who had visited Warsaw and Prague in 1946, now toured the neighbouring capitals and concluded pacts of friendship, mutual aid, and far-reaching economic exchanges with Bulgaria on 27 November 1947, Hungary on 8 December, and Romania on 19 December. On the occasion of the Bulgarian treaty Tito declared: 'We shall establish cooperation so general and so close that

---

[369] Cf. Seton-Watson (n. 349), pp. 219–26; R. F. Byrnes (ed.), *Yugoslavia (East Central Europe under the Communists)*, New York, 1958; E. Zellweger, 'Staatsaufbau und Gesetzgebung der Föderativen Volksrepublik Jugoslawien 1945–1948', in *Osteuropa-Handbuch, Bd. Jugoslawien*, ed. W. Markert, Cologne/Graz, 1954, esp. pp. 122–36.

federation will be a mere formality... We must find a new way to link our destinies together, to share all our resources in future, in short to make our cooperation perfect in every respect.' Tito's remarks were apparently directed only towards Bulgaria, but Dimitrov privately emphasized the need for a federation of all the Danubian and Balkan states, and on 16 January 1948 he signed similar agreements with Romania.[370] The Communist governments concerned had, in a short space of time, created a close network of bilateral treaties with a view to eventual federation, and had gone almost as far in this direction as the non-Communist governments in exile had planned to do. But Dimitrov, in a state of euphoria after his return from Bucharest, let the cat out of the bag: the treaties, he said, were not 'ordinary pacts' but were 'acts of union'. This immediately brought an adverse reaction from the Kremlin.

Asked at a press conference in Sofia on 21 January 1948 about 'rumours' of a Balkan federation, Dimitrov at first replied evasively but then revealed his true intentions. 'The question of a federation or confederation is premature for us. It is not on the agenda at present, and therefore this question has not been a subject of discussion at our conferences. When the question matures, and it must inevitably mature, then our peoples, the people's democracies – Romania, Bulgaria, Yugoslavia, Albania, Czechoslovakia, Poland, Hungary and Greece – mind you, and Greece! – will settle it. It is they who will decide what it shall be – a federation or confederation – and when and how it will be formed.' This statement left the question of form to the future, but made no bones about the project of uniting Eastern Europe. It provoked a Soviet veto in unusually sharp terms, in a *Pravda* editorial on 29 January 1948: 'The editors of *Pravda* consider that these countries require no questionable and fabricated federation or confederation or customs union; what they require is the consolidation and defence of their independence and sovereignty by mobilizing and organizing internally their peoples' democratic forces.' Thus, as on the occasion of the rejection of the Marshall Plan, the Soviet Union insisted on the maintenance of national sovereignties so that it might be certain of controlling each state separately.[371]

---

[370] Texts of the treaties of friendship, mutual aid, and co-operation in B. Meissner, *Das Ostpaktsystem*, Berlin, 1955, pp. 30–5; Tito's statement in Sofia quoted from 'The Evolution of the Cominform 1947–1950', *World Today, Chatham House Review*, Vol. 6 (1950), p. 220, and from *Osteuropa-Handbuch* (n. 369), p. 162; for Tito's journeys and Dimitrov's statement for home consumption, see the authorized biography by V. Dedijer, *Tito Speaks*, London, 1953, pp. 314–16. See also A. B. Ulam, *Titoism and the Cominform*, Cambridge (Mass.), 1952, pp. 69–95; W. Hildebrandt, 'Die aussenpolitischen Beziehungen der FVRJ', in *Osteuropa-Handbuch* (n. 369), esp. pp. 160–5; H. F. Armstrong, *Tito and Goliath*, New York, 1951, pp. 211–16; Kühl (n. 342), pp. 103–5; Stavrianos, *The Balkans* (n. 341), pp. 801–38; Hoensch (n. 7), p. 404 f.

[371] Text of Dimitrov's statement and Pravda's retort in Dedijer, Tito Speaks (n. 370), pp. 322–4; quoted in Meissner, *Das Ostpaktsystem*, Berlin, 1955, p. 15 f., and Meissner, 'Sowjetische Hegemonie' (n. 348), p. 66 f. Dimitrov tried to tone down his statement, but in so doing remarked that at one time Austria had prevented a customs union between Bulgaria and Serbia. Stalin summoned him to Moscow and upbraided him before the Yugoslavs for having suggested that 'the Germans were in the way earlier, now it is the Russians' (M. Djilas, *Conversations with Stalin*, London, 1962, p. 135).

Stalin forthwith summoned the Bulgarian and Yugoslav Communist leaders to Moscow. Dimitrov obeyed, while Tito sent Kardelj, Bakarić, and Djilas to represent him. At a stormy meeting on 10 February Stalin berated the Balkan leaders: 'Such a federation is inconceivable. What historic ties are there between Bulgaria and Romania? None. And we need not speak of Bulgaria and – let us say – Hungary or Poland.' He also made it clear that 'no relations between the "peoples" democracies' were permissible that were not in the interests and had not the approval of the Soviet government'.[372] The Soviet Union was not prepared to tolerate a viable, autonomous Communist political structure in an area which it regarded as directly subject to itself. It preferred instead to forfeit its dominion over one of the countries concerned: as the accused Yugoslavs refused to recant their errors, the Tito regime was outlawed by the Cominform in June 1948. Dimitrov submitted, but died mysteriously on his next visit to Moscow in July 1949. In all the East-European countries, leaders who had shown support for federal plans were disgraced and in many cases executed after show trials: Gomulka, Rajk, Patraşcanu, Markos, Kostov; each satellite in turn was compelled to break off trade relations and denounce its treaties with Yugoslavia.[373]

This episode is important, firstly because it shows that the East-European leaders were as conscious as those of Western Europe that the days of small nation states were past, and secondly for the light it throws on Soviet policy. Tito and Dimitrov were orthodox Communists from the political and ideological points of view, and the union they proposed was one of peoples' democracies governed on a strictly one-party Communist basis. The Soviet veto thus demonstrated clearly that Moscow objected to *any* federal union west of its borders: the Kremlin had no desire to see an independent, viable community, whether Communist or not, that answered to modern needs and might dispute its claim to European hegemony. From the satellites' point of view it was ironical that their only means of self-protection in the future lay in the national sovereignty which Stalin had invoked as a pretext to prevent their uniting. All mention of federalism was erased from their propaganda and replaced by emphatic references to national sovereignty, simply in order that they might preserve at least a measure of autonomy in the face of Soviet hegemonism.[374]

---

[372] Djilas, op. cit., p. 134 f.; Dedijer (n. 370), p. 325 f.

[373] Cf. sources quoted in n. 370; summary in Hildebrandt, p. 164 f., and Hoensch, pp. 413–18; R. Fischer, 'Tito contra Stalin', *Der Monat*, 1949, No. 7; E. Halperin, *The Triumphant Heretic. Tito's Struggle against Stalin*, London, 1958, p. 78 f. On Dimitrov's death see R. Fischer, 'Starb Dimitrov zur rechten Zeit?', *Die Zeit*, 19.8.1949. Those generally in the know were sure that 'Dimitrov was liquidated for having preached the idea of federation' (information from *von Auer*, 22.5.1964). For a similar account see P. S. Wandycz, 'Quest for Unity', in J. Lukaszewski (ed.), *The People's Democracies after Prague*, Bruges, 1970, esp. pp. 80–93.

[374] The only kind of 'federation' that was certainly considered by Stalin in his last years and at a later period of Comecon's existence was the incorporation of the 'peoples' democracies' into the Soviet Union. But this could only have meant absorption into the Soviet empire, for the Soviet

456 Revival of Plans for Federation

As the Sovietization of the East-European countries proceeded apace, we may form an opinion of what happened to pro-European groups in Romania and elsewhere by looking at the example of *Austria*, although in that country the Soviet Union was only one of four occupying powers, in fact as well as in theory. After the Red Army entered Vienna in April 1945 the Soviet Union unilaterally set up a provisional government under the Socialist Karl Renner, with a Communist minister of the interior. However, after the election in November, in which the right-wing People's Party (ÖVP) obtained 85 seats, the Socialists 76, and the Communists only 4, Leopold Figl of the People's Party formed a government with a Social-Democratic minister of the interior, which for the next seven years manœuvred adroitly between the occupying powers.[375] By late summer 1946 a body called Freunde der Vereinigten Staaten von Europa (Friends of the United States of Europe) had formed a Provisorisches Gründungskomitee der Europa-Union, Sektion Österreich (Provisional Founding Committee of Europa-Union, Austrian Section). The name indicates a connection with the Swiss Europa-Union; a 'provisional general secretariat' was established at Feldkirch (Vorarlberg) in the French Zone. This group, however, was not only forbidden to send representatives to the Hertenstein conference in September 1946 or the UEF meeting in Amsterdam in April 1947,[376] but on 4 September 1947 they were obliged to send the UEF a message which could only have been dictated by Soviet opposition to federalist ideas. It ran:

'The Austrian Ministry of the Interior has secured the prohibition of our organization on the strength of a law dating from 1867. The Ministry regards our work for European union as a danger to Austria's state interests. Comment on this is no doubt superfluous. Please support us in our struggle.'[377]

Union with *c.* 180 million inhabitants in 1948, was more than twice as populous as the other seven states put together; the East-European area, including Yugoslavia but without the Baltic States, Eastern Poland, and Bessarabia, had a population at that time of 87.3 million. If the East-European countries have so far escaped this fate, it is not because they have succeeded in asserting their national sovereignty but because the Kremlin fears the foreign and especially the internal consequences of such incorporation: it would dangerously strengthen particularist trends in the multinational Soviet state and would greatly weaken the dominance of the Great Russian people in the Soviet empire. Cf. Meissner (n. 348), p. 70.

[375] Cf. A. Wandruska, "Österreichs politische Struktur. Die Entwicklung der Parteien und politischen Bewegungen" in H. Benedikt (ed.), *Geschichte der Republik Österreich*, Munich, 1954, pp. 285–485; W. L. Sterman, *Die Sowjetunion und Österreich 1945–1955. Ein Beispiel für die Sowjetpolitik gegenüber dem Westen*, Bonn, 1962; W. B. Bader, *Austria between East and West 1945–1955*, Stanford, Calif., 1966.

[376] 'The German and Austrian participants whose names had been announced could not take part in the meeting, as they were refused exit visas' (H. G. Ritzel, 'Der Geist von Hertenstein', *Europa*, Vol. xiii, No. 10, Oct. 1946, p. 1). 'The Austrian federalists sent a telegram to say they were joining the UEF, but were unable to send a delegation to Amsterdam' (A. Marc in *Lettre-Circulaire*, No. 8, 25.4.1947, p. 1).

[377] Letter of 4.9.1947 from Josef H. Klein, secretary-general of 'Europa-Union, Austrian Section', to Action Européenne, Amsterdam, i.e. Brugmans (*BEF Archives*, E. Actie). Confirmed by DPD report, 3.12.1947: 'The Austrian movement of the Europa-Union . . . has been banned. The

To sum up: there is no question but that the same conclusions were drawn from the catastrophe of the Second World War in Eastern as in Western Europe. But in 1946–7 the East-European countries had no opportunity to take part in reviving the idea of European unity. Soviet domination made the prospect hopeless, and any attempts in that direction were at once suppressed. These countries were too weak to play a part in sustaining the UEF concept of a 'Third Force', which was consequently doomed to failure. Only the large East-European *émigré* communities were able to lend support to the European Movement, as we shall see in Chapter VI. In the US sphere of influence west of the Iron Curtain, advocates of European federation were free to form associations and carry on propaganda for their ideal, which had previously been flouted by both Roosevelt and Stalin. This was the first great measure of assistance that the USA afforded them, in accordance with its libertarian principles.

Austrian ministry of the interior has declared that its aims are contrary to law, since under the Control Council agreement Austria is not permitted to surrender its political independence.' Cf. above at n. 234, for the similar fate of the only German federalist association within the Soviet purview. It was not until April 1949 that an 'Austrian Council of the European Movement' could be founded by the deputy E. Ludwig: cf. chap. VI/2 (in vol. 2).

CHAPTER III

Limitation to Western Europe; Effects of the Developing East–West Conflict (May–December 1947)

1. Breakdown of Co-operation between the Superpowers; Effect on their Attitude towards European Union

The failure of the two world powers to reach agreement on essential questions at the Paris meeting of the Council of Foreign Ministers in the summer of 1946 brought home to world public opinion for the first time that the US and the Soviet Union might be unable to organize world peace on an agreed basis as they had promised, and that the tension between them might well increase.[1] The general state of unease encouraged the federalists, who had fallen silent as long as the superpowers appeared to be of one mind in their domination over Europe, to put forward once again their views about the lessons to be drawn from the world catastrophe. In the countries not occupied by the Soviet Union, the revived associations and organs of opinion were free, as before, to advocate European political union as a contribution to the world peace settlement. The groups which formed the UEF and genuinely reflected the ideas of the wartime Resistance put forward the concept of a 'Third Force' as described in chapter II, and were the only ones whose planning took full account of Eastern Europe in this way; they envisaged the federation of the whole of Europe as an area of peace, a neutral zone between the two world powers. They were unrealistic in so far as they underestimated Europe's weakness and supposed that the Soviet Union, like the US, would withdraw and allow its peoples to decide their own fate once again.[2] It is especially important to note that the idea of European union was a spontaneous reaction, on the part of the associations concerned, to the fact that the sufferings of war and the subsequent Balkanization of Europe had reduced nationalism to an

---

[1] Cf. above, chapter II/1, pp. 291–6; the sketch, there given, of conditions created by the two superpowers is here extended through 1947.
[2] Cf., in chap. II, especially p. 309 f. and the section on the concept of a 'Third Force', pp. 380–5.

absurdity. The challenge existed, and the response was formulated on the European plane, before the open dissension between the wartime allies introduced new external factors which contributed to the realization of the federalist ideal.

The crucial question in the winter of 1946/7 was how the world powers would react to the revival of federalist ideas and how their attitude would be affected by the development of their mutual relations, particularly as regards the unsolved problem of Germany. The West-European governments, at grips with economic disruption and serious payments problems, were at pains to avoid taking up any serious attitude towards the question of federalism.[3] As for Moscow and Washington, their first reactions appeared, as will be seen, to be as firmly hostile as they had been in 1943, when Roosevelt had condemned European union as harmful to the cause of Russo-American friendship. But from the middle of January 1947 that friendship was affected by events of key significance. The first of these was the ruthless behaviour of the Communists over the test case of the Polish elections. The US became increasingly restive at the high-handedness of Soviet power politics. Till now, the Rooseveltian 'policy of postponement' had been pursued in the hope of achieving permanent concord with the Russians; with the decision to abandon it came increasing support for the idea of European union. It is necessary therefore to go back a little in time and briefly review the developments in world politics during January–May 1947, the effect of which was gradually brought home to the European public in and after Marshall's speech of 5 June; how the Europeans then reacted will be studied in the remainder of this chapter. The decisions taken by the world powers in 1947 made it a year of decision for the whole post-war structure of Europe also.

(A) US FOREIGN POLICY COMES TO FAVOUR A REGIONAL SECURITY ORGANISATION

The sacrifices of war had imbued the Americans with a strong determination not to repeat Wilson's failure of 1919–20 but to succeed this time in bringing about a 'One World' peace settlement reflecting the 'American dream', in which all nations could live together in harmony. Only the strength of this hope can explain the patience and caution with which the US government endeavoured for so long to achieve a lasting agreement with the Russians, in accordance with Roosevelt's concept of a long-term co-imperium with the newly recognized world power in the East. Byrnes, the guardian of Roosevelt's legacy in foreign affairs, had to a large extent accepted the fact that the US government's recognition at Yalta of the

---

[3] Cf. the summary at the beginning of section 2 below. The West-European governments only began to react after Marshall's speech at Harvard on 5 June 1947, i.e. after both world powers, as will be seen, had thoroughly considered the idea of European union and defined their attitude towards it.

Soviet Union's right to a secure Western frontier was interpreted by Stalin as sanctioning a policy of political expansion. In all matters of controversy, especially Germany, Byrnes had patiently followed the 'policy of postponement' so as to neglect no possibility of coming to terms with the Soviet Union.[4] This, however, in no way prevented Stalin from continuing a policy of ruthless expansion and high-handed behaviour in all areas occupied by the Red Army. The State Department saw more and more clearly that Russia was a totalitarian state with revolutionary aims, and from the spring of 1946 onwards Truman, 'tired of babying the Soviets', had taken a firm line against further Soviet expansion. None the less, throughout 1946 Byrnes stuck fast to the Rooseveltian hope that a global settlement might eventually be reached with the Soviet Union, beside which regional problems seemed unimportant. As time went on Washington grew accustomed to a state of continuous tension, but no new policy came to replace the old. Byrnes's policy of 'patience with firmness' was intended ultimately to lead to a friendly settlement; Stalin flattered this hope by withdrawing from Iran and paying lip-service to 'co-operation' between the world powers, which had brought him such large dividends, but at the same time he went on Sovietizing Eastern Europe and kept up the pressure in Germany and China. In the autumn of 1946 Byrnes, supported by the Democratic majority of 'progressive internationalists' and the isolationist wing of the Republican party, persuaded Congress to approve the peace treaties with Finland, Hungary, Romania, and Bulgaria, which in practice sealed the Soviet domination of Eastern Europe in defiance of the Yalta agreement.[5]

At this point, however, Truman, already dissatisfied with Byrnes's 'passive and obviously ineffectual tactics',[6] must have decided that it was time for a drastic change in American foreign policy, which was everywhere on the defensive and threatened the country with isolation. If the peace treaties with the Axis satellites were the best result of the 'policy of

---

[4] Cf. chapter I/1 above, with full references, especially the characterization of the 'American dream' in J. W. Spanier, *American Foreign Policy since World War II*, New York/Washington, 1972[4], pp. 14–23; summary in M. Geiling, *Aussenpolitik und Nuklearstrategie, Eine Analyse des konzeptionellen Wandels der amerikanischen Sicherheitspolitik gegenüber der Sowjetunion 1945–1963*, Cologne/Vienna, 1975, pp. 17–27.

[5] Cf. chapter II/1, pp. 282–96, with detailed references; the continued US demobilization must especially be borne in mind. Byrnes repeated his formula to the Cleveland Council on World Affairs as late as 11.1.1947: '. . . fostering of a common fellowship. . . . We live in one world' (*Documents on American Foreign Relations, Vol. ix: Jan. 1–Dec. 31, 1947*, ed. R. Dennert and R. K. Turner, Princeton, 1949, p. 4). Byrnes's biographer G. Curry, who defends him to the utmost, states that he 'went to the limit to conciliate the Russians' (*James F. Byrnes*, New York, 1965, p. 312); cf. more fully chap. I, n. 12.

[6] Geiling (n. 4), p. 34. A similar dissatisfaction led to the formation of 'realist' groups in the State Department, Congress, and parts of the governmental and journalistic élite who opposed the 'progressives' and 'isolationists' of the old policy and advocated a 'realistic' alternative. Cf. K. J. Thompson, *Political Realism and the Crisis of World Politics. An American Approach to Foreign Policy*, Princeton, 1960; H.-P. Schwarz, *Vom Reich zur Bundesrepublik*, Neuwied/Berlin, 1966, p. 63 f.; Geiling, p. 32 f., n.

postponement', after all the patience that had been shown and all the official and unofficial pleas for observance of the Yalta agreement, free elections, and human rights in Eastern Europe, then that policy was manifestly bankrupt and contrary to US interests. Paradoxically, Truman was given an opportunity for a change of course by the elections to the 80th Congress in November 1946, which dramatically reversed the party balance by giving the Republicans large majorities in both Houses. Since Vandenberg's speech in February the Republican party had moved away from Taft's 'free hand' policy to a more 'realist' approach; Rooseveltian Democrats were now a minority in the Senate, and Vandenberg became chairman of the Foreign Policy Committee.[7] Meanwhile there were further danger signals on the horizon.

One of these was the predictable outcome of the Polish elections. Britain had gone to war in defence of Poland's independence in 1939; Roosevelt and Churchill had made the question of a free, representative, and democratic government for Poland (not that of its frontiers) a test case of Stalin's intention to observe the Yalta agreement, and had insisted on the acceptance of four non-Communist ministers and the promise of free elections. However, after the Polish Peasant party led by Mikolajczyk refused to join the Communist-dominated 'democratic bloc' in June 1946 it was subjected to a wave of terrorist murders and arrests, and, despite constant protests by the British and Americans, the Russians and their Polish henchmen made certain by violence and deception of all kinds that the 'bloc' was victorious at the elections of 19 January 1947. This was regarded throughout the world as a sign that the wartime alliance had collapsed.[8] In the UN Atomic Energy Commission the US government in June 1946 introduced the Baruch plan for effective world-wide control of atomic energy by a UN agency, and undertook that if such an agency was set up the US would destroy its own atomic bombs and production plants; the Russians, however, were working feverishly to develop their own bomb and refused to accept international control.[9] Apart from the Soviet occupation of foreign countries, the winter of 1946/7 saw Communist expansion in Korea, China, Greece, and the Near East, the strengthening of the

---

[7] Before the election there were in the House of Representatives 243 Democrats and 190 Republicans, in the Senate 57 Democrats and 38 Republicans; after the election the figures for the House were 246 Republicans and 188 Democrats, for the Senate 51 Republicans and 45 Democrats. Among the latter the old Rooseveltians under H. Wallace became a minority, as Democratic support developed for the new foreign policy under Senators Tom Connally and William Fulbright. On the Republican leaders, cf. A. H. Vandenberg Jr. (ed.), *The Private Papers of Senator Vandenberg*, Boston, 1952; for the isolationist credo of the chairman of the Republican Senate Policy Committee, see A. Taft, *A. Foreign Policy for Americans*, New York, 1951; cf. J. T. Patterson, *Mr Republican: A Biography of Robert A. Taft*, Boston, 1972.

[8] See S. Mikolajczyk (chap. II, n. 352), esp. chap. 14; also G. Rhode, 'Polen als "Volksdemokratie" ', in *Osteuropa-Handbuch. Polen*, Cologne, 1959, pp. 223–35; E. van der Beugel, *From Marshall Aid to Atlantic Partnership, European Integration as a Concern of American Foreign Policy*, Amsterdam/London/New York, 1966, p. 22; and elsewhere.

[9] Cf. the relevant sections of H. Volle and C.-J. Duisberg, *Probleme der internationalen Abrüstung. Die Bemühungen der Vereinten Nationen um internationale Abrüstung und Sicherheit 1945–1961*, 2 vols., Frankfurt, 1964. This was the last chance of replacing the nuclear arms race by a system of control, as the latter was no longer applicable to later developments: cf. H. Kissinger, *Nuclear Weapons and Foreign Policy*, New York, 1957, pp. 211–12.

French and Italian Communist Parties, etc.; and the propsects of Communism in Europe were enhanced by acute material hardship and the threat of economic collapse. Everything suggested that the Soviet Union was embarking on a second phase of expansion at the expense of countries that had not yet known Communist rule.[10]

In order to express in personal terms his determination on a change of policy (though he had not yet decided what the new policy should be), Truman in mid-December took up an offer of resignation which Byrnes had made earlier. On 7 January 1947 it was announced that Byrnes would shortly retire, and on the 21st he was succeeded as Secretary of State by General George C. Marshall, the wartime Chief of Staff of the US Army, in whom Truman had absolute confidence and whose appointment he had envisaged for months past.[11]

The occasion for an official declaration of the new policy, and to some extent for deciding what it should be, was furnished on 21 February when two notes were received from the British Embassy in Washington. These announced that Britain, on account of its economic weakness, could no longer support the Greek government but must withdraw from that country within forty days, and that she could no longer supply equipment and economic aid to Turkey. Both Greece and Turkey were under Soviet pressure at this time. In August 1946 the Russians had addressed a note to Ankara repeating demands for strategic bases, the cession of territory in the Caucasus, and the replacement of the Montreux Convention by joint Russo-Turkish control of the Straits; in Greece, the rebellion led by the Communists and clearly inspired by Moscow had flared into open civil war from the end of 1946. The American recipients of the British notes, as their almost unbroken testimony makes clear, were united in perceiving the historic importance of the hour: Britain found herself unable any longer to exercise her role of leadership even in Europe, no real power existed between Washington and Moscow, the world had become bipolar.

[10] Cf. E. O. Czempiel, *Das amerikanische Sicherheitssystem 1945–1949*, Berlin, 1966, p. 191 f.; H.-P. Schwarz (n. 6), pp. 209–11; M. D. Schulman, *Stalin's Foreign Policy Reappraised*, Cambridge (Mass.), 1963, pp. 3–15; Z. K. Brzezinski, *The Soviet Bloc: Unity and Conflict*, Cambridge (Mass.), 1967, pp. 4 f.; on p. 45 Brzezinski points out that Zhdanov, in his speech on the twenty-ninth anniversary of the October Revolution (7.11.1946), expressly reasserted the doctrine, which had been dormant since 1938, of the inevitable division of the world into two hostile camps. On the economic distress in Europe, see p. 470 f.

[11] On Byrnes's offer of resignation on medical advice in April 1946 (which did not take effect, as he recovered) and Truman's immediate enquiry of Marshall as to whether he would be prepared to take Byrnes's place, cf. Curry, *James F. Byrnes* (n. 5), p. 208 f.; on Byrnes's final resignation and continuance in office till 20 Jan. 1947, see ibid., pp. 293–7 and 390 f. On Marshall, cf. R. H. Ferrell, George C. Marshall (= vol. xv of the series *The American Secretaries of State and their Diplomacy*), New York, 1966 (outline account of his mission to China from Dec. 1945 to Dec. 1946, pp. 20–34); on his years as Chief of Staff, 1939–45, see the definitive biography by F. Pogue, *George C. Marshall, Vol. 2: 1939–1943*, New York, 1966. His great gift of leadership is best portrayed by Dean Acheson, his Under-Secretary of State, in *Present at the Creation. My Years in the State Department*, New York, 1969, pp. 213–16. Acheson, a man of brilliant intellect and no less integrity than Marshall, was an admirable complement to his chief.

The Washington leaders reacted with the unanimous decision not to tolerate a strategic vacuum but to take over the British commitments, making clear to the world that Greece and Turkey were a test case and that the US was determined to withstand any further Soviet expansion.[12] On 27 February, on the joint advice of the State, War, and Navy Departments, Truman received leading representatives of both parties in Congress and told them the position. Marshall presented the issue in a single sentence: 'The choice is between acting with energy or losing by default.' Acheson painted a vivid picture of the change brought about in the world situation by unilateral Soviet expansion since the end of the war, arguing that if Greece collapsed, with predictable consequences in Turkey, the Middle East, Italy, and France, US security would be directly endangered. Vandenberg expressed the opinion that Congress would cooperate 'if the President will say that to the Congress and the country'.[13] At a joint session of the two Houses on 12 March Truman delivered a special message in which he not only asked for $400,000,000 for emergency aid to Greece and Turkey but urged the need for a whole new foreign policy in the light of world conditions. Key passages of the speech were:

One of the primary objectives of the foreign policy of the United States is the creation of conditions in which we and other nations will be able to work out a way of life free from coercion. This was a fundamental issue in the war with Germany and Japan ... Totalitarian regimes imposed on free peoples, by direct or indirect aggression, undermine the foundations of international peace and hence the security of the United States. The peoples of a number of countries of the world have recently had totalitarian regimes forced upon them against their will. The Government of the United States has made frequent protests against coercion and intimidation, in violation of the Yalta Agreement, in Poland, Rumania and Bulgaria ... [Totalitarianism] relies upon ... fixed elections and the suppression of personal freedoms. I believe that it must be the policy of the United States to support free peoples who are resisting attempted subjugation by armed minorities

---

[12] Cf. especially, as an authentic source, the account, regarded on all sides as reliable, by Joseph M. Jones, then a member of the 'inner circle' of the State Department: *The Fifteen Weeks (February 21–June 5, 1947)*, New York, 1955, pp. 3–7; ibid., pp. 106–11, sketch of Marshall's qualities as a leader; p. 130 'virtual unanimity of view'; Acheson (n. 11), p. 217 f.; Beugel (n. 8), pp. 23–7; H. Feis, *From Trust to Terror. The Onset of the Cold War 1945–1950*, New York, 1970, pp. 175–83 (outline of developments in Greece and Turkey), 191 ff. (origin of the Truman doctrine); Geiling (n. 4), pp. 37–41; Spanier (n. 4), p. 29 f.: 'February 21 was thus a historic day. On that day Great Britain, the only remaining power in Europe, acknowledged her exhaustion. Now all of a sudden there was no power to protect the United States, but the United States itself; no one stood between this country and the present threat to its security. All the other major powers of the world had collapsed – except the Soviet Union. . . . The cold fact of a bipolar world suddenly faced the United States.'

[13] Acheson (n. 11), p. 219; Vandenberg (n. 7), p. 338 f.; Jones (n. 12), p. 141 f.; Geiling (n. 4), p. 39 f. On events in Greece, see especially W. H. McNeill, *The Greek Dilemma: War and Aftermath*, Philadelphia, 1947, id., *Greece. American Aid in Action 1947–1956*, New York, 1957; S. G. Xydis, *Greece and the Great Powers 1944–1947*, Thessaloniki, 1963; E. O'Ballance, *The Greek Civil War 1944–1949*, New York, 1966; O. Iatrides, *Revolt in Athens. The Greek Communist 'Second Round' 1944–45*, Princeton UP, 1972.

or by outside pressures ... The free peoples of the world look to us for support in maintaining their freedoms. If we falter in our leadership, we may endanger the peace of the world – and we shall surely endanger the welfare of our own Nation.[14]

We are not concerned here with the fact that what became known as the 'Truman doctrine' was deliberately couched in terms of wider application than Greece and Turkey, so that it heralded a new departure in foreign policy; nor is it our purpose to discuss whether it was fortunate to assert the ideological reasons for putting a stop to Soviet expansionism in relation to countries that were not themselves well qualified to pass an ideological test. These points were exhaustively debated – far more so than the literature would suggest – in the two months that followed before the Greek–Turkish Aid Act was passed by a two-thirds majority of the House of Representatives and a three-quarters majority of the Senate.[15] The decisive factor was Truman's determination to give aid and comfort to nations that wished to avoid the fate of Eastern Europe, in all parts of the world in which further Soviet expansion was possible, and to prevent such expansion by a resolute policy of 'containment', as it came to be called after the appearance of Kennan's anonymous article in *Foreign Affairs* for July 1947. Truman's decision can only be compared in importance with Wilson's request to Congress in April 1917 for a declaration of war on Germany, which put an end to America's century-old policy of isolationism.[16] For the

---

[14] Full text in *Congressional Record of the United States, 80th Congress, Vol. 93: 1st Session,* p. 1980 f.; *Public Papers of the Presidents of the United States: Harry S. Truman, 1947,* Washington, DC, 1963, p. 177 f.; *Documents on American Foreign Relations,* vol. 9 (1947), p. 6 f. For the genesis of the speech, preliminary drafts, etc., see details in Jones (n. 12), *passim;* summary in H. S. Truman, *Memoirs, ii. Years of Trial and Hope 1946–1952,* Garden City, NY, 1956, p. 104 f.; Acheson (n. 11), pp. 220–3. All important diplomatic texts also published in *Foreign Relations of the United States* (abbrev. *FRUS*), *1947, Vol. V: Greece,* Washington, 1973.

[15] Within the Administration, only Kennan thought Truman's message went too far: cf. Acheson (n. 11), p. 221, and later in detail G. F. Kennan, *Memoirs, 1925–1950,* Boston/Toronto, 1967, pp. 313–24. Useful accounts of the Congress debates in Jones (n. 12), pp. 178–98, Ferrell (n. 11), pp. 84–98, and Acheson (n. 11),. pp. 223–5. Opposition and 'No' votes came from left-wing 'internationalist' Democrats and right-wing 'isolationist' Republicans. On the extension of the scope of the doctrine beyond Greece and Turkey, cf. Czempiel (n. 10), p. 263, who explains it in terms of the announcement of a new foreign policy; similarly A. B. Ulam, *The Rivals. America and Russia since World War II,* London/New York, 1974[2], p. 125 f.; a balanced view in Feis (n. 12), pp. 195–207.

[16] Cf. L. Halle, *The Cold War as History,* London, 1967, pp. 109 f. and 117 f. On 31.1.1947 George F. Kennan sent to James Forrestal, Secretary of the Navy, a memorandum on the nature of Soviet power. With Forrestal's agreement and that of the publications committee of the State Department (as Marshall had asked Kennan in February to head a planning staff in that Department from May onwards), the memorandum appeared at the end of June as an article in the July number of *Foreign Affairs,* entitled 'The Sources of Soviet Conduct'; it was signed merely 'X', but the press discovered the author's identity within ten days. The article had an effect on the US public similar to that produced in the State Department a year earlier by Kennan's long telegram from Moscow (cf. chap. II/1, p. 289). It called for 'a long-term, patient but firm and vigilant containment of Russian expansive tendencies', exerting uniform counter-pressure 'at every point where they show signs of encroaching upon the interests of a peaceful world'. Full text in G. F. Kennan, *American Diplomacy 1900–1950,* Chicago, 1951, pp. 107–24; cf. Kennan (n. 15), pp. 354–67.

purpose of this study, however, it is more important to note that the negative policy of containment as framed in March 1947 was not yet accompanied by any positive or constructive element; democratic freedoms were to be protected, but there was no suggestion as to how regions of the world were to be politically organized. The US government, indeed, was uncertain at this time of the precise scope of its new foreign policy and how far it would be acceptable to Congress and the public. Accordingly Marshall set out for his first international conference, the Council of Foreign Ministers in Moscow, to explore once again the possibility of long-term co-operation with the Soviet Union.

At the fourth meeting of the Council, from 10 March to 24 April 1947, Marshall, Bevin, and Bidault, accompanied by large staffs, negotiated patiently for six weeks at forty-four plenary sessions to discover whether at least the central feature of the 'One World' policy could be salvaged, namely the joint control of Germany, and whether agreement over Germany might help to solve other problems also.[17] The Soviet government, as before, persisted in putting forward maximum demands, hoping either to secure their acceptance or to gain time while preventing the economic recovery of Western Europe – taking advantage, understandably enough, of the US 'policy of postponement' which had already secured them the whole of Eastern Europe in return for practically no concessions. To provide a basis of negotiations Marshall renewed Byrnes's proposal of July 1946 for a four-power pact against German aggression – not limited to twenty-five years, however, but, in accordance with Molotov's demand at the time, providing for joint control over a period of forty years and offering to set up governmental arrangements for the whole of Germany.[18] Motolov, however, throughout the conference refused to budge an iota from the three main Soviet demands, which he presented as an unalterable condition of any agreement. These were:

1. Reparations to the value of $10 billion from the current production of all four zones, to be guaranteed by a German government strictly supervised for the purpose. This ignored the fact that the population of the Western Zones was, at that time, barely able to survive with the aid of American subsidies. In vain Marshall pointed out that the German economy was closely involved with that of

[17] The meeting of the Council of Foreign Ministers was the subject of a full report in an early number of *Europa-Archiv*, vol. 2 (1947), pp. 671–774; Soviet statements in V. M. Molotov, *Problems of Foreign Policy. Speeches and Statements, April 1945–November 1948*, Moscow, 1949, pp. 341–453. The most detailed report by a participant is that of the US ambassador W. Bedell Smith, *My Three Years at Moscow*, Philadelphia, 1950, pp. 211–99; the most exact account is in B. Meissner, *Russland, die Westmächte und Deutschland*, Hamburg, 1954, pp. 105–31; also Feis (n. 12), pp. 208–20. US documents now published in *FRUS* (n. 14), *1947, Vol. II: Council of Foreign Ministers*, Washington, 1972, pp. 234–491.

[18] Cf. chap. II/1 at n. 19. Molotov objected strongly to the proposal in July 1946, no doubt because a long-term US presence in Europe in the form of a military guarantee was incompatible with the Kremlin's true aims in Europe. In 1947 Molotov refused to discuss the proposal and would talk of nothing but the Soviet demands.

Europe as a whole, and that if they continued policies which would make Germany 'a congested slum or an economic poorhouse in the centre of Europe' it would make European recovery an impossibility. Since this was exactly what Molotov wanted, he did not yield an inch.[19]

2. At every stage Molotov repeated the demand that 'the industry of the Ruhr, which constitutes a paramount part of Germany's war potential, should be placed under the joint control of the four Allied Powers', after the pattern of four-power control of Berlin and with the supervised nationalization of all 'monopolistic industrial and financial concerns'.[20]

3. Molotov also insisted at every turn on the 'real democratization' of the Western Zones and the need to carry out 'land reform throughout Germany, transferring the big Junker estates to the peasantry'; the German monopolies must be dispossessed and their plant made over to the German state, which should be democratized under the control of the four allies. Above all, German representative bodies should comprise 'not only members of parties but also of trade unions and other anti-Nazi organizations' which had proved reliable instruments of Bolshevization in the Soviet Zone under the leadership of the SED (the Communist-controlled Socialist Unity Party).[21]

In the light of these demands, the intended effect of which was especially clear if they were considered as a single whole, the Western delegations finally came to three main conclusions:

1. The Soviet Union would only agree to a solution of the German question that was more or less certain to bring about complete Soviet control and domination of all Germany, and consequently hegemony over the rest of Europe.

2. The Soviet leaders were only interested in Germany as a means of preventing European economic recovery: it was clearly in their interest that Western Europe should continue to decline economically under non-Communist governments.

3. Their chief method of securing this end was to drag out the argument over Germany as long as their maximum demands were not met. Marshall was especially convinced of this after an interview with Stalin in which the latter said that 'compromise would come after people had exhausted themselves in dispute'.[22] On the day after his return home, Marshall summed up the situation in a broadcast:

---

[19] Cf. quotations from Molotov in Meissner (n. 17), pp. 126–9; Marshall's reply of 31.3.1947 in *Vital Speeches of the Day*, Vol. 13, No. 13, New York, 15.4.1947, p. 398 f.

[20] Molotov's remarks on 17.3.1947 and 11.4.1947 in op. cit. (n. 17), pp. 361 f. Many references also in *FRUS 1947/II* (n. 17), see Index.

[21] Cf., with full quotations from Molotov, Meissner (n. 17), pp. 115–17 and 123–5. There was also a sharp exchange as to whether the Oder–Neisse frontier was provisional or final: Meissner, pp. 107–12. Although it had been agreed to discuss Austria, Molotov evaded the issue by arguing about German assets there, because if agreement were reached on an Austrian settlement the Russians would have no pretext for keeping their troops in the Danube area: cf. *FRUS 1947/II*, p. 373 f.

[22] Report by James Reston in *New York Times*, 29.4.1947 (cf. Ferrell [n. 11], p. 70). The US delegation's impressions on these three points were accurately summarized in Jones (n. 12), pp. 221–4; similarly Beugel (n. 8), p. 34 f.; also Kennan (n. 15), p. 325, and H. Herzfeld, *Ausgewählte*

The German negotiations involved not only the security of Europe and the world but the prosperity of all of Europe ... We were faced with immediate issues which vitally concerned the impoverished and suffering people of Europe who are crying for help ... We cannot ignore the factor of time involved here. The recovery of Europe has been far slower than had been expected. Disintegrating forces are becoming evident. The patient is sinking while the doctors deliberate. So I believe that action cannot await compromise through exhaustion.[23]

The US Administration had thus arrived at the conclusion which they had so long denied, that the German question could only be considered in a European context. It remained to be seen, however, whether they would endorse the positive concept of European union which the Europeans had themselves evolved.

(B) THE AMERICANS BEGIN TO ENDORSE PLANS FOR EUROPEAN UNITY

In the autumn of 1946 the State Department and the American public felt no enthusiasm for the idea of European union which was being revived on the Continent itself. One or two voices were raised in its favour,[24] but neither the public nor the State Department under Byrnes wished to abandon the hope of 'one world', and it was thought unrealistic and premature to discuss European union until at least agreement had been reached with the Russians over peace terms for Germany. Hence American reactions to Churchill's Zurich speech were predominantly sceptical in tone.

The *New York Herald Tribune* criticized Churchill for excessive haste in proffering an olive branch to Germany and actually treating it as a future leading power in Europe. Walter Lippmann read Churchill's proposal as an 'offer to the Germans' which would only be acceptable to others if Germany was partitioned in a peace treaty in such a way that its parts could take their individual place in a union of

---

Aufsätze. Festgabe zum 70. Geburtstage, Berlin, 1962, p. 359. The delegation were also affected by their personal experiences in Moscow: the terrorized air of the population, the secret police's bugging-devices in hotels, the fact that important conversations could only be carried on out of doors, etc.: cf. Ferrell (n. 11), pp. 60–2.

[23] Text of Marshall's broadcast in Department of State, *Germany 1947–1949*, Washington, 1950, p. 57 (quotation). It was an important factor that Bidault, already embittered by Molotov's refusal to agree to France annexing the Saar, came to the same conclusions as to the true aims of Soviet policy: cf. p. 497 f.

[24] William C. Bullitt, who had warned against Soviet expansionism ever since serving as ambassador in Moscow, was the only political figure of note who in 1946 urged the US 'not only to defend the western democracies of Europe from armed attack by the Soviet Union but also to help them to unite for military and economic defence. . . . The doors of the European Federation should be kept open to all European states which are not puppets and have democratic governments' (W. C. Bullitt, *The Great Globe Itself,* New York, 1946, p. 195 f.). Intellectuals were affected by A. Guérard's brilliant plea in *Europe Free and United,* Stanford, Calif., 1945. From October 1946 to 1948 Clarence K. Streit, Owen Roberts, and John F. Schmidt published in *Freedom and Union. Journal of the World Republic* articles of the 'New Federalist' calling for an Atlantic federation of all democracies including the US (cf. their book *Publius II, The New Federalist,* New York, 1950).

European nations.[25] The US military authorities in Germany were also apprehensive of the effect of prematurely encouraging the Germans; they had reacted adversely to the 'breathless haste' with which German federalist groups spoke of securing equality of rights for Germany.[26]

At the beginning of 1947, however, things began to change as a result of Byrnes's dismissal and the accumulation of press reports about the Communist take-over in Eastern Europe and the destitution, stagnation, fear, and insecurity on the West-European Continent. American public opinion began to favour the idea of European union, and within three months it was completely converted. Contributory factors were Churchill's impressive articles in *Collier's Weekly* and Coudenhove's publication in the US of the results of his poll of parliamentarians, which suggested that the idea was not a mere utopia but a practical possibility.[27] Of outstanding importance, however, in view of the Republican majority in both Houses, was a speech delivered by John Foster Dulles, adviser on foreign affairs to the Republican candidate for the Presidency, on 17 January 1947 in the ballroom of the Waldorf Astoria hotel in New York. His subject was America's interest in European union, and it was believed that the text had been approved beforehand by Senator Vandenberg and Governor Dewey.[28] It was the more effective by reason of its clear definitions and because the problem was stated in terms of US traditions.

Dulles briefly outlined the extension of Soviet domination, which 'was checked in 1946 when it had already gone so far that persistence would have jeopardized the peace'. Still more dangerous than territorial expansion was the second Soviet challenge of subversive revolution fostered by economic misery, especially in Western Europe. In 1947 we shall still need the ability to say 'no'. We shall still need to provide some relief. But we shall need more than that. Negation is never a

---

[25] A similar line was taken in a 'Ten-point Programme for European Economic Recovery' published in Washington at the beginning of December 1946 by the American Planning Association, an independent research institute run by well-known industrialists and workers' leaders: it called for the full resumption of Ruhr coal production and other measures of relief for Germany, renewal of trade relations especially with Eastern Europe, etc., but made no approach to the idea of European union (DPD, 4.12.1946).

[26] The European associations were 'strongly suspected' of using vague pan-European terminology in order to 'further the aims of German national egoism, so recently overthrown': thus, e.g., *Der Tagesspiegel*, 22.2.1947.

[27] Cf., in chap. II, Churchill's article at n. 81 and Coudenhove's enquiry at nn. 333-7; also R. Coudenhove-Kalergi, 'A Parliament for Europe' (speech to the *New York Herald Tribune* High School Forum, 7.3.1947), in *Vital Speeches of the Day*, Vol. 13, New York, 15.4.1947, pp. 399-401, using the figure of 612 'Yeses' and only 12 'Noes'; id., *An Idea Conquers the World* (German, *Eine Idee erobert Europa*), London, 1953, p. 275 f.

[28] Cf. Jones (n. 12), p. 220; J. C. Campbell, *The U.S. in World Affairs 1945-1947*, publ. for Council on Foreign Relations, New York, 1947, p. 471; M. Beloff, *The United States and the Unity of Europe. A Brookings Institution Study*, New York, 1963, p. 20; Beugel (n. 8), p. 33 f. During the war J. F. Dulles was foreign-affairs adviser to the Federal Council of American Churches and co-author of the 'Six Pillar' memorandum advocating European federation; cf. Introduction, n. 109. See H. P. van Dusen (ed.), *The Spiritual Legacy of John Foster Dulles. Selections from his Articles and Addresses*, Philadelphia, 1960; biography esp. by M. Guhin, *John Foster Dulles: A Statesman and His Times*, New York (Columbia Univ. Press), 1972. Dulles's papers are in Princeton University Library.

permanent substitute for creation, and no nation is so poor as a nation which can give only dollars. The need is of spiritual and intellectual vigour and the leadership which that bestows ... Whoever deals with Europe deals with the world's worst fire hazard. Repeatedly it bursts out in flames. Twice within the last thirty years the edifice has virtually burned to the ground. The human and material losses have been colossal and irreparable. After each past conflagration the structure has been rebuilt substantially as before. Statesmanship can do better than go on repeating that folly. The trouble is not hard to find. Our founders diagnosed the situation many years ago. Alexander Hamilton put it in these historic words: 'To look for a continuation of harmony between a number of independent, unconnected sovereignties in the same neighbourhood would be to disregard the uniform course of human events and to set at defiance the accumulated experience of ages.'

Not only did our founders diagnose the trouble; they found for themselves the remedy. They placed matters of concern to all under an administration responsible to all. The war victors will do well to have that formula in mind. Then, when they plan the future of Germany, they will think more in terms of the economic unity of Europe and less in terms of the Potsdam dictum that Germany shall be 'a single economic unit'.[29]

The effect of this speech in the US was similar to that of Churchill's Zurich speech in Europe. Under the headline 'Power Tilt Hits Boom to Federate Europe' the *Christian Science Monitor* wrote on 27 January, referring to Dulles and the European federalists: 'The rapidly developing concept of European federation is running head-on into the colossal East–West struggle for world power and influence.' Sumner Welles wrote in the *Washington Post* of 5 February: 'Europe desperately needs some effective form of political and economic federation'; Dorothy Thompson, in the *Washington Star* of 11 February: 'Above all the U.S., out of her own wonderful experience of the Union of States, should support a European confederation plan.' *Life* magazine commented on 17 March that: 'To Dulles, as to more and more thinking people, our policy should be to help the nations of Europe federate as our States federated in 1787.' Walter Lippmann, the most influential of all commentators at that time, called in the *New York Herald Tribune* of 20 March for a 'European Economic Union', and suggested that Soviet reparations claims should be bought off by large loans. The idea of European union gained ground and encountered scarcely any opposition from then on, corresponding as it did to an essential part of the American tradition.[30]

[29] The argument that Germany must be considered in the European context was especially effective. 'Of course there should be an economic unification of Germany. But the reason for that is also a reason for the economic unification of Europe. A Europe divided into small economic compartments cannot be a healthy Europe. All of Europe's economic potentialities need to be used and European markets should be big enough to justify modern methods of cheap production for mass consumption.' J. F. Dulles, 'Europe must federate or perish', in *Vital Speeches of the Day*, Vol. 13, New York, Feb. 1947, pp. 234–6.

[30] The few examples of newspaper comment that can be given here are quoted partly from press-cutting files of the Council on Foreign Relations, partly from Beugel (n. 8), p. 101 f. For the

Although it appeared at first that European federation was essentially a theme of Republican policy, within a short time it received bipartisan support: the prominent Democratic Senator Fulbright, together with Senator Elbert Thomas of Utah, moved a resolution on 21 March, proposed in identical terms in the House of Representatives by Congressman Hale Boggs of Louisiana, which stated concisely that 'The Congress favours the creation of a United States of Europe within the framework of the United Nations.'[31] This was about six months after the European federalists had agreed on their basic programme and Churchill had issued his call to unity in Zurich, thus reviving the plans carefully worked out by the European Resistance movements. Fulbright, speaking in the Senate on 7 April, formulated a decisive American motive: 'This country cannot tolerate the expansion of Russia to the point where she controls, directly or indirectly, all the resources and manpower of Europe, Asia and Africa.' Democrats and Republicans in both Houses called on the State Department to take active steps to promote European union, without which the European countries could not hope for an independent future; this pressure from the legislature, as Max Beloff states, 'was to be fairly consistent for the next three years'.[32]

At this stage there was as yet no sign of the Truman administration endorsing this constructive concept. They were, however, decisively affected by the accumulation during the spring of alarming news concerning the West-European economy. On 5 March William Clayton, Under-Secretary for Economic Affairs in the State Department, first pointed out to senior members of the government that as a result of 'hunger, economic misery and frustration' most of the European countries were 'on the very brink and may be pushed over at any time; others are gravely threatened'.

---

underlying tradition, cf. George Washington to General Lafayette: 'We have sowed seeds of liberty and union that will spring up everywhere on earth, and one day, taking its pattern from the United States of America, there will be founded the United States of Europe' (*The Writings of George Washington*, ed. W. C. Ford, New York, 1889–93, vol. 9, p. 2847).

[31] *Congressional Record, 80th Congress, Vol. 93; 1st session*, pp. 2418 and 2425. On 31.3.1947 Senator Wiley moved to amend the wording to 'a United Democratic States of Europe . . . , to consist of nations which respect the political, economic, social and religious liberties of their respective citizens'. This, as Wiley explained, was to indicate that the 'foreign-dominated people of the Soviet satellite states' would not be eligible until they had developed democratic institutions (ibid., p. 2848). The resolution was referred to the Foreign Affairs Committee, but was not passed owing to Marshall's intervention (see note 42 below). Again following Marshall's objection, it was not inserted into the ERP bill of 31 March 1948. But in the amending act, approved on 19 April 1949, a declaration was included stating that it was 'the policy of the people of the United States to encourage the unification of Europe. (cf. Beugel, n. 8, pp. 103 and 115; Beloff, n. 28, pp. 27, 35, and 38).

[32] Beloff (n. 28), p. 20; Beugel (n. 8), pp. 100 f. and 103. Gasteyger (n. 31), p. 94; DPD report, 8.4.1947; Coudenhove, *An Idea* . . . , p. 277. On 22 April Coudenhove was able at last to announce the formation of an 'American Committee for a Free and United Europe', with W. Fulbright as its first president; the vice-president was former ambassador W. Bullitt (DPD, 24.4.1947). For Marshall's different tactical approach to the resolution, see n. 42 f.

Economic collapse, beginning in Greece and France, could lead to the rapid spread of Communist regimes; a massive programme of US financial and technical aid was necessary, otherwise 'affairs will become so hopeless that the seeds of World War III will inevitably be sown'.[33] After an extremely cold winter the fragmented European economies, struggling to recover from the war, had more and more evidently reached a point of stagnation which might at any moment turn into a decline. The 3 billion dollars' worth of UNRRA aid and the credits of billions of dollars granted to the West-European countries in 1945/6 were sufficient to restart the economies but the recovery was, since February 1947, drastically slowing down and by the spring of 1947 the loans were almost exhausted. In France, Belgium, and Holland industrial production was with difficulty raised to about 85 per cent of the pre-war level by the end of 1946, in Italy to 60 per cent; in Britain and Scandinavia the level was slightly higher than pre-war. A major handicap was the absence of the normal contribution of the German economy, where production was stuck at around 36 per cent of what it had been in 1936. Altogether the sixteen countries which were to be beneficiaries of the Marshall Plan had achieved 83 per cent of pre-war production, with an increase of 23 per cent from the first to the last quarter of 1946; during this period, however, the total of profits and funds for investment had risen by only 1 per cent. The national incomes of the sixteen totalled 46 per cent of that of the US, whereas their population was nearly twice as great. In the spring of 1947, instead of further recovery, there were alarming set-backs in all areas, owing chiefly to the continued shortage of coal, rising prices of raw materials, and the world-wide dearth of foodstuffs. To avoid collapse Europe had to maintain a steady volume of imports at rising prices which it could no longer afford. In 1947 the US balance of payments attained a surplus of 10 billion dollars, that of the Europeans a deficit of 7.5 billion.[34] 'Cassandra speaking' was the title of an impressively factual article in which Walter Lippmann sounded the alarm in the *New York Herald Tribune* on 5 April:

There is still some time left to prepare measures against the great post-war crisis which is developing in Europe and will surely, if it is not checked and prevented, affect the whole world ... The crisis is developing because none of the leading nations of Europe – Great Britain, France, Italy, Germany – is recovering from

---

[33] Text in E. Clayton-Garwood, *Will Clayton: A Short Biography,* Austin (Univ. of Texas Press), 1958, pp. 115–18. Clayton's note did not yet include the element of European integration. Its importance as the first initiative towards a comprehensive aid programme is emphasized by Acheson (n. 11), p. 226; Ferrell (n. 11), p. 280 f.; and Beloff (n. 28), p. 27 f.

[34] Cf. the detailed analysis of the economic crisis in Europe in 1947 by S. E. Harris, *The European Recovery Program,* Cambridge (Mass.), Harvard Univ. Press, 1948, esp. summaries and tables with the above-quoted figures on pp. 30 f., 41–51, 92, 168 f., and 249; further details and analyses in the sources quoted in Introduction, nn. 11–15; for Britain's rapidly widening 'dollar gap' despite large credits, see chap. I/3 at nn. 138–40. Europe's economic distress in the spring of 1947 is also fully described in Feis (n. 12), pp. 227–36.

the war, or has any reasonable prospect of recovery with the means at its disposal and on the plans and policies on which it is now working. The nations of Europe are eking out a precarious existence. They are staving off the collapse of their currencies and of their present standards of life, not by successful production but only by using up their dwindling assets and the loans, the subsidies and doles which come from Canada, the United States, and in small amounts from the few other solvent countries. The danger of a European collapse is the threat that hangs over us and all the world. I do not believe I am exaggerating ... The truth is that political and economic measures on a scale which no responsible statesman has yet ventured to hint at will be needed in the next year or so. To prevent the crisis which will otherwise engulf Europe and spread chaos throughout the world, the measures will have to be very large – in Europe no less than an economic union, and over here no less than the equivalent of a revival of lend-lease.[35]

Recognition of the situation was already crystallizing when General Marshall returned from Moscow on 28 April. Convinced by his experience there that the Kremlin, wishing to prolong the economic crisis of Western Europe, had no interest in arriving at joint decisions, Marshall gave instructions that detailed proposals for US action to solve Europe's problems should be prepared. This resulted in the production within the State Department of three basic memoranda, the ideas in which found expression five weeks later in the Harvard speech and the Marshall Plan. These developments have often been described and can be summarized here very briefly. On 8 May Under-Secretary of State Dean Acheson made a speech at Cleveland, Mississippi, giving the basic economic facts and pointing out that if the US exported goods and services to the value of $16 billion per annum – a month's output – but imported only $8 billion worth, the question was 'How are foreigners to get the dollars to cover a likely deficit of $8 billion in the next year?' The best way to restore world economic stability was to concentrate on Europe, including Germany; 'European recovery cannot be complete until the various parts of Europe's economy are working together in a harmonious whole.'[36] Meanwhile there were circulating in the State Department parts of a memorandum by H. van Buren Cleveland, Charles Kindleberger, and Ben T. Moore; this

---

[35] The *New York Herald Tribune* article was much reprinted and quoted: cf. Beloff (n. 28), p. 20 f., and Beugel (n. 8), p. 39; also H. Lüthy, *The State of France*, London, 1955, pp. 352–3. Lippmann developed his argument in a further article in the *Herald Tribune* on 1.5.1947, foreshadowing essential features of the Marshall Plan: 'We should suggest to the European governments that they meet together, agree on a general European programme of production and exchange of imports and exports to the outer world, and that they arrive at an estimate of the consolidated deficit for as much of Europe as can agree to a common plan. Such a consolidated deficit will be smaller than the sum of the separate national deficits. Moreover . . . it would be a refreshing innovation to make our contribution not to many separate governments but to Europe. . . . Thus [the contribution] . . . would serve not merely to relieve suffering but as a premium and inducement to the unification of Europe' (Beugel, p. 40).

[36] Text of speech in *Department of State Bulletin XVI*, Washington, 1947, p. 991. Cf. Acheson (n. 11), p. 227 f.; Jones (n. 12), pp. 24–30 and 206; Ferrell (n. 11), p. 105 f.; Beloff (n. 28), p. 26 f.; Beugel (n. 8), p. 47 f.

document, prepared for a Foreign Aid Committee set up in March, was the first in the State Department to put forward the idea of European union.

The memorandum stated that there was an urgent need to preserve democratic Western Europe from economic collapse. An agreement with the Soviet leaders on acceptable terms was desirable, but it would only be possible when the US had shown its determination 'to go ahead with a consistent and adequate recovery programme for non-Communist Europe with or without the U.S.S.R.'. But a merely economic programme would be no less inadequate than a merely anti-Communist motivation, for which most of the West-European governments in any case felt too weak and too dependent on Moscow's goodwill. 'Non-Communist Europe must also be provided with positive goals to help fill the present ideological and moral vacuum'; and European union was the best, if not the only positive aim that could be suggested. 'There is a possibility of developing tremendous emotional drive in Western Europe behind the supranational ideal of European unity.' Moreover the US proposal would avoid hurting nationalist feelings if it were couched 'in terms of a European recovery plan which stresses the raising of European production and consumption through the economic and functional unification of Europe'. The Soviet Union and the East-European countries must certainly be invited to take part in the recovery programme, partly to maintain the traditional economic links between Eastern and Western Europe and partly to impress on the Kremlin that it was in its interest to seek agreement with the US on European affairs.[37]

The Policy Planning Staff under George F. Kennan, which Marshall set to work the day after he returned from Moscow, produced a memorandum of 23 May which agreed that a US offer should purport 'to combat not communism, but the economic maladjustment which makes European society vulnerable to exploitation by any and all totalitarian movements and which Russian communism is now exploiting'. The US should not themselves formulate 'a programme for the economic revitalization of Europe: this is the business of the Europeans. The formal initiative must come from Europe.' For political and economic reasons (not further specified in the memorandum) the programme should 'be a joint one, agreed on by several European nations'. The project could be put to the whole of Europe in the ECE, 'but then it would be essential that this be done in such a form that the Russian satellite countries would either exclude themselves by unwillingness to accept the proposed conditions or agree to abandon the exclusive orientation of their economies'. The

---

[37] A preliminary version of this memorandum (Interim Report of 21.4.1947, describing itself as a 'hasty analysis') is the first item in the Marshall Plan documentation in *FRUS 1947* (n. 14), *Vol. III*, Washington, 1972, pp. 204–19 ('this report led directly to Acheson's Mississippi speech, written by Joe Jones', ibid., p. 243). The final version, dated 12.6.1947, is not given in *FRUS* (cf. ibid., p. 243), but is quoted at length in Jones (n. 12), pp. 149–201 and 243 f.; summaries in Beloff (n. 28), pp. 21–6, and Beugel (n. 8), p. 44 f. The authors recommended that the plan be supervised by the ECE, partly in order to facilitate Soviet assent: cf. chap. II, n. 23.

memorandum was, as Acheson observed, on the cautious side.[38] Clayton, on the other hand, who returned from some weeks' stay in Europe on 19 May, submitted a paper urging speed and resolution. 'Europe is steadily deteriorating. The political position reflects the economic. One political crisis after another merely denotes the existence of grave economic distress. Millions of people in the cities are slowly starving.' He was presenting a somewhat generalized picture of what was the Central- and South-European situation in order to stimulate quicker action from his government. He went on to state that the remaining gold reserves in Europe would be exhausted by the end of the year. Failing substantial aid there would be a collapse that would also involve the US in a depression. There must be a 'strong appeal to the American people to sacrifice' and a grant to Europe of '6 to 7 billion dollars' worth of goods a year for three years', especially coal, grain, and shipping services.

'This three-year grant to Europe should be based on a European plan which the principal European nations, headed by the U.K., France and Italy, should work out. Such a plan should be based on a European economic federation on the order of the Benelux Customs Union. Europe cannot recover from this war and again become independent if her economy continues to be divided into as many small watertight compartments as it is today.' Thus an economic federation was again postulated. Clayton, on the other hand, was against using institutions such as the ECE. 'We must avoid getting into another UNRRA. The United States must run this show.'[39]

On the basis of these memoranda Charles E. Bohlen, Marshall's special assistant, prepared a draft which, after amendments by Clayton, Acheson, and the Secretary of State, became the text of the speech delivered by Marshall at the Harvard commencement ceremony on 5 June. In it he promised the Europeans massive aid towards economic recovery on condition that instead of each country expressing its wants separately they agreed on a joint programme, inaugurating a new period of European economic co-operation. The short speech, brilliant in its simplicity, began with a five-minute outline of Europe's plight on the lines of the Clayton

---

[38] Acheson (n. 11), p. 231. The Kennan memorandum did not refer to European federation, but proposed strict conditions for East-European participation; it suggested that the US embassies in Europe be instructed to take soundings and that there be full discussion with the UK, which should formally initiate the proposal. Full text in *FRUS* (n. 37), pp. 223–9; extracts previously published in Jones (n. 12), pp. 249–54; H. B. Price, *The Marshall Plan and its Meaning*, Ithaca, NY, 1955, pp. 21–4; also, with an account of its origin, in Kennan (n. 15), pp. 325–38. Cf. J. Reiss, *George Kennans Politik der Eindämmung (Studien zur europäischen Geschichte aus dem Friedrich-Meinecke-Institut der Freien Universität Berlin*, Bd. 2), Berlin, 1957; summaries in Beloff (n. 28), p. 29 f., and Beugel (n. 8), p. 42 f.
[39] Text of memorandum 'The European Crisis', based on notes written during the return flight on 19 May, dated 27 May (when it was submitted to Marshall), published in Clayton-Garwood (n. 33), pp. 119–21; also in *FRUS* (n. 37), pp. 230–2. As is often the case nowadays with definitive publications of documents on major questions, *FRUS* does not add to the sum of knowledge on the prehistory of the Marshall Plan. On this subject, besides the works quoted above, see W. C. Mallalieu, 'The Origins of the Marshall Plan', *Political Science Quarterly*, 73 (1958), pp. 481–504; Feis (n. 12), pp. 237–44.

memorandum. 'The remedy', Marshall continued, 'lies in breaking the vicious circle and restoring the confidence of the European peoples in the economic future of their own countries and of Europe as a whole ... Our policy is directed not against any country or doctrine but against hunger, poverty, desperation and chaos. Its purpose should be the revival of a working economy in the world so as to permit the emergence of political and social conditions in which free institutions can exist.' In the remaining three minutes of his address Marshall struck a note of caution more in accordance with Kennan's thinking:

> Before the United States Government can proceed much further in its efforts to ... help start the European world on its way to recovery, there must be some agreement among the countries of Europe as to the requirements of the situation and the part those countries themselves will take in order to give proper effect to whatever action might be undertaken by this Government. It would be neither fitting nor efficacious for this Government to undertake to draw up unilaterally a programme designed to place Europe on its feet economically. This is the business of the Europeans. The initiative, I think, must come from Europe. The role of this country should consist of friendly aid in the drafting of a European programme and of later support of such a programme so far as it may be practical for us to do so. The programme should be a joint one, agreed to by a number, if not all, of the European nations.[40]

The decisive breakthrough, giving a fresh depth of content to the new foreign policy, was that the negative purpose of 'containing' Soviet expansion was henceforth supplemented by the positive and constructive one of strengthening regions of the world for their own benefit and that of the global economy. The message for Europe was that its divisions and internal quarrels were a major cause of its distress, and that only by overcoming them could it achieve economic and therefore political stability. The advice that the European governments, beset by troubles, had refused to listen to when it was proferred by the federalists in their respective countries was now repeated by one of the two superpowers: 'Unite!' The Marshall Plan promised that if they did so the US would meet their combined deficit as a contribution to reviving the European economy and, it was hoped, rendering their countries immune to further Communist subversion and expansion. The sober, rational terms in which the plan was presented, and the prospect it offered of a fresh attempt to reach agreement with the Soviet Union, made it an outstanding example of successful

---

[40] Full text in *Department of State Bulletin,* June 15, 1947, p. 1159 f.; *Documents on American Foreign Relations, Vol. IX: Jan. 1–Dec. 31, 1947,* Princeton, 1949, pp. 9–11; *In Quest of Peace and Security, Selected Documents on American Foreign Policy 1941–1951* (Dept. of State Publ. 4245), Washington, 1951, pp. 93–5; Jones (n. 12), pp. 281–4; Beugel (n. 8), pp. 49–52. It was important in drafting the speech, though only incidental to our present purpose, that Congress should not be offended by a *fait accompli* or feel that its hands had been tied by promises. Congressmen could not object to the statement that if the Europeans jointly asked for help, the Administration would consider sympathetically what aid was practicable; cf. Acheson (n. 11), p. 234.

statecraft.[41] Marshall's formulation implied two further decisions which careful interpretation brought to light in due course:

1. The speech did not imitate the precision with which two of the three preceding memoranda had advocated a 'European economic federation' or an early customs union as the first stage towards political union. Marshall did not use the word 'federation' but spoke only of 'agreement among the countries of Europe' on a joint programme. On 4 June, the day before the speech, Marshall took care to explain this in a letter to Senator Vandenberg, describing his attitude to the resolution proposed by Fulbright 'that the Congress favours the creation of a United States of Europe'. Marshall wrote that he personally shared this view:

I am deeply sympathetic towards the general objective of the Resolution ... Of course the United States wants a Europe which is not divided against itself, a Europe which is better than that it replaces ... But we should make clear that it is not our purpose to impose upon the peoples of Europe any particular form of political or economic association. The future organization of Europe must be determined by the peoples of Europe ... [However,] the United States welcomes any initiative which may be taken by the peoples of Europe within the framework of the United Nations to ensure greater cooperation among themselves to expedite the reconstruction and restoration of the economy of Europe as a whole.[42]

The genuineness of Marshall's sympathy for the idea of a United States of Europe is borne out by the tenor of his Harvard speech and, for instance, by his address to a Governors' conference at Salt Lake City on 14 July 1947: 'Thinking back on the development of our Federal Union, ... Americans should have a keen and sympathetic understanding for the efforts now under way in Europe to overcome the limitations of national barriers.' He was resolved, however, not to impose any particular solution, and did not accept the view expressed by Fulbright in the Senate on 13 June: 'I am greatly encouraged by the letter, although I think that under the circumstances as they now appear in Europe it is unduly timid and cautious ... I do not agree that we should as a matter of policy always leave the initiative to other nations.' Fulbright went on to say that as practically all the Europeans had asked for US aid, and as in their present disunited condition they were 'no good risks either to repay loans or even to survive as democratic states, I am unable to see why the suggestion that they get together and form some kind

---

[41] More critical recent versions of events are still laudatory of Marshall's initiative; some, however, over-emphasize the 'contrast' with the Truman doctrine, whereas it was rather a development away from local economic aid closely linked with the containment of Communism, and towards the idea of mutual aid on a European basis. Halle (n. 16), p. 129 f., speaks of Marshall's 'statesmanship' in that his proposals were not 'cast in the form of a challenge to Moscow'; similarly Czempiel (n. 10), p. 265 f.: not directed against Russia, but European reconstruction for the sake of world economy; Ulam (n. 15), p. 127: an act of self-denial on America's part, as no 'reward' could be expected for years.

[42] 'Perhaps the authors of the Resolution might consider adding a preamble along these lines': Marshall to Vandenberg, 4.6.1947, given to the press on 10.6.1947; before me is a hectographed document, Dept. of State, For the Press, June 10, 1947, No. 469. Reproduced with some omissions in Beugel (n. 8), p. 103 f. For Fulbright's resolution, see n. 31 f.

of political and economic unity as part of the bargain is dictation or undue influence'.[43]

This difference persisted for some years, with the Administration taking a cautious attitude and many members of Congress urging the need for European federation. During his two years as Secretary of State Marshall adhered strictly to the policy of not offering the Europeans any definite advice as to the form their 'association' should take. This was perhaps a pity from the federalist point of view, but it was an impressive exhibition of restraint. It is not impossible that, while Marshall wished to help Europe to recover economically and to be immunized against Communism, and thought that a measure of European co-operation to this end was in the American interest, he did not want to be instrumental in bringing about a strong political federation that might one day give trouble to the US. Be that as it may, he gave an impulse towards effective economic co-operation and promised in addition to support any European initiative towards union.[44] This, in any case, was the contrary of the time-honoured 'divide and rule' policy adopted by the Russians – it was left to the European governments to decide for themselves what degree of 'association' they wanted.

2. On 28 May, in a final discussion with his advisers before the Harvard speech, Marshall made a point of considering once again whether the proposal should be addressed to the whole of Europe or only to the non-Communist states. Acheson, Kennan, Clayton, and Bohlen all took the view that Europe's economic recovery must not be made dependent on Soviet agreement, so that the Russians could torpedo it at will; on the other hand, the offer of co-operation should be addressed to the Russians in a final attempt to reach agreement with them. It was realized that they were unlikely to agree to lay open their economy in this way, but it was important to make them come into the open so that the US should not bear the responsibility for dividing Europe. Marshall personally decided on this course, while including in his speech a warning against obstruction:

---

[43] Marshall in Salt Lake City, 14.7.1947: *Documents on American Foreign Relations, Vol. IX: Jan. 1–Dec. 31, 1947,* Princeton, 1949, p. 166 f.; Fulbright in the Senate, 13.6.1947: *Congressional Record, 80th Congress, 1st session,* p. 6957 f.; quoted in Beugel (n. 8), p. 104 f.

[44] Cf. his statement at n. 42. It is to be noted in this connection that there was as yet no question of a security pact with Europe, such as was concluded shortly afterwards with the Latin-American states in a much more 'political' application of the new regional principle: in the Inter-American Mutual Assistance Treaty signed at Rio de Janeiro on 2 Sept. 1947 the nineteen American republics undertook that 'an armed attack by any State against an American State shall be considered as an attack against all the American States' (text in *Dept. of State Bulletin,* Washington, 21 Sept. 1947, pp. 565–7). On the interpretation of this treaty as a victory of the regional over the universal principle, cf. E. S. Furniss Jr., 'The United States, the Inter-American System and the United Nations', *Political Science Quarterly,* 65 (1950), pp. 415–30, esp. 424. Significantly it was the Senate which, in the Vandenberg resolution of 11.6.1948, later proposed the creation of a similar security pact in the Atlantic area (cf. chap. VI/1 in vol. 2).

Any government that is willing to assist in the task of recovery will find full cooperation, I am sure, on the part of the U.S. Government. Any government which manœuvres to block the recovery of other countries cannot expect help from us. Furthermore, governments, political parties or groups which seek to perpetuate human misery in order to profit therefrom politically or otherwise will encounter the opposition of the United States.

It was open to the Soviet Government, however, to regard the last two sentences as not applying to them, and to present themselves as 'willing to assist in the task of recovery'. In a statement to the press on 12 June Marshall expressly confirmed that the Harvard offer applied to 'all countries west of Asia', including the Soviet Union; the latter was welcome to join in, provided it accepted its share of joint obligations under the recovery programme.[45] It was now up to the Soviet Union to decide whether it would co-operate with the US and the European countries and what part a European union might play in the development of East–West relations.

(C) THE SOVIET UNION AGAIN REJECTS PLANS FOR EUROPEAN UNITY

The change in US policy and the Marshall offer undoubtedly presented the Soviet leaders with a difficult decision. They were completely unprepared for the prospect of such a substantial contribution to European recovery, linked with the constructive idea of European co-operation in the common interest. Their policy had so far been to prevent any close union of European countries and any solution of the German problem that did not give them *de facto* hegemony over all Germany.[46] By thus fostering economic chaos, and by a reparations policy which saddled the Americans with the task of keeping Germany at subsistence level, they hoped to weaken Western Europe to the point of exhaustion and induce the Americans to wash their hands of European affairs. This prospect, for which Stalin had been understandably hoping in view of Roosevelt's isolationist remarks at Yalta, was overthrown by the new US policy.

The part played in Soviet calculations by the question of European unity becomes especially clear if one considers how the Soviet Union had reacted in the preceding months to the reactivation of federalist plans. Having derived enormous profit from forbidding and hindering all attempts at unification, and having eradicated all such plans from Allied post-war planning since 1942–3, the Russians had no hesitation in firmly

---

[45] Similar accounts of the discussion on 28.5.1947 iin Acheson (n. 11), p. 232, and Kennan (n. 15), p. 342; for text of Harvard speech, see n. 40; press statement of 12.6.1947 in Price (n. 38), p. 21. Further evidence for the genuineness of the offer to Russia, esp. Clayton's statement, cf. below, n. 56; there is no basis for suppositions to the contrary, which also appeared in the press at that time. A 'Summary of Discussion' of 28.5.1947 is in *FRUS 1947/III*, pp. 234–6.

[46] Cf. Moscow meeting of Council of Foreign Ministers, 10.3.1947–24.4.1947, p. 465 f.

opposing the European idea when it was revived by the federalist groups and in Churchill's speeches. Faced with the internal anxieties of a dictatorship, they found it natural to practise a foreign policy of 'divide and rule'; and it had long appeared to them that the best way to 'prove' the Marxist thesis of the inevitable decline and collapse of the capitalist world was to preserve the disunion and consequent economic distress of the European states. On the day after the publication of Churchill's Zurich speech, Radio Moscow made the Soviet position clear. There were, it declared, two tendencies in world politics, that of democratic respect for state sovereignty and that of an anti-Soviet coalition. Churchill, the chief representative of the latter, wanted to launch a new war against the Soviet Union by means of a Franco-German combination under British and American patronage, in a desperate attempt to maintain the predominance of Anglo-Saxon capitalism.[47] Thus given their cue, all the Communist newspapers in Western Europe launched violent attacks against the 'warmongers'. For this purpose they played on all the hopes that had been encouraged since 1943 for a lasting peace under the aegis of friendly cooperation between the two superpowers, and also did their best to revive and exploit nationalist sentiment of all kinds.

Barely five days after the Zurich speech, Stalin himself gave two interviews which were typical of the Soviets' appeal to 'one world' feelings that had stood them in such good stead, and which also bore witness to the effect created by the revival, though as yet purely in theoretical terms, of the idea of European unity. Stalin declared that only political adventurers could talk of a new war or accuse the Soviet Union of planning further expansion. He firmly believed in the possibility of friendly competition between the Western democracies and the Soviet Union, which sought to develop the best cultural and commercial relations with every country in the world. The government daily *Izvestiya* responded in similar terms to the establishment of the United Europe Committee in London: 'The creation of a bloc of European states, no matter under what colours, cannot be reconciled with the principles of international co-operation.'[48] The theme of 'one world' solidarity as a recipe for peace was reinforced by the encouragement of nationalist feeling. Newspapers in the Soviet Zone of Germany, for instance, did not oppose the European idea on the ground that the Germans must first prove themselves good Europeans, but on the contrary made violent appeals to German nationalism, which from now on they made it their business to revive. Any attempt to bring about European unity would, they argued, 'mean in practice the complete dismemberment of Germany into two parts'. The *Berliner Zeitung*,

---

[47] *Neue Zeitung* and *Frankfurter Neue Presse*, 23.9.1946. The *Tägliche Rundschau* (Berlin) of 8.12.1946 stated in an article signed by 'H. Poljanow' that the idea of a Western bloc was 'essentially directed against the people' (*volksfeindlich*) and an attempt to 'consolidate reactionary forces'; similarly the *Tägliche Rundschau* of 18.12.1946 and 7.2.1947, and *Neues Deutschland* of 28.1.1947.
[48] Stalin quoted in *Die Weltwoche*, Zurich, 27.9.1946. He spoke highly of the friendly relations between Britain and the Soviet Union, which indeed had much to do with the stagnation of Bevin's foreign policy (cf. chap. I/3, pp. 173–89). *Izvestiya* quoted from DPD, 25.1.1947; the article went on to say that 'Any plan that would exclude the Soviet Union from participation in European affairs is a political anachronism.'

reporting on the Eutin congress in June 1947, called the advocates of European union 'the arch-enemies of a united Germany'.[49] In this way, on the tacit and cynical assumption that the Soviet Union would not permit the territories in its own sphere of influence to take part in a European union, the motive of preserving German unity became the local variant of the Kremlin's policy of stirring up nationalist feeling in every quarter so as to keep the European states divided among themselves. At the same time, of course, *L'Humanité* in Paris and the Communist papers in other West-European capitals continued to preach against German nationalism as the supreme danger to be fought at all costs.[50]

Apart from negative appeals to old-fashioned nationalism, Soviet propaganda had difficulty in producing rational objections to the European idea. The Russians took care not to refer to the federalists' aim of including the whole of Europe, of which they were well informed through their West-European missions; again on the tacit assumption that the East-European countries would, as a matter of course, be debarred from taking part, they declaimed against 'war-mongering ideas of a Western bloc' which would 'once again split into two camps the world that was to have been unified by the United Nations Organization'.[51] The Red Army newspaper *Krasnaya Zvezda*, in particular, made much use of slogans to the effect that plans for European union were an 'incitement to a new war', or, as *Pravda* wrote on 19 February: 'The revival of the old, bankrupt Pan-European idea and similar long-discredited formulas is a sign of extreme political clumsiness.' *Pravda* warned France, Belgium, and the Netherlands to give a wide berth to ideas of European union or even mutual tariff concessions, which were a plot to infringe their national sovereignty and 'bring part of Europe under the sway of the British Empire'.[52]

Further articles followed up this theme, which took pride of place in a pamphlet by the leading Soviet propagandist Alexander Galin, distributed in many languages in March 1947. 'The freedom-loving nations have disposed of one

---

[49] *Tägliche Rundschau*, 20.5.1947; on 21.5.1947 the paper quoted the *Daily Herald's* criticism approvingly under the headline: 'Churchill wants a divided Europe' (Churchill will ein geteiltes Europa). *Berliner Zeitung* quoted from DPD, 25.6.1947.

[50] 'Hitler wanted to include France in a coalition against Soviet Russia; has Churchill really not heard that we rejected such ideas?' (*L'Humanité* according to *Badische Zeitung*, 21.9.1946 and 18.10.1946). To complete our necessarily limited selection of press comment (cf. p. 433), see especially the Communist parties' views quoted in chap. IV (in vol. 2).

[51] *Tägliche Rundschau*, 20.5.1947. For Russian knowledge of UEF ideas, e.g. through Military Government in Karlshorst, Smirnov's reports, etc., cf. chap. II at n. 230 f. For the Soviet attitude to plans for European union in general, cf. M. Beloff, 'The Russian View of European Integration', in *The Great Powers*, London, 1959, p. 130 f. (P. Le Gall, 'L'URSS et l'unification européenne', in *Revue française de science politique*, No. 1, Feb. 1967, pp. 28–46, covers only the rejection of the Briand plan and the period from 1950).

[52] *Krasnaya Zvezda* and *Pravda* of 19.2.1947 as reported by the *New York Times'* Moscow correspondent, 20.2.1947. The *Pravda* article occupied a page and a half and was signed by Otto Kuusinen, member of the presidium of the Supreme Soviet; it advised West-European countries to 'save their sovereignty and economic independence' by concluding pacts with the Soviet Union as Poland, Czechoslovakia, etc. had done. It was also published in pamphlet form: O. V. Kuusinen, *O pretendentakh na opeku nad narodami Evropy*, Moscow, OGIZ, 1947.

Limitation to Western Europe 481

would-be *Führer* of Europe; why should they now need a *Führer* of the British brand? ... British Imperialism will not succeed ... by creating a "New Order" in Europe on the Churchill pattern. The peoples of Europe do not want a split under the label of union.' The argument was especially hollow as Churchill himself had only urged the Continentals to unite among themselves and had not envisaged British membership, while Bevin and the rest of the British government were at this time firmly opposed to the idea of European union.[53]

Once again, this time for decades to come, the Soviet leaders had thrown away the chance of anticipating the US initiative, endorsing the federalist ideal, and working for the recovery and unification of what could have been a 'progressive' Europe friendly to the USSR. Given a little more understanding of economic needs and recognition of the Europeans' right to live their own lives free from Soviet hegemony, the Kremlin might have secured for itself a prosperous neighbour of strongly Socialistic and pro-Russian tendencies. Instead, heedless of the Europeans' most elementary needs, the Soviets saw no way of consolidating their own vastly extended empire except by slandering and obstructing efforts to unite any part of Europe. This policy found ideological backing in Lenin's dictum that a union of Europe would prevent its collapse and must be combated, as it would diminish the attraction of Communism. There was thus from the start virtually no chance that the Soviet Union would respond favourably to Marshall's offer and join in a recovery programme on the basis of collective planning, which might rapidly bring about the economic stabilization of Europe and also strengthen the ties between its Western and Eastern parts.

(D) THE PRELIMINARY PARIS CONFERENCE ON THE MARSHALL PLAN, AND MOSCOW'S VETO

Marshall's offer was welcomed by Bevin in a speech to the Foreign Press Association in London on 13 June; this was a response to Marshall's stipulation that 'the initiative must come from Europe', and a reflection of the fact that Britain's 'dollar gap' was the most serious in any European country. Bevin declared that Marshall's offer 'will rank, I think, as one of the greatest speeches made in the world's history', and, referring to the question of Soviet participation, declared that 'when the U.S. throws a

---

[53] Cf. chap. I, pp. 181–9, chap. II, p. 320 f., and chap. III, p. 492 f. A. Galin, 'Europe: Split or United?' in *Foreign Affairs*, vol. 25 (1947), pp. 408–20 (quotations, pp. 416 and 419 f.). Similarly the SED paper *Neues Deutschland* on 6.4.1947, in an article entitled 'An Indian Europe?', denounced federal plans as a means to British domination of the Continent. 'As to the federalist principle, the most sacrosanct aspect of the idea, a parallel with India is entirely appropriate. The very same Churchill advocates a similar system for the "pearl in the British crown" ' (quoted from W. Cornides, 'Die Anfänge des europäischen föderalistischen Gedankens in Deutschland 1945–1949', *Europa-Archiv*, 6 (1951), p. 4243).

[54] Bevin on 13.6.1947, reported in *The Times* of 14.6.1947, quoted in J. and G. Kolko, *The Limits of Power. The World and United States Foreign Policy 1945–1954*, New York, 1972, p. 361.

bridge to link East and West it would be disastrous for ideological or other reasons to frustrate the U.S. in that great endeavour'. The Western response evidently threw Moscow into some confusion. *Pravda* did not react until 16 June, when it described Marshall's offer as merely another version of the Truman doctrine, 'political interference by means of dollars' in the internal affairs of other states.[54] On the afternoon of 17 June, Bevin arrived at Paris and handed to the French government a note stating that the 'United Kingdom enthusiastically welcomes the inspiring lead given to the United Kingdom and to the peoples of Europe by the United States' Secretary of State in his speech at Harvard on 5 June'.

The note stated 'it was desirable that if possible the plan should relate to Europe as a whole', and suggested that 'the British and French Governments should set up before the end of June a small body of experts drawn from a representative group of European countries, e.g. the United Kingdom, France, Poland, Czechoslovakia, Belgium or the Netherlands (for Benelux) and Denmark ... As soon as possible the proposal to appoint a Committee of Experts should be notified to all other European Governments (except Spain), who would be invited to co-operate.' On the evening of the 17th, as Bevin reported six days later to his Cabinet, 'M. Ramadier, M. Bidault and myself had a useful informal discussion, as a result of which we found we were in agreement on many points of substance. We both recognised the importance of the Marshall proposal and the urgency of taking the initiative and preparing a report at a very early date on the steps necessary to achieve European reconstruction. We agreed that the initiative must be taken by the European Governments outside the framework of the United Nations, since to remit the task of preparing the plan to the Economic Commission for Europe could only result in delay.' But 'it became clear in the course of the discussion that the French Ministers, and in particular M. Ramadier, regarded it as essential, because of the internal situation in France, that before any definite decisions were taken between us the Russians should be given the opportunity of joining in our deliberations'. In the formal talks of 18 June Bevin and Bidault decided upon a cordially worded invitation to Molotov; they also agreed on an agenda for the meeting with him, and to set up a Franco-British preparatory committee.[55]

On the evening of the 18th the invitation was sent to Molotov for 'a meeting of the British, French and Soviet Foreign Ministers ... at a place to be agreed in order to discuss these problems'. On the 19th Clayton in Washington appealed to the Russians to take part in the work of

---

[55] *Public Records Office*, Cab. 129, vol. 19, pp. 225–8: Report from Bevin, 23 June 1947, 'on my recent conversations with the French Government'; including as Annex A 'Note by United Kingdom Delegation', 17 June, on p. 226, and as Annexes E and F 'Draft Record of Meeting held in M. Bidault's Office at 6 P.M. on Wednesday 18th June, 1947' and 'Draft Record of Second Meeting Held in M. Bidault's Office at 6 P.M. on Wednesday 18th June, 1947'. The report itself (pp. 225–6) left no doubt that it was the French who were pressing the most for the immediate invitation to Molotov, and that later 'the French appear to be angling for a procedural conference of European powers', whereas Bevin would have preferred 'that two or three sponsoring powers should take upon themselves the responsibility of issuing invitations to selected individuals'. Bevin concluded 'the results of the meeting are not as positive as I would have hoped'.

European reconstruction, while Bevin declared in the Commons that Europe must press forward with or without the Soviet Union.[56] All this, in conjunction with Moscow's undoubted need for credits to support its own recovery, evidently strengthened the hand of those in the Kremlin who thought the American offer should be accepted or at least discussed through diplomatic channels. There were several reasons why the Soviet leaders could not bring themselves to veto the plan at once: the advantages it offered to the distressed areas of the East-European glacis, the risk that a refusal on their part would help the Americans to a special position in Western Europe, and the fact that responsibility for the split-up of the wartime coalition would be seen to rest on the Soviet Union alone. Accordingly on 22 June Molotov agreed to meet for a discussion with Bevin and Bidault in Paris on the 27th.[57]

Thus British and French diplomacy, like that of the US, was at pains to carry the Russians along and to avoid any responsibility for their non-participation. Bevin and Bidault may privately have thought that an effective programme could only be drawn up if the Russians did not take part,[58] but their actions gave no hint of this. Their fear was rather that active Russian opposition, supported by strong Communist parties in Western Europe, might endanger the planned recovery. They refused to acquiesce in a partition of Europe, hoping instead that co-operation in the task of reconstruction, arduous though it might be, would bring East and West together again. In preliminary conversations in London in the last week of June, senior Foreign Office officials emphasized to their Continental opposite numbers that important questions such as the liberalization of trade must not be touched on for fear of arousing Russian apprehensions.[59]

Hopes were at a high pitch when Molotov, accompanied by eighty-nine experts, arrived in Paris on 27 June, and during the first two days of talks it seemed possible, despite the ungracious tone of his remarks, that he enjoyed some latitude which would permit a compromise. In his first

---

[56] Bidault's official invitation to Molotov is reproduced in Ministère des Affaires Étrangères, *Documents de la Conférence des Ministres des Affaires Étrangères de la France, du Royaume Uni et de l'URSS tenue à Paris du 27 juin au 3 juillet 1947*, Paris, 1947, p. 15 f.; Clayton's appeal of 19.6.1947 cited from Kolko (n. 54), p. 361; Bevin in the House of Commons on the 19.6.1947, reported in *The Times* of 20.6.1947, quoted in Beugel (n. 8), p. 58. Cf. also *FRUS 1947/III* (n. 37), pp. 254–63.

[57] For probable advocacy in the Kremlin, see esp. A. B. Ulam, *Expansion and Coexistence*, New York, 1968, pp. 432–6. Difficulties of the Soviet recovery programme: in 1946 gross industrial production was 17% down on 1945 and about 40% below the 1940 level: cf. *Geschichte der Sowjetunion 1917–1957* (chap. II, n. 4), Berlin, 1960, p. 661. For the wishes of the East-European countries, see n. 62 below.

[58] D. Wightman, *Economic Cooperation in Europe*, New York, 1956, p. 29. According to Ferrell (n. 11), p. 113, they both told the US ambassador in Paris on 18 June that they secretly hoped the Russians would refuse (now confirmed by *FRUS 1947/III*, p. 260).

[59] Confirmed by Beugel (n. 8), who was present, p. 60. Federalist groups, above all, were inspired by Molotov's arrival in Paris to hope 'that the differences will be overcome and the basis soon created for economic co-operation among European states. This will be the quickest way to avoid the danger of Germany splitting into an Eastern and a Western half' – thus, as an example of many, a broadcast talk given from Stuttgart by Henri Bernhard on 30.6.1947: *Bernhard Archives*, Europ. Aktion file).

speech on 28 June he welcomed Marshall's offer of economic aid while pointing out that 'it is known that the U.S. is likewise interested in using its credit possibilities for expanding its foreign markets'. But, he went on, the Franco-British proposal that the conference should decide upon 'drawing up a comprehensive economic programme for the European countries' was unacceptable, because 'internal economic matters are the sovereign affair of the peoples themselves, and other countries must not interfere in these internal affairs'. He proposed that each country should be allowed to conclude bilateral credit agreements with the US, and would not hear of any German participation. Nevertheless, on 29 June Molotov proposed the setting-up of an 'Assistance Committee' composed of representatives of France, Britain, the USSR, and 'certain other Russian countries'; this, however, was only to co-ordinate the needs of individual states, in the first instance those which 'were subjected to German occupation and contributed to the common victory', and was to scrutinize carefully any conditions that might be attached to US aid. Bevin and Bidault, on the other hand, insisted on the need for the European states to submit a joint, 'consolidated' economic programme. In a last effort at compromise on 1 July Bidault emphasized that the necessary joint programme could be worked out without any violation of national sovereignty. But on the same day a telegram from Moscow was brought to Molotov, after reading which he took no further part in the discussion.[60] On 2 July he took the floor and categorically rejected the Franco-British proposals as contrary to the principle of national sovereignty; thereupon he withdrew from the conference.

It was clear, Molotov said, that if the proposals were accepted, 'European countries will become subsidiary states and will forfeit their former economic independence and national sovereignty in favour of certain strong Powers ... What will then remain of the economic independence and sovereignty of such European countries? ... Such a course is contrary to the interests of the European countries, because this may lead to renunciation of economic independence, which is incompatible with the preservation of national sovereignty... The Franco-British proposal ... would lead to no good. It would lead to Great Britain, France and the group of countries which follow them separating themselves from the other

[60] Thus Bevin according to W. Bedell Smith (n. 17), p. 198; similarly Acheson (n. 11), p. 234, who adds: 'I suspect that Molotov must have thought that the instruction sent him was stupid; in any case, the withdrawal of the Russians made operations much more simple.' Molotov's statements and proposals are given in *Problems of Foreign Policy* (n. 17), pp. 457–70 and 609–11. Bevin reported to his Cabinet that Molotov 'refused to consider any course except that of presenting the United States with a statement of each country's requirements. Any other course, he said, would mean interference, political and economic, in the internal affairs of the participating countries', and Bevin concluded: 'Had the Russians decided to come in, even on our terms, the opportunities which they would have had to delay and obstruct would have been almost unlimited; so that from a practical point of view it is far better to have them definitely out than half-heartedly in.' (PRO, Cab. 129, vol. 19, p. 266: Memorandum to the Cabinet, 5th July, 1947,' Foreign Ministers' Talks on Marshall Offer'). The statements of all delegations are summarized in Ministère des Affaires Etrangères, *Documents* ... (n. 56). Cf. also *FRUS 1947/III* (n. 37), pp. 296–309.

countries of Europe, which would split Europe into two groups of states and create fresh difficulties in the relations between them.'[61]

After Molotov's departure Bevin and Bidault invited twenty-two European governments (i.e. every country except Spain and Germany) to attend a conference in Paris on 12 July to discuss Marshall's offer. All fourteen countries outside the Soviet orbit accepted, and the East Europeans also made it clear that they were not disposed to fall in with Molotov's veto. The Czechoslovak government on 7 July unanimously voted to accept the Franco-British invitation. The Polish government had informed Washington at the end of June that they were prepared to work out a joint economic plan with all European governments, and had sent their minister of foreign trade to Paris, as had Finland and Yugoslavia. The Hungarian Telegraph Agency announced on 7 July that the Hungarian government had unanimously decided to take part in the European economic programme and had asked the Soviet military government for permission to accept the invitation to Paris on 12 July. Clearly it was not Marshall's offer that split Europe in two, since the East-European countries were only too anxious to accept; the Soviet Union itself made Molotov's parting threat into a reality by putting severe pressure on the East-European governments to refuse the Franco-British invitation or revoke their acceptance of it.

Jan Masaryk, the Czechoslovak foreign minister, was summoned to Moscow with Prime Minister Gottwald on 8 July to receive the order to reverse their decision; after the journey he remarked: 'I went to Moscow as the Foreign Minister of an independent sovereign state; I returned as a lackey of the Soviet government.' On 9 July Yugoslavia and Bulgaria declined the invitation; the Bulgarian refusal was announced by Radio Moscow before the cabinet in Sofia knew that they had taken a decision. On 10 July the Czechoslovaks and Hungarians refused, with the significant explanation that their participation 'would be regarded as an unfriendly act against the Soviet Union'; on 11 July came refusals from Romania, Albania, Poland, and Finland.[62]

Stalin, with his basically hostile approach, regarded it as unthinkable to accept the proposed co-operation with the US and the European countries in a way that would genuinely permit the latter's recovery. Molotov's aim

---

[61] Molotov (n. 60), p. 465 f. For contemporary comment, cf. 'Molotov or Marshall', *The Economist*, 5.7.1947. On the failure of the three-power conference and the interpretation of the Soviet refusal, cf. esp. T. H. White, *Fire in the Ashes. Europe in Mid-Century*, New York, 1953, pp. 37–41; Shulman (n. 10), pp. 13–51; Ulam (n. 15), pp. 128–32; Beugel (n. 8), pp. 60–3.

[62] Cf. Summary in J. K. Hoensch, 'Sowjetische Osteuropapolitik 1945–1955', in *Osteuropa-Handbuch. Sowjetunion Aussenpolitik Bd. 1*, Cologne/Vienna, 1972, p. 401 f. On Czech and Polish reactions, cf. H. Ripka (foreign-trade minister of Czechoslovakia in 1947), *Eastern Europe in the Post-War World*, London, 1961, pp. 73–5; Masaryk quotation from R. Bruce Lockhart, *My Europe*, London, 1952, p. 125; on Hungary's readiness to accept, see esp. S. D. Kertesz, 'Hungary in International Affairs since 1945', in E. C. Helmreich (ed.), *Hungary (East-Central Europe under the Communists)*, New York, 1957, p. 23 f. For details of government reactions in Eastern Europe, cf. V. Auriol, *Journal du septennat, Vol. 1: 1947*, Paris, 1970, p. 338 f., and reports from the US ambassador in *FRUS 1947/III* (n. 37), pp. 313–27.

in Paris was seen to have been merely to obtain bilateral credits on a 'shopping-list' basis while continuing to obstruct joint planning; when this attempt failed, Stalin at once called a halt. His chief practical motive as regards the East-European countries was the fear that by taking part in planning on a European scale they would again be exposed to the 'Western capitalist' influences which had just been eradicated, as Stalin thought, by military conquest and the seizure of power by native Communists. By compelling the East-European governments to decline the offer despite their elementary economic needs and their almost unanimous wishes, Stalin at the same time laid the basis for the division of Europe from an organizational point of view. By excluding the satellites from international trade based on the division of labour he ensured the economic and political domination of Moscow. The Warsaw conference of September 1947, at which the Cominform was set up, openly proclaimed the principle of the irreconcilable enmity between the 'socialist' and 'imperialist' camps.[63]

The effect on Europe of the breach of 2 July 1947 was accurately summed up by Herbert Lüthy in 1954: 'Molotov had vetoed, not just the Marshall plan, ... or any particular methods or proposals of Mr Bevin or M. Bidault, which he had not even begun to discuss; but the general principle of European cooperation, the idea of an organized Europe and of any kind of contact between his own clients and the Western world. Moreover he did this in the name of the antiquated principle of national sovereignty, while simultaneously demonstrating the deeper meaning that this "national sovereignty" had for Moscow by calling off, as if they were dogs which had gone astray, the governments of Poland and Czechoslovakia, which were more than ready to take part in the proposed conference. With this there began the tremendous post-war contest in which the United States backed the unification and reconstruction of western Europe while the Soviet Union gambled on its disunity and collapse. Many partial successes have been gained in this contest, but no decision; and the struggle continues.'[64]

From the point of view of the movement for European unity, the following three points should be noted at this stage:

---

[63] For this interpretation, see esp. Hoensch (n. 62), p. 402; Shulman (n. 10), pp. 42–55; D. Geyer, 'Von der Kriegskoalition zum Kalten Krieg', in *Osteuropa-Handbuch. Sowjetunion* (n. 62), p. 363 f. At the Cominform conference the West-European Communist parties were accordingly given the special task of 'raising high the banner of the defence of the national independence and sovereignty of your countries' (speech by Zhdanov, 23.9.1947; see Gasteyger (n. 31), p. 181). On this point and the execution of the order by the West-European CPs see chap. IV/2 (in vol. 2).

[64] Lüthy (n. 35), p. 353 f. A similar contemporary comment in *Die Neue Zeitung*, 14.7.1947: 'The Soviet Union has succeeded in stirring up a wave of distrust and fear of its policy, such as no one in the US or Britain would have dreamt of a few years ago. . . . The progressive political and economic decline of Europe meant that the hegemony of a great power over the Continent appeared as an increasingly sinister threat. It is to Molotov's moral disadvantage that he was unable to oppose any constructive idea to that of Marshall, who raises no claim to domination over Europe but merely seeks its autonomy. Molotov's assertion that a joint European economic authority would prevent the self-determination of European peoples is in flagrant contradiction to Soviet interference in the affairs of the East-European countries.'

1. The concept of unification, revived by European groups since the autumn of 1946, had been examined by the governments of the two superpowers, who after full deliberation and discussion took up a position for or against it, before a single one of the twenty-two European governments in office in the winter of 1946/7 – especially the British and French, on whom most depended – had given it any serious consideration, let alone endorsed the aims of the federalists in their respective countries. This was a further illustration of the fact that decisions of world-wide importance were henceforth being taken outside Europe.

2. The Soviet Union had categorically opposed the European idea and had, from 1945 onwards, protested against the slightest semblance of closer contact among West-European countries on the ground that it meant the formation of a 'Western bloc directed against the U.S.S.R.' Moscow had nothing constructive to offer Europe, only the doctrine of national sovereignty as a cloak for its 'divide and rule' policy, which was a recipe for speedy economic ruin. By dint of opposing the Europeans' most elementary needs the Soviet Union had actually created an anti-Soviet 'Western bloc', not least by forbidding contact of any kind between its satellites and the West.

3. The US Administration and Congress had come to favour the European idea in the context of their new policy of organizing security on a regional basis and encouraging the restoration of world trade. This meant a radical change in the prospect for European union. In Europe's state of prostration the idea could scarcely have had any chance of influencing practical politics as these were conducted by the superpowers, if one or other of those powers had not taken it up and promoted it.[65] Thanks to US economic aid and military protection (on a treaty basis from 1949 onwards) the West Europeans were able to set about making unification a reality. The veto imposed by the superpowers in 1945/6 had been lifted as far as the Marshall Plan countries were concerned. The course of events now depended primarily on the attitude of West-European governments and political and social groups, and it remained to be seen whether these would provide a motive force or act as a brake in their turn.

Thus the idea of European union did not owe its origin to the gradual development of the cold war, the Soviet Union's expansionist policy, and the American decision to withstand it. The European idea, as has been shown, arose long before, as an increasingly strong reaction on the part of Europeans to the tragic events of the Second World War. But, on the other

---

[65] And, until such time as the idea is realized, it remains indicative of Europe's weakness since the two world wars that it can only take major steps in that direction under the protection and with the consent of at least one of the world powers. That consent was forthcoming in the ensuing months and years, in the setting of the developing East–West conflict. Cf. the further outline of the global background in chaps. V/1 and VI/1 (in vol. 2), beginning with the unsuccessful fifth and last meeting of the Council of Foreign Ministers in London from 25 Nov. to 15 Dec. 1947.

hand, Soviet expansionism and the US decision to support European co-operation had the joint effect of limiting that co-operation to Western Europe and making it a factor in the negotiations conducted by West-European governments.

2. The West-European governments and the Impulse given by the Marshall Plan
by Wilfried Loth

In 1944–7 the aspiration to European unity, born of the experience of the Second World War, had not yet asserted itself in the West-European countries as a whole. One of its chief motivations at the outset had been the desire for a peace settlement more stable than that achieved after the war of 1914–18; but in 1945, owing to the Soviet government's attitude, this motive operated against federalism instead of in its favour. The Soviets were categorically opposed to European union in any form, and this deterred federalists from taking any decisive steps towards overcoming national particularism, lest instead of promoting the unification of Europe they succeeded only in sealing its division.[66] For lack of a feasible alternative, under the dominance of the two new world powers there was seen in all European countries a reactivation and consolidation of the traditional faith in nationalism which had been shaken by the war. Some of the national governments consciously favoured this development; others, finding that mutual co-operation was ruled out, gave up hope of joint planning for European recovery and tried – inevitably without success – to meet the threat of economic and political chaos on a purely national basis.

The abstention from intra-European co-operation, due to the latent US–Soviet tension, had catastrophic effects. As the London *Economist* wrote in a remarkably perceptive article on 31 May 1947: The margin between recovery and collapse throughout Western Europe is dependent at this moment upon massive imports from the U.S. ... If the dollars that are so desperately needed could somehow be represented not merely as assistance to the improvident but as the foundation of some good constructive purpose, then there might be a greater chance of eliciting a favourable response ... If the difficulties in the way are simply the unreasonable recalcitrance of the Europeans, let the U.S. use its great power to knock their heads together and impose agreement; there are plenty of Europeans who would welcome American 'dictation' if it were for a good cause.[67]

In July, Molotov's 'No' to the Marshall Plan made it clear that Europe and the world were already split in two. This liberated the forces working

[66] Cf. the summing-up of this state of affairs by Bevin and Spaak in chap. I, pp. 181 and 260; also chap. I/3–7, analyses of the behaviour of the West-European governments from 1945 to the spring of 1947; continued in the text above.
[67] *The Economist*, 31.5.1947, quoted from Beugel (n. 8), p. 56 f.; interesting also as a British view of the controversy between Fulbright and Marshall over 'dictation' (cf. at n. 43). On the economic situation, cf. references at n. 33 f. and W. Lippemann, 'Cassandra Speaking', 12.4.1947, at n. 35.

for European union from the dilemma that had paralysed their action: they were confirmed in their ideas and supported in practice by US pressure for the pooling of European resources, and were spurred on by the increasingly evident hopelessness of trying to deal with economic chaos on a purely national footing. Thus the general conditions for some measure of political and economic integration in Western Europe had radically improved as compared with 1944/5; but, at the same time, nationalistic doctrines, institutions, and habits were still in evidence and had taken on a new lease of life since 1945. Consequently the governments in the summer of 1947 were again confronted, as at the end of the war, by the question whether and to what extent they should acknowledge and foster the impulses towards European unity. It was for them to decide whether the Marshall Plan should be the first step towards a genuine union of Western Europe or should only be used to give a temporary boost to the national economies, and whether, given the inevitable consolidation of the Western camp as a whole, Europe would still be able to play an independent role in the future.

(A) THE BRITISH REACTION: DELAY INSTEAD OF LEADERSHIP

Great Britain seemed destined to play a key part in the forging of European union (or West-European, as it now was): in the crucial situation of 1947 many West Europeans expected important initiatives to be taken by the only remaining European great power. The Herter Committee, set up by the US Congress to explore ways and means of carrying out the Marshall Plan in Europe, believed that only Britain possessed 'the past experience and the present economic resources and political stability necessary for bold and imaginative leadership'.[68] Even though the State Department planners had rejected the idea of acknowledging Britain's 'special relationship' by giving her a special role in the execution of the recovery programme,[69] the British reaction was of key importance to the Continental governments. At a time when the fact of the East-Europeans' exclusion had hardly yet sunk in, no one in Western Europe was able and willing to imagine the joint recovery programme without British participation; union and cooperation in Western Europe were only possible to the extent that they were accepted by the British government.

[68] US Select Committee on Foreign Aid, *Final Report on Foreign Aid,* Washington, 1948, quoted in R. Mayne, *The Recovery of Europe 1945–1973,* New York, 1973[2], p. 156. R. W. G. Mackay wrote similarly to Coudenhove-Kalergi in August 1947: 'The creation of a European Federation in the next five years is more in the hands of Great Britain than anyone else. If Bevin would only take the lead at Paris now he could convert the present Paris Conference into a Conference for European Federation' (27.8.1947, *Mackay Archives*).
[69] Cf. references in n. 75.

490 Limitation to Western Europe

The British reaction to Marshall's offer was decisively affected by the dramatic worsening of the UK economy in the spring of 1947. As a result of the hard winter and of American inflation, which reduced the real value of the US loan of December 1945 by 25 per cent, the credits had been used up far more quickly than expected. When sterling was made convertible on 15 July 1947 in accordance with the loan agreement, the reserves from the loan dwindled by $1,300 million in four weeks, so that convertibility had to be suspended on 20 August; the credit had now sunk to $400 million.[70] Britain's admission on 21 February 1947 that she would not be able to discharge her military and economic commitments to Greece and Turkey after 31 March – the announcement which furnished the occasion for the Truman doctrine – was a cry for help which made only too clear the collapse of Britain's position as a world power. In this situation Marshall's offer could only be regarded as a lifeline which must be grasped as firmly as possible without a moment's delay.

'The position of the United Kingdom', as the intra-governmental 'Committee on European Economic Co-operation' confirmed in a memorandum delivered on October 1947,

> is a very difficult one ... Before the war we earned dollars by our surpluses with other countries. To-day the world shortage of dollars is such that the surpluses are not convertible into dollars. It is this that makes it impossible for us to balance our dollar payments even though we obtain an overall balance of payments ... Such a situation may well lead to a progressive frustration of our efforts to get ourselves back on to our feet. Our productive power will be reduced, first by lack of foodstuffs to nourish our people, second by non-availability of raw materials.

The efforts to secure the British supplies would lead 'to a further distortion of the world economic structure and a breakdown of even that part of multilateral trading which still survives ... The answer then must clearly be that we need assistance from the United States, and we need that assistance in 1948 if not sooner.'[71]

For this reason, Bevin's first concern after Marshall's speech of 5 June was to prevent the Soviet Union from taking part in the recovery programme in a way that would reduce the scope and speed of American aid. He could not openly oppose Soviet participation, however, on account of those elements in the Labour Party who believed that 'Left understands Left' and were once again denouncing Churchill's plans as designed to form an anti-Soviet bloc;[72] moreover, Bevin did not want European public opinion to blame him for dividing Europe in two.[73] 'We are glad to know that

---

[70] Cf. M. A. Fitzsimons, *The Foreign Policy of the British Labour Government 1945–1951*, Notre Dame, Indiana, 1953, p. 92; Kolko (n. 54), p. 365; Harris (n. 34), pp. 252–9.
[71] Cf. p. 462 f.
[72] Thus, e.g., the *Daily Herald* of 15.5.1947. The East-European press hastened to give prominence to these criticisms: e.g. *Neues Deutschland*, 18.5.1947 and 19.5.1947.
[73] PRO Cab. 129, Vol. 21. Memorandum by the Minister for Economic Affairs, 7.10.1947.

misunderstanding has been removed by including Russia in the American proposal', he declared on 13 June in his first public comment on Marshall's offer. However, when issuing the invitation to the Soviet Union to attend a preliminary three-power conference in Moscow, Bevin – like Bidault – assured the Americans on 19 June that he would make no concessions to the Russians that might jeopardize the consent of Congress to the aid programme; he also opposed the idea of operating the programme through the Economic Commission for Europe and thus giving the Soviet Union a chance to obstruct it. On the same day he stated clearly in the House of Commons that 'the guiding principle that I shall follow in any talks will be speed ... I shall not be a party to holding up the economic recovery of Europe by the finesse of procedure, or terms of reference, or all the paraphernalia which may go with it. There is too much involved.'[74] When Clayton, the US Under-Secretary of State, came to London on 24 June to discuss the form of the aid programme with the British before the three-power conference, Chancellor of the Exchequer Hugh Dalton tried to convey to him that 'we are something more than just a bit of Europe' and that Britain hoped to be offered at an early date a substantial bilateral aid agreement with the US. When Molotov said 'No' on 2 July to the proposal for a European plan Bevin was much relieved, and not disappointed as were many Continental Socialists and some members of the Labour Party. 'Looking back on those apparently interminable discussions', he reported to the Cabinet, 'I am confident that our conversations were doomed from the start in the sense that there was never any prospect of getting Soviet collaboration except on M. Molotov's unacceptable terms. Moreover, had the Russians decided to come in, even on our terms, the opportunities which they would have to delay and obstruct would have been almost unlimited; so that from a practical point of view it is far better to have them definitely out than half-heartedly in. That was why I insisted from the outset on thrashing out the differences of principle between us and making that the breaking point. Any other tactics might have enabled the Soviet to play the Trojan horse and wreck Europe's prospects of availing themselves of American assistance.' Together with Bidault, he went ahead energetically and invited all European governments except those of Spain and the Soviet Union to confer in Paris on 12 July in order to provide the Americans with the joint answer for which they had asked.[75]

[74] Bevin's speech of 13.6.1947 to the Foreign Press Association in London, reported in *The Times*, 14.6.1947: cf. n. 54. Assurance to Washington: see Wightman (n. 58), p. 35. Speech in the Commons: *Weekly Hansard, House of Commons, Vol. 438,* 19.6.1947, cols. 2353 and 2356. On this and Clayton's visit, see *FRUS 1947/III* (n. 37), pp. 260–94.
[75] Attempts to get preferential treatment for Britain: H. Dalton, *High Tide and After: Memoirs, 1945– 1950,* London, 1962, quotation, p. 256; cf. Ferrell (n. 11), pp. 114–17. Bevin to the Cabinet: PRO Cab. 129, Vol. 19, Memorandum by the Secretary of State for Foreign Affairs, 5th July, 1947. Invitation policy: cf. the final communiqué signed by Bevin and Bidault on 3 July 1947 in *L'Année politique 1947,* p. 354: 'It is essential to draw up as quickly as possible a programme covering

Although Bevin had stressed to Molotov the need to draw up a co-ordinated European plan instead of separate 'shopping lists', he had no intention in practice of permitting interference in national economic planning. The aim 'to see how best we can take advantage of this great proposal of the United States'[76] was not, in his opinion, likely to be achieved by uniting the (West) European national economies. On the contrary, as he wanted to lay his hands on American funds as quickly as possible, any attempt to link the plan with a European customs union or some communal arrangement among the recipient countries seemed to him an extra obstacle and a needless complication. From this point of view even the US pressure for closer association between the European states was a serious embarrassment. To overcome it was the second main aim of Bevin's Marshall Plan policy; and accordingly the second Paris conference was dominated by the problem of how to get as much out of the Americans as quickly as possible while making the minimum concession to their desire for European unity.[77]

Certainly the Marshall offer encouraged all those in Britain who had supported European union in any form. The United Europe Movement, officially constituted on 14 May 1947, was at the height of its prestige; Churchill was urging more emphatically than ever that now was the time to take steps towards European union. During the foreign-policy debate of the House of Commons on 19 June 1947 the Conservative speakers unanimously backed Churchill's view. The chief spokesman, Anthony Eden, welcomed the Marshall offer as stimulating 'the first steps towards that united Europe which my right hon. Friend the leader of the Opposition has so much at heart'. The offer, he said, should be of use for 'creating a prosperous and integrated association of countries of Europe', which would be 'a magnetic attraction for all' other countries not yet wishing to participate, i.e. the Eastern hemisphere. His colleague Peter Thorneycroft went even further, advocating a 'united Europe', not 'carrying out a policy independent of Russia and the United States of America', but defeating Communism by building up a great area of prosperity. 'Europe ... has to choose today between whether she shall become incapable of playing that role or sacrifice something of her individual sovereignty. If some sovereignty is not sacrificed, I do not see how Europe will be able to recover.' Robert Boothby also emphasized the necessity of the 'economic

---

Europe's needs and also its resources.' In direct opposition to Bevin's desire to get the aid programme going without Soviet participation was the rejection of the Marshall Plan by the 'Keep Left' group, by then on the defensive, under Konni Zilliacus, who declared in the Commons that the Plan was an expression of America's 'containment' policy, threatening the progress of Socialism in Europe and of understanding with the Soviet Union; if Europe became dependent on dollar imperialism it could no longer mediate between East and West (*Weekly Hansard, House of Commons*, Vol. 446, col. 443 f. and vol 450, col. 1345 f.).

[76] Speech on 13.6.1947 (n. 74).
[77] Cf. chapter III/3.

integration of Western Europe' without Soviet participation; and Richard Law added that 'perhaps the best way to secure Russian collaboration and create a totally united Europe is to get to work as quickly as we can on that part of Europe which we can influence and which shares with us a common standard of values'.[78] From the Labour Party side, R. W. G. Mackay was indefatigable in reminding the government of the chance afforded by the US proposal:

I should have hoped that the Marshall talks would have given the Foreign Secretary and the Minister of Economic Affairs the opportunity not so much to bother about a shopping list of what Europe was to spend in America, but to work out with the European Ministers a political structure for Europe in the next two years. We can build up in that time a Federation of Western Europe ...[79]

The General Council of the United Nations Association, on which all political parties were represented, urged the government to endorse the US desire for 'a coordinated economic plan for all Europe including Great Britain and the Soviet Union'.[80] Among the Conservative opposition hopes were expressed for at least an economic union of Continental heavy industry. There was, said Hugh Molson, MP, 'the greatest possible opportunity for a revival of the industry of Europe as a whole, if you integrate the industries of Belgium and Luxembourg, of Lorraine and the Saar'; only thus could Europe make 'the fullest possible use of its own resources'. From this point of view it was also perceived that the inclusion of West Germany in the recovery programme and the projected economic union was indispensable. As Harold Macmillan said: 'The economic interdependence of Western Germany and Europe must be recognized. The Ruhr, the Saar, Lorraine and Luxembourg are interdependent, and together they form the greatest industrial unit in the world.'[81]

[78] *Weekly Hansard, House of Commons*, vol. 438, 19.6.1947, col. 2254, 2256 (Eden), 2280 (Thorneycroft), 2333 (Boothby), and 2349 (Law). For the foundation of the United Europe Movement, cf. pp. 328–30.

[79] *Weekly Hansard, House of Commons*, vol. 443, 28.10.1947, col. 753. For Mackay's general concept, cf. p. 198, and pp. 616–21. The shift of emphasis in motivation for European unity as a result of the Marshall Plan is illustrated by Mackay's insistence on its economic advantages: West–European federation 'would give a free trade area for all, which would also provide freedom for the movement of population so that we can get goods and populations moving about to the places of industry where they are needed' (ibid.; similarly Mackay on 6.8.1947; *Weekly Hansard*, vol. 441, cols. 1584–7).

[80] Quoted from A. and F. Boyd, *Western Union*, London, 1948, p. 92. Soon after June 1947 the UNA ceased to maintain, as even Bevin had at the beginning, the attitude of welcoming Soviet participation. The announcement of the Marshall Plan gave a great impetus to British ideas of European union, as is shown by the appearance of several works at this time: S. D. Bailey, *United Europe, A Short History of the Idea*, London, 1947; V. A. Firsoff, *The Unity of Europe; Realities and Aspirations*, London, 1947; D. McLachlan, *Towards Western Union*, London, 1948; A. D. Marvis, *Prospects for Closer European Economic Integration*, London, 1948. Max Beloff introduced classic US federalist principles to the British public in an edition of *The Federalist; or The New Constitution*, by Alexander Hamilton, James Madison, and John Jay, ed. with an introduction and notes by M. B., Oxford, 1948.

[81] Molson: *Weekly Hansard, House of Commons*, vol. 441, 4.8.1947, col. 1028; Macmillan, ibid., col. 1012. Molson urged the government to overcome French resistance to integration including the fostering of West-German resources.

Bevin, and with him the Labour government, agreed that the Western Zones of Germany must be included in the recovery programme. It was not disputed in Britain in 1947 that, as Anthony Eden said, 'the Potsdam agreement can no longer be regarded by us as having any validity in so far as it concerns the economic treatment of Germany'.[82] With the agreement of 29 May 1947 setting up the Economic Council at Frankfurt and the five Administrative Agencies for Bizonia, Britain had fallen into line with US policy for Germany and taken a decisive step towards the reorganization of the Western Zones with a view to their integration in a European recovery programme. But the Labour government still objected to including the Ruhr in an integrated West-European economy, on the ground that they might wish to nationalize its industry as part of the British Zone—which promoted the sharp comment from Macmillan that 'national socialism' of this kind would be 'wholly disruptive of the European economy'.[83]

To all appeals for greater co-ordination Bevin replied with vague assurances that the European economy must certainly be treated as a whole and that world federation was the ultimate aim.[84] At the same time he gave his officials strict instructions that any attempt to include the British economy in a European order was to be blocked by referring to Britain's Commonwealth ties: as Sir Oliver Franks, the head of the British delegation to the Paris conference, expressed it, the Commonwealth 'had the effect of making the United Kingdom an extra-European as well as an intra-European power'. Christopher Mayhew, parliamentary under-secretary at the Foreign Office, declared in the Commons that: 'It would be wrong to support a scheme such as this well-known scheme for the United States of Europe merely because it aims at the elimination of sovereignty... At present these schemes are premature and more likely to lead to disunity than to unity in Europe.'[85] In other words, what really prevented Britain from grasping the renewed opportunity to take the lead in Europe was not, as Bevin pretended,[86] the insufficiency of her national potential, but rather her imagined excess of strength: the hope that, aided by Commonwealth resources, she could obtain more as a junior partner of the US than as the leader of Europe. Bevin himself eventually realized in

---

[82] *Weekly Hansard, House of Commons*, vol. 443, 21.10.1947, col. 20.
[83] Ibid. (n. 81). Cf. Rolf Steiniger, 'Reform und Realität. Ruhrfrage und Sozialisierung in der anglo-amerikanischen Deutschlandpolitik 1947/48', *VfZG*, 27 (1979), pp. 167–240.
[84] Cf. his speech in the Commons, 19.6.1947, and statement to the press, 13.6.1947 (both n. 74); in the latter he said: 'I am in favour ultimately of the establishment of a world parliament directly elected.' Cf. also the discussion of world parliament proposals in chap. I/3, p. 173.
[85] Franks reported in *The Times*, 16.8.1947; quoted in Mayne (n. 68), p. 156. Mayhew in *Weekly Hansard, House of Commons*, vol. 443, 27.10.1947, col. 2400.
[86] In his speech in the Commons on 19.6.1947 (n. 74), replying to criticism that he had not pressed on towards European unity, Bevin said: 'What could I offer? I had neither coal, goods nor credit... I have had nothing with which to negotiate.' For the modification of Bevin's position, cf. chapter III/3 below.

September/October 1947 that a European 'Third Force' under British leadership would be necessary to save British independence and he supported therefore the idea of a European Customs Union, but he failed to convince his colleagues in the Cabinet of this project; the efforts for a reconstruction of British industry within a narrow nationalistic framework prevailed.

(B) FRANCE: A CHANGE OF COURSE, BUT WITH HESITATIONS

In France too, the political determination to assume the leadership of the unification process was not yet forthcoming. It had existed among many members of the political intelligentsia during the post-Liberation months of 1944, but was discouraged by the prestige of Gaullism and the latent polarization of Europe. France's aspiration to great-power status appeared, it is true, increasingly illusory; Bidault, with his demands for the dismemberment of Germany, Rhineland separatism, and a large share of reparations, was stubbornly though patiently resisted by the Americans and British and finally snubbed by the Russians at the Foreign Ministers' meeting in Moscow in April 1947. But the aims and methods of the Quai d'Orsay remained unchanged, and France increasingly took her stand on principles divorced from reality. The 'European' associations had as yet no more than a marginal influence on the French political outlook and government policy. The parties concentrated on the problems of overcoming economic distress and establishing a new constitutional order, and refrained from tackling what seemed insoluble problems of foreign relations.[87]

But in the course of 1947 internal developments made it possible to escape from the rigid premisses of Gaullist foreign policy. The election of Vincent Auriol to the Presidency on 16 January brought to an end the struggle over the new constitution, and it seemed at first that the tripartite coalition of Christian Democrats (MRP), Social Democrats (SFIO), and Communists (PCF) which had reached agreement on the constitutional compromise would also provide successive governments for the Fourth Republic. However, as both the MRP and the PCF endeavoured to extend their influence within the coalition at the expense of the other parties, the tripartite experiment broke down in a very short time, a result not altogether desired at the time by either of these parties.[88]

The MRP scored the first success by weakening the Communists' role in the coalition. By playing on the need for US economic aid and American

---
[87] Cf. chap. I/4, pp. 214–30, and chap. III/1, n. 23.
[88] For an instructive summary of the following, cf. J. Duroselle, 'The Turning-Point in French Politics: 1947', in *Review of Poliics*, 13 (1951), pp. 302–28, and documentation of events in *L'Année politique*, vol. 3, 1947, Paris, 1948.

mistrust of Communist influence in France, the MRP saw to it that the first regular government of the new regime, under the Socialist Paul Ramadier, included members of the old liberal (Radical) party and the more or less conservative Independents; this meant that the Communists were no longer needed to form a majority. The Communist leaders accepted this state of affairs so as not to deprive themselves of all influence on the government's foreign policy. In the ensuing weeks, however, they came under increasing pressure from the party rank and file, who no longer wished to be identified with the government's wage-freeze policy, its *rapprochement* with the Western allies,[89] and the conflict with Ho Chi Minh's forces in Indochina which had been going on since December 1946. In response to this pressure from below and in the hope of strengthening their position in a government reshuffle, the Communist leaders provoked a crisis on 4 May by withholding support from Ramadier in the National Assembly. The premier, however, did not resign but replaced the Communist ministers by representatives of the other parties, a move subsequently endorsed by a narrow majority of the National Council of the SFIO. Although the Communists hoped to re-enter the government as late as the autumn of 1947, the SFIO and MRP stood fast and refused them any further concessions.[90]

From this point onwards the Socialists and Christian Democrats saw themselves, together with right-of-centre groups, as forming a 'third force' whose role was to defend the Republic against threats from both Left and Right. The enemy on the Left were the Communists, whose credibility as democrats was increasingly called into question and who were ordered to play the part of an intransigent opposition by the Cominform conference at the end of September 1947.[91] Meanwhile de Gaulle, who had been working since May 1946 for the establishment of a strong presidential regime, in April 1947 founded the Rassemblement du Peuple Francais, which soon grew into a mass movement firmly opposed to Communism and to party politics in general; in the municipal elections of 19 October 1947 it polled up to 40 per cent of votes in the larger constituencies.[92] The 'third force' was not only attacked from outside but constantly threatened from within. The SFIO, to which not only the premier but the largest number of ministers belonged, had become *de facto* a minority in a centre-right coalition, so that there was a cleavage between Socialist expectations and the government's increasingly liberal-conservative policy. After months of violent criticism from the ranks of his own party Ramadier fell

---

[89] Cf. p. 497 f.
[90] Cf., with detailed references, W. Loth, 'Frankreichs Kommunisten und der Beginn des Kalten Krieges. Die Entlassung der kommunistischen Minister im Mai 1947', *VfZG*, 26 (1978), pp. 9–65.
[91] Cf. the instructive account by the then representative of the Italian Communists: E. Reale, *Avec Jacques Duclos au banc des accusés,* Paris, 1958; on the significance of the Cominform conference, see also n. 63.
[92] Cf. *L'Année politique 1947,* pp. 194–6 and 363 f.

from office in November 1947, as Guy Mollet, the secretary-general of the SFIO, decided to support him no longer. The choice of Robert Schuman of the MRP as Ramadier's successor made it clear that the centre of gravity had shifted to the right.[93]

Thus internal developments, reinforced by changes on the international scene, had brought about a situation in which de Gaulle and the Communists were allied in opposition to the government as far as foreign affairs were concerned. Within the government itself, advocates and opponents of the existing policy were more or less equally balanced. The latter were as yet outnumbered, especially in the SFIO, but Bidault and others were coming to see that the methods so far adopted in order to strengthen French influence had failed. The upshot was a gradual reversion towards the Resistance movement's ideas for European unity, frequently seen from now on as a potential means of enhancing France's national greatness.[94]

The decisive factor in Bidault's change of policy was the attitude of the Soviet delegation at the Foreign Ministers' meeting in Moscow. While basically opposed to Communism, he had believed until then that he could reach an understanding with the Russians on the basis of joint opposition to Anglo-American encroachments in Europe; but on returning from Moscow he changed his tune completely, repeating on all occasions: 'C'est fini, c'est fini! Tout accord avec la Russie est impossible. Il n'y a plus d'alliance et d'union des trois Grands, plus de possibilité d'entente avec les communistes. C'est une ère nouvelle qui commence. Il faut en tirer toutes les conséquences.'[95] Bidault was convinced that the French attempt to mediate between the superpowers was a failure, that all co-operation with the Communists at home or with the Soviets in foreign affairs must be broken off, and that it was illusory to seek to build up Europe as a 'Third Force' equidistant between the Big Two.

For these reasons, when the Marshall offer was announced Bidault took up a far more decided position than Bevin – who had to take account of left-wing Labour views – as regards excluding the Soviet Union from the operation of the aid programme; only under pressure from his Socialist fellow-ministers did he accept Bevin's proposal for a preliminary conference

[93] Cf. R. Quilliot, *La S.F.I.O. et l'exercice du pouvoir 1944–1958*, Paris, 1972, pp. 244–56, and W. Loth, *Sozialismus und Internationalismus. Die französischen Sozialisten und die Nachkriegsordnung Europas 1940–1950* (= *Studien zur Zeitgeschichte, hrsg. vom Institut für Zeitgeschichte*), Stuttgart, 1977, pp. 139–42 and 149–55.
[94] On the change of French foreign policy in 1947, see, in general, K. Hänsch, *Frankreich zwischen Ost und West. Die Reaktion auf den Ausbruch des Ost–West-Konfliktes 1946–1948*, Berlin/New York, 1972; also Loth (n. 93), pp. 156–76, on the Socialists' attitude. There is, however, still no detailed over-all analysis of French foreign policy after the announcement of the Marshall Plan.
[95] Quoted from G. Elgey, *La République des illusions 1945–1951*, Paris, 1965, p. 282. President Auriol noted in his diary that: 'La situation est d'autant plus difficile que Bidault, depuis son retour d'URSS, est devenu anticommuniste au point que Francisque Gay a demandé à Ramadier de le modérer': Auriol (n. 62), p. 205 (1.5.1947).

between Britain, France, and the Russians.[96] Relieved by Molotov's walk-out, at the Paris conference of the sixteen Bidault endeavoured, like Bevin, to secure American aid as quickly as possible, but differed from him in advocating close co-operation among the European countries concerned. 'It is time to create Europe (faire l'Europe)', he declared to the National Assembly on 20 June, 'to rescue it from its distress and restore it to a proper place in world councils. This depends primarily on France, whose chief interests are European. In collaboration with the other European nations who are disposed to keep us company, we shall see to it that these interests are safeguarded and this mission accomplished.'[97] Bidault, to be sure, had not suddenly become an advocate of European federation; his idea was for an association in which France would hold a predominant place. But this was more than Bevin was disposed to allow, and there was thus an inevitable conflict at the Paris conference between the two principal foreign ministers of Western Europe.[98]

Bidault, as his statement made clear, believed in a West-European organization but had no intention of sacrificing the traditional aims of French foreign policy. When, at the beginning of July 1947, the military governors, Generals Clay and Robertson, agreed on a new industrial plan providing for 10.7 million tonnes of steel production per annum for Bizonia instead of the previous 7.8 million for the whole of Germany – a measure which followed naturally from the inclusion of Western Germany in the European recovery programme – the Quai d'Orsay reacted with a violent though ultimately ineffective diplomatic and publicity campaign under the slogan 'Nous d'abord, l'Allemagne après'.[99] Bidault saw himself in a dilemma, as France had to be defended against Soviet expansionism and also against a revived Germany; he was unable to resolve the contradiction between France's traditional policy of national security and the use of Germany's potential to assist European recovery.[100]

The contradictions and weaknesses of Bidault's policy played into the hands of his opponents both in his own party, the MRP, and among the Socialists. At the third MRP congress on 13–16 March 1947 the call for a radical change of foreign policy was heard for the first time, when the delegate Trémieux declared: 'The French government ought to have

[96] At the cabinet session of 18.6.1947 Ramadier said to Bidault: 'Si vous vous arrêtez sur le Rhin, ce sera un tout petit canton, le but sera manqué. Il est essential qu'il y ait, pour le moins, une certaine participation de l'Union soviétique et une part entière des États satellites'; quoted from Loth (n. 93), p. 148; see also ibid., p. 147.
[97] *Journal Officiel, Débats,* 29.6.1947, p. 2291.
[98] Cf. section by A. Milward, pp. 507 ff.
[99] Cf. Schwarz (n. 6), p. 722 f.; supplemented by Loth (n. 93), p. 170 f.
[100] As A. Grosser observes in *La IVe République et sa politique extérieure,* Paris, 1961, p. 207: 'On ajoute une politique nouvelle à la politique ancienne avec laquelle elle est logiquement incompatible, et on va se trouver contraint d'accepter les inconvénients cumulés des deux politiques sans pratiquer réellement ni l'une ni l'autre.'

unified its Zone with those of the Allies in order to make a Western Germany with its capital at Frankfurt, which would be part of the European federation.'[101] So as not openly to disavow Bidault, the majority of the foreign-policy committee at the congress did not allow a resolution to be passed in this sense; but the advocates of a 'European' solution of the security problem were by now strong enough to bring about the adoption of a resolution acknowledging the federal principle: 'Pour la sécurité et la prospérité de toutes les nations d'Europe il convient de préparer dès maintenant l'instauration d'un fédéralisme des patries et de la solidarité des peuples.' Along with this statement, which for the first time committed the whole party to a federal union of Europe, the resolution included an expression of support for Bidault, whose task was to ensure that 'Germany is made incapable of harmful action'.[102]

The Socialists, too, saw in the Marshall Plan a chance to alter the course of French foreign policy. On 6 July, four days after Molotov left Paris, the National Council of the SFIO declared that 'the governments of the Old Continent would act in the supreme interest of all its peoples by seizing the unique opportunity of General Marshall's offer to come to an understanding among themselves for the establishment of a plan of European reconstruction. A general agreement, even on a limited basis (même limité), would be a first step towards a Europe that would henceforth be more than a purely geographical notion.'[103] The Socialists saw Europe as a 'Third Force' between East and West, an 'instrument of *rapprochement*, mutual understanding and reconciliation between the two opposed blocs';[104] Europe, under the joint leadership of France and Britain, would be the home of democratic Socialism between Soviet totalitarianism and American capitalism.

The two main parties of the French government coalition differed in their precise attitude towards the two world powers; they had not clearly thought out the federal principle or the implications of European unity as regards the German problem. Nevertheless, their support of the 'Third Force' idea provided a basis on which France could develop a European policy. The rejection of Gaullist demands at the Foreign Ministers' meeting in Moscow, the removal of the Communist brake on government policy, and the increasing prevalence of pro-European ideas in the MRP

---

[101] 'Pour que l'entente régionale de l'Europe-Ouest vive, il faut que la France fasse une politique constructive et admette l'entrée de l'Allemagne dans cette entente': Trémieux in *MRP, IIIe Congrès national. Compte rendu, Commission de politique extérieure*, p. 664, quoted in M. Brun, *La Politique du Mouvement Républicain Populaire à l'égard de l'Europe de 1945 à 1950*, Mémoire de diplôme (typescript), Geneva, 1974, p. 36 f.

[102] *IIIe Congrès*, ibid., p. 757, quoted in Brun (n. 101), p. 39 f.; for discussion at the Congress, see ibid., pp. 35–42.

[103] 'Résolution sur la reconstruction de l'Europe', *Le Populaire*, 8.7.1947, quoted in Loth (n. 93), p. 51.

[104] Thus L. Blum, 'La Troisième Force internationale', *Le Populaire*, 6.1.1948. For similar ideas in the UEF, see pp. 380–5.

and SFIO made it possible, before the end of 1947, for France to support the conception of a joint European recovery programme such as that implied by the Marshall Plan and to propose initial steps towards a union of Europe over and above mere international co-operation.

In the summer of 1947 Ramadier publicly announced France's interest in a unified Western Europe. 'The time has indeed come when Europe must take shape or disappear', he declared on 13 July; on 28 September he said that he well knew 'that it is not easy to establish such a new and unique constitution as that of a united Europe, but I am certain that this is what we must do'; only thus could 'European civilization, the mother of world civilization', be preserved; only thus could Europe continue to exist as an independent political and economic force, that Europe 'without which the balance will be disturbed'.[105]

This unprecedented public statement of French readiness in 1947 to support the advance towards communal institutions in Europe prepared the way for the French government in the summer of 1948 to take the initiative which led to the creation of the Council of Europe.

(C) FIRST STEPS IN ITALY, BELGIUM, AND THE NETHERLANDS

In *Italy* the inception of the Plan policy and the formation of Western Europe coincided with the conclusion of the peace-treaty negotiations and the country's reappearance on the stage of world politics. Without intending it, and at first even without knowing it, Italy had no sooner recovered her freedom of action than she found herself in the Western camp; the parties' hopes for a new order in Europe[106] could henceforth only be expressed in the endeavour to build up a West-European organization in the Western world.

By an accident of the internal struggle for power rather than by any deliberate intent, the Christian Democratic party (Democrazia Cristiana – DC) under De Gasperi's premiership became the standard-bearer of Italy's new West-European policy. In January 1947 the Socialist party split on the issue of co-operation with the Communists, Nenni and Saragat being respectively for and against; this effectively diminished its importance in the three-party coalition, leaving the Communists (PCI) and the DC confronting each other as the two strongest parties. After the signature of the peace treaty De Gasperi, pressed by both wings of his party to terminate the coalition with the PCI, no longer felt obliged to pursue a policy of 'anti-Fascist unity' for the sake of the goodwill of the victorious Allies; this removed an important reason that had till then deterred him from acceding to the wishes of his rank and file. Provoking a government

---

[105] 13.7.1947; speech at Albertville, *Le Populaire*, 15.7.1947; 28.9.1947: speech at Mulhouse, *Le Populaire*, 29.9.1947.
[106] Cf. chap. I/6, pp. 250–8.

crisis on 13 May 1947 he tried to escape the direct confrontation with the Communists by enlarging the coalition to include Republicans, Liberals, and the new Social Democratic party (the PSLI under Saragat). The Republicans and the PSLI refused, however, and with the tacit consent of the Liberals De Gasperi formed a purely Christian Democratic cabinet on 31 May. This government, the fourth presided over by De Gasperi, included Sforza as foreign minister and Einaudi as deputy premier and finance minister, both as 'experts' and not party representatives. It was regarded strictly as a caretaker regime to ensure the transition to peacetime conditions of full demcracy and economic normalization.[107]

The idea of European union had enjoyed strong support in the Italian parties since the end of the war, and Marshall's appeal to overcome national particularism could be expected to meet with a widespread response. On 12 June Sforza welcomed the US offer. 'We are grateful', he said in a broadcast to the American public, 'for the far-sightedness that inspired General Marshall's speech at Harvard'. Later he observed that the Marshall Plan

puts the initiative for reconstruction in the hands of the countries of Europe; it requires the maximum coordination of efforts; and it makes the economic factor dominant over all other considerations. That is to say, it substitutes organized international production for the chaos which exists in the Europe of the so-called independent states. It does not anticipate events by urging a political unification of Europe.[108]

In clear contrast to the British and French governments, the Italians from the beginning laid less stress on the immediate receipt of American aid than on the essential need for European union as a condition of economic recovery. In telegraphic instructions to the principal Italian embassies on 16 June Sforza stated that from then on his government would do its utmost to collaborate.[109]

In his speech at the opening session of the Paris conference on 12 July – Italy had only been admitted on a footing of equality after the government had promised to use all its efforts to secure the ratification of the peace treaty – Sforza again emphasized his country's readiness for constructive co-operation in Europe. America's intervention in Western Europe had given the opportunity for unity.

[107] Cf. G. Vaccarino, 'Die Wiederherstellung der Demokratie in Italien (1943–1948)', *VfZG*, 21 (1973), pp. 285–324, E. Di Nolfo, 'Problemi della politica estera italiana 1943–1950', *Storia e politica*, Jan.–Feb. 1975.
[108] C. Sforza, 'Italy, the Marshall Plan and the "Third Force" ', *Foreign Affairs*, vol. 26, Nos. 3–4 (April–July 1948), New York, 1948, pp. 450–6, quotation p. 451. Broadcast of 12.6.1947 quoted from L. Graziano, *La Politica estera italian nel dopoguerra*, Padua, 1968, p. 91; for Italian reactions to the Marshall Plan, see ibid., pp. 91–5, and F. R. Willis, *Italy Chooses Europe*, New York, 1971, pp. 18–25; E. Rogaté, 'L'influenza die federalisti sulla politica europea dell'Italia', in: M. Bonanni (ed.), *Le Politica estera della Repubblica italiana*, Milan (Eidzione di Communità) 1967, pp. 455–84; on the Italian parties' favourable attitude to the European idea, see chap. I/6 (B), pp. 252–8.
[109] C. Sforza, *Cinque anni a Palazzo Chigi. La politica estera italian dal 1947 al 1951*, Rome, 1952, p. 44. For the transmission of the message in Washington, see *FRUS 1947/III* (n. 37), p. 254.

'We have no right not to unite ... If we do not succeed in this, it may be that our glorious Europe ... will again become, as it was 6,000 years ago, a small, poor, insignificant peninsula of Asia.' The Italian people well understood that every effort of its government to set the country on its feet 'would be fruitless without simultaneous European co-ordination'. In a dramatic appeal reflecting the seriousness of the situation, he addressed the governments whose most urgent concern was to lay hands on American funds: 'We are at a supreme turning-point of world history. We are on the eve of a transformation of the old world.' On 15 July, the last day of the Ministers' meeting, Sforza emphasized his point once again: no national sacrifice was too great for a united Europe; it was not merely 'desirable' to limit national sovereignty, as his Belgian colleague Spaak had said, but 'a supreme necessity'.[110]

Unlike Bevin in Britain and Bidault in France, the Italian government understood the immediate task before them not as helping to create a European–American Western bloc but, in accordance with the ideas of the Italian Resistance, as a step towards converting Europe into a zone of peace and thus removing the cause of confrontation between the two world powers. Truman's appeal for 'free world' unity was answered by Augusto Monti on behalf of the MFE, in terms that were typical of the Italian attitude in the spring of 1947:

For Europe, unfortunately, Truman's message offers the inescapable prospect of being divided into two camps – one for America, the other for Russia – and becoming the scene of a new conflict, this time caused by American intervention in Europe's affairs ... The time has come, therefore, for Europe to answer the call of history and complete the search for its lost unity by organizing itself into a single whole ... neither for America nor for Russia, but for Europe's own sake.[111]

On 22 July 1947, three weeks after Molotov's departure from Paris, the Italian ministerial committee for economic reconstruction held a session at which Einaudi, Del Vecchio, Fanfani, Merzagora, Vanoni, and others were present, and which noted that it was 'in Italy's interest to keep the Marshall Plan area open to the East-European countries and make every effort to encourage the tendency on the part of some of those countries to intensify relations with the West of Europe'; in any case, existing trade relations with Poland, Czechoslovakia, Yugoslavia, and the other Balkan countries should be strengthened.[112]

[110] Ibid., pp. 51–3.
[111] A. Monti, 'L'Europa risponde a Truman', *L'Unità europea*, Nos. 7–8, Turin, 20.4.1947, p. 1.
[112] In accordance with the view that the problem of reconstruction should be solved on a European basis, the committee also recommended that 'Germany as a productive economic unit' should be restored and that German production should not be hampered by large reparations deliveries or the international Socialization of the industry of the Ruhr. Report of the ministerial committee dated 22.7.1947, communicated by Prof. Rugiero Moscati, chief archivist of the Italian Foreign Ministry, at the ninth congress of German and Italian historians at Salerno, 15–17.6.1971. There is an inaccurate German translation of his lecture in R. Moscati, *Die Ära de Gasperi, Von der Diktatur zur Demokratie, Deutschland und Italien in der Epoche nach 1943*, Brunswick, 1973, pp. 82–101, above quotation p. 94 f. Similarly Sforza, in his speech in Paris on 12 July 1947, urged that the West Europeans should de everything to make it possible for the East-European countries to co-operate in the work of reconstruction: Sforza (n. 109), p. 52. For Italian reservations concerning a Western bloc, cf. *Italia e Stati Uniti durante l'amministrazione Truman*, Milan (Franco Angeli), 1976.

Limitation to Western Europe 503

The division of Europe, however, was by now unavoidable, and in Italy itself polarization continued. The Communists, although favourable in principle to the peace treaty with the Allies,[113] used the ratification debate in the National Assembly on 24–9 July to demonstrate, by abstention from the vote, their disapproval of the country's pro-Western orientation. Without directly attacking the Marshall Plan – this did not happen until after the establishment of the Cominform in October – but in clear disavowal of the government's support for European unification, Togliatti called for 'a policy determined and inspired only by our national interests'.[114] The Nenni Socialists, who had been chary of European union from the outset for fear of jeopardizing their unity of action with the Communists, were now also convinced that the Italian proletariat could not be led into the fold of US capitalism; they showed solidarity with the PCI, walked out of the Assembly before the vote, and proclaimed Italy's strict neutrality between East and West, at the same time declaring war on the unification movement.[115]

Emphasizing the new alignment, De Gasperi's government took up a strong pro-European position in the ratification debate, and used the prospect of a new order under the aegis of the Marshall Plan as an additional argument for accepting the peace treaty. As Sforza put it, only ratification could create 'a climate of trust and co-operation with those European powers which, like ourselves, wish to create Europe'. The alternative of destroying the treaty might well mean the destruction of Italy, as she would then be excluded from the Marshall Plan. Only by ratification, said Einaudi, 'can we attend the councils of nations with our head held high, and advance with determination and without delay towards the creation of a new European world'. The Social Democrat Canepa said that in order to rebuild Italy it was essential to terminate the armistice regime.[116] No one as yet declared plainly that, for the time being at any rate, Europe could only be created within the Western

---

[113] Cf., e.g. Togliatti in the ratification debate on 29.7.1947: 'The treaty is what it is. I do not think we can change a single comma of it'; *Atti e documenti dell'Assemblea Costituente, discussioni*, Rome, 12 vols., 25 June 1946–31 January 1948; here vol. vi, p. 6411.
[114] Ibid., p. 6419.
[115] Cf. declaration of principle of the PSI deputy Ivan Matteo Lombardo: *Atti e documenti* (n. 113), vol. v, p. 259. Against Nenni's insistence on national neutrality, Altiero Spinelli argued that only by a federation of European states 'in which the "independence" of each state is limited' could Italy and the rest of Western Europe avoid being enslaved to America or Russia. The choice was not between bondage and neutrality, but between bondage and freedom; freedom could only be achieved if 'nationalism, whether neutral or not, was superseded by a federation of the free peoples of Europe.' A. Spinelli, 'Nenni e la neutralità', 30.10.1947, in *Dagli stati sovrani agli stati uniti d'Europa*, Florence, 1950, pp. 241–5.
[116] Sforza: *Atti e documenti* (n. 113), vol. vi, pp. 6161–9; Einaudi: ibid., pp. 6422–6; Canepa: ibid., pp. 6177–81. The arguments against ratification were summarized by Benedetto Croce: 'We Italians who care for our country's honour . . . cannot approve the spirit of this diktat, because it would mean approving something we know to be untrue and part of the transient sickness of the times' (ibid., pp. 6169–72). Cf. Mario Albertini, 'L'amore dell'Italia nell'Europa', *Lo Stato moderno*, 5.10.1947, quoted in L. Levi and S. Pistone, *Trent'anni di Vita del M.F.E.*, Milan, 1973, p. 42.

camp; but Italy herself, with the polarization between advocates and opponents of the Marshall Plan, had contributed to making the East–West conflict in Europe a reality.

In *Belgium*, events in 1947 afforded a double parallel to those in Italy from the 'European' point of view. Here too, the internal situation developed in such a way that the Communists were no longer able to block a pro-European policy, and the Marshall Plan gave the government an opportunity to show much greater readiness than its powerful neighbours to take positive steps towards European unity. In Belgium, too, it was the Christian Democratic party (PSCB) that brought about the change in internal politics. On 11 March 1947 Van Acker's coalition of Socialists (PSB), Communists, and Liberals broke up owing to dissension over coal subsidies. The PSC, whose calculations paid more heed to international developments than those of the Italian DC, decided for the time being to sink their disagreement with the Socialists over the Royal question[117] and to make themselves available for a 'grand coalition' of Christians and Socialists. Despite the mistrust of the anticlerical wing of the PSB, Paul-Henri Spaak managed to form a cabinet on this basis on 26 March without either Liberals or Communists.[118]

On the day of Molotov's departure from Paris, Victor Larock, political director of the Socialist-party organ *Le Peuple* and afterwards foreign minister, wrote: 'Europe at this moment is at the crossroads. The US aid proposal presents the Continent with a decisive choice. Either it will choose the road of co-operation and ignore the claims of national particularism, or it will try once again, in defiance of experience and reason, to reconcile state sovereignties with the Continental solidarity that is imperatively needed.'[119]

Under pressure of economic distress and the advance of the Eastern superpower into Europe, the two main Belgian parties became firm supporters of the Marshall Plan in its original sense: as a way of helping Europe to recover economically and embark on unification under the protection of the Western great power. Larock's words expressed the opinion of the whole government, and at the Paris conference of the sixteen Spaak was able to argue for the fullest possible implementation of the co-operation clause.[120]

In the *Netherlands* the Communist and Liberal parties stood in opposition to each other from mid-1945 onwards; the Catholic People's

---

[117] Cf. chap. I/6, p. 262.
[118] Cf. W. Verkade, *Democratic Parties in the Low Countries*, Leiden, 1965, p. 212.
[119] V. Larock, 'La Reconstruction de l'Europe', *Le Peuple*, 2.7.1947, quoted in G. Marchal-Van Belle, *Les Socialistes belges et l'intégration européenne*, Brussels, 1968, p. 11. As early as 17/18.4.1947, *Le Peuple* had described European union as the only solution of the German problem. 'L'entente franco–allemande doit être la pierre angulaire d'une large coopération européenne sans laquelle les conditions économiques, sociales et politiques de la paix ne se réaliseront pas' (Marchal-Van Belle, ibid.).
[120] Cf. J. Willequet, *Peul-Henri Spaak. Un homme des combats*, Brussels, 1975, p. 159 f.

Party (KVP) and the Labour Party, who formed the ruling coalition, were, however, hampered in carrying out internationalist policies owing to a revival of nationalism in political circles.[121] The Marshall Plan strengthened their hand but did not enable them, as in Belgium and Italy, to set a course in favour of European federation. Marshall's offer was, however, followed in the first instance by the creation of the Benelux organization as an independent political force. The Netherlands, Belgian, and Luxemburg governments in exile had, in September 1944, agreed to conclude a customs union; attempts to put it into practice in 1946 were a failure,[122] but in 1947 all three countries manifested a stronger political determination to overcome the obstacles due to differing economic traditions, and to set an example of regional integration in expectation of the European recovery programme.

On 14 March 1947 the three governments agreed at The Hague to make preparations to bring the customs union, modified in some details, into force on 1 January 1948; at the same time the community was given additional strength and efficacy by a 'presidential council' of the chairmen of the three customs-union agencies and a permanent secretariat under a secretary-general. On 13 and 14 May the three premiers agreed in Brussels on further measures with a view to full economic union; on 6 July a new commercial treaty was concluded between the Netherlands and the economic union of Belgium and Luxemburg; an agreement of 29 August conferred reciprocal rights on Dutch and Belgo-Luxemburg workers in respect of social legislation; by 29 October the ratification process was completed, so that the common tariff in fact came into force at the beginning of 1948.[123]

In anticipation of their integration the three countries presented a common front at the CEEC conference in Paris. Generally through Dr Hirschfeld, their spokesman on the executive committee of the conference, they argued for the free convertibility of European currencies, the inclusion of West-German industry in the recovery programme, the increase of German production and the development of German trade, and closer co-ordination in all economic matters, including industry, agriculture, and currency policies. The Dutch in particular urged the other delegations to take up a firmer attitude towards co-ordination, and saw to it that the final report of the conference contained an appendix on the German question.[124]

However, although the Dutch government under Louis Beel pressed for more co-operation in Western Europe, they hesitated to endorse the

[121] Cf. chap. I/6, pp. 265–8.
[122] Cf. ibid., p. 267 f.
[123] Cf. the basic account in J. E. Meade, *Negotiations for Benelux: an Annotated Chronicle 1943–1956*, Princeton, 1957, here pp. 17–23.
[124] Cf. H. M. Hirschfeld, 'Conception and Origin of the Marshall Plan', *Road to Recovery*, The Hague, 1954, p. 13 f.; confirmed by US reports in *FRUS 1947/III* (n. 37), pp. 333 f., 342, 394, 407, and 425 f.

idea of an actual federation that was now once again being openly discussed. In a major foreign-policy debate in the Lower House on 20 November 1947 Van Boetzelaer, the foreign minister, stated that co-operation in clearly defined areas and with precise aims was certainly desirable, but at the present time a European federation would degenerate in practice into a West-European bloc, which would be incompatible with the long-term objective of world-wide international co-operation. The Dutch public still saw their country's economic future as bound up with Indonesia, and they hesitated to link themselves too closely to their European neighbours. Like the Italian government and the French Socialists, the Dutch believed that the breach between East and West was not yet complete; but, unlike them, they drew the conclusion that an understanding with the Soviet Union should still be given priority over the organization of Western Europe. In the long run this position was untenable, for the Dutch government's policy of West-European co-operation itself did much to consolidate the West and widen the rift between West and East; in the short term it expressed the uncertainty brought about by the change in relations between the great powers. Summing up his views in November 1947, Van Boetzelaer said he thought it necessary to 'wait and see whether the near future will produce some measure of clarification of the political situation in Europe'.[125] The Netherlands went less far in the course of 1947 than Belgium or Italy, but further than France or, especially, Britain felt able to do.

(D) A NEW QUALITY OF UNIFICATION POLICY

As this review of the situation following the Soviet refusal will have shown, there was still considerable resistance, though varying in strength from one West-European country to another, to a closer co-ordination of the national economies, and still more to a political federation. All of them were interested first and foremost in harnessing American aid to their own economies as quickly and effectively as possible. An increasing number of political groups were aware that economic union could increase the efficacy of aid, but as yet these groups were unable to affect national policies. Nevertheless, 1947 was the year in which the movement for European unity became a real and important factor in European

---

[125] Tweede Kamer, 20.11.1947, p. 444, quoted in S.I.P. Van Campen, *The Quest for Security. Some Aspects of Netherlands Foreign Policy 1945–1950*, The Hague, 1958, pp. 42 and 43 f. The cautious attitude of the Dutch public towards European unity was reflected for example in the programme of the Labour party (PvdA) approved on 26 April 1947: this favoured a world order in which 'every state must be prepared to transfer part of its sovereignty to higher institutions', but as regards Europe it only said that 'there must be room for regional groupings under the international rule of law' – a standpoint no less non-committal, as far as the problems of 1947 were concerned, than Bevin's lip-service to a world parliament. *Parlement en Kiezer 31 (1947–1948)*, The Hague, 1948, p. 110 f.

politics. The nature and scope of the breakthrough may be characterized in three ways. Firstly, since official thinking had given up the idea of a community between East and West, the concept of unity was no longer formally excluded from political planning; it was no longer the case that every initiative towards union was inhibited by concern for Soviet objections to it, which were wrongly conceived to be defensive only. Secondly, the idea of European union became a function of American planning; only now, it must be emphasized, was the policy of unification also part of the policy of rallying and stabilizing the 'West', i.e. the Atlantic community that was coming into being. Thirdly, this greatly increased the importance of the concept of unity in terms of practical politics. As will be made clear, the federalist associations ceased to be marginal and became influential vehicles of public opinion; pro-European forces acquired greater importance in and among the parties; the governments were compelled to acknowledge the principle of European co-operation and to concern themselves for the first time with the idea of European union. The swing-round of American foreign policy in 1947 brought about what no one could have expected since 1945; the movement for European union had been offered a fresh opportunity.

3. The Committee of European Economic Co-operation (CEEC) and the Advent of the Customs Union
by Alan S. Milward[126]

(A) THE NATURE OF THE PARIS CONFERENCE

In his speech at Harvard University in which he announced the programme of American aid to Europe Marshall had laid particular stress on the need for a co-ordinated European response to this aid. This was a fundamental aspect of State Department planning. The intention in Washington was to use dollar aid as a lever to create a more economically and politically 'integrated' Western Europe. Beyond this sweeping generalization, however, no American plans had at the time of Marshall's speech been formulated in any proper detail for implementing so bold a policy. In this sense Marshall's speech was an act of high policy and an act of high policy only. The British Ambassador in Washington had been forewarned of the speech and given relatively specific hints that Washington would like to see as an immediate response the formation of some sort of European organization which would co-operate with whatever American organization would administer the aid programme.[127] Immediately after

---

[126] The author would here like to express his genuine gratitude to Stiftung Volkswagenwerk, whose financial support made it possible to use archives in the Netherlands, in Norway, and in the United States as well as certain records of OEEC itself.
[127] PRO, T236/782, Washington to London, 2 June 1947. Bevin's apparently dramatic response to the news of Marshall's speech was considered, expected, and in accordance with American hints.

Marshall's speech William L. Clayton, the Secretary for Commerce, was sent to explain the new course of American foreign policy in London and Paris.

Given the diverse strands of ideas and pragmatism about European integration which had come together to influence American policy, it was surely unfortunate that it should have fallen to an absolute liberal freetrader like Clayton to prepare the ground in London and Paris for the European organization. In the event most of his conversations in Paris took more the form of listening to storms of protest about British–American agreement for some degree of industrial revival in the Bizone, and in London his visit did more to induce British opposition than support for America's aims. In spite of the confusion of American ideals and the misguided missionary determination to simplify European issues, what was at stake was fundamentally an issue of pragmatic policy-making. The plan for the combined recovery of Western Europe and Western Germany was in the first place a practical response to Washington's perception of the danger to its own strategic interests, whatever genuine chords of idealism it might cause to vibrate in America and Europe. It was essential therefore that the practical problems of imposing such a policy on Western Europe should be firmly faced. The immediate lowering or even abolition of tariff barriers was not one of these. Discussion of such an objective only confused the political and economic relationship between the United States and the United Kingdom, which was in itself the first practical problem to be solved, because American policy in Europe was based on the assumption that British support was essential to its success.

The abrupt ending of Lend-Lease in 1945 had been understood in London as a direct attempt by the United States to assert its power over Britain. Making support for America's multilateral trade policy the price of the dollar loan had led to further resentments and fears for the success of British full-employment policy. These had been assuaged by the open recognition of Britain's importance to European and world recovery implied by the acknowledgement of sterling's international status in the Anglo-American Financial Agreements. Washington's new policy now seemed to be denying Britain's world role, and Clayton's over-enthusiastic talk of European integration also implied a serious threat to the domestic economic objectives of the Labour government. Britain had reached the due date under the Financial Agreements when sterling must become convertible against the dollar. The date itself mattered little, for the limited degree of convertibility to be attained had been already more or less reached, but the foreign-exchange reserves could already be seen to be suffering under the shock. At the same time, at the trade negotiations at Geneva, where Clayton was the chief American negotiator, the United States was pursuing its frontal attack against trade 'discrimination' of which British imperial preferences appeared to be the most objectionable form.[128] The American administration had in fact only succeeded in getting Congress to accept the possibility of lower American tariffs against the pledge that British imperial preferences would also go.

Bevin protested to Clayton that American policy would mean that Britain would now be 'just another European country'.[129] As such it would have no protection from the next United States slump. The United States might then change policy again and leave Britain helpless. Bevin's policy was to get the United States to accept that the United Kingdom should have a special interim position for some years rather than have to seek its dollars from the same common pool as its European neighbours.[130] Later, as the exchange crisis worsened, Bevin privately indicated to the American ambassador, Douglas, his unwillingness that Britain should have to seek financial support on the same terms as other European countries. Douglas reported:

> He suggests personally and informally the possibility that the International Bank might be able to provide this relief to the tune of a billion dollars which, he believes, will be sufficient to carry them over the hump by the middle of next year, and which, he believes, will place Britain in a position where she can provide assistance to France and play her role in Germany.[131]

To participate on equal terms, Bevin feared, in a European recovery programme would be against British economic and political interests. Rather it was Britain who should take the lead in promoting the recovery of Western Europe. This would not be through any programme of political unification, but through limited measures of economic co-operation such as the sectoral industrial agreements being worked out between Britain and France. 'The British', Bevin said, 'did not want to go into the programme and not do anything ... This would sacrifice the "little bit of dignity we have left".'[132]

The concept of Western-European economic integration, in however limited a form, did not offer any immediate relief to Britain's economic difficulties, and it raised all manner of complicated issues concerning British relationships with the Empire and Commonwealth and the world-wide nature of British trade. The interministerial 'London Committee'

---

[128] Britain had agreed to participate in the trade negotiations which led eventually to the General Agreement on Tariffs and Trade (GATT), as a condition of the dollar loan.
[129] *FRUS, 1947/III*, p. 271. Meeting of Clayton with Members of British Cabinet, 24 June 1947.
[130] *Ibid.*
[131] NA, SD, 841.51, Box 5837, Douglas to Washington, 25 July 1947. There would not have been the slightest chance of getting such a proposal through the American administration, let alone Congress, and the size of the proposed loan would certainly not have allowed the United Kingdom to 'provide assistance to France'. It was, furthermore, twice the balance of dollars still available to the International Bank for lending at that date (United States, Senate Papers, 50th Congress, 2nd Session), *European Recovery Program, Report of the Committee on Foreign Relations on S.2202*, 26 February 1948.
[132] *FRUS, 1947/III*, p. 281. Second Meeting of Clayton with British Cabinet Ministers, 25 June 1947.

which was set up to guide the British delegation to the Paris conference put the matter succinctly in its brief:

This is an artificial means of getting assistance for U.K. We are not economically a part of Europe (less than 25 per cent of our trade is with Europe); the recovery of continental Europe would not itself solve our problem; we depend upon the rest of the world getting dollars (U.K. and Europe's deficit with U.S.A. are only half the world dollar shortage).[133]

This was in line with the Treasury's analysis of Marshall's proposals, wherein the failure of any European recovery programme to remedy the shortage of gold and dollars in third markets was seen as the first weakness. The second was that any such proposals would be slow to come into operation, and the third that they were explicitly anti-Soviet and as such might not be greeted with overwhelming enthusiasm by all Western-European countries.[134] The Foreign Office did not think the United States would so quickly be able to bypass its own brain-child, the United Nations, and events were to prove this view not without foundation.[135] Not only was American policy of dubious economic and political benefit to Britain, but its execution was also attended with much uncertainty.

The logical response was Anglo-French co-operation. The State Department wanted a purely European initiative in response to Marshall's speech. What exactly was meant by this was made clear in informal statements and contacts over the next two months. It could not be so earlier, because the precise governmental mechanisms of the Marshall Plan took at least that time to work out in Washington before they even went to Congress. But the idea that there should be a European organization which would play a parallel role with whatever administrative structures were created in the United States, and that this organization should also be a vehicle for integrating Western Europe, had been decided already and remained central. That was one reason why Marshall's speech was couched in the terms it was. Both in London and Paris it seemed essential to take joint control over that organization from the start. The intention of such control was to blunt the force of American policy and to turn the European organization into something less threatening to both British and French aims.

When Bevin travelled to Paris to meet Bidault immediately after Marshall's speech, it was not merely to consider the terms of the invitation to the Soviet Union. The State Department's own decisions had already meant that the Soviet Union would not be excluded from the offer of aid; but neither Bevin nor Bidault, any more than Marshall, wanted Soviet participation in the programme unless it were entirely on Western terms,

---

[133] PRO, FO 371/62579, Memorandum for the Paris Delegation, 15 July 1947.
[134] PRO, T236/782, 'Programme of European Reconstruction', 6 June 1947.
[135] Ibid., 'Brief for Mr. Bevin for his discussions with M. Bidault', n.d.

and neither expected it.[136] It was in this meeting at Paris that the basic structure of the common European organization was first discussed, and the preliminary ideas and decisions that emerged there were to determine not only the nature of the grand European conference to be held, but also much of the structure of the Organization for European Economic Cooperation (OEEC), which eventuated from the conference almost one year later. Both parties to the Paris talks agreed that the detailed work of a European conference should be done by a series of technical committees whose functions would be limited to working out the details of Europe's dollar deficit and of possible areas of economic co-operation, which would be limited and non-committal. Originally, technical committees were proposed to deal with transportation, energy, food and agriculture, and iron and steel.[137] When the conference met, two similar committees were formed to deal with timber and with manpower, the latter to meet the requests of the Italians. The detailed components of the dollar deficit would have to be put together in the conference by two further committees, a Balance of Payments Committee and a Committee of Financial Experts. These were not firmly decided upon in the Paris talks, although the need for such a format was overwhelming in view of the emerging American decision to estimate the total of dollar aid against Western Europe's balance of payments deficit with the dollar zone. The second committee derived its importance from the American emphasis on reducing the barriers to intra-European trade and payments as a further step to integration. The decisions on the structure of the European conference were therefore fluid, able to be modified in detail as American ideas emerged more clearly and to meet the as yet unknown wishes of the other countries who would attend. The principle, however, that the work would be done in separate committees empowered to handle no more than technical details was firmly decided, and that was the important issue. Wider questions of European unity would be entirely out of place at such a level.

The second principle which was also determined at the Anglo-French meeting was that these committees should be supervised by a much smaller executive committee of no more than five countries, which would draw up the specific proposals to be presented to the conference and liaise with the Americans. This body, which when the conference met was to become formally the Executive Committee of the Committee of European Economic Cooperation (CEEC), was designed as the main instrument for Anglo-French domination of the proceedings. The arrangement was

---

[136] 'Had Mr. Bevin travelled to Paris with a staff of experts to talk with M. Bidault for two days so that they could send an invitation to Mr. Molotov to join them?', D. Wightman, *Economic Cooperation in Europe,* (London, Allen and Unwin, 1956), p. 34.
[137] France, Ministère des Affaires Étrangères, *Conference des Ministres Étrangères de la France, du Royaume-Uni, de l'URSS* (Paris, 1947), pp. 10–12, Bidault to Bonnet, 10 June 1947.

sanctioned by Clayton on condition that Italy, which was likely to sympathize more closely with American policies, was also a member.[138] The appointment of the other two members was left to the British and French, but one place obviously had to be filled from Benelux. Britain insisted that any Benelux representative be Dutch.[139] In fact, by previous arrangement the Benelux countries had agreed amongst themselves to support their attempt at complete union by sending a joint delegation to the conference, so that the Dutch representative on the Executive Committee, H. M. Hirschfeld, served as representative of all three.[140] The last place, after much argument, went to Scandinavia as a bait to induce the Scandinavian countries to participate fully. The choice eventually fell on Norway, because it was by no means certain that Sweden would need or request dollar aid. This was a decision of much importance, for Norway was to be thrust into playing a crucial role in the first months of the attempt at a European organization precisely at the time when the internal debate over her own foreign policy was at its most intense. In the later history of OEEC the composition and title of the Executive Committee was to be slightly widened to cope with changed political realities, but it remained an instrument to guarantee the control of the larger European powers.

It may well be true, as van der Beugel recounts, that many of the participants in the technical committees, by being brought together in this common enterprise, acquired a wider comprehension of the common nature of European economic problems and even developed not only a certain feeling of affinity with each other, but also a degree of solidarity against their own national governments at moments when these governments did not show the same comprehension.[141] But they had little power to exert direct influence upon their governments. Only Italy chose a representative of ministerial status as head of its delegation and as its representative on the Executive Committee.[142] The other countries

[138] *FRUS, 1947/III,* p. 292, Meeting with Clayton of members of the British Cabinet, 26 June 1947. The idea of such an Executive Committee came originally from the French: PRO, FO 371/62568, conversation between Franks and Alphand.
[139] MBZ, 610.302, Foreign Ministry to Ministry for Economic Affairs, 3 July 1947.
[140] H. M. Hirschfeld served throughout the thirties and the war as the head of the economic department of the Javasche Bank. Director-General of Commerce and Industry and Secretary-General in the Netherlands Department of Economic Affairs 1947–52, a figure of central importance both in the formulation of reconstruction policy in the Netherlands and in the history of the Benelux union. Chairman and director of many companies. He was born in Germany.
[141] E. H. van der Beugel, *From Marshall Aid to Atlantic Partnership,* (Amsterdam, 1966), pp. 71–2. The author was himself one of the Netherlands delegates to the Paris conference but, although his work is the only account of the conference so far in print which is based on access to original materials, it is so careful to gloss over all matters of serious difference between the United States and Western Europe as to be almost as misleading as revealing.
[142] Pietro Campilli, who served in a wide range of ministerial and governmental positions from 1947 onwards. He eventually became president of the European Investment Bank. A banker and bank administrator, he had retired from public life on the Fascist seizure of power, although this did not prevent his making a highly successful private business career. He was a friend of De Gasperi and closely shared his political views.

appointed senior civil servants who were already closely involved in the formulation of national reconstruction policy, but who remained only the executants and advisers of their ministers. Thus before the conference began the stage was set for a fundamental opposition between the far-reaching hopes and ambitions of the United States and the machinery of the conference, which had been designed to thwart these ambitions. This opposition was to persist throughout the conference and throughout the first years of OEEC. There were occasional American victories, but they were small ones and eventually Washington began to pursue the grail of European integration by other routes.

One reason for this, as much as the fact of European opposition, was that the workings of the conference and of OEEC were to reveal to Washington how gravely it had simplified and even overlooked divisions in Western Europe which rested on profoundly different political choices. From the moment the conference met there began a learning process in Washington which was to forge a more realistic set of political aspirations there. To that extent the Anglo-French collaboration was constructive rather than the reverse. Yet it did not rest on any genuine agreement about the future organization of Europe. On the contrary, the conference was very soon to reveal yawning chasms of disagreement. The most obvious was that the United Kingdom could see more loss than gain from involvement in any process of Western-European unification, whereas for France such a policy was the immediate alternative to the preferred policy of the division and permanent economic enfeeblement of Germany. Should this solution to her relations with Germany prove impossible to obtain, and Marshall's speech was one of the strongest indicators that this would be so, the idea of incorporating 'western Germany' into an integrated Western Europe whose conditions and terms would be first defined by France and her allies offered a solution to the same problem. This solution had already been sketched out by the Socialist Party and certain adherents of the MRP.[143] France's attempts to manœuvre towards a solution of her future relationship with Germany which, while leaving her with sufficient security, would still be acceptable to America, were to limit Anglo-French collaboration at Paris to little more than their original collusion over the purely technical structure of the intended European organization.

The relationship of the United States to Britain and France was thus likely to be complicated and difficult once the conference met. Both London and Paris with reason regarded Washington's attitude to the conference as an attempt to exercise power without responsibility. America

---

[143] K. Hänsch, in *Frankreich zwischen Ost und West. Die Reaktion auf den Ausbruch des Ost–West–Konfliktes 1946–1948,* (Berlin, 1972) is prepared to claim by means of a cybernetic model that this alternative solution was inevitable once the United States and Russia were in dispute. For details of the political formulation of the alternative see W. Lipgens, 'Innenfranzösische Kritik an der Aussenpolitik de Gaulles 1944–46' in *Vierteljahrshefte für Zeitgeschichte,* vol. 24, 1976.

did not intend to participate in the conference, but intended to make it clear throughout what sort of political reconstruction in Europe was required in return for Marshall Aid. When the conference did not produce the sort of results Washington wanted, the heaviest diplomatic pressures were brought to bear on it and the blame inevitably was laid at the door firstly of the British and secondly of the French. But there was another set of diplomatic problems raised by the new American policy from which Washington had so far been relatively free. All the smaller West-European countries would be at Paris. For the first time questions about the reconstruction of Europe were to be handled outside the framework of the great-power conferences. What would be the attitude of the smaller powers?

The exclusion from all decision-making about Germany had been particularly resented in Brussels and The Hague. There anxious eyes were turned on the ailing Germany economy and angry protests were beginning to be aimed at Allied policy. The Paris conference was seen as a chance to bring pressure to bear on the greater powers over the German question. The Anglo-French attempt to dominate the procedure and structure of the conference only stoked the fires of resentment the more, and these circumstances no doubt made the task of formulating a common Benelux policy easier. The first element of this common policy was that the growth of European output must be as rapid as possible. Translated into action, this meant that United States aid should not be used to subsidize long-term capital investment plans such as the Monnet Plan – the purpose of which was to create over a four- to five-year period new comparative advantages for the French economy at, as Belgium saw it, the expense of countries, like Belgium, seeking to maximize output as quickly as possible. Dollars should be made available as soon as possible, but only for the immediate short-term utilization and maximization of European productive resources. This would effectively maintain Belgium's lead in the recovery process, and prevent her capital-goods export markets from being captured by the output from modernized French plant while she was herself persisting with older plant. Secondly, dollar aid must be secured in order to back a plan to introduce currency convertibility and multilateral trade in Western Europe as quickly as possible. Intra-European trade was fundamental to the Benelux countries' economy, and already Belgium was running into export difficulties because of her surpluses with virtually all European countries, which, in a network of bilateral trading agreements, could not be compensated by her import surpluses from outside Europe. This was the origin of the Belgian payments proposals at the Paris Conference which, after long argument and much alteration, eventually were transmuted into the first post-war European payments agreement.[144] Thirdly, the greater powers must be forced to put the

---

[144] See p. 530 ff.

German question on the agenda of the Paris Conference. Ruhr coal output must be increased, and once the over-all level of industrial output had reached the level foreseen in the Level of Industry Agreement Benelux must at once press for higher levels. Internal economic policy in Germany must be governed by these 'European' principles and taken out of the hands of the occupying powers.[145] All this meant that the proposed structure of the conference would also have to be changed so that all countries attending should be present on all the committees.[146]

The attitude of the neutral powers was likely to be the most antagonistic to US policy, the more so as their need for dollars in July 1947 was much less acute and there was little economic leverage which Washington could exercise over them. Because Norway made the same economic assumptions it tended to take its stance with the neutrals and, indeed, by virtue of the position it was given on the Executive Committee once the conference met it was forced into being their spokesman. The Norwegian Foreign Minister, Halvard Lange, told the cabinet on 17 June that it would be better not to participate in the American programme if this were economically feasible.[147] Until the end of May Norway's foreign-exchange reserves had been increasing. The anticipation was that they would decline in 1948 because of the increasing demands made by imports and shipping charges, but that as the Norwegian merchant marine was restored to its very large pre-war size the flow of invisible earnings would enable Norway to reach safety in 1949. The planned rate of improvement in the standard of consumption was in any case lower from 1948 onwards. The conviction that this medium-term forecast would not go awry and leave Norway dependent on dollar aid has to be seen in the context of the general fervour and exaggerated optimism which pervaded the small group of Keynesian economists and statisticians who had devised the first Norwegian National Budget. They were confident that national-income accounting and improved knowledge of the economy would enable the Norwegian Labour Party to pursue a radically different set of reconstruction policies, in which full employment would be a first objective and some measure of gross over-all planning of resources and rewards a second. Their own remarkable abilities probably blinded them to the coming international threats to the exchange reserves, on which in the initial stage a very high proportion of capital investment depended.[148]

---

[145] MBZ, 601.302, 'Ontwerp-Memorandum betreffende het standpunt van België, Luxemburg en Nederland in te nemen op de Conferentie in Parijs . . .', 10 July 1947.
[146] MBZ, 601.302, Netherlands Embassy in London to Foreign Ministry, 10 July 1947.
[147] H. Pharo, 'Bridgebuilding and Reconstruction, Norway Faces the Marshall Plan' in *Scandinavian Journal of History*, i, 1976, p. 134.
[148] A. Bourneuf, *Norway, The Planned Revival*, Harvard Economic Studies, vol. 106, (Cambridge, Mass., 1958) is the most comprehensive account so far of Norwegian post-war domestic policy. The author was herself a member of the Economic Co-operation Administration mission in Norway. A more detailed study based on a wider selection of documentary material is currently being prepared in the University of Oslo by Trond Bergh, for whose help, as for that of Helge Pharo, the author would like here to express his thanks.

The issue was confused by uncertainties about the East–West split. Norway had thrown its support energetically behind the United Nations and hoped to find her security there rather than in full allegiance to an American power bloc. Common sense suggested it was better, given the economic assessment, to assume a non-committal attitude to the Paris proceedings. Norway and Sweden therefore championed the cause of the United Nations Economic Commission for Europe (ECE), which already represented all European countries, as the European organization to handle Marshall Aid. At the start of the Paris conference they pressed this point vigorously; at the end of the conference they objected to a new permanent European organization because there already was one. It was entirely unacceptable to the United States to use the ECE in such a way; that would have been to repeat the experience with UNRRA. If there were to be any Eastern-bloc countries in the new organization they would have to be defectors from that bloc.[149]

Lastly, American and West-European relationships were confused by the fact that two of the countries which attended the conference, Greece and Turkey, were not only not in Western Europe but were also already receiving military aid under separate legislation from the United States. Both strongly resented being incorporated into a more general aid programme and did strikingly little to help in the formulation of that programme at Paris. The issues of West-European integration discussed there had virtually nothing to do with them, yet the pretence, and sometimes the actuality, was that their aid depended on the resolution of such issues. Both became members of the European Recovery Programme, and it would be fair to say that for most of the other members they were a thorough nuisance throughout. Their delegations were a source of constant complaint from the other delegations, because they could scarcely be bothered to provide the statistical information required by the Programme with any more than a flimsy pretence of subscribing to its operations. Their governments persisted in making direct representations about aid to Washington. There was already a separate American aid agency, the United States Economic Mission to Greece. On a per capita basis Greece had already received more dollar aid than even the United Kingdom since the end of the war, and the Paris conference could only appear in Athens as a threat to this situation.[150] The separate problems of Greece and Turkey lie outside the scope of this book, but it is worth emphasizing that they often intruded in a most disruptive way into the economic arguments

---

[149] Five of the sixteen countries which came to the Paris conference were not as yet members of the United Nations.

[150] Over the period 1 July 1945–30 June 1947 Greece had received $99.3 per inhabitant in grants and loans, the United Kingdom $94.8. The Greek receipts were mostly grants, those of the United Kingdom loans. US, *Senate Papers, 50th Congress, 2nd Session, Report of the Committee on Foreign Relations on S.2202*, 26 February 1948. In addition Greece had received about £29 million in military aid from Britain and had had about £40 million of sterling debt cancelled.

over Western Europe because of their inclusion in a common framework of American aid.

When sixteen countries ultimately sent delegations to Paris on 12 July for the conference which took to itself the name Committee of European Economic Cooperation (CEEC), their heterogeneity must surely have impressed at least as much as the similarities in their position.[151] Five had colonial empires, two had less than one million inhabitants, two had important armies, one was occupied by two of the others, and two had been neutral powers for more than a century. Two had per capita national incomes clearly exceeded only by that of the United States, four were still underdeveloped economies. Some has based their recovery on planning and stringent controls, others had been ardent advocates of decontrol and a *laissez-faire* economy. Some had a world-wide pattern of trade and investment, for others their international economic connections were overwhelmingly with the European Continent. The one country whose affairs had more than any other been responsible for the conference was not represented there at all.

There were as yet no German organs of government which the Americans could reasonably expect to provide German representatives at Paris. The possibility existed that the Bizone and the French zone of occupation might be represented by the occupying forces. The Benelux countries would have welcomed some form of representation of Germany as a way to initiate discussion on Allied economic policy there.[152] But the most that was acceptable was that the military administrations in the occupation zones should be required to provide the necessary statistical information on the same terms as the national governments officially represented at Paris. The central problem was bound to be that of the German economy, but in the event this problem arose at once in so unintended a way as to bring it immediately into focus as the central issue in European integration.

During the conference American policy on the objectives of Marshall Aid and the methods of its administration was elaborated in detail. The rather vague role which the European organization was originally to play came to be defined in such a way that CEEC was seen in Washington as an extremely important potential step towards West-European political integration, indeed as a West-European government in embryo. This section is not concerned with the formulation of American policy on European integration, but only with the European response to that policy. It must, however, be emphasized here how ambitiously far-reaching American hopes and plans for the Paris conference were. The State Department wanted that conference to give birth to a permanent European organization which would quickly bring together the West-European

---

[151] Austria, Belgium, Denmark, France, Greece, Iceland, Ireland, Italy, Luxemburg, the Netherlands, Norway, Portugal, Sweden, Switzerland, Turkey, and the United Kingdom.
[152] MBZ, 610.302, 'Laatste ontwikkeling van de conferentie te Parijs', 12 September 1947.

countries into a close economic association, and it wanted that association to be a stepping-stone towards some form of political integration.

The likely difficulties in the way of such ambitious plans for CEEC have been sketched here. How they worked out in practice must now be shown.

(B) THE PROBLEM OF GERMANY

The Anglo-American consultations on increasing the permitted levels of industrial output in specific sectors in the Bizone, which had been under way since April, took place against the background of total opposition in France to such a plan and to almost every other aspect of Allied policy in Germany. The day on which General Clay officially informed Washington that final agreement on a revision of the permitted levels of industry in the Bizone had been reached, 12 July, was the same day that the official opening ceremonies of the Paris conference were performed. Clayton had already received the full blast of French objections to these negotiations. Bidault had told him that France, Belgium, and Luxemburg would, with the implementation of the Monnet Plan, be capable of meeting all the requirements of Western Europe.[153] Clayton's task in Paris had been to persuade the French government to give full support to what Washington hoped would be a new era of Western-European economic co-operation, but Bidault maintained that if the new figures for German industry were publicly announced the sixteen-nation conference in Paris would be doomed to failure and 'there would be no Europe'.[154] To come to any agreement about Germany before the Paris conference had itself reached decisions would 'be to give priority to the reconstruction of Germany over the reconstruction of France'.[155] A successful outcome of the conference had been put into jeopardy before the conference had even begun.

When it did begin its real work the situation was made even more tense, because it seemed to offer to the smaller West-European countries their first opportunity to participate in any international decisions about the fate of Germany. For the most part the harsh economic logic of 1947 meant that they would espouse an even speedier reconstruction of Germany than Britain and the United States had tentatively agreed on. At the plenary session on 17 July the Benelux delegation put their brief into practice and demanded that the level of economic recovery in Germany be considered by the conference as an inescapable part of the European recovery plan, and in the Executive Committee the Benelux delegate, Hirschfeld, insisted even more strongly on these points. For Benelux, he complained, the 'currency curtain' in Germany (the refusal of the Joint Export-Import

---

[153] The author is indebted to Miss F. Lynch for making available from her University of Manchester PhD thesis transcripts of Clayton's conversations in Paris, as well as for much other practical help with French sources.
[154] *FRUS, 1947/II*, pp. 983–6, Gimbel, *The Origins of the Marshall Plan* (Stanford, 1976), p. 228.
[155] Ibid., p. 992.

Agency which controlled the Bizone's external trade to increase its volume of intra-European trade for fear it would accumulate soft currencies instead of dollars) was as bad a problem as the Iron Curtain, and he described Allied policy in the Bizone as 'totalitarian'.[156] Although the British and French representatives insisted that this was not the business of the conference, the Italian delegate supported the Benelux position on the grounds that Germany was the major market for Italian exports as for Benelux exports. Even the Norwegian representative, while insisting on restrictions being maintained on those areas which competed directly with Norwegian interests – fishing, whaling, shipping, and shipbuilding – spoke in favour of an accelerated German recovery and for much wider consultations with the smaller powers about policy in Germany.[157] The French took the same attitude to this as they had to US policy. If the conference proposed increasing German output beyond the 'level of security', France, Alphand declared, would take 'an entirely negative position'.[158]

The British, who had been the first and most ardent in their desire to increase the permitted German level of industry, now began to retreat and to persuade the Americans to do likewise. The problem in Washington, however, was that although the State Department was at least prepared to consider such a move in order to save its new European policy, the Army was not, for it was purely concerned with Germany. Marshall managed to persuade the new Secretary for the Army, Kenneth C. Royall, to sign an agreement postponing publication of the revised figures until 1 September so that the French could make representations in Washington.[159] But the French government got wind of the agreement through some rash Army publicity in Germany, and redoubled their protests at the apparent uselessness of any representations they might make. Bidault threatened to resign if there were no change of policy.[160] Although the Marshall–Royall agreement had stipulated that no other power be consulted on the level-of-industry agreement, the State Department had nevertheless to ask that the agreement be modified so that there could be tripartite talks in London with the French. At Paris the technical committees which were compiling statistical information on Western-Europe's economic situation and needs had come to a standstill because the French delegates were not prepared to consider any figures for coal, coke, or steel which differed from the original Potsdam agreements on the level of industry in Germany.

Any effective progress and the publication of the joint report to Congress, which in American eyes was the indispensable final outcome of the Paris

---

[156] MBZ, 610.302, Verslag van der vergadering van het Comité Executif dd. 15 Augustus 1947, 15 August 1947.
[157] Ibid.
[158] PRO, FO 371/62568, Draft Record of 2nd Meeting of CEEC, 17 July 1947.
[159] J. Gimbel, *The Origins*, p. 236 ff.
[160] General Clay threatened to resign if there were a change of policy.

meeting, had now also to depend on the discussions about Germany which would take place quite separately. The conference had scarcely been set in motion before it had stuck fast on the obvious, dangerous, and unavoidable reef which lay across its route. Thenceforward any settlement in Germany had to be by agreement with France, and any progress towards a joint European agreement on the use of American aid in reconstruction had to depend on the settlement in Germany. When the Benelux delegation was preparing its proposals for an intra-European payments system to be submitted to the Paris conference, Hirschfeld asked Clayton if such proposals should be based on the existing Bizone level of industry agreement and received an answer which was 'exceptionally vague'.[161] The Franco-German problem at last occupied the centre of the stage; European integration would only become a part of the play in so far as it was related to solving the dilemma of the main actors and the main plot.

The main plot took place in August away from Paris, where the delegations of the sixteen nations continued to busy themselves with organizing the completion of the statistical questionnaires prepared by the French, while they awaited the outcome of the talks on Germany. There were two sets of talks, the suddenly called tripartite talks in London and the so-called 'coal conferences' between the British and the Americans in Washington which had been previously arranged. The central problem of the tripartite talks was, from the American standpoint, to get the French to agree to the revised German output figures so that the report from Paris to Congress could at least appear to be based on them, and, from the French standpoint, to get the United States and Britain to modify their proposals for the future of the Ruhr and Germany. However, the problem of the Ruhr was also the immediate concern of the 'coal conferences', from which the French were excluded. The Americans were determined to use this occasion to change British plans for the socialization of the Ruhr mines. There was agreement between the State Department and the Army that by raising such larger issues the British were distracting the attention of miners from what should be their main job, getting coal, and, as well, were making political decisions about the future nature of 'Western Germany' which might be unacceptable to the American public and were certainly unacceptable to General Clay. The French attitude was that socialization of the mines by the *Land* government of Nordrhein–Westfalen would only be a temporary halting-place on the way to nationalization by a future West-German central government, which they regarded as more menacing than returning them to the control of private industry. For France, therefore, internationalization of the Ruhr had to have the essential ingredient that the mines should be managed by foreign managers, whatever ultimate supervisory and control powers the occupation authorities might retain.

---

[161] MBZ, 610.302, 'Besprekingen met de Undersecretary of State Clayton op 31 July 1947'.

Before the tripartite talks began the French had obviously decided that all they could salvage from the situation was a plan for the 'internationalization' of the Ruhr and Rhineland, rather than their separation from Germany. Within the ambit of such a plan it might be possible still to make the necessary German resources available for the Monnet Plan, and also combine such a policy with a more general European Recovery Plan. So long, however, as the French meant by this French managers in the Ruhr concerns it was not likely to win acceptance. Bevin was perfectly willing to see an international supervisory body, which would include not only France but also Benelux, brought into existence for the Ruhr, and was prepared to urge such a policy on the United States, always supposing that France would merge her occupation zone with the Bizone.[162] The American reponse could hardly have been less encouraging; the US government 'felt that no further price should be paid to France in this matter'.[163]

From this uncompromising position the Americans had to move. The French delegation was eventually told that the United States would give 'sympathetic consideration' to any proposal for an international Ruhr authority which would exercise some control over the allocation of the Ruhr's resources.[164] This assurance came only from the Ambassador in London and the State Department was extremely cautious about what it wrote on the question. With good reason, for the precise nature of the Ruhr authority would be all-important. Would it be an international board with direct management powers in the works themselves, or a remote international control board with few direct executive powers? There was a third possibility which briefly emerged in these talks and which was eventually to provide the solution after three more years of dispute, viz. an internationally supervised cartel which would include the French and Benelux firms.[165] The French had only a vague assurance that when there were talks on this issue the United States would consider benevolently one of these solutions. The American negotiators said they would recommend such talks immediately after the London talks, but the State Department did not accept this recommendation once the London talks had broken up. There was no need to make any more concessions at the time than were necessary to produce the report from Paris. But France did win a further concession, that the Washington 'coal conversations' would be followed at once by tripartite discussions in Berlin on the revision of the Moscow sliding scales for coal allocation within the framework of reparations. Much had been left unsettled, however. No decision had been taken, for example, about the Saarland. Furthermore it was to

[162] PRO, FO 371.65399, Meeting in the Secretary of State's room, 8 August 1947.
[163] PRO, FO 371/65201, Conversation between Bevin and Douglas, 18 August 1947.
[164] *FRUS, 1947/II,* pp. 1041–2, Caffery to Marshall, 19 August 1947.
[165] Ibid., p. 1022, Clayton to Marshall, 7 August 1947.

emerge almost at once that the 'wider' talks would not be held until America was ready, which meant waiting until the next meeting of the Council of Foreign Ministers in London at the end of November had come to its universally expected failure. France signed the final communiqué of the London tripartite talks 'with serious hesitation'.[166] Although the Paris conference could now proceed on the basis of the revised level of industry agreements for Germany, France did not cease to criticize those agreements. The Benelux delegates at Paris drew the conclusion from the tripartite talks that as far as Germany was concerned the United States and Britain 'did not yet know what they wanted'.[167]

The Washington 'coal conferences' were a more decisive event. Their outcome, although Bevin denied this, was the effective defeat of the British plans to socialize the Ruhr mines. At their conclusion there began at once in Berlin a series of tripartite coal talks intended to adjust the Moscow sliding scales in order to allow for the incorporation of the Saarland into France, so that its coal output could be considered as wholly at the disposal of the French economy. These talks began before formal agreement was reached at the Paris conference on the official report to be issued, and before they began the important principle was established that coal-consumption figures should be linked to the output figures in each zone of Germany. This was a major issue, for the proposed Paris report would have to have two separate sections on Germany, one for the Bizone and one for the French zone. It was also established that coke allocation from Germany should be a fixed proportion of coal allocations. All these, although they might seem matters of detail, were important concessions to the French position, and it was on this series of concessions that the Paris conference waited. The US government had originally set a deadline of 1 September for the successful conclusion of the Paris conference. This was why the agreement between Marshall and Royall not to publish the details of the revised level-of-industry agreement for the Bizone had been arranged to expire at that time. But, in large part because of the French determination to win further concessions on Germany, this deadline could not be met.

As the deadline of 1 September for publishing the new figures approached, however, it became increasingly clear that French policy towards Germany was not the only obstacle towards an effective conclusion to the Paris conference. As far as Germany was concerned, the best Washington could hope for by that date from the Paris conference was that it would not flaunt its disagreements over Germany before Congress nor, which might be worse, publish a report simply omitting all mention of German recovery. But it also became clear that what was likely to emerge from the Paris meeting would be far short in other ways of the sort of document which the American administration hoped to see as backing for the Marshall Aid

[166] PRO, FO 371.65201, Minutes of the 4th Meeting of the Tripartite Talks, 27 August 1947.
[167] MBZ, 610.302, 'Bespreking met Sir Oliver Franks', 31 August 1947.

legislation in Congress. It is therefore necessary to trace the evolution in Paris of the conference which Washington had hoped might be the first step towards West-European integration.

(C) THE PAYMENTS PROBLEM

One of the most noticeable differences between the reconstruction periods after the two world wars was the complete difference in the behaviour of exchange rates. After 1918 the major trading currencies fluctuated wildly against each other. These fluctuations were the outcome of market quotations, however, and the currencies could always be bought and sold at the rate quoted at any one time. The rapid spread of exchange controls from 1929 onwards and their universal use during the Second World War meant that by 1945 there had already been a long period when this was not the case. Most currencies now had a carefully maintained fixed rate of exchange, and in order to maintain it government-controlled bodies would allocate specific allotments of foreign exchange for specific foreign transactions. Post-war plans for a more flexible international monetary system were themselves based on the idea of maintaining stable rates of exchange between currencies for long periods. When a country participated in the International Monetary Fund it had to register a 'par rate' for its currency there. Major foreign transactions during the thirties had in many countries also been supervised and controlled by other methods, and perhaps as much as one-third of the world's foreign trade had come to be conducted by short-term trade agreements between two countries, usually for no longer than one year, to exchange specific quantities of goods at specified prices. Such agreements were designed to equalize the flow of foreign transactions and payments between pairs of countries, so that they usually included also all other forms of currency transactions, such as interest payments on investments, as well as foreign trade in commodities. As foreign trade revived in Europe at the end of the war, bilateral agreements of this kind were the main force behind its revival. In unsure and unpredictable circumstances they protected the fixed values of European currencies against each other (although not always at an economically justifiable level), and obviated the alarming swings in trade and payments which had characterized the reconstruction period after 1918 and had been one of the reasons for the instability of production and trade in that time. There was a deliberate avoidance in most countries of attempts to stabilize exchange rates by deflationary internal fiscal policies. Bilateral trade and fixed exchange rates were seen as corner-stones of economies which would have more control over their own destiny and be built on full employment and a wider availability of welfare. Fixed exchange rates were in fact part of the aspirations to a better world, for which the war had been fought. Bilateral trading agreements, however, were thought of in most countries as merely a temporary safeguard until some stability and a fixed post-war pattern of international trade and payments had emerged. Even so, by 1947 a far greater proportion of the world's trade was being conducted through such restrictive devices than in the thirties, especially in Europe, which was still by far the greatest generator of international trade.

The restrictions imposed by bilateral agreements were on one level practical and immediate. All such agreements strictly limited the volume of debt which any country could accumulate against another in either of their currencies over a short period of time. The margin of permissible debt once reached, it was necessary to make all further payments in gold or hard currency. In the post-war world this normally meant dollars or Swiss francs, both of which were jealously hoarded. As foreign trade between European countries expanded after the war, it therefore tended to be increasingly subject to sudden interruptions when particular countries reached their agreed margins of debt against others and cut off all further imports from the suppliers in question, rather than part with gold or currencies that formed part of their reserves. On another level the restrictions imposed by bilateral agreements were abstract and theoretical, a perfectly functioning flow of international trade and payments would presumably have meant that international trade would have flowed in different directions, and from an economic point of view more 'efficient' directions than those into which it was constrained by such carefully detailed inter-governmental agreements. This, however, was not so convincing an argument in Western Europe after the experience of the inter-war years as it was in the United States, which had, in any case, historically interfered far more through high tariffs with the 'efficient' flow of international trade than Western-European countries.

None the less the extraordinary growth of output and exports during the war in the United States had convinced American governments that a thriving post-war world and a prosperous America's place in that world depended on the creation of an efficient multilateral trade and payments system in which the international debts and surpluses of countries could be offset against each other in a comprehensive world balance, much as they had been before 1914. Such a system would alone permit American foreign trade and domestic output to exist at the new, much higher levels they must maintain in order to support the prosperity which the war had brought. As the plans for a peaceful post-war world order collapsed, these ideas were still seen as fundamental to a prosperous Western bloc. Firstly, full recovery in Europe would mean that higher levels of output would be turned through a multilateral payments system into a higher level of European exports, and, in so far as this also would apply to Western-European exports to the United States, the huge post-war American export surpluses to Western Europe would be brought into balance also through an almost world-wide mechanism. European countries asked themselves what it was they would export to the United States, and were less convinced that there would be an international balance of payments which would enable the system to cope with America's huge trade surpluses. Secondly, the freest possible flow of goods and payments between Western-European countries had now come to be seen in Washington as a desirable objective in itself. If political union between the Western-European countries could not yet be obtained, a liberal view of the world suggested in Washington that such union might in fact be the ultimate outcome of a complete liberalization of intra-West-European foreign transactions. If a West-European customs union was out of the question, a comprehensive West-European payments system was the next best thing. It should in theory have the same effects in expanding the market, 'rationalizing' production within the larger market, and raising productivity to the levels prevailing in the American market. One market might become one state. An intra-European payments system became therefore an important political objective in Washington, and its political importance tended to obliterate the uncertainties of the economic theory underlying it. Thirdly, as America's needs for a militant ideology of its own became so acute from 1947 onwards, the theoretically greater economic efficiency of a large market and a multilateral payments system came to be seen by many in Washington as a fundamental aspect of political democracy and 'a free society'. Several major figures in the Economic Cooperation Administration, Averill Harriman and Paul G. Hoffman in particular, appear to have been entirely unable to distinguish between the possible theoretical advantages of a multilateral payments system in Europe from the standpoint of economic efficiency, and such a system as one of the bases of a free, democratic, Western society based on fundamental human liberties. This confusion between freedom of economic and political action was to make the pressures on CEEC and its successor organization, OEEC, to construct an intra-European multilateral payments system so strong that arguments over the techniques of international payments within Europe often dominated for long periods the proceedings of the new European organization.

When Europe's post-war economic problem was designated in Washington as a production problem, the assumption underlying that phrase was that if West-European output could increase, a more efficient mechanism of international trade and payments would lead to a rapid mutual expansion of wealth in Western Europe and North America and also to a trade and payments equilibrium between the two continents. In Western Europe the economic problem was usually seen as a much more limited one, the problem of where to obtain sufficient foreign exchange to finance the imports needed to sustain the very rapid increases in output which had taken place everywhere except in Germany since 1945, and by 1947 were beginning to occur even there.[168] By comparison with the period

[168] The idea that economic recovery in Western Germany was dependent on the currency reform of 1948 is one of the most persistent myths of the post-war world. Economic recovery there, although

after 1918, European economies made a remarkably vigorous recovery after 1945. There was in some of them an observable decrease in the rate of growth of both output and foreign trade in the spring of 1947 which coincided with the change in American foreign policy and tended to be seen in Washington as making Western Europe more vulnerable to the threat of a Communist take-over. A thorough economic analysis of the so-called crisis in Western Europe in 1947 which played so great a part in bringing Marshall Aid into being can hardly be made here.[169] But its main component was the failure of planning for the post-war world to take into account the Americans' massive temporary need to make dollars, the only extensively used hard currency, available to finance their own export surpluses. The rate of growth of production in Europe was so rapid that no devices could prevent the world shortage of hard currency from forcing the major European importers to cut back on their imports in the summer of 1947. Europe's economic problems in fact stemmed more from the successes than from the failures of post-war production. The American view that a fundamental change in the mechanisms of intra-European trade would produce an immediate benefit in terms of increased European output therefore ran directly counter to the view of many European countries that such changes, although no doubt theoretically and practically desirable in the medium term, would in the short term be useless and dangerous unless the fundamental structural disequilibria in world trade were first corrected, a responsibility which fell heavily on the United States and of which recycling dollars through Marshall Aid was but a first and insufficient acknowledgement.

From what different standpoints the parties approached the issue may be briefly seen from a consideration of attitudes to the Sterling Area. From the standpoint of the British government the Sterling Area was an expansionary force in world trade and a way of overcoming the international structural disequilibria. It offered the possibility of multilateral settlements to a group of nations representing a significant part of total world trade.[170] British imports in 1947 were by themselves almost the equivalent of United States imports. What was more, most British purchases of primary

---

at a very much lower level than elsewhere in Western Europe, began well before that date. The process is traced for the Bizone in W. Abelshauser, *Wirtschaft in Westdeutschland 1945–1948*, (Stuttgart, 1975) and the parallel process for the French zone in M. Manz, *Stagnation und Aufschwung in der französischen Zone von 1945–1948,* Dissertation (Mannheim, 1968).

[169] The author is engaged at the moment on precisely such a study and hopes to publish his conclusions in a much more fully substantiated form shortly.

[170] The trade of the United Kingdom, the United States, and Canada with the Sterling Area alone amounted in 1947 to roughly 8.5 per cent of world imports and 7.0 per cent of world exports. Estimates of the value of world trade are taken from W. S. and E. S. Woytinsky, *World Commerce and Governments* (New York, 1955), p. 39. There are two good accounts of the pattern of Sterling Area trade and settlements, P. W. Bell, *The Sterling Area in the Post-war World* (Oxford, 1956) and United States Economic Co-operation Administration, *The Sterling Area. An American Analysis* (London, 1951).

goods were carried out through bulk purchasing agreements over several years and Britain thus offered what underdeveloped primary exporters most required, guaranteed longer-term markets. By contrast private trade in the United States offered no such guarantees.[171] From the standpoint of the United States, however, the Sterling Area was the biggest obstacle in the way of an intra-European payments agreement. It encouraged the flow of trade of Europe's largest international trader away from the Continent itself and was, furthermore, associated with the structure of British imperial preferences, which were seen both as a fundamental barrier to American trade and, by 1947, as a fundamental barrier to European economic integration also.

In London the Sterling Area was seen as an indispensable foundation-stone of Britain's post-war edifice. It would have been strange had it been otherwise, for, as the world shortage of dollars squeezed ever tighter on expanding international trade, the idea was inescapable that Britain was at least part of a large multilateral trading area facilitating access to a variety of foodstuff and raw-material imports which did not need to be purchased in dollars. The economic interest of the Labour government in the Empire and Commonwealth was fired by the possibility which it seemed to offer of economic independence from the United States. In the post-war world its possible advantages seemed even greater than in the thirties because of the disappearance of the food surpluses of some European national economies and because of the structural alterations in the pattern of world trade.

Before 1939 there were substantial European food surpluses which were traded almost entirely within Europe. Foodstuffs and fodder had in fact accounted for a quarter of intra-European trade, and of this much the largest proportion was made up of the exports of underdeveloped Eastern and South-Eastern Europe. The greater difficulty which underdeveloped countries had in recovering from the damage done to their agriculture in wartime meant that these European food surpluses were simply not available in the same quantity immediately after the war. The arrival in power there of governments whose development plans were focused exclusively on policies of extremely rapid industrialization probably meant, however, that these surpluses would never again appear in the same quantity. The political division of Europe between the two power blocs in 1947 exaggerated this. Western Europe became dependent for food and fodder imports almost entirely on extra-European sources. Since the agriculture of the even poorer underdeveloped economies outside Europe was still slower to recover from the war, that meant dependence at first on

---

[171] These guarantees were the better inasmuch as primary exporters probably had more confidence in the British government's expressed intention to maintain full employment than in that of the US government. The American downturn in 1949 saw both a steep increase in unemployment and a sharp reduction in primary imports.

the Dollar Area for most of the food and fodder imports. This was a major component in forcing Western-European countries to accept dollar aid whatever their views. The Sterling Area offered Britain some relief from this situation.

Before the war the pattern of intra-European trade had also depended on the trade surpluses which most European countries had with the United Kingdom. Basically it was the sterling earnings in Britain of European exporters which had enabled them to run trade deficits with Germany, as most of them did. In this sense a high level of intra-European trade had depended on a high level of exports from Continental Europe to Britain, which, in turn, was also dependent on a high level of British exports outside Europe. Because most European countries concentrated their efforts after the war on the speediest possible reconstruction of their industrial sectors, this led at once to a high import demand for capital goods and semi-manufactures as well as the retention of a high proportion of domestic output. Given the shortage of dollars such policies attracted exports in particular from those countries which could replace the former main supplier of such goods in European trade, Germany, and which had been able to recover earlier than others, namely Belgium and Britain. One consequence was that the long-standing position of the two greatest European traders in intra-European trade was reversed; Britain now had trade surpluses with Continental Europe, and Germany had deficits. In fact the increase in British exports to Continental Europe was roughly the equivalent of the fall in German exports to the same destinations. Such a reversal of the usual pattern of settlements would be but a temporary one if 'West Germany' were permitted the same level of recovery as other European countries. But should this occur, the capacity of Western Continental Europe to settle its trade deficits with North America would again be dependent to some extent on its capacity to do so by means of exports to Britain and the Sterling Area. Intra-European trade could in fact only increase in volume within a pattern of extra European settlements, and there was little or nothing in a purely intra-European payments agreement to facilitate this.

At the same time, the British and Belgian export surpluses to other European countries made any pattern of multilateral settlements in Europe harder to construct. This was especially the case with Belgium, which settled its large import surplus from the United States through an export surplus to every other European country. Within intra-European trade a Belgian franc was almost as valuable as a dollar, and it was hard to conceive any functioning pattern of intra-European payments until Belgian trade within Europe had settled into a different pattern.

In the two years before Germany surrendered the United States had a balance of payments surplus of $16,700 million, the major part of which was attributable to the growth of its exports to Europe. At the same time, with many of its sources of imports endangered the country became increasingly independent of those imports. After the war it was the only adequate source of supply for a wide range both of manufactured goods and of food. Europe, in return, could export little to the United States except luxury products. There was little to spare, and lower levels of productivity, together with currencies whose par rate against the dollar was usually much overvalued, meant that few European goods were competitive on American markets. As a problem it was not new, it was simply transposed in scale. Whereas the United States had an export surplus with Europe in commodity trade of $760 million in 1938, in 1946 it had one of $3,307 million and in the first half of 1947 of $2,444 million.[172] Europe's problem was to acquire the dollars or gold to sustain these enormous trade deficits with America.

Before the war these dollars had been earned in two ways. Firstly they came from European exports to extra-European areas which had earned dollars in the United States by exporting raw materials there, especially the Netherlands, East Indies, and Malaya. Secondly, they came from Europe's invisible earnings from investment, shipping, and insurance. The capacity of Asia to earn dollars was drastically reduced by the destruction of the war, the internal strife after the war, the fall in United States raw-material imports, and the shift during the war of those imports to the Caribbean and Latin America. In 1947 the United States had an export surplus to Asia more than twice as large as the import surplus she had run with the same area in 1938.[173] The extent of the drop in Europe's invisible earnings due to the sale of dollar investments to pay for the war, the destruction of shipping, and the loss of business cannot be accurately estimated. But the United States and Britain were still the only effective carriers of goods on the required scale in 1947, and the total receipts of Western-European countries from invisible earnings even in 1950–1 were only about nine per cent of the value of their 1938 exports, whereas in 1938 they had been about one-third.

The evidence therefore in the first place points strongly to the conclusion that the relative weakness of intra-European trade was due to the major disturbances of the pattern of world trade which had taken place.[174] Some

[172] United Nations, Department of Economic Affairs, *Economic Report 1948* (Geneva, 1948), p. 16.
[173] United Nations, Department of Economic Affairs, *Major Economic Changes in 1948* (Lake Success, 1949), p. 25.
[174] *Intra-European Trade as a Proportion of Europe's Foreign Trade*

	Exports	Imports
1913*	68.7	57.5
1927*	63.2	52.4
1938†	63.0	55.0
1947†	55.0	37.0

*The six major European foreign traders only (Belgium, France, Germany, Italy, Netherlands, United Kingdom). W. S. and E. S. Woytinsky, *World Commerce*, op. cit., pp. 74–5.
†United Nations, Department of Economic Affairs, *A Survey of the Economic Situation and Prospects of Europe* (Geneva, 1948), p. 31.

part of these disturbances might eventually be corrected by the growth of European production, for, although the prices of European goods were uncompetitive, almost all countries might well prefer to buy from Europe for some time rather than spend dollars. Nevertheless, in a situation when over the whole period 1945–9 the United States ran an over-all surplus of $30,000 million, it is clear that even if a more flexible European payments system could have been devised an increase in intra-European trade would have made little difference to the obstacles in the way of the growth of international trade which was essential to Europe's continued recovery. American foreign policy thus not only came into direct conflict with the economic realities of the situation both of Europe and of the world but also, in emphasizing so heavily the need for a 'freer' system of trade in Europe, offered no solution to the central problem of achieving equilibrium in the international economy; indeed, in the eyes of some European countries it threatened to make that equilibrium even more remote. This could not have been more appositely shown than by the history of the brief period of convertibility of sterling which coincided with the earlier weeks of the Paris conference. The new arrangements could not survive the severe deterioration in the British balance of payments in 1947, which was reflected in the concurrent trade and payments crises of the other Western-European countries. Convertibility was suspended on 20 August. Whatever the errors, both of commission and omission, made by the British government in moving towards convertibility[175] which, had they been avoided, might perhaps just have enabled convertibility to survive, the incident could not but be taken as a measure of the disequilibrium in world trade and the dangers attendant on moving towards a more flexible system of payments.

The natural consequence of American pressure was also to open a divide between those European countries, most obviously Belgium, which stood to gain from the immediate easing of the restrictions imposed by bilateral trade, and those which had most to fear, of which Britain was the most obvious example, having access to the more flexible arrangements of the Sterling Area, whose common reserves might well be endangered once more if forced into convertibility with other European currencies. Already the bilateral arrangements in Europe were imposing a curb on the growth of Belgian exports, and one of the points in the common Benelux programme had been to press for a more flexible payments system. Accordingly one of the Belgian delegates to Paris, M. Hubert Ansiaux, proposed to the committee of financial experts a system of transferability between the currencies of the CEEC countries which would eliminate gold and dollars from intra-European trade. Any such system would have depended on the United States providing some kind of dollar backing for

---

[175] They are excellently analysed in R. M. Gardner, *Sterling-Dollar Diplomacy* (Oxford, Clarendon Press, 1956), p. 316 ff.

European currencies transferred in excess of the credits provided for in the existing bilateral agreements, so that these proposals would probably involve a specific allocation of American aid for this purpose. Ansiaux discussed his proposals in London on 23 July and with Dutch and French experts who visited London a few days later. Neither the Bank of England nor the Treasury thought they would work or that they would be acceptable in Washington.[176] Their view, which, it soon appeared, was shared by the Americans, was that the inflationary policies of the French government would in any case make any such scheme out of the question.

Yet few countries depended more on trade expansion than the United Kingdom, and on the long-term objectives both Britain and Belgium were in agreement. Treasury policy was to try to achieve transferability between sterling and other European currencies over a four-year period providing there was a greater harmony of economic and especially monetary policy in Europe. How this was to be achieved was by no means clear. British officials appeared to be thinking very much in terms of bringing pressure to bear on France to end inflation and thus create a moment for convertibility when a convertible franc would be 'stable'.[177] There they were on exceptionally shaky ground. In trying to draw up a compromise on the Belgian proposals the Treasury excused a sentence in the suggested compromise, which began, 'An end shall be put to all inflationary expansion of credit', by indicating that it was aimed at France. Sir Stafford Cripps, the Minister for Economic Affairs, minuted on the memorandum 'No. This is on the slippery slope of servitude' and at its foot that the phrase was *'totally unacceptable to me'*.[178] The British government was no more willing than France to place restrictions on domestic economic policy in the interests of easing intra-European trade, especially, it might be added, to further a plan which would obviously ease Belgium's payments problems first and foremost.

It was agreed that Ansiaux's proposals should go forward to the Executive Committee at the end of July in a substantially different form. The insistence on immediate convertibility should be dropped and the request for specific American funds to back up the scheme not mentioned. The proposals were thus little more than an open invitation to all the countries to discuss alternative schemes. Even so they did not meet with an enthusiastic reception. 'The Norwegians said that the Benelux proposal is all rubbish because it would take many, many years before most European currencies can become convertible.'[179] The outcome of the discussion, none the less, was that CEEC set up a Committee on Payments

---

[176] Congress was not likely, the Bank of England thought, to put up money for 'a second Marshall Plan', PRO T 236/794, Bank of England to Treasury, 22 July 1947.
[177] PRO, FO 371/62565, Treasury Memorandum, 'Monetary Integration', 2 August 1947.
[178] PRO, T 236/794, Memorandum by Sir D. Waley, 29 July 1947.
[179] Ibid., Waley to Playfair, 1 August 1947.

Agreements to take over the work so far done by the Financial Experts Committee and try to produce a workable scheme.

The Norwegian opposition had been much more absolute than the British. As soon as the British government became aware, as it did at more or less the same time, that the French were going to support proposals in CEEC for a customs union,[180] it supported the payments discussions and the establishment of the Committee on the grounds that it was less threatening and closer to Britain's original policy on European reconstruction than the leap in the dark which a customs union represented. The agreement to set up the Committee on Payments Agreements had been virtually taken at the Anglo-Benelux-French discussions in London on 29 July, and the proposal to the Executive Committee was largely a formality.[181]

The Committee on Payments could not be faced with the same deadline as CEEC, and indeed there would have been no point since the assumption now was that dollar aid would not be specifically provided for a payments scheme. This assumption was correct. The American government had decided that aid for such a purpose would constitute an admission to Congress that IMF had failed as an instrument of international reconstruction.[182] There were, no doubt, larger considerations swaying this decision also. What Washington wanted was a dramatic political gesture, if possible a customs union. The British argument was that monetary and economic co-operation in Western Europe leading to currency convertibility as soon as that was 'safe' would do more to increase intra-European trade than the proclamation of a customs union. In Washington it often seemed that progress towards a payments agreement was a method of postponing a customs union indefinitely. The Belgians presented the proposals as a first step towards a customs union, but they were in fact heavily in Belgium's own interests; the United States would have been making dollars available to support exports of expensive Belgian steel to Western Europe in order to fund Belgian imports from the United States.[183]

This was the crux of the discussions in the Payments Committee. Any proposed payments agreement backed by Marshall Aid was likely to favour either debtors or creditors at the expense of the other. The idea of a 'stabilization fund' soon disappointed when it was realized the United States was not going to contribute. What was left was a variety of different Belgian proposals to try to use as far as possible each dollar of Marshall

---

[180] See p. 549.
[181] PRO, T 236/794, Waley to Playfair, 1 August 1947, Notes on discussions.
[182] Truman Library, President's Committee on Foreign Aid, Box 11, 'Second Memorandum Concerning the Financial Program to be Elaborated by the European Economic Cooperation Committee', 26 July 1947.
[183] American steel was cheaper on European markets in 1947 than Belgian steel, but domestic demand for steel was still so high in the United States in 1947 that exports only took place through deliberate diversion by the government.

Aid twice, once to finance intra-European trade deficits and then to finance Europe's over-all trade deficit with the USA.[184] They were trying to reach a solution where, for example, to consider at random any two countries, France would get more dollars than her total trade deficit with Belgium, Belgium less than her total deficit with the USA, and France would make up the difference. There were fundamental objections to any such approach to backing a settlements plan with Marshall Aid. Not the least was that no one in Europe yet knew what form Marshall Aid would take. Nor did any country want to give up a direct dollar in return for an indirect dollar based on a hypothetical foreign-trade calculation at a time of wildly swinging trade balances. This last fact, of course, only served to underline that no one could know under such a scheme how many dollars would be needed. The United Kingdom made an equally unlikely proposal, that existing balances be frozen for four years and the credit margins of all existing agreements extended, a policy in line with the Treasury's objectives but hardly likely to appeal to creditor countries.[185]

The Belgian representatives tried not to lose sight of the wider political objectives of their proposals. They hoped for a pooling of European reserves and even for a European bank to manage these reserves. The bank would have been intended to function as a superior European central bank, more like the Federal Reserve System than merely a clearing bank for international settlements as the Deutsche Verrechnungskasse had been during the war or the Bank for International Settlements was to become.[186] Any idea which involved pooling the Sterling Area reserves and the Sterling Area common dollar-pool with any common European reserve through the mechanism of unconditional sterling convertibility into other Western-European currencies could not have the slightest chance of success, especially in August 1947. The events of that month did not leave their impact only on British attitudes. Ole Colbjørnsen was not speaking merely for the Norwegian delegation when he summed up the situation for the American experts in the Washington conversations which followed CEEC.

Then came the 20th of August with its lesson. The 35 days' period of convertibility from the 15th of July to the 20th August had finished and we saw the whole question more in the light of the realities of the situation. So, if the United Kingdom has certain doubts now with regard to going too far and too quickly, it is the same or corresponding consideration as was already in the minds of several delegations during the Paris conference and in the meetings of financial experts there.[187]

---

[184] The best of the studies on this subject is W. Diebold Jnr., *Trade and Payments in Western Europe*, (New York, Harper and Row, 1952), which also serves as a valuable guide to officially published information.
[185] PRO, T 236/799, Proceedings of the Payments Agreements Committee, n.d.
[186] Ibid.
[187] Truman Library, President's Committee on Foreign Aid, Box 3, Washington Conversations, 22 October 1947.

The Belgian proposals could hardly have been made against a less favourable background. At the same time the exchange crisis had driven home the lesson, although not yet fully in Washington, that European dollar deficits with America were but one aspect of a world-wide international payments difficulty. The most sensitive barometer of that difficulty was the Sterling Area's reserves because they were the reserves, also, of such a large part of non-European trade. Of the other countries only France and Italy were prepared to support the Belgian proposals, but their support was contingent on British agreement, no great commitment on their part.[188]

The report of CEEC was in fact notable for the way it emphasized that problems of intra-European trade and payments could only be solved in a world, rather than a European, context.[189] It made no specific recommendations. The Committee on Payments Agreements could not come to an agreement until 18 November, and the agreement which it did produce, the First Agreement on Multilateral Monetary Compensation, was of little importance.[190] The full agreement covered only France, Italy, and the Benelux.[191] These countries agreed to make settlements between themselves automatically out of surpluses and deficits in each other's currencies for one year, the period of the agreement. Most other CEEC countries agreed to such compensations, but not automatically. An agent was appointed under the scheme to make proposals to these countries for such 'compensations' when the time for settlement came round and they agreed to 'entertain' such suggestions. A curious aspect of the whole affair was that the agent was the Bank for International Settlements in Basle, which had originally been set up to handle the transfers of reparations under the abortive Young Plan and had survived the thirties and the war as a vestigial trace of earlier mistakes. There was no worthwhile procedure for including third currencies in the settlements, so that the agreement was little more than a narrow extension of the bilateral agreements and a vague promise of a multilateral system to come. Since certain countries, such as Belgium, were either creditors or debtors to the group as a whole, the possibilities for settlements without involving third countries ('second category compensations') were absurdly small. In its one year of existence the agreement covered no more than about $1.7 million out of debts totalling $762.1 million.[192] It is sometimes argued that the agreement was the first

---

[188] PRO, T 236/798, Waley to Hall-Patch, 27 September 1947.
[189] Committee of European Economic Cooperation, *General Report,* vol. i (Paris, 1949). 'But the action which the participating countries can take is limited. The power to correct the maladjustment is not theirs alone. . . . The solution of the world problem is decisive for the participating countries' future,' p. 57.
[190] The text is published in Bank for International Settlements, *18th Annual Report* (Basle, 1948).
[191] The Bizone joined when the agreement was close to expiry.
[192] R. W. Bean, 'European Multilateral Clearing' in *Journal of Political Economy,* vol. 56, 1948, pp. 403–15.

step towards the European Payments Union, which all the countries would eventually form. The distance between the two agreements in form and circumstance was extremely wide, and such an interpretation is surely to read far too much into the chronological succession of historical events.

(D) LABOUR AND THE MANPOWER CONFERENCE

It was understandable that discussions in the committee on manpower should have been dominated by Italian policy initiatives. The mere compilation of a statistical report on labour was insufficient to meet the Italian government's wishes, and Italy pressed hard and ultimately successfully for an international conference on European manpower. The abandonment of many of the interventionist policies of the Fascist government in industry and agriculture brought the problem of how Italy's long-lasting problem of massive regional underemployment might be solved in a more liberal framework. It was made worse by the generalized unemployment which the stern financial policies pursued by Einaudi from September 1947 onwards produced. Except in Germany and Italy, over the whole of Western Europe conditions of high demand and full employment were still to some extent regulated by domestic and foreign controls, while governments determinedly pursued policies of economic expansion. Germany, of course, did not have the freedom to make this choice. Italy did, but chose deflation and decontrol instead.[193] This brought its rewards eventually in terms of trade surpluses with the other European countries whose expansionist policies attracted imports in spite of the battery of trade controls. But its corollary was the mounting level of unemployment and the abandonment of any real attempt to solve the problem of regional underemployment and underdevelopment inside Italy. The solution was sought, as it had been before 1921, outside Italy. Since, however, there was no longer the freedom of international labour migration which had characterized the years before 1914, this solution meant formal European or international agreements permitting and controlling Italian emigration. This was a major interest of the Italian government in European economic co-operation.

Italian pressure produced disagreements in the manpower committee which are clear from its contribution to the CEEC report.[194] It recommended policies of full employment and at the same time that immigration agreements should be signed with countries with labour surpluses. This could hardly have meant Germany; the political difficulties would have been too great on both sides. In reality the only such agreement that did exist was one between France and Italy. In France the Monnet Plan was

[193] M. de Cecco, 'Economic Policy in the Reconstruction Period, 1945–1951' in S. J. Woolf (ed.), *The Rebirth of Italy 1943–50* (London, 1972).
[194] Committee of European Economic Cooperation, *Technical Reports*, vol. ii, (Paris, 1947), p. 437 ff.

predicated on a high level of labour imports into French industry, and it was at first supposed that this could only be achieved by massive immigration.[195] Two agreements were signed with Italy, in March and November 1946, of which the second foresaw the immigration of 200,000 Italians into France in 1947. In fact only about 50,000 arrived, but this did not slow down the achievement of the plan's targets. Already it was becoming evident that the need to import labour was smaller than had been thought. About 479,000 foreign workers, other than seasonal agricultural workers, migrated into France over the years 1946–9, over half of them Algerian.[196] Algerian immigration was not subject to the same rigorous official controls as that from Italy and Algerian workers received lower wages. France in fact had already come to appreciate by the time of the CEEC conference that she had little to gain from the free movement of labour between herself and Italy. There were, it seems, also strong reservations in the French government about the political persuasions of the Italian workers selected for France. As Tarchiani, the Italian Ambassador in Washington, 'laughingly' told the State Department, 'It might be good for his country if it could ship its Communists to France.'[197]

The Italian representatives could get no further on the labour committee of CEEC than an agreed statement of general health and social-security provisions to be applied to the recruitment of foreign workers. As compensation it was agreed by CEEC that the countries should attend a special international conference to be called by the Italian government in Rome in January 1948, where the issues would be reconsidered. This conference was intended to give special consideration to the transfer of miners and agricultural workers. Here was another pointer to the failure of co-operation in this direction. Italy wished to export unskilled labour, but the demand in Europe was largely and increasingly for skilled labour.

When the Manpower Conference met in Rome the tide had set even more strongly against Italy's hopes. CEEC had estimated that the immediate labour need in Western-Europe (omitting Germany) was about 700,000 workers. The estimates presented at Rome in January were for only 380,000.[198] There was free movement of labour between most European colonies and the mother territories, as also between Ireland and the United Kingdom, and this, together with the already rapidly developing attraction of labour from the agricultural sector in all European economies, had led to a very active period of labour movement which had made little impression on Italy's labour surplus. The Italian government estimated

---

[195] The plans and figures are discussed in G. Tapinos, *L'Immigration étrangère en France,* Institut national d'études démographiques, Travaux et Documents, Cahier No. 71 (Paris, PUF, 1975), pp. 1–46.
[196] Ibid., p. 29.
[197] Truman Library, Clayton Office Files, Memorandum of Conversations, Visit of Tarchiani to Matthews, 1 July 1947.
[198] NA, SD, 840.50, Box 5648, Manpower Conference, Provisional General Report.

that it had 1.7 million workers 'available' for emigration.[199] The British delegates had insisted in the Manpower Committee that all manpower questions should be handled only within CEEC and that no new organization be formed. They were horrified that it might control Irish emigration to Britain. Their attitude to the Italian proposals for a large international organization to deal with European labour transfers was frankly hostile and that of the other countries scarcely more welcoming.[200] The Rome Conference rejected the Italian proposals and, had it not been for a late concession by France, the conference would have been a complete failure. The French delegates proposed that a special committee be formed solely for the purpose of day-to-day administration of Italian migration to France. This solution included an agreement that the French government might consider in future allowing the committee to administer Belgian and Portuguese migration to France. As the United States observer commented to his government, the conference *had* to produce something and that was probably why Britain agreed to this feeble change on condition that the committee remained part of CEEC and had no independent life.[201] In return Britain won the establishment of a parallel committee to deal with displaced persons, the great majority by now Poles in camps in the Bizone and Britain. Even this innocuous agreement, an utter failure from the Italian point of view, was accepted with more reluctance by Sweden and Switzerland than by the United Kingdom.[202]

The experience of the Manpower Committee was only distinguished from that of the other technical committees by the fact that it gave rise to an international conference, however abortive. As soon as any issue arose involving co-operation at a level of significant importance where government might be involved, the issue was quickly avoided. The technical committees of CEEC were the precursors of the subsequent fact-gathering and analysing activities of OEEC. They were a useful innovation in the European economy but they could not function on any higher level. Their task was to prepare the basic information for the chapters in the report to be submitted to Congress, no more, and only the Manpower Committee very briefly and ineffectively broke those bounds.

---

[199] Until the currency reform in June 1948 unemployment was a relatively meaningless concept in West Germany. Once the reform had introduced money wages as the norm, numbers in registered employment fell steeply, so that at the end of June 1949 there were 1,237,712 officially unemployed in the Bizone. (OMGUS records, Institut für Zeitgeschichte, Dk. 113.001, 'Unemployment and Underemployment in the Bizonal Area of Germany'.) There were about 300,000 displaced persons still in camps in Europe at the time of the Manpower Conference. Such figures put Italy's problems in perspective, as well as the extent of European co-operation on economic policy in these years.
[200] NA, SD, 840.50, Box 5650, Confidential Report on International Manpower Conference, n.d.
[201] Ibid., the observer was Val Lorwin, the distinguished labour historian.
[202] Ibid.

(E) THE DECISIONS OF CEEC IN SEPTEMBER

As the detailed information came in, the Balance of Payments Committee and the Executive Committee of CEEC began in mid-August to compile the required report. By then the Americans had let it be known that they were envisaging aid over a period of four to five years, and that the aid would be roughly the sum necessary for Western Europe to achieve a trade and payments equilibrium with North America by the end of that time. Compiling the total requests produced a sum of $29,200 million over a four-year period. That was more than two and a half times the total that had been made available in both grants and loans by all United States sources, including UNRRA relief funds and 'relief' disbursements by the occupation forces, between the end of the war and Marshall's speech. It was much more than Washington had been envisaging. Furthermore, the method of compilation was exactly what Washington had least wanted. The draft report was unable to demonstrate any real steps towards a rationalized integration of the separate economies, and it was considered in the State Department, and would certainly be considered in Congress, that that was one reason why the bill was too high. The costs of capital-equipment imports for reconstruction in each country had, for example, been accepted without any investigation into how far the imports were competitive or complementary. There was no specific provision anywhere in the draft report for any form of common allocation of resources or common recovery planning. Each country's recovery plans over the four-year period, and the role of dollar imports in those plans, had been considered as sacrosanct.

Worst of all from the American viewpoint, the draft report apparently contained no provision whatsoever for a continuing 'European organization' after the conference had ended. The Scandinavian countries, although accepting under protest that the aid requests should be drawn up in Paris and not by the ECE, were opposed to creating any permanent rival to the United Nations body. More important, the conclusions reached by the tripartite talks on Germany were so far from definitive that the French were as yet uncommitted to a continuing European organization, no doubt in the hope that a more favourable agreement might still be reached on the terms on which Germany would be included.

On 22 August the Committee which had been formed in the State Department to supervise progress on the Marshall Plan recommended that the CEEC report should be jointly screened by all the participating countries to reduce the sum of aid requested. This meant that the deadline for the publication of the report, 1 September, which had been set by the agreement between Marshall and Royall over the publication of the revised Level of Industry Plan, would not be met.[203] Two days later Under-

---

[203] *FRUS, 1947/III*, p. 369, 'Minutes of Meeting on Marshall "Plan" ', 22 August 1947.

Secretary Lovett told Marshall that: 'Progress so far is disappointing in that all that has come out so far is sixteen shopping lists which may be dressed up by some large-scale but very long-term projects such as Alpine power, etc.'[204]

The official phrase for the American attitude towards the conference's proceedings had been 'friendly aid'. The reality behind this phrase now appeared. From Lovett's rejection of the draft report to the final disorderly break-up of the conference, direct American pressure on the European countries became intense. Two State Department officials, Charles Bonesteel and George Kennan, were sent to Paris to reinforce the efforts of the ambassadors in Paris and London, and Clayton came from Geneva to reinforce the offensive. The complaints which this group formulated were fairly specific. Firstly, the sum requested in aid was too large, because there had been no rational co-operative exercise which might reduce it. Secondly, even this sum would not produce equilibrium between Western Europe and North America at the end of four years, again because no proper co-operative effort had been made to do so. This was not a point made merely to enforce the political pressures for integration. The persistent harping on the idea of a planned use of dollar aid to make Western Europe independent of dollar payments showed how strong the current of isolationist thought in American policy still was in the autumn of 1947, and how that policy was partly based on a dangerous international economic misconception. Trade and payments equilibrium between Western Europe and North America would enable Congress to consider the European Recovery Program as a programme with a firm end in sight and not far away. But such an equilibrium could not have been combined with the level of recovery the United States wished to promote in Western Europe, and if achieved it would have harmed the economic interests of both areas in the rest of the world, because one area's imbalances with the other had always been a motor of the growth of international trade, particularly in periods when that trade had expanded most rapidly. When the international payments system worked most efficiently it had depended on the ability of North America and Western Europe to settle their balances through their economic links with the rest of the world. Thirdly, some of the commodity estimates were considered to be based on excessively optimistic assumptions. There would not, for example, it was argued, be any possibility of Europe finding in the prevailing world shortage the quantities of steel scrap and even finished steel which were claimed as

---

[204] *FRUS, 1947/III*, p. 372, Lovett to Marshall, 24 August 1947. Robert A. Lovett, decorated as a pilot after the First World War. Educated at Yale, Harvard, and the merchant bankers Brown Bros., Harriman. Became special assistant to Henry J. Stimson in 1940. Assistant Secretary of War for Air, 1941–5. Appointed Under-Secretary in the State Department, July 1947. Secretary for Defence, 1951–3. It would be impossible to have a better claim to represent the American establishment.

essential imports in the draft report. This point was already being particularly emphasized by the so-called Harriman Committee which had been set up to consider the impact of a European aid programme on the American economy, and it has to be remembered that there were still controls on steel allocation within the United States in 1947. Fourthly, there had been no proper consideration of the role of each country's longer-term national capital investment programmes as a part of European recovery as a whole. Some of them, it was thought, did not belong. Fifthly, there was nothing in the report about measures to promote internal financial stability in the European economies. It was clear to all that inflation added to imports, but of course some countries, France in particular, had deliberately chosen such a path to recovery. To demand that all countries pursue roughly similar monetary policies in order to reduce the estimated total of dollar aid to support imports, and no doubt to make integration easier, was to tread very dangerous political ground and showed how far-reaching American aims were. Sixthly, there was no specific provision in the draft report for any multilateral trade and payments system between the European economies. Lastly, the report remained silent on the institution of a continuing European organization to oversee the recovery programme.[205]

These points when formulated were put directly to the Executive Committee, which met with the five Americans. There was one point on which it hardly seemed possible for any concessions to be made to the Americans, no matter how strong the pressure. The British and French members of the Executive Committee, Franks and Alphand, both explained that it was impossible and pointless for the report to produce a figure for aid which would represent equilibrium between Western Europe and North America in 1952.[206] On the other issues there was no alternative but to make concessions and hope that the price of aid might not be more than the conference could bear. The Executive Committee agreed to reconsider the report and to prolong the conference past the deadline of 1 September. But on one issue the Norwegian delegate, Ole Colbjørnsen, dissented from the Americans and his colleagues.[207] The other members of the

---

[205] *FRUS, 1947/III*, p. 391, Caffery to Washington, 31 August 1947.

[206] Sir Oliver Franks, later Lord Franks. A professor of philosophy in Glasgow University who had had a meteoric rise within the Civil Service during the war. Permanent Secretary in the Ministry of Supply, 1945–6, Ambassador to the United States, 1948–52. Later a bank director and Provost of Worcester College, Oxford. He was well liked in the State Department.

Hervé Alphand. Son of an ambassador. In charge of negotiating French commercial agreements in the Ministry of Finance from 1937. In charge of economic affairs in the 'Liberation Committee' in 1941, and appointed head of the Economic Section of the Foreign Ministry in 1944. Almost a friend of General de Gaulle. Like Franks he became Ambassador in Washington (1956–65). Served as Secretary-General in the Foreign Ministry until 1972. He was heartily disliked in the State Department.

[207] Ole Colbjørnsen. Became leader of the Norwegian delegation only in August, when it became clear in Oslo that the issues involved would not be confined to the purely technical. Before the war a

Executive Committee gave their purely personal opinion that it would be necessary to provide for 'a continuing organization', but Colbjørnsen on behalf of his own country and Sweden expressed 'full reservations'.[208]

Through the first week in September each country separately deleted certain requests for aid which had been intended to cover capital-goods imports, but this process was no nearer an approach to international co-operation than the one which had included them in the first place. In any case, even when it was complete the draft report still contained a larger sum for capital-goods imports than the Americans thought appropriate. At the same time a fixed percentage cut was made on the total of each country's aid requests, a process which deliberately avoided what the Americans had wanted, the mutual screening of each country's requests by all the others. The American contingent in Paris gave stern advice to Washington that the State Department should prevent the submission of the report in the form in which it was likely to emerge and should require the national governments to give fresh instructions to their Paris delegations.[209] Lovett accepted this drastic policy and recommended 'that the work to date not be considered as constituting a programme'.[210] A mighty and urgent effort was now made to bring pressure to bear on all the European capitals. The public stance that the Europeans were to be left free to formulate their own aid requests was exchanged for the reality of strong political pressure. The CEEC report to Congress would have to be shaped by the Americans as much as, or more than, by the European countries. In the context of these events of the end of August and early September the claim, still often made, that the Soviet Union could also have participated in Marshall Aid can be seen as the nonsense that it is. The same events revealed how determinedly America was prepared to try to wield her economic power to restrict the individual freedom of action of the European countries. How far she could succeed in doing so, however, was another question which remained to be answered.

It is impossible to read through the State Department committee papers without being impressed by the immensity of the effort of public persuasion which the Administration felt it had to undertake to ensure that the European Recovery Programme would pass Congress. After the long eclipse of the State Department's influence under Roosevelt its resurgence was inseparably linked to the new European policy. This was doubtless a good incentive to tackle seriously the business of making sure that things

---

journalist specializing on economic affairs for *Arbeiderbladet*. Counsellor in the Washington Embassy, 1940–6. From 1949 to 1967 in charge of the economic aspects of defence policy. Author of brochures on planning and Socialism. Better known for his endless initiatives and enterprises than for the fruition to which they came.

[208] *FRUS, 1947/III*, p. 391, op. cit.
[209] *FRUS, 1947/III*, p. 405, Caffery to Washington, 5 September 1947.
[210] NA, SD, RG 353, Box 27, 'Remarks by Lovett to Interdepartmental Committee on the Marshall Plan', 9 September 1947.

did not go wrong once the legislation reached Congress, and that in itself was a powerful motive for forcing a report which would do more to persuade Congress of the definitive nature of the European Recovery Programme. In so far as the gap between Congress's expectations of European integration and the more realistic ones of the State Department was a wide one, and in so far as the State Department's own expectations were not noticeably realistic in the first place, the outcome of pressure on the European countries was always likely to be that the Europeans would subscribe to forms of words which, not being followed by the action they seemed to promise, would only lead to greater disillusionment in both Congress and State Department afterwards. The one commitment now asked for which could not be covered by words without ensuing action was the undertaking to form a 'continuing organization', and insistence on this by the United States, an insistence which was not in the circumstances avoidable, made a collision certain.

The United Kingdom was still supporting a position where the technical committees of CEEC would be discontinued and their work transferred to the Economic Commission for Europe.[211] Such a decision would leave the possibility that the other committees could be recalled or revived if the other governments eventually decided this to be practical.[212] Norway supported this position. France and Italy were in favour of agreeing to reconvene CEEC once Congress had passed the aid bill. That would give time for the promised talks on the Ruhr and Rhineland to be held, and would permit France to keep the German settlement as the precondition of European integration. Benelux was more cautious but eventually supported the Franco-Italian position.[213] The Americans had suggested that a delegation from CEEC should visit Washington to help present the report to Congress, an idea which Colbjørnsen described as 'dangerous and unnecessary'.[214]

All delegations were agreed that CEEC could not continue to meet for a much longer time and draw up a new report. The divisions of opinion had therefore to be patched over in one way or other in a very short time and

---

[211] PRO, FO 371/62580, UK Delegation to London, 5 September 1947. CEEC had collated information which the United Nations had not had access to. But the Commission's first comprehensive surveys of the European economy, *A Survey of the Economic Situation and Prospects of Europe* (Geneva, 1948) and *Economic Survey of Europe in 1948* (Geneva, 1949), supervised by Gunnar Myrdal, were far more professional and dispassionate than the report of CEEC. Their appearance created a minor alarm in Washington because they constituted a trenchant and scholarly critique of American economic policy. The State Department in turn commissioned a critique of these reports from the International Bank for Reconstruction and Development: K. Varvaressos and R. Zafiriou, *The Report of the Economic Commission for Europe 'Economic Survey for 1948', A Summary and Comments* (May, 1949) which was not officially published, wisely, for it is neither a very strong nor a convincing refutation.
[212] PRO, FO 371/62565, Minute by UK Delegation, 31 August 1947.
[213] PRO, FO 371/62580, UK Delegation to London, 6 September 1947.
[214] Ibid.

under constant American pressure, which went as far as requesting the British government to join with Washington in a joint statement condemning the report.[215] The 'London Committee', now in a weak position, instructed the British delegation to concede that both the plenary conference (CEEC) and the Executive Committee be 'temporarily' maintained in an inactive state until Congress had concluded its debates on Marshall Aid.[216] On 7 September the Norwegian delegation heard that the British had changed their mind.[217] It was now useless to cling to the idea that a recovery programme would be operated through the United Nations. Norway had to make a crucial choice. The nature of that choice has given rise to a debate in Norway as to whether it was made on political or economic grounds. The harsh truth was beginning to be realized that the foreign-exchange reserves were no longer sufficient, after the exchange crisis of August, to enable Norway to continue with her reconstruction programme without dollar aid.[218] To plan that almost one half of net capital formation in 1947 would come from the balance of payments deficit, as the National Budget for that year had done, had been to give hostages to fortune in a year of such severe international disequilibrium. The moment of decision came when Britain finally accepted a purely Western-European organization instead of the United Nations organization which she had originally supported, and in that sense it is true that the decision was a political one. It is not necessarily true, however, that had it not been for Britain's change of position Norwegian domestic economic policy would have enabled Norway to remain independent of dollar aid; indeed the evidence is more to the contrary.[219]

Clayton and Douglas attended the meeting of the Executive Committee on 10 September, where Clayton insisted that CEEC meet for a further month and produce another report. The Executive Committee unanimously refused. The discussion was 'extremely confused' and its only result was that Clayton suddenly jumped to his feet and stormed out of the meeting. 'It was really a very strange performance', as Hirschfeld reported.[220] Bidault's reaction was that it was 'quite intolerable' and that 'he would not yield to pressure of this nature'.[221] Alphand told the chief Swedish delegate to CEEC, Hammarskjöld, that it was impossible for the French government to accept all the American demands because of the

---

[215] Ibid., FO to UK Delegation, 8 September 1947.
[216] Ibid., London Committee to UK Delegation, 8 September 1947.
[217] UD, 44.2/26, Bind V, Colbjørnsen to Sunnanå, 7 September 1947.
[218] Pharo, 'Bridgebuilding', op. cit., p. 140 suggests that on 7 September the Norwegian delegation received an estimate revising Norway's estimated future foreign-exchange reserves upward by about 70 per cent.
[219] E. Brofoss, in 'The Marshall Plan and Norway's Hesitation' in *Scandinavian Journal of History*, vol. 2, no. 3, 1947, argues otherwise. He was Minister of Commerce at the time.
[220] MBZ, 610.302, 'Laatste ontwikkeling van de conferentie te Parijs', 12 September 1947.
[221] PRO, FO 371/62582, UK Delegation to FO, 11 September 1947.

internal political situation in France.²²² The Norwegian delegation reported to Oslo that 'The American demand means we should write a new report at American dictation.'²³³

In spite of the evident need for dollar aid in most countries, American demands had brought the conference to deadlock. In retrospect it can be seen that the American position, although very strong, was not so strong as the more determined integrationists in Washington had assumed. Mainly this was because of the urgency of different problems to which Marshall Aid was now seen as the answer. The spiteful Soviet reaction to the CEEC conference, the attempt to mobilize trade-union opposition to Marshall Aid in France and Italy, and its implications, had greatly increased American nervousness about 'red' governments in Paris and Rome. After the first flush of enthusiasm over Marshall's speech and the calling of the Paris conference, the size and complexity of the issues at stake in the new policy soon became alarmingly apparent. On the most optimistic calculations Marshall Aid was not now likely to flow to Europe until the early summer of 1948, partly because of the unsettled problems in Germany, partly because the varying interests of the European countries had emerged so starkly at Paris, and partly because Congress itself would need to see some of these issues resolved before it would vote such large sums and sanction the new direction of foreign policy. Meanwhile UNRRA aid would be virtually coming to an end at the close of 1947. Once the decision had been made to launch the American diplomatic offensive against the recalcitrant CEEC, the assumption had been that CEEC would now not produce its report for another month, and on that basis the State Department's original timetable was in tatters. On 6 September the Department therefore recommended to Truman that urgent aid should be given to some European countries before the details of 'the long-term programme' had been worked out; this statement was released four days later to the press, two days before the breakdown of the Paris conference.²²⁴ The countries chosen for 'Interim Aid' were France, Italy, and Austria, and the aid was intended to bridge the gap before Congress sanctioned the European Recovery Programme. Interim Aid was free of all the conditions and negotiations on which Marshall Aid was dependent, and the task of convincing Congress was undertaken by Truman himself on 17 November. Interim Aid was presented by Marshall to the joint session of the Senate Foreign Relations Committee and the House Committee on Foreign Affairs as an aspect of 'the long-range programme', but even so 'essentially a

---

[222] UD, 44.2/26, Henvendelsen fra amerikanerne, 12 September 1947. Dag Hammarskjöld served in the Riksbank 1936–45 and after 1940 was Director of the Foreign Exchange Office. Became the second Secretary-General of the United Nations in 1953 until his death in a plane crash in Africa in 1961.
[223] UD, 44.2/26, Norwegian delegation to Oslo, 12 September 1947.
[224] *FRUS, 1947/III*, p. 410, Lovett to Truman, 6 September 1947.

relief programme' and not a little Marshall Plan.[225] None the less, the need for Interim Aid to support what Washington considered the three governments most threatened by Soviet tactics showed quite clearly that the Western-European countries still had some bargaining power.

The two days after Clayton departed so brusquely from the discussions with the Executive Committee were filled with a flurry of telegrams and confused private meetings whose main purpose was to persuade both Clayton and Bidault to take less extreme positions.[226] Monnet apparently persuaded Bidault, and Douglas Clayton.[227] Eventually the Americans enumerated six points which, while still leaving a report which 'fell far short' of being acceptable to 'the American people', would, if the Europeans agreed to them, allow matters to proceed without the CEEC meeting for a further month and writing a new report.[228] The six points were much less of a commitment to integration than the earlier American demands. The countries were to obligate themselves to the group as a whole to attain the production targets for certain commodities covered in the report. The financial section of the report was to be rewritten to avoid all suggestion that financial 'stabilization' might be postponed until aid had been received and output increased. The report was to lay greater emphasis on the elimination of barriers to intra-European trade. The requests for items of capital equipment were to be carefully separated from other forms of requests for aid. The conference was not to be 'adjourned', but only 'recessed'. Once the Marshall Aid bill passed Congress the European countries were to accept a firm undertaking to form a permanent European organization.[229]

When these six points were presented to the Executive Committee it agreed that CEEC should meet for one more week, at the end of which the report would be published as a 'first' report, but not, as the Americans tried to insist, as a 'temporary' report.[230] Most of the points were met by blurring the issues in the text of the report. The second point was directed chiefly at France, but, although the fourth chapter of the report stated that no country could expect aid without 'stabilizing' the economy, French

---

[225] USA, Senate Papers, 80th Congress, 1st session, Report No. 771, Calendar No. 825, *European Interim Aid Act of 1947*, 21 November 1947, p. 9.

[226] These events are glossed over by van der Beugel, op. cit., p. 81, in a half-page of hurried, misleading discretion. They conflict with his general theme that European integration arose from American–European harmony, an idea quaintly sanctioned by Henry Kissinger in the introduction.

[227] PRO, FO 371/62582, UK Delegation to London, 11 September 1947. On the American side the negotiations are covered in *FRUS, 1947/III*, pp. 391–446.

[228] *FRUS, 1947/III*, Caffery to Washington, 12 September 1947.

[229] Ibid.

[230] The Foreign Office however objected to the use of 'first', and the report was eventually published in each country as Committee of European Economic Cooperation, vol. i, *General Report*, vol. ii, *Technical Reports*. As soon as it was published it was bathed in positive propaganda from Washington, but it is an unimpressive document from the economist's point of view, and the uneasy political compromises it represented cry aloud from every section. It was easy to criticise in Congress.

internal domestic policy showed little change in 1948. This sort of cosmetic operation could not cover properly the last two points, which required a specific commitment. Both Britain and Norway had, however, already decided that they must abandon their opposition to a continuing organization, and only the neutral countries were now prepared to resist. On 17 September the Swedish delegation returned from Stockholm prepared to accept a weakened version of the sixth point, which was accepted by the Americans.[231] The report was publicly accepted in a brief ceremony on 22 September by the ministers who had formally opened the conference. Norway stipulated that the report be submitted to the Storting before her acceptance became official.

Although circulated with fanfares of publicity as a great step forward in European co-operation, the report was a long way from what the Americans had desired. The commitment of the European countries, furthermore, was obviously less than the wording of the report vaguely implied it to be. The report dwelt on examples of intra-European co-operation such as the Scandinavian customs-union discussions, which were certain to be amongst the most fruitless of all possible diplomatic negotiations, the Franco-Italian customs-union discussions which, as will be seen, were in fact directed towards a quite different kind of European integration from that desired in Washington, and on a variety of trivial schemes for industrial and transport co-ordination. It did incorporate the revised level of industry figures for the Bizone in the general commodity analyses. On the over-all problem of Germany, however, it offered only a two-and-a-half page Appendix, accurately pointing out that

> The incorporation of the Western Zones of Germany into the plans elaborated by the Conference, while essential for practical economic reasons, inevitably created considerable difficulty, because a number of fundamental policy decisions with regard to the German economy, which lie beyond the scope and competence of this Conference, have not yet been taken.[232]

Otherwise the Appendix was a splendid compilation of all possible conflicting views, sometimes represented in the same sentences. The output of the Ruhr coalfield was to be used to contribute both to European and to German recovery, but 'the German economy must not be allowed to develop to the detriment of other European countries as it has in the past'.[233] Any arrangements affecting Germany's international trade were to be incorporated into the European Recovery Programme, and the German tariff was to be liberalized to conform to the principles of the proposed International Trade Organization.

Throughout the disputes over the report the Americans had not

---

[231] *FRUS, 1947/III*, pp. 435–6.
[232] Committee of European Economic Cooperation, vol. i, *General Report* (Paris, 1947), p. 69.
[233] Ibid.

abandoned the idea that CEEC delegates should come to Washington to help in the presentation of the report to Congress as a visible sign of intra-European and of American–European co-operation. This was settled by the United States agreeing to accept some of the 'technical' experts as participants in the Washington discussions. The CEEC representatives who took part in the 'Washington conversations' which began on 9 October did not know what to expect in advance. They need not have been too apprehensive. Most of the meetings were specialized discussions on such issues as productivity, capital-investment projects, balance-of-payments problems, and so on, and all were carefully structured beforehand to prevent any issues arising on which such relatively low-level delegates would have not been empowered to speak.[234] At the outset the delegates were addressed in a somewhat lordly way by Lovett, who made clear how much was still undecided in planning the European Recovery Programme. As a public-relations exercise the discussions probably did very little to convince Congress and their main use was probably in bringing home to the members of the Interdepartmental Committee on the Marshall Plan certain economic weaknesses in the State Department's ideas. On the issue of European integration virtually nothing was said. Once more the main plot focused on the forthcoming conference on the Ruhr which the French had been promised.

To regard the CEEC as the starting-point of post-war European economic integration is to take a prejudiced view of recent history. What the Paris conference did was to force each West-European country to take a stance on the question, something which they had so far been able to avoid. The formal conference itself, it is clear, was much less of a success for European or for European–American co-operation than it has normally been depicted to be. Indeed, it aggravated the opposition in Western Europe to integration under American pressure and in the ways pursued by the American government. But that is simply to consider what happened in the specific framework of CEEC itself. One consequence of American pressure was that the European governments tried to negotiate their position on European integration away from American pressures and influence, which meant away from CEEC in Paris. A powerful motive for depoliticizing the new European organization was precisely that it was so subject to American economic and political pressures. Away from Paris, however, and away from the Paris conference a separate set of purely European negotiations began. These concerned the formation of separate West-European customs unions and also the formation of a general West-European customs union. This was of course a major political objective in Washington; but, as will be seen, the Europeans by no means

---

[234] There are complete records in PRO, FO 371/62671–5 and in Truman Library, Papers of the President's Committee on Foreign Aid.

meant the same thing by 'customs union' as Washington did. One motive for pursuing the idea of a European customs union away from Paris and CEEC was that it did seem to offer a possible defence against American pressures and, politically at least, it contained the germ of a purely European solution to the Franco-German problem, which was still unsolved at the 'recession' of the CEEC.

(F) THE ADVENT OF THE CUSTOMS UNION

The history of the European Customs-Union Study-Group has been so far entirely unwritten. The Group originated in a French proposal submitted to CEEC that the conference should consider the possibility of a Western-European customs union. Diebold, the only historian to pay the Group even the slightest attention, concludes after a brief discussion that it 'has been pretty much a backwater of European economic cooperation. How seriously its founders took it is hard to say. Once started it went on, as organizations will. Launched separately from the OEEC, it has had few connections with that main centre of Western European economic cooperation.'[235]

On the evidence then available to Diebold, this was not an unfair judgement. The technical discussions of the Group were almost entirely confined to preparing the theoretical ground for a possible common external tariff, a subject which did little in itself to engage the real fears or interests of the governments involved, since no actual tariff bargaining on particular commodities was as yet in sight and the theoretical statements emanating from the Group committed nobody to any particular course of action if such bargaining were to eventuate. All this, however, was but the scenery for intense discussion of the possibilities at a higher level.

It is not simply because the basis of the present European Economic Community is its common external tariff, and because it is in essence a common market, that the existence of discussions to this end in 1947 must have had significance. The European Customs-Union Study-Group had a greater importance than that. It was in the context of the customs-union discussions that the shape and nature of the first European Economic Community emerged. It was in fact a much more significant step on the road to the Treaty of Rome than CEEC, OEEC, or the European payments agreements. It was there that a practical, realistic basis for limited European political and economic integration as a solution to certain specific Western-European problems first emerged. The geographical shape and the economic nature of the future European Community first took shape there, and it was there, and not in Paris, that the outline of the future Treaty of Rome was first delineated.

[235] W. Diebold, *Trade and Payments*, op. cit., p. 317.

The French proposal at CEEC that there should be a Western-European customs union incorporating a smaller group of countries than the sixteen assembled in Paris was the first break in the Anglo-French agreement to control the proceedings there. It sprang from the earlier Italian proposals for a customs union with France. These had not been particularly welcome in Paris except as the germ of an idea which, on a larger scale, might be an alternative solution to France's future relationship with Germany. Accordingly, after warning the British beforehand that he would do so, Alphand proposed at a private luncheon on 2 August to the Benelux delegation that they should consider joining a customs union with France and Italy within the next five to seven years.[236] For the British delegation and government this was a serious blow to the security of their policy in Paris. It opened at once the possibility of a major breach in the Anglo-French alliance as a result of which, firstly, American policy might well gain a hold and which might, secondly, lead to a solution of the German problem through a restructuring of the European alliances and economies to Britain's detriment. In 1947 of course such a threat still seemed remote. Britain still had firm enough control in Germany, and the proposed customs union hardly offered in that year any economic threat to the British economy. None the less, the French proposals brought Franks immediately back to London for urgent consultations.

The exact degree of priority which these proposals had in French foreign policy is not easy to assess. At no stage did the French government seriously contemplate a customs union with Italy alone: the Franco-Italian negotiations were intended to define the principles and mechanisms of a larger common market. The biggest contrast in domestic economic policy between any of the CEEC nations was that between France and Italy. Whereas Italy pursued an increasingly deflationary policy of monetary 'soundness', France pursued a policy of high levels of public expenditure and accepted the associated inflationary tendencies on the assumption that they would eventually be mopped up by a fuller utilization of factors. The consequences of such conflicting monetary policies on the franc–lira exchange rate were by themselves enough to make a genuine Franco-Italian customs union seem most implausible. The nature of the first French recovery plan, and the extensive and complex trade controls which enforced it, made the approach to Benelux an unexpected one. But this was to misjudge the ultimate purposes of the Monnet Plan, the intention of which was to bring the French economy to a level of competitiveness where it could once more pursue what seemed the only feasible long-term policy for sustained growth, conversion to a more open economy. In the judgement of the British delegation Alphand's proposals had been motivated more by an immediate desire to stand well with the Americans than by

[236] PRO, FO 371/62522, UK Delegation to London, 2 August 1947.

any real intention of restructuring Western Europe. The French government, they thought, were frightened at the thought of having to wait until early summer 1948 for aid and wanted to be sure of 'Interim Aid' to bridge the gap.[237] This was to prove a shallow judgement, however. The French proposals were in fact a logical response to Marshall's speech and to Bidault's disillusionment with the Soviet Union after the Moscow Council of Foreign Ministers. If Germany could not be kept permanently weakened, it was necessary to feel out a political way to incorporate a revived German economy in a safe European framework. But in the circumstances of August 1947, with so much in Germany still to be decided, the steps were bound to be fumbling and uncertain, no more perhaps at first than a tentative exploration of a still only remotely possible alternative.

It is necessary at this stage to explore in some detail the formulation of British policy towards the French proposals. For Europe, for Britain, and for the United States the major question was whether Britain would participate in such a customs union. Suggestions for customs unions and for joint planning between the French and British economies had emanated from Paris on several occasions since the end of the war, but the British government, although giving priority to financial help to the French government in terms of foreign-trade credits, had been very cool indeed about any closer form of economic association. There was, however, an important and growing body of opinion within the Foreign Office which supported the idea of some form of British association with or even participation in a European economic bloc, and under the pressure of events during the autumn and winter this crystallized into support for participation in a European customs union. The motives of course were political, not economic. The economic ministries were flatly opposed to the idea. There thus opened up in Britain the fundamental divide between the apparent political advantages and the apparent economic disadvantages of membership of a West-European customs union, a divide which was to dominate the formulation of British policy towards the Common Market for the next thirty years and which perhaps still dominates it.

In such a situation the decisions and opinions of ministers were of crucial importance. Under the pressure of Soviet reaction to CEEC and Marshall Aid, Bevin came to see a European customs union as not merely a desirable but even a necessary basis for the West-European defensive alliance which had such high priority in his foreign policy. Between August 1947 and February 1948 he gradually changed his position so that he became an ardent advocate of a European customs union as a basis for Western Union. This was not exactly what the French intended by a European customs union, and indeed, as will be seen, opinions varied

---

[237] PRO, FO 371/62552, UK Delegation to London, 4 August 1947.

widely as to what the precise nature of such a customs union should be. The opposition of the economic ministers in the British Cabinet remained, however, implacable. Eventually Bevin let the matter drop, overtaken as it was to some degree by the speed with which the alternative defence and cultural structures associated with the Brussels Pact and the origins of NATO were formed. In retrospect the question must be asked whether the ultimate decision not to participate in the formation of the first proposed West-European customs union was not a vital moment in British history when a wrong turning was taken.

It is impossible to read through the voluminous documentation on the formation of British policy on this issue without realizing that everyone involved was aware of being faced with a historical choice of great moment. It was the almost unanimous opinion of civil servants, as well as of the few academic economists who were consulted, that customs unions would automatically lead to much closer forms of political union and to the harmonization of the very wide range of economic policies in Europe which, in the two years after 1945, had represented important differences in national political choices. The historian may well take a more cautious line here. The history of the Zollverein, as of the Dual Monarchy, shows that customs unions may very well survive for long periods of time while their constituent parts retain certain quite different internal economic policies and a wide range of independent political powers. Nor does it show that these differences are necessarily eroded over the duration of time: whether they are or not depends on the nature of continuing political choices. Once the nature of the customs union and the political powers with which it has been endowed are defined, there is not necessarily any inherent irresistable dynamic for further development along these lines. The recent history of the European Economic Community has been a severe disappointment to liberal federalists just for that reason. None the less there was an almost universal conviction in Britain that membership of a European customs union would be an irreversible political step – irreversible, at any rate, except by a dangerous and certainly final act of policy, and thus by a political decision as far-reaching as any in the country's history. In those circumstances the attraction of the economic status quo was naturally strong. The status quo in 1947 – almost great-power status, the Commonwealth, the Empire, the Sterling Area, and, not least, the greater apparent possibilities for increasing trade and exports which all these represented, and thus the long-term continuation of expensive domestic economic policies and even perhaps of eventual emancipation from American economic tutelage – all this did not then seem as fragile as in retrospect it now seems.

The London Committee was well aware that participation in CEEC might involve the need to take a stand on the question of a European customs union, and it had appointed a subcommittee to determine the policy to be pursued in Paris. The subcommittee received negative advice from the Board of Trade and the Treasury. It is important, however, to distinguish between the opinions of these two ministries.

No intelligent opponent of the customs union would find any real merit in the Board of Trade's attitude. It was devoid of the most rudimentary elements of proper economic analysis, and amounted to no more than a statement of outright and unthinking protectionism.

It would mean (as would *ex hypothesi* be its intention) the decline of industry here in favour of its competitors elsewhere, with all the attendant dislocation. All the difficulties in fact, but on a larger and wider scale, that our own development area policy is aimed at minimizing. This seems politically unthinkable in a European world in which all Governments are increasingly feeling their way to methods of planning aimed at mitigating the effect on their citizens of the more extreme rigours of the free interplay of economic forces.[238]

Even as this opinion was being formulated, the discussions over the first reconstruction plan in France must have been moving towards a consideration of how French plans for the future could be integrated into a European tariff union. Underlying the Board of Trade's attitude was not merely the successful experience of wartime planning and controls in Britain, but a deep-seated fear that important sectors of British capital-goods production, particularly steel and chemicals, would need permanent protection once the limits on the volume of German industrial production were removed.

The Treasury's objections, on the other hand, were not so much based on considerations of domestic policy. The central consideration, as with the payments negotiations, was that British reserves were also the Sterling Area reserves. Anything which might endanger the size of these reserves would threaten the recovery both of Britain and of the world, the more so as extra-European trade was more important to that recovery than intra-European trade. Deeper still lay the suspicion that one aspect of United States policy was an attack on the position of the City of London and an attempt, not just to gain access for United States exports on easier terms to markets where British goods had formerly dominated, but also to secure much of London's international business in invisibles for New York. Everything turned on the extent to which these reserves might be safeguarded in a European agreement. The Treasury's first priority was to establish a stable pattern of trade and exchanges in Europe. This would, it was assumed, be followed by convertibility of West-European currencies. Once this had been attained, there would be no objection in principle to a general lowering or removal of intra-European tariffs. For the Treasury, therefore, a European customs union in 1947 was at best irrelevant, at worst a threat to the British position, and almost certainly unworkable. In

---

[238] PRO, FO 371/62552, Board of Trade, note, 'Customs Union for Western Europe', 30 June 1947.

the longer run, however, once the Sterling Area was safe from American diplomatic pressures, it might prove a logical step.[239]

The advice which the London Committee received from its special sub-committee on the question reflected these opinions. 'We see', the subcommittee wrote, 'many and insuperable objections to any proposals for a customs union of which the United Kingdom would be a member'.[240] These objections were that unless the Commonwealth were a member the whole structure of British–Commonwealth trade would be destroyed; that British trade might decline; that insufficient political thought had been given to the question; that it would mean the harmonization of economic policies; and that it would create strategic problems. The subcommittee's advice, which was in essence the brief for the British negotiators at Paris and, later, Brussels, was: 'We conclude, therefore, it is not in our interest to encourage the idea of a European Customs Union of which the United Kingdom would be a member, and that in any case a general Western European Customs Union is out of the question as a matter of practical politics.'[241]

Only six days after this opinion had been recorded, Alphand proposed to the Executive Committee of CEEC that discussions should now begin among the members on the formation of a customs union. The deputy leader of the British delegation, Sir Edmund Hall-Patch, was (although he had the opposite reputation amongst the Americans) sympathetic to the idea of British membership in such a customs union. 'There is', he wrote to Bevin' 'a well-established prejudice in Whitehall against a European Customs Union. It goes back a long way and is rooted in the old days of free trade. It is a relic of a world which has disappeared, probably never to return.'[242] In Hall-Patch's view, with which it is difficult to quarrel, the Board of Trade had developed a technique for blocking all rational discussion by stating the choice as though it were between two opposites and as though a European customs union would have to mean the dissolution of *all* imperial trading arrangements. Bevin should, Hall-Patch suggested, initiate a more thorough inquiry into how far this was so, and he concluded with a direct appeal to his minister.

Now, as a result of the Marshall proposals, European imaginations have been fired. The financial position of Europe is so desperate that there is a chance, which may never recur, to break down the barriers which are hampering a trade revival in Europe. It may even be possible to go some way towards the integration of the European economy comparable to the vast industrial integration of the United

---

[239] Treasury opinion is summed up in the replies to the request from the Foreign Office for guidance on advice to ministers in PRO, T 236/808, London Committee, Sub-Committee on Integration of Europe, 16 July 1947.
[240] Ibid, 23 July 1947.
[241] Ibid.
[242] PRO, FO 371/62552, Hall-Patch to Bevin, 7 August 1947.

States which Soviet Russia is busy trying to emulate. If some such integration does not take place Europe will gradually decline in the face of pressure from the United States on the one hand and Soviet Russia on the other. The possibilities of European integration were revealed by what Hitler was able to do in four short years for his own nefarious purposes. If we can achieve for peaceful purposes what he attempted to do, with some success, for warlike purposes, we may set in motion an economic renaissance in Europe which will go far to solve our own difficulties. The stakes are high and the problems to be solved are enormous, but if there is one chance in a hundred of doing something effective we should not let that chance go by.'[243]

This minute was followed by an urgent visit from Franks to both Bevin and the London Committee to seek more exact instructions in the new circumstances. Franks listed to the Committee the various possibilities of action which he thought might satisfy the United States, and suggested that a customs union was not necessarily the worst option in so far as Britain, by joining now, might be able to retain Dominion trade preferences even though this would be against American wishes. He got short shrift. The Board of Trade's chief representative insisted that the necessary conditions for a customs union were political and economic stability, stable exchange rates, and a large measure of agreement on economic and political questions. 'The lack of these conditions made a European customs union in the foreseeable future quite impracticable.'[244] If this totally depressing view of Europe's future was not exactly in accord with the fears on which the argument for protection was based, the contradiction was made more apparent by the Bank of England's revelation at the same meeting that yet another large industry would be threatened by such proposals, since British textiles would not be able to compete against revived Italian production. Ministers decided that Britain should co-operate in the talks but avoid any commitment.[245]

In the previous summer Bevin had asked for an exploration of the economic possibilities of a Franco-British customs union which other countries might eventually join, but the Board of Trade had declined the request. In January 1947 the Cabinet had decided to review the whole range of policy options in case the proposals for an International Trade Organization miscarried. As a result of this a brief report under very circumscribed terms was commissioned from a small and acceptable group of economists under Sir Denis Robertson. It was completed at the end of August. Its conclusions were that if ITO failed there would be better means than a full customs union of achieving such measures of economic integration with Europe as the United Kingdom might desire. If ITO succeeded these means would not be permitted, whereas a customs

---

[243] Ibid.
[244] PRO, FO 371/62565, Minutes of the London Committee, 9 August 1947.
[245] PRO, FO 371/62552, Minutes of Ministerial Decision on 8 August 1947 on UE 7194/5132/53.

union might, and to that extent the report was not unenthusiastic about the possible gains from a European customs union. A smaller Western-European customs union without Britain would, it concluded, be harmful to British interests. However, the report encouraged the idea that the United Kingdom had more to gain economically from a customs union with less developed economies. The Board of Trade was able reasonably to draw from it the conclusion that, 'a Customs Union consisting of a number of primary producing countries with a wide diversity of unexploited resources would be likely to be to the advantage of the United Kingdom; likewise a Customs Union consisting of countries whose industries were primitive compared with those of the United Kingdom'.[246] Nevertheless, Board of Trade opinion was modified to the extent that if a European customs union showed signs of being organized without Britain, 'the risks inherent in our non-participation or killing the scheme by abstention might outweigh the disadvantages of participation.'[247]

The official position did not change. But the analysis of policy options was now an altogether more urgent and serious matter. On 3 September Bevin brought it before the public when he addressed the Trades Union Congress at Southport and seemed, although in rather vague terms, to be advocating a customs union which would embrace the Empire and perhaps other states. His motives were made clearer in a personal letter to Attlee two days later. He wished to re-establish Britain's position in the world and to free Britain from financial dependence on the United States. One way to do this was, he suggested, to draw on the raw-material resources of the Commonwealth and Empire, either through a customs union or a Commonwealth economic council. It might seem that such a letter would indicate that the die was cast against the arguments increasingly coming from the Foreign Office, but this was not so. In the first place the means Bevin now proposed were beyond the realm of practical politics and soon to be shown to be so. What was of more significance, therefore, was Bevin's reason for giving priority to the imperial solution for independence from America.

> I fear, however, we shall not achieve this purpose solely by selling manufactured goods to a world which is becoming increasingly industrialised and that multilateral trade may not suffice. It may come too late or not be wide enough to help us. We must have something in the way of raw materials as well as manufactured goods with which to buy our own food and other requirements in other countries.[248]

In short, a customs union in which Britain retained imperial preferences would admirably serve Britain's diplomatic aims.

---

[246] PRO, FO 371/62554, B.O.T. Memorandum, 'A European Customs Union or Unions', 10 October 1947.
[247] Ibid.
[248] PRO, FO 371/62554, Bevin to Attlee, 5 September 1947.

Nowhere in the opinions which had come from the economic ministries was there any hint that there might be advantages to be won from concentrating a greater proportion of foreign trade on the developed economies. Long-term studies of the pattern of foreign trade show that one tendency of the foreign trade of developed economies is that an increasing proportion of their exports flows to other developed economies.[249] One measure of the competitiveness of developed economies in the post-war world has been the relative rate of increase of the proportion of their manufactured exports which does go to such markets and, conversely, it might be suspected that a tendency for manufactured exports to be concentrated on less competitive, protected, colonial markets does not augur well for the future. Even seen strictly from the contemporary viewpoint of the British government, the financial and economic problems of the United Kingdom were only to be solved by a long-sustained increase in exports. There was a rapid growth in extra-European exports in the immediate aftermath of the Second World War, and, what is more, given the payments and exchange problems which prevailed in Europe, the mechanisms of exporting within the Sterling Area were simpler than those of exporting to Europe. But it is not easy to envisage how the growth of Dominion and colonial imports from Britain could by themselves have quickly enough satisfied the requirement for export growth provisionally set in 1944, whatever the importance of the supply of primary imports obtained from the same source.

Be that as it may, the Cabinet decided on 25 September to set up an Interdepartmental Committee to consider the feasibility of a customs union with the colonies or even with the Commonwealth.[250] In the Cabinet discussions Cripps insisted that such a study should get first priority over any study of a European customs union. Both the Minister of State for Commonwealth Relations (Arthur Henderson) and the Parliamentary Under-Secretary for the Colonies (Ivor Thomas), brought in for the occasion, pointed out that neither Dominions nor colonies were likely to be too interested in these proposals, and the whole Cabinet appears to have agreed that the idea was unlikely to be a realizable one.[251] In such circumstances alternative forms of economic association were hardly dead, no matter how fearfully they were regarded.

The same issues were considered by the Economic Policy Committee of the Cabinet, essentially the Cabinet without its less important members, on 7 November. Bevin put forward the Foreign Office viewpoint and indicated that the policy of opposing a European customs union was disappointing to the Foreign Office. He gave his opinion that it was

---

[249] The best demonstration of this is in A. Maizels, *Industrial Growth and World Trade* (Cambridge, 1963).
[250] PRO, FO 371/62554, Memorandum of Cabinet discussions, 25 September 1947.
[251] PRO, CAB 129 10 77 (47), 25 September 1947.

'essential that Western Europe should attain some measure of economic unity if it was to maintain its independence as against Russia and the United States'.[252] The tenor of the ensuing discussion was that multilateralism in the framework of ITO was better than any more restrictive solutions, and that if anything was envisaged in the form of special imperial economic links it would be wiser to keep any efforts in this direction secret from the United States. Bevin's obvious interest in some form of Western-European association met with no sympathy from the heads of the economic ministries. Harold Wilson, President of the Board of Trade, thought the British delegation should try to divert discussion away from the concept of a customs union, and Cripps actually argued that 'as far as concerned the United Kingdom, the first stage should be the creation of a Customs Union with the colonial Empire'.[253]

It is hard to see how any Commonwealth or Empire country would have welcomed such a policy, and this was the conclusion already emerging from the inter-departmental study-group which had been set up. Not only did most such countries want higher levels of protection for their manufacturing sectors, but their primary exports already usually entered Britain duty-free under imperial preference schemes. If ITO were to succeed preferences would in any case have to be renounced, and the United States would probably oppose an imperial customs union as old preferences writ large. 'Balancing the considerations set out above', the committee concluded, 'we feel bound to conclude that a Commonwealth Union, while probably desirable in itself, is unlikely to be realizable under existing conditions'.[254]

There was nothing to suggest, however, that, if ITO failed, the United Kingdom would have to renounce all imperial preferences in opting for a European union. The threat to imperial preferences came, rather, from the Geneva trade negotiations. The situation in the autumn of 1947 was that most French colonies received tariff preferences from France, although for some this did not apply to all goods. Their own tariff policy towards French goods varied through almost every possibility. Portugal imposed lower duties on all colonial imports and received the same preferences in return virtually throughout her empire. Belgium was still a duty-free market for her colonies. The Netherlands imposed tariffs on theirs. The future Benelux tariffs were to be a compromise between the two positions.

The only way in which the tariff adjustments that would make a closer economic association with Western Europe possible could be discussed in time with all Commonwealth and Empire countries was at the continuation of the international trade talks in Havana in November. The only country not to indicate unease there, when the discussions took place, was Canada.

[252] PRO, FO 371/62740, Meeting of the Cabinet Economic Policy Committee, 7 November 1947.
[253] Ibid.
[254] PRO, FO 371/62723, UK Study Group on Customs Unions, 3 November 1947.

Otherwise 'suspicion was the keynote of a very lukewarm meeting'.[255] The British government was unable, of course, to give the slightest indication of what extent of preferences might still be retained in a European customs union. The French were anxious to acquire British support to amend the proposed ITO charter at the last moment in order to keep the door open for preference schemes which would be part of a European customs union. Their attitude was that 'the Americans would find it easy to fall in with an extension of preferences in the sacred cause of forming a Customs Union'.[256] When these discussions were also taken up informally at Havana the French 'appeared to take it for granted that, if the United Kingdom entered a Western European Customs Union, it would be a *sine qua non* that the Imperial preference system should be continued in one form or another'.[257]

The idea of an imperial customs union had died almost as soon as it had been born, although the negative conclusions of the inter-departmental committee had not been submitted to ministers by the end of the year. What was left? A Western-European customs union including Britain in which it might not be necessary to abandon imperial preferences could still be part of a new structure of western security and might be the future basis of British and European independence of America.

This was the conclusion towards which Bevin rapidly moved in the autumn of 1947. He had asked in 1946 for due consideration of the possibility of an Anglo-French customs union. As the real economic weakness of the United Kingdom was fully brought home to him in 1947, he had snatched at the grander imperial solution. He was not a man to linger long over impossible solutions. At the latest by February 1948 he had fully espoused the cause of a Western-European customs union. On 22 January 1948 he spoke, again in somewhat imprecise terms, on the subject in the House of Commons. On 28 January it was decided to draw up a Foreign Office paper 'forcefully stating the political and strategic arguments for a Western European Customs Union'.[258] On 24 February the Foreign Office filed an argued exposé of his views by Bevin himself.[259]

Strategic safety depended, Bevin argued, on a closer Western-European association. It was essential to aim at building a powerful association of democratic states linked by traditional affinities and by a common determination to resist any attempt on their independence. The purpose of this association was to halt and possibly even turn back what Bevin called 'the flow of the Communist tide'. But such an association by itself, he argued, would be ineffective unless the economic situation of all countries involved, including the United Kingdom, improved. This depended on establishing

---

[255] PRO, FO 371/62754, Havana Delegation to London, 29 November 1947.
[256] Ibid., Stevens to Marton, 6 December 1947.
[257] Ibid., Havana Delegation to London, 14 December 1947.
[258] PRO, FO 371/71766, Minute by R. B. Stevens, 11 February 1948.
[259] Ibid., note by Bevin, n.d., received 24 February 1948.

secure sources of raw-material supply and on a harmonious development of all the West-European economies on that basis.

In western Europe itself we cannot hope to find any substantial alleviation of our food import problem. On the other hand, the colonial resources of the United Kingdom, France, Belgium, Holland, and Portugal, can in time be mobilized so as to constitute a valuable addition to our sources of supply. In the industrial field, moreover, we cannot afford to contemplate unregulated growth, if for no other reason than our concern for the future of the German economy ... In my view, our best hope of securing the political future of western Europe – above all of France and Germany – better even than through treaties and mutual defence arrangements is to help construct so closely woven an economic pattern that the constituent elements in it simply cannot afford to fall apart.[260]

But what sort of arrangements would best achieve this end? He reviewed all existing arrangements and rejected them as insufficient. CEEC was the best of them but, in Bevin's view, it could well break apart as soon as 'the lure of the American dollar has ceased to exercise its spell'.[261] An extension of imperial preferences to Western Europe or a West-European customs union were the only satisfactory alternatives. The first would be only a half-way house, apart from being a breach of ITO. There were certainly difficulties in the way of the second. But its advantages outweighed them. No other solution would contribute the same political and economic strengthening of Western Europe, none had the same permanence, none would produce the same measure of economic integration, even union. Such a customs union would allow medium-term planning, it would have a favourable effect in the United States, it would prevent the formation of regional unions which were not based on a genuine reduction of trade barriers, and, above all, it would establish the United Kingdom once more as the leader in Europe.

'I propose, therefore', he concluded, 'that the United Kingdom should take the lead in promoting and inspiring a European Customs Union on the broadest possible basis. Such a Union should comprise at least the United Kingdom, France, Benelux, West Germany and Italy; the addition of Scandinavia, Switzerland, Portugal and perhaps later Spain would be desirable but may be impracticable.'[262]

Stevens was quite justified in writing to Havana at the end of 1947 that, 'As for the Western European Customs Union project, in itself I do not think it is true to say this is dying so far as the UK is concerned, and I do not think that any member of the Interdepartmental Study Group here would wish to dissent from this statement as a reflection of the mood of the Group as a whole ...'[263] But what chance was there that those ministers

[260] Ibid.
[261] Ibid.
[262] Ibid.
[263] PRO, FO 371/62754, Stevens to Marton, 20 December 1947.

who had earlier rejected the idea in favour of an anachronistic and wholly unpractical solution would now support it?

The indecisiveness of British policy was easily perceived by the other CEEC nations. Their actions had to be based on their judgement about the likely outcome of this debate in Whitehall. As the indecision and the effort to keep all options open persisted, and as the other CEEC participants came increasingly to feel that the decision in Britain would ultimately be a negative one, the position of British leadership at Paris was inevitably weakened. For Britain an unexpected outcome began to appear: a smaller customs union without Britain began to seem a more realistic solution, not to Europe's immediate economic problems, but to the much wider issue of European reconstruction. There is certainly much to support the argument that a European customs union had nothing immediately to offer to the process of economic recovery in Britain, whatever its possible advantages in the longer run. But was it such a threat to British industry in 1947 as to make it in itself, setting aside all other policy options, a *dangerous* policy? Surely it was not.

Whether a Western-European customs union in which all the colonies of the member states received some form of imperial preference would in fact have been acceptable to American diplomacy was not put to the test. But as the negotiations stood in January 1948 it is hard to see that they contained any serious threat to the future development of the British economy. Indeed, if a future of high growth-rates, increasing output, and increasing exports were assumed, which is what did actually occur over the next twenty years and which is, in addition, what made the domestic economic policies of the government feasible, membership on such terms in a European tariff-free zone might well have been seen as bringing economic advantages. It is a well-known, even hackneyed, critique of bureaucratic policy formulation that it never looks to the long term, but in this case it applies with some force. The longest period of future time the Treasury envisaged during the whole process of decision-making was four years, and only within that time-scale were the decisions made there sound and logical.

There are two further criticisms that need to be made. One is that there was at the heart of British policy formulation a lack of awareness of how far a customs union might appeal on the Continent as a way of drawing a definitive line under a lamentable period in the history of Western Europe; and, secondly and much more importantly, there was also a lack of awareness of how possible the creation of such a union by an act of political will actually was. Of course these criticisms cannot be separated from the failure to think positively about the possible long-run economic advantages of a customs union in a period of sustained economic growth. It was the background economic conditions that eventually made the West-European customs union such a success within its own limits, and made the British decision look like one which had not taken all factors fully into consideration. In short, the lack of awareness both of what was desired and what was possible in Western Europe was also a failure of the imaginative capacity to think on a long-term basis. It was, in the end, going to be much easier for industrialists and farmers in France, Italy, the Benelux, and Western Germany to agree on a set of complicated economic deals which made a common external tariff possible if they did not have the British to bother about. That ought not to have been so hard to see even in 1947. After all, no one in Britain doubted that the recovery of German industry was certain. If it were to recover it had to do so in some framework of common agreement with French and Belgian interests, an agreement which might well ignore British producers in order to make the necessary arrangements possible. There was in fact a failure in London to understand the logic of European reconstruction, however accurate the understanding of European recovery.

The Benelux delegates made no immediate reaction to the French proposals other than to indicate once more that since, for them, the recovery of Germany was a prerequisite for their own sustained recovery, any such union must contain the possibility that 'West Germany' should be able to join; in addition they suggested that Switzerland should be invited. Hirschfeld himself felt that this might be the historic moment to embark on such a course, but the difficulties seemed overwhelming. Could Germany be brought into the scheme and the existing very high German tariffs be lowered to a level acceptable to Benelux? Were not the French tariff proposals for the Geneva trade conference higher than previous high French tariffs? Above all, would Britain join?[264] Hirschfeld's instructions were to go no further and no faster than the United Kingdom in the customs-union discussions.[265] It was of no interest to Benelux to join a French-dominated customs union, although for Belgium alone the case might well have been different. For the Netherlands either Britain had to be a participant or that as yet unborn political entity, West Germany. No customs union which did not enable the Netherlands to take at least the same share of the transit trade of Britain and Germany as it had had in the 1930s offered a very enticing prospect to that country. On the other hand the union only made sense for France if it included Benelux. A union with Italy alone 'was of no great practical interest to France'.[266]

The Italian delegation took the opportunity to issue a general statement to the Executive Committee in praise of a regional customs union as a first step towards a larger union. 'We would conclude that customs unions are the most generally accepted form and the one which best meets with the project for a better international organization of trade. Can we prepare to

[264] MBZ, 610.32, Netherlands Delegation to The Hague, 3 August 1947.
[265] PRO, FO 371/62552, UK Delegation to London, 11 August 1947.
[266] PRO, FO 371/62554, UK Delegation to London, 17 September 1947. Statement by Alphand.

finalize an agreement which unites in one single customs area the countries subscribing to the Marshall Plan?'[267] This was to be followed by a further declaration in the same tone on 18 August.[268]

Once the policy of the British delegation had been laid down by ministers on 8 August, Franks, following out a plan to try to retain the initiative, suggested that the whole conference should set aside three days for internal discussion of the question with those countries not represented on the Executive Committee. This was how the oddest of the regional customs-unions proposals arose, that between Greece and Turkey. The British delegation gave a lunch to the Greek and Turkish delegations and suggested that they might themselves consider a regional customs union.[269] It had already become apparent that the less developed economies were overwhelmingly concerned with preferential access for their primary exports to the European markets. For them a customs union achieved no more than a system of intra-European preferences and, as far as their developing manufacturing sectors were concerned, was more dangerous. The Irish were by no means sure that they would even take part in any further discussions.[270] When the Greeks and Turks made the same points, Franks stressed the insistence of the United States on steps towards a customs union. Feeling no doubt that it was well worth avoiding the possible loss of American support, both delegations agreed to refer the matter to their governments. As Franks put it to his own government, 'it seems to me that if we can organise a little demonstration of this kind from South Eastern Europe it could do no harm'.[271]

The British delegates had outlined their official position to their French colleagues and proposed the formation of a European Customs-Union Study-Group on 10 August which would meet in Brussels away from the American influence in Paris and have an independent life of its own. The French were reluctant to accept this procedure. Monnet, who took part in this discussion, insisted that it would not satisfy the United States.[272] The British government sought to reassure itself in Washington that State Department opinion was divided and that not all Clayton's colleagues believed in the practicability of an immediate liberal customs union as he did.[273] Ambassador Douglas gave his opinion that both Britain and Western Germany should be members of the proposed customs union and thus make it acceptable to the other members.[274] Eventually the British decided

[267] OECD; CCEE/26, Déclaration du délégué italien faite au Comité-Exécutif, 5 August 1947.
[268] MBZ, 610-32, Déclaration du délégué italien au Comité de Coopération Économique Européenne, 18 August 1947.
[269] PRO, FO 371/62552, UK Delegation to London, 13 August 1947.
[270] Ibid.
[271] Ibid.
[272] Ibid. UK Delegation to London, 10 August 1947.
[273] Ibid., UK Delegation to London, 15 August 1947.
[274] Ibid., Record of Conversation with Douglas by Makins, 15 August 1947.

Limitation to Western Europe 563

to place their proposal for a separate European Customs-Union Study-Group before the full conference, and it was discussed in plenary session of CEEC on 23 August. Norway had already indicated its opposition. A customs union, their delegation told Franks, would need many years to complete.[275] At the plenary session of the CEEC the Norwegian delegates, supported by Sweden, maintained that extra-European trade was as important for recovery as increasing intra-European trade, and that any discussion of a customs union should be conducted only within the framework of the Economic Commission for Europe which was a less politically divisive organization than the present conference. The Swiss were clearly not carried away with enthusiasm either, and their delegation spoke guardedly only in favour of 'freeing intra-European trade'.[276] The consequence of this lack of unity was that the invitations to the Study-Group were not confined to the CEEC participants but went also to all who had received the invitation to the original conference, including Byelorussia. This was intended to strengthen the Study-Group's position, giving it an apparent independence from the more direct American pressures, although, in the event, the only outsiders to attend were certain 'observers' from Commonwealth countries.

The question of whether participation in a European customs union would infringe Swedish neutrality had not arisen in CEEC, because the Swedish-Norwegian alliance had put forward its opposition to the American demands there on other grounds. The Swedish delegation was in any case shielded by Norway's position on the Executive Committee. None the less the Scandinavian bloc followed the ensuing debate in Switzerland, as well as they could, with great interest. The Swiss Federal Council's policy appears to have been to amend the Study-Group's terms of reference so that it should also consider all other ways to increase the level of intra-European trade. The hope was that in this way it would be diverted towards the more immediately attainable goal of a more flexible payments system, and thus not force Switzerland to choose between neutrality and a customs union. Furthermore Switzerland's position as a hard-currency creditor meant that her immediate problem, like that of Belgium, was to fund her own exports. There began in Switzerland an internal debate on this question whose outcome was not to be known until October.

There were two separate sets of customs-union negotiations already in existence before the first meeting of the European Customs-Union Study-Group. The first consisted of the negotiations between Italy and France. A French delegation visited Rome in the third week of September. Its leaders gave their opinion that 'it was now or never',[277] but they made no

---

[275] UD, 44.2/26, Bind IV, 'Oversikt over arbeidet pr. 11 August 1947', 12 August 1947.
[276] PRO, FO 371/62550, UK Delegation to London, 23 August 1947.
[277] PRO, FO 371/62554, Conversation between Commercial Counsellor in Rome and Drouin, 23 September 1947.

attempt to minimize the genuine difficulties, of which the most obvious were (a) that the French government's political interest was in the larger union and (b) that the exchange rate between the two currencies, thanks to the diametrically opposite financial policies the governments were pursuing, bore little relationship to the real price structure of the economies. The second negotiation was in Scandinavia. The opposition of Norway and Sweden to the customs union raised once again the idea of a separate Scandinavian union. In late August the Scandinavian ministers met to consider their attitude to the new direction which European affairs had taken. Lange and the Swedish ministers agreed that the question of a European customs union should only be examined by established international organs, i.e. those of the United Nations.[278] The Danes objected that this would put Scandinavia in the position of having to carry the burden of American disapproval for the 'failure' of the Paris conference. The Norwegians insisted that their attitude was 'the outcome of mature considerations and could not be changed'.[279] The Danish representatives said the same. At this point Lange played the card of Scandinavian co-operation, suggesting that they discuss how far they could nevertheless co-operate economically and put forward a common policy. In this impasse the distant idea of a regional Scandinavian customs union was kept alive, though it was no more than a way of saving face and refusing to admit to the world the reality of profound Scandinavian disunity.[280]

Denmark's comparative advantage in processed food exports would be useless were she excluded from a European customs union, although to be of value to her such a union must embrace Britain or Germany or both. A Scandinavian union made little difference to her. Indeed, merely removing tariffs on intra-Scandinavian trade would have made very little difference to Sweden either.[281] On 12 September Denmark joined the European Customs Union Study-Group. Norway, impelled by the logic of its own national economic development, still sought a different direction. Norwegian history suggested that an open economy might well run grave dangers of arrested development and might incur very severe regional problems in the less favoured areas. To lower Norwegian tariffs, Lange feared, would be to flood the country with Swedish manufactures and Danish food. In his opinion, 'This would ruin Norwegian farmers and

---

[278] UD, 44.2/26, Bind V, 'Møte den utvidede utenrikskomité', 1 September 1947.
[279] Ibid.
[280] There are only the briefest accounts of the proposed Scandinavian customs union. I. Svennilson, 'Det internordiska vareutbytets problem' in *Utrikes Politik*, March 1948, pp. 23–30, and G. Stolz, *Tollunioner* (Bergen, 1948), discuss the possibilities.
[281] Tariffs were very low in both Sweden and Denmark, the real barriers to trade being non-tariff barriers, and the proportion of their foreign trade with Scandinavia was also very low. Norway's level of tariff protection was distinctly higher. The market created by a Scandinavian customs union would only have had 14.4 million consumers, and intra-Scandinavian trade amounted to only about 12 per cent of the total foreign trade of the three countries.

create industrial unemployment necessitating a large-scale population shift to fishing, shipping, woodcutting which, even if ultimately successful would be a long, disheartening process.'[282] Iceland played 'on the whole a negative role'[283] in the intra-Scandinavian discussions. That is to say it sided with the Danes.[284] Its delay in joining the Study-Group appears to have been largely accidental. The split between the Scandinavian countries was not to be healed by further considerations. When they met again in February 1948 their positions were further apart. Undén, the Swedish Foreign Minister, insisted that a customs union had nothing to do with Marshall Aid, and Hammarskjöld insisted that Sweden could never agree that the United States should be the arbitrators in intra-European questions. The Danish government disagreed completely and wanted the others to send full representatives to the European Customs-Union Study-Group.[285]

The Swiss debate resulted in an attitude no more encouraging than that of Norway. On 7 October the Federal Counsellor for Foreign Affairs issued a long statement reflecting the Swiss dilemma. Switzerland did not dare not to take part in the Study-Group because it could not risk economic isolation, but

it would be to give ourselves up to dangerous illusions to imagine that the creation of a customs union would being health in Europe. To wish to make an economic unity of Europe in the shape of a customs union would contribute nothing to its economic reconstruction. It would only be a centralization, a sort of levelling downwards, whose drawbacks would quickly show themselves to be greater than its benefits. From the economic viewpoint as well, Europe's strength lies in its diversity. It is necessary to try to harmonize the national economies, not to unify them, ...[286]

When the Study-Group first met on 10 November discussions with the Benelux and the Danish representatives showed that they were not necessarily opposed to the United Kingdom keeping its preference schemes within a European customs union, or even maintaining certain tariffs between itself and the other members of a European customs union. Belgium in fact was positively in favour, since this appeared to present the best possibility of competing in sterling-area markets outside Europe, which were otherwise extremely difficult to penetrate, and this outweighed Dutch opposition to the idea.[287] In formal session the issue did not arise,

---

[282] NA, SD, 840.50, Box 532, Oslo to Washington, 6 February 1948.
[283] NA, SD, 840.50, Box 5646, Telegram from Reykjavik, 8 January 1948.
[284] UD, 44.2/26, Bind V, 'Møte den utvidede utenrikskomité', 1 September 1947.
[285] UD, 44.2/26, Bind VII, 'Ekstraktgjenpart av referat fra Utenriksministermøtet i Oslo 23–24 februar 1948'.
[286] Département Politique Fédéral, Information et Presse, Exposé de M. le Conseiller Petitpierre sur l'attitude de la Suisse vis-à-vis du plan Marshall, 7 October 1947.
[287] PRO, FO 371/62755, UK Delegation to London, 'First Meeting of Customs Union Study Group'.

for, whatever the wide range of government discussion, the Group itself was considering only the principles of a common tariff.

Both the Netherlands and Denmark insisted strongly that a customs union must include Germany and also, if possible, Britain. Neither had any choice but to wait on the British decision and to bring as much pressure as possible to bear on the great powers to lay the basis for a German recovery. For Denmark the proposed union offered better access to the British market, and that was its main advantage. The Danish attitude was 'profoundly sceptical of the ultimate attainment of a Western European customs union on a wider basis'.[288] Sweden and Norway sent only observers to the Group, and unambivalent opposition came from Ireland, representing the standpoint of the underdeveloped countries seeking higher tariff protection. 'Alone of all the delegations, the Irish dared to speak of tariffs as though they were not original sin.'[289]

As for the more important powers, they were temporarily united in pushing forward. The French, reported the British delegation, 'appear genuinely to have reached the conclusion that the only real salvation of Europe in the long run lies this way'.[290] If the British enthusiasm fell some way short of that they nevertheless, under the influence of the rapid developments in the Foreign Office, encouraged the group to move faster than it had thought to do in its theoretical studies.

The effects of their attitude was to harden the Dutch attitude towards the French, which might otherwise have weakened to accommodate Belgian wishes. The American Ambassador at The Hague reported quite correctly that: 'The Netherlands government would not welcome, and in fact would resist, efforts either by French or American governments to persuade Netherlands to enter into customs union with France (alone or with Italy).'[291] The pressure which the Belgians could bring to bear was muted by the obvious threat which a customs union posed to Benelux itself. Already the complete economic union of Benelux was threatened by the very large Netherlands payments deficits and the Dutch inability to continue to absorb Belgian exports.[292] Over most of its recent history the Netherlands had usually had payments deficits with both France and Italy, compensated for by trade surpluses with the United Kingdom. In 1947 the Netherlands was still running a large deficit with Britain but, looking to the future, a customs union without Britain might have halted the Benelux union in its tracks and might well have set it in reverse. Nevertheless the Dutch continued to support a European customs union as the best ultimate

---

[288] Ibid.
[289] Ibid.
[290] Ibid.
[291] *FRUS, 1948/III*, Baruch to Marshall, 7 February 1948.
[292] The net Dutch trade deficit in 1947 with Belgium–Luxemburg and the Belgian Congo was 229.7 million guilders, second only in size to the deficit with the USA, M. Weisglas, *Benelux* (Amsterdam, 1949), Statistische Bijlage, Table IV.

solution to the problem of sustained European recovery and the best way to reintegrate into this a revived German economy.

The Franco-Italian negotiations, which presumably remained 'of no particular interest' to the French government, were still pursued outside the framework of the Customs-Union Study-Group, perhaps because the French saw them as a lever towards a wider customs union as a stage in reconstruction. As the French delegation put it in a statement before CEEC on 27 August,

> As far as customs union is concerned it does not seem as though essential decisions could be taken in a study-group. These decisions are the task of governments and a study-group, in our opinion, if it can or wants to do a useful job, must suppose the problem solved ... If Europe can become viable we are absolutely convinced that that must be in an economic framework very different from the one we have known so far. It would serve no purpose to revert exactly to the same conditions. We are utterly convinced that we should arrive in the end at the same problems, the same dangers and perhaps the same cataclysm.[293]

It was in this spirit that the French government, before CEEC broke up in September, issued a statement declaring its readiness to take part in customs-unions negotiations with any of the participating countries.[294] The Italian delegation expressed its general agreement and support for this policy, and the two governments set up a Joint Commission to report on their own proposed customs union.[295]

In fact the Commission's report also dealt with a wider issue, viz. what difficulties would arise from a full economic union of the two countries, and yet the report was published in January.[296] This report like the later ones is well characterized by Diebold as making only 'rare acknowledgements of the role of competition'.[297] There were sections on how to form market-sharing agreements in third markets for foodstuff exports, on industrial agreements to limit competition, on the sharing of merchant-shipping services, on the forming of agreements to limit competition between ports, and on the limitations to be imposed on movements of labour and capital. Whether it would eventually be possible to agree on all these compromises was left to be seen. In February 1948 both cabinets agreed to press ahead, and on 20 March Bidault and Sforza met at Turin to sign their acceptance of the Commission's report and to initiate a new commission to implement it.

---

[293] OECD, CCEE/54, Déclaration du délégué de la France au Comité de Coopération sur les unions douanières, 27 August 1947. This is a translation from the French text, rather than the official English text, in order to render the form of expression nearer to the manner of the original.
[294] The statement is printed in CEEC, *General Report,* op. cit., vol. i, ch. iv, paragraph 98.
[295] Ibid., paragraphs 99, 100.
[296] Commission Mixte Franco-Italienne pour l'Étude d'une Union Douanière, *Rapport Final,* (Rome, 1948).
[297] W. Diebold, *Trade and Payments,* op. cit., p. 361.

Even by the date of this much dramatized meeting in Cavour's house at Turin, the unresolved contradictions in French policy were beginning to tug against this tremendous haste. It was not only that the first French priority was a wider customs union than just that of France and Italy, it was also that there was a more fundamental issue about what type of customs union was wanted. The liberal idea of an entirely unregulated market with a common external tariff hardly offered France the security against the German economy which she sought from a customs union. If the main purpose were to build an economic framework in Europe capable of containing and controlling a revived Germany, the proposed customs union might have to look very different. In this case it would be necessary to negotiate a set of separate deals between producers in different sectors, such that what emerged would look more like an officially and internationally regulated cartel sheltered by a common protective tariff. This second approach would alone satisfy French security needs and would still create, perhaps more easily, the European political institutions which a rising tide of opinion and a certain degree of internal conviction in the French government itself seemed to demand.

The negotiations with Italy were aimed therefore at this second type of customs union. Already the publication in France of the report of the first Joint Commission had been delayed because of opposition from French industrialists.[298] The new Joint Commission included representatives of industry and agriculture and served as a vehicle to organize a much wider set of consultations between many specialized groups of producers, which lasted throughout 1948. This was entirely the opposite approach from that of the European Customs-Union Study-Group, which continued to discuss the basic principles and likely effects of a 'pure' customs union. It did so because this was the wish of Britain and of Benelux. Even if the opposition of the economic ministries in Britain to the customs union were to diminish, membership of the alternative type of customs union, a loosely structured European producers' cartel, would require from Britain a break with the Commonwealth and Empire too drastic to be contemplated. Benelux, furthermore, supported the British position not merely in order to escape the French embrace but also because the main interest there too was in a more open and liberal union. It may be that the Benelux countries' experience of a Common Economic Council maintaining and regulating a battery of trade and production controls within a common tariff had not convinced them that this was the best path to complete economic union, an ideal which indeed now seemed to be receding rather quickly in the Low Countries. Italy could only waver between these two positions.

Thus the meetings of the European Customs Union Study-Group were

---

[298] NA, SD, 840.50, Box 5646, Caffery to Washington, 13 January 1948.

not only faced with Britain's indecision but were also condemned to temporary stalemate because of the Benelux adherence to the British model of a pure liberal customs union in Europe, with imperial and colonial preferences but without internal regulations on the European markets. This would only worsen the prospect of France's future economic problems with Germany and was unacceptable in Paris. None the less the issues had not only been defined but important decisions had in effect been made about the future. A more regulated European customs union, could its precise economic terms be defined and could Benelux be persuaded to participate, had emerged as an independent French policy for reconstructing Western Europe. Its geographical boundaries had been more or less defined apart from the doubt over whether Denmark would join, a question to which the answer depended more on events in Britain and Germany than in Copenhagen. As for the British, their indecision was now more likely to result in the organization of a less liberal union. For how long would Benelux wait for the negative decision from London? And once that negative decision came in 1948, there was little Benelux could do but move in the direction of the French idea of the customs union while seeking to modify it. Britain was not, economically, an indispensable member of the union; waiting to be brought on stage was the *deus ex machina*, West Germany. For Benelux the Study-Group had 'a more far-reaching and a longer-term purpose than the joint organisation'.[299] By the autumn of 1948 the Benelux representatives were already privately canvassing the suggestion that they might now enter a purely Continental customs union. When in West Germany the newly created Administrative Economic Council (*Verwaltungsrat für Wirtschaft*) was informed of the nature of the discussions, the German politicians (finding themselves in much the same situation as Italy) were 'barely restrained from making an immediate demand for the adoption of a Customs Union at once'.[300] The *deus ex machina* was moving to bring about the eventual dramatic climax, in which Britain would scarcely be on the stage, of the Schuman Plan and the Treaty of Rome.

4. Decisions at the Montreux Congress of the UEF

The US government decision to support the recovery and unification of Europe, with Marshall's offer of generous help if the Europeans would draw up a joint recovery programme, and the general background, confirmed by other sources, of American approval of the idea of European

[299] PRO, T 236/780, Meeting of the Preparatory Commission for the Economic Committee of the International Study Group on a European Customs Union, 6 March 1948.
[300] PRO, T 236/781, Third Meeting of the Economic Committee of the International Customs Union Study Group, 19/23 October 1948.

union, created an entirely new situation for those who had long been champions of that idea and who were organized in private pressure groups and associations under the umbrella of the Union Européenne des Fédéralistes. The veto exercised by the two superpowers had now been clearly revoked by one of them, which instead was pressing the European governments to plan concerted action. For the first time since 1943, when Roosevelt decreed that it should be ruled out of American post-war planning,[301] the idea of European union was a potentially significant political factor. The gap between imagination and reality had been bridged, and the possibility of fulfilment was within reach. A situation had developed in which the *anciens régimes* of the national states could be forced to take notice of the European idea by the combined pressure of US policy from above and the federalist associations from below. The UEF leaders were prompt to perceive their opportunity.

On 18 June 1947 Alexandre Marc, as secretary-general of the UEF, addressed his last *Lettre-Circulaire* to its twenty-one member associations. In it he pointed out that 'our cause, after being dismissed as a utopia by so-called realists, is now suddenly the focus of political attention. The sensational offer of the US Secretary of State, General Marshall, Bevin's important speech and his discussions with Bidault, Clayton's explanatory comments – all these signs, among others, show that the federal cause is in the very forefront of political actuality. This is sufficient reason why all member associations and organizations of the UEF should redouble their activity. We are convinced that governments, left to themselves, will not be capable of seizing the opportunity offered to Europe and will not arrive at the only proper solution, that of European federation within a global confederation, unless they are pressed to do so by public opinion, which must be informed, shaped and directed by authorized spokesmen of the federalist cause.'[302]

Marshall's offer in its original form had aroused the hope among all member associations of the UEF that joint planning with the East-European countries and the Soviet Union would after all prevent the division of Europe into two blocs, making possible a federation of all Europe which would keep the two world powers apart but maintain friendly co-operation with both of them. When this unique opportunity of realizing the UEF's original idea of an all-European 'Third Force' was torpedoed two weeks later by Molotov's 'Nyet' and Moscow's refusal to allow the East Europeans to join in the plan, the UEF federalists were grievously disappointed; in Leon van Vassenhove's words, 'Un grand espoir est né, et aussi une grande désillusion.'[303]

---

[301] Cf. Introduction, pp. 72–7.
[302] *Lettre-Circulaire*, No. 11, Paris, 18.6.1947 (*CEC Archives, Geneva*, UEF file), p. 1 f. On Alexandre Marc, who was succeeded as secretary-general by Raymond Silva on 16.7.1947, cf. chap. II, nn. 65, 162, and 192. For the twenty-one member associations of the UEF from eight countries, see chap. II/5, n. 190; the further history of the UEF is now taken up from that chapter.
[303] *L'Action fédéraliste européenne*, No. 7, Aug. 1947, p. 49. For the previous 'foreign policy' programme, formulated chiefly at the Amsterdam meeting in Apr. 1947, cf. chap. II/5, pp. 380–5. Marshall's offer addressed also to Eastern Europe and the Soviet Union, cf. chap. III/1, p. 477 f.; for the Soviet veto, pp. 483–6.

Marshall's offer and the Soviet reaction called for important decisions by the federalist associations, united in the UEF, which had come into existence in all major West-European centres. They faced the same two problems as the governments, but in reverse order of importance. In the first place, Marshall had been careful to speak in public only of 'some agreement among the countries of Europe as to the requirements' of a joint recovery programme, whereas the pamphlet issued in May 1947 by the UEF Central Committee had declared that 'the ruinous and destructive system of state sovereignty must first be done away with'.[304] Were the federalists really to support the West-European governments in their incipient efforts to achieve 'some agreement' in economic matters, when their own aim was to rebuild European society on federalist principles with the object of creating a unified federal state? Secondly, ought they to do so when the Soviet veto on East-European participation meant that any move towards European union was bound to give the appearance of constituting a Western bloc, which the UEF had hitherto condemned? The answers to these questions were worked out at the First Ordinary Annual Congress of the UEF which had for several months past been scheduled to take place at Montreux in August 1947, and at which the federalist principles were carefully re-examined.

(A) THE CONCEPT OF A FEDERAL EUROPEAN SOCIETY AND ECONOMY

At its foundation meeting in December 1946 the UEF had decided to hold its first congress 'in August 1947, in Switzerland'. The choice of venue was partly suggested by the provision in the Hertenstein programme for a European federation on the Swiss model; it also symbolized neutrality between East and West; moreover the world federalists were also holding their first congress in Switzerland in the same month. The decision was confirmed at the Amsterdam meeting, when Henri Genet, a municipal councillor of Lausanne and vice-chairman of the Swiss Europa-Union, was elected chairman of the central committee of UEF. Preparations reached their final stage with the transfer of the secretariat to Geneva at the beginning of July and the appointment of Silva as secretary-general: in a letter of 22 July he announced that the congress would be held at Montreux from 27 to 30 August, and circulated the draft agenda.[305] The local preparations and financing were in the hands of an 'organizational

---

[304] UEF pamphlet *Pour bâtir l'Europe*, Paris, (May) 1947; cf. chap. II/5, n. 174.
[305] Cf. resolution of the inaugural assembly dated 15.12.1946, chap. II/5 at n. 162; endorsement by the enlarged central committee in Amsterdam on 15.4.1947, at n. 190; appointment of Raymond Silva at n. 192; announcements in his *Lettre-Circulaire*, No. 13 of 22.7.1947, p. 1 f. (*CEC Archives, Geneva*). The congress agenda was several times amended thereafter: cf. Brugmans's letter of 26.7.1947 from Geneva to Marc on the addition of a speech by de Rougemont, special sessions on Germany, trade unions, etc. (*UEF Archives, Paris*).

committee for Montreux' under Genet's direction. Unexpectedly, the Swiss government made a contribution to the substance of the debate: in a speech on 1 August, the national holiday, M. Petitpierre, the Federal Councillor for Foreign Affairs, followed the lead given by De Gasperi and Sforza by endorsing the idea of a federal union of Europe:

We feel more strongly than ever that our fate is bound up with that of Europe. Our country is no longer bordered by four states that counterbalance each other. Today the whole of Europe lies between two powers that are superior to it in strength. Europe's own dissensions have deprived it of the dominant position it once enjoyed in the world. If Europe, despite all its sufferings, still cannot grasp the necessity of a union based on its common civilization, it is in danger of becoming a prey to others and ceasing to be master of its own fate. Although today we no longer have to defend ourselves against an external enemy, we must in our own interest take an active part in all efforts to create this unity of Europe ... We can only hope that the federal idea will also be realized on the international plane.[306]

On its four working days from 27 to 30 August the UEF congress was attended by about 150 delegates duly accredited by member associations; on grounds of expense, and to reduce the burden of work, they had been asked to observe a limit of about twenty delegates per country; in addition there were about fifty 'observers' and journalists and, at the main public sessions, audiences of several hundred. Among the regular delegations were, for the first time, a strong Italian team comprising almost the whole founding group of the MFE, and six Germans. Altogether thirty-two associations and ten countries were represented: Austria, Belgium, Denmark, France, Germany, Great Britain, Italy, Luxemburg, the Netherlands, and Switzerland.[307] Only eight months after the founding of the UEF, the congress was a highly impressive manifestation of its international standing and intellectual level. The standard of debate was high, and once again it proved possible for representatives of different national,

---

[306] Text in *Europa. Organ der Europa-Union*, Vol. XIV, No. 10, Basle, Sept. 1947, p. 2. Ibid., No. 9 (beginning), Aug. 1947, p. 1, appeal for donations by the 'organizational committee for Montreux' of Europa-Union: 'To make possible the participation of those short of funds or representing countries lacking in foreign exchange, we shall hire army barracks and army kitchens. . . . Ten days ago the position of the German delegation, who actually have no foreign currency, was discussed in Paris, and two French organizations spontaneously offered to pay the expenses of one German each during the Congress. And are we neutral, well-fed Swiss to hang back?' Several Swiss firms, in response to this, contributed between 100 and 1,000 Swiss francs (*EU Archives, Basle,* Montreux file).

[307] At a preliminary meeting of the central committee the task of verifying credentials was entrusted to H. Schiess. The committee also laid down the procedure for election to commissions and approved a draft of statutes for the congress's consideration (Procès-Verbal de la réunion du Comité Central le 25.8.[1947] à 15.30 h. à Montreux, *CEC Archives, Geneva,* UEF file). The Italian delegation, of which A. Spinelli was again a member (cf. at n. 321), was led by Ignazio Silone; for the six Germans, cf. n. 323. In addition to the twenty-one associations represented at Amsterdam (chap. II/5, n. 190) the following were at Montreux: the German Europa-Union, Europa-Bund, and Liga für Weltregierung (World Government League) (the official membership applications of these bodies began to run from the date of the congress in accordance with the UEF Statutes), the Austrian Europa-Union, three Italian splinter groups (cf. chap. III/5, n. 416), and five new smaller French and Belgian groups (cf. at n. 339).

philosophical, party-political, and social outlook – often after lively controversy, especially in late-night committee sessions – to demonstrate their attachment to federalism by achieving unanimous agreement on resolutions of considerable import. The real achievement of the congress was that it did not weaken the federal principle but strengthened and clarified it, while answering 'Yes' to the two questions of basic policy and also formulating concrete aims for the immediate future. It gave practical application to the philosophical principles expounded by Denis de Rougement in a general talk on 'L'attitude fédéraliste', given on the eve of the congress.

Taking as his starting-point a 'concept of European man' based on the idea of a 'person' in contrast to an isolated individual, and a community of persons in contrast to the omnipotence of a totalitarian state, Rougemont put forward the following principles as applicable to the present situation of Europe. A federation can only come about if the participants renounce any form of 'organizing hegemony' and attachment to a cut-and-dried system, since 'fédérer, c'est tout simplement arranger ensemble, composer tant bien que mal ces réalités concrètes et hétéroclites que sont les nations, les régions économiques, les traditions politiques'. Federalism knew no minority problems, for it recognized every group, however small, as irreplaceable in quality or function; it loved for their own sake the immensely varied European groups that came together for their own protection. Federation was historically overdue; it would be created by uniting persons and groups, not by acts of central governments. 'Today there are two camps, two policies, two basic human attitudes. Not the "Left" or the "Right", which are nowadays scarcely distinguishable in their manifestations; not Socialism or capitalism, one aspiring to be national and the other state-directed.' The two attitudes were 'totalitarianism and federalism, a threat and a hope. This is the antithesis that dominates our age, the real drama compared to which everything else is secondary or illusory.'[308]

The proceedings of the congress can be briefly described. In the opening session on the morning of 27 August, after a speech of welcome by the Swiss, Dr Henri Brugmans, chairman of the executive bureau, delivered a 'Report on general policy' which examined with thoroughness and precision the application of federalism to immediate problems and to a large extent determined the further course of the conference. The Marshall Plan, the Soviet refusal, the remaining possibilities of European federation, its relation to the German problem and to nationalization, especially that of heavy industry – on all these points Brugmans outlined solutions which

---

[308] Speech of 26.8.1947 in Palais des Sports, Montreux, officially opening the congress: D. de Rougemont, 'L'attitude fédéraliste', first printed in *Revue économique et sociale*, Lausanne, Oct. 1947; reprinted with texts of all the main speeches, statutes, reports, and resolutions in the collective volume: Union Européenne des Fédéralistes, *Rapport du premier congrès annuel de l'U.E.F., 27–31 août 1947, Montreux*, Geneva, n.d. (Nov. 1947, 141 pp.), pp. 8–16. Dutch translation of the volume, omitting some shorter speeches: *Montreux-Inleidingen, rapporten en resoluties van het grote congres der Unie van Europese Federalisten te Montreux 26–30 augustus 1947*, Amsterdam (Keizerskroon), n.d. (end of 1947, 132 pp.), with introduction by H. Brugmans: de Rougemont's speech, pp. 6–20.

were developed in the ensuing days.[309] The debate on the report in the afternoon, at which Larmeroux took the chair and important contributions were made by Goriely, Spinelli, and others, showed that Brugmans's theses were acceptable as a basis; committees were then appointed. In the evening Professor Allais gave the first of a series of public lectures on economic problems which were continued next morning under Henry Hopkinson's chairmanship; in the afternoon Ernst von Schenk, Robert Aron, and Hans Deichmann spoke on the German question. On Friday the 29th a plenary meeting chaired by M. A. Rollier discussed reports from the legal and economic committees and the committee on Germany; after the adoption or rejection of amendments, resolutions were passed unanimously. In the evening Frances Josephy, Grégoire Gafencu, and W. B. Curry spoke on 'different Aspects of Federalism'. On the 30th, with Voisin in the chair, the finance committee's report, the statutes, and the General Policy Resolution were fully discussed and approved and a central committee was elected. In the evening a concluding ceremony took place at the Palais des Sports, with addresses by Duncan Sandys, Gordon Lang, M. Vergnolles (the mayor of Paris), Van der Leeuw (former Dutch minister of education), and Dr Brugmans.[310]

The essential aim of the congress was to produce not general declarations

---

[309] The speech, which deserves to rank among the few outstanding examples of oratory in post-war Europe, ended with the words: 'It is less than a year since the first conference of European federalists was held at Hertenstein, not far from here. We have come a tremendous way since then, and, if we all wish to do so, we can make still greater progress in the coming year. I am not going to end on a rhetorical note: I only express the hope that European federalism may emerge from this Congress more united, better equipped, more aggressive and more realistic. Pour le reste, l'avenir n'est à personne – l'avenir est à Dieu.' Printed in full in H. Brugmans, 'Positions fondamentales du fédéralisme européen'', *Revue économique et sociale*, Lausanne, Oct. 1947; also in the collective volume (n. 308), pp. 17–29; Dutch translation (n. 308), pp. 21–39; a slightly shortened version in *La Nef*, Vol. 4, No. 35, Oct. 1947, pp. 61–72; again in H. Brugmans, *Vingt ans d'Europe. Témoignages 1946–1966* (= *Cahiers de Bruges*, N.S. 16), Bruges, 1966, pp. 53–67. Extracts from the speech are given below: on nationalization, n. 317; on the Marshall Plan and the Soviet refusal, at n. 320; on the German question, at n. 324.

[310] References to the speeches and resolutions on economic and constitutional questions follow; for those on the Marshall Plan and Germany, see section (B); for finances and statutes, section (D). The proceedings of the conference are described by participants in: A. Marc/R. Silva, UEF *Lettre-Circulaire*, No. 14, Geneva, c.5.9.1947 (*GEC Archives, Geneva*); F. L. Josephy, 'Policy and Constitution. EUF delegates work hard', *Federal News*, No. 151, Oct. 1947, pp. 9–11; (H. G. Ritzel), 'Der Kongress der UEF in Montreux 27.–30.8.1947', *Europa*, Vol. xiv, No. 11, Oct. 1947, p. 2 f.; A. Voisin, 'Les Fédéralistes à Montreux', *La Fédération, Revue de l'ordre vivant*, No. 33, Oct. 1947, p. 29; R. Silva, 'Le Fédéralisme en marche', *Cahiers du monde nouveau*, 4 (1948), No. 12 (Jan.), pp. 75–84; L. van Vassenhove, 'Le Congrès de Montreux. Physionomie générale', *L'Action fédéraliste européenne*, No. 8/9, Oct./Nov. 1947, pp. 3–7; J. F. Köver, 'Der Föderalismus als Kraftquelle der politischen Entwicklung. Randbemerkungen zu den Föderalisten-Kongressen in Montreux und Gstaad', *Die Friedens-Warte*, 47 (1947), pp. 306–12 (pp. 309–11 deal with the UEF congress, but are partly misleading); D. de Rougemont, 'The Campaign of the European Congresses', *Government and Opposition*, 2 (1966/7), pp. 329–49, here pp. 334–6. Also in all autumn bulletins etc. of the member associations, esp. fully e.g. in *Il Mondo europeo*, No. 51, Rome, 15.9.1947, *Numero speciale dedicato al congresso di Montreux dei federalisti Europei*. Fairly full reports also appeared in the daily press, esp. *Le Monde, Journal de Genève*, and *Tagesspiegel*, 29.8.1947–1.9.1947.

but concrete applications of federalism to economic and social life. The Amsterdam resolutions were somewhat vague in this respect, but economic questions were vital in the distressed Europe of 1947. It was important, moreover, both for the sake of intellectual clarity and because UEF adherents were a mixture of Socialists, Christian Democrats, Liberals, and Independents, to demonstrate that old-fashioned conceptions of socio-political 'left' and 'right' were in fact irrelevant to federalism.[311] This involved a profounder formulation of the federal principle, resting in its turn on the thesis, disputed by no one at the congress, that the centralized nation state had impeded the free functioning of groups that were part of itself and also the necessary co-operation and division of labour among nations. The General Policy Resolution expressed the point thus:

> The federal idea constitutes a dynamic principle which transforms all human activities. It brings with it not only a new political framework [as between nations] but also new social, economic and cultural structures [within nations]. Federalism is a synthesis, and it is made up of two elements indissolubly linked: organic solidarity and liberty, or, put differently, the expansion of human personality in every sphere of daily life. Thus co-ordinated, liberty ceases to mean exploitation, or solidarity to be a justification for dictatorship. True democracy must be a pyramid of solidarities from bottom to top, working harmoniously at every stage. But federalism makes liberty the very principle of this organization, a principle at the same time European and of universal application, which will safeguard and promote spiritual diversity, political tolerance, the security of the individual, the free enterprise of persons and of groups, functional decentralization and self-government.[312]

The detailed application of this principle to economic and social affairs was discussed by Maurice Allais, the French economist, in his address on the first evening of the congress, which was full of substance and lasted over two hours. It is not possible here do full justice to its wealth of ideas, which found expression in the Economic Policy Resolution by way of drafts formulated by Allais and discussed exhaustively by the congress. The federal autonomy of groups, he said, required free enterprise and

---

[311] For the Amsterdam formulations, cf. chap. II/5 at n. 181. The view that the opposition of 'left' and 'right' had lost its meaning was often put forward by Spinelli, cf. chap. I/2 at nn. 42 and 43; it was reformulated at Montreux by D. de Rougemont, see at n. 308.

[312] This – in its brevity and precision the best definition of the basic principle of post-war European federalism that has so far been offered – was completed by extracts from D. de Rougemont's speech (n. 308): 'Federalism can only spring from the abandonment of any idea of organizational hegemony on the part of one of its component elements, and any insistence on a system.' To federate Europe meant to co-ordinate the multiplicity of groups while preserving the initiative of each of them, and this must be a dynamic, progressive process. The General Policy Resolution and the Economic Policy Resolution are reproduced in the collective volume: UEF, *Rapport du premier congrès* . . . (n. 308), pp. 129–36 (the above quotation, p. 132 f.). They were printed many times, e.g. in *L'Action fédéraliste européenne*, No. 8/9, Oct. /Nov. 1947, pp. 113–21; *Die Friedens-Warte*, 47 (1947), pp. 319–24, etc.; English text in *Federal News*, No. 152, Nov. 1947, and Boyd, *Western Union*, London, 1948, pp. 141–8; Dutch in translation of collective volume (n. 308), pp. 115–20 and 126–9; Italian in *Il Mondo europeo*, No. 51, Rome, 15.9.1947; German, so far only part of the Policy Resolution in *Europa-Archiv*, 6 (1951), p. 4250.

competition and the maximum 'economic decentralization for the free circulation of people, goods and capital'; federal solidarity meant the planned limitation of profits and their distribution as evenly as possible. Allais opposed a 'planisme concurrentiel' to nineteenth-century *laissez-faire* on the one hand and twentieth-century 'planisme autoritaire' on the other. He condemned the destruction of the market by state sovereignty, and spoke at length of 'economic aspects of federal union'; this required the services of outstanding economic experts, whom their countries would never part with unless there were simultaneous progress towards political union.[313] Allais's basic arguments were endorsed by Daniel Serruys, for many years a French economic minister; Europe could achieve undreamed-of prosperity only by 'creating a unified economic will' to permit the free circulation of people, goods, and capital. The trade unionist Theo Chopard, speaking on 'Syndicalisme et fédéralisme', said that federal union offered the trade unions, as a typical federal group, the best opportunity of achieving wage autonomy in agreement with employers' associations and without state intervention; they were the destined champions of European federalism, provided they remained independent of political parties which aimed at concentrating power and suppressing personality.[314]

All these ideas were embodied in the Economic Policy Resolution, which concisely expressed the federalist combination of objectives in the economic and social field. After referring to the tragic consequences of war and unrestricted national sovereignty, it ran:

Conscious ... of the great lowering of living standards resulting from the artificial barriers set up by sovereign states to the division of labour on an international level;

Conscious of the impossibility of achieving economic democracy while each state can apply the fatal principle of absolute national sovereignty,

The European Union of Federalists declares:

1. There is no effective solution for the economic and social problems which afflict Europe except the institution of an economic federation, implying the transfer

---

[313] Allais was Professeur d'économie générale at l'Ecole Nationale Supérieure des Mines de Paris and at Paris University; M. Allais, 'Aspects économique du fédéralisme', repr. in the collective volume (n. 308), pp. 33–37; in the Dutch translation (n. 308), pp. 81–114; in *L'Action fédéraliste européenne*, No. 8/9, Oct./Nov. 1947, and elsewhere. His combination of the ideas of social planning and a free economy were intended to have the effect expressed by A. Voisin: 'We confess that M. Allais's vocabulary sometimes strikes us as too Leftist and his views too reminiscent of classical liberalism. Nevertheless . . . his report aroused the enthusiasm of the congress: it offered at last a coherent set of proposals, and showed a sincere effort to get away from antiquated systems' (*La Fédération*, No. 33, Oct. 1947).

[314] D. Serruys's address, 'La circulation des richesses', and T. Chopard's, 'Syndicalisme et fédéralisme', repr. in collective volume (n. 308), pp. 58–68 and 79–91; Dutch translation (n. 308), pp. 65–80 and 45–64; Serruys's also in *L'Action fédéraliste européenne*, No. 8/9, Oct./Nov. 1947; Chopard also in *Revue économique et sociale*, Lausanne, Oct. 1947. There was not time at Montreux for a separate resolution on trade unions and federalism; a text was worked out and approved at the second UEF congress in Rome, Nov. 1948 (cf. chap. V/7, in vol. 2).

by the sovereign states of a part of their present economic powers to a federal authority;

2. Any self-sufficient or totalitarian economic organization is completely incompatible with the fundamental objectives of federalism;

3. To fit in with these objectives, an economic organization must:

(a) rest on a radical decentralization of economic power at all stages;

(b) promote the maximum division and specialization of labour and of individual and group enterprise;

(c) carry out the necessary planning, especially in the spheres of currency and credit, the organization of markets, capital and labour, insurance against unemployment, accidents while at work, sickness and old age, general and technical education, town planning, etc.;

(d) in particular, facilitate the definition of goods and services, their rationalization and agreement of their qualities, improvement in conditions of labour, collective organization of research, the diffusion of economic information, control of monopolies of whatever description, etc.;

4. Such an economic organization, based on the free and autonomous action of individuals and enterprises within the framework of a market economy, together with a planning structure which would assure a fair division of wealth and the suppression of all income not corresponding to a service, present or past, rendered to the community, brings with it the fundamental advantages of a free economy and at the same time those of concerted policy designed to achieve an economy that is more equitable and more efficient.

5. An economic federation of this type should be able, with the shortest possible delay, to promote the free circulation of goods, capital and men which is indispensable for the realization of the high standard of living which present-day technical progress makes possible.[315]

Because of existing distortions these objectives could not be realized at once, but transitional measures were necessary. These, however, 'cannot be effectively applied unless efforts are made to achieve a federation which is both economic and political'; for – and here the UEF, in August 1947, made a point which it took decades of experience to bring home to all concerned – 'it would be idle to imagine that attempts at reciprocal economic agreements between sovereign states could themselves lead to a true European federation'. The resolution went on to say that progress towards economic union required the transfer of clearly defined essential functions to a European federal authority; individual states would retain all the powers that were not expressly surrendered, 'and, in any case, all rights the exercise of which has no repercussions on the other federated

---

[315] 'Motion de politique économique' in the collective volume: UEF, *Rapport du premier congrès* . . . (n. 308), pp. 129–31; see also n. 312. The only German translation known to me is in *Europa,* Vol. xiv, No. 12, Nov. 1947, p. 2. This is clearly based on a version circulated on the last day of discussion, in twelve points instead of fourteen, and so does not include the final amendments; points 3 and 4 were not yet separately numbered but figured under 2, except for 3(d) which was added at the end of the debate; apart from this only a few clarifying additions were made.

states'. The resolution specified in detail the rights that must be transferred to the federal authority.[316]

There followed a further example of the federalists' abandonment of 'antiquated ideas'. Paragraph 12 declared that 'These principles of economic organization are compatible with a collective economy so long as that in its turn is not one which is contrary to the spirit and methods of federalism' – i.e. it must be one which does not concentrate power in the state but promotes group economic activity and autonomy. 'Experience alone can show which of the two forms of property, private or collective, is, in the present state of the political and economic evolution of the peoples, the most effective in each sphere.'[317] The Economic Policy Resolution ended with an appeal to 'all Europeans to hasten by their activities the establishment of a federation of the different states of Europe, which alone will enable that Continent to escape the destruction and economic subjection with which it is threatened and to enter a period of prosperity which will leave far behind the immense advance of the nineteenth century'.

The General Policy Resolution emphasized the variety of possible ways of beginning with the association of persons and groups in professional, economic, and cultural activities of all kinds. As the preamble declared,

The interdependence of nations has become such that it is no longer possible to confine political, economic and social realities within state frontiers. So-called sovereign states are powerless to solve their problems and, in seeking purely

---

[316] These went further than has yet been achieved in the EEC, on account of national vetoes. Paragraph 10 declared that the delegated powers 'must include:

(a) the right to regulate matters of currency;

(b) the right to make laws regarding internal trade (i.e. within the Federation) and external trade relations;

(c) the right to make laws on the question of movement of capital both inside and outside the Federation;

(d) the right to take transitional measures designed to ensure at the earliest possible moment the free circulation of federal citizens within the area of the Federation:

(e) the right to make laws dealing with movement of persons where that entails the crossing of the frontiers of the Federation (emigration and immigration);

(f) the right to regulate the conditions of the production and distribution of armaments and atomic energy, within the framework of international agreements of universal application;

(g) the right to organize communications and to fix fares and freight charges;

(h) the right to raise the taxes essential to the functioning of the Federation and for the carrying out of large public works;

(i) the right to handle all economic questions relating to associated non-self-governing overseas territories.'

[317] Brugmans in his opening speech had already made it very clear that the problem of 'nationalization' must be considered in the light of economic, social, and political aspects taken together. 'If nationalization increases productivity we are for it; if not, why should we be?' If it served to promote 'social democracy, the rediscovery of joy in labour, the sharing of responsibility for work done in common', well and good. But 'why must the state be the natural repository of power (dépositaire naturel); why not the municipality or . . . canton? . . . Nothing, we believe, has been more fatal to the workers' movement than this mania that causes us to go for national solutions as though hypnotized, to identify Socialism with Socialization and the latter with bureaucratic state administration. . . . When these "nationalizations" foster the virus of nationalism – and they often do – we must frankly say that they are reactionary' (H. Brugmans, 'Positions fondamentales . . .', n. 309, in collective volume, p. 25 f.).

national solutions, succeed only in plunging their peoples into despair, causing their citizens to lose their personal liberties, and thus creating a dangerous situation which may at any moment lead to a terrible and possibly final catastrophe.

Federalists must therefore take every opportunity to work for the autonomy and co-ordination of groups without regard to frontiers, and must 'declare firmly and without compromise that national sovereignty must be abated'.

Part of that sovereignty [the resolution added] must be entrusted to a federal authority assisted by all the functional bodies necessary to the accomplishment, on the federal plane, of its economic and cultural tasks, whether in whole or in part. In particular this authority must possess:

(a) a government responsible to the peoples and groups and not to the federated states

(b) a supreme court capable of resolving possible disputes between member states of the federation;

(c) an armed police force under its own control, whose task will be, without prejudice to a world security organization, to uphold federal decisions.

Except on these conditions, any attempts to set up unions of an exclusively economic or cultural character are doomed to failure.[318]

(B) THE DECISION TO MAKE A START WITH WESTERN EUROPE

At the beginning of his opening speech Dr Brugmans put the fundamental question arising from the change in the world political situation. He said: 'Two new developments have taken place since our Amsterdam meeting: the Marshall proposal and the collapse of the three-power conference. Are our previous ideas still tenable in the light of these facts? What should be the attitude of European federalists towards them? The second principal issue was to answer the painful and difficult question: in view of the categorical Soviet rejection, should the federalists envisage an initial union of Western Europe only, as they had so far been unwilling to do, and thus reluctantly contribute to the institutional as well as the political division of Europe? The Soviet Union had forbidden the East Europeans to take part in the movement towards unity, and would evidently oppose, as before, a similar movement confined to Western Europe. An all-European 'Third Force' was thus ruled out for the foreseeable future, while a union of Western Europe would in practice be dependent on Marshall Aid and

---

[318] 'Motion de politique générale' in collective volume: UEF, *Rapport du premier congrès* . . . (n. 308), preamble p. 132, main provisions p. 134 f. As regards examples of necessary 'functional organs' and as a step towards creating them, the congress unanimously approved the 'Rapport de la Commission juridique' presented by Prof. A. de la Pradelle: this recommended the establishment of an 'Office juridique du fédéralisme européen' in which jurists from all member states should draft proposals for the necessary federal institutions and norms ('au premier rang le statut . . . des droits de la personne': ibid., p. 120). The congress also approved D. de Rougemont's 'Rapport de la Commission d'éducation et de culture', proposing a 'Centre fédéraliste européen d'éducation et de culture' in which specialists and groups from the member countries would plan 'the development of education in a federalist sense' and the increase of cultural exchanges (ibid., p. 122 f.).

therefore on American protection. Many federalists found this unacceptable as late as the beginning of August; Leon van Vassenhove had expressed himself in this sense in the latest number of his journal, which congress members had before them.

While deploring Molotov's opposition to joint European economic planning, van Vassenhove argued that existing difficulties on the government level could not in the long run alter the will of the peoples. If the East Europeans should ever 'unequivocally let it be understood that they wished to have nothing to do with their brothers in the West, then the European federalists would have to draw a line and make a fresh start by creating Western Europe. But that day will never come. The European idea is a reality and is imperishable . . . That is why it is all-important not to accept the notion of half a Europe . . . What prevents the union of Europe at the moment is not any resistance on the part of peoples, but the unfavourable international situation. But diplomatic constellations alter; the European idea remains.'[319] Van Vassenhove's advice was thus to ignore the developments to which Brugmans had referred, to proclaim the European idea as the will of nations, and to wait in the hope that the world situation would change for the better.

Brugmans, on the other hand, pointed out in his opening speech that the federalist movement must be neither opportunistic nor utopian, but must 'take account of the facts and come to terms with reality'. The first fact to be taken account of was that the Americans, tired of pouring money into a bottomless pit, had urged the Europeans to come together – to the shame, Brugmans added, of the European governments, who 'had to be called to order from across the Atlantic before they discovered where theiry duty and interest lay'. The danger, he went on, was that either Europe would succumb to US domination or, if European discord persisted, the Americans would be disillusioned and relapse into isolationism. The only way of averting either danger was for Europeans to unite. 'Our position could be much stronger if the Russians had not forbidden the East Europeans to join in creating the European community'; but this was the second hard fact, and 'these countries today cannot pursue a foreign policy without the approval of the Soviet Union'. There was still no question, Brugmans emphasized, of forming blocs or acquiescing in separation from 'our brothers in the East', but for them too the policy he advocated was the only hope. The die was cast, and 'the first nucleus of European union must crystallize without them: without the East, but on no account against it!'

---

[319] Cf. discussion of the idea of all Europe as a 'third force', chap. II/5, pp. 380–8. L. van Vassenhove, 'Les peuples avec nous!' *L'Action fédéraliste européenne*, No. 7, Aug. 1947, pp. 3–20, above quotation p. 11 f. Thrown into despair by the fact that the original 'third force' programme had become utopian, van Vassenhove was a personal victim of the Soviet veto: his valuable periodical came to an end with issue No. 10 of Feb. 1948, and he ceases to be mentioned in UEF sources. Köver (n. 310), p. 309 f., speaks of a motion in van Vassenhove's sense being proposed but defeated in the political committee. Köver is the only author of a report on the congress who himself disagreed with its decision; from this point of view his account is partly misleading.

The UEF [he went on] will take no decisions that ignore the aspirations of Eastern Europe; it will never accept a breach that is contrary to the manifest interests of all concerned. The East Europeans will always be able to count on the UEF's full understanding, and we shall do all in our power to promote meetings, exchanges of ideas, goods and persons ... We believe that Russian Communism with its censorship, its political police and its inquisition can never be an adequate and permanent form of society for European peoples, whether of East or West. We all have, and wish to preserve, a rebellious and freedom-loving temperament, and if we were never in a position to say 'No' to government or administrative measures, to academic art or official science, then Prague, Vienna, Paris and London would be dead cities. But the fact that our fundamental structures differ from those of the Russians does not exclude respect and friendship, on our side anyway ... A good-neighbourly policy towards the USSR? Certainly! But abandonment of our European personality? Never! Consequently: 'We refuse to be the standard-bearers of an ideological anti-Soviet campaign'; but 'We must start by making federalism a reality where it is possible to do so.'[320]

In the general debate which followed, this realistic view was most firmly supported by Altiero Spinelli, who pointed out that the obstacles to European federation derived firstly from the existing relations between Europe and the two superpowers and secondly from the nationalistic attitudes of European governments. The world powers had divided Europe into spheres of influence but were now unable to 'achieve the necessary compromises'. The European governments stood 'in various relations of dependence or subjection towards them, but it can be said without exaggeration that they are all rapidly becoming puppets in the world-wide political game of the two great powers', and it was chiefly this fact which had so far 'discouraged the federalists' initiative'. It was now clear, however, that the East-European countries were 'compelled to follow prescribed courses in external and internal affairs', and that it was 'impossible in practical terms to fight for a federation embracing the whole of Europe'; the countries in the Western or American zone, on the other hand, enjoyed 'a certain freedom of action' and were, above all,

---

[320] H. Brugmans, Positions fondamentales ... (n. 309), in the collective volume, pp. 17–22. It will be recalled (cf. chap. II/7 at n. 358) that Brugmans was completely disillusioned by his second visit to Prague in July 1947; before the congress began he made a last, unsuccessful effort through the Czechoslovak legation in Berne to get permission for a Prague group to attend (information from *Brugmans*, 23.4.1964). Köver is particularly misleading in this connection. However, Brugmans went to the limits of 'good-neighbourliness' towards the Soviet Union in his anxiety that there should be nothing anti-Soviet about the congress. The UEF Archives contain a 'Message de l'autre côté du rideau de fer' addressed to the congress by a 'Comité de libération des peuples opprimés de l'U.R.S.S.' (no names given), denouncing the 'enslavement of the East-European nations', the NKVD tortures, etc. and appealing to the congress to 'be realists, not lovers of peace at any price; have the courage to adopt a resolution warning the world of the danger of Bolshevism that is engulfing Eastern Europe'. In an accompanying letter of 3.9.1947 to Silva, the Comité de libération deplore the fact that Brugmans 'chose not to communicate it [the message] to the assembly. You will not succeed in creating a European union by means of an ostrich policy, by kowtowing to the "father of all peoples" and suppressing the voice of nations enslaved by the wickedest tyrant of all ages' (*UEF Archives, Paris*, Corr., vol. 137).

democratic. 'Nothing is more painful than to recognize that the Europe of our ideals, the cradle of justice and liberty, today extends to only a portion of the Continent. Its area will certainly diminish, and European civilization will become only a memory, unless we succeed in uniting at all events the part which remains to us.'

The US wanted to 'preserve their high standard of living and productivity, and they cannot do so if the rest of the world is plunged in misery. America's policy must therefore be to open up the sealed-off, autarkic national markets, with closed economies planned on a national basis. It is in America's own interest to see Europe prosper and to promise help to European nations on condition that they manage to develop a rich, free, co-ordinated economy. This is the main object of the Marshall Plan, and it offers the European democracies an opportunity that they should seize and make the most of ... But America cannot herself create such a union, and if the European states miss their opportunity she will be more and more impelled to depart from the liberal path and adopt the imperialist alternative ... To maintain its position of strength in a Europe incapable of autonomous life, the US would have to turn each country into an economic, political and military protectorate ... A European federation, even a partial one, will possess that independence *vis-à-vis* America that the Western states can no longer achieve individually. Such a federation can further restrain and finally do away with the pernicious policy of spheres of influence ... it can gradually bring back the values and institutions of democratic civilization to those countries which have departed from them.' The decisive battle from now on was against the second obstacle, that of nationalist governments, and it was important to make clear to the public mind 'who is for a free Europe and who is against it'.[321]

The great achievement of the congress was that in the ensuing days it discussed these crucial questions exhaustively and answered them in terms of a definition of the federal principle itself. The General Policy Resolution spelt out the arguments in much more detail than the formulations proposed on the opening day, and in this form they spoke for themselves. After referring to the basic principles of autonomy and solidarity, the Resolution went on: 'A federation is a living phenomenon which grows bit by bit from the association of persons and groups. In this sense it can be said that European federation is already being slowly constituted ... Here there may be economic agreement; there a new relationship is established. Here a supranational functional organism takes shape; there a group of small countries forms a customs union [Benelux]'. Against this background

'we affirm the possibility of setting out immediately on the road to a supranational European organization. The gravity of the position in which Europe finds herself

---

[321] Speech at Montreux, 27.8.1947, printed in A. Spinelli, *Dagli stati sovrani agli stati uniti d'Europa*, Florence, 1950, pp. 230–9; cf. Spinelli's analyses of the situation in 1945/6 in chap. I/7, p. 279f.; on the significance of his reappearance as regards the reactivation of MFE, see chap. III/6, pp. 628–33. Georges Goriely referred in the general debate to the undisputed example of Spain: the undemocratic regime could not be accepted into a federation, but a resolution should acknowledge the Spanish people's desire to be free and to co-operate with Europe (Ritzel, n. 310, p. 2).

demands that a beginning shall be made towards federal organization wherever it can be attempted, wherever the people still have some liberty of action and decision, wherever public opinion can have some effect on government action. It would be a crime not to seize the opportunities offered by the present political situation to start from today building a European federation wherever such a start is possible. Not to take advantage of opportunities which present themselves is to condemn ourselves to sterile impotence, to turn our backs on reality, to betray our duty as citizens of Europe ... It is in this spirit that we approve ... the effort at *rapprochement* made by sixteen nations of the old Continent, as a result of the Marshall proposals ...'

As regards Eastern Europe, the resolution declared that 'Such a nucleus federation must remain open to all the peoples, even those who for the moment, whether for internal or external reasons, are unable to join. That is why, even if a European federation can at the beginning unite only some of the states of Europe, the European Union of Federalists will never accept as a *fait accompli* the division of Europe into two hostile blocs. To start our efforts at unification in the West of Europe means, for the West, escaping the risk of becoming the victim of power politics, restoring to Europe, at any rate partially, her pride in her legitimate independence, and holding out a hand to the peoples of the East to help them to rejoin the other peoples in a free and peaceful community.'[322] This firm but balanced statement made it possible to avoid the dangerous stagnation that would have overtaken the federalists if they had stuck fast to the Amsterdam programme in the changed situation of the summer of 1947.

Finally, like the Amsterdam meeting, the Montreux congress of the UEF passed a separate resolution on the German question. The executive bureau had taken early steps to arrange for German participation; Dr von Schenck, the member of the executive responsible for German questions, sent twenty invitations to German representatives in June; six of these were given exit visas by the occupation authorities just in time to attend the congress, in which they took full part on a footing of equality.[323]

---

[322] 'Motion de politique générale' in the collective volume: UEF, *Rapport du premier congrès* ... (n. 308), pp. 133–5; for translations and further references, cf. n. 312. The resolution further declares: 'Action in the direction of co-operation ... in that part of the European Continent where it is immediately possible does not imply – and we insist on repeating this clearly and forcefully – that we accept as final the division of Europe into two parts, which is in process of being effected. We know that it is impossible in the final event to achieve a closely knit Europe for which life is possible unless all its constituent countries, north, south, east and west, pool their complementary qualities and economies. We know, too, that the traditions and culture of each one of these peoples are part and parcel of the common European heritage. We are determined, therefore, to strive by every means in our power to maintain or to re-establish at the earliest possible moment that exchange of ideas, persons and goods without which Europe must remain divided and reduced in stature. And we affirm that only the fundamental principles of federalism, implying recognition and respect for diversity and for liberty, will allow each country and each people to attain to a political and social expression satisfactory to its structure, to its way of life and thought, to its traditions and to its needs.'

[323] For the Amsterdam resolution on Germany, cf. chap. II/5 at n. 186 f.; for E. von Schenck's invitation of twenty delegates during his important tour of Germany and the German associations in June, cf. chap. III/6, p. 650 f. The six who came to Montreux were: Dr Hans Deichmann, Dornholzhausen/Obertaunus; Karl Gerold, editor of the *Frankfurter Rundschau*; Wilhelm Hermes,

Brugmans in his opening speech made two points about Germany: (1) the right course was not to 'federalize' German industrial potential but to create 'autonomous European authorities' (*régies*) for the coal and heavy industry of the whole of north-western Europe, and (2) an end should be put to the absurd exclusion of Germans from European cultural contacts.[324] In a debate on Germany on 28 August Ernst von Schenck briefly described the devastation of the country, psychological as well as physical, and the general discouragement that prevailed; Robert Aron gave a moving account of the disappointments of the thirty-year-old generation, to whom only the creation of a European community could give a new purpose in life; Hans Deichman, on behalf of the German delegates, spoke of the despair and remorse of his fellow-countrymen and declared that their only hope for the future lay in the European movement and the help and sympathy of European federalists.[325] Next afternoon the congress discussed and adopted with slight modifications a draft Resolution on the German Question prepared by the German delegates and experts of other nationalities. This was a thoughtfully worded document of a kind that was still quite unusual in mid-1947, dealing with the application of federal principles to Germany and combining immediate recommendations with long-term solutions. It declared that if the occupation policy only turned the occupation zones more and more into military and strategic protectorates of the world powers it would be impossible to create a European federation, which alone offered 'the necessary security against another European war'.

'Such a federation must include a restored Germany which, like all other European nations, must permanently surrender a large part of its sovereignty.' Only a European federation could ensure the effective neutralization of Germany and bring about a satisfactory solution of 'the frontier problems that have arisen as a result of Germany's aggression and capitulation'. The German economy must be rebuilt as soon as possible; but an all-European economic organization was a necessary guarantee of German and European recovery. The resolution declared that 'the organic reconstruction of German social, cultural, economic and political life' should be promoted 'within a system of self-government built up from below',

---

Mönchengladbach; Wilhelm Kasting, Berlin-Pankow; Obermedizinalrat Dr Pitsch, Freiburg i. Br.; Konsul a.D. J. Stocky, Köln-Lindenthal; cf. Köver (n. 310), p. 310; information from *von Schenck*, 23.8.1961 (Hermes arrived only on the last day of the congress); information from Schinzinger, 7.8.1954 (Pitsch took his place as representative of the Europa-Bund).

[324] H. Brugmans, 'Positions fondamentales . . .' (n. 309), in the collective volume, p. 27 f.: 'Innumerable Germans, imbued with European culture and goodwill towards Europe, have been waiting in vain for regular contact with the intellectual life of the outside world. Not only should this contact no longer be prevented, but it should be encouraged and organized in a systematic and clear-sighted way, under the direction and supervision of a competent body. What is called the re-education of Germany is not a privilege of the victors or the occupying powers or a burden imposed on them; it is a responsibility of the whole European and human community.'

[325] Best account of the three speeches in Ritzel (n. 310), p. 2; Aron and Deichmann also in van Vassenhove (n. 310),p. 5 f. Dr Hans Deichmann, member of a German wartime Resistance group, at this time belonged to the Hesse *Land* association of Europa-Union and was a protégé of von Schenck (information from *von Schenck*, 23.8.1961).

and that 'the German people must no longer be isolated from world-wide, and especially European, cultural forces and spiritual movements'. Finally the basic decision of the congress, that a beginning should be made in Western Europe, was logically applied to Germany: 'As long as it remains impossible to include all Germany in a European federation, at least those parts of the country that are able to do so should be allowed to join in a federation of free peoples', as a 'first step towards the integration of Germany as a whole into a united Europe'.[326]

This application of the federal principle to the German problem was fully in accordance with the ideas that had been worked out by the Resistance movements. The General Policy Resolution added a specific proposal in line with its thesis that federation should be a spontaneous process based on the integration of groups and local entities. 'The Saar and the Ruhr should be centres of economic co-operation undertaken for the benefit of all Europeans, and progressively extended to include all European resources and means of production. Thus, day by day, an effort could be made to put an end to the arbitrary divisions which obstruct the amelioration of the countries of our Continent ...' As Brugmans rightly observed in a subsequent review of the Montreux congress, 'This was a high point, perhaps *the* high point, in the history of the UEF. If we read the texts we really find in them everything that has since taken place in Europe, ... including several practical proposals like those which came to be embodied in the Schuman Plan.'[327]

(C) THE WORLD FEDERALISTS' CONGRESS AT MONTREUX

Finally, the UEF spelt out its views once again on the application of federal principles beyond Europe and the place of a federated Europe in the world. This was the more appropriate as all the leading members of UEF and many of the other delegates had just taken part in the Congress of the Movement for World Federal Government (MWFG), held at Montreux from 17 to 24 August. It will be recalled that since the Luxemburg conference of 1946, at which the MWFG was set up, most of the member associations of UEF had joined the movement for world federation, believ-

---

[326] 'Motion sur la question allemande' in the collective volume: UEF, *Rapport du premier congrès*... (n. 308), p. 127 f.; Dutch translation of the volume (n. 308), pp. 121–3; Italian version in *Il Mondo europeo*, No. 51, Rome, 15.9.1947; German in *Die Friedens-Warte*, 47 (1947), p. 318 f.; also in *Europa. Mitteilungsblatt des Europa-Bundes* (ed. Theo Merten), No. 2, Oct. 1947, p. 2 f., and in *Propaganda- und Informationsdienst der Europa-Union*, ed. by Propaganda Dept., Hagen-Haspe, Nov. 1947, p. 3. At the suggestion of the Dutch delegation it was agreed at Montreux to hold a 'representative working meeting' on the German question in Germany itself, so that the problem could be 'thoroughly discussed with the participation of those most interested' (quoted in *Mitteilungsblatt des Europa-Bundes*, No. 2, Oct. 1947, p. 1). This decision was the nucleus of the 'UEF meeting on Germany' at Homburg in May 1948: cf. details in chap. V/4 (in vol. 2).

[327] 'Motion de politique générale' in the collective volume, p. 134; H. Brugmans, 'Het begin van een beweging', *Europa in Beweging*, The Hague (BEF), 1968, p. 17. For the election of three Germans to the central committee of the UEF, cf. section (D) below, at n. 340. That section contains our critical assessment of the congress as a whole.

ing as they did that a federal world government was the ultimate solution to the problem of world peace. Their disagreement with the US secretary-general of MWFG, Tom O. Griessemer, and the Swiss Dr Max Habicht, who held that regional federations were on the whole an obstacle to world federation, was incompletely recognized in the final resolution passed at Luxemburg, which said that 'Many of us advocate, as a step towards [world federal government], the formation of Regional Federal Unions, and in particular the United States of Europe.'[328] Pending clarification of this issue at the world federalists' congress, which was also set for August 1947 in Switzerland, most of the European associations, including Federal Union in Britain, had not contributed financially to Griessemer's umbrella organization but only to the UEF.[329] They hoped at Montreux to secure fuller recognition of their view that regional and world federation should complement each other.

The US associations for world federation held a congress in February 1947 at Asheville, North Carolina, at which six of them merged to form the group of United World Federalists, henceforth the largest. The 327 delegates did not discuss the question of regional versus world federation, but debated chiefly whether they should aim at reforming the UN or bypassing it and working for the convocation of a world constituent assembly. The relevant passage in their final declaration ran (in retranslation): 'We shall work, first and foremost, to turn the UN into a world government with powers which, while limited, are sufficient to prevent war – a world government exercising direct powers over individuals in matters within its competence.'[330]

The MWFG congress at Montreux, attended by about 300 delegates, spent five days in debating a confused miscellany of statements and opinions, but was able to adopt a unanimous resolution on 23/24 August. The Americans sent a sizeable delegation, which spoke mainly in the sense of the Asheville statement. A few delegates came from Canada, New Zealand, South Africa, Palestine, Turkey, and Scandinavia, but the most numerous were naturally the West Europeans; they included at least 100

---

[328] Cf. account of the Luxemburg conference in chap. II/2, especially Miss Josephy at n. 56 and concluding resolution at n. 57. We may quote again the formulation of the standpoint of the founders of UEF: 'We see world federation as the crown of regional organizations. . . . We wish to create a united Europe that is ready to enter a world federation. . . . What we do not intend to do is to give up the idea of a federal Europe if world federation is delayed' (van Vassenhove, Jan. 1947; see above, chap. II, n. 163).

[329] Cf. Ritzel, 25.1.1947, to Tom Griessemer, New York: the managing committee of the Swiss Europa-Union had agreed in principle to join the World Federalist Association but pointed out that there could hardly be any question of paying a subscription, as they intended to contribute to the European secretariat (*EU Archives, Basle*, World Federation documents). In reply to Griessemer's complaint that 'some organizations were giving money to the European and not to the World movement', Federal Union decided 'that this could not be done until the £250 for the European Union had been obtained' (*Federal Union Archives*, Meeting of the Executive Committee, 28.2.1947 and 28.3.1947, p. 3 in each case).

[330] Cf. Weltstaatliga (Munich), Circular No. 2, July 1947. A convenient introduction to the chief writings and trends of the American world federalist movement is in E. Senghaas-Knobloch, *Frieden durch Integration und Assoziation* (= *Studien zur Friedensforschung Bd. 2*), Stuttgart, 1969, pp. 26–45.

students, chiefly from France and the Netherlands. After lengthy discussion of the statutes of the umbrella organization[331] there followed a general debate, in which little sign of basic agreement appeared by 23 August. The Asheville consensus in favour of reforming the UN was opposed by a large British group, which put forward the 'Usborne plan' worked out in July by Henry Usborne and ten other Labour MPs. This stated that: 'The existing organization of the United Nations, under the terms of its Charter, appears unable to make this change in time to prevent war ... since the Charter makes such amendments impossible without unanimous Great-Power assent. It seems, therefore, that another World Organization to replace UNO must speedily be created which has the necessary powers.' For this purpose, in all countries where it was possible, arrangements should be made to hold unofficial elections in the summer of 1950, on the basis of one representative per million inhabitants, for a 'People's World Constituent Assembly' which should set to work in Geneva in the autumn of 1950 to draft a World Charter.[332] Besides this plan, which went into much detail as regards the organization of voting etc., other proposals for action were submitted by twenty-six speakers. The Resolutions Committee under the chairmanship of Edith Wynner put forward a draft by Victor Collins MP, in the sense of the Usborne plan, which was sharply criticized. Its opponents then met under Miss Josephy's chairmanship and, with Collins's help, produced a draft which was adopted with surprising unanimity as the 'Montreux declaration' of 23 August. It offered a judicious blend of realism and idealism, clear definition of principles, and balanced recommendations as to various courses of action; above all, however, it endorsed the UEF view that regional federations were to be welcomed as intermediate stages.

---

[331] Accounts of the congress in: *AEP-Information No. 2075: Die Ergebnisse des ersten Weltföderalisten-Kongresses*, Paris, 26.8.1947 (three hectographed pages); J. K. Killby, 'World Federalists Confer', *Federal News*, No. 151, Oct. 1947, pp. 2–8; L. van Vassenhove, 'A Montreux: Le Mouvement universel pour un gouvernement fédéral mondial', *L'Action fédéraliste européenne*, No. 8/9, Oct./Nov. 1947, p. 8; Köver (n. 310), here p. 311 f.; F. L. Josephy, 'La Conférence de Montreux', *Cahiers du monde nouveau*, Vol. 4, No. 1, Jan. 1948, pp. 85–8. In telegrams welcoming the congress, Ernest Bevin once again applauded 'the idea of a World Government' and Albert Einstein emphasized its necessity for the purpose of controlling atomic energy; four members of the Soviet Academy of Sciences retorted that the idea of world government was altogether reactionary at a time when capitalism and Socialism stood in opposition to each other (*New York Herald Tribune*, 20.8.1947; *Tagesspiegel*, 20.8.1947 and 26.8.1947; *Wiesbadener Kurier*, 26.11.1947; DPD, 1.12.1947).

[332] Text of the 'Usborne plan' as submitted to the congress in *Federal News*, No. 149, Aug. 1947, pp. 1–5; the world constituent assembly was to draft by the summer of 1951 a constitution for a world federal government with exclusive authority over armed forces, atomic energy, peace-keeping, and a world bank. One of the proposed articles ran: 'When 50 per cent of the nations of the world, representing 50 per cent of the peoples of the world, have ratified this Charter, the Legislative Authority described herein shall be set up.' For: 'We cannot wait to set up World Government, under the provisions described in its Charter, until *all* the nations have ratified. If we were to do that we would be perpetuating a veto.' The idea was thus clearly to avoid the Soviet veto by beginning with a 'world' government limited to a region.

The declaration stated that 'the UN as at present constituted is incapable of preventing the rush towards war. We world federalists are convinced that the creation of a federal world government is the key problem of our time ... The choice is not between a free and a planned economy or between capitalism and Communism, but between federalism and imperialism.' The principles of agreement must be: '1. Universal membership. The Confederation must be open to all peoples and nations. 2. Limitation of national sovereignty and transfer to the Confederation of the legislative, executive and judicial powers necessary to world government. 3. Direct enforcement of law upon individuals, whoever and wherever they may be, within the limits of federal authority; guarantee of the rights of man, and repression of all attempts against the security of the Confederation.' This was a clear statement defining the limits of the necessary powers. Among the necessary means were also enumerated: sole control by the Confederation of (4.) armed forces and (5.) atomic energy, and (6.) direct taxation for federal purposes. Endorsing the UEF viewpoint, the declaration stated that the formation of regional bodies was compatible with the ultimate aim. 'Regional unions, provided they are not an end in themselves and do not tend to develop into rigid blocs, can and should contribute to the proper working of the Confederation.' Recommended action included persuading governments and parliaments 'to turn the UN into a world Confederation', and also working to bring about a world constituent assembly.[333]

Thus the world federalists' congress did in the end achieve significant results. All the associations agreed on a clear-cut declaration; the Europeans recognized, as the UEF later expressed it, that a world confederation was the final objective, and the non-Europeans accepted the idea of regional federations as stages towards, and organic components of, a future world government. In contrast to the dissension at Luxemburg the two groups were now in agreement, with the European federalists clearly in the ascendant. The position was reflected in the concluding election of officers of the MWFG, which took place on a democratic basis in accordance with its statutes. Of a Council of thirty-one members, more than half were European federalists and eleven were also members of the UEF Central Committee; the Europeans included Jean Larmeroux, who was elected chairman of the Council by a large majority. Out of nine members of the smaller Executive Bureau of MWFG, six were also members of the UEF Central Committee.[334] Although this proportion could not be maintained

---

[333] The clearest account of the debates is in Killby (n. 331), pp. 5–7, and Josephy (n. 331), p. 86. French text of the 'Déclaration de Montreux' in Josephy, p. 86 f., and *L'Action fédéraliste européenne*, Nos. 8/9, Oct./Nov. 1947, p. 122 f.; German in *Die Friedens-Warte*, 47 (1947), p. 317 f.

[334] List of members of Council as given by Killby (n. 331), p. 8; those who belonged to the Executive Bureau are marked with an asterisk; those who also belonged to the Central Committee of the UEF (see list at n. 339) are in italics: *Jean Larmeroux* (chairman), Ota Adler, M. Astier, *Dr H. Brugmans, *Jean Buchmann,* Fred Carney, *Edward T. Clark (vice-chairman), Victor Collins, Ugo Damiani (vice-chairman, member of parliament), Prof. G. Gabbrielli, *Henri Genet*, T. O. Griessemer, *Miss F. L. Josephy*, *H. Koch, *Revd. Gordon Lang* MP (chairman of executive), Prof. Reginald Lang, *Philip Lessermann, *Alexandre Marc*, *Dr H. R. Nord*, *T. Hatt Olsen*, Santi Paladino, *Abbé H. Groués-Pierre (member of parliament), Emery Reves, Mrs Sangiorgi, Lt.-Col. Sarrazac-

in the congresses of subsequent years, there was no rivalry after Montreux between the two organizations. The MWFG regularly congratulated the UEF on its successes; its own prospects of being a significant force in politics were in any case remote in view of the collapse of the 'one world' principle between 1945 and 1947.

In Britain, Federal Union provided an example on a smaller scale of harmonious co-operation between global and European federalists. Its first large meeting after Montreux was held in Hampstead Town Hall on 6 October 1947, with C. E. M. Joad in the chair and over 400 people present; Victor Collins, Hopkinson, and Miss Josephy gave complementary talks on the theme of 'One Europe – One World'. On 2 November the National Council drew up a 'Statement on the Expansion of Policy' which began with the words: 'The general principle to be borne in mind is the need to abate national sovereignty.' It urged that this be put into effect at all possible levels: 'recruitment and control by the Security Council of a supranational force'; 'creation of an Atomic Development Authority'; 'to transform the U.N. General Assembly from a delegate into an elected body'; 'to strengthen and give executive power to all the functional organs of UNO' (sc. the FAO, ILO, etc.). In addition it proclaimed support for regional federations 'calculated to reduce the number of sovereign states ... Such surrenders of sovereignty by individual nations provide both an example to others and practical experience in the functioning of supranational government.'[335]

On 30 August, a week after the MWFG resolution was adopted at Montreux, the UEF congress in its turn expressed a considered view, in its General Policy Resolution, of the application of federal principles on a world scale. It declared that: 'From the very beginning the cause of European Federation has deliberately been set within a world perspective.' Recognizing that *rapprochement* between the continents needed to be developed, the resolution went on: 'That is why from now on we are determined to fight for the establishment of world organizations capable of averting disaster and of establishing world peace.' World peace could only be secured, and a world dictatorship prevented, by 'federalism everywhere,

---

Soularge, M. Schroeder, *Henry Usborne MP, Carlo Vergani, Miss M. M. Wingate, Harris Wofford, Miss Edith Wynner.

[335] *Josephy Archives*, Report J, p. 56, on the meeting of 6.10.1947; text of statement of 2.11.1947 in *Federal News*, No. 153, Dec. 1947, p. 9 f. The 'Second World Congress of the World Movement for Federal World Government' (2. Weltkongress der Weltbewegung für föderative Weltregierung) (Luxemburg, 5–10.8.1948; report in *Münchner Merkur*, 22.9.1948) and the Third ditto (Stockholm, 28.8.1949–4.9.1949; cf. pamphlet, *Weltprobleme und ihre Lösung. Eine Zusammenfassung der wichtigsten Dokumente und Resolutionen des 3. Weltkongresses der Weltbewegung für föderative Weltregierung . . .*, Deutscher Zentralausschuss für Weltregierung, Cologne, n.d.) confirmed the approval of regional federations, the Third Congress with the words: 'It is clear that all actions designed to limit national sovereignty must be supported by world federalists' (ibid., p. 15). However, the intensification of the Korean war made the 'World Constituent Assembly' of 1950 a fiasco: cf. *New York Times*, 6.1.1951. The regional principle was again firmly endorsed at the Fifth Congress in Copenhagen, Aug. 1953: cf. *Europa-Archiv*, 8, 1953, p. 6070. There will not be any further occasion to trace the fortunes of the world movement, which was doomed to failure as long as the continents remained at such different stages of development and the Soviet Union continued to be what it was.

federalism on every plane and at every stage of human society from the bottom to the top'. More fully:

The aim of federalism is to establish a World Federal Government. That aim will be reached only by simultaneously organizing on all planes: inside each country, between neighbouring peoples, between nations of the same continent, between regional federations – in such a way as never to lose sight of the objective of the free co-ordination of the parts in the diversity and harmony of the whole. That is to say, we no more want a hermetically sealed Europe than a divided Europe. Our motto is and remains: One Europe in One World.[336]

(D) POSITION OF THE UEF AFTER MONTREUX

The UEF congress from 27 to 30 August 1947 was an impressive demonstration that within nine months of its creation the umbrella association of European federalists had achieved a stable organizational basis and had developed its doctrine to an important extent. The chief results of the congress, and the key questions arising out of it, were:

1. As regards structure, the congress confirmed and strengthened the federal arrangements that had governed the organization from the beginning and were contested by none of its member associations. The statutes, which were the fruit of six months' deliberation, were approved unanimously after a single hour of concentrated debate on 30 August, instead of taking up three days of discussion like those of the world federalists. Article 1 defined the UEF as the umbrella association of all organizations which shared the objectives 'laid down in the federalist declarations of Hertenstein and Luxemburg and the Amsterdam and Montreux resolutions'. The chief provisions of Article 2, concerning the functions of the UEF, have been cited in our account of the Amsterdam proceedings, including the happy formulation of the relationship between the umbrella association and its members, based on solidarity and 'subsidiarity'.[337]

---

[336] 'Motion de politique générale' in the collective volume, p. 135; cf. point 14 of the economic resolution: 'The extension of the application of the above principles to a wider field than European federation is eminently to be desired.' Two weeks later, Brugmans wrote in his private 'Bilan de l'U.E.F.' that it was difficult 'to make proper use of our victory over the world federalists' (12.9.1947, *Brugmans Archives*). In a letter to the present author (in German) he explained this as follows: 'The "victory" consisted in the fact that we had secured the principle of a "world confederation of regional federations" and also a pro-European majority on the Executive. But the victory was no use because we had too few forces to make use of it; the world federalist movements were utopian as far as most of their members were concerned, and co-operation with Churchill at The Hague was practically incompatible with world federalist ideas' (information from *Brugmans*, 15.3.1966).

[337] Cf. chap. II/5 before n. 189, where points (1) to (3) of Art. 2 will be found. Further tasks were enumerated as follows: '(4) to enlist the co-operation of all personalities whose intellectual influence or specialized knowledge may enable them to help the federal idea to victory; (5) to represent European federalists in newly created representative world organizations; (6) to support, as appropriate, the efforts of national federalist movements to organize federalist structures in their own countries; (7) to develop federalist activity and propaganda especially by creating federalist documentation centres and supranational study-groups and by promoting the formation of national co-ordinating committees.'

Articles 3–5 provided that the UEF would have its headquarters at Geneva, that it was established for an indefinite time, and that its scope extended to the whole of Europe. Articles 6–11 contained liberal provisions concerning membership and withdrawal from the association. Articles 12–25 described the general assembly (congress) as the policy-making body, the managing functions of the central committee and executive, and the secretariat; all these were to be organized on a democratic basis with due respect to the wishes formulated by member associations. Finally, Articles 26–30 contained lucid provisions for the administration of property.[338] Elections to the Central Committee at Montreux revealed a high degree of unanimity and brought about a more balanced membership, especially as regards German and Italian participation. An alphabetical list of the thirty members also shows the twenty-one principal member associations:

Adler (Ota)	Federal Union	Great Britain
Brugmans (Henri)	Europeesche Actie	Netherlands
Buchmann (Jean)	Rassemblement fédéraliste	Belgium
Genet (Henri), chairman 1947	Union Européenne (Europa-Union)	Switzerland
Gérard (Francis)	Comité pour une Fédération Européenne et Mondiale	France
Ghinst (J. van der)	Institut d'Économie Européenne	Belgium
Hermes (Wilhelm)	Europa-Union	Germany
Hopkinson (Henry L.)	Federal Union	Great Britain
Hytte (Claude-Marcel)	Cercles socialistes, fédéralistes, et communautaires	France
Josephy (F.L.)	Federal Union	Great Britain
Kasting (Wilhelm)	Pan-Europa-Bund	Germany
Koch (Henri)	Union fédérale	Luxemburg
Kogon (Eugen)	Europa-Bund	Germany
Lang (Revd. Gordon)	Federalist Group of the House of Commons	Great Britain
Larmeroux (Jean)	États-Unis du Monde	France
Lewandowski (Rudolf)	Europa-Union	Austria
McDermot (Niall)	New Europe Group	Great Britain
Marc (Alexandre)	La Fédération	France
Milo di Villagrazia (A.)	Associazione Federalista Europea	Italy
Nord (Hans R.)	Europeesche Actie	Netherlands
Olsen (Thomas Hatt)	En Verden	Denmark

[338] Full text of Statutes in UEF; *Rapport du premier congrès* . . . (n. 308), pp. 113–19. These carefully thought-out Statutes functioned for a decade without friction. Their lucid, democratic formulation within the first months of the UEF's existence contrasts favourably with the unintended delay of the corresponding process in the early history of the umbrella European Movement (cf. chap. VI/2, in vol. 2).

Limitation to Western Europe

Rifflet (Raymond)	Cahiers Socialistes	Belgium
Rossi (Ernesto)	Movimento Federalista Europeo	Italy
Schenck (Ernst von)	Europa-Union	Switzerland
Schiess (Henri)	Europa-Union	Switzerland
Silone (Ignazio)	Movimento Federalista Europeo	Italy
Silva (Raymond)	Europa-Union	Switzerland
Usellini (Guglielmo)	Movimento Federalista Europeo	Italy
Verkade (Wilhelm)	Europeesche Actie	Netherlands
Voisin (Andre)	La Fédération	France

Altogether this represented an international assemblage of intellect and talent devoted to federalism that could not have been matched anywhere in Western Europe in 1947.[339] It was significant that in addition to 5 members each from France and Britain, 4 from Switzerland, and 3 each from Belgium and Holland, there were now for the first time 4 Italians (those newly elected being three of the ablest members of the old MFE who did not belong to the Campagnolo group) and 3 Germans: Hermes, chairman of Europa-Union, Kasting (precisely because the UEF leaders knew of his close relations with Soviet military government), and, at the special instance of von Schenck, Dr Eugen Kogon, who was not actually present at Montreux, for the Europa-Bund. This was probably the first occasion since the war on which Germans were elected to the governing body of an international association.[340] The new Central Committee held its first meeting at Montreux on 31 August and unanimously chose an executive bureau from among its members; Brugmans retained the office of chairman, Silva was confirmed as the new secretary-general, and the membership was completed by a leading Italian representative. Thus the executive consisted of:

---

[339] UEF, *Rapport du premier congrès* . . . (n. 308), p. 111; cf. list of the twenty-one CC members elected at Amsterdam, chap. II/5 at n. 190. One British, French, Belgian, and Dutch member was replaced by a compatriot in each case; of these, Voisin and Lang were particularly valuable for their qualities of leadership. For personal details, see Index. H. Genet remained chairman for 1947: A wish to hold the 1948 congress in Italy was expressed, and the Italian delegation undertook to reply within two months. The answer was 'Yes', whereupon the well-known writer and Socialist deputy Ignazio Silone became chairman for 1948 (cf. also Procès-Verbal de la Réunion, first session of the newly elected CC, with twenty-five members present, Montreux, 31.8.1947, *DGAP Archives*, E 791.71, p. 2).

[340] For the significance of the reappearance of leaders of the old MFE, cf. chap. III/6, p. 629. Kasting, who 'maintained too close relations with the Russians for our taste' (information from *Verkade*, 2.9.1954; cf. his statement at Montreux, chap. II, n. 223), was not allowed by the Russians to attend any further session of the CC. Kogon, editor of *Frankfurter Hefte* and, through the USE-Liga, now a member of the Europa-Bund (cf. chap. II/6, n. 246), had been visited shortly before by von Schenck, who persuaded him to take a leading part among the German federalists (information from *von Schenck*, 23.8.1961; cf. details in chap. III/6, n. 474), At the CC session on 31.8.1947 Hermes 'thanked the UEF on behalf of the German delegation for the honour conferred on him and the other Germans by their election to the Central Committee and treatment on an equal footing with all other members' (Procès-Verbal . . . , n. 339, p. 2).

Chairman and delegate for East-European countries   Dr. H. Brugmans
Secretary-General   R. Silva
Director of the Institutional Department   A. Marc
Deputy Secretary-General   H. Koch
Delegate for English-speaking countries   F. L. Josephy
Delegate for German-speaking countries   Dr E. von Schenck
Delegate for Romance-language countries   G. Usellini

In the next fourteen months the work of the UEF was chiefly carried forward by this steering group.[341] As regards finances, instead of the provisional system by which a proportion of a fixed sum was assessed upon each country, the Montreux congress unanimously adopted a graduated system based on the size of member associations. In each financial year (beginning on 1 July) each association with up to 2,000 members paid a sum equal to the number of members multiplied by the average national wage for a quarter of an hour's work, according to the ILO table (thus eliminating disparities due to the actual purchasing power of currencies, the level of real wages, etc.). For larger associations this sum was progressively reduced: by a third if the membership was between 2,000 and 50,000, by two-thirds up to a membership of 100,000, and by nine-tenths if the membership exceeded that figure. In this way every association had an incentive to increase its membership and thus have a greater proportion of its funds available for further recruitment in its own country; at the same time, the finances of the UEF were placed on a solid footing.[342]

---

[341] Unanimous election of Executive Bureau in Procès-Verbal (n. 339), p. 1; result also announced in *Lettre-Circulaire*, No. 14, c.5.9.1947 (*CEC Archives, Geneva*, UEF documents); this circular also asked for the scripts of Montreux speeches so that they could be printed. *Lettre-Circulaire*, No. 15, Geneva, n.d. (c.10 Oct. 1947), stated that the *Rapport du premier congrès* . . . (n. 308) would be issued on 15.11.1947. It also drew attention to the special number of *Cahiers du monde nouveau*, just published under the title *La Bataille de la paix*, with contributions from all the UEF leaders; and addressed a questionnaire to all member associations for information concerning present addresses, lists of officers, etc. When these were received, c.Feb. 1948, the propaganda booklet which had been in preparation since April (first hectographed version, *Fédérer les Fédéralistes*, cf. chap. II/5, n. 174) was printed in a large edition: Union Européenne des Fédéralistes, Geneva, n.d. (c.Feb. 1948, twenty pages, copies in all Archives). Pp. 1–3 gave a short history of the UEF from Hertenstein to Montreux; pp. 4–9 the Montreux resolutions on general policy and economics, the former abridged; pp. 10–15 lists of member associations and committees (drawn upon in the following accounts for the respective countries), pp. 16–20 a programme summary under the heading 'Freedom – Welfare – Peace', with the motto: 'Aucune solution ne peut plus être trouvée dans le cadre national.'

[342] For the previous temporary system, cf. chap. II/5, nn. 165 and 191. 'Rapport de la Commission financière' in UEF, *Rapport du premier congrès* . . . (n. 308), pp. 124–6. It gave as an example: 'Let us take a Swiss member association. The average hourly wage in Switzerland is about 2 frs., or 50 c. for a quarter-hour. A Swiss association of under 200 members pays the minimum, i.e. 100 frs. per annum. An association of 2,000 members pays 1,000 frs.; one of 20,000 pays 7,000 frs.; one of 50,000 pays 17,000 frs.; and one of 100,000 pays 30,000 frs. Above 100,000 the rate per member is 5 centimes.' The unanimous adoption of the proposal is noted by Silva at the CC session of 31.8.1947, Procès-Verbal (n. 339), p. 3; this also records the acceptance of the finance committee's report for the past half-year, and appointment for the coming year of a committee consisting of Formiggini

Now that the organizational basis had been firmly laid, the increase of membership was indeed the main objective, since it alone could place the association on the map and give it a voice in practical politics. The leaders of the Resistance and of the resultant federalist movements believed that the 'peoples' wanted a federated Europe and a thorough reform of society on federal lines: 'Les peuples avec nous'; their hopes therefore centred on grass-roots mobilization and the rapid development of a democratic mass movement. The question was whether and how this could be achieved. Denis de Rougemont estimates that at the time of the Montreux congress the total membership of associations under the UEF umbrella was something over 100,000, which more or less tallies with our information regarding each association. This was a respectable figure, but not a politically impressive one when divided among eight countries. At the Central Committee meeting on 31 August 'Hopkinson mentioned Ireland, Iceland, Greece and Portugal as other countries where movements might be brought into being'; but Silva underlined the 'prime necessity of working hard to enlarge the associations of which the UEF is composed'.[343]

Considering ways and means, Brugmans drew up for his own use, twelve days later, a 'Bilan de l'U.E.F.' in which he noted as obstacles: 'A conspiracy of silence concerning the UEF in the major newspapers and among the general public of several countries ... There is a shortage of fully reliable, intelligent collaborators who are devoted to the idea of federalism, ... a lack of certainty as to the immediate programme.' As remedies he envisaged: 'Large public meetings to be organized at once' in all large cities; 'co-operation with professional bodies with the object of promoting federalist solutions, e.g. in trade unions, co-operatives, churches, universities ... Concentrate our efforts on about a dozen European cities and country areas so as to turn these into citadels and centres of a "Stakhanovite movement for Europe." '[344] In any case, now that policy and organization had been firmly settled, the great objective was to create a mass movement. Meanwhile, as Brugmans rightly noted on the credit side:

2. 'European federalism possesses a doctrine of its own.'[345] The speeches and committee reports and the three long resolutions of the Montreux

---

(Italy), Ravey (Switzerland), and Monnier (France). Eight weeks after Montreux, Brugmans pointed out in *Lettre-Circulaire,* No. 16, Geneva, 27.10.1947, that so far only the Italian MFE had sent its contribution (*CEC Archives, Geneva*); others followed, however, and the financial situation became stable.

[343] D. de Rougemont, 'The Campaign . . .' (n. 310), p. 338; Procès-Verbal (n. 339), p. 1. The CC at this session did not produce any recipe for action, apart from Voisin's advice that 'links between national associations should be strengthened, perhaps even to the point of a merger [in each country]: this would make recruitment easier and prevent the confusion of public opinion that arises when too many groups are pursuing the same object' (ibid., p. 2).

[344] H. Brugmans, 12.9.1947, 'Bilan de l'U.E.F.' (*Brugmans Archives*). After the sentence quoted above, the note concluded with the words: 'There must be an uninterrupted campaign with constant harassment of governments by petitions, resolutions, etc.' – which presupposed that a mass movement already existed. Cf. the discussion of methods under point 2 above.

[345] Brugmans's 'Bilan de l'U.E.F.', 12.9.1947 (*Brugmans Archives*, two typed pages) listed on the credit side: '1. All federalist movements are organically united. 2. European federalism possesses a

congress amounted to a comprehensive exposition of federalist ideas. A close examination of non-federalist European movements such as the UEM and the ELEC showed that their answers to the most urgent political and economic problems consisted in pragmatic suggestions for improved inter-state co-operation, customs union, the reduction of economic barriers, etc.; they did not see these problems as a symptom of the crisis of nationalism and the need for a radical reform of social structures. By contrast, the UEF had evolved a cogent, unified theory of federalism which took account of wartime experience and the post-war crisis in all spheres of life and proposed systematic reforms of a constitutional and socio-political kind. Starting from a definition, rooted in Christian and Socialist tradition, of the natural relationship between the individual and society, and combining the views of all its member associations in a manner accepted by all, the UEF offered a diagnosis of the universal crisis and the political and social reforms by which it could be overcome. The General Policy Resolution was based on strict formulations of federalist doctrine, but its conclusions were by no means doctrinaire or isolationist, perfectionist or sectarian; they provided concrete, realistic, and evolutionary answers to the crucial political problems of Europe, the East–West conflict, nationalization, the German question, etc. Taking account of the world federalists' views, the Resolution also offered a definitive application of federalist views in the global context. The political and economic resolutions constituted a far-reaching application, in socio-political terms, of the principle of co-operation between autonomous groups and of the free circulation of persons, goods, and capital throughout the area of the economic federation, which must therefore be empowered to legislate centrally for internal and external trade, immigration and emigration, currency matters, and certain types of large enterprise. The various documents in no way confined federalism to its constitutional aspects, but again and again expressed the basic conviction of all participants as to the need, within this broad context, to transcend the sovereignty of nation states.[346]

Here again, a key question was how to transform the existing structures with their national and centralist distortions into a healthy, decentralized,

---

doctrine of its own. 3. The UEF has gained a firm footing in Switzerland, politically and materially. 4. We have reached a *Modus vivendi* with the "rival" associations. 5. We have largely infiltrated the world federalists. These are important achievements, which give us a base to work from.' As to 5., cf. nn. 334–6; as to 4., see chap. III/7, pp. 661–3.

[346] On the definition of the federalist principle, cf. at n. 312; on social and economic applications, at nn. 315–7; on the German question, at n. 325 f.; on world-wide peace-keeping, at n. 336. In his 'Bilan' of 12.9.1947 Brugmans admitted that 'our programme is as yet incomplete', and gave as an example the lack of an 'action programme for European overseas territories' (*Brugmans Archives*). These were covered a year later in the UEF draft constitution, which provided that their relation of dependency should be replaced by federal or associative links and that they should meanwhile be placed under a 'European Trusteeship Council': cf. chap. V/7, in vol. 2.

European federal order. It was possible to begin to answer this question inasmuch as federal doctrine presented a clear set of objectives embracing local self-government, autonomous economic associations, sectional professional organizations, etc., building up through viable regional systems to the European level in accordance with the principles of subsidiarity and solidarity. This implied an integrational method based on functionalism, but conceived from the outset in terms of a unified economic, social, and political system; the basic motive force would consist in the encouragement it provided to self-administering bodies of all kinds. The expectation, as de Rougemont describes it, was that the representatives of 'creative forces' – industrialists and trade unions, agrarian and co-operative associations, municipal councils, parliaments, youth movements, churches, etc., etc. – would, as soon as they had grasped their own interest in federalism, be able to form themselves into European 'estates' after the fashion of 1789, presenting 'cahiers de revendications' and, as the debate proceeded, assuming the role of a constituent assembly. The UEF, putting its faith in these 'forces réelles', had initially not given much thought to methods of political integration in the narrower sense, or worked out how the existing national structures, which were meanwhile digging themselves in once more, could be got to support or acquiesce in such initiatives; in federalist eyes the 'anciens régimes' were crumbling and could not withstand the onslaught of the 'forces réelles'. In the event, however, it turned out that these forces were not disposed to challenge the existing order, or did so only at a later date and to a partial extent.

The General Policy Resolution had concluded with the words: 'It is further essential that we should take along with us all the popular forces, all the healthy forces which are active in the different countries, without any exception whatsoever: trade unions, professional organizations, intellectuals, political associations and parties which are working for a better society, universities and churches. By fulfilling all these conditions federalism will accomplish its mission and build a new world at the service of humanity and of peace.'[347]

3. However, unquestionably the most important political result of the Montreux congress, given the international situation in the summer of 1947, was the UEF's decision to begin with Western Europe, in accordance with the doctrine that 'A federation is a living phenomenon ... Here there may be an economic agreement ... there a group of small countries forms

---

[347] 'Motion de politique générale' in the collective volume (n. 308), p. 136. The Rapport de la Commission financière already provided that: 'Les grandes organisations professionelles, syndicales ou parlementaires qui donnent une adhésion collective à l'U.E.F. sont considérées comme des membres "correspondants" ' and should not pay regular contributions. Cf. D. de Rougemont, 'The Campaign ...' (n. 310), p. 336; a thorough analysis in E. B. Haas, *The Uniting of Europe. Political, Social and Economic Forces 1950–1957*, Stanford, 1968², pp. 532–50. Cf. also the UEF conception of the Hague Congress of 1948 as a meeting of 'states general', chap. V/3; the development of methods of political integration in the narrower sense at the Rome congress, chap. V/7; and our analysis in 'Conclusions' (all in vol. 2).

a customs union.' The gravity and significance of the decision were fully recognized in all speeches and resolutions passed at the congress. Taking into account Marshall's offer of aid on condition that the Europeans worked out a joint plan, and also the Soviet Union's veto on East-European participation, the UEF, although bitterly disappointed, faced the reality of the situation and resolved to begin with Western Europe despite the aversion it had hitherto felt to creating a 'Western bloc'. 'The gravity of the position in which Europe finds herself demands that a beginning shall be made towards federal organization wherever it can be attempted, wherever the people still have some liberty of action and decision, wherever public opinion can have some effect on government action.' Almost all the delegates found it a painful and difficult decision to renounce, for the time being, the prospect of union with the East Europeans, but the Soviet Union had left them no choice.[348]

Brugmans, in his 'Bilan', noted as a heavy item on the debit side 'The failure of our attempt to break through in the East'. True to the statement in the political resolution that 'the European Union of Federalists ... will never accept as a *fait accompli* the division of Europe into two hostile blocs', Brugmans noted privately that it was 'Necessary to visit Poland and Finland, if only to show the flag and reserve possibilities for the future. Reach agreement if possible with East-European *émigrés*, so far as they are not committed to a bloc policy or a "war of liberation". Meanwhile, prepare the way very carefully for a visit to Moscow. Try to persuade the Russians that European federalism may one day be a card they might wish to play in order to save face.'[349]

The federalists at Montreux realized that in view of the Soviet veto and domination of Eastern Europe it would be a long time before the rest of the Continent, now in a state of prostration, could become a 'Third Force' in world politics. This part of Europe, which belonged to the US sphere of influence, could not, in the nature of things, fully put into effect the ideas of the Resistance movements; it offered a less impressive political goal and was less fitted to capture the imagination of a wide public. Thanks to Soviet imperialism a beginning in Western Europe was the only realistic solution, but it reduced the momentum and psychological appeal of the federal movement. Had the UEF taken a different course it would have deprived itself of any influence on events and gone into the political wilderness; hence the emphatic language of the political resolution: 'It

---

[348] Cf. analysis of speeches and resolutions under (B) above, nn. 319–22. Our analysis of the evolution of UEF ideas, and of its previous concept of the whole of Europe as a neutral 'Third force' (cf. chap. II/5), should go some way towards filling the gap of which Roy Willis complains: 'Little attempt has been made by scholars to set the European integration movement in its Cold War setting. The parameters of Cold War rivalry have been largely taken for granted' (Introduction to *European Integration*, ed. R. Willis, New York, 1975, p. xi). The UEF's struggle with this predicament, unlike that of the 'unionist' groups, was proportionate to the gravity of the European situation.

[349] H. Brugmans, 12.9.1947, 'Bilan de l'U.E.F.' (*Brugmans Archives*). In the next ten years Brugmans failed to get a visa for this purpose: the Soviet Union was not interested.

would be a crime not to seize the opportunities offered by the present political situation to start from today building a European federation wherever such a start is possible.' After all, Europe west of the Iron Curtain comprised over three-quarters of the Continent's population – more than that of North America or the Soviet Union – and, if genuinely federated, could in time take its place as a power of similar rank.

But this situation led in turn to a further problem. The federalists' decision to begin with Western Europe meant that for the next two years they adhered more firmly than in the past to the view that Britain and Scandinavia must from the outset be fully associated with 'Europe' in the reduced sense of the term. Had it been possible to set about unifying the whole of Europe, it is probable that the UEF would have limited its sights to a Continental union without full British membership; this would have made sense psychologically, in view of Britain's different experience of the late war. But now that Eastern Europe was out of bounds, the federalists were loath to diminish the area of the West; they were, moreover, influenced by Britain's prestige as the only European victor nation and by its having taken the lead in organizing the European reply to Marshall's offer.

Spinelli himself declared at Montreux: 'Our gaze and our hopes are indeed now directed above all towards Britain, which possesses the necessary authority and prestige to launch an appeal to Europe, sunk in its post-war chaos, similar to the appeal it addressed to France in the chaos of her defeat in 1940. I fear that the first difficulties cannot be surmounted without a British initiative.' According to Silva, the British delegation at Montreux made a 'déclaration fondamentale' to the effect that 'Britain was an integral part of Europe and would take part, to the full extent of its resources, in the federal organization of the Continent; it was also more closely linked with the Commonwealth than ever, but these links were fully compatible with British membership of a federated Europe.'[350] If such a statement was actually made it was an irresponsible exaggeration of the attitude of the British public towards European federation and was liable to raise false hopes, as the next few years were to show.

The position, to which the UEF clung at this period, that British initiative and full membership were necessary raised a tactical problem of some importance. Would it prove possible to convert the Labour Party leaders to a policy of federal European union? Brugman's note of objectives

[350] Spinelli at Montreux, 27.8.1947, quoted from A. Spinelli, *Dagli stati sovrani agli stati uniti d'Europa*, Florence, 1950. p. 238 f. Silva refers to the alleged British statement in his report (n. 310), p. 83, but it is not mentioned in the other congress reports. According to Ritzel (n. 310), p. 3, Hopkinson, who was head of the Conservative parliamentary secretariat in the UK and was in the chair at Montreux on 28.8.1947, 'expressed the conviction that Britain was prepared and destined to play an important part in the context of European federalism'. This was confirmed by 'Churchill's recent speech'; but 'Britain was only a part of the great Commonwealth, which must also be won over to federalism.' Possibly Silva turned this personal 'conviction' into a formal 'declaration' by the British delegates. Duncan Sandys, in his speech at the final ceremony, said that Britain was 'resolved to play her part as a fully committed and active member of the European family of nations', but this was primarily in the context of economic co-operation (cf. collective volume, n. 308, p. 103 f.). Cf. p. 666 f.

included: 'Energetic steps to contact the Labour Party ... strike at the highest level (frapper la tête) ... See Bevin and Attlee.' When this hope proved illusory and the interviews did not come off, the UEF, still convinced that British membership was essential, found itself obliged to work with Churchill and the 'unionists'.[351]

5. Federalist Groups among Parliamentarians; Foundation of the European Parliamentary Union

The change in the world situation after the failure of the Foreign Ministers' meeting in Moscow in April 1947, and the US government's decision to support European union, led to the formation of the first groups of federally minded members of West-European parliaments. Many of these, no doubt, had long been discontented with the unimaginative policies of national governments, and some, as private persons, had belonged to federalist groups; but in view of Russo-American policy they had hitherto seen no realistic prospect of influencing their governments or parties. From the middle of May, however, as the economic situation grew more and more disastrous and as the 'One World' policy was obviously a failure, while the new trend of US policy was signalled by Acheson's Cleveland speech etc., for the first time since 1944 there was a real possibility of the idea of European union playing a part in current politics. As a result the first federalist groups of MPs began to form, and tentative contacts which had begun in February 1947 led in some cases to the formal constitution of pro-European parliamentary groups. On 26 May 1947 Léon Blum, who had been premier of France up to the previous January, showed his sensitivity to current trends by publishing a leading article in *Le Populaire* – the first of its kind by him since September 1945 – entitled 'L'unité européenne', in which he wrote:

A world-wide plan would clearly be too ambitious, but it is not hard to imagine a European one. Among the European states there is an interlocking of interests and a community of needs that suffice to make Europe into a unit *vis-à-vis* the rest of the world ... My ideas are very similar to the plans for a United States of

---

[351] H. Brugmans, 12.9.1947, 'Bilan de l'U.E.F.' (*Brugmans Archives*), where he added 'Noyer Félix-le-poisson'. In this connection Brugmans wrote to the author: 'As you see, the illusory hope of winning over the Labour Party was still alive. When it collapsed, co-operation with Churchill was the only political option that remained . . . "Felix the Cat" was our nickname for Churchill. We thought of him as both a danger and an opportunity. An opportunity, because he gave enormous publicity to the European idea; a danger, because he wanted to revive the *Ancien Régime* instead of doing away with it' (information from *Brugmans*, 15.3.1966). Hans Bauer, chairman of the Swiss Europa-Union, 'stayed in England for several weeks exploring the British attitude towards Europe'; on 19.10.1947 he reported to a meeting of delegates of his association in Basle that he had reached 'very favourable conclusions' (*Europa*, Vol. xiv, No. 12, Nov. 1947, p. 1). On the debates with unionist groups in the Co-ordination Committee and for the meaning of the term 'unionist' in the European context, cf. chap. III/7, pp. 657–84; on the development of the UEF and its federalist programme prior to its second congress in Rome, cf. chap. V/7 (in vol. 2).

Europe or a European federation which have taken shape in the last few months ... In accordance with either conception, European planning could serve as a basis for the international aid campaign ... It is possible that in the sphere of European organization we may sooner or later have to make up our minds to the absence or voluntary non-participation of the USSR, just as in French internal politics we put up with the voluntary withdrawal of our Communist comrades.[352]

Pro-European members of the various parliaments naturally began by contacting fellow-members who belonged to the same party, and this soon led to contacts with foreign MPs of similar party affiliation. Representatives of the Christian Democratic parties which had come to the fore so surprisingly in Continental Western Europe met in Switzerland from 27 February to 2 March 1947 to discuss possibilities of supranational co-operation; this led to a congress at Chaudefontaine near Liège and the foundation on 1 June of the Nouvelles Équipes Internationales (NEI) as a loose umbrella organization representing the European Christian Democratic parties, with the MRP deputy Robert Bichet as its secretary-general. The official theme of the congress was 'The Social Situation of the Workers'; talks about Europe went on behind the scenes only, because the party leaders in each country had not yet made up their minds, let alone reached unanimity on the subject. From the end of 1947, however, when its second congress (on the subject of Germany) was in preparation, the NEI managed to achieve co-ordinated support for the idea of European union.[353] On the Social Democratic side, pro-European left-wing groups – the French led by Marceau Pivert, while the British were members of the Independent Labour Party, including Bob Edwards – met in London on 22–3 February 1947 to discuss 'political co-operation for Europe'. At a congress on 21–2 June at Montrouge near Paris these groups founded a Comité International pour les États-Unis-Socialistes d'Europe; a full year later, after the accession of further Social Democratic elements, it was renamed the Mouvement Socialiste pour les États-Unis d'Europe (MSEUE). The speeches and final resolution at Montrouge,

---

[352] L. Blum, *L'Œuvre de Léon Blum* (ed. Société des Amis de Léon Blum), vol. vii: *1947–1950,* Paris, 1963, p. 20 f. For the Communists' exclusion from the government on 5 May, cf. p. 497 above; for the significance of Blum's appeal in *Le Populaire* of 27 May urging European Socialist parties to adopt a common standpoint regarding 'the United States of Europe and European federation' (ibid., p. 23), cf. chap. IV/1 in vol. 2. Also at the end of May 1947, Hans Bauer began a leading article with the words: 'There has never been so much written about European federal union as since the lamentable end of the Foreign Ministers' conference in Moscow. Everywhere, as if at an agreed signal, we hear the slogan: United States of Europe! But there was nothing prearranged about this, nor did there need to be: the Moscow failure was an alarm signal that every European understands.' The two extra-European powers, he went on, had no thought but for themselves; 'Europe means nothing in their counsels as long as she lies at their feet like a mangled corpse'; the only solution was for Europe to 'draw the conclusion that she must unite and become a new factor in world deliberations' (*Europa,* Vol. xiv, No. 7, June 1947, leading article, p. 1.)

[353] Cf. chap. IV/3 (in vol. 2) for further details of the origin, composition, congresses, etc. of the NEI, which can only be fully evaluated as part of the general analysis of the attitude of the Christian Democratic parties to the idea of European union.

reflecting the views of individual Socialists and not of their respective national parties, laid down firmly that 'the transfer of national sovereignties to a federal organism is essential in order to bring to an end the political and economic chaos of Europe'.[354] The importance and effectiveness of these first international contacts on a party basis cannot be properly estimated without taking into account the divergence of view between individual members and the national party executives, which, in nearly all the West-European countries, did not take up an unambiguous position as regards European union until well into 1948. For this reason they will be discussed more fully in Chapter IV, which deals with the evolution of party attitudes in general.

For the present the focus is rather on the all-party groups of pro-European members of West-European parliaments. Since the change in the international climate made it possible for the idea of European unity to play a part in practical politics, contacts took place among members of all persuasions (except the Communists) whose enthusiasm for the European cause outran that of their respective party executives. This led to the formation of 'Groupes parlementaires fédéralistes' in the French and British parliaments and, after the summer recess, in those of the Benelux countries and Italy; individuals who already belonged to federalist associations were the most active, but many other MPs whose attention had been absorbed for two years past by the problems of national recovery now showed interest in the wider European perspective. These groups differed from the associations discussed hitherto, inasmuch as they were not 'pressure groups' of individuals but consisted of elected members of national parliaments. However, by reason of their all-party character they closely resembled the existing associations, and they soon became an important part of the movement for European union.

(A) FEDERALIST GROUPS IN THE WEST-EUROPEAN PARLIAMENTS

In Paris, as Alexandre Marc announced in the UEF's *Lettre-Circulaire,* the 'Constitution officielle du Groupe parlementaire fédéraliste français' was drawn up at the Palais Bourbon on 19 June 1947. A communiqué stated that: 'The Group has been established by about eighty members of the National Assembly and the Council of the Republic (i.e. the Senate) ... 'Professor Rivet described to his fellow-members, with great success, the idea and present possibilities of federalism.' A *Bureau* (executive committee) was unanimously elected as follows:

---

[354] English text of resolution in A. and F. Boyd, *Western Union,* London, 1948, p. 80 f. For the origin of this pro-European Socialist movement, the congresses referred to, a fuller account of the Montrouge resolution, etc., cf. chap. IV/1 (in vol. 2), where the ambivalent position of the Socialist parties is studied.

602   Limitation to Western Europe

Chairmen: Paul Rivet, SFIO, vice-chairman of the foreign-affairs committee of the National Assembly.
Vice-Chairmen: Henri Barré for the SFIO, Edmond Michelet for the MRP, Edgar Faure for the Rassemblement des Gauches; Édouard Bonnefous, chairman of the foreign-affairs committee of the National Assembly, for the UDSR; Gustave Alric for the PRI; Réne Coty for the Groupe Indépendant.
Secretaries-General: Raymond Triboulet (Independent) for the National Assembly; Mlle Anne-Marie Trinquier (MRP) for the Council of the Republic.[355]

The composition of the committee was thus admirably non-partisan from the start: it included prominent spokesmen on foreign affairs belonging to all parties except the Communists, who, in Paris as elsewhere, refused to participate; politically it was of special importance that the members included the chairman and vice-chairman of the foreign-affairs committee of the Assembly. The list of deputies who belonged to the Group itself at the beginning of July 1947 was less balanced from the party point of view; as it has not been published elsewhere and is of interest in the context of party history, it is appended here.[356] Over half the members

[355] Press communiqué (including names of officers), Paris, 19.6.1947 (*BEF Archives*, Brugmans corr.); Marc's announcement in UEF *Lettre-Circulaire*, No. 11, Paris, 18.6.1947, p. 2 (*CEC Archives*, Geneva). Preparations had been going on for at least a month: cf. R. Silva in *Fédérer les Fédéralistes*, May 1947, p. 4, quoted in chap. II at n. 196. The same members of the Bureau are listed in a MUCM (MWFG) communiqué of 2.3.1948 (*BEF Archives*, secr.). In 1949 R. Coty became chairman instead of P. Rivet, and Bonnefous was replaced by H. Teitgen (*EM Archives, Bruges*, EPU folder; cf. A. Greilsammer, *Les Fédéralistes européens en France depuis 1945*, hectographed thesis, Paris, 1972, p. 220).

[356] 'Députés à l'Assemblée Nationale – Membres du Groupe Fédéraliste:

M.R.P.
MM. Bessac Abel
    Bichet Robert
    Boisdon Daniel
Mlle Bosquier Henriette
MM. Buron Robert
    Cayol Raymond
    Chevigné (de) Pierre
    Coste-Floret Alfred
    Coudray Georges
    Courtecuisse
    Dhers Pierre
    Duforest Armand
Mme Dupuis José
MM. Duveau Roger (appar.)
    Farine Philippe
    Fonlupt-Esperaber Jacques
    Furand Jacques
    Gosset Paul
    Guérin Maurice

    Guillant André
    Guyonard Joseph
    Ihuel Paul
    Lacaze Henri
    Laurent Raymond
    Lecrivain Servoz Albert
Mme Lefebvre Francine
MM. Lespès Henri
    Liquard Émile
    Louvel Jean
    Lucas Maurice
    Menthon (de) François
    Michelet Edmond (M. du bur.)
    Mont Claude
    Monteil André
    Noël André
    Orvoen Louis
    Palewski Jean Paul
Mme Peyroles Germaine
MM. Pflimlin Pierre

belonged to the MRP group in the Assembly, of which they constituted just under a third. The proportion of Independent deputies who belonged to the federalist group was almost a half; of the Radicals barely a quarter, of the PRL (Parti républicain de la Liberté) a fifth, but of the Socialists only one in thirteen and of the UDSR (Union démocratique et socialiste de la Résistance) only one in eight: i.e. the right wing of the Assembly was considerably more strongly represented than the left. Altogether at this time the federalist group numbered ninety-nine deputies, or barely a sixth of the whole Assembly. In the same way, rather more than half the senators

	Pierre-Grouès Henri (abbé)		Edgar-Faure (M. du bur.)
	Poimboeuf Marcel		Garavel Joseph
Mme	Poinso-Chapuis Germaine		Giacobbi Paul
MM.	Roques Raymond		Godin Henri
	Scherer Marc		Julien Jules
	Schumann Maurice		
	Terrenoire Louis		*INDÉPENDANTS*
	Tinaud Jean-Louis	MM.	Bougrain Patrice
	Truffaut Pierre		Coty René (M. du bur.)
	Viard Paul		Courant Pierre
	Viatte Charles		Crouzier Jean
	Villard Jean		Delachenal Joseph
	Wasser Joseph		Errecart Jean
			Lalle Albert
	S.F.I.O.		Mallez Henri
MM.	Le Bail Jean		Pantaloni
	Gorse Georges		Recy (de) Antoine
	Guyon Raymond		Temple Emmanuel (M. du bur.)
	Jeuve Gérard		Thesten Paul
	Lapie Pierre-Olivier		Triboulet Raymond (M. du bur.)
	Laurent Augustin		*P.R.L.*
	Minjoz Jean	MM.	Betelaud Robert
	Rivet Paul (Président)		Brusset Max
	U.D.S.R.		Desmaison (de) Olivier
MM.	Bonnefous Édouard (M. du bur.)		Frédéric-Dupont Édouard
	Petit Eugène – dit Claudius		Joubert Auguste
	Mondon Raymond		Laniel Joseph
			Mutter André
	RADICAUX–SOCIALISTES		*ACTION PAYSANNE*
MM.	Anxionnez Paul	MM.	Antier Paul
	Bene Maurice		Bardoux Jacques
	Chevallier Jacques		
	David Jean Paul		*SANS LISTE*
	Delbos Yvon	MM.	Capitant René
	Dupuis Marceau		Simonnet René .'

The above list was appended to a circular letter addressed by the group at the beginning of July 1947 to pro-European members of other parliaments (*BEF Archives,* Brugmans corr.). For the numerical strength of different parties in the Assembly, see F. Goguel and A. Grosser, *La Politique en France,* Paris, 1970, p. 337.

who belonged to the group were MRP members;[357] altogether the group numbered sixty-one senators, or just on a fifth of the Upper House. The group did not as yet put forward a programme of its own, but in a circular to other West-European parliamentarians at the beginning of July it declared its adherence to the principles of the UEF:

'Le groupe fédéraliste du Parlement français, travaillant en étroite liaison avec le Comité Français de Coordination des Mouvements fédéralistes (9 rue Auber, Paris IXe), et avec l'Union Européenne des Fédéralistes (Palais Wilson, Genève), vous prie de transmettre son fraternel salut aux parlementaires de votre pays.' The French group hoped for contacts and visits. 'Our basic views are defined in the important resolutions passed at the Amsterdam meeting (11–16 April) and in the booklet *Pour bâtir l'Europe*; both these texts are attached. The UEF will be

---

[357] 'Conseillers de la République – Membres du Groupe Fédéraliste:

M.R.P.
MM. Aguesse Georges
Boudet Pierre
Boyer Jules
Cardin André
Coudo du Foresto Yvan
Debray André – Henri
Delmas Jules (Général)
Fournier Émile
Gargeminy Paul
Gerber Marc
Grimal Marcel
Hyvrard Jules
Jacques-Destrés
Janton Victor
Jacuen Yves
Jayr René
La Gravière Emmanuel
Lauret François
Lienard Henri
Manditte Jacques (de)
Menu Roger
Ott Barthelemy
Pezet Ernest
Poher Alain
Poisson Émile
Rehault Hippolyte
Mme. Rollin Simone
MM. Sempe Augusto
Tresintin Pierre
Mlle Trinquier Anne-Marie (M. du bur.)
MM. Vourc'h Jean Antoine
Voyant Joseph
Walker Maurice

S.F.I.O.
MM. Barré Henri (M. du bur.)

Bechir
Bene Jean
Boyer Max
Carcassonne Roger
Charley Gaston
Chatagnier Joseph
Diop Alicune
Soldani Édouard

U.D.S.R.
M. Brunet Louis
Mme Saunier Claire

RADICAUX–SOCIALISTES
MM. Brunhes Julien
Casser Jules
Felice Pierro (de)
Lafay Bernard
Monnet Henri
Mme Patenotre Jacqueline
M. Pinton Auguste

RÉPUBLICAINS INDEPENDANTS
MM. Bonnefous Raymond
Delfortrie Pierre

P.R.L.
MM. Alric Gustave (M. du bur.)
Boisrond Jacques
Mme Devand Marcelle Simone
MM. Jean-Jullien
Pernot Georges
Rochereau Henri

R.G.R. (Apparenté)
MM. Durand-Reville Gabon
Marin-Tabouret.'

(List attached to circular letter of July 1947, see n. 356).

holding its general congress at Montreux from 27 to 31 August,' and the group intended to send a large delegation.[358]

Within a year the Paris group had doubled its membership, and on 19 March 1948 it introduced a motion in the Assembly for the summoning of a European constituent assembly; this, as will be seen, marked the definite emergence of the federal idea as a factor in current political negotiations.[359]

In London there had been since the war period a loose association of MPs who were also members of Federal Union or were close to it. A 'Federalist Group of the House of Commons' was officially formed some time in the second half of 1946, a letter from Mackay having stated: 'We are beginning to organize a group of Labour M.P.s ... to do something to secure a European Federation.' In February 1947, as already mentioned, the group put down a motion calling on the government 'to affirm Britain's readiness to federate with any other nations willing to do so on the basis of a federal constitution to be agreed by a representative constituent assembly'; this obtained seventy-two signatures, nearly all from the Labour left, but was brusquely rejected by the Attlee government on 27 February.[360] The group's chairman was the Revd. Gordon Lang, an

---

[358] Undated circular of 'Groupe Parlementaire Fédéraliste, Parlement Français', signed 'Secrétaire général du Group'; presumably of early July, as it invites visits especially to coincide with the forthcoming visit of a British delegation (cf. chap III/7, p. 660 f.); significantly, the UEF is mentioned prominently but there is no reference to Coudenhove-Kalergi's activity; carbon copy sent to Grugmans, *BEF Archives,* Brugmans corr.

[359] Cf. chap. V/2 (in vol. 2), where details will be given; meanwhile, with text, E. Bonnefous, *L'Idée européenne et sa réalisation,* Paris, 1951, p. 190 f.

[360] R. W. G. Mackay (cf. Index) to R. Coudenhove-Kalergi, 12.6.1946 (*Mackay Archives*). For full text of the motion, see chap. II at n. 87; for the government's rejection, chap. I at n. 186 The six authors of the motion and the original fifty-two co-signatories can presumably be reckoned as members of the Federalist Group. The authors were A. S. Champion, D. L. Lipson, J. Parker, E. Roberts, H. Usborne, and E. Willis; the co-signatories were the Labour MPs:

A. C. Allen	J. Kinley
W. H. Ayles	Rev. G. Lang
T. W. Burden	Lt. B. Levy
F. A. Cobb	Lt.-Col. M. Lipton
V. J. Collins	F. Longden
Wing-Commander G. Cooper	R. W. G. Mackay
R. H. S. Crossman	J. P. W. Mallalieu
A. Edward Davies	G. McAllister
N. N. Dodds	H. G. McGhee
M. Edelman	H. M. Medland
M. Foot	I. Mikardo
Captain R. J. Gunter	R. Morley
Flt.-Lt. J. E. Haire	J. D. Murray
C. L. Hale	Mrs M. E. Nichol
J. Harrison	Major Poole
H. E. Holmes	E. Porter
H. Hynd	W. T. Proctor
F. E. Jones	Lt.-Col. D. R. Rees-Williams
E. M. King	J. Reeves

idealistic pacifist and an enthusiast for closer international ties of all kinds, who was an honorary secretary of Churchill's United Europe Movement, a member of the UEF executive and also of the executive of the Movement for World Federal Government. Several names of the signatories of the February motion, from Victor Collins to Usborne, showed that here too ideas of world federation were still in the ascendant. The group's existence and title were of importance in the spring and the summer of 1947 because of the encouragement they offered to the founders of the Paris group and MPs in other countries. But the name was misleading inasmuch as it was still a Labour-dominated and not a truly non-party group; while Marshall's offer and Molotov's refusal opened up the practical possibility of union on a West-European but certainly not on anything like a world-wide basis. These difficulties led to a crisis in the autumn, as a result of which Lang resigned and the group, as will be seen, was reformed into an 'All-Party Europe Group' – this time correctly named – under Mackay's chairmanship.[361]

In the parliaments of Italy and the Benelux countries the first half of 1947 also witnessed contacts across party lines and associations among deputies who held federalist views or belonged to member associations of the UEF. Thus Campagnolo informed the UEF meeting at Amsterdam that sixty members of the Italian constituent assembly belonged to MFE and were working as a group for European union. However, as will be seen, the formal establishment of European federalist groups with executives and a sizeable number of adherents did not come about until the autumn and winter of 1947/8.[362] In the early summer of 1947 – except in Paris, where a genuinely representative parliamentary group was formed – the member associations of UEF were either not strong enough to influence or win over all the deputies who had answered 'Yes' to Coudenhove's

G. O. Roberts	Major V. F. Vernon
C. Royle	G. D. Wallace
P. L. E. Shurmer	Major W. T. Wells
A. M. Skeffington	Colonel G. E. C. Wigg
T. C. Skeffington-Lodge	W. L. Wyatt
I. O. Thomas	V. F. Yates
M. Turner-Samuels	

(Source: S. D. Bailey, *United Europe: A Short History of the Idea*, London, 1947, p. 32). I have not been able to discover any archives of this group.

[361] For the group's conversations on 12–16.5.1947 with French federalists (including six founder members of the Paris parliamentary group), cf. chap. II at n. 198. On 12.9.1947 Coudenhove-Kalergi wrote in a letter encouraging Mackay: 'As long as King and Lang are at the head, they are nothing but puppets of Sandys'; on 10.11.1947 Mackay informed Coudenhove that King had been given a government appointment and that the majority of the Labour group now wanted him, Mackay, and not Lang as chairman (both in *Mackay Archives*). There is no other information concerning the crisis. For the formation of the All-Party Europe Group on 17.12.1947, see p. 620 f.

[362] Campagnolo's statement reported by van Vassenhove, 'A travers l'Europe', *L'Action fédéraliste européenne*. No. 6, July 1947, p. 44. No archives of this early group could be traced. For the groups established in the autumn and winter of 1947/8, cf. at nn. 381–5.

enquiry, or else they did not make a particular effort to do so. Silva, it is true, had included among the tasks listed in *Fédérer les Fédéralistes* that of 'establishing federalist parliamentary groups in all countries'.[363] But the UEF put little trust in the old political parties of outdated centralist national states, preferring to rely on the 'forces réelles' – the federal aspirations of local and economic associations, their potential assumption of a 1789 role, etc. Brugmans in his 'Bilan' spoke in somewhat aloof and patronizing terms of 'Recruiting parliamentarians to all our commissions, committees, etc., but recognizing clearly that they represent an "ancien régime" which has a paralysing effect. Make sure they do us no harm.'[364] The gap thus left open was filled by the purposeful action of Coudenhove-Kalergi.

(B) CREATION OF THE EUROPEAN PARLIAMENTARY UNION, AND ITS CONGRESS AT GSTAAD

As mentioned in chapter II, Richard Coudenhove-Kalergi returned to Europe from America in June 1946 and stayed for five months. In view of the federalist associations which had come into being since the war he decided not to revive the Pan-Europa-Union as a mass movement, but instead circularized all West-European parliamentarians with the question 'Are you in favour of the establishment of a European federation within the framework of the United Nations?' Apparently in April 1947, before leaving New York for the second time, he wrote to the members of parliament who had by then answered 'Yes', and who numbered about a sixth of the total, suggesting that they join with other pro-Europeans to form 'Parliamentary Committees for European Federation' in their respective parliaments.[365]

On 28 April, elated by the favourable reception of the European idea in the United States, he addressed an 'Appeal to all Europeans' from on board the *Queen Elizabeth*, in which he declared that Europe's misery and inability to find peace would 'continue as long as the world persists in trying to rebuild it on the basis of

---

[363] May 1947, p. 4; cf. chap. II, n. 196. The twenty-page programme booklet *Union européenne des fédéralistes*, Feb. 1948, also noted as a task: 'susciter la formation de groupes parlementaires fédéralistes. Le Secrétariat général favorise les contacts entre ces divers groupes et leurs rapports avec les Mouvements fédéralistes.'

[364] 'Bilan de l'U.E.F.' 12.9.1947 (*Brugmans Archives*). Brugmans explained to the author: 'We realized that the parliamentarians, as organs of the national state, stood for the most progressive part, relatively speaking, of the *ancien régime*. We therefore had to prevent their being ensnared by the conservative Europeanists, but we did not expect anything really revolutionary from them' (information from *Brugmans*, 15.3.1966).

[365] For Coudenhove-Kalergi's first post-war stay in Europe from 18 June to 15 November 1946, and his poll of West-European parliamentarians, cf. chap. II/7, pp. 435–41. The idea of forming parliamentary groups was first mentioned in his notes on 27.1.1947 (cf. ibid. at n. 335). In his printed report on the Gstaad conference, *Toward a Constituent Assembly for Europe* (EPU, Gstaad, Dec. 1947, p. 9), he states that he put the suggestion of forming such groups to those who had answered 'Yes' to his enquiry on 26 April before his final departure from New York; similarly R. Coudenhove-Kalergi (n. 27), *An Idea Conquers the World*, p. 273; German version, *Eine Idee erobert Europa*, Vienna/Munich, 1958, p. 286. I have not found any letters confirming this, however.

the outdated principles which have twice ruined our generation; unrestricted national sovereignty, national tariffs and currencies, the arms race and international hatred. We appeal to you to put an end to this state of things by at once setting about the creation of the United States of Europe – with a supreme council and a supreme court, a single police authority and human rights common to all, a European market and a European currency. Not all the states of Europe are today free to unite. But Britain and France with some of their neighbours can and should go ahead ... It is the task of Europe's parliaments to take the lead in this decisive battle.'[366]

The first definitive response to Coudenhove's letter came from the Greek constituent assembly, where a non-party Committee for European Federation was set up in May or June 1947 with the former minister Leon Maccas as its chairman (there was at that time no Greek association affiliated to the UEF); by June, 41 per cent of members of the assembly had answered 'Yes' to Coudenhove's enquiry. Moves towards the formation of similar committees took place in Italy and Belgium. In Italy, given the inactivity of the MFE under Campagnolo, the moving spirit was the Christian Democratic member of the constituent assembly, Enzo Giacchero; in Belgium, where the federalists were divided among themselves, the lead was taken by Georges Bohy, chairman of the Socialist party in the Chamber. In Rome and Brussels, and soon afterwards in Paris, The Hague, and London, the parliamentary groups included original members of the UEF and also MPs whose interest was first aroused by Coudenhove's appeal.

At the suggestion of Greek and Italian deputies Coudenhove arranged a preliminary conference at his home at Gstaad on 4–5 July 1947. This was attended by about twenty parliamentarians: eleven Italians, some Greeks and Belgians, the Swiss Radical Democrat Ernst Boerlin, member of the *Nationalrat*, and the Danish Liberal deputy Søren Olesen.[367] It was decided

---

[366] Text in Deutsche Nachrichten-Agentur report, 28.4.1947, and *Munzinger Archives*, 24.7.1947; evidently scarcely noticed by the press. His statement therein that by 28 April he had collected 646 'Yeses' from parliamentarians and 14 'Noes' suggests that his second enquiry, together with the suggestion about parliamentary groups, may have been launched after his arrival in Europe in May. Fuller information on the whole subject of this chapter could no doubt be gathered from Coudenhove-Kalergi's papers, which were for a long time inaccessible and, after many moves, are now in the custody of Dr Vittorio Pons near Geneva. In the month in which this book was completed he kindly invited the author to examine them, but unfortunately he was unable to do so.

[367] Information on the formation of groups and the Gstaad meeting in July from R. Coudenhove-Kalergi, *Rapport sur l'Union Parlementaire Européenne*, Gstaad, 7.9.1947 (circulated to the congress as a printed document), p. 5. This does not indicate how many attended the meeting; it does not mention any British, French, or Dutch MP, so evidently none came. The only other sources concerning the meeting are: the 'Rapport sur les travaux . . .' (n. 368 below); a list of the eleven Italian participants (little known apart from Giacchero: two Christian Democrats, two Socialists, two Qualunquists, three Liberals, and F. Parri; *EM Archives, Bruges,* EPU folder); and an extract from Coudenhove's welcoming speech, French text in *L'Action fédéraliste européenne*, No. 7, Aug. 1947, p. 62; English in *New York Herald Tribune*, 6.7.1947 ('The aim of our conspiracy is to organize throughout Europe parliamentary majorities strong enough to compel the governments to execute our programme'). Cf. R. Coudenhove-Kalergi, *An Idea* . . . (n. 365), pp. 279–81 (German p. 295); O. Philip, *Le Problème de l'Union Européenne*, Paris/Neuchâtel, 1950, p. 185 f.

to set up an umbrella organization, the European Parliamentary Union (EPU), as soon as seven national groups had been constituted. Maccas was elected chairman of a 'Conseil préliminaire', with Bohy as vice-chairman, Giacchero and Olesen as further members, and Coudenhove-Kalergi as secretary-general. It was also decided to follow up the circularizing of deputies, to press on with the formation of parliamentary committees, and to convoke at Gstaad by 8 September a 'preliminary European parliament' on the basis of one member per million of population.[368] An important pre-condition of its success was achieved at a first meeting of the leaders of all existing pro-European associations in Paris on 20 July 1947, when Maccas was able to persuade the heads of UEF, ELEC, and UEM to recognize the EPU as an organization in its own right; they also agreed to urge all existing parliamentary groups of federalists – in particular the French and British, whom Coudenhove had not yet been able to contact – to send representatives to the 'preliminary European parliament' at Gstaad.[369]

This 'parliament', which was in effect the first EPU congress, met at Gstaad from 8 to 10 September 1947. It was attended by 114 active parliamentarians from ten West-European countries – a number which testifies to the enthusiasm of the different national groups for contacts and joint action, and also the co-operation and goodwill of the groups founded by UEF, especially in France. The numbers indeed varied greatly from one country to another: France alone sent 43 members (including such important names as E. Bonnefous, R. Coty, F. de Menthon, F. Gay, M. Guerin, F. Leenhardt, André Mutter, André Noel, P. Pflimlin, and Paul Reynaud), and Italy 39 (including L. Benvenuti, F. Colitto, Ugo Damiani, Enzo Giacchero, Guglielmo Giannini, G. R. Perez, and T. Zerbi). The French and Italians comprised almost three-quarters of the

---

[368] Coudenhove-Kalergi, *Rapport sur l'union* . . . (n. 367), p. 5, and 'Rapport sur les travaux de la Conférence Parlementaire Européenne à Gstaad, les 4 et 5 juillet 1947', evidently drawn up by him immediately after the July meeting (one typed page, *BEF Archives*, Brugmans corr.); this said that a committee under Giacchero had been appointed to work out a 'European charter' to be discussed at the 'preliminary European parliament'. At a press conference at Berne on 20 June Coudenhove said:'This parliament, as the supreme moral authority on the Continent, will continue its activity until the day when it can transfer its mandate to a European constituent assembly freely elected by the peoples of Europe' (*von Schenck Archives,* UEF documents). The deputies at Gstaad evidently thought this premature, opting instead for a three-day session. Maccas wrote on 5 July to Churchill and Léon Blum, inviting them to become honorary presidents of the EPU in accordance with a unanimous decision reached at Gstaad. After enquiries by Sandys, Churchill replied on 1.9.1947: 'I would prefer to hold over my reply to your kind invitation . . . until the new body is formally constituted' (*EM Archives, Bruges,* EPU folder). Blum's reply is not known but was probably also negative, as Coudenhove wrote to Sandys on 25.8.1947 that he was considering Paul-Boncour as the second honorary president (ibid.).

[369] According to a statement signed in Paris on 20.7.1947 by Retinger, Courtin, Brugmans, and Maccas, the Comité de Liaison set up at the Paris meeting (cf. chap. III/7, pp. 657–64) 'has decided to appeal to all European parliaments and especially all federalist parliamentary groups to undertake that they will participate in the EPU congress at Gstaad from 8 to 10 September 1947' (*EM Archives, Bruges,* EPU folder).

total; of the remaining 32, 10 were from Brussels and 7 from The Hague, only 4 from London (Labour MPs E. M. King and R. Mackay, Conservatives Sir Peter Macdonald and Sir Walter Smiles), 2 each from Greece and Denmark, and 1 each from Sweden and Austria.[370] In addition there were at least 80 'observers' and journalists; among these were Duncan Sandys and Somerset de Chair from Britain and a group of East Europeans, notably Gafencu and Ninčić, former foreign ministers of Romania and Yugoslavia, and Dr von Auer, former chairman of the foreign-affairs committee of the Hungarian National Assembly. After an opening address by Maccas, Coudenhove once more expounded his basic ideas:

The question is no longer: 'Shall Europe unite?' The question is now: 'How can Europe be united before it is too late?' There are but three answers to this question: by agreement among governments; by a bloody revolution; by parliamentary majorities. Since a quarter of a century we are waiting for a Union of Europe accomplished by its governments. But only a single attempt was made – and failed ... No European federation is possible unless its member states transfer some of their sovereign rights to a federal authority ... We have every reason to fear that the conference of the Sixteen, as soon as it will leave its present stage of statistics and platonic recommendations, will meet with the same obstacles as Briand's initiative. To wait until the European governments take the initiative to limit their proper sovereign rights would mean to wait for the outbreak of World War III ... The danger [is] that one day the peoples of Europe lose their patience and take the solution of the European question into their own hands. Such a revolution, even if it were to lead to European union, threatens to destroy the foundations of our glorious civilization. On account of these difficulties of governmental action and these dangers of revolutionary methods, the only chance left for European union is a parliamentary initiative ... Our programme is clear: First, we must mobilize, throughout Europe, parliamentary majorities in favour of federation and organize them, beyond all party politics, into strong groups; second, we must co-ordinate these groups by means of the European Parliamentary Union; then we must call, as soon as possible, a constitutive assembly for Europe, elected by its parliaments; and finally we must have its charter accepted by our majority groups.[371]

---

[370] A complete list of names is annexed to the printed report on the congress, *Toward a Constituent Assembly for Europe*, EPU, Gstaad, Dec. 1947, p. 15. The total is 114; the figure 'over 200', current in the press at the time and in subsequent literature, must be based on a total given by Coudenhove at the press conference, which included 'observers'. For the Dutch and Belgian deputies, see below, nn. 381 and 382. The Greeks were Maccas and Nicolas Phocas, the Danes Karl Boegholm and S. Oleson; Erik Arrhen was a member of the Swedish Upper House, and Dr E. Ludwig was chairman of the foreign-affairs committee of the Austrian parliament. It may be noted that by now Coudenhove had collected over 1,700 affirmative replies to his enquiry: cf. chap. II/7 at n. 340.

[371] For the 'observers', cf. *Toward* ... (n. 370), p. 10. Text of 'Opening Address at the European Parliament by Richard Coudenhove-Kalergi', Gstaad, 8.9.1947 (hectographed in *Mackay Archives*). Others who spoke at the opening session were Paul Reynaud, G. Giannini, and the leaders of national delegations: King, Coty, Giacchero, Bohy, Roolvink, Boerlin, Arrhen, and Boegholm. Messages of welcome were received from, among others, Bevin and Churchill, Teitgen and Coste-Floret, de Gasperi and Sforza, Beel and Boetzelaer, the Luxemburg prime minister and president of

As all reports emphasize, the debates took place in 'a cordial and courteous atmosphere'; they were imbued with a sense of inter-parliamentary fellowship, and provided a first example of the practical feasibility of a European parliament. Differences of opinion were fully ventilated, but at no time did the MPs of a particular country vote *en bloc*, and the final declaration was adopted unanimously.[372] It was repeatedly pointed out that the League of Nations had failed because it was no more than a diplomatic conference, and that the present task was to create a federation of peoples with a common parliament. It was debated whether a European constituent assembly should consist of delegates of national parliaments or be directly elected; the Belgian deputy Arthur Gilson was especially in favour of the latter method. Concentrating on Coudenhove's ideas, the congress passed over some important matters in silence; for example, it 'gave the German problem a wide berth', in contrast to the boldness and determination with which the UEF congress had recently tackled it in a European spirit.[373] Nor do the sources indicate that there was much discussion of the Soviet veto on the participation of East-European countries, whose representatives were not present and had, for the most part at least, not been invited.[374] Without any heart-searching on the lines of the UEF debate at Montreux, the congress evidently decided in a matter-of-fact spirit to confine itself to projects of West-European union; the East-European countries were not mentioned in the resolutions, except by implication in the reference to a community 'comprising all states that are prepared for cooperation'.[375] Again, there was nothing

---

the Chamber (Pierre Dupont and Émile Reuter), the presidents of the two houses of the Swiss parliament, the president of the Norwegian Odelsting, and the vice-president of the Czechoslovak parliament (*Toward* . . . , p. 10).

[372] Reports on the congress are: E. Bonnefous, 'Aurons-nous un Parlement Européen?', *Le Monde*, 14.9.1947; 'Europäische Rettungsversuche', *Die Weltwoche*, 26.9.1947; L. van Vassenhove, 'A Gstaad', *L'Action fédéraliste européenne*, Nos. 8/9, Oct./Nov. 1947, pp. 9 (quotation)–11; J. F. Köver, 'Der Föderalismus . . .' (n. 310), here pp. 307–9; R. Coudenhove-Kalergi, *Vers un parlement de l'Europe*, Gstaad, n.d. (end of Sept. 1947), pp. 9–11; English version Toward . . . (n. 370), pp. 9–11: id., *An Idea* (n. 365), pp. 279–83 (German, pp. 296–9. The German and English versions of this book differ in various respects).

[373] On the debates (with Gilson quotation), see van Vassenhove (n. 372), p. 10. Quotation concerning Germany from *Die Weltwoche*, 26.9.1947; although the German *Landtage* were in being, Coudenhove did not invite any of their members (information from *Coudenhove-Kalergi*, 14.4.1954).

[374] Questioned on this point, Coudenhove said he had invited Czechoslovak and Finnish deputies because these were the only two East-European countries with whose parliamentarians he was in personal touch. Köver (n. 372), p. 308. But Coudenhove writes of those present at Gstaad (*Eine Idee* . . . (n. 365), p. 297). 'I only knew a few of them personally.'

[375] Cf. chap. III/4 on the UEF congress. The *New York Herald Tribune* wrongly surmised on 10.9.1947 that a proposed speech of Mackay's had been cancelled because 'Mackay is an advocate of Russian participation in a European federation.' Mackay had long seen eye to eye with Coudenhove on the Soviet question, and on 27.8.1947 wrote to him concerning the conference programme that it was a question of setting up the United States of Western Europe, with 'a government directly elected by the people' and with 'power to make laws for the peace, order and good government of the territory covered by the Federation, and in particular power to legislate

corresponding to the UEF's enumeration of the social, economic, local, etc. spheres in which federal associations ought to be cultivated if the edifice culminating in a political federation was to be strong and durable. At the same time, the 114 parliamentarians from ten countries took a bold and important step when, following Coudenhove's lead, they proclaimed the logical and straightforward concept of a conscious democratic act of inauguration and the *via aurea* of the 'early convocation of a European constituent assembly'. What Spinelli in 1944, and other federalists since then, had seen as an objective to be reached by stages was now brought back into the forefront of attention by the assembled members of ten parliaments who declared it to be the essential democratic basis of the whole enterprise. This was in fact the congress's great achievement. The 114 deputies had for the first time shown by example that successful co-operation between them was possible; they had proclaimed the objective of a federal constitution for Europe and, as true parliamentarians, they advocated a constituent assembly as the legitimate democratic way of achieving it. All this had a powerful effect in launching the European idea as a fact of political life. The final resolution, passed unanimously, declared that:

The European Parliamentary Conference appeals to all members of European Parliaments to use their power and influence with governments and with people to attain the following objectives: 1. to set up as soon as possible a European Regional Group, according to the spirit of Article 52 of the United Nations charter; 2. to constitute a Commonwealth under the name of United States of Europe, embracing all states that are ready to join and aiming at the inclusion of all of Europe; 3. to call as soon as possible a Constituent Assembly for Europe, charged with the drafting of a federal Constitution; this Assembly shall be elected either by the national Parliaments or directly by the people; its draft Constitution shall be submitted to the European states, who shall be free to accept or to reject it. To assure these aims, the Conference invites the Members of Parliaments: 1. to organize in every Parliament non-partisan groups favouring federation, destined to constitute powerful and dynamic majorities working for the federation of Europe.[376]

---

with respect to external affairs, defence, essential services, money and finance, customs and excise'. A letter of 12.9.1947 from Coudenhove to Mackay, expressing regret for 'the attitude the British delegation took towards you and your speech', indicates that the speech was cancelled because the other British MPs did not wish to be associated with such far-reaching federal proposals (both letters in *Mackay Archives*).

[376] The resolution further called on parliamentarians: '2. to assure as strong a support as possible for all recommendations and discussions towards an ever increasing economic co-operation, aiming at an economic union of Europe, and for all other measures assuring co-operation and collaboration among European states'; and appealed 'to all spiritual and moral leaders, to mothers and to teachers, to foster the spirit of international brotherhood and solidarity' (French text in *Vers un parlement* [n. 372], p. 13; English in *Toward* . . . [n. 370], p. 11 f.). While general support was to be canvassed in this way, there was no suggestion of weakening the principal aim of 'calling as soon as possible a Constituent Assembly for Europe', or making it conditional on progress in other respects.

Limitation to Western Europe 613

The last day of the congress, 10 September, was devoted to the organization of the EPU itself. A Provisional Executive Council of fifteen members was elected, with a very even distribution of seats from the national and party points of view. The chairman was Georges Bohy, leader of the Socialist group in the Belgian Chamber; vice-chairmen were the Greek Social Democrat Leon Maccas, the Italian Christian Democrat Enzo Giacchero, the French Independent René Coty and the Labour MP, E. M. King; parliamentary secretaries were the Dutch Liberal A. H. V. Hacke and the French MRP senator, Anne-Marie Trinquier. R. Coudenhove-Kalergi, the only non-parliamentarian, was secretary-general; the other Council members were Erik Arrhen (Swedish Conservative), Ernst Boerlin (Swiss Radical Democrat), Édouard Ludwig (Austrian People's Party), E. G. M. Roolvink (Dutch Catholic Party), Arthur Gilson (Belgian Christian Socialist), F. Leenhardt (French Socialist), Peter Macdonald (British Conservative), and Guido Russo Perez (Italian Qualunquist Party).[377] This gave a balance of five Socialists, five Christian Democrats, and five Liberals or Conservatives; Italy, Belgium, the Netherlands, and Britain had two Council members each, France three, and Austria, Switzerland, Sweden, and Greece one each. On a motion by Coty the Council was given the task of drafting statutes and preparing for the next congress, and 'in the meantime, in the spirit of the Resolutions adopted by the Conference', it was to take 'every initiative that may promote the cause of European Federation'. Committees were set up for legal, economic, cultural, propaganda, and social-security matters. The parliamentarians could congratulate themselves on having created a promising association for the purpose of bringing about European union, and it would now be their aim to secure actual majorities for this end in their national parliaments.

The Council met for the first time at Gstaad on 13–14 December 1947, and decided to hold the next EPU congress at Interlaken on 8–11 September 1948, under the title 'Parliamentary Congress for the Constitution of a United States of Europe'; it was to be attended by representatives of national groups in the ratio of one deputy per million of population. A constitution for Europe was to be drafted meanwhile by a legal committee under the chairmanship of François de Menthon (an MRP deputy, former minister, and professor of law at the Sorbonne); its secretary was

---

[377] List in *Vers un parlement* (n. 372) and in *Toward* . . . (n. 370), p. 2. The distribution of offices was discussed on the previous evening by the leaders of the ten delegations, when Sandys, who was present as King's interpreter, argued for the appointment of two secretaries-general, one parliamentarian and one non-parliamentarian. Coudenhove said he would resign if this was accepted, and at Coty's instance it was decided that he (Coudenhove) should be sole secretary-general 'under the control of the Board' (Coudenhove-Kalergi, *An Idea* . . . (n. 365), p. 282; more fully in German original, p. 297; also Coudenhove in a letter of 12.9.1947 to Mackay, who left the conference earlier: *Mackay Archives*).

A. H. V. Hacke. The congress was to submit the draft, when approved, to the national parliaments for adoption.[378]

The Council also invited the comments of national groups on a draft, prepared by de Menthon, of statutes for the EPU. It appointed Mlle Trinquier secretary of the economic and social committee, and Coudenhove secretary of the propaganda committee. It invited national groups to set up similar bodies and send their chairmen to take part in the EPU committees on their respective subjects. As regards other European associations: 'While preserving our independence, essential for our very special task on an exclusively parliamentary level, we should try to entertain cordial relations with all movements inspired by principles similar to our own', in accordance with the circumstances of each country. It was also unanimously decided that the post of vice-chairman vacated by E. M. King (who had been appointed to a British government post) should be filled by R. W. G. Mackay, chairman of the newly founded Labour group for European Federation (cf. p. 618 f. below). The Council discussed the design of a flag – the old Pan-European symbol, a red cross in a golden sun on a blue ground; it became clear in this connection that Coudenhove's obstinacy in such matters would create problems for EPU in the future.[379]

(C) FEDERALIST PARLIAMENTARY GROUPS IN THE BENELUX COUNTRIES AND ITALY; THE ALL-PARTY EUROPE GROUP IN THE HOUSE OF COMMONS

Not much source material has been found concerning the work of the individual federalist groups in the national parliaments. Their principal achievement, which consisted in the simultaneous tabling in several West-European parliaments, on 19 March 1948, of parallel proposals for the summoning of a constituent assembly for Europe, will be discussed later.[380]

In the parliaments of the three Benelux countries groups of considerable

---

[378] Report on the closing session of 10.9.1947, appointment of committees, and Coty resolution in *Toward*... (n. 370), p. 11 f.; ibid., p. 13 f., text of resolutions passed by Council, 13–14 December 1947. The Council meeting was also attended by committee members F. de Menthon and Charles Viatte (MRP) and Germain Rincent (French Socialist), three Belgian PSC members, and two Dutch deputies (cf. at nn. 381 and 382);. 'liste des participants à la réunion du Conseil Exécutif' of EPU, Gstaad, 13–14.12.1947). The documents were sent to Mackay by Coudenhove on 17 Dec. with the request to 'take an active part in the drafting of the Federal Constitution for Europe. Please get in touch with M. Fr. de Menthon and M. Hacke to assure a close co-operation with the Juridical Committee' (*Mackay Archives*). For the draft constitution prepared by those mentioned and its adoption at the Interlaken congress, cf. chap. V/6 (in vol. 2).

[379] Text in *Toward*... (n. 370), p. 11 f. A somewhat shorter but substantially identical French version (one typed page), with the draft statutes, was sent by Coudenhove to Mackay on 17 Dec. (*Mackay Archives*). The statutes declared that: '1. The EPU is an association open to all parliamentarians of European countries who accept the present Statutes... 2. The object of the EPU is the earliest possible realization of a European Federation. For this purpose the EPU will endeavour to create a permanent community under the title "United States of Europe", composed of all the European countries which accept this aim and with the determination ultimately to unite the whole of Europe. 3. Any freely elected member of a European parliament may become a member of the EPU...' Arts. 5–13 comprised detailed regulations for the Congress and Council.

[380] Cf. chap. V/2 (in vol. 2). Archival records of the groups might still be found amongst papers left by their chairmen or in national parliamentary or party archives.

standing were formed, with a good balance of party membership. The *Belgian* 'Groupe parlementaire fédéraliste' was probably founded as early as the summer of 1947; in any case Georges Bohy, the leader of the parliamentary Socialist party (PSB), attended the Gstaad congress as the group's chairman and, as such, was elected chairman of the EPU as a whole. The second most prominent member of the Belgian group was the Christian Social (PSC) deputy Arthur Gilson, who was also elected to the EPU executive, while other PSC representatives – Albert Coppé, Léopold Deschepper, and Henry Lambotte – attended the December meeting as committee members. The Belgian group was thus supported by members of both the two largest parties.[381] In the *Netherlands* Second Chamber (Lower House) the chief members of the federalist group were E. G. M. Roolvink of the Catholic People's Party and the Liberal A. H. W. Hacke, both of whom were elected to the EPU executive; N. S. C. Tendeloo (Socialist) and J. Fokkema (Anti-Revolutionary Party) attended the December meeting as committee members, showing that the group included members of all the main parties.[382] The *Luxemburg* group is the only one for which the exact number of members is known: at the beginning of 1948 it comprised 75 per cent of all deputies (40 out of 51; this proportion is probably untypical of the others). The chairman was Mme Émilie Reuter, Speaker of the Chamber, with Hubert Clement, the Deputy Speaker, as vice-chairman.[383]

In the *Italian* constituent assembly, as would be expected and as has already been mentioned, many deputies were members of the MFE on a personal basis; under the influence of world political developments, others seem to have joined them by June 1947 to form the Gruppo Parlamentare Federalista, which sent thirty-nine deputies – the second largest delegation – to the Gstaad congress. Their chairman, the Christian Democrat Giacchero, declared at the congress that most members of the Italian government were members of the group.[384] However, if the source is to be relied on, it was not until February 1948, in connection with a meeting of the foreign-affairs committee, that the non-party group was formally

---

[381] 'Liste des Participants à la réunion du Conseil Exécutif' of EPU, Gstaad, 13–14.12.1947 (*Mackay Archives*). The Gstaad congress on 8–10 Sept. was also attended by the Belgian deputies A. de Keuleneir, A. J. Deschepper, G. Develter, Hilaire Lahaye, and Eugène Mauriau (*Toward* . . . [n. 370], p. 15). These, and the five mentioned above, may be regarded as forming the inner circle of the Belgian group.

[382] 'Liste des Participants . . .' (n. 381). The Gstaad congress on 8–10 Sept. was also attended by the Dutch deputies A. Fortanier-de Wit, J. R. Schmal, and van Tets. These, and the four mentioned above, may be regarded as forming the inner circle of the Dutch group; the date of its foundation is not known, but was probably in the autumn of 1947.

[383] MUCM (MWFG) press announcement of 2.3.1948 by Henri Koch of Luxemburg, who was then head of the MUCM press department at Geneva (*BEF Archives,* Secr.).

[384] Cf. above, nn. 362 and 367; Giacchero at Gstaad, reported in van Vassenhove (n. 372), p. 10 (quotation). L. Levi and S. Pistone, in *Trent'anni di vita del Movimento Federalista Europeo*, Milan, 1973, p. 42, refer to Einaudi and his speech of 29.7.1947 (cf. n. 116): 'Il più illustre esponente del Gruppo Parlamentare Federalista alla Constituente'.

constituted or re-established; it then comprised 210 deputies ranging from Socialists to Monarchists. Of all the national groups mentioned so far it was certainly the strongest, since it included the leading deputies of all parties except the Communists and the Nenni Socialists.

Among its members were former ministers Bonomi and Parri, the foreign minister Count Sforza (Republican), the ministers of education and finance (Gonella and Pella, both Christian Democrats); Gronchi, the chairman of the parliamentary Christian Democrats, and Piccioni, their secretary-general; Micheli and Cingolani, Christian Democrats and former ministers; Lucifero, secretary-general of the Liberal party, and Corbino, a former minister of that party; Saragat, the Social Democratic leader, Gasparotto, a former minister, and Treves and Persico, also of that party; the Qualunquist leader Giannino and deputies Colitto, G. R. Perez, and Tumminelli; the Nenni Socialists Pieri and Tonello; the Unionist Damiani, and the Monarchist Bergamini.[385]

In the *British* House of Commons, as has been demonstrated, the original Federalist Group under the Revd. Gordon Lang consisted almost entirely of Labour members; it was as a whole strongly in favour of world federation, but was represented at Gstaad in September only by King and Mackay.[386] The change in the world political situation in July 1947 thrust the idea of world federation into the background; pro-European members sought a more specific expression of their views, and the Continental example pointed to the formation of an all-party group. Ronald W. G. Mackay, the leading spirit of the reorganization, was at this time forty-five years old. An economist and a convinced European federalist of long standing, he at once grasped the supreme importance of Marshall's offer as an opportunity to bring about European union. In July he drew up a 'Memorandum on Britain's Economic Future' which was eventually sent to all Labour MPs, expounding the basic facts that world trade had been in decline since 1913 and above all since 1930 because of restrictions due to the policy of European nation states; that US production, having multiplied fivefold, was choking in dollar surpluses, and that world trade could not revive unless Europe recovered economically, for which purpose it must unite. Mackay's fifth and final point was:

That the economic problems which confront Great Britain confront the other industrial states of Europe, if not all the states of Europe, for each of whom it is essential that their market or trading area be extended; that to this end we should secure a federation of as many of the states of Europe, including Great Britain, as will come together; that such a federation should have power over trade, customs and currencies at least, so that the effective area of trade for each of the states

---

[385] Names given in MUCM press communiqué (n. 383), which referred to the foreign-affairs committee meeting and stated: '. . . a été constitué le groupe parlementaire fédéraliste italien, qui a recueilli 210 adhésions'. L. Levi and S. Pistone (n. 384) state on p. 109 that the 'Gruppi Parlamentari per l'Unione Europea' were at once refounded in the newly elected parliament on 18.4.1948; they then consisted of 104 senators and 169 deputies, the respective chairmen being Parri and Giacchero.

[386] Cf. at nn. 360 and 361; for the strength of the British representation at Gstaad, cf. at n. 370.

members of the federation will be large enough and sufficiently self-sufficient for mass production to be successful as is the case in the U.S.A.[387]

Mackay was handicapped by having no personal base in the Labour Party, whether of the academic or of the trade-union variety; but he was respected on all sides as a man of honest conviction and an independent economic expert, the best brain of the Labour Left.[388] His standing was enhanced by a brilliant speech in the Commons on 6 August, in which he opposed the Conservatives with vigour but also berated the Labour government for thinking 'only in terms of short-term remedies'; the fact was that 'for 50 years this country has lived on the fat which has come from its external investments', which had now disappeared, and that the present crisis was the culmination of the whole process of decline since 1913. After analysing the stages of this process he called on his hearers to recognize that Britain was now 'a small country';

The second thing is bluntly to face the fact, and why not face it and get rid of this cant and humbug going around the country, that we can still go on living as we did 50 years ago? We are a small country which is not big enough to mass-produce, and you cannot survive in the 20th century unless you have a market big enough to mass-produce. The only way to do that is to set up in Western Europe a customs union and a common currency ... If a free-trade market of 200 million people is brought about, you will create an area within which there is an ample source of supply for raw materials and which is big enough to give this country and Europe the markets needed for survival ... It may be a bit of a come-down for this country to regard itself as a European state, but that is the way to build up an economic structure for Europe. I ask the Government to think of this much more seriously than they have done.[389]

---

[387] Cf. chap. I/2 for Mackay's chairmanship of Federal Union in 1941, and biography, ibid., n. 112; as advocate in Oct. 1945 of European union on the lines of the USA and USSR, cf. chap. I/3 at n. 137; for his New York press conference in April 1947 and its influence on the change of US opinion, cf. Chap. I/3 at n. 204. His 'Memorandum on Britain's Economic Future' (forty-three typed pages; covering sheet dated 14.7.1947, preface dated 17.6.1947, hence written between these dates; *Mackay Archives,* EPU folder) was supported with numerous statistics which, in supplemented form, were appended a year later to a comprehensive work summing up his argument: R. W. G. Mackay, *You Can't Turn the Clock Back,* London, 1948, pp. 341–54 (cf. discussion of this in chap. V/5, in vol. 2).

[388] Information from *Hart,* 7.10.1974. Hart described Mackay as a liberal middle-class Socialist who was not concerned with creating a position of personal power but believed in the force of rational argument; his influence thus remained limited, although he was respected on all sides as a thinker of absolute integrity. Mackay corresponded occasionally with Coudenhove from 1946 onwards (*Mackay Archives*); his first contact with Brugmans was when he sent the latter a copy of his book on 22.5.1947. Brugmans replied on 26.6.1947 hoping they would meet and expressing confidence that 'we will be able to discuss many things in a spirit of complete understanding' (*BEF Archives,* Brugmans corr.).

[389] *Parliamentary Debates. House of Commons,* Vol. 441, 6.8.1947, No. 158; offprint in *Mackay Archives,* p. 5 f. Against the background of the Paris economic conference this speech made so strong an impression that Mackay could write to Coudenhove on 27.8.1947: 'I think I am now getting a majority of the British Labour Party to think along these lines, and I don't want to do anything which is going to prevent them coming to a conclusion on this matter in the next six months or so. That is where the Churchill business is so awkward.' Mackay's ideas, expressed in this letter, on the *political* objectives of federation – peace-keeping, defence, foreign policy – have been quoted in n.

For three months after this speech Mackay strove indefatigably to gain acceptance of his views among Labour MPs in the first instance, before proceeding to reconstitute the federalist group. On 1 September, with reference to the August debate which had shown the necessity 'to look again at our foundations', he sent all Labour MPs a copy of his book *Federal Europe* (1940) with a memorandum stating that 'The creation of a federation of Western Europe with Britain as a member state is the most urgent question confronting the British people today.' As effective federation with the Dominions was impossible, 'Great Britain must either associate herself in an economic and political union with the other states of Western Europe, or completely abandon her present standard of living.'[390] By the beginning of November Mackay was able to announce that King (acting in place of the Revd. G. Lang, who was ill) had agreed to summon a meeting of the Federalist Group, which had not assembled for some time, 'to consider a European Federation'; King, who had accepted a government post, would then relinquish his position in the Group. Mackay fully intended to form an all-party group on the EPU model; however, he was strongly opposed to Churchill and wanted in the first place to create a Labour group similar to its predecessor, but with a firm commitment to European federation. 'I want to get this movement backed by the Labour Party in Britain; that, to me, is what matters.'[391] After a preliminary meeting, twenty-one Labour members agreed on 2 December 1947 'to form an unofficial group of the members of the Parliamentary Labour Party who are interested in promoting the economic and political integration of Europe'. Mackay was elected chairman of this 'Europe Group', John Hynd and Christopher Shawcross its vice-chairman and secretary respectively. The group decided to begin by preparing 'various papers for study'. 'It was emphatically affirmed that the group would have no association with the Churchill group ... The prime objective of the group will be to ascertain whether a positive British socialist foreign policy may be

---

375 above; they suggest that it was for tactical reasons that Mackay stressed economic arguments in the Commons debate.
[390] He added that the German problem could only be solved 'under the control of a European government'. The Paris conference had only dealt with proposals for a European customs union, 'but if anyone considers a customs union seriously, they will realize that it would be idle to suppose that it could ever be established within a purely economic framework. The political structure would have to be brought up alongside.' Memorandum sent with covering latter of 1.9.1947 and a copy of *Federal Europe* (cf. chap. I/2, n. 112): *Mackay Archives*, EPU folder.
[391] Mackay to Coudenhove, 10.11.1947. The latter had encouraged him on 12.9.1947 'to set up a new parliamentary committee strongly based on Labour' and able to send delegates to the next EPU congress 'ready to give up some elements of national sovereignty, which cannot be expected from the Sandys group'. On the other hand he wrote on 11.11.1947, in reply to a letter from Mackay which has not been preserved, saying that he was 'so glad' to hear of Mackay's plan to form an all-party group and advising him to contact Sir P. Macdonald and Sir A. Salter (all in *Mackay Archives*, EPU folder).

constructed on the principle of European Union and, if so, to secure the adoption of such a policy.'[392]

At the group's next session on 16 December, however, Mackay produced a working paper which went further in two respects. He proposed that studies be made of particular aspects of European federation, and that a short memorandum 'setting out the basic ideas of a European Federation' be submitted to all Labour MPs as a 'basis of agreement'; also that a letter be sent to E. Shinwell, the party chairman, seeking agreement in principle to the creation of a Socialist pro-European movement open to public membership. These proposals were approved; subjects for study were allotted to different members of the group, and the letter as drafted by Mackay was sent off to Shinwell:

'For some time we have been aware of the grave consequences, both to this country and to Europe, resulting from the monopoly of the United Europe idea now enjoyed by Churchill and his followers. Some of us have close contacts with European Socialists and they all ask the same questions: "Why do you let him pervert the one idea which brings some hope of salvation? Why doesn't the Left have its own campaign?" We believe that these questions must be answered by the establishment of a Committee composed of Socialists, both from outside and inside Parliament, and drawn from all sections of the Party and the Movement, specifically devoted to conducting a campaign for a European Union.' The Committee could of course only conduct the campaign in Britain with the 'consent and encouragement of the National Executive'; on the other hand it could discuss on its own account possibilities 'which Cabinet Ministers cannot at present commit themselves to. We feel that if such an organization is not established in the near future, a golden opportunity will be missed both for educating public opinion in Britain and for rallying the Socialist forces in Europe. These latter, owing to the fatal tactics of the Communists, have now a real chance of reviving democratic Socialist leadership, and this will be increased if they know that in Britain the ideas for which they fight are being actively propagated.'[393] This was an accurate appraisal

---

[392] Europe Group, record of meeting on 2.12.1947, signed C. Shawcross. The preliminary meeting, called by King on 13.11.1947, was attended by thirteen MPs, who agreed that the question of closer links among European states deserved 'careful investigation', and issued a collective invitation to the meeting on 2.12.1947 (both documents in *Mackay Archives*). The news of the reconstituted Labour group must have spread at once, for A. Marc wrote to Mackay from Geneva on 15.12.1947: 'With great pleasure we learned of the formation, in the House of Commons, of the European Committee'; he enclosed documents of the UEF Montreux congress and proposed co-operation (ibid.).

[393] Mackay's 'Draft Proposals for activities of the Europe Group' (three typed pages) and draft letter to Shinwell submitted to the group on 16.12.1947: 'Minutes of Meeting held on Tuesday 16.12.1947', with decision to send the letter (all in *Mackay Archives*). Those present are given as R. Mackay (in the chair), W. H. Ayles, W. Coldrick, A. Crawley, R. H. S. Crossman, M. Foot, H. Hughes, J. Hynd, F. Longden, Leah Manning, G. H. Oliver, R. T. Paget, A. M. F. Palmer, H. Pursey, C. Shawcross, T. C. Skeffington-Lodge, A. L. Symonds, and the Revd. G. S. Woods. At subsequent meetings the names of Foot and Longden do not recur, but additional regular attenders were: Barbara Castle, R. Chamberlain, F. Fairhurst, John Haire, Leslie Hale, R. Hamilton, P. Holman, S. Segal, S. Silverman, Julian Snow, and W. N. Warbey. At the end of 1947 Shawcross wrote to all Labour MPs enclosing a brief account of the meeting of 16.12.1947 and inviting them 'to join the Group and to send their names as soon as possible to the Secretary. The Group now has 40 members' (*Mackay Archives*).

of the position of Continental Socialists. The Labour leaders apparently did not reply to Mackay's appeal, however, and the non-party approach which he also organized was all the more important in consequence.

Mackay had let it be known that an all-party group for European federation was in process of being formed, and at the session of the Labour group on 16 December he urged his fellow-members to join in good numbers so that it could be under their control 'rather than allowing it to get into the hands of the Churchill people'. On 11 December Mackay and Shawcross had in fact joined with the Conservatives P. Macdonald and Smiles and an Independent member, Sir A. Salter, to invite all MPs who had answered 'Yes' to Coudenhove's enquiry to attend an all-party meeting on the 17th to consider the creation of an all-party group. The Labour group, in accordance with Mackay's advice, 'decided that as many members as possible should attend the all-party meeting ... with a view to its becoming a group representative of the Socialist majority in the House'.[394]

The all-party meeting on the 17th, at which Sir P. Macdonald gave an account of the Gstaad congress, was attended by eight Labour members, four Conservatives, and one Liberal. 'Owing to the small number of members present (due to pressure of other business at the time) it was decided to form a temporary All-Party Parliamentary Committee for the provisional purpose of (a) drawing up a statement of proposals' as regards the work of a permanent all-party group, and (b) calling a 'larger all-party meeting with the object of deciding whether a permanent Group of this kind should be formed'. Mackay was elected provisional chairman, and C. Shawcross and P. Roberts joint secretaries.[395] The All-Party Parliamentary Group for European Federation seems to have been formally constituted in January 1948 or on 2 February, when Georges Bohy, the chairman of EPU, visited London under Mackay's auspices.[396] On 18 February it held

---

[394] Minutes (n. 393), p. 2; invitation of 11.12.1947; Mackay's 'Draft Proposals' (n. 393), p. 2. Mackay added the suggestion that a motion might be drafted 'to be put down and for time to be got for a discussion of the whole question in the House' (all in *Mackay Archives*). Thus in mid-December 1947 Mackay put forward the idea of an all-party motion on Europe, which materialized on 19.3.1948. All his activity in the interim was a preparation for this; cf. chap. V/2 in vol. 2.

[395] 'Minutes of an All-Party Meeting', 17.12.1947. Those present were Labour members S. Cooper, L. Hale, P. Holman, H. Hughes, R. W. G. Mackay, H. Pursey, C. Shawcross, and A. L. Symonds; Conservatives J. R. H. Hutchinson, Sir P. Macdonald, M. Phillips Price, and P. G. Roberts; and the Liberal, Sir H. Morris-Jones. In the discussion Sir P. Macdonald stated that the Inter-Parliamentary Union had various proposals for contact and that 'the British Section of the IPU would give its blessing to the proposed group ... of EPU concerned only with the definite objective of promoting a European Federation' (*Mackay Archives*).

[396] No record of the foundation has yet been traced. Minutes of the Labour group and a letter of 27.1.1948 from Mackay to Prime Minister Attlee show that Bohy arrived in London on 30.1.1948 and lunched at the House of Commons on 2 February with members of the All-Party Group, after which he addressed a meeting of members of the Parliamentary Labour Party. Between lunch and the meeting he saw Attlee for an hour (Attlee's private secretary to Mackay, 29.1.1948; all in *Mackay Archives*).

a session with Mackay in the chair, this time with numerous Conservatives present, which decided *inter alia* that 'the EPU should be approached to become sponsors to the Hague Conference'.[397] Meanwhile, in January and February the Labour 'Europe Group' held at least five or six meetings to discuss 'functional' and 'federalist' methods; this work will be described in Chapter V/2, as it formed a basis for the motion tabled on 19 March. Meanwhile close co-operation grew between Mackay and R. Boothby, the chief European federalist on the Conservative side. On the basis of these developments the All-Party Group reached agreement on 3 March on the text of a motion which was signed between then and the 19th by 133 MPs (all of whom presumably belonged to the Group), including 68 Labour members, 53 Conservatives, 5 Liberals, and 7 Independents; by the end of April the signatures numbered 190.[398] Mackay, with his two-pronged strategy, had mobilized parliamentary opinion among all parties in favour of European federation to the maximum extent permitted by British insularity and Bevin's anti-Europeanism. The result did not amount to a majority, but the Group did all it possibly could to foster the idea of European union in the British parliament.

Altogether, within six months of June 1947, federalist groups were formed by pro-European parliamentarians in Britain, France, the Netherlands, Belgium, Luxemburg, Italy, and Greece; in each group all parties were represented except the Communists, who consistently refused to take part. In the Scandinavian countries attempts to form such groups proceeded with difficulty, while in Spain, Portugal, and Eastern Europe they were out of the question. On the Continent these groups were formed from the outset on a non-party basis, as those concerned realized that the urgent need for union took precedence over party objectives; in Britain, on the other hand, the first associations of MPs were on a party basis, and the All-Party Group was formed at a relatively late stage. From early 1948 onwards the all-party parliamentary groups were an important part of the movement for European union. There was long debate over the question whether they should be affiliated to the UEF or, later, to the European Movement, or form an independent association under the EPU; this issue took two years to resolve, during which time the groups were mainly concerned with the task of converting their own party executives.[399]

---

[397] According to minutes of a meeting of the Labour group on 24.2.1948; it appears from these that fewer Labour than Conservative members attended the meeting of 18.2.1948, the minutes of which have not been found. For the preliminaries to the Hague congress (7–10.5.1948), cf. chap. V/3 (in vol. 2).

[398] See chap. V/2 (in vol. 2) for an account of the full debate in the Labour group and Mackay's letter of 26.2.1848 to 'My dear Bob' (Boothby, both in *Mackay Archives*), and of the all-party motion of 19.3.1948 for a European constituent assembly. On Boothby, cf. chap. I, nn. 175 and 205; on the general background to Bevin's ban on the European idea, cf. chap. I/3, pp. 166–200.

[399] On the efforts of the federalist groups within their own parties, cf. chap. IV (in vol. 2), In chaps. V/3 and VI/2, also in vol. 2, will be discussed the question of affiliation with the pro-European associations, the fate of the EPU and its incorporation in the European Movement in the summer of

Except in Luxemburg, the groups did not even succeed in recruiting all members of parliament who had answered 'Yes' to Coudenhove's enquiry. They were, so to speak, non-party clubs comprising at first only a quarter or a third of the members of their respective parliaments; some of them were convinced federalists, while others were only beginning to envisage the problems of European unification from the standpoint of essential economic co-operation. Nevertheless, the formation of these parliamentary groups meant that the idea of European federation had established itself in the opinion-forming centres of West-European political life.

6. Formation of National Federalist Associations in Western Europe

As has been seen, the change in the international situation following the Moscow deadlock and the US appeal to Europeans to pool their resources had made the question of union a live political issue in Western Europe, while the East-European countries were finally sealed off by the Soviet rejection of the Marshall Plan. From June 1947 onwards, many West-European parliamentarians reacted by forming pro-European associations among themselves. The federalist groups which had so far been the champions of the European cause were faced with difficult problems, to which provisional answers were formulated in August 1947 at the Montreux congress of their umbrella organization, the UEF. Forced to abandon the hope that Europe as a whole might be made into a neutral zone between East and West, the UEF accepted the necessity of making a beginning 'wherever it [could] be attempted', i.e. in Western Europe, with the impetus provided by the US initiative and the changed political climate. Partly in compensation for the enforced limitation of plans to Western Europe, the Montreux congress emphasized the need for integral federalism and a genuine union embracing all spheres of life, and also took the view that in current circumstances it was essential to secure the full participation of Great Britain.[400]

At this juncture it is necessary to examine the effect of these developments and of the Montreux decisions on member associations of the UEF in particular countries. Thanks to the opportunities offered by the political situation, the associations flourished considerably in the second half of 1947 and also made progress towards unity among themselves.

1949, a development in which Mackay played a large part. Chap. VI/7 (in vol. 2) describes the formation of a similar 'German Parliamentary Group of the European Movement' in the Bundestag soon after it first assembled on 10.11.1949; the first secretary of this group was Fritz Erler.
[400] Cf. chap. III/4.

(A) FRENCH FEDERALIST GROUPS AND THE CONSEIL FRANÇAIS POUR L'EUROPE UNIE

As described in Chapter II, larger and smaller groups of French federalists arose in fruitful diversity from mid-1946 onwards. The need to confine the immediate objective to Western Europe was especially painful to them, as they had generally conceived of a united Europe as a 'Third Force' independent of both superpowers and promoting peace between them. On the other hand, integral federalism was strongly represented in France by La Fédération and the Cercles socialistes, and their gradualistic ideas fitted in well enough with the fact, recognized at Montreux, that Europe would have to be unified by geographical stages.

The fresh impulse given by the new political situation to the movement for European unity found expression in France in the creation of the Conseil français pour l'Europe unie. René Courtin – a man of liberal views, a professor of law, and a co-director of *Le Monde* – was in touch with Coudenhove-Kalergi and Duncan Sandys, secretary of Churchill's United Europe Movement; with encouragement from the former he had endeavoured since June 1946 to form a group of politicians and other leading personalities in support of European union, but up to May 1947 he had encountered a good deal of difficulty and scepticism.

In December 1946 Sandys wrote to Coudenhove-Kalergi 'It is difficult to make any progress at the moment in France', the main reason being French fear of a revived Germany.[401] Among those who did not share Bidault's nationalistic approach to the German problem, the Socialists were sympathetic in principle to Courtin's initiative but were deterred by its close links with Churchill's movement, since the Labour Party disapproved of the latter and the SFIO leaders did not want to get out of step with their British colleagues.[402] Courtin, on the other hand, wished to avoid forming an 'unbalanced' committee of parliamentarians representing only the MRP and the Radicals; so, having received a rebuff from the Socialists in the spring of 1947, he set out to form a provisional, non-political committee composed of business leaders, journalists, and churchmen.[403]

By 10 July 1947, however, Courtin was able to send Sandys a list of twenty-six leading personalities, including Socialists and other politicians, who had agreed in principle to serve on an enlarged committee. These were:

---

[401] Sandys to Coudenhove-Kalergi, 4.12.1946, *EM Archives, Bruges*.

[402] Churchill wrote to Blum on 24.1.1947 expressing the hope 'that a French Group may be formed on parallel lines [to the UEM], so that Britain and France can keep in touch with each other on the further steps that may be taken' (*EM Archives, Bruges*); however, Blum conveyed a negative reply to Churchill's emissary, Commander King-Hall. André Philip asked Courtin and Michel Debré, who was pressing for an answer, to allow him time for reflection; after a trip to London in mid-February 1947, he told them 'que les choses s'arrangeront en Grande-Bretagne et [il] espère d'ici deux mois nous donner son appui' (Courtin to King-Hall, 20.2.1947, *EM Archives, Bruges*; the same, 11.2.1947, ibid.). On 17.5.1947 Courtin informed Sandys: 'J'ai eu depuis notre rencontre [in Nov. 1946] une conversation avec M. Blum, sympathique mais toujours hésitant' (*EM Archives, Bruges*).

[403] Courtin to King-Hall, 20.2.1947, *EM Archives, Bruges*.

Radicals: Paul Bastid, Édouard Herriot, René Mayer.
MRP: Paul Coste-Floret, François de Menthon, Edmond Michelet, Pierre-Henri Teitgen.
SFIO: Robert Lacoste, Minjoz, Francis Leenhardt, André Le Troquer.
Independent: Paul Reynaud.
Church leaders: Cardinal Saliège, archbishop of Toulouse; Fr. Chaillet, editor of *Cahiers du témoignage chrétien*; Pastor M. Boegner, president of the French Protestant Federation.
Academicians: Raymond Aron, Jean Bayet, Paul Claudel, André Kaan, André Siegfried, Edmond Vermeil.
Others: Michel Debré, founder of the École Nationale d'Administration; Pierre Denis, president of the Banque Française d'Outremer; André Monnier, former prefect.

The inaugural assembly of the Conseil français pour l'Europe unie, held at Courtin's house on 16 July, elected Herriot as honorary president and André Siegfried, Paul Bastid, Paul Reynaud, and Pierre-Henri Teitgen as vice-presidents. Paul Ramadier subsequently became a vice-president, while Courtin was appointed 'délégué-général' and *de facto* manager.[404]

The Conseil did not draw up any programme at this meeting, held shortly before the summer recess, nor did it do so in the following months. Its *design for Europe* can therefore only be described with some caution. According to a manifesto drafted by Courtin in January 1947, the group's aim was a 'federation of the nations of Europe', which were too small individually to achieve economic recovery or provide for their own defence; they must unite to form 'one Europe with a single currency and economic policy, a single army and diplomatic service'.[405] Thus Courtin's own views were firmly supranational, and he approached the future members of the Conseil on this basis. On the other hand he was in close touch with Duncan Sandys, who hoped to turn the Conseil into the French branch of the UEM, reflecting Churchill's 'unionistic' ideas based on co-operation as opposed to federation. The Conseil, loosely organized as it was, did not take up a firm position on this matter, but certainly all its members regarded the Anglo-French *entente* as the nucleus of the future Europe and desired to co-ordinate their efforts with those of the UEM – though they

---

[404] 'Liste des personnalités ayant bien voulu donner leur adhésion au Comité français pour l'Europe unie dans le cadre de l'O.N.U.', *EM Archives, Bruges*; Courtin to Sandys, 10.7.1947, ibid.; René Courtin, 'France, Angleterre, Europe', *Réforme*, 2.8.1947 (describing establishment of the Committee); reports by AEP 18.7.1947, *Le Monde* 19.7.1947, *The Times* 19.7.1947, *Der Kurier* 19.7.1947, *Daily Mail* 20.7.1947. On 22.7.1947 the list of names, unaltered, was sent by D. Sandys to all members of the British UEM as constituting the 'French United Europe Committee" (*EM Archives, Bruges*).
[405] 'Manifeste du Comité provisoire français pour l'Europe unie dans le cadre de l'O.N.U.', 24.1.1947, *EM Archives, Bruges.*

made it clear that they would like to see more Labour Party members joining the latter to offset Churchill's predominance.[406]

As to *Europe's position in the world*, Courtin at the beginning of 1947 saw it as a 'Third Force'. 'Europe must neither be America's bridgehead against the East, nor a Russian spring-board against the US; ni bloc occidental, ni bloc oriental.' A European federation should include Germany and should encourage a more progressive colonial policy; thus, alongside the USA and USSR, there would be a third viable Continental unit, with a stabilizing effect on relations between the other two: 'United Europe is the first condition of world peace.'[407] On the other hand co-operation with Churchill's organization, especially after the Soviet rejection of the Marshall Plan, meant that united Europe must be considered as part of the developing organization of the Western hemisphere. On this point too, the Conseil as such did not arrive at a firm conclusion.

The *structure* and *methods* of the Conseil help to explain the relative vagueness of its programme. Its members, who came to number something like 100,[408] were all prominent public figures who could not themselves devote much time and energy to the council's activities. Courtin's object was rather to select individuals who already played a key part in public affairs, so as to introduce the European idea into the mainstream of French politics and publicity. In due course, after initial difficulties,[409] the Conseil began to function as intended, and by the beginning of 1948 the idea of European union was taken far more seriously in France than it had been eight months earlier.

Among federalist movements with a broader membership, La Fédération continued to take first place. The Comité de coordination des mouvements fédéralistes français, under André Voisin's chairmanship, set up its headquarters at the office of La Fédération at 9, rue Auber, thus emphasizing

[406] As will be seen later, a delegation of British pro-Europeans led by Lord Layton visited Paris on 17–21 July 1947 for talks with members of the Conseil français; the group included Sandys, L. S. Amery, Lord Beveridge, the Labour MP E. M. King, the Conservative MP R. Boothby, Lady Violet Bonham Carter, president of the Liberal Party, and the Revd. Gordon Lang, chairman of the federalist group in the House of Commons. From the talks it soon became clear that there were different views on the question of federalism versus 'unionism'. Courtin observed: 'The difficulties persist, but we can and must find a solution' (*Réforme*, 2.8.1947; cf. n. 404). For details of the delegation's visit, cf. at nn. 516–20. Pressure for Labour participation, e.g. Courtin to Sandys, 31.7.1947 (*EM Archives, Bruges*).
[407] 'Manifeste . . .' (n. 405).
[408] O. Philip (n. 367), p. 182.
[409] Despite Sandys's pressure the Conseil could not do much during the summer recess of 1947. Courtin tried unsuccessfully to organize a mass demonstration in November 1947 with the help of Churchill, who was willing, and Blum, who as before would not co-operate unless the Labour Party was involved. In December 1947 a 'Mouvement français pour les États-Unis d'Europe' was founded under the chairmanship of Raoul Dautry for the purpose of giving the Conseil the mass support it needed, but this group soon had to give way to the French member association of the UEF. Cf. Courtin to Sandys, 31.7.1947; Sandys to André Noël, 6.8.1947; Jacques Bassot to Sandys, 30.10.1947; *EM Archives, Bruges*; on Dautry, see Philip (n. 367), p. 216.

the latter's predominance and its increasing tendency to absorb smaller and less substantial groups. An examination of its monthly journal *La Fédération* shows that discussion within the association in the second half of 1947 was increasingly concerned with international aspects. Its contributors were well aware of the opportunities offered by the new international situation and the beginnings of official interest in European co-operation; they supported the latter, but in a critical spirit and without ever losing sight of federalist principles.

La Fédération was prompt to welcome the Marshall Plan as a means of giving practical content to federalism. 'The need to draw up a joint plan as a condition of enjoying American aid should promote a "community" spirit and bring about at least the first stage of federalism in the economic sphere.' The Soviet rejection and the consequent division of Europe were to be expected: 'It is impossible to see how the totalitarian structure of its economy could permit the Soviet Union to engage in permanent close co-operation with countries of an entirely different structure.' For Western Europe, on the other hand, the Marshall Plan was 'the last chance ... In France, our rulers unfortunately seem to place all their hopes in the miraculous shower of dollars ... Shall we ever come to understand that this secular Heaven, studded with all its forty-eight stars, will only help us if we help ourselves? ...The Sixteen have drawn up a balance sheet of their needs and resources – that was the first step. Now they must align their economies, harmonize their national plans and prepare to enter into customs unions after the Benelux model. When they do that, they will discover that economics are not everything. The European economic area, this side of the Iron Curtain at any rate, will only take shape and come to life by means of common political, administrative and cultural institutions.'[410] The gradualistic philosophy of integral federalism made it possible to aim at ultimate union while realistically taking account of actual possibilities.

The most detailed exposé of federalist thought in the light of the new situation in Europe was produced by the Cercles socialistes, fédéralistes, et communautaires pour une république moderne (CSFC), led by Claude-Marcel Hytte, who played a key role at Montreux as rapporteur of the General Policy Resolution. In a series of five articles published in the association's journal *La République moderne* in the summer of 1947, Victor Atalant described the viewpoint of integral federalism in relation to Europe.

In opposition to doctrinaire stubbornness and extremism, Atalant emphasized the need for 'empirical organization, proceeding from the simple to the complex. The first stage is to unite nations, hitherto isolated, into regional federations; this may serve as a testing-ground of true federalism and also provide an increasingly substantial element of balance between the USA and the USSR – both of which are still very imperfect federations, as is shown by their overt antagonism to each

---

[410] Quotations from: 1. Claude Saint-Jean, 'Exhortations à l'Union', *La Fédération*, No. 30, July 1947, p. 28; 2. id., 'Le laborieux été européen', *La Fédération*, Nos. 31–2, Aug.–Sept. 1947, p. 36; 3. Editorial, *La Fédération*, No. 33, Oct. 1947, p. 1. In Aug. 1947 *La Fédération* reported at length on the visit of British pro-Europeans (cf. n. 406); in Oct., on the development of American capitalism as a future partner of united Europe; in Dec., on Germany and the need to integrate it in the work of reconstruction.

other.' If the Europeans do not want to be crushed in the latent struggle, which may one day be an open conflict, between the two world powers, they must unite for self-defence; and this too is the only way of ensuring a peaceful future for Germany. 'In present circumstances the federated area must clearly be confined in the first place to Western Europe and to a few nations which are sufficiently akin to form a preliminary union. But its success and power of attraction will be so great that other nations will join the original nucleus and extend the federation to the borders of Europe, so that the Continent may be born again and live in freedom between America and the Soviet Union.'[411]

In Atalant's view West-European federation would not be achieved by old-fashioned political parties, whose horizons were bounded by the nation state, but by a mass movement bringing pressure to bear on governments. The spirit of federalism should be fostered by encouraging impulses of all kinds towards unity and co-operation, and all attempts to override national autarky in however small a way. The Marshall Plan offered 'the chance of achieving a first degree of union'; it guaranteed 'co-operation and compromise', if not as yet 'planning or unity', and was therefore a first step towards federation even if some European states remained outside it. The journal was at pains, however, to disclaim any idea that it had joined a pro-American faction. 'The salvation of Europe depends on Europeans alone; only they can assert European unity against the cleavage imposed from without, and free the Continent from American tutelage as well as from Soviet dependence.'[412] Although federation had to begin in Western Europe, it was hoped that the movement would eventually become strong enough to make the Continent independent of both world powers.

The smaller federalist associations likewise hoped, in 1947 and at the beginning of 1948, that US aid would not prevent Europe becoming a 'Third Force'. The Comité d'Action Internationale spoke in an internal discussion paper of the 'unique opportunity' of a supranational experiment by way of West-European co-operation, which could now not be refused; on the other hand, the paper observed that 'agrarian Eastern Europe is a natural counterpart to the industrial West'. The Comité français pour une Fédération européenne et mondiale (CFEM), headed by Francis Gérard, at its general meeting on 15 February 1948 welcomed 'any step towards uniting those parts of Europe that are already prepared to join in a European federation'; at the same time, the door must be left open for the East Europeans and Europe must be protected from the 'tutelage of big international combines'. The Comité d'Action fédérale et sociale, founded

---

[411] V. Atalant, 'Le problème de la fédération européenne', *La République moderne*, Nos. 27/8, 15.5./1.6.1947 (first quotation); ibid., No. 29, 15.6.1947 (second quotation).
[412] V. Atalant, 'Le problème de la fédération européenne', *La République moderne*, No. 30, 1.7.1947 (first quotation); 'Nos positions: Le fédéralisme européen', editorial, *La République moderne*, No. 41, 15.12.1947 (second quotation). The text has 'indépendance', evidently an error for 'dépendance'.

at this time by Jean-Pierre Gouzy,[413] favoured the 'organic unity of Western Europe through the working-out of a federal system', but hoped that the influence of diplomats of all nationalities would be superseded by that of the 'broad masses'.[414]

In October 1947 Alexandre Marc summarized the attitude and hopes of French federalists after Montreux as follows. A European community 'should in itself be a bridge – not only geographically but above all in political, social and spiritual terms; a bridge, not a compromise – between the two hostile systems which, by their own inner logic, can only ignore or oppose each other'. Such a community, 'in one of the most dangerous areas of our planet, must kindle the living flame of federalism, whose power and radiance, transcending all frontiers, will help to set the world on the path of supranational collaboration'.[415] Altogether, the French federalists did not by any means reject the chance of making a start in Western Europe, but they were not prepared on that account to relinquish their broader objectives. Relying, as can be observed, with excessive confidence on the power of the federalist ideal, they believed that Western integration was compatible with the creation of an independent Europe.

(B) REVIVAL OF THE MOVIMENTO FEDERALISTA EUROPEO AFTER MONTREUX

Among French federalists, the conflict between the principle of universality and the alternative of beginning with Western Europe was avoided thanks to a gradualist philosophy and, eventually, by unanimous *de facto* agreement on the second course. In Italy, on the other hand, the choice was at first a matter of open dissension.

The 'maximalist' school of thought which prevailed at the first national congress of the Movimento Federalista Europeo (MFE) in October 1946 favoured a strategy of converting the masses so as to create a Europe of

---

[413] Jean-Pierre Gouzy, b. 1925, studied political science and literature; journalist; member for a time of the Resistance-based UDSR, later secretary-general of the UFF and UEF; from 1968 chairman of French national committee of the European Movement; see A. Greilsammer, *Les Fédéralistes européens en France depuis 1945*, thesis, Paris, 1972, p. 319.

[414] Comité d'Action Internationale: C. Monnier, J. Joetzlin, 'Plan pour servir à l'élaboration d'un Manifeste', 28.10.1947 (*BEF Archives*, Brugmans corr.). CFEM: 'Résolution' in *Le Document fédéraliste*, No. 6, May 1948. Comité d'Action fédérale et sociale: UEF circular letter No. 18, 14.4.1948, based on a report by J. P. Gouzy.

[415] A. Marc, 'Le Fédéralisme et la Paix', in 'Bataille pour la paix', *Cahiers du monde nouveau*, 1947, no. 6, pp. 249–55; quotations here, pp. 252–3. This article was soon translated into German under the title 'Der Föderalismus und der Friede' in F. A. Kramer (ed.), *Der Kampf um den Frieden*, Coblenz, 1948, pp. 172–8. Several other scholarly French journals discussed European federalism in Oct.; Gaston Goldschild and Maurice Klein wrote in the *Revue socialiste* on 'Une nécessité: la construction de l'Europe' (Nov., pp. 435–45); similarly Georges Scelle, 'Le Fédéralisme et l'Europe occidentale', *Revue politique et parlementaire*, Dec. 1947, pp. 209–16; Jean Lucien-Brun, 'Vers une fédération européenne?', *Études*, pp. 239–42; Louis Marlio, 'L'heure de la Fédération Européenne', *Revue hommes et mondes*, Sept. 1947, pp. 1–18; all testifying to the stimulus given to federalist ideas by the inception of the Marshall Plan in France.

peoples, if necessary without the help of governments and even in spite of them; the federation, moreover, should include all European nations, East and West. Professor Campagnolo, the new secretary-general, was an advocate of this 'revolutionary' federalism, but his attempt to put it across led to a crisis in the MFE leadership: after an initial increase in membership five splinter groups seceded from the movement in protest against Campagnolo's intransigence. These were:

> Movimento Autonomista di Federazione Europea (chairman Tullo Tulli, secretary-general Veniero Spinelli);
> Associazione Federalista Europea;
> Movimento Italiano per la Federazione Europea;
> Movimento Unionista Italiano;
> Movimento Unionista Europeo.

Campagnolo did not encounter much sympathy on the international plane either; at the Amsterdam meeting of April 1947 he was not elected to the Central Committee of the UEF, the 'Italian' seat being filled by Dr Milo di Villagrazia of the Associazione Federalista Europea. The MFE was by this time no more than a debating society.[416] It was led back into the realm of practical politics by the 'minimalists' headed by the founder members Altiero Spinelli and Ernesto Rossi, after the announcement of Marshall's offer and the beginnings of co-operation in the CEEC. Previously the lack of concrete encouragement for any kind of federalism had operated in favour of Campagnolo with his verbal extremism; but the weakness of his position was increasingly clear as economic co-operation began to transcend national boundaries and as Italian foreign policy, under Count Sforza,[417] came to be firmly oriented towards Europe. At the UEF congress in Montreux at the end of August 1947 Altiero Spinelli, who had just returned to federalist activity after being secretary-general of the Partito d'Azione, made an impressive speech which gave the decisive impulse towards making a start in Western Europe.[418] Together with others of like mind he set about transforming the MFE into a pressure group with the object of backing specific moves towards European unification.

A clear sign of the Italian federalists' change of heart was given at a mass meeting on 26 October 1947 at the Teatro Eliseo in Rome. The audience of over 2,000 was addressed by ex-premier F. Parri (Partito d'Azione), Einaudi of the Liberal party (minister of the budget), Professors Calamandrei and Salvemini,

---

[416] On the Venice congress, Oct. 1946, cf. chap. I/7 above, pp. 275–8; on the Amsterdam congress, attended by Campagnolo, cf. chap. II/5, n. 195. For other Italian federalist groups, see list of addresses in *L'Europe unie dans un monde uni,* UEF pamphlet, Geneva, 1948, p. 12, and A. A. Young, 'Federalism in Italy', *Federal News,* No. 148, July 1947, p. 8.
[417] Cf. chap. III/2, p. 501 f. On assuming office in Feb. 1947 Sforza is reported to have said: 'I have become the foreign minister of a European nation-state, and I shall do all I can to make my post superfluous. (*Junior Magazin, Sonderheft Europa,* Aschaffenburg, 1953, p. 2; not verified, however).
[418] Chap. III/4, p. 581 f.

and Ignazio Silone, formerly chief editor of *Avanti* and subsequently leader of the United Socialist Party (PSU). All these speakers approached the problem of European unity not from an abstract, ideal point of view but in the light of the actual situation in 1947. Salvemini deprecated 'European union *à la* Churchill', and Silone urged the necessity of doing away with national sovereign states. 'The real issue today is not whether the nations of Europe should keep their sovereignty or improve their lot by uniting; the question is rather, shall they unite and thus try to survive, or is each of them to come to grief separately in its own way?' Silone then developed for the first time his well-known thesis of the nationalization of European Socialism: 'The assessment of political parties will have to be revised in many ways when they are judged in terms of concrete initiatives for European unity or the federation of groups of European peoples. The present-day designations of "Right" and "Left" will then prove to be arbitrary labels.'[419]

In opposition to Spinelli and the increasingly numerous advocates of a change of policy in the direction of 'realism', Professor Giacomo Devoto of Florence summed up the maximalist arguments in a majority report of the executive council of the MFE prepared in December 1947 for the movement's second National Congress, to be held in February 1948. Those who wanted to take up Marshall's initiative and make a start in Western Europe were guilty of 'underrating the totalitarian nature of the West and over-emphasizing totalitarian manifestations in the East'; the result of their policy would be, 'not to strike a blow simultaneously at war and totalitarianism in general, but to open a rift by striking indirectly at a particular form of totalitarianism and increasing the risk of war'. The Marshall Plan must therefore 'be approved inasmuch as it calls for a degree of economic co-ordination in a supranational area and requires a corresponding surrender of sovereign rights, but not in so far as it has the effect of restoring vigour to a mutilated part of Europe with potentially aggressive aims'.[420] The maximalists were rendered politically impotent by the European dilemma of 1947: the fact that by uniting part of the Continent they would be helping to crystallize its division, and by putting federal principles into practice they would be bolstering a social order based on liberal capitalism. With the objective of all-out federalism in mind, they were not disposed to pay the price of supporting European union under the aegis of the Marshall Plan.

Devoto's report, representing the Campagnolo point of view, was opposed in a memorandum by Rossi which, on behalf of a minority of the executive, argued that Devoto was confusing true federalists with 'those who

---

[419] All five speeches were republished in *Europa federata*, by F. Parri and others, introduction by Ernesto Rossi, Milan (Nov.) 1947; Salvemini has been quoted more fully in chap. II at n. 118. Silone continued: 'The nation state . . . , at the very time when it ought to be absorbed into larger political units, has received a tremendous accretion of strength. Its power is monstrous'; for 'The distribution of economic profit . . . depends on the state's laws', and the Socialists took their bearings by this nationalist horizon.

[420] *Il Mondo europeo*, Nos. 58/9, Bologna, 15.1.1948; circulated as a special offprint for the MFE's second national congress (15–17.2.48), pp. 3–5.

claim to be such but in reality stand for Churchill's imperialist ideas – that is, they want to see Western Europe united under British patronage into an anti-Soviet bloc, a weapon in the hands of Britain and the USA against the USSR'. As against this, Rossi and those who thought like him wanted to create 'a Western European federation in which all the participating countries have equal rights, and which may cover a larger or smaller area' according to whether Britain joined in, or Spain and Portugal became democratic, or it proved possible to include all or part of Germany.

US policy, Rossi continued, undeniably showed imperialistic features, but they were of little account compared with the political vision of a peaceful Europe 'capable of checking Soviet expansion by its own power'; moreover, a federal union of Western Europe would make it possible to avert the 'danger of American colonization'. Should the Soviet Union refuse to be convinced of the peaceful character of the federation, that was still no reason to give up the attempt and to stand idly by while the Russians created a 'zone of small countries under their economic and political influence'. Federalism meant peace, but peace in freedom.[421]

Against Devoto's policy of passive expectation, whether inspired by scepticism, prudence, or sheer vagueness and lack of ideas, Rossi urged that the federalists should take resolute action in Western Europe and address themselves realistically to its actual problems – that of Germany, for instance, or that of determining the extent of their collaboration with other groups working for unity.

At the national congress of MFE, which took place at Milan from 15 to 17 February 1948, Spinelli and his friends succeeded in bringing the majority round to the views expressed in Rossi's memorandum. In its final resolution the congress defined its ultimate *objective* as 'a federal union of states with a supranational government directly elected by, and directly responsible to, the citizens of the federated countries'. As to *Europe's position in the world,* the resolution pointed out that 'if a beginning is not made at once with the federation of at least part of Europe, provided personal and political liberties are respected there, the great imperialist powers cannot be prevented from gradually extending their domination over the whole Continent'. A federal Europe, although helped to recover by American aid, would not only safeguard the US against Soviet encroachment but would also protect the Soviet Union against American economic expansionism, and would thus 'contribute decisively to détente'. The Italian federalists, under Spinelli's influence, had thus reached a similar position to their French opposite numbers. Both groups believed sufficiently in the dynamics and attractiveness of the federalist movement to feel sure that even though a start had to be made in Western Europe

---

[421] Op. cit. (n. 420), pp. 5–11. Rossi continued to argue for 'territorial gradualism, beginning with the states which can most easily join the federal pact, and extending to further areas as and when circumstances prove favourable'; but he opposed the 'functional approach' which would renounce the immediate objective of supernationality. He believed this latter to be the maximalists' intention, in view of their reluctance to come out openly for making 'a start in Western Europe'.

alone – or perhaps for that very reason – they could still avoid the twofold risk to which Devoto had drawn attention, viz. that (1) the creation of a bloc would increase the danger of war and (2) the connection with American capitalism would prevent the establishment of a Socialist-federalist order within the states concerned.

The principal decision of the Milan congress was to agree on a *plan of campaign* in the light of these conclusions: viz. that the MFE would henceforth base its policy on the definite prospects of unity offered by the Marshall Plan and 'with the help of democratic political forces, [would] induce governments to direct their foreign policy towards the immediate creation of European federal institutions'. Nothing more was heard of Campagnolo's 'revolutionary' plans for a mass movement against parties and governments; the Milan congress adopted, once and for all, the policy of forming a pressure group within the parliamentary system. After a thorough discussion in which the contradictory theses were openly presented by two opposing camps, the MFE had conformed to the Montreux decision and was thus once again ready to co-operate with the other member associations of the UEF.[422]

The transformation by which the MFE became an ordinary pressure group instead of a 'revolutionary' but basically unpolitical 'mass' movement which did not even enjoy mass support was symbolized by A. Spinelli's appointment, in June 1948, to replace Campagnolo as secretary-general. From now on the movement reverted to the *Purpose* laid down in its statutes of October 1946, that of 'promoting the formation of political institutions able and empowered to perform the legal act of creating a new European federal state, as soon as the necessary historical conditions have developed':[423] in other words, it was set on a gradualist course and would press for the realization of the federal principle whenever historical circumstances made it opportune to do so.

A number of organizational decisions were taken. Milan was to be the movement's headquarters, and branches were to be set up in localities 'where there are at least ten registered members'. Their chief task consisted in publicity, recruitment, and, where appropriate, the formation of groups in particular firms or among members of a given trade or profession (Art. 8). The 'national centre' of the movement consisted of the national executive with a maximum membership of fifteen, with an advisory central council composed of all chairmen of regional

---

[422] Quotations from Political Resolution of the MFE's second national congress, 15–17.2.1948, printed as a pamphlet in March 1948 (*Spinelli Archives*); reproduced in L. Levi and S. Pistone (ed.), *Trent'anni di vita del Movimento Federalista Europeo*, Milan, 1973, pp. 100–2. MFE's 'return' to effective participation in UEF was heralded by Brugmans's appearance at this congress and his speech on the European situation, which contributed to the victory of Spinelli and his group (cf. MFE letter to Brugmans, 11.2.1948, *UEF Archives, Paris*, corr. 1948, Italy).
[423] Cf. text in *L'Unità europea*, Nos. 19/20, Turin, 25.10.1946. On the MFE's change of course under Spinelli, see also G. G. Boot, *L'Azione politica del Movimento Federalista Europeo dalla resistenza all'istituzione della C.E.C.A.*, dissertation, Turin, 1969/70, here p. 53.

centres and secretaries of provincial centres. The council appointed the secretary-general and four other members of the executive. According to information published by the UEF in April 1948, on 31 January – and thus before the increase in membership that followed later in that year – the MFE had seventy-seven branches in thirteen regions with a total of 12,027 members; this is the biggest membership attested with precision for any European federalist association at that time.[424]

With this comparatively large number of members the MFE was in a position to plan *activities* that were genuinely calculated to arouse public opinion and influence decisions in parliament and the administration. The MFE was an effective force in the journalistic world: its fortnightly *Il Mondo europeo* had a regular circulation of 8–10,000 copies;[425] the Turin branch published *L'Unità europea*, while an internal bulletin (*Bollettino d'informazioni del MFE*) appeared from July 1947 to December 1948. Public meetings reinforced the campaign; following that of 26 October 1947, another large rally at the Teatro Eliseo in Rome was held on 26 January 1948.[426] Before the parliamentary election of 18 April 1948 the MFE appealed to all candidates to sign a petition for an international parliament to decide upon 'methods and procedures for the early convocation of a Constituent Assembly of the United States of Europe'; 630 affirmative replies were received, so that large groups of federalist deputies were formed as soon as the new parliament assembled.[427] The MFE's policy of working for European union under the aegis of the Marshall Plan had paid off; by the spring of 1948 there was a genuinely influential Italian movement in support of the federal ideal.

(C) DISSENSIONS AMONG BELGIAN GROUPS

In France, Italy, and other West-European countries the practical possibility of union, due to altered international circumstances, led to a

[424]
Regions	Branches	Number of members
Piedmont	18	2,780
Lombardy	18	3,658
Venezia Giulia	3	32
Emilia	4	184
Liguria	2	2,622
Tuscany	4	498
Umbria	5	77
Marches	1	17
Apulia	1	47
Latium	3	546
Campania	2	115
Sicily	6	360
Veneto	10	1,091
13 regions	77	12,027 members

Source: UEF, *Lettre-Circulaire*, No. 18, Geneva, 14.4.1948.
[425] According to *Il Mondo europeo*, Nos. 58/9, 1/15.1.1948, p. 11.
[426] Op. cit., n. 425.
[427] Cf. Levi/Pistone (n. 422), p. 109; more fully, n. 385.

marked revival of the various independent federalist groups and to their fusion into nation-wide organizations affiliated to the supranational UEF. In Belgium, by contrast, several groups continued to exist separately during the second half of 1947, and attempts to combine them into a single large, effective association were as yet unsuccessful.

As previously noted, the first of these groups to come into existence was the *Union Fédérale (section belge)*, founded on 1 December 1945 in the house of the Liberal deputy Ernest Demuyter. This group regarded itself as a branch of the British Federal Union, and a member of its executive, Baron Antoine Allard, took an active part in the Hertenstein conference and the subsequent developments leading to the foundation of the UEF.[428] Its aims, however, were evidently closer to those of the world federalists in Federal Union than to the members of that body who put European federation first. How strongly they were actuated by uncritical pacifism can be seen from their 'propaganda plan':

All doctors should hang in their waiting-room an appeal to mothers to support the banning of war. A poster with a light-coloured cross on a red ground, circumscribed with the words 'Stop War' in all languages, should be affixed to 'every wall in every country', and the automobile clubs of all countries should distribute badges of the same design. Members of the association wearing 'Stop War' badges should parade through city streets on Sundays. Great rallies of cyclists should attend the world federalists' congress in August, bringing the emblem from every country in Europe; and so on.[429]

The rising international tension after the Foreign Ministers' meeting in Moscow was naturally a great set-back for this group, which was unable to adjust itself to the practical possibility of 'making a start with Western Europe'. At Montreux, Allard was not re-elected to the central committee of the UEF. When, shortly after Montreux, an attempt was made to form an umbrella organization of Belgian federalists, Union Fédérale under Allard's leadership 'was unable to agree to the proposed statutes, especially the aim of "One Europe" etc.', and from then on the group ceases to figure as a member association of UEF.[430]

---

[428] Cf. chap. I, n. 377, and chap. II at nn. 55 and 190. At Amsterdam in April 1947 Allard was elected to the UEF central committee, together with Jean Buchmann and Raymond Rifflet as founders of other Belgian federalist groups (cf. below, nn. 432 and 435).

[429] A 'Stop War' poster was to be hung up in all hairdressers' shops in the world by a 'Fédération Internationale des Coiffeurs'; an anti-war film would be shown in every cinema in the world, and so on. Plan entitled 'Propagande Générale' sent by A. Allard to Brugmans, 20.2.1947, *BEF Archives*, Brugmans corr.; other material belonging to this group could not be traced.

[430] Not re-elected at Montreux, cf. n. 339 above; quotation concerning rejection of umbrella organization (cf. n. 437) from J. Buchmann's statement of 4.12.1947 to Brugmans (*BEF Archives*, Brugmans corr.); not listed as member of UEF, see the latter's policy document of *c*.Feb. 1948, Geneva, p. 10. The group probably changed its title to Union Fédérale Mondiale, Bruxelles, when the chairman Maurice Cosyn (who has been mentioned as a collaborator of Allard's) attended the Stockholm congress of MWFG in Sept. 1949 (cf. *Weltprobleme und ihre Lösung*, Lige-Verlag, Cologne, 1949, p. 23).

Evidently for similar reasons, a group called the *Ligue unioniste européenne* enjoyed only a brief existence. Its founder, Robert Debande, approached Brugmans at the beginning of June 1947 with a programme which moved the latter to comment: 'Do you really believe the Soviet leaders would agree that part of their federation should transfer part of its sovereignty to a non-Soviet institution?' Nothing was heard of this group after the autumn of 1947.[431]

Jean Buchmann, a lawyer who was elected to the UEF central committee at Amsterdam, now came into prominence with an association called the *Rassemblement federaliste*, which he had founded at the end of 1946 and which unambiguously accepted the necessity of 'starting with Western Europe'. Buchmann was an influential member of the Christian Social Party (PSCB), and his group contained a strong Flemish element. It used as its mouthpiece a weekly (afterwards monthly) paper, *États-Unis d'Europe*, founded independently by the journalist Ram Linssen; he and his immediate associates, however, were directly affiliated to the UEF. The journal was housed and partly financed by the Institut d'Économie Européenne, which was likewise a member of UEF in its own right; its director, Professor Van der Ghinst, was elected to the UEF central committee at Montreux in Allard's place.[432]

Among the Socialists the most widely active group was that of the *Cahiers socialistes*, a journal founded at the end of 1944 with Raymond Rifflet as its chief editor; other important contributors were G. Ernestan, G. Jaeger, Maurice and G. Van den Dale. Contrary to the majority view of the Parti Socialiste Belge (PSB) at that time, the group were strongly in favour of a supranational European federation; they made this clear in August 1946, when they also pleaded for the inclusion of Germany:

'The victors in Europe cannot maintain their standard of living, and the vanquished are in total misery. But there is a way to avoid the impending catastrophe, and that is for Europe to unite all its forces.' Germany could not be kept at a lower economic and political level than the rest of Europe; the only chance of saving Europe lay in 'increased co-operation on the basis of Germany enjoying equality of rights'. 'La fédération européenne n'est pas une élucubration wilsonienne, elle est une réalisation imposée par la nécessité de sauver l'Occident.' And federation

---

[431] Debande to Brugmans at the beginning of June, not preserved; Brugmans to Debande, 13.6.1947; 15.6.1947, Debande to Brugmans, stating that the Ligue dated back to March 1942 and that he was prepared to join a Belgian co-ordination committee (*BEF Archives*, Brugmans corr.). On 3.7.1948 Debande announced that the 'Ligue unioniste européenne belge' was obliged to cease functioning (*BEF Archives*, Secr.).

[432] Cf. J. Buchmann to Brugmans, 4.12.1947; one of his chief collaborators was R. Gubbels (later of MSEUE), Buchmann, Van der Ghinst, and Rifflet (cf. n. 339) were elected to the UEF central committee at Montreux. Other archives of the group have not been traced; copies of the journal *États-Unis d'Europe* only from 1948 (cf. n. 438). Lists of member associations of UEF agree in mentioning the above three bodies, together with Union Fédérale and Cahiers Socialistes (= Action européenne, section belge), as the five Belgian groups: UEF, *Fédérer les Fédéralistes* (mimeographed, May 1947), p. 1; J. Larmeroux, 'Bilan des forces fédéralistes européennes', *Cahiers du monde nouveau*, Vol. 3, No. 7 (July 1947), p. 246; and Annexe III, Associations Fédéralistes, ibid., p. 309 f.

would very soon produce concrete results, both in the economic and in the political sphere.[433]

At the beginning of 1947 this group was prepared to merge with an association called Synthèses and headed by Maurice Lambilliotte, a representative of the Walloon trade unions and economic adviser to Paul-Henri Spaak; the joint association was to be called 'Action européenne, section belge', and to be based on the Theses of the Dutch Europeesche Actie. But in June, when the *Cahiers socialistes* hailed the Marshall Plan as a great opportunity to set European countries on the way towards economic federation and recovery, Lambilliotte backed out of the merger because the Walloon trade unions were anxious to co-operate with the Communists and still hoped for an accommodation with the Soviet Union.[434] During the summer Rifflet, who had been called the 'great driving force of Belgian federalism', was temporarily inactive for health reasons. At the end of October, when the PSB was beginning to talk cautiously of the 'economic restoration of Europe' under the Marshall Plan, which could be 'much facilitated by mutual aid among the countries concerned and their organization into an economic whole', Rifflet in a major article in the *Cahiers socialistes* again proclaimed the objective of 'a true economic democracy in a European federation formed by free consent'.

This article argued that the 'old Western world' was in a tragic situation following the overthrow of 'all power relationships that prevailed in the world of 1939', the awakening of colonial peoples, and the predominance of the two superpowers, with the USSR standing for 'authoritarian planning' and the 'habit of absolute power', while the Americans with their 'esprit très matérialiste' were only interested in technical achievement. As for Europe, 'Seule, et combien imparfaitement, elle unit dans une multitude de consciences lentement façonnées au cours des siècles un minimum de respect de la personne ... et les ressources matérielles capables de les mettre en valeur.' Europeans could only expect help in preserving their freedom and dignity, which were daily ebbing away, if they would 'replace the fatal rivalry among their states by co-operation and division of labour in accordance with present-day needs'. The motive force of the 'European revolution' must be the 'unity of the working world'. The ultimate end was world federation, but European federation was a necessary stage towards it; for if the League of Nations and the UN so far had been ineffectual, it was because they were 'superimposed on social and national contradictions that ought first to have been resolved'.[435]

---

[433] R. Denys, 'Comprendre son temps', *Cahiers socialistes,* No. 11, Aug./Sept. 1946; the *Cahiers socialistes. Revue bimestrielle indépendante de critique sociale* appeared from 1944 to 1953, when it merged with *Socialisme*; quotation from G. Marchal and Van Belle, *Les Socialistes belges et l'intégration européenne,* Brussels, 1968, p. 19 – an informative study as regards the party's attitude.
[434] Report by Dr J: W. M. Schröder, 'Stand van Zaken der contacten – België', 27.7.1948 (*BEF Archives,* Secr.), mentioning van Caeneghem as the chief collaborator with Synthèses; archives of the group itself have not been traced; on the Theses of Europeesche Actie, cf. chap. I, nn. 103 and 107 f.
[435] R. Rifflet, 'La Révolution européenne', *Cahiers socialistes,* No. 18, Nov. 1947, pp. 1–10 (quotations, p. 1 f., 4 f. and 7 f.). For Rifflet's illness and the description of him as the 'driving force of Belgian federalism', see Dr Schröder's report (n. 434). For an account of the party majority, see 'Rapport du Bureau du P.S.B. an Congrès des 25–26–27 octobre 1947', quoted in G. Marchal-Van

During Rifflet's illness, and before the UEF congress at Montreux, Jean Buchmann attempted to unite all these Belgian groups under a co-ordinating committee composed as follows:

General Director (*Responsable general*):	J. Buchmann
Secretary:	J. Toint
Representatives of:	
Cahiers socialistes	G. Jaeger
États-Unis d'Europe	R. Linssen
Institut d'Économie Européenne	Prof. Van der Ghinst
Ligue Unioniste Européenne	R. Debande
Rassemblement Fédéraliste	R. Gubbels
Union Fédérale	Baron A. Allard.[436]

On his return from Montreux, Buchmann tried to convert the committee at its second session into a 'Mouvement populaire' by merging its constituent groups; it was in fact transformed into a *Rassemblement fédéraliste*, described as a 'federation of movements', but, as already mentioned, Allard's Union Fédérale refused to join. Maurice Hamesse, an industrialist who had been persuaded to finance the movement, did his best to develop it into a genuine association with local branches and (doubtless oversimplified) propaganda, but this proved unwelcome to most of the groups, and before the end of the autumn the organization had dissolved.[437]

Hamesse, on his own account, continued his efforts to build up a mass movement, which he now called '*Mouvement d'Action et de Propagande* (MAP). The secretary was J.-B. van Craenenbroeck; many local branches were set up, and numerous functions organized. Linssen's *États-Unis d'Europe*, in a much improved format and with a larger circulation, became the movement's official journal. Contact was made with the Belgian group of the European Parliamentary Union under Bohy and Gilson. But, failing cooperation from the leading 'integral' federalists, the movement's publicity took on a diluted, 'unionistic' flavour, as part of a speech by Hamesse indicates: 'Europe, the most densely populated part of the world, has lost its agricultural areas ... The only solution is to unify our Continental and colonial resources ... Witness the fine example of federalism that Belgium

---

Belle (n. 433), p. 21; cf. analysis in vol. 2, chapter IV: The *Cahiers socialistes* team, consistently with their principles, were co-founders in Feb. 1947 of the Mouvement pour les États-Unis socialistes d'Europe, and afterwards became its Belgian branch.

[436] Reported in UEF, *Lettre-Circulaire*, No. 13, Geneva, 22.7.1947, p. 3, with the premature comment: 'We cannot applaud this decision too strongly' (*DGAP Archives*, UEF files); Brugmans had probably helped to bring it about, cf. chap. II at n. 194.

[437] Report by J. Buchmann, 4.12.1947 (*BEF Archives*, Brugmans corr.), describing the September meeting, the formation of a 'Rassemblement' without Allard's group, and the failure of this attempt to create an umbrella organization; Buchmann withdrew, remarking that it was 'impossible de fonder une action sérieuse et efficace sur une collaboration avec des théosophes et des marchands de tapis' (ibid.). According to Schröder (n. 434), the main reason was the incompatibility between Buchmann and Hamesse.

is prepared to give by the creation of Benelux. This spirit of human solidarity may be the beginning of moral renewal and the revival of hope.'[438]

Meanwhile Buchmann and other federalists who had withdrawn from the short-lived umbrella organization formed a new group known at first as the 'Troisième force ... comprenant non des représentants des forces de base mais des personnalités "représentatives"' – an élitist group intended to influence the political parties and major newspapers. Rifflet, now restored to health, endeavoured to put it on a broader basis, and at the beginning of April 1948 it took shape under his and Buchmann's direction as the *Mouvement Belge pour les États-Unis d'Europe,* incorporating the Belgian section of MSEUE (Mouvement Socialiste pour les États-Unis d'Europe; Ernestan and Gubbels) and the Christian Democratic NEI (Nouvelles Équipes Internationales: Heyman and Lohest).[439] Owing to the dissensions among Belgian federalists and their inability to form an effective umbrella organization, the groups connected with periodicals which came out strongly for European union from the autumn of 1947 onwards, such as *Les Documents de L'Action Sociale Catholique, La Relève, Streven,* and *De Gids op Maatschappelijk Gebied,* sought direct affiliation to the UEF.[440]

(D) CREATION OF THE DUTCH BEWEGING VAN EUROPESE FEDERALISTEN

In June 1947, when the Marshall Plan was announced, there were two Dutch federalist associations in being. By far the larger was *Europeesche Actie* (EA), founded on 29 January 1945, during the German occupation, by Hylkema, Salinger, and Verkade. In May–June 1946 the EA, of which a full account has already been given, was joined by two other groups – Federale Unie under Nord and Wery, and Neerlands Toekomst under S. J. van Embden – on the basis of the agreed programme embodied in

---

[438] Report on various activities of the MAP in Jan,-Feb. 1948, and the Hamesse quotation, in UEF, *Lettre-Circulaire,* No. 18, Geneva, 14.4.1948, p. 6. For the meaning of the term 'unionist' in the European context, cf. p. 665 below. As to *États-Unis d'Europe,* Vol. 2, No. 8 of May 1948 is extant (four pages of large newspaper size), with articles by R. Silva ('Le Fédéralisme européen peut sauver la paix'), M. Lambilliote ('Énergie et crédit, bases de l'édification d'une Union Économique Européenne'), M. Hamesse and J. B. van Craenenbroeck ('Europese Federatie of algemene ondergang'), and others. Contacts between the Belgian group and EPU (cf. n. 121 above) according to Schröder (n. 434), who sums up: on the one hand, an expensive propaganda machine without integral federalists, on the other – integralists without a basic organization.

[439] Buchmann's report of 4.12.1947 to Brugmans (n. 437) on the 'Troisième force'; its secretary J. Toint observed to Brugmans on 13.12.1947: 'L'Europe ne peut être sauvée que par une entente sérieuse entre les élites de ce qui peut constituer la troisième force' (*BEF Archives,* Brugmans corr.). On the refoundation and merger of the Belgian group of MSEUE with NEI (described more fully in chap. IV), see Schröder's report, concluding with the hope that there might at last be a 'possibility of serious collaboration between the Dutch and Belgian federalists'.

[440] The UEF's printed pamphlet (Geneva, spring 1948), on p. 11 under 'Belgium', mentions the above periodicals as 'associées', and the Mouvement d'Action et de Propagande and the Mouvement Belge pour les États-Unis d'Europe as regular member associations. For further developments in Belgium, see chap. V/5(C) in vol. 2.

the Theses of Europeesche Actie. The association, envisaged at that stage as a supranational one, elected Henri Brugmans as its chairman with Salinger as secretary; the chairman and secretary of the 'Netherlands section' were de Beaufort and Meilof Yben. In the summer of 1946 Europeesche Actie was one of the strongest federalist associations in Europe, with energetic, far-seeing leaders and a clear and detailed programme, and accordingly it played a prominent part in the creation of an umbrella organization of European federalists: Brugmans was elected president of UEF, and that body held its first meeting at Amsterdam in April 1947.[441] Because of these international links, the formation of local branches of EA was suspended between May and August 1947 while basic issues were discussed in committees; conversations took place with a view to uniting with the other Dutch group, and parts of the resolutions of the UEF congress were drafted in Montreux.

During this period a policy pamphlet *De enige Uitweg* was issued, an enlarged version of the Theses which was chiefly Brugman's work. It argued that only by uniting could Europe cease to be a 'plaything of the two non-European world powers'; that it must be organized as a neutral 'Third Force' from the Atlantic to the eastern frontier of Poland; and that to ensure internal equilibrium it should be composed of 'freely formed regional federations'. The pamphlet also emphasized that united Europe was not an alternative to a world organization, but a contribution to it.[442]

The other, smaller movement was the Europese Federative Beweging (EFB). The date of its foundation is not known but was probably in the winter of 1946/7, before it became known that Europeesche Actie was organizing the Amsterdam meeting. While EA consisted chiefly of professional economists, theologians, and journalists, EFB was exclusively an academic body concerned with promoting the European idea in universities. An 'Appeal for European federation' circulated in the spring of 1947 listed as members of its 'advisory council' Professor F. J. M. Duynstee of Nijmegen University, Professor C. A. Mennicke, director of the international school of philosophy at Amersfoort, and Professor J. Tinbergen of the Economic University at Rotterdam.[443] The Appeal spoke

---

[441] Cf. chap. I/2(D), esp. at nn. 96–110, and chap. II/2 and 5. The Theses influenced the Hertenstein programme, the work of Verkade's committee of Europeesche Actie for German affairs, and the Amsterdam resolution on Germany (ibid.).

[442] *De enige Uitweg, uitgegeven in samenwerking met de 'Europese Actie'*, Amsterdam (Keizerskroon), 1947: pp. 3–5 foreword by H. Brugmans, 6–27 policy statement, 28–36 review of European associations by W. Verkade, dated 15.6.1947. This was a last formulation of the 'third force' programme, before Brugmans's second visit to Prague (cf. chap. II at n. 358) and before the change to 'making a start in Western Europe' (cf. chap. III/4(B). In the summer of 1947, at a time for which records are not available, Dr Salinger withdrew from the leadership of Europeesche Actie, partly because he disapproved of raising credit without cover and partly because he was fully occupied with the Secretariat of European Industrial Associations which he had successfully re-established at The Hague (information from *Salinger*, 28.9.1974).

[443] Leaflet *Oproep tot Europese Federatie*, four printed pages, undated, but evidently issued before the Marshall Plan and contact with EA, in the spring of 1947 (*BEF Archives,* Europ. Actie). No other

of the unity of European culture, endangered by wars and nationalism, and declared that European union was essential on 'elementary economic grounds' and as a counterweight to the non-European world powers. An annexed 'Basic Programme' described EFB as 'an organization working for European federation as part of a world federation, in order (a) to offer disoriented Europeans a new, viable prospect for the future; (b) to overcome the fatal chauvinism of European nations and prevent wars; and (c) to establish a strong co-operative unit to replace the present fragmentation into a multiplicity of powerless states'. The aim of the organization was to help bring about 'a clear popular decision in all European states in favour of a voluntary union'. Without referring specifically to obstacles created by the superpowers or going into ways and means of setting up a European federation, the programme defined its principles as follows:

'1. The European federation shall include all nations which can be regarded as belonging to Europe and which decide to accede of their own free will. 2. The nations of the federation may unite with non-European nations to form larger federations or a world federation.' They may: 3. enter into sub-federations, 4. continue to maintain overseas possessions, 5. enjoy autonomy in domestic matters.

6. All national governments shall transfer an equal portion of their sovereignty to a federal European government in the interest of Europe as a whole. 7. In the formation of the federal European government and its institutions each of the participating nations shall enjoy a fair share of authority so as to ensure that they all take part in decisions affecting the whole community. 8. The federal government shall be organized in such a way as to prevent domination by one or more member countries. 9. Every citizen of a member state shall enjoy citizenship of the federation as well as of that state. 10. The federation shall guarantee to all its citizens the enjoyment of democratic liberties and shall have a supreme representative body composed of deputies elected by the nations. 11. The federal European government has the task of watching over the general welfare of the federation and shall pursue a policy adapted to the common needs of member nations in economic, social, cultural and educational matters.[444]

Although the aims of the two groups were clearly similar, the talks held to discuss a merger at first ran into difficulties; but, after the Montreux conference was over, they succeeded thanks to determination and sacrifices on the part of Europeesche Actie. The merger was effected at a joint general meeting in the De Kroon restaurant at The Hague on 4 October 1947; Brugmans made a speech on 'the international responsibility of

---

material of this group could be traced. The more active younger members were J. E. van Dierendonck, E. Lopes Cardozo, and P. van Schilfgaarde (information from *Verkade*, 27.9.1974; confirmed by result of merger discusions, cf. n. 445).

[444] *Oproep tot Europese Federatie* (n. 443), p. 3 f. A final point 12 stated that the European federal government should 'promote the individual citizen's sense of responsibility towards the community and his enthusiasm for the realization of common aims'.

Limitation to Western Europe 641

European federalism', and the combined association took the name Beweging van Europese Federalisten (BEF). Besides agreeing to forgo its own title, the EA conceded more or less equal representation on the new committee: Prof. Duynstee and Dr Brugmans became vice-chairmen with equal rights, while the chairman, Prof. C. D. J. Brandt, had previously not been closely associated with either group. Even the secretariat was divided between Dierendonck (for administration) and Meilof Yben (for organization), until this arrangement was given up after a year as unpractical. The chairmanship of the smaller 'committee of management', however, went to P. van Stam, an experienced member of EA.[445] The meeting approved new statutes, considerably altered from those of 1945; EA's plan to become a supranational organization was abandoned and the new BEF was clearly designated as the Dutch member association of UEF, democratically constituted on the basis of local groups. Article 2 on the aims of the association, based clearly on UEF's Montreux resolutions, gave a precise definition of the federal principles by which the BEF was to be guided:

(a) The existing tensions between nations can only be overcome by adopting federalism as a guiding principle. (b) Federalism as a basis of economic, political and cultural organization means that every problem must as far as possible be solved by those whom it affects, through the creation of a joint institution with powers that correspond exactly to the scope of the problem. (c) In international affairs this means that all problems that the nations concerned can only solve jointly are dealt with by creating supranational institutions with power to take binding decisions in matters within their province. (d) On the national plane this means that economic, political and cultural tensions are relieved by promoting the independence of the parts [smaller communities]. (e) it is vital for European nations in particular to solve their common problems by means of a European federation.[446]

As soon as the BEF was founded, intensive publicity and a drive for new members began. Between 5 and 11 October Van Stam presided over

---

[445] As regards the merger negotiations: 'For a time people tried to invent political differences, but it became clear that we all really had the same object' (H. Brugmans, 'Het begin van een beweging', *Europa in Beweging*, The Hague, 1968, p. 19). The nature of the difficulties can be seen from P. van Stam's complaint of 26.9.1947 to J. E. van Dierendonck that the latter had tried to alter to his own advantage agreements already reached on organizational matters. Invitation and agenda of inaugural meeting to Brugmans, 26.9.1947 (both *BEF Archives*, E-Aktie). Composition of new general committee and smaller committee of management in BEF, *Chaos in Europa*, publicity pamphlet, no place of origin given, Nov. 1947, p. 6; members of the smaller committee, besides P. van Stam, were Senator Kerstens and Kaars Sijpesteyn (cf. n. 447), J. C. van Brockhuyzen, H. M. Lange, Ders, E. Lopes Cardozo, Dr H. R. Nord, Dr P. van Schilfgaarde, J. F. Verhey-Neumeyer, and W. Verkade.

[446] BEF Statutes, mimeographed, as adopted at inaugural assembly on 4.10.1947, in *BEF Archives*, Secr.; these were submitted to the Ministry of Justice for approval, returned a year later with requests for amendment, amended by the national assembly of the BEF in April 1949, resubmitted, and finally published in *Nederlands Staatscourant* 4, Sept. 1950, No. 171; Art. 2 also printed in Nederlandse Raad der Europese Beweging, pamphlet No. 1, *Ontstaan, Doel en Werkwijze*, The Hague, Oct. 1950, p. 26 f.

the formation of branches in ten cities. One fact of crucial importance was that Brugmans secured the services of an able financier, *Dipl.-Ing.* J. C. Kaars Sijpestein, who as treasurer to the movement succeeded in procuring funds on a large scale.[447] A series of effective publications were brought out in rapid succession by a well-known publishing house: a well-drafted manifesto entitled *Chaos in Europe*; an exposé of policy by Brugmans, *Chaos of orde?* (Chaos or Order?); a volume containing the speeches and resolutions of the Montreux conference; and the final report of the CEEC conference in Paris.[448] The 'five points' of policy were not altered by these publications; the statement of policy *Wat willen de Federalisten?*, published and reprinted several times in 1948, was still based on the original Theses, but some points were more sharply defined.

As to the *design for Europe*, the manifesto made it clearer that the federal principle also protected the legitimate interests of individual member nations.

Napoleon and Hitler tried to impose centralized unity on Europe by military force, but history showed that the European peoples' love of freedom would not allow this. Federalism points the way to a unity in which essential liberties are preserved. On the one hand, there must be voluntary union for the protection of joint interests by a federal European government. Nation-states must confer adequate powers on this government by restricting their own sovereignty. On the other hand, each state must retain the right to order its own affairs in its own way...

We want a Europe that is united, but not regimented; a Europe that can stand on its own feet thanks to the collaboration of its members; a Europe in which the unhindered exchange of goods and services leads to greater prosperity; a Europe in which democratic freedoms and social justice are guaranteed to all. We want a state of Europe that is open to all peoples who feel themselves to be Europeans and freely decide to participate on a community basis; a Europe friendly to both East and West and ready to cooperate with all.[449]

---

[447] Brugmans relates that: 'Some talks of mine aroused the interest of J. C. Kaars Sijpestein, manager of the linoleum works at Krommenie. He had worked in the past with Coudenhove-Kalergi and was much impressed by Churchill's Zurich speech. . . . He helped us to obtain necessary funds. . . . Without him there would have been no European federalist movement in the Netherlands' (Brugmans, 'Het begin . . .' (n. 445), p. 18 f.). Van Stam's report on his tour, and letters of application from new members on the basis of the merger, in *BEF Archives,* Secr.

[448] BEF; *Chaos in Europe,* Nov. 1947, eight-page pamphlet (cf. n. 445); H. Brugmans, *Chaos of orde? Europa's eigen Taak,* Amsterdam (Keizerskroon), Dec. 1947, 16 pp.; *Europa één in een verenigde wereld. Montreux, Inleidingen, rapporten en resoluties van het grote congres der Unie van Europese Federalisten te Montreux 26.–30. Aug. 1947,* Amsterdam (Keizerskroon), Dec. 1947, 132 pp.; *Marshall-Rapport, Verslag van de Commissie van Zestien te Parijs,* Amsterdam (Keizerskroon), Jan. 1948, 96 pp.

[449] BEF, *Chaos in Europa* (n. 445), pp. 3 and 6. The statement of principles in Art. 2 of the Statutes, quoted at n. 446, continued: '(f) The European federation must be open to all peoples who feel themselves to be European and, of their own free will and through their appropriate institutions, indicate their desire to participate on a community basis. (g) The European federation shall guarantee to all peoples and national groups within its territory the forms of organization necessary to enable them to preserve their own character and manage their own affairs. (h) Each member nation shall have an appropriate say in the regulation of matters of common interest by the institutions of the European federation.'

As regards the *plan of campaign*, following on the Montreux resolution an argument was put forward by Brugmans in particular; if the European countries, threatened by economic collapse, could not refuse the aid offered by Marshall, yet rightly feared that it might make them dependent on the US, the only way for them to avert this danger was to unite.

The question, therefore, is this. In our dire necessity we cannot refuse American aid, but how can we accept it and so use it as to derive the maximum benefit while neutralizing the risks as far as possible? This is the only question, and the answer is clear. We must do our utmost to bring pressure to bear in all possible quarters so that the economic co-operation on which governments are embarking with evident reluctance may become a constructive reality ... Without unity, Europe cannot assert itself against any power – including the USA.[450]

As to the *aims of the association*, the manifesto declared that: 'the BEF is not a political party. Representatives of all political trends and religious beliefs may find in it a platform for their European aspirations.' Brugmans again gave expression to his view that, while the BEF could not create supranational institutions, many social forces might 'have much to hope for from a European federation. Our task is to awaken all these forces to their proper task, to unite and stimulate them and make them politically effective.'[451]

The BEF's multifarious activities were not confined to the publication of literature. A press bureau headed by van Broekhuizen began to send out articles to provincial daily papers, and the numerous local branches in course of formation were urged to invite the press to all their public meetings and see that they were well reported. The BEF's monthly journal, *Nieuw Europa*, which still exists, was published from November 1947; the editor, P. C. Heiser, was also in charge of its distribution. Successful contacts were made with other bodies: the Dutch trade-union association agreed to draw the attention of all its members to the BEF's activities and to publish its articles in their journal. A UEF circular reported:[452]

'Our Dutch comrades have already established 16 branch associations ... Their latest activities are: 3.1.1948, conference on the German problem; 29.1., mass meeting at The Hague, Dr Brugmans addressing an audience of 1,000; public meetings at Maastricht, 2.2.; Hengelo, 3.2.; Rotterdam, 16.2.; Haarlem, 25.2.; 8.3., mass meeting in the Concertgebouw, Amsterdam, with 2,300 present; 11.3., public meeting at Arnhem,' etc.

---

[450] H. Brugmans, *Chaos of orde?* (n. 448), p. 7 f. This pamphlet, which e.g. Sijpestein also distributed in his factories, prompted the Communists to issue a counter-pamphlet arguing that it was 'impossible to unite Europe under the capitalist system' (copy sent by Sijpestein to Brugmans, 31.12.1947; discussed in chap. IV/2, in vol. 2).
[451] BEF, *Chaos in Europa* (n. 445), p. 5; Brugmans, *Chaos of orde?* (n. 448), p. 15.
[452] Instruction by Broekhuizen, c.Nov. 1947, on branches' relations with the press; letter of 30.12.1947 from central Dutch trade-union organization to van Stam; much organizational information in annual report of the BEF executive, March 1949 (all in *BEF Archives*, Secr.); UEF, *Lettre-Circulaire*, No. 18, Geneva, 14.4.1948, p. 10 (*UEF Archives*).

644   *Limitation to Western Europe*

At the beginning of 1948 the association of Dutch federalists was thus one of the best organized and most effective in Europe. Its next major task was the preparation of the Hague Congress of all organizations working for European union – an enterprise involving sacrifices from which the BEF itself was to suffer.[453]

(E) UNIFICATION OF EUROPEAN FEDERALIST GROUPS IN THE WESTERN ZONES OF GERMANY

The timidly developing political forces in Germany had more difficulty than those of other countries in obtaining a clear picture of the international scene. This was partly due to the policy of the occupying powers, who allowed the German press to present only a glossed-over account of the increasing tension between the major Allies, and who continued to ban intellectual exchanges between Germany and the rest of Europe.

Another factor in the Germans' isolation was that it was psychologically much harder for them to accept the frustration of the hope that the four Allies would agree on a peace settlement for Europe. It was equally hard for Germans to face the fact that the Soviet Union was beginning to cut its Zone off from the rest of Germany, having found it impossible either to exploit German resources in agreement with the Western powers or to Communize the whole of Germany and turn it into a pro-Soviet state. These alarming changes came as a shock to public opinion in the Western Zones, inadequately informed as it was, and to its justified sense of national unity. After the failure of the Moscow conference of foreign ministers the American and British authorities had endowed Bizonia with more or less effective institutions,[454] but it was not yet clear that this was more than an emergency measure, welcome in itself, to prevent complete economic stagnation and misery. Hans Ehard, the prime minister of Bavaria, invited the prime ministers of all the other *Länder* to attend a conference at Munich

---

[453] For a further account of the BEF, see chap. V/5(D) in vol. 2. An account of the British Federal Union would logically belong here, to complete the sketch of West-European groups, but the chief events in its history as far as the autumn of 1947 have already been described in chap. III/4 on Montreux (at n. 335). An association of long standing, it continued at this time to carry on not very effective activities in the field of public speaking, without undergoing any organizational change as did the other West-European groups in consequence of the Montreux decisions.

[454] Bizonia was set up on 1.1.1947, but initially with neither legislative nor executive organs (six advisory agencies were established in different cities, 'to avoid any justification for charges by our colleagues of political amalgamation': L. D. Clay, *Decision in Germany*, London, 1950, p. 168). However, by a British-American agreement of 29.5.1947, which came into force on 10.6.1947, it was given a kind of parliament, the legislative Economic Council, and its various offices were concentrated in Frankfurt am Main to form an effective executive. Decisive motives for the change were that the European economic crisis had assumed alarming dimensions and that it was desired to link the German and European economies. The Allies believed that the Russians wished to gain time to exploit the crisis, and resolved that if necessary they would take steps to restore the European and German economy, without the Russians and even in opposition to them. Cf. esp. J. Gimbel, *The American Occupation of Germany – Politics and the Military*, Stanford, 1968, pp. 113–16.

on 5 June 1947; those from the Soviet Zone staged a demonstrative walk-out, but similarly it was not yet evident that this signified a permanent check to Ehard's initiative.[455] The foreign ministers were due to meet again in London at the end of November, and it was vaguely hoped that this time the victors would at last reach agreement on Germany's future.

The Germans, however, had grasped the fact that their future must be part of a new European order, and this awareness gave them hope of deliverance. Marshall's speech of 5 June was seen more and more as a turning-point that would at last lead to co-operation among European states and open the minds of governments to the idea of sharing the work of reconstruction.[456] The first fruit of the Marshall offer, hailed with relief in Germany, was the US and British decision to revise the Level of Industry Plan. Dismantling was not terminated but was at least limited, and the various detailed provisions made it clear that the policy was to enable Germany once more to 'make its indispensable contribution to the economic recovery of the whole of Europe'.[457] Thus Marshall's speech and the opening of the Paris talks had the effect, in Germany as elsewhere, of stimulating ideas for European union and encouraging federalist groups. While the scope of Molotov's refusal was not yet fully realized, the US offer and the efforts in Paris to organize co-operation in the first instance among West-European states prompted German as well as other federalists to redouble their activity and to seek union among themselves so as to be better fitted for the tasks that lay ahead.

After the first attempt at uniting the German federalist groups had been torpedoed by Wilhelm Hermes, secretary-general of Europa-Union,[458] it was the leaders of the international UEF who encouraged the other German associations to join forces. On 28 May 1947 Alexandre Marc addressed a circular letter 'aux fédéralistes allemands' stating that the UEF hoped a German delegation would attend its congress at Montreux in August; such a delegation must be 'régulièrement constituée', and it

---

[455] Cf. articles by W. Grünewald, 'Die Münchener Ministerpräsidentenkonferenz 1947, Anlass und Scheitern eines gesamtdeutschen Unternehmens. Meisenheim 1971', and E. Krautkrämer, 'Der innerdeutsche Konflikt um die Ministerpräsidentenkonferenz in München 1947', in *VfZG*, 20 (1972), pp. 154–74; id., 'Ergänzende Bemerkungen zur Münchener Ministerpräsidenten-Konferenz 1947', *VfZG*, 20 (1972), pp. 418–21; M. E. Foelz-Schroeter, *Föderalistische Politik und nationale Repräsentation 1945–1947, Westdeutsche Länderregierungen, zonale Bürokratie und politische Parteien im Widerstreit*, Stuttgart, 1974, pp. 103–33; R. Steiniger, 'Zur Geschichte der Münchner Minister-präsidenten-Konferenz 1947', *VfZG*, 23 (1975), pp. 375–453.

[456] Cf. H. Bernhard's speech quoted in n. 59 above, and numerous comments in all daily papers in June 1947. Heile, in his speech at Eutin (p. 429 above), said with reference to the Marshall Plan: 'We follow the call: "Nations of Europe, Unite!' . . . In the history of Germany, of Europe and of all mankind there has never been so momentous an hour, one so full of the greatest possibilities, as that in which we are now living.'

[457] Text of 'Revised Plan for Level of Industry in the Anglo-American Zones', 29.8.1947, in Beate Ruhm von Oppen, *Documents on Germany under Occupation 1945–1954*, Oxford University Press, 1955, pp. 239–45. See also F. R. Allemann, *Bonn ist nicht Weimar*, Cologne, 1956, p. 55 f.

[458] Cf. chapter II/6, p. 427; the present account continues from there.

was accordingly for the German federalists to reach agreement among themselves. Marc proposed that they appoint a German co-ordinating committee in which 'all serious movements' should be represented by one or two delegates each.[459]

As has been seen,[460] a meeting of all pan-European associations in Germany was held at Hanover on 12 July in response to UEF's appeal. The following groups were represented:

> Europa-Union, Mönchengladbach
> Pan-Europa-Union, Hamburg
> USE-Liga, Ascheberg
> Deutsche Liga für föderalistische Union Europas, Schwerte
> Europäische Volksbewegung, Hamburg
> Pan-Europa-Bund, Berlin
> Europäische Aktion, Stuttgart
> Union-Europa-Liga, Munich
> Liga für Weltregierung (Föderalistische Union), Cologne
> Vereinigte internationale Freunde, Hamburg
> Europäische Gemeinschaft, Kachtenhausen (Lippe).[461]

The participants saw it as the task of the conference not to draw up detailed programmes but to clarify the aims of the respective groups and thus decide which of them could unite to form a larger association. Good progress was made in this direction. The representatives of the Liga für Weltregierung and the Internationale Freunde were the only ones who gave priority to world government as opposed to European union, and it was unanimously decided that they (as well as the Weltstaatsliga of Munich, which was not represented) should not be included in the proposed national association.[462] As to the Europäische Volksbewegung under Herbert Ritter, while this group was willing to join in a merger, the others decided promptly and firmly that it was not eligible, since the joint association must preserve a non-party character, whereas the Volksbewegung was a neo-Nazi body with political aspirations.[463] The representatives of

---

[459] UEF, 'Aux fédéralistes allemands', 28.5.1947 (*Gérard Archives*); cf. chap. II at n. 318. In reply to a question by Wilhelm Kasting, Alexandre Marc said. 'It is not at all the case that the Europa-Union (Mönchengladbach) has been recognized by us as the only valid movement for Germany' (Marc to Kasting, 2.6.1947, *von Schenck Archives*, UEF).

[460] Cf. chap. II/6, p. 430.

[461] List in Europa-Liga, *Mitteilungsblatt*, July 1947 (*Merten Archives*), and in Europa-Union, *Informationsdienst*, 29.8.1947. Apart from Vereinigte Internationale Freunde, which is mentioned nowhere else and which immediately dropped out as explained above, all these groups are described on the basis of their archives in chapter II/6, pp. 388–415. The student body Europäische Gemeinschaft, being purely academic in scope, did not join in the organizational merger: cf. chap. II, n. 264.

[462] 'Contact is useful for the purpose of developing the federal principle, which is a basis of co-operation with like-minded foreigners in the case of both "world citizens" and pan-Europeans. For the rest, the two organizations should be built up separately.' Dr Merten commented thus on the Hanover conference in Europa-Liga, *Mitteilungsblatt*, July 1947: *Merten Archives*, USE-Liga file.

[463] Merten, loc. cit. (n. 462); in *Der Kurier*, 14.7.1947, he wrote: 'When Ritter started to inveigh against the existing political parties ("they are all a menace to the nation") and argued that his own group should be represented in parliament, he was almost unanimously opposed by his pan-European colleagues.'

all other groups unanimously agreed to join forces and to form a co-ordinating committee composed of two members of each, so as 'to combat the harmful fragmentation of the work of informing the German public, especially young people, and educating them to think in European terms'.[464] The committee was to hold its first meeting at Frankfurt am Main on 1 August, for the purpose of 'formally completing the merger'.[465]

This purpose, however, was not fully achieved at the Frankfurt meeting. The largest association, Hermes's Europa-Union, there proposed the appointment of a 'merger committee' on which the associations would be represented in proportion to their numbers. The other groups, however, came to the conclusion that this was a tactical delaying measure inspired 'solely by personal ambition and egotism, and not conducive to the common purpose'.[466] Accordingly the following groups:

Deutsche Liga für föderalistische Union Europas, Schwerte
Europäische Aktion, Stuttgart
Pan-Europa-Union, Hamburg
USE-Liga, Ascheberg
Union-Europa-Liga, Munich

resolved to merge forthwith into a joint association called 'Europa-Bund. Gemeinschaft deutscher Verbände für europäische Föderation'. Henry Bernhard was provisionally elected its first chairman, while Dr Theo Merten, Kurt Rompf, and Edmund Wertheimer, chairmen of the existing individual associations, became members of the executive.[467] On 22–3 August, also in Frankfurt, the new association held its first congress of *Land* delegates. The policy guide-lines agreed on this occasion showed the homogeneity of the federated groups and thus confirmed the necessity and appropriateness of the merger.

Design for Europe. The Europa-Bund 'takes as its starting-point the fact that the age of nation states is at an end. Europe must unite or perish. In economic matters, too, our Continent has become too small for the traditional forms of coexistence.' In clear reference to Marshall's speech and with explicit mention of the Paris talks then going on, the guide-lines declared that it was 'the task of all European peoples to be ready for the impending development of Europe'. Unification was only possible, however, 'if all its members strive towards unity and surrender certain

---

[464] Text in Europa-Liga, *Mitteilungsblatt,* July 1947. Unfortunately the full text of the minutes could not be traced; extracts quoted from Europa-Union, *Informationsdienst,* 29.8.1947.

[465] Minutes quoted by DPD, 12.7.1947. The original intention to appoint a joint delegation to the UEF congress at Montreux was not carried out; 'It will be left to the individual organizations to send representatives to Montreux, if travel difficulties can be overcome'; DPD, 12.7.1947.

[466] Steinhorst in Europa-Union, *Informationsdienst,* 29.8.1947; Paneuropa-Union circular, No. 4, 2.8.1947.

[467] On 1.8.1947 Freiherr von Rheinbaben was also elected to the executive; but in the course of August, as the Europa-Union used his name as a basis for attacks, he withdrew (with discreet help from Bernhard) so as not to harm the association. He was now in any case more deeply involved in founding an association of expellees from the Eastern territories; cf. correspondence between him, Bernhard, and Pulides in Aug.–Sept. 1947, *Bernhard Archives,* Europa-Bund file.

traditional rights of sovereignty to the higher community, which in turn is not an end in itself but should promote endeavours to form a world government'. The federal principle must also be applied within states: 'a federal Germany is a necessary pre-condition of a federation of European democracies'.

Europe in the world. Against Molotov's rejection of the Marshall Plan, the Europa-Bund emphasized that 'the future federation of European democracies stands for nothing but the welfare of Europe and will not let itself be manœuvred into opposition to any European or non-European power'.[468] In the September number of the movement's new journal *Europa* Dr Theo Merten endorsed the Theses of Europeesche Actie: 'the Eastern boundary of a United Europe lies at the point where human beings begin to be valued only as members of a collectivity. In the West, Britain is unquestionably European in culture and intellectual outlook.'[469] The issues involved by 'starting with Western Europe' were not yet examined, at all events not publicly.

Plan of campaign. The Europa-Bund saw its task as clearly related to the governmental negotiations over the Marshall offer. As Merten wrote in November: 'The historic conferences are bringing us close to the new political and economic order in Europe, so rapidly and unmistakably that we are fortunate to have an organization ready to hand and capable of educating the public mind in the right direction.'[470] The Europa-Bund thus set itself a twofold strategy: on the one hand, European union must be promoted through government negotiations; on the other hand, public opinion must be mobilized so as to provide support for government policies both in and outside parliament.

The purpose of the organization was already implied in this objective: 'The Europa-Bund has set itself the task of propagating the European idea in Germany and providing a basis for European thoughts and attitudes.' Its aims were universal: it was 'independent of all party doctrines and organizations, an organization for people of all professions'; it sought 'links with other European groups' and desired to admit to its membership the isolated Europa-Union. It was to be organized on federal lines: the central association, a 'working community of *Land* associations', was 'solely to provide uniformity, especially in matters of ideology and recruitment, and to represent the Europa-Bund *vis-à-vis* other German bodies

---

[468] *Europa-Bund: Leitsätze, Organisatorische Grundlagen, Satzung,* hrsg. v. d. Hauptgeschäftsstelle Hamburg (*c.* Aug. 1947), *Federal German Archives,* Kardorff papers, 72; also in *Europa, Mitteilungsblatt des Europa-Bundes,* 1.9.1947. Bernhard's speech on the meeting of delegates of the Europa-Bund, 17.10.1947 (cf. n. 475 below); published as No. 1 of the *Schriftenreihe des Europa-Bundes:* H. Bernhard, *Werdendes Europa,* Hamburg, n.d.; quotations, pp. 11 and 14.

[469] From a political point of view 'the initiative as regards joining a European federation rested with Britain alone'. 'Organisation und Programm der Europa-Bewegung' in *Europa,* first number of Sept. 1947 (*Merten Archives*).

[470] 'Einheit ist not!' *Europa,* Nov. 1947 (*Merten Archives*).

and foreign organizations, leaving the main substance of the work to be done by the *Land* associations, which should be as independent as possible'.[471] The total membership of the Europa-Bund, as Bernhard announced at the delegates' congress, was over 10,000.[472]

Activities. The delegates' congress of 22–3 August 1947 took decisions on the appointment of specialized committees, a competition for the compilation of a 'European reader', and a recommendation to parliamentarians in all the West-German *Länder* that talks and courses should be arranged in schools to popularize the European idea.[473] At the second congress, held in Frankfurt on 17–18 October, it was decided to set up further committees of experts to 'make preliminary studies for the solution of European problems in so far as they concern Germany'. A committee on matters affecting the Ruhr and Saar was set up under the joint chairmanship of C. Driewer (secretary of the Chamber of Commerce and Industry at Essen) and Dr Eugen Kogon (at Merten's particular suggestion);[474] also a committee on German constitutional matters under R. Proske, a committee for economic union, and one for cultural co-operation.[475]

The formation of the Europa-Bund in the autumn of 1947 gave a definite impetus to the European movement in the Western Zones of Germany. Personalities and professional associations that had held back because of the multiplicity of federalist bodies now appealed to the public to support the Bund, their attitude being also influenced by the Marshall Plan negotiations. Such an appeal was signed at Münster, for instance, by chairmen of chambers of commerce, industry, and crafts from all over Westphalia, the rector of the University, chairmen of expellee associations, etc., including Theodor Blank and Wilhelm Deist for the trade unions: 'Germany, destroyed by nationalism, is called on to renounce power

---

[471] *Europa-Bund: Leitsätze* ... (n. 468).
[472] *Der Kurier*, 25.8.1947.
[473] *Europa, Mitteilungsblatt des Europa-Bundes*, 1.10.1947; *Der Kurier*, 25.8.1947.
[474] Dr Eugen Kogon, born 2.2.1903, attended the right-wing Catholic Othmar-Spahn-Schule; he afterwards spent seven years in a concentration camp, which altered his political convictions. In the Sozial-Republikanischer Arbeitskreis (cf. p. 238) he gave an address on 9.1.1946 on 'The national problem', arguing that society was coming to the end of the concluding phase of nationalism, in which it was 'only a dogma, with no sense of value behind it'; in future the national destiny was not to be a power factor but to play a 'Grecian' role within a larger structure (*Cornides Archives*, file on Sozial-Republikanischer-Arbeitskreis). Editor of the *Frankfurter Hefte*, which appeared monthly from April 1946, and author of *Der SS-Staat* (English translation, *The Theory and Practice of Hell. The German Concentration Camps* ... , London, 1950), he was known throughout Germany as a convinced federalist. A member of Dr Merten's USE-Liga (cf. chap. II, n. 246), he soon also joined the Bund deutscher Föderalisten (cf. p. 653) with the object of bringing about federalism in Germany itself. Through the USE-Liga he became a member of the Europa-Bund and was made available for the Hessian *Landesverband* – all information from *Kogon*, 11.10.1961, *DGAP Archives*, E 790/Korresp. Ernst von Schenck, who visited him in the summer of 1947, recognized his dedication to federalism and decided that he was the right man to lead the movement in Germany; over Hermes's opposition he got Kogon elected to the UEF central committee at Montreux, thus decisively influencing the course of the German movement for a united Europe.
[475] The Europabund youth organization was also reorganized, with its own secretariat in Hamburg, Fuller account in *Europa. Mitteilungsblatt des Europa-Bundes*, second number of Oct. 1947; on the 'European Academy', see DPD, 3.11.1947, and *Munzinger Archives*, 20.5.1948.

650 Limitation to Western Europe

politics and to serve the cause of renewing the traditional community of the Western world.'[476] In the same way, fresh forces rallied to the *Land* associations in Bavaria, North Rhine–Westphalia, Schleswig–Holstein, and Württemberg–Baden, which had come into being without friction on the basis of previous regional groups. In August new *Land* associations were formed for Hesse (under the chairmanship of Rüdiger Proske, a member of the staff of *Frankfurter Hefte,* and a business man named Froechte, an old supporter of Coudenhove)[477] and for South Baden (under Schinzinger);[478] in September for Lower Saxony, under Generaldirektor Klages.[479] The *Land* association for North Rhine–Westphalia was especially active at this time; here Dr Merten succeeded by his energetic policy in establishing the Europa-Bund as *the* Pan-European organization, and also founded a number of local groups.[480]

The political orientation of the Europa-Bund leaders and their endeavours to 'federate the federalists' were vindicated when no fewer than twenty German pro-Europeans were invited to the Montreux congress of the UEF,[481] which elected to its central committee Eugen Kogon of the Europa-Bund, Wilhelm Hermes of Europa-Union, and Kasting of the Berlin Pan-Europa-Bund.[482]

It was meanwhile becoming increasingly clear that the only real reason why Europa-Union remained outside the merger of all other German federalist groups lay in Hermes's political ambitions. His tactics had been to protract the merger negotiations while Europa-Union continued to grow, so that it would in the end clearly predominate over the other groups and the leadership of the German national association would thus, automatically as it were, fall to Hermes himself. But, while the Europa-Bund now invited Europa-Union to join it and, at the delegates' congress in October, authorized its sub-formations to form 'regional unions without delay with corresponding formations of Europa-Union',[483] the latter body did not respond: its 'merger committee' set up at Eutin, meeting on 18

---

[476] Appeal dated 1.10.1947, in *Europa. Mitteilungblatt des Europa-Bundes,* 1.10.1947.
[477] Cf. v. Radowtiz corr., Aug. 1947, in *DGAP Archives,* E 791.71/D.
[478] Cf. p. 390; he was not present at Frankfurt, but joined the organization later, the delay being due to the isolation of the French Zone; cf. correspondence with Dr Pulides, Aug.–Sept. 1947, *Bernhard Archives,* Europa-Bund file.
[479] Cf. report in *Europa, Mittelungsblatt des Europa-Bundes,* 1.10.1947.
[480] Cf. reports in the *Mitteilungsblatt des Europa-Bundes,* edited by him, Sept.–Nov. 1947.
[481] These were : Wilhelm Hermes (Europa-Union), Max Dominicus (Europa-Union), Wilhelm Heile (Europa-Union), Joachim Berringer (Europa-Union), Werner Lenz (Pan-Europa-Jugend), Heinz Kosfeld (Union Junges Europa), Friedrich Freiherr Schilling von Canstadt, Alexander Mitscherlich, Bernhard Kolanczyk Jr. and Sr. (Pan-Europa-Bund), Wilhelm Kasting (Pan-Europa-Bund), Walter Henrich (Union Europa Liga), Bruno Maass (Union Europa Liga), F. Nothardt (Europa-Aktion), Herbert Hillringhaus (Die Kommenden), M. Rebholz (Die Kommenden), F. Bogler, Hans Deichmann, Prof. Hartner, Eugen Kogon, and Konsul Stocky. List in *Federal German Archives,* Heile papers, vol. 98. Not all those invited received permission to travel to Montreux; for those who did, see n. 323.
[482] Cf. *Europa, Mitteilungsblatt des Europa-Bundes,* first number of Oct. 1947, and nn. 323 and 474. Kogon was one of those who were invited to Montreux but could not get there.
[483] Full account in *Europa, Mitteilungsblatt des Europa-Bundes,* second number of Oct. 1947.

August at Cologne under Hermes's chairmanship, resolved 'to desist from further negotiations with a view to union with the newly founded Europa-Bund'.[484]

The member groups of Europa-Union, however, showed little sympathy with their chairman's personal ambition. In the autumn of 1947 local and regional groups began of their own volition to merge with the Europa-Bund, e.g. in Detmold, Bielefeld, North Westphalia, and especially in the French Zone.[485] This development threatened to leave the central secretariat at Mönchengladbach in a state of complete isolation, and on 23 September Hermes[486] felt obliged to visit Bernhard in hospital and propose a merger of the two organizations.

On 20 November, accordingly, Berringer and Hasemann for Europa-Union, Maass and Schmitz of Solingen[487] for the Europa-Bund, and Meinberg for the Bielefeld unification group agreed that the two associations would unite at all levels to form the 'Gemeinschaft Europa-Bund/Europa-Union'. Joint meetings of members at district level would prepare the merger from below, and meetings at all levels would ensure a fully democratic reorganization.[488] This procedure was duly carried out in the

[484] In line with his usual rather unscrupulous publicity methods, he also stated that the SPD had forbidden its members to join the Europa-Bund; shortly afterwards, however, he had to admit that the SPD's Meinberg decision had meanwhile been restricted to the Berlin Paneuropa-Bund. DPD, 19.8.1947 and 22.8.1947; *Nouvelles de France*, 19.9.1947. On the Meinberg decision, see chap. IV/1, in vol. 2.

[485] As early as 20 August the Europa-Union local branches (*Kreisgruppen*) at Detmold and Bielefeld joined to form working groups with their opposite numbers of the Europa-Bund. Shortly afterwards one of the biggest local groups of Europa-Union in Westphalia, that at Tecklenburg, joined the Europa-Bund as a body. Thereupon the Europa-Union delegates for the district (*Bezirk*) of North Westphalia, meeting at Münster on 1 Sept., addressed a demand to Mönchengladbach to the effect that if the merger with the Europa-Bund was not completed by 1 October, local groups should be free to join the Europa-Bund. At the same time the Kreis group at Wuppertal joined the Europa-Bund (Merten to Bernhard, 9.9.1947, *Bernhard Archives*, Europa-Bund file). The situation developed similarly in the other *Länder*, especially in the French Zone, where Kolwes on 1 August had just received a licence for a *Landesverband* of Europa-Union. Here 'Schinzinger, representing the Europa-Bund for the *Länder* Rhineland–Palatinate, Baden, and South Württemberg, lost no time in merging the groups under his authority in the French Zone, on the basis of negotiations with Kolwes (Coblenz) and Hummel (Freistett), representing the Europa-Union in their areas' (Schinzinger, 17.7.1954, in *DGAP Archives*. For the licence, cf. DPD, 4.8.1947 from Mönchengladbach and 31.8.1947 from Coblenz). The leaders of the *Land* group for Lower Saxony appealed to all their members in Sept. to 'suppress dissension and present a firm front', as Hermes had announced merger negotiations. At the *Land* assembly on 24–5.9.1947 the group expressed its unanimous desire for a merger, which must not be hindered by personal or formal considerations (circulars, nos. 4 and 8, *Federal German Archives*, Heile papers, vol. 67).

[486] Hermes was accompanied by, and probably under pressure from, Dipl.-Ing. J. Berringer, chairman of the Bavarian *Landesverband*. For the 'Ellwangen conversation', see Europa-Union, *Informationsdienst*, 29.8.1947, *EU Archives*; summarized in Bernhard's telegram of 24 Sept. to Merten, *Bernhard Archives*, Europa-Bund file.

[487] Maass was second chairman of the Bavarian *Landesverband* of the Europa-Bund; Schmitz was chairman of its North Rhine/Westphalian *Landesverband* in succession to Dr Merten, who concentrated on press relations and public speaking.

[488] The formulation of individual points, now conducted democratically with merger committees at all levels, conformed closely to the Bielefeld working group's decisions of 10.11.1947; cf. *Mitteilungsblatt der Gemeinschaft Europabund-Europaunion*, Ascheberg, Nov. 1947.

course of the winter. Discerning observers like von Schenck of the UEF noted that the process itself led to a relaxation of centralism, increased spontaneity and independence on the part of local groups, and thus to a stronger infusion of the federalist spirit.[489] This effect of the merger was scarcely less important than the fact that a single body representing all German supporters of the European idea at last existed or was coming into being. The centralist tendency for which Hermes had stood was in principle overcome, and the pro-European movement in Germany was itself being reorganized on federal principles. By February 1948 matters were far enough advanced for the new 'Europa-Union' to be formally constituted, with Bernhard and Hermes as co-chairmen with equal rights; its headquarters were fixed at Stuttgart, with Erich Rossmann as secretary-general.[490]

Hermes made another attempt to outmanœuvre his former rivals of the Europa-Bund in the new organization, with the result that Bernhard withdrew from the chairmanship on 31 March 1948;[491] but, as will be seen in vol. 2,[492] the process of democratization had gone so far that there was no longer room for personal ambitions of this kind. Hermes's behaviour in regard to the merger should not be allowed to obscure the good qualities which enabled him to play an essential part in creating the European movement in Germany during 1947, and which no one described better than Schinzinger: 'He was courageous and indefatigable, full of vigour in speech and action, and above all he possessed a keen sense of the importance of organizational matters, which Bernhard lacked, as did Kogon after him.'[493]

Before it became clear whether the merger of associations in the Europa-Bund would be successful and produce an effective national movement, an organization of a special kind had come into being in the French Zone, which was still to a large extent isolated from events in Bizonia. As has been described, the weekly *Der Rheinische Merkur*, published at Coblenz from April 1946, was devoted to the cause of federation in Germany and Europe. One of its themes was that the Rhineland, as a historic part of Germany, should have independent political status within a German federation and at the same time strengthen the no less historic bonds that linked it with the West of Europe.[494] F. A. Kramer, the editor of

---

[489] 'Report to Executive Bureau of the UEF on Activity and Situation in Germany' by E. von Schenck, 27.12.1947; *Schenck Archives,* UEF file.
[490] Cf. *Westdeutsches Tageblatt,* 25.2.1948; *Sopade-Informationsdienst,* Apr. 1948, p. 125. In a report of 20.2.1948 to Bernhard, Hermes said the merger of most of the *Landesverbände* was completed, but the situation in Berlin was quite unclear (*Bernhard Archives,* Europa-Union file). For details, see chap. V/4 in vol. 2.
[491] Cf. Bernhard to J. Sandner (Carlsruhe), 14.4.1948; *Bernhard Archives,* Europa-Union file.
[492] In chap. V/4, vol. 2.
[493] Schinzinger, 7.8.1954, *DGAP Archives.*
[494] Cf. chap. I/5, p. 241 f.

Der Rheinische Merkur, had contacts with many who thought on these lines, and through Catholic federalists in the Rhineland he also had connections with Protestant federalists in Lower Saxony.[495] On 17 August 1947 representatives of both groups, meeting at Bad Ems, resolved to form an association called the Bund Deutscher Föderalisten.

This body included surviving supporters of two associations dating from the Weimar republic, the Reichs- und Heimatbund Deutscher Katholiken and the (Guelphic) Bund Deutscher Föderalisten. It was inspired by a Christian and federalist tradition which had flourished in Lower Saxony, the Rhineland, and South Germany since the days of Joseph von Görres and had survived the Prussian triumph of 1866; its chief theorist was Constantin Frantz. The inaugural manifesto of the new association declared that the opportunity had now again presented itself to 'place the internal government of Germany on its natural and historical basis' and to create a federal system 'in the spirit of the classic nineteenth-century federalists'. The principles of free self-government should be applied to every part of the political and social system, and Germany should in this way be reintegrated into the European community.[496] An appeal was thus made to the rich tradition of a native German theory of federalism, which had from the outset also possessed a European and universal character.

The manifesto was signed by a number of eminent personalities including Ludwig Alpers, chairman of the Guelph party in Weimar times, Peter Altmeier, prime minister of the Rhineland–Palatinate, Dr von Brentano, H. Hellwege, Hoegner, Kogon, Kramer, Naumann, editor of *Neues Abendland*, Pechel, editor of the *Deutsche Rundschau*, and Helena Schmittmann, widow of the Rhineland federalist murdered in 1934. A. Süsterhenn, minister of justice of the Rhineland–Palatinate, played an especially active part in making the movement a success.

The Bund Deutscher Föderalisten remained on a élite basis and at no time canvassed mass support. Its chief aim was to ensure that the federal principle was recognized in the forthcoming consultations on the recreation of the German political system above the level of the *Länder*. The association was imbued with federalist principles, and the 'integral federalists' among its members saw it as an urgent need to assert those principles in German internal affairs.[497] Its influence was chiefly exerted through the CDU constitutional committee at Ellwangen, of which Brentano was chairman and Süsterhenn a member, and afterwards through the constitutional congress at Herrenchiemsee, which produced a draft of what later became the Basic

---

[495] For details of the origin of the Bund Deutscher Föderalisten, cf. W. Ferber, 'Der Föderalismus in Deutschland', *Die Friedenswarte*, vol. 50, 1950.

[496] Inaugural manifesto of the Bund Deutscher Föderalisten, *Rheinischer Merkur*, 26.8.1947.

[497] The association was for a time in danger of over-emphasizing the federal principle in favour of the *Länder*, almost to the point of separatism. But it managed to steer clear of this danger by making clear that it was opposed to centralism on a *Land* basis (a tendency which generally went with separatism) and was in favour of a national federal state intermediate between the *Länder* and a European federation.

Law (Constitution) of the Federal Republic of Germany.[498] The association naturally also worked from the outset for a federation of Europe; it was chary, however, of pro-European organizations which aimed too exclusively at a union of European states and were less ready to make federalism a reality in Germany itself.[499] It was this integral federalism which caused the association to gravitate towards the UEF,[500] while sensibly refraining from linking its fortunes with the other German groups. The UEF central committee accepted the Bund Deutscher Föderalisten as a member on 17 January 1948. On the same day they also admitted the Cologne Liga für Weltregierung, thus once more making clear their desire to see the federal principle applied at all levels – local, regional, national, European, and world-wide.[501]

Apart from *Der Rheinische Merkur*, there came forward in the autumn of 1947 a number of writers who expounded federalist ideas both systematically and historically and favoured advocating their application to both German and European affairs. Especially clear and forceful publications were *Der Föderalismus* by Walter Ferber and *Laiengespräche über den Staat* by Ferdinand Kirnberger, formerly Hessian minister of justice and president of the Katholischer Akademikerverband; both these were members of the Bund Deutscher Föderalisten.[502] Many politico-literary monthly journals also published articles advocating federalism and European federation. In particular almost every number of *Frankfurter Hefte*, published by Eugen Kogon and Walter Dirks with Rüdiger Proske as assistant editor, contained a fresh exposition of federalism as an inescapable consequence of the democratic principle.

Democracy could only be a success if self-governing institutions were built up organically from below, the level of decision-taking being as low as possible in every case. The journal was opposed either to depriving the *Länder* of power or to over-stressing their role in a separatist fashion. In the same way, it warned against creating either a European Leviathan or a loose confederation of states without sufficient power of its own; it wished to see the federal principle applied uniformly at all levels. In the first issue in April 1946 Walter Dirks wrote: 'We proclaim the end of the sovereign national state'; he went on to demand an 'europäische Konföderation', without specifying the exact degree of federation that this implied. 'Europe, the poor Continent, can only stand for something if it pulls itself together and unites; it must organize on a planned basis the use of its natural resources, means of production and manpower.'[503]

[498] The federalist principles of the Basic Law are largely based on the work of members of the Bund Deutscher Föderalisten; cf. chap. V/4, in vol. 2.
[499] All from statements by Dr E. Kogon, 11.10.1961, and ex-minister Dr A. Süsterhenn, 28.10.1961.
[500] Cf. Schenck to UEF Executive, 27.12.1947, *von Schenck Archives*, UEF file.
[501] Report of session of the UEF central committee in *Lettre-Circulaire*, No. 17 of 5.2.1948.
[502] W. Ferber, *Der Föderalismus*, Augsburg, 1947 (2nd ed., 5,000, 1947), F. Kirnberger, *Laiengespräche über den Staat*, Augsburg, 1947.
[503] W. Dirks, 'Die Zweite Republik', *Frankfurter Hefte*, 1/I (1946), pp. 12–24, quotations p. 16 f. Cf. also C. Münster, 'Abbau der nationalen Souveränität', *Frankfurter Hefte* 6 I (1946), pp. 1–3; E. Kogon, 'Demokratie und Föderalismus', *Frankfurter Hefte* 6 I (1946), pp. 66–78.

In *Neues Abendland* H. Schmittmann argued that the nation must be 'organized on a basis of respect for personality' and that internal federation was the pre-condition of a peace-loving European community of nations; in *Neues Europa* Rudolf Amelunxen advocated a federal European 'Third Force' with Germany as an equal partner; in several numbers of the *Stuttgarter Rundschau* H. Bernhard developed his ideas on the United States of Europe; in *Die Wandlung* Carlo Schmid urged that Germany should agree to the internationalization of the Ruhr for the sake of Franco-German *rapprochement*, which was the key to European unity; in the *Merkur* Denis de Rougemont argued for 'political structures of a federalist stamp'.[504]

In contrast to periodicals, the idea of European federation was by no means predominant in books published in Germany in 1947 on historical and political subjects. There was indeed a tendency, as there had been ever since the cataclysm of 1945, to stress the common Western inheritance;[505] the need for co-operation in Europe was also clearly recognized by many writers who, however, did not draw federalist conclusions;[506] those who did so to the full extent numbered perhaps a quarter of the total.

Ernst Friedländer and O. Lehmann-Russbueldt, for instance, spoke expressly of the need for European union, but meant by this only a 'unionist' confederation. Kurt Karl Doberer's *United States of Germany*, published in London in 1944, pleaded for federalism in Germany and Europe, as did Erwin Kohl, who also advocated 'subsidiarity': 'The state must enjoy only so much power and authority as is essential in the common interest of all.' Herbert Hörhager argued similarly in *Wesen und Praxis der übernationalen Staatenordnung*, the first of a series of works published by the Liga für Weltregierung. F. A. Kramer's articles in *Der Rheinische Merkur* were collected into a volume entitled *Politische Leitsätze*; Heinrich Ritzel popularized the Hertenstein programme, and Hans Ehard, prime minister of Bavaria, advocated the decentralization of Germany and its incorporation in a European federation.[507]

[504] E. Schmittmann, 'Demokratie als personale Volksordnung', *Neues Abendland*, March 1947, pp. 1–3; R. Amelunxen, *Neues Europa*, 2 (1947), Nos. 5 and 9; H. Bernhard, 'Französische Friedensvorschläge', *Stuttgarter Rundschau*, 1947, No. 2,; id., 'Deutschland in Europa', ibid., No. 4; C. Schmid, 'Das deutsch-französische Verhältnis und der Dritte Partner', *Die Wandlung*, 2 (1947), pp. 792–805; D. de Rougemont, 'Die Krankheiten Europas', *Merkur* 1 I (1947), pp. 17–26. The idea of a federally organized, independent Europe based on a common cultural inheritance was developed in *Merkur* in the winter of 1947/8 in opposition to Lionel Curtis's conception of a democratic Western community including the Commonwealth and the US: L. Curtis, 'Vereintes Europa', *Merkur*, i (1947), pp. 641–9; J. von Kempski, 'Föderalismus und Unitarismus', ibid., pp. 817–28; K. Schmid, 'Europäische Union', ibid., pp. 649–54; K. Geiler, 'Union der Demokratien', ibid., pp. 654–61; L. Ziegler, 'Imperium europaneum', *Merkur*, ii (1948), pp. 115–20; G. de Reynold, 'Was ist Europa?' ibid., pp. 120–5.

[505] Cf. W. Feitner, *Die abendländischen Vorbilder und das Bild der Erziehung*, Godesberg, 1947; J. Ebbinghaus, *Zu Deutschlands Schicksalswende*, Frankfurt, 1947[2]; W. Eichler, *Schicksalsfragen für Deutschland*, Stuttgart, 1947; A. Mauer, *Bekenntnis zu Europa*, Wiesbaden, 1947.

[506] Cf. e.g. *Die Neutralität Deutschlands und der Friede; Unmittelbarkeit des Friedens und Unteilbarkeit Deutschlands; Zur völkerrechtlichen Lage Deutschlands; Zur künftigen deutschen Gesamtverfassung;* all in the series *Schriften der Heidelberger Aktionsgruppen zur Demokratie und zum freien Sozialismus*, Heidelberg, 1947. For the meaning of the term 'Unionist' in the European context, cf. p. 665 ff.

[507] O. Lehmann-Russbueldt, *Europa den Europäern*, Hamburg, 1948 (completed in Aug. 1947); E. Friedländer, *Das Wesen des Friedens*, Hamburg, 1947; K. K. Doberer, *Die Vereinigten Staaten von Deutschland*, Munich, 1947; 'Reconciler' (= Erwin Kohl), *Die letzte Chance, Deutschland und die*

Some of these writers, like *Der Rheinische Merkur*, used the term 'Europe' from the outset as synonymous with the linking of Germany to her Western neighbours in the first instance. But in 1947 even they did not as yet fully grasp the implications of 'starting in the West', and this was even more true of writers and associations who, like the UEF, thought in terms of a 'Third Force' comprising the whole of Europe. For reasons already mentioned, both of a psychological character and because of insufficient information, the elimination of the East-European countries was scarcely understood at this stage; still less did German observers face the crucial question whether, as the UEF eventually decided, a beginning should be made by unifying Western Europe and hence including Western Germany only. In any case the associations were busy at this time with their merger problems. Only in 1948, at the Homburg congress, did the German pro-Europeans come to grips with the problem of the temporary restriction of European unity to the West.[508]

The official press in the Allied military zones voiced the suspicion that the European idea might be used as a cover by forces that were chiefly interested in the revival of German power. In was indeed the case that, during the war, the German Resistance movement had been ever more clearly obliged to desire the defeat of its own country, so that after 1945 a demand for European federation implied at the same time 'equality of rights' for Germany; whereas the federalists in other European countries were more and more obliged to work against the sovereignty of their respective nations. (Only when Germany recovered her sovereignty, from 1955 onwards, did the situation of federalists in Germany begin to resemble that in other countries from this point of view.) However, the Allied authorities in their scepticism failed to realize that, as has been shown, almost all the original German pro-European associations fully and expressly recognized the danger of 'putting Germany first'; they refused to have anything to do with neo-Nazi fellow-travellers, and genuinely wanted to do away with national sovereignty in Europe in order to create a supranational federation. The sceptics also failed to see that, as Lord Beveridge and Ernst von Schenck had pointed out, the Germans could only come to terms effectively with the past if they had some hope for the future: what was needed was a new political beginning with new objectives.[509] The misunderstanding was due in part to the fact that

---

Vereinigten Staaten von Europa, Hamburg, 1947; H. Hörhager, *Föderalismus, Wesen und Praxis übernationaler Staatenordnung*, s.l.n.d. (*c.*1947); F. A. Kramer, *Politische Leitsätze*, Coblenz, 1947; H. Ehard, *Freiheit und Föderalismus*, Munich, 1947; id., *Die europäische Lage und der deutsche Föderalismus*, Munich, 1948; H. G. Ritzel, *Europa und Deutschland, Deutschland und Europa*, Offenbach, 1947. Less clearly based on federalist principles, but more or less specifically envisaging the decentralization of Germany and its integration in a united Europe were: W. Schmidt, *Das Reich ist tot – Aufruf zur Gründung des europäischen Bundes*, Stuttgart, 1946; E. Reger, *Vom künftigen Deutschland*, Berlin, 1947; H. Dietrich, *Auf der Suche nach Deutschland, Probleme zur geistigen, politischen und wirtschaftlichen Erneuerung Deutschlands*, Hamburg, 1946¹, Stuttgart, 1947².

[508] Cf. chap. V/4 in vol. 2.

[509] Cf. quotations from Beveridge and von Schenck, chapter II, note 205. Newspapers of the Allied authorities: cf. *Der Tagesspiegel* 22.2.1947, *Nouvelles de France* 19.9.1947, *Die Welt* 16.3.1948.

individual members of the Allied Control Commission themselves thought in terms of national sovereignty which had been discarded by federalist groups in Germany and other countries.

7. The International Committee of the Movements for European Unity

Since the autumn of 1946 the federalist groups for European union which had arisen spontaneously in many centres had made contact with one another, and by the beginning of 1947 almost all such groups in the West-European Continental countries had become affiliated to the umbrella organization of the UEF. Except in Belgium they had also united on the national level, either in a single association (as in Switzerland, Italy, and the Netherlands) or under a co-ordinating committee, as in France, while the German associations had combined to form the Europa-Union. The UEF leaders, all of whom were former Resistance fighters of the generation aged 35–40, wanted not only a federal European state but a thorough decentralization and reform of society on federal lines; they generally mistrusted the existing political parties, in which none of them personally played a leading part. The doctrine elaborated at the Montreux congress envisaged a revolutionary mass movement and a mobilization of grass-roots opinion; by the summer of 1947 'UEF already grouped together 28 movements, comprising 100,000 subscribing members'.[510]

Alongside the UEF, as has been shown, there were four other groups, considerably smaller in numbers but led by prominent politicians of an older generation who, after the catastrophe of war, wanted in their own way to overcome national antagonisms and work for European co-operation, integration, or union. These groups, and their dates of formation were: in January 1947, the United Europe Committee (known as the United Europe Movement from May onwards) under Churchill's chairmanship; in March, the Ligue Indépendante de Coopération Européenne (from June onwards the LECE, or in English ELEC) under the former Belgian premier van Zeeland; on 5 July, the European Parliamentary Union (EPU), with Coudenhove-Kalergi as its secretary-general and an executive composed of ex-ministers and heads of parliamentary parties; and on 16 July, the Conseil français pour l'Europe unie under ex-premier Herriot. Of these, only the EPU had a programme that envisaged federal union and the summoning of a constituent assembly; with its groups of federalist parliamentarians, it had a larger membership than the others. The other

---

[510] D. de Rougemont, 'The campaign of the European congresses' (translated from French), *Government and Opposition*, vol. 2 (1966/7), p. 338. The total given by de Rougemont, who belonged to the inner circle of the UEF from Montreux onwards, agrees well enough with the figures ascertained by us as far as possible for each association. On the UEF generally, see especially chaps. II/5 and III/4.

committees, although some individual members might be federally inclined, confined themselves officially to vague formulas: they wanted to 'increase and cultivate opportunities for co-operation among European nations' (ELEC), 'ensure to the government of the day wide support for any action which tends towards European unity' (UEM), and in general to evolve pragmatically towards a confederal union. The members of each committee numbered no more than 20–40, but all belonged to the ruling circles of their countries: political and social leaders, ex-ministers (nearly half of the members), and parliamentarians; as Duncan Sandys remarked with satisfaction of the Conseil français, they were 'influential and highly representative'.[511]

In a situation in which none of the governments had yet endorsed the European idea, it was essential to achieve co-ordination between these groups and the UEF so as to prevent rivalry, overlapping, and the confusion of public opinion. Brugmans had tried to get the UEM and EPU to become member associations of the UEF; and Marc asked Sandys on 20 June if he would agree to the UEM being listed by the UEF as a 'mouvement associé'.[512] Sandys and Coudenhove, however, would not hear of this; in their view it was for the groups of young, idealistic amateurs to associate themselves with the work that seasoned politicians were doing in their own committees. This difficulty in relation to the UEF became less important as the centre of gravity shifted towards other groups which were concerned from the outset with uniting Western Europe only, the Soviet rejection of the Marshall Plan having shown that Eastern Europe was out of bounds for the time being.[513] At that stage Duncan Sandys seized the initiative with a view to co-ordinating these groups.

---

[511] Sandys to all members of UEM Executive Committee, 22.7.1947 (*EM Archives, Bruges*). Cf. the discussion of these groups in chaps. II/3 (UEM, quotation p. 331, and ELEC, quotation p. 338), III/5 (EPU), and III/6, pp. 623–5 (Conseil Français). It was not yet widely known that besides these groups a pro-European association of left-wing Socialists and another of Christian Democrats had been in the course of formation since June 1947. Cf. n. 548 f., and (in the context of political parties) chap. IV/1 and 2, in vol. 2.

[512] For Brugmans's attempts, cf. chap. II at n. 338 f. and 501. A. Marc addressed his enquiry to Sandys on 20.6.1947, enclosing a copy of *Fédérer les Fédéralistes*. On 24.6.1947 Sandys replied: 'As regards the inclusion of the UEM in the list of movements associated with the UEF, this is, of course, not strictly correct, though I consider that some closer association between us is very desirable. I should be very pleased to discuss with you how this could best be done.' From this correspondence and another at the same time with Voisin (both in *EM Archives, Bruges*) it appears that Sandys went to Paris on 30 June–1 July for a preliminary talk with the leaders of other groups about the agreement of 20 July (cf. n. 521).

[513] Brugmans noticed the shift of emphasis at once, as he showed in a letter of 14.7.1947 to Mrs E. Dangerfield. Herriot and his friends, he wrote, were trying 'to organize a French committee in the style of Mr Churchill's. They also adhere to the *comité de coordination*, but it must be our constant preoccupation to prevent the French movement from sliding to the right. It will be specially difficult now after the failure of the first Paris conference (*BEF Archives*, Brugmans corr.).

(A) FOUNDATION OF THE LIAISON COMMITTEE IN PARIS, 20 JULY 1947

For external reasons and in accordance with his own political conviction, Sandys took as the setting for his efforts the Journées Franco-Britanniques which had for some time been planned to take place in Paris from 17 to 20 July. At the end of 1946 he had impressed on Coudenhove his view that owing to French fear of Germany it was 'absolutely essential that Britain and France should, in the first place, come out as the joint founder members of the European movement'.[514] It had been agreed that a British delegation should return the visit of the twenty-eight French federalists, led by Voisin and accompanied by Brugmans, who had come to London on 12–16 May at the invitation of Federal Union and the UEM and had attended the mass meeting at the Albert Hall. The invitation to Paris was issued by the Comité français de Coordination des Mouvements fédéralistes. and Voisin was in charge of all preparations. Sandys was at pains to see that the British delegation consisted chiefly of representative political members of UEM, and had urged Courtin to hasten the establishment of the Conseil français (which took place formally on the day before the British arrival), so as to reduce the existing predominance of the federalists.[515]

The delegation which arrived at Le Bourget airport on the afternoon of 17 July consisted of twenty-nine persons led by the eminent Liberal peer Lord Layton, proprietor of the *News Chronicle*. Other members were the ex-ministers L. S. Amery, Leslie Hore-Belisha, Walter Elliot, and Duncan Sandys (all UEM and Conservative); Conservative MPs R. Boothby, J. Hutchison, and W. Teeling; Labour MPs A. J. Champion, H. J. Delargy, E. King, Gordon Lang, W. T. Proctor, S. Segal, and D. Granville West; the Liberal MP W. Butcher and the prominent Liberals Lord Beveridge, Lady V. Bonham Carter, and Lady Rhys Williams; ex-MPs, S. King-Hall and T. B. Martin, both representing the UEM; for the executive of Federal Union, O. Adler, H. Hopkinson, Prof. C. E. M. Joad, Miss Josephy, and Keith Killby; finally Prof. D. Brogan of Cambridge, the Roman Catholic Bishop Edward Myers, and J. M. Richardson, president of the Bath Council of Christian Churches.[516]

---

[514] Sandys, as his biography shows (cf. chap. II, n. 77 f.), was especially concerned about reconciliation with Germany. On 4.12.1946 he wrote to Coudenhove-Kalergi after a visit to Paris: 'I was greatly impressed with the importance of handling the question of Germany's future with great tact. There are too many people in France who still regard Germany and not Russia as the real power.' Hence, as quoted above, 'Britain and France should come out as the joint founder members of the European movement. Subsequently, after agreeing amongst themselves upon the plan of action, they should together invite the Germans' (*EM Archives, Bruges*, CFEU file).

[515] For the French federalists' visit to London on 12–16 May 1947, cf. chap. II, n. 193; organization of the return visit to Paris, cf. esp. Voisin's letter to Sandys of 15.7.1947; establishment of the Conseil Français hastened under pressure from Sandys, cf. Courtin to Sandys, 10 and 31 July ('Je vous ai toujours dit que si je constituais notre comité en juillet, c'était uniquement pour vous rencontrer'); all in *EM Archives, Bruges*. Inaugural meeting on 16.7.1947, cf. at n. 404.

[516] The list is given here as it appears in the fullest account written retrospectively by one who took part in the visit: K. Killby, 'Diversity and Unity. Paris Conference', *Federal News*, No. 149, Aug. 1947, pp. 11–14. In UEF *Lettre-Circulaire*, No. 13, Geneva, 22.7.1947, p. 3, R. Silva reproduced a

On the evening of the 17th a ceremonial reception was given by Jean Larmeroux for over 400 people including 100 French MPs. Paul Rivet, chairman of the parliamentary federalist group, emphasized the need for the pooling of sovereignties; Brugmans and Mme Peyrolles, vice-president of the Assemblée Nationale, declared that federalism was the one hope for mankind. Lord Layton replied that the British delegation had come 'to affirm the great support in Britain for European unity'. Next day the visitors were received in the morning by H. Genet on behalf of the UEF, and at noon in the Assembly by E. Herriot. The latter extolled Anglo-French friendship and the duty of the two countries to 'build Europe', while Amery in his reply spoke chiefly of 'a plan of economic cooperation'. On the 19th the delegates were received by M. Vergnolle, the mayor of Paris, whose speech of welcome was replied to by Miss Josephy, and on the morning of the 20th a farewell reception was given by J. Bassot on behalf of La Fédération; on both these occasions stress was laid on the idea of federal union.[517] Daytime sessions took place in the Maison des Alliés; on the 18th the German question was discussed, and on the 19th the problems of creating a common market. Issues of principle were also ventilated; René Courtin gave the clearest account of these debates:

'The British were convinced of the need for speedy German recovery... The French rejected the idea of any priority for the aggressor... The other controversy was this: the French, both of the Right and Left, unanimously held that Europe cannot be built unless every nation is prepared to yield part of its sovereignty to a common authority. We were extremely firm on this. Our view was shared by the members of Federal Union, ... but others of the British team, especially the Conservatives..., thought that united Europe should be constructed on the same basis as the British Commonwealth, the states all preserving their sovereignty while freely harmonizing their policy and legislation. I need not say that these views seem to us highly unrealistic (*singulièrement théoriques*).'[518] Thus began the crucial debate which was to dominate the next few years.

At the conclusion of the last working session, under Lord Layton's chairmanship, the following declaration was adopted:

---

list sent by Sandys to Voisin on 26.6.1947 and including four more MPs, three Labour and one Liberal. These are not mentioned in any other report and were evidently prevented from attending at the last moment.

[517] Details and brief summaries of speeches in Killby, loc. cit.; reports in *Le Monde*, 19.7.1947 and 22.7.1947; *The Times*, 19.7.1947 and 21.7.1947; DPD, 21.7.1947; extracts from Lord Layton's speech in *Daily Mail*, 19.7.1947; from Amery's in *La République moderne*, 32, 1.8.1947, p. 9.

[518] R. Courtin, 'France, Angleterre, Europe', *Réforme*, 2.8.1947; a similar account headed 'Des désaccords subsistent' in *La République moderne*, 32, 1.8.1947, p. 9. Fullest report of the sessions by M. Richard, 'Les Journées Franco-Britanniques de Paris', *La Fédération*, Nos. 31/2, Aug./Sept. 1947, pp. 2–4; on p. 2 Lord Beveridge is reported as saying: 'Des membres de tous les partis, venus à titre individual, considèrent la fédération – incluant le transfert d'une part des souverainetés nationales – comme la condition nécessaire d'une paix mondiale'; the British team had come to Paris 'pour discuter les méthodes capables de rendre effective l'idée des États-Unis d'Europe'.

The prosperity and peace of our Continent, the preservation of its civilization and democratic principles require a united Europe. In many people's opinion it is too early to decide whether the new organization of Europe should take the form of a close federation or some other kind of union. But, whichever institutional solution is finally adopted, in any case it will be essential for elements of national sovereignty to be pooled so that a genuine, effective union may be created ... In the work of European construction that lies before us, the duty and honour of the initiative belong jointly to France and Britain.[519]

On the evening of 19 July the UEM members of the British delegation conferred at Courtin's house with the Conseil français and, according to Sandys, agreed 'that the British United Europe Movement and the Comité Français pour l'Europe Unie should regard one another as sister movements and as far as possible conduct a joint campaign'.[520]

On the following day, and against this background, Sandys entertained the heads of the other associations to lunch at a restaurant on the Champs Élysées. He had invited them by a letter of 12 July to which was annexed 'a draft proposal which sets out the basis for a Coordinating Committee of the various Movements on the lines which I have discussed with each of them'; the letter expressed the hope that the recipients would come on the 20th with authority to reach agreement on the draft.[521] It was in fact signed with few amendments, thus inaugurating the history of what became the European Movement. Those who agreed on behalf of their organizations were:

For the Independent League: Dr Joseph Retinger and Daniel Serruys
For the UEF: Dr Henry Brugmans, Alexandre Marc, and Raymond Silva
For the EPU: Leon Maccas
For the UEM, British Committee: Gordon Lang and Duncan Sandys; French Committee: René Courtin and Andre Noël.

---

[519] The Marshall offer should be used 'To bring about a better economic organization of our Continent. Unfortunately several countries are at present unable to take part in the work, but that is no reason to abandon it. Time is precious, and we must go forward boldly with those who are able and willing to join us.' Text of motion in *La Fédération*, Nos. 31/2, Aug./Sept. 1947, p. 4. It is noteworthy that Sandys, who on 22.7.1947 sent out numerous typed letters reporting on the further proceedings (cf. n. 520), never mentioned this motion, the first part of which went too far to suit him.

[520] Sandys wrote thus in a letter of 22.7.1947 to all members of the UEM Executive, informing them of the results of the Paris meetings, and stating that the Conseil and the UEM had agreed to set up a 'Joint Propaganda Committee' and a 'Joint Policy Committee' and to organize a joint rally in the Vélodrome d'Hiver in Paris with Churchill and Blum as the main speakers; also 'that the two organizations should endeavour to secure the formation of similar representative committees in other European countries' (*EM Archives, Bruges*). These decisions, however, were not put into effect. The 'Joint Committees' never came into being, and the rally failed to take place because Blum, in the face of Labour opposition, would not agree to appear with Churchill (cf. n. 409). The plan to form 'sister committees' in other countries also failed; cf. H. Brugmans, 'Naissance d'une politique fédéraliste', *Les Cahiers de Bruges*, 1957/1, p. 66.

[521] Sandys wrote on 12.7.1947 in almost identical terms to Voisin, Marc, Maccas, and Retinger, and probably also to Brugmans, Courtin, and Coudenhove; however, there are no file copies of these invitations or of the 'draft proposal' (*EM Archives, Bruges*). The latter summarized the possibilities of co-ordination discussed in Paris on 30 June and 1 July: cf. n. 512.

Sandys opened the proceedings by pointing out how important it was to avoid duplication of effort; he added that preliminary talks had given ground for hope that agreement could be reached on the allocation of responsibilities and the founding of a European Liaison Committee as provided for in the draft. The course of the discussion has not been recorded; the 'Minutes of our meeting' afterwards circulated by Sandys listed only points of agreement and promises of help. Serruys offered the services of an experienced secretary (Paul Naudin) to run a branch office of the proposed Committee: he could circulate letters 'in a purely personal and unofficial capacity' and make practical arrangements for meetings. Maccas stated that the parliamentarians at the Gstaad congress 'would be entirely free to take such decisions as they thought fit in regard to the framing of the [EPU] statutes'; and all four organizations agreed 'jointly to issue an appeal to the various parliaments to give their support to the EPU, and to send representative delegations to the Congress at Gstaad'.[522] The agreement finally reached on the basis of Sandy's draft, slightly modified, was as follows.

1. In order to secure concerted action and to avoid unnecessary duplication between the principal Movements which are working in the international field to promote the cause of European unity, it has been decided to set up a European Liaison Committee composed of representatives of the following organizations:

Independent League for European Co-operation
European Union of Federalists
European Parliamentary Union
United Europe Movement (and associated movements).

2. The four organizations have accepted responsibility for different spheres of work as follows:

(a) *Independent League for European Co-operation*
The formation of a body of international experts on economic questions; the conduct of expert economic studies; the preparation of reports on economic subjects; the organization of conferences to discuss economic problems.

(b) *European Union of Federalists*
The co-ordination internationally of the national movements affiliated to it; the organization of conferences of representatives of those national movements; the production of literature and propaganda material for distribution to those national movements; generally the work of assisting those national movements to build up a mass membership.

(c) *European Parliamentary Union*
The organization of inter-parliamentary action; inter-parliamentary con-

---

[522] 'Minutes of a Meeting held in Paris on Sunday, July 20th, 1947', sent by Sandys on 22.7.1947 to all participants (for their official positions, see Index under the respective organizations) and to all members of the UEM Executive (*EM Archives, Bruges; Josephy Archives; UEF Archives*, etc.). Maccas was no doubt interested in getting a good attendance at the EPU congress at Gstaad on 8–10.9.1947 (cf. at n. 369), and Sandys wanted to influence the EPU (cf. n. 377). An appeal on the lines indicated was agreed on 20.7.1947 (cf. n. 524) and given to the press with the announcement of the formation of the Liaison Committee.

ferences; the initiation of action in the various Parliaments to secure support for the European cause.
(d) *United Europe Movement (and associated movements)*
The formation of a body of prominent public figures in each country; the organization of large public meetings of an international character: the direction of large-scale international propaganda (radio, films, newspapers, exhibitions, etc.).

3. The Movements will give to each other all possible assistance in discharging the responsibilities allotted to them. In the event of a Movement wishing to undertake activities other than those mentioned above, it will notify the others of its intention.

4. The Movements will, through the European Liaison Committee, exchange views upon the political situation and will seek, as far as possible, to agree upon the adoption of a common line of action.

5. The Committee will have no official staff or offices.

6. The Movements will endeavour in all important matters to act in consultation and agreement with each other. However, membership of the European Liaison Committee will, in the event of disagreement, not prejudice the freedom of action of the individual Movements.'[523]

This was a well-balanced preliminary agreement for mutual support, consultation, and division of labour. In order to take some account of the difference in membership numbers the two small groups of influential personalities, UEM and the Conseil français, figured as a single association with two committees; on the other hand their functions were described in fairly wide terms, while for the other three bodies they were defined more restrictively. This was not of great importance, however, as the Liaison Committee's decisions were not to be taken by a majority vote, and each association was free to inform the Committee of any extension of its activities. In the event of disagreement each association had full freedom of action, but the regular consultation that was provided for made possible a high degree of co-ordination in the common interest. Provided that this led to the overcoming of mutual distrust, the associations could be said to have achieved a confederal state among themselves. In the nature of things it could not be long before the question of a more effective unity was raised.

The press was informed in a joint statement that: 'In view of the present situation in Europe the associations [here followed their names] have decided to co-ordinate their efforts as far as possible while preserving their legitimate independence and freedom of action. For this purpose they have formed a Liaison Committee on a round-table basis, to examine the possibilities of co-operation in each specific case.'[524]

---

[523] The English text of the agreement was also sent by Sandys on 22.7.1947 to all participants and to members of the UEM Executive, the names of the above participants being added in typescript (*EM Archives, Bruges,* etc.); it has not previously been published; as to ratification, cf. at nn. 525 and 527.

[524] 'The Committee decided in particular to issue an appeal to all European parliaments . . .' etc.: here followed the agreed text concerning support for the EPU congress at Gstaad (cf. n. 522). The statement was printed e.g. in *Le Monde,* 22.7.1947; UEF, *Lettre-Circulaire,* No. 13, 22.7.1947, p. 2

On 22 July Sandys sent out the final text of the agreement under a covering letter asking the recipients to sign a confirmatory copy and return it to him. The first affirmative reply came from Retinger on the 29th, 'wishing only that this co-ordination may lead to an even greater unification of our joint efforts towards the constitution of a united free Europe'. Courtin replied on the 31st that he had 'signed at once' but would get his vice-chairman to countersign. Silva's reply was evidently delayed by the Montreux congress, but immediately afterwards, on 2 September, he returned a copy of the agreement signed by himself, Marc, and Brugmans on behalf of the UEF.[525] The EPU ratification, however, failed to materialize. In a letter of 25 August inviting Churchill once more to become honorary president of the EPU, Coudenhove wrote: 'The Agreement of July 20th stands. I do not consider the minutes a part of it. But I have every reason to doubt whether it can work, because the Federalists permanently violate its spirit by their unchanged hostility.'[526] After Churchill replied declining the invitation, the EPU executive unanimously decided on 7 September to 'postpone the question of ratification to a later date and to reserve full freedom of action'. Coudenhove, in communicating this decision, added that the EPU desired good relations 'with the three non-parliamentary groups which at present constitute your Liaison Committee'.[527] It was not long before the UEF for its part began to regret that the association which, next to itself, was most firmly committed to the idea of a federal Europe, had withdrawn from the co-ordination plan.

(adding that this was in accordance with a decision taken by the UEF Central committee on 16 July 'à l'unanimité moins 1 voix'); *La Fédération*, Nos. 31/2, Aug./Sept. 1947, p. 4; *L'Action fédéraliste européenne*, No. 7, Aug. 1947, p. 63 f.

[525] Retinger to Sandys, 29.7.1947; Courtin to Sandys, 31.7.1947; Silva to Sandys, 2.9.1947. The UEF reply proposed to add at the beginning of point 2: 'Subject to the reservations in paragraph 6 below, the four organizations have for the time being accepted . . .': i.e. they wanted to make it clear that the restrictive description of tasks was subject to the provision allowing complete freedom of action in the event of any difference of opinion (further correspondence on this point has not been preserved; all in *EM Archives, Bruges*, 'Int. Committee' file).

[526] Coudenhove-Kalergi to Sandys, 25.8.1947. On 15.8.1947 Silva had complained in a letter to Naudin that the programme of the EPU congress made no mention of the agreement of 20.7.1947 (both in *EM Archives, Bruges*, EPU file). On 8.8.1947 Brugmans wrote (in German) to Count G. Kanitz, who was in touch with Coudenhove: 'In this collaboration we reckon C.-K. to be the greatest hindrance . . . because his whole activity still bears altogether too personal a stamp. . . . On our side no personal or institutional *amour-propre* is in question. All we want is the best possible co-operation among all those working for European federation' (*BEF Archives*, Brugmans corr.).

[527] It was in these stand-offish terms that Coudenhove conveyed the decision (not until 18 Sept.) to P. Naudin (*EM Archives, Bruges*, 'Int. Committee' file); not to Sandys, whom (especially since the Gstaad congress, cf. n. 377) he regarded as his 'most dangerous opponent' – cf. his autobiography (n. 365) in the original German, *Eine Idee erobert Europa*, p. 293 f.; the English version does not mention the polemic with Sandys. For a fuller analysis of his motives, see p. 680 f.

(B) TENSION BETWEEN FEDERALISTS AND 'UNIONISTS'

Six weeks after the formation of the Liaison Committee the UEF had an opportunity at its congress at Montreux (27–31 August) to pursue conversations with the non-federalist associations. Duncan Sandys, Retinger, and members of the Conseil français attended the congress, and Daniel Serruys gave one of the main addresses.[528] On 28 August a debate between Duncan Sandys, Denis de Rougemont, Raymond Silva, and Raymond Aron, broadcast at the invitation of Swiss Radio, brought out more clearly than before the basic disagreements that existed within the Committee. De Rougemont described the argument in his diary that evening:

Sandys declares that the movement for European unity must be based on the Marshall Plan, and that economic integration must necessarily lead to military integration. According to him, we should confine ourselves to modest measures of cooperation arising out of consultations between governments. I speak immediately after Sandys, and urge that European action should arise from the militant movements, should hustle the cautious governments and should demand no less than a political federation, without which there can be no concerted economy or defence. Our disagreement is so blatant that the producer interrupts the recording to enable us to bring some harmony into our statements.[529]

As de Rougemont observed twenty years later, 'the difficulties and frustrations from which our movement was to suffer in the next three years were all implicit already in this first confrontation between the revolutionary drive of the federalists and the realistic tactics of the unionists'.

The federalistic conception of the UEF was formulated in detail at the Montreux congress. The speeches, reports, and three long resolutions presented a comprehensive doctrine offering economic, social, and constitutional remedies, based on federalist principles, for the crisis afflicting the system of nation states. The details need not be repeated here,[530] but it will be recalled how, in conversations outside the regular sessions, the idea of the 'European States-General' took shape at Montreux. This

---

[528] Cf. above at n. 314; de Rougemont, 'The campaign . . .' (n. 510), p. 332; Sandys wrote on 21.8.1947 to Brugmans that he would be glad to discuss matters concerning the new Liaison Committee with him at Montreux (*EM Archives, Bruges*). As nearly all those who had taken part in the first meeting on 20.7.1947 were present at Montreux, there apparently was a further meeting there designated as '2ème réunion', but no record of it exists. There is a full 'Procès-verbal de la 4ème réunion' held at Paris on 15.10.1947 (cf. n. 542), but no record has survived, or perhaps none was made, of the third, which probably took place some time after the EPU pulled out at the end of September.

[529] ' . . . (Which we manage to achieve, more or less, before resuming the debate in front of the microphone in the afternoon)': de Rougemont, 'The campaign . . .' (n. 510), pp. 332–3 (q.v. also for his retrospective view of this argument, typical of many later ones between federalists and unionists).

[530] Cf. analysis of the results of the congress in chap. III/4, esp. at nn. 311–18 (socio-political aspects) and at n. 346 f. (summary of doctrine).

idea was developed in a planning paper of 24 September. To quote de Rougemont again:

> We thought of quickly drafting those whom ... we called the 'live forces' of our countries: industrial, agricultural and employers' unions; cooperatives; magistrates and parliaments; youth movements; churches. Then of having them draw up their 'cahiers de revendications' [list of rights to be reclaimed from the centralized nation states] and appoint their delegates, who would come together in vast deliberative assemblies which would gradually turn into constituent assemblies, as agreement emerged on the new forms of a federal Europe. Permanent committees would study problems – juridical, social, economic, colonial etc. Their leaders would form the nucleus of a future European government.[531]

The non-federalist associations, i.e. the committees of political and social leaders, had no comparable doctrine but were sincerely devoted to the cause of a 'united Europe' which, in a very broad sense, they regarded as necessary. The UEM declared that its aim was 'to unite all the peoples of Europe' but that it was 'premature to define constitutional relationships'; the Ligue Indépendante wanted to 'promote understanding among European states' but for the time being to 'leave political aspects out of account'; and the Conseil français had refrained from publishing any kind of official programme.[532] Duncan Sandys, the moving spirit of all three groups during the next two years, evidently felt that the gap needed filling, since he gave an address at Chatham House towards the end of July 1947 setting out in clear and simple terms what he regarded as an integrated programme. When asked to speak at the conclusion of the Montreux congress he repeated parts of this address without alteration, and at the beginning of 1948 he showed his idea of its importance by suggesting that it be 'printed as the UE "Bible" now'.[533]

Sandys' 'Bible' began with the words: 'There are two really big dangers which confront Europe and the world, the danger of economic depression and the danger of war. I do not for a moment claim that a United Europe provides a complete answer to those two giant problems. I do, however, sincerely believe that

---

[531] De Rougemont, 'The campaign . . .' (n. 510), p. 336. Cf. references below to the 'States-General' plan, esp. Brugmans to Léon Blum, 3.11.1947, quoted in n. 547.

[532] Cf. analyses of policy statements in chaps. II/3 (quotations at nn. 91 and 112) and III/6 (at n. 405 f.).

[533] Typescript of address (nine pages), headed 'United Europe. Why and how', in *Sandys archives*, 'Speeches 1947–50'. A handwritten note 'June 1947 Chatham House' dates it a month too early, as it twice mentions the Paris conference of the Sixteen concerning the Marshall offer, which opened on 12 July; a *terminus ante quem*, on the other hand, is given by the identical passages (about a third of the London address) which Sandys used at Montreux and which are printed in *Rapport du premier congrès annuel de l'UEF* (n. 308), pp. 102–5. On the last page of the original is written in a different hand, probably T. B. Martin's: 'Comment on your proposal to have this printed as the UE 'Bible' now, 15.1.48: The style, length and general treatment are not right for our main pamphlet for widespread distribution at this stage' – i.e. some months after the Paris conference and shortly before receipt of draft resolutions for The Hague. 'The Executive Committee, who would have to be consulted about the form of the 'Bible' at this stage, would probably take the view that this doesn't go much further than the Albert Hall speeches' (*Sandys Archives*, ibid., p. 10).

if it were achieved, it would take us a very long way towards it.' For – he added at Montreux, quoting Dulles – Europe was 'the world's greatest fire risk. Establish prosperity and peace in Europe and you will have gone a very long way towards establishing them throughout the world.'[534] Much the longest part of the address was devoted to the question which countries should belong to 'United Europe', which Sandys rightly called 'a practical rather than a theoretical problem'. France must certainly belong, for historical and geographical reasons: 'her situation on the Continental mainland, her contribution to civilization, all these mark out France as one of the indispensable leaders of the new Europe. Equally, without Germany there can be no Europe. For the moment Germany is shattered, but she is not destroyed.' Instead of waiting for Germany to make a new bid for *Lebensraum*, she should be offered a share in the future of 'our European economy'. But it was asking a lot of France to expect her, after three invasions, to agree to Germany eventually sharing the leadership of Europe. 'There are two ways in which these legitimate French anxieties can be eased. First, the industry of the Ruhr, the core of Germany's war potential, must be placed under permanent international control. Secondly, France must be assured that there will be in the European Union another large Power upon whose friendship and good faith she can implicitly rely. There is of course only one such Power, and that is Great Britain. Unless Britain can convince France that she means to play her part as a full and effective member of the European family, the whole project will come to naught.' This was the first main theme of Sandys's political credo, his reason for advocating British participation. There must be no risk, however, of 'giving the impression that we are divorcing the Commonwealth to marry Europe'. It was possible fully to maintain Commonwealth ties, and the true interest of the Dominions demanded that Britain should play a full part in the 'creation of a United Europe'. 'The whole trend of opinion in the Dominions in recent months makes us confident that when in due course that issue is put, we shall have not only their tacit consent but their active encouragement.'[535] Russian participation was also desirable, but 'unhappily the Soviet government, by its fateful decision to turn down the Marshall offer, has for the present refused to take any part in European consolidation and recovery', and was moreover 'determined to forbid all cooperation from the countries in the Soviet sphere ... For the present we have to go forward with those countries which are free and willing to cooperate. In practice, that means the nations of Western Europe' – but the ultimate objective remained 'the unity of all the nations of all Europe'.

---

[534] In these opening and concluding sentences Sandys briefly summarized the first part of his London speech, arguing for European union as opposed to world federation: the latter was necessary in the nuclear age but was not yet possible because the continents were so unequally developed, whereas 'the peoples of Europe have very much in common with one another – history, culture, standard of living, experience and outlook'.

[535] For French co-leadership and German membership under the conditions stated, see pp. 3–4 of the London speech; terms of British participation (with 'readiness to assume the same responsibilities and obligations as any other European nation'), ibid., p. 5 f., adding that it would be to the general benefit to 'extend to the whole of Europe the preferences now enjoyed by Britain in the Dominions, and in return to accord to the Dominions throughout Europe the preferential treatment which they now receive in Great Britain'; also that the Dominions had every interest in arrangements which would prevent their having 'to shed the blood of their young men in European wars' every twenty years. On the need to 'make a start in Western Europe', see ibid., p. 6 f.

From Sandys's first main theme, that Britain must be a member of united Europe, it followed in his view that it was necessary to begin with modest measures of cooperation ... Doubtless we shall have to approach our objective by a series of steps ... There are those who think that straightaway the thorny question of drafting a federal constitution should be tackled. Others believe that Europe ought to be economically integrated before we grapple with any political problems. The truth, of course, is that the economic and political aspects are inseparable ... However, in face of the dramatic initiative of Mr Marshall it will no doubt be easier in the first place to broach this question from the economic angle. The European peoples must radically reorganize their economic relations. They must make rational use of their combined resources. Above all, they must create an internal market of sufficient size to make possible mass production methods.

There should be economic integration and commodities should be produced wherever it was most efficient to do so; 'but as soon as you start considering such things, military issues at once arise'. Since no nation could afford to make itself economically dependent on another without security guarantees, economic integration ultimately involved 'the creation of a single European defence force'.

Clearly complete unity will not in any case be achieved overnight. At first it may only be possible to adopt quite modest measures of cooperation among a restricted number of nations. But the important thing is to make a start. An attitude of cooperation, once initiated, becomes a habit, and the scope expands.[536] A group of nations working in harmony with one another will by their example attract others to them ... The obstacles which clog the way are complacency, shortsightedness and false patriotism. To help dispel these clouds of doubt and confusion ... is the task and duty of all who perceive the immensity both of the danger and of the opportunity.

Sandys certainly wanted 'European unity' so as to enable Western Europe, at least, to maintain itself after the catastrophe of war; he saw it also as an economic necessity and the only solution of the German problem, and he defended the cause with exceptional energy and candour for an Englishman at that time. His fundamental view was that France could not by herself achieve partnership with Germany and that success therefore depended on full British participation; in this way he went further than his father-in-law Churchill in advocating British membership. His idea of 'union' went beyond a customs union and included a 'European defence force', which he was one of the first to envisage. But, just because he wanted Britain to be part of Europe, he insisted on his other main theme that it was necessary to start with 'modest measures of cooperation'. From

---

[536] In the typescript of the London speech, pp. 8 and 9 (which Sandys repeated at Montreux with slight omissions) he crossed out this sentence *after* the Montreux congress and substituted: 'The first step is to institute a system of regular consultations between governments. Consultation will soon develop into cooperation. Cooperation in one sphere will spread to another.' A classic formulation of the 'cooperationist' instead of the federalist view.

the point of view of winning over British public opinion and converting governments he regarded Continental federalism as wholly premature and resisted it as far as possible. Both Sandys's basic assumptions may be called in question, however. As regards the first, France eventually showed itself prepared to join the European Coal and Steel Community and the EEC without Britain (though not until after 1950, and even then it balked at the European Defence Community). As to Sandys's second point, he failed to appreciate the lesson taught by experience, on the Continent and elsewhere, that the League of Nations had failed because it was purely consultative and that an efficient community is impossible without some pooling of sovereignty. While not denying this principle, he relegated its application to the future as far as Britain was concerned.

Replying to a reader's letter in the *Streatham News,* probably in September 1947, Sandys wrote as follows. 'Mr Lee has referred to my suggestion that a Union of Europe might begin in the first place as a loose association of states similar to the British Commonwealth. He maintains that a solution which does not tackle the problem of national sovereignties must fail ... My own view is that the more the rights of sovereignty can be merged and shared, the greater will be the prospects of peace and prosperity. But at the same time we must face the fact that nations are not, and rightly, prepared straight away to entrust their safety and stability to new and untried international institutions. The first precondition of any union of nations is mutual confidence and a common outlook. These cannot be created, they must grow. The first stage in this process is to foster the habit of regular consultation between European governments on intra-European and international problems. These include trade, finance, defence, foreign affairs, culture and education. For this purpose it is urgently necessary that formal intergovernmental consultative machinery should be set up. Out of this process of consultation there will emerge, I believe quite quickly, a sense of European solidarity and common purpose. When once a firm basis of confidence and joint experience has been laid, it would be reasonable to ask the nations of Europe to abate at any rate some part of their separate sovereignties.'[537]

This was the chief, though not the only difference between Sandys and the federalists on the Liaison Committee. The federalists were convinced that no 'process of consultation' among governments that remained fully sovereign could produce solidarity or an effective community; it was now, when the sufferings of war were still fresh in everyone's memory, that the decisive step of pooling some essential rights of sovereignty could and should be taken. Only thus could solidarity in action ever be achieved. Sandys, however, convinced of the need for British co-operation, held

---

[537] At present, 'to ignore the very real psychological and practical difficulties ... would destroy all hope of bringing this great project to fruition'. But, provided that 'we first create an atmosphere of mutual trust and a realization by the European peoples of their common interests, I am convinced that it will thereafter be possible to bring about some effective and far-reaching form of organic union' (*Sandys Archives,* Press Statements file; presumably dated September 1947, as filed among other statements of that month). He thus avoided the term 'federation' even as a description of the final goal.

back the federalists to the best of his ability so as to adjust the pace of development to the degree of insight which he perceived to exist in British governing circles.[538]

There were other important differences as well. The federalists still sought to avoid offending the Soviet Union and would have nothing to do with 'sterile anti-Communism'. In political and social affairs they were mostly on the Left, while the Committees stood more to the Right.[539] There was also an important sociological factor. The Committees were led by veteran politicians – Churchill, van Zeeland, Herriot, Serruys – and their members were peers, ministers, MPs, and other influential persons in their sixties; the UEF leaders, by contrast, were mostly under forty, had no particular social standing, and felt at a disadvantage in joint meetings. Two reminiscences give a picture of this. Retinger wrote in notes for his biography: 'The UEF members were much younger than those in the other movements, and as they had no experience or political responsibility they tried to forge ahead far more quickly than the rest of us.'[540] According to Brugmans in 1965: 'If Duncan Sandys had devoted his tireless energy, personal charm and incomparable sense of tactics to defending the federal standpoint (need for a truly federal government in particular areas etc.) instead of attacking it, then at least as many British as French MPs would have signed the pact, and we should have had a European federation in 1950.'[541] The misunderstanding lay in the fact that Sandys and those close

[538] He tried in particular to discourage the ideas that existed in the committees, especially the Conseil Français, of the need to pool sovereignty (cf. at n. 518 f.). On 6.8.1947 he wrote to André Noël asking him to bring pro-European elements of the MRP into the Herriot committee as opposed to forming a Christian Democratic association of their own, and added: 'I hope that you will secure the adoption by the MRP of the title "Europe unie" and not "États-Unis d'Europe". The use of the title "United States of Europe" implies the acceptance of a federation on the American model. There are many people who are in favour of European unity but are not yet prepared to accept any precise form of constitution. Apart from this, it is a great advantage from the point of view of propaganda that all supporters of this cause should use the same expression' (*EM Archives, Bruges,* CFEU file).

[539] Cf. quotations in n. 513 above, and the approach to Léon Blum at n. 547. Brugmans wrote on 20.10.1947 to Bettencourt, editor of *Journal de la France agricole,* welcoming their 'basic agreement that instead of sterile anti-Communism we should pursue a concrete, progressive policy inspired by federalist principles'. On 28.10.1947 Brugmans wrote to Christian Monnier that it was playing into the Communists' hands to strengthen the Right and to weaken the Socialists and trade unionists. 'Pourquoi, sous prétexte de "modération", faire le jeu de Moscou? Si la vraie bataille se livre à gauche (ce qui est objectivement incontestable), pourquoi nous affaiblir de ce côté?' (Both letters in *BEF Archives,* Brugmans corr.).

[540] J. Retinger, *Memoirs of an Éminence Grise,* ed. John Pomian, Sussex Univ., 1972, p. 214. The sociological aspect was emphasized by *Miss Josephy* in an interview with the author, 30.11.1974.

[541] *Brugmans* to the author, 8.5.1865. The same point was made more emphatically to the author by *Frenay* and *Marc,* both on 19.3.1964. Sandys, under Churchill's direction, had shown masterly skill in restraining the Continental federalists and keeping them within the bounds of British policy. Brugmans, on the other hand, stated on 23.4.1964 that Sandys genuinely wanted a united Europe but reacted to all pressure for a minimum federal programme with the 'British' arguments that there must first be an atmosphere of confidence, consultation must proceed by stages, Europe could only be created gradually. The differences between these retrospective judgements are a reflection of those that existed at the time and led to conflict at the UEF congress in Rome in 1948: cf. chap. V/7 in vol. 2.

to him estimated what was attainable in terms of British readiness and not of Continental aspirations.

The next meeting of the Liaison Committee on 15 October seemed quite successful from the federalist point of view. 'Dr Brugmans spoke of the need to create, as Alexandre Marc had proposed, an international council of leading personalities from all associations, as well as a co-ordination and action committee, with a permanent secretariat, to define tasks and get to work at once.' All those present agreed to this proposal, the purpose of which was to strengthen the loose confederal structure of the Committee by creating an effective instrument for joint action in support of the European cause.[542] Lucien de Sainte-Lorette, representing the Ligue Indépendante, wanted a discussion of proposals 'which may serve as the basis of a joint programme which should be agreed before the organization in question is finally set up'. Brugmans thereupon presented a draft declaration which embodied the basic points of the federalist programme and which, if it had been adopted, would have given the future European Movement a different shape:

1. United Europe must be governed by a central organization to which the participating states delegate part of their national sovereignty for specific common purposes.

2. United Europe must not exclude any state *a priori*, and must not enter into any commitment which would cause it to forfeit its independence *vis-à-vis* any state or group of states outside united Europe.

3. United Europe must respect obligations assumed under the UN Charter in respect of dependent territories, while associating them with the communal organization.

4. United Europe will guarantee the fundamental freedoms of the individual.

5. United Europe will co-ordinate initiatives to restore and develop the European economy.

6. United Europe will make it possible to raise workers' standard of living by rationalizing production and by an upward levelling of wages and salaries.

7. Currency stabilization is necessary to the economic health of Europe.

8. European life is based on spiritual values; Europe is concerned with the optimum development of the human personality, while elsewhere what counts is its maximum development.[543]

---

[542] 'Procès-verbal de la 4ème réunion', Paris, 15.10.1947. Present were: Brugmans and Voisin for the UEF; T. B. Martin, a former Conservative MP and organizational secretary of the UEM, representing Sandys; Courtin for the Conseil Français; Serruys, Retinger, and Gubbins for the Ligue Indépendante; P. Naudin and L. de Sainte-Lorette of the Ligue as secretaries of the Liaison Committee, and the banker Christian Monnier as an invited observer (*EM Archives, Bruges*, Int. Committee file). Commenting on the minutes, Brugmans told Naudin on 24.10.1947 that he had advocated 'un Comité Exécutif, travaillant sous la responsabilité du Conseil Européen et faisant, en effet, un travail de coordination et d'action' (*BEF Archives*, Brugmans corr.).

[543] 'Procès-verbal' (n. 542), p. 2. Brugmans formulated two of these points more precisely in his letter of 24.10.1947 to Naudin: '3. L'Europe unie doit mettre en commun et coordonner toutes les forces dont elle dispose pour exploiter la richesse naturelle de ses territoires d'outre-mer et augmenter le niveau de vie des populations indigènes. – 7. Une stabilisation monétaire concertée et conçue pour

Daniel Serruys expressed doubts as to point 3; all the associations were asked to study Brugmans's proposals and put forward their own. As regards the composition of the two new bodies, Retinger proposed that each country should appoint three delegates. The UEF representatives showed their tactical inexperience by taking no stand on this question, decisive though it was bound to be in a committee constituted on a federal basis. At Monnier's suggestion it was agreed that the number should be two each, so as not to have too large a total. In the closing debate as to the headquarters of the future joint secretariat, the federalists pressed for Geneva. Retinger stated that Sandys and van Zeeland preferred Paris; Monnier and Serruys also voted for Paris, which was chosen by a majority decision.[544]

The various proposals were to be finally decided on at the next meeting on 10 November. Brugmans, who evidently had misgivings as to the outcome, tried to improve his position beforehand. In a warning letter to Monnier he pointed out what a mistake it would be 'to relegate to second or third place men who have devoted their whole lives to the European cause'; what the movement most needed was not 'great personalities' who talked about Europe among other things, but down-to-earth workers for federalism.[545] In an attempt to organize support among the Socialists he first visited Marceau Pivert, SFIO chairman for the Seine department and leader of the Socialist left wing; he found him 'very well disposed' and noted that there was 'no danger of opposition between the États-Unis

---

l'ensemble de l'Europe unie est nécessaire à sa santé économique.' In other words, he wanted colonies and currency matters to be still more clearly subordinated to the supranational federal government referred to in point 1 (*BEF Archives,* Brugmans corr.).

[544] 'Procès-verbal' (n. 542), p. 3 f. In his remarks of 24.10.1947 (n. 542) Brugmans still did not notice the significance of the composition of the new bodies; true to his federal principles, he merely emphasized that 'l'organe exécutif serait paralysé s'il ne disposait d'une autorité et d'un pouvoir réel'. The banker Christian Monnier evidently played a key part during these weeks. In the spring of 1947 he had founded a Comité d'Action International with other bankers and J. Bassot. On 19 June its secretary, Ruth Ford, invited Sandys on behalf of the Centre to a lunch on 1 July during his visit to Paris, informing him that: 'The members of the committee are all eminent French industrialists of various denominations, who have got together to endeavour to promote international understanding, especially between England and France. They take a great interest in the "Union Européenne des Fédéralistes" and have assisted them financially in no small way' (*EM Archives, Bruges,* CFEU file). From then on Monnier pressed for closer links between the UEF and Sandys (cf. nn. 545 and 554). Cf. L. de Sainte-Lorette, *L'Idée d'union fédérale européenne.* Paris (Colin), 1955, p. 125: 'Sous l'impulsion' de C. Monnier etc. 'le Comité de Liaison étudia la possibilité de se transformer en Comité de coordination des mouvements'.

[545] Brugmans to Monnier, 28.10.1947, evidently agreeing with the latter's views: 'Ce serait une injustice criante de ne pas rendre hommage pleinement et intelligemment au rôle primordial que les fédéralistes joueront dans la concentration européenne. . . . Ce n'est pas M. van Zeeland, malgré son autorité, qui fera réussir cette chose immense, voyageant entre le Liban, l'Indonésie et New York. Il ne pourra jamais apporter à la cause la flamme, ni même le temps matériel qui sont nécessaires. Qu'il ait une place au premier rang, je le veux bien et je le demande, mais qu'on écarte ceux qui pratiquement seront les seuls ouvriers pour le travail écrasant de tous les jours – cela, jamais!' (*BEF Archives,* Brugmans corr.).

Socialistes and ourselves'.[546] Above all he wrote to Léon Blum in the hope of converting him to the UEF's main project, the 'States-General of Europe':

'The plan for a "European States-General", already communicated to you through Comrade Verdier, will be put into effect come what may.' There was a danger, however, that it would come about under Churchill's auspices. The alternatives therefore were: 'Either a predominantly Rightist European group, with a "Left alibi" thanks to a few Socialists lending their names to the project, ... or else the vigorous, unanimous co-operation of all comrades, proclaiming our Socialist solutions from a new, spectacular platform and unmasking the lack of constructive ideas on the right wing ... You, Sir, are the key to the problem. If you lend effective support to the European cause you will have the opportunity to lay down political conditions on which we shall easily reach agreement. In this way the threat of a split within the Party can be averted.' In conclusion he invited Blum to join an 'ad hoc committee for the convocation of the States-General'.[547]

If the 'grand old man' of Continental Socialism had acceded to this request it might inded have strengthened the federalists, but it was not to be. When Brugmans called on Blum he found him 'very tired'; not only did he get no positive answer to the memorandum sent through Verdier, but Blum 'began to mock at the federalist movement, calling us a quarrelsome lot (panier de crabes) and adding: "En France la seule chose sérieuse, c'est, Courtin."' Deeply disappointed, Brugmans returned to The Hague, where Kerstens told him that the Ligue Indépendante and the UEM had decided to torpedo his plans by themselves organizing a big European congress in that city.[548] Brugmans had to console himself with the fact that Sandys, whom he saw in London next day, was 'extremely cordial', assuring him that he accepted the States-General idea in principle and thought it fully compatible with the proposed congress. Brugmans

---

[546] Undated message (probably of 6.11.1947) from Brugmans at The Hague to Marc and Silva at Geneva, adding that according to Voisin his letter (evidently that in n. 545) had made a strong impression on Monnier. Brugmans went on to report a conversation with Blum which answers to the *aide-mémoire* of 3.11.1947 (cf. n. 547), and to discuss a proposal by Costa Gomez about federalist representation at the Latin-American conference at Bogotá, which he (Brugmans) also mentioned to Silva on 19.11.1947. The message ends with 'Ce soir départ pour Londres', where Brugmans arrived on 6.11.1947 (cf. n. 549). Original in *UEF Archives*.

[547] Brugmans, 'Aide-mémoire pour M. le président Léon Blum, Paris 3.11.1947', stating further: 'Nous voulons convoquer toutes les forces vives de l'Europe, et former une concentration plus ou moins comparable à l'"All-India Congress", qui, d'une part, se prononce pour un certain nombre de revendications précises, mais, d'autre part, laisse à tous une entière liberté d'action' (*BEF Archives*, Brugmans corr.).

[548] Report of both conversations to Marc and Silva (*c*.6.11.1947, cf. n. 546): 'j'ai pris conscience une fois de plus de la gravité de la situation. Ce soir départ pour Londres.' 'Minutes of a private meeting held in Brussels on 28th September, 1947. Present: Mr van Zeeland, Mr Kerstens, Mr D. Sandys, Dr J. Retinger', with the decision that the Ligue Indépendante and the UEM should combine into a single movement and that 'a Conference of between 500 and 800 prominent Europeans should be held at The Hague during the first weekend after Easter', organized by the London office of the UEM (*EM Archives, Bruges*, Int. Committee file). For the tactical importance of Sandys's decision to take charge of plans for the conference, cf. at n. 553 f.

also saw Retinger, who told him that 'le dictateur économique de ce pays, S[tafford] C[ripps], va venir et parlera à la Conférence-Congrès-États-Généraux', so that preparations for the event could be made by a joint committee with the support of the Socialist Chancellor of the Exchequer. This set Brugmans's mind at rest, and he remarked: 'Je pense que tout se présente assez bien.'[549]

(C) DECISIONS OF THE COMMITTEE AT ITS NOVEMBER/DECEMBER MEETINGS

At the decisive session of the Liaison Committee in Paris on 10–11 November Sandys was at pains to make matters easier for the federalists. Since his hope of establishing committees on UEM lines in various Continental capitals had proved illusory, he wished to maintain co-operation with the UEF provided he could turn the Liaison Committee into an instrument of his policy. His arrangements concerning the number of participants were no doubt intended to prevent the UEF from feeling they were in too much of a minority: those who attended were Brugmans, Marc, Silva, and Voisin for the UEF, Serruys, Retinger, and Gubbins for the Ligue, and only Courtin and Sandys for the 'United Europe Movements'.[550] Nothing was said about reforming the Committee or reducing its membership; the debate centred on how it could best perform its tasks. 'After full discussion, it was agreed that it was desirable that certain specific activities should be conducted jointly and that the necessary coordinating machinery should be set up for this purpose.' The delegates finally reached the following agreement, subject to confirmation by their respective associations.

1. *Participating Movements*

The undermentioned movements shall, in the first place, be invited to participate:

European Union of Federalists
Independent League for European Cooperation
United Europe Movements (British and French).

2. *Joint activities*

The following activities will be organized jointly:
(a) A Conference of representative Europeans to be held at The Hague in the spring of 1948.
(b) A European Youth Rally to be held in the late summer of 1948.
(c) Any necessary propaganda, meetings etc. in support of the above items.
(d) Other activities which it may be agreed to undertake together.

---

[549] Brugmans to Marc and Silva, dated 'Londres 7.11.1947'. 'Roux' (code-name for Sandys) had spoken of the need for 'une confiance mutuelle – aujourd'hui celle-ci existait de sa part'. On Cripps's offer of support, cf. also J. Retinger, *Memoirs* (n. 540), pp. 218 and 220. Brugmans added: 'Enfin voici un travailliste qui va se lancer. Vous voyez ce que ce serait si nous nous laissions débarquer!' He (Brugmans) would be in Paris on 9 Nov. (*UEF Archives, Paris*, Corresp. 137).

[550] 'European Liaison Committee. Minutes of meetings held in Paris on 10th and 11th November, 1947'; P. Naudin and L. de Sainte-Lorette were also present as secretaries of the Committee (*EM Archives, Bruges*, Int. Committee file).

3. *Coordinating Committee*

The direction of the above-mentioned joint activities will be undertaken by a Coordinating Committee composed of not more than four members of each participating movement, together with such additional members as the Committee may decide to co-opt ... [Chairmanship of the Committee was to alternate, and it was to elect a Secretary from among its members].

4. *Executive Committee*

Between the meetings of the Coordinating Committee, the responsibility for taking any necessary decisions beyond the normal competence of the Secretary will be entrusted to a small Executive Committee, which will be composed of representatives of the participating movements and the Secretary. The Executive Committee and its Chairman will be appointed for a period of one year.

5. *General Secretariat*

A general Secretariat will be constituted under the direction of the Secretary, with offices in Paris and London.

6. *Economic Committee*

The task of studying and advising upon economic matters will be undertaken by the Independent League for European Cooperation, which will have a separate Economic Secretariat for this purpose.

7. *Accession of Additional Movements*

The Committee may decide to admit to membership additional movements (such as the European Parliamentary Union and the United Socialist States of Europe Society) on such terms as it may think fit.

8. *Confirmation of Agreement*

This Agreement will be put into effect as soon as confirmation has been received from a majority of the movements named in paragraph 1.

An annexed Protocol contained the uncompromising provision that 'In the event of voting being necessary, each of the movements named in paragraph 1 of the Agreement will be entitled to four votes without regard to the number of representatives present at the meeting', and that for this and other purposes 'the French and British United Europe Movements will be recognized as separate movements'.[551]

In a discussion of the forthcoming congress at The Hague 'various titles' were mentioned. The federalists no doubt put forward their 'States-General' idea; Sandys agreed 'to defer this question until a later meeting'. He also suggested that Brugmans should 'prepare a paper containing detailed proposals for the allocation of invitations'. The federalists

---

[551] 'Agreement' and 'Protocol', together designated as ICP [International Committee Paper] 1, signed at 'Paris, 11th November, 1947' (*EM Archives, Bruges,* Int. Committee file). The UEF representatives soon found that the unobtrusive-looking Protocol laid the basis for future majority decisions in which Sandys could normally count on 12 votes against their 4. Sandys was influenced by (if he did not inspire) a letter of 3.11.1947 from Courtin saying: 'Je me borne à vous signaler qu'il est absolument nécessaire de prévoir, au Comité International de Liaison, une représentation séparée pour le Comité anglais et le Comité français. M. Serruys comprend du reste ma position qui doit être également la vôtre.' He also asked if Sandys and Miss Ford could have 'un déjeuner intime' with him on 8 Nov. (*EM Archives, Bruges,* USED).

presumably regarded this as a gain for their side, although the decision to accept or reject Brugman's draft rested with the Committee. Following up his draft policy statement of 15 October, by which he hoped to establish the supranational principle, Brugmans suggested that 'a short summary of aims' should be included in a communiqué to the press about the proposed Coordinating Committee; all he achieved, however, was to be asked to present 'his suggestions for consideration at the next meeting'. After all this it was only an apparent concession by Sandys that the composition of the new Executive Committee was provisionally fixed as follows: Sandys (chairman), Retinger (secretary), Brugmans, Silva, Courtin, and Serruys; for, although the UEF was to have two members on the Committee, it only had one vote in four.[552]

For the other associations the ratification of the eight-point agreement was only a matter of form; but the UEF delegates had to submit it to their Central Committee, democratically elected at Montreux, which met in Paris in full strength on 15 November. It was a difficult decision for the Committee to take, as either acceptance or refusal involved heavy risks. Brugmans recalled the origin at Montreux of the plan for a 'European States-General', expressing a broadly based popular decision and providing the nucleus of a future federal government. The other associations, he went on to say, had decided to hold a congress of leading European personalities at The Hague, and had invited the UEF Central Committee to take part. The representatives of the 'United Socialist States of Europe' had refused to attend a congress held under Churchill's aegis. Thanks to Sandys's manipulation of voting rights, the UEF was in a minority of one to three on the new committee.

However [Brugmans continued] if we refuse, what will happen? It seems to me difficult to call the States-General against the congress of The Hague. The others will have ample cover on the Left ... and we shall soon have to face serious financial difficulties ... Our own movements will disintegrate if we do not give them a clear goal. We would run the risk of becoming a sect. And in the meantime the others would act. The Right is enjoying an unexpected revival, the Communists have deliberately isolated themselves, and the 'third force' will either withdraw to its tent or join the 'great names' of 'united Europe' ... We could, doubtless, to a certain extent prevent the others from winning a complete victory at The Hague, but we could not succeed either, and we should have paralysed each other. Brugmans therefore proposed 'that the agreement prepared on 11 November should be ratified, provided however that the countries of Eastern Europe were invited; that permanent organs should be established at The Hague; and that the

---

[552] All from 'Minutes of meetings', 10/11 Nov. 1947 (n. 550), pp. 2 and 3; for Brugmans's policy statement, cf. at n. 543. One reason why the UEF could not assert itself more strongly is indicated by another point in the Minutes: Sandys agreed, 'subject to confirmation', that the expenses of the London section of the secretariat would be borne by the UEM, while Monnier, Serruys, and Courtin agreed to cover those of the Paris section.

delegates should be chosen by national committees without the Joint Committee having the right of veto'.[553]

De Rougemont recalled that, in the discussion which followed, each of the 18 members of the Central Committee who spoke (out of the 20 present) had the same fears and contradictory desires, however unequally divided: breaking with the party of leading personalities, which held the purse-strings and the press,[554] meant, on one hand, to run the risk of courting rapid destruction or of becoming a sect, ... and on the other to condemn The Hague to be simply a *trompe-l'œil* congress without any European future. But to go to The Hague under the auspices of a union vaguely outlined by Churchill instead of calling the Estates General – did this not involve running the risk of losing ... the creative and revolutionary dynamism which the federalist doctrine brought with it? Should we survive and risk losing the very reason for our existence (and not only the support of the socialists)? Or should we run the risk of isolation and dislocation and thus jeopardize the only chance perhaps for our federalist revolution to succeed? (The Left, youth and the others would follow.) UEF chose that day to take the risk of collaborating. It did so seemingly without enthusiasm, even with a certain pessimism among many, as if the decision already implied more than a concession: a kind of admission of the relative weakness of 100,000 sincere militants faced with a few former British and French ministers.[555]

---

[553] Minutes of session of central committee of UEF, 15.11.1947; Brugmans's speech quoted from de Rougemont, 'The campaign . . .' (n. 510). It was evidently still hoped that The Hague would lead to something like the 'States-General' idea. The political background to which Brugmans referred was that at the Italian, French, and British local elections in October the Communists had lost many votes on account of the Soviet rejection of the Marshall Plan, while the Italian Christian Democrats, the Gaullists, and the Conservatives had more or less doubled their respective shares of the poll (cf. DPD, 2.11.1947, *Der Kurier,* 22.11.47, under the headline 'Europe Moves to the Right'.

[554] There was a specific background to the twofold reference to financial difficulties in the event of refusal. This can be seen from Silva's report to C. Monnier on 19.11.1947 stating that 'grâce aux efforts déployés et selon la promesse que je vous ai faite personnellement, nous avons pu faire ratifier à l'unanimité par notre Comité Central l'accord conclu pour le Comité de Coordination Européenne', and going on to ask for money to pay for UEF attendance at its meetings (*BEF Archives,* Brugmans corr.). But this was no more than a subsidiary reason as far as the UEF idealists were concerned. Their main reasons were summarized in a letter from Brugmans to the present author, dated 15.3.1966 (in German): 'When the illusion of winning over the Labour Party collapsed, co-operation with Churchill became the only political possibility. . . . Our hope of swaying public opinion on our own account disappeared when the Churchill committee decided to organize a spectacular "gathering". It was clear then that we must either go along with that, and by so doing sacrifice part of the UEF's revolutionary appeal, or else organize a rival congress, which would have condemned us to a sectarian role.'

[555] De Rougemont, 'The campaign . . .' (n. 510), p. 338. Similarly H. Brugmans, 'Het begin . . .' (n. 327), p. 17 f.; 'We signed the agreement, and thus saved the UEF from becoming a sect of "conscientious objectors" (principiële secte). But it was a shock to our members to have to co-operate with what became, a year later, the "European Movement". They saw it as an embourgeoisement, a betrayal of our revolutionary efforts and a shift to the Right. Most of them, in consequence, never co-operated whole-heartedly with Sandys and his friends. But as it became clear that we for our part could not succeed in launching a dynamnic mass movement, many of us were prepared to form a European "pressure group" and thus save our essential objective. It was certainly not our original plan, but we chose the lesser of two evils. Silva and the writer of this article were strongly in favour of joining the European Movement; Marc was basically against it, and so were the Italian federalists.' The disagreement that thus arose came to a head at the UEF congress in Rome, cf. chap. V/7 in vol. 2; in Nov. 1947, however, Marc fully endorsed the decision (cf. n. 557).

On balance, however, the optimistic view prevailed; the UEF leaders decided to ratify the agreement, and to work during the coming weeks to give it a fair wind from their point of view. It was, after all, clear as a matter of practical politics that nations must first go through a stage of economic and political co-operation before they could federate, and the sooner that stage began, the better. Was it not sensible, therefore, to work with the unionist associations for the time being and, during the first stage, to do all they could to make federal ideas prevail? With this in view Brugmans insisted on the reintroduction of a clause in the agreement of 11 November designed in the long term to prevent a conservative predominance in the Co-ordinating Committee: 'Each movement in selecting its representatives will be expected to assist in ensuring that different shades of political opinion are adequately reflected in the committee.'[556] The more Socialists were on the committee, it was still thought, the more weight federalism would carry. Above all, the UEF hoped that the committee would soon include representatives of the new Comité international pour les États-Unis socialistes d'Europe. In a letter to Marceau Pivert, then chairman of that body, Marc gave a forceful summary of the UEF arguments:

We know, of course, that the committee is at present dominated by conservative elements. But:

1. We wish as soon as possible to bring about adequate representation of *all* European forces. Clearly this would not be achieved with a committee of the Right; but the important thing is that we should maintain our privilege of dynamic action, revolutionary vigour and boldness.

2. As regards the particular movement wrongly called the 'Churchill committee', we must remember that this UEM as a whole by no means reflects the political leanings of its chairman, but includes many liberal, socialist and trade-union elements ...

3. If we have decided to work with this UEM, as with the Ligue Indépendante and the Conseil français, it is by no means a 'union sacrée' but simply a way of achieving a particular end: the convocation of a large European congress that will at last enable Europe to decide its own fate.

4. In our view, co-operation between the UEF and any other association means simply that all Europeans have the right to make their views known (see 1. above); it certainly does not mean that we renounce the right to defend the liberating and genuinely revolutionary conception of federalism against all comers.

5. Those who are rightly disturbed by the conservative and reactionary tendencies of some elements on the Coordinating Committee should not disparage

---

[556] Cf. Brugmans to Silva, 19.11.1947; on 21.11.1947 the latter confirmed to him that the UEF central committee had insisted on reintroducing this provision (*UEF Archives,* Corresp. 137). On 19.11.1947 Sandys confirmed to Miss Ford that Brugmans was perfectly right: 'The clause was certainly agreed by us all and was included in the earlier versions. How it got left out of the final text, I do not know'; Miss Ford was to do her best 'to reinsert it and to explain that it was a mistake' (*EM Archives, Bruges,* Corresp. Paris Office; Sandys had engaged Miss Ford for the Paris office on 11 Nov.).

our efforts and shut themselves up in an ivory tower; they should hasten to stand by us so as to strengthen the cause we are defending and enable us to fight with the maximum chance of victory.[557]

But all appeals by Marc and Brugmans were in vain. Individual members of the Comité international pour les États-Unis socialistes d'Europe, especially the Resistance leader and confirmed federalist Henri Frenay, did their best to persuade their colleagues to join the Committee. But the British members particularly – as Frenay reported after a trip to London – 'fell into a kind of trance as soon as one mentioned the name of Churchill, and that was an end to any possibility of rational discussion'. Shortly afterwards, the executive of this Socialist body rejected a motion for accession by 9 votes to 7; it did not join the Committee until November 1948.[558] In February 1948, on the other hand, the Christian Democratic NEI – the other party-political body with European leanings, which had meanwhile come into existence – resolved to join the Committee, where it supported federalist objectives to an extent which surprised the UEF. By February 1949, after the Socialists too had joined, there was in fact a federalist majority on the Committee, which had by then developed into the European Movement.[559] The basic cause of this was, however, the UEF decision to work with the Committee, and the patience and devotion shown by its members.

Next to the Socialist committee, the UEF leaders in November 1947 placed their chief expectations in the European Parliamentary Union, which they hoped would soon join the Coordinating Committee and

---

[557] Marc's letter of 10.12.1947 to Pivert began by recalling that he had written to Robin on 21 Nov. and to Frenay on the 29th soliciting 'votre participation au Comité Européen de Coordination'. Referring to the points quoted, he calculated that the UEF was in a minority position on the Committee, since it could count on 'only 6 or 7' of the 16 votes. 'If, however, the États-Unis Socialistes d'Europe on the one hand, and the EPU on the other, were to join the Committee, then without being over-optimistic we could reckon on 12 or 13 votes out of 24.' He attached great importance to the Hague conference, 'réunion que nous avons la ferme volonté de transformer en États-Généraux d'Europe' – but this could only happen if the other federally minded associations joined in without delay (*BEF Archives*, Brugmans corr.).

[558] Cf. O. Philip (n. 367), pp. 190–2; H. Frenay, 15.12.1947, to Marcel Hytte and similarly to Marc on 12.12.1947 (both in *UEF Archives,* Corresp. 137). Thus it was the British Socialists in particular who prevented a positive decision, attaching more importance to party politics than to the European cause. Marc wrote to Frenay on 20.12.1947: 'I would not have agreed to the UEF joining the Coordination Committee if I had had any idea that the EUSE would commit the monumental blunder of leaving us in the lurch' (*BEF Archives*, Brugmans corr.). More on this organization in the context of political parties, chap. IV/1 in vol. 2.

[559] For the Christian Democratic NEI, see also chap. IV/3; this group, unlike the Socialists, had the advantage of not having a British section to contend with. For the victory of federalist ideas at the Brussels meeting of the International Council of the European Movement in Feb. 1949, cf. chap. VI/2 in vol. 2. It should be noted, as Marc pointed out to Frenay on 20.12.1947, that Sandys from the beginning agreed, though 'à contre-cœur', to the principle of the participation of the EUSE and all other associations working for European unity, even though it must weaken the position of the 'unionists' – thus in this respect he acted as a true European. The anticipatory reference to 1949 is intended chiefly to round off the interpretation of the UEF decision.

strengthen the federalist position. Some of the parliamentary groups, like the Groupe parlementaire fédéraliste français, had originally been connected with the UEF, and the EPU was set up at Gstaad in September 1947 with a definitely federalist programme. Brugmans and Marc rested their hopes on Anne-Marie Trinquier (MRP), who was elected parliamentary secretary of the EPU at Gstaad (together with Coudenhove-Kalergi), and on other confirmed federalists including Georges Bohy, the Belgian Socialist who was elected president of EPU. Could not these and other members of the elected executive of EPU, most of whom were federally minded, bring that body on to the Coordinating Committee during Coudenhove-Kalergi's second absence in the United States, from November 1947 to April 1948? In this hope, Marc wrote to Mlle Trinquier on 22 November urging her to mobilize her parliamentary colleagues and bring about the accession of the EPU,[560] while Brugmans added his weight to the argument: 'It would be intolerable if the parliamentarians were not co-sponsors of the Hague congress, which we believe ought to be something like the States-General. Can you not press your EPU colleagues to bear their share of the responsibility of organization?' But Silva promptly sounded a warning: they could 'at best hope for a few renegades among Coudenhove's parliamentarians', and should make every effort to reach agreement with the Count himself. No trace exists of any direct contact, or of the letters Coudenhove probably wrote expressing dissent. At all events, the EPU executive decided at its session of 13–14 December at Gstaad 'to maintain our independence, which is essential for our special task on a purely parliamentary level'.[561] The members of the executive did not want to reverse Coudenhove's policy behind his back, and their sense of propriety was reinforced by their position as parliamentarians. The main reason why the EPU held aloof was undoubtedly the fact that its founder, since the session of the 'Parlement Européen' at Gstaad, was still unwilling to join a co-ordinating committee which might neither accept his policy nor acknowledge his claim to leadership.

[560] Cf. Brugmans to Marc and Silva, 19.11.1947; Marc wrote to Brugmans on 20.11.1947 that it would be best 'de négliger le Comte (en tant que non-parlementaire) et de s'adresser directement aux parlementaires responsables de l'UPE'; similarly Marc to Mlle Trinquier, 22.11.1947, adding: 'We for our part can support your approach by having Rifflet talk to Bohy, Miss Josephy and Gordon Lang to King, and Brugmans and Verkade to Hacke' (all in *BEF Archives,* Brugmans corr.). For the federalist origins of important member groups of the EPU, cf. chap. III/5; for the above-named members of its executive, see esp. at n. 377.

[561] Brugmans to Mlle Trinquier, 27.11.1947 (*BEF Archives,* Brugmans corr.); Silva wrote to Brugmans on 21.11.1947 that he had had 'a very long talk with Anne-Marie [Trinquier], who is determined not to let him [Coudenhove] down' (*UEF Archives, Paris,* Corresp. 137). For the EPU council's decision, see above at n. 379; on condition that the EPU's independence was preserved, it promised 'cordial relations with all movements inspired by principles similar to our own'. Silva, who visited Georges Bohy shortly afterwards, persuaded him to agree to a co-ordinating committee of the EPU and UEF (this never actually met) but could not get him to join the International Coordinating Committee (Silva to Bohy, 22.12.1947; Brugmans to Bohy, 3.1.1948, mistakenly welcoming EPU accession to the Committee; *BEF Archives,* Brugmans corr.).

The result of his refusal was that in the next few years Coudenhove-Kalergi, the respected founder of the movement for European union between the wars, fell into isolation and relative insignificance. There were three main reasons for his attitude. In the first place, all reports describe him as highly authoritarian: the trials of his pioneering struggle during the past quarter-century were compensated for by an exaggerated sense of his own importance as leader. His idea of the world was an élitist, undemocratic one; the federalist groups of former Resistance fighters were alien to him, harbingers of the 'bloody revolution' against which he had warned at Gstaad, when he predicted that the peoples of Europe might one day lose patience and destroy the foundations of society. The society for which he feared was that of himself and his peers – ministers and parliamentarians, artists and aristocrats; he could not stomach the idea that former Resistance leaders might be as important to the European movement as himself.[562] On the other hand, among his social equals he saw Duncan Sandys as a 'distinguished adversary' (Gegenspieler von Format), and in his memoirs he referred to him as 'my most dangerous opponent, determined to supplant me in the leadership of the movement' – there was no doubt in Coudenhove's mind that he himself should be its leader as long as he chose. In March 1948, when the Hague congress was in the offing and he wrote to Churchill soliciting an invitation, Coudenhove laid down conditions that he was often to repeat in the future, viz. that he should be the first speaker after Churchill and that the Pan-European flag should be flown.[563] A final reason for mistrust was his belief that a federal system was essential but that Sandys did not really want one. A year later, when Sandys developed the Coordinating Committee into the European Movement and offered him one of the vice-presidencies, Coudenhove refused on the ground that he would not join a group 'which did not take a firm line in favour of a European federation ... under a federal Constitution and a federal Government'.

'I realize', Coudenhove wrote to Sandys on 18 January 1949, '[that] within your Committee there are supporters of a genuine European Federation', but they were in a minority and did not determine its policy. He felt the same basic objection in the autumn of 1947, when he wrote urging Mackay to bring together parliamentarians who 'should all be ready to give up some elements of national sovereignty, [which] cannot be expected from the Sandys group'.[564] But, in a situation which called for all pro-European groups to unite in the Coordinating Committee and

---

[562] Speech at Gstaad, 8.9.1947, quoted at n. 371. Information from *Spinelli*, 13.3.1961, who added that, while one could not have a real conversation with Coudenhove, he often surpassed the 'Young Europeans' in the clarity of his ideas. Marc, on 23.11.1963, described him severely to the author as 'egocentric and autocratic'. Cf. information from *von Schenck*, 23.8.1961, quoted in chap. II, n. 339. Similarly Retinger, *Memoirs* (n. 540), p. 214: 'He had every right to be considered as a pioneer of European unity, and notwithstanding other circumstances he wanted to be treated as such. We had the greatest respect for his past, but we thought his share ought to be the same as that of other participating Movements.'
[563] Coudenhove-Kalergi, *Eine Idee erobert Europa* (n. 365), p. 292 f. (not in the English version). For his letters of 16.2.1948 to Churchill and 15.3.1948 and 25.3.1948 to Sandys, which throw a particularly vivid light on his opinion of himself, see chap. V/3 in vol. 2.
[564] Coudenhove to Sandys, 18.1.1949 (photocopy in *CEC Archives, Geneva*; see further chap. VI/2 in vol. 2); Coudenhove to Mackay, 12.9.1947 (*Mackay Archives*).

combat the hesitations of governments, Coudenhove's personal attitude prevented him from following the example of the UEF and doing his best to aid the federalists to become a majority. His own prestige, and that of the parliamentarians who would have gone along with him, would have ensured the triumph of federalist ideas on the Committee at a much earlier stage.

As it was, the UEF failed to persuade further federally minded associations to join the Committee at its session in Paris on 13–14 December 1947. As a result, points of contention between the UEF and the unionists were naturally decided in the latter's favour. The UEF representatives, Brugmans, Silva, and Voisin, were faced by now fewer than thirteen 'unionists', including seven ex-ministers.[565] Under Sandys's chairmanship the Committee took note of the ratification of the agreement of 11 November by the four associations and formally constituted itself as the Joint International Committee of the Movements for European Unity (Comité International de Coordination des Mouvements pour l'Unité Européenne). The Executive Committee was definitively elected, consisting of Sandys (chairman), Retinger (secretary), Brugmans, Silva, Dautry, and Serruys.[566] The main business of the session was to make detailed preparations for the Hague congress. The UEF had to accept a majority decision that 'the Hague Conference should be entitled "Congress of Europe"' (and not 'States-General'); that Churchill should be invited to preside; that, while the associations might suggest who should be invited, 'the final decision and responsibility must rest with the International Committee', i.e. its non-federalist majority; and that 'leading figures' from political parties, organizations, and the professions should be invited from each country. Above all, the aims of the congress were so defined and the work of preparing material for it so regulated as to give us little scope as possible to the specific views of the UEF.

'It was decided that the purpose of the Conference was (1) to demonstrate in striking fashion the powerful and widespread support which already exists for the European idea; (2) to produce material for discussion, propaganda and technical

---

[565] 'Joint International Committee . . . Combined Minutes of three Meetings of the Main Committee held on 13th and 14th December' (*EM Archives, Bruges*, Int. Committee file). Present were: Dautry, Bastid, Courtin, Vermeil, and Noël for the Conseil Français pour l'Europe Unie; van Zeeland, Kerstens, Serruys, Retinger, Beddington-Behrens, and J. Delattre (for Senator Motz) for the Ligue Indépendante de Coopération Européenne; and Lord Layton and Duncan Sandys for the United Europe Movement.

[566] 'Combined Minutes (n. 565), p. 1. As compared with the provisional composition of the executive (cf. at n. 552), the only change was the replacement of Courtin by Dautry, as the latter, being in retirement, had more spare time. The change made things easier for Sandys, as Courtin (cf. at n. 518) had recently been taking a federalist line; cf. Dautry to Sandys, 19.12.1947, and Sandys's reply, 21.12.1947, in *EM Archives, Bruges*. As regards the Coordinating Committee, thus constituted, the minutes add that the UEM did pay the expenses of the London office of the secretariat (cf. n. 552), and the French committee members those of the Paris offce. Finally, it was agreed once more to invite Georges Bohy, chairman of the EPU, to join the committee (Minutes, p. 4 f.).

studies; and (3) to provide a strong new impetus to the campaign in all countries.' These limited objectives, amounting essentially to a demonstration for the purpose of influencing political parties, fell far short of the federalist idea of an assembly of 'living forces' demanding their rights from the nation states and laying the foundations of a federal policy and European institutions. The UEF was especially slighted as regards responsibility for preparing basic reports, three of which were to be discussed by sections of the congress. It was simply announced that (1) the Ligue Indépendante 'had decided the general lines of the Economic Report to be presented to the Conference; (2) the Conseil Français pour l'Europe Unie and the United Europe Movement, in collaboration with Dr Brugmans, were asked to undertake responsibility for the preparation of a draft political report for consideration by the Committee; and (3) Dr Retinger was asked to take steps to form a suitable group to prepare the necessary reports on the moral and cultural aspects of the European problem and, in this connection, to consult M. Denis de Rougemont.'[567]

Soon after, on 21 December 1947, Sandys circulated a draft of his own as a basis for the political report; the section on 'the ultimate goal of European unity' should, he proposed, 'explain in extremely general terms the various forms which this unity might take'. The UEF argued in vain that this section should at least make it clear that 'European unity can only be made effective by creating federal institutions to which nations have transferred portions of their sovereignty and which are therefore in a position to exercise real authority.'[568] Sandys, with his majority on the Committee, was able to ensure that the resolutions passed by the congress would be so vague as to be acceptable to all parties and as far as possible in line with British policy. In the drafting of reports and in the distribution of invitations he did his best to see to it that the congress would not proclaim to politicians and others, as the federalists would certainly have done, the essential truth that a pooling of sovereignty was the *sine qua non* of any real unification of Europe. It was Sandys's endeavour to obscure the chief lesson that Continentals had drawn from the failure of the League of

---

[567] 'Combined Minutes' (n. 565), pp. 2–4. The discrimination in procedure was obvious: the committee, that is to say Sandys, reserved to itself the final decision on the political report; Brugmans was allowed to help draft it, but the UEF was not even mentioned. At the next meeting of the executive committee on 30.1.1948, Silva and Voisin were only able to get agreement that 'UEF' should be substituted for 'Dr Brugmans' in the minutes of 14.12.1947. On the other hand they were prevented from using the term 'States-General': 'It was agreed that in order to avoid possible confusion, no oral or written statements regarding the Congress should be made by members of the Committee or the organizations they represent, without prior consultation with the General Secretariat'; in particular all statements should 'adhere to the agreed title, namely "Congress of Europe", and should employ no other designation' (Minutes of a Meeting of the Executive Committee, 30.1.1948, pp. 1 and 3, *EM Archives, Bruges,* Int. Com. File).

[568] D. Sandys, 'Suggested outline of Poliical Report', sent on 21.12.1947 to Dautry, Courtin, Brugmans, and Serruys; UEF, 'Rapport sur la Politique Générale' (IC/P/4 and 13 respectively in *EM Archives, Bruges,* Int. Com. file). The genesis of the political resolution, beginning with these texts, will be discussed in chap. V/3 in vol. 2, together with other details of preparations for the Hague Congress, from the session of 14.12.1947 onwards.

Nations and the catastrophe of the Second World War, and instead to focus attention on 'first steps' in which Britain could participate. So far did he water down the essential doctrine as almost to endanger the organization that he himself had just created with such energy and goodwill towards Europe. For a political pressure group of this kind loses its *raison d'être* if it conforms too closely to the basic consensus instead of pointing the way ahead.

Nevertheless, the setting-up of the International Committee and the planning of the Hague congress were no doubt a necessary phase in the history of the movement for European unity, which thus impinged for the first time on the mental horizon of post-war European governments. Given the anachronistic and unimaginative policies pursued by those governments since 1946–7, the plan for a massive demonstration of the 'European idea' was itself a portent for the future. The short, clear sentences of the communiqué which Sandys issued to the press after the meeting on 14 December, and which was published in most papers, stated that the associations for European union had 'decided to coordinate and harmonize their activity on the international plane and undertake some important activities jointly'. At a congress to be held at The Hague in May 1948, the most prominent representatives of political, economic, and cultural life would demonstrate their will to unite and would produce concrete proposals for the purpose. In this way it was becoming clear that the associations, which had so far been in a minority everywhere, could make an impression on governments and on a wide public. As Sandys put it: 'The fact that we have now created an effective instrument for joint action will considerably strengthen our appeal to the public and lend greater weight to our efforts.'[569] The formation of the European movement, a complex of many groups and diverse motives, had thus reached a point at which it was possible to take stock. It remained to be seen whether the movement could now gain a foothold in the practical politics of Western Europe, where the change of American policy had given it an opportunity. This depended above all on the attitude of the political parties, the appointed channels for the expression of opinions and policies within each nation.

---

[569] DPD, 15.12.1947, *Continental Daily Mail*, 16.12.1947, *Nouvelles de France*, 17.12.1947; cf. *The European Movement and the Council of Europe*, pub. by European Movement, London, n.d. (1949), p. 33 f.

Position at the End of 1947

To conclude this first volume, the main themes of our exposition are summarized here in seven points. These are not intended to present a comprehensive survey of the idea of European union; this will be given at the end of volume 2 (as indicated in the prospective table of contents, see p. xvi). The exposé which follows is neither complete nor systematic, but draws attention to some salient features of our analysis of the period from 1945 to 1947, indicating the chapters and sections in which these are more fully developed.

1. In 1945, the concept of European union had already been formulated, with all its essential features and motivations, in the post-war plans of nearly all the non-Communist Resistance movements and in the programmes of pro-European groups in the liberated countries (cf. Introduction, 1–3, and Chapter I/2). The necessity of union was seen as a lesson of the Second World War. The situation was dominated by two factors: the political and economic decline of the European countries, which had ruined one another in two wars of European origin waged in the course of a single generation, and the rise of the two new world powers, the USA and the USSR – themselves continental unions of the first magnitude, which joined hands in 1945 in the middle of devastated Europe and divided it into their respective spheres of influence. By the standards of the new age the European countries were no more than petty Balkan states, and their only prospect of survival lay in economic and political union. All studies of the situation in 1945 agreed that the failure of the League of Nations and the degeneration of nationalism into Fascism proved that consultative machinery was not enough and that Europe must be united in a true federation if it was to avoid internecine wars and make its voice heard in the world at large. It is mistaken to suppose that the movement for European union was merely a product of the later conflict between West and East, of Soviet threats and American inducements; it had long existed as a purely European reaction to the catastrophe into which the Continent was plunged by the system of nation states.

2. Initially all possibility of the European idea being put into practice, or even gaining wider support, was ruled out by the policy of the two victorious superpowers, whose troops were stationed in Europe and who decided all questions of importance. The two powers decreed that the European nation states should be restored, and promised that their own co-operation would ensure peace throughout the world. The Soviet Union had insisted that any idea of union among European states should be excluded from Allied post-war planning, and the US under Roosevelt's leadership had

acquiesced in this for the sake of continued Russo-American friendship. In the new bipolar system, Europe no longer counted as a power in its own right. The superpowers maintained their joint policy from mid-1945 to mid-1946, and the champions of European union endured twelve months of bitter disappointment and impotence, while nationalist ways of thought and bureaucracies entrenched themselves once more. If the world powers had continued to be of one mind in opposing European union and exerting a virtual co-imperium over the Continent, the Europeans would have had no further chance (cf. Introduction, 4 and 5, and chapter I, 1 and 7). In the summer of 1946, however, when differences between the superpowers and the risk of a conflict between them became increasingly evident, the pro-Europeans in Western Europe (those in the Soviet-occupied Eastern countries being debarred from self-expression) were again encouraged to propound the idea of federation as a solution to problems with which the superpowers were unable to cope, and as the true foundation of a world-wide peace-keeping system (cf. chapter II, 1 and 2).

3. The West-European governments, struggling desperately against economic chaos and obliged to recognize the tutelage of the world powers in matters affecting international peace, did not endorse the idea of union either in the first year after the war or in the second, by which time they could have done so. Suggestions to this effect in 1945 by Spaak, the Belgian foreign minister, and De Gasperi, his Italian colleague, were flatly rejected by the British and French, the only two governments which possessed a certain freedom of action. Germany and Italy, as defeated nations, had first to await a peace settlement, and the East-European countries under Soviet domination could only hope to preserve a measure of internal independence if they were careful not to offend the Soviet Union in external affairs. Even during and after the second post-war year, Bevin as foreign secretary was concerned solely to assert Britain's role as a third world power, albeit subordinate to the other two, and was not even prepared, like Churchill, to encourage the Continental countries to unite among themselves. Britain's experience was basically different from that of the other Europeans: she had escaped the wartime débâcle, and during the post-war years her attitude towards union was consistently negative. As to France, in 1944-5 large groups of advocates of federalism were held in check by de Gaulle's regime, with its reactivation of nationalist sentiment and its anachronistic policy towards the Rhineland. Even from mid-1946 to mid-1947, France's foreign policy was conducted by Bidault on a Gaullist, nationalist basis; only after the failure of the Moscow conference of foreign ministers was it possible for federalist, internationally minded elements to gain ground and prepare the way for the French initiatives of 1948 and 1950 (cf. chapter I/3-6 and chapter III/2).

4. Only the non-governmental associations of advocates of European unity made it possible for the conception inherited from the Resistance

movements to survive the dark years immediately after the war. Thanks to the federalists' writings, congresses, and personal self-sacrifice the idea of European union became a public issue once again, and this is the justification for the detailed treatment of their activities in the present volume. Subsequently they became second in importance to governments, but in the first post-war years they were the true pioneers and sustainers of the European ideal. From the autumn of 1946 onwards associations were founded and grew rapidly in almost all large centres, advocating European federation as a solution devised by the Europeans themselves. They called unanimously for a union of the whole of Europe as a 'Third Force' separating the two world powers, and for federal institutions with real authority as a pre-condition of effective European unity and independence. By the summer of 1947 all these groups had joined to form the Union Européenne des Fédéralistes, which evolved an impressive federalist programme as a political expression of personalistic philosophy (cf. chapter II/4–7, chapter III/4 and 6). Alongside the UEF, from January 1947 onwards smaller committees were formed in London, Brussels, and Paris under the leadership of eminent politicians, aiming at 'European unity' in a non-federative sense, beginning with economic co-operation and confined in the first instance to Western Europe; while Coudenhove-Kalergi brought together federal-minded parliamentarians in the European Parliamentary Union (cf. chapters II/3 and III/5).

5. The UEF leaders originally rested their hopes on three main presumptions. Firstly, they expected that the Soviet Union would show a realistic sense of the political and economic necessity for European union and would allow the East Europeans to join in, instead of keeping its heel on Eastern Europe and driving the West into the arms of the USA. Secondly, they hoped that all social democratic forces, especially the British Labour Party, would in their own basic interest opt for a European 'Third Force' with a social policy of its own. Thirdly, they hoped for a European mass movement of a quasi-revolutionary kind in which the 'living forces' of professional and regional associations, centred around the UEF, would assert their right to autonomy and break the constraint imposed by the centralized nation states. As none of these expectations were fulfilled, and as the Soviet stranglehold on Eastern Europe obliged the federalists to 'make a start in the West', they had to reconcile themselves to joining with more conservative groups and exerting pressure on European governments through the Joint International Committee of the Movements for European Unity (cf. chapter III, 4 and 7).

6. The courageous revival of the federalist associations in the autumn of 1946, with their propaganda and congresses, as well as Churchill's Zurich speech, reminded public opinion, and also the world powers, of the ideal of European union. The USSR remained implacably hostile and continued to pursue a 'divide and rule' policy under colour of upholding the principle

of national sovereignty. In the US, on the other hand, Congress and the Administration came round to the idea of regional security organizations and welcomed the signs of support for the federal concept in Europe itself – not on the part of governments, none of which had so far come out in favour, but on the basis of the attitude of private associations and the replies from parliamentarians to Coudenhove's organized enquiry. Thus the situation altered completely from the summer of 1947 onwards, in that one of the world powers recognized and encouraged the idea of European unity, gave free rein to its advocates in Western Europe, and, while offering urgently needed economic aid, pressed the recipients to put ideas of European co-operation into practice. Three-quarters of the European countries were able to accept the US offer, and for them the idea of union thus became, once and for all, an issue of practical politics: from then on the private associations from below, and American advice from above, combined to put pressure on governments to recognize the federalist ideal. Provided US support for the ideal continued, the extent to which it became a reality depended henceforth on the governments of Western Europe (cf. chapter III, 1 and 2).

7. By the end of 1947, therefore, a historico-political movement which had been at the nadir of its hopes two years earlier was close to achieving political success in Western Europe, thanks to its own maturity and increasing popular support on the one hand and, on the other, to a sudden change in the international scene. Its development was similar to that of all great historical movements. Individuals in pre-war days had first evolved the idea; later, private groups and associations had championed it despite all set-backs; now at last the movement had gained the support of all or most of the parties, the appointed channels of political opinion, and through them the realization of the European idea was in sight. In volume 2 a detailed study will be made of how the movement became part of the political scene, and how the different parties reacted to it. The partial fulfilment, albeit in a watered-down form, of the plan for a directly and democratically elected European Constituent Assembly will also be described.

APPENDIX

List of Archives Consulted

The Archives on which this book is based are listed on the left with abbreviated titles as used in the Notes; the right-hand column gives their full titles and location and a brief indication of contents.

Volume 2 will contain a detailed list of archival sources (showing documents quoted from the respective Archives), a list of written communications and notes of interviews with personalities concerned (referred to in the Notes as 'Information from ...'), and a bibliography.

Adenauer Archives	Papers bequeathed by Dr Konrad Adenauer, Stiftung Bundeskanzler-Adenauer-Haus, D 534 Rhöndorf, Germany (dept. of speeches and personal documents for 1945–50)
BEF Archives, The Hague	Archives of the Beweging van Europese Federalisten, Alexanderstraat 2, The Hague, Europese Beweging (documents of Europese Actie, Dec. 1944–Sept. 1947, and of the BEF, Oct. 1947–1950); two files of international correspondence by Prof. Dr Henri Brugmans, 1946–9.
Bernhard Archives	Papers bequeathed by Consul (retired) Henry Bernhard, in the possession of his family, Stuttgart (documents of Europäische Aktion, Jan.–July 1947; Europa-Bund, July–Dec. 1947; and Europa-Union, 1948–9)
BCEM Archives	Archives of the British Council of the European Movement, 1 Whitehall Place, London, SW1 (minutes of all Council meetings, Sept. 1948–50)
Brugmans Archives	Personal papers of Prof. Dr Henri Brugmans, deposited in the library of the Collège d'Europe, Bruges (relating to the UEF, 1946–9; cf. correspondence in BEF Archives)
CEC Archives, Geneva	Archives of the Centre Européen de la Culture (Denis de Rougement), Geneva (esp. files: Mouvement Européen: Conseils Nationaux, Union Paneuropéenne,

	Union Parlementaire Européenne, MSEUE, NEI, UEF, and Conférence culturelle, Lausanne)
CIDC Archives, Rome	Archives of the Centre International Démocrate-Chrétien d'Études et de Documentation, Rome (early history of the NEI)
Cornides Archives	Papers of Wilhelm Cornides, in the possession of his family, Bad Godesberg (on the foundation of Europa-Archiv, 1946, and the European Movement, 1948/9)
Dalton Archives	Papers of the Rt. Hon. Hugh Dalton in the archives of the London School of Economics, Library of Political Science (esp. relating to his leadership of the British delegation for negotiations on the foundation of the Council of Europe, 1948/9)
DGAP Archives	Archives of the Documentation Centre, Research Institute, Deutsche Gesellschaft für Auswärtige Politik (German Foreign Affairs Association), Bonn (press cuttings and material relating to the European Movement, its member associations and congresses, esp. two files on the UEF, 1946–50)
EM Archives, Bruges	Archives of the Mouvement Européen/European Movement (collected by Baron von Schendel), 1974, deposited in the library of the Collège d'Europe, Bruges (documents of the London International Secretariat, 1947–50, and the Secrétariat International, Paris, 1948–50; about fifty files for this period; also documents of all committees, member associations, and congresses)
EU Archives, Basle	Archives of the general secretariat of Europa-Union. Schweizerische Bewegung für die Einigung Europas, Basle (documents and correspondence, 1946–50)
Federal German Archives	Central Ministerial Archives of the Federal Republic of Germany, Coblenz (papers of Staatssekretär Prof. Dr H. Brill, Minister W. Heile, Frau K. von Kardorff-Oheimb, Gen. Sekr. Erich Rossmann, and others, also documents of the Deutsches Büro für Friedensfragen – relating to pro-European associations in Germany, 1946–50)
Federal Union (FU) Archives	Archives of Federal Union, British member association of the UEF, in the possession of Ota Adler, 13 Chester Square, London, SW1 (collection of leaflets and minutes of all meetings, 1945–50)

Appendix 691

GCEM Archives	Archives of the German Council of the European Movement (Deutscher Rat der Europäischen Bewegung), Am Markt 24, Bonn (foundation of the Council, executive committee papers, correspondence with member organizations and with the European Movement; two files of international correspondence by Dr Eugen Kogon, 1949–51)
Gérard Archives	Collection of Francis Gérard, Paris (relating to early French federalist groups, 1944–8)
IBU Archives	Archives of the Internationale Bürgermeister-Union für deutsch-französische Verständigung und europäische Zusammenarbeit (International Union of Mayors for Franco-German Understanding and European Co-operation), Deutsche Geschäftsstelle Stuttgart-Bad Cannstadt (reports of earliest conferences)
Josephy Archives	Collection of Miss F. L. Josephy, London (documents and correspondence of Federal Union, UEF 1946–50, Churchill's United Europe Movement, and the European Movement, 1947–50)
Lammers Archives	Collection of Heinrich Lammers, merchant at Eutin, on the Eutin congress of Europa-Union, 1947
Mackay Archives	Papers bequeathed by Ronald W. G. Mackay, Labour MP 1945–51, in the London School of Economics, Library of Political Science (papers and correspondence of R. W. G. Mackay, the British Parliamentary Europe Group, the EPU 1946–9, the Parliamentary Section of the European Movement 1949/50)
MBZ, The Hague	Ministerie van Buitenlandse Zaken, The Hague: Files of the Foreign Ministry for 1947, especially 610/302, 611/48: European reconstruction
Merten Archives	Archives of the publisher Dr Theo Merten, Darmstadt (collection of all circulars and information bulletins of USE-Liga, Europa-Liga, Europa-Bund, Gemeinschaft Europa-Bund und Europa-Union, and Ascheberg press service, 1946–8)
MFE Archives, Turin	Archives of the Piedmont secretariat of the Movimento Federalista Europeo (Prof. Dr Sergio Pistone), Turin. (Full collection of MFE publications, minutes, and documents of national congresses and meetings of the executive, 1945–50)

NA, Washington	National Archives of the United States, Washington DC: Decimal Files of the Department of State, 840.50, European Recovery General Records of the Department of State, Record Group 59, sep. 841.51, United Kingdom, 851.51, France Record Group 53, Records of Departmental and Interdepartmental Committees
NCEM Archives	Archives of the Netherlands Council of the European Movement, Alexanderstraat 2, The Hague (foundation of the Council, minutes of meetings, correspondence 1948–50)
OECD, Paris	Archives of the Organization of Economic Co-operation and Development (formerly OEEC), Paris: Papers of the Committee for European Economic Co-operation (CEEC) Actes de l'Organisation (OEEC)
OMGUS	Records of the Office of the Military Governor, United States, Institut für Zeitgeschichte, Munich. Photocopies of some of these records whose originals are still in the Washington Federal Records Center, United States
PRO, Cab. 128	Public Records Office, London: Cabinet Meetings Series for 1945–51; Minutes of Meetings and confidential Annexes, Vols. 1–4 (1945), 5–8 (1946), 9–11 (1947)
PRO, Cab. 129	Public Record Office, London: Cabinet Papers Series (Memoranda) for 1945–51, Vols. 1–5 (1945), 6–15 (1946), 16–22 (1947)
PRO, FO 371	Public Record Office, London: Files of the Foreign Office for 1945–8 (with File Number, esp.:) 49068-70 Anglo-French Relations, 1945 50921/22 Council of Foreign Ministers, 1945 53007/08 Western Bloc, Economic Prospects, 1946 57093 Moscow Foreign Ministers' Conference, 1946 59757/58 Britain and Western Europe, 1946 59911 France, Belgium and Holland, 1946 59953-55 Anglo-French Relations, 1946 62552-55 Customs Union, 1947 62563-67 Records of the 'London Committee', 1947

Appendix 693

	62568-70 CEEC Delegation Papers, 1947
	62579-85 CEEC, Records of Executive Committee, etc.
	62671-75 Washington Conversations, 1947
	62723/24 Customs Union Study Group, 1947/48
	62707/19/39 Washington Conversations, 1947/48
	62754 Customs Union Discussions, Havana
	62780 Continuance of Economic Cooperation
PRO, T 232	Public Record Office, London:
	Files of H.M. Treasury for 1947–8, esp.:
	10/14 Division of ERP aid
	15 Long-Term European Cooperation
	20 Sterling Area Planning
	24 Meeting of European Finance Ministers
	28 Visit of Chancellor to U.S.A.
PRO, T 236	Public Record Office, London:
	Files of H.M. Treasury for 1947–8, esp.:
	779/81 European Customs Union
	786/88 Customs Union Study Group
	794/7 Monetary Cooperation
	798/9 Multilateral Compensation
	804 Possible Customs Unions
	808 Sub-Committee on European Integration
Retinger Archives	Papers of Dr Joseph Retinger, secretary to Gen. Sikorski, at The Polish Library, 240 King St., London, W6 (documents and correspondence of ELEC, 1946–50, and the European Movement, 1948–50)
Rifflet Archives	Private archives of Prof. Raymond Rifflet, Brussels; Documents on Belgian pro-European groups, MSEUE, and the Belgian Council of the European Movement
Sandys Archives	Private papers of the Rt. Hon. Duncan Sandys (now Lord Duncan-Sandys; former government minister, chairman of Joint International Committee, 1947/8, and of Executive Committee of the European Movement, 1948–50), now in Churchill College, Cambridge. (Files of the Joint International Committee of the Movements for European Unity; files of the Hague Congress, May 1948; also of the Executive Committee of the European Movement, 1948–50, the Parliamentary Section, the Strasburg Bureau, 1949–50, etc.)

694 Appendix

von Schenck Archives	Private papers of Dr Ernst von Schenck, Basle (documents and correspondence relating to the foundation of the UEF and the work of its committee on Germany, 1946–9)
Schuman Archives	Papers bequeathed by Robert Schuman (at present being used by Prof. Raymond Poidevin), Metz (documents and correspondence on European politics, 1948–50)
Spinelli Archives	Private papers of Prof. Altiero Spinelli, Rome (documents and correspondence of MFE and UEF, 1946–50)
Truman Library	National Archives of the United States, Harry S. Truman Memorial Library, Independence, Missouri, Private Papers and Office Files of the following: Dean Acheson George M. Elsey Will Clayton Paul Hoffman Clark M. Clifford The President's Committee on Foreign Aid
UD, Oslo	Det Norske Utenriksdepartementet, Oslo, Files of the Foreign Ministry, esp.: 44.2/26, European Recovery Programme
UEF Archives, Paris	Archives of the Union Européenne des Fédéralistes, 6 rue de Trévise, Paris 9e (minutes of all meetings of the central committee, correspondence with member associations, 1947–50)
Verkade Archives	Collection of Dr. Willem Verkade, Arnhem (documents of Europeesche Actie and BEF, 1946–8)

In vol. 2, as government activities come into the foreground, more official archives will be used and listed.

Abbreviations of Names of Parties, Organizations, etc.

This is not a complete list of organizations and associations, but only of those cited in abbreviated form. Those marked with an asterisk are national or international governmental organizations; the remainder are political parties or non-governmental, private organizations.

BEF	Beweging van Europese Federalisten (Dutch association, continuation of EA)
Benelux	*(Economic union of) Belgium, the Netherlands, and Luxemburg
BHE	Bund der Heimatvertriebenen und Entrechteten (Association of those Driven from their Homes and Deprived of their Rights: German party)
BILD	Bureau International de Liaison et de Documentation
BIS	*Bank for International Settlements, Basle (banker to the OEEC, etc.)
CDU	Christian Democratic Union (German party)
CEC	Centre Européen de la Culture, Geneva
CEEC	*Committee for European Economic Co-operation
CFFE	Comité Français pour la Fédération Européenne (continued as C(I)FE(M); member of UEF)
CFTC	Confédération Française des Travailleurs Chrétiens (French trade union)
CFUE	Comité Français d'Union Économique et Fédérale Européenne (member of UEF)
CGT	Confédération Générale du Travail (French trade union, Communist-oriented from 1947)
C(I)FE(M)	Comité International pour la Fédération Européenne (in Jan. 1947 renamed Comité pour la Fédération Européenne et Mondiale; continuation of CFFE; member of UEF)
CMEA	*see COMECON
CNPF	Conseil National du Patronat Français (French employers' union)
COMECON	*Council of Mutual Economic Assistance (Soviet bloc)
CSFS	Cercles Socialistes, Fédéralistes et Communautaires (French group, member of UEF)
DC	Democrazia Cristiana (Italian Christian Democrats)

DGB	Deutscher Gewerkschaftsbund (German Trade Union Association)
DP	Deutsche Partei
EA	Europeesche (later spelling Europese) Actie: Dutch federalist group from 1944 to Oct. 1947, continued as BEF, member of UEF
ECA	*European Co-operation Administration of the United States (cf. ERP)
ECE	*United Nations Economic Commission for Europe (set up by UN in 1947)
ECSC	*European Coal and Steel Community
EDC	*European Defence Community (abortive treaty of 1952)
ELEC	European League for Economic Co-operation (in French LECE)
EM	European Movement: umbrella organization of movements for European unity, set up in Oct. 1948
EPA	*European Productivity Agency (established by OEEC)
EPU	European Parliamentary Union (in French UPE). The initials also stand for *European Payments Union (1950–9)
ERP	*European Recovery Programme (Marshall Plan)
EU	Europa-Union (Swiss federalist association, member of UEF)
EUF	European Union of Federalists (in French UEF)
FAO	*Food and Agriculture Association (inter-governmental agency related to the UN under Art. 57 of the Charter)
FDP	Free Democratic Party (German Liberals)
FU	Federal Union (British member of UEF)
GATT	*General Agreement on Tariffs and Trade (inter-governmental negotiating system)
IAR	*International Authority for the Ruhr
IBU	Internationale Bürgermeister-Union für deutsch-französische Verständigung und europäische Zusammenarbeit
ILO	*International Labour Organization (specialized agency related to the UN)
KPD	German Communist Party
KVP	Katholieke Volkspartij (Dutch Christian Democrats)
LECE	Ligue Européenne de Coopération Économique (name of former LICE from June 1948 onwards; in English ELEC)
LICE	Ligue Indépendante de Coopération Européenne (March 1947–June 1948; then named LECE)

MFE	Movimento Federalista Europeo (Italian group, member of UEF)
MLEU	Mouvement Libéral pour l'Europe Unie
MLN	Mouvement de Libération Nationale (French umbrella organization of non-Communist Resistance groups)
MRP	Mouvement Républicain Populaire (French Christian Democrats)
MSEUE	Mouvement Socialiste pour les États-Unis d'Europe
MUCM	Mouvement Universel pour une Confédération Mondiale (in English MWFG)
MWFG	Movement for World Federal Government (umbrella organization)
NATO	*North Atlantic Treaty Organization
NEI	Nouvelles Équipes Internationales (Christian Democratic federalists)
OEEC	*Organization for European Economic Co-operation
PCF	French Communist Party
PCI	Italian Communist Party
PLI	Partito Liberale Italiano
PRI	Partito Repubblicano Italiano
PRL	Parti Républicain de la Liberté (French right-wing party)
PSB	Parti Socialiste Belge
PSCB	Parti Social-Chrétien Belge (Christian Democrats)
PSI	Partito Socialista Italiano (Nenni Socialists, from 1947)
PSIUP	Partito Socialista Italiano di Unità Proletaria (to 1947)
PSLI	Partito Socialista dei Lavoratori Italiani (Social Democrats under Saragat's leadership, from Jan. 1947)
RGR	Rassemblement des Gauches Républicaines (French left-wing party)
RPF	Rassemblement du Peuple Français (Gaullists)
SFIO	Section Française de l'Internationale Ouvrière (French Socialists)
SPD	German Social Democratic Party (Sozialdemokratische Partei Deutschlands)
TUC	Trades Union Congress (British)
UDSR	Union Démocratique et Socialiste de la Résistance (French party)
UEF	Union Européenne des Fédéralistes (umbrella organization; in English EUF)
UEFE	Union Économique et Fédérale Européenne (member of UEF)

UEM	United Europe Movement (Churchill Committee, London)
UFF	Union Française des Fédéralistes (umbrella organization of French federalists from April 1948; member of UEF)
UFI	Union Fédéraliste Inter-Universitaire (section of UEF)
UNESCO	*United Nations Educational, Scientific, and Cultural Organization (specialized agency in relations with the UN)
UN, UNO	*United Nations (Organization; this word is not part of its official title)
UNRRA	*United Nations Relief and Rehabilitation Administration (1943–9)
UPE	Union Parlementaire Européenne (in English EPU)

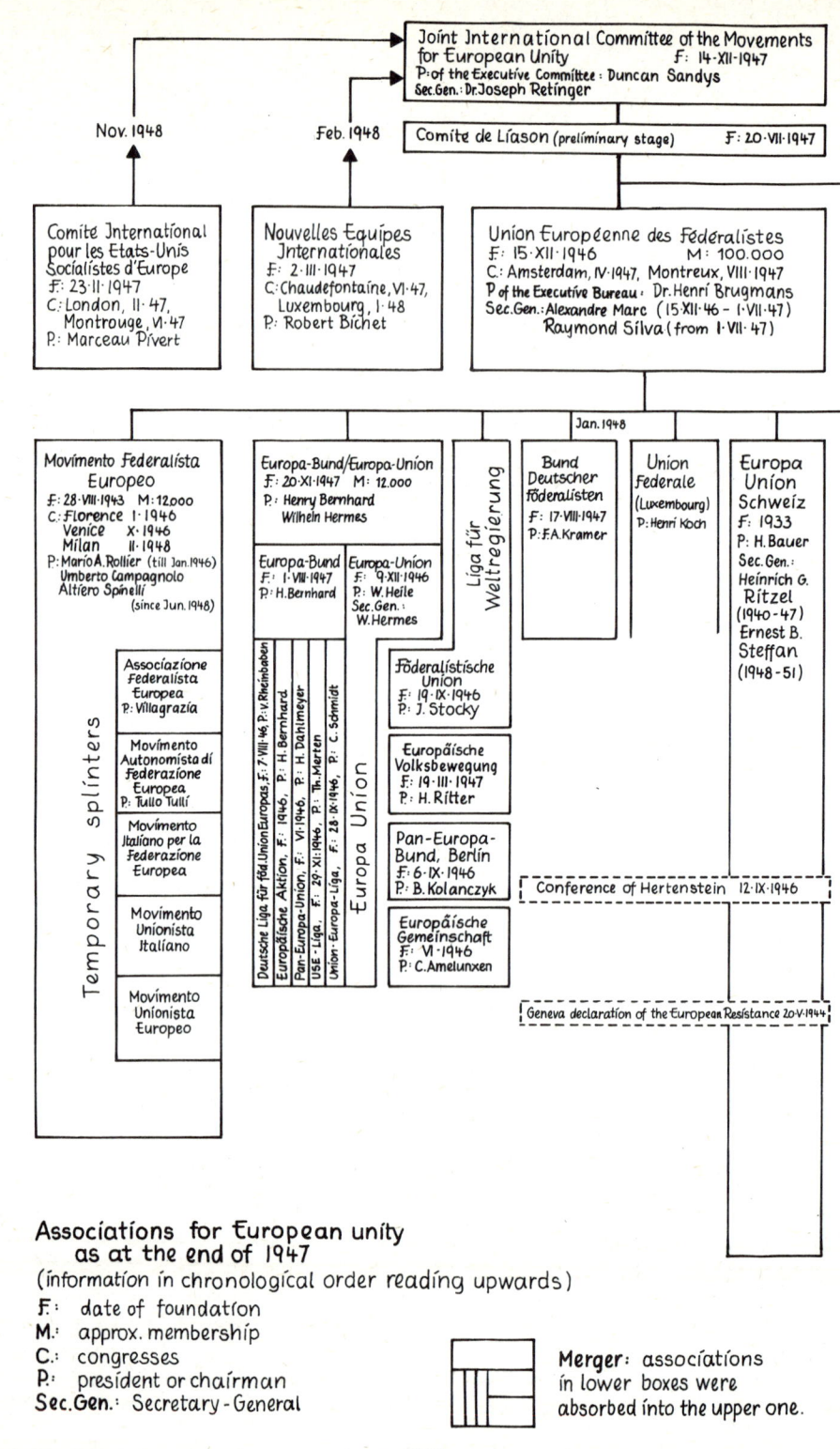

Joint International Committee of the Movements for European Unity
F: 14·XII·1947
P. of the Executive Committee: Duncan Sandys
Sec.Gen.: Dr. Joseph Retinger

Comité de Liason (preliminary stage) F: 20·VII·1947

Nov. 1948 — Feb. 1948

Comité International pour les Etats-Unis Socialistes d'Europe
F: 23·II·1947
C: London, II·47, Montrouge, VI·47
P: Marceau Pivert

Nouvelles Equipes Internationales
F: 2·III·1947
C: Chaudefontaine, VI·47, Luxembourg, I·48
P: Robert Bichet

Union Européenne des Fédéralistes
F: 15·XII·1946   M: 100.000
C: Amsterdam, IV·1947, Montreux, VIII·1947
P of the Executive Bureau: Dr. Henri Brugmans
Sec.Gen.: Alexandre Marc (15·XII·46 – 1·VII·47)
Raymond Silva (from 1·VII·47)

Jan. 1948

Movimento Federalista Europeo
F: 28·VIII·1943   M: 12.000
C: Florence I·1946
   Venice X·1946
   Milan II·1948
P: Mario A. Rollier (till Jan. 1946)
   Umberto Campagnolo
   Altiero Spinelli (since Jun. 1948)

Temporary splinters:
- Associazione Federalista Europea — P: Villagrazia
- Movimento Autonomista di Federazione Europea — P: Tullo Tulli
- Movimento Italiano per la Federazione Europea
- Movimento Unionista Italiano
- Movimento Unionista Europeo

Europa-Bund / Europa-Union
F: 20·XI·1947   M: 12.000
P: Henry Bernhard, Wilhelm Hermes

- Europa-Bund — F: 1·VIII·1947   P: H. Bernhard
- Europa-Union — F: 9·XII·1946   P: W. Heile   Sec.Gen.: W. Hermes

Europa Union (vertical labels):
- Deutsche Liga für Föd. Union Europas F: 7·VIII·46 P: v. Rheinbaben
- Europäische Aktion F: 1946, P: H. Bernhard
- Pan-Europa-Union, F: VI·1946, P: H. Dahlmeyer
- USE-Liga, F: 29·XI·1946, P: Th. Merten
- Union-Europa-Liga, F: 28·IX·1946, P: C. Schmidt

Föderalistische Union
F: 19·IX·1946
P: J. Stocky

Europäische Volksbewegung
F: 19·III·1947
P: H. Ritter

Pan-Europa-Bund, Berlin
F: 6·IX·1946
P: B. Kolanczyk

Europäische Gemeinschaft
F: VI·1946
P: C. Amelunxen

Liga für Weltregierung

Bund Deutscher föderalisten
F: 17·VIII·1947
P: F.A. Kramer

Union Federale (Luxembourg)
P: Henri Koch

Europa Union Schweiz
F: 1933
P: H. Bauer
Sec.Gen.:
Heinrich G. Ritzel (1940–47)
Ernest B. Steffan (1948–51)

Conference of Hertenstein 12·IX·1946

Geneva declaration of the European Resistance 20·V·1944

Associations for European unity as at the end of 1947
(information in chronological order reading upwards)

- F: date of foundation
- M: approx. membership
- C: congresses
- P: president or chairman
- Sec.Gen.: Secretary-General

Merger: associations in lower boxes were absorbed into the upper one.

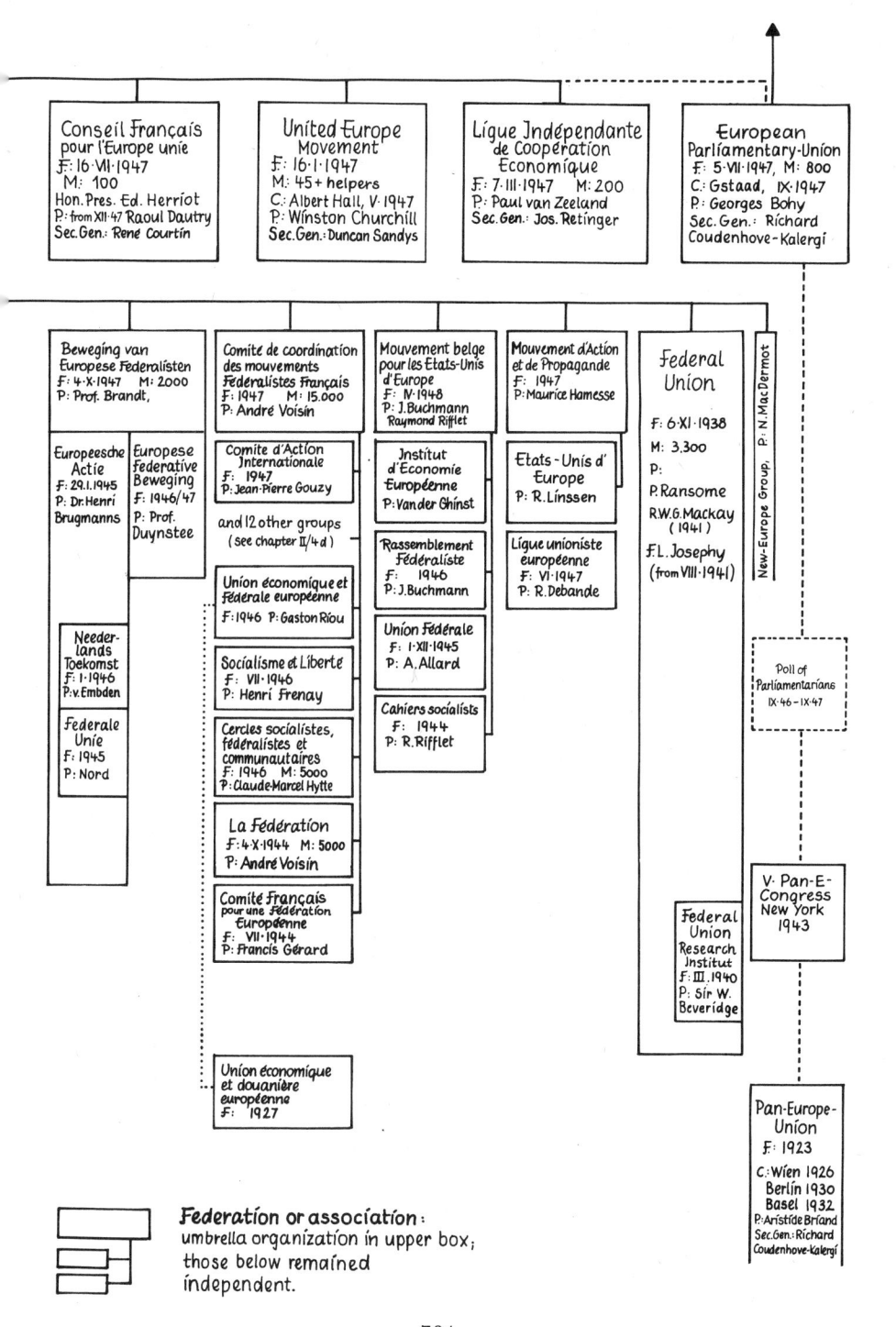

Conseil Français pour l'Europe unie	United Europe Movement	Ligue Indépendante de Coopération Économique	European Parliamentary-Union
F: 16·VII·1947 M: 100 Hon. Pres. Éd. Herriot P: from XII·47 Raoul Dautry Sec. Gen.: René Courtin	F: 16·I·1947 M: 45 + helpers C: Albert Hall, V·1947 P: Winston Churchill Sec. Gen.: Duncan Sandys	F: 7·III·1947 M: 200 P: Paul van Zeeland Sec. Gen.: Jos. Retinger	F: 5·VII·1947, M: 800 C: Gstaad, IX·1947 P: Georges Bohy Sec. Gen.: Richard Coudenhove-Kalergi

Beweging van Europese Federalisten	Comité de coordination des mouvements Fédéralistes Français	Mouvement belge pour les États-Unis d'Europe	Mouvement d'Action et de Propagande	Federal Union	New-Europe Group, P: N. MacDermot
F: 4·X·1947 M: 2000 P: Prof. Brandt,	F: 1947 M: 15.000 P: André Voisin	F: IV·1948 P: J. Buchmann Raymond Rifflet	F: 1947 P: Maurice Hamesse	F: 6·XI·1938 M: 3.300 P: P. Ransome R.W.G. Mackay (1941) F.L. Josephy (from VIII·1941)	

Europeesche Actie	Europese federative Beweging
F: 29.I.1945 P: Dr. Henri Brugmanns	F: 1946/47 P: Prof. Duynstee

Comité d'Action Internationale
F: 1947
P: Jean-Pierre Gouzy
and 12 other groups
(see chapter II/4d)

Institut d'Économie Européenne
P: Van der Ghinst

États-Unis d'Europe
P: R. Linssen

Neederlands Toekomst
F: 1·1946
P: v. Embden

Federale Unie
F: 1945
P: Nord

Union économique et fédérale européenne
F: 1946 P: Gaston Riou

Rassemblement Fédéraliste
F: 1946
P: J. Buchmann

Ligue unioniste européenne
F: VI·1947
P: R. Debande

Socialisme et Liberté
F: VII·1946
P: Henri Frenay

Union Fédérale
F: 1·XII·1945
P: A. Allard

Poll of Parliamentarians
IX·46 – IX·47

Cercles socialistes, fédéralistes et communautaires
F: 1946 M: 5000
P: Claude-Marcel Hytte

Cahiers socialists
F: 1944
P: R. Rifflet

La Fédération
F: 4·X·1944 M: 5000
P: André Voisin

Comité Français pour une Fédération Européenne
F: VII·1944
P: Francis Gérard

V. Pan-E-Congress
New York 1943

Federal Union Research Institut
F: III.1940
P: Sir W. Beveridge

Union économique et douanière européenne
F: 1927

Pan-Europe-Union
F: 1923
C: Wien 1926
Berlin 1930
Basel 1932
P: Aristide Briand
Sec. Gen.: Richard Coudenhove-Kalergi

Federation or association: umbrella organization in upper box; those below remained independent.

Index of Proper Names to Vol. 1

The Index includes names of persons, countries, and places, international organizations, parties, and associations. In the case of individuals, data will usually be found on the pages indicated as to their profession and the parties or associations they belonged to; short biographies of leading 'Europeans' are given in the footnotes. Authors of academic works are not included. Not all occurrences of place-names are given, especially when they merely indicate a person's origin; such names are given only in relation to political events, especially conferences. There is no entry for 'Europe' or 'Western Europe', as these are mentioned on almost every page. Parties are not listed under countries but under broad political headings (Christian Democratic, Liberal, Communist, etc.). For basic themes of the book, see the table of Contents and numerous references under the names of pro-European association, whose programmes are analysed in the text under the headings: 1. Design for Europe; 2. Europe in the World; 3. Plan of Campaign; 4. Purpose and Character of the Organization; 5. Forms of Activity. Cross-references to related entries are given in the usual way. Members of the British House of Commons and the French Assembly are designated 'MP' and 'Dep.' respectively. The German vowels ä, ö, ü are alphabetized as ae, oe, ue.

Index of Proper Names

Abetz, Otto 316
Ablass, Friedrich 388–90, 417, 421
Abraham (Brit. Captain) 305
Abs, Hermann J. 336
Absatz, Harald 390
Acheson, Dean 462 f., 472-4, 478, 599
Acker, Achille van 262, 504
Adenauer, Konrad 139, 237, 245 f., 417, 419, 689
Adler, Ota 151 f., 378, 588, 591, 659, 690
Aeppli, Hermann 117, 123
Africa 11 f., 74, 155, 197, 202
Agnelli, Giovanni 37
Aguesse, Georges (French Senat., MRP) 604
Alanbrooke, Field Marshal Lord 164, 332
Albania 26, 258, 441, 453 f., 485
Albers, Johannes 407
Albertini, Mario 503
Alexander I (Tsar) 29, 30
Alexander II (Tsar) 30 f.
Allais, Maurice 575, 576 f.
Allard, Antoine 261, 308, 314 f., 362, 364, 377, 634, 637
Allardi, Jean 359
Allen, Arthur Cecil (MP, Labour) 605
Alliance spirituelle des femmes pour la Paix (Fr. federalist group) 377
Allied Control Council 79 f., 213, 224, 231–3, 423
All-Party Europe Group (*or* All-Party Parliamentary Group for European Federation) 606, 619–21
Alpers, Ludwig 408, 653 f.
Alphand, Hervé 335, 512, 519, 540, 543, 549, 553
Alric, Gustave (Fr. Senat., PRI) 602, 604
Altmeier, Peter 653
Ambre, Helle 409
Amelunxen, Clemens 409 f., 417
Amelunxen, Rudolf 655
America *see* Latin America, Organization of American States, United States of America
Amery, Leopold Stennett 64, 193, 318, 326, 330 f., 345, 625, 660
Amsterdam 138, 639, 643
   Conference of the Central Committee of UEF (12.-15.4.1947) 313, 363, 367–83, 414, 431, 433 f., 456, 571, 575, 579, 590, 604, 629, 635 f., 639
André, Jacques 360
Andresen, Thomas 390
Angell, Norman 36
Antier, Paul (Dep., Act. Paysanne) 603
Antonelli (*Pseudonym for* Spinelli)
Anxionnez, Paul (Dep., Rad.) 603
Anxiaux, Hubert 530, 531
Armenia (Turkish) 176
Aron, Raymond 222 f., 624, 665
Aron, Robert 42, 316, 350, 352, 355 f., 358, 370, 574, 584

Arrhen, Erik 610 f., 613
Ascheberg (Westphalia) 403–6, 426 f.
Asheville (North Carolina), Congress of the United World Federalists (Feb. 1947) 586 f.
Asia 14 f., 22, 26 f., 68, 74, 121 f., 133, 146, 197, 284 f., 311
Association for European Cooperation (1926–32) 40, 416
Associazione Federalista Europea (Italian federalist association) 377, 591, 629
Astier de la Vigerie, Emmanuel-Raoul d' 588
Atalant, Victor 626
Attlee, Clement Richard 159 f., 165 f., 168, 174, 599, 620
Auer, Paul von 449 f., 455, 610
Augsburg 411
Auriol, Vincent 127, 215, 219 f., 439, 495, 497
Australia 12, 34, 99, 144, 155
Austria 31, 43, 69, 175, 236, 365, 438, 445, 449 f., 456, 466
Ayles, Walter Henry (MP, Labour) 605, 619
Azerbaijan 285

Baccarini, Paride 275
Badoglio, Pietro 110, 115, 247 f., 255
Baer, M. de (General) 147
Bailey, Gerald 261
Bainville, Jacques 205
Bakarić, Vladimir 455
Baltic lands 7, 10, 13–16, 26–32, 65–8
Bardet, Gaston 355
Bardoux, Jacques (Dep., Act. Paysanne) 603
Bareth, Jean 302, 311, 350, 353, 355
Barnes, George N. 43
Barré, Henri (Fr. Senat., SFIO) 328, 602, 604
Barth, Erwin 429
Barth, Karl 139
Barthélemy, Joseph 37
Baruch, Bernhard 461
Basle, 43, 117, 120, 123 f., 300 f., 314–16, 361 f., 420, 599
Bassot, Jacques 349 f., 353, 376, 378, 625, 660, 672
Bastid, Paul (Dep., Rad.) 624, 682
Bauer, Hans 117, 120–3, 240, 298, 300 f., 305 f., 308, 315, 343 f., 599 f.
Bauer, Leo 239
Bauer, Otto 442
Baumel, Jacques 126, 129
Bavaria 69, 71, 234, 650, 651
Baxter, Arthur Beverley (MP, Cons.) 152
Bayet, Jean 624
Beaufort, Jonkheer François W. L. de 135 f., 142, 639
Bechir (Fr. Senat., SFIO) 604
Beck, József 442
Beck, Ludwig 51
Beddington-Behrens, Edward 332, 336–38, 341, 682

Index of Proper Names 705

Beel, Louis J. M. 265 f., 505, 610
Beguin, Albert 316
Behrens, Karl Christian 390
Beilhartz (Fr. socialist) 359
Belgium (*see also* parties, places of conferences, names of associations) 7 f., 12, 67, 78, 85, 102, 104, 165, 171, 181, 201, 245, 258–63, 267 f., 273, 318, 335 f., 367, 438, 349 f., 471, 493, 504–6, 514, 517 f., 528–31, 534, 557, 559, 561, 563, 608, 613–15, 633–8 657
Belley (Fr. world-federalist) 361 f.
Beloff, Max 470, 493
Benazet, Paul 360
Benda, Julien 20, 42
Bene, Jean (Fr. Senat., SFIO) 604
Bene, Maurice (Dep., Rad.) 603
Benelux (Economic Union of Belgium, the Netherlands and Luxembourg) 67, 268 f., 505, 512, 517–19, 521 f., 534, 559, 561, 566, 568 f., 614 f., 626, 638
Beneš, Eduard 67, 70 f., 443, 447, 449
Beneš, W. 448
Benninghaus, Ursula 408–10
Benvenuti, Ludovico 609
Bergamini, Alberto 616
Berle, Adolf jr. 337
Berlin, 40, 51, 79, 139, 232, 235–7, 243 f., 293, 323, 392–9, 419 f., 428, 466, 521 f.
Bernanos, Georges 43
Berne 118, 123 f., 300, 305, 439 f.
Bernhard, Henri 374, 410, 412–15, 425 f., 483, 647–52, 655, 689
Berringer, Joachim 424, 427 f., 429, 650 f.
Berry, Rev. Sidney Malcolm 326
Bertholet, Hanna 56
Bertrand, Jeanne 359
Bessac, Abel (Dep., MRP) 602
Betelaud, Robert (Dep., PRI) 603
Bettencourt, André 670
Beugel, E. H. van der 512
Beuve-Méry, Hubert 222
Beveridge, Sir William 143, 332, 386, 625, 656, 659 f.
Bevin, Ernest 105, 167 f., 175–89, 260, 322, 327, 432, 465, 479, 481–6, 490–4, 497 f., 506 f., 509–11, 521 f., 550–9, 570, 587, 599, 621, 686
Beweging van Europese Federalisten (BEF, Dutch federalist association) 641–4, 689, 694
Bewegung Vereinigte Staaten von Europa— USE-Liga, *see under* USE-Liga
Beyreis (trade-union leader in Schleswig-Holstein) 390
Bialystok 69
Bichet, Robert (Dep., MRP) 600, 602
Bidault, Georges 180, 183, 205 f., 211, 213, 225, 228 f., 266, 346, 465, 467, 482–6,

491, 495–9, 510 f., 518 f., 543, 545, 550, 567, 570, 623, 686
Bielefeld 404, 651
Binapfl, Dr (Regensburg) 411
Bismarck, Otto von 239, 286
Blank, Theodor 649
Bled (Dimitrov-Tito agreement, 1947) 453 f.
Bloch, Joseph 305
Block, August 417
Blücher, Franz 416 f.
Blum, Léon 38, 40, 42, 49, 102, 109, 126, 170, 185 f., 214 f., 223 f., 228 f., 269, 358, 499, 599, 609, 623, 625, 661, 666, 670, 673 f.,
Bobzin (Dr. Hamburg Pan.-E.) 390
Boegholm, Karl 609 f.
Boegner, Pastor Marc 624
Boel, Baron René 340
Boerlin, Ernst 608, 610, 613
Boetzelaer van Oosterhout, Carel Godfried W. H. Baron van 506, 610
Boggs, Hale 470
Bogler, Franz 650
Bogomolov, Alexander G. 336
Bohlen, Charles 71, 474, 477
Bohy, Georges 609 f., 613, 615, 620, 637, 680 f., 682
Boisdon, Daniel (Dep., MRP) 602
Boisrond, Jacques (Fr. Senat., PRI) 604
Boissier, Léopold 262
Bondy, François 56, 115, 131, 161, 279, 305
Bonesteel, Charles 539
Bonham-Carter, Violet 328, 332 f., 625, 659
Bonn 408–10, 419
Bonnefous, Edouard (Dep., UDSR) 602 f., 609
Bonnefous, Raymond (Fr. Senat., Rep. Indép.) 604
Bonomi, Ivanoe 248, 256, 439, 615
Bonte, Florimond 216, 221, 226
Boothby, Robert (MP., Cons.) 177, 182, 326, 621, 625, 659
Borsody, S. 445
Bosquier, Henriette (Dep., MRP) 602
Boudet, Pierre (Fr. Senat., MRP) 604
Bougrain, Patrice (Dep., Indép.) 603
Bourdet, Claude 51, 54, 359
Boyd Orr, Sir John 153
Boyer, Jules (Fr. Senat., MRP) 604
Boyer, Max (Fr. Senat., SFIO) 604
Brailsford, Henry Noel 145
Brandt, C. D. J. 641
Braun, Otto 240
Brazil 12
Brentano, Heinrich von 653
Bretton Woods 175
Briand, Aristide (Briand Plan) 4, 40–2, 50, 70, 214, 318, 335, 345, 360, 400, 610
Bridgeman, D. H., 261
Britys, M. (Czechoslovak émigré) 369 f.
Brizon, Paul 127, 131, 223

706 Index of Proper Names

Brockhuizen, J. C. van 641, 643 f.
Brogan, Sir Denis 659
Brogle, Otto 118, 123, 305
Broschkowski, Bernhard 390, 426
Brown, Ernest 326
Brüning, Heinrich 41
Brugmans, Henri 26, 33, 136–42, 264, 267, 270 f., 299, 304–8, 314–16, 328 f., 342 f., 354, 362, 365–9, 374, 369–80, 415, 420, 439 f., 446–8, 451, 571, 573 f., 578–81, 584, 585, 588, 591–3, 594–7, 599, 607, 609, 617, 634 f., 637–43, 659–61, 664, 670–80, 682 f., 689
Brunet, Louis (Fr. Senat., UDSR) 604
Brunhes, Julien (Fr. Senat., Rad.) 604
Brussels 213, 260 f., 318, 335–8, 504 f., 553
  Brussels Congress of the International Council of EM (25-28.2.1949) 23 f., 302, 679
  Brussels Pact (Five-Power-Treaty 17.3.1948) 22, 88
Brusset, Max (Dep., PRI) 603
Buchheister, Erwin 429
Buchmann, Jean 377, 588, 591, 634 f., 637 f.
Bucknell, R. Barry 151, 156
Budapest 445, 449 f.
Bülow, Bernhard W. von 38
Bürgel, Rudolf 419
Bulgaria 10, 26, 29, 77, 96 f., 169 f., 175, 287, 292, 295 f., 365, 441, 444 f., 451–55, 460, 463, 485
Bullitt, William Christian 71, 73, 76 f., 467, 470
Buls, Arthur 421
Bund Deutscher Föderalisten 407 f., 649, 653 f.
Burckhardt, Carl Jacob 5 f.
Burden, Thomas William (MP, Labour) 605
Buron, Robert (Dep., MRP) 602
Butcher, Walter Herbert (MP, Liberal) 659
Butler, Sir Harold 336–8
Butler, Richard Austin 182
Byelorussia 563
Byrnes, James F. 174–6, 181, 192, 213, 256, 283, 287–91, 293 f., 301, 386, 432, 459 f., 461, 465, 468
Byzantium 13 f., 27 f.

Cabiati, Attilo 37
Cadogan, Sir Alexander 260
Cahiers Socialistes (Belgian federalist association) 262, 592, 635–7
Caillaux, Joseph 38
Calamandrei, Piero 108, 629
Campagnolo, Umberto 275–8, 300–3, 312, 315 f., 344, 362, 364, 375, 377, 592, 606, 629–32
Campilli, Pietro 512
Camus, Albert 124–6, 129, 347
Canada 12, 34, 155, 158, 175, 472, 526, 557
Canepa, Giuseppe 503
Capitant, René (Dep. Sans Liste) 603
Carcassonne, Roger (Fr. Senat., SFIO) 604

Cardin, André (Fr. Senat., MRP) 604
Carlsruhe 414 f.
Carmiggelt, Jan S. 132 f.
Carney, Fred 312
Casser, Jules (Fr. Senat., Rad.) 604
Castle, Barbara (MP, Labour) 619
Catherine II (Empress) 29 f.
Catlin, George Edward Gordon 327
Catoire, Jules 225
Catroux, Georges 209, 211, 213
Cayol, Raymond (Dep., MRP) 602
CDU see under Christian Democratic Parties
CEEC see Paris, Conference of the Sixteen
Centre d'Action (Geneva) 116, 123
Cercles socialistes, fédéralistes et communautaires (French federalist association) 356–8, 361, 377, 591, 623, 626
Chaillet, Pierre, S. J. 370, 624
Chamberlain, Ronald (MP, Labour) 619
Chambers, Paul 332
Champion, Arthur Joseph (MP, Labour) 328, 605, 659
Chaning-Pearce, Melville 64, 142
Charles-Roux, François 338
Charley, Gaston (Fr. Senat., SFIO) 604
Chastagnier, Joseph (Fr. Senat., SFIO) 604
Chastenet, Jacques 338
Chateau, Pierre 359
Chaudefontaine (near Liège), 1st Congress of NEI (1.6.1947) 600
Chevalier, Jacques (Dep., Rad.) 603
Chevigné, Pierre de (Dep., MRP) 602
China 73 f., 99, 171, 285, 287, 324, 460 f.
Chiti-Batelli, Andrea 276
Chopard, Théo 576
Christian Democratic Parties 46 f., 182, 273 f., 456, 575, 600 f., 613–16, 677, 679, 690
  Belgium (PSCB) 261–3, 504, 614–16, 635, 638
  France (MRP) 126, 216, 218 f., 225–9, 495–8, 512 f., 517, 529, 557, 561, 566, 602–4, 623 f., 670, 677
  Germany (CDU/CSU, Zentrum) 235–7, 245 f., 403, 417, 422, 425
  Italy (DC) 111, 247 f., 251 f., 254 f., 273, 500, 503, 608, 612 f., 615 f., 677
  Netherlands (KVP, Anti-Revolutionary Party) 135, 268 f., 370, 505, 613–15
  in Eastern Europe 446–8
Churchill, Sir Winston Spencer (see also Fulton speech and Zurich speech) 43, 58, 63 f., 67 f., 71–4, 76 f., 83, 96, 107, 145 f., 167, 181–3, 186, 202–6, 208–12, 217, 231, 256 f., 260, 289–91, 308 f., 317–34, 341–6, 360, 365, 379, 386, 388 f., 398, 403, 413, 432–4, 440, 468, 470, 479–81, 490, 590, 599, 606, 609, 618, 620, 623 f., 625, 630 f., 642, 661, 664, 668, 670, 676 f., 686 f.
Cingolani, Mario 616

Císař (Czechoslovak émigré) 147
Clark, Edward T. 588
Claudel, Paul 624
Clauzel, Comte Bertrand (Fr. author) 360
Clay, Lucius 233, 498, 518-20
Clayton, William 470, 474 f., 477 f., 482, 491, 508 f., 512, 518, 520 f., 539, 543-5, 562, 694
Clement, Hubert 615
Clemminck, C. H. 136
Cleveland, Ohio 435
  Mississippi 472 f.,
Cleveland, Harald van Buren 472
Cobb, Frederick Arthur (MP, Labour) 605
Coblenz 164, 652
Colbjørnsen, Ole, 533, 540-2
Coldrick, William (MP, Labour) 619
Cole, George D. H. 194 f.
Colitto, Francesco 609, 616
Collinet, Michel 126, 130, 222
Collins, Victor J. (MP, Labour) 587-90, 605
Cologne 386-8, 407 f., 425, 602, 651
Colorni, Eugenio 109-11, 115, 253 f.
COMECON 296, 455
Cominform 191, 503
Comité d'Action fédérale et sociale (Fr. federalist group) 627 f.
Comité d'Action Internationale (Fr. European group) 628, 672
Comité de Liaison (20.7.-12.12.1947, continued as Comité International de Coordination des Mouvements pour l'Unité Européenne, both forerunners of European Movement) 659-64, 669-72, 674 f., 682 f.
Comité français de Coordination des Mouvements fédéralistes 347-9, 604, 627, 659 f.
Comité Français pour la Fédération Européenne 58, 114, 116, 124-31, 218 f., 303, 308 f., 311, 347-9, 362, 377, 591, 627
Comité International de Coordination des Mouvements pour l'Unité Européenne (13 Dec. 1947 – Oct. 1948, forerunners of European Movement) 674 f., 682 f.
Comité International pour les États-Unis Socialistes d'Europe (from Oct. 1948 *see under* Mouvement Socialiste pour les États-Unis d'Europe) 359, 379, 600, 672 f., 675, 679
Comité (International) pour une Fédération Européenne et Mondiale, *see* Comité Français pour la Fédération Européenne
Commonwealth 182, 527, 551
Communist Parties 59 f., 70-2, 78, 86, 102, 186, 195, 206, 274, 295 f., 320, 359 f., 433, 455 f., 462, 486, 621, 670, 676
  Belgium (PCB) 258-63, 504, 636
  France (PCF) 206, 214, 216, 223-30, 347, 355 f., 495-7, 603
  Germany (KPD) 236 f., 292, 425, 428 f., 480 f.

Italy (PCI) 109 f., 248 f., 255
Netherlands 266, 504, 643
in Eastern Europe 442, 446, 456
Connally, Senator Tom 73, 461
Conseil français pour l'Europe unie 333, 623-6, 657-60, 663 f., 666, 670, 683
Conservative Parties 21, 204, 612-16, 676
  France (Indépendants, PRL, RPF) 227, 495 f., 601-4, 613-15, 624, 677
  Germany (DP, DRP) 237, 401, 417
  Great Britain (Conservative Party) 166, 200, 326 f., 331 f., 494, 613, 617 f., 659 f., 677
  Italy (monarchists, Partito dell'Uomo Qualunque) 248 f., 608, 613, 615
Cooper, Duff 64, 179, 183
Cooper, Commander Geoffrey (MP, Labour) 605, 620
Cooperative Movement 167
Coppé, Albert 615
Coquet, Lucien 42
Corbino, Epicarmo 616
Cornides, Wilhelm 238, 391, 438, 690
Corsten, Hermann 407
Coste-Floret, Alfred (Dep., MRP) 602
Coste-Floret, Paul (Dep., 1947-55, Minister, MRP) 126, 610, 624
Cosyn, Maurice 305, 312, 634
Cot, Pierre 221 f., 226
Coty, René (Dep., Indép.) 602 f., 609, 613 f.
Coudenhove-Kalergi, Count Richard Nikolaus 39-44, 67, 117, 318 f., 343, 364, 389 f., 392, 408, 416 f., 432, 435-40, 442, 444, 468, 470, 489, 605-14, 617 f., 620, 622 f., 657-9, 661, 664, 680-2, 687 f.
Coudo du Foresto, Yvan (Fr. Senat., MRP) 604
Coudray, Georges (Dep., MRP) 602
Council of Europe 22, 67, 75, 88 f., 319, 322, 324, 436
Council on Foreign Relations (New York) 66
Courant, Pierre (Dep., Indép.) 603
Courtecuisse (Dep., MRP) 602
Courtin, René 609, 623-5, 659, 660 f., 664, 676, 682
Craenenbroeck, J. B. van 637 f.
Crawley, Aidan Merivale (MP, Labour) 619
Cripps, Sir R. Stafford 531, 556 f., 674
Croce, Benedetto 503
Crosby, Oscar T. 43
Crossman, Richard H. S. (MP, Labour) 189-91, 605, 619
Crouzier, Jean (Dep., Indép.) 603
Cuneo 212
Cunningham, Sir Andrew (British Admiral) 332
Curry, William Burnlee 64, 147, 574
Curtis, Lionel 44, 53, 142, 326, 655
Curtius, Julius 42
Cyprus 12
Cyrenaica 170

Index of Proper Names

Czechoslovakia 10, 66, 70, 96, 103, 115, 295, 341, 365–7, 438, 441, 447 f., 485 f., 502, 581, 611 f.

Dahlmeyer, Heinz 388 f., 391, 422, 425 f., 428
Daladier, Edouard 63
Dale, G. van den 635
Dal Pra, Mario 276
Dalton, Hugh 167, 174, 491, 690
Damiani, Ugo 558, 609, 616
Dandieu, Arnaud 316
Dangerfield, E. 658
Danilevsky, Nikolai 30
Dautry, Raoul 335, 625, 682 f.
David, Jean Paul (Dep., Rad.) 603
Davies, Albert Edward (MP, Labour) 605
Davies, Forest 76
Davies, Leigh (MP, Labour) 166
Davies, Lord David 43, 63 f.
Dawson, Christopher 20, 26
DC *see under* Christian Democratic Parties
Dean, Vera Micheles 61
Debande, Robert 635–7
Debray, André-Henri (Fr. Senat., MRP) 604
Debré, Michel 623 f.
de Chair, Somerset 610
De Col (Italian federalist, Milan) 277
Dedijer, Vladimir 454 f.
De Gasperi, Alcide 85, 248, 254–8, 269, 273, 500–3, 512, 572, 610, 686
Dehio, Ludwig 239
Deichmann, Hans 574, 583 f., 650
Deist, Wilhelm 649
Delachenal, Joseph (Dep., Indép.) 603
Delaisi, François 39
Delargy, Hugh James (MP, Labour) 659
Delattre, J. (Belgian LECE) 682
Delbos, Yvon (Dep. Rad.) 603
Delfortrie, Pierre (Fr. Senat., Rep. Indép.) 604
Delmas, Jules (Fr. Senat., MRP) 604
Delp, Alfred, S. J. 55, 238
Del Vecchio, Gustavo 502
Demangeon, Albert 19, 39
Democrazia Cristiana (DC) *see under* Christian Democratic Parties
Demuyter, Ernest 261, 634
Denis, Pierre 624
Denmark 56, 59, 102, 138, 365, 369 f., 438 f., 482, 517, 564, 566, 572
Denys, R. 636
Deschepper, A. J. 615
Deschepper, Léopold 615
Desmaissons, Olivier de (Dep., PRI) 603
Dessailly, Robert 359
Deutsche Friedens-Gesellschaft 407
Deutsche Liga für föderalistische Union Europas, Schwerte 401–4, 421, 425, 646
Devand, Marcelle Simone (Fr. Senat., PRI) 604

Develter, G. 615
Devoto, Giacomo 630–2
Dewey, Thomas 468
Deznai, Viktor 451
Dhers, Pierre (Dep., MRP) 602
Didier, E. 117
Diebold, William Jr. 548, 567
Dierendonck, Johannes E. van 311, 640 f.
Dimitrov, Georgy 451–5
Diop, Alioune (Fr. Senat., SFIO) 604
Dirks, Walter 243, 654
Djilas, Milovan 455
Doberer, Kurt Karl 655
Dodds, Norman Noel (MP, Labour) 605
Dönitz, Karl 231
Dominicus, Max 418, 422, 429, 650
Douglas, 509, 521, 543, 545, 562
Doyen (French general) 212
Drasdo, F. (German Europa-Union) 418 f.
Driewer, C. (Essen) 649
Dubois, Pierre 35
Dubreuil, Hyacinthe 354
Duclos, Jacques 226, 496
Dünner, Helene 123
Düsseldorf 390 f. 419
Duforest, Armand (Dep., MRP) 602
Duisburg 428
Dulles, Allen W. 243
Dulles, John Foster 66, 174, 336, 468–70, 667
Dumbarton Oaks (Conference, 21.8.-7.10.1944) 80, 99, 215, 220, 264
Dunkirk, British-French treaty (4.3.1947) 188, 229
Dupont, Pierre 611
Dupuis, José (Dep., MRP) 602
Dupuis, Marceau (Dep., Rad.) 603
Dupuis, René 42
Durand, Julien 360
Durand-Reville, Gabon (Fr. Senat., RGR) 604
Duveau, Roger (Dep., MRP) 602
Duynstee, F. J. M. 639, 641

Eastern Europe (countries occupied by the Soviet Army in 1945) 6, 8, 15–17, 26, 77–9, 85 f., 95–7, 134, 168 f., 175, 195, 272 f., 285 f., 292, 295 f., 318–20, 326, 336 f., 360, 365 f., 381–5, 396, 398, 405, 424, 439 f., 441–57, 460, 463, 473 f., 477 f., 482–5, 502, 579–83, 597 f., 611, 621, 667, 686
Ebbinghaus, Julius Karl 655
Ebeling, Hans 132
Eberhard, Fritz 413
ECE 295 f., 477 f., 516, 538
ECSC 86
Edelmann, Maurice (MP, Labour) 605
Eden, Anthony (Lord Avon) 59, 65, 69–71, 76 f., 106, 150, 161, 164, 173, 180, 259, 324, 492, 494
Edwards, Bob 600

Edwards, Philip 148, 151
EEC (European Economic Community) 86, 89, 155, 551, 578, 669
Een Verden (Danish federalist association) 370, 377, 591
EFTA 59
Eggebrecht, Axel 421, 423
Ehard, Hans 644, 655
Eichler, Willi 58, 127, 129, 407, 655
Einaudi, Luigi 49, 109, 255, 258, 439, 502 f., 535, 615, 629
Einsiedel, Horst von 243
Einstein, Albert 36, 101, 587
Eisenhower, Dwight D. 203
Elfes, Wilhelm 422
Elliot, Walter 659
Ellis, Bishop S. Edward 326
Ellwangen 651, 653
Embden, S. J. van 138, 141, 638
Emrich, Louis 243
Erler, Fritz 622
Ernestan, G. 635, 638
Ernst, E. (Swiss lawyer) 123
Errecart, Jean (Dep. Indép.) 603
Estonia 15 f., 28 f., 68 f., 288, 441
Estournelles de Constant, Paul Henri Baron d' 214
États-Unis d'Europe (Belgian federalist group) 302 f., 637
États-Unis du Monde (French federalist association) 311, 361, 362, 377, 591
Europa-Bund (German federalist association) 404, 411, 414, 431, 572, 591 f., 648, 691
Europäische Aktion (German federalist association, Stuttgart) 412–14, 425, 647 f.
Europäische Föderalistische Union, Cologne (from 3.6.1947 Liga für Weltregierung) 385, 406–8, 430
Europäische Gemeinschaft (German federalist group, Münster) 385, 408–10, 646
Europäische Volksbewegung Deutschlands, Hamburg 399–401, 646
Europäischer Zollverein 40–2, 335, 442, 445
Europa-Liga (short-lived merger of German organizations 12.4.–10.5.1947) 425–430
Europa-Union (German federalist association) 389, 404, 411, 415–31, 572, 591 f., 646–52
Europa-Union (Austrian federalist association) 304, 456 f., 572
Europa-Union, Swiss movement for the unification of Europe 23, 43, 89, 117–24, 298–314, 341–4, 362, 375, 377 f., 415–18, 429, 445 f., 571, 591 f., 599, 637
European Advisory Commission 76
European Customs Union Study Group 548, 562–5, 568
European Federation Campaign Council (British federalist association) 162

European League for Economic Cooperation (ELEC) *see* Ligue Européenne de Coopération Economique
European Parliamentary Union (EPU) 199, 437 f., 607–14, 618, 620 f., 637, 657 f., 661–4, 675, 679–82, 687, 691
Europeesche Actie (Dutch federalist association) 23, 33, 131–42, 265, 299 f., 303–5, 362, 366, 368, 377, 408, 412–15, 591 f. 638, 648
Europese Federative Beweging (Dutch federalist association) 311, 639–41
Eutin (Congress of the German Europa-Union 21.–23.6.1947) 396, 418, 424 f., 429 f., 480, 650
Evatt, Herbert V. (Australian Minister for External Affairs) 99
Ewer, W. N. 191

Fabian Society 167
Fairhurst, Frank (MP, Labour) 619
Falck, Enrico 336
Fancello, Francesco 253
Fanfani, Amintore 502
Farine, Philippe (Dep., MRP) 602
Faure, Edgar (Dep., Rad.) 354, 602 f.
FDP *see under* Liberal Parties
Febvre, L. (French author) 335
Fechner, Max 236
Fecker, R. 422
Federale Unie (Dutch federalist association) 136–8, 265, 638
Federalist Group of the House of Commons (*see also* All-Party Europe Group) 379, 591, 605 f., 616–21
Federal Union (British federalist association) 43, 64, 142–53, 160 f., 198, 261, 269, 300, 303 f., 324–7, 362, 377–9, 401 f., 406, 420, 586 f., 589, 591, 605, 617, 634, 644, 659 f., 690 f.
Fédération, La (French federalist association) 131, 311 f., 346 f., 349–55, 361 f., 377, 591 f., 623, 625 f., 660
Feierabend, Ladislaus 70
Feldkirch (Vorarlberg) 456
Felice, Pierro (Fr. Senat., Rad.) 604
Ferber, Walter 241, 654
Ferrat, André 124–30, 347
Ferrero, Guglielmo 20
Fidler, Jack 152, 327
Figl, Leopold 456
Fimmen, Edo 38
Finidori (Mme) 311
Finland 15 f., 29 f., 52 f., 78, 292, 295, 365, 441, 460, 485, 597, 611
Firsoff, V. A. 493
Fischer, Helmut 422
Fischer, Ruth 452, 455

710 Index of Proper Names

Fisher of Lambeth, Lord (Archbishop of Canterbury) 328
Fleissig, Andreas 41
Florence 254, 275 f., 278, 630
Floyd, David 58
Fokkema, J. 615
Fonlupt-Esperaber, Jacques (Dep., MRP) 602
Foot, Michael (MP., Labour) 189–91, 366, 605, 619
Ford, Ruth 672, 675
Formiggini 593
Forrestal, James 464
Fortanier-de-Wit, A. (Dutch deputy) 615
Fortoul (French Socialist) 359
Fournier, Emile (Fr. Senat., MRP) 604
France (see also parties, places of conferences, names of associations) 4, 7 f., 12, 32, 37, 39–41, 49–51, 54 f., 58, 63–7, 77 f., 84 f., 99, 102, 104, 109, 115, 124–31, 146, 157, 159 f., 164, 171, 180, 183, 187 f., 201–30, 235, 242, 245, 247, 257, 260 f., 263, 267, 269, 271–3, 280, 294, 311 f., 319–21, 324, 328, 335–8, 344 f., 346–61, 369–71, 379 f., 385, 411, 433–5, 467 f., 471, 474, 480, 482, 484, 495–500, 506, 509, 513, 517–22, 529, 533–7, 542, 544, 549, 552, 559, 561, 566, 568 f., 572, 587, 592, 608 f., 613, 621, 623–28, 633, 661, 668 f., 672, 686
Frankfurt 236, 238, 426, 494, 499, 600 f., 644
Franks, Sir Oliver 494, 512, 522, 540, 549, 554, 562
Frantz, Constantin 241, 408, 653
Frédéric-Dupont, Edouard (Dep., PRI) 603
Freiburg im Breisgau 390, 415
Frenay, Henri 51, 53, 124, 127, 359, 440, 679 f.
Friedländer, Ernst 655
Frings, Cardinal Joseph 139
Froechte (merchant in Frankfurt) 650
Fuglsang, Peter 429
Fulbright, J. William 101, 461, 470 f., 476, 488
Fulton (Churchill's speech) 181, 290 f., 318, 365
Funk, Fritz 41
Furand, Jacques (Dep., MRP) 602

Gabbrielli, G. 588
Gafencu, Grégoire 442, 445, 449–51, 574, 610
Galen, Count von 407
Galin, Alexander 480 f.
Ganz, A. 428
Garavel, Joseph (Dep., Rad.) 603
Gardini (Italian emigre) 147
Gargominy, Paul (Fr. Senat., MRP) 604
Garnett, James C. Maxwell 64
Garosci, Aldo 275 f.
Gasparotto, Luigi 616
Gasser, Adolf 118, 305, 352, 413
Gaulle, Charles de 58, 67, 102, 130, 170, 174, 179, 181, 201–18, 220 f., 224 f., 227–9, 256, 260, 269, 271–4, 318, 322, 346 f., 359, 361, 540, 686
Gauvain, Jean 223
Gay, Francis 497, 609
Gazier, Albert 219
Geiler, Karl 655
Geineder, Heinrich 411
Gelpke, A. (Swiss economist) 123
Gemaehling, Jean 359
Genet, Henri 123, 377, 572, 588, 591, 660
Geneva 40, 50, 123, 302, 315, 378 f., 438, 508, 557, 561, 571, 587, 591, 672
  Conference of Resistance fighters (31.3., 29.4., 20.5. and 7.7.1944) 50 f., 54–7, 62, 112 f., 115 f., 124 f., 148, 157, 296, 303, 313, 363, 444
Gérard, Francis 125 f., 304, 314, 347–9, 362, 364, 369, 374, 377, 591, 627, 691
Gerber, Marc (Fr. Senat., MRP) 604
Gerlach, Fritz 43
Germany (German question, Weimar Republic, Western zones of occupation etc.; see also parties, places of conferences, names of associations) 4–10, 17 f., 37, 41 f., 43 f., 46, 51 f., 54–7, 65 f., 68–71, 77–83, 103–5, 115, 121, 126, 128, 133, 138 f., 140 f., 144–6, 157, 159, 164, 179 f., 180, 188, 191–3, 205, 208–13, 216 f., 224–8, 230–48, 266 f., 271, 278–80, 292–4, 296, 301 f., 315 f., 319 f., 353, 368 f., 374, 381, 385–431, 438, 460–3, 465 f., 468, 471, 478, 480, 483, 485, 495, 513–22, 525, 528 f., 535 f., 538, 549 f., 559, 561, 564, 566, 568, 571 f., 574, 583, 585, 625–7, 635, 644–56, 667, 686
Gerold, Karl 583
Ghinst, J. van der 261, 591, 635, 637
Giacchero, Enzo 608–10, 613, 615
Giacobbi, Paul (Dep., Rad.) 603
Giannini, Guglielmo 609 f., 616
Gibson, George 326, 328, 332
Gide, Charles 40, 335
Gilson, Arthur 611, 613–15, 637
Ginzburg, Leone 115
Giscard d'Estaing, Edmond 335, 338
Glaser, František 447
Gniffke, Erich 236
Godin, Henri (Dep., Rad.) 603
Goedhart, Franz J. 136
Goedhart, Gerrit J. van Heuven 52
Goerdeler, Carl Friedrich 51
Görres, Josef 653
Goldschild, Gaston 628
Gollancz, Victor 232, 326, 328, 331, 404
Gomulka, Wladyslaw 455
Gonella, Guido 616
Goriely, Georges 574, 582
Gorse, Georges (Dep., SFIO) 221, 603

Index of Proper Names 711

Gosset, Paul (Dep., MRP) 602
Gottfurcht (German emigre) 147
Gottwald, Klement 447, 485
Gouin, Felix 180-2, 228 f.
Gouzy, Jean Pierre 628
Granada 25
Granville-West, Daniel (MP, Labour) 659
Gratry, Auguste-Josephe 214
Great Britain (*see also* parties, places of conferences, names of associations) 4, 7 f., 12, 40 f., 43, 45, 58 f., 63-5, 68-81, 84 f., 89, 102 f., 108 f., 113, 120, 126, 133, 140, 149, 155-66, 172-89, 207, 210 f., 217 f., 220-3, 227, 234, 245, 247, 261, 263, 269, 279, 308, 319-34, 337, 341-5, 369, 371, 385 f., 388 f., 395, 406, 408, 415 f., 424, 431, 434, 438, 461, 463, 471, 474, 479, 482, 489-95. 498, 508-10, 512 f., 516 f., 520, 522, 527-31, 533, 536 f., 542 f., 546, 549-66. 572, 592, 598, 608, 613, 616-22, 667, 684
Greaves, H. R. S. 64
Greece 26, 66, 77 f., 89, 107, 126, 173, 176, 190, 192, 285, 304, 326, 438, 441, 444, 452, 454, 461-4, 471, 490, 516 f., 562, 594, 613, 621
Green, Georges 162
Griessemer, Tom O. 312 f., 586, 588
Grillparzer, Franz 37
Grimal, Marcel (Fr. Senat., MRP) 604
Gromyko, Andrei 80, 99, 106
Gronchi, Giovanni 616
Gross, Feliks 442 f.
Grosso, Giuseppe 254
Grotewohl, Otto 236
Grotkopp, Wilhelm 40
Groza, Peter 450
Gruffydd, William John (MP, Labour) 153
Grumkow, Prof. von 390 f.
Gstaad 607 f., 613-16, 680 f.
    1st Congress of EPU (8.-10.9.1947) 437 f., 609-14, 620, 662-4
Guardini, Romano 20
Gubbels (Belgian federalist) 635, 637 f.
Gubbins, Sir Colin 336, 338, 671, 674
Guérard, Albert 467
Guérin, Maurice (Dep., MRP) 126, 129, 602, 609
Guillant, André (Dep., MRP) 602
Guillaume, H. A. 409
Gunter, Raymond Jones (MP, Labour) 605
Guyon, Raymond (Dep., SFIO) 603
Guyonard, Joseph (Dep., MRP) 602

Haase, Paul 403
Habicht, Max 312 f., 586
Hacke, A. H. V. 613-15, 680
Haire, John Edwin (MP, Labour) 151, 605, 619
Hale, Charles Leslie (MP, Labour) 605, 619 f.
Halévy, Daniel 354
Halfmann, Bishop Wilhelm Hermann 390
Halin, Hubert 52
Hall-Patch, Sir Edmund 184 f., 553
Hamburg 139, 235, 374, 385, 388-92, 399 f., 425-7, 430, 646
Hamel, Joseph 335
Hamesse, Maurice 637 f.
Hamilton, Alexander 109, 469
Hamilton, Commander Innes 151
Hamilton, Roland (MP, Labour) 619
Hammarskjöld, Dag 543, 565
Hankey, R. M. A. 185
Hanover 139, 236, 394, 397, 416 f., 430 f., 646
Hantos, Elmer 40, 335, 442
Harriman, Averell 78, 97, 334, 525
Harris, Seymour Edwin 471
Harrison, James (MP, Labour) 605
Hart, Norman J. 162
Hartner, Willy 650
Harvey, Oliver C. 171, 182 f.
Haselmayr (German general) 43
Hasemann, Walter 417 f., 422 f., 425, 429, 651
Hauriou, André 51, 220 f.
Havana 557-9
Heidorn, M. (SDP deputy in the Hamburg Parliament) 369, 374
Heile, Wilhelm 40, 241, 389, 397, 401 f., 408, 416-19, 422-9, 650, 690
Hein, Benno 422
Heinemann, Friedrich 401, 425
Heiser, P. C. 643
Hellmann (Hamburg Pan-E.) 422, 425
Hellwege, Heinrich 417, 653
Hellwig, Wilhelm 417 f., 422, 425 f.
Helmore, J. R. 185
Henderson, Arthur 556
Henrich, Walter 650
Henseler, E. (Swiss lawyer) 123, 241
Hermes, Andreas 236
Hermes, Wilhelm 393-7, 416-31, 583, 591 f., 645-7, 651 f.
Herrenchiemsee 242, 653
Herriot, Edouard 41, 360, 624, 657, 660, 670
Hersent, Georges 360
Hertenstein Conference of European federalists (15.-22.9.1946) 23, 33, 139, 277, 299, 303-12, 314 f., 317, 358, 363 f., 365, 383, 409, 413, 419 f., 422 f., 426, 431, 571, 574, 590, 593
Herter, Christian A. 493
Hervé, Pierre 223 f.
Heuss, Theodor 237, 403
Heyman 638
Hillmann, W. 288
Hillringhaus, Herbert 650
Hinchingbrooke, Viscount (MP, Cons.) 188
Hirschfeld, Hans M. 512, 518, 520, 543, 561
Hitler, Adolf (Hitler's Europe etc.) 2, 10, 15, 17, 25, 32, 42, 44-6, 66, 68 f., 72, 82, 103,

712 *Index of Proper Names*

118, 161, 269, 291, 303, 317, 374, 480, 554, 642
Hobbes, Thomas 32
Ho Chi Minh 496
Hodža, Milan 70, 442, 449
Hoegner, Wilhelm 120, 240, 422, 653
Hörhager, Herbert 655
Hoffman, Paul G. 525, 694
Hoffmann, Karl 418, 422
Hofmannsthal, Hugo von 5, 20, 37
Holman, Percy (MP, Labour) 619 f.
Holmes, H. E. (MP, Labour) 605
Homburg, Bad, Germany, UEF conference (May 1948) 585, 656
Hopkins, Harry 94, 232 f.
Hopkinson, Henry L. (MP, Cons.) 370, 377, 574, 589, 591, 594, 598, 659
Horabin, Tom (MP, Labour) 148, 153
Hore-Belisha, Leslie 164, 659
Hughes, Hector (MP, Labour) 619 f.
Hugo, Victor 214
Hull, Cordell 73, 75, 233
Hummel, Karl 426 f., 651
Hungary 13, 21, 25 f., 32, 77, 175, 292, 295, 365, 369, 438, 441, 445, 448–50, 453, 460
Huntingdon, Lord (MP, Labour) 148, 161
Hutchinson, James Riley Holt (MP, Cons.) 620, 659
Hylkema, O. T. 132, 134, 137, 142, 638
Hynd, John Henry (MP, Labour) 127, 129, 153, 605, 618 f.
Hytte, Claude-Marcel 356–60, 362, 375, 377, 591, 626, 679
Hyvrard, Jules (Fr. Senat., MRP) 604

Iceland 517, 565, 594
Ickes, Harold L. 73
Ihuel, Paul (Dep., MRP) 602
ILO 443, 589, 593
IMF 532
Independent League for European Cooperation, *see* Ligue Indépendante de Coopération Européenne
India 12 f., 33, 153, 155, 176, 192, 311, 481
Indo-China 12, 496
Indonesia 12, 107, 265 f., 506
Institut d'Economie Européenne (Belgian federalist association) 261, 591, 635, 637
Interlaken, 2nd Congress of EPU (8.–11.9.1948) 560
Internationales Koordinations-Komitee der Verbände für die Einigung Europas, *see* Comité International de Coordination des Mouvements pour l'Unité Européenne
Iran 97, 103, 107, 171, 176, 284 f., 288, 291, 296, 460
Ireland 438 f., 517, 536, 594

Italy (*see also* parties, places of conferences, names of associations) 7 f., 42–8, 52, 56 f., 71, 77–9, 85, 96, 102, 104, 108–17, 134, 147, 202, 212, 246–58, 274–8, 292, 295, 311, 358, 369, 438, 471, 474, 500–6, 512, 517, 529, 534–7, 542, 544, 549, 559, 561, 566, 568, 572, 592, 606, 608, 613, 621, 633, 657, 686
ITO 554, 557, 559
Ivan III (Tsar) 27
Ivan IV (Tsar) 27

Jaccard, René 116
Jacques-Destrés (Fr. Senat., MRP) 604
Jäckh, Ernst 43
Jäger, G. 635, 637
Janton, Victor (Fr. Senat., MRP) 604
Janvier, Emil 46
Jaouen, Yves (Fr. Senat., MRP) 604
Japan 5, 7, 9, 15, 38, 73, 97, 170, 175
Jas, F. 137
Jaspers, Karl 240 f.
Jászi, Oscar 445
Jay, John 109
Jayr, René (Fr. Senat., MRP) 604
Jean-Julien (Fr. Senat., PRI) 604
Jennings, Ivor W. 64, 144
Jeuve, Gérard (Dep., SFIO) 603
Joad, Cyril Edwin M. 144–8, 150 f., 589, 659
Joetzlin, J. (Fr. business man) 628
Joint International Committee of the Movements for European Unity, *see* Comité International de Coordination des Mouvements pour l'Unité Européenne
Jones, Frederick E. (MP, Labour) 605
Jones, Joseph M. 468 f., 472, 474
Josephy, F. L. 136, 145–53, 310–16, 324–7, 354, 362, 365 f., 370, 377 f., 393, 407, 574, 588 f., 591, 593, 659 f., 670, 680, 691
Jostock, Paul 374
Joubert, Auguste (Dep., PRI) 603
Jourdain, Paul 360
Jouvenel, Bertrand de 350, 354
Jouvenel, Henri de 42 f.
Juchhoff, Rudolf 407
Jürgensen, Jean-Daniel 49
Julien, Jules (Dep., Rad.) 603
Jung, Carl Gustav 122

Kaan, André 624
Kaars Sijpestein, J. C. 641 f.
Kaiser, Jacob 237, 246, 383, 393, 396 f., 398
Kalinov (Russian Colonel) 7
Kanitz, Count G. 304, 315, 664
Kant, Immanuel 4
Kardelj, Edvard 455
Kardorff-Oheimb, Katharina von 392, 396–9, 584, 690

Index of Proper Names

Karnel, K. 448
Kasting, Wilhelm 393-9, 428, 584, 591 f., 646, 650
Katkov, Mikhail Nikiforovich 30
Kauffmann, Herbert 418, 422
Kempff-Berthelot (Mme, UEFE) 360
Kempski, Jürgen von 655
Kennan, George F. 66, 69, 288 f., 464 f., 473 f., 477, 539
Kerensky, Aleksandr Fedorovich 31
Kerstens, Pieter 336, 338, 641, 673, 682
Keuleneir, A. de 615
Keynes, John Maynard 174 f., 207
Keyserling, Count Hermann 20
Kiev 13 f., 26 f.
Killby, Keith 151, 153, 327 f., 367, 376, 659
Kimber, Charles 143-5, 147, 150
Kindleberger, Charles 472
Kindt-Kiefer, J. J. 118, 124
King, Evelyn Mansfield (MP, Labour) 151, 188, 311 f., 324, 326, 370, 376 f., 605 f., 610 f., 613, 616, 618, 625, 659, 680
King-Hall, Commander Stephen 148, 326, 439, 623 f., 659
Kinley, John (MP, Labour) 605
Kirnberger, Ferdinand 654
Kissinger, Henry 545
Klaesi, L. 118, 123
Klages (managing director) 650
Kleffens, Eelco N. van 265
Klein, Friedrich 406
Klein, Josef H. 456
Klein, Maurice 628
Kleinemeyer (pastor) 404
Kluthe, Hans Albert 147
Koch, Christa 429
Koch, Alison 310
Henri 310, 362, 367, 369 f., 377 f., 588, 591, 593, 615
Kocher, Walter 124, 446
Koch-Weser, Erich 40, 403
Koeth, Joseph 40
Kogon, Eugen 239, 368, 403, 591 f., 649 f., 652-4, 691
Kohl, Erwin 655
Kolanczyk, Bernhard 383, 392-9, 407, 650
Kolwes, Paul G. 410 f., 422, 427, 651
Königsberg (Kaliningrad) 32, 69
Konsbruck, Guillaume 336, 338
Kooy, P. van der 138
Korea 285, 461, 589
Korver, C. J. de 132
Kosfeld, Heinz 650
Kossuth, Lajos 450
Kostov, Traicho D. 455
Kramer, F. A. 239-41, 652 f., 655
Krattiger, Hans 123
Kraus, Herbert 43
Kraus, Karl 20

Kredel, Heinrich 422
Kreisau Circle 47, 51 f., 54 f.
Krofta, Kamil 452
Kronsten (Polish emigré) 147
Kučera, J. M. 447
Kuusinen, Otto W. 480

Labour Party *see* Socialist Parties, Great Britain
Labour "Europe Group" (*see also* All-party Europe Group) 617-20
Lacaze, Henri (Dep., MRP) 602
Lacoste, Robert (Dep., SFIO) 624
Lacour-Gayet, Jacques 335
Lacroix, Jean 130, 222
Länderrat (US occupation zone) 234
Lafay, Bernard (Fr. Senat., Rad.) 604
La Gravière, Emmanuel (Fr. Senat., MRP) 604
Lahaye, Hilaire 615
Lalle, Albert (Dep., Indép.) 603
La Malfa, Ugo 336
Lambilliotte, Maurice 636, 638
Lambotte, Henry 615
Lammers, Heinrich 429, 691
Lamour, Philipp 316
Landauer, Carl 304
Lang, Gordon (MP, Labour) 326, 332, 574, 588, 591 f., 605 f., 616, 618, 625, 659, 661, 680
Lang, Reginald 588
Lange, Halvard 515, 564
Lange, H. M. 641
Laniel, Joseph (Dep., PRI) 603
Lapie, Pierre-Oliviér (Dep., SFIO) 603
Laragnini, Aldo 300
Larmeroux, Jean 311, 361-4, 370, 377, 588, 591, 660
Larock, Viktor 504 f.
Laski, Harold 43, 167, 189-91
Latin America 33, 74, 100 f., 477, 673
La Tour du Pin, René de 350
Latvia 15 f., 29 f., 68 f., 288, 441
Laurent, Augustin (Dep., SFIO) 603
Laurent, Raymond (Dep., MRP) 602
Lauret, François (Fr. Senat., MRP) 604
Lausanne 123, 300, 306, 315
Lavigne, Jacques 359
Layton, Lord (Walter) 58 f., 64, 127, 149, 152, 156, 182, 326, 334, 625, 669, 682, 685
League for European (Economic) Cooperation, *see* Ligue Européenne de Coopération Economique
League of Nations 3 f., 11 f., 36 f., 40 f., 49-51, 53, 63 f., 82, 100 f., 109, 116, 133, 149, 159, 162, 223, 226, 259, 264, 271, 322, 378, 402, 611, 636
Leahy, William (US admiral) 76, 203
Le Bail, Jean (Dep., SFIO) 603
Lebanon 107, 208 f., 212, 220 f.
Lebrec, Léon 360

714 Index of Proper Names

Lecrivain Servoz, Albert (Dep., MRP) 602
Ledermann, László 118
Leenhardt, Francis (Dep., SFIO) 609, 613, 624
Leenhouts, A. 136
Leeuw, Gerardus van der 574
Lefebvre, Francine (Dep., MRP) 602
Le Foyer, Lucien 360
Lehmann, Max 36
Lehmann-Russbueldt, Otto 655
Leibniz, Gottfried Wilhelm 109
Leiden 132
Lenin, Vladimir Ilyich 3, 70, 481
Lenz, Werner 650
Leopold III, King of the Belgians 262
Lerat (Fr. Socialist) 359
Leroy, Maxim 354
Lespès, Henri (Dep. MRP) 602
Lessermann, Philip 588
Le Troquer, André (Dep., SFIO) 624
Levy, B. (MP, Labour) 605
Levy, Louis 162
Levy, Paul M. G. 272
Lewandowski, Rudolf 591
Lhuillier, René 311, 349, 356, 361, 363
Liberal Parties 21, 41, 145, 271 f., 393, 575, 608 f., 612–16
  Belgium (PLB) 261–3, 336, 504, 613–16
  France (Radicaux-Socialistes and UDSR) 220, 229, 359 f., 496 f., 601–4, 613 f.
  Germany (FDP) 237, 241, 389, 416 f., 419, 421 f.
  Great Britain 145, 157, 166, 332 f., 620 f., 625, 659 f.
  Italy (PLI and PRI, *see also* Partito d'Azione) 248 f., 255, 336, 501, 504 f., 608 f., 615 f., 629
  Netherlands (VVD) 504 f., 613–15
  in Eastern Europe 443, 448–51
Libya 258 f., 285
Lichnowsky, Prince Karl Max 36
Lie, Trygve 436
Lienard, Henri (Fr. Senat., MRP) 604
Lienert (Fr. Socialist) 359
Liga für Weltregierung, Cologne 407 f., 572, 646, 654 f.
Ligue Européenne de Coopération Economique (European League for Economic Cooperation—ELEC) 334–41, 595, 609, 658, 661–4, 666, 671, 673, 678, 682
Ligue Indépendante de Coopération Européenne *see* Ligue Européenne de Coopération Economique
Ligue pour les États-Unis d'Europe (French federalist association) 361
Ligue Unioniste Européenne 635, 637
Lindsay, Lord (Kenneth) 188, 326
Linhardt, Hanns 406
Linssen, Ram 302, 306, 635, 637
Lippmann, Walter 467, 469, 471 f.
Lipson, Daniel Leopold (MP, Independent) 328, 605
Lipton, Marcus (MP, Labour) 605
Liquard, Emile (Dep., MRP) 602
Lithuania 14–16, 28 f., 68 f., 288, 441
Lloyd, G. 312
Lo Bue, Francesco 275
Locarno (Treaties, 1925) 4
Loebe, Paul 40, 392
Löwenthal, Richard 195
Lohest, Albert 638
Lombardo, Ivan Matteo 503
London 17, 40, 70, 85 f., 146, 149, 186, 267 f., 325, 328 f., 337 f., 366–9, 379, 479, 481, 483, 517–19, 521 f., 532, 552, 581, 600, 605 f., 620, 659 f., 666 f., 673–5, 687
  1st Meeting of the Council of Foreign Ministers (11.9.–2.10.1945) 105, 169 f., 175, 213, 268, 317
  1st General Assembly of the UN 106 f., 178
  5th Meeting of the Council of Foreign Ministers (25.11.–15.12.1947) 487, 645
Longden, Fred (MP, Labour) 605, 619
Lopes, Cardozo, E. 640 f.
Lorraine 493
Los Rios, Fernando de 436
Lothian, Lord Philip 143–5
Loucheur, Louis 40
Louvel, Jean (Dep., MRP) 602
Lovett, Robert A. 539, 541, 547
Lublin (Committee) 77, 95, 210 f.
Lucas, Maurice (Dep., MRP) 602
Lucerne 123, 305
Luchair, Jean 316
Lucien-Brun, Jean 628
Lucifero, Roberto 616
Ludwig, Eduard 457, 610, 613
Lübeck 428
Lüthy, Herbert 486
Luetkens, Gerhart 67
Lugard, Frederick D. 144
Lugt, Anton P. W. von 132
Luxemburg 67, 199, 226, 245, 259 f., 267, 304, 362, 369, 438–40, 493, 505, 572, 621 f.
  Federalist Conference (13.–16.10.1946) 310–14, 347 f., 352, 362 f., 407, 586, 588, 590
  2nd World Congress of MWFG (5.–10.9.1948) 586
Luzzatto (Italian émigré) 147
Lyons 50, 52, 58, 116, 124–6

Maas Geesteranus, Henry 313, 364, 377
Maass, Bruno 412, 650 f.
Maccas, Leon 608–10, 613 f., 661 f.
MacDermot, Niall 162, 591
MacDonald, James Ramsay 36
Macdonald, Sir Peter (MP, Cons.) 610, 613, 618, 620

Index of Proper Names

Mackay, Ronald William Gordon (MP, Labour) 64, 109, 144 f., 148, 152 f., 157–9, 182, 198 f., 343–5, 436, 489, 493, 605 f., 610, 612 f., 616–22, 681, 691
Mackenzie King, William Lyon 164
Macmillan, Harold 177, 332, 337 f., 494
Madagascar 12
Madison, James 109
Maier, Reinhold 237
Maigne, Jean 227
Malaya 529
Mallalieu, Joseph Percival William (MP, Labour) 605
Mallez, Henri (Dep., Indép.) 603
Mallon, James Joseph 326
Manchuria 3, 285
Manditte, Jacques (Fr. Senat., MRP) 604
Mangin, Robert 117, 361
Mangoldt, Hermann von 243
Maniu, Julius 450 f.
Mann, Thomas 67, 101
Manning, Leah (MP, Labour) 619
Mansholt, Sicco Leendert 139, 264
Marc, Alexandre 42, 314–16, 329, 350, 352, 358, 362–70, 375–85, 393, 397, 430, 571 f. 588, 591, 593, 601, 628, 645 f., 658, 661, 664, 671, 673, 677, 679, 681
Marcel, Gabriel 350, 354 f.
Marin, Louis 217, 226
Marin-Tabouret (Fr. Senat., RGR) 604
Maritain, Jacques 67
Markos, Vafiadis 455
Marlio, Louis 628
Marshall, George C. 462–7, 475–8, 481 f., 484 f., 490, 492 f., 497, 501, 519, 521 f., 539
 Marshall Plan (Harvard speech 5.6.1947, *see also* Paris, Conference of the Sixteen) 9, 175, 189–200, 250, 258, 268, 337 f., 429 f., 435, 440, 448, 454, 459, 471–5, 478, 486–8, 493, 499 f., 502–5, 507–10, 513, 531, 538, 544 f., 547, 550, 553, 562, 565, 573 f., 579–82, 597 f., 606, 616, 622, 625, 628, 630, 632 f., 636, 638 f., 643, 645, 647–9, 665–8, 677
Martin du Gard, Roger 43
Martin, Thomas Ballantyne 332, 659, 666, 671
Marx, Karl 31
Masaryk, Jan 336, 485 f.
Matthews, Walter Robert 326
Maulnier, Thierry 354
Mauriau, Eugène 615
Maurras, Charles 205
Maxwell-Fyfe, Sir David 326
Mayer, Daniel 126, 215, 217, 219, 225, 273
Mayer, René 624
Mayhew, Christopher 187, 191 f., 197, 494
McAllister, Gilbert (MP, Labour) 605

McGhee, Henry George (MP, Labour) 605
McNeil, Hector 197
Mecklenburg, Adolf Friedrich 429
Medland, Hubert Moses (MP, Labour) 605
Meggle, Armand 360
Meilof Yben, J. 142, 639, 641
Meinberg, Bad (SPD resolution, 22.04.1947) 427, 651
Meinberg (EU chairman at Bielefeld) 651
Meinecke, Friedrich 239
Meinecke (Oldenburg, Pan-E.) 390, 422
Mennicke, C. A. 639
Menthon, François de (Dep., MRP) 602, 609, 613 f., 624
Menu, Roger (Fr. Senat., MRP) 604
Merten, Hugo 403, 405
Merten, Richard 336
Merten, Theo 403–6, 413, 425–7, 430 f., 585, 646–8, 651, 691
Merzagora, Cesare 502
Métadier, J. 147
Meyerhoffer, Paul 312
Meyer-Sevenich, Maria 404
Meynen, Johannes 139
Michelet, Edmond (Dep., MRP) 602 f., 624
Micheli, Giuseppe 616
Middelhauve, Friedrich 416
Migel, J. A. 312
Mikardo, Ian (MP, Labour) 191, 605
Mikolajczyk, Stanislaw 446
Milan 112, 115–17, 247, 274–6, 302
 Founding conference of MFE (27./28.8.1943) 112–15, 125 f.
 2nd Congress of MFE (15.–17.12.1948) 631–3
Millar, F. Hoyer 178 f., 183
Milo di Villagrazia, Antonio 371, 377 f., 591, 629
Minjoz, Jean (Dep., SFIO) 603, 624
Mitchell, Leslie 152
Mitrinović, Dimitrije 162
Mitscherlich, Alexander 650
Möller, Nicolaus 417 f., 422
Mönchengladbach 420–6, 651
Molden, Otto 238
Mollet, Guy 195, 228, 497
Molotov, Vyacheslav Mikhailovich 70 f., 75, 105, 169 f., 176, 210, 284, 286–8, 293, 384, 465–8, 482–6, 488, 491 f., 499, 502, 511, 580, 606, 648
Molson, Arthur Hugh (MP, Cons.) 493
Moltke, Count Helmuth James von 33, 44, 47 f., 53, 60, 109
Mondon, Raymond (Dep., UDSR) 603
Mongols 13 f., 26–8
Monnet, Henri (Fr. Senat., Rad.) 604
Monnet, Jean 185, 207, 514, 518, 521, 535, 545, 549, 562
Monnier, André 624

Monnier, Christian 378, 594, 628, 670 f., 673
Mont, Claude (Dep., MRP) 602
Monteil, André (Dep., MRP) 602
Montesquieu, Charles de 22
Monti, Augusto 115, 275 f., 502
Montreux, 1st Congress of UEF (27.-30.8.1947) 24, 33, 84, 162, 313, 363, 370, 373 f., 378, 384, 398, 446, 448, 462, 571-85, 622 f., 626, 628, 632, 634, 637, 640, 647, 650, 657, 665-7, 676
   Congress of MWFG (17.-24.8.1947) 585-90
Montrouge (near Paris), 1st Congress of MSEUE (21./22.6.1947) 600
Monts, Count Anton 36
Moore, Ben T. 472
Morgenthau, Henry 293
Morley, Ralph (MP, Labour) 605
Morocco 12 f., 404
Morris-Jones, Sir H. (MP, Liberal) 620
Morrison, Herbert Stanley 113, 166 f.
Moscow 13 f., 27 f., 31, 69, 78, 86, 102, 209 f., 223, 283, 289, 383, 453, 484, 597
   Conference of Foreign Ministers (Oct. 1943) 71 f., 75
   Conference of Foreign Ministers (Dec. 1945) 105 f., 175 f., 176, 181 f., 213, 283, 287 f., 294
   4th Meeting of the Council of Foreign Ministers (10.3.-24.4.1947) 229, 423, 439, 465-7, 472, 497, 499, 521, 550, 599 f., 634, 686
Motz, Roger 336, 338, 682
Mounier, Emmanuel 42, 126
Mouskhely, Michel 33
Mouvement Belge pour les États-Unis d'Europe 638
Mouvement d'Action et de Propagande (MAP, Belgian federalist association) 638 f.
Mouvement Socialiste pour les États-Unis d'Europe (from Oct. 1948) (for Feb. 1947 until Oct. 1948 see Comité International pour les États-Unis Socialistes d'Europe) 349, 359, 600, 637 f., 679, 690, 693
Movement for World Federal Government (MWFG) 311-13, 585-90, 634
Movimento Autonomista di Federazione Europea (Italian federalist group) 629
Movimento Federalista Europeo (MFE) 52, 56 f., 108-17, 124, 251 f., 269, 274-8, 300 f., 303, 362, 502 f., 592-4, 606, 608, 629-32, 691
Movimento Italiano per la Federazione Europea (Group 1947/8) 629
Movimento Unionista Europeo (Group 1947/8) 629
Movimento Unionista Italiano (Group 1947/8) 629
Mozer, Alfred 139 f., 304, 306, 309
MRP, *see under* Christian Democratic Parties
Müller, Ernst (Berlin) 427, 429

Müller, Vincenz 237
Müller-Wiemers (Hamburg Pan.-E.) 422
Münch, Hermann 390, 392
Münster 385, 403 f., 408-10, 649, 651
Münster, Clemens 654
Munich 385, 447, 644
Murray, Professor Gilbert 326
Murray, James Dixon (MP, Labour) 605
Mussolini, Benito 43, 56, 110, 247 f.
Mutter, André (Dep., Act. Paysanne) 218, 603, 609
Myers, Bishop Edward 659

Nadai, H. 305
Nagy, Ferenc 448 f.
Napoleon I 29, 35, 122, 642
NATO 477, 551
Naudin, Paul 335, 338, 662, 664, 671, 674
Nauheim Circle 190
Naumann, Friedrich 416
Naumann, Johann W. 653
Neerlands Toekomst (Dutch association) 142, 638
Nenni, Pietro 115, 253 f., 258, 500, 503, 616
Netherlands (*see also* parties, places of conferences, names of associations) 7 f., 12, 37, 48 f., 58, 67, 102, 104, 107, 115, 130-42, 157, 165, 173, 201, 245, 247, 259 f., 263-8, 272, 303, 369, 438 f., 471, 480, 482, 504, 572, 592, 613, 621, 638-44
Neumann, Luis 124, 315
New Commonwealth Society 43, 63 f., 311, 318, 418
New Europe Group (British federalist association) 162, 377, 591
Newlands, H. M. L. 151 f.
New York 66, 198, 438, 443, 468, 552, 607
   3rd Meeting of the Council of Foreign Ministers (4.11.-11.12.1946) 185, 294-6
Nichol, Muriel Edith (MP, Labour) 605
Nicholas I (Tsar) 30
Nicolson, Harold 64
Nietzsche, Friedrich W. 36
Ninčić, Momčilo 610
Nipperdey, Hans C. 407
Nippold, Otfried 36
Nitti, Francesco Saverio 38
Nice 359 f.
Noël, André (Dep., MRP) 602, 609, 661, 670, 682
Noël, Léon 335
Nord, Hans R. 136 f., 141, 299, 304, 312, 314, 366 f., 377, 381, 384, 588, 591, 638, 641
Norway 56, 59, 67, 102, 115, 164, 194, 201, 259, 306, 365, 438 f., 512, 515-17, 563-6
Nothardt, Fritz 413 f, 650
Nouvelles Equipes Internationales (NEI) 600, 638, 679, 690

Novgorod 27 f.
Nutting, Anthony 188, 192

Oberkirch, Alfred 226
OEEC 9, 88, 507, 511–14, 525, 537, 548
Olesen, Søren 608–10
Oliver, George Harold (MP, Labour) 619
Olivier, Sir Laurence 332
Ollenhauer, Erich 427
Olsen, Thomas'Hatt 370, 377, 588, 591
Organization of American States (OAS) 65, 100, 120, 137, 424, 477, 673
Ortega y Gasset, José 21, 26, 39
Orvoen, Louis (Dep., MRP) 602
Ott, Barthélemy (Fr. Senat., MRP) 226, 604

Paget, Reginald Thomas (MP, Labour) 619
Palewski, Jean Paul (Dep., MRP) 226, 602
Palmer, Arthur Montague Frank (MP, Labour) 619
Pan-American Union, *see* Organization of American States (OAS)
Paneuropa-Bund (federalist group in Berlin) 383, 393–9, 420, 430, 446, 591, 604, 646 f., 650 f.
Paneuropa-Union (1923–38, *see also* Coudenhove-Kalergi) 39–44, 214, 388 f., 392, 442, 607, 681
Paneuropa-Union (German federalist association, Hamburg 1946–7) 383, 388–93, 400, 404, 417, 421 f., 425–8, 646 f.
Pantaloni (Dep., Indép.) 603
Paris 3, 17, 40, 85 f., 202, 204, 208 f., 216, 292, 313, 315–17, 337 f., 351 f., 359 f., 437, 450, 483, 581, 605 f., 608 f., 625, 659–2, 671 f., 674 f., 682
 Federalist Conference (22.–25.3.1945) 116, 126–30, 307, 316, 347
 2nd Meeting of the Council of Foreign Ministers (25.4.–15.5. and 15.6.–12.7.1946) 183, 196, 292–4, 318, 335, 347 f., 361–4, 367, 385, 458
 Conference: Bevin, Bidault, Molotov (28.6.–2.7.1947) 485–8, 491 f., 497, 504
 Conference of the Sixteen (CEEC, 12.7.–22.9.1947) 485, 489, 493 f., 497–9, 501 f., 505 f., 510 f., 514–25, 535–60, 567
Parker, John (MP, Labour) 148, 153, 328, 605
Parmelee, F. 312
Parri, Ferruccio 111, 256, 272, 608, 616, 630
Parties (in Europe) *see under* Christian Democratic, Communist, Conservative, Liberal, Socialist
Partito d'Azione (Socialist–Liberal) 111, 115, 252 f., 272, 629
Partito dell'Uomo Qualunque, *see* Conservative Parties, Italy
Party, Democratic (USA) 73 f., 290 f., 460 f., 464, 470 f.

Republican (USA) 73, 289 f., 460 f., 464, 470–3
Passani, Pierre 360
Passy, Frédéric 214
Patenotre, Jacqueline (Fr. Senat., Rad.) 604
Patrascanu, L. (Romanian Communist leader) 455
Paul-Boncour, Joseph 102, 124, 220 f., 360, 439, 609
Peasant parties (in Eastern Europe) 294 f., 441–3, 446–52
Pechel, Rudolf 653
Peguy, Charles 316
Pella, Giuseppe 616
Perez, Guido Russo 609, 613, 616
Pernot, Georges (Fr. Senat., PRI) 604
Persico, Giovanni 616
Peter I (Tsar) 14, 28
Peters, Hans 392
Petit, Eugène, *dit* Claudius (Dep., UDSR) 603
Petitpierre, Max 572
Petkov, Nikola 452
Peyer, E. E. V. de 151
Peyroles, Germaine (Dep., MRP) 602, 660
Pezet, Ernest (Fr. Senat., MRP) 225, 304, 604
Pflimlin, Pierre (Dep., MRP) 602, 609
Philip, André 126, 130, 218–20, 623
Philip, Olivier 354
Phocas, Nicolas 610
Picard, Max 302
Picard, Roger 341
Picardo, Orazio 255
Piccioni, Attilia 616
Pieck, Wilhelm 236
Pieri, Gino 616
Pierlot, Hubert 259, 262
Pierre-Grouès, Abbé Henri (Dep., MRP) 588, 603
Pinder, John 331
Pinton, Auguste (Fr. Senat., Rad.) 604
Pitsch, Dr (Freiberg) 390, 584
Pitt, William (the Younger) 61
Pius XI (Pope) 351, 374
Pius XII (Pope) 54
Pivert, Marceau 600, 672, 678
Plato (Dr, Hamburg—perhaps Dr Robert Platow, commercial journalist) 415 f.
Poher, Alain (Fr. Senat., MRP) 604
Poimboeuf, Marcel (Dep., MRP) 226, 603
Poincaré, Raymond 4, 205, 207, 219, 286
Poinso-Chapuis, Germaine (Dep., MRP) 603
Poisson, Emile (Fr. Senat., MRP) 604
Poland 10, 13–16, 21, 27–32, 52, 56, 65–71, 76–9, 96, 103, 115, 133, 169, 186 f., 201, 210, 259, 295, 365, 441–6, 454, 461, 463, 480, 482, 485, 502, 597, 639
Pons, Vittorio 608
Poole, Cecil Charles (MP, Labour) 605
Porter, Edward (MP, Labour) 605

718 Index of Proper Names

Portugal 12, 40, 45, 59, 173, 247, 517, 557, 559, 594, 621
Potsdam (Conference 17.7.–2.8.1945) 82, 97, 103–6, 128, 130, 186, 210 f., 235, 256, 271, 285, 288, 292, 469, 519
Pradelle, A. de la (Fr. prof.) 579
Prague 153, 194, 360, 445, 447 f., 453 f., 581
Price, M. Phillips (MP, Cons.) 620
Price, Sir Henry 337
Priester, Karl Heinz 401
Pritt, D. N. 191
Privat, Edmond 118
Proctor, William Thomas (MP, Labour) 605, 659
Proske, Rüdiger 649 f., 654
Proudhon, Pierre-Joseph 136, 214, 311, 316, 350, 356, 361, 373 f.
Pünder, Hermann 387
Pulides, P. (Dr, Hamburg Pan-E.) 388, 390, 647
Pursey, Harry (MP, Labour) 619 f.
PvdA (Partij van de Arbeid), see Socialist Parties

Qualunque(ist), see Conservative Parties, Italy
Quartara, Giorgio 41
Quay, Jan Eduard de 136
Quidde, Ludwig 36

Radowitz, Hugo Wendt von 392, 650
Rajk, László 455
Ramadier, Paul 229 f., 482, 496–500, 624
Ransome, M. Patrick 64, 142 f., 145 f., 152, 327
Rassemblement fédéraliste (Belgian federalist association) 377, 591, 635, 637
Rathenau, Walther 37
Ravey, Paul 378, 594
Rawnsley, Derek 142
Reale, Eugenio 496
Rebholz, M. (Freiburg) 650
Recy, Antoine de (Dep., Indép.) 603
Rees-Williams, David Rees (MP, Labour) 605
Reeves, Joseph (MP, Labour) 605
Regensburg 411
Reger, Erik 656
Rehault, Hippolyte (Fr. Senat., MRP) 604
Reichsarbeitsgemeinschaft Deutscher Föderalisten, see Bund Deutscher Föderalisten
Renner, Karl 40, 442, 456
Reston, James B. 99, 466
Retinger, Joseph 335–8, 341, 609, 661, 664 f., 670–4, 676, 682 f.
Reuter, Emil 611, 615
Reves, Emery 101, 136, 407, 588, 609 f.
Reynaud, Paul 63, 183, 354, 439, 610, 624
Rheinbaben, Wilhelm von 401 f., 416 f., 422, 426–8, 647
Rhineland 183, 521, 542
Rhys-Williams, Lady Juliet Evangeline 326, 337, 659
Richard, Max 349 f., 352 f., 354, 660

Richardson, John Macdonald 328, 659
Rifflet, Raymond 377, 592, 634–8, 680, 693
Rincent, Germain 614
Rio de Janeiro (Interamerican Mutual Assistance Treaty, 2.9.1947) 477
Riou, Gaston 311, 335, 360–2, 364, 377
Ripka, Hubert 448, 485
Ritter, Gerhard 233
Ritter, Herbert 399–401. 646
Ritzel, Heinrich Georg 120–5, 240, 303–10, 315, 364, 418–20, 422, 427–9, 574, 655
Rivet, Paul (Dep., SFIO) 219 f., 601–3, 660
Robbins, Lionel 64, 142, 144
Roberts, Emrys (MP, Liberal) 328, 605
Roberts, G. O. (MP, Labour) 604
Roberts, Owen J. (US judge) 101, 136, 467
Roberts, Peter Geoffrey (MP, Cons.) 620
Roberts, Wilfrid (MP, Liberal) 177
Robertson, Sir Brian 498
Robertson, Sir Denis 554
Robin, Jacques 679
Rochereau, Henri (Fr. Senat., PRI) 604
Rockefeller, David 336
Röpke, Wilhelm 239, 280 f.
Rollier, Mario Alberto 48, 111–17, 574
Rollin, Simone (Fr. Senat., MRP) 604
Romains, Jules 19 f., 37, 42
Romania 10, 33, 68, 77, 95, 103, 175, 287, 292, 365, 441, 445, 449, 453–5, 460, 463, 485, 610
Rome 27, 109, 114, 247 f., 254 f., 278, 302, 343, 536 f., 608
  2nd Congress of UEF (7.–10. Nov. 1948) 122, 374, 377, 379, 576, 596, 670, 677
Romein, Jan 12, 48, 131
Rompf, Kurt 390, 426 f., 647
Romrée de Vichenet, Comte de 260
Ronald, Sir Nigel 178, 105
Roolvink, E. G. M. 610, 613, 615
Roosevelt, Elliot 296
Roosevelt, Franklin Delano 64 f., 69, 71–80, 94, 155, 174, 181, 202 f., 211 f., 233, 256, 287, 291, 457, 459–61, 478, 541, 685
Rops, Daniel 316, 352
Roques, Raymond (Dep., MRP) 603
Roselli, Carlo 43
Rosenfeld, (Dr, Hamburg Pan-E.) 389
Rosenfeld, Oreste 228
Rossi, Ernesto 47 f., 56 f., 108 f., 115 f., 160, 275, 278, 582, 594, 596, 629, 631, 677
Rossi-Doria, Manlio 115
Rossmann, Erich 652, 690
Rotten, Elisabeth 118
Rotterdam 639, 643
Rougemont, Denis de 24, 42, 302, 316, 571, 573, 575, 579, 596, 655, 665 f., 683
Rousseau, Madeleine 359
Rouzand (Dr, Fr. Socialist) 359
Rovan, Joseph 227

Index of Proper Names 719

Rowe-Dutton, E. 185
Royall, Kenneth C. 519, 522, 538
Royle, Charles (MP, Labour) 606
Rudloff, H. 421, 427
Rueff, Jacques 335
Rütten, E. 418
Ruhr district 142, 178, 180, 183, 208, 215, 224, 280, 293, 304, 468, 493 f., 502, 520 f., 541, 546 f., 585, 655, 667
Ruini, Menccio 257
Rumbold, A. 179 f.
Russell, Lord (Bertrand) 326
Russia until 1917 (from 1917 *see* Soviet Union) 13 f., 26–31, 34, 62, 69

Saar territory 123, 192, 208, 235, 267, 304, 493, 521 f., 585
Saillant, Louis 217, 335
Saint-Jean, Claude 626
St. Petersburg (Leningrad) 28 f.
Sainte-Lorette, Lucien 335, 338, 671, 674
Saliège, Cardinal Jules-Géraud 624
Salinger, Hans Dieter 62, 132–41, 299, 304–6, 308, 312, 314 f., 364, 374, 408–10, 413 f., 420 f., 447, 638 f.
Salis, Jean Rodolphe von 118
Salle, Bertrand de la 223
Salt Lake City (Marshall's speech, 14.7.1947) 477
Salter, Sir Arthur 64, 332, 337, 618, 620
Salvemini, Gaetano 108, 343 f., 629 f.
Salzmann (*Landeshauptmann* Münster) 404
Sanders, D. W. 152
Sandner, Julius 374, 414 f.
Sandys, Diana (Churchill's daughter) 323
Sandys, Duncan (Lord Duncan-Sandys) 323–7, 332, 360, 366 f., 369, 379, 433, 437 f., 574, 598, 606, 609 f., 613, 623 f., 658 f., 661–3, 665–70, 674–8, 681–4, 693
San Francisco (Conference, 25.4.–26.6.1945) 99–102, 106, 130, 221 f., 224, 271
Sangiorgi 588
Sangnier, Marc 214
Saragat, Giuseppe 248, 500. 616
Sargent, Sir Orme 155, 179, 185
Sarrazac-Soularge, Colonel Robert 589
Sassen, Emmanuel, Marie Joseph A. 370
Saunier, Claire (Fr. Senat., UDSR) 604
Scandinavia (*see also* Denmark, Finland, Iceland, Norway, Sweden) 8, 13, 25 f., 59, 65, 84 f., 89, 134, 140, 247, 300, 339, 439 f., 471, 559, 586
Scelle, George 43, 131, 360, 628
Schaeffer, Fritz 237
Schenck, Ernst von 303 f., 306, 369–73, 377–9, 382, 384, 386, 402, 415, 440, 574, 583 f., 592 f., 649 f., 652, 656, 694
Scherer, Marc (Dep., MRP) 603
Schermerhorn, Willem 136 f., 139, 264 f.

Schiess, Heinrich 123 f., 308, 315 f., 362 f., 370, 377, 572, 592
Schilfgaarde, P. 641
Schilling von Canstadt, Friedrich 640 f., 650
Schinzinger, Albert 388, 390, 412, 426, 584, 650–2
Schmal, J. R. 615
Schmid, Carlo 43, 271, 655
Schmidt, Carl F. 410 f.
Schmidt, John F. 467
Schmidt, P. J. 136
Schmittmann, Benedikt 241, 653
Schmittmann, Helena 655
Schmitz-Lenders, Bruno 397, 420 f.
Schmitz, (Solingen, member of Pan-E. executive) 390, 651
Schneider, Reinold 240
Schröder, J. W. M. (Dutch federalist) 636, 638
Schroeder, M. (MWFG) 589
Schubart, Wilhelm 240
Schücking, Walther 36
Schultz van Haegen, J. H. 117
Schulze-Boysen, Harald 316
Schumacher, Kurt 139, 236, 244 f., 428
Schumacher-Hellmold, Otto 422
Schuman, Robert 497, 694
  Schuman Plan (9.5.1950) 88, 199 f., 323, 585, 694
Schumann, Maurice (Dep., MRP) 216, 220 f., 228, 272, 569, 603
Schuschnigg, Kurt von 301
Schwarz, Hans-Peter 87, 189 f., 196
Schwennicke, Carl-Hubert 399
Schwerte a.d. Ruhr 401–403
Scolefield, Allen 153
Secrétan, Daniel 378
Segal, Samuel (MP, Labour) 619, 659
Seipel, Ignaz Karl 40 f.
Semenov, Vladimir Semenovich 384, 394 f.
Sempe, Augusto (Fr. Senat., MRP) 604
Séraut, Paul 354
Sering, Paul, pseudonym of R. Löwenthal, q.v.
Serre, Philippe 360
Serruys, Daniel 335 f., 338, 340, 360, 576, 661, 665, 671 f., 675 f., 682 f.
Sforza, Count Carlo 43, 113, 258, 439, 501 f., 567, 572, 610, 616, 629
Shawcross, Christopher 618–20
Sheridan, S. F. 151
Shillan, David 162
Shinwell, Emanuel 619
Shotwell, James T. 66
Shurmer, Percy Lionel Edward (MP, Labour) 606
Siegfried, André 360, 624
Siemsen-Vollenweider, Anna 118, 304 f., 308, 315 f., 429 f.
Sikorski, Wladyslaw 66, 335, 442 f.
Silone, Ignazio 115, 253 f., 377, 572, 592, 630

720 Index of Proper Names

Silva, Raymond 118, 364 f., 367 f., 377–81, 434, 570 f., 574, 581, 592–4, 598, 661, 664–74, 676 f., 680, 682 f.
Silverman, Sydney (MP, Labour) 619
Simonnet, René (Dep. San Liste) 603
Skeffington, A. M. (MP, Labour) 606
Skeffington-Lodge, Thomas Cecil (MP, Labour) 606, 619
Sligting, Jan F. 132, 134 f.
Smiles, Sir Walter (MP, Cons.) 610, 620
Smirnov, Andrey 394 f., 480
Smith, Walter Bedell 465
Smithers, M. P. W. 145
Smuts, Jan Christiaan 164, 320, 345
Snow, Julien (MP, Labour) 619
Socialisme et Liberté (Fr. federalist group) 359
Socialist Vanguard Group 58, 67, 127, 162 f.
Socialist Parties (see also Comité International pour les États-Unis Socialistes d'Europe) 21, 41, 86, 181 f., 194 f., 197 f., 200, 272 f., 309, 332 f., 335–58, 400, 422, 456, 573, 575, 578–600, 612–16, 670, 673, 676 f.
 Belgium (PSB) 194 f., 258–63, 504, 608, 613–16, 635 f., 638
 France (SFIO) 42, 127, 170 f., 181, 194 f., 215 f., 219–21, 225, 227–30, 347, 356, 358–61, 495–500, 602–2, 613 f., 623 f., 672
 Germany (SPD) 41, 127, 195, 236 f., 244, 292, 425, 427 f., 651
 Great Britain (Labour Party) 64, 112, 127, 144 f., 160, 162–7, 187, 189–95, 320, 326–8, 333, 365, 433, 490, 493, 598 f., 605 f., 610 f., 613, 616–21, 623, 625, 659, 661, 677, 687
 Italy (PSIUP, Jan. 1947 PSI and PSLI) 110, 115, 248 f., 253 f., 501, 503 f., 615 f., 630
 Netherlands (PvdA) 135 f., 139, 194 f., 264–6, 269, 505 f.
 in Eastern Europe 441–56
Soddy, Frederick 162
Sofia 454
Soldani, Edouard (Fr. Senat., SFIO) 604
South Africa 12, 164, 311, 586
South America, see Latin America
Soutou, Jean-Marie 56, 119
Soviet Union (see also Russia until 1917, Eastern Europe, Communist Parties, places of conferences) 2–8, 14–17, 22, 31 f., 34, 44, 49, 55 f., 58 f., 68–86, 89, 94–9, 102–7, 112, 134, 146, 155 f., 161, 163–7, 169, 174–80, 184–7, 189–91, 194, 196, 201, 205, 209, 211, 215, 218, 222–4, 227, 234, 279, 281, 283–93, 296, 301, 308 f., 319–21, 324–7, 330, 339, 342, 344, 349, 353, 357, 365, 367, 382–5, 395, 397, 402, 407, 431, 436, 443, 445, 453, 458–63, 473, 475, 478–81, 483, 485, 487, 491–3, 497, 502, 510, 541, 550, 554, 557, 579, 581, 589, 597 f., 600, 617, 625–7, 631, 644, 670, 685–7

Spaak, Paul-Henri 52, 67, 85, 164, 178, 188, 259–63, 335, 488, 504, 636, 686
Spain 25, 37, 45, 59, 102, 126, 133, 190, 247, 358, 482, 485, 491, 559, 582, 621
SPD see under Socialist Parties
Spellman, Cardinal Francis Joseph 74
Spengler, Oswald 19
Spinelli, Altiero 47 f., 56 f., 108–17, 126, 129, 154, 252, 269, 271, 274, 440, 503, 572, 574–6, 582, 598, 612, 629–32
Spinelli, Veniero 629
Spinelli-Hirschmann, Ursula 109, 126
Stalin, Joseph V. 3, 7, 15 f., 32, 59 f., 68–79, 96, 99, 169, 176, 202 f., 209 f., 256, 278–80, 283, 286–8, 291, 296, 301, 384, 445–7, 453, 457. 460 f., 478 f., 486
Stalingrad 71
Stam, P. van 641–3
Stanley, Oliver 326, 328, 331
Stassen, Harald 296
Stauss, Adolf 392
Steed, H. Wickham 142
Stefan, Werner 403
Stefani, Gaston 33
Steffan, Ernest B., 123 f., 306
Steinbüchel, Theodor 240
Steinhorst, Karl 421 f., 426 f., 429, 647
Steltzer, Theodor 54 f., 417
Sternberger, Dolf 239
Stern-Rubarth, Edgar 40, 335
Stettin 16, 290
Stettinius, Edward 79, 203
Stevens, Roger 184 f., 559
Stier, Hans Erich 406
Stikker, Dirk 264
Stimson, Henri J. 73, 539
Stockholm, 3rd World Congress of MWFG (28.8.–4.9.1949) 589
Stocky, Julius 324, 395 f., 406–8, 584, 650
Stökl, Günther 27
Stolper, Gustav 234
Strabolgi, Lord 150, 152
Stránsky, Miloš 448
Strasser, Otto 43
Strauss, Walter 316
Strecker, Reinhard 403
Streit, Clarence K. 34, 64, 136, 467
Stresemann, Gustav 4, 40, 412
Struye, Paul 259 f.
Stuttgart 234, 237, 293, 386, 401, 428, 483, 652 f.
Süsterhenn, Adolf 241 f., 653
Sudeten district 232
Sukarno, Ahmed 266
Sulyok (leader of the Hungarian 'Freedom party') 450
Sweden 28 f., 45, 59, 194, 310 f., 365, 438, 512, 516 f., 537, 563–6, 613
Switzerland (see also parties, places of conferences, names of associations) 8, 43, 56–9, 108, 117 f., 122–4, 240, 300, 304, 307,

Index of Proper Names

310 f., 313 f., 319, 358, 363, 369, 378 f., 405, 420, 434, 438-40, 517, 537, 539, 561, 563, 565, 571 f., 592, 595, 613, 657
Syke (near Bremen) 416-19, 426
Symonds, Arthur Leslie (MP, Labour) 619 f.
Synthèses (Belgian federalist group) 636, 638
Syria 107, 156, 174, 208 f., 220 f., 224
Szapiro (Polish emigré) 147

Taft, Robert A. 290, 461
Tanguy, Charles 359
Tarchiani 536
Tatarescu, George 450
Tecklenburg 651
Teeling, William (MP, Cons.) 659
Tehran ('Big Three' Conference) 71, 74-7, 202
Teitgen, Pierre-Henri 126, 602, 610, 624
Temple, Emmanuel (Dep., Indép.) 603
Tendeloo, N.S.C. 615
Terrenoire, Louis (Dep., MRP) 603
Tessier, Gaston 216
Tets, van 615
Tewson, Harold Vincent (Secretary-General of TUC, 1946-60) 337
The Hague 134-6, 268, 304, 306, 308, 337, 366, 383, 413 f., 446, 566, 590, 639 f.
  European congress (7.-10.5.1948) 340, 596, 675, 684
  Peace conferences, 1899 and 1907, 36
Thesten, Paul (Dep. Indép.) 603
Thierry, A. 37
Thomas Aquinas 24, 316
Thomas, Elbert D. (US Senator) 101, 470
Thomas, Fleury 360
Thomas, Ivor Owen (MP, Labour) 556, 606
Thompson, Dorothy 469
Thorez, Maurice 206
Thorneycroft, Peter 492
Tildy, Zoltán 448
Tinaud, Jean-Louis (Dep., MRP) 603
Tinbergen, Jan 639
Tito (*or* Broz), Josip 59, 285, 451-4
Togliatti, Plamiro 503
Toint, Jacques 637 f.
Tonello, Tommaso 616
Toscanini, Arturo 436
Toynbee, Arnold J. 11, 16 f., 104
Trémieux (delegate to MRP party congress) 499
Tresintin, Pierre (Fr. Senat., MRP) 604
Trevelyan, Charles 36
Treves, Paolo 616
Triboulet, Raymond (Dep., Indép.) 602 f.
Trieste 16, 32, 81, 258, 280, 290, 292
Trinquier, Anne-Marie (Fr. Senat., MRP) 370, 602, 604, 613 f., 680
Trocquer, Yves le 42
Trotha, Carl Dietrich von 243
Trott zu Solz, Adam von 66
  Werner von 239
Truchy, Henri 42, 360
Truffaut, Pierre (Dep., MRP) 603
Truman, Harry S. 98 f., 105, 124, 158, 163, 181, 212, 256, 287-91, 296, 301, 308, 460-4, 476, 482, 502, 544
Tulli, Tollo 629
Tumminelli, Michele 616
Turin 115, 275, 302, 567 f.
Turkey 26, 29 f., 65, 77, 192, 285, 462, 490, 516 f., 562, 586
Turner-Samuels, Moss (MP, Labour) 606

UDSR *see under* Liberal Parties
Ukraine 14-16, 26-33
Ulbricht, Walter 234-6
UN (United Nations Organization) 50, 57, 73-6, 79, 98-101, 105 f., 124, 130, 163, 173, 181, 185, 186 f., 218-21, 260, 265, 282, 297, 339, 348, 434, 438, 493, 510, 516, 538, 543, 564, 607
Undén (Swedish Foreign Minister) 565
Union Economique et Douanière de l'Europe 39-41, 313, 334 f., 360, 442, 445
Union Economique et Fédérale Européenne (French federalist association) 335, 360 f., 377, 445
Union-Europa-Liga (German federalist association, Munich) 385, 410-12, 432, 647 f.
Union Européenne (French federalist association) 359 f., 431-4, 458
Union Européenne des Fédéralistes (UEF) 24, 33, 83 f., 88, 122, 131, 162, 308, 310, 314, 347, 358, 362-80, 393-8, 401, 420, 431, 569-99, 604, 634, 639, 641, 645, 647, 649, 656 f., 665-80, 687
Union Fédérale (Belgian federalist association) 261 f., 303, 308, 362, 377, 634 f., 637
Union Fédérale (federalist association in Luxemburg) 362, 377, 591
Union Fédérale Mondiale (French federalist association) 361 f.
Union "Junges Europa" 650
Union Universelle pour la Paix (French federalist group) 361
United Europe Movement 186 f., 323-34, 341, 365-7, 381, 433, 595, 606, 623 f., 657-63, 666, 674, 682
United Kingdom, *see* Great Britain
United Nations Association 493 f.
United States of America (*see also* Party: Democratic, Republican, *and* places of conferences) 2-8, 12, 17, 33 f., 36 f., 40, 44, 49, 55, 62-8, 71-89, 94, 102-7, 145, 155-8, 164, 166, 174, 177, 184 f., 189, 191, 196, 198, 213, 222, 247, 279, 281, 283, 290, 301, 319, 326, 329 f., 431, 436, 457-67, 473, 475, 484, 486, 502, 508-10, 512 f., 516-22, 524, 526-30, 532 f., 537, 540, 547, 550, 552, 554, 557, 559, 562, 587, 617, 625 f., 631, 685, 688

Index of Proper Names

UNRRA 77, 80, 104, 250, 295, 471, 474, 516, 538, 544
Unruh, Fritz von 43
USA *see* United States of America
Usborne, Henry C. (MP, Labour) 151, 153, 312, 327 f., 587-9, 605 f.
USE-Liga, Ascheberg 403-6, 421, 425 f., 646 f., 691
Usellini, Guglielmo 115, 276, 592 f.
USSR *see* Soviet Union

Valéry, Paul 19, 34 f.
Vandenberg, Arthur M. 181, 289 f., 461, 468, 476-8
Vanoni, Ezio 502
Vansittart, Lord 178 f.
Vassenhove, Léon van 118 f., 187, 271, 300-3, 305, 310, 315 f., 342-5, 363 f., 369-71, 374 f., 377, 439 f., 570, 574, 580, 606
Vedel, Georges 354
Veit, Otto 403
Venice 252, 277 f., 629
Ventotene, Manifesto di 47 f., 108-11, 113 f., 126, 252
Verdier, Robert 126 f., 129, 347, 673
Vereinigte internationale Freunde (World federalist group, Hamburg) 646
Vergani, Carlo 589
Vergnolle, Henri 364, 574, 660
Verhey-Neumeyer, J. F. 641
Verkade, Willem 132, 134-42, 299, 304 f., 364, 369, 592, 638 f., 641, 680, 694
Vermeil, Edmond 624, 682
Vernon, Wilfrid Foulston (MP, Labour) 606
Versailles (Peace treaty, 1919) 4 f., 206, 214
Viannay, Philippe 46, 53
Viard, Paul (Dep., MRP) 603
Viatte, Charles (Dep., MRP) 603, 614
Vichy 202
Viénot, André 220 f.
Vienna 40, 194, 442, 456, 581
Villard, Jean (Dep., MRP) 603
Villey, Daniel 280
Villiers, Georges 350
Visser 't Hooft, Willem A. 54, 56-8, 115
Vital-Mareile (Fr. federalist) 352
Vojaksch (Czechoslovak émigré) 147
Voisin, André Raymond 312, 328, 349 f., 353 f., 362-4, 370, 376, 379, 592, 594, 625, 648 f., 661, 671, 673, 682 f.
Volpelière (Mme, CFFE) 305 f., 308, 314 f., 348
Voroshilov, Kliment Yefremovitch 448
Vorrink, Koos 139
Vourc'h, Jean Antoine (Fr. Senat. MRP) 604
Voyant, Joseph (Fr. Senat., MRP) 604
Voyenne, Bernhard 350, 358
VVD (Volkspartij voor Vrijhijd en Democratie), *see under* Liberal Parties
Vyshinsky, Andrei 453

Walker, Maurice (Fr. Senat., MRP) 604
Wallace, George Douglas (MP, Labour) 606
Wallace, William H. 66, 73, 432, 461
Warbey, William Noble (MP, Labour) 619
Ward, Barbara 22
Warsaw 3, 16, 26, 29, 77, 95, 272, 446, 486
Washington 522, 533 f.
Washington, George 470
Wasser, Joseph (Dep., MRP) 603
Weber, Alfred 20, 39
Wehberg, Hans 37, 107, 276, 305, 313
Welles, Sumner 65 f., 435, 469
Wells, William Thomas (MP, Labour) 606
Weltstaatsliga (Munich) 586, 646
Wennigsen 236, 244
Werfel, Franz 436
Wertheimer, Edmund 411 f., 647
Wery, R. F. 136 f., 638
Wesseling, J. C. 369
Westerhuf, G. 136
Westminster, economic conference of the European Movement (20.-25.4.1949) 340
Westphal (pseudonym), *see* Kluthe
Wettstein, Georg 123
Wheare, K. C. 144
White Russia 14-16, 26-9; *see also* Byelorussia
Wiedemann, Günther 427
Wigg, George Edward Cecil (MP, Labour) 606
Wijffels, Franciscus Cornelis Marie 136
Wiley, Alexander 470
Wilde-Schulze, Harry 415
Wilhelmina (Queen of the Netherlands) 264
Willems, G. W. 137
Willis, Eustace (MP, Labour) 328, 605
Wilson, Harold 557
Wilson, Thomas Woodrow 3, 37 f., 98, 459, 464
Winant, John G. 77
Wingate, Monica 151, 327, 589
Wirth, Josef 240 f.
Wofford, Harris 589
Woods, George Saville (MP, Labour) 619
Woolf, L. 190
Wootton, Barbara 142-5, 147
World Federalists Inc. 312
Woytinski, Wladimir 38
Wrench, Sir Evelyn 64
Wyatt, Woodrow Lyle (MP, Labour) 606
Wynner, Edith 587-9

Yalta ('Big Three' Conference) 77-9, 94 f., 99, 104, 127-9, 176, 186, 191, 203, 208 f., 211-13, 256, 271, 283, 295, 459, 461, 463
Yates, Victor Francis (MP, Labour) 606
Young Plan 534
Yugoslavia 10, 56 f., 67, 77, 96, 115, 211, 258 f., 280, 285, 365, 369, 441, 449, 452-5, 485, 502, 610

Zaksas, Gilbert 124–6, 129
Zanker (Augsburg, UE–Liga) 411
Zeeland, Paul van 337–42, 439 f., 670, 672 f. 682
Zerbi, Tommaso 609
Zhdanov, Andrei 385, 462, 486
Ziegler, Leopold 20, 655

Zilliacus, Konni 145 f., 153, 189, 492
Zurich 19, 123, 253, 319
   Churchill's speech (19.9.1946) 309 f., 317–23, 330, 343, 386–8, 403, 432–4, 469, 479, 687
Zulawski, Zygmunt 186
Zurcher, Arnold J. 436